Encyclopedia of

Literary Critics and Criticism

Volume 1

Encyclopedia of

LITERARY CRITICS AND CRITICISM

Volume 1
A–K

Consultant
John Sutherland

Edited by
CHRIS MURRAY

FITZROY DEARBORN PUBLISHERS
LONDON • CHICAGO

FITZROY DEARBORN PUBLISHERS
919 North Michigan Avenue – Suite 760
Chicago, IL. 60611
USA

or

310 Regent Street
London W1R 5AJ
England

Editors: Edith Summerhayes and Radojka Miljevic
Proofreaders: Edith Summerhayes and Nicola Bennett
Researchers: Michael Brett and Rowland Hughes
Indexer: Drusilla Calvert

British Library Cataloguing in Publication Data
Encyclopedia of literary critics and criticism
1. Criticism – Encyclopedias 2. Critics – Encyclopedias
I. Murray, Chris
801.9′5′03

ISBN 1-57958-144-7

Library of Congress Cataloging in Publication Data is available.

First published in the USA and UK 1999

Typeset by Florence Production Limited, Stoodleigh, Devon
Printed and bound in Great Britain by The Bath Press, Bath

CONTENTS

INTRODUCTION

In 1894 the celebrated French poet Stéphane Mallarmé gave a lecture in Oxford on the "state of French poetry." He began with an irony clearly meant to tease his august Anglo-Saxon audience: "I am indeed bringing news. The most surprising news ever. Nothing like it has ever happened before. They have been tampering with the rules of verse . . . *On a touché au vers.*" In an essay published in his collection *Blindness and Insight: Essays in the Rhetoric of Contemporary Criticism* (1971), the Belgian-born American critic Paul de Man gave this remark a modern gloss: "*On a touché à la critique*" (they have been tampering with criticism). De Man (being equally ironic) continued: "Well-established rules and conventions that governed the discipline of criticism and made it a cornerstone of the intellectual establishment have been so badly tampered with that the entire edifice threatens to collapse." Or so it seemed.

Certainly profound changes have occurred in literary theory and criticism (and therefore teaching), largely as a result of the growing influence of other disciplines – notably linguistics, philosophy, political thought, and psychoanalysis. Increasingly students have had to acquire a working knowledge of a wide range of theories and concepts, including – to cite only the more familiar examples – the linguistics of Ferdinand de Saussure (as developed by Roland Barthes and other structuralists); Marxist thought (as interpreted by Georg Lukács, Walter Benjamin, Louis Althusser, or Terry Eagleton); Freudian concepts (as reinterpreted by Jacques Lacan); and phenomenology (as expounded by Martin Heidegger or Hans-Georg Gadamer). And at the end of the 1960s there was a development that seemed to undermine all theories: the subtle and elusive "deconstruction" practiced by the French philosopher Jacques Derrida (and the later Barthes) introduced the notion that there can be no final and fixed point for meaning – that the interpretation of a text (and this applies to critical texts themselves) involved the endless "free play" of meanings.

As theories, concepts, and analytical techniques have proliferated, the four key elements of the "critical square" – author, reader, text, and society – have been subjected to searching analysis, the emphasis differing according to the theory. Some developments seem to threaten the most fundamental concepts of literary study. The "author," for example, has been one of the most surprising casualties, the death of the author having been announced by Roland Barthes in 1968. Far from being an independent agent whose thoughts, feelings, and intentions, skilfully expressed, give a text its meaning (a meaning to be made explicit by the critic), the author can be seen as an "ideological construct," a point of intersection (made possible by language) between the personal and the public, the conscious and the unconscious. (It is interesting to note that the death of the author has been challenged not only by more "traditional" critics, but also by feminists and postcolonial critics [among others], who believe that any weakening of the concept of a free and responsible "subject" has dangerous political implications.)

At the same time, Barthes grants the reader far greater power and autonomy (he saw the relationship between author and reader as parallel to the political and economic relationship between producer and consumer): "The birth of the reader must be at the cost of the death of the Author." This new emphasis on role of the reader can also be seen in theories mainly indebted to phenomenology, such as Reader-Response Criticism.

Those critics who have focussed on the text have generally shown a strong desire to bring a new rigor and discipline to the study of literature; to make it, in effect, scientific. Rejecting "merely subjective" responses to literary texts, they concentrate on identifying the basic features common to all works of literature. Structuralists and semioticians, for example, search for the fundamental structural elements that give a text meaning; narratologists anatomize stories of all kinds (from *Oedipus Rex* to *Cinderella* and comic strips) to discover the basic units (and the rules for combining them) used in generating narratives; and stylisticians analyze literary texts to produce a wealth of grammatical and semantic data.

Here the main influence is clearly linguistics, in particular the structuralist theory of Ferdinand de Saussure, which has cast new light on the close relationship between language, society, and culture. Language, it is argued, can be seen as a self-sufficient system in which meaning is determined not by a correspondence between language and the world, but by the structure of the system itself. As a consequence, language is not a mere reflection of the world, but the very means by which "reality" – the individual, society, and the world – is constituted. What has made Saussure's theory so influential is that it provides a model of communication that can be applied to a wide range of subjects, from fashion and advertising to mythology and architecture; social, cultural, and intellectual phenomena can, in effect, be read as "texts." This theory reached its logical conclusion (some might say its *reductio ad absurdum*) in Jacques Derrida's celebrated and provocative claim: *Il n'y a pas de hors-texte* (there is nothing outside the text).

Those critics who focus on the social context of literature have also been able to draw on structuralist theory, though their main influences are Marxism and sometimes psychoanalysis. Their theories often reveal a determination to expose the ideological or "political" foundations of literature. As the products of a specific society, works of literature, it is claimed, will inevitably embody not only that society's values and perceptions, but also its unadmitted conflicts, prejudices, and contradictions. Literature, furthermore, can be seen as having an "unconscious," and it is the critic's function to bring to light the repressed and unacknowledged elements beneath the apparent (the "conscious") subjects and themes of a work. This approach has helped to establish a range of critical theories that focus on reinterpreting Western literature in terms of the ways in which it has systematically ignored or silenced certain groups – such as the working classes or the poor (the focus of Marxist criticism), women (feminism), homosexuals (gay or queer criticism), and ethnic groups (postcolonial and black criticism).

As Paul de Man observed, some have taken a decidedly pessimistic view of developments: criticism, it is claimed, caught up in a general collapse of moral and intellectual values, has either been reduced to a form of scholasticism, to a labyrinthine study of theories of theories, or it has become absorbed into other disciplines, such as social theory, political thought, or linguistics.

For many others, however, the edifice of criticism is not about to collapse. Basic assumptions and deeply rooted values have been challenged and some rejected. But the

many new theories, concepts, approaches, and techniques that have emerged have also brought a new vitality, range, depth, and intellectual rigor to literary criticism. This has meant that criticism, in its turn, has been able to influence other disciplines, including philosophy, history, social and political analysis, anthropology, and legal studies. Even deconstruction, which was initially seen as entailing a wholesale rejection of the fundamental principles of the humanities, has been absorbed into teaching practice, providing (according to Robert Scholes' influential *Textual Power: Literary Theory and the Teaching of English*, 1985), "an extremely sophisticated and powerful set of procedures" for scrutinizing not only literature but also the teaching of literature.

Moreover, modern developments have brought new insights to criticism's continuous dialogue with its own past (a past that stretches back to Plato), and have also encouraged an engagement with non-Western traditions – a development which, rich in promise, is only just beginning.

It is this broad diversity of literary criticism and theory past and present, Western and non-Western, that is explored in the *Encyclopedia of Literary Critics and Criticism*.

Aim and scope

The aim of the *Encyclopedia of Literary Critics and Criticism* is to provide a clear, wide-ranging, and authoritative guide to literary theory and criticism past and present. There are in total 374 entries, ranging from 800 words to 14,500, on individuals, theories, and concepts. Indexes and cross-references are provided to help readers explore themes systematically, and all the entries have bibliographies and suggestions for further reading.

The first edition of the encyclopedia appeared in 1987 as the *Critical Survey of Literary Theory*, published by Salem Press. For this new edition, every one of the existing entries has been revised and updated, and in addition, 117 new entries have been written.

The most distinctive feature of the *Encyclopedia of Literary Critics and Criticism* is its scope. Firstly, it covers the whole history of Western literary theory and criticism, and also has entries on non-Western traditions. This means that it provides readers with accounts not only of all the familiar figures of literary criticism (such as Aristotle, Longinus, Sir Philip Sidney, Dr Johnson, Matthew Arnold and so on) but also of a wide range of lesser-known figures – figures who, seldom dealt with in detail elsewhere, can be of great significance in research, either in themselves or as background to other figures and topics. From the Middle Ages, for example, there is Fulgentius, Alan of Lille and Geoffrey of Vinsauf, from the Renaissance Lodovico Castelvetro, Antonio Minturno, Julius Caesar Scaliger, George Gascoigne, and George Puttenham.

Secondly, as these few examples indicate, the scope of the encyclopedia is not restricted to the critics who have had an impact on literature in English – there are also entries on a wide range of writers who have been important for their own national traditions. They include (to give just a few examples): François de Malherbe, Joachim du Bellay, Ferdinand Brunetière, Théophile Gautier, Charles-Augustin Sainte-Beuve, and Paul Valéry in French literature; Nikolai Dobroluibov, Vissarion Belinskii, Dmitrii Pisarev, and Nikolai Chernyshevskii in Russian literature; Johann Wolfgang von Goethe, Johann Gottfried Herder, Gotthold Ephraim Lessing, Friedrich Schiller, Franz Grillparzer, and Hugo von Hofmannsthal in German literature; Dante, Giuseppe Mazzini, Benedetto Croce, and Francesco De Sanctis in Italian literature; Benito Jerónimo Feijóo y Montenegro, Ignacio de Luzán y Claramunt, Marcelino Menéndez y Pelayo, and Miguel de Unamuno y Jugo in Spanish literature.

Moreover, as already indicated, the entries include some from outside the Western tradition. At a time when the Eurocentric view of the world is being challenged, it was felt essential to represent several non-Western traditions, namely the Arabic (four entries), the Japanese (six), the Chinese (five), and the Indian (four). There are also entries on modern African literary criticism.

This international range allows readers not only to consider concepts and approaches new to the Western tradition, but also to discover intriguing parallels and points of contact – between, for example, ancient Indian literary theory and the deconstructive approach of the contemporary French thinker Jacques Derrida (see, for example, the entry on Bhartrhari.)

Finally, the encyclopedia includes many thinkers and writers who are not known primarily for their literary theory, but whose works have had an important impact on our understanding of either literature or literary criticism. Examples include: the theologian Saint Augustine, the poet Geoffrey Chaucer, the philosophers Georg Wilhelm Friedrich Hegel, Friedrich Nietzsche, and Henri Bergson, the anthropologists Claude Lévi-Strauss and Clifford Geertz, the novelists Marcel Proust and Thomas Mann, and the communications theorists Marshall McLuhan and Jean Baudrillard.

Entries and structure

The 374 entries appear in alphabetical order and are of four kinds (for the complete list of entries see page xv).

1. Individuals. There are 292 entries on individuals (ranging from 2,000 to 4,000 words), all of them having the following structure: **Biography**; **Influence** (in effect a concise statement of their distinctive achievement); and **Analysis**, which forms the body of the entry. At the end of each entry there is also a comprehensive list of the individual's books and essays in **Principal criticism.** The section **Other major works and literary forms** contains a short account and listing of a writer's non-critical works, such as poetry or autobiography. In **Further reading** the contributors suggest a selection of books or essays on their subject. Finally, a number of cross-references to other entries in the encyclopedia are given under **See Also**.
2. Chronological Surveys. The 15 entries on major literary periods and literatures (5,000-14,500 words) form a concise history of Western criticism from Plato to postmodernism. There are three entries on the twentieth century, and four on non-Western traditions.
3. Theories and approaches. These 28 entries (from 2,000 to 4,000 words) provide accounts of many of the major theories, approaches, and movements in literary criticism, such as Black Literary Theory and Criticism, Deconstruction, Dialogic Criticism, Narratology, Phenomenological Criticism, Russian Formalism, and Semiotics.
4. Concepts. Slightly shorter than the other entries (800-1,200 words), these 39 entries discuss a number of the key concepts in literary criticism, including the erotic, intertextuality, metonymy, pastoral, style, the sublime, and translation.

The links between entries can be explored in a number of ways.

1. Firstly, there is (a) **Entries by Category** (page xix), in which all the entries are listed alphabetically in the four categories described above: Individuals, Chronological Surveys, Theories and Approaches, and Concepts; and (b) a **Chronological List** (page xxiii) of individuals, with their dates and a description of them.

2. Secondly, almost all of the entries (whether on individuals, periods, theories, or concepts) have **See Also** at the end of the essay identifying related entries. The range varies according to the entry; they are not meant to provide exhaustive references but to start lines of enquiry.
3. Thirdly, there are two indexes. The **Subject Index** provides a detailed listing of proper names, concepts, theories, themes, and titles. The **Title Index** gives a complete listing of the books cited in the "Principal criticism" section of the articles on individuals. These important works of the subject are given in their original language and in translation, where there is one. The author of the work is given in the entry too.

To take an example, we can consider the Bulgarian-born French writer Julia Kristeva. "See Also" at the end of the essay refers the reader to several other writers whose ideas are related to hers, either by influence or similarity (Luce Irigaray, Toril Moi, and Jacques Lacan); to critical approaches and theories of which her work forms a part (Feminist Criticism, Psychoanalytic Criticism, Semiotics); to a concept that plays an important role in her work (intertextuality); and – to set her work in a broad national tradition – an historical survey (French Literary Theory: Twentieth Century). Because each of these entries has its own set of "See Also" references, the reader can quickly build up an increasingly detailed map of links and parallels.

Similarly, the Subject Index – which covers individuals, concepts, theories, and titles – provides a list of every meaningful occasion when Kristeva or her works are cited throughout the encyclopedia. And if only a title is known – *Pouvoirs de l'horreur*, for example – the Title Index can be consulted to identify both the author and the translation.

CHRIS MURRAY

NOTE ON TRANSLITERATION

Russian: The system of transliteration from Cyrillic used in this volume is that of the Library of Congress, without diacritics, except for place names where the English forms are used, e.g. Moscow. Names of people and characters, except when featured in translated titles, follow the Library of Congress transliteration (thus "Fedor Dostoevskii" and "Lev Tolstoi").

Arabic: A simplified version of the standard transliteration of Arabic names and terms is employed, whereby long vowels are indicated but diacritical dots omitted. The signs ' and ' stand for a glottal stop and a laryngeal consonant respectively, peculiar to Arabic. The former sign is also used to distinguish combinations of two consonants (as in Is'hāq) from digraphs (as in Rashīq).

Chinese: Wade-Giles is used.

CONTRIBUTORS

Michael Adams
Patrick Adcock
Jacob H. Adler
Owen A. Aldridge
James R. Andreas, Sr.
Andrew J. Angyal
Norman Araujo
Raymond M. Archer
Stanley Archer
Stephen M. Ashby
Bob Ashley
Dorothy B. Aspinwall
Bryan Aubrey
James R. Aubrey
Ehrhard Bahr
James Baird
Joseph O. Baker
Simon C. Baker
Thomas Banks
Laura Stone Barnard
Peter Barry
Thomas F. Barry
Thomas O. Beebee
Richard P. Benton
Terry D. Bilhartz
Cynthia A. Bily
Carol Bishop
Paul Bishop
Harold Branam
Gerhard Brand
Michael Brett
Jean R. Brink
Susan Briziarelli
J. R. Broadus
Michael J. Büsges
Joseph A. Buttigieg
Theodore J. Cachey, Jr.
Edmund J. Campion
Peter Carravetta
Margaret H. Childs
Dennis C. Chowenhill
Lina L. Cofresi
William Condon
John J. Conlon
Deborah Core,
Mark E. Cory.
Liselotte M. Davis
Frank Day
Robert F. Denton
John F. Deredita
R. P. Draper
Bruce L. Edwards
Robert P. Ellis
Thomas L. Erskine
Clara Estow
Thomas H. Falk
Robert J. Forman
Robert J. Frail
Margot Frank
Camille Garnier
Diana Gosselin Nakeeb
William H. Green
William Griffin
Giovanni Gullace
M. A. R. Habib
Jennifer Ham
William S. Haney, II
Stella Harvey
Greig E. Henderson
Sean Homer
Pierre L. Horn
Mark Houlahan
Rowland Hughes
Barbara L. Hussey
Shakuntala Jayaswal
Karen A. Kildahl
Wm. Laird Kleine-Ahlbrandt
Dwight A. Klett
Paula Kopacz
Charles S. Kraszewski
Elizabeth Kuhlmann
William LaHay
Carl Landauer
Philip Leonard
Leon Lewis
Janine Liladhar
James Livingston
Perry D. Luckett
R. C. Lutz
A.W. Lyle
John D. Lyons
Mark R. McCulloh
William McDonald
Hugh McLean
John McLeod
Kerrie L. MacPherson

Martha Manheim
Emerson R. Marks
John Marks
Joss Marsh
Bronwen Martin
JoAnne Liebman Matson
Charles E. May
Laurence W. Mazzeno
Anthony Mellors
Sara Mills
Leslie B. Mittleman
Robert A. Morace
Francis J. Morris
Simone Murray
William Nelles
K. M. Newton
Emma Coburn Norris
Peter Nosco
George O'Brien
Robert M. Otten
Lisa Paddock
Nicholas O. Pagan
Robert J. Paradowski
David Patterson
William E. Pemberton
George F. Peters
Christopher L. Picard
Susan L. Piepke
Domenico Pietropaolo
Johann Pillai
Lorraina Pinnell
Ernest R. Pinson
Wayne Pounds
David Powell
Norman Prinsky
Charles Pullen
Glyn Pursglove
Michael L. Quinn
Victor J. Ramraj
Thomas Rankin
Tina M. Rhein
Felizitas Ringham
Vicki K. Robinson
Carl Rollyson
Paul Rosefeldt
Joseph Rosenblum
Donya Samara
Nancy Scerbo
Barry P. Scherr
Marilyn V. Schuler
Steven P. Schult
Alison M. Scott
Joan Corey Semonella
Matt Senior
Rodney Sharkey
Narain Govind Sharma
Richard Sheldon
Michael Sherberg
John C. Sherwood
Bryan C. Short
R. Baird Shuman
Thomas J. Sienkewicz
Armand E. Singer
Genevieve Slomski
Marjorie Smelstor
David P. Smith
Gilbert Smith
Katherine Snipes
Joanna Stephens
Davd R. Stevenson
Paul Stuewe
James Sullivan
Roy Arthur Swanson
Spurgeon Thompson
Michael Tilby
Jan Udris
Raynalle Udris
Larry W. Usilton
John Van Cleve
George Van Devender
Geert Jan Van Gelder
Dennis Vannatta
Scott Vaszily
Anne R. Vizzier
William T. Walker
John Wilson
Maryk Royden Winchell
John D. Windhausen
Johnny Wink
Michael Witkoski
Gregory Woods
Eugene P. Wright
Karin Wurst
Vincent Yang
Clifton K. Yearley

ALPHABETICAL LIST OF ENTRIES

ENTRIES BY CATEGORY

Individuals

William Empson
Desiderius Erasmus
Martin Esslin
Benito Jerónimo Feijóo y Montenegro
François de Salignac de La Mothe-Fénelon
Leslie Fiedler
Stanley Fish
E. M. Forster
Michel Foucault
Northrop Frye
Fulgentius
Margaret Fuller
Hans-Georg Gadamer
John Gardner
George Gascoigne
Henry Louis Gates, Jr.
Théophile Gautier
Clifford Geertz
Gérard Genette
Geoffrey of Vinsauf
Stefan George
Sandra M. Gilbert and Susan Gubar
Giambattista Giraldi Cinthio
René Girard
Johann Wolfgang von Goethe
Witold Gombrowicz
Stephen Gosson
Johann Christoph Gottsched
Rémy de Gourmont
Antonio Gramsci
Robert Graves
A. J. Greimas
Franz Grillparzer
Friedrich Gundolf
Geoffrey H. Hartman
Hāzim al-Qartājannī
William Hazlitt
Stephen Heath
Georg Wilhelm Friedrich Hegel
Martin Heidegger
Heinrich Heine
Johann Gottfried Herder
Hugo von Hofmannsthal
Norman N. Holland
Arno Holz
Gerard Manley Hopkins
Horace
Hu Shih
Victor Hugo
T. E. Hulme
David Hume
Roman Ingarden
Luce Irigaray
Wolfgang Iser
Saint Isidore of Seville
Roman Jakobson
Henry James
Fredric Jameson
Randall Jarrell
Hans Robert Jauss
Samuel Johnson
Ben Jonson
Lord Kames
Kamo no Mabuchi
Immanuel Kant
John Keats
Hugh Kenner
Frank Kermode
Heinrich von Kleist
L. C. Knights
Annette Kolodny
Murray Krieger
Julia Kristeva
Jean de La Bruyère
Jean de La Fontaine
Jean-François de La Harpe
Jacques Lacan
D. H. Lawrence
F. R. Leavis
Gotthold Ephraim Lessing
Claude Lévi-Strauss
C. S. Lewis
Liu Hsieh
David Lodge
Longinus
Iurii Lotman
Lu Chi
Percy Lubbock
Lucian
Georg Lukács
Anatolii Lunacharskii
Ignacio de Luzán y Claramunt
Macrobius
François de Malherbe
Stéphane Mallarmé
Thomas Mann
Filippo Tommaso Marinetti
Jacques Maritain
F. O. Matthiessen
Giuseppe Mazzini
Jerome J. McGann
Marshall McLuhan
Marcelino Menéndez y Pelayo
John Stuart Mill
J. Hillis Miller
Antonio Minturno
Toril Moi
Michel Eyquem de Montaigne
Motoori Norinaga
Es'kia (Ezekiel) Mphahlele
Ngugi wa Thiong'o
Friedrich Nietzsche
Charles Olson
Walter J. Ong
Walter Pater
Marjorie Perloff
Petrarch
Luigi Pirandello
Dmitrii Pisarev
Plato

Chronological Surveys

Theories and Approaches

Concepts

CHRONOLOGICAL LIST OF INDIVIDUALS

c. 427 B.C.–347 B.C.	Plato	Greek philosopher
384 B.C.–322 B.C.	Aristotle	Greek philosopher
c. 305 B.C.–240 B.C.	Callimachus	Greek scholar and poet
106 B.C.–43 B.C.	Cicero	Roman writer and rhetorician
78/54 B.C.–7 B.C.	Dionysius of Halicarnassus	Greek teacher and rhetorician
65 B.C.–8 B.C.	Horace (Quintus Horatius Flaccus)	Roman poet and writer
1st century A.D.	Longinus	Greek theorist
c. 35 A.D.–c. 96 A.D.	Quintilian (Marcus Fabius Quintilianus)	Roman rhetorician and teacher
c. 120 A.D.–after 180 A.D.	Lucian	Greek writer and critic
187 A.D.–226 A.D.	Ts'ao P'i	Chinese poet
3rd century A.D.	Bharata	Indian dramatic theorist
205 A.D.–270 A.D.	Plotinus	Greco-Roman philosopher
261 A.D.–303 A.D.	Lu Chi	Chinese Poet
354 A.D.–430 A.D.	Saint Augustine (Aurelius Augustinus)	Christian scholar, philosopher, and writer
c. 375 A.D.–c. 422 A.D.	Macrobius	Latin philosopher and writer
c. 465 A.D.–c. 522 A.D.	Liu Hsieh	Chinese philosopher and theorist
c. 500–600	Fulgentius	Christian Latin writer
c. 560–636	Saint Isidore of Seville	Spanish theologian and scholar
7th century	Bhartrhari	Indian grammarian and philosopher
9th century	Anandavardhana	Indian theorist
c. 884–c. 945	Ki no Tsurayuki	Japanese critic and editor
?–c. 948	Qudāma Ibn Ja'far	Arabic theorist and philologist
?–1087	'Abd al-Qāhir al-Jurjānī	Arabic theorist and grammarian
1110(/1130)–1203	Alan of Lille (Alanus de Insulis)	French philosopher and poet
c. 1200–?	Geoffrey of Vinsauf	English scholar
1211–1285	Hāzim al-Qartājannī	Arabic theorist, grammarian, and poet
1265–1321	Dante (Durante Alighieri)	Italian poet
1304–1374	Petrarch (Francesco Petrarca)	Italian poet and writer
1313–1375	Giovanni Boccaccio	Italian writer
1320–1388	Nijō Yoshimoto	Japanese poet
c. 1343–1400	Geoffrey Chaucer	English poet
1466?–1536	Desiderius Erasmus	Dutch theologian, scholar, and critic
1470–1547	Pietro Bembo	Italian scholar and poet
1478–1550	Giangiorgio Trissino	Italian poet and scholar
1484–1558	Julius Caesar Scaliger	Italian-French scholar and writer
1500–c. 1574	Antonio Minturno (Antonio Sebastiani)	Italian critic and scholar
1504–1573	Giambattista Giraldi Cinthio	Italian playwright and theorist
1505–1571	Lodovico Castelvetro	Italian critic and playwright
1522–1560	Joachim du Bellay	French critic, poet, and translator
c. 1525–1577	George Gascoigne	English writer and critic
c. 1530–1590	George Puttenham	English critic
1533–1592	Michel Eyquem de Montaigne	French essayist and writer

1554–1586	Sir Philip Sidney	English poet and critic
1554 (baptized)–1624	Stephen Gosson	English critic and writer
1555–1628	François de Malherbe	French poet, writer, and translator
1561–1626	Francis Bacon	English statesman, philosopher, and essayist
1573–1637	Ben Jonson	English poet, playwright, and critic
1606–1684	Pierre Corneille	French dramatist and critic
1621–1695	Jean de La Fontaine	French writer
1631–1700	John Dryden	English poet, critic, and translator
1636–1711	Nicolas Boileau-Despréaux	French critic and poet
1639 (baptized)–1699	Jean Racine	French playwright and writer
c. 1643–1713	Thomas Rymer	English critic, translator, and editor
1644–1694	Matsuo Bashō	Japanese poet, traveler, and teacher of poetry
1645–1696	Jean de La Bruyère	French writer, critic, and translator
1651–1715	François de Salignac de La Mothe-Fénelon	French theologian and writer
1668–1744	Giambattista Vico	Italian philosopher
1671–1713	Third Earl of Shaftesbury (Anthony Ashley Cooper)	English writer and critic
1672–1719	Joseph Addison	English essayist and critic
1676–1764	Benito Jerónimo Feijóo y Montenegro	Spanish writer and critic
1683–1765	Edward Young	English poet and critic
1688–1744	Alexander Pope	English poet, translator, and critic
1694–1778	Voltaire (François-Marie Arouet)	French writer and critic
1696?–1782	Lord Kames (Henry Home, Lord Kames)	Scottish jurist, legal historian, philosopher, and critic
1697–1769	Kamo No Mabuchi	Japanese writer and philologist
1698–1783	Johann Jakob Bodmer	Swiss critic, historian, and translator
1700–1766	Johann Christoph Gottsched	German critic and philosopher
1702–1754	Ignacio de Luzán y Claramunt	Spanish writer and critic
1709–1784	Samuel Johnson	English writer, editor, and lexicographer
1711–1776	David Hume	Scottish philosopher
1712–1778	Jean-Jacques Rousseau	Swiss-born French writer, critic, and social theorist
1713–1784	Denis Diderot	French editor, writer, and theorist
1717–1768	Johann Joachim Winckelmann	German art historian and critic
1719–1789	Giuseppe Baretti	Italian-English critic and lexicographer
1722 (baptized)–1800	Joseph Warton	English critic and poet
1724–1804	Immanuel Kant	German philosopher
1727–1790	Thomas Warton	English critic and poet
1729–1781	Gotthold Ephraim Lessing	German critic and playwright
1729–1797	Edmund Burke	Irish-born writer and politician
1730–1801	Motoori Norinaga (Ozu Norinaga)	Japanese writer and philologist
1739–1803	Jean-François de la Harpe	French writer and critic
1744–1803	Johann Gottfried Herder	German writer
1749–1832	Johann Wolfgang von Goethe	German poet, novelist, playwright, and critic
1759–1805	Friedrich Schiller	German poet, playwright, and theorist
1766–1817	Madame de Staël (Anne Louise Germaine, Baroness of Staël-Holstein)	French critic and writer
1767–1845	August Wilhelm Schlegel	German translator and critic
1770–1831	Georg Wilhelm Friedrich Hegel	German philosopher
1770–1850	William Wordsworth	English poet
1772–1829	Friedrich Schlegel	German critic and writer
1772–1834	Samuel Taylor Coleridge	English poet and critic
1775–1854	Friedrich Wilhelm Joseph Schelling	German philosopher, writer, and critic
1777–1811	Heinrich von Kleist	German writer and playwright
1778–1830	William Hazlitt	English critic and essayist
1780–1819	Karl Wilhelm Ferdinand Solger	German philosopher and critic
1783–1842	Stendhal (Marie-Henri Beyle)	French novelist
1783–1852	Vasilii Zhukovskii	Russian poet, translator, and critic
1788–1824	Lord Byron (George Gordon, sixth Baron Byron)	English poet and critic
1788–1857	Joseph von Eichendorff	German poet, writer, and critic
1788–1860	Arthur Schopenhauer	German philosopher

1791–1872	Franz Grillparzer	Austrian dramatist and critic
1792–1822	Percy Bysshe Shelley	English poet
1795–1821	John Keats	English poet
1797–1856	Heinrich Heine	German poet and writer
1799–1837	Aleksandr Pushkin	Russian poet and writer
1802–1885	Victor Hugo	French novelist, poet, and playwright
1803–1882	Ralph Waldo Emerson	American essayist and critic
1804–1869	Charles-Augustin Sainte-Beuve	French critic and writer
1805–1872	Giuseppe Mazzini	Italian critic and essayist
1806–1873	John Stuart Mill	English writer, critic, and polemicist
1809–1849	Edgar Allan Poe	American writer and poet
1810–1850	Margaret Fuller	American critic and social reformer
1811–1848	Vissarion Belinskii	Russian critic
1811–1872	Théophile Gautier	French writer and critic
1817–1883	Francesco De Sanctis	Italian critic, translator, and essayist
1819–1900	John Ruskin	English social and cultural critic
1821–1867	Charles Baudelaire	French poet and critic
1821–1881	Fedor Dostoevskii	Russian novelist
1822–1888	Matthew Arnold	English poet and critic
1828–1889	Nikolai Chernyshevskii	Russian critic and writer
1828–1893	Hippolyte-Adolphe Taine	French critic and writer
1828–1910	Lev Tolstoi	Russian novelist and writer
1836–1861	Nikolai Dobroliubov	Russian critic and poet
1837–1909	Algernon Charles Swinburne	English poet and critic
1838–1906	Aleksandr Veselovskii	Russian critic and translator
1839–1894	Walter Pater	English critic and writer
1840–1868	Dmitrii Pisarev	Russian critic
1840–1893	John Addington Symonds	English critic
1840–1902	Émile Zola	French novelist, writer, and critic
1840–1922	Giovanni Verga	Italian writer and critic
1842–1898	Stéphane Mallarmé	French poet and critic
1843–1916	Henry James	American novelist and critic
1844–1889	Gerard Manley Hopkins	English poet and Jesuit priest
1844–1900	Friedrich Nietzsche	German philosopher
1845–1933	George Saintsbury	English critic, historian, and biographer
1849–1906	Ferdinand Brunetière	French critic
1851–1935	A. C. Bradley	English critic
1852–1935	Paul Bourget	French writer and critic
1854–1900	Oscar Wilde	Irish writer, dramatist, and essayist
1856–1912	Marcelino Menéndez y Pelayo	Spanish writer and critic
1856–1918	Georgii Plekhanov	Russian writer and theorist
1856–1950	George Bernard Shaw	Irish dramatist and critic
1857–1913	Ferdinand de Saussure	Swiss linguist
1858–1915	Rémy de Gourmont	French writer and critic
1859–1941	Henri Bergson	French philosopher and writer
1863–1929	Arno Holz	German critic and poet
1864–1936	Miguel de Unamuno y Jugo	Spanish philosopher, writer, and critic
1865–1933	Irving Babbitt	American critic, translator, and editor
1865–1939	William Butler Yeats	Irish poet, dramatist, and critic
1865–1945	Arthur Symons	English writer and critic
1866–1952	Benedetto Croce	Italian philosopher and critic
1867–1936	Luigi Pirandello	Italian playwright and writer
1868–1933	Stefan George	German poet, critic, and theorist
1871–1922	Marcel Proust	French novelist and critic
1871–1945	Paul Valéry	French writer and poet
1874–1929	Hugo von Hofmannsthal	Austrian poet, dramatist, and critic
1875–1933	Anatolii Lunacharskii	Russian writer and critic
1875–1955	Thomas Mann	German novelist and writer
1876–1944	Filippo Tommaso Marinetti	Italian writer and critic
1879–1965	Percy Lubbock	English critic and writer

1879–1970	E. M. Forster	English novelist and critic
1880–1931	Friedrich Gundolf (Friedrich Gundelfinger)	German writer and critic
1880–1934	Andrei Belyi (Boris Nikolaevich Bugaev)	Russian writer and critic
1882–1941	Virginia Woolf	English novelist and critic
1882–1973	Jacques Maritain	French religious philosopher and critic
1883–1917	T. E. Hulme	English poet and theorist
1885–1930	D. H. Lawrence	English novelist, poet, and critic
1885–1971	Georg Lukács	Hungarian theorist and critic
1885–1972	Ezra Pound	American poet and critic
1886–1956	Ernst Robert Curtius	German scholar and critic
1886–1959	Boris Eikhenbaum	Russian theorist
1886–1963	Van Wyck Brooks	American critic and writer
1886–1967	R. S. Crane	American critic
1888–1965	T. S. Eliot	American-born English poet, dramatist, and critic
1888–1974	John Crowe Ransom	American critic and poet
1889–1976	Martin Heidegger	German philosopher
1891–1937	Antonio Gramsci	Italian writer and political theorist
1891–1962	Hu Shih	Chinese critic
1892–1940	Walter Benjamin	German writer, critic, and theorist
1892–1957	Erich Auerbach	German-born American scholar
1892–1973	J. R. R. Tolkien	South African-born English novelist and scholar
1893–1968	Sir Herbert Read	English writer, poet, and critic
1893–1970	Roman Ingarden	Polish philosopher
1893–1979	I. A. Richards	English critic, writer, and linguist
1893–1984	Viktor Shklovskii	Russian critic
1894–1943	Iurii Tynianov	Russian theorist
1895–1970	Vladimir Propp	Russian folklorist and critical theorist
1895–1972	Edmund Wilson	American writer and critic
1895–1975	Mikhail Bakhtin	Russian theorist and critic
1895–1978	F. R. Leavis	English critic
1895–1985	Robert Graves	English poet, writer, and critic
1896–1948	Antonin Artaud	French writer, actor, and playwright
1896–1966	André Breton	French poet and theorist
1896–1982	Roman Jakobson	Russian-born American linguist and theorist
1896–1982	Mario Praz	Italian writer on literature and art
1897–1962	Georges Bataille	French writer and editor
1897–1993	Kenneth Burke	American writer and critic
1898–1956	Bertolt Brecht	German playwright and critic
1898–1963	C. S. Lewis	English writer, critic, and scholar
1898–1989	Malcolm Cowley	American editor and critic
1898–1990	Dámaso Alonso	Spanish poet and critic
1898–1998	Owen Barfield	English critic, writer, and teacher
1899–1979	Allen Tate	American writer and critic
1899–1986	Jorge Luis Borges	Argentine writer, poet, and critic
1900–	Hans-Georg Gadamer	German philosopher and critic
1900–1968	Yvor Winters	American critic and poet
1901–1978	F. W. Bateson	English literary critic and editor
1901–1981	Jacques Lacan	French psychoanalyst and theorist
1902–	Georges Poulet	Belgian critic and theorist
1902–1950	F. O. Matthiessen	American critic and editor
1903–1969	Theodor Adorno (Theodor Wiesengrund)	German critic and philosopher
1903–1995	René Wellek	Austrian-born American theorist
1904–1965	R. P. Blackmur	American critic and poet
1904–1969	Witold Gombrowicz	Polish critic and writer
1905–1975	Lionel Trilling	American critic and writer
1905–1980	Jean-Paul Sartre	French philosopher and writer
1905–1989	Robert Penn Warren	American teacher, critic, poet, and novelist
1905–1991	Fredson Bowers	American bibliographer, editor, and critic
1906–1984	William Empson	English critic and poet
1906–1994	Cleanth Brooks	American critic and editor

1906–1997	L. C. Knights	English critic and scholar
1907–1973	W. H. Auden	English-born American poet and essayist
1907–1975	William K. Wimsatt, Jr.	American critic and editor
1907–1997	Leon Edel	American biographer, critic, and editor
1908–	Claude Lévi-Strauss	Belgian-born French anthropologist and theorist
1910–1970	Charles Olson	American critic and poet
1911–	Luciano Anceschi	Italian philosopher and critic
1911–1980	Marshall McLuhan	Canadian critic and writer
1912–	M. H. Abrams	American critic and editor
1912–	Walter J. Ong	American essayist and critic
1912–1991	Northrop Frye	Canadian critic and theorist
1913–	Paul Ricœur	French critic
1914–1965	Randall Jarrell	American poet, critic, and teacher
1915–1980	Roland Barthes	French writer and cultural critic
1916–	Eric Bentley	English-born American critic, writer, and translator
1917–	Leslie Fiedler	American critic and writer
1917–	Ian Watt	English critic
1917–1992	A. J. Greimas	Lithuanian-born French semiotician
1918–	Martin Esslin	Hungarian-born English drama critic
1918–1987	Richard Ellmann	American biographer and critic
1918–1990	Louis Althusser	French political philosopher
1919–	Frank Kermode	English critic and writer
1919–	Es'kia (Ezekiel) Mphahlele	South African writer and critic
1919–1983	Paul de Man	Belgian-born American critic
1921–	Wayne C. Booth	American critic and teacher
1921–1988	Raymond Williams	Welsh critic and writer
1921–1997	Hans Robert Jauss	German literary theorist
1922–	Alain Robbe-Grillet	French novelist, writer, and theorist
1922–1993	Iurii Lotman	Russian critic and theorist
1922–1995	Donald Davie	English poet and critic
1923–	René Girard	French cultural critic
1923–	Hugh Kenner	Canadian critic
1923–	Murray Krieger	American critic
1923–1985	Italo Calvino	Italian novelist, editor, and critic
1925–1995	Gilles Deleuze	French philosopher
1925–1997	Andrei Siniavskii ("Abram Tertz")	Russian writer and critic
1926–	Michel Butor	French writer and critic
1926–	Clifford Geertz	American cultural anthropologist and critic
1926–	Wolfgang Iser	German theorist
1926–1984	Michel Foucault	French philosopher and writer
1927–	Norman N. Holland	American critic
1928–	J. Hillis Miller	American critic and editor
1929–	Jean Baudrillard	French cultural critic
1929–	Geoffrey H. Hartman	German-born American critic and editor
1929–	George Steiner	French-born American critic and writer
1930–	Harold Bloom	American theorist and critic
1930–	Jacques Derrida	French philosopher and critic
1930–	Gérard Genette	French critic and editor
1930–	Luce Irigaray	Belgian-born French psychoanalyst, writer, and critic
1931–	Marjorie Perloff	American critic
1932–	Malcolm Bradbury	English novelist and critic
1932–	Umberto Eco	Italian writer, semiotician, and critic
1933–	Christopher Ricks	English teacher, critic, and editor
1933–	Susan Sontag	American essayist, critic, and novelist
1933–1982	John Gardner	American novelist, translator, and critic
1934–	Fredric Jameson	American critic and theorist
1934–	Wole Soyinka	Nigerian playwright, poet, and novelist
1935	David Lodge	English novelist and critic

1935–	Edward Said	Palestinian-American cultural critic
1936–	Sandra M. Gilbert	American critic
1937–	Hélène Cixous	French writer, theorist, and critic
1937–	Jerome J. McGann	American critic, editor, and theorist
1938–	Stanley Fish	American critic
1938–	Ngugi wa Thiong'o	Kenyan writer
1939–	Tzvetan Todorov	Bulgarian-born French theorist
1940–	Jane P. Tompkins	American critic and educator
1941	Annette Kolodny	American critic
1941–	Julia Kristeva	Bulgarian-born French critic and theorist
1942–	Gayatri Chakravorty Spivak	Indian cultural critic
1943–	Terry Eagleton	English critic, writer, and editor
1944–	Jonathan Culler	American critic
1944–	Susan Gubar	American critic
1946–	Stephen Heath	English critic, editor, and translator
1950–	Henry Louis Gates, Jr.	American critic and editor
1953–	Toril Moi	Norwegian theorist and critic

A

‘Abd al-Qāhir al-Jurjānī

Arabic theorist and grammarian

Born: Gurgān (Iran); date unknown
Died: Gurgān (Iran); 1087

Biography

Abū Bakr ‘Abd al-Qāhir Ibn ‘Abd ar-Rahmān al-Jurjānī was born on an unknown date in Gurgān (Arabicized to Jurjān), ancient Hyrcania, at the southeast corner of the Caspian Sea; a place that he never left in his lifetime. Very little is known of his life, apart from the names of some of his teachers and his pupils. A Persian writing in Arabic, he became a famous authority on grammar to whom people traveled from afar in order to be his pupils, as is mentioned by his contemporary al-Bākharzī, in his biographical anthology *Dumyat al-qasr* (the palace's statue), where some of his poetry is also quoted. A later biographer, al-Qiftī, praises him yet calls him "stingy" with his knowledge, by not exhausting a subject even though he was capable of doing so. Al-Qiftī links this with the frequency of the theme of "blaming the world and its people" in his poetry, expressing a dim view of his times. On the one hand, this criticism is understandable, seeing that some of the topics that ‘Abd al-Qāhir dealt with in an essayistic manner were later systematized and greatly elaborated, and that some of his works on formal syntax are, indeed, concise; on the other hand, it is unjust because when he writes on other topics, notably on the effects of imagery in poetry, he takes great pains to make his reader understand him, since in his analysis he is more penetrating and more exhaustive than any other Arabic literary critic before or after him.

Influence

During his lifetime ‘Abd al-Qāhir was famous especially for his works on formal syntax, such as his *al-‘Awāmil al-mi'a* (one hundred syntactical agents), *al-Jumal* (sentences), and his several commentaries (one being in thirty volumes) on *al-īdāh* (the elucidation) by Abū ‘Alī al-Fārisī. In later times, however, it is his contribution to stylistics and literary theory (particularly the literary and stylistic aspects of syntax and the study of poetic imagery) that ensured his reputation, which today is as high as ever. The importance of his two main works in this field was understood not long after his death, and is noticeable, for instance, in the important Koranic commentary by the great grammarian and philologist az-Zamakhsharī (died 1144). Recast in the shape of systematic textbooks, his ideas were fundamental in the formation of *‘ilm al-balāgha*, "the science of eloquence," as it was studied through countless commentaries and compendia in the course of some seven centuries. Having been buried, as it were, under this mass of scholasticism, his original works were unearthed and studied again thanks to the important Islamic reformer, the Egyptian Muhammad ‘Abduh (died 1905). In the past decades ‘Abd al-Qāhir has been described, notably by Kamal Abu Deeb, as anticipating modern Western theorists (Samuel Taylor Coleridge, Ferdinand de Saussure, I. A. Richards, and Noam Chomsky, among others).

Analysis

Opinions are divided as to which of ‘Abd al-Qāhir's two main critical works was written first. In accordance with what became the customary sequence in the traditional study of rhetoric or eloquence, his *Dalā'il* will be discussed first. Its title, *Dalā'il al-i‘jāz* (intimations of inimitability), shows that it is meant as a contribution to an important problem in Islamic studies that was studied from the eighth century, the "inimitability," or the miraculous nature, of the Koran. This miracle (serving as a proof of Mohammed's prophethood) was to be found, according to the majority of scholars, in its style. The theological concerns of ‘Abd al-Qāhir, which have recently been emphasized by Margaret Larkin, have often been overlooked; perhaps understandably, since in most parts of his two major books he is dealing with grammar and poetry. It is true that the Koran is often quoted in the *Dalā'il*, yet the number of poetic quotations is much larger. This, in itself, would not make it a book on literary topics, since poetry normally figures largely in any work on linguistics. Yet, a glance at ‘Abd al-Qāhir's poetic quotations makes it clear that he did not write the *Dalā'il* as first of all a book on language, for it contains many lines by the so-called modern poets from the eighth to the tenth centuries, whereas grammarians (including ʿAbd al-Qāhir in his strictly linguistic works) would restrict themselves to early poetry of the "Arab" (in the sense of Bedouin Arabs), until the beginning of the eighth century.

The *Dalāʾil*, together with the "science of syntactical meanings" (*ʿilm al-maʿānī*) of which it became a founding text, has long been thought of as part of rhetoric rather than linguistics. Lately, however, scholars of the history of Arab linguistics, with some justification, tend to see it as belonging to linguistics, where the *ʿilm al-maʿānī* provides the necessary semantic and stylistic elements that are largely absent from the formal traditional study of syntax called *ʿilm an-nahw*.

After a few introductory chapters including an apology for poetry, never wholly superfluous in pious Muslim circles, ʿAbd al-Qāhir explains that he is not satisfied with the ideas on eloquence current in his day. He is particularly unhappy with the prevalent view that "meaning/content" and "expression/linguistic form" can and should be studied separately. Instead, he argues, stylistic qualities and defects are a result of the linking of words, syntactically and semantically, which he calls *nazm*, "composition, construction." Literally meaning "ordering, stringing (as of pearls on a necklace)," this term was already employed as a synonym of *shiʿr*, poetry as "bound speech" in contradistinction to *nathr*, "prose" (literally, "scattering"); no doubt the ambiguity of the term helped to consolidate the position of poetry as the prime source of eloquence (barring, naturally, the Koran). A specific configuration of interrelated expressions and meanings he calls the *sūra*, "form" of the utterance (note that the transliteration employed here does not differentiate between this term and the word meaning "Koranic chapter"). Aware of the many layers of the word "meaning" (*maʿnā*), he makes a distinction between the surface meaning of an utterance and a deeper intention, which he calls "the meaning of the meaning" (*maʿnā l-maʿna*).

The main part of the *Dalāʾil* is concerned with a variety of types of sentences (such as interrogative, negative, or restrictive), the linking of sentences, ellipsis, and so on; all this in a somewhat rambling fashion but with great subtlety. Toward the end he addresses in more detail the problem of the Koranic miracle, to which he also devoted a separate treatise, *ar-Risāla ash-shāfiya* (the adequate treatise).

In the *Dalāʾil* some attention is given to tropes. It is to these that he devoted his *Asrār al-balāgha* (the mysteries of eloquence). He differs greatly from his predecessors who wrote on figures and tropes in that he is not content with listing many of them with a brief definition and quoting examples; instead, he analyzes a limited number of essential tropes in great depth, taking pains to explain their aesthetic effects on the hearer and subtly distinguishing between various types. At length he explains why figurative or tropical speech (*majāz*) is very often more effective in conveying ideas than literally true statements (*haqīqa*). One of the reasons, apart from the delight naturally taken in discovering strange and hidden similarities between disparate concepts, is that the mental effort required for the interpretation enhances our appreciation, just as joy on finding something is increased when one has had to look for it. He constantly addresses the reader – a personal element that was soon weeded out in the scholastic refashioning of his ideas. Though not especially noted as a poet, his own rather wordy prose style is distinctly literary and remote from the much drier prose of those who systematized his ideas. The great majority of his illustrations are taken from poetry, particularly the great "modern" poets who were innovators in their imagery: Abū Tammām, al-Buhturī, Ibn al-Muʿtazz, and al-Mutanabbī. Although he has been described as anticipating Coleridge's concept of "organic unity," it should not be thought that he was interested in the "unity" of a literary work as a whole: his scope is limited to the single image or conceit, or at most to a passage containing a series of linked images.

Such an image or conceit may take the form of a comparison or simile (*tashbīh*), in which two concepts are compared. It is distinguished from a type that he calls *tamthīl* ("likening," "analogy," or "providing a parable") which requires more analysis, since it is based on analogy which is sentence-based, and not on the mere juxtaposition of two terms; such as in the comparison of "those burdened with the Torah but who do not carry it" to an "ass carrying books" (Koran, 62:5), or when one likens a group of equally noble men to "a ring of cast metal" in which all parts are equal. Metaphor (*istiʿāra*, literally "borrowing" or "loan") similarly may be divided on the same basis into two types. A related subdivision of metaphor concerns the presence or the absence of a substratum for the *secundum* (the second term) of the implied comparison. Thus, in the verse by the pre-Islamic Labīd, "on a windy morning, when its reins are in the hand of the North wind," there are no objects corresponding to either "reins" or "hand," which are "lent" to the morning and the wind respectively.

Simile may also be divided and classified differently, for example on the basis of whether it involves sensually perceived objects or intellectual concepts in the first or the second term of a comparison, or both. Alternatively, they may be divided into the straightforward type, in which a common attribute is found in a higher degree in the second term of a comparison, and the reversed simile, which is occasionally effective, as when one says "The sun is as bright as the Caliph's face" instead of the more normal "The Caliph's face is as bright as the sun." Such poetic pretending became increasingly frequent in Arabic and Persian poetry. It may take the form of a figure that has been termed "fantastic etiology" (*taʿlīl*), providing a fictitious reason, as when Orion is said to have girded himself for the king, or roses are described as blushing, feeling outshone by the narcissus. This is a kind of *takhyīl*, creating a poetic image or illusion, which is one of the essential elements of poetry.

Principal criticism

Asrār al-balāgha (the mysteries of eloquence), 1954 (Hellmut Ritter, editor; with English summary)
Die Geheimnisse der Wortkunst (Asrār al-balāġa) des 'Abdalqāhir al-Curcānī, 1959 (Hellmut Ritter, translator)
ar-Risāla ash-shāfiya (the adequate treatise), in *Thalāth rasā'il fī i'jāz al-Qur'an* (three treatises on the inimitability of the Koran), 1968, and as an appendix to *Dalā'il al-i'jāz*, 1984
Dalā'il al-i'jāz (intimations of inimitability), 1984 (Mahmūd Muhammad Shākr, editor)

Further reading

Abu Deeb, Kamal. "Studies in Arabic Literary Criticism: the Concept of Organic Unity," in *Edebiyât*. 2 (1977), pp. 57–84.
——. *Al-Jurjānī's Theory of Poetic Imagery*, 1979.
Ait al-Ferrane, Mohammed. *Die Ma'nā-Theorie bei 'Abdalqāhir al-Ǧurǧānī (gestorben 471/1079): Versuch einer Analyse der poetischen Sprache*, 1990.
Baalbaki, R. "The Relation between naḥw and balāġa: A comparative study of the methods of Sībawayhi and Ǧurǧānī," in *Zeitschrift der Arabischen Linguistik*. 11 (1983), pp. 7–23.
Cantarino, Vicente. *Arabic Poetics in the Golden Age: Selection of Texts Accompanied by a Preliminary Study*, 1975.
Larkin, Margaret. *The Theology of Meaning: 'Abd al-Qāhir al-Jurjānī's "Theory of Discourse,"* 1995.
Weisweiler, Max. "'Abdalqāhir al-Curcānī's Werk über die Unnachahnlichkeit des Korans und seine syntaktisch-stylistischen Lehren," in *Oriens*. 11 (1958), pp. 77–121.

GEERT JAN VAN GELDER

See also Arabic Literary Theory; Hāzim al-Qartājannī; Qudāma Ibn Ja'far

M. H. Abrams

American critic and editor

Born: Long Branch, New Jersey; July 23, 1912

Biography

Meyer Howard Abrams was born to Joseph and Sarah Shanes Abrams in 1912. Except for a year (1934–1935) as a fellow at Cambridge University in England, he obtained all of his formal training at Harvard University, receiving the bachelor of arts degree in 1934, the master of arts in 1937, and the doctor of philosophy in 1940. His work at Harvard was the foundation of his scholarly career, as his honors thesis was published as his first book, *The Milk of Paradise*, and an expanded version of his doctoral dissertation became *The Mirror and the Lamp*. In 1937 Abrams married Ruth Gaynes, with whom he had two daughters. Abrams taught at Harvard until 1945, when he joined Cornell University, becoming Frederic J. Whiton Professor of English in 1960, Class of 1916 Professor in 1973, and professor emeritus in 1983.

Abrams has received many awards and prizes, including the Christian Gauss Prize for *The Mirror and the Lamp* in 1954 and the James Russell Lowell Prize for *Natural Supernaturalism* in 1972. He has been a Rockefeller, Ford, and Guggenheim fellow and a guest lecturer at the Royal University of Malta, Indiana University, Cambridge University, and the University of Toronto, among others. In 1977 he was a Visiting Fellow at All Souls' College, Oxford. He is also an advisory editor of the publishing firm of W. W. Norton and Company and a member of the advisory council of scholars of the Library of Congress.

Influence

Abrams' work as a historian and interpreter of the Romantic movement, not only in Britain but also in Germany and France, is so vast and pervasive that it is difficult to classify it. He is a literary critic, an aesthetician, a historian of ideas, a philosopher, and a theologian. Abrams' work in the Romantic period has helped readers and critics to recognize it as the beginning of the modern age and to view it as a continuing influence on human life, not as a dead period lost in the past.

Abrams has extended his influence into the classroom through his editorship of *The Norton Anthology of English Literature*, which is often used in survey courses of English literature. His *A Glossary of Literary Terms* frequently provides students with their first exposure to the language of literary criticism.

Analysis

Abrams has stated that he has no critical method other than intuition and personal judgment, that is, his own sense of what literary works and philosophical concepts are proper to help explain and elucidate a work of art, theory, or idea. When intuition and judgment are informed by such immense erudition as that of Abrams, the result resembles a great tree which sends out in many directions roots in the form of references to earlier writers and branches in the form of comments on the connections between the Romantics and such twentieth-century authors as D. H. Lawrence, James Joyce, and Wallace Stevens.

In *The Mirror and the Lamp* and several critical essays, Abrams explains the shift from the eighteenth-century neoclassical view of a work of art as a mimetic imitation of reality (the mirror) to the Romantic view of a work of art as a reflector of the mind of the artist (the lamp) which helps not only to shed light on the world but actually to define it, a shift which has led to the modern view of art and, for that matter, to the modern view of our relationship to the universe and our role in it. Yet instead of comparing the Romantic writers to those theorists of art who immediately preceded them, such as Samuel Johnson and Sir Joshua Reynolds, Abrams begins his discussion with Plato and Aristotle and discusses every aesthetician from ancient times to the Romantic period and beyond, linking the Romantics with their Victorian descendants, such as John Stuart Mill, John Ruskin, Matthew Arnold, and Walter Pater.

In the course of this lengthy survey, Abrams points out how the concern of those who think about art began to move from the work of art itself to the relation between the work of art and the audience and finally to the relation between the artist and the work of art. In the nineteenth century it became clear that artist, art, and audience could not be separated, as many neoclassical and earlier theorists had assumed, but must be seen as parts of a process resulting in a unity. This view, presented most powerfully in Samuel Taylor Coleridge's *Biographia Literaria* (1817), led to the modern organic view of art which is now embraced by almost every thinker on the subject, even those who deny importance to either the artist or the audience.

Two analogies help to clarify this change. In an essay on William Wordsworth, Abrams points out that while the eighteenth century had thought of words as being like clothing for ideas, the Romantic poets insisted that words were the incarnation of ideas. The metaphor of clothing typifies the eighteenth-century approach to art as assemblage based on critical recipes, while Wordsworth's theory is based on a unity of thought and expression. Clothes may be removed and considered separately from that which they contain, but incarnation involves fusion of idea and expression into a third, new, and indivisible unity.

This view of art found most apt expression in Coleridge's comparison of the work of art to a plant, a living entity which draws sustenance from both the earth and air and converts it by a mysterious process into new growth which is vitally interrelated both with itself and with the environment around it, returning nourishment to that which had nurtured its growth. Cut off a part of the plant, and that part will die, just as the parts of a properly made poem cannot be taken from their created context and retain their power. Merely to assemble supposingly pleasing parts into a whole without thought of the total form or total impact Coleridge called the operation of fancy, while to make the observed world into a new whole was an act of vision aided by the poet's imagination, a faculty analogous to the mysterious growth processes of a plant.

The plant metaphor was a challenge to what the Romantics saw as the dark forces of scientific rationalism and Enlightenment epistemological theories of association, which, by viewing the physical world as a set of objects independent of humankind and learned of in a fragmentary way, doomed people to be severed from the world in which they live. The consequences of that separation were obvious in the growing social and psychological problems of the Industrial Revolution.

Abrams explains the philosophical challenge which the Romantics offered to that increasingly discrete view of humanity and nature in his other huge scholarly work, *Natural Supernaturalism*, which deals with the content of the Romantic movement as *The Mirror and the Lamp* had dealt with its form and theories of art. The link between the two books is the Romantic poets' recognition that art is not mere ornamentation and instruction but an expression of humanity's living soul. During the seventeenth and eighteenth centuries the advance of science and philosophy had driven religion into a corner and reduced it to the status of a myth, but spiritual impulses had not disappeared and had emerged in the secularization of former religious feeling in the guise of art. The Romantics set about the task of doing what their aesthetic theory demanded, making art the vehicle for what had formerly been religion.

Natural Supernaturalism borrows its title from Thomas Carlyle, who used that phrase to describe the attempts of the Romantic poets to find religious meaning in people's association with nature and first focuses on Wordsworth's "Prospectus" (1814) for *The Recluse*, the long philosophical poem which the poet never completed. The empiricism and rationalism of the eighteenth century having dramatized humanity's estrangement from nature (what the twentieth century would come to call alienation), the Romantics, and Wordsworth in particular, recognized that we live in a world fallen out of a state of unity and harmony with nature, a state which must be restored if humanity is again to thrive and grow. As Abrams had begun his book on Romantic aesthetics with Plato, he returned to the biblical writers to explain our fallen state, as did the Romantics themselves. Other integrative poets, such as Edmund Spenser and John Milton – who attempted to explain the reasons for people's sense of separation and despair and also to bring humanity back into a proper, complete, and fulfilling relationship with all creation – also illuminate Abrams' explanations, as they served as models for the Romantics, particularly Wordsworth, William Blake, and Percy Bysshe Shelley.

As Wordsworth stated in his "Prospectus," the role of the poet is to reunite humanity with all creation by an act of mind and imagination and thereby reintegrate the personality whose shattering had been exemplified in the biblical story of the Fall. When people began to think pluralistically, the first separate object they discovered was their own self apart from the world, and science and utilitarianism had compounded this error. Biblical sources, however, also provided in the Book of Revelation the model for the reunification of humanity with itself and with nature through the apocalyptic account of the end of this world and the establishment of a new kingdom of God. For the early Romantics, the French Revolution, with its insistence on the importance of the individual and the rights of humanity, was seen as the earthly sign of such a millennium, but the Reign of Terror disillusioned thinkers all over Europe.

The French Revolution had failed precisely because it was secular and insufficiently spiritual. Wordsworth, who described his personal encounters with the Revolution in *The Prelude* (1799, 1805, 1850), came to realize that the kingdom of God is within us and attempted in his poetry a record of a spiritual journey which ended in the same place where it began, with humanity in and a part of creation, but with the difference that people, through an act of imagination aided by the experience of art, return to their previous position, but with a new awareness, informed by spiritual values, of what they and the world are. The form of the Romantic spiritual journey is not a circle, which is unfulfilling since it ends where it begins, but a spiral, which moves to the same point but on a higher level, incorporating, assimilating, and understanding all that has been experienced.

Coleridge contributed to the new vision not only with his poetry and aesthetic theories but also with an attempt to bring science into the reintegrative plan with the theory that the universe is composed of the powers of light and gravitation, which, brought into a right relationship, produce life and unity. Shelley thought that artists must be active participants in the social and political affairs of humankind in order to bring about necessary changes leading to spiritual enlightenment on this earth, and Blake differed from the integrative theory only in his view that the phenomenal world is a sham and that the true condition of both people and the universe is spiritual. In Blake's view, to strengthen the spirit was to build Jerusalem, another biblical model for the expression of essential unity.

Abrams' work is not without some flaws; he tends to regard a text's meaning as evident, preferring to discuss the philosophical implications of that meaning as he perceives it rather than to investigate other interpretive possibilities. Also, he writes mostly about Wordsworth and Coleridge, preferring to leave extensive discussion of Blake and Shelley to such friends and colleagues as Northrop Frye and Harold Bloom. He has written little on John Keats, whose sensuous approach to poetry does not fit his own philosophical bent, and almost nothing on Lord Byron, whose humor and irony undercut the visionary and apocalyptic stance of the other Romantics, although Abrams once proposed another volume focused on Byron as counterpoint to the arguments raised in *The Mirror and the Lamp* and *Natural Supernaturalism*. Yet these shortcomings, if that is what they are, are balanced by his extensive commentary on G. W. F. Hegel, Friedrich Schlegel, Friedrich Hölderlin, Novalis, and other German Romantics, whose impact on and similarity to the views of the English Romantics is sometimes overlooked or minimized.

After the publication of *Natural Supernaturalism*, Abrams continued to issue essays on the poets and movement which he treated so expertly in that work and in *The Mirror and the Lamp*, but he has also written a number of articles which defend not only the Romantic poets but literature itself from the attempts of logical positivists and deconstructionists to reduce literature to a merely linguistic game with no reference outside itself. Abrams has reaffirmed continually his basic belief that literature is above all by human beings and addressed to human beings, in an attempt to enrich and enliven human existence.

Principal criticism

The Milk of Paradise: The Effect of Opium Visions on the Works of De Quincey, Crabbe, Francis Thompson, and Coleridge, 1934, second edition 1970
The Mirror and the Lamp: Romantic Theory and the Critical Tradition, 1953
The Poetry of Pope, 1954 (editor)
A Glossary of Literary Terms, 1957, fifth edition 1987
Literature and Belief, 1958 (editor), includes "Belief and the Suspension of Disbelief"
English Romantic Poets: Modern Essays in Criticism, 1960, second edition 1975 (editor)
"Five Types of Lycidas," 1961
The Norton Anthology of English Literature, 1962, fifth edition 1987 (editor, with others)
"English Romanticism: The Spirit of the Age," 1963
"Structure and Style in the Greater Romantic Lyric," 1965
"Coleridge, Baudelaire, and Modernist Poetics," 1966
Natural Supernaturalism: Tradition and Revolution in Romantic Literature, 1971
"What's the Use of Theorizing About the Arts?" 1972
Wordsworth: A Collection of Critical Essays, 1972 (editor)
"Coleridge and the Romantic Vision of the World," 1974
"A Note on Wittgenstein and Literary Criticism," 1974
"Rationality and Imagination in Cultural History: A Reply to Wayne Booth," 1976
"The Limits of Pluralism II: The Deconstructive Angel," 1977
"Behavior and Deconstruction: A Comment on Morse Peckham's 'The Infinitude of Pluralism,'" 1977
"How to Do Things with Texts," 1979
William Wordsworth: The Prelude, 1799, 1805, 1850, 1979 (editor, with others)
The Correspondent Breeze: Essays on English Romanticism, 1984
Doing Things With Texts: Essays in Criticism and Critical Theory, 1989
"The Transformation of English Studies, 1930–1995," 1997

Other major works and literary forms

In addition to the books and essays listed above, M. H. Abrams has published many other critical essays and reviews, the most significant of which are collected in *The Correspondent Breeze* and *Doing Things With Texts*. He is known primarily if not exclusively as a literary critic.

Further reading

Booth, Wayne C. "M. H. Abrams: Historian as Critic, Critic as Pluralist," in *Critical Inquiry*. II (Spring, 1976), pp. 411–445.
——. "History as Metaphor: Or, Is M. H. Abrams a Mirror, or a Lamp, or a Fountain, or . . .?" in *High Romantic Argument: Essays for M. H. Abrams*, 1981. Edited by Lawrence Lipking.
Culler, Jonathan. "The Mirror Stage," in *High Romantic Argument: Essays for M. H. Abrams*, 1981. Edited by Lawrence Lipking.

Ende, Stuart A. "A Bibliography of M. H. Abrams," in *High Romantic Argument: Essays for M. H. Abrams*, 1981. Edited by Lawrence Lipking.
Lipking, Lawrence, ed. *High Romantic Argument: Essays for M. H. Abrams*, 1981.
McFarland, Thomas. "A Coleridgean Criticism of the Work of M. H. Abrams," in *High Romantic Argument: Essays for M. H. Abrams*, 1981. Edited by Lawrence Lipking.

JAMES BAIRD

See also Coleridge; Romanticism; American Literary Theory: Twentieth Century

The Absurd

"The Absurd" as a theoretical term slowly evolved out of European existentialism and became an umbrella expression for a certain type of experimental modernist theater. Existentialism gathered currency as a philosophy in France in the 1940s after the publication of Jean-Paul Sartre's celebrated *L'Être et le néant* (1943; *Being and Nothingness*, 1956) which propounded the first atheist philosophy of human freedom. In Sartre's view, humankind is "condemned to be free" in a godless world. In this divine vacuum we must then construct our own values. In other words, the purposeless, absurd nature of existence is a tabula rasa on which we must invest our own meaning and imprint our own ethical system. Sartre also illustrated the philosophical impulse of *Being and Nothingness* in works such as the novel *La Nausée* (1938; *Nausea*, 1949) and in the obliquely political drama *Les Mouches* (1943; *The Flies*, 1947). In its treatment of the common, or habitual, environment as a strange, unfamiliar place his creative work bears some affinity with that of Franz Kafka and Albert Camus who, in *Die Verwandlung* (1915; *Metamorphosis*, 1915) and *La Peste* (1947; *The Plague*, 1948) respectively, explore the effect on the human mind when it is confronted with bizarre circumstances which presuppose an entirely random or godless world.

Each of these experimental writers emphasized the notion of absurdity as an inescapable aspect of life and paved the way for Martin Esslin's appropriation of this perspective to describe complementary experimental shifts in the theater. The critical view in question is expounded in Esslin's groundbreaking work *The Theatre of the Absurd* (1964) and also in *Samuel Beckett: A Collection of Critical Essays* (1965). Taken together these works consolidate the view of Samuel Beckett as the canonical absurdist writer. Moreover, they also represent the first comprehensive critical evaluation of experimental European theater in which Esslin identifies meaninglessness as the constant dominant in the work of such diverse authors as Eugène Ionesco, Jean Genet, Harold Pinter, and Robert Pinget. For example, Esslin writes that in comparison to the Aristotelean notion of the "good play" with a clear cause/effect/resolution structure, an absurdist work seems often to have "neither a beginning nor an end." Further, he believes that "if a good play relies on witty repartee and pointed dialogue, [the absurdist one] often consist[s] of incoherent babblings." Faced with drama that lacks the determinate contextual structure inherited from ancient Greek tragedy – a structure that is still present in most traditional dramatic production – Esslin is forced to speculate that a writer like Beckett is concerned with conveying "the author's sense of ... anxiety when confronted with the human condition, and his despair at being unable to find a meaning to existence." Thus, Esslin proposes "the Absurd" as an organizing term for categorizing a variety of drama in which transparent meaning is not clear and in which the action does not conform to conventional theatrical expectations. He also makes the point that

> Most of the incomprehension with which plays of this type are still being received by critics and theatrical reviewers, most of the bewilderment they have caused and to which they still give rise, comes from the fact that they are part of a new, and still developing stage convention that has not yet been fully understood and has hardly ever been defined.

This quotation is revealing for two reasons. Primarily, Esslin does not follow his own dictum wherein the plays are "a still developing stage convention" which has not yet been "fully understood" as this would require a certain "opening up" of interpretative possibility; an allowance of heterogeneous significance and the production of multiple meanings. Rather, he attempts to categorize diverse works on the basis of their similarities and not their differences. In this regard, and although it is persuasive and instructive, his theoretical approach is at odds with a current and prevailing trend in literary theory in which the primary goal of examination is the identification and recognition of difference and plurality. Changes in theoretical approaches predicated on poststructuralism's recognition and prioritization of the principle of play have resulted in a critic like Jean-François Lyotard commenting that "in Beckett's theatre, silence and a certain indefiniteness suggest that something is at stake." In this formulation, Esslin's view that an absurdist work seems to have "neither a beginning nor an end" or that it "often consist[s] of incoherent babblings" is a reduction or foreclosure on the possible meanings, or significance, of Beckett's work. Put simply, Beckett's work is not an exercise in absurdity or meaninglessness but a creative act the significance of which has not as yet been articulated, and may not indeed be explainable. This does not however signify that the work is meaningless; rather, it becomes the site of productive, interpretative play.

As a further example of cultural shifts altering the nature of absurdist aesthetics, Vaclav Havel, during his presidency of the Czech Republic, occasionally wore a T-shirt showing the gagged face of Beckett accompanied by the written caption that "If Samuel Beckett had been born in Czechoslovakia we would still be waiting for Godot." Havel elaborated on the meaning of this slogan when he said that

> One can wait in different ways. The way in *Waiting for Godot*, incarnation of waiting for universal liberation and salvation, occupies one of the extremes of a vast range of possible forms of waiting. For many of those who, like us, lived in the Communist era, waiting was often or even permanently of a kind very close to this extreme form.

However, from the experience of the sheer intensity of this waiting Havel has drawn a lesson regarding the virtue of patience in politics, and of allowing history to operate in its own time:

> In a word, I thought that time was mine. I had made a serious mistake. The world, being and history are governed by their own time, on which we can intervene creatively but which no-one can ever dominate.

Put another way, he believes that by "intervening creatively" on time, writers such as Beckett and himself can undertake modest imaginative exercises in which time is respected for its possibility. A work like *Waiting for Godot*, for all of its lack of any immediate clarion cry toward political mobilization or collective and decisive political action, nonetheless makes an inscription in time that will be carried forward by time itself. If the inscription remains open and is not an attempt to overcome time, it respects the openness of time itself. In other words, one, or a hundred creative authors cannot change the world, but an inscription made in respect of time leaves open the possibility of the world's alteration, and, with it, the return of critical possibility to the site of absurdist theater.

Further reading

Elam, Keir. "Catastrophic Mistakes: Beckett, Havel, The End," in *Samuel Beckett Today/Aujourd'hui*. 3 (1994), p. 5. (Originally printed in *La Repubblica*, November 4, 1992.)

Esslin, Martin. *The Theatre of the Absurd*, 1961.

Hinchliffe, Arnold P. *The Absurd*, 1972.

Lyotard, Jean-François. "Return upon the Return," in *Toward the Postmodern*, 1993. Edited by Robert Harvey and Mark S. Roberts.

McMullan, Anna. *Theatre on Trial*, 1993.

Wilkinson, James D. *The Intellectual Resistance in Europe*, 1981.

RODNEY SHARKEY

See also Artaud; Esslin; Sartre

Joseph Addison

English essayist and critic

Born: Milston, England; May 1, 1672
Died: London, England; June 17, 1719

Biography

Joseph Addison was born into a modest clerical family in Milston, Wiltshire, on May 1, 1672. His father was to go on to a more important position as the Dean of Lichfield Cathedral and was to provide his son with a first-class education, at the great public school, Charterhouse, and then at Oxford University, where Addison distinguished himself as a Latin poet and a classical scholar. He was a Fellow at Magdalen College from 1697 to 1711. His literary gifts and his allegiance to the Whig Party led to his being financially supported as a young man of promise by Charles Montagu, later the Earl of Halifax, and he traveled under such patronage throughout Europe between 1699 and 1703. He began to write poetry with a Whiggish political bent on his return to England, and in 1704, he was elected to the most fashionable Whig club, the Kit-Kat.

In 1705 he collaborated for the first time with Richard Steele, helping him to revise a comedy, *The Tender Husband: Or, The Accomplished Fools* (1705). In the same year he traveled on a diplomatic mission to Hanover, where the groundwork was being laid for the succession of the Hanover ruling family to the throne of England, if Queen Anne were to die childless. He became a senior government secretary in 1706 and remained in service until the Whigs fell in 1710. Such duties were minimal, and he was engaged in writing constantly; he wrote an opera libretto, *Rosamond* (1707), to prove that Englishmen could compete with the Italians, and it had a respectable three-night run. He became a Member of Parliament in 1708 and remained in the House until 1719.

In 1709 Addison joined Steele in *The Tatler*. In 1711 they came together again with *The Spectator*. This time Addison was the major contributor, and the journal built on and surpassed the popularity of *The Tatler*, running in total to five hundred and fifty-five issues. In 1713 Addison had his greatest theatrical success with *Cato*. After the death of Queen Anne and the fall of the Tory government, he received further government appointments, and in 1717, a year after his marriage to the Countess of Warwick (and partly as a result of it), he was made Secretary of State, a post which he was forced to give up in 1718 because of failing health. His daughter Charlotte was born in 1719, and he died on June 17, 1719, at Holland House, Kensington, in the center of fashionable London.

Influence

What Addison wrote about the arts is often interesting and sometimes important, but his real contribution lies in the way he wrote it. Nothing quite like Steele and Addison's journals of social and critical commentary had been published before. Together, they may be seen as the inventors of the modern popular magazine. The idea that serious, as well as trivial, ideas could be discussed intelligently and amusingly and that literary, philosophical, and aesthetic ideas, quite free from patronizing tone, could be made accessible to the educated public was met with general praise by the British readers. Addison's systematic, as well as occasional, discussions of John Milton, wit, theatrical taste, the ballad, and literary, musical, and visual arts in general were to have an enormous influence on British middle-class taste, not only in the eighteenth century but also well into the nineteenth.

Analysis

Addison's criticism must be seen in the context of his work as a popular journalist, since much of his commentary on the arts lies in *The Spectator*. *The Spectator* (like all of his nonpolitical writing) was a cultural phenomenon mirroring several different aspects of Addison's training, beliefs, and ambitions. It was, in the first instance, a fulfillment of his classical training, founded on the belief that literature has a duty to educate through pleasing. That old Horatian idea is a constant in *The Spectator* and *The Tatler* articles, brought up to date by Addison and Steele's awareness of the fact that in the first years of the eighteenth century there was a rapidly developing desire among the rising and expanding middle classes (many of them with connections to the financial and mercantile life of London) for guidance in how to live better lives, not only morally but also materially and aesthetically. The people of the middle classes wanted, in short, someone to tell them how to choose, how to make their lives civilized, and the development of the popular press was a response to that desire.

Connected to this social movement were the philosophical ideas of the great Whig theorist John Locke, who in his *An Essay Concerning Human Understanding* (1690) and in *Some Thoughts Concerning Education* (1693) had, stunningly, simplified the mystery of human knowledge by proving that all that was known came from five senses and that by exposing those senses to the best of everything, the perfectly educated, civilized human being could be manipulated into ideal maturity. It was to become the basis for all future educational theory, but Addison saw that it could be used outside the world of formal education, that it could be the basis for a commercially successful form of literature which would supplement education by constant, low-key instruction through anecdote and fictional example. Part of the attraction was the cheerful manner in which Addison and Steele went about their ambitious (some might say presumptuous) task of civilizing an entire society, or, at least, those members of it who could afford the modest charge for the paper – and its circulation was surprisingly high for the time. The Restoration period had been an age of tough satire, and that movement was to be carried on with great success by writers such as Jonathan Swift and Alexander Pope, but there was a movement after the turn of the century to a gentler kind of criticism, a belief in the idea that errant behavior was best met by gentle laughter (at its most theoretical, it shows up in Anthony Ashley Cooper, Earl of Shaftesbury's *Characteristicks of Men, Manners, Opinions, Times*, published in 1711), and by offering refined, knowledgeable guidance with Horatian grace rather than with Juvenalian harshness.

Addison was the master of this sophisticated, tender paternalism, and it can be seen not only in his social essays but also in his critical essays, which always have a strong sense of social pertinence. In *The Tatler* papers, Addison had occasionally introduced the idea that literature, however modest, had the obligation to discuss virtue and doctrine, but he never allowed such serious obligations to take the easy charm out of the papers, and his choice of artistic subjects was strongly influenced by the knowledge that gentlemen, in the long tradition of courtesy and social obligation, would and could talk sensibly about art.

When he took the position of leadership with *The Spectator*, Addison seized the opportunity for extended critical discussion. John Milton's *Paradise Lost* (1667), despite its Puritan associations, was very popular in the early eighteenth century, and Addison devoted seventeen articles to Milton's epic, beginning with issue 267 of *The Spectator* and ending with issue 369. Given the intervening articles on all sorts of topics, one might suppose that Addison's audience would grow weary of such prolonged attention to a single work, but the eighteenth-century reader liked long poems and was particularly impressed by the epic. It is not surprising, then, that Addison should begin with four essays in which he argued that Milton's poem could stand with those of Homer and Virgil. If the early-eighteenth-century British writer, with his shyness about deep feeling and his general inclination to skepticism, seemed unable to write the epic and contented himself with some of the finest mock epics ever written, readers still believed that there was a hierarchy of excellence in literature and that the epic stood first. Addison's detailed attention to Milton proved very popular and was to establish the central critical and popular attitude toward that poem which was to last well into the nineteenth century.

This same awareness of what the public wanted as well as needed appears repeatedly in Addison's criticism. The intrusion of Italian opera on the English stage, which the English found fascinating, silly, confusing, and impossible to resist, provoked him beyond sly disdain to a series of articles in which he proposed the repudiation of the new, foreign craze for a return to tragedy as the great dramatic form, at once just as entertaining and intellectually and morally more valuable. The constant moral bent of his criticism is especially strong in these essays, and his commitment to conservative ideas of how tragedy works is balanced by his appreciation for ways in which British tragic playwrights break the rules to artistically fruitful ends.

His deep knowledge of the classical literature and criticism is constantly in action in his criticism, but it never hampers the play of what is essentially a neoclassical sensibility, as deeply influenced by the thinkers of his own time as by those of the distinguished past. His discussions, social or literary, are deeply influenced by Locke, not only by the way in which Locke suggested that humans collected ideas and then rearranged them in their minds but also by the way in which Locke's ideas could be used to examine the nature of how literature worked on the human being. His series on the imagination, on the Sublime, on True and False Wit, on medieval literature, all have touches of Lockeanism about them. Yet they also indicate that Addison had more than an admirable mix of classical learning and contemporary neoclassical conservatism, with its emphasis on rules tempered by common sense and tasteful discrimination.

If Romanticism jumped fully grown out of William Wordsworth and Samuel Taylor Coleridge's preface to the *Lyrical Ballads* (1800 edition), there were plenty of signs that it was coming, particularly through the last half of the century. Indeed, the attempt to bring feeling back into literature, which the Restoration writers had rigorously expunged, was tentatively explored at some length in Addison's essays, and any attempt to trace the rising interest in feeling, in tenderness, in deep emotion, must begin with his work. If Addison confirmed the basic neoclassical ideas of how literature worked for the betterment of humankind, how it represented by example how people conducted themselves as social animals, his Neo-Platonic tendency to see art as going beyond social to spiritual proportions was to lead him to discuss the way in which art went beyond the mind to the feelings. This is where Addison's work leads, rather than simply confirming old ideas.

Addison may scurry back to the shelter of the reason too often to be a true innovator, as he does in accepting the idea that the pleasures of the understanding which art provides are superior to the pleasures of the imagination, but the cat was slipping out of the bag, and those pleasures were to become stronger as the century progressed. His mixing of Lockean ideas about the importance of the "eye" in experience with Longinian ideas of the Sublime led him to anticipate the work that Edmund Burke did almost fifty years later in his essay "On the Sublime and Beautiful," part of a major movement in British arts toward a new emphasis on the feelings.

Even more immediately revolutionary was Addison's serious consideration of certain kinds of literature which were judged unworthy of civilized attention. In issue 419 of *The Spectator*, he retrieves the fantasy world of fairies, witches, and demons and brings in Shakespeare to prove how such subjects can be made respectable. In issues 70 and 74 of *The Spectator*, he praises the old ballad "Chevy Chase," and he comes back to unsophisticated, seemingly primitive medieval work again in issue 85. This breaking with the established canon to champion unfashionable works of obvious feeling and simplicity is a confirmation of his independence and a mark of his creative energies as a critic.

Addison was never entirely satisfied with instructing his society in all that is best, although he certainly did that. He tended, if with some temerity, to lead his readers into areas of experience which they had not contemplated. Certainly his interest in how literature works, and in how some old kinds of literature, such as the ballad, might be read within the wider context of such theories of artistic experience, was to aid immeasurably in the widening of the technical, thematic, and tonal range of literature later in the century. If it can be said that Addison displayed what were the central judgments on literature in the first quarter of the century, it can also be said that he suggested where literature was going and that he was, in large part, responsible for preparing the readers of that society to adjust to the new literature of feeling.

He also provided the model for the journal of informed opinion which suggested that the arts were of concern to the modestly educated human being, not only because they carried messages of social and ethical moment but also because they added to the richness of life. Twentieth-century journals such as *The Atlantic, Harper's Magazine*, and the present-day version of *The Spectator* in England carry on that distinguished tradition of providing informed comment on life and the arts without the impediment of pedantic obfuscation. Addison taught an entire society that an understanding of the arts belonged, as he said, to the tea table and the coffeehouse, as well as to the library and the schoolroom, and that such understanding could be expressed with wit and charm.

Principal criticism

Essays in *The Tatler* (1709–1711), *The Spectator* (1711–1712, 1714), and *The Guardian* (1713)

Other major works and literary forms

Joseph Addison began his literary career as a poet, first in Latin and later in English, and as a critic of classical literature. This was his most limited work, but it was, in miniature, an indication of the depth of his scholarship, which would provide him with the background for his most popular and most famous work as a critic of the arts. Addison was also something of a playwright, and his tragedy *Cato* (1713) was very popular. In addition, he had a long and effective career as a political essayist with publications such as *The Freeholder: Or, Political Essays* (1715–1716). It is also important to remember that he was, in and out of collaboration with Sir Richard Steele, a major commentator on British society and that the scope of *The Tatler* and *The Spectator* was enormously wide-ranging in topics which extended from aesthetic criticism to the minutiae of social and personal conduct.

PLAYS
Rosamond, 1707 (libretto; music by Thomas Clayton)
Cato, 1713
The Drummer: Or, The Haunted House, 1716

POETRY
To Mr. Dryden, 1693
A Poem to His Majesty, 1695
Praelum Inter Pygmaeos et Grues Commisum, 1699
A Letter from Italy, 1703
The Campaign, 1705
To Her Royal Highness, 1716
To Sir Godfrey Kneller on His Portrait of the King, 1716

NONFICTION
Remarks upon Italy, 1705
Dialogues upon the Usefulness of Ancient Medals, 1721
Letters, 1941 (Walter Graham, editor)

TRANSLATIONS
Fourth Georgic, 1694 (of Virgil's *Georgics*)

MISCELLANEOUS
The Freeholder: Or, Political Essays, 1715–1716
The Miscellaneous Works, 1914 (A. C. Guthkelch, editor)
The Spectator, 1965 (Donald Bond, editor)

Further reading

Bond, Richard P. *"The Tatler": The Making of a Journal*, 1971.
Elioseff, Lee Andrew. *The Cultural Milieu of Addison's Literary Criticism*, 1963.
Evans, James E., and John N. Wall, Jr. *A Guide to Prose Fiction in "The Tatler" and "The Spectator,"* 1977.
Ketcham, Michael G. *Transparent Designs: Reading, Performance and Form in The "Spectator" Papers*, 1985.
Otten, Robert M. *Joseph Addison*, 1982.
Smithers, Peter. *The Life of Joseph Addison*, 1968.

CHARLES PULLEN

See also Dryden; Johnson; Neoclassical Literary Theory; Pope

Theodor Adorno

(Theodor Wiesengrund)

German critic and philosopher

Born: Frankfurt am Main, Germany; September 11, 1903
Died: Visp, Switzerland; August 6, 1969

Biography

Theodor Adorno was born Theodor Wiesengrund in 1903 in Frankfurt am Main, Germany. His mother, the daughter of a German singer and a French army officer (whose Corsican and originally Genoese ancestry accounts for the name Adorno, the name by which Theodor was known after his emigration from Germany), was a talented singer from whom he inherited a love of music; his father was a successful wine merchant of Jewish extraction. While attending secondary school, Adorno studied privately with Siegfried Kracauer, the German historian and social critic. From 1925 to 1928 he studied music with Alban Berg and Eduard Steuermann in Vienna. Returning to the University of Frankfurt in 1928, Adorno wrote his qualifying paper on the aesthetics of Søren Kierkegaard.

In 1931 he became a lecturer at the University, where he became involved with the Institut für Sozialforschung (Institute for Social Research) and published numerous articles in its journal, *Zeitschrift für Sozialforschung*. The Institute was established by a group of radical Marxist scholars whose goal was to assess modern society through an interdisciplinary study of its cultural and philosophical phenomena. Soon after Adolf Hitler's rise to power, the Institute moved to the United States; Adorno officially joined in 1938, when he moved to New York City. In 1941 Adorno moved to Los Angeles and continued to write prolifically, although most of his manuscripts remained unpublished until after his return to Germany in 1949. While in Los Angeles, he renewed his acquaintance with Arnold Schönberg and assisted Thomas Mann with the musical sections of his novel *Doktor Faustus* (1947; *Doctor Faustus*, 1948). He became assistant director of the Institute for Social Research in 1950 and codirector, with Max Horkheimer, in 1955. He continued to teach and publish numerous essays and books until his death in Visp, Switzerland, in 1969.

Influence

Adorno was among the first cultural critics to propose a consistent theory of popular culture and to analyze the various aspects and functions of the modern cultural market, mass cultural consumption, and what he and Max Horkheimer called the "culture industry" (the task of which is to supply the cultural market with products specifically designed to induce a state of relaxation or escape). In essays written as early as 1941, Adorno describes the need of the masses for distraction as both a product and a result of the existing capitalist economy.

Analysis

Probably the first lesson one learns from reading Adorno's literary criticism (or any of his cultural criticism) is that any attempt to codify or systematize his work is bound to fail. One of his major philosophical works, *Negative Dialektik* (1966; *Negative Dialectics*, 1973), illustrates the reasons for this. The self-contradictory term "negative dialectics" is meant to affirm the idea and value of an ultimate synthesis, while negating its existence in individual instances. Adorno argues that every theory about the world, as it is formed, tends to become reified by the mind and to be invested with the prestige and permanency of an object, thus effacing the very dialectical process from which it emerged. It is this optical illusion of the substantiality of thought which negative dialectics attempts to dispel.

Thus, Adorno's negative dialectics is not Marxist dialectical materialism in the conventional sense of the term. Reviving Karl Marx's "materialist" critique of G. W. F. Hegel, Adorno, as well as his colleagues at the Institute for Social Research, believed that there was no ontological primacy of spirit over matter, nor a logical priority of the thinking subject over the material object. Consequently, they sought a principle which would legitimize both the intellectual comprehension of the world and its radical critique; they also relentlessly attacked the opposition between culture and a superior sphere of human endeavor and material existence as a lesser aspect of the human condition.

The goals and methods of the Institute (later known as the Frankfurt School), as well as the historical situation out of which it arose, are important factors to consider in any discussion of Adorno's work. Under the directorship of Max Horkheimer, Adorno's longtime colleague and collaborator, the Institute's theorists focused on the interdisciplinary nature of "social research." This social research, however, is not to be confused with sociology or *Geisteswissenschaft* (cultural sciences) as practiced in German universities, which fostered a tradition of treating intellectual history in a social vacuum. Rather, Adorno and fellow members of the Frankfurt School devoted themselves to what became known as *kritische Theorie* (critical theory).

Using the dialectical method, critical theory's practitioners engaged in a dialogue with both other schools of Marxist thought and with a changing historical situation (the success of the Russian Revolution and socialism's advance eastward). The two poles of critical theory's dialectic (as opposed to Hegel's dialectic between subject and object, or mind and matter based on the primacy of the absolute subject) were praxis (more specifically, the relation of theory to praxis) and reason (*Vernunft*, or an appreciation of the dialectical relations beneath surface appearances). Praxis, in the sense in which it is used here, has been defined as

> a kind of self-creating action, which differed from the externally motivated behavior produced by forces outside man's control . . . . One of the earmarks of *praxis*, as opposed to mere action, was its being informed by theoretical considerations.

One of the Institute's major tasks was to explore how the social and cultural order could be transformed through praxis.

Sharing the interdisciplinary goals and methods of the Institute for Social Research, Theodor Adorno, in his role as a critic of modern culture, investigated many forms outside literature:

> The task of criticism must not be so much to search for the particular interest-groups to which cultural phenomena are to be assigned, but rather to decipher the general social tendencies which are expressed in these phenomena and through which the most powerful interests realize themselves. Cultural criticism must become social physiognomy.

What distinguishes Adorno's sociology of art from its more orthodox Marxist counterparts (the theory of Georg Lukács, for example) is its refusal to reduce cultural phenomena to an ideological vehicle of class interests. In Adorno's view, art not only expresses and reflects social tendencies but also serves as the last preserve of individual subjectivity in the face of historical forms which threaten to crush it. A dialectical critique of art, Adorno argues, "takes seriously the principle that it is not ideology in itself which is untrue but rather its pretention to correspond to reality."

In a widely read essay entitled "On Commitment," published in 1962, Adorno argues that Bertolt Brecht's plays are fundamentally flawed, both aesthetically and politically, by the author's heavy-handed political didacticism and oversimplified presentation of such realities of the contemporary world as capitalism, Fascism, or Communism. Even more destructive is Brecht's tendency to "preach to the converted," to distort "the real social problems discussed in his epic drama in order to prove a thesis." Echoing Friedrich Engel's injunction (in a letter to Ferdinand LaSalle, May 8, 1859) that "the more the author's views are concealed the better for the work of art," Adorno goes on to say that "the gravest charge against commitment is that even right intentions go wrong when they are noticed, and still more so, when they then try to conceal themselves." Critics of Adorno have pointed out that his treatment of "committed" writing is often narrow and one-sided; in attacking polemics, Adorno himself turns polemicist.

In this same essay attacking the theory and practice of "committed" literature in the works of Jean-Paul Sartre and Bertolt Brecht, Adorno praises Franz Kafka and Samuel Beckett as true models of a critical, revolutionary art. Instead of the artificially reconciled and positive outlook of the directly "political," Beckett's "dissonant" (exhibiting a state of unresolved tension) and "negative" art refuses to pacify and console.

> Kafka's prose and Beckett's plays, or the truly monstrous novel *The Unnamable*, have an effect by comparison with which the officially committed works look like pantomimes . . . . By dismantling appearance, they explode from within the art which committed proclamation subjugates from without, and hence only in appearance. The inescapability of their work compels the change of attitude which committed works merely demand.

Adorno believed that Beckett was the one truly outstanding literary figure to emerge after World War II, and he even intended to dedicate *Ästhetische Theorie* (1970; *Aesthetic Theory*, 1986) – published posthumously – to the author.

In a 1959 essay on *Fin de partie* (1957; *Endgame*, 1958), Adorno describes Beckett's work as a continuation of Kafka's relentless reminder of the death of personality in the contemporary world; still, this abandonment of selfhood had now advanced further. In Adorno's view, Beckett's work is not ahistorically "existential" but powerfully suggestive of the absence of the self.

> Instead of excluding the temporal from existence, . . . [Beckett] subtracts that which time – the historical trend – is in reality preparing to annul. He extends the trajectory of the subject's liquidation to the point where it shrinks to the here-and-now. . . . History is excluded because it has dried up the power of consciousness to conceive history: the power of memory. . . . All that appears of history is its result, its decline.

Adorno writes that in Beckett's art "all that remains of freedom is the impotent and ridiculous reflex of empty decisions."

Equally pessimistic is Adorno's famous statement on the place of art in the modern world: "To write poetry after Auschwitz is barbaric." He meant that even art that is "dissonant" is inadequate, because it contains hopeful language and imagery which have the power to elicit aesthetic enjoyment. The horror vanishes; the sound of despair becomes a "hideous affirmation." Yet the work of Beckett (and Arnold Schönberg) provides a glimpse of hope by its capacity to express even the slightest of contemporary society's horrors. In Adorno's view, as long as their discordant sounds are heard and appreciated, their artistic power would enable them to keep alive the possibility of a "consonant" utopia in their honest acknowledgment of its absence.

In his discussion of the modern novel, Adorno argues that traditional bourgeois realism is no longer a historically viable option. Only the type of fragmentation of personality and narrative "standpoint" as appears in the works of such writers as Marcel Proust, James Joyce, or Robert Musil, for example, could adequately represent the extent of individual alienation, torment, and impotence in contemporary life. Telling a traditional realistic story from a single narrative perspective would nullify collective guilt and suggest that the individual still has independent meaning and power in society. On the other hand, modern novelists who disjointedly interrupt narration, present it from multiple perspectives, reveal the power of objects in the unconscious or thoughts of powerless "characters," and construct the whole through associational logic of the parts are more "truthful" in their representation of contemporary life, according to Adorno. Yet these novelists' techniques must serve to demonstrate, in a potentially critical way, the disintegration of individual subjectivity.

One legacy of Adorno's (and the Frankfurt School's) critique of modern culture is that it enriched and challenged traditional Marxist criticism and better equipped it to assess both the modernist revolt and the crisis of liberal bourgeois society in the postwar era. In twentieth-century Western culture, a culture in which traditional art is reduced to what Adorno and Horkheimer in *Dialektik der Aufklärung* (1947; *Dialectic of Enlightenment*, 1972) call "the culture industry," that is, to a form of mere entertainment, Adorno points out that the artist is obliged to create works which demand intellectual activity of themselves and of the audience.

In stressing the need for formal preoccupations and self-reflectiveness in both art and criticism, in rejecting the classical notion of organic unity, romantic subjectivity, or realist "reflection," and in emphasizing the fragmentary, ephemeral, and relativist nature of "truth" (although remaining primarily rooted in the Austro-German cultural tradition), Adorno eventually came to accept much of what the modernist revolt had attempted to achieve.

Principal criticism

Noten zur Literatur, 1958–1974 (4 volumes; partially translated as *Notes to Literature*, Vol. 1, 1991) (Rolf Tiedemann, editor; Shierry Weber Nicholsen, translator)

Other major works and literary forms

While *Noten zur Literatur* is the best-known product of Theodor Adorno's lifelong interest in literary criticism, Adorno is perhaps even better known for his essays and book-length studies in philosophy, popular culture, aesthetics, and sociology. Also a musical composer and theoretician, he published influential books on the philosophy and sociology of modern music. Adorno (along with Herbert Marcuse, a Frankfurt School colleague) was also fascinated by Freudian psychoanalytic theory and published several essays on its relationship to the social sciences.

NONFICTION

Dialektik der Aufklärung, 1947 (with Max Horkheimer; *Dialectic of Enlightenment*, 1972)

Philosophie der neuen Musik, 1949 (*The Philosophy of Modern Music*, 1973)

Prismen: Kulturkritik und Gesellschaft, 1955 (*Prisms*, 1967)

Negative Dialektik, 1966 (*Negative Dialectics*, 1973)

Ästhetische Theorie, 1970 (*Aesthetic Theory*, 1986)

Gesammelte Schriften, 1970– (20 volumes)

Further reading

Benjamin, Andrew, ed. *The Problems of Modernity: Adorno and Benjamin*, 1989.

Buck-Morss, Susan. *The Origin of Negative Dialectics*, 1977.

Harding, James Martin. *Adorno and "A Writing of the Ruins": Essays on Modern Aesthetics and Anglo-American Literature and Culture*, 1997.

Hohendahl, Peter Uwe. *Prismatic Thought: Theodor W. Adorno*, 1995.
Ingram, David. *Critical Theory and Philosophy*, 1900.
Jameson, Fredric, ed. *Marxism and Form*, 1971.
Jarvis, Simon. *Adorno: A Critical Introduction*, 1998.
Jay, Martin. *The Dialectical Imagination*, 1973.
Lichtheim, George. *From Marx to Hegel*, 1971.
Lunn, Eugene. *Marxism and Modernism*, 1982.
Roblin, Ronald, ed. *The Aesthetics of the Critical Theorists: Studies on Benjamin, Adorno, Marcuse, and Habermas*, 1990.
Varadharajan, Asha. *Exotic Parodies: Subjectivity in Adorno, Said, and Spivak*, 1995.

GENEVIEVE SLOMSKI

See also Benjamin; Brecht; Frankfurt School; Lukács; Marxist Theory and Criticism

Aestheticism

The term "aestheticism" refers to the notion that all art must be autonomous – *ars gratia artis* or "art for art's sake" – that is, art should never be "useful" as such: artistic creation may not serve any ulterior purpose, be it religious/moral, political/ideological, or social/humanitarian. Art has traditionally been regarded as being of educational import, as imitative of nature (mimesis), of divine inspiration, or (as craft) merely decorative. Didactic art (which teaches some kind of moral/ethical point), religious art, or tendentious art (which argues for/against some kind of prevailing social or political condition) represent the antithesis of autonomous art. American writer Upton Sinclair's famous "muckraking" novel *The Jungle* (1906), which attacked the terrible conditions of the Chicago meat-processing industry, would be an example of such tendentious art. In many instances, however, aestheticism is indeed associated with an epistemological (and therefore ultimately "religious") goal, that is, art – in its creation by the artist and its reception by the viewer – leads to the perception or apprehension of some kind of vision of "authentic reality." Aestheticism is closely related to the rise of twentieth-century modernism and is in many respects an outgrowth of nineteenth-century German philosophy and literary Romanticism. In its European heyday around the turn of the twentieth century, the proponents of aestheticism were considered to be decadent elitists who lived in distant "ivory towers," ultimately divorced from the real concerns of everyday middle-class people.

Classical aesthetics had demanded that all art be educational as well as entertaining. Aestheticism – art as an end in itself – is strictly a modern phenomenon, a product of sociological changes in Western civilization in general and Kantian philosophical Idealism in specific. With the advent of the Renaissance and the rise of the modern city, the sense of a village community with people performing multiple functions gave way to a sense of professional specialization and individuals began to regard themselves as belonging to specific occupations within society. With such specialization also came the need to justify one's activities with respect to the group. Not serving any obviously practical purpose within the community, artists came to regard art – and here "art" is to be distinguished clearly from decorative arts or crafts produced by artisans – as an end unto itself. The intellectual justification for this view of art came at the end of the eighteenth century in the Idealistic philosophy of Immanuel Kant. In the *Critique of Judgment* (1790), Kant discusses aesthetics: art – the "aesthetic idea" as distinct from logical thought – functions in a completely autonomous realm, completely free from both the physical necessity (nature) and moral duty (divine law) which usually define the boundaries of the human spirit. Within this aesthetic domain of absolute freedom, the human imagination reigns supremely and the artist becomes something of a creative divinity within a "universe" of his or her own conception. Art as the sole province of human autonomy is thus justified as an end in and of itself and the artist serves as a kind of religious/seer figure. The artist is discussed here as being a "genius," often a solitary individual, isolated from bourgeois society, who lives and creates on his or her own terms. Weimar "neoclassicist" Friedrich Schiller took up Kantian ideas in a number of his own philosophical writings on aesthetics, the most notable being his *On the Aesthetic Education of Man* (1795) in which he argues that art (and the act of aesthetic contemplation) as a disinterested and harmonious union of nature and spirit (or feeling and form) educates humanity to a state of moral autonomy and spiritual freedom. German Romantic writers such as Ludwig Tieck and Novalis who were in revolt against rationalist/neoclassical aesthetics also embraced both the artistic freedom and the illustrious station of the artist implicit in Kant's Idealism. The German Romantic movement quickly spread to England, France, and the United States, to writers ranging from William Wordsworth and Charles Baudelaire to Edgar Allen Poe. With this exalted self-justification of artistic creation as imaginative freedom, art assumed a privileged position as a mode of perception unique to human experience.

The first clear expression of aestheticism came with Théophile Gautier in the Preface to his 1835 novel *Mademoiselle de Maupin* in which he declared that art was in no way to be useful, and Poe did likewise with his definition of art as the creation of "Beauty" in his aesthetic treatise *The Poetic Principle* (1850). Baudelaire maintained throughout his poetry, novels, and letters the primacy of aesthetic experience as a mode of apprehending ultimate reality and this epistemological goal constituted (ironically) the realistic thrust of his writing. The French Symbolists – Stéphane Mallarmé, Paul Verlaine, and Arthur Rimbaud – asserted the centrality of the aesthetic idea (in opposition to rational discourse) as sensuous "symbol" through which everyday reality was to be both clarified and transcended. In the spirit of Poe (and Arthur Schopenhauer), poetic language was to incorporate the disinterested (or abstracted) emotion and beauty to be found in music. Later French poets – Paul Valéry, Guillaume Apollinaire, and André Breton – continued the impetus of aestheticism into the modernist twentieth century.

English Romanticism – John Keats and John Ruskin – with its high valuation of Beauty as an end in itself as well as the glorification of the artist's subjectivity as a privileged mode of perception, prepared the way for the aesthetic movements of the 1880s and 1890s. The Pre-Raphaelites (and the later international Art Deco movement as well) valued art and beauty not so much as a mode of perceiving truth or reality but rather in their more decorative and utilitarian function. The influence of Walter Pater's writings on British aestheticism during the last decades of the nineteenth century cannot be underestimated. Pater extolled art as a mode of sensuous perception superior to mere analytical explanation. Oscar Wilde, Lionel Johnson, Arthur Symons, and the early William Butler Yeats all owe a profound debt to the former's work. Symons also helped to spread the influence of the French Symbolists – especially Baudelaire, Mallarmé, and Verlaine – among British poets.

In the twentieth century aestheticism came to be associated with modernist doctrines of the absolute autonomy of the work of art – its essentially non-referential/non-mimetic nature – and its absolute meaning as formal structure. Its complement in literary criticism was to be found in the American New Criticism school of the 1940s and 1950s which examined literary texts primarily as formal structures of language. With the advent of political and social activism in the 1960s which dictated that art be socially relevant, that is, it should reflect social, economic, gender-based, and historical realities, the aesthetic frame of mind came into disrepute.

Further reading

Anderson, Mark M. *Kafka's Clothes: Ornament and Aestheticism in the Habsburg Fin De Siècle*, 1992.

Beckson, Karl E., ed. *Aesthetes and Decadents of the 1890s: An Anthology of British Poetry and Prose*, 1992.

Chai, Leon. *Aestheticism: The Religion of Art in Post-Romantic Literature*, 1990.

Dellamora, Richard. *Masculine Desire: The Sexual Politics of Victorian Aestheticism*, 1990.

Iser, Wolfgang. *Walter Pater: The Aesthetic Movement*, 1987.

Johnson, Robert Vance. *Aestheticism*, 1968.

Loesberg, Jonathan. *Aestheticism and Deconstruction: Pater, Derrida, and De Man*, 1991.

Mason, Stuart. *Oscar Wilde and the Aesthetic Movement*, 1970.

Psomiades, Kathy Alexis. *Beauty's Body: Femininity and Representation in British Aestheticism*, 1997.

THOMAS F. BARRY

See also Baudelaire; Gautier; Pater; Swinburne; Symbolism; Wilde

Alan of Lille

(Alanus de Insulis)

French philosopher and poet

Born: Lille, Flanders; between 1110 and 1130
Died: Cîteaux, France; 1203

Biography

Alanus de Insulis (Alan of Lille or Alain de Lille) is thought to have been of French origin. He was born at Lille in Flanders, now Belgium, sometime between 1110 and 1130. Much of his career was spent in Paris and at Montpellier as a teacher. His patron was Count William VIII of Montepellier, a retainer of Pope Alexander III. Alan achieved great renown in his day. Besides praising his literary achievements, several contemporary references and legends cite his fearsome debating ability and his outspoken, dramatic statements on such diverse topics as education, theology, and morality. A thirteenth-century portrait shows him wagging a finger at a colleague. His scholarship was such that his contemporaries called him the "doctor universalis" and "doctor ille famosus." He was mentioned by Otto of St. Blaise as living in Paris in 1194, but, according to Alberic de Trois Fontaines, he died in 1203 at the abbey of Cîteaux. The Cistercian monks at his abbey did not teach at universities, so it may be presumed that he entered the order late in life. The epitaph on his tombstone asserts that he knew everything there was to know.

Influence

Alan was one of the most accomplished poets and philosophers of his time. He was highly skilled in the devices of rhetoric so important to the complex style of the late twelfth century; his philosophical content, rather than being highly original, is peculiar to his age, a reflection of the Platonism of the School of Chartres. He read directly from the classical and medieval authors, rather than through intermediate commentators, and his familiarity with their work was profound. His major works, sixteen of which are extant – poems, treatises, and sermons – served as models for scholastic poetic expression far beyond his own time into the English Renaissance. He was considered by scholars of the thirteenth century as one of the greatest literary figures of the age.

Analysis

Because Alan's learning was so vast and his ideas so wide-ranging, a study of the influences upon him is difficult. First, his Platonism and classicism seem most indebted to the School of Chartres, particularly to Bernard of Chartres, William of Conches, John of Salisbury, and, most of all, Bernard Silvestris of Tours and Thierry of Chartres, who wrote, respectively, *De mundi universitate* (c. 1136) and

Heptateuchon (c. 1140). The latter presents a description of the seven liberal arts that is very similar to Alan's classification of them in *The Anticlaudian*, while the former describes a Platonic Nature as a reflection of the mind of God, and "Noys" as the Neo-Platonic Logos or Divine Thought, concepts that are almost identical to those of Nature and Noys in *The Anticlaudian*. Both Alan and Bernard Silvestris even describe Reason as using three mirrors to examine the secret images of the mind of God. Other general similarities between the two works can be seen in their accounts of a trip through the stars and descriptions of the angels, the five senses, and the ultimate goals of creating a perfect man. Bernard likely was Alan's teacher, but Alan surpassed him in the use of allegory, classical background, and poetic skill.

Like other Chartrians, Alan despised the moderns and preferred the ancients; references to classical sources abound in his works. A complete list of these would be very lengthy, but the most important are Lucan, Horace, Ovid's *Metamorphoses* (c. A.D. 1–8), Virgil's *Aeneid* (c. 29–19 B.C.) and *Georgics* (c. 37–29 B.C.), and Cicero's *De natura deorum* (44 B.C.), *De oratore* (55 B.C.), *De finibus* (45 B.C.), and *Academica* (45–44 B.C.). His knowledge was at first hand, not acquired through a set of commentators, as was so common among writers of the time.

Last, patristic sources and influences were numerous and included Jerome, Augustine, Pope Gregory the Great, and especially Boethius. *The Consolation of Philosophy* (c. 523–524) served as the model for *The Complaint of Nature*; it also inspired many sections of *The Anticlaudian*. Alan's description of concord is like the description of universal love in *The Consolation of Philosophy*, book 2, meter 8; his criticism of the nobility of race is similar to that in book 3, prose 6; and his image of Fortune's wheel certainly was inspired by that of Boethius, as were so many others in the Middle Ages.

Alan's Platonic scholastic humanism is evident throughout his work. In *The Anticlaudian*, the natural world is depicted as logically and formally ordered as the reflection of the mind of God. This epic poem of 4,400 lines of classic hexameter, with a prose and verse prologue, tells of Nature's quest to create a perfect man. So far, she has been unable to accomplish this goal because, even with the help of the virtues, she cannot create a soul for man. She decides to send Prudence through the cosmos to the Empyrean Heaven to ask God's help. The cart in which Prudence travels is built by the Seven Liberal Arts, drawn by five horses that represent the five senses, and guided by Prudence's sister, the charioteer, Reason. Alan's account of the journey emphasizes the ordered Platonic universe. Nearing her destination, Prudence is unable to complete her trip alone; she must accept the guidance of Theology and Faith. Finally, she reaches the Empyrean Heaven, where the angels, the blessed souls, the Virgin, Christ, and God the Father live by the light of the supercelestial sun. God grants Prudence the soul needed to finish Nature's creation of man, and she returns home. When man is completed, he is attacked by the vices sent by Alecto from Hades, but they are all defeated.

The Anticlaudian is valuable for its description of the cosmic order as it was understood in the late twelfth century. It is conventionally medieval; the poem may be read as either a theological allegory of the mind's ascent to God or as a sort of Platonic science-fiction journey through the universe. It includes a lengthy list of astronomical and general scientific questions which, unfortunately, remain unanswered in the text. The work, however, implies that a major field within astronomy is astrology, a study of the powers of celestial bodies. It also hints at a heliocentric universe in which the sun rules and has authority over the planets and stars.

Not all of Alan's writings, however, were solely indebted to the School of Chartres. In the "Sermone sphaera intelligibili," he describes an infinite universe in which God is everywhere and the world has no bounds, as described in the *Aesclepius* (c. 50–300) and the *Liber XXIV philosophorum* (c. 50–300), works that reflect the teachings of the Hermetic School. Following what may be considered Hermetic doctrine, Alan suggests that all things are good since they have been created by God, an idea that was not at all universal during the twelfth century. *The Anticlaudian* also reflects this belief in the goodness of creation. Indeed, it was intended as a response to Claudian's poem *In Rufinum* (396), in which the character Rufinus is created by the Vices and the Furies. Alan's Antirufinus, on the other hand, is entirely good, created by the Virtues and by God.

These ideas combine with the Chartrian view of the nature of causality, as described in *The Anticlaudian*, in which God is the efficient cause and the final cause, which give a thing its being and its end, but He is not the formal cause, which gives the thing its characteristics. Noys, or Divine Thought, acts as the efficient and final causes, subject to God's approval. This Platonic concept of God as the Form of forms should not be confused with the Christian Trinity or with pantheism. Noys is not the Holy Spirit, nor is the mind of God within all natural forms.

The style, too, of Alan may be seen as peculiarly characteristic of the late twelfth century, although it continued to be highly respected long after. It exemplifies the aesthetic which sought complexity by employing as many rhetorical figures and abstruse devices as the writer could summon to describe a single idea. Alan's poetry is crowded with images, synonyms, and devices of repetition, even where it counsels succinctness. Although Alan embraced a style filled with allegory, didacticism, and rhetoric, he nevertheless produced excellent satire, lyric description, and epigram.

Thus, Alan's work manifests a world-view drawn from many ancient sources and described in the preferred scholastic style. First, there is the ordered medieval universe with a Platonic Heaven, but often the natural world is seen hermetically as being perfect and infinite, since it is God's creation. Third, Alan seems to know of but does not necessarily accept the Aristotelian notion of God as a sphere whose center is everywhere and whose circumference is nowhere; in Alan's time, Aristotelian thought had not yet gained preeminence. Finally, human reason governs, at least up to the void beyond the stars. Man is rational with the potential to be suprarational. Indeed, Alan's is a humanistic medieval world-view, not original but incorporating the major ideas of the twelfth century.

The influence of Alan of Lille as a Neo-Platonist lasted for hundreds of years. Resting largely on *The Complaint of Nature* and *The Anticlaudian*, his reputation as an accurate commentator and compiler of classical philosophy has remained strong into the twentieth century. Although his style has been described as repetitive and tedious, he is the most notable poet of his generation.

Many writers of England and continental Europe have been influenced by Alan's style and ideas. Albert von Stade, Geoffrey of Vinsauf, and Giraldus Cambrensis borrowed from Alan's description of the beauty of Prudence in *The Anticlaudian*, a passage from which Petrarch may also have borrowed in composing his tributes to Laura. An analysis of *The Anticlaudian*'s influence upon Dante's *The Divine Comedy* (c. 1320) has also been presented and debated. Another argument suggests a possible echo of *The Anticlaudian* in John Milton's invocation to divine light in book 3 of *Paradise Lost*. The single indisputable reference to *The Anticlaudian* in English literature is made in Geoffrey Chaucer's *The House of Fame* (1372–1380), when the narrator claims that he has thought "on Marcian" (Martianus Capella, one of Alan's chief sources), "and eek on Anticlaudian/ That sooth was hir descripcioun/ Of al the heveneis regioun."

Alan was a revered poet, often praised by subsequent writers. *The Anticlaudian* was glossed twice before 1231, by Alan's pupil Ralph de Longo Campo and by William of Auxerre. A school manuscript from the fifteenth century shows the study and glossing the work continued to receive. Poets of the thirteenth century such as John of Garland, Otto of St. Bastien, and Henry of Ghent called Alan one of the great poets of their age, while Henry d'Andeli, Eberhardus Alemannus, and Hugo von Trimberg considered him popular and prolific.

His reputation continued into the fourteenth century and became even more wide-ranging. Robertus Holkot called him "Magnus," and Chaucer, who cited him twice, undoubtedly read his work in French. A fourteenth-century German text of Alan is extant, and an Italian grammarian cites his work as an example of excellent meter. Such evidence indicates the accessibility of his work in all of Europe.

In the fifteenth century Alan was described by Hartmann Schedel as "Alanum autem doctorem celeberrimum; cognomento Universalem," and in 1500 Johannes Trithemius wrote that Alan was a "doctor in omni scibili fuit profundissimus" and listed sixteen of his works. Manuscripts of his work were widely circulated along with those of Augustine, Boethius, Isidore of Seville, and the Venerable Bede, and his ideas influenced Nicholas of Cusa, René Descartes, and Blaise Pascal. Even though Alan concluded *The Anticlaudian* with a curse of death on his envious detractors, he did not arouse such detractors. Rather, he was highly regarded, even overrated, for centuries after his time.

Principal criticism

Passages in *Anticlaudianus, sive de officio viro boni et perfecti libri*, c. 1180 (*The Anticlaudian of Alain de Lille*, 1935), and *Liber de planctu naturae*, c. 1180 (*The Complaint of Nature*, 1908)

Other major works and literary forms

Fourteen other major works of Alan of Lille are extant. Most are untranslated treatises and sermons with unknown dates of origin. All are significant because they shed light upon Alan's Christianity and Platonism; of particular importance are *De fide catholica contra haereticos libri*, *Liber in distinctionibus dictionum theologicalium*, and *Regulae theologicae* (all twelfth century).

NONFICTION

De fide catholica contra haereticos libri
De sex alis cherubim
Dicta mirabilia, seu memorabilia
Doctrinale minus, alias liber paraolarum
Elucidatio in Cantica Canticorum
Liber in distinctionibus dictionum theologicalium
Liber poentitentialis
Liber sententiarum
Regulae theologicae
Rhythmus de Incarnatione Christi
Rhythmus de natura hominis
Sermones alii
Sermones octo
Summa de arte praedicatoria

The above were published in the twelfth century.

Further reading

Baumgartner, M. *Die Philosophie des Alanus de Insulis im Zussamenhange mit den Anschauungen des ewölf*, 1896.

Cornog, William Hafner. Introduction to *The Anticlaudian of Alain de Lille*, 1935.

Evans, G. R. *Old Arts and New Theology: The Beginnings of Theology as an Academic Discipline*, 1980.

Quilligan, Maureen. "Allegory, Allegoresis, and the Deallegorization of Language: The Roman de la Rose, the De Planctu Naturae, and the Parlement of Foules," in *Allegory, Myth, and Symbol*, 1981, pp. 163–186. Edited by Morton-W. Bloomfield.

Trout, John M. *The Voyage of Prudence: The World View of Alan of Lille*, 1979.

VICKI K. ROBINSON

See also Geoffrey of Vinsauf; Medieval Literary Theory

Dámaso Alonso

Spanish poet and critic

Born: Madrid, Spain; October 22, 1898
Died: Madrid, Spain; January 25, 1990

Biography

Dámaso Alonso was born in Madrid on October 22, 1898. After receiving his elementary and secondary education in private Catholic schools, he entered the Universidad de Madrid with the intention of studying the sciences. He soon changed to philosophy and letters, perhaps through the influence of his friend, the poet Vicente Aleixandre. His studies toward the bachelor's degree and the doctorate, which he completed in 1928, were directed by the illustrious professor of philology Ramón Menéndez Pidal.

By the time he received his doctorate, Alonso had already published a book of poems and several stories and translations, had collaborated extensively in the publication of the leading journal of philology in Spain, the *Revista de Filología Española*, and had lectured at several major universities. At the Seville Atheneum in 1927, Alonso presented a lecture on the work of Luis de Góngora. In the same year, *La lengua poética de Góngora*, based on his doctoral dissertation, received the National Prize for Literature.

In 1929 Alonso married Eulalia Galvarriato, a young writer. In 1933 he became a professor at the Universidad de Valencia, later moving to the Universidad de Madrid, where he was awarded the distinguished professorship vacated by the retirement of Menéndez Pidal.

Through his public lectures and the publication of many books of literary criticism, philological studies, and poetry, Dámaso Alonso became one of the most influential scholars of the twentieth century in Spain. He served as editor of the *Revista de Filología Española* and as president of the International Association of Hispanists. In 1968 he was elected unanimously to the directorship of the Real Academia Española de la Lengua. When he announced his plans for retirement in 1975, the members of the academy refused to accept his resignation, insisting rather that he continue, aided by a newly appointed assistant director.

Alonso remained as director until 1982. He died in Madrid on January 25, 1990.

Influence

Alonso is recognized as the initiator of the twentieth-century rediscovery and reevaluation of the Spanish Baroque poet Luis de Góngora and as one of the leaders of a group of poets who came to be called the "Generation of '27" because of their participation in the commemoration of the three-hundredth anniversary of the death of Góngora. Primarily because of the work of Alonso, the poetry of Góngora was rescued from oblivion and became a significant part of the established canon of Hispanic literary studies. Through his literary studies, Alonso established a new tradition in Spanish critical methodology, based on a careful and thorough textual analysis grounded in philological principles.

Analysis

Throughout his career as a literary critic and as a poet, Alonso developed and refined an eclectic approach to the creation of poetry and the critique of poetic art. His theory incorporates to some degree many of the dominant trends of twentieth-century literary theory – Russian Formalism, American New Criticism, structuralism, semiotics, and reader-oriented criticism.

The most extensive development of Alonso's critical method is presented in the work that is generally considered the most important of his career, *Poesía española*. As the culmination of years of study and teaching of various poetic texts from sixteenth- and seventeenth-century Spanish literature, this book is a systematic formulation of the methods and techniques that Alonso had developed in his previous essays and books.

Poesía española is a formulation of Alonso's attempt to understand and explain the phenomenon of the reading experience. For Alonso, the text represents a communication between the intuition of the poet and that of the reader. To understand that act of communication, Alonso proposes an analysis from three distinct perspectives, which he identifies as the points of view of the reader, the literary critic, and the stylistic critic. The experience of the reader with the poetic text is primarily intuitive and influenced somewhat by the reader's unique personal condition. The literary critic, confronting the text with more skill, is able to concentrate on the intuitive experience and express it more clearly. The stylistic critic, approaching the text objectively rather than intuitively, attempts an analysis of the structural and linguistic elements that make the text a unique work.

The objective approach of the stylistic critic makes use of the techniques of structural linguistics to confirm the existence in the text of specific elements that contribute to the intuitive experience of the poem. Alonso calls the poetic text the *signo* (sign), which consists of two principal elements, the *significante* (signifier) and the *significado* (meaning). The *significante* is the complex of objective elements in the text, such as the syntactical and rhythmic patterns, the particular vocabulary used, the patterns of sounds. The *significado* is the effect produced by the *significante*, the complex of objective elements. In Alonso's theoretical formulation, this "meaning" is not an abstract concept, but the poetic reality portrayed by the poem, the experience produced by a reading of the poem. It is, in effect, the fictional, poetic equivalent of a real-life experience.

Through this formulation of three interdependent approaches to the literary work, Alonso reaffirms the critical theory that he had proposed in a less definitive form in his previous work. The initial knowledge of a literary work is primarily intuitive. The objective analysis of the text serves to confirm the intuitive knowledge, to verify that the reception of the literary work, though influenced by the reader's subjective response, is indeed determined by the elements present in the text itself.

While Alonso had a definitive influence on critical methodology in twentieth-century Spain, his initial contribution to literary criticism proved to be of enormous significance in the development of the established canon of Hispanic studies. His early interest in the work of Luis de Góngora led him to propose two ideas that represented extraordinary departures from interpretations that were then current among students of Spanish literature. In his Seville lecture and in his dissertation, later published as *La lengua poética de Góngora*, Alonso disputed the evaluation of Góngora as a poet who first wrote popular, accessible poetry and later turned to a convoluted, esoteric style that became almost incomprehensible. Alonso argued convincingly that the two types of poetry – the straightforward popular verse and the elitist, stylized compositions – were produced throughout Góngora's career.

Alonso's reevaluation of Góngora led him to the insight that the entire history of Spanish poetry is characterized not primarily by the realistic and popularized, as was generally proposed, but by the concurrent existence of both the popular and the learned traditions. The difficult, esoteric poetry of Góngora was not an aberration, but the extreme expression of a tradition that has existed throughout the history of Spanish poetry.

Alonso continued throughout his career to analyze and elucidate the importance of the works of Góngora, always approaching the artistic work from the dual perspective of the literary historian and the textual critic. In doing so, he established a trend in literary studies that represents a significant departure from the two principal directions of criticism in Spain, the historical and the Romantic. Literary history had consisted of little more than a process of cataloging and classifying literary works and explaining in general terms the characteristics of literary movements. Romantic criticism had emphasized the thematic and stylistic characteristics of literary works as expressions of the emotions of the writers themselves.

Alonso revolutionized literary criticism in Spain by applying the methods of linguistic analysis to the texts for the purpose of clarifying the significant traits of a particular literary tradition and placing the text within that tradition. For Alonso, the proper role of literary history is to identify the traditions within which particular writers worked and to provide a narrative of the continuum represented by the recurrence of those traditions. This can be done only through careful analysis of the texts, the result of which should be the discovery of the means through which the writer drew from an established tradition to create an original work of art.

This critical approach is evident in *La poesía de San Juan de la Cruz (desde esta ladera)* and, later, in *Vida y obra de Medrano*. Through an analysis of the linguistic structures of the poetry of Saint John of the Cross, Alonso reveals the way in which the mystic poet elaborated on the texts of a little-known mediocre imitator of Góngora and on the erotic imagery of the Song of Songs, creating a unique poetic text that blends the popular and learned traditions. In the same manner, Alonso shows how Francisco de Medrano, while imitating other writers, created from their themes and concepts an innovative poetic vision through his own stylistic devices.

Alonso continued throughout his career to emphasize the importance of the intuitive experience. Until the late 1950s, his primary interest lay in a linguistically oriented analysis of the features of the literary text. After about 1960, however, he began to express more interest in the text's expression of human values than in its formal characteristics. He came to devote more attention to the poetry of his contemporaries, such as Jorge Guillén, Vicente Aleixandre, and Pedro Salinas. This shift of emphasis can be explained in part by the fact that by the 1950s Alonso's methodology was firmly established, whereas it had been considered somewhat revolutionary when he was publishing his earlier work.

The success of Dámaso Alonso's efforts to change the direction of literary criticism and to promote a reevaluation of the Spanish literary tradition was a result of the sound philological and historical foundation of his theories and the eclectic nature of his approach. Alonso succeeded in achieving a balance between an approach that would exclude the subjective response of the reader and one that would deny the independence of the literary work in favor of the reader's personal experience with the text.

Principal criticism

Soledades de Góngora, 1927
La lengua poética de Góngora, 1935
La poesía dramática en el "Don Duardos" de Gil Vicente, 1939
La poesía de San Juan de la Cruz (desde esta ladera), 1942
Ensayos sobre poesía española, 1944
Vida y obra de Medrano, 1948–1958 (2 volumes)
Poesía española: Ensayo de métodos y límites estilísticos, 1950
Seis calas en la expresión literaria española (prosa, poesía, teatro), 1951
Estudios y ensayos gongorinos, 1955
Menéndez Pelayo, crítico literario, 1956
De los siglos oscuros al de oro, 1958
Dos españoles del siglo de oro, 1960
Góngora y el "Polifemio," 1960–1961 (2 volumes)
Primavera temprana de la literatura europea: Lírica, épica, novela, 1961
Del siglo de oro a este siglo de siglas, 1962
Cuatro poetas españoles: Garcilaso, Góngora, Maragall, Antonio Machado, 1962
Para la biografía de Góngora: Documentos desconocidos, 1962
En torno a Lope: Marino, Cervantes, Benavente, Góngora, los cardenios, 1972

Other major works and literary forms

Although Dámaso Alonso gained prominence primarily through his hundreds of articles and many books of literary criticism, he is also recognized as one of the significant poets of twentieth-century Spain. In the 1920s he was active in a group of poets who cultivated "pure" poetry. His most important poetry, published in the 1940s and 1950s, concentrates on the conflict between people's material existence and their desire to transcend their human limitations. Alonso's interest in the elitist, complex poetry of the Golden Age in Spain was complemented by his attraction to certain English writers, which led him to publish translations of works by James Joyce, William Butler Yeats, Gerard Manley Hopkins, T. S. Eliot, and D. H. Lawrence.

POETRY
Poemas puros: Poemillas de la ciudad, 1921
Oscura noticia, 1944
Hijos de la ira, 1944 (*Children of Wrath*, 1970)
Hombre y Dios, 1955
Gozos de la vista, 1955–1957

TRANSLATIONS
El artista adolescente, 1926 (of James Joyce's novel *A Portrait of the Artist as a Young Man*)
Poemas, 1946 (of poems by T. S. Eliot)
Antología de poetas ingleses modernos, 1963 (of poems by Gerard Manley Hopkins, William Butler Yeats, and D. H. Lawrence)

Further reading

Book Abroad. XLVIII (1974), pp. 231–320. Special issue on Dámaso Alonso.
Debicki, Andrew. "Dámaso Alonso's Views on Poetry," in *Hispanic Review*. XXXIV (1966), pp. 111–120.
——. *Dámaso Alonso*, 1970.
Guillén, Jorge. *Language and Poetry*, 1961.
Insula (February 1991). Special issue on Dámaso Alonso.

GILBERT SMITH

Louis Althusser

French political philosopher

Born: Birmandreïs, Algeria; October 16, 1918
Died: La Verrière, France; October 22, 1990

Biography

Louis Althusser was born in Birmandreïs, Algeria, on October 16, 1918. He was brought up by his extremely pious mother in a very traditional Roman Catholic environment. He studied at the Lycée du Parc, Lyons, in France, from 1936 to 1939, where he joined the Young Christian Students movement. Althusser prepared for the prestigious École Normale Supérieure (ENS) and came sixth in the highly competitive entrance exam in July 1939. However, he was called up for military service in September of that year and did not take his place at the École. He was captured in the summer of 1940 and was to spend the rest of the war as a prisoner in Schleswig-Holstein. It was during these years of captivity that Althusser began to lose his Catholic faith and to suffer the bouts of depression that were to plague him for the rest of his life.

After his release from captivity, Althusser resumed his formal education and in 1948 came first in his year for the *agrégation* in philosophy; interestingly, in the light of his subsequent desire to expunge the remnants of Hegelianism from Marxist philosophy, his thesis was on *The Notion of Content in Hegel's Philosophy*. After successfully completing the *agrégation*, Althusser was appointed as a teacher at the ENS and remained there for the rest of his working life. He was promoted to Secretary of the École in 1962. In 1948 he joined the Communist Party of France (PCF) and was to remain a lifelong party member.

Althusser was first hospitalized for depression in 1946 and thereafter with increasing frequency throughout his life, eventually being diagnosed as a manic-depressive with periods of melancholy. He was subjected to a range of treatments from ECT (electroconvulsive treatment) to antidepressive drugs and spent many years in psychoanalysis with René Diatkine, but his mental torment never lifted. In November 1980, in a period of extreme depression, he strangled his companion of thirty-five years, Hélène Rytman. They had met in the winter of 1945; Hélène was already a heroine of the French Resistance at that time and was to become a prominent dissident within the PCF. A crucial figure in Althusser's embracing of Communism, Hélène was herself a highly respected sociologist and supported Althusser intellectually and emotionally. After her death, Althusser spent the last ten years of his life in and out of hospital while composing his autobiography, *The Future Lasts a Long Time* (published in 1992), but he was never to fully regain his health. He died at the age of seventy-two in hospital at La Verrière, in the department of Yvelines, France, of a heart attack on October 22, 1990.

Influence

Althusser burst onto the intellectual scene in the mid-1960s with the publication of two extraordinarily influential books, *For Marx* and *Reading Capital* (both published in France in 1965). In these two works Althusser proposed nothing less than a systematic re-reading of Marx, a re-reading that would retrieve Marxism's true revolutionary potential, define it as the science of history, and finally offer a critique of Stalinism from within the PCF itself. *For Marx* and *Reading Capital* immediately achieved international recognition and Althusser became the most important Marxist philosopher of his day, influencing a whole generation of political activists and radical theorists from philosophy and sociology through literary and film studies to feminism. "Structural Marxism" (a definition Althusser himself would always reject), or "Althusserianism," as it became known, crossed the disciplinary boundaries and through its critique of "humanism" and "historicism" would lay the intellectual foundations for much of what we now understand as "poststructuralism." Through his critique of the authoritarian and orthodox thinking of the traditional Communist Left in France, Althusser profoundly influenced the political events of May '68, but through his refusal to leave the Party, as many of his comrades did, May '68 would also mark the beginning of his intellectual eclipse. With the publication in 1970 of his seminal essay on ideology, "Ideology and Ideological State Apparatuses," Althusserianism gained a new lease of life into the early 1970s, but after 1968 Althusser was never again to achieve the intellectual status and influence that he had enjoyed in 1965.

Analysis

Althusserianism essentially comprised of three closely interrelated objectives. First, Althusser insisted on the need to subject Marx's texts to a symptomatic reading, that is to say, that we should not read Marx superficially, choosing a reference here or a quote there to suit our own purposes and political agendas, but rather we should read the text closely and identify the *problématique* the text seeks to address. The notion of the *problématique*, or problematic, is that ideas or concepts do not exist in isolation but within specific theoretical and ideological frameworks. Thus the meaning of a given concept will depend not only upon other ideas present in the text, but also upon the ideological context from which those ideas arise but which may in themselves be absent from the text. To identify a given problematic, therefore, is in a sense to identify the "unconscious" elements at work within that text. The purpose of such a reading was to establish an epistemological break in the works of Marx between his early "humanist" texts, which Althusser saw as inherently ideological, and the later "scientific" work such as *Capital*. It was only on the basis of this later work, argued Althusser, that we could begin to establish Marxism as the true science of history.

Secondly, according to Althusser, Marx inaugurated a revolutionary new form of philosophy, what he called the "theory of theoretical practice." In brief, the theory of theoretical practice sought to reconcile an epistemology (the theory of knowledge) which recognized the inevitably historical, social, and theoretical character of science with a realist insistence on the existence of "real objects" independent of human minds and irreducible to theory. Althusser almost immediately revised this initial conceptualization of theoretical practice and would consistently return to the self-criticism and reformulation of this notion throughout his career.

Thirdly, and most importantly, Althusser sought to elaborate a nonreductive and noneconomistic theory of the social formation of capitalism. This involved four significant developments of Marxist theory: (1) the rejection of the Hegelian legacy of the dialectic in favor of a new theory of contradiction and overdetermination, or multiple causality; (2) discarding the vulgar Marxist model of the economic base determining the ideological superstructure in favor of a theory of structural causality that would respect the relative autonomy of the different levels and spheres of society; (3) the rejection of the Hegelian, teleological account of history according to which Communism was the inevitable product of history in favor of a theory of structural transition; and finally, (4) the reconceptualization of ideology as a subject's imaginary relations with their real conditions of existence.

Althusser's reconstruction of Marxism provoked strong and often hostile reactions both at the time of writing and subsequently. Many Marxists today accept that his insistence on the priority of *Capital* over Marx's earlier work, particularly the *Economic and Philosophical Manuscripts of 1844*, is fully justified and that a new materialist theory of history does indeed begin to emerge from Marx's work post-1845. However, Althusser clearly overstated the extent to which the humanist aspects of Marx's thought, that is, the notion of human nature and a distinct human essence, were erased from his work. Indeed, there is no textual evidence within Marx's mature work to support the claims that Althusser made for it in this respect. In his later work, particularly his attempt to reformulate the notion of a theory of theoretical practice in the form of philosophy as "class struggle in theory," Althusser succeeded only in creating more theoretical problems than he had sought to resolve. Philosophy appeared, on the one hand, to be the answer to everything, and, on the other, the answer to nothing. Finally, Althusser's critique of Stalinism and the Party, when it came in 1978 ("What Must Change in the Party"), was devastating and according to Gregory Elliott is probably Althusser's finest word; but it came too late. The vast majority of the young activists of May '68 had by this time moved on from Althusserianism, through Maoism to political quietism, while academically Marxism had been superseded by psychoanalysis, deconstruction, and poststructuralism.

The subject of ideology

Althusser's work contains a number of brief excursions into the theory of ideology from around 1964 or 1965 onwards, but it was not until the publication in 1970 of "Ideology and Ideological State Apparatuses" that the question of ideology became central to the Althusserian project. What has become known as "the ISAs essay" is in fact in two parts, the bulk of it being concerned with what Althusser calls the ideological and the repressive state apparatuses, whilst the shorter section proposes what is known as the theory of ideological interpellation. The two parts of this essay are not in fact linked and, as subsequent critics have pointed out, they are theoretically incompatible. Within the

Marxist tradition there are numerous definitions of ideology, which can be reduced to two broad definitions. First, there is the notion of ideology as "false consciousness" and, second, the notion of ideology as class affiliation. The first "epistemological" definition (in the sense that it speaks from a position of knowledge superior to that which is being categorized as ideological) sees ideology as essentially a question of illusion, mystification, and distortion of thought. The second definition conceptualizes ideology as the specific world-view of given historical social classes. Althusser's radical break with previous conceptions of ideology was his attempt to shift the debate away from questions of false consciousness to issues of a subject's "lived" relationship to his or her conditions of existence.

Ideology, argued Althusser, has little or nothing to do with questions of consciousness; indeed it is profoundly unconscious. Ideology is not a set of ideas, not a system of beliefs or a political program through which subjects are indoctrinated. Ideology is rather a system of representations, a system of images, concepts, and, above all, "structures" which are not imposed upon our consciousness, but are lived. Ideology is a matter of a subject's lived relation to their world: it appears as conscious only on condition that it remains unconscious. An ideology fails the moment we recognize it as ideological. In short, ideology for Althusser represents a subject's imaginary relation to his or her real conditions of existence. The importance of Althusser's reformulation, therefore, has been to shift ideology away from its epistemological definition, away from notions of false consciousness and the "true" representation of reality, to the function of representation itself. It transformed the debate over ideology from questions of consciousness to questions of representation and the subject's constitution as an ideological subject within the system of representation.

Althusser drew from these conclusions two important and related theses: (1) there is no practice except by and in an ideology, and (2) there is no ideology except by the subject and for the subject. In other words, it is the subject and not consciousness that is the central category of ideology. The subject is constitutive of all ideology, but at the same time ideology has the function of "constituting" concrete individuals as subjects. This tautology, or double constitution, that is to say, the constitution of ideology by a subject who is always-already ideologically constituted, is, for Althusser, the precise function of ideology. To put it another way, we are constituted as ethical, political, or economic subjects rather than some abstract notion of an individual with an essential essence or human nature. At the same time, we are always-already within ideology, there can be no subjectless ideology. Althusser suggested that this double constitution took place by a process of hailing or interpellation and gave the example of a policeman calling someone on the street. When the policeman calls out "Hey, you there!" and someone turns around and recognizes that they are being addressed, they are in that precise moment constituted as subjects of the law. They are transformed from being abstract individuals into specific kinds of subjects.

Althusser and literary studies

Althusser's reformulation of the concept of ideology was to have wide-ranging influence throughout cultural studies because it pointed to the way in which texts embodied particular ideologies, not in terms of their content or their overt political message, but in relation to their form and the way in which they constituted specific kinds of reading or viewing subjects. This project is best exemplified in the pages of the British film journal *Screen* in the mid-1970s and the North American feminist film journal *Camera Obscura*. But it also left its mark on literary theory through the work of Pierre Macherey in France, Terry Eagleton in Britain, and Fredric Jameson in the United States.

Pierre Macherey was a young colleague of Althusser who published the first explicitly Althusserian study in the field of literary studies, *A Theory of Literary Production* (1966). Macherey's text is essentially a study in the ideology of form, that is, a study of the received forms of literary criticism which tend to substitute "ideal interpretations" for the text under analysis. Macherey argued that criticism seeks to resolve all the contradictions, ambiguities, and absences in a text and restore to it its "full" and "proper" meaning; in this way literary criticism comes to replace the text itself with its own "normative" value judgments. For Macherey, therefore, the objective of Marxist criticism was to resist and expose the ideological nature of traditional forms of criticism by revealing the incompleteness, discrepancies, and silences within the text. Macherey's project was to remain itself incomplete as he developed his work in other directions, but he did establish a distinctively Althusserian problematic in literary studies – that is, the proper object of any Marxist criticism as the study of the ideology of literary form.

Terry Eagleton was to continue this endeavor in the first work of Althusserian criticism in English, *Criticism and Ideology* (1976). As with Macherey before him, Eagleton criticized the inherently ideological character of previous forms of literary criticism, especially the liberal humanism of F. R. Leavis and the socialist humanism of his own mentor, Raymond Williams. Eagleton then sought to define what he saw as the proper concerns of a materialist criticism that could break with the ideological character of both literature and criticism and produce "a science of the text." *Criticism and Ideology* was a ground-breaking text in contemporary Marxist criticism and crucial for the dissemination of Althusserian ideas amongst literary theorists but, as with Macherey, Eagleton would shortly abandon what he later described as the rather "bloodless writing" of his Althusserian period and return to the tradition of socialist humanism represented by Williams.

Probably the most sustained attempt to utilize the Althusserian theory of ideology for the study of literary form has been Fredric Jameson's *The Political Unconscious: Narrative as a Socially Symbolic Act* (1981). In a long and closely argued opening chapter, Jameson sought to reconcile Althusser's antihistoricism with his own Hegelianism through a reformulation of Althusser's structural causality as structural historicism. In a complex and multilayered analysis, Jameson identifies the different levels of ideological meaning, or determinate contradiction – the textual, the social, and the historical – in a range of texts. Above all, Althusser provides a theory of the subject which, argues Jameson, has always been lacking in Marxism. The weakness of Althusser, however, is that he only conceives of ideology working on individual subjects and lacks any theory of "class consciousness." The Althusserian theory of ideology therefore must be supplemented, argues Jameson, with a renewal of utopian thinking which allows us to situate the subject not only in his or her alienated present but also at the other end of history in some imaginary, classless future.

Principal criticism

Montesquieu: La Politique et l'histoire, 1959 (*Politics and History: Montesquieu, Rousseau, Hegel and Marx*, 1972)
Pour Marx, 1965 (*For Marx*, 1969)
Lire "Le Capital," 1965 (with Etienne Balibar; *Reading Capital*, 1970)
Lénine et la philosophie, 1969 (*Lenin and Philosophy and Other Essays*, 1971)
"Idéologie et appareils idéologiques d'état," in *La Pensée*. 151 (June, 1970), pp. 3–38. Translated as "Ideology and Ideological State Apparatuses," in *Lenin and Philosophy and Other Essays*, 1971
Philosophie et philosophie spontanée, 1974 (*Philosophy and the Spontaneous Philosophy of the Scientists and Other Essays*, 1990)
Éléments d'autocritique, 1974 (*Essays in Self-Criticism*, 1976)
Écrits sur la psychanalyse: Freud et Lacan, 1993 (*Writings on Psychoanalysis: Freud and Lacan*, 1996)

Other major works and literary forms

Louis Althusser is best known as a political philosopher. However, he wrote two autobiographical works that provide an insight into both his intellectual development and his troubled personality: *Les Faits* (1976; the facts) and *L'Avenir dure longtemps* (1992), both of which appear in *The Future Lasts a Long Time* (1994).

Further reading

Benton, Ted. *The Rise and Fall of Structural Marxism: Althusser and his Influence*, 1984.
Callinicos, Alex. *Althusser's Marxism*, 1976.
Clarke, Simon, et al. *One-Dimensional Marxism: Althusser and the Politics of Culture*, 1980.
Eagleton, Terry. *Criticism and Ideology*, 1976.
Elliott, Gregory. *Althusser: The Detour of Theory*, 1987.
——. *Althusser: A Critical Reader*, 1994.
Jameson, Frederic. *The Political Unconscious: Narrative as a Socially Symbolic Act*, 1981.
Kaplan, E. Ann, and M. Sprinker, eds. *The Althusserian Legacy*, 1993.
Macherey, Pierre. *A Theory of Literary Production*, 1966.
Thompson, E. P. *The Poverty of Theory and Other Essays*, 1978.

SEAN HOMER

See also Eagleton; French Literary Theory: Twentieth Century; Gramsci; Ideology; Jameson; Marxist Theory and Criticism

American Literary Theory to 1900

The settlers of New England came to America on a mission to establish, in John Winthrop's words, "a city on a hill." While they were never as "puritanical" as their reputation has led later generations to believe, the religious nature of their errand encouraged them to enforce strictly their own moral codes, and to demand unwavering allegiance to the doctrines of their church. Claiming to be a people of the Word, these early Puritans tolerated little deviation from orthodoxy. The society they created, though undoubtedly devout, was not conducive to the open exchange of ideas and freedom of expression which generally are necessary for the development of a rich literary tradition.

It is not that the Puritans lacked literary sensibilities. Even in the seventeenth century, virtually all New Englanders of both sexes and all classes were literate. Establishing Harvard College only six years after arriving in the wilderness, Puritans expected those in authority to seek higher learning. Most writers of the period were college graduates with strong classical backgrounds. The clergy, also well trained in the humanistic tradition, filled their sermons not only with Scripture but also with frequent illustrations from classical poets and orators. Poetry, in particular, received Puritan approbation because its ethical and moral qualities often reinforced the truth of Scripture. Puritans, in sum, did not despise the literary arts, but they did insist that literature be used always to embrace their particular understanding of religious orthodoxy.

The earliest expression of what could be called literary criticism in America appeared in 1640 in the preface to the *Bay Psalm Book*, the first work published in the New World. In an attempt to defuse potential criticism of this translation, the Puritan minister Richard Mather (1596–1669) wrote:

> If therefore the verses are not always so smooth and elegant as some may desire or expect; let them consider that Gods Altar needs not our pollishings: Ex. 20. for we have respected rather a plain translation, than to smooth our verses with the sweetness of any paraphrase, and so have attended Conscience rather than Elegance, fidelity rather than poetry, in translating the hebrew words into english language.

With these words, Mather articulated the prevailing Puritan preference for clarity over poetic quality. The Bible, according to Mather, should be allowed as much as possible to speak for itself. Minor alterations for the sake of meter were permissible, but the trimmings must not interfere with the message.

Mather's comments were neither original nor distinctively American. At least since the publication of William Perkins' *The Art of Prophesying* (1592; translated from the original Latin into English in 1606), Puritans had insisted that ministers preach and write in a plain style, deliberately avoiding traditional rhetorical ornamentation and arrangement. The sermon, which was the most published literary genre of colonial times, was expected to be clear, convincing, and persuasive. Like all forms of literature, it was intended to instruct, not delight. Eloquence was a virtue so long as it did not inflame the passions or detract from the simple truths of Scripture.

Puritans in both Old and New England measured the fine arts with a religious standard: great poetry and prose were those works that effectively taught those eternal truths which all humankind needed to know. The Reverend Cotton Mather's remarks concerning the study of poetry, "Let not what would be sauce rather than food for you engross all your application," reflected the underlying Puritan ambivalence toward all the arts. While they did not denounce literature as intrinsically evil, neither did they view it primarily from an aesthetic point of view. Throughout the colonial era, Puritans read, quoted, and critiqued the literary giants of the past, but their criticism was largely judicious in nature.

By the early decades of the eighteenth century, new methods and ideas from Europe increasingly were exerting an influence upon American minds. Gradually the mysterious religious world of the Puritans was being replaced with the rational, mechanical universe of Sir Isaac Newton, René Descartes, John Locke, and Voltaire. The enlightened concept of the world as a machine, and of God as its divine mechanic, encouraged thinkers to look to reason for their inspiration, and to natural law for the bases of their criticism. Confident that literary laws governed correctness in style just as physical laws governed nature, eighteenth-century intellectuals on both sides of the Atlantic sought regularity, formality, and decorum in the art of writing.

In America, however, the "Age of Reason" was no more friendly to the development of a literary tradition than had been the former age of superstition. Benjamin Franklin (1706–1790), the ablest American representative of the Enlightenment, urged Americans to learn how to "express themselves clearly, concisely, and naturally without affected Words or high-flown Phrases." He admitted, however, that the fine arts had little place in American society. "To America," Franklin wrote, "one schoolmaster is worth a dozen poets, and the invention of a machine or the improvement of an implement is of more importance than a masterpiece of Raphael." "Nothing is good or beautiful," he concluded, "but in the measure that it is useful." The enlightened Franklin, like his Puritan forefathers, viewed literature primarily in functional and utilitarian terms.

The colonial confrontation with England that culminated with the war for independence and the establishment of a new government dominated the thoughts and concerns of Americans during the second half of the eighteenth century. These events inspired the publications of scores of epic poems which praised the greatness of the young republic and promised that America at last was in the process of acquiring a heroic history. Yet, despite this outpouring of nationalistic sentiment, American literary theory during the period remained largely dependent upon the rules and models of the great English neoclassicists Alexander Pope, John Dryden, Jonathan Swift, and Samuel Johnson.

The best-known examples of what may be called "American neoclassicism" are found in the writings of a group of Yale College graduates known as the Connecticut Wits. These authors, who included John Trumbull (1750–1831), Timothy Dwight (1752–1817), David Humphreys (1752–1818), and Joel Barlow (1754–1812), placed relatively less emphasis upon the ancient classics as literary models and were more receptive to the Romantic idea of progress than were their more conservative English counterparts. In other details, however, these representative Americans perpetuated traditional neoclassical themes. As critics, they valued decorum, formality, and elegance in diction, and order and design in poetry. They criticized Romantic poetry for its lack of clarity, blank verse for its "too near resemblance to Prose," and fiction for failing to enhance the mental or spiritual development of the reader. Often strongly moral and judicious in nature, these critics viewed literature in utilitarian terms. To Trumbull, as to many of his colleagues in America, the grand purpose of literature was "to ennoble the soul, purify the passions, and give the thoughts a better turn . . . to add dignity to our sentiments, delicacy and refinement to our manners."

England's Romantic revolt against the literary forms of the eighteenth century, exemplified in the work of Samuel Taylor Coleridge, William Wordsworth, and Lord Byron, was slow to reach America. Most early-nineteenth-century Americans rejected the extreme subjectivism of the Romanticists, for they believed that it represented a lack of restraint and stood for the release of pent-up emotions which if not suppressed would have a deleterious effect upon the structure of society. Still insisting upon the moral and social obligations of the creative arts, most American publicists decried poetry which indulged in pure sensuousness and criticized the dynamic Romanticism of fiction authors who seemed to glorify the emotions and triumphs of antisocial characters. Throughout the early decades of the new century, American critics commonly complained about the supernaturalism of Coleridge, the melancholy of Byron, the morbid imagination of Johann Wolfgang von

Goethe, and the social irresponsibility of Friedrich Schiller and Edward Bulwer-Lytton. At least until 1830 the overriding American literary temper was rather conservative.

While unimpressed with the more subjective and sensuous tendencies of the Romantic movement, early-nineteenth-century Americans generally approved of other literary trends associated with European Romanticism. Several prominent Americans of the period, for example, revolted against heroic couplets and formal diction, while others expressed a heightened interest in Romantic themes such as physical nature, the nonclassical past, and the activities of ordinary people. Most also embraced the notions of progress and freedom from the tyranny of a monarch and his privileged classes. The receptivity of Americans to these aspects of the Romantic impulse was owing to a variety of influences, some local in nature and others international.

A practical factor contributing to the growing popularity of certain phases of British Romanticism was the appearance after 1815 of numerous literary periodicals which discussed Romantic themes. Magazines such as the *North American Review* (established in 1815), *New York Mirror* (1824), *American Quarterly Review* (1827), *New England Magazine* (1831), and *Knickerbocker Magazine* (1835) made possible reviews of foreign books and provided space for the critical evaluation of British literary developments. Moreover, the absence at this time of an international copyright law made it more profitable for booksellers to copy and reprint European books and magazines than to peddle those authored by Americans. Consequently, in 1820 only 30 percent of the works published in the United States were by American writers. While the number and percentage of American publications rose rapidly during the second quarter of the century, the economic realities of the publishing business temporarily discouraged the development of native literary talent and encouraged Americans to look to England for their best examples of literary achievement.

A counterinfluence which lessened the impact of foreign thought on American literary development was the rising spirit of nationalism. The swelling of national pride, in part a reaction to General Andrew Jackson's military victory over the British at New Orleans and the surprising successes of American diplomats in negotiating a favorable conclusion to the War of 1812, spurred American efforts to produce a literature that could be called genuinely American. Extreme nationalists, such as James Kirke Paulding (1778–1860) and Edward Everett (1794–1865), called for a new democratic literature totally freed from the rank, fashion, and authority of the aristocratic past. These patriots not only insisted that a democracy could produce literary greatness but also confidently predicted the coming of a new national literature that would rival that of the Augustan Age.

Less militant nationalists also issued a declaration of independence from English authority. Writing in the "Era of Good Feelings," Edward Tyrrell Channing (1790–1856) insisted that the primary task of American criticism was to save American poetry from being merely a bad imitation of foreign authors. In making a similar comment on the novel, critic John Neal (1793–1876) praised James Fenimore Cooper's *Lionel Lincoln* specifically because it was "a brave, hearty, original work . . . crowded with real American characters; alive with American peculiarities; got up after no model, however excellent; woven to no pattern, however beautiful; in imitation of nobody, however great." Similarly, in his pompous discourse "The Importance and Means of a National Literature" (1830), William E. Channing (1780–1842) criticized America's overdependence upon English books and lack of familiarity with the literature of continental Europe. These critics, no doubt galled by the general disrespect given to American writers by their British colleagues, were in no mood simply to embrace European standards as their own.

One manifestation of American literary nativism at this time was the tacit agreement among many American critics to refrain from captious criticism of American works. William Cox (1805?–1847), who contributed 168 critical essays to the *New York Mirror* between 1828 and 1848, argued that American critics should act more "as friendly assistants than as dogmatic censors." Similarly, Washington Irving (1783–1859) insisted that the critic be not like the spider spinning a web but like "the honest bee, that extricates honey from the humblest weed." Writing a short time later, Henry Wadsworth Longfellow (1807–1882) also advocated more sympathetic criticism of fellow Americans. "Many critics," he complained, "are like wood-peckers, who, instead of enjoying the fruit and shadow of a tree, hop incessantly around the trunk, pecking holes in the bark to discover some little worm or other." While few American critics ever admitted offering praise when it was not due, many did accept Edward Everett's dictum to be silent when they could not commend.

For most American critics, however, especially after the anti-British animosity following the War of 1812 subsided, the creation of an American national literature did not require them to reject totally their British and European heritage, or necessarily to defend their fellow American artists. William Cullen Bryant, writing in 1818, told American poets not to expect an American audience "merely because they [the poems] are written by an American, and are not decidedly bad." Arguing against the erection of a protective tariff around the works of native authors, Bryant defended the right of the critic to show the young writer "what we expect from him," insisting that for the sake of future poets "it is as necessary to point out the faults of his predecessors, as to commend their excellences." In 1819 even the nationalistic R. H. Dana, Sr. (1787–1879), of the *North American Review* warned: "It is not yet time to empty our shelves of European lumber to make way for American writers, – there is still room enough for these in the vacancies left. An American library would, we fancy, be rather a sorry and heart-sickening sight to a literary man." While these critics acknowledged that inadequacy of previous literary expressions for the new nation, as a rule the more moderate nationalists desired to incorporate as much of the old into the new as was possible. They wanted to create an American literary tradition that was an extension of European culture. While highly patriotic, their nationalism drove them to seek a literature of merit which would have international significance and would match the greatness of America's political experiment.

Given the priority Americans gave to political matters, it is not surprising that internal partisan strife as well as international quarrels often shaped American criticism. The *North American Review*, whose founders were Federalist in politics and neoclassical in literary taste, tempered its nationalism and sustained its attack on Romantics longer than some of its rival periodicals. In contrast, the *United States Democratic Review*, established twenty years later by Democrats with a tendency toward Romanticism, supported a vigorous nationalism and vehemently condemned both foreign writers and American Whigs for their lack of sympathy for democratic ideals. Similarly, *The Whig Review* (1845) deliberately set out to destroy James Fenimore Cooper (1789–1851), largely because of his well-known association with the Democratic Party. American criticism was not produced in a vacuum by men of Olympian detachment. On the contrary, the political biases of critics, editors, and magazine owners frequently had a discernible impact on their criticism.

Virtually all early national critics, whether extremist or moderate in their nationalism, believed that authors should make American literature as native as its sources permitted. For a few this meant creating a new American language and using American dialects. More typically, however, this simply required seeking inspiration from American landscapes, selecting American themes and settings, depicting everyday life on the frontier and the customs and mores of the American Indian, contrasting American ideas and institutions with European ones, or drawing upon the richness of the American past. While not requiring writers to break completely with British traditions or to renounce their methods and standards, American critics during the second quarter of the century increasingly did expect authors to select subjects appropriate for a democratic people.

Another factor which contributed to the transition to Romanticism was the continuing popularity in America of the ideas of the Scottish commonsense philosophers who reacted against standards of taste based strictly upon the authority of neoclassical historical principles. Between 1815 and 1835, for example, the "associational principle" of the Scottish rhetorician Archibald Alison (1757–1839) had a great influence upon American critical theory. According to Alison, the emotion called beauty, which proceeds from viewing a landscape or piece of art, comes not from qualities immediately perceptible in the object itself, but from the train of agreeable ideas with which the object is associated by the imagination of the reviewer. In asserting that beauty is the result of ideas associated with objects by the imagination, Alison unwittingly gave impetus to the development of the concept of subjectivity. To literary critics, this concept undermined the neoclassical notion that humans have a common nature toward which works of art should be directed. It also led to the conviction that the essence of great literature rested more in its ability to kindle the imagination than in correct technique.

In America, the "associational principle" also provided critics – already consumed with nationalistic sentiment – with further reason to demand that authors use distinctively American material that was rich in associations for the reader. Samuel Knapp (1783–1838), William Tudor (1779–1830), and like-minded critics of the era argued that merely describing American scenes or pasting American names on scenes that were in no respect American was not enough. For them, great literature required the use of words drenched with historical associations, such as the bravery and the high ideals of the struggle for independence, which would stir the imagination of the reader.

The swing from neoclassicism to Romanticism in American criticism is perhaps best seen in the career of one of the ablest critics of the period, William Cullen Bryant (1794–1878). Unlike many of his colleagues, who were reluctant to approve of the works of Wordsworth and Coleridge, Bryant echoed all the main motifs of Romantic theory. From his first critical essay, "On the Use of Trisyllabic Feet in Iambic Verse" (1819), to the end of his career, Bryant condemned the "balance and wearisome regularity" of American neoclassical poets, which, he argued, "allows just as much play and freedom to the faculties of the writer as a pair of stilts allows to the body." To Bryant, poetry was not imitative art but suggestive art, which dealt as much with the imagination and the emotions as with the intellect. The "great spring of poetry," he insisted, is emotion, and great poetry is that which both touches the heart and teaches "direct lessons of wisdom." Poetry, he proclaimed, by lifting its hearer "to a sphere where self-interest cannot exist," incites a greater love of nature and one's fellow human. Bryant, much like his European predecessors Alison and Wordsworth and in anticipation of a future generation of American critics, emphasized the close association between poetry and nature, and how the study of poetry leads to greater religious sentiment.

By the middle decades of the nineteenth century, the Romanticism of Wordsworth and Coleridge, as well as that of the Germans Goethe, Immanuel Kant, and Friedrich Schelling, was well entrenched within American criticism. Each of the major magazines of the period – the transcendental *The Dial*, the nationalistic *United States Democratic Review*, the conservative *The Whig Review*, and the sentimental *Southern Literary Messenger* – was in varying degrees Idealist and organicist. Between 1840 and 1870 American critics in all regions of the nation generally viewed the world as a living organism, not as a mechanical clock. Clearly the science of biology had replaced Newtonian physics as the schoolmaster of American criticism.

The clearest example of the Romantic impulse in American literary theory is found in the works of members of the Transcendental Club, a group which included Amos Bronson Alcott (1799–1888), Theodore Parker (1810–1860), Margaret Fuller (1810–1850), Henry David Thoreau (1817–1862), Jones Very (1813–1880), and William Henry Channing (1810–1884). One of the founders of this network of congenial New Englanders was Ralph Waldo Emerson (1803–1882), a one-time Unitarian minister who, during a visit to Europe in 1832, came under the influence of Wordsworth, Coleridge, and Thomas Carlyle. In 1836, the same year the Transcendental Club was formed, Emerson published his first significant work, *Nature*. This essay, which has been called the "philosophical constitution of Transcendentalism," contains the seeds of Emerson's later works: his love of nature, pantheism, optimism, mysticism, and extreme individualism.

For Ralph Waldo Emerson and other Transcendentalists, art was nature idealized, and the poet was a prophet who in submitting to the streams emanating from the Over-Soul, created works of beauty which reflected the central Idea of the universe. In Emerson's theory of literature, artistic greatness lay not in talent but in self-surrender and in a willingness to let the Over-Soul inform the human spirit. "Good poetry," Emerson wrote, "sounds as if [it were] copied out of some invisible tablet in the Eternal Mind." The creative genius, thereby, was one who had "found the verse, not made it." This concept of literature as a revelation from the Over-Soul led Emerson inevitably to connect good artistry with that which expressed universal truth and espoused high moral ideals.

An advocate of "transcendental criticism," Emerson insisted that the fundamental law of criticism was that "every scripture is to be interpreted by the same spirit which gave it birth." Since poems are merely corrupt versions of an archetypal text, the function of the critic is to make the text tally with the archetype. To accomplish this task, the critic must share with the author the mystical experience of the poem, and commune with the Over-Soul. Only then is the critic able to attempt to rectify any errors in the text which the poet may have committed because of lack of vision. Thus, for Emerson, criticism was itself art – the expression of an idea intuitively received from the Over-Soul.

Only a handful of mid-nineteenth-century Americans escaped the pulls of both cultural nationalism and Transcendentalism, but among those notable few was perhaps the greatest of all American critics, Edgar Allan Poe (1809–1849). In striking contrast to most of his contemporaries, Poe repeatedly attacked the narrow nationalism and groundless mysticism of American critics. In his two most significant works of criticism, "The Philosophy of Composition" (1846) and "The Poetic Principle" (1850), Poe outlined his well-known doctrine of "art for art's sake." In these and other pieces, Poe argued that the sole function of criticism was to identify the structural errors in the text, not to promote any personal or national agenda. Similarly, Poe rejected the popular notion that the purpose of literature was to instruct and please. Labeling this concept "the heresy of the didactic," Poe adamantly insisted that poetry was concerned solely with beauty. Taste alone was the single legitimate basis for critical judgment. The critic's task was to analyze the text, not to test the validity of the author's ideas.

With a tactlessness that often alienated other writers of the period, Poe also attempted to shock American readers away from their naive belief in inspiration. Denying Emerson's claim to transcendental knowledge, Poe could not conceive of thoughts beyond the control of language. Poetry was not a mystical imitation of the external world. Instead, it was the product of a conscientious craftsman who paid careful attention to details of expression. "There is no greater mistake," Poe insisted, "than the supposition that a true originality is a mere matter of impulse or inspiration. To originate is carefully, patiently, and understandingly to combine." Insisting that all novel conceptions "are merely unusual combinations," Poe defined the poetic genius as a mathematician with rare combinatory powers.

Poe also broke from the mold with his insistence that the end of art was not truth but pleasure. To create pleasure, a work of art must provoke an emotion of excitement. This requirement demanded that poems be brief (less than one hundred lines in length) and have organic unity. Every word must be carefully chosen to create a single mood. "In the whole composition," Poe insisted, "there should be no word written, of which the tendency, direct or indirect, is not to the one pre-established design." While not immediately embraced by his contemporaries, Poe's literary theory, which called attention to the problems of form, design, and literary craftsmanship, had a profound influence upon the subsequent development of criticism both at home and abroad.

Perhaps the last outstanding personality of American Romantic criticism was Walt Whitman (1819–1892). In a lengthy preface to his 1855 edition of *Leaves of Grass*, Whitman outlined a theory of poetry which he held throughout his long and productive career. According to Whitman, the American poet must reflect the spirit of his or her nation, "must incarnate its geography and natural life and rivers and lakes" and its "free American workmen and workwomen." Like Emerson, Whitman deemphasized the distinction between works of art and works of nature and viewed the poet as the high priest of literature. The poet, he asserted, was a proclaimer of truth who must "hold up high to eyes of land and race the eternal antiseptic models, and dauntlessly confront greed, injustice, and all forms of that wiliness and tyranny whose roots never die." Literature was not an end in itself but a means to social and religious reform. Also like Emerson, Whitman stressed originality, individuality, and self-reliance. The poetic genius was not confined to literary laws; instead, Whitman wrote, "a great poet is followed by laws – they conform to him." To Whitman, the best poetry was written freely, simply, naturally, "without meter, rhyme or other ornament," and expressed themes that were appropriate both for the America of his day and for centuries in the future. Ultimately, Whitman assessed literary merit according to the ethical and spiritual depth of the work and its ability to "tally and express nature in its cosmos fullness." To Whitman, "nature," in the final analysis, "is the only complete and actual poem."

Ironically, America produced its most truly national literature at the very moment when sectional hostilities were propelling the nation toward the Civil War. It is also ironic that after the Civil War, which politically reunified the nation, American cultural unity began to disintegrate. During the 1870s, American men and women of letters were torn between the new promises of science and the older world of dreams. While the great Romantics of a previous era – Emerson, Longfellow, John Greenleaf Whittier (1807–1892), James Russell Lowell (1819–1891) – remained active and exerted a considerable influence upon a number of prominent critics of the period, younger writers bolted from the principles of Romanticism and groped for an aesthetics that could accommodate an increasingly scientific and empirical age. The literary world was divided between the Progressives, who revered "science" and "reality," and the Traditionalists, who, fearful of scientific determinism and literalism, sought to retain a more idealistic philosophy of literature.

Among the leading critics of the "genteel tradition" who remained strongly influenced by the Romantic tradition were Edmund C. Stedman (1833–1908), Thomas Bailey Aldrich (1836–1907), George E. Woodbury (1855–1930), and Bayard Taylor (1825–1878). In criticism, the most noteworthy representative of this group was Stedman, a New York stockbroker and editor of the prestigious *Century Magazine*. As the first American critic to concern himself with the influence of science on thought, Stedman sought to blend the earlier idealism with the more current Spencerian notions of progress in an attempt to reconcile science and literature. In his theory of poetry elaborated in *Victorian Poets* (1875), *Poets of America* (1885), and *The Nature and Elements of Poetry* (1892), Stedman, like Poe, emphasized beauty and rhythm. While the spokesman for the declining genteel tradition, in championing the cult of beauty and idealizing Alfred, Lord Tennyson, Stedman also reflected the transition in America from an essentially ethical to an aesthetic criticism.

Stedman's bold predictions for a poetic renaissance, however, never materialized. Instead, during the last quarter of the century, the novel (or as William Dean Howells preferred to call it, the "prose romance"), became the most vital literary form of the age. In the capable hands of a younger generation of authors and critics – William Dean Howells (1837–1920), Henry James (1843–1916), Bret Harte (1836–1902), Mark Twain (1835–1910), Hamlin Garland (1860–1940), and others – the wide possibilities of the novel were explored in both theory and practice. For critic-novelists such as Harte and Twain, the novel offered the opportunity to entertain with humorous story lines filled with local color. For them, prose which failed to interest the reader in its story, or which lacked consistency of plot and character, lacked true artistic merit. More militant realists such as Garland, on the other hand, used the novel to portray the harshness and social injustices of life in a noble attempt to "hasten the age of beauty and peace by delineating the ugliness and warfare of the present." In developing his theory of "veritism," Garland called upon writers to put aside all models and be true to themselves, always speaking the truth by depicting "normal people, unarranged landscapes, and colors that are not 'harmonized.'"

The individual credited with the greatest influence upon the American novel was William Dean Howells. From the time of his editorship at *Harper's Magazine* in 1886 until his death in 1920, Howells examined and commented on most major publications and remained one of the most potent voices in American criticism. Early in his career, Howells labored to make realism the legitimate successor to the Romantic novel. Realism to Howells meant "truthful treatment of material," although his own prudish standards and his keen business sense as editor of a magazine with a primarily female readership led him to admit that only part of the truth was fit to print. Howells also had little sympathy for the "naturalism" of Émile Zola, which he characterized as an obsession with only the ugly, the abnormal, the exaggerated, and the diseased.

Howells expected the critic to be gentle, never harsh or arrogant, always recognizing that literature was not static but progressive, not simply the imitation of masterpieces but a true reflection of living men and women. For Howells, the proper critical method was scientific, not impressionistic. He insisted that the office of the critic was "to ascertain facts and traits of literature, not to invent or denounce them; to discover principles, not to establish them; to report, not to create."

Unlike many of his predecessors, Howells' preference for the American theme did not outlaw the use of foreign materials. Neither did Howells support those who advocated the development of the "great American novel." Recognizing the great cultural diversity of the United States, Howells noted that all America could be expressed only in a novel conceived as an encyclopedia, "with a force of novelists apportioned on the basis of our Congressional representation, and working under one editorial direction."

The only individual to rival Howells as the master of late-nineteenth-century criticism was Henry James. In comparison to his contemporaries, such as Howells or the local-color writers, James placed less emphasis on the subject and more upon technique, form, prose style, and structural problems. "We must grant the artist his subject, his ideas . . . ." James wrote, "our criticism is applied only to what he makes of it." While also a realist, unlike Howells, James expressed little concern for the plain, unvarnished facts of life. Instead, James was primarily interested in the skill of the artist in giving the work a "feeling" or "spirit" of reality. Known in his own novels for his realistic psychological penetration and analysis, as a critic he expected writers to produce "the illusion of life." Labeling life itself as "all inclusion and confusion," James asserted that the task of the novelist was to bring pattern and meaning to life by probing its depths, not simply by transcribing its surface.

By the end of the century, American criticism had gone full circle. From an early cultural dependence upon Old World ideas, critics in the United States, during its first century of independence, developed, or at least struggled to develop, a genuinely national literary tradition. Once this tradition was secured, the aggressive cultural nationalism was tempered, and the lines of American and European criticism began again to follow parallel paths. This convergence was evidence that, at long last, American criticism had reached full maturity.

Further reading

Brown, Clarence Arthur, comp. *The Achievement of American Criticism: Representative Selections from Three Hundred Years of American Criticism*, 1954.

Clark, Harry Hayden, ed. *Transitions in American Literary History*, 1953.

Dauber, Kenneth. *The Idea of Authorship in America: Democratic Poetics from Franklin to Melville*, 1990.

Howard, Leon. *The Connecticut Wits*, 1943.

Moss, Sidney P. *Poe's Literary Battles: The Critic in the Context of His Literary Milieu*, 1963.

Parks, Edd W. *Ante-bellum Southern Literary Critics*, 1962.

Perosa, Sergio. *American Theories of the Novel: 1793–1903*, 1984.

Pritchard, John P. *Criticism in America*, 1956.

Rice, Grantland S. *The Transformation of Authorship in America*, 1997.

Smith, Bernard. *Forces in American Criticism*, 1939.

Stafford, John. *The Literary Criticism of "Young America": A Study in the Relationship of Politics and Literature*, 1952.

Stovall, Floyd, ed. *The Development of American Literary Criticism*, 1955.

Wellek, René. *A History of Modern Criticism: 1750–1950*. Vol. 3, *The Age of Transition*, 1965.

Whalen-Bridge, John. *Political Fiction and the American Self*, 1998.

TERRY D. BILHARTZ

See also Emerson; Fuller; James; Poe

American Literary Theory: Twentieth Century

Nineteenth-century American literary criticism had been preoccupied with a number of themes, such as searching for and expressing a national identity, formulating organicist, transcendental, and Romantic conceptions of art, struggling against commercialism and mechanism, debating the relative virtues and possible compromise of romance and realism, of tradition and originality, as well as the autonomous or didactic nature of literature. Some of these concerns were inherited by twentieth-century American literary criticism. Reacting against the romance fiction of figures such as Nathaniel Hawthorne and Herman Melville, William Dean Howells had expressed a theory of realism in *Criticism and Fiction* (1891). Another realist around the turn of the century was Hamlin Garland who advocated "veritism," a local literature based on individual insight and committed to truth. In his "A Plea for Romantic Fiction" (1901) and *The Responsibilities of the Novelist* (1903), Frank Norris identified the limitations of realism and advanced a manifesto of naturalism in the vein of Émile Zola.

The quest for national identity and an American tradition was continued in works such as John Macy's *The Spirit of American Literature* (1913), which urged a separation of literature and morality, and Randolph Bourne's *Youth and Life* (1911), which argued that tradition should be revaluated and its positive elements utilized in defining the central aspects of American culture. Similarly, in *America's Coming of Age* (1915), Van Wyck Brooks called for a review of the past and the formulation of a viable tradition which might sustain American writers. The attack on commercialism and philistinism was continued both by Brooks and by publications such as *Civilization in the United States* (1922), a collection of pieces by thirty authors. Another major American critical voice around the turn of the century was that of W. C. Brownell who, somewhat influenced by Matthew Arnold, sought to establish literary criticism as a serious, substantive, and original activity in its own right, rather than as merely adjectival upon works of art. Later works in this vein, concerning the uses to be made of an American past and the connection between literature and criticism, included Howard Mumford Jones' *The Theory of American Literature* (1948) and Vernon L. Parrington's *Main Currents in American Thought* (1927–1930). Also current in the early twentieth century was impressionism, perhaps best represented by the work of James Gibbons Huneker and H. L. Mencken. Both men attacked Puritanism and insisted on addressing the aesthetic elements in art as divorced from moral considerations. Other notable names of this period include George Edward Woodberry who viewed literature as instrumental in the achievement of humanity, and George Santayana whose *The Sense of Beauty* (1896) attempted to ground criticism on a psychological basis.

The New Humanists

Many of these critical impulses and concerns underlay a wide-ranging polemic initiated by the so-called "New Humanists." Led by Harvard professor Irving Babbitt and including figures such as Paul Elmer More, Norman Foerster, and Stuart Sherman, the New Humanists were conservative in their cultural and political outlook, reacting against what they saw as a relativistic disorder of styles and approaches characterizing early-twentieth-century America. They rejected the predominant tendencies stemming from the liberal-bourgeois tradition: a narrow focus on the present at the expense of the past and of tradition; unrestrained freedom in political, moral, and aesthetic domains; a riot of pluralism, a mechanical exaltation of facts, and an uninformed worship of science. As Babbitt put it, "Man has gained immensely in his grasp on facts, but . . . has become so immersed in their multiplicity as to lose that vision of the One by which his lower self was once overawed and restrained." Indeed, for Babbitt, the problem of the One and the Many, of perceiving unity in the diversity of our experience, was "the ultimate problem of thought . . . ."

Babbitt's ideas represented one side of a newly awakened debate between Ancients and Moderns, a debate often grounded in educational concerns. Babbitt opposed reformists such as Harvard University President Charles Eliot and John Dewey who urged that the college education system should be brought into line with prevailing bourgeois scientific and economic interests. Babbitt, somewhat incoherently, sees these interests as descended primarily from Jean-Jacques Rousseau, as the father both of democracy and Romanticism. In *Rousseau and Romanticism* (1919) and other works, Babbitt seeks to oppose Romantic "excess" (which for him comprehends the bourgeois traits noted above) with classical moderation and restraint, with a focus on what is "normal" and "universal" in human experience, and especially with a return to tradition in the seeking of moral and aesthetic value. Babbitt sees the literary criticism of his time as pervaded with the disease of impressionism; as against this, he calls for objective judgment and impersonality based on comparative and historical methods.

The influence of the New Humanists reached its peak in the 1920s and waned during the 1930s when they were challenged both by rival humanists such as Lewis Mumford, by more liberal-minded critics such as Edmund Wilson, Allen Tate, and R. P. Blackmur, by philosophers such as George Santayana who pointed to their inconsistencies, as well as by the left-wing and Marxist critics discussed below. Other schools of criticism also rejected the New Humanism: the Chicago School, the New York Intellectuals, and the New Critics reacted against the New Humanists' subordination of aesthetic value to moral criteria and their condemnation of modern and innovative literature. Perhaps the single most important circumstance behind the eclipse of the New Humanists lay in social conditions in America during the 1930s: the depression, widespread unemployment and suffering caused by economic collapse, perhaps generated a need for more socially conscious criticism rather than New Humanist criticism which had focused on perfecting the individual.

However, the New Humanists exerted a profound impact on the most influential American (and later British) critic of the twentieth century, T. S. Eliot, whose early ideas owed a great deal to their emphasis on tradition, classicism, and impersonality. Eliot was also indebted to later nineteenth-century French poets and particularly to Ezra Pound and the Imagist movement. Pound assumed a broad range of critical roles: as poet-critic, he promoted his own work and the works of figures such as Robert Frost, James Joyce, and Eliot; he translated numerous texts from Anglo-Saxon, Latin, Greek, and Chinese; and, associating with various schools such as Imagism and Vorticism, he advocated a poetry which was concise, concrete, precise in expression of emotion, and appropriately informed by a sense of tradition. As a result of his suggestions, Eliot's major poem *The Waste Land* (1922) was radically condensed and transformed. Eliot took his so-called theory of "tradition" from both Babbitt and Pound. This theory claimed that the major works of art, both past and present, form an "ideal order" which is continually modified by subsequent works of art. The central implication here was that contemporary writers should find common ground with that tradition even as they extended it. Eliot effectively succeeded in redefining the European literary tradition, continuing the New Humanists' onslaught against the Romantics, and bringing into prominence Dante, the Metaphysical poets, and the French Symbolists. Eliot also advanced an "impersonal" notion of poetry, whereby the poet expresses not a personality but a precise formulation of thought and feeling such as is lacking in "ordinary" experience. The poet, according to Eliot, employs an "objective correlative," whereby objects and events in the external world are used to express complexes of thought and emotion. In terms of literary history, Eliot held that a "dissociation of sensibility" had set in after the seventeenth century which entailed a disjunction of various human faculties such as reason and emotion which had previously been integrated within a unified sensibility. Eliot's ideas bore an ambivalent relationship with the claims of the New Criticism. On the one hand, he believed that the aesthetic dimension of works of art is irreducible; on the other, he believed, with increasing insistence throughout his career, that art is irreducibly bound to its social, religious, and literary context. The ideas of Pound and Eliot have had a lasting influence but their most forceful impact occurred between the 1920s and the 1940s.

While Eliot and Pound were urging a return to classical values, the decade of the 1930s in America witnessed the rise of a number of distinct critical modes: left-wing and

Marxist criticism, the New Criticism, the Aristotelian criticism of the Chicago School, and the so-called New York Intellectuals. All of these were in various ways underlain by the Great Depression of the 1930s.

Marxism

During this decade of economic collapse, Marxism became a significant political force. Socially and politically conscious criticism had a long heritage in America, going back to figures such as Walt Whitman, William Dean Howells, and Ralph Waldo Emerson and running through the work of writers noted above such as John Macy, Van Wyck Brooks, and Vernon L. Parrington. Notable Marxist critics of the 1920s and 1930s included Floyd Dell, Max Eastman, V. F. Calverton, Philip Rahv, and Granville Hicks. Eastman and Dell edited the important radical journal *The Masses* and then *The Liberator* (1918–1924). Both produced works of literary criticism, Dell relating literary history to social causes and Eastman unorthodoxically treating poetry as a distinct domain. Calverton and Hicks were perhaps the most prominent of the Marxist critics; the former founded *The Modern Quarterly: A Journal of Radical Opinion* (1923), which later became *The Modern Monthly*. In *The Newer Spirit* (1925) he urges that aesthetic judgments are conditioned by a reader's background and that a work must be interpreted and judged in relation to the social structure which generated it. In *The Liberation of American Literature* (1932) Calverton interprets the tradition of American literature in terms of Marxist categories such as class and economic infrastructure. Granville Hicks became a Communist during the depression and in his *The Great Tradition* (1933) he assesses American writers in terms of their social and political awareness and their relevance to social progress and their contribution to the development of proletarian awareness and literature. In other works, Hicks had acknowledged that literary achievement and ideological disposition were not intrinsically related. This period saw the growth of a number of other radical journals as well as the voicing of revolutionary views by non-Marxist critics such as Kenneth Burke and Edmund Wilson. The latter's most influential work, *Axel's Castle* (1931), traced the development of modern Symbolist literature, identifying in this broad movement a "revolution of the word," which might open up new possibilities of thought and literature.

New criticism

Liberal critics such as Vernon L. Parrington and F. O. Matthiessen employed a historical approach to literature but Matthiessen insisted on addressing its aesthetic dimensions. This formalist disposition became intensified in both the New Criticism and the Chicago School. The term "The New Criticism" was coined as early as 1910 in a lecture of that title by Joel Spingarn who, influenced by the expressionist theory of art expounded by the Italian philosopher Benedetto Croce, advocated a creative and imaginative criticism which gave primacy to the aesthetic qualities of literature over historical, psychological, and moral considerations. Spingarn, however, was not directly related to the New Criticism which developed in subsequent decades. Some of the important features of the New Criticism originated in England during the 1920s in the work of T. S. Eliot (as noted earlier) as well as in seminal studies by I. A. Richards and William Empson. Richards' *Principles of Literary Criticism* (1924) advanced literary-critical notions such as irony, tension, and balance, as well as distinguishing between poetic and other uses of language. His *Practical Criticism* (1929), based on student analyses of poetry, emphasized the importance of "objective" and balanced close reading which was sensitive to the figurative language of literature. Richards' student William Empson produced an influential work, *Seven Types of Ambiguity* (1930), which was held up as a model of New Critical close reading.

Across the Atlantic, New Critical practices were also being pioneered by American critics known as the Fugitives and the Southern Agrarians, who promoted the values of the Old South in reaction against the alleged dehumanization of science and technology in the industrial North. Notable among these pioneers were John Crowe Ransom and Allen Tate who developed some of the ideas of Eliot and Richards. Ransom edited the poetry magazine *The Fugitive* from 1922 to 1925 with a group of writers including Tate, Robert Penn Warren, and Donald Davidson. Other journals associated with the New Criticism included *The Southern Review*, edited by Penn Warren and Cleanth Brooks (1935–1942), *The Kenyon Review*, run by Ransom (1938–1959), and the still extant *The Sewanee Review*, edited by Tate and others. During the 1940s the New Criticism became institutionalized as the mainstream approach in academia and its influence, while pervasively undermined since the 1950s, still persists. Some of the central documents of New Criticism were written by relatively late adherents: W. K. Wimsatt and Monroe Beardsley's essays "The Intentional Fallacy" (1946) and "The Affective Fallacy" (1949) (it is worth noting, in this context, the enormous influence of E. D. Hirsch's book *Validity in Interpretation*, published in 1967, which equated a text's meaning with its author's intention); Austin Warren's *The Theory of Literature* (1949); W. K. Wimsatt's *The Verbal Icon* (1954); and Murray Krieger's *The New Apologists for Poetry* (1956). The seminal manifestoes of the New Criticism, however, had been proclaimed earlier by Ransom who published a series of essays entitled *The New Criticism* (1941) and an influential essay "Criticism, Inc.," published in *The World's Body* (1938). This essay succinctly expresses a core of New Critical principles underlying the practice of most "New Critics," whose views often differed in other respects. As Ransom acknowledges, his essay is motivated by the desire to make literary criticism more scientific, precise, and systematic; it must, says Ransom, become a "serious business." He urges that the emphasis of criticism must move from historical scholarship to aesthetic appreciation and understanding. Ransom characterizes both the conservative New Humanism and left-wing criticism as focusing on morality rather than aesthetics. While he accepts the value of historical and biographical information, Ransom insists that these are not ends in themselves but instrumental to the real aim of criticism, which is "to define and enjoy the aesthetic or characteristic values of literature."

In short, Ransom's position is that the critic must study literature, not *about* literature. Hence criticism should exclude: (1) personal impressions, because the critical activity should "cite the nature of the object rather than its effects upon the subject"; (2) synopsis and paraphrase, since the plot or story is an abstraction from the real content of the text; (3) historical studies, which might include literary backgrounds, biography, literary sources, and analogues; (4) linguistic studies, which include identifying allusions and meanings of words; (5) moral content, since this is not the whole content of the text; (6) "Any other special studies which deal with some abstract or prose content taken out of the work." Ransom demands that criticism, whose proper province includes technical studies of poetry, metrics, tropes, and fictiveness, should "receive its own charter of rights and function independently." Finally, in this essay and other works, Ransom insists on the ontological uniqueness of poetry, as distinct from prose and other uses of language. All in all, he argues that literature and literary criticism should enjoy autonomy both ontologically and institutionally. His arguments have often been abbreviated into a characterization of New Criticism as focusing on "the text itself" or "the words on the page."

The Chicago School

Another group of critics, known as the Chicago School or the Neo-Aristotelians, began formulating their central ideas around the same time as the New Critics were voicing their manifestoes. In the 1930s departments of humanities at the University of Chicago were undergoing a radical transformation in an attempt to revive them and make them institutionally more competitive with the sciences. Six of the figures later known as the Chicago critics were involved in these changes: R. S. Crane, Richard McKeon, Elder Olson, W. R. Keast, Norman Maclean, and Bernard Weinberg. These critics later produced the central manifesto of the Chicago School, *Critics and Criticism: Ancient and Modern* (1952), which both attacked some of the important tenets of the New Criticism and elaborated an alternative formalistic method of criticism derived in part from Aristotle's *Poetics* (c. 334–323 B.C.). In an earlier essay of 1934, Crane had anticipated (and influenced) Ransom's call that professional criticism should move from a primarily historical toward an aesthetic focus. However, Crane and the Chicago School generally diverged from the New Criticism in their insistence that literary study should integrate both systematic theory of literature (being informed by the history of literary theory) and the practice of close reading and explication of literary texts. Moreover, the Chicago School drew from Aristotle's *Poetics* a number of characteristic critical concerns, such as the emphasis on literary texts as "artistic wholes," the analytical importance of locating individual texts within given genres, and the need to identify textual and generic (as opposed to authorial) intention. Whereas the New Critics had focused attention on specifically poetic uses of language, irony, metaphor, tension, and balance, the Chicago School followed Aristotle in emphasizing plot, character, and thought. In general, the Neo-Aristotelians offered an alternative formalist poetics which acknowledged the mimetic, didactic, and affective functions of literature. The influence of this school, however, was overshadowed by the widespread adoption of New Critical dispositions throughout the American education system.

The New York intellectuals

Before discussing various other and more widespread reactions against the New Criticism, a few words should be said about the so-called New York Intellectuals. These were a group of critics who produced their most significant work between the 1930s and the 1960s and who wrote extensively for radical journals such as *Partisan Review*, *The New Republic*, *The Nation*, *Commentary*, and *Dissent*. Major figures in this group included Richard Chase, Irving Howe, Alfred Kazin, Philip Rahv, Lionel Trilling, Elizabeth Hardwick, Sidney Hook, Steven Marcus, Richard Poirier, Meyer Schapiro, and Susan Sontag. Taking the work of Edmund Wilson as a model, these writers considered themselves aloof from bourgeois society, commercialism, Stalinism, and mass culture; they viewed themselves as democratic socialists and wrote criticism with a social and political emphasis. They promoted literary modernism, and valued complexity, irony, and cosmopolitanism in literature. This broad critical movement (if such a diverse range of critical activity can be called such) was never institutionalized, though it was continued into the 1980s, confined within small circles.

Myth criticism

Much criticism since the 1950s can be regarded as an implicit impugnment of widely institutionalized New Critical practices. A sustained challenge came from structuralism and some of its descendants such as deconstruction. In the West, the influx of structuralism was to some extent anticipated in the work of the Canadian Northrop Frye, who was the most influential theorist in America of what is called Myth Criticism, which was in vogue from the 1940s to the mid-1960s and whose practitioners included Richard Chase, Leslie Fiedler, Daniel Hoffman, and Philip Wheelwright. Drawing on the findings of anthropology and psychology regarding universal myths, rituals, and folk tales, these critics were intent on restoring spiritual content to a world they saw as alienated, fragmented, and ruled by scientism, empiricism, positivism, and technology. They wished to redeem the role of myth, which might comprehend magic, imagination, dreams, intuition, and the unconscious.

They viewed the creation of myth as integral to human thought, and believed that literature emerges out of a core of myth, where "myth" is understood as a collective attempt on the part of various cultures and groups to establish a meaningful context for human existence. Frye's *Anatomy of Criticism* (1957) continued the formalist emphasis of the New Criticism but insisted even more strongly that criticism should be a scientific, objective, and systematic discipline. Moreover, Frye held that such literary criticism views literature as a system. For example, the mythoi of Spring, Summer, Autumn, and Winter gave rise to fundamental literary modes such as comedy, tragedy, irony, and romance. Given the recurrence of basic symbolic motifs, literary history is a repetitive and self-contained cycle. Hence the historical element ostensibly informing Frye's formalism is effectively abrogated, literature being viewed as a timeless, static, and autonomous construct.

Structuralism

Frye's static model, exhibiting recurrent patterns, is a feature shared by structuralist views of language and literature. Structuralism itself was imported into America from France during the 1960s and its leading exponents included Roman Jakobson, Jonathan Culler, Michael Riffaterre, Claudio Guillén, Gerald Prince, and Robert Scholes. Other American thinkers working in the field of semiotics have included C. S. Peirce, Charles Morris, and Noam Chomsky. The foundations of structuralism were laid in the work of the Swiss linguist Ferdinand de Saussure, whose insights were developed by the French anthropologist Claude Lévi-Strauss, Roland Barthes, and others. In his *Course in General Linguistics* (1916), Saussure distinguished *langue*, the system and rules of language, from *parole* or speech. It was the former, according to Saussure, which lent itself to synchronic structural analysis: the system of language could be analyzed at a given point in time as a set of interdependent elements (as opposed to a diachronic study which looked at developments over time). Moreover, Saussure attacked the conventional correspondence theory of meaning whereby language was viewed as a naming process, each word corresponding to the thing it names. Saussure urges that the sign unites not a thing and a name but a concept (signified) and sound-image (signifier). He argues that the bond between signifier and signified is arbitrary (and not natural) in that a concept is not intrinsically linked to a particular signifier. The meaning is determined by collective behavior or convention and is fixed by rules. Hence language is a system of signs and meaning itself is relational, produced by interaction of various signifiers and signifieds within that system. In addition to these insights, what Lévi-Strauss and others took from Saussure was an emphasis on linguistic features described as structures (Lévi-Strauss himself saw myth as a particular kind of language); they also stressed the deep structures underlying various phenomena and sometimes referred these structures to basic characteristics of the human mind. Also entailed in structuralist analyses is the antihumanist view that, since language is an institution, individual human agency is unprivileged, neither human beings nor social phenomena having essences.

Many of these principles underlay the methods of American structuralists. In his renowned study *Structuralist Poetics* (1975), Jonathan Culler explained that structuralist investigations of literature would seek to identify the systems of conventions underlying literature. Robert Scholes, in *Structuralism in Literature: An Introduction* (1974), sought a scientific basis for the study of literature as an interconnected system of various texts. Other key texts of structuralism in America included a special issue of *Yale French Studies* (1966), and volumes entitled *Structuralism* (1970), edited by Jacques Ehrmann, and *The Structuralist Controversy* (1970), edited by Richard Macksey and Eugenio Donato. Also influential in America was the work of Roman Jakobson who taught for many years at various American universities, and who worked out an influential model of communication as well as a distinction between metaphor and metonymy in the analysis of narratives.

Deconstruction

By the time that structuralism was introduced in America, it had already spawned its own critique in the work of the French thinker Jacques Derrida who for several years was affiliated with American universities. At the heart of Derrida's project was a concerted assault against what he termed "logocentrism," which he sees as pervading Western thought. Logocentrism is the attempt to center one's discourse on the stability of a "transcendental signified" outside of the discourse itself and acting as its foundation. Such transcendental signifieds include the Logos; the idea of substance, matter, Platonic forms, the Hegelian absolute, and the various hierarchical oppositions which sustain these, such as speech/writing, sense/intellect, body/soul, and center/margin. Structuralism itself, according to Derrida, was not free of these traits. In a seminal paper, "Structure, Sign, and Play in the Discourse of the Human Sciences," presented in 1966, Derrida argued that the notion of structure self-contradictorily entailed a notion of a center as both the foundation of, and external to, a given structure. In this paper, Derrida drew on the insights of Lévi-Strauss and also took from structuralism its foregrounding of language in conducting any type of analysis.

Derrida's influence in America was unparalleled in the latter twentieth century. His American disciples included the Yale critics Paul de Man, J. Hillis Miller, and Geoffrey Hartman as well as Barbara Johnson and, arguably, Harold Bloom. These critics applied and extended Derridean techniques such as searching for impasses or *aporiai* in various texts, displaying the hidden presuppositions and contradictions of literary and philosophical works, and demonstrating how their central claims and oppositions undermined themselves. In *Blindness and Insight* (1971), for example, de Man argues that the insights produced by critics are intrinsically linked to certain blindnesses, the critics invariably affirming something other than what they intended. De Man's *Allegories of Reading* (1979) explores the theory of tropes or figurative language, affirming that language is intrinsically metaphorical and that literary texts above all are highly self-conscious of their status as such and are self-deconstructing. Hence criticism inevitably misreads a text, given that figurative language mediates between literary and critical text.

Harold Bloom, also centrally concerned with the function of tropes in literature, is best known for his assessment of poetic tradition on the basis of the "anxiety of influence." Each writer, asserts Bloom, attempts to carve out an imaginative space free from overt domination by his or her predecessors; to this end, as Bloom argues in *A Map of Misreading* (1975), the writer assumes an Oedipal disposition, creatively misreading those predecessors or "fathers" by way of certain tropes such as irony, synecdoche, and metonymy.

Feminist approaches

Feminist criticism in America received a major stimulus from the Civil Rights movement of the 1960s, and has differed somewhat in its concerns from its counterparts in France and Britain, notwithstanding the undoubted impact of earlier figures such as Virginia Woolf and Simone de Beauvoir. A seminal work, *The Feminine Mystique* (1963), was authored by Betty Friedan, who subsequently founded the National Organization of Women in 1966. This widely received book expressed the fundamental grievance of middle-class American women, their entrapment within private, domestic life and their inability to pursue public careers. A number of other important feminist texts were produced around this time: Mary Ellman's *Thinking About Women* (1968), Kate Millett's *Sexual Politics* (1969), Germaine Greer's *The Female Eunuch* (1970), and Shulamith Firestone's *The Dialectic of Sex* (1970). Millett's influential book concerned female sexuality and the representation of women in literature. It argued that patriarchy was a political institution which relied on subordinated roles for women. It also distinguished between the concept of "sex," which was rooted in biology, and that of "gender," which was culturally acquired. Other critics in this tradition of examining masculine portrayals of women included Carolyn Heilbrun and Judith Fetterly.

A number of feminist texts have attempted to identify alternative and neglected traditions of female writing. These have included Patricia Meyer Spacks' *The Female Imagination* (1975), Ellen Moers' *Literary Women* (1976), and Sandra Gilbert and Susan Gubar's *The Madwoman in the Attic* (1979). The most influential work of this kind was Elaine Showalter's *A Literature of their Own* (1977), which traced three phases of women's writing, a "feminine" phase (1840–1880) where women writers imitated male models, a "feminist" phase (1880–1920) during which women challenged those models and their values, and a "female" phase (from 1920) which saw women advocating their own perspectives. Recent debates within American feminism, conducted by figures such as Showalter, Lillian Robinson, Annette Kolodny, and Jane Marcus, have concerned the relationship of female writers to male theories, the need for feminist theory and a female language, the relation of feminism to poststructuralist perspectives, as well as continuing problems of political and educational activism.

Also hotly debated has been the possible connection of feminism and Marxism. Michele Barrett's *Women's Oppression Today: Problems in Marxist Feminist Analysis* (1980) attempts to reconcile Marxist and feminist principles in analyzing the representation of gender. Other works in this vein include Judith Newton and Deborah Rosenfelt's *Feminist Criticism and Social Change* (1985), which also argues for feminist analysis that takes account of social and economic contexts. A notable recent development has been the attempt to think through feminism from black and minority perspectives, as in Alice Walker's *In Search of Our Mothers' Gardens* (1983) and Barbara Smith's *Toward a Black Feminist Criticism* (1977). Finally, significant contributions by lesbian critics include Mary Daly's *Gyn/Ecology* (1978) and Adrienne Rich's "Compulsory Heterosexuality and Lesbian Existence" (1980).

Other critical trends

A number of other critical tendencies enjoyed popularity in America between the 1970s and the 1990s. One of these is the so-called New Historicism, developed primarily by Stephen Greenblatt and influenced by Michel Foucault's insistence on viewing literary discourse within a larger social framework of political, religious, and other discourses, with especial emphasis on the fabric of power. New Historicists tend to emphasize the plural and discontinuous nature of history as well as the impossibility of an entirely detached and objective approach to the past. In other words, history itself is a series of texts. Reader-response theory has had its American exponents, such as Stanley Fish, Norman Holland, and David Bleich, who have generally located the meaning of a literary text within the interaction between text and reader, as framed by an institutional community of interpretation.

More recent trends in American criticism have included postcolonial and minority perspectives. A seminal influence on postcolonial criticism was Franz Fanon's *The Wretched of the Earth* (1964), as well as Edward Said's landmark work *Orientalism* (1978). These texts drew attention to "Third-World" struggles and dilemmas and the imposition of Western values and constructs upon other cultures. Other influences on postcolonial criticism have included Derrida's critique of Western metaphysics, and Antonio Gramsci's notion of political and cultural hegemony. Significant figures in this mode of criticism are Gayatri Spivak and Homi Bhaba. Minority perspectives have been advanced by figures such as Henry Louis Gates in his *Black Literature and Literary Theory* (1984) and *The Signifying Monkey: A Theory of Afro-American Literary Criticism* (1988). Gates draws attention to the complex inheritance of African-American writers as drawing on both Western and African traditions in the use of peculiar tropes.

Finally, it is worth noting the irony that, in an era where Marxism has often been viewed as "dead," America has produced a major Marxist theorist in the Hegelian tradition, Fredric Jameson, whose work has complemented the enormous popularity in America of the writings of the English Marxist Terry Eagleton. Jameson's major works, such as *Marxism and Form* (1971), *The Political Unconscious* (1981), and *Postmodernism, or the Cultural Logic of Late Capitalism* (1991), all attempt in their various ways to rethink the connections between literature and broader cultural/political contexts in terms of the dialectical categories of Hegelian Marxism, while drawing on psychoanalysis and various elements of structuralism and poststructuralism. The work of both Eagleton and Jameson highlights the fact that debate within the various branches of American literary theory is still very much alive. All in all, it is evident that American literary criticism has produced a rich native tradition while it continues to be enriched by external developments, in Europe and elsewhere, which have been adapted to American cultural, political, and educational contexts.

Further reading

Foerster, Norman. *American Criticism: Studies in Literary Theory from Poe to the Present*, 1928.
Glicksberg, Charles J. *American Literary Criticism 1900–1950*, 1951.
Leitch, Vincent B. *American Literary Criticism from the Thirties to the Eighties*, 1988.
Smith, Bernard. *Forces in American Criticism: A Study in the History of American Literary Thought*, 1971.
Spikes, Michael P. *Understanding Contemporary American Literary Theory*, 1997.
Stovall, Floyd, ed. *The Development of American Literary Criticism*, 1955.
Sutton, Walter. *Modern American Criticism*, 1963.

M. A. R. Habib

Anandavardhana

Indian theorist

Active: ninth century A.D.

Biography
Nothing is known of his life.

Influence
Anandavardhana's theory of *dhvani* (the power of suggestion) has long been accepted as canonical in the tradition of Sanskrit poetics. Immediately after its development certain theorists tried to challenge it, but without success. Most *dhvani* theorists following Anandavardhana, like Mammata, contributed mainly toward refining and explaining the theory but without adding anything of lasting significance. Anandavardhana belonged to the first period of Indian philosophy of art, that of formulation, which extended from the first century B.C. to 950 A.D. It was during this period that Bharata developed the theories of *bhava* (emotion) and *rasa* (aesthetic rapture). The second period ran from 950 A.D. to around 1150, a time of consolidation when *dhvani* was defended against its opponents. The final period extended to the seventeenth century, an era of exposition on the interconnections between *bhava*, *dhvani*, and *rasa*. Anandavardhana's influence dominated the latter periods and continues to be of relevance today. As Sushil Kumar De explains, "No other work on Sanskrit Poetics has indeed exerted so much influence as the *Dhvanyaloka*, which brought to a focus the tentative efforts of earlier thinkers, and by its thoroughness and masterly exposition eclipsed all its predecessors, dominating, as it did, thoughts of generations of theorists even down to the present time."

Analysis
Anandavardhana was the great ninth-century exponent of one of the four major schools of Indian literary theory, the school of *dhvani* or suggestion, and the author of the *Dhvanyaloka*. The three other schools were the *alankara* (poetic figures), *riti* (poetic rhythm or arrangement of word), and *rasa* (aesthetic mood or flavor). The *dhvani* school followed and marked a significant departure from the formalism of the *alankara* and *riti* schools. While the earlier theorists emphasized outward expression, Anandavardhana formulated and popularized a new interpretive approach emphasizing the inward content of a work, the *dhvani* or *rasadhvani*. He held that the real charm of poetry comes neither from its expression nor its expressed content, but rather from its suggested meaning which alone has the power to expand the reader's awareness toward greater unity. And while any reader can appreciate the expressed dimension of poetry, not everyone can necessarily appreciate its suggested content (*dhvani*). Anandavardhana

thus postulated a class of readers as *sahrdayas*, those who were competent to realize the suggested greatness of poetry in the timeless present of their own awareness. Even though the expressed form and content give rise to a suggested content, for Anandavardhana suggestion was of paramount importance and constituted the soul of poetry.

The *Dhvanyaloka*, which is also called the *Kavyaloka* or *Sahrdayaloka*, comes in two parts: the Karika consisting of verse and treating *dhvani*; and the Vrtti, generally expressed in prose with verse examples of the Karika. As De indicates, Anandavardhana is reputed to be the author of the *Dhvanyaloka*, but questions have been raised about the differences between the two parts. One argument is that the Karika contradicts certain aspects of the Vrtti and seems to have been written by an older writer with different opinions from those of Anandavardhana, who is accepted as the author of the Vrtti. Of the two parts of the *Dhvanyaloka*, the Vrtti is an exposition of the Karika, which seems to have come first and to belong to a tradition that predates Anandavardhana. But the Vrtti considerably elaborates on the bare outlines of the Karika, expanding, revising, and clarifying *dhvani* according to *alankara*, *rasa*, and other poetic elements not fully developed in the Karika. Hence Anandavardhava is distinguished from an unknown author called the Dhvanikara.

Though the origins of the *dhvani* school may be lost in obscurity, the Dhvanikara was the first to give the theory a systematic formulation as an interpretive method. His dates are unknown, but he does not seem to have lived much before Anandavardhana, his ostensible commentator. We know that *dhvani* belongs to an older tradition because the Dhvanikara was familiar with the earlier theories of *rasa*, *alankara*, and *riti*. He may also have been contemporaneous with the founders of the earlier schools, which could explain why *dhvani* though used to a certain extent by these schools was not fully accepted or even properly understood until a later time. Anandavardhana's commentary in the Vrtti is responsible for bringing about this acceptance and understanding and for establishing *dhvani* as a key principle of Indian literary theory.

The charm of suggested content gives poetry its real significance says Anandavardhana. He holds that *dhvani* can manifest itself in three forms: a fact (*vastu*), a poetic figure (*alankara*), or an emotional mood (*rasa*). This implies that there are three types of *dhvani*: *vastu-dhvani*, *alankara-dhvani*, and *rasa-dhvani*. But this division led to an apparent contradiction. At one point Anandavardhana says that *dhvani* in general is the soul of poetry, and then with apparent inconsistency claims that *rasa-dhvani* alone is the essence of poetry. This contradiction was resolved by Abhinavagupta, a commentator of the *Dhvanyaloka*, who argued that Anandavardhana was correct to privilege *rasa-dhvani*. He reasons that the other two forms of *dhvani*, *vastu* and *alankara*, as formal or material properties, can never be charming without the magic taste of *rasa*. The real charm of poetry, *rasa-dhvani*, is conveyed only by the power of *vyanjana* (suggestion), not by *abhidha* (denotation), *laksana* (indication), or *gauni* (secondary power), which were already known to the early grammarians. Anandavardhana's remarkable contribution to the tradition of Indian literary theory was this formulation of *rasa-dhvani*.

Anandavardhana further held that if the language of poetic figures did not augment the aesthetic taste of poetry (*rasa*), then the figure was reduced in status. For example, if the components of a trope (*alankara*), such as the objective word meaning (*artha*) and its conveyed knowledge (*sabda*), do not contribute to *rasa*, then the trope is a mere ornament. As such it belongs to the lowest type of poetry, *citra*, which being devoid of a suggested idea is not real poetry but the imitation of poetry. In this way Anandavardhana conceived of all the elements of poetry in relation to *rasa* (aesthetic rapture), which can be evoked only through suggestion (*dhvani*). Through *rasa-dhvani*, moreover, the reader or hearer has the experience of the word whole or *sphota*, which resembles the Neo-Platonic *logos*. *Sphota*, as defined by the grammarian-philosopher Bhartrhari, consists of a word as a whole conveyed by its component letters (*varnas*). The sequence of sounds of a word give rise to the meaning of the word whole, which flashes forth in the reader's mind. The eternal unity of sound and meaning in a word (*sphota*) is identified with Brahman as the ultimate reality. Through *sphota*, the reader or hearer engages in a three-in-one unity of absolute word, consciousness, and reality called *Sabda Brahman*.

This connection in a word between *dhvani* and *sphota* can be applied by analogy to poetry, as it was to a certain extent by the earlier *alankara* (trope) school of Indian critics. They showed how the formal devices or expressed parts of a poem can reveal a deeper sense. This unexpressed sense differs from the denotative and referential elements of a poem both in order of arrangement and in essence, and is thus called the *dhvani* (sound, echo, or tone) or *vyangya artha* (suggested content). As Anandavardhana pointed out, the term *dhvani* was sometimes used by the grammarians for the word or letters of a poem that reveal *sphota*. As the critic Mammata remarks in De, "the *dhvani* is, according to the grammarians, that word which reveals the all-important *sphota*, inasmuch as through it arises the knowledge of the word's meaning." Even though other grammarians were also applying the term *dhvani* not only to the expressed word but also to the suggested meaning that supersedes the one directly expressed, credit for developing *dhvani* into a fully-fledged and sophisticated theory goes to Anandavardhana.

Given the interrelation between suggestion and emotion, Anandavardhana further elaborated that poetry with emotion (*bhava*) as its theme was superior to other types of poetry. But an emotion cannot be expressed in an ordinary, direct way by words (*vacya*); it can be communicated to the reader only indirectly through its causes and effects, or through the context in which the emotion arises. Once this situation is conveyed to allow readers to apprehend the emotion, then they can experience the "exalted delight called *rasa*." Theorists who followed Anandavardhana and the *Dhvanyaloka* became known as the *navina* or New School of aesthetic interpretation, while earlier theorists such as Bhamaha of the *alankara* system generally became known as the Old School (*pracina*). For the *navina* school the difficulty was how to explain the transition for the reader from the expressed form of a poem to its unexpressed or inexpressible content (*dhvani*).

The basis of *dhvani*, then, is the power to convey meaning through suggestion in addition to communicating through overt expression. This suggested meaning (*vyangyartha*) differs from and exceeds the meaning conveyed explicitly by words (*vacyartha*). The emotional content of a poem can be expressed in language only when the poet describes a situation in a way that indicates to the reader its underlying emotion through the power of suggestion. The emotion (*bhava*) of a poem necessitates a suggested meaning (*dhvani* or *vyangyartha*). The New School (*navina*) compares the expressed form (*vacana*) and its suggested meaning (*dhvani*) of a poem to the body (*sarira*) and soul (*atman*) of a human being. *Dhvani* as the essence of a poem is its *atman*, while the expressed form with its words (*sabda*) and explicit meaning (*vacyartha*) is the situation of *dhvani* or its body (*sarira*). Unlike the Old School of poetics, which focused on the expressed form or body of poetry, the New School comments on how the reader transcends the explicit in order to reach the inner meaning suggested by a poem. This shift in emphasis from the formalism of the Old School to the exalted delight of the reader's experience in the New School, a shift from outer to inner elements, parallels the shift in contemporary Western literary theory from New Criticism and Russian Formalism to phenomenological criticism, reception theory, and reader-response criticism.

Just as the reader-oriented theories in the West sought a balance between the formal and rhetorical, objective and subjective elements, so the *navina* school of *dhvani* sought to clarify the value of inner expression suggested to the reader by a poem. For the Old School, the beauty (*sobha*, *carutva*) of a work determined its value, but for the New School the beauty of an expression is relevant not in itself, since the expressed form is subordinate to the suggested content, but only in serving to convey this suggested content. The criterion for judging beauty in poetry is the extent to which it is adequate (*ucita*) to take the reader to the emotion suggested by the inner meaning. For Anandavardhana, when we contemplate a beautiful object, we are led to the experience of freedom from all activity, including the desire or will to do anything but continue in this state of contemplation. The aesthetic object suspends our grasping for anything in the regretted past or anticipated future, opening a clearing for the awareness of a "unit of meaning" (*sphota*) in the timeless present. This stasis results not from the ornamental beauty or expressed content of a work but rather from the response it evokes through the power of suggestion (*dhvani*). Though rarely discussed in Western literary theory, this contemplative response (*rasadhvani*) leads the reader through the flavor of subtle emotions toward "liberation" or *moksha*. Sanskrit poetics differs from Western theory insofar as aesthetic experience (*rasa-dhvani*) is said to occur through an experience of *turiya*, the self as transcendental pure consciousness, which poststructuralism attempts to deconstruct. But how qualityless pure consciousness or unexpressed suggestion can be deconstructed has never been adequately explained – much less empirically proved. Entering the timeless present suggested by art continues to bring transpersonal revelations or translogical connections; a flash of truth or a moment of eternity.

Although modern science posits only one kind of empiricism and thus only one kind of truth, the sensory or material, Eastern cultures posit three (interrelated) kinds of empiricism – sensory, mental, and contemplative, as indicated by *rasadhvani*. For Anandavardhava, great works of art comprise an interrelationship of all three. The expressed form and content of a work correspond to sensory and mental empiricism, while the suggestion of a timeless freedom corresponds to the contemplative. Historically, the West has applied the principle of falsifiability, the criterion of valid knowledge, only to sensory empiricism and denied it to the other two. In the East, on the other hand, falsifiability has also been applied to mental and contemplative knowledge. That is, as in sensory empiricism, so in mental and contemplative empiricism one can apply the three strands of valid knowing: injunction (doing something), apprehension (collating results), and confirmation (testing these results) – or exemplar, data, and falsifiability. Bhartrhari emphasized that the individual's experience of a unit of meaning (*sphota*) constitutes a process of inner transformation, a *yoga* of spiritual development. This *yoga* is an injunction, its result is the apprehension of a meaning whole, and its test is the principle of adequacy (*ucita*) and the record of ancient texts such as the Vedas and the *Dhvayaloka*. Similarly, Anandavardhana felt that *dhvani* leads to an inner truth capable of evoking a palpable (testable) response in the individual. The theory of grammar and aesthetic rapture in Indian poetics thus constitutes an empirical approach to all three aspects of literature: the sensory, mental, and contemplative.

From the perspective of Anandavardhana's New School, then, the merit (*guna*) and defect (*dosa*) of poetry take on a new significance. These merits and defects, or the beauty and ugliness of a poem, refer ultimately to the fitness (*aucitya*) of an expression to suggest an emotion. Words are not beautiful or ugly in themselves but only to the extent they suit a suggested emotional content. As

T. P. Ramachandran observes, a word designating "sweetness" may be appropriate for the emotions of love or sorrow, but would "hinder rather than help the delineation of an emotion like fury." Similarly, the use of florid language, with long compounds and strident sounds, was always considered by the Old School to be a merit, but for the New School "floridity" was only a merit for the appropriate emotions such as anger and courage. Adequacy and beauty are thus to be determined not by reference to the expressed form or content of a poem but only to its suggested emotion. Ramachandran says: "To speak in terms of the metaphors of soul and body, once *bhava* (or *rasa*) [emotion or aesthetic rapture respectively] is regarded as the soul of poetic content, *gunas* [merit] in the expression come to be conceived of in the manner of qualities of the soul, such as bravery or charity, whereas the previous writers [the Old School] thought of *gunas* in the manner of embellishments of the body."

The value of Anandavardhana's New School of *dhvani* thus consists in elucidating how the expressed form and content of a work can lead the reader to the unexpressed, to the taste or relish (*rasa*) of the underlying poetic emotion (*bhava*), which in reality is inexpressible. This end, however, is not divorced from the expressive form. On the contrary, the literary dimensions of a work, its ornamental accouterments, and structural devices, contribute to the aesthetic effect. De emphasizes that suggestion should not be confused with the abstract hinting or total silence found in certain modern poems, or in the unexpressed defined as the indeterminable. Neither should the power of suggestion be confused with the poststructuralist notion of undecidability or indeterminacy caused by the free play of signifiers, which infinitely defers the possibility of stable meaning. In Sanskrit poetics the unexpressed is not thought of as something arbitrary, ambiguous, or indeterminate, but rather as having definite links with an expressive form. The ability to interpret the unexpressed, however, depends on the reader's subtle affinity for the essence of poetry. The connoisseur of suggestion, the *sahrdaya*, is adept at penetrating the expressed intricacies of a work and relishing its suggested import – the beauty of which emanates from the work as an aesthetic whole.

Principal criticism

Dhvanyaloka, with the commentaries of Abhinavagupta, Ramasaraka, and Mahadeva Sastri, 1940 (Pattabhirama Sastri, editor)
Dhvanyaloka-sangraha, 1973 (edited with translation and notes by K. Kunjunni Raja)
Dhvanyaloka, 1974 (edited with introduction, translation, and notes by K. Krishnamoorthy)

Further reading

Bhartrhari. *The Vakyapadiya*, 1971. Edited with translation by K. Raghavan Pillai.
Chakrabarti, Tarapada. *Indian Aesthetics and Science of Language*, 1971.
Chakravarti, P. K. *The Linguistic Speculations of the Hindus*, 1933.
Choudhuri, N. N. *Philosophy of Poetry*, 1959.
Coward, Harold. *The Sphota Theory of Language*, 1980.
Dasgupta, Surendranath. *A History of Indian Philosophy*, Vol. 1, 1963.
Datta, D. M. *The Six Ways of Knowing*, 1972.
De, Sushil Kumar. *History of Sanskrit Poetics*, Vols. 1 and 2, 1960 (second revised edition).
Dwivedi, R. C. *Principles of Literary Criticism in Sanskrit*, 1969.
Krishnamoorthy, K. *The Dhvanyaloka and Its Critics*, 1968.
Patanjali. *Yoga Sutras of Patanjali*, 1978. Translated by Rama Prasada.
Radhakrishnan, Sarvepalli. *Indian Philosophy*, 1962.
——, ed. and trans. *The Principle Upanishads*, 1992 (fifth edition).
——, and Charles A. Moore, eds. *A Source Book in Indian Philosophy*, 1957.
Ramachandran, T. P. *The Indian Philosophy of Beauty*, Part Two, 1980.
Sankaran, A. *Some Aspects of Literary Criticism in Sanskrit or The Theories of Rasa and Dhvani*, 1973.
Staal, J. F., ed. *A Reader on the Sanskrit Grammarians*, 1972.
Vedanta Sutras, The, with *Commentary* by Shankara, 1962. Translated by G. Thibaut.

William S. Haney II

See also Bharata; Bhartrhari; Indian Literary Theory

Luciano Anceschi

Italian philosopher and critic

Born: Milan, Italy; February 20, 1911

Biography

Luciano Anceschi was born in 1911 in the cosmopolitan city of Milan, in northern Italy. Demonstrating a precocious sensibility as well as a capacity to absorb theoretical material, he studied languages and classics before attending the University of Milan, from which he graduated in 1934 with a degree in philosophy. During those years, Anceschi studied under the philosopher Antonio Banfi, who was responsible for introducing Edmund Husserl, Georg Simmel, and neo-Kantianism to Italy. The theoretical framework of Anceschi's thesis, "The Idea of Pure Poetry," reflects his teacher's interests in a non-Idealist, more concrete and dynamic approach to literary texts as well as a "European" outlook, which under the Fascist regime had all but disappeared. Anceschi wrote reviews of young painters and poets and critical pieces on writers and theoreticians from France, Spain, and the United States, including Eugenio D'Ors, Paul Claudel, Jules Renard, and T. S. Eliot. He also worked with the poet Salvatore Quasimodo (who would win the Nobel Prize in Literature in 1958) on translations from the Greek and participated actively in the post-World War II debate on the status and purpose of literature and criticism. He became known as a "militant critic" alert to new phenomena, severe toward any dogmatic or parochial approach to aesthetic and critical theory, and a staunch believer in the artist's "reasons" as pivotal for the proper evaluation of individual works and necessary for a better grasp of the aesthetic process in general. Anceschi's son, Giovanni, went on to become an important visual and graphic artist in his own right in the 1970s. Anceschi's life had been centered on his career as professor and later chair of the faculty of aesthetics at the University of Bologna. A much-loved teacher and "the poet's friend," he retired in 1985 and now moves between Bologna and a summerhouse in the valley of the Enza River near Parma. He has continued his own work, overseeing the publication of his complete works, edited by former students.

Influence

Anceschi is the founder and most important interpreter of phenomenological criticism and poetics in Italy. Beginning with his pioneering *Autonomia ed eteronomia dell'arte* (1936), Anceschi introduced phenomenology to a literary community which for the first thirty years of the twentieth century lived under the spell of idealism, historicism, philological positivism, and impressionism. By showing how poetry always exhibits a reflective and operative component, he was able to reread the post-Renaissance tradition of literature in such a way as to illuminate the dynamic between creative texts and critical writings. For Anceschi, a poem is never isolated in an aesthetic vacuum, though historically there have been movements that sought precisely this "pure" poetry. On the other hand, reflection on art will always tend to contextualize and emphasize the "impure" elements of the text. Yet whether one is concerned with the essence of the text or with how to talk about it, the fact remains that problems raised by technical execution and availability of materials, in addition to authors' ideas about their own work, become crucial in order to understand not only the poet but also the critical commentary on his or her work. In fact, interpretation requires that the ideas, values, and aesthetic systems within which a given author works be taken into account, for these shape and ultimately permit, in various guises, the artist's production. The dialectic between autonomy and heteronomy is thus at work at all times.

With this "relational" model, critics were able to explore areas which the previous generation had branded as nonpoetic and of little interest, such as the Baroque, neoclassicism, the various avant-gardes, and other specific or "local" artistic phenomena. Since his appointment to the chair of aesthetics at the University of Bologna in 1952, Anceschi has had a strong influence on the literary theorists and critics who have studied at that university. In addition, he has acted as a catalyst for innovative voices emerging in the Italian cultural panorama. Worthy of mention here is the literary journal *Il Verri*, which he founded in 1956 and through which the militant critic promoted both theoretically and editorially the two neo-avant-garde movements of the early 1960s known as *I Novissimi* and *Gruppo 63*. In the early 1970s his critical method was reformulated and is known today as New Critical Phenomenology.

Analysis

A number of contemporary critics have said that all Anceschi's theoretical ideas are contained in his first important work, *Autonomia ed eteronomia dell'arte*, and that most of his subsequent publications represent variations and developments of key notions in that book. The statement is both true and false. It is true insofar as the discovery, made in this first book, of an invariant law of reason that oscillates between the motives of the practical and circumstantial and the exigency of an ideal organic system of values, informs most of the critic's production. It is false insofar as the development and application of an interpretive model are precisely what allow it to disclose new insights, to open untried areas to research and refine the method: without the second, more practical part, the mere stating of an idea would be an idle and ephemeral discovery.

For Anceschi, the transcendental principle that governs critical awareness requires reason to be theoretically autonomous and universal. At the same time, however, a text or artwork needs to be considered in its concreteness and in its partiality with respect to a greater order of things and phenomena. What links the two apparently unrelated poles is a phenomenology of the critical act which can account for the great diversity of aesthetic phenomena while being methodologically rigorous. This double exigency allows Anceschi to discover, compare, and reassess poetic currents and aesthetic schools in their true historical and social context. At the same time, he is able to posit new characterizations given the fact that his method must be guided by "limit ideas," or hypothetical constructs which research either validates or rejects. So if this method reappears, with various refinements, in all of his works, then it is true that his first book contains the seed of all of his later thought.

Moreover, in works subsequent to 1936, Anceschi unearths aesthetic theories where there were none before. For example, in *Da Bacone a Kant* (1972), Anceschi demonstrates that the discipline of aesthetics, which according to the extremely influential philosophy of Benedetto Croce was founded by Giambattista Vico in Italy and Alexander Gottlieb Baumgarten in Germany, can actually be said to have originated in England, beginning in the sixteenth century. At the level of poetry and poetics, Anceschi had claimed as much in his first book, but in this later book he sets out to prove it at the level of the history of ideas. It is more than a question of how one reads and what method one employs, for, according to Anceschi, if one were to refrain from accepting as categorically valid only the ideas expressed by theoreticians of aesthetics, one would be in a better position to gauge any "reflection on art," whether it comes from a natural philosopher and statesman, such as Sir Francis Bacon or Thomas Hobbes, a poet, such as Sir Philip Sidney, or an essayist, such as Joseph Addison.

It can be said, in fact, that this concept is one of the great contributions of Anceschi, for it is akin to discovering that the aesthetic and poetic map of the modern era can be redrawn and can show meanings where first there were critical blanks. Starting with the observation that, since Plato, art has been held to be both a freedom from constraints or reason (as in *Ion*) and a need to be functional and useful (as in the *Republic*), Anceschi demonstrates that this polarity hides a dynamic tension whereby art tends at the same time toward complete autonomous freedom and toward a conscious disclosure of life and reality. For the post-Renaissance period, this means being able to trace the emergence of the historical notions of *l'art pour l'art* and "pure" Symbolist poetry back to the English Metaphysical poets. In the course of demonstrating how this is possible, the critic discloses a remarkable genealogy of conscious and textual continuities. Along this route, one encounters passages from the Elizabethans and the various poetics of neoclassicism, the crucial role played by Samuel Taylor Coleridge in circulating Kantian concepts among artists, the first explicit theorization of pure poetry with Edgar Allan Poe's essay "The Philosophy of Composition" (1846), and, finally, the "return" of the notion of pure poetry back to Europe where it found its last and greatest "systematizers" in Charles Baudelaire, Arthur Rimbaud, and Paul Verlaine. Throughout – and this is what makes Anceschi's approach always revealing – attention is paid to the different ways in which each poet adapts and develops an inherited idea of poetry and how these same ideas by themselves create a "current" or school.

In a book which came out in 1968, *Le istituzioni della poesia*, Anceschi develops theoretical models of how poetries interact, calling them "institutions." These are essentially working models derived from the actual history of literature, which serve as critical frameworks or aesthetic principles. Institutions exhibit a tripartite structure: a concern with a technical and pragmatic account of language, attention to communication or being "useful" in some way, and dependence on other models, interdisciplinarity, and "tradition." The description of the interaction among the three orientations can be based on what the poet or the text show as being primary or secondary in any of the three areas. Yet it is always a question of reading the text directly, focusing on what it actually says: this prevents the mechanical imposition of the critical grid on the work of art, for Anceschi never forgets that there are "methods," not one universal, unique method. Examples of institutions are "negative capability" (in John Keats), "objective correlative" (in T. S. Eliot and Eugenio Montale), and "poetic of the object" (the Italian *crepuscolari* of the early twentieth century). According to Anceschi, a poet can claim to have been influenced by a particular poetic institution, such as "objective correlative," and not by its alleged main exponent, such as Eliot, and be correct. In Italy at least, several poets in the 1930s and 1940s were attentive to the technical and thematic concerns which a poetic of relation between subject and object brought out, but were less interested in the overall aesthetic of its main theorizer, namely Eliot. Bearing in mind the obvious differences, the institution of poetry or poetics in Anceschi's phenomenological sense is the analogue of what in the language of hermeneutics is called a canon, in stylistics a dominant trope, in rhetoric an influential topos.

The actual principles or tenets of literary interpretation that can be extracted from Anceschi's writings can be described as follows. His preliminary assumptions include the beliefs that, first, there is no opposition between philosophy and criticism; second, interpretation creates and constitutes its field of research; third, the critic's attitude and vision must be organic and disposed toward some yet-unseen order or system; and fourth, interpretation is always aware philosophically of its steps, that is, it proceeds phenomenologically and is therefore also metacriticism. He also assumes that criticism entails making a "choice" within predetermined limits, that there are no absolute, unchanging, or dogmatic models or methods, and that the question should not be what is art, which belies a totalizing, metaphysical posture, but how is it that this work of art is possible or that certain influences are possible and others are not. Though it can be said that some of these tenets are common to other contemporary approaches, most notably hermeneutics, especially as concerns the avoidance of totalizing principles and the possibility that history is always reinscribed in the critic's discourse, phenomenological criticism is still tied to a Kantian idea of transcendental reason. Anceschi's noteworthy contribution to this major stream flowing into contemporary criticism consists in bending Immanuel Kant, Husserl, and his own teacher, Banfi, to attribute more importance to the reasons of art, to the pragmatic aspect of the phenomenon of art. The contribution consists also in loosening up the categories to the point of not questioning the grounds of what art is (unless it was part of studying how one particular artist defined it, his "explicit poetic") but focusing attention rather on how art may be understood in its making and becoming (what its "implicit poetic" might be).

Principles are generally followed by practical rules of application, which represent the modalities of this approach in the field. In Anceschi's case, this is particularly important, since he never tired of repeating "to the texts themselves." To sum up the various and at times interlocking steps involved, the critic must then suspend judgment before facts or phenomena, especially when dealing with absolutes, and actuate a phenomenological reduction. This requires that the critic deal with the phases of phenomenology individually, that is, by first stating the thesis of the problem, second, making a survey of the situation (*rilievi di situazione*), third, deferring judgment when analyzing as many secondary "established" opinions and sources as possible, and finally, reconstructing the problem by creating a model hypothesis on the basis of the data available, ensuring that the new critical elaboration is more a "reading" of the work of art in question than a confutation of other already advanced critical stances. It can be observed that in this type of criticism it is important to reconstruct the problem and to provide what Anceschi calls the "horizon of the situation," or context of the work of art, as well as the original pragmatic intent of the artist. Anceschi is not interested in the psychology of the artist, but in how he or she thinks in order to get the work done. This means paying attention to the problems the artist encounters and solves as a work is brought to completion. This approach permits the critic to recover the "projecting individuality" and its "situational predeterminations," both of which are necessary for interpretive coherence and to keep the critic's own opinions out of the picture. The critic's judgment is not abolished; it is merely postponed until one reaches the appropriate stage to effect it. At that point, the actual assessment will be guided by the ordering principle of transcendental reason underlying the relationships among the elements analyzed. For Anceschi, judgment cannot be arbitrary because it is exercised within a specific field, called "horizon of available choices," which in turn is made up of what has emerged from the research as the "horizon of comprehension." Finally, and closing the hermeneutic circle, the "law of integration" that girds all critical operations will now permit the attribution of a "sense" on the basis of what Anceschi calls an "open systematicity." If the critic's task is ultimately to attribute meaning to a text or phenomena, it is crucial to avoid the temptation to offer "definitive" interpretations. If one follows the above steps, dogmatisms of all types, demagogy, cynicism, and personal opinion will be kept off the critical path.

The undeniable flexibility of Anceschi's critical phenomenology can be seen also when he turns his attention to critics and their theories. In *Da Ungaretti a D'Annunzio* (1976), one can study how, with the above "rules" of method, the main traits of several other approaches can be charted, for example, the criticism of philosophers, poets, essayists, scientists, writers, and, most notably, that of structuralists such as Tzvetan Todorov and Roman Jakobson or poets such as T. S. Eliot and Paul Valéry.

Principal criticism

Autonomia ed eteronomia dell'arte, 1936
Saggi di poetica e di poesia, 1942
Idea della lirica, 1945
Del barocco ed altre prove, 1953
Poetica americana, e altri studi contemporanei di poetica, 1953
Barocco e novecento, 1960
Le poetiche del novecento in Italia, 1962
Fenomenologia della critica, 1966
Il modello della poesia, 1966
Le istituzioni della poesia, 1968
Da Ungaretti a D'Annunzio, 1976
Il caos, il metodo, 1981
Che cosa è la poesia?, 1982

Other major works and literary forms

In addition to the above, Luciano Anceschi wrote works on interpretation, aesthetics, and the history of aesthetic and poetic concepts. Consequently, though he is best known as a philosopher-critic concerned with the evaluation of poetry, his writings cover areas such as systems of aesthetics and poetics, the history of specific stylistic forms, the importance of new writers, the development of the relationship between philosophy and literature, the impact of literature on society, and the comparative study of criticism. He also wrote important introductions to the works of numerous poets and visual artists. Several of these pieces have been republished as chapters in books listed above.

NONFICTION
L'estetica dell'empirisimo inglese, 1959
Progetto di una sistematica dell'arte, 1962
Tre studi di estetica, 1966
Da Bacone a Kant, 1972

TRANSLATIONS
Il bosco sacro, 1946 (of T. S. Eliot's collection of essays *The Sacred Wood*)

Further reading

Barberi Squarotti, Gorgio. "Anceschi," in *Grande Dizionario Enciclopedico UTET*, 1967.
Barilli, Renato. "L'estetica fenomenologica di Anceschi," in *Per un'estetica mondana*, 1964.
Carravetta, Peter. *Il problema del metodo e la prospettiva ermeneutica*, 1983 (dissertation).
De Angelis, Valentina. *L'estetica di Luciano Anceschi*, 1983.
Gentili, Carlo. *Nuova fenomenologia critica*, 1981.
Macrí, Oreste. *Realtà del simbolo*, 1967.
Patrizi, Giorgio. "Reading Anceschi's Poetics for the New Turn of the Century," in *Forum Italicum*. (1992), pp. 583–588. Translated by Harsha Ram.
Rossi, Lino. *Situazione dell'estetica in Italia*, 1976.

PETER CARRAVETTA

See also Croce; Phenomenological Criticism; Praz

Arabic Literary Theory

The history of Arabic literary theory and criticism spans at least twelve hundred years, or more if one includes the scattered opinions dating from pre-Islamic times (from c. 500 A.D. to the time of the Prophet Mohammed, who died in 632) which were collected and recorded in the first few centuries of the Islamic period. The indigenous tradition is strongly linked with the study of the Arabic language and its stylistics; literary theory and rhetoric overlap to a large extent, the latter having the sense of elocution rather than the art of persuasion. The Greek tradition was known, if imperfectly understood, through translations of and commentaries on Aristotle's *Poetics* and *Rhetoric*. A few attempts at a synthesis between the Arabic and the Greek traditions remained isolated. From the end of the nineteenth century, when "classical Arabic literature" gradually turned into "modern Arabic literature," the various forms and schools of Western theory and criticism were increasingly adopted and to some extent adapted.

The phrase "literary theory and criticism" seems to imply that there is such a thing, or concept, as "literature." Even in the modern world this can lead to endless discussion; yet, for all practical purposes, modern Arabic has such a concept, called *adab*, which in most contexts is the equivalent of "literature." For the classical (or "medieval," or "pre-modern") period things are more difficult: though *adab* may have many meanings, including "good manners" and "erudition," none of them is "literature." Nevertheless there is something that might be called "literariness," and which is the object of traditional Arabic theory and criticism. It is strongly linked with the "pure" and correct classical Arabic language, to some extent an artificial language which is nobody's mother tongue. Texts that use elements from the spoken language, such as some forms of poetry, were rarely discussed by the critics; the great historian Ibn Khaldūn (died 1406) was an exception when he argued that eloquence was not necessarily absent from "popular" or "vulgar" poetry. The *Thousand and One Nights* and similar popular collections of stories or epic poems, which were orally transmitted and, if written down, then with an admixture of the spoken language, were wholly ignored by Arab theorists and critics until well into the twentieth century, in the wake of Western admiration.

CLASSICAL ARABIC LITERATURE

The oldest Arabic literature, a substantial body of pre-Islamic Bedouin poetry and some scattered stories, proverbs, aphorisms, speeches, and oracles, all of it preserved orally for a considerable period, would certainly have been lost for posterity, for all its splendor and forcefulness, but for the appearance of a unique text between A.D. 610 and 632. The Koran (Qur'ān) is, according to Muslims, God's uncreated speech, revealed to the Prophet Mohammed (Muhammad); its acceptance as the central text in a new religion which became a new civilization had far-reaching consequences. Islam spread rapidly and widely; Arabic became the first or second language of many groups ethnically non-Arab, and its grammar and vocabulary were studied and codified. The Koran, though responsible for this process, was only of limited use: the main source for the consolidation of Arabic was pre-Islamic and early Islamic Bedouin poetry, which was eagerly collected, recorded, and studied, and highly valued for its aesthetic and ideological qualities. The oral tradition of Bedouin poetry continued, and seemed to be dying out only in the twentieth century; yet the philologists were not interested in poetry by Bedouins made after about 730, having derived from the older generations what they needed. At the same time, urban poetic genres were developed, together with new prose forms that may be called literary.

Poetry certainly remained, until today, the Arabic literary form *par excellence*. The beauty of its language and images were appreciated, but its aesthetic function was rarely the only one, for its power in society was sought (praise or self-praise) or feared (satire and invective). If there is one quality on which Arabs (soon a linguistic rather than an ethnic designation) pride themselves, it is eloquence.

Traditional literary criticism

Scattered critical remarks on particular poems or on the nature and functions of poetry in general from pre-Islamic and early Islamic times were collected in works such as *al-Bayān wa-t-tabyīn* (eloquence and exposition) by the great prosaist al-Jāhiz (died 868 or 869), or in the many works on poets, with sections on individual poets, such as *Tabaqāt fuhūl ash-shu'arā'* (the classes of master poets) by Ibn Sallām al-Jumahī (died 846 or 847) and *ash-Shi'r wa-sh-shu'arā'* (poetry and poets) by the polymath Ibn Qutayba (died 889). The first monograph that could be called a work of literary theory was a short treatise on tropes and figures of speech, *al-Badī* (the novel style), by the Abbasid prince 'Abd Allāh Ibn al-Mu'tazz (died 908), himself one of the most important poets of his time. He demonstrates that the stylistic and rhetorical embellishments which were consciously sought and frequently employed in the new urban genres were in fact anticipated to some extent in older poetry and prose. He lists seventeen kinds, including metaphor, paronomasia, antithesis, apostrophe, parenthesis, feigned ignorance, and simile. His examples are taken from the Koran, prose sayings, and poetry. This work set a trend, for countless works were produced over the centuries that follow the same pattern, swelling the number of tropes and figures originally studied by Ibn al-Mu'tazz more than tenfold. Although some attempts were made to systematize these many figures by classifying them into categories and hierarchies (for example, figures of thought versus figures of expression), this tradition of studying rhetorical figures, called "the science of *badī*" after the book by Ibn al-Mu'tazz, remained rather unsystematic, the anthological interest of many of its representants outweighing their theoretical importance.

A number of interesting works of practical criticism, with some explicit theorizing, were written in connection with a few controversial poets. Abū Tammām (died 845) startled his audience and offended his critics with his daring metaphors and conceits and with his fondness for antithesis and paronomasia. His "artificial," mannered style was often contrasted with the "natural" style of his younger contemporary al-Buhturī (died 897). Their poetry is compared and contrasted in great detail in an extensive monograph entitled *al-Muwāzana* (the balancing) by the critic al-Āmidī (died 987). Several monographs were devoted to al-Mutanabbī (died 965), by many considered the greatest Arabic poet in Islamic times, yet controversial, partly because of his excessive self-esteem and alleged heretical leanings. The critic, poet, and *qādī* (judge) 'Alī Ibn 'Abd al-'Azīz al-Jurjānī (died 1002) wrote his *al-Wasāta* (the mediation) as an attempt to refute most of these criticisms, arguing, among other things, that one should not judge the quality of poetry on the basis of the religious opinions expressed in it. A large part of this work deals with real or presumed *sariqāt*, "thefts": forms of plagiary and borrowing, or "intertextuality," a topic that has always received much attention from critics and theorists, several books being wholly devoted to it ("the plagiarisms of X"). In all this the scope of attention is small: critics focus on particular lines, on individual figures, tropes, or conceits, on short passages, rather than on whole poems. This is, at least partly, explained by the nature of Arabic poetry and its mode of existence: poems do not usually tell stories, lines tend to be semantically and syntactically independent or at least potentially so; in anthologies and works of criticism whole poems are quoted far less often than short fragments. Moreover, the poetic genre with the highest status has always been the *qasīda* or "polythematic" ode, which combines modes that, at least at first sight, do not strongly cohere, for instance elegiac love lyric followed by desert description and praise or self-praise, perhaps with invective. The coherence or unity of a literary work, deemed so important in the Western tradition at least since the Romantic era, is discussed relatively little in traditional Arabic theory and criticism. That many Arabic poems are in fact carefully structured as wholes was not demonstrated until quite recently, in the wake of the structuralist approach to literary works, by Arabists both from the West and the Arab world.

The first works that could be called "poetics" were written in the first half of the tenth century. Qudāma Ibn Ja'far (died c. 948) discusses poetry in his *Naqd ash-shi'r* (the criticism of poetry) in a manner that shows he is acquainted with methods of logical analysis derived from the Greeks. He studies its constituent elements (meaning, expression, meter, and rhyme) and their interaction, hoping thereby to develop a method of testing poetry and distinguishing good from bad, just as true and bad coinage are distinguished; the term *naqd* means "assaying (coinage)" and in modern Arabic still means both "criticism" and "cash." His contemporary Ibn Tabātabā (died 934), unlike Qudāma a poet himself, wrote *'Iyār ash-shi'r* (the standard, or touchstone, of poetry), the title similarly deriving from the field of testing money. Less systematic than Qudāma's work, it consists of a series of thoughtful essays on the "essence" of poetry and its production, on good versus bad verse, on comparisons, and so on; more than others he stresses the coherence of a poem. Both Qudāma and Ibn Tabātabā subscribe to the idea, almost universal in Arabic theory, of the basic dichotomy between *ma'nā* (meaning or content) and *lafz* (the linguistic expression of form). Theorists may differ as to which element they consider more important.

A useful "encyclopedia" of poetry and poetics was written by the North African poet Ibn Rashīq (died 1063 or 1071). His *al-'Umda* (the support) deals with poetry in almost all its aspects: its status and functions, its nature, its formal structures, its themes, genres, diction, forms of borrowing, and its defects, a large part being devoted to figures and tropes. Like many other writers on poetry, Ibn Rashīq finds it necessary to include a defense or apology for poetry. The Koran, after all, seems to condemn poets (sura 26: 224–227: "The poets – the erring ones follow them. Do you not see how they roam in every wadi? And that they say that which they do not? – Except those that believe . . ."). Fortunately, there are many reliable reports about the Prophet Mohammed enjoining poets among his followers, notably Hassān Ibn Thābit, to support his case with stinging invective and forceful vaunting verse. Poetry was often condemned for its irreligious or frivolous nature: much of it deals with love, mostly illicit, often (from the ninth century) homoerotic; Arabic literature boasts a very large body of bacchic verse, notwithstanding the Muslim prohibition of alcohol consumption. Finally, much poetry is scandalously vituperative or blatantly obscene. In the light of this, and in view of the popularity of poetry in all its kinds, medieval Muslim society as a whole seems remarkably tolerant. In the last resort, poets could always defend themselves, saying, with the Koranic verse just quoted, "that they say that which they do not."

Critics who restrict themselves to the discussion of poetry are far fewer in number than those who, like Ibn al-Mu'tazz, deal with both prose and poetry. The title of a work by Abū Hilāl al-'Askarī (died after 1010), *Kitāb as-Sinā'atayn* (the book of the two arts), meaning the stylistics of poetry and prose, is significant – as is the fact that its original title was *san'at al-kalām* (the art of speech), indicating that the art of eloquence is essentially identical for prose and poetry. This is evident also from another title, the influential *al-Mathal as-sā'ir fī adab al-kātib wa-sh-shā'ir* (the familiar proverb: on the knowledge required from chancery scribe and poet) by Diyā' ad-Dīn Ibn al-Athīr (died 1239). Even books written specifically on prose writing, for instance *Husn at-tawassul ilā sinā'at at-tarassul* (the good expedient toward the art of letter writing) by Mahmūd Ibn Sulaymān al-Halabī (died 1325) are full of quotations from poetry. Prose to literary theorists meant epistolography (*kitāba* or *inshā'*) or oratory (*khitāba*) and focused on style and eloquence, the art of narrative being virtually ignored, not because it was absent but, on the contrary perhaps, because it was ubiquitous, popular, and not restricted to the literary elite.

A contemporary of Ibn Rashīq, but living in the east of the Islamic world, was the perceptive literary theorist ʿAbd al-Qāhir al-Jurjānī (died c. 1087). He was a linguist who wrote some books on grammar. His fame, however, rests mainly on two books on the stylistic aspects of syntax and on imagery, important not only for their intrinsic merit but also because they turned out to be seminal works that lie at the basis of the "scholastic" treatment of *ʿilm al-balāgha*, "the science of eloquence." He does not restrict himself to poetry, indeed his work on the stylistics of syntax is entitled *Dalāʾil al-iʿjāz* (intimations of [the Koran's] inimitability) and his book on imagery is called *Asrār al-balāgha* (the mysteries of eloquence); but in both poetry is his most important source. One of his merits, besides his great subtlety of analysis, is that he transcends the customary rigid dichotomy between *lafẓ* and *maʿnā*, "expression/form" and "meaning/content."

His books consist of series of essays rather than a well-ordered sequence of ideas. It was left to other scholars to fashion his ideas into systematic form and textbook format. For the later eleventh century saw the rise of the *madrasa*, "school" or rather "college" for students, first of all of religious law but embracing language and rhetoric too. A very popular textbook was *Miftāḥ al-ʿulūm* (the key to the sciences) by as-Sakkākī (died 1229), which deals with morphology, formal syntax, stylistic syntax (now called *ʿilm al-maʿānī*, "the science of [grammatical] meanings"), and imagery (now called *ʿilm al-bayān*, "the science of exposition"), to which the remaining embellishments of speech (*ʿilm al-badīʿ*) form a short appendix. The book closes with chapters on logic, prosody (poetic meters), and rhyme. Even more popular was a very concise condensation of the subject matter of ʿAbd al-Qāhir's two books *Talkhīs al-Miftāḥ* (the epitome of the key) by al-Khaṭīb al-Qazwīnī (died 1338). Short enough to be learned by heart, it became the object of countless commentaries, supercommentaries, and versifications and its influence can still be discerned in schoolbooks of the twentieth century.

To some extent this field of literary and linguistic studies became ossified, its dryness being relieved only by those authors who raised the literary character of their texts by incorporating many examples taken from poetry and prose. There was usually some interaction between the scholastic and systematic method of *ʿilm al-balāgha* and the less scholarly, more amateurish approach of *ʿilm al-badīʿ*. They have in common that they are not exclusively concerned with poetry, that they show little interest in the "essence" of poetry or in its genres, themes, and modes, such as panegyric, elegy, invective, love-lyric, bacchic, gnomic, epideictic, to name some of the main ones. There exist, it is true, numerous works of an anthological character in which the material is arranged thematically, the themes often coinciding with poetic modes and themes; however, generally they contain little if any systematic criticism or theoretical reflection.

The role of the Koran

"The science of eloquence (*balāgha*)," says al-Khaṭīb al-Qazwīnī in the introduction of his *Talkhīs al-Miftāḥ*, "is one of the most exalted and most subtle sciences, since by means of it one may learn the subtleties of the Arabic language and discover the ways in which the composition of the Koran is inimitable." The inimitability of the Koran (*iʿjāz al-Qurʾān*) had long been a dogma of orthodox Islam. A true prophet should "prove" his mission by a miracle that could not be imitated, according to Muslim opinion. Moses, living in a time when magic was much esteemed, changed his staff into a snake; Jesus performed medical wonders in an epoch when medical science flowered. Finally, in Mohammed's days a more intellectual and abstract miracle was necessary; his contemporaries, proud of their unmatched eloquence, were convinced by the miracle of the Holy Book, God's uncreated literal speech. The miraculous nature of the Koran was much discussed and most theologians agreed that it resided above all in its style. It is a text *sui generis*, neither poetry nor prose, nor even (according to Muslim Arab specialists) to be compared to the oracular utterance in rhymed prose (*sajʿ*) of the pre-Islamic soothsayers, even though some parts of it may sound not very different.

An authorative work on this topic is *Iʿjāz al-Qurʾān* (the inimitability of the Koran) by the jurist and theologian al-Bāqillānī (died 1013). Although the miraculous superiority of the Koranic style cannot, he argues, be analyzed properly by means of studying its figures and tropes, at least it is demonstrated by comparison with human products. To this end he contrasts it with two poems generally deemed masterpieces, a very famous pre-Islamic ode by Imraʾ al-Qays and a "modern" ode by al-Buḥturī, going out of his way to find fault with them.

It may seem something of a paradox that a text the genre of which is unique and unrepeatable, and the style of which is pronounced inimitable, should be so central in a tradition of stylistics, rhetoric, and poetics. On the whole, it seemed to have had little adverse effect on the development of this tradition. Koranic scholars used the terminology and techniques of literary scholars to analyze features of the Koran, and the latter rarely failed to use Koranic examples to illustrate figures and tropes. Many scholars were theologians and erudite literary specialists at the same time: the two medieval Muslim types of intellectual, the *ʿālim* (religious scholar) and *adīb* (man of letters), often overlap. Early discussions on controversial Koranic passages contributed simultaneously to the development of dogma and poetics: thus anthropomorphic expressions such as "the hand of God," or God seating Himself on His Throne, could be explained as forms of figurative language.

The Koran was "inspired" or revealed to Mohammed by the archangel Jibrīl (Gabriel). Early poets believed, or pretended to believe, that they were inspired by *jinn*, demons. Although belief in *jinn* is part of orthodox Islam and one might have expected some kind of islamicized "inspiration" to have been incorporated in literary theory, this did not happen, perhaps because one shied away from the presumed origins of poetry as a form of magic. The subject was taken up by the Andalusian poet Ibn Shuhayd (died 1035) in his *Risālat at-tawābiʿ wa-z-zawābiʿ* (treatise of familiar spirits and demons), which belongs as much to imaginative belles-lettres as to literary criticism. That emotion (joy, anger, sorrow, and other affects) could be a source of poetic inspiration was recognized but was not elaborated in any detail by the theorists.

The Greek tradition

The ancient Greek philosophers and scientists, above all Aristotle, were greatly revered in Islam, and their influence is difficult to overrate. Aristotle's works were translated and studied by many scholars. Several of the great philosophers writing in Arabic clothed their own theories in the form of commentaries on Aristotle's texts. In the case of his *Rhetoric* and *Poetics*, the translators and commentators were seriously hampered by their lack of understanding of Greek literature, drama as a serious literary form being unknown in Arabic. They could choose between introducing Greek words in Arabic, such as *tarāghūdhiyā* and *qūmūdhiyā*, and trying to find Arabic not-so-near equivalents, such as speaking about *qasīda* (polythematic ode), panegyric, and satire, standing for dramatic play, tragedy, and comedy, respectively. The former method, followed by Ibn Sīnā (Avicenna, died 1037) and others, could only alienate the general reading public ("Everything he [Ibn Sīnā] says is stuff and nonsense and useless for those whose language is Arabic," as one critic grumbled); the latter approach, chosen by Ibn Rushd (Averroës, died 1198), was bound to baffle the same readers.

The Muslim philosophers did not consider the study of rhetoric and poetics as part of literary studies. In the East, the two corresponding Aristotelian works formed part of the *Organon*, the books on logic. Rhetoric and poetry are two forms of persuasion and demonstration, similar (and in terms of logic inferior) to strictly logical demonstration or dialectic discourse. Rhetoric achieves its effect by means of incomplete syllogisms (enthymemes) and poetry by means of imagery, such as metaphor. For all their regard for the ancient Greeks, the Arabs were not interested in their poetry and belles-lettres, and usually not even aware of their existence, convinced as they were of their own superiority in this respect. Not surprisingly, Greek literary theory in Arabic garb remained confined largely to circles of *falāsifa* and *mutafalsifūn*, philosophers and dabblers in philosophy, and failed to make any great impact on the indigenous tradition. Nevertheless, at least a few brave attempts were made at a conciliation and synthesis. The most sophisticated of these is *Minhāj al-bulaghā' wa-sirāj al-udabā'* (the path of the eloquent and the lamp of the lettered) by the poet Hāzim al-Qartājannī (died 1285), who was active in Spain and North Africa. His poetics came too late to have much influence.

THE MODERN PERIOD

There is a tradition of letting the modern history of the Arab world begin in 1798, when Napoleon temporarily occupied Egypt, an event that served as a catalyst for many new developments and changes. Modern Arabic literature, however, can only be said to arise toward the end of the nineteenth century. Writers and critics took fresh impulses from two directions: obviously, from the West (meaning mostly France and Britain), but also from the earlier stages of their own literary past, jumping, for instance, over centuries of glosses and commentaries to original and seminal texts that had been lost from sight. Thus the important religious reformer and modernist Muhammad ʿAbduh (died 1905) reintroduced ʿAbd al-Qāhir al-Jurjānī's works as teaching material at the Azhar University. The old textbooks on *balāgha* (eloquence) were rewritten and simplified and are still being used for the study and appreciation of the classical literary heritage. Others, wholly or partly rejecting the critical heritage, wholeheartedly adopted Western critical ideas, methods, and schools.

Some critics espousing Western ideas applied them to classical as well as contemporary literature, such as the very influential Tāhā Husayn (died 1973) and his pupil Muhammad Mandūr (died 1965). A leading role in the spread of concepts such as *iltizām* ("commitment") was played by the literary journal *al-Ādāb*, founded in Beirut in 1953. As in the classical period, many poets wrote on poetics and criticism, an outstanding example being Adūnīs (Adonis, pen name of ʿAlī Ahmad Saʿīd, born 1928 or 1930). A glance at the Egyptian journal *Fusūl* shows the extent to which Arab critics of today are keeping abreast of the latest fashions in European and American literary criticism, applying these to modern and "heritage" literature alike, coining many a new Arabic term in the process, for example *tafkīk* (formerly merely "fragmentation," "decomposition," now also "deconstruction") and *tanāss* (newly formed from the word *nass*, "text," and a pattern denoting mutuality, hence "intertextuality").

Further reading

Abu Deeb, Kamal. "Literary Criticism," in *ʿAbbasid Belles-Lettres*, 1990. Edited by Julia Ashtiany et al.

Adonis [ʿAlī Ahmad Saʿīd]. *An Introduction to Arab Poetics*, 1985. Translated by Catherine Cobham.

Ajami, Mansour. *The Neckveins of Winter: The Controversy over Natural and Artificial Poetry in Medieval Arabic Literary Criticism*, 1984.

——. *The Alchemy of Glory: The Dialectic of Truthfulness and Untruthfulness in Medieval Arabic Literary Criticism*, 1988.

Allen, Roger. "The Critical Tradition," in his *The Arabic Literary Heritage: The Development of its Genres and Criticism*, 1998.

Cachia, Pierre. *The Arch Rhetorician, or The Schemer's Skimmer: A Handbook of Late Arabic badī drawn from 'Abd al-Ghanī an-Nābulsī's* Nafaḥāt al-Azhār 'alā Nasamāt al-Asḥār, 1998.
Cantarino, Vicente. *Arabic Poetics in the Golden Age: Selection of Texts Accompanied by a Preliminary Study*, 1975.
Heinrichs, Wolfhart. "Literary Theory: The Problem of its Efficiency," in *Arabic Poetry: Theory and Development*, 1973. Edited by G. E. von Grunebaum.
——. *The Hand of the Northwind: Opinions of Metaphor and the Early Meaning of isti'āra in Arabic Poetics*, 1977.
——. "Literary Criticism," "Rhetoric and Poetics," and "Rhetorical Figures," in *Encyclopedia of Arabic Literature*, 1998. Edited by Julie Scott Meisami and Paul Starkey.
Ouyang, Wen-chin. *Literary Criticism in Medieval Arabic-Islamic Culture: The Making of a Tradition*, 1997.
Van Gelder, G. J. H. *Beyond the Line: Classical Arabic Literary Critics on the Coherence and Unity of the Poem*, 1982.

GEERT JAN VAN GELDER

See also 'Abd al-Qāhir al-Jurjānī; Ḥāzim al-Qartājannī; Qudāma Ibn Ja'far

Archetypal Criticism

In literary terms, an archetype is a recurrent figure, action, image, or other element that is found in literary texts from different times and places. Fundamental to archetypal criticism is the belief that behind the accidental details of individual works of literature lie archetypal patterns and structures, and that it is to the presence of these literary archetypes that such texts owe much of their power.

Though there are recognizable antecedents in the works of, for example, Giambattista Vico, Johann Wolfgang von Goethe, and F. W. J. Schelling, archetypal criticism is essentially a phenomenon of the twentieth century and can be said to have developed, at least initially, through the application to literary studies of the work of two of the century's most seminal thinkers, Sir James Frazer (1854–1941) and Carl Gustav Jung (1875–1961).

Frazer's major work was *The Golden Bough*, which appeared in twelve volumes between 1890 and 1915. In it Frazer examines a huge number of myths from many times and places – from the preclassical era to modern times, from Australia and Asia to the Mediterranean and America – employing an essentially comparative method and seeking to demonstrate their essential similarities. The effect of Frazer's work and that of his many followers was (intentionally or otherwise) to suggest that myth and ritual, however various their occurrence in time and place, followed certain recurrent patterns. The earliest sustained application in the literary field of Frazer's work seems to have been that of a number of scholars, mainly based in Cambridge, England, of the classics. In many of the writings of Jane Harrison, Gilbert Murray, F. M. Cornford, and others, the example of Frazer prompted a new way of looking at classical texts. These scholars shared the belief that the mythical narrative of the life-force's victory over death, as seen primarily in the cycle of the seasons, lay at the roots of drama and poetry. Cornford, for example, traced underlying mythical patterns in the narratives of Thucydides and sought to demonstrate the origins of Greek comedy in the fertility rites of the year-spirit; Murray discerned myths of the death and rebirth of gods in Greek tragedy (and in *Hamlet*); Jane Harrison (in *Ancient Art and Ritual*, 1913) insisted that "art and ritual . . . have a common root, and that neither can be understood without the other. It is at the outset one and the same impulse that sends a man to church and to the theatre" (understanding a ritual as a stylized reenactment of a myth). The work of these "Cambridge Ritualists," as they have become known, offered powerful encouragement to other critics and scholars to interpret a whole range of literary texts in the light of their resemblances to mythological characters, narratives, or situations.

Jung argued for the existence of two layers in the human unconscious. One is the personal unconscious, the contents of which are collected from the individual's experience during the course of his or her own life. The other is the collective unconscious, the contents of which are inherited and common to the species. The collective unconscious is made up of archetypes, primordial images (or, perhaps better, structural patterns) that have existed since the earliest days of humankind. They are not, of course, directly available to our conscious minds, and can be "seen" only when clothed, by the conscious mind, in the materials of conscious experience. Jung himself paid the greatest attention to such archetypes as the anima and the animus, the great mother, the child, the self, and the shadow. In his *Wandlungen und Symbole der Libido* (1911–1912; *Psychology of the Unconscious*, 1916) Jung analyzed such underlying structures in Henry Wadsworth Longfellow's *Hiawatha*; in another essay, "On the Relation of Analytical Psychology to Poetic Art" (1922; collected in *Contributions to Analytical Psychology*, 1928), he argued that in the effective use of such archetypes the poet lifts his or her poem "above the occasional and the transitory into the sphere of the ever-existing." Acceptance of Jung's hypothesis suggests that one of the jobs of criticism should be the discovery in works of literature of the presence (veiled by the accidentals of the particular texts) of such "primordial images." Such a search was undertaken in early works of Jungian criticism, such as Maud Bodkin's *Archetypal Patterns in Poetry* (1934). She saw her work as an examination of Jung's hypothesis (her opening sentence refers to Jung's essay of 1922), a hypothesis she understood in the light of the anthropological research referred to above – declaring that she would "use the term 'archetypal pattern' to refer to that within us which, in Gilbert Murray's phrase, leaps in response to the effective presentation in poetry of an ancient theme. The hypothesis to be examined is that in poetry – and here we are to consider in particular tragic poetry – we may identify themes having a particular form or pattern which persists amid variation from age to age, and which corresponds to a pattern or configuration of emotional tendencies in the minds of those who are stirred by the theme." Bodkin proceeded to offer studies of the "rebirth archetype" in Samuel Taylor Coleridge's "Rime of the Ancient Mariner," of the archetypes of heaven and hell in "Kubla Khan," the poetry of William Morris, Virgil, and Dante Alighieri, of the "image of Woman" in John Milton, Dante, and Goethe, of the "images of the Devil, of the Hero, and of God" in a number of poets (including Percy Bysshe Shelley), and of "the patterns in Sacred and Contemporary literature," involving discussion of, *inter alia*, William Shakespeare, D. H. Lawrence, Virginia Woolf, and T. S. Eliot. Bodkin's work remains stimulating, though inevitably now seeming rather dated and limited by a certain interpretative rigidity. The forerunner of much Jungian archetypal criticism, it is open to the same criticism that can be directed at many of its successors – that in largely ignoring distinctions of period and genre, literary and historical convention, such criticism is always in danger of sidestepping the complexities of individual texts or replacing those texts by broader and broader generalizations. The whole school, however, can be said to have facilitated our own time's understanding of the claims of William Blake: "The Nature of Visionary Fancy, or Imagination, is very little Known, and the Eternal nature and permanence of its ever Existent Images is consider'd as less permanent than the things of Vegetation and Generative Nature; yet the Oak dies as well as the Lettuce, but Its Eternal Image and Individuality never dies, but renews by its seed; just as the Imaginative Image returns by the seed of Contemplative Thought."

Extending and developing strategies based on these anthropological and psychological models (to which, of course, there were other contributors than Frazer and Jung, too numerous to be mentioned here), critics have discussed the presence and effect of many archetypal motifs in a wide range of literary texts; these have included archetypal characters or figures (the hero, the Ulysses figure, the trickster, the Don Juan figure, the rebel, the Beatrice figure, the maiden in distress, the magician, and so on), archetypal places (such as the paradisiacal garden, the labyrinth, the underworld), creatures and plants (such as the rose, the serpent, the lion), and archetypal actions (the quest, acts of redemption such as a sacrificial death, the descent into the underworld, the seasonal cycle, and so on). Many important archetypes are discussed and illustrated in the *Dictionnaire des mythes littéraires* (1988, edited by Pierre Brunel; *Companion to Literary Myths, Heroes and Archetypes*, 1992). The texts and authors illuminated by the methods of archetypal criticism have been many and diverse, from those to whom the approach might seem obviously suited (such as Dante, Blake, Novalis, and William Butler Yeats) to those to whom its relevance might seem more doubtful (such as Henry James, Charles Dickens, and Joseph Conrad).

The Canadian critic Northrop Frye was responsible for a major attempt to systematize the insights of archetypal criticism, and to locate it within a larger system of ideas about literature and literary criticism. Though influenced by both anthropological and Jungian schools, Frye's version of archetypical criticism was dependent on neither. His belief was that literary archetypes were the structures which made up and gave coherence to literature as a whole, and, as such, were purely literary phenomena. In his relatively early work on Blake (notably in *Fearful Symmetry: A Study of William Blake*, 1947) Frye interpreted the poet's work as essentially organized around a single, recurrent archetypal narrative (or myth), that of creation, fall, redemption, and apocalypse. That temporal narrative is seen to be counterpointed with, as it were, four spatial paradigms – a redeemed apocalyptic world, a world of unfallen Nature (apprehensible only imaginatively), a fallen landscape of time and space, and a demonic world. The ultimate literary archetype is the narrative of the hero's quest through these four levels. In the essays gathered in *Fables of Identity* (1963) and, more comprehensively, in his *Anatomy of Criticism* (1957), Frye developed these ideas in the direction of a synoptic statement about literature as a whole. The book is made up, after a "Polemical Introduction," of four essays: "Historical Criticism: Theory of Modes," "Ethical Criticism: Theory of Symbols," "Archetypal Criticism: Theory of Myths," and "Rhetorical Criticism: Theory of Genres." The archetype is a concept of fundamental importance to the whole project. The *Anatomy of Criticism* seeks to establish a view of literature in which its history can be seen as the evolving treatment of an original, mythic archetype through four further modes – romance, the high mimetic, the low mimetic, and the ironic. Frye understands literature in terms of an order in which myth marks one extreme and naturalism the other. He defines an archetype as "a symbol which connects one poem with another and thereby helps to unify and integrate our literary experience. And as the archetype is the communicable symbol, archetypal criticism is primarily concerned with literature as a social fact and as a mode of communication. By the study of conventions and genres, it attempts to fit poems into the body of poetry as a whole." The archetype is thus central to Frye's perception of literary order. Nowhere is this clearer than in the third essay of the *Anatomy of Criticism*, where Frye identifies four structuring archetypes, corresponding to the four seasons. These are "the Mythos of Spring: Comedy," "the Mythos of Summer: Romance," "the Mythos of Autumn: Tragedy," and "the Mythos of Winter: Irony and Satire." Frye identified distinct phases within each of these archetypes and illustrated their presence in a wide range of literary texts. The *Anatomy of Criticism* has proved a highly influential (and controversial) book, nowhere more so than its vision of archetypal criticism. Frye's own version of archetypal criticism is an important element in later books of his, such as *A Natural Perspective: The Development of Shakespearean Comedy and Romance* (1965), *The Return of Eden: Five Essays on Milton's Epics* (1965), *A Study of English Romanticism* (1968), *Spiritus Mundi: Essays on Literature, Myth, and Society* (1976), *The Great Code: The Bible and Literature* (1982), *The Myth of Deliverance: Reflections on Shakespeare's Problem Comedies* (1983), and *Words with Power: Being a Second Study of 'The Bible and Literature'* (1990). Frye's work, especially in *Anatomy of Criticism*, can be seen as enabling many later developments in literary criticism, and it is fitting that Julia Kristeva should praise Frye's work as a "rediscovery . . . of [the] polyphony, which . . . characterizes the Western imagination" and should judge that "Frye bestows on us an exceptional experience, rich in erudition and wisdom, which not one of us has yet equalled."

Later archetypal criticism has been influenced by the work of the American analyst James Hillman (1924–), who has drawn on a rich tradition of literary and philosophical texts, including figures such as Plotinus, Proclus, Marsilio Ficino, Vico, Blake, and the twentieth-century Islamist Henri Corbin (1903–1978) who has explored, and articulated for Western readers, the Islamic concept of the *mundus imaginalis*, which has affinities with the Western tradition of the archetype (though there are also important differences) and which offers exciting possibilities for the analysis of literary texts. Hillman sees the archetypal as part of the very activity of imagination, an insight developed in a series of important books (notably *Re-Visioning Psychology*, 1975, and *Archetypal Psychology: A Brief Account*, 1983) and in the pages of the journal *Spring: An Annual of Archetypal Psychology and Jungian Thought*, which Hillman revived in 1970.

Recent years have seen the emergence – indeed flourishing – of a school of feminist critics and theorists who have drawn on Jungian models, while "correcting" the male bias implicit in much of his work. Writers such as Annis Pratt and Estella Lauter have extended the horizons of archetypal criticism in exciting ways, relating its concerns to questions about gender and language in ways that have helped to make visible connections between Jungian thinking on the archetypal and many of the most modern schools of literary theory and criticism. Lauter's *Women as Mythmakers* (1984) is a particularly illuminating study of the transformation of traditional myths by American poets such as Anne Sexton and Diane Wakosi. Judith Kroll's *Chapters in a Mythology: The Poetry of Sylvia Plath* (1976) also demonstrates the continuing value of archetypal approaches, used in full awareness of other, later, critical methodologies, rather than in isolation or with inappropriate rigidity. Far from being exhausted, archetypal criticism seems full of new possibilities and well able to make important contributions to the future understanding of the literary imagination and its products. It cannot, any more than any other critical approach, offer any kind of absolute or universal answers, as perhaps some of its early adherents wrongly hoped; but its methods and its insights certainly deserve recognition in any balanced picture of criticism as a whole.

Further reading

Ackerman, Robert. *The Myth and Ritual School: J. G. Frazer and the Cambridge Ritualists*, 1991.
Bodkin, Maud. *Archetypal Patterns in Poetry*, 1934.
Doll, Mary A. *Beckett and Myth: An Archetypal Approach*, 1988.
Frye, Northrop. *Anatomy of Criticism: Four Essays*, 1957.
Gould, Eric. *Mythical Intentions in Modern Literature*, 1981.
Hamilton, A. C. *Northrop Frye: Anatomy of His Criticism*, 1990.
Kristeva, Julia. "The Importance of Frye," in *The Legacy of Northrop Frye*, 1994. Edited by A. A. Lee and R. D. Denham.
Lauter, Estella. *Women as Mythmakers: Poetry and Visual Art by Twentieth Century Women*, 1984.
——, and Carol Schreier Rupprecht, eds. *Feminist Archetypal Theory: Interdisciplinary Revisions of Jungian Thought*, 1985.
Pratt, Annis V. *Archetypal Patterns in Women's Fiction*, 1981.
van Meurs, Jos, and John Kidd. *Jungian Literary Criticism, 1920–1980: An Annotated Critical Bibliography of Works in English*, 1988.
Vickery, John B., ed. *Myth and Literature: Contemporary Theory and Practice*, 1966.
——. *The Literary Impact of 'The Golden Bough,'* 1973.

GLYN PURSGLOVE

See also Fiedler; Frye; Graves; Psychoanalytic Criticism

Aristotle

Greek philosopher

Born: Stagirus, Chalcidice, Greece; 384 B.C.
Died: Chalcis, Euboea, Greece; 322 B.C.

Biography

Aristotle was born in 384 B.C. at Stagirus in the Chalcidice, Greece. He was the son of Nicomachus, physician at the court of Amyntas II of Macedonia. Aristotle's youth at Amyntas' court fostered a lifelong interest in the natural sciences which not only led to his works on pure science but also suggested the analytic method employed in his nonscientific works, including *De poetica* (c. 334–323 B.C.; *Poetics*).

In 368 or 367 B.C. Aristotle enrolled in Plato's Academy, the Athenian philosophic school to which Aristotle remained attached until his teacher's death in about 348 B.C. During this twenty-year time span, usually referred to as Aristotle's "First Athenian Period," Aristotle laid his philosophical foundations, clearly set in Platonism. Even if

Aristotle in later years felt compelled to disagree at times with his master, Aristotle's respect for and debt to Plato are firm.

After Plato's death, Aristotle left Athens and began his so-called Middle Period (c. 348–336 B.C.), spent mostly under the patronage of two absolute Hellenistic rulers, Hermeias (tyrant of Atarneus and Assos in Mysia in modern Turkey) and Philip II of Macedonia. Hermeias' enlightened government fostered an active intellectual center which attracted not only Aristotle but also Callisthenes of Olynthus (Aristotle's nephew) and Theophrastus (Aristotle's most illustrious student). Aristotle married Pythias, Hermeias' niece and adopted daughter, by whom Aristotle had a daughter, Pythias. At Philip's court, Aristotle became the tutor of Philip's son, Alexander (the Great). Several of Aristotle's zoological and political works have been dated to this Middle Period, including the extant *Tōn peri ta zōia historiōn* (*Zoology*).

Aristotle's Second Athenian Period begins with his return to Athens in 335 B.C. and the founding of his own philosophic school, the Peripatos, and lasts until his death in 322 B.C. Most of his extant works, including *Poetics*, were written during this time. After the death of his wife, Aristotle had a son, Nicomachus, by a woman called Herpyllis. The death of Alexander in 323 B.C. led to anti-Macedonian movements in Greece, and Aristotle, as a non-Athenian Macedonian sympathizer, was charged with impiety and forced to leave Athens for Chalcis, where he died the next year. Theophrastus succeeded Aristotle as head of the Peripatos.

Influence

Aristotle's *Poetics* is the earliest known and only extant Greek technical handbook of literary criticism. Not only does Aristotle's work mark the beginning of the Western tradition of formal literary criticism, but it also contains, in chapters 20 through 22, the beginnings of a scientific grammar. Aristotle was certainly innovative in applying the tools of physical science – critical observation and the analytic method – to literary studies, and Aristotle's interest in the psychological effects of art (*catharsis*) was, in many ways, ahead of his time and presaged modern psychological studies.

Poetics served as a rigid dramaturgical code from the Italian Renaissance through the late eighteenth century and has continued to be a point of departure for literary theory and poetic composition. No other single text, except perhaps the Bible, has appeared in more editions and exerted a greater influence on Western poetic, especially dramatic, criticism than has this frequently misunderstood treatise by Aristotle. It is unfortunate that the reputation of *Poetics* rests especially on misreadings of the work by generations of critics from the Renaissance onward; these misreadings have tended to cloud the work's genuine and lasting contribution to literary theory: its critical and analytic study of tragedy as a genre. Aristotle has given modern Western literature not so much a set of rules as, rather, a compelling interest in the mechanics of poetic composition and in tragic form and its psychological effect.

Analysis

Aristotle's scientific devotion to form and structure and his deductive approach to literature, and to tragedy in particular, can be appreciated through a brief summary of *Poetics*. The extant *Poetics* devotes twenty-six chapters to tragedy and epic poetry. A second book, on comedy, is lost. In the introductory first chapter, Aristotle states that the work is arranged *kata physin*, "according to the order of nature," by first principles, namely the different aspects of *mimesis*, or imitation. Aristotle applies the term *mimesis* to all the arts, including literature, music, and painting, and does not mean, as the English translation "imitation" may imply, mere copying but rather a process of art as an imaginative representation of appearances, a concept which has the Platonic forms as a source.

In chapters 1 through 3, different types of *mimesis* are distinguished according to their first principles: the means, object, and manner of imitation. The means of *mimesis* are the materials used to create the work. Aristotle lists four means of imitation for the arts: form or shape, color, and sound, which is subdivided into *rhythmos* (rhythm), *harmonia* (harmony), and *logos* (speech). Of the fine arts, painting uses form and color, while literature, which relies on sound, can be divided into several groups, including those which use both *rhythmos* and *logos* (verse, for example) and *logos* alone (prose).

Aristotle lists three objects of *mimesis*: action, agent, and moral qualities (*spoudaios*, or "noble and serious," and *phaulos*, or "base and trivial"). The manners of imitation as outlined in *Poetics* conform to the modern classifications of first person (lyric), second person (dramatic), and third person (narrative). Thus, Aristotle's reliance on a deductive, analytic approach to the fine arts is evident from the very first chapters of *Poetics*.

The origins of poetry are discussed in chapters 4 and 5. First, Aristotle presents a brilliant discussion of the human psychological need for *mimesis* or improvisation, the effect of which is an intellectual satisfaction, the pleasure of recognizing the relationship between the object imitating and the object imitated. Aristotle then provides a brief but informative history of drama in Greece, which has also made *Poetics* an invaluable source on the origins of Greek drama.

In chapter 6, Aristotle turns to tragedy, which absorbs his attention until chapter 22, and, in a famous passage, defines tragedy as "a *mimesis* of an action which is *spoudaios*, complete, and has a certain magnitude; with seasonings of *logos*, different kinds being found in the various parts; dramatic not narrative in form; completing, through pity and fear, a *catharsis* of these emotions." By "seasonings of speech," Aristotle means rhythm, harmony, and song; by "different kinds found in the various parts," Aristotle is referring to the standard combination in Greek tragedy of song (rhythm and harmony) in the choral parts and dialogue in verse alone (rhythm) in the spoken parts. The *mimesis* of tragedy is then divided, according to means, manner, and object into six parts: diction and song (means), spectacle (manner), and plot, character, and thought (objects). Of these six parts, by far the most important to Aristotle is *mythos* (plot), to the structure and emotional effects of which he devotes chapters 7 through 18.

It is in this central section of *Poetics* that Aristotle presents his statements concerning a unified and probable plot, from which Renaissance scholars derived the three unities and the principle of verisimilitude. Crucial to the Aristotelian concept of *mythos* are the terms *peripeteia* (reversal), a change of an action to its opposite, and *anagnorisis* (recognition), a change from ignorance to knowledge. A simple tragic plot is one without either reversal or recognition; a complex plot has either reversal or recognition or both. The perfect tragedy, in Aristotle's scheme, is one in which a reversal is linked with a recognition and which shows a person who is neither exceptionally good nor bad and who experiences a reversal from good fortune to bad, as a result of *hamartia* (a mistake or error).

In chapters 20 through 22 Aristotle turns to *lexis* (diction). This discussion of phonetics, of parts of speech and their function, and of types of words and metaphors contains the basic elements of a preliminary scientific grammar. Chapters 23 through 26 are devoted to epic and consider the similarities of epic and tragedy, several problems of criticism, and, finally, the superiority of tragedy to epic.

The term *catharsis* is probably the single most influential and misunderstood term in *Poetics*, and Aristotle's own exposition of that term is so incomplete as to have made many critics argue for a more detailed discussion in the lost second book. Unfortunately, no single English word satisfactorily translates the several broad connotations of the Greek word *catharsis*: "medical purgation, evacuation, or secretion," "ritual cleansing," "intellectual clarification," and, even, "the pruning of trees, the winnowing of grain, and the clearing of land." Commentators in the Renaissance and seventeenth century generally favored the interpretation of *catharsis* as a "cleansing" and saw the cathartic process of tragedy as a purifying of the spectators of undesirable or excessive emotion. The term thus gained a didactic, morally improving sense not found in Aristotle, who mentions only pleasure and not utility as the effect of tragic *mimesis*.

The nineteenth-century work of Jacob Bernay *Zwei Abhandlungen über die aristotlische Theorie des Dramas* (1880) was instrumental in transferring emphasis from purification to the medical meaning of physical secretion. In this context, *catharsis* is connected with the ancient concept of the four humors and the cathartic process is understood in a psycho-physical sense: just as the body secretes excess fluids, the dramatic process causes the release of the spectator from the emotions aroused by the tragedy. The effect of this release on the spectator is pleasure.

A more recent and equally plausible interpretation of the Aristotelian term, developed in the twentieth century, especially by Leon Golden, is that of *catharsis* as a clarification, as an intellectual procedure, an insight into the mimetic process, into the relationship between the imitating object (the tragedy) and the imitated object (reality) and between the tragedy and the world of universals, Platonic forms. Whether Aristotelian *catharsis* refers to a physical secretion or to an intellectual clarification, it is generally accepted that the term should not be interpreted, as it was in the Renaissance, in a moral context, that is, as a process of ethical purification.

Hamartia is another Aristotelian term which has often been misunderstood and which requires special analysis. The primary meaning of the Greek word is derived from archery: "to miss the mark" and, hence, "to err or fail." Aristotle uses this term to refer to a false belief or an error of the mind which causes the tragic hero to err in deed. Since Aristotle clearly excludes evil from the character of the tragic hero, this error must be seen as unintentional and not a "sin" or "crime" in the modern, and especially Christian, sense. Thus, acceptable translations of *hamartia* are "tragic error" or "tragic mistake." The concept of *hamartia* as a "tragic flaw" or weakness of character is probably a result of Samuel Henry Butcher's influential late-nineteenth-century essay *Aristotle's Theory of Poetry and Fine Art* (1894) and is not what Aristotle intended to mean, even if "tragic flaw" has come to be a useful term in modern criticism. It is another irony of *Poetics* that *hamartia* as a "tragic flaw" can be applied more successfully to such modern dramas as Eugene O'Neill's *Desire Under the Elms* (1924) and Henry de Montherlant's *La Reine morte* (1942; *Queen After Death*, 1951) than can Aristotle's *hamartia* as a "tragic error" to fifth-century B.C. Athenian tragedy.

In *Poetics* Aristotle displays a particular admiration for plays with a complex plot, that is, plays with either *peripeteia* or *anagnorisis*. As fifth-century B.C. examples of simple plots, Aristotle cites Aeschylus' *Prometheus desmōtēs* (date unknown; *Prometheus Bound*), Sophocles' *Aias* (early 440s B.C.; *Ajax*), and Euripides' *Mēdeia* (431 B.C.; *Medea*); as examples of complex plots, he mentions Aeschylus' *Choēphoroi* (458 B.C.; *Libation Bearers*), Sophocles' *Oidipous Tyrannos* (c. 429 B.C.; *Oedipus Tyrannus*), and Euripides' *Iphigenia ē en Taurois* (c. 414 B.C.; *Iphigenia in Tauris*). A survey of extant Greek tragedies shows that the complex plot is not necessarily common: of the seven surviving plays of Aeschylus, only *Libation Bearers* is complex. Of the seven plays of Sophocles, only *Élektra* (418–410 B.C.; *Electra*) and *Trachinai* (435–429 B.C.; *The Women of Trachis*) can be added to the *Oedipus Tyrannus*. In the last decades of the fifth century B.C. plots of recognition became increasingly common, especially in Euripides' corpus.

Besides *Iphigenia Among the Taurians*, the complex plots of Euripides include *Alkēstis* (438 B.C.; *Alcestis*), *Hekabē* (425 B.C.; *Hecuba*), *Iōn* (c. 411 B.C.; *Iōn*), *Helenē* (412 B.C.; *Helen*), *Élektra* (413 B.C.; *Electra*), *Bakchai* (405 B.C.; *Bacchae*), and *Iphigeneia ē en Aulidi* (405 B.C.; *Iphigenia in Aulis*).

Aristotle's preference for complex plays cannot be made into a rigid standard of good fifth-century B.C. dramaturgy, for Aristotle's theories of tragedy were developed more than fifty years after the deaths of Sophocles and Euripides and more than a century later than the earliest extant tragedy of Aeschylus. Consequently, fifth-century B.C. tragedies were not written to conform to Aristotelian standards and must, in general, be interpreted independently from *Poetics*. This is not to suggest that Aristotle should be ignored in the study of Greek tragedy. Quite the contrary, Aristotelian terminology and theory represent a significant historical stage in the interpretation of Greek tragedy, but it is important, in such a study, that the errors of neoclassicism be avoided and that *Poetics* not be regarded as a rule book for fifth-century B.C. tragedy.

The Greek play which comes closest to fitting the Aristotelian ideal of tragedy is *Oedipus Tyrannus*, and, indeed, it is this play which Aristotle cites prominently in chapter 11 of *Poetics* as containing the best form of recognition, one accompanied by reversal. The plot of this play is clearly complex, with both a recognition by Oedipus of his true identity and a sudden reversal, Oedipus' blinding and fall from power. In chapter 13 Aristotle also refers to the character of Oedipus (but without specifically mentioning the Oedipus of Sophocles) as an example of the ideal tragic character, one neither very good nor very bad, whose reversal is caused by *hamartia*.

While Sophocles' Oedipus does possess the moral stature required in a tragic character by *Poetics*, it has been a great misfortune that Aristotle said no more about *hamartia* and Oedipus, for there has been little modern critical agreement as to the exact nature of the *hamartia* of Sophocles' Oedipus. The character's "tragic mistake" could be the slaying of an old man at a crossroads many years before the events of the drama, or it could be Oedipus' intellectual pride and stubborn determination to discover the murder of Laius. The ambiguity is not only a result of Aristotle's failure to specify Oedipus' *hamartia* but also, more important, a result of the fact that Sophocles himself did not compose a play centered on Aristotelian *hamartia*. The dramatic emphasis of Sophocles' *Oedipus Tyrannus* is rather on irony, on a movement from Oedipus' ignorance to the knowledge of his true identity as murderer and son of Laius. Thus, even in the play which Aristotle admires so highly, not all the terms of *Poetics* are critically significant. Aristotle's emphasis on *peripeteia* and *anagnorisis* is useful, to a certain degree, in the interpretation of *Oedipus Tyrannus*, but the term *hamartia* adds little to the play besides controversy.

Application of Aristotelian terminology to other extant Greek tragedies yields similar results. It is not Aristotle's terminology but his emphasis on plot, his careful analysis of form and character, which is the lasting contribution of *Poetics* to literary criticism.

Together with *Ars poetica* (c. 17 B.C.; *The Art of Poetry*) of Horace, as well as with the tragedies of Seneca and the comedies of Terence, Aristotle's *Poetics* became a major influence on Renaissance drama and dramatic theory. The first visible modern use of *Poetics* as a model can be found in early-sixteenth-century Italian plays which were both imitations of Greek tragedy and early attempts to create Aristotelian *catharsis* of pity and fear. On a theoretical level, *Poetics* provided Renaissance literature with an awareness of genre which had been lacking in medieval literature and with a foundation upon which to create great literature. As the influence of medieval scholasticism, and hence of Aristotelian philosophy, waned in the sixteenth century, Aristotelian literary criticism as interpreted especially by Italian commentators became more and more popular and came to serve as a guide for European tragedy from the mid-sixteenth century until the end of the eighteenth century. While Aristotle had never intended his analytic study of tragedy to become a set of rules, he nevertheless became a literary dictator for sixteenth-century Italian critics who sought in antiquity the standards for great literature.

The Italian critics, heavily indebted to Horace's utilitarian principle of *utile et dulce* (useful and pleasant), inferred several poetic and dramatic principles from *Poetics*. First, Aristotelian *mimesis* was interpreted by Renaissance critics as imitation of the ancient Greek and Latin literatures so greatly admired in this period. *Catharsis* was another Aristotelian term misinterpreted in the Renaissance. For Aristotle, the goal of poetry was pleasure alone, and *catharsis* was a physical process of purgation; sixteenth-century didacticism, however, springing equally from Horace's *The Art of Poetry* and Christian morality, made utility a primary poetic goal and Aristotle's *catharsis* an ethical purification, an ennobling of character. Aristotle's belief that a tragic character should be *to homoion* (true to life) became in the sixteenth century the principle of decorum: that only certain types of characters should be depicted on the tragic stage and that these characters should act and speak in a manner appropriate to their station. The Italians also expanded Aristotle's statement that art imitates nature into the principle of verisimilitude (*vraisemblance* in French), which taught that the actions of a tragedy should have the appearance of probability or likelihood.

The most infamous misreading of Aristotle concerns the rule of the three unities, sometimes wrongly called the Aristotelian unities, of action, time, and place. Of these, only unity of action is authentically Aristotelian. Unity of time is mentioned in *Poetics*, but only as a possibility, not as a rule, and unity of place was a Renaissance addition. In the early seventeenth century, especially in the French theater of Pierre Corneille and Jean Racine, these unities, together with the principles of tragic decorum and verisimilitude, became rules of dramatic composition which were proclaimed as Aristotelian, advocated by the neoclassical critics, and followed by playwrights well into the next century.

Despite frequent misreadings of *Poetics*, the esteem which the sixteenth-century Italians held for Aristotle has ensured his literary approach and critical vocabulary a permanent place in modern critical theory. Even after the dramatic principles of the neoclassical period were abandoned, Aristotelian critical terms continued to be discussed, often by writers only vaguely aware of their ancient source, and it has become nearly impossible for modern critics of Western literature to discuss poetry and drama without introducing, consciously or unconsciously, Aristotelian concepts.

For example, William Wordsworth, whose particular poetic achievement was a substitution of everyday themes for the classical tradition, was nevertheless widely read in the ancient literatures and very conscious of his literary debt to these works. While Wordsworth rarely employed Aristotelian terminology, his poetic theories demonstrate the continuing influence of Aristotle. Without using the word *catharsis*, Wordsworth adopted as his own poetic principle a variation on the Aristotelian term when he described the effect of poetry as "establishing that dominion over the spirits of readers by which they are to be humbled and humanized, in order that they may be purified and exalted" in "Essay Supplementary to the Preface to *Poems*" (1815).

Aristotelian criticism did not develop in the United States until the nineteenth century, when certain poets and critics, such as Edgar Allan Poe, began to assimilate Aristotelian concepts and later writers, such as Ralph Waldo Emerson and James Russell Lowell, embraced many of Aristotle's poetic principles. The early-twentieth-century critic Irving Babbitt was particularly influential in reintroducing classical principles, including those of *Poetics*, into both American and British literature, and Aristotelian literary concepts have left a strong mark on such modern writers as T. S. Eliot, W. H. Auden, and Eugene O'Neill.

Principal criticism

De poetica, c. 334–323 B.C. (*Poetics*)

Other major works and literary forms

Aristotle's works are divided into two categories: the exoteric or published pieces written in a flowing style for wide circulation, and the esoteric or private books written in a choppy and unpolished style and probably intended for restricted circulation within the Peripatos, Aristotle's philosophical school.

Aristotle's exoteric works are lost, unless the extant *Athenaiōn politeia* (c. 329–328 B.C.; *The Athenian Constitution*) is included among the public works. Most of the surviving esoteric works are philosophical or scientific in scope, but several, including *Poetics*, are devoted to rhetoric, literature, and the arts. Aristotle also compiled several didactic collections, which are now lost, including the constitutions of Greek states, barbaric customs, and lists of victors at the Olympic and Pythian contests and at the dramatic festivals at Athens.

NONFICTION

The works listed here date to Aristotle's Second Athenian Period (335–322 B.C.), except for *Zoology*, which is dated to the Middle Period (c. 348–336 B.C.):

Analytica priora (*Prior Analytics*); *Analytica posterioria* (*Posterior Analytics*)
Aporemata Homerika (*Homeric Problems*)
Aristotelous peri geneseōs kai phthoras (*Meteoroligica*)
Athenaiōn politeia (*The Athenian Constitution*)
Peri Psyches (*On the Soul*)
Ethica Nicomachea (*Nicomachean Ethics*)
Metaphysica (*Metaphysics*)
Organon (English translation)
Physica (*Physics*)
Politica (*Politics*)
Technē rhetorikēs (*Rhetoric*)
Tōn peri ta zōia historiōn (*Zoology*)
Topica (*Topics*)

Further reading

Aristotle. *Poetics*, 1968. Edited by D. W. Lucas.
Butcher, Samuel Henry. *Aristotle's Theory of Poetry and Fine Art*, 1951 (revised edition).
Cooper, Lane. *The "Poetics" of Aristotle: Its Meaning and Influence*, 1923, 1963.
Else, Gerald F. *Aristotle's "Poetics": The Argument*, 1957.
——. *Plato and Aristotle on Poetry*, 1986.
Golden, Leon, and O. B. Hardison, Jr. *Aristotle's "Poetics,"* 1968.
——. *Aristotle's Poetics: A Translation and Commentary for Students of Literature*, 1981.
Grube, G. M. A. *The Greek and Roman Critics*, 1965.
Halliwell, Stephen. *The "Poetics" of Aristotle: A New Translation and Literary Commentary*, 1987.
Lear, J. *Aristotle*, 1988.
Spingarn, Joel. *History of Literary Criticism in the Renaissance*, 1963 (second edition).

THOMAS J. SIENKEWICZ

See also Classical Greek and Roman Literary Theory; Mimesis; Plato

Matthew Arnold

English poet and critic

Born: Laleham, England; December 24, 1822
Died: Liverpool, England; April 15, 1888

Biography

Matthew Arnold was born on December 24, 1822, in the village of Laleham, in the Thames valley, England. He was the eldest son of Thomas Arnold, headmaster of Rugby School, and Mary Penrose Arnold. After being educated at Winchester College and Rugby School, Arnold won a classical scholarship to Balliol College, Oxford University, which he entered in 1841.

He graduated with a B.A. degree in 1844, and a year later he was elected Fellow of Oriel College. After traveling in France and Switzerland during 1846, he moved to London in 1847 to accept a post as private secretary to Lord Lansdowne, a minister in the government.

Two years later he published his first collection of poems, and in 1851 he married Frances Lucy Wightman. In the same year he was appointed inspector of schools, a position which he held until his retirement in 1886. This position involved him in much travel throughout England and Wales, inspecting elementary schools and training colleges.

In 1857 he was elected to the position of professor of poetry at Oxford, a part-time post which required him to give three lectures annually. He held this position for ten years. In October, 1883, he began a lecture tour of the United States, which lasted until March, 1884. He died of a heart attack on April 15, 1888.

Influence

During his lifetime and for fifty years after his death, Arnold exerted a pervasive influence on literary theory. Indeed, T. S. Eliot remarked that informed literary opinion in the early twentieth century was largely formed by Arnold. Arnold represented many things, both to his contemporaries and to his successors: he was the Victorian apostle of "culture" (as opposed to "anarchy"), the definer of nineteenth-century poetic taste, and the defender of humanistic values in an increasingly utilitarian and materialistic age. He reminded the literary world of the ideals of classical literary theory, and he expanded the basis of English criticism, using foreign literature as a touchstone for the evaluation of English writers. As a defender of "disinterestedness" in criticism, declining to be an advocate of any particular poetic school or partisan cause (even his own), he outlined a lofty, if difficult, ideal which much subsequent criticism has attempted to follow.

Analysis

Arnold made his debut as a literary theorist with the publication of his preface to the first edition of *Poems*, in October, 1853. It was in part a reply to a critical review of his poetry by his friend Arthur Hugh Clough, which appeared in *The North American Review* in July, 1853. The main thrust of Arnold's argument is his rejection of the subjective basis of Romanticism and a call for a return to the objective, classical ideal. Because the ancients regarded choice of subject and action as paramount, Arnold argues that these two are the only basis on which narrative and dramatic poetry can be constructed. The action must appeal (and here Arnold strongly echoes William Wordsworth's preface to *Lyrical Ballads*, 1800) to the "great primary human affections: to those elementary feelings which subsist permanently in the race." It is in this way, according to Arnold, that the ancient Athenian audience expected to be moved by their drama, and he identifies "unity and profoundness of moral impression" as the chief source of the continuing vitality of the ancients. Whereas the Greeks were always aware of the whole, modern literature pays too much attention to the parts. This error is at the root of the confusion Arnold sees in contemporary poets: expression predominates over action, instead of the other way round.

Following Aristotle, Arnold states that poetry is interesting because it imparts knowledge through imitation or representation. Yet conveying knowledge is not of itself enough. Poetry must also "convey a charm, and infuse delight." The poet must add to the happiness of humanity; all art – and here Arnold quotes Friedrich Schiller – "is dedicated to Joy." The effect on the reader is of great importance. No enjoyment can be found, for example, in a work that prolongs "a continuous state of mental distress . . . unrelieved by incident, hope, or resistance." Indeed, the reason Arnold abandoned writing poetry was that he believed that he was unable to live up to this standard. He judged his own poem "Empedocles on Etna" harshly because it was "morbid," and he omitted it from *Poems*. Its subject was not suitable because it could not bring joy.

Arnold held high expectations of what poetry should do. In addition to bringing joy, it should bring strength, offer consolation, and have power to edify and ennoble. Arnold thought that poetry could relieve what Wordsworth called "the burthen of the mystery"; through poetry humankind can come to terms with and master the oppressive nature of life. Poetry in this sense is therapeutic; Arnold hails Wordsworth, for example, for his "healing power," and comments on the "tonic and fortifying" quality of Homer's poetry. Living in an age when traditional religious beliefs were in decline, Arnold believed that poetry could fill the gap. Religion had failed because it had relied too much on historical facts, which were now being called into question. Yet poetry and religion meet in the sphere of conduct and moral feelings, since religion is "morality touched with emotion." Arnold thought optimistically that more and more people would turn to poetry, as they formerly had to religion and philosophy, to interpret the world for them.

Poetry for Arnold is "a criticism of life," a definition which he frequently reiterated and which has been much discussed. Eliot complained that the definition was "frigid to anyone who has felt the full surprise and elevation of a new experience of poetry." The word "criticism" is perhaps slightly misleading. Arnold does not mean rational analysis but a sympathetic understanding or interpretation of life, a representation of things as they are but with an implicit moral evaluation. The best "criticism of life" through poetry will be of direct use to people; it will make life bearable, it will give "consolation," and it will answer the question of how to live. It is in this sense that Arnold defines poetry, in his essay on Wordsworth, as "the application of ideas to life."

A more extended definition appears in Arnold's essay on the minor French poet Maurice de Guérin, which was included in *Essays in Criticism*. Poetry is distinguished by its "interpretative power." This power has two aspects. First, it awakens "a wonderfully full, new, and intimate sense of [things], and of our relations with them." Readers can thus penetrate the essential reality of objects and feel harmony with them. This intuitive knowledge, which is distinct from rational philosophical analysis, satisfies and calms the spirit; it is superior to the explanations of science because it appeals not only to the intellect but to the whole person. Arnold calls this first power of poetry "natural magic." He likens it to Adam's ability to name the animals (Genesis 2:19). (This comparison recalls Arnold's statement in his essay on Wordsworth that "poetry is nothing less than the most perfect speech of man, that in which he comes nearest to being able to utter the truth.")

If the first power of poetry deals with the external world, the second power appeals to the internal world. It expresses "the ideas and laws of the inward world of man's moral and spiritual nature." This power Arnold calls "moral profundity." The idea that poetry must satisfy and guide people's moral instincts is central to Arnold's entire literary theory. He does not, however, use the term "moral" in a narrow, didactic sense. Poetry instructs by revealing the underlying truth about things; its moral profundity consists of its ability to resonate with a person's innate sense of the natural laws of the universe. Once again, Arnold refers not so much to the rational intellect alone as to an intuitive understanding in which all the faculties take part (what he called elsewhere the power of "imaginative reason").

Taken together, these two powers of poetry – "natural magic" and "moral profundity" – give people a sense of unity; they reconcile them, not only to themselves but also to the universe at large. Arnold names William Shakespeare, Lucretius, and Wordsworth as possessing this power.

In "The Study of Poetry" (in *Essays in Criticism: Second Series*), Arnold returned to the idea of moral profundity. His essay attempts to describe how poetry may be justly evaluated. One must be wary, he says, of confusing true poetic value with an estimate which leans too heavily on the historical importance of the poem (rather than its intrinsic worth) or merely on its personal importance. He argues that great poetry always exhibits truth and "high seriousness." According to these criteria, Geoffrey Chaucer cannot be ranked with the greatest writers. Although there is strength and joy to be gained from his work, and he expresses truth in his representation of the world, he lacks "high and excellent seriousness." It is only this seriousness, which Homer, Shakespeare, and John Milton possess, that "gives to our spirits what they can rest upon."

Arnold suggests that the best way of judging excellence is to have at one's command some short passages from the great masters (he selects Dante, Shakespeare, Homer, and Milton) and to use them as a "touchstone" with which to evaluate other poetry. Concrete examples are superior to the abstractions of critics. This "touchstone theory" has been the subject of much discussion, and Arnold has sometimes been accused of a rigid insistence on certain objective standards. This judgment, however, springs from a misunderstanding. Arnold refers, as usual, to an intuitive feeling for greatness rather than the application of an inflexible rule; the critic must allow himself or herself to be penetrated by the power of these passages, to feel the presence in them of high poetry. This experience will enable him or her to catch the essence of what great poetry is and avoid giving a falsely high estimate of other, inferior, poetry.

In "The Function of Criticism at the Present Time," Arnold put forward his influential theory of criticism, using the term in a broad sense to include commentary on social, political, and religious questions. Central to his theory is the concept of "disinterestedness." The critic must absorb and disseminate "the best that is known and thought in the world" with a lack of partisan concern and practical involvement. Criticism must embrace "the Indian virtue of detachment"; it must be removed from the stream of everyday life. Only through this free, disinterested, and objective play of the mind can the critic "see things as they are" and so become a beneficial force in society. Without this disinterestedness, truth and culture would be impossible. With it, the critic could create a "current of true and fresh ideas" which would pave the way for a new flowering of creative power in a subsequent age.

Arnold was without doubt the most influential literary critic of his time, and the most important critic since Samuel Taylor Coleridge. For half a century his influence was perhaps almost as great as that of Aristotle. Eliot commented that Walter Pater (who attended Arnold's lectures on poetry when he was an undergraduate at Oxford), Arthur Symons, and Leslie Stephen, among others (such as A. C. Bradley and I. A. Richards), adopted Arnold's critical assumptions. In the United States, Henry James was an enthusiastic admirer, and Irving Babbitt and Paul Elmer More adopted many of Arnold's ideas as they developed the "New Humanism," which was scornful of Romanticism and looked back to classical models, but without Arnold's "disinterestedness." In sum, Arnold's influence has been such that his biographer can plausibly claim that an understanding of Arnold is "more useful to us than an understanding of any other Englishman of the last [nineteenth] century."

There are several main aspects of this influence. First, Arnold played a major part in shaping and standardizing the literary taste of the period. Second, he encouraged a more cosmopolitan outlook in English literary criticism.

His continual references to world literature, and his insistence that the critic should master at least one literature other than his or her own, extended the range of twentieth-century criticism. Third, he spoke directly to the collective need of the time, for example, in his attempt to reconcile rationalism and faith in his social and religious writings (the equivalent of his attempt to balance reason and feeling, or reason and imagination, in his literary criticism). Fourth, his defense of literature, in a world increasingly dominated by study of the natural sciences and the pursuit of technology, has become a classic statement of the value of the humanist tradition. His belief that literature alone is able to relate the findings of science to "our instinct for beauty, our instinct for conduct" speaks to the modern need, felt even more acutely than in Arnold's day, to relate the parts of knowledge to the whole.

Principal criticism

Preface to *Poems*, 1853
On Translating Homer, 1861
Essays in Criticism, 1865
On the Study of Celtic Literature, 1867
Discourses in America, 1885
Essays in Criticism: Second Series, 1888

Other major works and literary forms

In addition to his work as a literary theorist and critic, Matthew Arnold was one of the major poets of the Victorian Age. He published several volumes of poetry, including *The Strayed Reveller and Other Poems* (1849), *Empedocles on Etna and Other Poems* (1852), *Poems* (1853), and *New Poems* (1867), which included what some regard as his finest poem, "Dover Beach." He also made his mark as a social critic, particularly in *Culture and Anarchy* (1869) and *Friendship's Garland* (1871), and he wrote religious works, such as *Literature and Dogma* (1873), *God and the Bible* (1875), and *Last Essays on Church and Religion* (1877).

PLAY
Merope: A Tragedy, 1858

POETRY
The Strayed Reveller and Other Poems, 1849
Empedocles on Etna and Other Poems, 1852
Poems, 1853
Poems: Second Series, 1855
New Poems, 1867
Poems: Collected Edition, 1869

NONFICTION
Culture and Anarchy, 1869
Friendship's Garland, 1871
Literature and Dogma, 1873
God and the Bible, 1875
Last Essays on Church and Religion, 1877
Civilization in the United States, 1888
The Complete Prose Works of Matthew Arnold, 1960–1976 (R. H. Super, editor)

Further reading

Bloom, Harold, ed. *Matthew Arnold*, 1987.
Bush, Douglas. *Matthew Arnold: A Survey of His Poetry and Prose*, 1971.
Carroll, Joseph. *The Cultural Theory of Matthew Arnold*, 1982.
Donovan, Robert A. "The Method of Arnold's *Essays in Criticism*," in *PMLA*. LXXI (1956), pp. 922–931.
Eliot, T. S. "Matthew Arnold," in *The Use of Poetry and the Use of Criticism*, 1933.
Garrod, H. W. *Poetry and the Criticism of Life*, 1931.
Madden, William A. *Matthew Arnold: A Study of the Aesthetic Temperament in Victorian England*, 1967.
Neiman, Fraser. *Matthew Arnold*, 1968.
Peltason, Timothy. "The Function of Matthew Arnold at the Present Time," in *College English*. 56, no. 7 (November, 1994), pp. 749–765.
Pinkney, Tony. "Matthew Arnold and the Subject of Modernity," in *Critical Survey*. 4, no. 3 (1992), pp. 226–232.
Trilling, Lionel. *Matthew Arnold*, 1949.

BRYAN AUBREY

See also Literary Theory in the Age of Victoria; Mill; Ruskin; Sainte-Beuve

Antonin Artaud

French writer, actor, and playwright

Born: Marseilles, France; September 4, 1896
Died: Ivry, France; March 4, 1948

Biography

Antonin Artaud was born on September 4, 1896, in Marseilles, France. In 1901 he suffered an attack of meningitis, which probably led to the nervous condition that would plague him the rest of his life. His youth was spent in and out of mental wards or under the private care of psychiatrists. In 1920 he went to Paris to begin his career as an actor. While in Paris, Artaud published a volume of poetry, wrote for various literary journals, and joined and later rejected the Surrealist group. In 1926 he founded his own theater, the Théâtre Alfred Jarry, but his bizarre productions were poorly received and the attempt was a failure. Venturing into film acting, in 1927 Artaud gave moving performances in Abel Gance's *Napoléon* (1927) and Carl Theodor Dreyer's *La Passion de Jeanne d'Arc* (1928; *The Passion of Joan of Arc*, 1928). While continuing his film career, Artaud embarked on a second unsuccessful attempt to form an innovative theater.

Frustrated by these failures, Artaud sailed to Mexico, where he lived with the Tarahumara Indians and participated in their peyote rituals. In 1936 he returned to Paris, and later sailed to Ireland with a cane he believed to be Saint Patrick's. After altercations with authorities in Ireland and a violent scene on his homeward passage, Artaud was confined to a series of mental asylums. During this time his famous work *The Theatre and Its Double* was published. After spending nine years in mental asylums, Artaud was released and reaccepted into the artistic community with his 1947 poetry recitation at the Vieux Colombier. Artaud's final performance, a radio drama, was censored in 1948. Soon afterward, on March 4, 1948, Artaud died of anal cancer.

Influence

Artaud's criticism of language and his theories of signification have sparked commentaries from many poststructuralists, ranging from semioticians to deconstructionists, but most especially in the writings of Jacques Derrida. In addition, Artaud's theories on the nature of insanity have influenced the writings of psychologist-philosophers such as R. D. Laing and Michel Foucault. Yet Artaud's greatest influence has been in the area of contemporary theater. Along with Bertolt Brecht, Artaud is one of the most influential theorists of the modern theater.

Analysis

Because Artaud was not a systematic thinker, his literary criticism is encouched in a series of oracular pronouncements, mystical rhapsodies, and ranting invectives. Out of such writings, one has to sift through numerous inconsistencies and highly symbolic utterances in order to discover Artaud's poetics, a poetics of pain and passion. In his writing Artaud defines the nature of the poet, the poetic process, the technique of poetry, and poetry's ultimate aim. Finally, Artaud focuses on what he believes to be the consummate art, the theater, and sets forth a blueprint for a revolutionary one that would eventually reshape the focus of contemporary theatrical performance as well as modern drama theory.

For Artaud, the poet is a visionary who, through his suffering, is able both to gain insight into the mysteries of Being and to create a living work of art that is intensely moving and uniquely redemptive. Artaud's poet "visualizes and makes concrete his ideas and images more intensely and with more telling appropriateness than [do] other people." He cannot write a poem "outside the spasm and sob of the heart, a poem that has not been *suffered*." Artaud criticizes both Lewis Carroll and Samuel Taylor Coleridge for not involving themselves in "the uterine existence of suffering in which every great poet has been immersed." For Artaud, "Everything that is not a tetanus of the soul, . . . like the poems of Baudelaire or Poe, is not true and cannot be accepted as poetry." True poets must pay the price for their genius: they are "the outcast, the poisoned, . . . the executed criminals of language who suffer ruin in their writing." They are pitted against a hostile society, a society who would "flagellate in secret the true heart of the suffering poet." Artaud's poet is a sacrificial victim, a true shaman who experiences the terrors of demoniac forces and exorcizes them in order to purify himself and his community.

Either through reverie or through a drug-induced state, the poet plummets into the depths of his being and delves into the dark, sinister labyrinth of his unconscious in order to emerge with the true poetic utterance, "the screams of a tortured world." During this process, the poet is seized by a spasm of conflicting emotions, ranging from the sublime to the terrifying. To create true poetry, the poet destroys all logical associations and eschews abstract words, which have become bankrupt of their affective power. The poet accomplishes this feat by dream reveries. According to Artaud, "All those who dream . . . without suffering from a feeling of unbearable nostalgia after plunging down into a fertile subconscious are swine. Dreaming is true." Artaud's dream world, however, is played out on a nightmarish landscape revealing man's "taste for crime, for his erotic obsessions, [and] his savagery."

Other than dreams, the poet focuses on disruptive images, images which do not ordinarily fit together. These evocative images prevent readers from forming stereotyped associations and force them to formulate new perceptions. They also defy rational analysis: "Whatever belongs to the realm of the image cannot be subjected to reason; it must remain within this realm, or be annihilated." When poetry juxtaposes such disparate images, the reader is jolted out of his or her conscious reflection and experiences into a subconscious awareness. As Artaud states, "True psychic situations stem from the clash of objects and gestures."

Artaud's poetics abolishes aesthetics and style. Images of violence, scatological references, and sadistic scenes intermesh with metaphysical speculations. Words are transformed into incantations, nonsense syllables, neologisms, and blasphemous puns. Artaud's poetics is that of chaos: "When poetry isn't somewhat anarchic, when it lacks fire and incandescence, . . . it isn't poetry."

Nevertheless, Artaud's poetics is not simply one of disruption. For Artaud, the aim of poetry is purgation, transformation, and redemption. True poetry acts directly on the nervous system of the reader in the same manner as musical vibrations charm a snake. Through experiencing a poetry of violent sensations, readers are jolted out of their ordered, rational, and complacent existence in order to confront the hidden terrors of their own beings and, finally, to emerge cleansed and whole. "Poetry, which restores order, first resuscitates disorder, a disorder full of inflamed elements; thrusting these elements against each other, it brings them to a single point of flames, gestures, blood and screams."

Artaud found theater the ideal medium for carrying out his theories. Instead of a dramatic literature dependent on dialogue, ideas, and character revelations, Artaud foresaw one using myth, ritual, and spectacle. Drama would no longer be dependent on the written text: instead, an inspired director using the physical language of the theater (gestures, sound, music, lights, bodies in space) would create a mass spectacle that would surround and overwhelm an audience.

Strange sounds, screams, shrieks, and incantations would be accompanied by bizarre musical instruments "producing sound or noises that are unbearably piercing." Lights would pour across the stage and auditorium in pulsating waves creating "sensations of heat, cold, anger, fear." Modern dress would be replaced by symbolic, ritual garb. The box set would disappear, transformed into a world populated by "manikins, enormous masks, [and] objects of strange proportions," such as puppets "ten feet high" and "musical instruments tall as men."

In order to make full use of ritual space, the traditional building would give way to a found space, "some hangar or barn." Sitting in swivel chairs in the middle of the room, the audience would be surrounded by a performance taking place in every corner of the building and on galleries and catwalks above them. Artaud wished "to make space speak, to feed and furnish it."

Artaud also wished to take theater beyond psychological realism concerned with individual or social problems and to produce cosmic dramas of mythic proportions, focusing on cataclysmic events, such as social upheavals or natural disasters. Individual characters would be replaced by characters "enlarged to the statures of gods or monsters." Such a powerful spectacle would not be a series of random effects but a well orchestrated performance in which all the elements of the theater would coalesce to produce an awe-inspiring event.

Artaud called his theater the Theater of Cruelty, not so much because it featured violent and catastrophic events, but because it focused on the meta-physical cruelty of human beings trapped in a cycle of determinism. For Artaud, cruelty is inherent in the human condition: in his vision, humanity is caught in a web of fate and evil is inescapable.

In his visionary theater, Artaud found the perfect medium for his new poetics. His Theater of Cruelty would emphasize suffering artists, destroy the tyranny of written language, transcend rational thinking, and jangle the nerves of the spectators, who would be buffeted and battered through a sensory experience that would act as a sort of shock therapy, leaving them both purged and cleansed.

Although unable to put his theories into practice or gain acceptance for them in his own lifetime, Artaud would have considerable influence on subsequent generations. His theories on the impotence of the spoken language and his call for a language of gesture are embodied in the works of such leading absurdist playwrights as Samuel Beckett, Eugène Ionesco, and Jean Genet. Genet's dramas, moreover, display many of the ritual qualities espoused by Artaud. Artaud has also directly influenced the leading practitioners and theoreticians of the modern avant-garde theater. His vision of an environmental theater taking place in a nontraditional space, involving a high degree of audience participation, and emphasizing the qualities of an occult ritual has influenced Jerzy Grotowski and his Polish Laboratory Theatre, Julian Beck's Living Theatre, Richard Schechner's Performance Group, and Peter Brook's Theatre of Cruelty. Everything from happenings to street theater, from performance art to the theater of images, somehow bears the mark of Artaud.

Principal criticism

Correspondance avec Jacques Rivière, 1924 (*Correspondence with Jacques Rivière*, 1965)
"L'Évolution du décor," 1924 ("The Evolution of Decor," 1976)
"L'Activité du Bureau de Recherches Surréalistes," 1925 ("The Activity of the Surrealist Research Bureau," 1976)
"À la grande nuit: Ou, Le Bluff surréaliste," 1927 ("In the Dark: Or, The Surrealist Bluff," 1968)
"Le Théâtre Alfred Jarry," 1927 ("The Theatre Alfred Jarry," 1976)
L'Art et la mort, 1929 (*Art and Death*, 1968)
Le Théâtre et son double, 1938 (*The Theatre and Its Double*, 1958)
Les Lettres de Rodez, 1946 (*Letters from Rodez*, 1960)

Other major works and literary forms

Antonin Artaud, an eclectic writer, wrote Surrealist poetry in such works as *Tric-trac du ciel* (1923; *Heavenly Backgammon*, 1965) and *L'Ombilic des limbes* (1925; *Umbilical Limbo*, 1964). His play *Le Jet de sang* (1925; *The Jet of Blood*, 1963) is a series of nightmare images culminating in a swarm of scorpions pouring forth from under a woman's dress. His one attempt at the Theater of Cruelty, *Les Cenci* (1935; *The Cenci*, 1969), is loosely based on Percy Bysshe Shelley's *The Cenci* (1819) and features a Don Juan figure who unequivocally embraces evil. The drama is filled with violent action, rhythmic chants, and ritualistic dances. Artaud's film scripts, most of which were never produced, foreshadow the later developments of the surrealistic film. His other works include historical novels, articles on drugs, writings on religion and politics, pseudoanthropological studies, and attacks on modern psychiatry. His critical works reach beyond literature and into the fields of art, music, cinema, and theater.

NOVELS

Héliogabale: Ou, L'Anarchiste couronné, 1934 (*Heliogabalus: Or, The Anarchist Crowned*, 1976)

PLAYS

Le Jèt de sang, 1925 (*The Jet of Blood*, 1963)
Les Cenci, 1935 (*The Cenci*, 1969)

POETRY

Tric-trac du ciel, 1923 (*Heavenly Backgammon*, 1965)
L'Ombilic des limbes, 1925 (*Umbilical Limbo*, 1964)
Le Pèse-nerfs, 1925 (*The Nerve Scales*, 1968)
Artaud le Mômo, 1947 (English translation, 1976)

NONFICTION

D'un voyage au pays des Tarahumaras, 1945 (*A Voyage to the Land of the Tarahumara*, 1976)
Van Gogh: Le Suicidé de la société, 1947 (*Van Gogh: The Man Suicided by Society*, 1949)

Further reading

Barber, Stephen. *Antonin Artaud: Blows and Bombs*, 1993.
Bermel, Albert. *Artaud's Theatre of Cruelty*, 1977.
Costich, Julia F. *Antonin Artaud*, 1978.
Esslin, Martin. *Artaud*, 1976.
Goodall, Jane. *Artaud and the Gnostic Drama*, 1994.
Greene, Naomi. *Antonin Artaud: Poet Without Words*, 1970.
Hayman, Ronald. *Artaud and After*, 1977.
Knapp, Bettina. *Antonin Artaud: Man of Vision*, 1969.
Pluka, Gene A. *Antonin Artaud and the Modern Theater*, 1994.
Rowell, Margit. *Antonin Artaud: Works on Paper*, 1996.
Sellin, Eric. *The Dramatic Concepts of Antonin Artaud*, 1968.
Stout, John C. *Antonin Artaud's Alternate Genealogies: Self Portraits and Family Romances*, 1996.

PAUL ROSEFELDT

See also Absurd; Esslin; Surrealism

W. H. Auden

English-born American poet and essayist

Born: York, England; February 21, 1907
Died: Vienna, Austria; September 28, 1973

Biography

Wystan Hugh Auden was born on February 21, 1907, in York, England, the third son of a doctor and a mother who was a graduate of London University. In 1908 the family moved to Solihull, a suburb of Birmingham, where Auden's father had been appointed to the County Hospital (he later became school medical officer and Professor of Public Health at the University of Birmingham). From 1915 to 1920 Auden attended St. Edmund's, a preparatory school at Hindhead, Surrey, and from 1920 to 1925 Gresham's School, Holt, Norfolk. At the age of eighteen he went to Christ Church College, Oxford, where he enjoyed a reputation for intellectual brilliance and was the leader of a group of promising writers including Christopher Isherwood, C. Day Lewis, Louis MacNeice, and Stephen Spender. He graduated in 1928 with a third-class degree; in the same year his first volume of poetry was published, *Poems*, on a private press owned by Spender.

Between 1928 and 1929 he spent a year abroad in Berlin, and from 1930 to 1935 he taught at Larchfield Academy, near Glasgow, and the Downs School, Colwall, Herefordshire. In 1935 he worked for some months with the General Post Office Film Unit under John Grierson, and in the summer of 1936 he made a visit to Iceland with MacNeice, out of which came their joint volume *Letters from Iceland* (1937). From January to March 1937 he went to Spain in support of the Republicans fighting against General Franco in the Spanish Civil War. His main concern, however, in the 1930s was with the writing of poetry and, in collaboration with Isherwood, poetic dramas such as *The Dog Beneath the Skin* (1935) and *The Ascent of F6* (1937). With Isherwood he also visited China in 1938 as an observer of the Sino-Japanese War, their impressions being published in the joint volume *Journey to a War* (1939). The two writers left England for America in January 1939 and remained there throughout World War II – Auden settling in New York, and becoming an American citizen in 1946.

In the 1940s Auden's interest shifted from politics to religion; he was much influenced by Søren Kierkegaard, and adopted a broadly Christian position. While in America, Auden also undertook various teaching posts at universities, including Ann Arbor and Swarthmore. From about 1946 his thoughts turned to Europe again. He regularly visited Ischia in Italy, and later moved to Austria, where, in 1957, he bought a house at Kirchstetten, near Vienna. He divided his time between Austria, New York, and Oxford, having been elected Oxford Professor of Poetry (a five-year part-time post) in 1956. His partner in these years was Chester Kallman, with whom he wrote various opera libretti for the composers Stravinsky and Hans Verner Henze. He died in a Vienna hotel on September 28, 1973, after giving a poetry reading at the Austrian Society of Literature.

Influence

Auden was more influential as a poet than as a critic. His criticism was essentially an offshoot of his poetry, though enhanced in quantity, and perhaps in quality, by his incidental activities as a university teacher and a lecturer to various foundations. As he wrote in 1937, "The writing of poetry is always a more complex thing than any theory we may have about it. We write first and use the theory afterwards to justify the particular kind of poetry we like and the particular things about poetry in general which we think we like." Auden belongs to the great tradition of poet-critics from John Dryden through Samuel Taylor Coleridge and Matthew Arnold to T. S. Eliot who, because they use their practitioner's interest in their art to fuel their criticism, write with an energy and insight – and sometimes partisanship – which distinguishes their work from the more balanced, but often more pedestrian, work of the professional critic. His commitment to liberal left-wing views in the 1930s made him a powerful and influential advocate of poetry with a social conscience, and his cultivation of a highly versatile craftsmanship, especially in the postwar period, made him an equally effective advocate of formal, rhyming, rhetorically structured verse as against inspirational free verse of the D. H. Lawrence/William Carlos Williams/Charles Olson school. But he was also catholic in taste, and, despite his interest in the detailed techniques of verse, much given to generalizing and theorizing in a wide diversity of fields, providing outlines of theses which subsequent critics would gratefully pick up and develop in a more academic manner.

Analysis

In his essay "Reading," Auden's answer to the question "What is the function of the critic?" is to set out six tasks: (1) to introduce readers to literature they did not know before; (2) to revalue an author or work; (3) to engage in comparison, and (4) interpretation; (5) to throw light on the nature of artistic creation; and (6) to consider its relation to other intellectual pursuits. The first three demand scholarship and the second three insight, and all, significantly, he calls "services." For Auden criticism is essentially the handmaid of literature; it is a facilitator and mediator rather than an arbitrator or dictator. In that sense he is an old-fashioned critic. Although he responds to the modernist influence of T. S. Eliot by insisting that the object of attention should be the work of art rather than the author (or, at most, the author in his or her professional, authorial activity, not in his or her private life), he is neither a Leavisite moralist nor a Barthesian demoter of the author. He has a share in the great twentieth-century critical shift from "appreciation" to analysis of the "text," and he can sound almost contemporary when he asserts that the purpose of poetry is "by telling the truth, to disenchant and disintoxicate"; but it is typical of him that when referring to practical criticism as exemplified in the work of I. A. Richards and William Empson he should concede that it is "a fascinating game in itself," yet wonder "whether its educational use is other than to convince readers that a poem must be read carefully and often to get its full value." Auden's respect is for the work of art itself, to which the critic is firmly subordinated as a servant.

The first of Auden's functions is represented in his own work by, for example, his essay on Marianne Moore and the chapter on the Icelandic sagas in his T. S. Eliot Memorial Lectures (published as *Secondary Worlds*, 1968). He gains the reader's attention for Moore by approaching her head-on via her use of syllabic meter. By rehearsing his own process of initiation into the peculiarities of the verse, and a tone of voice that he intriguingly labels "pure 'Alice,'" he induces a similar experience in the reader, before going on to analyze the distinctive qualities of her animal poems. With the Icelandic sagas the approach is more oblique, partly because they are being treated in a context of "secondary worlds" (the semi-independent imaginative worlds created by writers), and partly because the argument he wishes to pursue about their differentiation from the better-known worlds of heroic literature entails preliminary summary of the latter. The effect is to enable the reader to pass more easily from the known to the unknown, and to feel a greater, and more exciting, sense of newness when the saga world is reached.

The second function is perhaps best illustrated by his brilliant essay on Lord Byron's *Don Juan*. Critical opinion had already shifted from emphasis on the Byron of *Childe Harold* to the Byron of the later verse, and to that extent Auden is not innovatively revaluing. His own discovery of Byron came during his Iceland visit and issues most notably in the poem *Letter to Lord Byron*. The essay on *Don Juan*, however, makes its mark not only by characterizing in prose the license-within-order which Auden imitates so effectively in his own poetry of the *Letter*, but by singling out "the authentic poet in Byron" as "Byron the Friend," and claiming him as a poet of comedy rather than satire.

Comparison and interpretation are also incidental to the examples already cited of introduction and revaluation. Despite his fondness for ingenious categorization and generalization (virtues which sometimes become a vice in him), Auden rarely keeps his categories watertight. But it is in pieces like "Balaam and His Ass" and "Music and Shakespeare" that the third and fourth functions are seen to come into their own. "Balaam and His Ass" is an important study which has as its theme the relation between Master and Servant in European literature. Although it seems at times to be verging on a semi-philosophical, semi-theological discourse on the meaning of love, Auden's finger is still kept firmly on the artistic creations by which the theme is explored. Its core is a series of interpretations and comparisons of "myth"-figures (not figures from myth or mythology, but literary creations who have acquired the evocative status of myth), including such diverse examples as Don Quixote and Sancho Panza, Don Giovanni and Leporello, Phineas Fogg and Passepartout, and Bertie Wooster and Jeeves. The list – which is not exhaustive – is symptomatic of the catholicity of Auden's taste and the strength of his imaginative-connective powers.

Finally, the nature of artistic creation and its relationship to other pursuits is seen again in *Secondary Worlds* and in "The Poet and the City." The latter is essentially a lament for the modern condition, in which, according to Auden, the artist is divorced from society. Once again, with his fondness for categorization, Auden specifies four "aspects of our present Weltanschauung" which make for the isolation of the artist: (1) loss of belief "in the eternity of the physical universe"; (2) loss of belief "in the significance and reality of sensory phenomena"; (3) loss of the sense that there is "a norm of human nature which will always require the same kind of man-fabricated world"; and (4) the virtual "disappearance of the Public Realm as the sphere of revelatory personal deeds." His argument is that belief as such is so radically undermined that people no longer feel themselves to be living in that personally meaningful universe which is vital to the artist. The artist is almost archaic, with the result that "the mere making of a work of art is itself a political act." In a world of managers and management, artists are a reminder that "the managed are people with faces, not anonymous members." Nevertheless, his conclusion is not a political one. Rather it is the seemingly bizarre assertion of "the right to play, the right to frivolity," in other words, the right to engage in a form of nonproductive, yet essentially creative activity that allows human beings to be their own humane end, not the mere means to others' material ends.

Principal criticism

Education Today and Tomorrow, 1939 (with T. C. Worsley)
The Enchafed Flood, 1951
The Dyer's Hand and Other Essays, 1963
Secondary Worlds, 1968
Forewords and Afterwords, 1973
W. H. Auden: Prose 1926–1938, 1996 (Edward Mendelson, editor)

Other major works and literary forms

Although this is not the place to discuss W. H. Auden's major work, as a poet, it is appropriate to mention those poems in which he also functions as an unprofessional, free-ranging critic of literature and art. Among these are "Who's Who," "Musée des Beaux Arts," "The Novelist," "The Composer," "Rimbaud," "A. E. Housman," "Edward Lear," "In Memory of W. B. Yeats," "In Memory of Ernst Toller," "Voltaire at Ferney," "Herman Melville," "At the Grave of Henry James," "Ode to the Medieval Poets," and, in a class of its own, "The Sea and the Mirror." "Who's Who" sardonically and epigrammatically mocks the kind of criticism that is defected away from the work of art itself to a sentimental version of the artist's private life ("A shilling life will give you all the facts"); "A. E. Housman," with something of the same young man's flippant wit, juxtaposes the dry "Latin Scholar of his generation" with the very different poet of *A Shropshire Lad*. More mature judgments are made in the poems on Yeats and James. "In Memory of W. B. Yeats" is a great poem in its own right, in which, as in John Milton's *Lycidas*, the poet considers his own vocation as a writer and the fate of the work of art as "words of a dead man" which posthumously will be "modified in the guts of the living." "At the Grave of Henry James" is a valedictory tribute to a "Master of nuance and scruple," but also an elegantly judged comment on the dangers besetting the writer who defies populism, and, still more so, the need for a proper artistic balance between "the disciplinary image" and "eddying Muddle," between "Proportion" with its "alpine chill" and the poet's own "loose impromptu song."

"The Sea and the Mirror," subtitled "A Commentary on Shakespeare's *The Tempest*," is a long poem, and among the most difficult that Auden wrote. Although it is called a commentary on Shakespeare's play, and does have much to add to the body of Auden's Shakespearean criticism (which includes the prose essays "The Globe," "The Prince's Dog," and "Brothers and Others"), it is more a meditation by Auden on the theme of art versus life than strictly an interpretation of *The Tempest* – relevant as that theme is to Shakespeare's play. Each of the main characters in *The Tempest* becomes a persona speaking through an essentially Audenesque poem (or, in the case of Caliban, a prose discourse), and these personae are dialectical aspects of Auden's own responses to a work of art which has traditionally been taken as a supreme artist's farewell to, and winding-up of, his artistic career. The imperfection of art's power – as manifested, for example, in Prospero's apparent failure to trigger repentance in Antonio, and also in the nature of Caliban, on which nurture will not stick – generates an overall sense of disillusionment and near cynicism, notwithstanding the lyrical idealism of Ferdinand and Miranda. The possibility of redemption is suggested by oblique reference to the Supreme Artist who is God. This possibility, however, lies outside the human world of art, to which the work of both Shakespeare and Auden belongs, and raises the question of art's limitations vis-à-vis religion. Auden agrees with T. S. Eliot in rejecting art as a substitute for religion; art is placed firmly in the fallen world. Surprisingly, much of this is discussed by Caliban in a speech which, almost perversely it would seem, is cast in the highly mannerist convoluted style of the late works of Henry James. In this respect Auden goes deliberately against his Shakespearean model. Shakespeare's special language for Caliban is tactile, sensuous, and mythopoeic; Auden's radically different strategy sets up an inherent contradiction between the animality of Caliban and Jamesian sophistication which underscores the unregenerate nature of human art even at its most elaborate.

MISCELLANEOUS
Collected Poems, 1976 (Edward Mendelson, editor)

Further reading

Brooks, Cleanth. "Auden as a Literary Critic," in *A Shaping Joy*, 1971. Reprinted in *Critical Essays on W. H. Auden*, 1991 (George W. Bahlke, editor).
Carpenter, Humphrey. *W. H. Auden: A Biography*, 1981.
Davenport-Hines, Richard. *Auden*, 1995.
Fuller, John. *A Reader's Guide to W. H. Auden*, 1970.

R. P. DRAPER

See also British Literary Theory: Twentieth Century; Eliot

Erich Auerbach

German-born American scholar

Born: Berlin, Germany; November 9, 1892
Died: Wallingford, Connecticut; October 13, 1957

Biography

Erich Auerbach was born into a Jewish family in Berlin in 1892. In 1910 he graduated from the French Gymnasium in Berlin and began to study law at the University of Berlin. His law studies brought him to Freiburg, Munich, and finally to Heidelberg, where he received his doctorate of law in 1913. In the spring of 1914 he began to study philology until his studies were interrupted by World War I. Wounded on the front in 1918, Auerbach returned to study Romance philology in Berlin. In 1921 he completed a dissertation directed by Erhard Lommatzsch at the

University of Greifswald on the early Renaissance novella in France and Italy. From 1923 until 1929 he held a position at the Prussian State Library. In 1929 he was awarded the chair of Romance philology at Marburg University but was forced to retire from his post in 1935 by the laws of the Third Reich.

Auerbach sought refuge in Istanbul, where he taught at the Turkish State University and wrote his magnum opus, *Mimesis* (1946). He wrote this immense volume on the literature of the West without the benefit of a large university library, and he claimed that the book would never have been completed had he had access to a fuller library. In 1947 Auerbach came to the United States and, after teaching briefly at Pennsylvania State University, joined the faculty of Yale University in 1950, where he taught in the French department until his death in 1957.

Influence

Auerbach was one of those products of the Weimar Republic – along with Erwin Panofsky and the members of the so-called Frankfurt School – who attained prominence only in American exile. In Germany, Auerbach was a respected young Romance philologist, but in the United States he became one of the key figures in the relatively new field of comparative literature. Although his method integrated a close reading of texts with historical and cultural analysis (akin to German *Geistesgeschichte*), he was most appreciated by the New Critics, with their purely textual methodology. His most important work, *Mimesis*, had already attained the status of a classic in the 1950s. It has remained a classic, finding a wide readership in the humanities. In the 1970s and 1980s his name was invoked again, this time by writers of the "new literary history," who were seeking a path away from the textuality of deconstruction.

Analysis

Auerbach's criticism represents a powerful blend of close textual reading and contextual analysis. Academic literary criticism in Germany at the turn of the century was dominated, as were the other disciplines of the humanities, by what was called *Geistesgeschichte*, the examination of the "spirit" of particular cultures in particular epochs. Literature was seen as an expression of the general cultural orientation of the Germans in the eighteenth century or the Italians in the fifteenth century. German scholars working in the Romance languages, however, were influenced by the French practice of explication, a close reading of individual textual passages. Thus, Auerbach, who was a German scholar of Romance literature, mixed the native German tradition of *Geistesgeschichte* with French explication.

Mimesis represents this blend with particular mastery. Auerbach opened each chapter with a long passage, often two pages long, drawn from the texts that would provide the focus for the chapter. Although his analysis varied from chapter to chapter, Auerbach would follow these passages with a close examination of the text. In a number of cases, he provided an analysis of the rhetorical structure of the passage. It was not unusual for him to explain, as he does in his discussion of the medieval *Chanson de Roland*, that, except for one temporal hypotaxis, "everything else is in the form of principal clauses, juxtaposed and opposed like blocks, with a paratactic independence still further emphasized by mention of the speaking subject each time." Auerbach, however, made skillful transitions from his close textual analyses to historical discussions that showed his sensitivity to the change of cultural values from one epoch to the next.

Auerbach's orientation in *Mimesis* is often viewed as sociological. The book's emphasis on realism in literature has sometimes been understood as an interest in the reflection of society. Although Auerbach showed in places an interest in the literary reflection of social structure and social mores, it is important to understand that his definition of literary realism was extremely broad, allowing him to discuss authors who are rarely thought of as realists. Indeed, there is no single definition of *Wirklichkeit* (reality) in Auerbach's criticism. Sometimes by "reality" Auerbach means social reality, other times he means the reality of the senses, and still other times he means psychological reality, as he does in his discussion of the internal monologues of twentieth-century modernists. The fact that there are differences in the forms of realism is established in the famous first chapter of *Mimesis*, "Odysseus' Scar." There Auerbach contrasts the interest of Homer's *Odyssey* (c. 800 B.C.) in the sensuous "foreground" – all the visual details of the environment – to the lack of such a foreground in the biblical story of the sacrifice of Isaac. In the episode from Genesis, Auerbach argues, the reader is not even told in which direction Abraham turns when he hears the voice of God; rather than a detailed foreground, the focus is entirely on the "background." By distinguishing between types of realism in his first chapter, and among forms of realism in his general discussion, Auerbach shows a strong commitment to historicism; different cultures, Auerbach believed, were concerned with different conceptions of reality and adopted different conceptions of reality. Auerbach's understanding of culture can be traced to the imprint of German *Geistesgeschichte*, with its belief in the individual "spirit" of each culture. Yet Auerbach took that concept a step further. As a result of his highly developed historical sensitivity, he changed his critical method in *Mimesis* from chapter to chapter. Moving from text to text, he believed that he must also alter his critical focus.

Auerbach's historicism did not lead to relativism, for Auerbach's criticism was marked by important normative values, and the hero of his scholarship from the 1920s until his death was Dante. Dante was a constant preoccupation, and it was in his work with Dante that Auerbach developed one of his principal methodological concepts: figuration.

In his most explicit discussion of figuration, "Figura," Auerbach distinguished figuration from allegory. He argued that allegorical symbols are merely conventional signposts for transcendental ideas or essences. They have no life or reality of their own. By comparison, a figure has a full existence separate from its signification. Thus, the figural signifier is more than a signpost; it has a historical concreteness which the allegorical signifier does not. "The two poles of the figure," Auerbach wrote in 1938, "are separate in time, but both, being real events or figures, are within time, within the stream of historical life." The figures in Dante's *La divina commedia* (c. 1320; *The Divine Comedy*), then, are not merely lifeless allegorical symbols. Rather, Dante breathes life into them. For that reason, Auerbach gave his book on Dante the title *Dante: Poet of the Secular World*, which would be better translated as "Dante: Poet of the Earthly Realm."

The concrete, historically situated world is central to the chapter on Dante in *Mimesis*, "Farinata and Cavalcante." The two Florentines portrayed by Dante in canto 10 of the *Inferno*, Farinata degli Uberti and Cavalvante de' Cavalcanti, were full of earthly vitality in their infernal home. They were, in fact, so full of life and the Florentine culture they left behind that Auerbach described their appearance as an "irruption of a different realm" in Hell. Yet, despite their earthliness and the historical concreteness of other characters in Dante's *The Divine Comedy*, Auerbach wanted his reader to understand that they are also representative of a transcendental order, that of God's justice. Auerbach took both poles of the figuration seriously. If many readers of Auerbach identify his interest in the concrete historical world and its reflection in literature, Auerbach was also deeply concerned with transcendental realms, whether or not they were religiously framed. The "reality" of the sacrificing of Isaac was not so much a concrete historical reality as a transcendental reality of religious truth.

The figural union of two separate realms represented by Dante's verse took on special significance for Auerbach. Although he made no explicit statement about the importance of Dante or the concept of figuration for the formulation of his massive study of realism in Western literature, Auerbach's argument in *Mimesis* is defined by his attitude toward figuration. If *Mimesis* is a book with centrifugal forces pulling on it in different directions, it still articulates a central argument: that Western literature can be viewed in terms of an alternating dominance by and liberation from the classical doctrine of the levels of style. The doctrine of the levels of style stipulated that literature was to be written on higher and lower planes: an elevated style should reflect an elevated subject, while a lower style should reflect more base subject matter. Thus, there should be no intrusion of the mundane aspects of ordinary life in literary works written on an elevated plane.

Auerbach asserted, however, that there were certain periods in the history of Western literature in which the doctrine of the levels of style was in decline. Many of his readers were aware that the realism of nineteenth-century France, freely mixing different styles and subject matter, represented a decline in the fortunes of the high classicism of seventeenth-century French literature. Yet Auerbach insisted that a similar break in the ascendancy of the doctrine of the levels of style took place in medieval literature, and, as it turns out, Dante was one of the heroes of that development. Although Auerbach demonstrated an appreciation for cultural variation, he showed a personal distaste for the sterility of the classical model, and he was particularly fond of those literary works which blended freely from the higher and lower realms.

In his criticism, Auerbach was not interested in national literary development. Rather, he was occupied with the literature of the West, and there were important historical reasons for his version of literary history. When Auerbach wrote *Mimesis*, he was in exile from his native Germany. Consequently, he defined literary history in terms of a general European development rather than in terms of specific national histories. His *Mimesis* may, in fact, be seen as an effort to identify a culture in which he saw himself as an insider, and that culture was, for him, no longer German. Auerbach's identification with Western culture and his anxiety about its health during World War II made their appearance powerfully in the last sentences of *Mimesis*:

> Nothing now remains but to find him – to find the reader, that is. I hope that my study will reach its readers – both my friends of former years, if they are still alive, as well as all the others for whom it was intended. And may it contribute to bringing together again those whose love for our Western history has serenely persevered.

In these passionate lines, Auerbach expressed his emotional commitment to the culture of the West and its literary tradition. The aspect of this literary tradition which seemed most important to him when writing *Mimesis* was its "Europeanness." That impression was reinforced by an essay Auerbach wrote in the 1950s, "Philologie der Weltliteratur" (1952). There Auerbach turned to Johann Wolfgang von Goethe's notion of "world literature," with its belief in the organic interaction of Europe's several national literatures, and he expressed a deep commitment to the cosmopolitan pluralism represented by Goethe's concept. In addition to his commitment to the "Europeanness" of European literature, Auerbach was also committed to its literariness, to the fact that it was produced for and by a cultivated elite. Auerbach's concern with the cultivated, highly literate public of the European past assumed prominence in his *Literary Language and Its Public in Late Latin Antiquity and in the Middle Ages*. The threat to Western culture in the 1950s was no longer National Socialism; instead, it was the very loss of a literary public. If it seems ironic that the same Auerbach who showed so much interest in the mixture of high and low styles wrote in praise of a cultivated elite, it should be remembered that even when he referred to the use of lower literary styles, he was referring to its use in "serious" literature. His concept of European culture was always highly literate.

As a whole, Auerbach's critical corpus represents tremendous erudition and at the same time an emotional commitment to erudition. His criticism showed a clear preference for literature which blended higher and lower styles, and that was a result of Auerbach's commitment both to an ideational realm and to the concrete, historical world. His work took as its focus the historical development of Western literature, and that focus derived from his commitment to historical understanding, his devotion to Western culture, and finally his belief in the power of literature.

Principal criticism

Zur Technik der Frührenaissancenovelle in Italien und Frankreich, 1921

Dante als Dichter der irdischen Welt, 1929 (*Dante: Poet of the Secular World*, 1961)

"Figura," 1938 (in *Archivum romanicum*)

Neue Dantestudien, 1944

Mimesis: Dargestellte Wirklichkeit in der abendländischen Literatur, 1946 (*Mimesis: The Representation of Reality in Western Literature*, 1953)

Introduction aux études de philologie romane, 1949 (*Introduction to Romance Languages and Literature*, 1961)

Vier Untersuchungen zur Geschichte der französischen Bildung, 1951

Literatursprache und Publikum in der lateinischen Spätantik und im Mittelalter, 1958 (*Literary Language and Its Public in Late Latin Antiquity and in the Middle Ages*, 1965)

Scenes from the Drama of European Literature, 1959

Other major work and literary forms

Erich Auerbach was known primarily for his literary criticism, although he did occasional translations.

TRANSLATION

Die neue Wissenschaft über die gemeinschaftliche Natur der Völker, 1925 (of Giovanni Battista Vico's *Scienza nuova*)

Further reading

Bahti, Timothy. "Auerbach's *Mimesis*: Figural Structure and Historical Narrative," in *After Strange Texts*, 1985. Edited by G. Jay and D. Miller.

Green, Geoffrey. *Literary Criticism and the Structures of History: Erich Auerbach and Leo Spitzer*, 1982.

Gronau, Klaus. *Literarische Form und gesellschaftliche Entwicklung: Erich Auerbachs Beitrag zur Theorie und Methodologie der Literaturgeschichte*, 1979.

Holdheim, Wolfgang. "Auerbach's *Mimesis* as Historical Understanding," in *Clio*. X (Winter, 1981), pp. 143–154.

Holquist, Michael. "The Last European: Erich Auerbach as Precursor in the History of Cultural Criticism," in *Modern Language Quarterly: A Journal of Literary History*. 54, no. 3 (September, 1993), pp. 371–391.

Landauer, Carl. "*Mimesis* and Erich Auerbach's Self-Mythologizing," in *German Studies Review*. XI, no. 1 (February, 1988), pp. 83–96.

Lerer, Seth, ed. and introd. *Literary History and the Challenge of Philology: The Legacy of Erich Auerbach*, 1996.

Wellek, René. "Auerbach's Special Realism," in *The Kenyon Review*. XVI (1954), pp. 299–307.

CARL LANDAUER

See also Mimesis; Realism

Saint Augustine

(Aurelius Augustinus)

Christian scholar, philosopher, and writer

Born: Tagaste, Numidia; November 13, 354
Died: Hippo Regius, Numidia; August 28, 430

Biography

Augustine was born Aurelius Augustinus on November 13, 354, at Tagaste in the Roman proconsular province of Numidia (now Algeria). His mother, Monica, a staunch Christian who became a saint of the Catholic church, was as eager for her son's education and secular advancement as she was that he embrace Christianity; she was without doubt the single most important influence in Augustine's life. Patricius, Augustine's father, remains an elusive figure; Augustine describes him in the *Confessions* as *tenuis municeps* (a townsman of slender means).

A good man and devoted father, Patricius was not a Christian. Even so, he was as anxious as Monica for Augustine's advancement and worked hard to secure the best education he could for his son. Thus it was that Augustine received a provincial version of a classical Roman education at nearby Madauros (the modern Mdaourouch). For at least his last year there Augustine seems to have received some financial support from Romanianus, a local grandee. The training Augustine received was in rhetoric, a "gentleman's education" suitable only as preliminary for the teaching profession, since law courts no longer followed the old forms of public speaking.

By 371 Augustine had gone to Carthage to pursue his studies and to teach. He acquired there the worldly sensuality he would condemn in his later life. The *Confessions* records the death of Patricius (probably about 372) while Augustine was still at Carthage. Augustine's illegitimate son, Adeodatus, was born about this time (c. 373). Augustine returned to Tagaste in 375 and taught there for a year, but a year later was back in Carthage, where he remained until 383, when he sailed for Rome. In 384 he was teaching rhetoric in Milan and was joined by Monica in the spring of the following year. He immersed himself in philosophy during this period, reading the Neo-Platonists, especially

Plotinus. Augustine came under the influence of Ambrose and was baptized a Christian at Milan, to his mother's delight, in March, 387.

It may have been the death of Monica in 387, followed in 390 by the deaths of his son and of his friend Nebridius, which influenced Augustine to found a monastery at Hippo, the Bishopric of Numidia. He was ordained a priest there in 391 and was appointed its bishop in 395. Augustine spent these mature years producing nearly one hundred important works which helped form the teachings of his church. He died at Hippo on August 28, 430.

Influence

Historical accident coupled with Augustine's natural brilliance have made him a pivotal figure of textual criticism. He was among the last generation to be educated according to the classical Roman methods, which emphasized literature and rhetoric. Though Augustine himself taught briefly in Rome, he clearly sensed the changing times, and this realization coincided almost exactly with his conversion to Christianity. Literature could no longer exist as pure fiction; Horace's injunction that literature should be *dulcum* (sweet) and *utile* (useful) was no longer satisfactory in a world awaiting Christ's imminent return.

It was for this reason that Augustine came to believe that all written language should serve God: *logoi* (words) must mirror the *Logos* (the Word). This idea, that language needed a referent outside and beyond itself, is the origin of what in the Middle Ages would be called the allegorical method.

Analysis

Augustine's unique ideas on the purposes literature should serve sprang from a synthesis of the historical period in which he lived and the education he received. Tagaste, his place of birth, touted itself as "the most resplendent" in its official communiqués; despite this self-applied epithet, the town was in fact part of the fertile North African backwater of the old Roman Empire, part of what is now the depleted high country of southern Algeria. Wealth as well as the reins of municipal government remained in the hands of estate owners, whose lands surrounded a hub of small Numidian towns. The area was inhabited by people in every sense pioneers: tough, often rude, but with a deep respect for imperial Roman forms, including Roman educational methods. These individuals had, indeed, established Madauros, the town in which Augustine would receive his earliest training, as the region's educational center. Schooling there was conservative in the extreme – in other words, useless for an agricultural area; such schools produced rhetoricians, not farmers.

H. I. Marrou in his *Histoire de l'éducation dans l'antiquité* (1948; *A History of Education in Antiquity*, 1956) and Augustine himself in his *Confessions* provide vivid accounts of the rote methods such schools employed. The subject matter was literature, in Latin rather than Greek; it was memorized, dissected by syntax and parsing, and ultimately debated. No mathematics or science was available, except by special arrangement. For a bright but poor boy such as Augustine, there was essentially only one career option: that of *rhetor*, a teacher of rhetoric. (Not even law courts used the epideictic or formal style by the early fourth century.)

Augustine was a brilliant student and followed this curriculum with ease. His teachers quickly recognized his talents, and Augustine was much taken by his primary school text, Virgil's *Aeneid*, his lively imagination enabling him to identify with Aeneas. Aeneas' worldliness and travels must have had great appeal to a boy so obviously a leader himself. That the *Aeneid*'s first four books are set at Carthage, only two hundred miles northeast of Tagaste, added to the poem's immediacy. The *Aeneid* continued to feed Augustine's imagination in his early teaching career as well. His identification with Aeneas remained strong when he wept at Carthage's theater spectacles and stood in awe of its art, every bit as much as Aeneas when he looked at the walls of Dido's Carthage.

It was probably during Augustine's brief teaching career in Milan (384–385) that he recognized that his approach to literature was inadequate. Literal explication of a text, which he taught his students to do, yielded its mechanical underpinnings, but any search for a higher meaning that was also true was essentially fruitless. Dido's tears at Aeneas' departure for Italy, though they might cause a sensitive reader to cry, are fictive, and so the reader's response is compounded falsehood. This developing theory ran counter to the bibliomantic cult which had sprung up around Virgil's works as early as the first century of the Christian era. It affected Augustine's teaching as well. He came to believe that the most he could accomplish by continuing to teach in the traditional way was to "seduce" his students with beautiful but false words.

Hearing Ambrose, Bishop of Milan, preach during these years further developed Augustine's ideas. Ambrose was neither a great stylist nor an epideictic speaker, yet what he said held meaning beyond the words themselves. With his background in rhetoric, it is logical that Augustine attempted to discover similar hidden meanings in secular literature. It was with this goal in mind that he journeyed to Cassiciacum, probably the modern town Cassiago near Lake Como in the foothills of the Italian Alps, in September, 386. For a brief time at least, Augustine might have envisioned establishing a Neo-Platonist philosophical community there. He brought several bright young friends and students with him, read the works of Plotinus, concentrating on Plotinian methods of exegesis, discussed the nature of the soul, and wrote several critical works, *Contra academicos* (386; *Against the Academics*), *De beata vita* (386; *The Happy Life*), and *Soliloquia* (386; *Soliloquies*), during this period.

It is significant that the two most familiar episodes described in Augustine's *Confessions* – his conversion to Christianity and the death of Monica (both at Ostia, the port of Rome) – took place between March and September of 387. Recalling both well into his maturity, he presents them in terms which allow them to stand as examples of his allegorical method. The voices Augustine heard in the garden crying *Tolle, lege!* ("Take up, read!") may have been those of children at some game, but for him the words held a higher meaning: to check his tears, open the New Testament, and read the injunction in Matthew 19:12 against those who live worldly and sensual lives. When Augustine read the *Aeneid* as a schoolboy, when moved by the theater spectacles at Carthage, he could merely cry. Because he recognized the personal hidden meaning of the Scripture he read at Ostia, he could check his emotions and act.

This notion of the higher meanings of words finds more complete development in the conversation Augustine has with his mother shortly before her death. They talk first of small things, pleasant in themselves but unimportant. Then the words stop, and for one brief moment it seems to each that they have touched upon the Divine itself, the One who is the Word. By 401, then, Augustine's ideas on the use of language had come to full flowering. He was ready to denounce the *Aeneid* as *dulcissimum spectaculum vanitatis* (the sweetest spectacle of vanity), his choice of words implying abandonment of the literary text which had formed him as well as the *spectacula* of Carthage which had seduced him. Never one for halfway measures, he came to believe that all *logoi* (words) needed to find their ultimate referent in the *Logos* (God).

Augustine's exegesis of the first two chapters of Genesis demonstrates his method in a more formal way. At its most basic level, the text explains creation; even as it does this, it shows through its symbolic language that the human race is vulnerable to corruption and sin. Still, it transcends this level to make a personal statement concerning every individual's vulnerability even as it holds out the possibility of individual justification in the Creator. This explication, appearing at the conclusion of the *Confessions*, also stands as a symbol of Augustine's verbal maturity, of his own rebirth.

If all *logoi* need serve the *Logos*, there would have to be a new literature to replace the old. False *logoi* were an ever-present danger, for heterodoxy can appear easily in an infant church. Moreover, it was imperative to produce this new literature quickly, for the return of Christ could be imminent. Thus it was that Augustine's ideas about the form literature should take became an inseparable part of everything he wrote. Since, for example, he and most who would read him were well-acquainted with the *Aeneid*, the *Confessions*, although prose, follows the archetypal journey motif, with Augustine as the true embodiment of the false Aeneas.

Like Aeneas, Augustine was goaded to Italy from Carthage, by God's prodding rather than pure fate, and like Aeneas Augustine had to leave people and a way of life he loved. Augustine, also like Aeneas, sees the establishment of a city as his personal destiny. The City of God would replace that of Rome, marking the irreversible Western course of empire. The journey Augustine made was thus what could be called an odyssey of the soul, circular like that of Odysseus, the Greek prototype of Aeneas, because it concluded in North Africa where it had begun. It was like the *Aeneid*, too, because of its epic scope, circumstances, and its goal, but unlike that of Aeneas it was true, a journey which every human being takes and which for every committed Christian ends successfully. Augustine's theories on literature had a profound influence on developing the more systematized allegorical methods of the Middle Ages. One sees their full implications in the allegorical levels of Dante's *La divina commedia* (c. 1320; *The Divine Comedy*), a secular poem with a personal and collective spiritual meaning.

Principal criticism

Contra academicos, 386 (*Against the Academics*)
De ordine, 386 (*On Order*)
De musica, 389 (*On Music*)
De magistro, 389 (*On the Teacher*)
De sermone Domini in monte, 394 (*Commentary on the Lord's Sermon on the Mount*)
Confessiones, 397–400 (*Confessions*)
Annotationes in Job, 400
De Genesi ad litteram, 401–415

Other major works and literary forms

Saint Augustine is familiar to many readers through his *Confessions*, a carefully limited autobiography which traces his movement toward spiritual maturity. The *Confessions* considers episodes from Augustine's youth, but unlike modern autobiography limits such narratives so that they logically climax in his acceptance of Christianity at Ostia in Italy. Moreover, its allegorical exegesis of Genesis, the first book of the Old Testament, provides the most accessible example of Augustine's critical methods, this in a work not ordinarily classified as literary criticism.

In his mature years, particularly after his return to North Africa and after his appointment as Bishop of Hippo, Augustine was concerned with combating heterodoxy in the early Christian church. As a consequence, he abandoned the classically written criticism and philosophy of his youth to write what in modern times would be called philosophy of religion. His *De doctrina Christiana* (books 1–3, 396–397, book 4, 426; *On Christian Instruction*) and *De Trinitate* (c. 419; *On the Trinity*) are two of the best-known examples of this form. Throughout his life, but especially in these later years, Augustine wrote letters, most intended for publication, to far-flung correspondents. The consuming passion of these years was, however, his massive

De civitate Dei (413–427; *The City of God*), a synthesis of his learning as well as his prophecy of a new Christian world order which would surpass that of Rome and overturn that of the Vandals, who by the time of Augustine's death had extended their influence into the very heart of what was Roman Numidia.

NONFICTION
De beata vita, 386 (*The Happy Life*)
Soliloquia, 386 (*Soliloquies*)
De immortalitate animae, 387 (*On the Immortality of the Soul*)
De vera religione, 391 (*Of True Religion*)
De doctrina Christiana, books 1–3, 396–397; book 4, 426 (*On Christian Instruction*)
De civitate Dei, 413–427 (*The City of God*)
De Trinitate, c. 419 (*On the Trinity*)

Further reading

Bourke, Vernon J. *Wisdom from St. Augustine*, 1984.
Brown, Peter. *St. Augustine of Hippo*, 1967.
Chadwick, Henry. *Augustine*, 1986.
Evans, Gillian. *Augustine on Evil*, 1982.
Forman, Robert J. *Augustine and the Making of a Christian Literature: Classical Tradition and Christian Aesthetics*, 1995.
Hawkins, Ann Hunsaker. *Archetypes and Conversion: The Autobiographies of Augustine, Bunyan, and Merton*, 1985.
Kirwan, Christopher. *Augustine*, 1989.
McWilliam, Joanne, Timothy Barnes, et al., eds. *Augustine: From Rhetor to Theologian*, 1992.
Morrison, Karl Frederick. *Conversion and Test: The Cases of Augustine of Hippo, Herman-Judah, and Constantine Tsatsos*, 1992.
Schnaubelt, Joseph C., and Frederick Van Fleteren. *Collectanea Augustiniana*, 1990.

ROBERT J. FORMAN

See also Classical Greek and Roman Literary Theory; Medieval Literary Theory; Plotinus

The Author

The tradition

The concept of the author has traditionally occupied a stable and fixed position in literary criticism, the author being seen as the sole originator of a written work. The author is that figure who brings the necessary vision, creativity, and skill to the production of the work. Moreover, through experience and intellect, knowledge of the world, living in a certain time and space (that is, having a biography), and the ability to translate all these factors into a literary/linguistic medium, the author is the creator from whose unique interiority the work emerges. As the originator and controller of the idea, the author inscribes the text with an inviolable authority and authenticity: authority because of a certain "ownership" of the idea, and authenticity because of the relationship between the individual author and meaning. Roland Barthes clarifies this when he states: "The *explanation* of a work is always sought in the man or woman who produced it as if it were always in the end through the more or less transparent allegory of the fiction, the voice of a single person, the *author* 'confiding' in us." (Barthes, along with Michel Foucault, will launch an aggressive attack on this notion. See below.)

In a certain sense, these propositions suggest a type of theology or a system of belief which sanctifies the author's position as the singular and indisputable maker of the work. Without such an identifiable author the work itself may be called into question (hence the ongoing quests of many scholars to "authenticate" a text, to ascribe it to a particular author). For example, William Shakespeare's name and biography function to validate his writing or to demarcate it as *his* and nobody else's. As Michel Foucault claims, to discover that Shakespeare did not in fact write the sonnets would radically alter the reception and status of the poems. In other words, the author is inseparable from the text and is perpetually alive *within* it, yet paradoxically *outside* it.

These assertions can be expressed as a *humanist* or *structuralist* proposition which pivots on the classical Cartesian conception of the unitary subject, the individual man or woman possessed of an autonomous, self-knowing, and coherent consciousness largely uncoerced by political, historical, or cultural circumstances. With this in mind, "the subject/author is the originating consciousness" with "authority for meaning and truth"; meaning and truth are then delegated to the text. In this sense, truth resides within or "behind" the text (quoting from Sarup Madan's *An Introductory Guide to Post-Structuralism and Postmodernism*). In humanist and structuralist terms, authorial consciousness is thus the fundamental psychic condition in the creation of a work.

The challenge

While the traditional (humanist/structuralist) understanding of the author still has currency in the fields of language and literature, its legitimacy is under constant challenge. The most notable challenge came in 1968 from Roland Barthes' *poststructuralist* critique, "The Death of the Author." In this essay, Barthes announces the demise or "death" of the author. Paralleling this authorial descent is the ascent of writing; the author cedes control and authority over the work, which is now assumed by *language* itself. With the death of the author comes the life of language. Barthes maintains that at the very moment of writing – the *present* of writing – the language takes primacy and the author metaphorically evaporates. Moreover, once language leaves the realm of the intellect to become writing, it is now *exterior* to the author. In this sense, he routs the notions of the author's singular interiority to which the traditional and structuralist propositions adhered. According to Barthes, the author is only the mediator or the conduit between idea and language, its arterial vehicle, its *scriptor*: "[T]here is no other time than that of the enunciation and every text is eternally written here and now." As a result, the privileged position that the author held in the past has been assumed by language and the author's transcendental or theological positioning is now desanctified. A corollary to the ascendancy of language and the death of the author is the "birth of the reader." Once the idea is transmitted into language, it is now in the domain of the reader, or as Barthes says: "[A] text's unity is not in its origin but in its destination . . . the birth of the reader must be at the cost of the death of the author."

Michel Foucault's 1969 essay "What is an Author?" echoes Barthes in several ways, particularly by questioning the sovereignty of the author. Foucault argues that the author is a *construction of discourse*, where discourse is a body of knowledge inscribed in a specific vocabulary and governed by institutional "rules" and interests, as in psychoanalysis or literature for example. While Foucault does not agree that the author or writing subject is dead – "the subject should not be entirely abandoned" – he nonetheless relegates the author to a function of discourse, what he calls "*the author-function*," a mediating role. Foucault argues that the author is not the originator of a text, but because that text does not exist in isolation but is part of a wider discourse, so too is the author a part of that discourse. In this sense, the author cannot claim exemption from or be transcendental to the discourse but functions *within* it. As a genealogist of power, Foucault would consider the originating author, the author as Authority, even as God, as an expression of power which must be resisted. He imagines "a culture where discourse would circulate without any need for an author. Discourses, whatever their status, form of value, and regardless of our manner of handling them, would unfold in a pervasive anonymity. . . ." Another poststructuralist, Jacques Derrida, takes Foucault's and Barthes' propositions even further by decentering and destabilizing the very notion of language itself in *Of Grammatology* (1967). Likewise, the structuralist-Marxist Louis Althusser in his seminal essay "Ideology and Ideological State Apparatuses" opposes the assumption that the individual and author is the final guarantor of meaning.

The challenge to the challenge

While poststructuralism has posited a compelling platform against the author's status as the unmediated consciousness at the origin of a work, its argument has been seriously challenged by current writings in feminism, gay and lesbian, and minority studies, as well as postcolonialism. At the basis of this challenge is the idea that the author's subjectivity or *identity* is crucial to a fuller understanding of how systems of oppression (including language itself) operate to erase a particular *voice* or a particular identity. For example, many feminists, and most notably the French feminists Luce Irigaray and Hélène Cixous, believe that language is fundamentally patriarchal. In order to redress this, woman must "write herself" into language, that is, position her subjectivity at the/as the center of a text. Similar politically charged arguments for the crucial connections between author and text are made by gay, lesbian, and minority writers who have been marginalized not only within mainstream society but within the institution of language and literature also. The primary task of these writers is to make their *distinct* voices audible which can only be achieved through a unique, interior perspective. The writing subject, the author, as a representative of an oppressed class or group of people, is therefore vital to this project. Likewise, the postcolonial subject categorically affirms the political, social, and cultural necessity of the "speaking- and writing-self." The death threats leveled against the Anglo-Indian novelist Salman Rushdie and the Bangladeshi feminist writer Taslima Nasreen vividly illustrate the resilience – and the importance – of the concept of "the author," and the complexity of the relationship between author and text.

Further reading

Althusser, Louis. "Ideology and Ideological State Apparatuses," in *Critical Theory Since 1965*, 1986. Edited by Hazard Adams and Leroy Searle.

Barrett, Michele. *Women's Oppression Today*, 1980.

Barthes, Roland. "The Death of the Author," 1968, reprinted in *Image, Music, Text*, 1977.

Burke, Sean. *The Death and Return of the Author*, 1992.

Cixous, Hélène. "The Laugh of the Medusa," in *Critical Theory Since 1965*, 1986. Edited by Hazard Adams and Leroy Searle.

Foucault, Michel. "What is an Author?," 1969, reprinted in *Language, Counter-Memory, Practice*, 1977.

Harland, Richard. *Superstructuralism*, 1987.

Madan, Sarup. *An Introductory Guide to Post-Structuralism and Postmodernism*, 1989.

Owen, Craig. *Beyond Recognition: Representation, Power, and Culture*, 1992.

Spivak, Gayatri C. *Outside in the Teaching Machine*, 1993.

LORRAINA PINNELL

See also Barthes; Foucault

B

Irving Babbitt

American critic, translator, and editor

Born: Dayton, Ohio; August 2, 1865
Died: Cambridge, Massachusetts; July 15, 1933

Biography

Irving Babbitt was born on August 2, 1865, in Dayton, Ohio, one of three children born to Edwin Dwight Babbitt and the former Augusta Darling. His father was a physician and a partner in a business school; his mother died when he was eleven. After his mother's death, the family moved often, going as far east as New York City before finally moving back to Cincinnati, where he graduated from high school in 1881. Because of lack of funds, he did not attend college until 1885, when he enrolled at Harvard University. There he studied languages, including French, German, Spanish, Italian, Greek, and Latin.

After he graduated with high honors in classics, Babbitt took a job at the College of Montana, but in 1891 he resumed his language studies, first in Paris, then in 1892 at Harvard, where he met Paul Elmer More with whom he founded and led the school of literary criticism that became known as American Humanism or the New Humanism. After he received his master's degree, he briefly taught modern languages at Williams College before he returned to teach French and comparative literature at Harvard. In 1900 he married Dora May Drew, with whom he had two children. During his Harvard teaching career he traveled to England and France, served as visiting professor at several universities (among them Yale, Stanford, and the Sorbonne), and was reunited with More when the latter joined the Harvard faculty in 1926. Babbitt became a corresponding member of the French Institute in 1926, when the controversy over his New Humanism began in earnest. During his last years he continued his writing and lecturing despite declining health. In 1932 he delivered a lecture before the American Academy of Arts and Letters, to which he had been elected in 1930. He died in 1933.

Influence

Babbitt's humanism, founded in part on Matthew Arnold's classical humanism, was directed against other fashionable schools of criticism – Marxist, Freudian, naturalistic – that held less exalted views of humankind's potential. The conflict between the New Humanists and their critics became more than a literary one. Because their views derived from different perceptions of humankind, the controversy was a cultural and political one that filled the pages of serious contemporary journals. In fact, Babbitt was himself the subject of many books and articles in the 1920s and 1930s. So significant was he as a scholar and teacher that the opposition had to counter his arguments and all critics had to confront the questions he asked about modern science, psychology, politics, and culture.

When T. S. Eliot described himself, with some reservations, as a disciple of Babbitt in *Selected Essays* (1932), he was not alone. Norman Foerster, Russell Kirk, Yvor Winters, Allen Tate, Harry Levin, Milton Hindus, and Newton Arvin are among the many literary critics whose work reflects Babbitt's influence. As a writer and teacher at Harvard University, Babbitt influenced two generations of literary critics, and his stature was officially acknowledged by Harvard when it created in 1960 the Irving Babbitt Chair of Comparative Literature. Considered by many of his contemporaries as a modern Samuel Johnson, Babbitt changed the course of literary criticism, shifting its emphasis from expressions of "good taste" to a study of the relationship of literature to culture.

Analysis

During Babbitt's lifetime the United States experienced revolutionary changes as the nation became increasingly urban and industrial and as millions of immigrants entered the country. These profound changes made the nineteenth-century gospel of taste untenable. The growing prestige of the scientific world-view fostered experimentation and relativism and created a gulf between ethics and aesthetics. Conventional morality and social custom were threatened by Darwinian evolutionary theories and by Freudian psychology, which stressed the primitive and irrational side of humanity, now considered far less than the exalted beings made in God's image. These changes accelerated after World War I, which was followed by rebellion, unconventionality, and individualism as the nation and its writers spurned traditional values and adopted the doctrine of relativism, the negation of absolute standards.

Babbitt, whose classical education at Harvard made him an anachronism in such a culture, retreated to the past in order to find a more congenial world-view, one that included decorum (exercise of control), moderation, and morality. From his historical perspective, the modernity he criticized had its roots in late-eighteenth-century Romanticism, with its advocacy of individualism. When he sought a literary critic who could serve as a model for his own critical endeavors, he reached back to Gotthold Ephraim Lessing, the German classicist whose *Laokoon: Oder, Über die Grenzen der Malerei und Poesie* (1766; *Laocoön: An Essay on the Limits of Painting and Poetry*, 1836) inspired Babbitt's *The New Laokoon*. He believed that he and Lessing were similar in several respects: both were critical of the contemporary literature that reflected the unfettered imagination and a lack of moral seriousness. As Lessing attempted to discriminate between what he called the "truly classic" and the "pseudo-classic," Babbitt "attempted to discriminate between the truly classic and the romantic." For Babbitt, the truly classic resided in Christian humanism, Aristotle and Greek classicism, and the Buddhist and Confucian philosophies. (In *Rousseau and Romanticism* he pointed out how Aristotle, Confucius, and Buddha all serve as examples of a positive and critical humanism.) As a result, Babbitt's literary criticism is closely tied to philosophy and faith.

From the Greeks, Babbitt took the notion that a person has two selves, one the "natural" self of impulse and desire, the other the "human" self that embodies the power to control the other self. To become "human," one must restrain everything excessive in one's "natural" self and observe proportion in values. Babbitt's belief in the "dualistic" nature of people (also, to be sure, a fundamental tenet of Christianity) included a basic battle of good and evil within each person. People must control their animal nature, must bend their emotions and imagination to reason in order to fulfill their human self, to achieve decorum, to fit into universal law.

For Babbitt, Jean-Jacques Rousseau's Romanticism, which was based on faith in a person's innate or natural goodness, was at fault because it ignored the person's nature, exalted his or her "self-expression" (the product of the undisciplined imagination), and repudiated the "very idea of an ethical center" in its concern with individuality. Writers influenced by such views are led, according to Babbitt, to such absurdities as child worship. Of William Wordsworth, who called the child of six "Mighty Prophet! Seer blest!", Babbitt wrote: "To set up the spontaneity of the child as a substitute for insight, to identify wonder with awe, romance with religion, is to confuse the very planes of being." The Romantics, in fact, excelled at only one thing, self-advertisement, as they sought to express themselves, rather than "humanize" themselves, as classicists did, by constant reference to accepted standards.

Closely allied to Romanticism, according to Babbitt, is naturalism, which originated with Francis Bacon, who emphasized science. Babbitt believed that naturalism and Romanticism dehumanize people because both philosophies regard the person as a product of natural forces, not as a being self-made through moral struggle and deliberate choice. The naturalist has an essentially "romantic" imagination, moreover, because he or she is idealistic, but his or her "inverted" idealism leads him or her to portray not the loveliness but the ugliness of human nature: "It [naturalism] finds a sort of morose satisfaction in building for itself not castles but dungeons in Spain." Babbitt objected not only to the subject matter of the naturalists but also to their mechanistic philosophy. He criticized Theodore Dreiser's *An American Tragedy* (1925) because in his rejection of free will and moral responsibility Dreiser stressed only a person's natural self.

Another target of Babbitt was humanitarianism, which he distinguished from humanism. Humanitarianism was allied with utilitarianism, calculation, and mechanization and was tied to the study of people by the quantitative tools of physical science. In effect, it was "laboratory sociology" and served to further a person's material progress without taking into account his or her ethical or moral development. Since humanitarianism also stressed the individual's "impulses," those desires that Babbitt believed should be checked, it was humanism without a concern for standards. When applied to higher education, as it was at Harvard under the leadership of Charles William Eliot, it led to the elective system and the credit counting deplored by Babbitt, who saw in these "abuses" Baconian quantification and Rousseauistic idealization of adolescent potential. Babbitt's condemnation of humanitarianism both as a literary tendency and as a trend in higher education is typical, for his "criticism" was of both literature and life, which he saw as integrally related.

Babbitt was as unsparing in his criticism of contemporary literary criticism as he was of contemporary literature, and he was particularly hostile to H. L. Mencken, whose literary criticism he termed impressionistic. According to Babbitt, Mencken's literary judgments were "impressions," his "gustos" and "disgustos" entirely the individual, transient response of a critic without the standards that would allow him to achieve a "correct scale of values" and the ability to see things "proportionately." Without the "inner life" associated with a person's controlling human self, the critic's response can only be dictated by the current fads and fashions. Lacking a broad knowledge of literary history, the "tradition" T. S. Eliot invokes in "Tradition and the Individual Talent," the critic makes voguish judgments which will inevitably change as literary fashion changes.

The critic's writing may even be affected by the literature under scrutiny, and in fact Mencken's writing shared the disillusioned cynicism of the contemporary writers he championed.

Babbitt was accustomed to controversy over literary criticism, for his humanistic criticism had been overshadowed at Harvard by the philological criticism practiced by his colleagues. For Babbitt, philology was the scientific reduction of literature to its historical and mechanical parts, and the elevation of quantitative measures over literary and ethical values. The scientific method, which originated in Germany, was valuable, but Babbitt believed that the specialized skills produced obscure facts which were erroneously considered more important than ideas. Similarly, Babbitt had reservations about the historical method then in vogue, for he believed that historicism neglected the moral importance of issues and focused instead on mere externals. Rather than using history to explain literature, as often was the case, critics should use literature to explain history – in this view Babbitt was paraphrasing Aristotle. Both men were primarily concerned with the text, rather than with the writer or writer's milieu, ultimately focusing on the dualism within the work, the play of understanding on imagination.

Babbitt used "imagination" and "understanding" to correspond to the "natural" self and the "human" self, but he expressed this dualism or dichotomy in a variety of related ways. The natural self is also related to the "Many" (since imagination changes with fashions), with the relative, the transitory, and the body (seat of the emotions); the human self is associated with the "One," the absolute, the external, and the spirit. While he claimed that a balance between the two was necessary, his work clearly established the primacy of the human self, which is "good," as opposed to the natural self, which is "evil." Of the three levels of experience – the religious, the human (good), and the animal (evil) – people should obviously occupy the human level while also supporting the religious level because it reinforces ethics and morality.

Babbitt extended his basic dichotomy to literary art, which he also divided into opposites. The "inner form" of art, the content, he associated with the human self; the "outer form," technique, he categorized with the natural self. The "soul" of literature, for Babbitt, was its inner form, while the "outer" form, while necessary to distinguish art from pure didacticism, was less important. Babbitt's problem is the interplay between the two selves, for one self must be checked by the other through an "inner check," a "higher will" not associated with God or the natural person but somehow related to both. Unwilling to accept religious "received truth," for his humanism was more secular than religious, he was also unable to use the individualism that he associated with naturalism and the lowest level. Consequently, the reason that a particular writer is a humanist or a romantic is not always readily apparent.

Because of this vagueness in terminology, it is somewhat difficult to define Babbitt's critical theory, which he provided primarily in a negative way. That is, he did not really provide a positive measure against which he measured literature and found some humanistic and some romantic. Instead, he condemned modern literature, all that literature written since the mid-eighteenth century. Consequently, the reader must construct a theory from a series of preponderantly negative opinions by a critic out of touch with the contemporary literature he abhorred. In a relativistic age, he championed the absolute, and his aristocratic and intellectual effort to restore morals to art left him outside mainstream American thought.

Because, as Thomas R. Nevin writes, "few men were ever so remote by disposition as Babbitt was from his time," Babbitt had relatively few followers, although many critics modified some of his ideas: T. S. Eliot's "Tradition and the Individual Talent" is one of the more notable examples. Certainly there is no appreciable contemporary school of literary criticism associated with ethical or humanistic criticism. In fact, criticism and literature seem to have moved to frankly "romantic" criticism (reader response), to European-inspired Freudian and Marxist criticism, and to semiotics, the minute study of facts, rather than ideas – all are trends he would have deplored. Yet there is renewed interest in Babbitt, not as a literary critic but as a cultural critic whose political views have found favor with American conservatives. *Irving Babbitt in Our Time* (1986), a collection of essays by political conservatives, largely ignores Babbitt's literary criticism, focusing instead on his political and cultural views, which are used to attack contemporary political liberalism. For example, Babbitt criticized higher education for its failure to supply students with classical standards of excellence – that charge has been made since the 1980s. In addition, Babbitt's insistence on "standards" and on the need for moral and ethical education have been resurrected by conservatives like William Bennett seeking to change the course of American civilization. Their intent differs little from Babbitt's, for he also saw literature as a means of reshaping culture.

Principal criticism

Literature and the American College: Essays in the Defense of the Humanities, 1908
The New Laokoon: An Essay on the Confusion of the Arts, 1910
The Masters of Modern French Criticism, 1912
Rousseau and Romanticism, 1919
On Being Creative and Other Essays, 1932
Spanish Character, and Other Essays, 1940

Other major works and literary forms

In addition to the books listed above, most of which treat literary criticism within the broader context of religion, education, and culture, Irving Babbitt wrote *Democracy and Leadership* (1924), which is a humanistic response to humanitarianism (distinguished from humanism), utilitarianism, and romanticism in politics. Because he is more properly described as a critic of culture than of literature per se, Babbitt's criticism is integrated so that his essays on religion, particularly on Buddhist thought, and on higher education also relate to literature and culture. In fact, his controversial essays, many of which appeared in *The Atlantic Monthly* and *The Nation*, were scarcely less important than his books; even his book reviews of contemporary literary criticism embody his critical beliefs. Of the many book reviews he wrote, most of which concerned literary criticism and French literature, perhaps the most important were those of two books by Paul Elmer More, who was his colleague and friend, as well as a fellow advocate of the humanistic school of criticism. In his essays Babbitt developed his humanistic credo, extending it to its application to sociology and politics, embroiling himself in a critical battle with educationist John Dewey and with liberals and Marxists. In other essays, notably "Buddha and the Occident," Babbitt revealed the extent to which his humanistic philosophy was pervaded by Buddhism and other Eastern religions. Because of the scope of his interests, the acidity of his attacks on contemporary culture, and the frequency and volume of his criticism, Babbitt was at the center of critical controversy during much of his life.

NONFICTION
Democracy and Leadership, 1924

TRANSLATION
The Dhammapada, 1936

EDITED TEXTS
Introduction à l'Histoire de la Littérature Anglaise, with an Essay on Taine, by Hippolyte Taine, 1898
Souvenirs d'Enfance et de Jeunesse, by Ernest Renan, 1902
Zadig and Other Stories, by Voltaire, 1905
Phèdre, by Jean Racine, 1910

Further reading

Altieri, Charles. *Act and Quality: A Theory of Literary Meaning and Humanistic Understanding*, 1981.
Brennen, Stephen C., and Stephen R. Yarborough. *Irving Babbitt*, 1987.
Eliot, T. S. "The Humanism of Irving Babbitt" and "Second Thoughts About Humanism," in *Selected Essays*, 1932.
Hindus, Milton. *Irving Babbitt's Literature and the Democratic Culture*, 1994.
Hoeveler, J. David, Jr. *The New Humanism: A Critique of Modern America, 1900–1940*, 1977.
McKean, Keith F. *The Moral Measure of Literature*, 1961.
Manchester, Fredrick, and Odell Shepard, eds. *Irving Babbitt, Man and Teacher*, 1941.
Mercier, Louis J. A. *The Challenge of Humanism*, 1933.
Nevin, Thomas R. *Irving Babbitt: An Intellectual Study*, 1984.
Panichas, George A., and Claes G. Ryn, eds. *Irving Babbitt in Our Time*, 1986.

THOMAS L. ERSKINE

See also American Literary Theory: Twentieth Century; Arnold

Francis Bacon

English statesman, philosopher, and essayist

Born: London, England; January 22, 1561
Died: London, England; April 9, 1626

Biography

Francis Bacon was born on January 22, 1561, at York House in London, to Sir Nicholas Bacon, Lord Keeper of the Seal of England, and his second wife, Ann (née Cooke). In 1573 Bacon entered Trinity College, Cambridge, which he left in 1576 for Gray's Inn, thus beginning a legal career.

After a short time in France, Bacon settled at the Inn and was called to the bar in 1582, two years before he began an ambitiously undertaken political career that commenced with his membership in Parliament. Nevertheless, his career stalled under Queen Elizabeth, whom he apparently offended during a parliamentary debate regarding regal subsidies in 1593. His long period of relative political inactivity under the queen, however, gave Bacon time to write; it was during this period that he produced the first ten of his *Essayes* and the *Advancement of Learning*.

Bacon's political fortunes changed in the reign of James I; he was knighted in 1603 and attained the high position of Lord Keeper in 1617, before he was made Lord Chancellor and Baron Verulam and, ultimately, Viscount St. Albans in 1621, at the age of sixty.

His fall came when old enemies charged him with bribery; he admitted the charges, resigned from office, was briefly imprisoned, and was banished from the court. He made slow progress at rehabilitation, but at the time of his death, in 1626, he had not yet received full royal pardon from the new king, Charles II.

Influence

An important figure of the English Renaissance, and as such one of the men who helped to shape the foundations of modern thought, revolutionizing the medieval patterns of reasoning and critical thinking, Bacon was the first to use English instead of Latin for a philosophical treatise with his *Advancement of Learning* and thus demonstrated the fitness of the vernacular language for theoretical discourse. Bacon's reputation as a literary theoretician, however, has shifted during the centuries since his death.

In the past, the radical nature of his professed refutation of Aristotelian dialectic and Scholasticism was at times overestimated. His originality and accuracy and the practical influence of his inductive method of logical reasoning have been found to be less extraordinary than scholars of the eighteenth and early nineteenth centuries wished to believe.

Recent critical interest in formal structure and the politics of language, however, have led to a reassessment of

Bacon's relevance as a critic of language. In this light, Bacon's critique of traditional dialectic as prescribing a strategy of persuasion rather than of discovery contains a theoretical argument which is central to critical trends such as poststructuralism and deconstruction.

Analysis

In popular opinion, the body of work of Sir Francis Bacon has been associated with science, and the methods of scientific discovery in particular, rather than with literary theory or criticism. The eighteenth century hailed him as the father of modern science, and the German philosopher Immanuel Kant referred to Bacon's *Novum Organum* as the work of "one of the greatest physicists of modern times." Yet Voltaire called the same book "the scaffold on which the English have built their philosophy"; it was unfortunate for them, he added, that they later abandoned Bacon's ideas.

The academic specialization and distinction between such fields as natural science, philosophy, and literature that are taken for granted today were unknown to previous eras. Scholars in Renaissance times, Bacon's era, prided themselves on a universal approach to all areas of human understanding; therefore, an ideal method would be based on a theoretical framework that could be applied to problems of natural science as well as to questions of morality, philosophy, or poetry to obtain a "truthful" answer.

For an appreciation of Bacon's work in relation to the study of literary theory, one must keep in mind further the deep rooting of the idea of "text" within all intellectual activity since the dawn of Western civilization and the beginning of Greek philosophy. Aristotle's highly abstract scientific methodology for the understanding of his world is closer to a literary strategy for the unraveling of a mysterious text than to the modern idea of scientific experiment and practical research and development.

What Bacon had to offer, then, was an intellectually audacious plan for the universal restructuring of the methods by which to obtain knowledge. The blueprints for this plan are outlined in his *Advancement of Learning*, *Novum Organum*, and lesser writings, all of which were planned to be collected in what Bacon called *The Great Instauration*, a work he never completed.

As a Renaissance man, Bacon designed his theory as an open rebellion against the medieval tradition of Scholasticism, which itself was rooted in its understanding of the Greek classics. In place of the traditional Aristotelian logic (or "dialectic" in the modern sense), Bacon put what he perceived to be his own "inductive method." He sharply attacked traditional and commonplace manifestations of Scholastic dialectic. Bacon fiercely objected to the conventional a priori scheme of deductive logic, whereby the scholar tried to reason his way "down" from a generally accepted "truth" to more and more specific manifestations of that truth (basically performing a series of descending syllogisms), until a seemingly irrefutable answer to an original question (such as "What is virtue?") presented itself "logically."

In the place of this deductive scheme, Bacon put his own inductive method, which operates in precisely contrary fashion, by ascending, or reasoning upward, from a collection of specific details to the most general truth. In *Novum Organum*, Bacon demonstrates his method by using the example of "heat" and the question of its final definition.

First, according to Bacon, the philosopher-scientist has to compile what is basically an empiric table of positive evidence and what he calls a "table of affirmatives": all things which emanate heat will be listed.

Second, Bacon stresses the necessity of compiling a table of negative evidence, or "negative instances"; the theoretician was weary of the methods of some of his contemporaries who obtained quick results by neglecting this step. Only when the second table has been compiled can the process of negative elimination of possible definitions or answers to the original question begin, and the philosopher-scientist start his or her critical analysis.

A third table is created, that of "comparison, *majus et minus*" (more and less). Here, all possible evidences for or against the existence of heat in an object are discussed. For example, while land animals have body heat, fish have none; thus, "being in a living body" cannot be a definition of heat, and this cause is entered in a "preliminary table of exclusions." In the end, Bacon arrives at the conclusion that the smallest common denominator for heat (the most general statement about it) is "motion": "Heat is Motion," motion that is "expansive, restrained, and acting in its strife upon the smaller particles of bodies – a motion which, while it expands all ways, has at the same time an inclination upwards."

Bacon's partisan insistence on the inductive method as the only way to achieve scientific knowledge brought about his initial fame in Europe, but also brought down his overall reputation when his achievements were examined by later scholars. The nineteenth-century critic John Nichols, in his biography, *Francis Bacon: His Life and Philosophy* (1888–1889), focused on the extent of Bacon's achievement, showing convincingly that Bacon's theories are often too bold, his claims about their sphere and precision overstretched. Furthermore, according to Nichols, Bacon seemed unaware of the essential necessity of his method's deductive counterpart, the formulation of an audacious hypothesis – the sign of a true genius – against which empirical data can be tested. Yet even though Bacon's theory has not fully withstood the test of time, his voice has proved to be very influential indeed.

It was Bacon who first gave intellectual dignity to the practical side of every scientific endeavor, and the persuasiveness of his voice helped contemporary and subsequent scholars to break with the exclusive focus on theory in natural philosophy which had kept the Greek and medieval philosophers from a practical, rewarding look at nature.

In the field of literature, Bacon's overall stress on the importance of sense perception and collection of practical data earned for him the homage of the renowned eighteenth-century French encyclopedists Denis Diderot and Jean d'Alembert, who revered him as one of the philosophical fathers of their enterprise to take down in writing and thus organize and make accessible all human knowledge. In the late eighteenth century, the German philosopher Gottfried Wilhelm Leibniz praised Bacon's theoretical writings for the crucial influence they had exerted on his own reform of the science of language, a reform which began with Leibniz's rejection of the belief that all languages must originate in Hebrew (according to the Scriptures, the division of language started with the building of the tower of Babel). It was Bacon who led Leibniz to the conviction that philology "must be conducted on the same principles as those of the exact sciences, beginning from the languages best known to us, and so ascending step by step to those more remote."

Roughly two hundred years later, Bacon's thoughts again fascinated scholars of language. After a period of declining interest in his ideas, critics began to notice with fresh interest Bacon's implicit view that the natural world can be seen as representing a large, arcane text which needs deciphering by humanity. Expressing a desire to acquire knowledge, that is, to decipher a hidden code or find a magic key to the understanding of his universe, Bacon constructed theories that are valuable not so much as a practical means in themselves, but for their demonstration of an acute awareness of the linguistic problems facing the explorer of knowledge.

With the Scholastics of the Middle Ages and the philosophers of antiquity, Bacon shares a belief that all teaching, philosophizing, and gaining of knowledge is primarily a linguistic act: that is, an act of using language to express, speculate on, or describe a way toward new scientific findings. Thus, Bacon and his intellectual predecessors work from a theoretical position which has been described by critic Lisa Jardine in her book *Francis Bacon: Discovery and the Art of Discourse* (1974) as

> a view of language as providing a perfect map for process and change in nature. Dialectic is . . . seen as analysing natural relations as embodied in discourse, and manipulating language to gain insight into the natural world.

It was the possibility of using language "to gain insight" that triggered Bacon's revolt against reformist Scholastic dialectic and led to his formulation of his own inductive method. Bacon, as well as contemporaries such as the logician Jacob Degen Schegk, can be credited with the discovery that the humanist textbooks of dialectic (which he most likely read) had stripped the subject of its classical double function of providing a strategy for the teaching as well as for the gaining of knowledge. Seeing dialectic as valuable only as a strategy of persuasion, Bacon, however, did not stop at discarding conventional deductive dialectic as a tool for the discovery of scientific knowledge; in a rather cynical fashion, he also affirmed the use of dialectic in conjunction with rhetoric for what might today be called political propaganda, public relations, advertisements, or special pleading.

Thus, the ongoing reevaluation of the theoretical relevance of Bacon's work grounds him much more strongly in the intellectual tradition of his time and deemphasizes the extent to which he was familiar with natural philosophers and their methodologies, but also takes the sting out of earlier findings which showed Bacon to be not very original at all. Instead, Bacon's intellectual rebellion is reaffirmed, although the target has been discovered to be not so much Aristotle and deductive logic as contemporary textbook applications of the sophisticated system of theory which the Scholastics derived from the Greeks.

Jardine convincingly argues that Bacon had received a conventional education at Cambridge under the "professed Aristotelian" Everard Digby, whose limited understanding of the crucial subtleties of his subject made him one of the implied objects of Bacon's later attacks. In their efforts to gear universities such as Cambridge toward their new aim – the education of worldly gentlemen-students who could write an argumentative piece of literature (as, for example, the profession of law required from its adepts) – the humanist reformers had stripped academic subjects of all "irrelevant" subtleties. Masters such as Philipp Melanchthon and Rodolphus Agricola had written new textbooks for the study of "logic," or dialectic, emphasizing ways to present an argument in an intellectually satisfactory fashion and test an opponent's argument for weaknesses or incoherencies. Thus, dialectic had become almost exclusively a method of presentation rather than of philosophical discovery; all the final truths and the a priori axiomatic knowledge so important for the deductive method were not subject to critical debate themselves, but were taken as unchallengeable wisdom.

Because Bacon could see the shortcomings of this old approach to knowledge, he began the formulation of a radical new one; nevertheless, as Jardine has observed, he found some good use for the traditional system of thinking. His own "persuasive" work, his *Essayes*, offers perfect examples of the art of argumentation. His exegesis of classical parables demonstrates his belief that this literary form could be put to use whenever some truth had to be communicated to a wide audience. Bacon emerges as a clever literary critic who was able to discern theoretically how language can be used as a system or strategy for persuasion; with this discovery, he prefigured modern skeptics and critics of everything from the capitalist system to the theory of mass communication and advertising.

It is in the light of Bacon's critique of his conventional theoretical education that contemporary Marxist critics have rediscovered this Renaissance statesman and philosopher, whose thoughts about language, whose view on the necessity and possibility of a practical theory for scientific progress and discovery, and whose own practical literary work earned for him renewed respect at the close of the twentieth century. Thus the British critic Charles Whitney reaffirms Bacon's "modernity":

> As [Frank] Lentricchia's critique of de Man helps us to see, Bacon calls our attention most of all to the ideological aspects of modernity: the senses in which society's networks of power at once constitute and "coopt" cultural production. . . . clearly Bacon's call to intellectual revolution does find a context in the new class of rising, proto-bourgeois administrators of which he is a leading member. . . . In any case, although his vision is ideologically constituted and limited, although his language is compromised and his motives ambiguous, the energy and the depth of Bacon's vision provide example, encouragement, and direction for others attempting to scramble out of the rhetorical quicksand in which they flail, and to seize and redirect the power of official rhetoric and patterns of thought.

Principal criticism

The Two Bookes of Francis Bacon of the Proficience and Advancement of Learning, Divine and Humane, 1605 (enlarged as *De Augmentis Scientiarum*, 1623, best known as *Advancement of Learning*)
De Sapientia Veterum, 1609 (*The Wisdom of the Ancients*, 1619)
Instauratio Magna, 1620 (*The Great Instauration*, 1653)
Novum Organum, 1620 (English translation, 1802)
Historia Ventorum, 1622 (*History of Winds*, 1653)
Historia Vitae et Mortis, 1623 (*History of Life and Death*, 1638)
Sylva sylvarum, 1627
Valerius Terminus, 1653 (*View of Form*, 1734)

Other major works and literary forms

During his lifetime, Francis Bacon was widely renowned for the worldly wit of his *Essayes*, which were published in 1597, and again, because of their popularity, in 1612 and 1625, both times with significant enlargements. Bacon also wrote works of history and law and translated psalms into English; his last, unfinished work, *New Atlantis* (1627), caps his lifelong achievements as a writer on the subject of scientific discoveries.

POETRY
The Poems of Francis Bacon, 1870

NONFICTION
Essayes, 1597, 1612, 1625
A Declaration of the Practices and Treasons Attempted and Committed by Robert, Late Earle of Essex, 1601
The Historie of the Raigne of King Henry the Seventh, 1622
New Atlantis, 1627
"The Elements of the Common Lawes of England," 1630
"The Learned Reading of Sir Francis Bacon upon the Statute of Uses," 1642

TRANSLATIONS
The Translation of Certaine Psalmes into English Verse, 1625

MISCELLANEOUS
The Works of Francis Bacon, 1879–1889 (7 volumes; James Spedding, Robert Leslie Ellis, and Douglas Benon Heath, editors)

Further reading

Anderson, Fulton H. *Francis Bacon: His Career and His Thought*, 1962.
Bowen, Catherine Drinker, and Dominic J. Balestra (introd.). *Francis Bacon: The Temper of a Man*, 1994.
Farrington, Benjamin. *The Philosophy of Francis Bacon*, 1964.
Formigari, Lia. *Language and Experience in 17th Century British Philosophy*, 1988.
Jardine, Lisa. *Francis Bacon: Discovery and the Art of Discourse*, 1974.
Nichols, John. *Francis Bacon: His Life and Philosophy*, 1888–1889 (2 volumes).
Schuler, Robert M. *Francis Bacon and Scientific Poetry*, 1992.
Snider, Alvin. *Origin and Authority in 17th Century England: Bacon, Milton and Butler*, 1994.
Stillman, Robert E. *The New Philosophy and Universal Languages in 17th Century England: Bacon, Hobbes and Wilkins*, 1995.
Whitaker, Virgil K. *Francis Bacon's Intellectual Milieu*, 1962.
Whitney, Charles. *Francis Bacon and Modernity*, 1986.

R. C. LUTZ

See also Montaigne; Renaissance and Restoration Literary Theory

Mikhail Bakhtin

Russian theorist and critic

Born: Orel, Russia; November 16, 1895
Died: Moscow, U.S.S.R.; March 7, 1975

Biography

Mikhail Bakhtin was born on November 16, 1895, in Orel, just south of Moscow. His father's position as a bank manager took the family to Odessa, where Bakhtin entered the university in 1913. A year later he transferred to St. Petersburg University and studied philology under Russia's leading intellectuals. He graduated in 1918 and taught school in Nevel. It was during his two-year stay in Nevel that he published his first article.

In 1920 Bakhtin moved to Vitebsk, where he continued to teach; there he married Elena Okolovich. While in Vitebsk, his osteomyelitis grew worse, and in 1924 he moved to Leningrad; in 1938 he would lose a leg as a result of his disease. During the 1930s Bakhtin wrote several works published under the names of friends. In 1929 he published *Problemy tvorchestva Dostoevskogo* (problems of Dostoevskii's creative works), which was well received. Soon afterward, however, he was arrested for his involvement in a Christian group and was exiled to Kazakhstan for six years.

In 1936 Bakhtin taught at the Mordovian Pedagogical Institute in Saransk. The following year he moved to Kimry, where he finished a book on Johann Wolfgang von Goethe. One copy of the manuscript was lost, however, during the German invasion, and the only other copy Bakhtin burned as cigarette paper during World War II, when he wrote his book on François Rabelais. In 1946 he returned to Saransk, where he taught until 1961. His book on Fedor Dostoevskii came out in a revised edition in 1963 and won for Bakhtin substantial renown.

In 1969 he returned to Moscow, where he enjoyed the acclaim that many believed was long overdue. Scholars and intellectuals flocked to his side throughout the years before his death on March 7, 1975.

Influence

In spite of the fact that Bakhtin's impact on literary theory began to be felt only in his later years, his influence has run deep and wide. The French critic Tzvetan Todorov, for example, has declared him to be the twentieth century's greatest literary thinker. Wayne C. Booth has said that, if Bakhtin is correct, then much of what Western critics have been doing is either mistaken or trivial, or both. Taking discourse or the word as his focal point, Bakhtin joins a philosophy of language with a philosophy of literature. As a result, his works on Dostoevskii and Rabelais, for example, have led to a major reconsideration of those and other authors, including Miguel de Cervantes, Denis Diderot, Aleksandr Pushkin, Lev Tolstoi, and James Joyce.

Bakhtin's thought has had a significant impact on a number of schools of criticism, most notably the Paris, Tel Quel, and Tartu semiotics schools. His broadest influence on literary history has arisen from his ideas regarding the history of literature and especially the development of the novel. Because he views the novel not as a genre but as a force of interaction between language and life, he has taken modern theorists beyond the traditional boundaries of literary theory. His conceptual innovations have led to an examination of literature's relation to social hierarchy, institutional authority, and linguistic interaction. Consequently, Bakhtin's influence has extended beyond literary theory and into the general study of texts in nearly every area of the humanities.

Analysis

In the 1920s, when Bakhtin was laying the conceptual foundations for the development of his thought, the mainstream of Russian literary theory was dominated by the Russian Formalists. Like the structuralists after him, Bakhtin agreed with the Formalists' emphasis on language, but he disagreed with two positions fundamental to the Formalists' view of literature: first, that a text is merely the sum of its devices, an object crafted by the artist; and, second, that a literary work is to be assessed strictly on its own terms, without reference to the social or historical circumstances surrounding it. While the Soviet Marxists condemned the Formalists for ignoring the ideological aspects of literature, Bakhtin, in turn, resisted the Marxist tendency to reduce literature to ideology. "The study of verbal art," he insists in *The Dialogic Imagination*, "can and must overcome the divorce between an abstract 'formal' approach and an equally abstract 'ideological' approach." In Bakhtin's view, form and idea are of a piece. The formal aspects of literature are part of its message, and the nature of its message determines the form it assumes. Further, according to Bakhtin, the ideological atmosphere or the historical milieu in which the work arises has a bearing on its form and content.

Such a view is grounded in Bakhtin's dialogic concept of language and literature. A novel, for example, is neither an isolated artifact nor a static mirror held up to society; rather, it is an active and interactive system of discourse "structured on an uninterrupted mutual interaction with the discourse of life." The novel, in other words, not only reflects the forces of dialogic exchange but also is itself such a force. As the embodiment of the forces of interaction, discourse in the novel revolves around encounters between various voices or ideas. "The idea begins to live," says Bakhtin in *Problems of Dostoevsky's Poetics*, "only when it enters into genuine dialogic relationships with other ideas. . . . The idea is a *live event*, played out at the point of dialogic meeting between two or several consciousnesses." The critical juncture of space and time or the threshold where such an encounter occurs is what Bakhtin calls the "chronotope" in the novel. The chronotope is where word encounters alien word, and each emerges transformed by the other. Discourse in the novel, therefore, not only represents but also is itself the object of representation; the "hero" of a novel, in Bakhtin's view, is the word. In the novel, the hero's struggle is the struggle of an idea to come to life through dialogic interaction.

A given idea or outlook on the world is couched in a certain discourse. Because the novel consists of a multitude of discourses, it rests on a diversity and a plurality of languages. Addressing this point, Bakhtin introduces the concepts of heteroglossia and polyglossia. Heteroglossia, or the variety of discourses, makes up the underlying condition of any utterance, literary or otherwise. It is the locus of similarities and differences among languages that both draws them together and pulls them apart, the centripetal and centrifugal forces of discourse. Both within the novel and outside the novel, heteroglossia situates a given utterance in a specific social, historical, and ideological context. Says Bakhtin in *The Dialogic Imagination*, "Authorial speech, the speeches of narrators, inserted genres, the speech of characters are merely those fundamental compositional unities with whose help heteroglossia [*raznorechie*] can enter the novel." The linguistic features of a novel, therefore, are of a piece with its stylistic aspects. As Bakhtin himself points out, "such a combining of languages and styles into a higher unity is unknown to traditional stylistics."

Central to that "higher unity" which characterizes the novel is polyglossia, or the plurality of languages, discourses, and voices interacting within the framework of the text. Bakhtin argues that "polyglossia and the *interanimation of languages*," in fact, made it possible for the novel to emerge as a literary form, because only the multiplicity of languages can free language for dialogic self-examination. Without intercultural and, along with it, interlinguistic exchange, a given language cannot free itself from the monological, hierarchical language of myth and epic. The dialogic discourse that goes into the making of the novel comes to life only when the language of the familiar encounters the language of the alien.

In addition to polyglossia, Bakhtin cites a second element "of decisive importance" to the rise of the novel: laughter. In laughter, language becomes its own object of representation and of critical examination through "the ridiculing of another's language and another's direct discourse." Laughter, according to Bakhtin, is thus the key to freedom. Freeing language from the authoritarian monologism of myth, laughter "destroys the epic," Bakhtin declares in *The Dialogic Imagination*, "and in general destroys any hierarchical (distancing and valorized) distance." Laughter undermines the epic through the "parodic-travestying forms" it assumes in literature, and these forms prepare the ground for the novel. In *Rabelais and His World*, Bakhtin claims that by the time of the Renaissance, laughter had taken on a philosophical meaning, whereby the world is demythologized and seen anew. Of particular interest to him in this connection is what he calls "carnival laughter," festive and universal, at once affirming and denying, burying and reviving.

As expressed through the rogue, the clown, and the fool – those who are free "to be 'other' in this world" – laughter influences "the positioning of the author himself within the novel (and of his image, if he himself is somehow embedded in the novel), as well as the author's point of view." The rogue, the clown, and the fool thus provide the novelist with a mask from which he may engage life in a dialogue. Through these three figures, the novel becomes the stage for the encounter between word and alien word. As the genre whose subject is discourse, the novel is the laughing genre, that is, not a genre at all but a force. Holding such a view of the novel, Bakhtin attaches great significance to the Menippean satire in the evolution of the novel. In *Problems of Dostoevsky's Poetics*, for example, he argues that "the 'inappropriate word' – inappropriate because of its cynical frankness, or because it profanely unmasks a holy thing, or because it crudely violates etiquette – is . . . very characteristic for the menippea." The menippea is the "genre of 'ultimate questions'" because it calls into question the ready-made truths of official monologism. Thus the menippea combines laughter and polyglossia to enable the author to put the needful question to himself and to his hero.

The relation between author and hero is a major point of concern for Bakhtin, as evidenced by his essay "Avtor i geroi v esteticheskoi deiatel'nosti" (1924; "Author and Hero in Aesthetic Activity," 1988). In this essay Bakhtin examines the relation between author and hero in terms of a dialogue between one consciousness and another. Accordingly, he regards the character as an event, and not as an object that can be filled into a predetermined category, a view which a Formalist approach might suggest. This dynamic notion of character is of particular importance to Bakhtin's revised book on Dostoevskii, in which he asserts that self-consciousness "presupposes a radically new *authorial position* with regard to the represented person . . . . At issue here is precisely the discovery of a *new integral view on the person* – the discovery of . . . 'the man in man.'" One way in which Bakhtin describes "the man in man" is to call it "that internally unfinalizable something in man." This "something" is what gives the novel its open-endedness.

Self-consciousness and open-endedness are fundamental features of what Bakhtin terms "the polyphonic novel," which, says Bakhtin in *Problems of Dostoevsky's Poetics*, "*is dialogic through and through*." Polyphony is a system of voices or ideas that engage one another in an unending process of summons and response. Bakhtin views the characters in Dostoevskii's novels as persons born of ideas, and the interactions among them are interactions among ideas. The message which finally emerges from Dostoevskii's polyphonic novels, Bakhtin believes, is that the ultimate word of the world and about the world is forever yet to be uttered. While Bakhtin initially argued that polyphony belonged to Dostoevskii's novels alone, he later changed his position and acknowledged the establishment of polyphony throughout world literature. The important point for Bakhtin, then, is not that polyphony is peculiar to Dostoevskii's novels but that it is a distinguishing feature of the novel in all of its dialogic dimensions.

In Bakhtin's view, the primary dialogic dimension of the novel is rooted in its concern for truth; truth is the stake in the novel's interaction with life. Explaining what is fundamental to the "genre" of the novel, Bakhtin writes,

> At the base of the genre lies the Socratic notion of the dialogic nature of truth, and the dialogic nature of human thinking about truth. The dialogic means of seeking truth is counterposed to *official* monologism, which pretends to *possess a ready-made truth*.

> . . . Truth is not born nor is it to be found inside the head of an individual person, it is born *between people* collectively searching for truth, in the process of their dialogic interaction.

Truth, as Bakhtin conceives of it, lies more in process than in outcome, more in seeking than in finding. Truth is that which is yet to be revealed. It is situated in an open-ended, unfinalized third position between or above speaker and listener. Bakhtin makes this point in his essay "Problema teksta v lingvistike, filologii, i drugikh gumanitarnykh naukakh" (1959–1961; "The Problem of the Text in Linguistics, Philology, and Other Human Sciences," 1986), asserting that every dialogue proceeds against the background of a third position that is invisibly present. As the horizon of possibility for what is yet to be uttered, as well as the realm of all past utterances, the "third," or the position of truth, sustains the movement of dialogue. Such a view of truth as the primary concern of the novel makes the reader's role an active one, whereby the reader must sort through not only the author's word but also those voices that resound in the author's word and in his or her own ideology.

Bakhtin's concept of a third position raises a question that is central to his theories of literature and language: who is speaking? His response, simply stated, is that the word itself speaks. A novel may be written by a given author, but the word breathed into it comes from an atmosphere of language consisting of a multitude of discourses. In this connection Bakhtin draws a distinction between the author as person and the author as creator, with the changeover occurring in what he calls "the aesthetic event." The person becomes a creator when language becomes its own object of representation, as it does in the novel. From a dialogic standpoint, the language of the novel is situated neither in the author nor in the reader but in an interactive system of discourse between the two. This third position of discourse is what lends open-endedness both to the novel and to the critical response it invokes. "The work and the world represented in it," Bakhtin writes in *The Dialogic Imagination*, "enter the real world and enrich it, and the real world enters the work and its world as part of the process of its creation, as well as part of its subsequent life, in a continual renewing of the work through the creative perception of listeners and readers." While a novel may be finally finished, it remains forever unfulfilled.

Placing the reader in a position of active response, Bakhtin places the reader in a position of responsibility. Because the novel's most basic concern is a concern for truth, the readers in their response to the text decide not only something about the work at hand but also about the truth of themselves. Bakhtin thus draws aesthetics out of its normal confines and makes it an existential matter, and he does so beginning with his first essay, "Iskusstvo i otvetstvennost'" (1919; art and responsibility), in which he declares that, although art and life are not one and the same, they must become one in the wholeness of the reader's responsibility. It is important to note that, just as the novel remains unfinalized, so does the issue of the reader's responsibility. Each word contains a summons and calls for a response. Once uttered, a word becomes "the dead flesh of meaning," as Bakhtin puts it, and must be resurrected in a new movement of response.

It is not by chance that the language of many of Bakhtin's works on literary theory and discourse has Christological connotations. His approach to meaning in language and literature parallels his Christian views on the death and resurrection of the God-man. In the book attributed to Valentin Voloshinov but probably authored by Bakhtin, *Marxism and the Philosophy of Language*, it is argued that when meaning is buried under the language of a given theme, it must once again be brought to life through the renewed dialogic response of the reader or listener. In his or her interaction with the text, moreover, the reader encounters much more than a lifeless literary structure. In *The Dialogic Imagination*, Bakhtin observes, "the text as such never appears as a dead thing; beginning with any text, . . . we always arrive, in the final analysis, at the human voice, which is to say we come up against the human being." To interact with a human voice, Bakhtin believes, is to interact with a human life. Human life consists of this dialogic process, by which the human being constantly becomes more than what he or she is at any given moment. When dialogue ends, everything ends. To cease becoming, Bakhtin asserts in "Author and Hero in Aesthetic Activity," means spiritual death.

Bakhtin's lifelong endeavor has been depicted as a religious quest for the nature of the word. His legacy and influence on subsequent thinkers lies perhaps more in his quest and his questions than in any answers or conclusions he may have drawn. Placing his accent on dialogic response, on human responsibility, and on spiritual life, he puts a question to his reader: where are you? His reader must respond not with any of the fixed formulas or ready answers of theoretical isms but with his or her own human voice, that is, with his or her own life. Just as the novel, according to Bakhtin, transforms generic forms and structures, so does his literary theory undermine the closed systems of literary criticism. The reassessment of language and literature that has resulted from his work has led to a reassessment of literary theory itself. Those who have been influenced by Bakhtin view theory in dialogic terms; that is, they see theory as a participation in the creation of literature, as well as a part of the creation of the theorist. The critic's relation to the text has a bearing on his relation to himself and to others. Bakhtin might add that it also includes his relation to God.

While Bakhtin's long-term legacy is perhaps yet to be determined, he has at least drawn aesthetics out of the realm of passive appreciation and academic curiosity. Under his influence, the aesthetics of verbal art is joined with the ethical and spiritual dimensions of human life. Whereas Søren Kierkegaard divided the aesthetic, the ethical, and the religious into separate stages along life's way, Bakhtin joins them into a human unity. If, as Bakhtin claims, the novel carries on an uninterrupted dialogue with life, then any theory of the novel must do the same. If, as Bakhtin argues, the author's creation of a hero is part of a process of self-creation, then the critic's response to author and hero also entails such a process. Indeed, if, as Bakhtin asserts, a quest for truth lies at the base of the novel, then so does it become the basis of literary theory as influenced by him. Addressing not simply the characteristics but the metaphysics of literature, as well, Bakhtin has led literary theory beyond its traditional confines to include such diverse disciplines as epistemology, sociology, and linguistics. Indeed, the term he himself uses to portray his activity is not "literary theory" but "philosophical anthropology"; others have described it as an "existentialist philology." In any case, the impact of Bakhtin's thought has been felt throughout the human sciences, and his legacy may well go to the heart of human life.

Principal criticism

Problemy tvorchestva Dostoevskogo, 1929
Problemy poetiki Dostoevskogo, 1963 (*Problems of Dostoevsky's Poetics*, 1973, 1984)
Tvorchestvo Fransua Rable i narodnaia kul'tura srednevekov'ia i Renessansa, 1965 (*Rabelais and His World*, 1968)
Voprosy literatury i estetiki, 1975 (*The Dialogic Imagination*, 1981)
Estetika slovesnogo tvorchestva, 1979
Speech Genres and Other Late Essays, 1986
The Architectonics of Answerability, 1988
Art and Answerability: Early Philosophical Essays by M. M. Bakhtin, 1990
Toward a Philosophy of the Act, 1993

Other major works and literary forms

In addition to the books listed above, there are three major works ascribed to other authors but which were probably written by Mikhail Bakhtin. One is a critical study by Pavel Medvedev titled *Formal'nyi metod v literaturovedenii: Kriticheskoe vvedenie v sotsiologicheskuiu poetiku* (1928; *The Formal Method in Literary Scholarship*, 1978). The other two works were published under the name Valentin Voloshinov: *Freidizm: Kriticheskii ocherk* (1927; *Freudianism: A Marxist Critique*, 1973) and *Marksizm i filisofiya iazyka* (1929; *Marxism and the Philosophy of Language*, 1973). The major literary figures with whom Bakhtin was concerned included not only Fedor Dostoevskii and François Rabelais but also William Shakespeare, Johann Wolfgang von Goethe, Nikolai Gogol', and Lev Tolstoi. Some student notes on Bakhtin's lectures have appeared in print and include discussions of Andrei Belyi, Fedor Sologub, and Aleksandr Blok. The subject matter of his essays is as broad as his knowledge; among the disciplines he examines are philosophy, linguistics, philology, psychology, and sociology. Although Bakhtin is known primarily as a literary theorist, he is the probable author of "Sovremennyi vitalism," an article on vitalism attributed to the biologist I. I. Kanaev, and in 1934 he published "Opyt izucheniia sprosa kolkhoznikov," a short piece on collective farming.

NONFICTION
Freidizm: Kriticheskii ocherk, 1927 (probable author, as Valentin Voloshinov; *Freudianism: A Marxist Critique*, 1973)
Formal'nyi metod v literaturovedenii: Kriticheskoe vvedenie v sotsiologicheskuiu poetiku, 1928 (probable author, as Pavel Medvedev; *The Formal Method in Literary Scholarship*, 1978)
Marksizm i filisofiia iazyka, 1929 (probable author, as Valentin Voloshinov; *Marxism and the Philosophy of Language*, 1973)

Further reading

Clark, Katerina, and Michael Holquist. *Mikhail Bakhtin*, 1984.
Emerson, Caryl. *The First Hundred Years of Mikhail Bakhtin*, 1997.
Holquist, Michael. *Dialogism: Bakhtin and His World*, 1990.
Lodge, David. *After Bakhtin: Essays on Fiction and Criticism*, 1990.
Morson, Gary Saul, ed. *Bakhtin: Essays and Dialogues on His Work*, 1986.
Morson, Gary Saul, and Caryl Emerson, eds. *Rethinking Bakhtin: Extensions and Challenges*, 1989.
Morson, Gary Saul, and Caryl Emerson. *Mikhail Bakhtin: Creation of a Prosaics*, 1990.
Patterson, David. *Literature and Spirit: Essays on Bakhtin and His Contemporaries*, 1988.
Studies in Twentieth Century Literature. IX (Fall, 1984). Special Bakhtin issue.
Todorov, Tzvetan. *Mikhail Bakhtin: The Dialogical Principle*, 1984.
University of Ottawa Quarterly. LIII (Winter, 1983). Special Bakhtin issue.

DAVID PATTERSON

See also Dialogic Criticism; Grotesque; Ong; Russian Formalism

Giuseppe Baretti

Italian-English critic and lexicographer

Born: Turin, Italy; April 24, 1719
Died: London, England; May 5, 1789

Biography

Giuseppe Marc' Antonio Baretti, also known as Joseph Baretti, was born on April 24, 1719, in Turin, Italy. The eldest of four sons of an architect, he was encouraged by his family to train for the Jesuit priesthood but instead, as quite a young man, began the travels that would eventually lead him to England. After living in several Italian cities, he arrived in London in 1751.

Baretti's life in England was inextricably linked to his friendship with Samuel Johnson. Like Johnson, he was fascinated by language and soon established himself as an authority on Italian language and literature and an able lexicographer. Bilingual in Italian and English, he was also quite fluent in Spanish and French. After a brief return to Italy (1760–1766), where he published a critical journal for several years, he reestablished himself in Johnson's circle. A particularly close friend of Baretti was Sir Joshua Reynolds, the painter and first president of the Royal Academy of Arts. Baretti served as the Secretary for Foreign Correspondence at the academy during Reynolds' term (1768–1790).

Baretti was employed as a tutor in the household of Henry Thrale, a friend and patron of Johnson, during the 1770s. He acted as interpreter for Thrale and Johnson on a tour of France in 1775. In the previous year, he had refused a position as a professor of Italian at Trinity College, Dublin, preferring to remain "a kind of demi-Englishman." He was awarded a royal pension in 1782. Giuseppe Baretti died in London on May 5, 1789, and was buried in Marylebone.

Influence

As a member of Johnson's circle in London, Baretti was directly involved in some of the most significant intellectual and literary movements of the eighteenth century, particularly the study of language and the relationship between language and literature. His earliest English works, on Italian literature, served to advance the study of Italian in general and of the works of Dante in particular among the English. Perhaps his best-known critical work, *Discours sur Shakespeare et sur Monsieur de Voltaire* (discourse on Shakespeare and on Mr. Voltaire), furthered the appreciation of William Shakespeare by Italian writers, even though it was written to refute Voltaire's criticism and was therefore intended for a French readership.

In short Baretti served on two fronts by virtue of his linguistic abilities and his appreciation for the literatures of several nations. Although he condemned the excessive trend toward the pastoral among Italian poets, his role as a bridge between the English and Italian languages and cultures laid the foundation for much of the fascination with Italy that marked the Romantic poets of the next generation in England.

Analysis

To understand Baretti as a critic, one must take into account his dual identification as an Italian and a "demi-Englishman." While the two overlap frequently – most notably in his lexicographical works – it is essential to consider his career as a critic with respect to two national literatures and at least two languages. While he was neither a brilliant nor a highly original critic, his talents as a linguist are indisputable, and it was this linguistic mastery, plus a keen appreciation of vernacular literature, that shaped Baretti as a critic and allow his critical writings to merit continuing interest.

From the earliest stages of his literary career, Baretti demonstrated a passionate commitment to Italian literature and a disdain for passing literary fashions that might either damage the national literature itself or persuade Italians that their literature was insignificant compared to that of another nation. For Baretti, the works of Dante represented all that was finest in the Italian vernacular literary tradition, and it is to Dante that he continually returns when praising or defending his native literature. He was particularly contemptuous of the attacks of French critics, notably Voltaire, on the so-called decadence of Italian literature and culture. Indeed, his celebrated essay, *Discours sur Shakespeare et sur Monsieur de Voltaire*, is less concerned with praising Shakespeare than it is with impugning Voltaire's ability to read either English or Italian literature in the original. By contrast, Baretti singles out for praise those writers, such as John Milton, who have learned foreign languages and are able to appreciate literature written in those languages; his regard for Milton is apparent in his suggestion that the English writer may have been influenced by Dante in the composition of *Paradise Lost* (1667, 1674) – like *La divina commedia* (c. 1320; *The Divine Comedy*), an epic poem of Christian redemption.

During the years from 1763 to 1765, Baretti edited and published a journal of literary criticism entitled *La frusta letteraria* (the literary whip) while residing in Venice. Adopting the pseudonym Aristarco Scannabue (Aristarco the ox-slayer, or dunce-killer), he took on as his principal target the Arcadian movement among Italian poets. The Arcadian Academy was a loosely organized yet influential group of pastoral poets and would-be poets that had been founded in Rome at the end of the previous century. Members assumed suitably classical names – Sylvanus, Thyrsis – and dedicated themselves to penning poetic evocations of Arcadia, the mythic realm of pastoral bliss. In the mid-eighteenth century Italian poetry and poetic drama were still heavily influenced by the Arcadians, though the dominance of the academy itself had waned. Baretti viewed the Arcadian movement as disastrous and dangerous. Not only was far too much of the poetry being published simply doggerel but also, more important, Italian literature was losing a sense of moral force. As Aristarco Scannabue, Baretti undertook more than literary criticism: he reintroduced his countrymen to their once-formidable literary tradition.

It is not surprising that Baretti should choose the device of a literary journal as a forum for his critical writing. While living in England, he had become an admirer of that country's literary journals, principally *The Spectator* but also *The Rambler* and *The Idler*. *La frusta letteraria*, though inferior to its prototype, was clearly modeled after *The Spectator*, and its editor had observed and attempted to implement the particular qualities of English critical writing: namely, that literature should possess moral and didactic qualities in addition to art.

While it is certain that Baretti's theory of criticism was influenced by Johnson and other English writers of his circle (notably Oliver Goldsmith), it is quite probable that Baretti's own interests and talents as a linguist and a reader of several national literatures enabled him to appreciate the didactic possibilities and moral authority that literature might, and should, possess. Again, he needed to look no further than Dante to find Italian literature that could teach, guide, and entertain. Yet Baretti was no chauvinist; he demonstrated his approval of many works written in languages other than Italian that can both instruct and delight. The plays of Shakespeare and Pierre Corneille, the prose of Miguel de Cervantes, the works of Johnson – all of these are studied by Baretti the linguist, enjoyed by Baretti the reader, and held up as paradigms by Baretti the critic.

Baretti's talents as a multilingual critic and his highly personalized sense of duty concerning the reform of literature in his native country prevent the modern reader from placing him neatly within the confines of a distinctive movement or school of criticism. Despite his admiration for Corneille and his association with Johnson, he cannot be called a neoclassicist; his attacks on the Arcadians reveal him as one who is not inclined to believe that the makers of literature need look to Greece and Rome for their inspiration. Nor is it probable that his intellect was of the caliber to appreciate the subtleties of neoclassical theory. It is equally inaccurate to portray him as a kind of pre-Romantic, despite the fact that the Romantic affinity for Italian language and culture was no doubt enhanced by the introduction of that language and culture to the English literati by Baretti himself. Finally, it is unjust to describe him solely in terms of Johnson's circle, despite the fact that it is in the context of their association that Baretti is principally studied.

Rather, Baretti's work as a critic, and indeed his life both in Italy and in thirty-two years as "a kind of demi-Englishman," were shaped and guided by his intense awareness of the richness and integrity of modern languages as the foundations of equally rich national literatures. In his native country, his tireless promotion of the Italian literary heritage and his condemnation of all contrivance and frivolity that might be unworthy of the heirs of Dante undoubtedly contributed to the assertion of a vital, indigenous Italian literary voice in the late eighteenth and nineteenth centuries. In his adopted country, a land he found after long residence to be "no less agreeable than familiar," Baretti's tripartite mission as teacher, lexicographer, and critic brought Europe to London and made the journey in the opposite direction a pleasing prospect indeed.

Principal criticism

A Dissertation upon the Italian Poetry, 1753
Remarks on the Italian Language and Writers, 1753
La frusta letteraria, 1763–1765 (as Aristarco Scannabue, 2 volumes)
Preface to *Tutte le opere de Niccolò Machiavelli*, 1772
Discours sur Shakespeare et sur Monsieur de Voltaire, 1777
Scelta di lettre familiari, 1779
Tolondron, 1786

Other major works and literary forms

In addition to his literary criticism, Giuseppe Baretti is perhaps best known for his lexicographical works. His two-volume *A Dictionary of the English and Italian Languages* (1760) remained the standard such work until the twentieth century. His *A Dictionary, Spanish and English and English and Spanish* (1778) and his numerous works on grammar and phraseology were all well received during his lifetime. Baretti also translated Ovid's poetry into Italian (1742) and Samuel Johnson's *Rasselas* into French (completed in 1759 but never published). He published several accounts of his travels, notably *A Journey from London to Genoa* (1770), and also published his correspondence with his brothers (1762–1763).

POETRY
Le piacevoli poesie di Giuseppe Baretti torinese, 1750

NONFICTION
The Italian Library, 1757
A Dictionary of the English and Italian Languages, 1760 (2 volumes)
A Grammar of the Italian Language, 1760
Lettre familiari a' suoi tre fratelli Filippo, Giovanni, e Amedeo, 1762–1763 (2 volumes)
An Account of the Manners and Customs of Italy, 1768
A Journey from London to Genoa, 1770
A Dictionary, Spanish and English and English and Spanish, 1778

TRANSLATION
Degli amore di P. Ovidio, 1742 (of Ovid's poetry)

Further reading

Bondanella, Peter, and Julia Conaway Bondanella, eds. "Baretti, Giuseppe," in *Dictionary of Italian Literature*, 1979.
Collison-Morley, Lacy. *Giuseppe Baretti, with an Account of His Literary Friendships*, 1909.
Curley, Thomas. *Samuel Johnson and the Age of Travel*, 1976.
Gallup, Donald C. *Giuseppe Baretti's Work in England*, 1939.
Iamartino, Giovanni. "The Lexicographer as a Biased Witness: Social, Political, and Religious Criticism in Baretti's English Italian Dictionary," in *Aevum: Rassegna di Scienze Storiche, Linguistische, Filologiche*. 64, no. 3 (Sept.–Dec., 1990), pp. 435–444.
Lubbens van der Brugge, C. J. M. *Johnson and Baretti*, 1951.
Robinson, Duncan. "Giuseppe Baretti as 'A Man of Great Humanity,'" in *British Art 1740–1820: Essays in Honor of Robert R. Wark*, 1922, pp. 81–94. Edited by Guilland Sutherland.
Wellek, René. "The Italian Critics," in *A History of Modern Criticism: 1750–1950*, 1955.

NANCY SCERBO

See also Johnson; Neoclassical Literary Theory

Owen Barfield

English critic, writer, and teacher

Born: London, England; November 9, 1898
Died: Forest Row, England; December 14, 1998

Biography

The youngest of four children, Arthur Owen Barfield was born in 1898 in Muswell Hill, North London, to a prosperous and largely self-educated legal solicitor, Arthur Edward Barfield. His mother, née Elizabeth Shoults, was interested sufficiently in women's issues to become a suffragette. In 1917 Barfield won a scholarship to Oxford University, but his entrance into Wadham College was delayed by military service in the Royal Engineers.

At the university, Barfield began his celebrated and productive friendship with C. S. Lewis, a fellow student. In 1921 he completed his B.A. and began reading works by Rudolf Steiner, the founder of spiritual science (anthroposophy). For the next decade, collaborative argument with Lewis and an intensifying interest in Steiner energized and shaped Barfield's intellectual development. He married Christian Maude Douie in 1923; the couple adopted two children, acting as foster parents to a third.

"For economic and for other reasons," Barfield says, he joined his father's law firm in 1930, becoming a partner in 1934. Until 1964 he was a practicing solicitor, occasionally writing or lecturing on anthroposophy while maintaining contact with Lewis and a circle of his literary friends at Oxford known as the "Inklings" – the group included J. R. R. Tolkien, Neville Coghill, and Charles Williams, among others.

Retirement freed Barfield to devote himself entirely to writing and lecturing. A Fellow of the Royal Society of Literature, he held visiting professorships at various colleges and universities in the United States and Canada, including Brandeis University and the University of Missouri. He died at Forest Row, East Sussex, on December 14, 1998.

Influence

"To Owen Barfield: Wisest and Best of My Unofficial Teachers" reads the dedication of C. S. Lewis' *The Allegory of Love* (1936), the book that made Lewis' critical reputation. The distinguished medieval and Renaissance scholar's repeated public expressions of gratitude served in fact to draw needed attention to Barfield's work, especially during the quarter century when the practice of law limited his output. Clearly, Lewis' own subsequent understanding of metaphor and myth is the product of his prolonged contact with Barfield during the 1920s and later. Nevertheless, Barfield's influence extends beyond his being the key intellectual figure behind the criticism of Lewis.

His relation to Rudolf Steiner's anthroposophical thought is crucial and curious. Simply put, much of what Barfield had arrived at analytically, Steiner claimed to have experienced directly in the practice of his spiritual science. Conventionally minded critics and students of philosophy are clearly put off by Barfield's frequent and unapologetic celebrations of Steiner's views, but these views occupy a critical position in his thinking. His efforts to secure for them a wider hearing were in fact central to his career as a writer and a thinker.

It will, however, be primarily as an extension of the Coleridgean imagination that Barfield's effect on the mind of the twentieth century will be judged. His work seeks to validate analytically and to transform Samuel Taylor Coleridge's insight into the nature of consciousness and the relation of aesthetic experience to knowledge.

Analysis

At the center of Barfield's thought, providing a focus for an impressive spectrum of linked illuminations, is his concept of the evolution of consciousness. Implicit in this idea is his understanding of how consciousness itself works; how it formulates representations (ideas or images) of the outside world; how its participation in the outside world generates and completes that world's reality, while realizing its own; and how awareness of the changing meaning of words reveals not merely semantic growth or decay, but also the evolving mind of the past and of the world it possessed and partially created. There are no contrasting earlier and later versions of his views; there is instead a progressively more ambitious application of this deeply pondered idea to ever-wider reaches of thought:

> If evolution of consciousness is the thread you hold in your hand, . . . it winds a long course through literature to language, through language to history, through history to prehistory and the antecedent unity of man and nature, and back again from there to such matters as psychology, philosophy, and religion.

His investigation of his own intense response to the language of lyric poetry (particularly to the language of the English Romantics) enabled him to pick up this thread in *Poetic Diction*.

His starting point is to answer the question, what really happens when the individual encounters poetic diction? The answer: "A felt change of consciousness, where 'consciousness' embraces all my awareness of my surroundings at any given moment, and 'surroundings' includes my own feelings. By 'felt' I mean to signify that the change itself is noticed, or attended to." Aesthetic pleasure occurs at the actual moment of the change and its significance is not limited to a warm glow or a tingle (though it may induce that kind of reaction). A manifestation of the mind's passage from one plane of consciousness to another, the experience of pleasure "considered as an action" is knowledge, "considered as a state" is wisdom. The quality of everyday experience of the outside world depends entirely on what the mind brings from within to the sense-data or to the language which precipitates the experience. Aesthetic experience – particularly, though not exclusively, the kind realized by the assimilation of metaphor – allows the individual to bring more than could be brought before and creates a faculty enabling the observation of what could not be observed before and the recognition of previously occult resemblances and analogies. In the grandiloquent language of Coleridge, it is "a repetition in the finite mind of the eternal act of creation in the infinite I AM." Barfield more modestly labels it a form of participation of the knower in the known. It obviates the distinction between subject and object and suggests how altogether misleading is the idolized image engraved in the mind of so much post-Renaissance science and thought, a picture of a world wherein inert phenomena – the only and ultimate reality – are peered at longingly by an isolated human consciousness sealed inside a vacuum of meaninglessness. This experience with poetry, he noted in his preface to *Romanticism Comes of Age*, left him with two strong impressions: "Firstly that the poetic or imaginative use of words enhances their meanings and secondly that these enhanced meanings may reveal hitherto unapprehended parts or aspects of reality. All this seemed to promise a way out of the vacuum."

Examining changes of meaning in words as they develop in and through languages, long recognized as a useful way of detailing more precisely the history of thought, offered to Barfield the more valuable possibility of grasping the history of thinking, of understanding how the vanished individual minds of the past gave birth to language that realized participation in their world and (in William Wordsworth's phrase) both "perceived and half-created" it. To intuit the role Barfield allots the imagination in the history of thinking, the faculty's overall relation to reality must first be understood. He does not believe that *esse est percipi* (to be is to be perceived). His idealism is objective, and the force of that qualifier can be best understood by noting the following train of thought put forth in *Saving the Appearances*. The word "rainbow" signifies a consciously shared representation, the outcome of the sun's light striking particles and stimulating sight. The reality of a rainbow exists outside subjective consciousness, but the individual only knows it when he or she either experiences the word's meaning or participates through the sense of sight in the outside phenomena (light striking particles of moisture). Yet science has demonstrated that all matter, a tree, for example, consists of "particles" – "the atoms, protons and electrons of modern physics . . . now perhaps more generally regarded, not as particles, but as notional models or symbols of an unknown supersensible or subsensible base." If these particles are there and are all that is there, then, since the particles are no more like the thing called a tree than the raindrops are like the thing called a rainbow, it follows that the appearance of a tree is just as much a shared collective representation as is a rainbow. The whole nonego, outside world – which science investigates, and which presumably existed in the past – is a system of shared or collective representations realized imagistically in the consciousness by the imagination's participation in sense experience, which is another name for language. For Barfield, in the beginning of consciousness was the word.

Yet the words of the past differ from those in the present. What words name as things, sensible or insensible, the past perceived as representations or images. The difference between image and thing lies in the fact that "an image presents itself as an exterior expressing or implying an interior, whereas a thing does not." Semantic history reveals that an overwhelming proportion of what are now regarded as abstract words (such as the word "spirit") referred at one time either to a solid sensible object or to some animal or human activity. (The Latin *spiritus* meant "breath" or "wind.") It is tempting but unhistorical to make the easy assumption that out of the limited and specific meanings of primitive language there grew – via the intervention of metaphor – new meanings whose metaphorical origins were forgotten. Such a hypothesis nevertheless involves a disabling contradiction: at every stage, as the investigator moves backward in the history of language, he or she finds it becoming more and more figurative; to make this theory work, however, he or she must assume a period – still further back – when language was not figurative at all. Barfield argues that it would be far more coherent to imagine a time when *spiritus* or its Greek root or older forms "meant neither *breath*, nor *wind*, nor *spirit*, nor yet all three of these things, but when they simply had *their own old peculiar meaning*," a single meaning encompassing these ideas, that crystallized later in the evolution of consciousness into separable meanings and into others as well, for which by the Greco-Roman period different words had been found. At stake here is Barfield's understanding of the relation of words – the names or terms affixed to representations – with the outside world itself. It may be believed that early words were the names of sensible material objects and nothing more, but

> in that case, you must suppose the "sensible objects" themselves to have been something more; you must suppose that they were not, as they appear to be at present, isolated, or detached, from thinking and feeling. Afterwards, in the development of language and thought, these single meanings split up into contrasted pairs – the abstract and the concrete, particular and general, objective and subjective.

Barfield argues that throughout the prehistorical and historical course of the evolution of consciousness, the price paid for the development of human analytical power has been the loss by the perceiving ego of that experience of unity with the world outside, in the world of nature. Stages of the loss are registered in the history of language. Unconscious of relation – lacking the words to name it and thus call it into being – primal language reported that unity as direct perceptual experience. Concomitant with an increase in the awareness of separate phenomena, an awareness of things whose representational qualities were no longer realized, the ego's consciousness of the gap between the knower and the known intensified, culminating in the painful sense of a growing alienation that has marked the apprehension of the four last centuries. Adumbrations of primal unity still echo affectingly in antique forms of language. There still remain the ancient myths; modern consciousness, driven to inventing specious explanations for their power, remains ignorant that myths are in fact the "ghost of concrete meaning." These echoes aside, in the present time

> it is the language of poets, in so far as they create true metaphors, which must restore this unity conceptually, after it has been lost from perception. Thus, the "before-unapprehended" relationships of which Shelley spoke, are in a sense "forgotten" relationships. For though they were never yet apprehended, they were at one time seen. And imagination can see them again.

In aesthetic experience, Barfield holds, it does so with pleasure.

His 1952 preface to the second edition of *Poetic Diction* affirms that the book's intention was to present "not merely a theory of poetry, but a theory of knowledge." His epistemology had been born of his experience with English Romantic poets. Romanticism, however, had a philosophy as well as a literature, and his examination of its intellectual roots took him back to Johann Wolfgang von Goethe and to the German Idealists of the nineteenth century. As a consequence, he was more and more drawn to Coleridge's thinking, which had assimilated vitally the Idealism of the German school and – in its emphasis on the creative role of the imagination – had anticipated and shaped his own. Barfield's discovery of Rudolf Steiner permitted him to test his own inferentially developed ideas about "the point at which philosophy borders on psychology" against those of a thinker who claimed direct knowledge of an experience with a world that transcended the ordinarily perceived one. Steiner had elaborated his reflections on that experience into his voluminous teachings on spiritual science or anthroposophy which Barfield has described as "nothing less than Romanticism grown up."

Although his emphasis on the participation of the knower in the known may appeal to poststructuralist textual critics, it is not as a theorist or tactician of any particular school of literary criticism that Barfield makes his impact on the twentieth-century mind; it is as the projection of the living thought of both Steiner and Coleridge. In his philosophically oriented criticism, the mystically derived insight of Steiner is probed analytically and made available to the uninitiate; simultaneously, the driving originality of Coleridgean aesthetic thought on the polarity of imaginative experience and the need for at-oneness with nature is transformed into a challenging critique of modern science and theology.

Principal criticism

History in English Words, 1926
Poetic Diction: A Study in Meaning, 1928
Romanticism Comes of Age, 1944, revised 1966
Speaker's Meaning, 1967
What Coleridge Thought, 1971
"The Rediscovery of Meaning" and Other Essays, 1977

Other major works and literary forms

Though he presents "a felt change in consciousness" effected by aesthetic contact with poetry as his intellectual starting point, Owen Barfield's ideas on literature to a considerable extent derive from – are really a by-product of – his philosophical understanding. Attempting, therefore, to place his published works into the usual categories – literary theory, psychology, philosophy, or history – yields more than the usual misleading arbitrariness. Listed above are books in which his primary, though not exclusive, subjects are language, imagination, and meaning, that is, the individual's experience of conscious knowing. The two collections *Romanticism Comes of Age* (1944, revised 1966) and *"The Rediscovery of Meaning" and Other Essays* (1977) contain essays that explore language-triggered aesthetic and epistemological experience. They also contain much more. Spanning forty years of reflection, these essays illuminate from different angles Barfield's concept of the role of the imagination in the evolution of human consciousness, and the consequences of that evolution on the understanding of physical nature, philosophically conceived reality, time, and history.

From the same viewpoint, *Saving the Appearances: A Study in Idolatry* (1957) examines provocatively the premises of post-Renaissance Western science. *Worlds Apart: A Dialogue of the 1960s* (1963) and *Unancestral Voice* (1965), both modeled loosely on Plato's dialogues, reflect on among other things the modern individual's difficulty in integrating perceived meanings into patterns of philosophical or theological knowledge. *History, Guilt, and Habit* (1979) returns to the exploration of the central question in which all of Barfield's intellectual interests have been rooted – the meaning of human experience in time.

NOVEL
This Ever Diverse Pair, 1950 (as G. A. L. Burgeon)

PLAY
A Poetic Drama in Four Acts, 1983

NONFICTION
Saving the Appearances: A Study in Idolatry, 1957
Worlds Apart: A Dialogue of the 1960s, 1963
Unancestral Voice, 1965
History, Guilt, and Habit, 1979

CHILDREN'S LITERATURE
The Silver Trumpet, 1925, 1986

Further reading

Adey, Lionel. *C. S. Lewis's "Great War" with Owen Barfield*, 1978.
Fulweiler, Howard W. "The Other Missing Link: Owen Barfield and the Scientific Imagination," in *Renascence: Essays on Value in Literature*. 46, no. 1 (1993), pp. 39–55.
Grant, Patrick. "Belief in Thinking: Owen Barfield and Michael Polanyi," in *Six Modern Authors and Problems of Belief*, 1979.
——. "Owen Barfield as Literary Man and Anthroposophist," in *Seven: An Anglo-American Literary Review*. III (1982), pp. 113–125.
Kranidas, Thomas, and Jeanne Clayton Hunter. "Introduction" in *A Barfield Sampler*, 1994.
Mood, John J. "Poetic Language and Primal Thinking: A Study of Barfield, Wittgenstein, and Heidegger," in *Encounter*. XXVI (August, 1965), pp. 417–433.
Morris, Francis J., and Ronald C. Wendling. "Coleridge and 'the Great Divide' between C. S. Lewis and Owen Barfield," in *Studies in the Literary Imagination*. 22, no. 2 (1989), pp. 149–159.
Potts, Donna. *Howard Nemerov and Objective Idealism: The Influence of Owen Barfield*, 1994.
Reilly, R. J. *Romantic Religion: A Study of Barfield, Lewis, Williams, and Tolkien*, 1971.
Sugerman, Shirley, ed. *Evolution of Consciousness: Studies in Polarity*, 1976.
Tennyson, G. B. "Owen Barfield and the Rebirth of Meaning," in *The Southern Review*. V (January, 1969), pp. 42–57.

FRANCIS J. MORRIS

See also British Literary Theory: Twentieth Century; Lewis

Roland Barthes

French writer and cultural critic

Born: Cherbourg, France; November 12, 1915
Died: Paris, France; March 26, 1980

Biography

Roland Barthes was born on November 12, 1915, in Cherbourg, France. At the age of nine, he moved with his mother to Paris. After he completed his *baccalauréat* in 1934, his studies were interrupted by the onset of tuberculosis. For more than a decade, illness became a way of life. In the sanatorium, Barthes read, studied, and formed stimulating friendships.

Shortly after his release in 1945, he taught French in Romania and later in Egypt, where he met A. J. Greimas, who introduced him to modern linguistics. Returning to Paris, Barthes published *Writing Degree Zero* in 1953, thus launching his career as an iconoclast and champion of the avant-garde. Subsequently, he published a series of essays on contemporary culture as well as articles on the New Novel and other literary subjects. These were then collected in *Mythologies* and *Critical Essays* and marked the beginning of his work in semiology, the science of signs.

When Barthes applied his methodology to classical literature in *On Racine*, he sparked a controversy which brought him to the forefront of the French intellectual scene. He became the object of an attack by Raymond Picard, a traditional academic, who made Barthes the symbol of all that seemed radical and irreverent in the new criticism. Barthes responded with *Criticism and Truth*, in which he justified a structuralist science of literature. By the late 1960s, structuralism had become an established method of literary study, and Barthes one of the most sought-after of French intellectuals.

At this point Barthes began to move away from structuralism, and his next works earned for him a reputation as a versatile writer. In 1976 he became chair of literary semiology at the Collège de France, a position he held until his death in 1980 from injuries suffered when he was struck by a van.

Influence

Although any label applied to the elusive Barthes can represent only a moment in his varied career, he is best known as a French structuralist. The goal of the structuralist's activity, according to Barthes, is to reconstitute the literary work in order to reveal its rules of functioning, the set of conventions that make meaning possible. This was a radical departure from traditional criticism with all that it took for granted about the fullness of the literary work and its plenitude of meaning. Barthes proclaimed the "death of the author" and advocated an "emptiness of language." His was a controversial position: a measure of his influence in literary studies has been the resistance his ideas have encountered, particularly in Great Britain and the United States, where structuralist studies of literature have been viewed as dangerously antihumanistic. Nevertheless, Barthes permanently altered the status of literary criticism by calling attention to how naively its practitioners have relied on "what-goes-without-saying."

As the primary spokesperson of the *nouvelle critique* of the 1950s and 1960s, Barthes furthered the cause of literary modernism. By using works of avant-garde writers such as Alain Robbe-Grillet, Michel Butor, and Philippe Sollers to illustrate certain exemplary characteristics of contemporary literature and by praising their resistance to reading, he did much to contribute to the critical acceptance of experimental fiction.

Analysis

Possibly the best account of the successive enthusiasms of Barthes' career as a literary theorist is offered by the critic himself in his book *Roland Barthes by Roland Barthes*, wherein he reflects on the three major moments in his career: his transformation from mythologist to semiologist/structuralist to self-proclaimed hedonist. One factor remains constant, however, throughout these metamorphoses, and that is a necessity to avoid orthodoxy (what he calls *doxa*). This imperative has its origins, not simply in a desire to be different, but in the view of literature advanced in Barthes' earliest works, specifically *Writing Degree Zero* and *Critical Essays*.

To some extent, Barthes' *Writing Degree Zero* answers a statement that Jean-Paul Sartre made on the purpose of literature in *Qu'est-ce que la littérature?* (1947; *What Is Literature?*, 1949). In that work, Sartre deplores the excesses of modernist writing, which he calls a "cancer of words." He insists that literature has a moral obligation of political commitment. The mission of the writer, he states, is to bear witness to the world in transparent prose that is engaged with reality. In such writing, words should be used to reveal the world and not to call attention to themselves. Barthes, on the other hand, denies the possibility of a transparent prose. He sees all literary language as an engagement with the institution of literature, which is one of the ways culture orders the world. Consequently, writing promotes a myth of literature. It is the moral obligation of committed literature to demystify itself by pointing out its own artifice, indicating the arbitrariness of the sign. Anything else, in Barthes' terms, is existential bad faith. The best literature, then, is self-reflexive, contending with itself as literature. In a neutral, "zero degree" of writing, it points to its own surface and makes no pretense of depth. Its motto, Barthes proposes, should be *Larvatus prodeo* (I advance indicating my mask).

This nonreferential writing is a marginal activity, an exercise in negation tending toward silence and seeking a promised land where literature is no longer necessary. It aims to destroy itself as a language object and exists only as "the figure of its own problem." Literature is truth, Barthes concedes, but its truth lies in asking real questions to which it is powerless to respond. As examples of authors who achieve a problematic mode of writing, Barthes cites Gustave Flaubert's consciousness of fabrication, Marcel Proust's postponement of literature by endless declaration of an intention to write, Stéphane Mallarmé's identification of literature and the theory of literature, the Surrealists' multiplication of the meaning of the word object, and Alain Robbe-Grillet's neutrality of language.

Barthes dreams of a world which would be "exempt from meaning." The image he calls domination and death, the novel an intentional murder. Even antiliterature, however, is not permanently exempt from meaning and order, as it eventually represents a new meaning and a new tradition. The result: a new flight, a new trajectory. If today's antiliterature is tomorrow's orthodoxy, a paradox Barthes acknowledges, the irreverent criticism of the moment often becomes the gospel of the future. Keenly aware of that, Barthes left his projects somewhat incomplete in favor of new perspectives – many of which were inherent in his work from the beginning.

The urge, so apparent in Barthes' early work, to demythologize literature and expose its underlying assumptions found fuller expression in *Mythologies*. This work, although mainly concerned with contemporary cultural phenomena, illuminates in retrospect some of Barthes' previous statements on literary history and his arguments for a neutral mode of writing. A myth, according to Barthes, operates by confusing nature and history. It thus translates bourgeois norms, which belong to culture, to self-evident laws of nature, thereby reinforcing social stereotypes and making them appear inevitable. These myths, masquerading as "what-goes-without-saying," conceal an ideology. At that time, Barthes believed that an intellectual could take political action by exposing these myths as delusions. Hence the position on literature that informs *Mythologies*: writing promotes a myth of literature which can have social significance. Seeking a tool for exposing and understanding how myth functions, Barthes turned to semiology, the science of signs, and the related practice of structuralism.

It was as a structuralist that Barthes had the greatest impact on the practice of literary criticism. During the 1960s he was the most influential proponent of this controversial method of literary study, which originated with the linguistic theories advanced by Ferdinand de Saussure at the beginning of the century. As an early advocate of a science of signs, Barthes found useful Saussure's distinction between *langue*, the linguistic system, and *parole*, the individual utterances of a language. This model allows the structuralist to reconstruct the system of distinctions and conventions that give meaning to cultural phenomena. Barthes explains the "structuralist activity" as "a mode of thought (or a 'poetics') which seeks less to assign completed meanings to the objects it discovers than to know how meaning is possible." Structural analysis of literature does not elucidate the text; rather, it seeks to comprehend the work's system, its rules of functioning.

It is easy to understand how this becomes for Barthes a moral goal, given his inclination to demystify. It is also clear just how radical such an activity might appear to more traditional critics. For one thing, structural analysis refuses to look for secret meanings or to explain the text. The implications of such denial of meaning are revolutionary, as Barthes recognizes in claiming that the refusal to

> assign a "secret" an ultimate meaning, to the text (and to the world as text), liberates what may be called an anti-theological activity, an activity that is truly revolutionary since to refuse to fix meaning

> is, in the end, to refuse God and his hypostases – reason, science, law.

Closely related to this refusal of God is Barthes' announcement of the death of the author. The reader now becomes the producer rather than the consumer of the text; the author is no longer the source of meaning. In *S/Z*, Barthes defines two types of texts, the readerly (*lisible*) and the writerly (*scriptible*). The readerly (or readable) text is the one that is easy to read: predictable, unself-conscious, transparent. It meets expectations. The writerly text must be composed as it is read, thus calling attention to the structuring activity of the reader. Structuralism examines what makes texts intelligible to a range of readers in various eras.

To Barthes, "dominant ideology" translates to "arrogant ideology," and his structuralist poetics scored a major victory (a troublesome idea to him) against the dominant ideology of the time. Traditional academic critics were understandably reluctant to give up the right to confer meaning on texts. Many of these critics resisted avant-garde literature, together with Barthes' irreverent speculations. In France, at least, there was an uneasy coexistence of new criticism and traditional scholarship – until Barthes' application of his methods to the works of Jean Racine in *On Racine* and his publication abroad of articles defaming dull academic criticism initiated a public debate.

Using Barthes as a scapegoat, Raymond Picard, a Sorbonne professor, protested the new criticism in *Nouvelle Critique ou nouvelle imposture?* (1965; *New Criticism or New Fraud?*, 1969). Barthes responded with a polemical book, highly unusual for him, entitled *Criticism and Truth*. Mockingly calling the academic criticism "old criticism" and accusing it of *a-symbolia*, he raises the same objections that he previously used against myth: the possession of a hidden agenda. Presuming to speak for the reader, traditional criticism, in Barthes' view, does not recognize the possibility that a text can have multiple meanings. Arguing, for example, that Racine is Racine, such criticism takes the what-goes-without-saying stance that Barthes so deplores. In this way, it pretends to objectivity while disguising dogma as common sense. Other forms of criticism, Barthes contends, admit their ideological allegiance (Marxism, semiology, psychoanalysis, phenomenology). The unacknowledged ideology of academic criticism is the desire to preserve the status quo, bourgeois consensus, popular opinion. Barthes' arguments were convincing to the extent that structuralism became not only acceptable but moreover the latest rage in academic circles – in short, the new *doxa*. It was then time for him to find a more marginal and less scientific approach to literary studies. Inquiring in *Roland Barthes by Roland Barthes*, "Who is still a structuralist?" he developed an ironic, poststructuralist attitude toward his former activity and proceeded to explore an aesthetics of pleasure in *The Pleasure of the Text*. This was perhaps the logical outcome of the prominence given to the reader's involvement in the text in structuralist criticism.

Barthes' revival of hedonism provided him with a new means of challenging intellectual orthodoxy, since whatever pleasure a reader could garner from a text was typically of no concern to the academy. In *The Pleasure of the Text*, Barthes outlines a theory of textual pleasure, converting the text into an object of pleasure, like any other, and abolishing the differences between the practical and the contemplative life. Each reader, or consumer, according to Barthes' typology, finds his own brand of textual pleasure. For example, the paranoid is a deep interpreter, the fetishist a seeker of fragments, the hysteric an enthusiast without critical detachment. The analysis of reading pleasure leads Barthes to posit an opposition between two types of texts, based on the reader's enjoyment. He makes a distinction between two kinds of pleasure: *plaisir*, which is the pleasure, comfort, and fulfillment that come from the readerly text, and *jouissance*, the rapture or ecstasy that proceeds from the text that imposes discomfort and unsettles the reader. One might expect Barthes to come out on the side of *jouissance*, in keeping with his earlier distinction between readerly and writerly works. Instead, he contends that textual pleasure results from finding ecstatic moments (loss, destruction) in a comfortable text, and in rendering postmodern works sufficiently readable for them to convey their sense of disruption. Barthes suggests here that neither culture nor its destruction is erotic, but the gap between them excites. He even goes so far as to suggest a theory of boredom, which he calls the threshold to ecstasy.

To assess Roland Barthes' lasting contribution to critical theory is to contribute unavoidably to a myth of Barthes. Most important, perhaps, he has enlivened the dialogue. His finest achievement is not an authoritative one. What Barthes does best is to challenge authority, and he does so by writing, like the literary works he praises, in the gap between culture and its destruction. It is, in some sense, a gap of his own making.

Ironically, a measure of his powerful influence has been, on one side, the angry reception his ideas have often encountered. Both imitated and scorned, he is seldom ignored. A testimony to his notoriety was a book published in 1978, *Le Roland-Barthes sans peine*, a parody which claimed to teach the reader how to speak Roland-Barthes in eighteen simple lessons. To the academic establishment, his theories are often tantamount to heresy, as the following assessment by Graham Hough shows:

> "Faut-il brûler Roland Barthes?" Surely not: even ten years ago when the question was first raised no one really wanted an auto-da-fé, and by the time Barthes's heresies fused into a dogma he had become necessary – as the archetype of a left-wing, left-bank, post-Sartrean orthodoxy, rumour of which has spread by now to the plains of Iowa and the slopes of Mount Fuji.

On the other hand, Susan Sontag called Barthes "France's most important writer-intellectual since Sartre," and Wayne Booth concedes that he is "the man who may well be the strongest influence on American criticism today." That influence has been to radicalize the discipline in a movement against meaning, against interpretation.

The main source of Barthes' influence has been structuralism, despite his attempted abdication as its leading advocate once it became a tradition in its own right. In his hands it became a tool for calling into question the way cultural events, and literature in particular, have meaning. The long-standing objection to structuralism has been its dehumanization of literature and its presumed refusal to make moral judgments. Yet, for Barthes, the denunciation of myths is itself a moral activity. His critical practice is to re-humanize the text by removing the authority of the author (and the critic as his interpreter) and emphasizing the experience of the reader.

Through his critical theorizing, Barthes also helped create a climate for the appreciation of avant-garde texts. These works are themselves often engaged in the very structuralist activity Barthes advocates – questioning the way in which they construct meaning. Barthes applauds those postmodern writers who function as critics within their works, thus blurring the distinction between "critical" and "creative" writing. Barthes himself is, in this respect, the quintessential postmodern writer.

Principal criticism

Le Degré zéro de l'écriture, 1953 (*Writing Degree Zero*, 1967)
Michelet, par lui-même, 1954 (*Michelet*, 1986)
Mythologies, 1957 (English translation, 1972)
Sur Racine, 1963 (*On Racine*, 1964)
Essais critiques, 1964 (*Critical Essays*, 1972)
La Tour Eiffel, 1964 (*The Eiffel Tower and Other Mythologies*, 1979)
Éléments de sémiologie, 1964 (*Elements of Semiology*, 1967)
Critique et vérité, 1966 (*Criticism and Truth*, 1987)
Système de la mode, 1967 (*The Fashion System*, 1983)
S/Z, 1970 (English translation, 1974)
L'Empire des signes, 1970 (*Empire of Signs*, 1982)
Sade, Fourier, Loyola, 1971 (English translation, 1976)
Nouveaux essais critiques, 1972 (*New Critical Essays*, 1980)
Le Plaisir du texte, 1973 (*The Pleasure of the Text*, 1975)
Roland Barthes par Roland Barthes, 1975 (*Roland Barthes by Roland Barthes*, 1977)
Fragments d'un discours amoureux, 1977 (*A Lover's Discourse: Fragments*, 1978)
Image-Music-Text, 1977
Sollers écrivain, 1979
La Chambre claire: Note sur la photographie, 1980 (*Camera Lucida: Reflections on Photography*, 1981)
Le Grain de la voix: Entretiens, 1962–1980, 1981 (*The Grain of the Voice: Interviews, 1962–1980*, 1985)
A Roland Barthes Reader, 1982 (Susan Sontag, editor)
L'Obvie et l'obtus, 1982 (*The Responsibility of Forms*, 1985)
Le Bruissement de la langue, 1984 (*The Rustle of Language*, 1986)
The Semiotic Challenge, 1988

Other literary forms

Many of Roland Barthes' works resist classification by genre, in keeping with his unorthodox critical perspective. In this regard, it should be noted here that several of the books listed above exemplify innovative applications of his critical methodology. Barthes' view of literature as one sign system among many allows him to extend his critical philosophy to cultural phenomena as diverse as wrestling, food, automobiles, and plastic in *Mythologies* and fashion advertising in *The Fashion System*. Following a trip to Japan, he wrote *Empire of Signs*. Sometimes classified as travel literature, with observations on chopsticks, sukiyaki, and transvestism, the book is, on another level, a critical "reading" of Japan. Barthes has also written meditations on photography and on the language of love. One of his most unusual projects is his "autobiography," *Roland Barthes by Roland Barthes*. Challenging the conventions of the genre, it is a critique of the writing self and also, as the author warns in an epigraph, a fiction, like all autobiography.

Further reading

Burke, Sean. *The Death and Return of the Author: Criticism and Subjectivity in Barthes, Foucault and Derrida*, 1992.
Culler, Jonathan. *Barthes*, 1983.
Lavers, Annette. *Roland Barthes: Structuralism and After*, 1982.
Lombardo, Patrizia. *The Three Paradoxes of Roland Barthes*, 1989.
Moriarty, Michael. *Roland Barthes*, 1991.
Sontag, Susan. "Writing Itself: On Roland Barthes," in *A Roland Barthes Reader*, 1982.
Thody, Philip. *Roland Barthes: A Conservative Estimate*, 1977.
Ungar, Steven. *Roland Barthes: The Professor of Desire*, 1983.
Wasserman, George R. *Roland Barthes*, 1981.

Barbara L. Hussey

See also Derrida; French Literary Theory: Twentieth Century; Intertextuality; Saussure; Semiotics; Structuralism

Matsuo Bashō

Japanese poet, traveler, and teacher of poetry

Born: In or near Ueno, Japan; 1644
Died: Ōsaka, Japan; November 28, 1694

Biography

Matsuo Bashō was born in 1644, in or near Ueno, in Iga Province, Japan (now part of Mie Prefecture). He himself adopted the nickname "Bashō" ("banana plant") after he had moved into a hut which had a banana tree growing alongside it. As a child he had been called Kinsaku, but when he came of age he was designated Matsuo Munefusa. He was the son of a low-ranking samurai (a member of the military caste). Evidently intending to follow in his father's footsteps, he entered the service of a higher-ranking local samurai, Todo Shinshichiro, becoming a page or personal attendant to the lord's son, Yoshitada, who was about the same age as Bashō. When not engaged in the practice of arms, Yoshitada was fond of writing the short Japanese poem called the *haiku* and had a "*haiku* name," Sengin. (The *haiku* is a three-line poem of 5–7–5 syllable lines, and although short it is highly suggestive in symbolic meaning.) Bashō was thus introduced to poetry, and he often joined his master in poetic composition, particularly in writing the linked *haiku* verses called *haikai*.

When Yoshitada died prematurely in 1666, Bashō was deeply unnerved. He resigned his position as page and began roaming the Kyōto area to investigate fashionable life in the capital, meanwhile zealously continuing to write *haiku*. In 1672, encouraged by the recognition he had received as a result of his *haiku* in the collection *Kai ōi* (1672; covering shells), Bashō moved to Edo (now Tokyo), evidently in search of job opportunities. Eventually, while working at odd jobs, he succeeded in establishing himself as a teacher of *haikai*, adopting the name Tōsei. He also became attracted to Zen Buddhism and began to study Zen under the priest Butchō (1642–1715). By 1680 Tōsei had enough good students to publish a volume called *Tōsei montei dokugin mijihkasem* (best poems of Tōsei's twenty disciples). He was, finally, making a name for himself as a *haiku* master. Eventually, however, he came to believe that his life, although simple, was "too worldly," and he began to practice his Zen Buddhism more assiduously. Zen advocated strict morality, rigorous self-discipline and self-denial, and meditation ("zen" means "meditation"), in an effort to reach a higher spiritual state in which one might achieve the condition of *hannya*, the highest form of intuition humans are capable of, and by which they are able to come directly into contact with basic reality itself.

Later in the year he acquired the small hut in the Fukagawa district of Edo which had the banana plant growing next to it. At this time Bashō and his disciples published an anthology of verse called *Minashigun* (1683; empty chestnuts). However, its general tone is hardly acceptable, for it suggests spiritual uncertainty and a strange urge to combat conventions by avoiding the hackneyed or commonplace. This set of mind eventually took the physical form of random travels. It appears that in these exercises Bashō hoped to regain both spiritual confidence and poetic discipline at one and the same time.

In the fall of 1684 Bashō left Edo and traveled westward along the southern coast to his native town of Ueno, where he arrived about a month later. At Nagaya he led a team of poets in composing five volumes of *haikai* (linked *haiku* verses) which bore the title *Fuyu no hi* (1684; the winter sun). Then he visited Nara, Ōgaki, Ōsaka, and Kyōto, returning to Edo the following summer. This journey resulted in Bashō's journal *Nozarashi kikō* (1685; *The Records of a Weather-Exposed Skeleton*, 1966).

In the fall of 1687 Bashō traveled to Kashima, a trip that resulted in a short travel diary, *Kashina kikō* (1687; *A Visit to Kashima Shrine*, 1966). This work shows Bashō cultivating the aesthetic ideal of *fūryū*, or "elegant artistry." Afterwards he set out on another long journey westward. This long trip of some ten months resulted in two more poetic diaries: *Oi no kobumi* (1690–1691; *The Records of a Travel-Worn Satchel*, 1966) and *Sarashina kikō* (1688; *A Visit to Sarashina Village*, 1966).

Bashō's last journey was a long trek to the most undeveloped part of Japan at that time – the northern area of Honshū. He made this trip of some 1,500 miles in a hundred and fifty six days, starting from Edo in the late spring of 1689. It was on this journey that he apparently evolved his famous aesthetic principle of *sabi*, or the scene of desolation that is endowed with the beauty of loneliness and quiet, introduced in terms of a "positive ideal." Although this aesthetic ideal was evidently originated by the early Kamakura *waka* poet Fujiwara Shunzei (c. 1175–?1250), it was especially cultivated by Bashō. The result of this particular journey was Bashō's best-known work, the masterly *Oku no Itosomichi* (1694; *The Narrow Road to the Deep North*, 1966), though it is relatively short and contains only about fifty of Bashō's fine *haiku*.

Influence

When Bashō died in Ōsaka, central Honshū, in 1694 of some sort of stomach ailment, he had, so it is said, around 2,000 students. He was the grand master of *haiku* and was considered responsible for having elevated it into a major art form. His impact on both the writing and the interpretation of *haiku* has been profound, his works bringing a new range and subtlety to Japanese poetics.

Among the chief members of Bashō's school were Yamaguchi Sodō (1642–1716), Enomoto Kikaku (1661–1707), and Naitō Josō (1661–1704). Several important *haiku* writers appeared during the late Tokugawa Period (1600–1868), also known as the Edo Period. Among these writers, the two most important were Yosa Buson (1716–1781) and Kobayashi Issa (1763–1828). Buson, considered a "flawless technician," endowed the *haiku* with a romantic quality by virtue of his aristocratic distinction. Issa, on the other hand, gave the *haiku* the accents of the common people because he loved the small and humble things of the world.

The status of the *haiku* as a lyric form was raised to a new level in the late nineteenth century and the early twentieth century not only in Japan but also in Britain and the United States. In about 1883, a young Japanese poet living in Tokyo named Masaoka Shiki (1867–1902) began to study the *haiku* seriously and soon began to write in this form. His aim was the reform of the *haiku*. He disapproved of the bulk of Bashō's *haiku*, and advocated freedom of diction and subject matter, insisting that the *haiku* be treated as serious literature. He stressed the importance of "realism" or "immediacy," and called this quality *shasei*, "a sketch from life." He founded the *haiku* magazine *Hototogisu*, and in time came to be recognized as one of the four masters of *haiku* along with Bashō, Buson, and Issa. One of his disciples, Takahama Kyoshi, became the most influential *haiku* poet of his day.

The "new" *haiku* soon attracted the attention of poets and critics in Britain and the United States and started the poetic movement Imagism, which began in about 1909 and lasted until about 1917. Imagism was strongly influenced by the aesthetic theories of T. E. Hume and the enthusiasm of Ezra Pound, who, with F. S. Flint, produced an "imagist manifesto," which was published in *Poetry Magazine* in 1913. This movement was an attempt to revitalize the language of poetry. Hume and Flint were English, as was the poet Richard Aldington. The American poets in the Imagist movement were Pound, T. S. Eliot, John Gould Fletcher, Hilda Doolittle (H. D.), Amy Lowell, William Carlos Williams, Carl Sandburg, and Wallace Stevens.

Analysis

The first poem Bashō composed in his "new style" was the now well-known "On a bare bough":

On a bare bough	*Kareeda ni*
A crow is perched–	*Karasu no tomarikeri*
Autumn evening.	*Aki no kure.*

But Bashō considered another *haiku* the "standard" for his "new style":

The old pond –	*Furuike ya*
A frog leaps in,	*Kawazu tobikomu*
And a splash!	*Mizu no oto.*

However, two other famous *haiku* of his may best be used to illustrate not only some of the essential aesthetic features of Bashō's style, but particularly its great power of suggestion in terms of cultural factors:

Altar of Benkei!	*Oi mo tachi*
Yoshitsune's sword! . . . oh fly	*Mo satsuki ni kazare*
The carp of May!	*Kami-nobori!*

and:

The summer grasses grow.	*Natsu gusa ya*
Of mighty warriors' splendid dreams	*Tsuwamonodomo ga*
The afterglow.	*Yume no ato.*

These *haiku* were the result of Bashō's visit to the village of Hiraizirmi, in northern Honshū. On this occasion the villagers were preparing to celebrate the national holiday called the Boys' Festival (*Tango no Sakku*). This day honors Japan's samurai hero Minamoto no Yoshitsune. From tall flagpoles in the village flutter great paper streamers made in the shape of carp, which are symbols of strength and perseverance. In alcoves in their homes, the villagers set out samurai dolls, miniature armor, samurai swords, and a few family heirlooms.

The tragic hero Minamoto no Yoshitsune (1159–1189) was the son of Minamoto no Moshitomo and the half-brother of Minamoto no Yoritomo, by a different mother. He was a principal figure in the Taira–Minamoto war, but in 1160, after the victory of the Taira clan over his own, Yoshitsune was exiled to the Chuzonji Temple. In 1180, when Yoshitsune heard that Yoritomo had begun to attack the Taira, he raised an army, joined the members of the Minamoto, and soon distinguished himself by his gallantry and by the bold strategies he employed in achieving his victories over the Taira.

However, when the ex-emperor Go-Shirakawa rewarded Yoshitsune handsomely for his endeavors, Yoritomo became madly jealous and henceforth sought to destroy his half-brother. Thus Yoshitsune spent the last years of his life as a fugitive from the envious Yoritomo. He was finally tracked down at his Koromogawa residence by a force of 20,000 warriors. Yoshitsune's faithful retainers Musashibō Benkei, the legendary warrior-monk, and Ise no Yoshimori, a crafty and short-tempered man, fought off the massive attack with superhuman effort to gain time for Yoshitsune, who inside the castle sought an honorable death by means of *seppu'ku* (ritual disembowelment at one's own hand). Thus Yoshitsune died, leaving the task of killing his wife and two children to the faithful Ise no Yoshimori. Prior to his suicide, Yoshitsune recited part of the Buddhist text the *Lotus Sutra*.

In his travel diary Bashō tells how he climbed up to the Takudate Castle on the hill overlooking Hiraizirmi. Also, in the "Golden Temple of Chuzonji" he views Yoshitsune's famous two-handed sword as well as Benkei's portable altar. He also remarks on "the carp of May," since these fish symbolize "the strength and endurance" of the samurai class.

What is clear from this account is that for Bashō the *haiku* could be far more than a concentrated image of a scene (a common assumption in the West); it was a poetic form that could bring together a wide range of social and cultural references. Bashō's approach to the *haiku* also highlights several technical features of the form. Apart from the *haiku* structure of three lines of 5–7–5 syllables, it was customary, for example, to employ a "season word" (*kigo*). Secondly, the poet might exploit a "pillow word" (*makura-ji*), the name of a famous place, person, or thing which has particular resonance. Finally, there is the use of the "cutting word" (*kireji*), a word which indicates a pause within the *haiku*. For instance, in the phrase "The old pond" (*Furuike ya*), the word "*ya*" is a "cutting word."

When Pound and Flint recognized the value of the *haiku* to invigorate Western poetry and promoted the Imagist movement, Pound defined an "image" as "that which presents an intellectual and emotional complex in an instant of time." And Flint set forth the following rules for the new movement: "Direct treatment of the 'thing' whether subjective or objective; to use absolutely no word that did not contribute to the presentation; as regarding rhythm: to compose in sequence of the musical phrase, not in the sequence of the metronome."

Major works

POETRY
Kai ōi, 1672 (covering shells)
Tōsei montei dokugin mijihkasem, 1680 (best poems of Tōsei's twenty disciples)
Minashigun, 1683 (empty chestnuts)
Fuyu no hi, 1684 (the winter sun)
Oku no Itosomichi, 1694 (*The Narrow Road to the Deep North*, 1966)

NONFICTION
Nozarashi kikō, 1685 (*The Records of a Weather-Exposed Skeleton*, 1966)
Kashina kikō, 1687 (*A Visit to Kashima Shrine*, 1966)
Sarashina kikō, 1688 (*A Visit to Sarashina Village*, 1966)
Oi no kobumi, 1690–1691 (*The Records of a Travel-Worn Satchel*, 1966)

Further reading

Aitken, Robert. *A Zen Wave: Bashō's Haiku and Zen*, 1978, reprinted 1985.
Barthes, Roland. *Empire of Signs*, 1982. Translated by Richard Howard.
Bashō, Matsuo. *Bashō's "The Narrow Road to the Far North" and Selected Haiku*, 1974. Translated by Nobuyuk Yuasa.
Blyth, Robert H. *A History of Haiku*, 1963–1964 (2 volumes).
Nitobé, Imago. *Bushidō: The Soul of Japan*, 1905.
Suzuki, Daisetz. *Zen and Japanese Buddhism*, 1938.
——. *Japanese Spirituality*, 1972. Translated by Norman Waddell.
Uedo, Makoto. *Matsuo Bashō*, 1970.
Varley, Paul. *Warriors of Japan as Portrayed in the War Tales*, 1994.

RICHARD P. BENTON

See also Japanese Literary Theory; Kamo No Mabuchi; Motoori Norinaga

Georges Bataille

French writer and editor

Born: Puy-de-Dôme, France; September 10, 1897
Died: Paris, France; July 8, 1962

Biography

Georges Bataille was born on September 10, 1897, in Puy-de-Dôme, near Reims, to a family of peasant stock. His father was blind and suffered paralysis in 1900. On the outbreak of World War I, Bataille fled with his mother and brother to his mother's family in Cantal. He was drafted in 1916 but was discharged a year later owing to ill health. He embraced Catholicism in 1914 and contemplated the priesthood, but abandoned his faith in 1920. In 1918 his first publication, *Notre Dame de Rheims*, appeared in pamphlet form, the same year in which he entered the School of Paleography and Library Science. On his graduation he was appointed a Fellow at the School of Advanced Hispanic Studies in Madrid, Spain. An important formative event at this time was his initiation to the spectacle of bullfighting. He witnessed the death of Granero, one of Madrid's most popular matadors.

In 1922 he was appointed librarian at the Bibliothèque Nationale, where he was a medieval specialist. In 1924 his involvement with the Surrealist movement began through his friendship with Michel Leiris. While his friendship with Leiris was to be an enduring one, his relationship with André Breton, the main spokesperson for Surrealism, would prove conflictual. He shared the Surrealists' interest in Sigmund Freud, and in 1927 he entered into psychoanalysis.

Bataille's first novel, *L'Histoire de l'oeil* (*The Story of the Eye*), variously described as erotic or pornographic, was published in 1928 under the pseudonym of Lord Auch. In the same year his interest in anthropology resulted in the publication of a review of a Paris exhibition of pre-Colombian artifacts. It was also in this year that he married his first wife, Sylvia Maklès. Their daughter, Laurence, was born in 1931.

In 1934 he attended a course on Hegelian phenomenology given by Alexandre Kojève which helped him to formulate his own interpretation of G. W. F. Hegel. That year also saw the beginning of a liaison with Colette Peignot, who wrote under the pseudonym of Laure. She notably inspired the character of Dirty in the semi-autobiographical novel *Bleu du ciel* (*Blue of Noon*), which was written in the 1930s but was not published until 1957. Her death in 1938 precipitated in Bataille a profound depression and a subsequent interest in yoga and meditation.

During the 1930s Bataille's interest in the sacred led to him setting up, with Michel Leiris and Roger Caillois, the secret society called Acéphale (1935), which purported to explore the place of the sacred in the contemporary world, and the College of Sociology (1937), which offered a public forum for the concerns of Acéphale, attracting the participation of many of the foremost intellectuals of the day. Both enterprises were disbanded with the advent of the war.

Ill health was a recurrent feature of Bataille's life, and in 1942 a bout of tuberculosis forced him to relinquish his post at the Bibliothèque Nationale. However he continued to publish extensively, and 1943 saw the publication of *L'Expérience intérieure* (*Inner Experience*), while another major work, *La Part maudite* (*The Accursed Share*), appeared in 1949. He also founded the review *Critique* in

1946, and remained its editor-in-chief until his death. He married his second wife, Diane Kotchoubey, in 1951 (their daughter, Julie, was born three years earlier), and published another major work, *L'Érotisme* (*Eroticism*), in 1957. He died in Paris on July 8, 1962.

Influence

A major and controversial figure in the twentieth-century French intellectual field, Bataille produced a remarkably eclectic œuvre which is widely considered a fundamental influence on the most prominent intellectual movements of the latter part of the century. Informed by Friedrich Nietzsche and G. W. F. Hegel, by Émile Durkheim and Marcel Mauss, by Marxism and existentialism, by Surrealism, psychoanalysis, and mysticism, his writings embrace the fields of philosophy and religion, anthropology and sociology, history and economics, as well as literature and art history. The transgression (a key Bataillean term) of boundaries implied by his interdisciplinary approach has led to his being seen as a precursor of structuralism. His claim that a book is "communication" and the author "only a link among many different readings" anticipates Roland Barthes' "death of the author." His paradoxical philosophy based on a concept of un-knowing (*non-savoir*) which challenges the idea of philosophy as a quest for certain knowledge establishes a continuum from Nietzsche through to poststructuralism. Jacques Derrida's reading of Bataille in *L'Écriture et la différence* (1967; *Writing and Difference*, 1978) helped promote recognition of the importance of Bataille's influence.

While Bataille's relationship with Surrealism was not unproblematic, his principal affinity with that movement was his commitment to the spirit of revolt inherited from Arthur Rimbaud, evident in his exploration of the limits of experience, which has prompted comparisons with writers such as the Comte de Lautréamont, Antonin Artaud, and the Marquis de Sade. The legacy of Sade is most apparent in the erotic content of his novels. The question of eroticism informs all aspects of his œuvre, contributing significantly to making this a central, rather than marginalized, matter of intellectual inquiry. Although he did not formulate a "theory of the body" as such, his situating of the body at the core of experience, and hence at the heart of philosophical inquiry, has had extensive impact. Another crucial area of influence relates to the sacred as approached by the French sociologists, notably Durkheim and Mauss. In particular, Bataille's concern with the place of violence in religion has notably informed René Girard's *La Violence et le sacré* (1972; *Violence and the Sacred*, 1977).

Analysis

Having entertained thoughts of entering a seminary during his youth, Bataille went on to expound a philosophy that was vehemently anti-Christian, yet declared itself intensely religious. Jean-Paul Sartre described him as "*un nouveau mystique*." He combined the influence of Nietzsche with that of Gnostics, Christian mystics, and tantric scriptures, as well as Hegel and Marx, all of which he was reading in the early 1920s. His interest in mysticism is evident in his concept of "inner experience," with the fundamental difference that Bataille rejects the notion of transcendence. He views human beings as constituted of "base materialism" and rejects the body/spirit dichotomy. The body is the means through which we experience the world, and while religious mysticism offers communion with something exterior to ourselves, namely God, inner experience is "a voyage to the end of the possible of man," an exploration of the limits of human possibilities apprehended in experiences such as love, eroticism, inebriety, madness, abjection, or poetry. Christianity, he argues, denies the true nature of our existence by its privileging of spirit over body, which obscures the fact that our ultimate reality is death. Inner experience opens onto what Bataille terms "the impossible," that is, communication with the unknown, an intimation of what lies beyond the possibilities of human limits. It has been compared with the idea of "the Real" in the psychoanalytic theory of Jacques Lacan, whom Bataille knew well.

While contesting orthodox religion and the notion of God, Bataille was profoundly interested by the sacred of archaic societies which was the subject of study by the French sociologists. This was the "authentic sacred" which had violence at its very core, and whose ambiguous nature encompassed the holy and the horrific, epitomized by the act of sacrifice. In 1923 he was introduced to Marcel Mauss' *Essai sur le don* (*The Gift*), published that year. This work inspired the essay "La Notion de dépense," which appeared in *La Critique sociale* in 1933. Mauss' seminal analysis identified the pivotal role of gift-exchange in archaic societies, emphasizing that it was not merely an economic transaction but a fundamental constituent of the entire social order, whose equilibrium it ensured. Of particular interest to Bataille was Mauss' description of the Potlatch ritual of Native American tribes. This ritual, which interrupted the normal exchange procedure in a manner comparable to the archaic festival, involved the excessive giving of possessions by one subgroup, and prestige and social hierarchy were determined by the quantity given. Bataille formulated a theory of a "general economy" that focuses on excess and consumption, in contrast with the focus on production and the amassing of wealth that underpins the capitalist system (in its pre-consumer society stage of development). Consumption could be divided into two parts. The first corresponds to what was required for the provision of basic human needs. The other consists of a nonproductive expenditure (*dépense*) comparable with the excess of the Potlatch, which Bataille regards as a ritual enactment of collective expenditure. In his view, this expenditure or loss responds to a primary human need for release of vital energy by transgressing the bounds of utility. He identifies its occurrence in symbolic forms such as jewelry (which, clearly influenced by Freud, he equates with excrement, "accursed material" destined to be wasted), sacrifice, competitive games, sexual activity divorced from reproduction, as well as art, poetry, and music. However, since it was a competitive activity that required reciprocity, the Potlatch was not an instance of disinterested gift-giving. Making a bridge with Marxism, Bataille sees its competitive nature as an origin of the class system. If orthodox religion is seen to collude with the oppression of capitalism, the authentic sacred, centered as it is on the violence of sacrifice, counters the profane world of the utilitarian. As an instance of destruction, *dépense* is also an intimation of death, and sacrifice its most complete manifestation.

While the master/slave dialectic is fundamental to Bataille's socioeconomic analysis, he does not accept Hegel's argument that work can be liberating. On the contrary, it is primarily a form of enslavement, albeit necessary for the effective functioning of society. As a utilitarian activity, work belongs to the sphere of project, whereas its contrary, play, belongs to the realm of the immediate and permits access to what he terms "sovereignty." Bataille's key notion of sovereignty evolved from the starting point of Hegel's mastery. Derived from the Potlatch as well as the conspicuous consumption of the aristocratic, "sovereign" class of feudal society, the power the term denotes lies in the fact that it has no purpose beyond itself. This is the common ground of all the "heterogeneous" states or activities such as laughter, tears, play, poetry, anguish, violence, drunkenness, or eroticism that are anathema to the servitude of utility and project. Sovereignty belongs to the realm of chance and opens onto un-knowing and the limitless. It is the only hope for humankind, for whom there is no redemption. Sovereignty can only be attained in the immediacy of experience; once it becomes a project, it negates itself. It is, therefore, unremittingly elusive.

Acéphale and the College of Sociology sought to further the investigations into the sacred embarked upon by the French sociologists. Like Durkheim, Bataille considers religion to be inextricably bound up with society, but where Durkheim insists on the division between the sacred and the profane, Bataille sees a dialectic, interactive relationship. And whereas Mauss views the decline of the sacred in industrialized society as a welcome development, Bataille contends that it alienates us from nature and our profoundest religious propensities. Importantly, the "complicit" relationship between taboo and transgression is severed, as a result of which the former becomes associated with "good" and the latter with "evil," a duality that Bataille contests. In archaic societies, he explains, taboo did not impose an absolute prohibition but rather set a limit necessary for the efficient functioning of society, which in particular required its members to work. (The relationship between work and play is analogous with that of taboo and transgression.) These prohibitions were ritually broken during periods of festival, whereby transgression performed a regulatory function without which taboo could not exist. The act of sacrifice represents the acme of sacred violence. Akin to the lifting of taboo that occurs in times of war, it is a collective crime holding the community together and regulating collective violence. It is a dramatic representation of life's interdependence with death.

Eroticism is another sphere of activity that manifests the interdependence of life and death. Bataille speaks in terms of continuity and discontinuity; we are discontinuous beings whose existence ruptures the continuity that pre-existed us and will exist after our death. We are eternally torn between seeking to preserve our discontinuous identity while simultaneously driven by nostalgia for the lost continuity. Communication, a fundamental desire that defines us as social beings, is at odds with the impulse to preserve our identity, and thus always constitutes a rupture. As the most intense instance of fusion with the other, sexual union epitomizes the conflict. Eroticism, as distinct from reproduction, is a form of disorder combining ecstasy with anguish that calls humanity's being into question. Insofar as it offers a glimpse of the lost continuity, it may be said to open onto death. It represents a state beyond life and death, revealing their ultimate oneness. In this respect it shares an affinity with sacrifice.

The convergence of disciplines that characterizes Bataille's thinking is reflected in his approach to literature. In *La Littérature et le mal* (1957; *Literature and Evil*, 1973) he discusses a selection of writers – Emily Brontë, Charles Baudelaire, Jules Michelet, William Blake, the Marquis de Sade, Marcel Proust, Franz Kafka, and Jean Genet – who in various ways engage in the problematic of the ambiguity of the sacred and probe the limits of experience. He underscores the notion of literature as a mode of transgression and as a challenge to the orthodox view of morality, qualifying it as "dangerous" and "irresponsible." The complementary relationship between good and evil is a major issue at stake: in Brontë and Blake, for example, it is seen to attain a kind of purity. In his reading of Brontë's *Wuthering Heights* evil is found to be "not only the dream of the wicked: it is to some extent the dream of the good." Violence is a recuperation of the innocence and freedom of childhood, a sovereign state located in the realms of the impossible. Evil is a revolt against the constraints of adulthood or, in the case of Blake, the subservience of work. An overlap with Bataille's economic analysis occurs when he draws a distinction between evil as a disinterested attraction toward death that is tied up with passion, and evil that is motivated by self-interest, the former being equated with "the accursed share" of pure expenditure, and hence the destruction of sacrifice.

Like sacrifice, literature is for Bataille an instance of intense communication and destruction. Drama, both tragedy and comedy, he asserts, is rooted in ancient sacrificial practice. The states of anxiety it provokes, whether these produce laughter or tears, are instances of rupture that attest to the reality of death. Poetry is the most authentic and violent form of literature. Bataille distinguishes between the type of poetry that is constrained by the exigencies of meter and linguistic artifice and poetry such as that of Baudelaire or Rimbaud that challenges the confines of words and penetrates the silence, "a word that is not a word," that underlies language, revealing the space of the unknown. In *Eroticism*, to illustrate how the fusion of discontinuous beings opens onto the continuity of death in sexual union, he quotes Rimbaud's verse "Elle est retrouvée./ Quoi? L'éternité./ C'est la mer allée/ Avec le soleil" ("It has returned. What? Eternity. It is the sea gone off with the sun" – Wallace Fowlie translation). Like eroticism, poetry is a kind of disorder that belongs to the sphere of play – its "sovereign violence" springs from childhood rather than the utilitarian domain of work, identifying it with *dépense*; it is beyond the teleological confines of logos and thus allows access to un-knowing. As a symbolic representation, however, it is only an evocation of sacrifice whose efficacy is limited to changing the order of words. It actualizes an instance of passage between the limited existence to which language is bound and the impossible. It is founded on a paradoxical destruction of language by language itself. As such, it encapsulates the elusiveness of sovereignty.

Thoroughout his life Bataille remained on the margins of the main intellectual and cultural movements that helped shape the first half of the twentieth century, yet his original engagement with these movements makes him an important witness of his time. His fascination with violence may be disconcerting but his work addresses the crucial question of the interaction of literature with the realm of taboo, and prompts reflection on the ethical uncertainties with which literature engages. Its enduring relevance to the literary critic is evidenced by the concern of many contemporary writers to recuperate something of the archaic sacred in a secular world.

Principal criticism

L'Expérience intérieure, 1943 (*Inner Experience*, 1988)
Le Coupable, 1944 (*Guilty*, 1988)
Sur Nietzsche, 1945 (*On Nietzsche*, 1992)
La Part maudite, 1949 (*The Accursed Share*, Vol. 1, 1988, Vols. 2 and 3, 1991)
Lascaux, ou la naissance de l'art, 1955 (*Lascaux or the Birth of Art*, 1955)
La Littérature et le mal, 1957 (*Literature and Evil*, 1973)
L'Érotisme, 1957 (*Eroticism*, 1962)
Les Larmes d'Éros, 1961 (*The Tears of Eros*, 1991)
L'Impossible, 1962 (*The Impossible*, 1991)
Théorie de la religion, 1973 (*Theory of Religion*, 1989)

Other major works and literary forms

L'Histoire de l'oeil, 1928 (*The Story of the Eye*, 1977)
Madame Edwarda, 1941 (*The Beast at Heaven's Gate*, 1956)
L'Abbé C, 1950 (English translation, 1983)
Bleu du ciel, 1957 (*Blue of Noon*, 1977)
Ma Mère, 1966 (*My Mother*, 1972)

Further reading

Derrida, Jacques. *L'Écriture et la différence*, 1967 (*Writing and Difference*, 1978).
Hollier, Denis, ed. *Le Collège de sociologie*, 1979 (*The College of Sociology*, 1988).
Sollers, Philippe, ed. *L'Écriture et l'expérience des limites*, 1968.
——, ed. *Bataille (Colloque de Cerisy)*, 1973.

Stella Harvey

See also French Literary Theory: Twentieth Century; Girard

F. W. Bateson

English literary critic and editor

Born: Styal, England; 1901
Died: October 16, 1978

Biography

Frederick Noel Wilse Bateson was an important figure in the development of English Studies as a subject discipline. He was a graduate of Trinity College, Oxford, beginning his undergraduate work as a student of classics and later switching to English. He spent part of his early career at Harvard, as holder of a Commonwealth Fellowship from 1927 to 1929, then moved to Italy, before finally returning to Britain and settling in the village of Brill, in Buckinghamshire, his main residence for the rest of his life. He became a lecturer in English at Oxford in 1947 but did not attain the established position of a College Fellowship (at Corpus Christi College) until 1963. In 1930, while still involved in postgraduate studies, he was invited to undertake the bibliographical work which eventually became the *Cambridge Bibliography of English Literature* ("*CBEL*"), of which he was the founder-editor. The work took ten years, and played a major part in the consolidation of English as a fully-fledged subject discipline within the humanities. Bateson spent periods in the later part of his career as a visiting professor at universities in the United States, including Cornell in 1958, Berkeley in 1960, and Pennsylvania State University in 1960, 1962, and 1964. An F. W. Bateson memorial lecture now takes place at Corpus Christi College, Oxford, in February each year.

Influence

Bateson's role in the development of English Studies is often eclipsed by that of his Cambridge counterpart F. R. Leavis, and there are a remarkable number of parallels between these two figures. The one spent his entire career at Cambridge, the other virtually the whole of his at Oxford. Both were widely influential within the discipline at large, but dissident "outsider" figures within their own universities, achieving full professional appointments and recognition remarkably late in their careers. Both founded influential journals which seem the very embodiment of the British approach to literary studies – Leavis' *Scrutiny* and Bateson's *Essays in Criticism* – and both exerted a major influence, not just as writers, but as teachers of whole generations of students who themselves went on to assume prominent positions within the profession. Both aimed for a robust plainness of style and a transparent empiricism of method, and both saw themselves as the spiritual successor of Matthew Arnold, a fatal allegiance in the 1970s, which ensured that both ended up as demonized "resisters of theory" in the eyes of the rising structuralist and post-structuralist generation of critics and theorists. However, the crucial difference between their contributions might be summed up by saying that while Leavis established the *critical* foundation of the discipline, Bateson made a major contribution to setting up its the *scholarly* foundation.

To be recognized as a fully-fledged field of study a subject discipline needs to produce major scholarly reference works which are the essential professional bedrock of academic disciplinarity. History, for instance, had the *Dictionary of National Biography* (the "*DNB*"), founded in 1882, and *CBEL* itself was modeled on earlier Cambridge reference works in history. From the 1920s onward, therefore, as the study of English literature replaced the study of the Greek and Roman classics as the key literary discipline in the humanities, Bateson was a leading figure in the growth and provision of the professional infrastructure for vernacular literary study. *CBEL* was first published in 1940, and remains a major source of bibliographic data, currently in its third edition. Bateson was also founder (in 1951) and first editor of the journal *Essays in Criticism*, and later the founder-editor of the "Longman Annotated English Poets" series.

But Bateson's role in the development of English Studies needs to be understood with some precision. The study of English *language* (as opposed to English *literature*) had long been accepted as a "proper" scholarly discipline. Its roots lay in the nineteenth-century German tradition of historical linguistics known as philology, which involved study of the origin and development of languages. English language study already had its major scholarly landmarks in place, including the academic editions of early texts produced by F. J. Furnivall's Early English Text Society ("EETS"), founded in 1864, and the *New English Dictionary*, edited by James Murray (and based on materials collected by the Philological Society) which had begun appearing in serial form in 1884. So when an English course was finally established at Oxford in 1894 it involved far more linguistic study (of Old and Middle English, for instance) than literary study, and was heavily dependent for its external prestige and internal self-image on the academic credibility which this linguistic (or "philological") emphasis provided. Bateson realized the illogicality of linking literary studies to the compulsory study of Anglo-Saxon and historical bibliography (the study of books and manuscripts as physical artifacts), and campaigned for a separation of language and literature at his own university. His campaign was only partly successful, and the link between the two remains in place at many of the large civic universities of Victorian foundation in Britain.

But early English Studies at Cambridge moved in an entirely different direction. In the 1920s when this Cambridge English School (which had been founded as recently as 1911) first became influential it centered on the work of F. R. Leavis, I. A. Richards, and William Empson, which began a radical shift from studying language to studying literature. This "Cambridge criticism" was based upon the "close reading" of "the words on the page": it was, perhaps, always most at home with the very shortest texts – William Blake's "London," William Wordsworth's "Lucy" poems, and the sonnet generally – not surprisingly, since the method involved minute attention to verbal nuance and association, often ignoring the wider context, whether historical, literary-historical, biographical, or generic. This method (disparagingly referred to by its opponents as the "lemon-squeezer school of criticism") was and is a marvelous pedagogic tool which, at its best, empowers students and facilitates an open-ended, seminar-based kind of teaching on which the subject discipline of English Studies still relies. But Bateson realized, shrewdly, that literary study could only afford to be divorced from its uneasy arranged marriage with language studies if it could be shown that scholarly rigor came from *within* literary study itself, and did not need to be grafted on from external sources like philology or (from the mid-twentieth century) linguistics, stylistics, and (later) structuralism.

Analysis

Bateson's view of the history of criticism is given in a piece which can be taken as his personal critical manifesto, the essay "The Function of Criticism at the Present Time" (named in honor of Matthew Arnold, of course) which first appeared in *Essays in Criticism* in January 1953 and forms the main concluding section of *English Poetry: A Critical Introduction*, first published in 1966 and reissued in 1978. He writes here that the Cambridge "textual revolution" of the 1920s and 1930s, spearheaded by Richards, Empson, Leavis, and T. S. Eliot, was "a glorious victory" which needed its "short reign of terror," during which no dissent was tolerated, to discredit once and for all the patriotic belletrist guff of late-Victorian and Edwardian criticism. But the revolution also involved critical losses, including "factual accuracy, awareness of historical background, linguistic expertise, and even sometimes the ability to write lucid English." In a sense, as Francis Mulhern argues in his book *The Moment of Scrutiny* (1979), "Bateson's journal marked the 'settlement' after the excesses of the 'revolution,'" seeking, as it did, to fuse "the innovations of the inter-war period with an older tradition of academic philology." Bateson's whole enterprise is the attempt to use these traditional *scholarly* qualities to counter what he saw as the "interpretive irresponsibility" of the new close-reading orthodoxy, the "irresponsibility" lying in the fact that often a striking interpretation of an individual word or line is offered which often "only retains its validity so long as the larger poetic context is excluded." This "larger poetic context" may consist of the run of sense of the rest of the poem, or the literary history of the genre in question, or even aspects of the nonliterary context of the poem. Either way, they are matters which a properly competent literary method ought not to ignore, or (indeed) be ignorant of.

In the wider context of the consolidation of "English" as an academic discipline, the dangers of this kind of "close reading" are apparent. Bateson's contribution was to realize that if the shift from language to literature were to achieve wide academic acceptance, then Cambridge criticism would need to be balanced by the kind of historical scholarship with which his own university of Oxford was closely associated. In his view, it could never be enough to be just a critic: rather, it is always necessary to be what he called a "scholar-critic," and always in that order, for in his book *The Scholar-Critic: An Introduction to Literary Research* (1972) he went so far as to say that "the scholar-critic must be a scholar, a researcher *before* he can become a really competent critic. There are, therefore, almost no reputable 'critic-scholars', *even if the adolescent self-identification with the literary hero of the moment is a necessary pre-requisite to what may seem to be pure scholarship*" (author's italics).

However, the phrases I have italicized here point to a problem and a contradiction in Bateson's line of thought: we must be scholars before we can be critics; yet few people (surely) are ever fired with an initial love of literature by early exposure to an approach which is primarily scholarly. Even so, Bateson's own prowess as a critic often seems distinctly limited: he had no interest in the novel, which he regarded (perhaps with the one-time classicist's innate distrust of the one kind of literature which was not invented in antiquity) as an inherently flawed literary form, one in fact which he bizarrely wished out of existence in a curious piece called "The Novel's Original Sin: A Lecture" which is the last essay in *Essays in Critical Dissent* (1972). Here he claimed at the start "not that the serious novel is dead, but that, with the exception of the satiric novel, it *ought* to be." In spite of the reprieve offered to satire (again favoring a classical form) this pronouncement must have startled the original auditors of the lecture, and it becomes clear that Bateson's taste, while pretty catholic in poetry, did not really embrace the novel, even as recreational reading. Likewise, his readings of Wordsworth and Blake are sometimes suspect, for he seemed, in the last analysis, to lack the instinctive sense of balance which is the prime requirement for those who walk the high wire of close reading, with or without the safety net of scholarship. For instance, in discussing Blake's "London" he inexplicably prefers the original word "dirty" to the later "charter'd" in the opening lines ("I wander thro each dirty street/ Near where the dirty Thames does flow"). He writes that "the explicit 'dirty' seems better to me than the more pretentious and obscure 'charter'd' " (*The Scholar-Critic*), eliminating a much debated word which seems to encapsulate the individuality and complexity of the whole poem.

Yet, paradoxically, Bateson's advocacy of scholarship was never total either. He did not, after all, found a journal called *Essays in Scholarship* and he realized quite clearly that literary studies can never live by scholarship alone: in an essay about the Oxford journal *Review of English Studies* (a journal which was, and remains, the defining "other" of his own *Essays in Criticism*), he writes of the need for "the wide-ranging generalisations without which the details of scholarship have little or no meaning outside themselves" (*Essays in Critical Dissent*), and he wisely remarks elsewhere that "a degree of anti-historicism is the price that has to be paid for the continuing vitality of an English literary tradition." It might be added that T. S. Eliot's notion of literary tradition embodies essentially the same insight, which is that the past has somehow to be shaped to the needs of the present if it is to remain alive, and that the trick of the truly vital contemporary poets is to make their predecessors speak anachronistically through themselves. His ultimate ambivalence, then, about both scholarship and criticism indicates a certain element of self-contradiction within Bateson's work, but these are intractable matters on which the best do well to lack all conviction, and he himself was always cheerfully willing to admit his own limitations: he saw Leavis as incomparably better than himself as a critic, but felt (quite justly) that he had the edge as a scholar.

Further, Bateson's relationship to "theory" is a complicated one. He detested any form of scholarship which had frozen into a "method" or a "system" that claimed to be able to offer critical salvation based on the application of formulae. This explains the series of "dissenting" episodes with all the emergent literary-critical hegemonies which appeared at various stages of his career as a academic: thus, he opposed the New Bibliography in the 1950s, literary linguistics and stylistics in the 1960s, and structuralism in the 1970s. The first of these, the New Bibliography, was consolidated in its modern form by R. B. McKerrow and W. W. Greg in the first thirty years of the twentieth century. It was "the science of the material transmission of literary texts," which claimed to be able to establish definitively what the author actually wrote. Its great achievements were establishing the order of composition of Shakespeare's plays, and deducing the precise operating procedures of the printing houses which preserved them for posterity. But the New Bibliography wanted to expand its empire, and like all new approaches within literary studies it was eager to convict all others of mere methodless impressionism. A typical claim (by Greg's American disciple Fredson Bowers) was that it could prove that Shakespeare wrote, in *Hamlet* I, ii, 129, of Hamlet wanting his "*sallied* flesh" to melt, not his "*solid* flesh." Bateson effectively challenges the physical evidence on which this claim is based, but his main point is that "the crux needs to be tackled with the appropriate tools, which are stylistic rather than bibliographical" (*Essays in Critical Dissent*). Bateson concludes that "solid flesh is better English, better Shakespeare, better poetry." Of course, one might reply that this does not disprove that Shakespeare wrote "sallied" rather than "solid," which is what the bibliographer set out to prove. What has happened is that Bateson has changed his scholarly hat for a critical one halfway through the argument – he shows, with conviction and élan, that "solid" is *critically* better than "sallied," but the scholarly point (concerning what Shakespeare actually wrote) is, at best, unproven. Yet Bateson's wider emphasis must surely stand: the claims of the bibliographic, scholarly approach to usurp and preempt criticism must be resisted, since otherwise literary study will tend to dwindle into pedantry and antiquarianism.

Bateson's argument with linguistics and stylistics began with Helen Vendler's review of Roger Fowler's *Essays on Style and Language* (1966) in his journal (*Essays in Criticism*, 1966). Fowler's riposte in the journal produced Bateson's editorial reply (he was not the sort of editor to stay on the sidelines merely ensuring the journal's impartiality) and began a lengthy debate between them which became emblematic of the mutually uncomprehending relationship between linguistics and literary criticism (*Essays in Criticism*, 1967 and 1968). His dispute with linguistics had essentially the same grounds as his grievance against the New Bibliography – he felt that it was claiming to supersede criticism and obviate critical judgment by substituting for it a "mechanical discovery procedure." The case was the same in the 1970s when he went to war with structuralism (in a lively polemic called "Is Your Structuralism Really Necessary?" in *The New Review*).

Bateson was a critic (or scholar-critic) who was at his best when on the attack. His general position in such large-scale polemical exchanges was always right, in spite of his mistakes of emphasis or detail, and he was never decisively refuted in confrontational polemic. The closest he came to it was in the dispute with Leavis which followed the publication of Bateson's essay "The Function of Criticism at the Present Time" in which he argued for his own brand of "contextual reading" in distinction to Cambridge "close reading." This procedure, he said, was more likely to achieve the Arnoldian goal of reaching "the object as in itself it really is." Leavis' magisterial reply was that whereas the literary work under consideration is a determinate entity tangibly present, the "context" is always an arbitrary construction which can never have an equivalent order of actuality.

In recent years the balance between scholarship and criticism which Bateson believed in so passionately has again been upset. The dominance of "theory" in the 1980s made textual criticism and close reading seem the epitome of conservatism, but the ebbing of the theoretical tide in the 1990s led not to the reinstatement of criticism, but to the resurgence of scholarship under the guise of a historicism (whether "old" or "new" makes little difference) which now seems so stiflingly pervasive in literary studies as to obscure any firm sense of what a distinctively literary-critical contribution to debate might consist of. Because theory had undermined the ontological status of the text, insisting upon its ineluctable provisionality and plurality, it is now commonplace to argue that (say) *King Lear* is actually an amalgam of various texts and various textual traditions, rather than a literary entity which is "simply there" as a "determinate entity" in Leavis' sense. In effect, this substitutes a never-static textual kaleidoscope for the older solid ground on which textual criticism could operate. For Bateson, what the student of literature most needs is learning and judgment. The intellectual pendulum which always swings between these two seems currently arrested at the former, but his example reminds us that the most fruitful state of affairs is the unresolved tension between the two which his own best work exemplifies.

Principal criticism

William Wordsworth: A Reinterpretation, 1954, 1956 (second edition)
Selected Poems of William Blake, 1957 (editor, with introduction and explanatory notes)
English Poetry and the English Language, 1961
The Poems of Alexander Pope, Vol. 3, ii: Epistles to Several Persons, 1961 (second edition)
English Poetry: A Critical Introduction, 1966, 1978
Alexander Pope: A Critical Anthology, 1971 (editor, with N. A. Joukovsky)
Essays in Critical Dissent, 1972
The Scholar-Critic: An Introduction To Literary Research, 1972
A Guide To English and American Literature, 1976 (third edition)

PETER BARRY

See also Bowers; British Literary Theory: Twentieth Century; Leavis; McGann

Charles Baudelaire

French poet and critic

Born: Paris, France; April 9, 1821
Died: Paris, France; August 31, 1867

Biography

Charles-Pierre Baudelaire's father was thirty-four years older than his wife and died when the poet was only five years old. His widow remarried in less than two years, this time to someone nearly her own age, the thirty-nine-year-old Jacques Aupick, an army captain with a brilliant career ahead of him. Aupick would become a general, an ambassador, and the military governor of the city of Paris.

Aupick was not a cruel man, despite Baudelaire's later comments; he was absorbed with his career and with his new wife and had increasingly less time to spare in satisfying the demands of his frequently obstreperous new charge. In 1833, when Aupick was assigned to military district headquarters at Lyons, he decided to enroll the boy in boarding school, an arrangement that would last for the next six years; unfortunately, the sensitive young Baudelaire hated institutionalization. In addition, when the family moved back to Paris, where he attended the Collège Louis-le-Grand, he so antagonized his teachers with his disrespectful behavior that they had him expelled; he completed preparation for his examinations at home with a private tutor.

In 1839 he entered the University of Paris law school but probably never attended class, preferring instead to lounge around the Latin Quarter cafés, where he drank heavily and arranged rendezvous with the local prostitutes. His troubled parents temporarily removed him from this environment by arranging a sea voyage to India, a trip intended to last at least a year, but Baudelaire returned in less than eight months, filled with the memory of exotic places and the images of strange and wonderful destinies and with his taste for dissolute living and reckless expenditure intact.

Shortly after his return, Baudelaire became eligible to claim the inheritance left to him by his father. This property he soon sold and, resuming his old life, managed to squander half the proceeds in less than two years. His extravagance so alarmed his parents that they had him declared a ward of the court and put under the supervision of a financial guardian who doled out a monthly allowance only large enough to keep the poet in modest circumstances. This financial arrangement lasted until Baudelaire's death some twenty years later.

Baudelaire wrote articles and poetry and dabbled in politics. He also participated in both the February and June revolutions of 1848 in Paris. Yet his persistent dissipation and inability to manage finances reduced him to squalid circumstances, which the small additional earnings from his publications did not change. Nor did the appearance of his masterpiece, *Flowers of Evil*, in 1857, bring him the fame or financial independence he craved. The book had a first edition of only thirteen hundred copies, and six of its poems were condemned by the public prosecutor as immoral, costing the author a fine of three hundred francs.

Despite financial problems and the ravages of drugs, alcohol, and venereal disease, the period was one of the most inspired of Baudelaire's life. Increasingly, however, he suffered from ill health, and in March, 1866, he was felled by a cerebral stroke from which he never recovered. The last year and a half of his life was particularly grim, a period of speechlessness alternating with terrible outbursts and gradual, persistent loss of all mental acuity. He died in Paris on August 31, 1867.

Influence

Baudelaire was imbued with the Romantic movement's imperative that truth lies in feeling and emotion, an "aspiration toward the Infinite, expressed by all the means available to the arts." Although his criticism did not receive much notice during his own lifetime, his imaginative ideas and provocative personal observations had an immense impact in shaping modern literary methodology.

Analysis

During the 1840s the Romantic synthesis, which had so dominated French culture during the previous generation, was under bitter attack. Its enemies, the realists, saw human existence in less chromatic terms: life was stark, harsh, impersonal, and scientific. The realists dismissed the Romantics as foolishly misguided in their love of the bizarre, in their optimism, and in their admiration for fantasy and the beauties of nature. The age of realism was a time of disillusion and loss of faith in progress.

Baudelaire exhibited some of the characteristics and values of both movements, but he remained a Romantic at heart. Though greatly attracted to a system that pretended to understand the world as it was, in all its filth and depravity, he also believed that the most important quest was the search for Beauty. Baudelaire was essentially a Platonist who held real poetry to be "completely true only in *another world*." This was also true of Beauty – providing that Beauty was strange and unconventional.

According to Baudelaire, a critic must be a constant traveler to distant lands, perpetually receptive to new ideas, new sensations, and new harmonies, even though it was impossible to catch up with "the multiform and multicolor beauty that moves in the infinite spirals of life." The contradiction could be resolved in part through imagination, which, as he wrote in the "Salon of 1859," "has taught man the moral meaning of color, of outline, of sound, and of perfume. . . . [Imagination] decomposes all creation, and from the materials, accumulated and arranged according to rules whose origin is found only in the depths of the soul, it creates a new world, it produces the sensation of the new." Baudelaire called imagination "the queen of truth . . . [in] a definite relationship with the infinite."

Baudelaire's contemporary reputation as a critic was completely eclipsed by the formidable presence of Charles-Augustin Sainte-Beuve, who set the Second Empire standard for literary criticism. About the only thing upon which the two agreed was a belief that great works had to enrich the human mind. Sainte-Beuve's approach was much less freewheeling, essentially pedagogical. He believed that the critic must base criticism on a fixed methodology and develop it into a true science, painstakingly explaining a literary work in terms of its author's personal background, its appropriate historical period, and its relevant psychological and sociological characteristics. Sainte-Beuve had abandoned his pretensions to being a poet and a novelist and worked primarily on criticism, leaving behind forty-eight volumes of reviews.

Baudelaire, however, never stopped being a poet. Poetry for him was the means by which the soul could glimpse the splendors beyond the tomb: "When an exquisite poem brings us to the verge of tears, those tears are not proof of excessive pleasure; they are rather evidence of an aroused melancholy, of a condition of nerves, of a nature which has been exiled amid the imperfect and which would like to take possession immediately, on this very earth, of a revealed paradise." Criticism he regarded as a vital extension of his poetry: "It is impossible," he wrote, "for a poet not to contain within himself a critic. Therefore . . . I consider the poet as the best of all critics." Nor did it matter what type of criticism: cultural values were universal. In this respect, Baudelaire saw no real distinction among the arts – painting, music, or literature: one form of creativity could not be philosophically divorced from another.

Among the writers of his own generation, Baudelaire had the greatest admiration for Poe, who, he said, was unsurpassed in his knowledge of the "harmonic conditions of beauty" and his sense of magic in telling about the "exceptions" in human life. Poe analyzed "whatever is most fugitive, he weighs the imponderable and describes, in a detailed and scientific manner the effects of which are terrible, all that imaginary world which floats around a high-strung man and leads him into evil." Baudelaire thereby expounded the principles which lay at the core of his own aesthetic doctrine.

He applauded Poe's attack on utilitarian poetry which disreputably pandered to the desires and tastes of the masses. He also joined him in condemning didactic poetry which purported to teach a lesson by fortifying the conscience, preaching a perfect morality, or proving something that is useful. He hailed Poe as a kindred spirit who believed that the only true poetry was that which excited and uplifted the soul, which through imagination could reveal "the inner and secret relations of things, the correspondences and the analogies."

In analyzing the works of Poe, Baudelaire stressed the importance of defining "beauty" and the importance of depicting melancholy, desire, and despair – all important elements in Baudelaire's own creative pantheon. Baudelaire said that poetry had no other goal but itself: "It cannot have any other, and no poem will be so great, so noble, so truly worthy of the name of poetry as that which will have been written solely for the pleasure of writing a poem." He also believed, however, that the critic, as should the poet, had to possess certain attitudes and beliefs about the world and his or her society.

A critic must be antibourgeois, with strong contempt for a society based on materialism. He or she also must be one "who does not wish to be elbowed by the crowd and who runs to the far east when the fireworks go off in the west." Finally, he or she must affirm the primordial perversity of humanity, realizing that everyone is born marked for evil: "Nature produces only monsters, and the whole question is to understand the word *savages*."

Baudelaire seemed unconcerned that his own self-righteousness about the nature of criticism was in principle little different from the moralism of those benighted critics who were "constantly recalling the artist to ancient beauty [and] questioning a poet or a novelist on the morality of his purpose and the merit of his intentions." Baudelaire even compounded this hypocrisy by admitting that criticism was an intensely subjective activity which in practice often justified strong personal likes and dislikes. Thus he paid Théophile Gautier egregious praise, calling him "the equal of the greatest in the past, a model for those who are to come, a diamond more and more rare in an epoch drunk with ignorance and materialism, in other words A PERFECT MAN OF LETTERS." He also poured exaggerated scorn on George Sand by dismissing her as stupid, dull, and garrulous: "Her ideas on morals show the profundity of judgment and the delicacy of feeling of a concierge or a kept woman."

At his best, however, Baudelaire was more sensitive and perspicacious. His appraisal of Gustave Flaubert's *Madame Bovary* (1857; English translation, 1886) revealed great insight into the novelist's relationship to his main character, whom Baudelaire perceived as the literary embodiment of Flaubert himself. Flaubert could only agree and told Baudelaire that he had "entered into the arcana of the work as if my brain were yours." Moreover, Baudelaire, unlike most contemporary critics, correctly saw Emma Bovary as a victim of "the sophisms of her imagination" rather than of sexual passion. This "ill-fated woman," he observed, "cares less about the visible, external imperfections and the glaring provincialisms of her husband than about that total lack of genius, that spiritual inferiority so clearly demonstrated by the stupid operation of the clubfoot." She was thus a creature more to be pitied than censured.

The scholar Henri Peyre claimed that no other poet compares with Baudelaire's greatness in the field of criticism, that no other has been able to combine such "intelligence and sensibility, analysis and synthesis, the exploration of the often troubled abysses of his own inner world and the ability to penetrate the universe of other creators." As important as Baudelaire's criticism has appeared to twentieth-century readers, however, it would hardly enjoy that prestige had it not been written by one of the greatest poets of the French language. The literary criticism which Baudelaire applied to others constituted an attempt to rationalize and explain his own creativity. Thus, an understanding of Baudelaire-the-critic is inseparable from an understanding of him as a poet, and to read his criticism is to partake of that considerable genius.

Principal criticism

"Salon de 1846," 1846 ("The Salon of 1846," 1964)
"Les Drames et les romans honnêtes," 1851 ("The Respectable Drama and Novel," 1964)
"L'École païenne," 1852 ("The Pagan School," 1964)
"Edgar Allan Poe, sa vie et ses ouvrages," 1852 ("Edgar Poe: His Life and Works," 1872)
"Exposition universelle, 1855," 1855 (English translation, 1964)
"Notes nouvelles sur Edgar Poe," 1857 ("New Notes on Edgar Poe," 1872)
"*Madame Bovary*," 1857 (English translation, 1964)
"Théophile Gautier," 1859 (English translation, 1964)
"Salon de 1859," 1859 ("The Salon of 1859," 1964)
"Réflexions sur quelques-uns de mes contemporains," 1861 (a collection of 10 articles; "Reflections on Some of My Contemporaries," 1964). These essays appear in English translation in *Baudelaire as Literary Critic: Selected Essays* (1964) and *Art in Paris, 1845–1862: Salons and Other Exhibitions* (1965)

Other major works and literary forms

Charles Baudelaire's renown comes from his collected poetry, presented as *Les Fleurs du mal* (1857, 1861, 1868; *Flowers of Evil*, 1909); the first edition contained a hundred and three poems; the second, appearing four years later, had a hundred and twenty-nine. Baudelaire once remarked that he had put into these poems all of his thoughts, all of his heart, all of his religion, and all of his hate. In addition to this work, he translated into French between 1847 and 1859 most of the stories of Edgar Allan Poe – some claim that Baudelaire's version of Poe's tales reads better than the heavily latinated text of the original – and between 1860 and 1865 he produced the bulk of his prose-verse, *Petits Poèmes en prose*, popularly known as *Le Spleen de Paris* (1869; *Poems in Prose*, 1905, also as *Paris Spleen*, 1869 and 1947).

NOVEL
La Fanfarlo, 1847

POETRY
Les Fleurs du mal, 1857, 1861, 1868 (*Flowers of Evil*, 1909)
Les Épaves, 1866
Petits Poèmes en prose, 1869 (also as *Le Spleen de Paris; Poems in Prose*, 1905, also as *Paris Spleen*, 1869, 1947)

NONFICTION
Les Paradis artificiels, 1860 (partial translation as *Artificial Paradises: On Hashish and Wine as a Means of Expanding Individuality*, 1971)
Le Peintre de la vie moderne, 1863 (*The Painter of Modern Life*, 1964)
Curiositiés esthétiques, 1868
L'Art romantique, 1868
Mon cœur mis à nu, 1887 (*My Heart Laid Bare*, 1950)
Journaux intimes, 1920 (*Intimate Journals*, 1957)
The Letters of Baudelaire, 1927
My Heart Laid Bare and Other Prose Writings, 1951
Baudelaire on Poe, 1952

TRANSLATIONS
Histoires extraordinaires, 1856 (of Edgar Allan Poe's short stories)
Nouvelles Histoires extraordinaires, 1857 (of Poe's short stories)
Aventures d'Arthur Gordon Pym, 1858 (of Poe's novel)
Eureka, 1864 (of Poe's poem)
Histoires grotesques et sérieuses, 1864 (of Poe's tales)

MISCELLANEOUS
Œuvres complètes, 1868–1870, 1961 (Y.-G. Le Dantec and Claude Pichois, editors)

Further reading

Bandy, W. T., comp. *Baudelaire Judged by His Contemporaries*, 1933.
Burton, Richard D. E. *Baudelaire in 1859: A Study in Poetic Creativity*, 1988.
Carter, A. E. *Charles Baudelaire*, 1977.
Gilman, Margaret. *Baudelaire the Critic*, 1943.
Holland, Eugene W. *Baudelaire and Schizoanalysis: The Sociopoetics of Modernism*, 1933.
Mayne, J., ed. *The Mirror of Art: Critical Studies*, 1955.
Mossop, D. H. *Baudelaire's Tragic Hero*, 1932.
Peyre, Henri, ed. *Baudelaire: A Collection of Critical Essays*, 1962.
Pia, Pascal. *Baudelaire*, 1961.
Porter, Laurence M. *Crisis of French Symbolism*, 1990.
Quennell, Peter. *Baudelaire and the Symbolists*, 1955.
Quinn, Patrick F. *The French Face of Edgar Poe*, 1954.
Raser, Timothy Bell. *Poetics of Art Criticism: The Case of Baudelaire*, 1989.
Rhodes, S. A. *The Cult of Beauty in Baudelaire*, 1929.
Sartre, Jean-Paul. *Baudelaire*, 1947.
Thélot, Jerôme. *Baudelaire: violence et poésie*, 1993.
Zimmermann, Melvin. *Visions du monde: Baudelaire et Cie*, 1991.

WM. LAIRD KLEINE-AHLBRANDT

See also Continental Theory; Gautier; Poe; Romanticism; Symbolism

Jean Baudrillard

French cultural critic

Born: Rheims, France; 1929

Biography

Although Jean Baudrillard once replied to a written request for information about his background with "no background," he has, on other occasions, willingly discussed his family origins, his grandparents who were peasants and his parents who worked for the civil service. For lack of an intellectual milieu at home, he worked hard in the lycée, a period he refers to as his "primitive accumulation," and pursued the traditional marks of academic distinction in France – admission to the École Normale Supérieure and conferral of the *agrégation*. He was not successful in these attempts and taught German in a lycée while writing a thesis in sociology under Henri Lefevbre at Nanterre, completed in 1966. He taught as an *assistant* and *maître-assistant* in sociology at Nanterre, one of the centers of radical thought that helped precipitate the 1968 student revolt, until his retirement from teaching in 1987. His first publications were reviews of German and Italian literature for *Les Temps modernes* and translations of Bertolt Brecht's theoretical writings and plays by Peter Weiss. He contributed to Guy Debord's situationist journal *Utopie* and, in 1975, was one of the founding editors of *Traverses*, along with Michel de Certeau, Louis Marin, and Paul Virilio. His first book, *Le Système des objets* (1968), echoes the title of Roland Barthes' *Système de la mode* (1967), with whom he taught at the École des Hautes Études. Combining Marxism and structuralism, the book argues that in late capitalism goods are consumed as signs, not as commodities that satisfy needs.

With the publication of *Le Miroir de la production* (1973; *The Mirror of Production*, 1975), *L'Échange symbolique et la mort* (1976; *Symbolic Exchange and Death*, 1993), *De la séduction* (1979; *Seduction*, 1990), *Simulacra et simulations* (1981; *Simulacra and Simulations*, 1994), *Les Stratégies fatales* (1983; *Fatal Strategies*, 1990), *L'Amérique* (1986; *America*, 1988), and *La Transparence du mal* (1990; *The Transparency of Evil*, 1992), Baudrillard synthesized the most important trends in French thought of the last thirty years (Marxism, psychoanalysis, structuralism, poststructuralism) and emerged as a major theoretician of postmodernism and critic of the media and technology. He is best known for his claim that, in the transition from an industrial age to an information age, Western societies have abandoned reality in favor of "hyperreality" and, with the proliferation of "simulacra" without originals, a new type of permissive yet coercive society is born which governs the masses by the manipulation of signs. All thought and lived experience are affected by this epistemic change: biology, metaphysics, linguistics, the media, and history all operate and are theorized according to the model of digital and fractal codes.

Since leaving Nanterre in 1987, Baudrillard has traveled widely and held guest lectureships in the United States, Italy, Spain, and Australia. In 1989 he was ranked by a poll (certainly an irony for a thinker who so regularly disparages polls in his writings) as the eighth most influential intellectual in France. He appeared on Bernard Pivot's *Apostrophes* television show and has published numerous articles on topics such as J. G. Ballard's *Crash* (1981), the Millennium (1987), the Gulf War (1991), and Dolly the cloned sheep (1997). A host of websites attests to Baudrillard's near cult status as disabused sage and guide to cyberspace and postmodernity. A pointed reference to *Simulacra and Simulations* in the Hollywood movie *The Matrix* (1999) confirms that this intellectual "terrorist" and "sharp-shooting Lone Ranger of the post-Marxist left" (*New York Times*) has made a lasting impression on public consciousness and popular culture. His most recent notoriety stems from being cited in Alan Sokal's *Intellectual Impostures* (1998), along with other postmodernist intellectuals, for inaccurate and fraudulent uses of science.

Influence

In a 1991 interview, Baudrillard named Friedrich Nietzsche as the "epicenter" of his work and mentioned in order Marcel Mauss, Sigmund Freud, Karl Marx, Ferdinand de Saussure, and Roland Barthes as other influences. Walter Benjamin, Marshall McLuhan, and Georges Bataille also figure prominently in his analysis of the media and primitive economies. Among contemporaries and peers, Baudrillard's work must be compared to that of Jacques Derrida, Michel Foucault, Julia Kristeva, and Jacques Lacan. In the area of linguistics, *Symbolic Exchange and Death* is a major poststructuralist critique of the sign comparable to other key works of the late 1960s and early 1970s: Derrida's *Of Grammatology* (1976), Foucault's *The Order of Things* (1970), and Kristeva's *Séméiotiké: Recherches pour une sémanalyse* (1969; researches for a semanalysis). The notion of the poetic in Baudrillard draws upon and is contrasted with the rhetoric of the Freudian joke (*Witz*) and the Lacanian unconscious. As an analysis of power, the body, and successive epistemological ages, Baudrillard's *Seduction* and *Oublier Foucault* (1977; *Forget Foucault*, 1987) engages and criticizes Foucault's *Discipline and Punish* (1977) and *History of Sexuality* (1984).

Much of Baudrillard's effectiveness as a critic results from his seductive writing style and deft combination of theory, art, literature, cinema, and analysis of popular culture. Key arguments are illuminated by references to Baroque stucco angels, Maori tribesmen, Søren Kierkegaard's *Diary of the Seducer* (1971), break-dancers in Manhattan, and strippers at the Crazy Horse in Paris. In his travel narratives and autobiographical writings, *America* and *Cool Memories* (1987), Baudrillard reveals himself to be, *tour à tour*: a wry observer and brilliant satirist of contemporary life, an arrogant and megalomaniac intellectual superstar, an acerbic critic of all liberal ideologies – feminism, multiculturalism, and environmentalism – not as a reactionary, but as a radical thinker convinced that his own critique of capitalist society is more revolutionary than all of the liberal "mirrors of production."

His irascible, irreverent humor cuts in many directions at once: he praises and ostracizes, delights in and abhors American technological culture; he is weary of the inescapably bourgeois outlook he finds in Europe, yet his whole enterprise is, in some sense, a *tour d'Europe*, a travelogue of Continental philosophy and the European cultural patrimony. Not since Roland Barthes has a French intellectual reached such a wide audience and made critical theory seem so appealing and relevant to everyday life.

The analysis of the walkman in *Cool Memories* shows Baudrillard in the full range of his style, imagination, and insight:

> We shall one day have dreams in walkman or video form, dreams to which we can add sound effects, which we can slow down or speed up, like television pictures, or play over a second time if we like them. Perhaps we'll even be able to tune in to other people's dreams on FM and converse by cable in our dreams? Dreams would at least have become a means of communication.
>
> Conversely, the music of the walkman penetrates your body like a dream. Neither inside nor outside, it passes behind your eyes like a cenesthesic tape. But we manipulate it. We no longer accept image or sensations unless we can manipulate them. We don't have any great expectations of the substance of images any more, but we expect everything of their tactile and digital manipulation.

Analysis

What Baudrillard shares with Nietzsche is a persistent criticism of Enlightenment rationality and liberal humanism. Nietzsche once compared the modern scientific ethos, with its narrow outlook and restrictive protocols, to a leech attached to a man's arm; in similar fashion, employing a deliberately disturbing and politically incorrect metaphor, Baudrillard writes in *Cool Memories* that the ideal humans imagined by technology are the handicapped, "because they are immobilized and therefore marked down for automation and remote control."

Another Nietzschean element in Baudrillard is his use of primitive, "savage" societies and their *symbolic* mode of thought, language, and economic exchange as a theoretical base from which to critique modern societies. In a passage from *Symbolic Exchange and Death*, which is emblematic of his entire work, Baudrillard describes a traditional Taoist butcher who dissects beef carcasses by cutting through the void between the joints: "The knife and the body are exchanged, the knife articulates the body's lack and thereby deconstructs it in accordance with its own rhythm." The butcher's technique is a model for properly analyzing any object or text, "in the Orphic dispersal of the body, in the anagrammatic dispersal of the poem." Baudrillard reads texts and dismantles existing paradigms according to the same prerationalistic logic of the Taoist butcher.

Baudrillard derived the idea of symbolic exchange from Marcel Mauss' *The Gift* (1925) which describes how potlatch is used to exchange goods and form sacred bonds in Polynesian societies. On feast days, neighboring tribes vie with one another in gift-giving: women, food, charms, land, labor, and services are freely given away in a symbolic display of largesse which obliges the receiver of the gifts to pay back in kind. Goods, animals, and humans are all considered to be "spiritual matter" in this exchange, which is prior to any consideration of need, use value, or economic advantage. Primitive exchange offers a more radical perspective from which to critique capitalist society than the Marxist concepts of use value, exchange value, and the political economy.

Baudrillard also saw in potlatch a signifying practice that offered as radical a critique of Saussurian linguistics as it had of Marxist economics. Variously referred to in different contexts throughout his work as "symbolic exchange," "poetry," "undivided speech," and "seduction," primitive signification is a kind of material and spiritual communication that violates the principles of classical linguistics. In *The Gift*, the Polynesians had described the unity brought about by symbolic exchange: "Our feasts are the movements of the needle which sews together the parts of our reed roofs, making of them a single roof, one single word." This conflation of words and things which joins together disparate elements to form a single word is analogous to the linguistic phenomenon of anagrams which Saussure had discovered in ancient Vedic and Germanic poetry. Just as the potlatch is a gratuitous giving away of goods prior to any regard for utility, so primitive poetry, like the Freudian *Witz*, is a gratuitous exchange of language for pure enjoyment, prior to any concern for meaning. "Poetry shatters the fundamental law of the human word." It disrupts the linearity of discourse and breaks down the meaning of individual words by the formation of anagrams. The repetition of sounds leads to a canceling of the surface meaning of the text and a revelation of the *anathema*, the name of the god or hero hidden in the text, which is taken apart phonetically and offered up, figuratively, as a sacrifice.

Baudrillard cites Stéphane Mallarmé's verse "Aboli bibelot d'inanité sonore" (Abolished the trinket of sonorous inanity) as an example of a poem which accomplishes the semantic and phonetic destruction of conventional meaning. Arthur Rimbaud's statement that the poem signifies "literally and in all senses" also sets poetry in opposition to linguistics. The poem is true *literally*, in the most reductive and denotative sense. Poetry constantly strives to motivate the sign, in opposition to the linguistic doctrine of the arbitrary sign, to effect a real connection between words and things. Certain poetic techniques, by focusing attention on sound, foreground the poem as an acoustic "thing." But the poem is also true in *all* senses; it reveals all of its meanings in a moment of linguistic "expenditure." It does not conceal any final, repressed, unconscious meaning. In this sense it is beyond psychoanalysis which always searches for hidden meanings, thereby reestablishing, ultimately, a stable relation between the signifier and the signified. Baudrillard thus situates poetry beyond any attempts to contain it theoretically – it exceeds linguists, psychoanalysis, and materialist theories of language. Poetry ends up being an "anti-matter" which, "far from making the thing appear, aims to destroy language itself as a thing." In *Symbolic Exchange and Death* he writes that poetry is, finally, an antimetaphysics:

> It is on condition that we see that fire, water, earth and air are neither values nor positive elements, that they are metaphors of the continual dissolution of value, of the symbolic exchange of the world – on condition that we see that they are not substances but anti-substances, anti-matter – this is the sense in which language may be said to reunite them, as soon as it has been torn from the logic of the sign and value.

Symbolic exchange is thus a poststructural theory that radically eschews all binarist and idealist accounts of language, including vulgar materialism. Rejecting Hegelian idealism and Marxist materialism, going beyond Saussure's structural account of meaning, radicalizing the treatment of words as things in Freud, Baudrillard insists that language must be the undivided medium of total exchange, the primitive "sewing" that pierces and stitches, that simultaneously does and undoes all thoughts and practices.

Starting with primitive societies, Baudrillard defines three successive sign-cultures which have evolved in the place of traditional societies and created semiotic practices that are progressively more artificial. Each culture is based upon a new concept of the sign and a characteristic simulacrum. (1) The Renaissance, dominated by the idea that human signs are "counterfeits" of the natural world. The model Renaissance simulacrum was stucco, the ubiquitous building material used in palaces and churches for sculpture and decoration. As a smooth, seamless medium it represents the Baroque ambition of capturing the entire cosmos in a uniform signifying substance. (2) The Industrial Revolution, modernism. The era of dialectical materialism and classical linguistics, the age of mechanical reproduction, the invention of photography and cinema, art forms which erode the distinction between an original, natural model and its copy. (3) The age of simulacra, postmodernism. Serial reproduction, followed to its logical conclusion, breaks down the distinction between original and copy. Increasingly, all reference is lost to the real and to origins. "Every Andy Warhol does this: the multiple replicas of Marilyn Monroe's face are of course at the same time the death of the original and the end of representation." Warhol's art destroys the distinction between an original portrait of Marilyn and any subsequent copies. The multiplication of many copies of the same image proves that there is no original portrait of Marilyn – only a piece of code, reproducible in endless images – and, perhaps, no original Marilyn herself, only a strand of DNA which could be cloned into endless copies of the original. The same logic of reproduction according to a code stands behind postmodern art and molecular biology. The "death of the original" also refers to the deadly and efficient nature of postmodern culture. The media hounded Marilyn to death, as it did Diana, Princess of Wales; both now live on in endlessly multiplied images that entice and sedate the masses, which mask real references to death behind an artificial immortality of images.

With the publication of *The Transparency of Evil* and *The Perfect Crime* (1994), Baudrillard added a fourth period to his scheme of semiotic evolution. At this stage, the "Xerox degree of culture," simulation imitates only other simulations. Adolescents (and adults) travel to theme parks to interactively reenact scenes from the films *Jurassic Park* and *Star Wars*. Real wars are fought, politically and militarily, as simulations of simulations. This ultimate disappearance of reality, leaving no traces or incriminating evidence, is the "perfect crime" which contemporary sign culture has committed.

Principal criticism

Le Système des objets, 1968
Le Miroir de la production, 1973 (*The Mirror of Production*, 1975)
L'Échange symbolique et la mort, 1976 (*Symbolic Exchange and Death*, 1993)
Oublier Foucault, 1977 (*Forget Foucault*, 1987)
De la séduction, 1979 (*Seduction*, 1990)
Simulacra et simulations, 1981 (*Simulacra and Simulations*, 1994)
Les Stratégies fatales, 1983 (*Fatal Strategies*, 1990)
"The Ecstasy of Communication," in *The Anti-Aesthetic: Essays on Postmodern Culture*, 1983 (Hal Foster, editor)
L'Amérique, 1986 (*America*, 1988)
Cool Memories, 1987
Selected Writings, 1988
La Transparence du mal, 1990 (*The Transparency of Evil*, 1992)
La Guerre du Golfe n'a pas eu lieu, 1991 (*The Gulf War Did Not Happen*, 1995)
Baudrillard Live: Selected Interviews, 1993
The Perfect Crime, 1994

Further reading

Gane, Mike. *Baudrillard: Critical and Fatal Theory*, 1991.
Genosko, Gary. *Baudrillard and Signs: Signification Ablaze*, 1994.
Jameson, Fredric. *Postmodernism, or the Cultural Logic of Late Capitalism*, 1991.
Kellner, Douglas. *Jean Baudrillard: From Marxism to Post-Modernism and Beyond*, 1989.
Sokal, Alan. *Intellectual Impostures*, 1998.
Sturrock, John. "Le Pauvre Sokal," in *London Review of Books*, July 16, 1998.

MATT SENIOR

See also Foucault; French Literary Theory: Twentieth Century; McLuhan; Postmodernism

Vissarion Belinskii

Russian critic

Born: Sveaborg, Finland; June 11, 1811
Died: St. Petersburg, Russia; June 7, 1848

Biography

The first of five children, Vissarion Grigorievich Belinskii was born on June 11, 1811, on the island of Sveaborg, or Suomenlinna, in Finland, which was then part of the Russian Empire. His father was a physician who served with the Baltic fleet before practicing in central Russia. Vissarion Belinskii spent many of his early years in Chembar, southeast of Moscow; under the Soviet government that city was later renamed in his honor. In 1825 he enrolled in a Gymnasium in Penza, the largest city in the province, but subsequently he was expelled for his failure to attend classes. Although in 1829 he was admitted to Moscow University, he made little progress with his academic work, and three years later he was forced to conclude his studies. All the while Belinskii had read widely and avidly in literary and philosophical works. He also had a knack for writing on short notice and at length on a variety of topics. His career as a literary critic got fully under way when he began work for journals in Moscow; in 1839 he moved to St. Petersburg, where many of his most important pieces were written. In 1843 he married Maria Vasil'evna Orlova, a teacher at a women's school; theirs was not a happy union, and Belinskii's domestic situation was troubled further by the death of their son Vladimir, at the age of four months, in 1847. Throughout his adult life, Belinskii was afflicted with tuberculosis, which progressively undermined his health even as he maintained an active and demanding career. After a period of travel in Western Europe, Belinskii weakened and died after his return to the Russian capital, on June 7, 1848.

Influence

During his lifetime, Belinskii set the tone for the critical reception of important works by major authors such as Nikolai Gogol' and Mikhail Lermontov. Indeed, many important writers were introduced to the Russian reading public in part through his reviews. He also formed literary circles which met for evening discussions of artistic and philosophical questions; he was on social terms with such disparate figures as Aleksandr Hertzen, Mikhail Bakunin, and Ivan Turgenev. Belinskii has been considered the first Russian thinker to combine literary theory with social criticism, and after his death his influence came to be widely acknowledged. His works had a particularly powerful effect on the radical intelligentsia, and he was cited as an example by Nikolai Chernyshevskii and Nikolai Dobroliubov. Among literary writers, the noted satirist Mikhail Saltykov-Shchedrin made use of Belinskii's precepts. Somewhat later, Marxist and other leftist thinkers found important affinities in his thought, and after the Bolsheviks came to power Belinskii's work was widely cited and studied. In the former Soviet Union he has been regarded as perhaps the most important precursor of socialist literary critics. The influence and vitality of his thought have also been recognized by most students of Russian and European literature, who have pointed to his significance alongside the novelists and poets of his time.

Analysis

For several reasons, Belinskii's work was markedly uneven. Most of his essays were composed for publication in journals; thus, relatively brief notices were produced alternately with longer, though somewhat repetitious, articles. His social and aesthetic theories, though bearing the hallmarks of philosophical influences that held sway in the Russia of his day, showed some variations over time and were expressed to the extent possible within the format of essays and book reviews. It is not entirely clear to what degree tsarist censorship, which during that period was relatively stringent, affected Belinskii's work. It would seem, in any event, that Belinskii was adept at finding guises by which his ideas could appear in print. In a broader perspective, Belinskii was called upon to assess the works of numerous writers at the beginning or at the zenith of their careers; though many of his judgments seemed sound at the time, to later readers some of his evaluations have appeared perhaps pitched too high or too low. Nevertheless, Belinskii's work has sufficient consistency and insight to allow for systematic generalizations about the whole.

Although in Russia some indigenous traditions of literary criticism had already been established, on a theoretical level aesthetic thought followed patterns established by German Idealism. During the third and fourth decades of the nineteenth century, Russian intellectual life was deeply affected by interpretive controversies over the application of such ideas. It has become common to depict Belinskii's outlook as having passed through several stages. For his knowledge of European thought he relied heavily upon translations, or oral accounts from people he knew; he was able to read French works in the original, but not German. Initially, Belinskii was impressed by certain notions of Friedrich Wilhelm Joseph Schelling, the objective Idealist philosopher whose vision of nature afforded an organic view of aesthetic creation. Belinskii also evidently borrowed Schelling's conception of genius – a term that appears relatively frequently in the Russian critic's writings. On the other hand, Schelling's conception of the divine manifestation in creative work found little response in Belinskii. After several years, and some pondering of other systems, including that of Johann Gottlieb Fichte, such views were supplanted by philosophical conceptions taken from G. W. F. Hegel; in some respects, Belinskii's thought remained in this mold for the rest of his life. On the most basic level, Belinskii found attractive the German thinker's emphasis on realistic and objective art; his reaction to Romanticism as an intellectual and aesthetic movement probably owed much to Hegel. His exposure to Hegel's ideas may also have led Belinskii to conceive of literary developments as determined by historical evolution. Nevertheless, Belinskii found Hegel's abstract rationalism somewhat forbidding, as well as overly detached from social and political questions. At times during his later career, Belinskii manifested some interest in leftist Hegelian trends in German thought even as he was occasionally attracted to the teachings of French Utopian socialism. While he did not establish a fully realized or entirely coherent aesthetic system, Belinskii's incorporation of philosophical concepts in his critical writing began to establish the relationship between ideology and literary writing that later was to be a basic concern for the Russian intelligentsia. At the same time, in contrast with some of his more partisan followers, Belinskii implicitly upheld the autonomy of art even when he insisted that it should have a definite social and moral stance.

In some of his longer essays, and in reviews of works where such concerns arose, Belinskii took up questions of moral and social interest in a searching evaluation of his country's problems and prospects. Historical studies interested him particularly, and, though expressions of conventional Russian patriotism sometimes occur in his treatment of works celebrating great battles and other major events, his views on cultural developments show a fine grasp of the problems confronting Russian literature. He had little taste for older epics or for the more superficial productions from the eighteenth century, but he took special notice of the contributions of earlier authors such as Mikhail Lomonosov and Gavrila Derzhavin. He also commented on the patterns of style that had emerged as the literary language had developed. He acknowledged as well the advances achieved by Nikolai Karamzin and Vasilii Zhukovskii, who toward the beginning of the nineteenth century paved the way for the emergence of modern Russian fiction and poetry. In a more general sense, the historical developments that Belinskii considered vital were the reforms of Peter the Great, which brought Russia out of medieval backwardness; the growth of the educational system under Catherine the Great he also cited with approval. Belinskii's assessment of his nation's past reveals his alignment with the Westernizing faction of Russian intellectuals, who encouraged innovations in a European style and who scorned the nostalgia of their opponents, the Slavophiles, for ancient Russian traditions. Moreover, though he did not pursue historical themes for their own sake, Belinskii's point of view reinforced his insistence that socially responsible literature must embrace certain historical tasks.

Belinskii aroused controversy with his denunciation of the influence exercised by the Orthodox Church. His own religious beliefs were not clearly defined; in places, he referred with apparently genuine respect to the life and teachings of Jesus Christ, but generally to suggest a fundamental contrast between early Christian doctrine and the actual practices of the later church. He severely criticized the narrow-mindedness and obscurantism of religious functionaries and commented caustically on the ignorance and credulity that characterized the lower clergy. His willingness to address religious themes in a literary context was consistent with the emphasis on social issues that became a central concern of his work; it also set him apart from authors and thinkers who treated such matters as separate, more elevated pursuits.

Belinskii's judgments of literary works almost invariably emphasized the universal significance of characters and situations: he also tended to have a higher regard for content than for form. He cited Friedrich Schiller frequently but drew from his poetry as much as from his aesthetic thought; Belinskii concerned himself largely with matters of artistic truth and was not particularly attracted to the German thinker's conception of the good and the beautiful. Belinskii's assessment of Johann Wolfgang von Goethe, who was discussed at many junctures, tended to fluctuate over time. While at various places he described the German author as a genius, some of Belinskii's judgments were inconclusive, often because of his difficulty in reconciling Goethe's aloofness from problems of the day with his own literary activism. Other idiosyncratic observations on Western literature can be found in his comments on Sir Walter Scott; Belinskii regarded his novels as exemplifying historical truth to a greater extent than most formal studies of past ages. He also had high praise for the works of certain French authors, some of whom he had translated himself. Among other curious judgments, Belinskii ranked the popular writer Charles-Paul de Kock as one of France's premier novelists.

In Russia, Belinskii was one of the most widely read critics of his time, and his pronouncements on major writers had great influence on the literary public's reception of new offerings. In many cases, Belinskii's assessments of authors of that period have been upheld by later critics. His reaction to Aleksandr Pushkin, however, was perhaps unusually diffident. He did find numerous reasons to praise the poet, notably in a series of eleven articles that began to appear six years after Pushkin's death. In considering most of Pushkin's works, Belinskii forthrightly acclaimed him as Russia's national poet, whose verse captured the ethos of his country while holding out a genuinely universal appeal. The distinction between Pushkin's compositions and those of other versifiers such as Zhukovskii was, according to this view, indicative of the growing maturity of Russian literature. Moreover, Pushkin's poetry displayed a concern for objective reality that Belinskii found exemplary. Belinskii expressed some reservations in his discussion of the essentially artistic intent of Pushkin's work; though he praised Pushkin for his sheer virtuosity, on other counts he judged that others, such as Lermontov, had achieved more in the actual content of their poetic works.

In some cases, Belinskii's reviews of works by his contemporaries showed a critical acumen that bordered on prescience. Lermontov's *Geroi nashego vremeni* (1840; *A Hero of Our Time*, 1854, originally as *Sketches of Russian Life in the Caucasus*, 1853) was derided by some for being uneven or insufficiently realistic, but Belinskii, in an article that helped secure for the novel its status as a major work, acclaimed it as a bright new star on the literary horizon. He contended further that the novel's alleged lack of unity actually manifested a deeper and more complex design. Although the story is narrated partly through a series of flashbacks, and features a protagonist (Grigorii Aleksandrovich Pechorin) who seemingly lacks positive qualities, Belinskii found this very dissonance a manifestation of the author's grasp of reality.

Belinskii also accorded a strikingly favorable reception to the works of Gogol'. He regarded several of the writer's short novels as superlative efforts which demonstrated an acute consciousness of current social problems. In his review of the first part of *Mertvye dushi* (1842–1855; *Dead Souls*, 1887), Belinskii acclaimed Gogol' as the foremost writer of his time. Belinskii considered the novel not so much a satire as an indictment of serfdom which achieved its purpose through its evocation of the petty and tyrannical features of the social system in the countryside. On this count particularly, Belinskii insisted on the grimly realistic character of Gogol''s work. Indeed, though his reviews greatly enhanced Gogol''s standing in serious literary circles, Belinskii never grasped Gogol''s characteristic use of fantasy and broad humor.

Belinskii's warm approval of Gogol' turned to bitter disillusionment after the publication of a collection of essays and letters, *Vybrannye mesta iz perepiski s druz'iami* (1847; *Selected Passages from Correspondence with Friends*, 1969). Displeased by the tone of religious conservatism that marked this work, Belinskii became involved in a heated exchange of views resulting in an open letter to Gogol', which became one of the most celebrated works of Belinskii's career; later, it was regarded as a nearly definitive statement of his beliefs. Belinskii began by asking whether he were dealing with the same author as before; he contrasted the sweeping and acute social commentary of Gogol''s fiction with his odd, belated efforts at reconciliation with the Church. Belinskii then launched a spirited attack on existing institutions. People in Russia generally, he contended, were not religious but superstitious, and most clerics had strayed far from the way of Christ. Serfdom and corporal punishment had degraded social institutions; it was only in literature that any life and progress had been seen. Only through civilization, enlightenment, and humaneness could Russia be redeemed; the mysticism and piety that Gogol' had sought late in life had already been found wanting.

In other cases, Belinskii took the measure of young authors whose careers were only beginning. He commented favorably on the first published works of Turgenev. His articles on the stories which subsequently were collected in the famous *Zapiski okhotnika* (1852; *Russian Life in the Interior*, 1855, best known as *A Sportsman's Sketches*, 1932) approvingly noted the author's deep thought and penetrating observation, but later Belinskii evinced dissatisfaction with Turgenev's somewhat detached stand on social issues. Yet he retained the other man's esteem, to the extent that in his memoirs Turgenev portrayed Belinskii in openly sympathetic terms.

Among Belinskii's later judgments, his reviews of the early work of Fedor Dostoevskii are memorable, both for the favorable reception he accorded Dostoevskii's first novels and for the withering disapproval he expressed for some of the author's later stories. Belinskii lavished great praise on *Bednye liudi* (1846; *Poor Folk*, 1887), which he cited for its depth and originality; even a tendency toward prolixity Belinskii was willing to forgive. He also found the spark of creative genius in Dostoevskii's short novel *Dvoinik* (1846; *The Double*, 1956), though he found this work in some ways to be imperfectly developed, owing too much to the fantastic. Disappointment set in, however, on both sides. Belinskii roundly criticized the stories "Gospodin Prokharchin" (1846; "Mr. Prohartchin," 1918) and "Khoziaika" (1847; "The Landlady," 1913), which he found monstrous and unworthy of their author. To be sure, there was much that was uneven in Dostoevskii's early work; it may be also that Belinskii's views oscillated more sharply than was warranted. In any event, though Dostoevskii had great respect for Belinskii at the outset of his own career, he later turned against the great critic; as his own views developed, he became particularly hostile to Belinskii's standpoint on spiritual issues. For that matter, where subsequent literature was concerned, many of Belinskii's followers came from groups with a rather different cast of mind, regarding criticism primarily as a means to elucidate social issues.

In certain ways, political conditions in Russia facilitated the eventual acceptance of Belinskii's views. Because the publication of openly political works was often restricted, literary criticism became charged with much wider implications, and it was common in some circles for fictional works to be assessed for their position on social concerns. Thus, Russian criticism often took on peculiarly polemical overtones. Under such circumstances, Belinskii's beliefs and methods seemed particularly appropriate. Although some variations in this pattern may be observed, arising from shifting government policies and changing literary tastes, conditions of this sort ultimately may have facilitated the dissemination of Belinskii's ideas in imperial Russia.

Because the government still found his ideas controversial, Belinskii's influence was muted during the years immediately following his death. For a time he was rarely mentioned in print, and his letter to Gogol' was suppressed. After about 1855, however, it became possible for his ideas to be discussed more openly, and his theories were taken as a point of departure for other thinkers. Perhaps the most important sign of his acceptance among certain literary critics was the publication of Chernyshevskii's *Ocherki gogolevskogo perioda russkoi literatury* (1855–1856; partial translation as "Essays on the Gogol Period of Russian Literature," 1953), which upheld Belinskii's judgments at many turns. Dobroliubov made an avowedly radical interpretation of Belinskii's ideas. Creative writers such as Saltykov-Shchedrin, who pointed to the hypocrisies and shortcomings of society, also found support in Belinskii's conceptions. For a time, thinkers of various political persuasions were attracted to Belinskii's views; Apollon Grigor'ev, a political moderate who cherished Russian nationalist ideals, incorporated some of Belinskii's ideas in his own highly influential theory of criticism. Other possibilities were suggested in the approach of Nikolai Mikhailovskii, who found Belinskii's works useful in promoting his application of populism to literary criticism. Increasingly, Belinskii's ideas became associated with leftist political thought.

During the later nineteenth century, the confluence of ideological trends leading to Russian Marxism seemed to favor certain interpretations of Belinskii's views, particularly where social issues were concerned. The first major Russian Marxist, Georgii Plekhanov, cited with approval Belinskii's views on the utility of art; he maintained that the autonomy of literary creation could be reconciled with considerations of usefulness, since great works by their nature would serve progressive ends. Enlarging upon Belinskii's precepts, Plekhanov applied a much more specific theory of social classes and class struggle to literary analysis; indeed, though he regarded this as an even greater failing among Chernyshevskii and others of his generation, Plekhanov reproached Belinskii for an inadequate sense of history. He judged that Belinskii had failed to conjoin his social theory, such as it was, with a broader conception of the unfolding processes of economic change. Other Marxist critics were somewhat more willing to make allowances for the conditions of time and place that limited Belinskii's views; he was regarded as the first Russian critic to deal with social questions directly. Belinskii's emphasis on content, as against form, in the assessment of literary works gained some following as well. Anatolii Lunacharskii, the first Soviet commissar of education, maintained that from a Marxist standpoint Belinskii's thought marked an important stage in the proper appreciation of literature; according to this view, Belinskii had anticipated the socialist tenet that art could serve as a catalyst for social change.

There had been some opposition to Belinskii's conceptions, notably among Symbolist and Russian Formalist theorists; they contended that his views constituted an unnecessary intrusion of social concerns into the domain of literature. It became increasingly rare, however, for this objection to be raised; uniformity eventually was imposed upon those writers who remained in the Soviet Union, while those who emigrated tended to deal with matters that were more congenial to them. After 1934, when Socialist Realism formally became the guiding doctrine of Soviet literature, Belinskii's importance for the development of Russian criticism was accepted beyond challenge. It became commonplace to regard him as one of the ideological progenitors of socialist literary theory. Yet some adjustments were made, unobtrusively and without comment, in ways that brought his original views more nearly in line with those of Soviet theorists. To some extent, this task was facilitated by the acceptance of classical works as part of Russia's literary heritage; thus, judgments of early writers became somewhat less constrained by ideological concerns, and criticism could be assessed on the basis of the literary issues that were involved. As a result, those cases in which Belinskii's views had been based predominantly upon artistic criteria could be considered in a like spirit. There has been a tendency as well among Russian scholars to regard Belinskii's philosophical stance as arising in part from the times during which he lived. The Hegelian elements of his thought have been considered important where it could be argued that they anticipated Marxism; alternately, some Russian writers have contended that during his later years Belinskii recognized the limitations of Hegel's philosophy and began to move away from an Idealist viewpoint. In other ways as well, Belinskii may have been made to appear more consistent than he actually was. Still, Belinskii's ideas have been made accessible by Russian specialists' numerous studies of the great critic and important scholarly editions of his works. Though elsewhere interest in Belinskii has not run quite so high, his importance in the development of Russian literature has been generally acknowledged, and Western scholarship has yielded searching and important studies of the problems and nuances of his critical writings.

Principal criticism

Sochineniia, 1859–1862 (12 volumes)

Polnoe sobranie sochinenii, 1953–1959 (13 volumes; partially translated in *Selected Philosophical Works*, 1948, and *Belinskii, Chernyshevsky, and Dobrolyubov: Selected Criticism*, 1962)

Other major works and literary forms

At times Vissarion Belinskii tried his hand at drama and poetry. These efforts achieved little distinction and are remembered largely for their association with Belinskii's critical studies, yet some insight as to his point of view as a writer may be discerned from ventures of this sort. His play *Dmitrii Kalinin* (1831), which has been read as an attack upon serfdom, was suppressed shortly after it appeared, and it may have had a part in the termination of Belinskii's university studies. Neither his verse compositions, of which only the short piece "Russkaia byl'" (1831) remains extant, nor his later play *Piatidesiatiletnyi diadiushka, ili strannaia bolezn'* (1838) received more than passing attention. Another area of concern to the great critic, however, was the development of a literary language, and to promote proper usage and style he wrote *Osnovaniia russkoi grammatiki* (1837). Early in his career, he also produced numerous translations from the French, including works of Charles-Paul de Kock and Alexandre Dumas, *père*.

PLAYS
Dmitrii Kalinin, 1831
Piatidesiatiletnyi diadiushka, ili strannaia bolezn', 1838

POETRY
"Russkaia byl'," 1831

NONFICTION
Osnovaniia russkoi grammatiki, 1837

TRANSLATIONS
Magdalina, 1833 (of Charles-Paul de Kock's novel *Madeleine*)
"Nyneshnee sostoianie muzyki v Italii (Pismo entuziasta)," 1833 (of an essay later published in Hector Berlioz's collection *Voyage musical en Allemagne et en Italie*)
"Vozdushnye zamki molodoi devushki," 1833 (of a short story from Jules-Gabriel Janin's collection *Contes fantastiques et contes littéraires*)
"Gora Gemmi," 1834 (of a piece from Alexandre Dumas, *père's* travel sketches *Impressions de voyage*)

Further reading

Berlin, Isaiah. "Vissarion Belinskii," in *Russian Thinkers*, 1978, pp. 150–185.
Bowman, Herbert E. *Vissarion Belinski, 1811–1848: A Study in the Origins of Social Criticism in Russia*, 1954.
Ginzburg, Lydia, ed. *On Psychological Prose*, 1991. Translated by Judson Rosengrant.
Mann, Yuri. "Vissarion Belinsky (1811–1848) for the 175th Anniversary of His Birth," in *Soviet Literature*. No. 7 (1986), pp. 152–158.
Olson, Kenneth J. "Belinskii's Misinterpretation of Gogol as a Social Critic," in *New Review of East-European History*. XIV (1974), pp. 131–141.
Ponomareff, C. V. "Configurations of Poetic Vision: Belinskij as an Idealist-Critic," in *Slavic and East European Journal*. XIV, no. 2 (1970), pp. 145–159.
——. "V. G. Belinskii's Romantic Imagination," in *Canadian-American Slavic Studies*. VII, no. 3 (1973), pp. 314–326.
Scherer, John L., Jr. "Belinskij and the Hegelian Dialectic," in *Slavic and East European Journal*. XXI, no. 1 (1977), pp. 30–45.
Smirnova, Zinaida Vasil'yevna. *The Socio-political and Philosophical Views of V. G. Belinsky*, 1955.
Stacy, Robert H. *Russian Literary Criticism: A Short History*, 1974.
Terras, Victor. *Belinskij and Russian Literary Criticism: The Heritage of Organic Aesthetics*, 1974.
Weber, Harry B. "Belinskij and the Aesthetics of Utopian Socialism," in *Slavic and East European Journal*. XV, no. 3 (1971), pp. 293–304.

J. R. BROADUS

See also Chernyshevskii; Dobroliubov; Dostoevskii; Pisarev; Veselovskii

Andrei Belyi

(Boris Nikolaevich Bugaev)

Russian writer and critic

Born: Moscow, Russia; October 26, 1880
Died: Moscow, U.S.S.R.; January 8, 1934

Biography

Andrei Belyi was born Boris Nikolaevich Bugaev on October 26, 1880, in Moscow, Russia. His father, Nikolai Vasilievich Bugaev, was dean of the faculty of science at Moscow University; his mother, Aleksandra Dmitrievna, was an aspiring socialite whose nervous, hypersensitive temperament often clashed with her husband's preference for scholarly pursuits. In his memoirs, Belyi attributed his precocious interest in language to the need to escape from his parents' constant bickering.

After spending his first ten years at home being educated under his mother's direction, Belyi completed his secondary education at Polevanov's Gymnasium between 1891 and 1898, and in the following year he entered Moscow University. There he studied both science and literature, finally settling upon philology as his area of specialization, while through his father he met such intellectual luminaries of the day as the philosopher Vladimir Solov'ev and the poet Aleksandr Blok. He also began to write and publish his own creative efforts, using the pseudonym "Andrei Belyi" in the accurate assumption that the avant-garde character of his work would provoke some harsh reaction, and by the time of his thirtieth birthday in 1910 was an active participant in literary society.

Following a period of absorption in occult subjects and travels in Europe and the Middle East with his wife, Asia Turgeneva, to whom he was married in 1910, Belyi spent the years between 1914 and 1916 studying anthroposophy with Rudolf Steiner in Dornach, Switzerland. He returned to Russia in 1916, leaving behind his wife and in effect terminating their relationship, and became active in the literary and political upheavals that accompanied the Russian Revolution. After spending the years between 1921 and 1923 in Berlin, he returned to the Soviet Union, where he spent the remainder of his life in increasing intellectual isolation. He experienced severe sunstroke in the summer of 1933, which led to his death in Moscow on January 8, 1934.

Influence

In general terms, Belyi's concern with the nature of literary language anticipated the stress such pioneering modernists as Stéphane Mallarmé and T. S. Eliot placed upon discovering the necessary relationships between words and objects. Although this aspect of his work was largely suppressed by the literary commissars of the postrevolutionary Soviet Union, Belyi's more technical contributions to the study of Russian prosody and poetics became the foundation of the Russian Formalist school of criticism. Even those Formalists who disagreed with his general theories, such as Viktor Zhirmunskii and Boris Tomashevskii, nevertheless recognized his significance as a scientific student of literary data.

Kiril Taranovskii and James Bailey are among the contemporary critics who have acknowledged Belyi's importance, and Vladimir Nabokov's commentary on Aleksandr Pushkin's *Evgenii Onegin* (1825–1833; *Eugene Onegin*, 1881) makes extensive use of his techniques. Belyi is among the very few critics of his generation to have worked out sophisticated procedures of literary analysis, as a result of which he is often referred to as an innovator – rather than merely paid polite homage as an "influence" – by researchers in such fields as statistical stylistics, metrical variation, and the study of rhythmical structure.

Analysis

In *The Fontana Biographical Companion to Modern Thought* (1983), edited by Alan Bullock and R. B. Woodings, Belyi's literary criticism is described as "wild, complex and brilliant." This is as good an introduction as any to a writer whose critical theories are often based upon broad analogies with music and religion yet also exhibit a scientist's concern for the study and interpretation of empirical reality. As a consequence, anyone looking for a precise articulation of basic rules and principles in Belyi's criticism will be sadly disappointed; those interested in a stimulating variety of exploratory hypotheses, however, will find him an abundant source of ideas and suggestions.

Belyi's early critical essays are best approached as a kind of thinking-in-progress rather than as polished statements of well-honed theoretical axioms. They should also be placed within the context of the Symbolist movement, whose French originators – Paul Verlaine, Charles Baudelaire, Stéphane Mallarmé, Arthur Rimbaud – sought to fuse words, images, and musical qualities into a unified literary whole. In his 1902 article "Forms of Art," Belyi suggested that music provided a model for the serious literary artist: its immediacy of impact and freedom from stereotyped correspondences with the external world made it the ideal vehicle of expression. At the same time, he was considering the relationships between colors and words, attempting to create a science of literature in which controlled stimuli would evoke predictable responses. Belyi's 1904 essay "Criticism and Symbolism" described Symbolist writers as "the final link in an endless chain of experiences – that central station from which new paths will lead."

Although many Symbolists became so obsessed with capturing the subtleties of aesthetic experience that they effectively removed themselves from contact with the rest of society, Belyi saw Symbolism as a potential alternative to the sterile conventionalities of established orthodoxies. In the introduction to his 1910 collection of essays *Simvolizm*, he affirms that "Symbolism is for me . . . a certain religious creed, having its own dogma," a dogma he goes on to define as "*the Verb become Flesh*." In one of the major essays in the book, "The Magic of Words," he writes of

> the world of verbal symbols by means of which can be illumined the mysteries of the world outside me and also the mysteries of the world inside me . . . . In the word, and only in the word, can I create for myself what is both outside and inside. "I" am the word . . . .

Although statements such as these may seem to augur merely some sort of vague literary mysticism, it must be emphasized that they are in fact the subjective, idealistic pole of a persona which was at the same time firmly rooted in objective reality. In 1909, for example, when Belyi was writing "The Magic of Words," he was also organizing a Rhythmics Society dedicated to the scientific study of Russian verse. If Belyi devoutly believed that words were magical, he meant this as a spur to discovering their hidden significances as well as a tribute to their latent powers: the mysteries of the word would yield only to those who worked hard at comprehending them.

That Belyi himself worked hard is evident from the three collections of his essays published in 1910 and 1911: *Lug zelenyi*, *Simvolizm*, and *Arabeski*. Of these, *Simvolizm* contains his most important general statements regarding literary theory and criticism, although *Arabeski*'s "Symbolism as a World View" (originally appearing in 1903) should also be mentioned. This article focuses upon Friedrich Nietzsche's affinities with Symbolism, but in addition includes a number of philosophical discussions of its vast potentialities: Symbolism is defined as "a method that unites the eternal with its spatial and temporal manifestations" and as a fundamental element in the process of artistic cognition.

Several of *Simvolizm*'s essays develop these and other ideas in Belyi's characteristically discursive but passionate prose. "The Magic of Words," for example, wanders all over the literary map in attempting to distinguish between the language of poetry and the language of everyday discourse, and often approaches occultism in its own linguistic flights of fancy:

> The process of naming spatial and temporal phenomena with words is a process of invocation. Every word is a charm. By charming a given phenomenon I am in essence subjugating it. Thus connections between words, grammatical forms, and figures of speech are in essence charms.

Sandwiched between outbursts of this sort, however, one also finds trenchant considerations of what makes language flower or wither, as well as highly technical analyses of word formation which give Belyi's philosophical ideas a foundation in observable fact. If it is often difficult to believe that the same person is responsible for such apparently antithetical kinds of literary criticism, it is nevertheless the case that Belyi viewed them as means to the same end.

A similar convergence of the seemingly divergent takes place in "Lyric Poetry and Experiment" (1911). On the one hand, Belyi wants to uncover the transcendental pattern which determines the actual manifestations of aesthetic impulses; on the other, he intends to demonstrate through formal analysis how this is realized within the structure of individual works of art. In the latter he is often successful, as here in his seminal remarks on a method of distinguishing between poetic styles:

> The relation between the figures and the intervals between them (standing for regular iambic verses), as well as between the figures themselves, marks the rhythmic individuality of the poet within the bounds of a given metric form.

It is difficult, however, to be quite so enthusiastic about Belyi's efforts to discover the more abstract laws governing the creation of literature, efforts which culminate in "The Emblematics of Meaning" (1909).

This very long, poorly organized, and at times impenetrably obscure essay presents Belyi in his most philosophically idealistic guise. He later wrote in his memoirs that he had flung the article together in great haste, and despite its periodic attempts to articulate a schematic outline of meaning, it continually dissolves into flights of rhetoric such as the concluding peroration:

> We must forget the present. We must recreate everything, and in order to do this we must create ourselves.
>
> And the only slope on which we may still clamber is ourselves.
>
> At the summit our "I" awaits us.
>
> Here is the answer for the artist: if he wishes to remain an artist but not cease to be a man, he must become his own artistic form.
>
> Only this form of creation still holds out the promise of salvation.
>
> Here lies the path of the art of the future.

Belyi's penchant for verbiage of this sort should not, however, blind one to the merits of his more down-to-earth critical writings of this period. In seeking a scientific rationale for his philosophical ideas, he developed techniques of formal literary analysis which are still being used by contemporary scholars. If his more recondite notions often seem rather hazy or even downright ridiculous, it must be remembered that Belyi thought of himself as a participant in a dynamic new movement, Symbolism, as well as a critic of literature; thus language which was itself dynamic, regardless of whether it met conventional standards of meaning, was one of the basic intentions of his literary work.

In the decade following 1910, Belyi somewhat revised his ideas about the nature of written discourse, and also admitted political elements into his thinking. Although he had previously been opposed to Marxism's materialist and determinist aspects, he hailed the 1917 Bolshevik Revolution as a long-needed sweeping-away of Russia's moribund past. Belyi believed that this change afforded an unprecedented opportunity to create a mass audience for advanced intellectual concepts, and in 1919 he organized the Free Philosophical Association as a means of increasing contacts between intellectuals and the working class. In an essay entitled "The Crisis of Culture," written between 1912 and 1918, he qualified the aesthetic absolutism of the 1910–1911 essay collections by distinguishing between two types of writers: there were those who sought escape within "the cube of culture," and those who were willing to face the turmoil of their times. Although Belyi's conception of the latter's function still stressed the creative and integrative powers of the word, he was clearly moving toward a more socially responsible view of the author's role in society.

Thus in the preface to his 1931 prose fantasy *Maski*, Belyi accepted the primacy of the cause of the social revolution while carving out a little space for himself with the concept of a "verbal dialectic," which he defined as a revolution of the word that ran parallel to broader social transformations. He also learned to cloak his more technical researches in the proper language, as in this passage from his study of Pushkin's poem "The Bronze Horseman," in *Ritm kak dialektika i 'Mednyi vsadnik,' issledovanie*:

> This is a fact of transformism: a fact of the third dialectical stage, the fact of the search for a principle and its departure from nomenclature. In this sense, my very interpretation of rhythm is a symbolic divorce from the Aristotelian scholasticism: rhythm – x, y, z – call it what you will; but: you will not be able to discover it in present-day terms, in the formal definitions of metre, until you can establish a correspondence between a variety of exceptions.

Introduced by the appropriate Marxist terminology – "the third dialectical stage" being the period of synthesis that follows the emergence of thesis and antithesis – Belyi is then able to go on and engage in the formal literary analysis he loved so well.

No discussion of Belyi's work would be complete if it failed to mention his imposing achievements as a writer of fiction, and not least because, in his later years especially, he was still able to express in his fiction ideas that would have been unacceptable as criticism. Thus novels such as *Moskovskii chudak* (1926) are full of essentially philosophical passages such as the following:

> At that moment he felt: linear time, history, bent tautly in a bow, were in the process of becoming – spiral time: everything was in motion, topsy-turvy: the past reflected had transformed all the projections of the future into a linear past: this past began to move, outstripping itself . . . .
>
> He understood: now no one would be able to grasp anything; the age of clear Aristotle was over.
>
> Heraclitus has risen!

Here Belyi's conception of the potential metamorphosis of everything into everything else, a fundamental Symbolist tenet to which he always remained faithful, finds expression in terms that would have been cause for censorship in a critical article.

Shortly after Belyi's death in 1934, the much more restrictive aesthetic guidelines of Socialist Realism – which demanded that artists act as servants of the state and explicitly promote the realization of a truly communist society – were imposed upon Soviet authors. In 1937 he was officially disparaged as a "comedian," and for decades thereafter neither his criticism nor his fiction was reprinted.

In the West, émigré critics such as D. S. Mirsky and Konstantin Mochulskii kept Belyi's reputation alive by praising the brilliance of his major fictional works. As these have appeared in translation and have been assimilated into the body of world literature, Belyi has been generally recognized as a major stylistic innovator whose place in Russian literature is analogous to that of James Joyce in English letters. His "wild, complex and brilliant" critical writings have always been considered an integral part of the history of the Symbolist movement, and his more technical methods of literary study are still used by specialists in the appropriate fields. Although for political and linguistic reasons it is difficult to gauge the extent of Belyi's influence, it seems safe to say that the intrinsic quality of his work will ensure that he remains a significant figure in the history of twentieth-century literature.

Principal criticism

Lug zelenyi, 1910
Simvolizm, 1910
Arabeski, 1911
Ritm kak dialektika i 'Mednyi vsadnik,' issledovanie, 1929
Masterstvo Gogolia, 1934
Selected Essays of Andrei Belyi, 1985

Other major works and literary forms

Andrei Belyi was a prolific writer who cut across conventional literary genres in his attempts to exemplify in prose and poetry the principles articulated in his literary criticism. The novels *Serebrianyi golub* (1909–1910; *The Silver Dove*, 1974), *Peterburg* (1913–1914; *St. Petersburg*, 1959; also known as *Petersburg*, 1978, 1995), and *Kotik Letaev* (1922; English translation, 1971) are among the works Belyi viewed as his most significant literary statements. His experiments in shorter prose fiction can be sampled in *Andrei Belyi: Complete Short Stories* (1979), and his poetry in *Pervoe svidanie* (1921; *The First Encounter*, 1979).

NOVELS
Serebrianyi golub, 1909–1910 (*The Silver Dove*, 1974)
Peterburg, 1913–1914 (*St. Petersburg*, 1959 also known as *Petersburg*, 1978, 1995)
Kotik Letaev, 1922 (English translation, 1971)
Moskovskii chudak, 1926 } published jointly as
Moskva pod udarom, 1926 } *Moskva*, 1968
Maski, 1931

SHORT FICTION
Andrei Belyi: Complete Short Stories, 1979

POETRY
Pervoe svidanie, 1921 (*The First Encounter*, 1979)

NONFICTION
Dramaticheskaia simfonia, 1902 (*The Dramatic Symphony*, 1986)
Formy iskusstva, 1902 (*The Forms of Art*, 1986)
Na rubezhe dvukh stoletii, 1930
Nachalo veka, 1933
Mezhdu dvukh revoliutsii, 1934 (autobiography)

Further reading

Alexander, Vladimir E. *Andrei Bely: The Major Symbolist Fiction*, 1985.
Elsworth, J. D. *Andrey Belyi: A Critical Study of the Novels*, 1983.
Janacek, Gerald, ed. *Andrey Belyi: A Critical Review*, 1978.
Key, Roger. *The Reluctant Modernist: Andrei Belyi and the Development of Russian Fiction, 1902–1914*, 1996.
Malmstad, John E. *Andrei Bely: Spirit of Symbolism*, 1987.
Maslenikov, Oleg. *The Frenzied Poets: Andrey Biely and the Russian Symbolists*, 1952.
Mochulskii, Konstantin. *Andrei Belyi: His Life and Works*, 1977. Translated by Nora Szalavitz.
Pyman, Avril. *A History of Russian Symbolism*, 1994.
West, James. *Russian Symbolism*, 1970.

PAUL STUEWE

See also Russian Formalism; Shklovskii; Symbolism

Pietro Bembo

Italian scholar and poet

Born: Venice, Italy; May 20, 1470
Died: Rome, Italy; January 18, 1547

Biography

Pietro Bembo was the scion of an eminent patrician family. His father, Bernardo Bembo, among the most important

Venetian political and cultural figures of his day, possessed one of Italy's richest private libraries and cultivated vernacular literature as well as the classics. Young Bembo obtained his humanistic preparation in Greek at the school of Costantino Lascaris in Sicily. One of the first books published by Aldus Manuzio, as part of that editor's Hellenistic program, was Lascaris' grammar, which was edited by Bembo upon his return to Venice. Bembo's edition of Petrarch's *Canzoniere* (written 1374, published 1470) in 1501 and his edition of Dante's *La divina commedia* (c. 1320; *The Divine Comedy*) in 1502 represented editorial break-throughs in the history of vernacular literature. The courtly *Gli Asolani* are contemporary with the beginning of Bembo's estrangement from Venice, which included lengthy and formative stays at the courts of Ferrara and Urbino.

While at Urbino, Bembo set his sights on papal patronage and an ecclesiastic career; his decision resulted in a kind of self-imposed exile from the Venetian Republic, where his literary ambitions were regarded with anxiety by his father and suspicion by his patrician peers. Bembo's courtly career culminated, at the height of the Renaissance, in his being named papal secretary, along with Jacopo Sadoleto, by the Medici Pope Leo X in 1513. Upon the death of his father in 1519, Bembo returned to Venice, eventually establishing himself at Padua, where, in 1522, he took religious orders. During this same period, he lived with Morosina, a woman he had known in Rome; with her he had three children. Bembo was named the historiographer of the Venetian Republic in 1530 and was made cardinal in 1539; he subsequently became bishop of Gubbio and Bergamo. He moved again to Rome in 1544 and died there three years later, after a fall from a horse. He is buried in the Church of Santa Maria sopra Minerva.

Influence

The exemplary character of Bembo's career and the profound influence of his works were celebrated in his own time by his most important contemporaries. The famous conclusion of Castiglione's *The Courtier*, completely dedicated to the fictional Bembo's dissertation on Neo-Platonic love, commemorates Bembo's authorship of the vernacular dialogue *Gli Asolani*. Ludovico Ariosto's praise in the *Orlando furioso* (1516, 1521, 1532; English translation, 1591) of Bembo, "who raised that pure and sweet idiom of ours out of vulgar dark usage, and shown us with his example what it should be," celebrated the principal linguistic and rhetorical authority of their generation. Iconographically, Titian's impressive portrait of 1540 depicts Cardinal Bembo shortly after his elevation.

Principally known today for his role in the Italian *questione della lingua* (language question), Bembo was the author of the decisive contribution to that debate, the *Prose della volgar lingua* (writings in the vernacular language). The work is generally acknowledged to be the most important and influential rhetorical-linguistic treatise in the Italian tradition after Dante's *De vulgari eloquentia* (c. 1306; English translation, 1890). The most famous example of the work's immediate success in the linguistic sphere is provided by Ariosto's substantial final revisions for the 1532 edition of the *Orlando furioso*, an edition which reveals the influence of *Prose della volgar lingua*. Florentine historian Francesco Guicciardini's annotations reveal its influence on his contemporary revisions of the *Ricordi* (1857), which was begun in 1513. While Castiglione's *The Courtier* contains an extensive and articulate rebuttal of Bembo's position on the language question, the language of *The Courtier* itself discloses in its revisions and final form a marked movement in the direction which Bembo was indicating. The pervasiveness of his influence extended into the poetic sphere, where the rhetoric outlined in the *Prose della volga lingua*, together with Bembo's own poetic practice in the *Rime*, epitomized Petrarchism for most of sixteenth-century Italy.

Analysis

Bembo's contribution is best understood against the background of the technological, cultural, and political factors which generally promoted the resolution of an Italian linguistic crisis that had reached its full maturity by the beginning of the sixteenth century. The technological advance of printing had rendered ever more apparent the need for a linguistic-rhetorical model. Within the cultural sphere, the recent triumph of humanistic Ciceronianism in Latin indicated the path of imitation which the vernacular might follow.

Bembo himself was the author of one of the period's major Ciceronian statements in his *De imitatione* of 1514, and his reform essentially transfers to the vernacular sphere the approach of humanistic rhetoric which had established Virgil and Cicero as the models for poetry and prose respectively. According to Bembo's vernacular program, the language of Petrarch and Giovanni Boccaccio was established as the proper object of imitation for poetry and prose. This essentially "literary" (and anachronistic) solution nevertheless represented a historically efficacious cultural response to the contemporary political crisis, which marked the beginning of more than three centuries of foreign domination and Italian political disunity.

Bembo's literary solution, which followed the theoretical model founded upon the example of fourteenth-century classics, had the force of historical necessity behind it. Indeed, the literary and linguistic unification promulgated by Bembo during the early decades of the sixteenth century represents the only kind of unification Italy would accomplish before political unification finally was achieved in 1870.

Bembo's militancy on behalf of the vernacular and his arguments in support of a humanistic literary solution to the vernacular linguistic crisis came up against, besides the resistance of purist partisans of the Latin, what has been termed the "courtier" school of thought as well as the proponents of the contemporary Florentine language. Book 1 of the *Prose della volgar lingua* represents Bembo's response and provides the theoretical bases for the specific rhetorical and grammatical guidelines which are advanced in later books. The dialogue takes place, according to the fiction, in 1503, within the bourgeois (not courtly) setting of the Bembo home in Venice. Bembo's brother Carlo, who died in 1503, acts as spokesman for Pietro's position, initially in response to the dialogue's eminent Latinist-Humanist, Ercole Strozzi, who, representing the resistance of the orthodox Humanists, calls into question Pietro's neglect of Latin in favor of the vernacular. Strozzi subscribes to the discredited notion, maintained in the fifteenth century by Leonardo Bruni (in opposition to Flavio Biondo), that the Roman vernacular and the contemporary vernacular are one and the same and that if the Romans had chosen Latin as the nobler tongue for writing, then modern Italians would do well to do the same.

Federigo Fregoso comes to the vernacular's defense, citing the authority of Cicero, who had promoted the "modern" Latin language against the Greek. Fregoso refutes the old Bruni thesis and argues that the vernacular had originally evolved out of a corrupted form of Latin following the barbarian invasions and the destruction of the empire, subsequently undergoing a process of distillation and improvement during the late medieval period of political liberty after centuries of foreign occupation. A third interlocutor, Giuliano de' Medici (who finds himself in the Bembo home, an exile from his native Florence because of the French invasion of 1494), intervenes at this point to interject the hope that Italy will never return to "speaking servilely," alluding to contemporary foreign invasions of the peninsula. Fregoso then continues his account, tracing the vernacular literary tradition to its origins in the Provençal troubadours.

In a disguised debate with Dante (whose *De vulgari eloquentia* he never mentions, though the *Prose della volgar lingua* in several passages reveals a knowledge of it), Bembo deemphasizes the importance of the Sicilian poets and denies them any role as an autonomous and transitional school in the history of the Italian lyric, favoring a lineage which traces the origins of the Italian vernacular lyric directly to the Tuscan poets. Bembo's claims that the "antichi toscani" were the first Italian poets and that they learned directly from the Provençal poets the "art of verse" represents historiographic support for his linguistic program, which made the fourteenth-century Tuscan writers Boccaccio and Petrarch linguistic and rhetorical models. Fregoso thus provides an articulated and historic lesson on the Provençal troubadours and the metrical forms and vocabulary transmitted from the Provençal lyric tradition to Italy.

Having defended the credentials of the vernacular vis-à-vis the Latin of the Humanists and having outlined its linguistic and literary history, Carlo Bembo next turns to address the problem of the model form of the vernacular. At this point, the debate on the language question is joined with the courtly school of thought, represented by Calmeta (Vincenzo Collo); subsequently, the position of the contemporary Florentines is defended by Giuliano de' Medici. The courtier school proposed and promoted the notion that the language of the courts, that is, the spoken language of the finest gentlemen at court, should serve as the rhetorical-linguistic model for the vernacular. In the version of this school's position attributed by Bembo to Calmeta, the court of Rome, as the most cosmopolitan and central, is recommended and this makes for an easy polemical target. Gentlemen from all Italy, and worse, "barbarians" from abroad, converge there. How could such an eclectic linguistic dissonance function as a model? In addition, courtly conversation had as yet produced no literature, no literary or linguistic model susceptible to imitation in the humanistic sense. Indeed, the political realities, the lack of a politically stable court anywhere on the peninsula had already rendered quixotic the realization of the courtly linguistic solution to the crisis.

The Florentine, Giuliano de' Medici, joins this attack on the language of the court and seconds Carlo Bembo's affirmation that the Florentine language is better suited than the Venetian for literary expression in the vernacular. Giuliano seems unaware that he and contemporary speakers of the Florentine language are the next targets of Bembo's vernacular humanism. Indeed, perhaps it is better not to be born Florentine, if one's aim is to attain vernacular eloquence, since one must unlearn the contemporary Florentine innovations which had corrupted that language since the linguistic golden age of Petrarch and Boccaccio. Boccaccio and Petrarch are anachronistically resurrected in opposition to the contemporary language of the Florentines at the conclusion of book 1, and these vernacular classics form the basis for Bembo's vernacular humanism.

Bembo turns to the presentation of a prescriptive rhetoric and grammar respectively in books 2 and 3. The rhetoric is most articulated and developed in the poetic field, based as it is upon Bembo's mature appreciation (following decades of study and a century of Petrarchism) of the poetry and language of Petrarch. The example of Boccaccio's *Decameron: O, Prencipe Galeotto* (1349–1351; *The Decameron*, 1620) for prose is less secure, and Bembo admits that prose might remain more open to contemporary Tuscan usage. The grammar in book 3 is prescriptive and generalizes norms derived from Bembo's study of the grammar of these and other Tuscan authors of the fourteenth century. In both the rhetorical and grammatical spheres, Bembo allows for difference and variation given the nature of literary language.

The first Florentine resistance to the expropriation or Italianization of the native tongue, represented fictionally at the close of book 1 of the *Prose della volgar lingua*, is perhaps best captured in Niccolò Machiavelli's *Dialogo intorno alle nostre lingue*, written in about 1515 (1730; dialogue or discourse concerning our language). This resistance, however, soon gives way to the different response of Guicciardini, fifteen years younger than Machiavelli. Paradoxically, Florence quickly becomes the great theoretical inheritor of Bembian vernacular humanism, a heritage maintained in works such as Benedetto Varchi's *Ercolano* (1570) and Leonardo Salviati's *Degli avvertimenti della lingua sopra 'l Decameron* (1584). The first of the European national linguistic academies, the Accademia della Crusca (founded 1582), and its influential dictionary, the *Vocabolario* (1612), was informed by explicitly stated Bembian principles which sought guidance for contemporary expression in the texts of the classic authors of the fourteenth century. Bembo's influence in the poetic field, deriving principally from the example of his *Rime*, was also pervasive, leading directly to the masterpiece of the genre, the *Rime* (1558) of Giovanni Della Case.

Principal criticism

De imitatione, 1514
Prose della volgar lingua, 1525

Other major works and literary forms

Pietro Bembo began his career in classic Humanist style with the Latin dialogue *De aetna* (1495) and maintained impeccable Humanist credentials in works such as the philological *De Virgilii Culice et Terentii fabulis* (1530), the Ciceronian manifesto *De imitatione*, and his epistolary as papal secretary. Bembo's vernacular production took as its point of departure the Neo-Platonic courtly dialogue on love: *Gli Asolani* (1505; English translation, 1954). During Bembo's residence at the court of Urbino (after 1506), his vernacular project expanded into tragic-heroic and comic registers respectively in a *canzone* ("Alma cortese, che dal mondo errante") commemorating the death of his brother Carlo and in the courtly *stanze* written for the carnival of 1507. During this same period, he celebrated the same court of Urbino immortalized by Baldassare Castiglione's *Il cortegiano* (1528; *The Courtier*, 1561), in the *De Guido Ubaldo Feretrio deque Elisabetha Gonzaga Urbini ducibus* (1530). Bembo's vernacular lyric poetry was painstakingly organized into a Petrarchan *canzoniere*: his *Rime* (1530) signals the start of mature Renaissance Petrarchism in Italy. After 1530 Bembo began to collect and revise all of his works, including his *Epistolarum familiarium* (1552) and his history of Venice in preparation for a definitive edition. He continued this revision and correction for the rest of his life, and the complete works, *Opere* (1729), edited by his literary executors, began to appear in Rome as early as 1548.

POETRY
Rime per festa carnascialesca, 1507
Rime, 1530
Carmina, 1533

NONFICTION
De aetna, 1495
De Guido Ubaldo Feretrio deque Elisabetha Gonzaga Urbini ducibus, 1530
De Virgilii Culice et Terentii fabulis, 1530
Epistolarum Leonis X nomine scriptarum libri XVI, 1535
Rerum Venetarum historiae libri XII, 1551
Epistolarum familiarium, 1552

MISCELLANEOUS
Gli Asolani, 1505 (English translation, 1954)
Lettere, 1548–1553 (4 volumes)
Opere, 1729
Prose e rime di Pietro Bembo, 1960

Further reading

Cachey, Theodore J., Jr. "Il pane del grano e la saggina: Pietro Bembo's 1505 Asolani Revisited," in *Italianist: Journal of the Department of Italian Studies, University of Reading*. 12 (1992), pp. 5–23.
Dionisotti, Carlo, ed. Introduction to *Prose e rime di Pietro Bembo*, 1960.
Fletcher, Jefferson Butler. *Literature of the Italian Renaissance*, 1934, 1964.
Forster, Leonard. *The Icy Fire: Five Studies in European Petrarchism*, 1969.
McLaughlin, Martin L. *Literary Imitation in the Italian Renaissance: The Theory and Practice of Literary Imitation in Italy from Dante to Bembo*, 1995.
Robb, Nesca A. *Neoplatonism of the Italian Renaissance*, 1935, 1968.
Symonds, John Addington. *The Renaissance in Italy*, 1886.

THEODORE J. CACHEY, JR.

See also Giraldi Cinthio; Renaissance and Restoration Literary Theory; Scaliger; Trissino

Walter Benjamin

German writer, critic, and theorist

Born: Berlin, Germany; July 15, 1892
Died: Port Bou, Spain; September 27, 1940

Biography

Walter Benjamin was born in 1892 in Berlin, Germany. His father was a well-to-do upper-middle-class Jewish art dealer who was able to provide not only for a fine secondary school education but also for the cost of a university education. Starting in 1912, Benjamin studied at universities in Freiburg, Berlin, Munich, and finally Bern, where he received his doctoral degree in philosophy and literature in 1919. In 1917 he married Dora Pollack; they had one son in 1918 and were divorced in 1930.

In 1915 Benjamin became acquainted with Gershom Scholem, a lifelong friend and adviser. Even after Scholem left Germany to become a professor of Jewish mysticism in Jerusalem, they remained in constant contact, exchanging hundreds of letters. Another friend, Theodor Adorno, whom Benjamin met in 1923 and with whom he also carried on an extensive correspondence, was to serve as the first editor of Benjamin's posthumously published works in 1955. In 1924 he met Asja Lacis, a Latvian Bolshevik and theater director who was instrumental in Benjamin's extensive studies of Marxist philosophy and in encouraging his trip to Moscow in 1926.

When Adolf Hitler came to power in Germany in 1933 Benjamin fled to Paris, a place he had often visited since his student days and whose literature and culture he valued highly. During these years he also visited the playwright Bertolt Brecht on numerous occasions in Denmark. When the Nazis invaded France, Benjamin had to flee once more. His friends at the Institute for Social Research (the institute had moved to New York) had obtained a visa for him to come to the United States via Lisbon, Portugal. In June, 1940, he left Paris for Lourdes. From there he crossed the Pyrenees from France to Spain on foot. When told by Spanish officials in the border town of Port Bou that he would be returned to France and the custody of the German military, he committed suicide on September 27, 1940. His dream to "be regarded as the foremost critic of German literature" was realized some fifty years later.

Influence

Benjamin's work has not directly influenced a particular school of criticism, but it has been very influential in shaping the concept of criticism in the late twentieth century in Germany and in England, while also affecting the work of some Marxist critics in the United States. His intellectual home base was the Institut für Sozialforschung (Institute for Social Research) in Frankfurt, Germany, with institute colleagues Theodor Adorno, Max Horkheimer, and other founders and members of that school. In England, the critic Terry Eagleton has written extensively and passionately on the impact that Benjamin had on revolutionary Marxist criticism. In the United States, the philosopher Martin Jay and a group of critics publishing in the periodical *New German Critique* have closely examined Benjamin's work and its role in contemporary criticism.

Analysis

The question of whether Benjamin is a Marxist literary critic was not only problematic during the last decade of his life but has also been an issue since his "discovery" in Germany in the late 1950s and in the United States in the late 1960s. Not unlike many Western European intellectuals who were attracted to the philosophical writings and speculations of Karl Marx and Friedrich Engels during the period following the Russian Revolution and the conclusion of World War I, Benjamin became an adherent of Communism without joining the Communist Party. The conversion to Marxism for Benjamin can be set in 1925. His three major works, *Der Begriff der Kunstkritik in der deutschen Romantik* (1919; the concept of art criticism in German Romanticism), *Goethes Wahlverwandtschaften* (1922; Goethe's *Elective Affinities*), and *Ursprung des deutschen Trauerspiels* (1925; *The Origin of German Tragic Drama*, 1985), as well as a host of shorter essays and reviews in the early years, show little or no influence of Marxism.

Benjamin was a convert to Marxism but remained highly critical of Communism. Believing that to decide in favor of Communism a person should see Russia, he visited Moscow from December 6, 1926, to February 1, 1927. These first-hand experiences are reported in his *Moscow Diary*. In this report, as well as in a number of later, shorter essays and letters, Benjamin reveals his disillusionment with the practice of Communism. Still, his commitment to the philosophical concepts of both Marxism and Communism remained strong for the rest of his life.

Unfortunately, Benjamin never wrote a definitive work on Marxist literary criticism. His views, therefore, must be culled from the many essays, fragments, letters, and reviews he wrote during his last decade and a half. Had he lived longer and in greater security, he might have finished his great "Passagen-Werk" (arcades project), a materialistic history and philosophy of the nineteenth century. One can only speculate about what might have been included in this unfinished opus. It is clear, however, that Benjamin did not restrict himself to an examination of only literary works; he considered the arts in general.

"The Work of Art in the Age of Mechanical Reproduction" examines the new role that the work of art has attained. Starting with the notion that "art has always been reproducible," as, for example, in the ancient stamping of coins or woodcut graphic art and medieval engravings and etchings, Benjamin cites the fact that lithography made the illustration of everyday life possible. This invention was quickly superseded, however, by the invention of photography, which made pictorial reproduction almost instantaneous. The subsequent inventions of film and sound film, in which a "process of pictorial reproduction was accelerated so enormously that it could keep pace with speech," provided for the reproduction of "all transmitted works of art." This development not only made a powerful impact on the public but it also created a new form of artistic expression.

To be sure, the photograph and film have taken from the work of art "its presence in time and space." That means that the new work no longer enjoys the authority of originality, of uniqueness, or of exclusive ownership. The "aura" of the work of art has been destroyed, yet it can now be received by an audience of many, in many places. The traditional concept of art has been transformed completely and the mechanically reproduced works of art have become the new media for the masses. The new audience has also a new function in the relationship of the new work of art; namely, they have become not only consumers but also participants and critics. Benjamin envisions films in which there will no longer be the "illusion-promoting spectacles" of the capitalistic film industry of his time but a union of the producer and the consumer of the work of art. He sees an example of this in some of the then-new Russian films in which "some of the players whom we meet . . . are not actors in our sense but people who portray themselves – and primarily in their own work process."

Another essay, "The Author as Producer," presented by Benjamin as a lecture in 1934 to the Institute for the Study of Fascism in Paris, also deals with the problem of the use of technological advances – as in film and theater – by the new, or progressive, artists. The views articulated in this essay are the result of many discussions Benjamin had with the German playwright Bertolt Brecht. He begins with the assumption that contemporary social situations demand that a progressive writer, in contrast to the "bourgeois writer of entertainment literature," recognize an alliance with the proletariat in the class struggle. Benjamin now seeks to define how the writer is to state "the correct political line," as well as create a work of artistic quality and resolve the conflict between content and form. Rather than accepting the dogmatic notion that "a work that shows the correct political tendency need show no other quality," Benjamin sets out to prove that "the tendency of a literary work can only be politically correct if it is also literarily correct."

The first part of this issue, the political tendency, is garnered from an examination of society. Advancing the Marx-Engels method of historical analysis of dialectical materialism, which posits that social and economic change can be effected only through a change of the forces of production or by the establishment of a classless society, the author's task is to recognize that the only correct political tendency is the revolutionary overthrow of those conditions of production. Benjamin, however, is not satisfied with asking only "what is the attitude of a work to the relations of production of its time?" He immediately goes on with the point that is of greater concern to him in this essay, namely, "the function the work has within the literary relations of production of its time." With this, Benjamin turns to the other part of the problem of the literary work, the literary tendency.

What literary tendencies bring about a progressive literary technique? Benjamin cites numerous examples. He identifies Sergei Tretiakov, an "operating writer," a journalist whose mission was "not to report but to struggle, not to play the spectator but to intervene actively." Tretiakov participated in the total collectivization of Russian agriculture when he went to the collective farms for an extended period and worked there as a journalist and propagandist. He not only worked to build up a successful farm but he also established reading rooms, edited newspapers, trained reporters, and introduced radio and motion-picture houses to the commune.

Tretiakov's book based on those experiences not only demonstrated the proper political tendencies for Benjamin but also, since it had a powerful influence on the further development of collective agriculture in Russia, demonstrated the proper literary tendencies as well. Benjamin does not apologize for selecting as his example a newspaper writer. He notes that from the work of this journalist there developed new writers at the commune with the final result that "the reader is at all times ready to become a writer, that is, a describer, but also a prescriber. As an expert . . . he gains access to authorship." This case, to be sure, is a concrete example of the "mighty process of recasting . . . the conventional distinction between genres, between writer and poet, between scholar and popularizer, but also revises even the distinction between author and reader."

Although Benjamin sees the Tretiakov example as decisive evidence of the author as producer, he believes that it is necessary to seek examples in other media to illustrate the revolutionary artist's mission to create or transform modes of artistic production. Phonograph records have made obsolete music in the concert hall in that they no longer limit artistic performances to the private property of only a few, but make them available to everyone. In a similar way, films and photography have changed the former modes of perception as well as the older techniques of artistic production and the relationship of the producer to the consumer.

Since this essay resulted from Benjamin's association with Brecht, it is understandable that he would discuss Brecht's "epic" theater at some length. Unlike the traditional theater that creates an illusion and involves the spectator emotionally in various segments of the plot, the epic – or new – theater is one of a narrative confrontation that forces the spectator to be a reasoning participant. The epic theater stages situations, rather than plots, and is frequently interrupted by songs. It develops in montages and incorporates devices from both modern communications media and the medieval theater tradition. Spectators are purposely distanced from the action so that they must observe the process of that action and the role the actor is performing. The spectator participates with astonishment, rather than satisfaction. The epic theater "is less concerned with filling the public with feelings, even seditious ones, than with alienating it in an enduring manner, through thinking, from the conditions in which it lives." The spectator is an active and critical participant in the performance of the theatrical event; the spectator has joined the author in the production.

Benjamin maintains that whereas traditional writers have served only a bourgeois public, revolutionary artists have incorporated their commitment to the social cause in their development of the artistic form, making the author and the reader or spectator into true collaborators.

From the plethora of fragments and essays, there is one small collection that reveals Benjamin as a cultural critic of enormous breadth and profound depth: "Paris, Capital of the

Nineteenth Century." Elsewhere, Benjamin had read literary texts, but here he was "reading" and providing his Marxist analysis of institutional structures of the city – the architecture of the arcades and boulevards, the panoramas made possible by Louis Jacques Mandé Daguerre, the world exhibitions in the industrial age, interior design in the living and working space – and an essay on Charles Baudelaire, the poet in revolt against the contemporary bourgeois society.

This collection, originally prepared as an outline for the "arcades project," demonstrates the idiosyncratic way in which Benjamin approaches his work. First, he identifies a particular "fact" and looks for the technological and sociological causes of "correspondences." Next, he advances an association of economic and political trends to the historical period under investigation, and, finally, he demands that the "fact" represent the secret desires of the ruling classes.

Benjamin's critics point out that he is wrong in his analysis, since he is dealing with static facts rather than sequential events. Benjamin seems to suggest that technical forces are the determining factors in history, rather than considering the role these forces play in the production process. The question that finally remains unanswered in his criticism of the work of art or literature is the way in which the criticism of the work can be directly and systematically linked, at one and the same time, as a mode of production and as a mode of experience. His friend and critic Theodor Adorno chides him for occasionally positing "correspondences" between isolated economic facts and isolated literary facts, suggesting a metaphorical relationship rather than the relationship between base and superstructure demanded by the Marxist critic. Indeed, there are flaws in Benjamin's understanding of Marxist literary criticism which he might have corrected in time. On the other hand, one could speculate, he might have eventually developed a theory of criticism apart from Marxist philosophy.

Principal criticism

"Moskau," 1927 ("Moscow," 1978)
"Der Sürrealismus," 1929 ("Surrealism," 1978)
"Zum Bilde Prousts," 1929 ("The Image of Proust," 1968)
"Der Autor als Produzent," 1934 ("The Author as Producer," 1978)
"Franz Kafka," 1934 ("Franz Kafka – On the Tenth Anniversary of His Death," 1968)
"Brechts *Dreigroschenroman*," 1935 ("Brecht's *Threepenny Novel*," 1978)
"Paris, die Hauptstadt des XIX. Jahrhunderts," 1935 ("Paris, Capital of the Nineteenth Century," 1978)
"Der Erzähler," 1936 ("The Story-teller: Reflections on the Work of Nikolai Leskov," 1968)
"Das Kunstwerk im Zeitalter seiner Reproduzierbarkeit," 1936 ("The Work of Art in the Age of Mechanical Reproduction," 1968)
"Über einige Motive bei Baudelaire," 1939 ("On Some Motifs in Baudelaire," 1968)
"Was ist das epische Theater?," 1939 ("What Is Epic Theater?," 1968)
"Über den Begriff der Geschichte," 1940 ("Theses on the Philosophy of History," 1968)
Moskauer Tagebuch, 1980 (*Moscow Diary*, 1986)

The essays listed above are translated in *Illuminations*, 1968, edited by Hannah Arendt, and *Reflections: Essays, Aphorisms, Autobiographical Writings*, 1978, edited by Peter Demetz. Other essays in English translation can be found in *Walter Benjamin: Selected Writings*, 1996–1999, edited by Marcus Bullock and Michael Jennings.

Other major works and literary forms

In addition to the selected essays on criticism cited above, Walter Benjamin wrote more than 3,000 items, including lectures, essays, book reviews, and translations. His complete works are published in a multivolume edition, the *Gesammelte Schriften* (1974–1985), edited by Rolf Tiedemann and Hermann Schweppenhäuser, initially in cooperation with the late Theodor Adorno and Gershom Scholem. Adorno and Scholem also edited Benjamin's vast correspondence, *Briefe 1, 1910–1928* and *Briefe 2, 1929–1940* (1978; *The Correspondence of Walter Benjamin, 1910–1940*, 1994). Although Benjamin's influence on Marxist criticism has been profound, the vast majority of scholars working on Benjamin are German-speaking, making the possibility of further English translations unlikely.

NONFICTION
Der Begriff der Kunstkritik in der deutschen Romantik, 1919
Goethes Wahlverwandtschaften, 1922
Ursprung des deutschen Trauerspiels, 1925 (*The Origin of German Tragic Drama*, 1985)
Charles Baudelaire: Ein Lyriker im Zeitalter des Hochkapitalismus, 1973 (*Charles Baudelaire: A Lyric Poet in the Era of High Capitalism*, 1973)
Versuche über Brecht, 1973 (*Understanding Brecht*, 1973)

Further reading

Arendt, Hannah. Introduction to *Illuminations*, 1968.
Brodersen, Momme. *Walter Benjamin: A Biography*, 1996.
Buck-Morss, Susan. *The Dialectics of Seeing: Walter Benjamin and the Arcades Project*, 1989.
Cohen, Margaret. *Profane Illumination: Walter Benjamin and the Paris of Surrealist Revolution*, 1993.
Demetz, Peter. Introduction to *Reflections: Essays, Aphorisms, Autobiographical Writings*, 1978.
Eagleton, Terry. *Walter Benjamin: Or, Towards a Revolutionary Criticism*, 1981.
Gilloch, Graeme. *Myth and Metropolis: Walter Benjamin and the City*, 1996.
Missac, Pierre. *Walter Benjamin's Passages*, 1995.
Nägele, Rainer. *Theater, Theory, Speculation: Walter Benjamin and the Scenes of Modernity*, 1991.
Roberts, Julian. *Walter Benjamin*, 1983.
Scholem, Gershom. *Walter Benjamin: The Story of a Friendship*, 1982.
Smith, Gary, ed. *On Walter Benjamin: Critical Essays and Recollections*, 1988.
Witte, Bernd. *Walter Benjamin: An Intellectual Biography*, 1991.
Wolin, Richard. *Walter Benjamin: An Aesthetic Redemption*, 1982.

THOMAS H. FALK

See also Adorno; Brecht; Eagleton; Gramsci; Lukács; Marxist Theory and Criticism

Eric Bentley

English-born American critic, writer, and translator

Born: Bolton, Lancashire, England; September 14, 1916

Biography

Eric Russell Bentley was born in industrial Lancashire, the son of a businessman, sometime mayor, and liberal politician, and a musical mother. A scholarship student, Bentley attended Bolton School, then studied under C. S. Lewis at University College, Oxford. Bentley's undergraduate activities included numerous performances, both dramatic and musical, and his studies culminated in a thesis on psychology and literary criticism. His graduate work at Yale University in comparative literature produced his first book, *A Century of Hero-Worship* (1944); this philosophical work grounded his critical career in a thorough understanding of modern social thought.

Bentley's first, troubled academic position was in the English department at the University of California at Los Angeles (from 1941 to 1942), where his disagreements with older colleagues were counterbalanced by his new acquaintance with Bertolt Brecht, Theodor Adorno, and the other Hollywood exiles of Nazi Germany. Bentley's second, more congenial appointment, from 1942 to 1944, was at Black Mountain College in North Carolina, where he produced his first translation of a Brecht play. Bentley then settled at the University of Minnesota, where he published *Bernard Shaw* (1947), *The Playwright as Thinker* (1948), and the critical anthology *The Importance of "Scrutiny": Selections from "Scrutiny," a Quarterly Review, 1932–1948* (1948).

Having established himself as an important new voice in drama scholarship, Bentley left Minneapolis for three years of travel and practice in the European theater, aided by a Guggenheim Fellowship. Apart from viewing a considerable number of plays, he signed on with productions such as Brecht's 1950 Munich staging of *Mutter Courage und ihre Kinder* (1940; *Mother Courage and Her Children*, 1941). Eventually Bentley became involved in productions at theaters as varied as the Zurich Schauspielhaus, the Abbey Theatre in Dublin, the university theater at Padua, and Max Reinhardt's Schloss Leopoldskron at Salzburg.

Bentley's teaching career resumed in 1952 with a coup of the first order: his simultaneous appointments as Brander Matthews Professor of Dramatic Literature at Columbia University and as drama critic for *The New Republic*. Bentley's subsequent critical writings on the stage were collected in *The Dramatic Event* (1954) and *What Is Theatre?* (1956); an expanded edition of the latter contains all of his reviews during the era, including a number of later commissioned pieces. Bentley interrupted his stay at Columbia twice. The first leave was for an appointment as the annual Charles Eliot Norton professor at Harvard University (1960–1961), the lectures for which he later expanded into his only theoretical study, *The Life of the Drama* (1964). Bentley also went to Berlin as an artist-in-residence on a Ford Foundation Fellowship. During his tenure at Columbia, he produced a truly prodigious number of collections, critical anthologies, and translations, as well as a further volume of critical writings, *"The Theatre of Commitment" and Other Essays on Drama in Our Society* (1967), and his recordings.

The next few years lack any particular coherence in Bentley's critical career, but they did include a new concentration on the writing of original plays. Among these was a very successful dramatization of the Hollywood McCarthy trials, *Are You Now or Have You Ever Been: The Investigation of Show-Business by the Un-American Activities Committee, 1947–1958* (1972), using material with which Bentley had earlier dealt in a collection entitled *Thirty Years of Treason* (1971). Bentley became active in the gay rights movement, openly declaring his homosexuality after an earlier domestic life that had included two marriages and the fathering of twin sons; the play which reflects this new interest is a treatment of Oscar Wilde's trial, *Lord Alfred's Lover* (1978). He also continued to publish his criticism, some of which was collected in *Theatre of War* (1972). Many of the plays take a premise from a favorite writer, while others, like the sketches written for *DMZ Revue* (1968), are frankly topical and political. Though his work has become increasingly personal, Bentley's reputation has continued to be consolidated, and he was celebrated in 1986 by a collection of essays marking his seventieth birthday entitled *The Play and Its Critic: Essays for Eric Bentley*, which included contributions from many leading scholars and personal documents such as his early letters of recommendation from C. S. Lewis. In 1998 Bentley lectured on Bertolt Brecht in New York, and his book *Bentley on Brecht* appeared to coincide with the writer's centenary.

Influence

Bentley's primary achievement has been his influence in forming the literary taste of two generations of British and American theater students. His importance has come not principally through his many critical and creative activities but through his work as an assembler of texts, selecting and editing plays for a number of anthologies that became standard texts in literature classes and the study of dramatic theory. Bentley began that editorial activity early in his career, and through a steady program of revision and republication, he has kept his choices of "great" plays before the public for almost forty years. Bentley has also exerted considerable influence as a teacher and lecturer, with forty years of university instruction and an uncounted number of occasional speeches to his credit. As a theorist Bentley offers little that is original, but as a tireless worker for his favorite authors, his impact on theater academia has been enormous.

Analysis

Bentley's first book, *A Century of Hero-Worship*, includes all the major concerns of his career except theater performance. His immediate concern, in the wartime context of the book, was the effect of the theory of the Superman upon social thought and the relation of the "heroic vitalists" to the politics of Fascism. Bentley manages to construct a vitalism that is not driven by a will to power but is characterized by a pragmatic approach to political problems, like the vitalism of William James and George Bernard Shaw. Bentley argues that Fascism is essentially mechanistic, not vital, and that democracy, rather than leveling people, places a value upon them that allows the hero, the excellent person, to emerge. His emphasis upon values later activated his response to the Vietnam War, contained in a number of essays from the 1960s, and his vocal defense of homosexual rights, especially in his essay on *Lord Alfred's Lover* in *Thinking About the Playwright* (1987). Bentley's criticism always responds in some way to the contemporary moment, though that response may be grounded in a very personal agenda.

Bentley's conclusion that Shaw's political philosophy was the most humane form of vitalism resulted from a close reading of a number of Shaw's plays. Bentley then expanded the material on Shaw in the book on heroism into a study that is still the most cogent political introduction to Shaw's work and provides the best view of the entire range of the playwright's thought. Bentley explains how the ambiguities and contemporary motives of Shaw's plays exist because "he stands for society against anti-social conspiracies, he stands for style against fashion, for man against the machinery of living and for life – 'life with a blessing' – against any particular 'idea' whatsoever." Though Bentley staunchly defends the organic integrity of the playscript in many comments throughout his career, his critical method is not the New Critical style of reading plays as closed objects, but the Marxist style of relating plays to their contemporary contexts, drawing links among plays and plotting the psychological dynamics of their reception. *Bernard Shaw* is by far Bentley's most complete treatment of a writer's body of work, yet the most fascinating aspect of the book is its insight into British political behavior, not its critical method. In his first statement of what he viewed as the ultimate goal of art – education – Bentley provides a link between the patient polemics of the Fabian Shaw and the urgent propaganda of Brecht when he concludes the book by noting, "The fact that Shaw really wrote because he 'had to' (and not to change the world) was fortunate in one respect: by not saving the world he saved his drama as art and, therefore, as teaching." To a certain extent Bentley saved Shaw, at least from other critics less sympathetic to Marxism, and he would do Brecht even greater service.

Though Bentley's political sympathies are socialist, his method of criticism deals less with broad, abstracted historical trends than with the individual's experience of history. This tendency is most pronounced in Bentley's work on Brecht, whom he met early in his career. Bentley's first treatment of Brecht's dramas, in *The Playwright as Thinker*, divided the work into four biographical phases. Yet this kind of historical rigor finally collapsed into a criticism that is highly anecdotal, in which Bentley the critic, through extended contact with the author, loses focus on Brecht's experience of history and writes instead about Bentley's experience of Brecht (not only in *The Brecht Memoir*, 1986, but also in large portions of *The Brecht Commentaries*, 1981). There was a kind of taut vigor in Bentley's early work on the *Lehrstücke* – such as the essay on *Furcht und Elend des dritten Reiches* (1938; *The Private Life of the Master Race*, 1944), which systematically responds to Thomas Mann's six criticisms of Brecht and then expounds the logic of Brecht's aesthetic of formal interruption – that is entirely missing from the memoir, which Bentley ends by quoting singer Lotte Lenya's endorsement of his own record albums: "It's quite wonderful to hear all those songs, and you do them so well that I am afraid you might become a close competition to me." Bentley's critical acuity, so pronounced in his ringing indictments of the Broadway theater, languishes in the shadow of his reverence for Brecht, so that in even his most trenchant collection of notes on Brechtian texts, in *Theatre of War*, Bentley ends up arguing too often in support of Brecht's intentions rather than analyzing the texts or their productions. Brecht's didactic plays were perfect material for the testing of Bentley's hypothesis that the goal of drama is teaching, or rather learning, yet his criticism of Brecht is dominated by reminiscence. As a treatment of the historical individual, the work on Shaw is far superior to the better-known comments on Brecht – comments which helped to create Brechtian idolatry in theater study.

If the shortcomings of Bentley's personal/historical method of criticism in the treatment of Brecht seem peculiar to that relationship, one should keep in mind Bentley's fascination with Pirandello's work, the product of a man Bentley did not know, and one whose Fascism he showed some reluctance to address. Bentley's thesis that the art reflects the man and his conviction about the excellence of Pirandello's work come to loggerheads in the case of the great author who was also an "authoritarian." The metaphysical commitments in Pirandello's plays about truth and illusion, reality and appearance, art and life, consistently produce for his relativist fields of difference an imposed order, arbitrary in its assignment of art to a higher plane of being. Yet Bentley does not connect this metaphysical commitment with Fascism because his own theory of art carries within it many of the same assumptions. Much of Bentley's early training in aesthetics is related to the thought of F. R. Leavis, the *Scrutiny* critic, perhaps the last major critic to use mystification as a means of justifying the use of personal taste as the ultimate critical criterion. Bentley, while lucid in his expositions of the relation of history to literature in the case of Shaw, had no recourse to historical argument in his analysis of Pirandello and so makes his endorsement on the basis of his own aesthetic preferences. In fact, Pirandello's *L'umorismo* (1908; *Humor*, 1966) is another of the dangerous forms of the "heroic vitalism" that Bentley goes to such lengths to decry in his first book. Yet Pirandello's vitalism is an aestheticized vitalism – almost, as Bentley notes in one essay, a version of Platonic idealism – that exposes how far Bentley's appreciation of the aesthetics of dramatic art is from his appreciation of political meanings. His concern with putting the matter "too philosophically" causes his consideration of Pirandello to stop when the playwright is still in midcareer, to praise the establishment of Pirandello's relativist identity theory without analyzing the abuse of power that it invites – which is dramatized in the later "myth" plays and lived in the events of Pirandello's political life.

There are many passages that illustrate the elevation of art to a spiritual plane in Bentley's work. His major book of dramatic theory, *The Life of the Drama*, for example, states:

> And this [drama] constitutes a supreme idealization of life, for it signifies a life which has a clear and unitary meaning, a direction, an utterly purposive movement toward an end. In this respect, dramatic art is one of the great wish-fulfilling dreams, for there is nothing human beings more ardently crave than to be persons in such a drama. In the Middle Ages, it was official doctrine that humanity did belong in such a drama; and so the art of drama represented a metaphysical fact. But this art has as great a poignancy – or greater – in an age like our own when the universe is generally felt to be unintelligible, amorphous, undramatic. For today art offers the only integrated drama, and we can be persons in a perfectly constructed Action only, it would seem, when we read or see a play.

To Bentley a play is still a way to gain access to a kind of ideal of beauty and absolute completeness of expression that has been effectively challenged and debunked by concepts of *différance*, the infinite play of semiotic textuality. He posits a closure for the artwork that is at odds with his best applied critical work, the developmental study *The Playwright as Thinker*. In that book Bentley notes of the avant-garde that "discoverers always think they have found the truth when what they have actually found is at best *a* truth, *a* formula, *a* new and fruitful approach." Unfortunately Bentley discounts the applicability of this principle to the act of reading the text; he talks about the text as written, about the process during which an authoritative meaning is inscribed, rather than about the text as read, when the process of communication actually takes place. That Bentley, interested in writing, should take such an approach is understandable, but that he should propose a kind of essential meaning for the play that readings only tend to approach, as is his premise in essays such as "Doing Shakespeare Wrong" from *In Search of Theatre* (1953), is a mistake that denies the vigor and creativity of the reading process. Such a position made Bentley a confident but unrelenting reviewer of performances.

Bentley's position as a critical theorist seems in fact to be surprisingly traditional, given his political views. *The Life of the Drama* is essentially a revision of Aristotle's *De poetica* (334–323 B.C.; *Poetics*) on its own terms; one part of the book reviews plot, character, dialogue, thought, and enactment (rather than spectacle), while the second part is a survey of the various fragmentations of comedy and tragedy that constitute the major forms of drama, including the often quoted chapters on farce and melodrama which hinge on the opposition between writing and performance. This conservative theoretical approach has aided Bentley to some extent in his secondary, but perhaps most important, critical project, the establishment of a canon for modern drama. Bentley edited two major, multivolume modern play anthologies, *From the Modern Repertoire* (1949–1956) and *The Modern Theater* (1955–1960), both of which persuasively altered accepted perceptions of the relative value of modern writers. Bentley also adjusted the antecedents of official modern drama by issuing comprehensive collections and collections of classic plays from different national literatures. In all cases Bentley is able to defend his selections in familiar terms; thus the books have gained wide acceptance and have greatly altered American perceptions of the history of dramatic literature.

Finally, it should be noted that Bentley is also an excellent stylist; the literary quality of his critical writing is so fine that even when he says something that seems wrong or arbitrary, he says it with such panache that one wants to believe it. Take as a parting example the tautological opening paragraph of Bentley's chapter on dialogue in *The Life of the Drama*:

> All literature is made up of words, but plays are made up of spoken words. While any literature may be read aloud, plays are written to be read aloud. It is because the drama presents men speaking that the theatre hires speaking men to communicate it. This is expensive. And nothing testifies more surely to people's interest in hearing words spoken than their willingness to pay for it.

Principal criticism

A Century of Hero-Worship: A Study of the Idea of Heroism in Carlyle and Nietzsche, with Notes on Other Hero-Worshippers of Modern Times, 1944 (also known as *The Cult of the Superman*, 1947)

The Playwright as Thinker: A Study of Drama in Modern Times, 1946 (also known as *The Modern Theatre: A Study of Dramatists and the Drama*, 1948)

Bernard Shaw: A Reconsideration, 1947, 1957
In Search of Theatre, 1953
The Dramatic Event: An American Chronicle, 1954
What Is Theatre? A Query in Chronicle Form, 1956 (revised and expanded as *What Is Theatre: Incorporating "The Dramatic Event" and Other Reviews, 1944–1967*, 1968)
The Life of the Drama, 1964
"The Theatre of Commitment" and Other Essays on Drama in Our Society, 1967
Theatre of War: Comments on 32 Occasions, 1972
The Brecht Commentaries, 1981
The Brecht Memoir, 1986
The Pirandello Commentaries, 1986
Thinking About the Playwright: Comments from Four Decades, 1987
Bentley on Brecht, 1998

Other major works and literary forms

Eric Bentley's work falls into a number of different classifications, only some of which can be considered types of literary criticism. In addition to books and articles on dramatic texts, his works include collections of reviews of performances, volumes of translations in which critical/interpretive choices are inscribed in the texts, volumes of adaptations in which his interpretive activities are more clearly evident, and original dramatic texts (many of which are based in historical events). As a translator, Bentley is acclaimed for his work on the plays of Luigi Pirandello and Bertolt Brecht. As an adapter, his work with texts by Pirandello and Heinrich von Kleist has been collected as "variations" on plays. Bentley's original scripts have been collected according to theme; the most important volumes are *Rallying Cries: Three Plays* (1977) and *Monstrous Martyrdoms: Three Plays* (1985). He has also translated and performed songs by Brecht and Wolf Biermann, and other incidental materials associated with his numerous anthologies and record albums. Bentley's original work has never achieved the prominence and respect accorded to his critical writings.

PLAYS
Are You Now or Have You Ever Been: The Investigation of Show-Business by the Un-American Activities Committee, 1947–1958, 1972
Rallying Cries: Three Plays, 1977
Lord Alfred's Lover, 1978
Monstrous Martyrdoms: Three Plays, 1985

TRANSLATIONS
Parables for the Theatre: "The Good Woman of Setzuan" and "The Caucasian Chalk Circle," 1965 (of Bertolt Brecht's plays *Der gute Mensch von Sezuan* and *Der kaukasische Kreidekreis*)

EDITED TEXTS
The Private Life of the Master Race: A Documentary Play by Bertolt Brecht, 1948
The Importance of "Scrutiny": Selections from "Scrutiny," a Quarterly Review, 1932–1948, 1948
From the Modern Repertoire, 1949–1956 (3 volumes)
The Play: A Critical Anthology, 1951
Shaw on Music, 1955
The Modern Theater, 1955–1960 (6 volumes)
Let's Get a Divorce and Other Plays, 1958
Six Spanish Plays, 1958
The Classic Theater, 1958–1961 (4 volumes)
The Genius of the Italian Theater, 1964
The Storm over "The Deputy," 1964
Songs of Bertolt Brecht and Hanns Eisler, 1966
The Theory of the Modern Stage, 1968
The Great Playwrights: Twenty-five Plays with Comments by Critics and Scholars, 1970 (2 volumes)
Thirty Years of Treason, 1971
La Ronde: Ten Dialogues by Arthur Schnitzler, 1978
Baal: A Man's a Man; and The Elephant Calf: Early Plays by Bertolt Brecht, 1983
Before Brecht: Four German Plays, 1985
Woyzeck by Georg Buchner, 1991
Pirandello: Plays, 1998

Further reading

Allen, Ralph G. "Eric Bentley's Most Recent Letter to the World," in *The New York Times Book Review*. LXXIV (March 30, 1969), p. 4.
——. "Liberal Paradoxes," in *The Times Literary Supplement*. May 25, 1973, p. 588.
Bacon, Leonard. "Heroes and the Heroic Cult," in *Saturday Review*. XXVII, no. 40 (1944), p. 14.
Bertin, Michael. *The Play and Its Critic*, 1986.
Chiaromonte, Nicola. "From Carlyle to Shaw," in *The New Republic*. III, no. 17 (1944), pp. 526–528.
Gassner, John. "The Play Is Still the Thing," in *The New York Times Book Review*. LXIX (October, 1964), p. 6.
Hook, Sidney. "Heroic Vitalism," in *The Nation*. CLIX, no. 15 (1944), pp. 412–414.
Suvin, Darko. "Eric Bentley: The Hero as Theater Critic," in *The Massachusetts Review*. IX, no. 2 (1968), pp. 350–358.
Visser, Colin, ed. *Re-Interpreting Brecht: His Influence on Contemporary Drama and Film*, 1990.
Weales, Gerald. "What a Life!" in *The Hudson Review*. XVIII, no. 1 (1965), pp. 142–152.

MICHAEL L. QUINN

See also Brecht; Esslin; Shaw

Henri Bergson

French philosopher and writer

Born: Paris, France; October 18, 1859
Died: Paris, France; January 4, 1941

Biography

Henri Bergson was born on October 18, 1859, in the Montmartre district of Paris to Michael Bergson and the former Katharine Levinson. His father came from a distinguished Polish family; his mother was an English Jew of Irish extraction. Henri's early childhood was spent in London, but when he was nine his family returned to Paris, where Henri entered the Lycée Condorcet. An extremely gifted student, he quickly manifested a mastery of both science and literature, and his initial intent was to pursue mathematics as a career. Upon graduation, however, he decided to study philosophy since that was a means of blending the precision of mathematical science with the speculations of imaginative literature.

In 1879 Bergson became a student at the École Normale Supérieure, the institution responsible for training teachers. After successfully passing his competitive examinations in 1881, he held a succession of teaching posts at various schools until he was appointed to the faculty of the École Normale Supérieure in 1898. From 1900 to 1921 he held the chair of philosophy at the Collège de France, where his lectures grew increasingly popular, attracting large audiences of both academics and nonacademics.

In 1891 he married Louise Neuburger, a cousin of Marcel Proust, and they later had a daughter. Bergson wanted to lead a quiet life with his family, but his growing celebrity often compromised his desire. He was elected to the Académie Française in 1914, and after World War I he devoted himself to international affairs and participated in diplomatic missions to Spain and the United States.

In the early 1920s arthritis forced Bergson to retire from his academic responsibilities. Awarded the 1927 Nobel Prize in Literature, he was unable to attend the ceremonies in Stockholm. His output slowed during the 1930s, and by the time of World War II his major work had been done. During the Nazi occupation of France, the Vichy government exempted Bergson from the decrees requiring Jews to resign from official posts, but, in a gesture of solidarity with his persecuted people, he quit his honorary chair at the Collège de France. During the final years of his life Bergson was attracted to the Catholic church, and had circumstances been different, he most likely would have converted. When he died in Paris at the age of eighty-one, he seemed to belong to a vanished age. Only twenty mourners attended the funeral of the man whom Paul Valéry eulogized as the last truly great symbol of the European intellect.

Influence

Bergson is best known for his influence on philosophers, for his anticipation of phenomenology and existentialism, and for his attacks on positivism, scientism, and evolutionism. He taught an entire generation new ways to think about time, memory, freedom, and life. He emphasized the superiority of intuition over intellect as a means of apprehending reality. He clarified the distinction between clock time and duration (time as one actually experiences it). Underlying all these teachings was his desire to free people from systems of materialistic determinism.

These ideas, developed in Bergson's philosophical writings, had a huge influence on literary theory. His treatment of time helped to create new forms of fictional narrative. His understanding of intuition and freedom opened the way for writers to seek deeper levels of motivation for their characters. In addition, Bergson had a direct influence on many young writers who were destined to become key literary figures of the twentieth century – among them, Marcel Proust, André Gide, Charles-Pierre Péguy, Paul Claudel, and Paul Valéry. Indeed, Proust admitted that he had profited from Bergson's analysis of time, and several critics have analyzed this influence on his great novel *À la recherche du temps perdu* (1913–1927; *Remembrance of Things Past*, 1922–1931, 1981). Bergson's influence has also been felt in the works of figures as diverse as George Bernard Shaw and William Faulkner.

Analysis

Bergson's philosophy was both a critique of scientific reason as the instrument of genuine knowledge, and a proposal of intuition and the immediate data of consciousness as the proper ways to such knowledge. During the nineteenth century the concern for objectivity by many writers led to a vision of the world that had no room for values directly experienced by people. Bergson countered this vision with a joyful belief that humanity could be liberated from the tyranny of materialism.

By the end of the nineteenth century positivism had provided a philosophy for naturalism, and this philosophy left its mark on literary criticism. The evolution of literary genres was explained in a way not too much different from Charles Darwin's explanation for the evolution of life. Bergson provided an alternative to these positivistic explanations. He was able to accomplish this task by building on his broad opposition to positivism and by centering his inquiry on the self and its direct intuitions. In his early work *Time and Free Will*, he tried to establish the idea of duration, or lived time, as opposed to the clock time of the scientists. If one grasps the data of consciousness directly, one no longer sees these data as quantities but as pure qualities, a continuous progression rather than a cinematographic succession of distinct events. Because people have been formed by positivistic ideas, they try to measure their states of consciousness and they give these states names. One believes that these events can be separated from one another like words, and one further imagines that they can be arranged one after the other as along a line. For example, people tend to spatialize time in this way. Bergson, however, revealed that time is not simply something quantitative and abstract, but a reality indissolubly linked with life and the human soul. Charles-Pierre Péguy was much impressed by Bergson's analysis of spatial time and pure duration. Péguy believed that a poet could capture the actual flow of time, transcending its mechanical division into units.

Bergson did not end his analysis with the immediate data of consciousness; he tried to discover a way of getting beyond them. For him the philosopher's job was to discover the deep reality behind the symbols given by intelligence. This quest for the knowledge lying beyond words Bergson called intuition, the direct awareness of a reality. Scientists cannot delve deeply into the essential nature of things, for deep reality remains beyond the grasp of the discursive mind. Great poets, however, can encounter the deeper forces of life, because they know nature through intuition, not reason.

Although Bergson's analysis of intuition had a profound influence on many writers, it met with resistance among philosophers. Jacques Maritain, for example, believed that it was folly to substitute intuition for intelligence; this approach destroyed the valid knowledge of real beings. Some literary critics pointed out how several of Bergson's youthful disciples misused his analysis of intuition. These disciples found it easy to write when writing was exempted from all logical norms, but what resulted was a loss of unity and coherence in their characters and an unintelligibility in their plots. Instead of the restoration of intuitiveness leading to spontaneity, for these writers, at any rate, it led to a glorification of the childish and the primitive.

Allied with Bergson's analysis of intuition is another immediate datum of consciousness, that of freedom. This was another way for Bergson to attack the scientistic philosophies of the nineteenth century, for he found that these philosophies logically led to ridding the world of human presence. For example, the mechanical world of molecules obeying rigid laws left no room for human freedom. Still, one knows that one is free and responsible, said Bergson, and when one pursues things freely, that action has no explanation other than one's own nature. Bergson regarded freedom not as the rational determination of a human act but as the spontaneous bursting forth of vital energy (*élan vital*) from the depths of the self, a creative but nonrational act expressive of the total personality. This doctrine of freedom was closely connected with his other views, for living time is the realm of free choice and new creations. A creative act is a way of breaking the servitude that matter imposes. This view of freedom continued to have an important influence on French writers throughout the twentieth century.

Another Bergsonian theme that had a huge influence on writers and literary critics is memory. As before, Bergson opposes a positivistic to an intuitive analysis of memory. For some scientists the brain is a factory manufacturing thoughts; for others it is an instrument that selects ideas from the past to enable one to interpret the present. To counter these explanations, Bergson seizes the intuition of the real and shows that the mind does not believe that a few pounds of gray matter can hold all the meaning of a person's life. He does not deny the power of the brain to sort out certain images useful for human activities, but the mind contains a person's entire past, all at once, independent of time. For Bergson memory has a vital and spontaneous, not simply a mechanical, character.

Time and memory are important themes in Marcel Proust's *Remembrance of Things Past*. Memory was one of the problems that most interested Proust in Bergson's philosophy. Proust was confronted with the problem of giving an adequate idea of the passage of time in his novel. He found that words were weak tools in describing events that took place over days or years. The real task of the writer, he believed, was to capture the motion of time without destroying it. To solve this problem Proust used Bergson's idea of duration to communicate the flux of life. Proust was able, through his sensitive memory, to tap an abundance of sense impressions of a vanished society and to bring into consciousness the motives behind the acts of his characters. In this way Bergson's ideas were the source for the creation of a new type of novel.

The work of Bergson that is closest to literary criticism is *Laughter*, his exploration of the aesthetics of comedy. In this essay Bergson states that the comic arises whenever the mechanical intersects with the vital, that is, whenever the vital human spirit, with all of its adaptability, becomes inelastic and fixed in mechanical rigidity. Thus Bergson regards laughter as society's defense against an adaptive failure. With its blend of the vital and the mechanical, Bergson's theory of laughter is consistent with his analysis of time and memory.

Bergson's influence on twentieth-century literary theory was important and wide-ranging, even though this influence is difficult to pin down. He taught an entire generation of writers to look at life from within. The many experiments by writers to delve beneath the static images of the self and to capture by new techniques the flux of consciousness owe much to him. Bergson's aim was to show that rationality can only be understood when referred to its dynamic source – the self – in action. Jacob Bronowski has written much about the habit of truth in science, but Bergson denounced habit as a form of passivity, and he emphasized that life is always seeking new adventures. Therefore his literary influence runs parallel to his philosophical one, both working toward a vital conception of thought and reality, freeing both philosophers and writers from traditional explanations, recovering a new spiritual universe that positivism and naturalism had ignored.

Principal criticism

Essai sur les données immédiates de la conscience, 1889 (*Time and Free Will: An Essay on the Immediate Data of Consciousness*, 1910)

Matière et mémoire: Essai sur la relation du corps à l'esprit, 1896 (*Matter and Memory*, 1911)

Le Rire: Essai sur la signification du comique, 1900 (*Laughter: An Essay on the Meaning of the Comic*, 1911)

Introduction à la métaphysique, 1903 (*An Introduction to Metaphysics*, 1912)

L'Évolution créatrice, 1907 (*Creative Evolution*, 1911)

Les Deux Sources de la morale et de la religion, 1932 (*The Two Sources of Morality and Religion*, 1935)

Écrits et paroles, 1957–1959

Œuvres: Édition du centenaire, 1959

Other major works and literary forms

Henri Bergson's principal literary form was the philosophical treatise, though his books ranged over a wide variety of subjects, including science, religion, morality, mysticism, and laughter. He wrote these works in styles that extended from the analytic to the rhapsodic. *Creative Evolution*, for example, has been called a poem about the drama of the evolution of life. Bergson wrote it in a style that intersperses observations from science with ingenious metaphors from the arts and humanities. Some found this intuitive style insightful and illuminating; others saw it as cloaking a lack of precision in Bergson's thought.

NONFICTION

Extraits de Lucrèce, 1884 (*The Philosophy of Poetry: The Genius of Lucretius*, 1959)
Quid Aristoteles de loco senserit, 1889
L'Énergie spirituelle, 1919 (*Mind-Energy: Lectures and Essays*, 1920)
Durée et simultanéité, 1922, 1923, 1926 (*Duration and Simultaneity with Reference to Einstein's Theory*, 1965)
La Pensée et le mouvant, 1934 (*The Creative Mind*, 1946)

Further reading

Alexander, Ian W. *Bergson: Philosopher of Reflection*, 1957.
Balsillie, David. *An Examination of Professor Bergson's Philosophy*, 1912.
Carr, H. Wilson. *Henri Bergson: The Philosophy of Change*, 1910.
Chevalier, Jacques. *Henri Bergson*, 1928.
Cunningham, Gustavus Watts. *A Study in the Philosophy of Bergson*, 1916.
Deleuze, Gilles. *Bergsonism*, 1988.
Dodson, George Rowland. *Bergson and the Modern Spirit*, 1913.
Gunn, John A. *Bergson and His Philosophy*, 1976.
Gunter, Peter A. "Henri Bergson: A Bibliography, 1911–1980," in *Philosophical Research Archives*. VII (1981).
Hanna, Thomas, ed. *The Bergsonian Heritage*, 1962.
Herman, Daniel J. *The Philosophy of Henri Bergson*, 1980.
Kolakowski, Leszek. *Bergson*, 1985.
Kumar, Shiv K. *Bergson and the Stream of Consciousness Novel*, 1963.
Lacey, A. R. *Bergson*, 1989.
LeRoy, Edouard. *The New Philosophy of Bergson*, 1913.
Lovejoy, A. O. *Bergson and Romantic Evolutionism*, 1914.
Luce, A. A. *Bergson's Doctrine of Intuition*, 1922.
Maritain, Jacques. *Bergsonian Philosophy and Thomism*, 1968.
Maurois, André. "Henri Bergson," in *From Proust to Camus: Profiles of Modern French Writers*, 1966.
Moore, F. C. T. *Bergson: Thinking Backwards*, 1996.
Mullarkey, J., ed. *The New Bergson*, 1998.
Papanicolaou, A. C., and P. A. Y. Gunter, eds. *Bergson and Modern Thought*, 1987.
Pilkington, A. E. *Bergson and His Influence: A Reassessment*, 1976.
Scharfstein, Ben-Ami. *Roots of Bergson's Philosophy*, 1943.

ROBERT J. PARADOWSKI

See also French Literary Theory: Twentieth Century; Proust

Bharata

Indian dramatic theorist

Active: third century A.D.?

Biography

Nothing is known of his life.

Influence

The *Natyashastra* (the science of drama) of Bharata, probably written around the third century A.D. (dates around three hundred years earlier and three hundred years later have been suggested), is one of the oldest works of Indian dramaturgy. Emerging in the context of Indian philosophy, it has had a tremendous impact on classical Indian theater and is beginning to influence the developing model of Western theater today, as suggested by Peter Malekin and Ralph Yarrow in their book *Consciousness, Literature and Theatre: Theory and Beyond* (1997). Although Bharata is said to be the author of this work, the name Bharata originally meant an actor in a drama, an expert in transformations or adopting roles. The *Natyashastra* contains about 5,600 verses and also comes in a shorter version of about two hundred verses. Although scholars have not discovered which of the two came first or their exact provenance, the tremendous influence of Bharata's book on dramaturgy and literary theory still prevails. Of its many chapters the most important is considered to be the sixth on *rasa*, defined as "aesthetic or imaginative experience." Bharata defines all aspects of drama in terms of *rasa*, stating that "Without *rasa* no dramatic device is of any importance." While Bharata may have drawn upon earlier dramatic texts in writing the *Natyashastra*, these do not seem to have been available to later writers. Indeed the first known commentary of the *Natyashastra*, that of Ubdhata, was not written until five hundred years after Bharata. The first imitation of the *Natyashastra*, the *Dasarupaka* of Dhanamjaya, was written in the tenth century.

Analysis

In writing the *Natyashastra*, Bharata was clearly familiar with a long tradition of plays, though unfortunately none survive. Bharata seems to have written his work for the benefit of directors and playwrights, though it is also of great value for actors. Unlike the author of the *Dhvanyaloka* and the main exponent of the *dhvani* (suggestion) school of criticism, Anandavardhana, Bharata was not concerned with founding a literary theory. He was more concerned with the technical aspects of the successful representation of plays on the stage than with plays only read and appreciated, yet his work is essential for anyone studying Sanskrit poetics. For the contemporary critic, however, the *Natyashastra* presents a problem of interpretation; Bharata's intentions have not always been clear even to the most astute commentator. One of the most influential classical commentators is Abhinavagupta, who wrote the *Abhinavabharati* on Bharata and the *Dhvanyalokalocana* on Anandavardhana. Bharata and his commentators gave rise to a distinction between dramatic criticism and literary criticism; the latter deals with the language of speech while the former deals with dramatic spectacle. Because spectacle and speech both occur on the stage, literary and dramatic criticism both appear in the *Natyashastra*. Hence many of the elements developed in Indian literary theory such as *rasa* also apply to Indian dramaturgy.

The theory of *rasa* that was so important for Bharata is closely connected to the doctrine of *atman* (the self as pure consciousness), which underlies the major tenets of Indian literary theory, such as *dhvani* (suggestion) and *bhava* (emotion). The Vedas and the Upanishads define the ultimate reality underlying the universe as Brahman, and the ultimate reality of the individual as *atman*, which are held to be identical in key statements (*mahavakyas*) such as "That thou art" (*Chandogya Upanishad*) and "I am Brahman" (*Brhadaranyaka Upanishad*). Ultimate reality for Indian philosophy is one, with the basis of the external world being the same as that of the knowing individual. Yet this unity is manifested more in the individual, as indicated by the expression *sat* (being)-*chit* (consciousness)-*ananda* (bliss). Only the self can reflect on its consciousness and bliss, even though they also exist in Brahman. The principle of *atman* in the Upanishads thus represents a transition from an outer view of reality to an inner view based on the self (*atman*). This metaphysical perspective has had great influence on Indian aesthetics, especially in the theory of *rasa* underlying the *Natyashastra*.

G. H. Tarlekar explains that *rasa* is the relish not of an emotion in real life but of a permanent emotional mode (*sthayibhava*) as represented through the imagination of the poet. Sushil Kumar De distinguishes between ordinary emotion (*bhava*), which may be pleasurable or painful, and a poetic sentiment (*rasa*), which transcends the boundaries of ordinary individual pain or pleasure to reach "pure joy, the essence of which is its relish itself." T. P. Ramachandran observes that *santa-rasa* (*santa* relates to *santi* or peace) gives one "not only a foretaste of the bliss of *moksha* [liberation] but also an insight into the nature and source of that bliss." Whether or not *rasa* leads successfully toward the experience of *moksha* depends on whether the theme of the work also deals with the nature and process of attaining *moksha*. If it does then the *rasa* is called *santa*. Many critical attempts have been made to explain the process of experiencing *rasa*, which involves the relation between *rasa*, *pratibha* (direct intuition), *sthayibhava* (latent emotional modes), and *dhvani* (suggestion). Abhinavagupta's formulation and development of *rasa* on the basis of Bharata's theory became the accepted standard and involved the experience of *turiya* (the fourth or transcendental state of consciousness). As K. C. Pandey writes, Abhinavagupta thought "that the *Santa Rasa* is the highest of all Rasas, because it is concerned with the highest objective of human pursuit and leads to final emancipation."

As developed by Bharata, Anandavardhana (the founder of the theory of *dhvani*), and Abhinavagupta, the theory of *rasa* conforms to several criteria. First, the emotional modes or *sthayibhavas* that comprise the content of a work are aesthetic (transpersonal) idealizations, since a particular (personal) emotion would not be a source of delight. Second, the means of communicating the *sthayibhavas* are indirect. While a "situation" may be presented directly as the work's content through primary signification, an emotion is presented indirectly through suggestion. And third, the *sthayibhavas* presented in the work must also be present in the spectator as the material cause of *rasa*. Ramachandran describes the Vedantic notion of *rasa*, as formulated by Abhinavagupta, as manifestation of the bliss of the spectator's self as *turiya*:

> *Rasa* ... is the manifestation (*abhivyakti*) of the intrinsic bliss of the self through the *sthayibhava* [basic emotions or moods latent in the mind] rendered free from barrier [ego-consciousness]. It is in this sense that the *sthayibhava* is said to be transformed into *rasa*. Like a mirror cleaned of dirt, the *sthayibhava* freed from the personal attitude reflects the bliss of the self, and this reflected bliss is called *rasa*.

The theory of *rasa* is thus concerned not with the direct representation of an emotional mode, the immediate referent, but rather with its aesthetic image: not with the expressed referent, but with the suggested "sense" of the work as a whole. *Rasa* defamiliarizes ordinary experience by means of figurative language, preventing the audience from identifying with a conventional referent or expression and thereby heightening their sense of aesthetic delight.

Bharata's dramaturgy differs significantly from Western twentieth-century schools of criticism such as Russian Formalism, structuralism, and poststructuralism. Whereas the former elicits aesthetic delight through the experience of expanded pure consciousness (*atman*) in which sound and meaning are united, the latter have little or no direct interest in metaphysical experience – except poststructuralism, which attempts to undermine it. Yet *rasa*, as a subjective experience objectified, is not a purely subjective or extralinguistic element, but rather involves the coexistence of feeling/intellect, unity/diversity, and is therefore extremely powerful. Its effects, value, and influence cannot be undermined merely through intellectual analysis.

According to Bharata, theater should not only entertain, grip the emotions, and challenge the intellect, it should also expand the mind of the audience toward pure consciousness (*atman*). By engaging an audience through a stimulating performance, theater should have the further and more significant impact of eliciting the experience of *atman* or *turiya* (transcendental pure consciousness). In this way, the long-term effects of theater would be to stabilize *atman* in the state of *moksha* (liberation) and thereby assist in the development of society toward utopia. Traditionally in Indian culture this aim was considered realistic and achievable.

The *Natyashastra*, as the classical Indian treatise on drama and theater, thus serves as a manual for two objectives: first, to expand the actor's awareness, and secondly to describe what an actor who has realized this expanded state can do spontaneously on stage to produce awareness-expanding effects on the audience. The *Natysashastra* and other works of Sanskrit dramaturgy, in describing the techniques of histrionic representation necessary for raising consciousness, emphasize not only physical techniques but also the representation of emotional modes or temperamental states so essential for creating aesthetic delight (*rasa*) in the audience. The actor develops a mode of acting (*sattvika abhinaya*) for portraying these modes of temperament (*sattvika bhava*). *Sat* is the eternal absolute. As mentioned above, pure consciousness in Sanskrit is known as *sat-chit-ananda*: the eternal absolute or being (*sat*), consciousness (*chit*), and bliss (*ananda*). *Sat* refers to the qualityless self beyond conceptual content, that pure witnessing awareness at the basis of all manifestations of thoughts, feelings, sensations, and perceptions. On the manifest level, *sat* is expressed in the term *sattva*, which is one of the three fundamental qualities (*gunas*) of nature, along with *rajas* and *tamas*.

As Rekha Jhanji states in *Aesthetic Communication: The Indian Perspective* (1985):

> *Sattva* which refers to the freedom from all willing is the state of detachment from the pragmatic world, and it is the state of pure knowledge. *Rajas* is understood in terms of all qualities of will and all the psycho-physical activities have their origin in terms of this quality. *Tamas* refers to the state of ignorance and lack of consciousness. The entire life of the individual represents the varied combinations of these three *gunas*. Beatitude and knowledge are associated with *sattva*; greed with *rajas*, and ignorance and illusion with *tamas*.

The balance between the three *gunas* can vary, leading to different temperamental modes. An excess of *tamas* can cause stagnation and suffering, just as a predominance of *sattva* can lead to increased happiness and ultimately to bliss consciousness. In ordinary life, therefore, the quality (*guna*) of *sattva* most closely approximates the quality of *sat* or pure consciousness. Bharata observes that when an actor or actress performs with *sattva* predominating in his or her awareness over *rajas* and *tamas*, then he or she will maintain a greater degree of *atman* (pure consciousness) in his or her performance and thereby stimulate a corresponding state of purity in the audience.

The Upanishads, Patanjali's *Yoga Sutras*, and other Vedic texts describe techniques available for increasing *sattva* and expanding awareness, techniques with which Bharata was of course familiar. Patanjali, for instance, describes *yoga* (unity) in terms of the purity of the body, the "one-pointedness of the mind," and the liberation of the spirit, with different methods prescribed for achieving each. *Yoga* in the body comes through specific physical postures (*asanas*); it comes in the mind through breathing exercises (*pranayama*), and in the spirit through meditation. In drama, as Daniel Meyer-Dinkgräfe observes, gesture as a means of theatrical representation (*angika abhinaya*) corresponds to *yoga asanas* as a means of purifying the body to sustain *sattva*, just as the control of breath, which is vital to performance in both East and West, corresponds to *yoga pranayama*. Because breath is associated with energy, it is crucial (as Phillip Zarrilli observes) for making "otherwise mechanical facial configurations" in which are "encoded the message pleasure/erotic or fury," "live with pleasure."

Zarrilli goes on to show that Indian dramaturgy does not involve a "suspension of disbelief" as in the Western tradition, for the actor and audience jointly conjure up a "power of presence" on the stage as "other," which, although histrionically embodied in the actor, in fact transcends the actor's limited ego. The dramatic figure thus constitutes a (transpersonal) suggested content (*dhvani*) suspended between audience and actor, an emotional mode (*rasa*) transcending the personal attitude of an historical individual. As the *Natyashastra* indicates, therefore, acting, like *yoga*, employs methods that condition the mind and body for eliciting and sustaining the state of pure consciousness (*turiya*). In this way Bharata's approach differs markedly from that of Western theater. As G. H. Tarlekar puts it,

> The Greek tragedy aimed at achieving violent purgation. The Indian conception of drama avoided tragedy and aimed at repose. Even in the tragic themes of the two plays of Bhasa, namely *Urubhanga* and *Karnabhara*, the ideal of a warrior, i.e. the obtainment of heaven if killed in the course of fighting, is aimed at . . . such plays also do not produce that perturbation of the mind which is effected by the Greek tragedy. . . . The Drama was meant to evoke Rasa. Rasa is so called because it is relished. Its meaning can be accepted as "aesthetic delight."

The "perturbation of the mind" mentioned here is the antithesis of *rasadhvani*. According to the *Natyashastra*, drama should induce the experience of the mind's transcending the perturbation of mental activity, settling down toward *turiya* – the ever-present witnessing awareness (*atman*) beyond the activity of thought. *Rasa*, moreover, is beyond the reach of expressed form, conjured up only by the suggestion (*dhvani*) of the latent (transpersonal) permanent emotional modes (*bhavas*).

Historically, dramatic performances in India as represented by the *Natyashastra* have their origins in religious rites and festivals. They may have involved dance and songs honoring Shiva and other deities. This ritual dance reflects the Indian notion of the play (*lila*) of the cosmos. As Malekin and Yarrow put it, *lila* is "the play of becoming, which is also *maya* – *not* illusion in the sense of simple unreality, but a world of appearance that is real on the phenomenal level only and veils its own ultimate unconditioned nature" (original emphasis). The emblem of the dancing Shiva, who is many-limbed and potentially androgynous, represents the Indian performance tradition as a play of forms (*lila*). Dramatic play, as Malekin and Yarrow observe, thus emphasizes the essential "transformability" of the theatrical enterprise. The play of the "subject" (*lila*) as conveyed through *rasa* (aesthetic rapture) presents all aspects of the transforming dramatic action to the consciousness of all the participants, performers and audience. The ultimate transformation, therefore, would be transcendence to a higher state of consciousness, with all participants moving from the perturbation of mental content (sensations, perceptions, emotions) to the stillness of pure awareness (*atman*). It is the stillness beyond the subject-object duality of observation, the blissful being of *sat-chit-ananda*, a candle flame in a windless place.

As part of its spiritual heritage, dramatic art was already well developed in India before contact with the Greeks followed the invasion of Alexander the Great in 326 B.C. In his *Astadhyayi*, dated around the fourth century B.C., Panini refers to the dramaturgy of two theorists, Krsasva and Silali. Moreover, legend has it that one of the disciples of Buddha, Sariputra, was so affected by a dramatic presentation that he renounced the world and became a Buddhist ascetic. Bharata claims that the dramatic is the highest form of art because it subsumes the attributes of all the others: lore, experience, spiritual discipline, science, craft, and art. In fact, the immense status of the *Natyashastra* in Indian thought led to its being called the "fifth Veda," for along with the four principle Vedas of Indian philosophy it has the power to induce spiritual enlightenment (*moksha*). Drama, moreover, unlike philosophy, which is dry and difficult, provides both instruction and entertainment, qualities that have enhanced its survivability and popular appeal in modern times. Today the dramatic arts in India are alive and well, with the Sanskrit plays of classical dramatists being performed by colleges, universities, and Sanskrit associations, all of which encourage national competitions. In the early 1990s Indian national television broadcast a thirty-part series on the epic the *Ramayana*, and in the 1980s the English director Peter Brook directed a nine-hour performance of the great Indian epic the *Mahabharata*.

Principal criticism

Natyashastra, with the commentary of Abhinavagupta, 1956 (M. Ramakrishna Kav, editor)

Further reading

Aranya, Swami Hariharananda. *Yoga Philosophy of Patanjali: Containing his Yoga Aphorisms with Commentary of Vyasa in Original Sanskrit*, 1981 (third edition). Translated by P. N. Mukerji.

Bharatamuni. *The Natya Shastra*, 1987. Translated by a board of scholars.

Bhat, G. K. *Sanskrit Dramatic Theory*, 1981.

Chakrabarti, Tarapada. *Indian Aesthetics and Science of Language*, 1971.

Dasgupta, Surendranath, and Sushil Kumar De. *A History of Sanskrit Literature, Classical Period*, Vol. 1, 1947.

De, Sushil Kumar. *History of Sanskrit Poetics*, Vols 1 and 2, 1960 (second revised edition).

Jhanji, Rekha. *Aesthetic Communication: The Indian Perspective*, 1985.

Malekin, Peter, and Ralph Yarrow. *Consciousness, Literature and Theatre: Theory and Beyond*, 1997.

Mankad, D. R. *Ancient Indian Theatre*, 1950.

Masson, J. L., and M. V. Patwardhan. *Aesthetic Rapture*, Vols. 1 and 2, 1970.

Meyer-Dinkgräfe, Daniel. *Consciousness and the Actor*, 1996.

Pandey, K. C. *Comparative Aesthetics*, Vol. 1, *Indian Aesthetics*, 1959; Vol. 2, *Western Aesthetics*, 1972.

Radhakrishnan, Sarvepalli, ed. and trans. *The Principle Upanishads*, 1992 (fifth edition).

——, and Charles A. Moore, eds. *A Sourcebook in Indian Philosophy*, 1957.

Ramachandran, T. P. *The Indian Philosophy of Beauty*, Part Two, 1980.

Shekhar, I. *Sanskrit Drama: Its Origin and Decline*, 1960.

Taimni, I. K. *The Science of Yoga (Patanjali's Yoga Sutras)*, 1961.

Tarlekar, G. H. *Studies in the Natyashastra*, 1991 (second revised edition).

Wells, H. W. *The Classical Drama of India*, 1963.

Zarrilli, Phillip B. "What Does it Mean to 'Become the Character': Power, Presence, and Transcendence in Asian In-Body Disciplines of Practice," in *By Means of Performance: Intercultural Studies of Theatre and Ritual*, 1990. Edited by R. Schechner and W. Appel.

William S. Haney II

See also Anandavardhana; Bhartrhari; Indian Literary Theory

Bhartrhari

Indian grammarian and philosopher

Active: mid-seventh century A.D.

Biography

Nothing is known of his life.

Influence

One of India's most prominent grammarian-philosophers, Bhartrhari is known to us today through his work rather than through biographical references. This obscurity conceals the lives of many Indian philosophers, partly because their work evolved out of an oral tradition and partly because their quest for eternal truth took precedence over their individuality. In his own quest, Bhartrhari's influence can hardly be overestimated. He formulated one of the earliest and most enduring theories of language through his Grammar School of transcendentalism, challenging the empirical or nominalistic schools of language such as those of Buddhism which questioned the validity of verbal discourse as a source of knowledge. The Mimamsa and Nyaya schools have in turn challenged Bhartrhari and the Grammar School but, together with Advaita (nondual) Vedanta, his remains a powerful description of language and its connection to the absolute. Bhartrhari, moreover, has influenced all the major schools of Indian literary theory, such as the schools of *alankara* (tropes), *dhvani* (suggestion), and *rasa* (aesthetic rapture). By explaining the way language transplants experience from speaker to listener, Bhartrhari's work continues to have relevance today and has been compared to the theory of deconstruction developed by the French philosopher Jacques Derrida.

Analysis

Just as mathematics underpinned Greek philosophy and culture, so language and its relation to consciousness underpin Indian philosophy. Since its beginning in the *Rig Veda*, Indian philosophy has held that language, particularly as used in rhetoric and poetry, has two dimensions, phenomenal and metaphysical. While Indian grammarians like Panini, Patanjali, and Bhartrhari were concerned with the outer, phenomenal dimension of language, they also explored the inner, transcendental dimension. As one of the great Indian grammarian-philosophers, Bhartrhari begins the *Vakyapadiya*, his major work, with a metaphysical study of language in relation to Brahman (Absolute) and consciousness, and then proceeds to explore the grammatical structure of ordinary usage. For classical Indian philosophy, the phenomenal structure of language – with its link between sound and meaning, name and form – and its metaphysical nature are not mutually exclusive but complementary, since language and reality are graded and with them, cognition. The connection between language, reality, and consciousness directly impinges on the Indian notion of creativity.

While (traditionally) the modern Western theory of language understands creativity in terms of a writer producing something new and original, the Indian understanding of creativity is rather different. As Klaus Klostermaier puts it (in Coward, 1978):

> The great creative geniuses of India, men like Gotama the Buddha or Shankara, take care to explain their thought not as creation but as a retracing of forgotten eternal truth. They compare their activity to the clearing of an overgrown ancient path in the jungle, not to the making of a new path.

The *rishis* or "seers" of the word in its metaphysical dimension, like the "seers" who cognized the Vedic texts, do not create something new but rather remember or rediscover a timeless, forgotten truth. Language, which is called *vak*, has an important place in the Vedas and is considered the support of Vedic gods like Indra, Mitra-Varuna, and Agni. *Vak* is also identified with Sarasvati, the goddess of wisdom, learning, and inspiration. The *Rig Veda*, moreover, identifies *vak* with Brahman (Absolute or Divine) and states that the number of words equal the manifestations of Brahman, since any particular word comprises a vibration or sound corresponding to a particular form of Brahman. As this concept is at the heart of Indian thinking on language and consciousness, and is unfamiliar to contemporary Western thought, it may be worth expanding it a little. It brings together three closely related beliefs: (1) that all the manifestations of the world, conceptual or physical, constitute forms (vibrations or sounds); (2) that through consciousness these forms can be experienced as meaningful; and (3) that the unity of sound and meaning is the basis of the word and therefore language. In other words, all manifest creation consists of sounds or vibrations (the "hum of the universe," the "music of the spheres"), and any sound can form part of a word (a unity of sound and meaning experienced on the basis of consciousness), which means there can be as many words as there are manifestations of Brahman. The nearest Western equivalent to this view is the Greek (and later Christian) concept of the *Logos*, expressed in the Bible as "In the beginning was the Word, and the Word was with God, and the Word was God" (John, I).

In the creation of Vedic hymns, the *rishi* is not an individual author but a "seer" (*drastr*) of an ever-present eternal truth which, like Brahman, is impersonal. As Aurobindo Ghose states, language in the Vedas is "rhythm not composed by the intellect but heard, a divine Word that came vibrating out of the Infinite to the inner audience of the man who had previously made himself fit for the impersonal knowledge." In the *Mandukya Upanishad* the initial vision of the Veda by the *rishi*, a vision of the whole or Brahman, is represented by the mantra AUM. This expression combines the three ordinary states of consciousness – awake, asleep, and dreaming – with the fourth state of transcendental consciousness (*turiya*). Thus the form of language (*vak*) ranges from expressions associated with the ordinary waking state to those associated with transcendental consciousness (*turiya*). Even though Brahman is unmanifest and transcendental, its closest manifest form is considered to be AUM.

In *Vakyapadiya*, Bhartrhari develops a theory of the integration between the outer word and its inner meaning. His position has become known as the *sphota* theory of language, *sphota* deriving from the Sanskrit term *sphut*, "to burst forth." With the term *sphota*, Bhartrhari designates the eternal word essence because it bursts forth through an illumination or sudden insight. He defines *sphota* as having two characteristics: that of being revealed by parts such as the letters, the word, and the sentence; and that of being a total, indivisible content. Each sound of a word's letters or syllables serves to express the totality of the word essence, with the qualitative difference that succeeding sounds affect the revelation of the word essence by making it deeper and more complete. The most significant experience of meaning, called *Vakyasphota*, occurs through the direct perception of the total sentence or proposition as a whole idea. The intuitive understanding of the sentence constitutes an experience of the absolute meaning or transcendental signified. But, as Coward explains, the *sphota* does not end with the sentence. It may be extended according to a hierarchy in which the sentence is an "unreal abstraction" of the paragraph, the paragraph an unreal abstraction of the chapter of the book, the book a part of a larger context, and so forth. These parts or differences relate to an underlying identity, the indivisible and eternal unity of sound and meaning in language identified with Brahman as the ultimate reality. This unity of the absolute word, consciousness, and reality is called *Sabda Brahman*.

For Bhartrhari *sphota* is the transcendent ground of language that combines the spoken syllables and the suggested meaning *(dhvani)*. In Bhartrhari's theory of communication, the speaker does not convey meaning to the listener; instead the spoken word acts as a catalyst to elicit a meaning already inherent in the hearer's mind. In poetry, the meaning of a poem is inherently present in the poet's consciousness just as it is in that of everyone else. The poet has the revelation or *sphota* of a unitary idea, which he then starts to examine for the purpose of communication. This expression occurs in a twofold process. The poet finds the objective meaning *(artha)* he wants to communicate and then connects it with the signifying words and phrases (*dhvani*) he uses. The objective or expressed value of the meaning *(artha)* combined with the suggested meaning (*dhvani*) are the two sides of the coin that constitute *sphota*, which for Bhartrhari is eternal and immanent in consciousness.

Bhartrhari's theory has been compared to language theories in the West, particularly the poststructuralism of Jacques Derrida. Structuralism and poststructuralism emerged out of the semiology of Ferdinand de Saussure, who revolutionized linguistics by studying language in itself (as a self-contained system in which meaning is created solely by the relationships between the elements of the system). Bhartrhari and Indian language theorists in general go a step farther by studying language both in itself, and in terms of its various manifestations at different levels of consciousness. According to Saussure's influential but misleading premise, there is no natural bond between a sign and referent, or within a sign between sound and concept. Saussure further broke with tradition by dropping the "diachronic," historical method of research for the "synchronic," atemporal method of studying the structure of language at a given period of time. Structuralism, as Christopher Norris notes, "took over from Saussure's idea that all cultural systems – not only language – could be studied from a 'synchronic' viewpoint which would bring out their various related levels of signifying activity." Derrida's poststructuralism, however, questioned the stability of this opposition by showing how the meaning of any given synchronic moment or structure is infinitely deferred across the diachronic plane – which applies even in a moment of revelation.

Bhartrhari and the Indian tradition take an altogether different approach. They posit a correspondence between different levels of language and consciousness, and conceive the subject and object of knowledge as forming an integrated whole that cannot be separated without falsification and misrepresentation. This approach takes into account the full diachronic and synchronic range of both subject and object. According to the *Rig Veda*, language (*vak*) consists of four levels which correspond to different levels of consciousness and which range from the spoken word to the subtlest form of thought in pure awareness (*turiya*). In the order of increasing unity of sound and meaning, name and form, these levels are *vaikhari*, *madhyama*, *pashyanti*, and *para*. As defined by Bhartrhari, *vaikhari vak* or outward speech is the most fully expressed temporal sequence of language and consists of a gap between sound and meaning. *Madhyama vak* or inward speech is associated with the mind or intellect and, like *vaikhari*, it also consists of a distinction between word and meaning, but as an inner thought the temporal sequence is less pronounced. These two levels of language comprise historical meaning in which the subject (knower) is separated from the object (known) by a spatio-temporal gap that must be bridged, although at these levels of language the bridge is never complete.

Pashyanti vak, the next innermost stage, consists of the word essence as a noumenal whole; it is without the temporal sequence and without the gap between word and meaning. This concept of language resembles that of phenomenologists like Edmund Husserl and the later Geneva School of critics (J. Hillis Miller, Georges Poulet, and Jean Starobinski) who tried to fathom the essence of a writer's consciousness and its connection to language through its appearance in the critic's consciousness. At this level of direct intuition, meaning transcends the dependency on phenomenalization and thus cannot be analyzed into parts as an ordinary expression. But the notion of an absolute unity of sound and meaning does not mean that the two are inseparable in an ordinary sense, however. That is, the meaning or transcendental signified of *pashyanti* differs radically from the notion of a transcendental signified in *vaikhari* and *madhyama*. The bond between signifier (sound) and signified (meaning) in *vaikhari* and *madhyama*, the two levels of language associated with the mind or intellect in ordinary waking consciousness, comprises an apparent unity of meaning (transcendental signified) which in fact is only a conceptual closure. On the other hand, in *pashyanti*, the level of language associated with pure consciousness (*turiya*), the bond between signifier and signified goes beyond conceptuality altogether and thus constitutes a true transcendental signified, a direct and open illumination of the word as an eternal wholeness. *Vaikhari* and *madhyama* belong to the mind as a field of conceptuality and difference, while *pashyanti* (and *para*) belong to consciousness emptied of its empirical phenomenological content. It follows that the spatio-temporal gap between sound and meaning in the lower two levels of language (*vaikhari* and *madhyama*) open them to a deconstructive critique, which postulates that meaning (the transcendental signified) is infinitely deferred by the spatio-temporal play of language. *Pashyanti*, being without this gap, exceeds deconstruction and the play of difference. Hence different levels of language manifest different degrees of wholeness or *sphota*.

So, whereas *vaikhari* and *madhyama* correspond to ordinary waking consciousness, *pashyanti* and *para* correspond to different aspects of transcendental consciousness. In their attempt to describe how the underlying essence of a writer's language appeared to a critic's consciousness, phenomenologists and the later reader-response critics conceived a theory of language and consciousness similar to Bhartrhari's, but they lacked an understanding of how language is different in different states of consciousness. For Husserl meaning predates language such that knowledge operates within a pre-understanding. He tried to imagine language that purely expressed consciousness, but this language, in the wake of the linguistic revolution from Saussure and Ludwig Wittgenstein to postmodern theorists, was considered to be solipsistic. For Bhartrhari, however, to experience the underlying essence of a writer's language is to experience language in its unified phase of *pashyanti*, which corresponds to transcendental consciousness always already residing in both writer and reader.

Bhartrhari does not mention *para vak* himself, although as the highest level of language it is first mentioned in the *Rig Veda* along with the other three. As Subramania Iyer points out, *para* consists of the same unity of sound and meaning found in *pashyanti*, but while the latter corresponds to *turiya*, known as *savikalpa samadhi* or temporary transcendental consciousness, the former corresponds to *nirvikalpa samadhi* or permanent transcendental consciousness. A further distinction is that in *pashyanti* the unity of sound and meaning contains an impulse toward phenomenalization, while in *para* the unity remains unmanifest. Thus a word thought or spoken in ordinary waking consciousness is only a partial expression of an eternal meaning or transcendental signified. The problem with the deconstructive notion of a transcendental signified is that it is not really transcendental to begin with. Rather it is merely a conceptual closure, which in terms of Indian language theory corresponds to the lower levels of language, *vaikhari* and *madhyama*. Language here constitutes a field of spatio/temporal difference, a field of conceptuality. On the other hand, *para* and to a lesser extent *pashyanti* constitute language associated with transcendental pure consciousness, a field of wholeness beyond the duality of space and time, subject and object. They have been likened to the Neo-Platonic *logos*. Because meaning here is transcendental and not produced by human utterance, it is not a temporal effect and therefore not perishable. Rather, it is that meaning said to be immanent in the sacred texts of cultures throughout the world.

In *Derrida and Indian Philosophy*, Harold Coward has brought to light important parallels between Derrida's deconstruction and traditional Indian philosophies of language and consciousness, including the two schools of Bhartrhari and Shankara. He says that Bhartrhari conceives of language and consciousness as being coextensive in a field of temporal sequence, and as constituting "the dynamic becoming of reality itself." Like Derrida, Bhartrhari sees difference, or the sequencing of time, as the nonlogocentric, nontranscendental originary state of language. As Coward discerns:

> Bhartrhari, like Derrida, sees sequencing or difference as the characteristic dynamic of language in all its levels [although Bhartrhari does not discuss *para*]. Even the innermost apparently unitive level of speech [*pashyanti*] is pregnant with the power of difference. As Bhartrhari puts in it his *vrtti*, *pashyanti vak*, though it is One, has the power to produce sequence within it. There is no pure presence or *logos* devoid of this pregnant power. For Bhartrhari the one Brahman is the *Sabdatattva* or Word-Principle.

The Word-Principle (*Sabdatattva*) is without temporal sequence, and as Brahman it represents for Bhartrhari the highest ontological level. Even though on this level, namely *pashyanti*, time is pure potentiality, one may still acquire a full perception of meaning.

Shankara, unlike Bhartrhari, includes the level of *para* in his theory of language. One of India's best-known philosophers who came a century after Bhartrhari (although some scholars place him 5,000 years ago), Shankara is the founder of the nondual or *advaita* school of Vedanta. Coward feels that Shankara seems to separate language from the real or Brahman. But Shankara's notion of Brahman can be understood as encompassing all aspects of language, from unity to the field of diversity. Some scholars, moreover, find that this theory may provide a fuller understanding of the link between language and consciousness than does Bhartrhari's theory of difference. Shankara defines *para* as the absolute unity of language, a unity that forms the basis of his nondual Vedanta. Coward interprets Shankara as postulating that Brahman or the real is separate from the differential structure of language, that difference constitutes ignorance (*avidya*) and therefore obstructs the real. But for Shankara, Brahman includes the full range of language, both its absolute unity in *para* and its differential manifestations in the other levels (or in *pashyanti* its potency for manifestation). Bhartrhari's theory cannot accommodate *para* as a level devoid of the impulse toward sequential manifestation, although the *Rig Veda* mentions all four as integral to language. It would thus be inaccurate to say that for Shankara language and the real are separate. Brahman does not, simply speaking, transcend history but rather encompasses all levels of reality, both absolute and relative. In Shankara's nondual theory, Brahman is by definition one with the universe, encompassing language in all of its aspects of unity and diversity. Even in the absolute unity of language, diversity exists in the virtual triad of name, form, and relationship.

Nonetheless, through *pashyanti vak*, Bhartrhari describes the science of grammar as a means to the realization of Brahman. He emphasizes the individual's experience of language as a process of inner transformation, a yoga of spiritual realization. His account of the individual's inner experience of language as a dynamic process resembles Derrida's theory of deconstruction as a dynamic oscillation between the polar opposites of meaning. But in Bhartrhari the sequence of words (Derrida's shifting polar opposites) is subordinate to a unified whole, whether of the sentence or a larger unity. To understand the meaning of a whole depends on an accumulation of its parts, which elicit in the individual a flash of illumination (*pratibha* or *sphota*). The *sphota* or flash of understanding of a meaning whole constitutes *Sabdatattva* – Brahman as the omniscient Word-Principle. This flash (*pratibha*) is ultimately of one's own inner self. Thus for Bhartrhari, as for many other Indian philosopher-grammarians, language is not only a means of communication (an epistemology) but also a vehicle for attaining self-realization or *atman* (an ontology). *Sphota* theory and the ancient science of grammar have had a profound influence on Indian poetics. *Sphota* underlies the major tenets of Indian literary theory, such as *rasadhvani* (suggested feeling), and continues to have relevance in a modern context, as seen in its similarities to the work of Derrida and its influence on writers like Rabindranath Tagore and Salman Rushdie.

Principal criticism

The Vakyapadiya, 1971 (K. Raghavan Pillai, editor and translator)
Vakyapadiya of Bhartrhari, 1977 (K. A. Subramania Iyer, translator)

Further reading

Chakrabarti, Tarapada. *Indian Aesthetics and Science of Language*, 1971.
Chakravarti, P. K. *The Linguistic Speculations of the Hindus*, 1933.
Coward, Harold G. *Bhartrhari*, 1976.
——, ed. *"Language" in Indian Philosophy and Religion*, 1978.
——. *Sphota Theory of Language*, 1980.
——. *Derrida and Indian Philosophy*, 1990.
Dasgupta, Surendranath. *A History of Indian Philosophy*, Vol. 1, 1963.
De, Sushil Kumar. *History of Sanskrit Poetics*, Vols. 1 and 2, 1960 (second revised edition).
Derrida, Jacques. *Writing and Difference*, 1978.
Ghose, Aurobindo. *On the Veda*, 1956.
Herman, A. L. "Sphota," in *Journal of the Ganganatha Jha Research Institute*. 19 (1963), pp. 1–21.
Iyer, K. A. Subramania, trans. *Sphotasiddhi of Mandana Misra*, 1966.
——, trans. *Vakyapadiya of Bhartrhari, with Commentaries Vrtti and Paddhati of Vrsabhadeva*, 1966.
——. *Bhartrhari: A Study of the Vakyapadiya in the Light of Ancient Commentaries*, 1969.
Krishnamacharya, V. V., ed. *Sphotavadda of Nagesa Bhatta*, 1946.
Norris, Christopher. *Derrida*, 1987.
Patanjali. *Yoga Sutras of Patanjali*, 1978. Translated by Rama Prasada.
Shankara. *Vivekacudamani*, 1988. Translated by P. Sankaranarayanan; commentary by Sri Candrasekhara Bharati.
Staal, J. F, ed. *A Reader on the Sanskrit Grammarians*, 1972.
Vedanta Sutras, The, with *Commentary* by Shankara, 1962. Translated by G. Thibaut.

William S. Haney II

See also Anandavardhana; Bharata; Indian Literary Theory

Biblical Criticism: Allegory and Typology

The Bible as literature

Biblical criticism is the source for most of the interpretive strategies that have been developed to explain and teach literature in the West over the last two thousand years. Long regarded as the source of religious inspiration for untold millions, the Bible continues to be examined for its rhetorical brilliance by critics such as Kenneth Burke and George Kennedy and for its value as literature by Northrop Frye, Frank Kermode, and Robert Alter. The Bible, contrary to the system of allegorical explanation eventually developed to render it coherent and comprehensive, is actually a collection of stories, a library of religious narratives, poetry, and homilies. The word "Bible" comes from the Greek *ta biblia*, meaning "little books." Story, as Claude

Lévi-Strauss and others have shown, is an integral structure of human language akin to myth. When people speak, they express and organize their experience as stories. Selected stories – or what Frye calls "myths," from the Greek *mythoi* meaning plots – compose and record a body of narratives that in turn may well provide a cultural matrix for a "people." When stories are edited, selected, and collected to represent the history, traditions, interests, and aspirations of a given culture, a canon is formed. If the canon is committed to script and is sufficiently vested with authority, it becomes "scriptural," that is sacrosanct and binding – what we call "sacred writ." When the scriptural canon becomes the object of collective veneration, an institutional religion develops around it, from *re-ligo* in Latin, meaning "to bind." Religious stories are then interpreted as parables and paradigms to be taken on faith, beyond their face value, as models not only describing but prescribing human allegiance and behavior. Characters in sanctioned religious story become types, its myths become archetypes, and its texts constitute a body of legal and religious doctrine against which the behavior of individuals comes to be assessed and judged. Most importantly, the myths and types of the emerging canon are seen ultimately to have been inscribed by the hand of God at crucial moments in the history of the emerging culture. The stories are not thought of as composed by religious prophets or teachers; they are transmitted through religious visions or rhapsodic communication between God and his prophets. The Bible's claim to truth then becomes, as Eric Auerbach claimed, "tyrannical." It admits no disputation and brooks no unofficial interpretation. This is not to say, however, that the Bible cannot be interpreted and judged as literature or story, maybe as "the greatest story ever told," and such interpretations continue to flourish today.

Once "holy writ" is acknowledged and its canonical stories collected, a class of scribes is trained to edit and interpret what comes to be thought of as the sacred texts, expound their teachings, and promulgate a definitive interpretation of the "scripture." The interpretation itself often comes to be recognized as sacrosanct – even written by God himself and only transmitted through his scribes. The doctrine of the institution or church that is ratified by the stories and their official interpretation is seen to be, as Cardinal Newman asserted in his *Essay on Development of Christian Doctrine* (1845), evolving to correspond to the hermeneutic or interpretive needs of the times. Revelation is ongoing and is communicated through the interpretive officers of the temple or church. The interpretations themselves, of course, must be submitted to a given body for authorization. Eventually a method is developed by the scribes or clerks that is offered as a scientific system designed to extract the meaning from the myth. The Bible itself comes to be regarded as, in Northrop Frye's words, a "great code" which must be deciphered and "explicated" or unfolded as a text. The Bible can be and has also been examined as a rhetorical text-persuasive, hortatory, and homiletic as well as an enjoyable if enigmatic narrative in its thrust and power. The rhetoric of religious writing, pioneered by Kenneth Burke, is a productive literary field at the moment as is attested by the various collections of essays recently devoted to the topic.

Old Testament midrash

The earliest form of Biblical criticism is called "midrash," a Hebrew word meaning "interpretation" which became the term for the official collection of critical writings devoted to the Old Testament or the "Torah." Midrash is the written interpretation of Old Testament discourse as opposed to the extension of such narrative in the oral tradition. It was accumulated in compilations of many volumes that span several centuries of biblical commentary. Midrash sustained and was bolstered by rabbinical authority. Over time, commentary on the sacred text itself became sacred and was subject to the scrutiny of religious elders. Midrash early on developed into a theological genre in its own right, increasingly nationalistic and devoted to propagating interpretations favorable to the rise of a Jewish identity and nation. Like most interpretive strategies to follow, midrash pursued a stratified approach to biblical myth and legend to keep hermeneutic possibilities open and evolving. Beginning with the legal interpretation of a given biblical passage, the commentary proceeded to expound the moral and religious implications. After the straightforward meaning of the text was discussed, a fanciful interpretation was offered anticipating the literal and spiritual readings of a biblical text in the allegorical exegesis of the Middle Ages. Over time the idea of a continuous revelation received from God became acceptable. It was thought that God communicated with a rabbinical commentator in much the same way that he did with Moses who witnessed Jehovah himself writing the ten commandments on two stone tablets.

Allegorical exegesis of the Bible

By the second century A.D., under the influence of Saint Paul, the Church Fathers developed a method of biblical criticism called allegorical "exegesis" as a way of dealing with both the Old Testament and pagan literature – Homer, Sophocles, Virgil, Ovid, Horace – which was the main subject of study in the schools of the late classical period. As in midrash, a given text, whether the *Book of Job* or Sophocles' *Oedipus Rex* (430–426 B.C.), was thought to have both a plain or literal meaning and a spiritual one, corresponding metaphysically to the crucial distinction between the body and the spirit. Drawing on the Pauline assertion that the letter kills while the spirit enlivens and inspires, allegorical theory privileges the implication of the text – the meaning that is enfolded or encoded in the superficial narrative – above the straightforward, self-evident meaning of the story. The term "allegory" derives from the Greek *allos*, meaning "other," and *agoreuein*, meaning "to speak." Commentators were schooled in discovering another, hidden meaning in a given text. The exegete passed quickly over what was variously called the "hull" or "chaff" to the "kernel" or "fruit" of the matter in the narrative. It was thought that God "spoke" through "enigma," through a puzzle that had to be solved by the commentator. The procedure was institutionally convenient as well, because authorities could extract whatever meaning was expedient to the needs of the Church while expounding on the scriptures. The institutional directive was then thought to be grounded in God's Word.

Allegory was analyzed by ancient rhetoricians such as Aristotle, Cicero, and Quintilian as a rhetorical trope of literature whereby a speaker or writer could say one thing and mean another. More technically, in allegory a given narrative becomes what Edwin Honig calls a "dark conceit," continuously expressing something beyond itself in a double narrative with an obvious and a hidden stratum of signification. Allegory, of course, privileges and empowers the commentator. In extracting the meaning from a biblical or literary text, he or she in a sense recomposes the text and supplements the meaning of the original author. Allegory is clearly a major precedent for the reader-response criticism of the late twentieth century and a method so compelling in its assumptions that it was applied liberally throughout all the arts and sciences of the trivium (grammar, rhetoric, logic) and the quadrivium (mathematics, music, geometry, astronomy) of late classical and medieval culture. Nature as well as history were interpreted as, and even called, "books" written, like the Bible, by God himself. In the allegorical explication of human history, we are not too far afield from Marxist doctrine which teaches that history is a coherent system of meaning that the dialectical materialist can read, predict, and possibly even control. To the medieval mind, highly trained in the methods of biblical exegesis, the universe was a text that demanded a trained exegete, and the entire educational system itself was constructed to teach the correct methods for reading and divulging universal mysteries.

Typology

A major form of both patristic and medieval allegory was called "typology." In typological readings of the Old Testament or pagan literature, narratives and characters were thought to anticipate or prophesy events and characters in the gospels. Jesus Christ was well aware of the process and put it to work in his own life and teaching. He was, as a rabbi and master, well versed in Old Testament doctrine and echoed the teachings of Ecclesiastes and Deuteronomy in his sermons and parables, adopted the preaching methods of Jeremiah and Isaiah, and emulated the lives of Old Testament prophets such as Noah and Jonah. In his own preaching, Saint Paul passed on the traditional methods of literary exegesis gleaned from both Hebraic and Hellenic sources. Interpreting Genesis allegorically, Paul speaks of Adam as a type of Christ, Eve as prefiguring Mary, and the Tree of Life as the anticipation of the Cross. The Old Testament Fall is viewed not so much as the beginning of human independence from God as the archetypal fall from God's grace that will be restored through the redemptive action of his son on the cross. In the Old Testament, Abraham is asked by God to sacrifice his son, Isaac, who is spared at the last moment. So, too, God is required to sacrifice his son, Jesus, who will be resurrected after the agony of the crucifixion.

Jesus taught that the promise of the Old Testament was fulfilled in the New Testament. Saint Augustine echoes the sentiment when he says in *On Christian Instruction* (396–397) "In the Old Testament the New Testament is concealed; in the New Testament the Old Testament is revealed." The gospel was considered true because its stories echoed and confirmed the prophecies of the Old Testament. Life, in short, was lived according to the book, the good Book. The Old and the New Testaments were thought of as two books facing each other like mirrors. This pattern of reflection is architecturally realized in the cathedrals of medieval Europe where the windows on the left depict Old Testament stories and figures which are adapted or interpreted pictorially in the corresponding windows on the right which were devoted to the New Testament. The window at the "binding" in the ambulatory at the back of the church depicted both Jacob's ladder in the Old and the flowering staff of Jesse in the New Testament, recounting in the process the genealogies of Old and New Testament prophets. When we are told in the gospels that Jesus asked why he had been "forsaken by God" on the cross, he is echoing the use of the phrase in the Book of Psalms. Jesus' behavior fulfills, in his own life, the general mission of the "suffering servant" in Isaiah. The suffering servant is mysteriously scorned by the community he comes to serve and is despised and punished by the authorities. Jesus tells us, therefore, that a prophet has no honor in his own land and has nowhere to lay his head, indicating that he is well aware of his fate as an instrument of God. In short, the Old Testament "figures forth" the New Testament, and the New is the key, through allegorical explication by proper authority, to the mysteries and the "enigma" of the Old. Through the system of allegory, old literature is made new, or, to put it in Geoffrey Chaucer's words, "new corn comes from old fields."

The allegorical reading of secular literature

The allegorical exegesis of pagan literature actually antedates both Hebraic and Christian exegesis. Ancient Roman rhetoricians read Homer allegorically to extract the prophecy that the Romans were actually descended from the ancient Homeric enemy of the Greeks, the relatively blameless Trojans, and Virgil followed suit in the *Aeneid* (29–19 B.C.). Jean Seznec and Erwin Panofsky have shown that late classical mythographers interpreted ancient Greek "characters" such as those examined by Theophrastus in his book of that title as "types" of great Roman leaders. In the first century Plutarch adopted this typological procedure as a method for producing his matched biographies linking up famous Greek and Roman leaders such as Theseus and Mark Antony, much in the same way that Paul likened Isaiah's suffering servant to Jesus.

The exegesis of classical and Christian scholars and theologians are combined and extended in Dante Alighieri's *La divina commedia* (c. 1320; *The Divine Comedy*), a Christian poem which is to be read, according to its author, as an allegory of the damnation, purgation, and ultimate salvation of the human soul. Dante was not the first Christian poet to have composed a book which is to be read as the "dark conceit" of the pilgrimage of the Christian to union with his or her maker, nor was he the last. Edmund Spenser's *The Fairie Queene* (1590–1609) and John Bunyan's *The Pilgrim's Progress* (1678) both derive from the same tradition and depend on the principles of allegorical exegesis plainly laid out in Dante's letter to a patron, Can Grande Della Scala. His "comedy," Dante explains, is "polysemous" in intention; it has many meanings organized in a hermeneutic grid. The first level of meaning is called "literal" which denotes the "subject of the work as it is accepted according to the letter." The second level of meaning is the "one obtaining through the things signified by the letter." The second level has three parts to it: the allegorical, moral, and anagogical. Appropriately for our purposes, Dante offers the following scriptural verse as an illustration of how the allegorical process is to be applied to secular literature. The verse is "When Israel went out of Egypt, the house of Jacob from a people of strange language, Judah was his sanctuary and Israel his dominion." The literal level is the historic meaning of the text from the Old Testament: the "departure of the Israelites from Egypt under the guidance of Moses." The allegorical or "other" meaning typologically anticipates the New Testament "redemption accomplished by Christ." The moral, or what was often called the "tropological" sense, has to do with the exemplary course of action suggested by the passage, namely, "the conversion of the soul from the woe and misery of sin to a state of grace." Finally, the anagogical or mystical sense refers the reader prophetically to things to come, "the departure of the consecrated soul from the slavery of this corruption to the liberty of eternal glory."

Early Modern and contemporary biblical criticism

Allegory fell out of fashion in the Early Modern period for two compelling reasons. The Protestant Reformation democratized the reading and interpretation of the Bible. Reformers like Martin Luther and John Calvin either translated or authorized translations of the Bible into the "vulgar tongue," the language spoken by the people, to break the stranglehold of the Roman Catholic Church on the Word of God. Secular allegory, which was often a thinly veiled attempt to interpret pagan texts as vehicles for Christian revelation, came to be seen as crudely mechanical and doctrinaire. The dominance of literary allegory which had held sway in literary criticism for more than a millennium was displaced in the nineteenth and twentieth centuries by symbolism, formalism, and eventually the current hermeneutic fashion of postmodernism.

Further reading

Alter, Robert. *The Art of Biblical Narrative*, 1983.
——, and Frank Kermode, eds. *The Literary Guide to the Bible*, 1987.
Auerbach, Erich. *Mimesis: The Representation of Reality in Western Literature*, 1953.
Burke, Kenneth. *The Rhetoric of Religion*, 1970.
Fishbane, Michael. *Biblical Interpretation in Ancient Israel*, 1985.
Fletcher, Angus. *Allegory: The Theory of a Symbolic Mode*, 1964.
Frye, Northrop. *The Great Code: The Bible as Literature*, 1983.
Honig, Edwin. *The Dark Conceit: The Making of Allegory*, 1966.
Kennedy, George. *New Testament Interpretation through Rhetorical Criticism*, 1984.
Morgan, Robert. *Biblical Interpretation*, 1988.
Panofsky, Erwin. *Studies in Iconology: Humanistic Themes in the Art of the Renaissance*, 1962.
Quilligan, Maureen. *The Language of Allegory: Defining the Genre*, 1979.
Sanders, James. *Canon to Community: A Guide to Canonical Criticism*, 1984.
Seznec, Jean. *The Survival of the Pagan Gods*, 1953.
Smalley, Beryl. *The Study of the Bible in the Middle Ages*, 1964.
Warner, Martin, ed. *Bible as Rhetoric: Studies in Biblical Persuasion and Credibility*, 1990.

James R. Andreas, Sr.

Black Literary Theory and Criticism

Introduction

"It is a peculiar sensation, this double-consciousness, this sense of always looking at one's self through the eyes of others, of measuring one's soul by the tape of a world that looks on in amused contempt and pity. One ever feels his two-ness, – an American, a Negro; two souls, two thoughts, two unreconciled strivings; two warring ideals in one dark body, whose dogged strength alone keeps it from being torn asunder." W. E. B. Du Bois (1868–1963) expressed this famous sentiment in 1903 in *The Souls of Black Folk*. Bearing witness to the pain of black peoples in a racially unequal world ruled by whites, but also to black peoples' strength in refusing to be vanquished in the face of intolerance and prejudice, Du Bois' identification of "double-consciousness" has, in contrasting ways, preoccupied attempts to theorize black cultures and modes of interpretation ever since. At first, black intellectuals tended to explore the possibility of identifying uniquely black forms of literary and critical practices grounded in fixed notions of racial difference, which acknowledged and restored fully-formed consciousness to black peoples. But in the light of the theoretical and political problems created by this approach, recent theoretical work has frequently proposed a distinctly black aesthetic as the product of certain kinds of language use, and not the consequence of fixed racial "essences." This attitude, which enthusiastically pursues the potential virtues of Du Bois' "double-consciousness," has become the bass-line of black literary theory and criticism as it is understood today.

Negritude, black consciousness, and interpretation

One of the first, and most influential, schools of thought which attempted to theorize black modes of culture and interpretation was Negritude, popular during the 1950s and 1960s especially in America, Africa, and the Caribbean. Negritude involved restoring to black peoples a sense of self-worth, stability, and dignity beyond white definitions of blackness, one that would replace the sense of a self "torn asunder" and under siege. In his comments of 1965 about distinctly black forms of interpretation, the Senegalese Negritude writer Léopold Senghor (1906–) proposed that black peoples throughout the world shared a particular way of representing and responding to reality derived from their common race. In contrast to the white world, which allegedly interprets reality with disinterested, objective detachment, Senghor posited that the black man "does not begin by distinguishing himself from the object, the tree or stone, the man or animal or social event. He does not keep it at a distance. He does not analyse it. Once he has come under its influence, he takes it like a blind man, still living, into his hands. He does not fix or kill it. He turns it over in his supple hands, he fingers it, he *feels* it." In depicting the ways in which black peoples related to the world in unique and privileged ways, Senghor and others made an important and valuable attempt to depict black peoples as having their own fully-formed consciousness and interpretative methods. Black peoples were urged to refuse to see the world through the eyes of others; black literature (oral and written), art, and culture, it was argued, expressed the specific nature of the black race in ways which were not visible to white ways of seeing. So, if Du Bois lamented the black self split by double-consciousness, then the Negritude writers attempted to heal the rift by refusing the "tape" of a contemptuous white world and asserting instead a racially rooted idea of black cultural expression and interpretative practice deemed unique and discrete from all others.

Much of what is understood today as black literary theory and criticism is both informed by and deeply critical of many of the assumptions of Negritude. Despite its attempts to restore dignity and value to black peoples and their myriad cultures, many black writers and critics have become increasingly uncomfortable with the ways in which Negritude continued to traffic in stereotypical representations of black peoples (such as Senghor's representation of the "sensual" black man) rather than challenge them. In addition, the chauvinistic attitudes which pervade some Negritude writings are unwelcome to black women; Senghor once remarked that black women were the "life-force" of black peoples and did not require liberation.

With the advent of structuralist and poststructuralist literary theory from the 1970s, critics began to doubt the revolutionary propensity of a black aesthetic which proposed fixed, "essential" forms of identity for black peoples, as well as treating black peoples in Africa, America, the Caribbean, and Britain as if they could all be easily unified as a common people or race. Rather than use the term "black" to signify unity, stable identity, roots, solidarity, and fixity, as had been the case, a new generation of critics influenced by Jacques Derrida, Mikhail Bakhtin, and others, began to reconstruct the term "black" as an exciting sign of plurality, shifting identities, routes, dissensus, and instability. Whereas Du Bois had used the notion of "double-consciousness" to measure the pain of being a black person in a white world, black intellectuals working in (and in-between) Britain and America seized upon ideas of doubling, fracturing, and movement as the conceptual building blocks of an exciting new black aesthetic. The shift emphasis from the fixed "roots" of race to the contingent "routes" of black language use is vital to understanding black literary theory and criticism today.

Black literary theory and criticism in America

A few examples from, inevitably, a much wider field serve as an example of this emphasis on plurality, partiality, and process in theories of a distinctly black aesthetic. In books such as *Figures in Black: Words, Signs, and the "Racial" Self* (1987) and especially *The Signifying Monkey: A Theory of Afro-American Literary Criticism* (1988), Henry Louis Gates, Jr., develops a theory of the black vernacular by attending specifically to language use in the work of black American writers ranging from Zora Neale Hurston to Alice Walker. Seizing upon the "trickster" figure in Yoruba belief systems, and its concomitant manifestation in South American, Caribbean, and black American writing, Gates argues that a distinctly black vernacular can be demonstrated in black writers' specific and inventive appropriation of standard English usage, a process which he terms "Signifyin(g)." Rather than identifying a black aesthetic outside white Western ways of seeing, Gates shows how black writers work within received language, disrupting standard meanings by such strategies as parody and pastiche, or by playing with the rhetorical and aural qualities of language. In a similar fashion, black literary texts often enter into an intertextual dialogue with others, appropriating and "doubling" their literary antecedents and generating new meanings from older texts. For these reasons, meaning in black American literature is always in motion, enabled and deferred by the antic rhetorical strategies of "Signifyin(g)." In a theory which owes as much to Bakhtin as it does to Yoruba beliefs, meaning is asserted as plural, partial, and always in process; never fixed, secure, or closed. Thus, Gates proposes a black American literary tradition and interpretative practice the "blackness" of which is not a result of fixed identities or common racial characteristics, but a consequence of historically situated and diverse forms of language use which interact cunningly, contingently, and critically with the received language of (white) America.

A major part of this arguably more flexible and open-ended approach to theorizing black literature and culture – an approach which is aware of the *diversity* of black cultural expressions – has been a sophisticated awareness of the relationship between racial and gender differences. This is the result of much important and pioneering work by black American women, such as bell hooks. Her groundbreaking book *Ain't I a Woman: Black Women and Feminism* (1982) explores the tense relations between racist and patriarchal modes of oppression, with particular reference to writing by and about black women in the late nineteenth and early twentieth centuries. In her depiction of black male complicity in patriarchy, hooks' work reveals the inner contradictions which continue to complicate life for black women, and hence she makes it impossible to posit the homogenizing and often chauvinist representations of black American communities found in Negritude or separatist writings. But she is also cautious when considering the critique of fixed, essential identities. In *Yearning: Race, Gender and Cultural Politics* (1991) she considers some of the dangers in cheerfully embracing theoretical ideas which declare the end to static notions of subjectivity, history, and identity, not least because this can detract attention away from the enduring politics of racial representations. Thus, in *Black Looks: Race and Representation* (1992) hooks memorably critiques the politics of a variety of representations of black women in mass culture, from *Vanity Fair* covers to Madonna videos, demonstrating that representation remains one of the most important modes of racism today, no matter how fleeting and unstable it might be.

Interestingly, both Gates and hooks have each recently written autobiographical texts about their childhoods (in *Colored People: A Memoir*, 1994, and *Bone Black: Memories of Girlhood*, 1997, respectively). This maneuver demonstrates how, in moving between the languages of "high" theory, autobiography, history, and memoir, contemporary black intellectuals continue to eschew the role of the "detached" academic, safely ensconced in the "ivory tower" and removed from the politics and experiences of the black communities beyond.

Black British cultural studies

A particularly influential critic in Britain is Stuart Hall, whose work has established many of the key ideas with which black British critics have worked. A Caribbean migrant to Britain in the 1950s, Hall has been a central figure in exploring and theorizing the fortunes of black Britons since the end of World War II. Like bell hooks, Hall's work engages with a variety of different cultural phenomena (literature, film, television, and so on). One of his most influential essays, "New Ethnicities" (1989), identifies two important moments in the representation and theorizing of black peoples in Britain. In the first, the black community is seen in homogenous terms as a singular body with a common and discrete identity. Hall argues that, during this moment, black writers and artists felt compelled to represent a common "black experience" to the white majority as part of a protest against racism and marginalization. Central to this was the representation of black peoples in stereotypical and positive terms. But in the second moment, this consensual and positive vision of the black community gives way to new ways of representing black peoples which challenge their seeming unity, and focuses instead on the differences in class, gender, religion, sexuality, and so forth, which make the black community internally diverse and conflictual. This recognition of diversity means that it is no longer possible for writers and artists to present one black individual as representative of the black community as a whole; instead, the differences of black peoples becomes the focus for attention, as conflicts within the black community are acknowledged and explored. It is this "new" sense of ethnicity – as internally multifarious, with individuals acknowledged as multifaceted rather than singular or fixed – which replaces the older paradigm of the representative black person who is black before he or she is anything else. In charting these two "moments" in the representation of black Britain, Hall is careful to point out that they can coexist at the same point in time, and reminds us that (as with Negritude) there may be historical situations when an assertion of a totalizing, fixed black identity is politically justified, despite its theoretical shortcomings.

The establishment of a more pluralized notion of black experience has been matched by new forms of representation. In his essay "What is this 'Black' in Black Popular Culture?" (1992), Hall attends to the ways in which black cultural production is marked by recognizable processes of hybridization, where artistic forms from many traditions and locations are mixed together to produce new, pluralized, and hybrid results. The focus on the formal impurity and hybridity of black popular culture, where appropriation is the key strategy of artistic (re)creation, became the presiding theme in theoretical work in 1990s. Kobena Mercer's book *Welcome to the Jungle: New Positions in Black Cultural Studies* (1994) looks at the ways in which a much more internally divergent and multifarious sense of the black community was expressed in the 1980s in Britain and America, with particular reference to the fortunes of gay and lesbian black peoples. And in *Black Women, Writing and Identity: Migrations of the Subject* (1994), Carol Boyce Davies argues for new forms of reading practices which derive their energy from the multiple journeys and subject-positions of black women. By appropriating existing literary theories and adapting them for the specific purpose of attending to the cultural productions of black women, Boyce Davies builds a "migratory" aesthetic by (in her words) "going a piece of the way" with received knowledge, putting it to new purposes. As with Gates' use of Bakhtin, Derrida, and others, her approach works with the theoretical insights of poststructuralism, selecting and adapting new ideas for the purposes of understanding specifically black reading and writing practices.

The "Black Atlantic"

One of the most valuable texts to emerge in the field of black literary theory and criticism is Paul Gilroy's *The Black Atlantic: Modernity and Double Consciousness* (1993), which perhaps captures best of all the sense of motion, multiplicity, and contingency that characterizes the different kinds of black literary theory and criticism current in Britain and America. The gesture to W. E. B. Du Bois in the subtitle exemplifies the heart of Gilroy's theory: the ways in which black peoples can utilize ideas and resources of others located at a different juncture in history or in another part of the world. In appropriating existing kinds of black cultural expression, black peoples alter both the form of these ideas as well as their content, revising and supplementing past meanings for the present. One of Gilroy's favorite examples is the way in which black music has been transfigured over successive decades: African music was adapted in slave songs, which in their turn became transformed in jazz and blues. The appropriation of existing black cultural expression emphasizes, first, the innovative, unpredictable, and untidy evolution of black culture, forever bringing past and present, here and there, into dialogue with each other as new forms of culture appear; and, second, the ways in which black peoples in any one place and time remain informed by the history of others in similar positions around the world. In these terms, Gilroy attempts to show how black culture is fresh and innovative, forever in process, yet always resourced by the histories of black peoples' experience and the geographically divergent locations where these histories occurred – without totalizing either "black peoples" and "black history," nor positing a fixed, essential black race or self.

As its title implies, *The Black Atlantic* suggests a black aesthetic which is "at sea," but not in the sense of being shipwrecked or off-course. The image of the "Black Atlantic" recalls the slave ships journeying between Africa, the Caribbean, America, and Britain, crisscrossing the Atlantic with their unholy cargo. But if these were the routes of a hideous traffic, Gilroy also reminds us that the same ships' routes were used by black radicals to circulate their ideas and build solidarity with black peoples across the globe. Similarly, as an aesthetic the "Black Atlantic" values the appropriation of the very systems of black peoples' oppression for new purposes, and foregrounds the shifting and untidy solidarities between different black peoples which go beyond purely national contexts. For Gilroy, "double-consciousness" marks the beginning of a valuable and exciting mode of critique, but one which does not deny the pain of black oppression that Du Bois identified almost a century earlier.

The frequent emphasis upon restless, unstable, and contingent ways of rendering, reading and (re)producing black cultural expression is central to black literary theory and criticism today. The fact that Du Bois' remark remains influential at the turn of a new century, but refashioned in ways he could never have predicted, perhaps exemplifies better than anything else the innovative spirit of appropriation which characterizes Gates' antic "Signifyin(g) Monkey" or Gilroy's non-essentialized "Black Atlantic," if not black literary theory and criticism in general.

Further reading

Arnold, A. James. *Modernism and Negritude: The Poetry and Poetics of Aimé Césaire*, 1981.

Boyce Davies, Carol. *Black Women, Writing and Identity: Migrations of the Subject*, 1994.

Du Bois, W. E. B. *The Souls of Black Folk*, 1903.

Gates, Henry Louis, Jr., ed. *"Race," Writing, and Difference*, 1986.

——. *Figures in Black: Words, Signs, and the "Racial" Self*, 1987.

——. *The Signifying Monkey: A Theory of Afro-American Literary Criticism*, 1988.

Gilroy, Paul. *The Black Atlantic: Modernity and Double Consciousness*, 1993.

——. *Small Acts: Thoughts on the Politics of Black Cultures*, 1993.

Hall, Stuart. "New Ethnicities" and "What is this 'Black' in Black Popular Culture?," in *Stuart Hall: Critical Dialogues in Cultural Studies*, 1996. Edited by David Morley and Kuan-Hsing Chen.

hooks, bell. *Ain't I a Woman: Black Women and Feminism*, 1982.

——. *Talking Back: Thinking Feminist, Thinking Black*, 1989.

——. *Yearning: Race, Gender and Cultural Politics*, 1991.

——. *Black Looks: Race and Representation*, 1992.

——, and Cornel West. *Breaking Bread: Insurgent Black Intellectual Life*, 1991.

Mercer, Kobena. *Welcome to the Jungle: New Positions in Black Cultural Studies*, 1994.

Morrison, Toni. *Playing in the Dark: Whiteness and the Literary Imagination*, 1992.

John McLeod

See also Gates; Postcolonial Literature and Theory

R. P. Blackmur

American critic and poet

Born: Springfield, Massachusetts; January 21, 1904
Died: Princeton, New Jersey; February 2, 1965

Biography

Richard Palmer Blackmur was born on January 21, 1904, in Springfield, Massachusetts, the son of George Edward and Helen Palmer Blackmur. The young Blackmur followed an unusual path to academic success. After leaving school at the age of fourteen, he educated himself while working in bookstores. He achieved success through intelligence, hard work, and powerful writing about serious subjects.

By the age of twenty-three, Blackmur had published his poetry in major magazines and journals, and in 1928 began to attract attention with essays in literary criticism. From 1928 to 1931 he served as associate editor of *Hound and Horn*, a respected literary magazine. In 1930 he married Helen Dickson; they were divorced in 1951.

In 1935 Blackmur published his first volume of collected essays, *The Double Agent*, followed in 1937 by his first collection of poetry, *From Jordan's Delight*. In 1936 he received a Guggenheim grant for a study of Henry Adams. His work on Adams began to shift his focus from specific works of art to the role of artist and critic in a mass society.

In 1940 Blackmur became poet Allen Tate's assistant in the Princeton University creative writing program. He spent the rest of his life at Princeton, receiving an appointment in 1948 to the department of English, where he became a professor in 1951. His essay and poetry collections appeared regularly throughout his life and continued to be published after his death, on February 2, 1965.

Influence

Blackmur's early critical analysis of such major figures as T. S. Eliot, James Joyce, and Ezra Pound shaped Anglo-American understanding of many of the masters of twentieth-century literature. Blackmur also had a lasting impact on the evolution of literary criticism. His major influence on his colleagues came through his helping establish as orthodoxy the need for a close reading of the text and his work on understanding the mix of rational and nonrational elements in the creative act. He was one of the originators of the New Criticism school, and he helped establish it within an initially hostile academic community. In the latter part of his career, he helped broaden critical focus by writing about a critic's responsibility in an age that had so fragmented culture that artists and readers no longer shared a common body of knowledge and assumptions.

Analysis

Blackmur's career flourished from the 1930s through the 1950s, the golden age of the New Criticism. He was one of its major figures, along with such people as John Crowe Ransom, Allen Tate, Cleanth Brooks, Robert Penn Warren, and Yvor Winters. The New Critics, influenced by T. S. Eliot and I. A. Richards, rebelled against a world dehumanized by science and industrial capitalism. In societies that allowed scant opportunity for people to combine intellect and feeling, the New Critics regarded literature, especially poetry, as a haven where alienated humanity might again experience the rich density of life. Although the unity of the school fades as one examines individuals, the New Critics emphasized the necessity of the close reading of the text and spurned criticism extrinsic to the work. Much of their surface unity came from their rejection of the historical, biographical, and psychological approaches to literature that dominated critical writing before the 1930s.

Although Blackmur shared these concerns, his focus and literary style differed from those of other New Critics. He came to believe that New Criticism had become facile, turning method into methodology.

Blackmur established his reputation with his early critical work on such poets as T. S. Eliot, William Butler Yeats, Wallace Stevens, e. e. cummings, and Marianne Moore; he wrote admirable studies of Henry James, James Joyce, Henry Adams, Thomas Mann, and others. His own thought was deeply influenced by Eliot, James, and Adams.

In his work on such figures, Blackmur stressed the necessity of a close reading of the text. He was one of the hardest working of all critics, carefully analyzing the "facts" of a poem, often using a variety of disciplines, and fitting his critical approach to the text at hand. As a poet, Blackmur understood the craft of writing and had superb taste in literature. He loved words and believed that the ability to communicate through them was the essential meaning of what it is to be human.

Blackmur believed that poets experienced reality through imagination and through reason. Imagination transformed ordinary experiences in a special way; reason brought order to the poetic images of those experiences and allowed them to be communicated. The critic also used reason and imagination. An artistic work consisted of "facts," which the critic approached through reason, and "gestures" (any unusual use of words that conveyed meaning beyond that ordinarily transmitted by them), which could be intuited through imagination.

The critic could only point to clues about the meaning of a poem; the reader must experience it directly. The critic properly left the "real work" to the reader; literary criticism could not distill the meaning for the reader. In *Language as Gesture*, Blackmur wrote:

> Analysis cannot touch but only translate for preliminary purposes the poem the return to which every sign demands. What we do is simply to set up clues which we can name and handle and exchange

> whereby we can make available all that territory of the poem which we cannot name or handle but only envisage.

The critic can discuss the "facts" or words but not "the imaginative product of the words which is poetry." Critics cannot act as vicars for poetry: "Poetry is idiom, a special and fresh saying, and cannot for its life be said otherwise; and there is . . . as much difference between words used about a poem and the poem as there is between words used about a painting and the painting. The gap is absolute."

Thus, Blackmur found uncommunicable mystery at the heart of a work of art, as in life itself. Lifting a veil on reality only revealed mystery; that was reality. Recognition of this mystery at the heart of art and life led Blackmur from his early focus on literary works to concern with the role of artists and critics in the twentieth century and finally to the crisis of modern society. His writing style after about 1940 became increasingly difficult and cryptic. It outraged some and amused others, but his admirers found method behind his seeming obscurity. One of Blackmur's favorite passages of poetry was in John Donne's third "Satyre": "On a huge hill,/ Cragged, and steep, Truth stands, and hee that will/ Reach her, about must, and about must goe." While some readers found Blackmur's later writing to be fuzzy, others understood that he was working at the limits of a language that required him to go roundabout to where "Truth stands," that forced him to use rational discourse to express the nonrational. The nonrational, to Blackmur, was the core of the human experience.

Writers, critics, and readers combined reason and imagination when they wrote, analyzed, and read literature. Yet forces unleashed by modernity fragmented reason and relegated imagination to the realm of the nonessential. Blackmur probed the nature of modern society and the calamity faced by alienated and degraded humans. He especially turned to such problems in essays collected in *Anni Mirabiles, 1921–1925, A Primer of Ignorance*, and *Henry Adams*.

Blackmur believed that in "Stanzas from the Grande Chartreuse," Matthew Arnold had captured the essence of Henry Adams' conception of himself and his society: "Wandering between two worlds, one dead,/ The other powerless to be born." Arnold's words fit Blackmur as well, although he may have lost the optimism that something better was waiting to be born. Blackmur believed that modernity had destroyed the core of Western civilization, the central beliefs that had explained to earlier generations the meaning of life, the beliefs on which they had ordered their existence. The principle of indeterminacy in mathematics and physics destroyed the already eroded foundation of moral absolutism; anthropology exposed the mystery of gods to the annihilating analysis of social science theory; and sociology "flattened us into the average of the lonely crowd."

Literature was one haven for besieged humanity, for there reason and imagination still could merge. The critic could serve by mediating between artist and reader, who were no longer the products of a shared culture: "This is the struggle between the old literacy and the new illiteracy, which is not ignorance but fragmented and specialized knowledge."

Blackmur believed, as did Henry Adams, that longing for the cultural unity that provided meaning to life was an essential human characteristic, but he also believed that life was meaningless. Whatever myths people used to hide the void were but temporary shields: "Indeterminacy is life," Blackmur wrote in *Anni Mirabiles, 1921–1925*. One must search, as did Adams, for a unifying principle, for "Truth," but never commit intellectual suicide by finding it, whether by accepting religion or any of the modern "isms." When T. S. Eliot turned to religion, Blackmur wrote: "We admire him, we cannot follow him." Although there was an elitist cast to Blackmur's work, he was fundamentally concerned with people and with their need to feel and express their humanity in the modern world.

Adams rather than Eliot remained Blackmur's guide. Pressed by the drive for conformity in the post-World War II era, the age of the Cold War and McCarthyism, Blackmur sketched the role of the intellectual, who "seeks truth and . . . plays with it":

> He will . . . keep himself a little outside the avowed interests of the society – or the institution – which he serves. His true allegiance will be to the contentious, speculative, imaginative nature of the mind itself and to the dark, problematical, reversible nature of the experience with which the mind deals. That is to say, his allegiance is to the whole enterprise of the mind, and far from being remote from it, it will move him from both without and within. That is why he will be skeptical of any particular commitment and will be rebellious to any attempt to make conformity a simple or narrow thing.

Blackmur is assured of a secure position in literary history, and many scholars believe that he will be at or near the head of the list of twentieth-century critics. Some literary historians rest their judgment on his early work that fell within the New Criticism school; others believe that his later essays, like the work of his mentor Henry Adams, will continue to resonate with those who confront the dilemmas humans face in the modern world, those who remain with Blackmur and Adams on the edge of the abyss, committing suicide neither physically by flinging themselves into it nor intellectually by fleeing from it into faith in some "ism."

Principal criticism

The Double Agent: Essays in Craft and Elucidation, 1935
The Expense of Greatness, 1940

Language as Gesture: Essays in Poetry, 1952
Form and Value in Modern Poetry, 1952
The Lion and the Honeycomb: Essays in Solicitude and Critique, 1955
Anni Mirabiles, 1921–1925: Reason in the Madness of Letters, 1956
Eleven Essays in the European Novel, 1964
A Primer of Ignorance, 1967
Henry Adams, 1980
Studies in Henry James, 1983
Selected Essays of R. P. Blackmur, 1986 (Denis Donoghue, editor)

Other major works and literary forms

Although R. P. Blackmur is best known for his literary criticism, he valued his poetry more. Allen Tate called *From Jordan's Delight* (1937) the best poetry collection of the decade. Many readers delight in his use of the language, while others find that the intellectual and analytical content of Blackmur's poetry crowds out its life.

POETRY
From Jordan's Delight, 1937
The Second World, 1942
The Good Europeans and Other Poems, 1947
Poems of R. P. Blackmur, 1977

Further reading

Bryant, J. A., Jr. "R. P. Blackmur: Making Peace with Disorder," in *The Sewanee Review*. XCVII (Winter, 1989), pp. 153–162.
Foster, Richard. "R. P. Blackmur: From Criticism to Mysticism," in *The New Romantics: A Reappraisal of the New Criticism*, 1962.
Frank, Joseph. "R. P. Blackmur: The Later Phase," in *The Widening Gyre: Crisis and Mastery in Modern Literature*, 1963.
Fraser, Russell. *A Mingled Yarn: The Life of R. P. Blackmur*, 1981.
Jones, James T. *Wayward Skeptic: The Theories of R. P. Blackmur*, 1986.
Pannick, Gerald J. *Richard Palmer Blackmur*, 1981.
Wain, John. "R. P. Blackmur," in *Essays on Literature and Ideas*, 1964.
Wellek, René. "R. P. Blackmur Re-examined," in *The Southern Review*. VII (July, 1971), pp. 825–845.

WILLIAM E. PEMBERTON

See also American Literary Theory: Twentieth Century; New Criticism

Harold Bloom

American theorist and critic

Born: New York, New York; July 11, 1930

Biography

Harold Bloom was born in New York City on July 11, 1930, the son of William and Paula Bloom, and grew up in the Bronx in a Jewish environment colored by the intellectual example of Talmudist ancestors. As a pre-teenager he discovered his love of poetry, Hart Crane and William Blake being his earliest favorites. He also discovered his possession of the astonishing memory which permitted him to retain, seemingly without effort, many thousands of lines of the greatest English verse.

As an undergraduate at Cornell University, Bloom studied under M. H. Abrams and became interested in the "pattern of displacement of religious models" which Abrams found in Romantic poetry. After graduating in 1951, Bloom went to Yale University. He received his doctorate in 1955 with a dissertation on Percy Bysshe Shelley that became his first published book. He rose rapidly through the academic ranks to become professor of English in 1965, De Vane Professor of the Humanities in 1974, and Sterling Professor of Humanities in 1983. In 1988 he was appointed Berg Professor of English at New York University (NYU), and he subsequently split his professional time between Yale and NYU. In 1958 he married Jeanne Gould, with whom he had two children.

Bloom's theoretical work was much influenced by the Yale milieu of the 1970s – especially by close intellectual contact with Paul de Man, Geoffrey Hartman, and John Hollander – as well as by the poet John Ashbery and others in his circle of New York literary contacts. He has received many honors for his work, including a 1985 MacArthur Foundation Prize. He is a member of the American Academy of Arts and Letters and the American Philosophical Society.

Influence

Bloom's work has influenced both academic literary studies and broader, more popular trends in cultural commentary. His academic influence, stemming from the theoretical work of the 1970s and early 1980s, lies in four areas. His studies of the "visionary" nature of high Romantic poetry have contributed greatly to subsequent reevaluations of the Romantic poetic tradition and its major figures. His famous theory of the "anxiety of influence" has changed the nature of influence studies; it has been found useful by feminist and cultural critics interested in describing the tension between oppressed and dominant literary voices. His "map of misreading" and numerous discussions of Sigmund Freud have reinforced and enriched the rhetorically oriented Freudian criticism brought into prominence by followers of Jacques Lacan. Finally, his system of tropes and theory of poetry as trope have added weight and direction to analyses of figurative language central to deconstruction and the other poststructuralist perspectives which Bloom himself came to eschew. Although Bloom has not attracted the number of apologists and interpreters that Northrop Frye, Kenneth Burke, Michel Foucault, Jacques Derrida, and certain other theorists have, the breadth and duration of his impact on American literary studies are unsurpassed.

Bloom's extra-academic influence stems from work of the 1990s in two areas: interpretations of the Western religious tradition and its cultural importance, and impassioned defenses of the canon of great works without which, according to Bloom, our civilization and our understanding of ourselves would be unthinkable. Both of these enterprises, along with pointed critiques of postmodern theory and cultural studies, endeared Bloom to conservatives during the "culture wars" of the 1990s, a period of heated political controversy over the incursion into high school and university humanities curricula of ethnic and other marginalized writers, deconstructive forms of analysis, and Marxist-based social criticism. Although Bloom by no means avoided the resulting publicity, his view of culture, indeed of life, remained so idiosyncratically literary as to prove inimical to political agendas of any stripe.

With his monumental 1998 book on Shakespeare, Bloom once again assayed a detailed study of an individual writer, this time using a more accessible and intuitive approach and clearer language than those which characterized his earlier author studies. In insisting on the surpassing importance of literature, in this case its "invention of the human," and in challenging both "French" and ideological approaches, Bloom ensured his continued status as one of the preeminent voices in the increasingly eclectic critical environment emergent at the close of the twentieth century.

Analysis

Bloom's voluminous, complex, and sometimes frustratingly obscure critical enterprise can best be understood in terms of its obsessive drive to define the irreducibly poetic nature of "strong" writing. What Frank Lentricchia calls Bloom's "desperate humanist effort" results from his pugnacious advocacy of poetry as a special form of knowledge; his ideas fly in the face of those modern theories – psychological, materialist, structural, linguistic, or philosophical – that treat literature as a subset of ordinary language or cultural conventions.

The special knowledge, termed "mythopoeia" in Bloom's early works, achieved by his favorite Romantic poets, defines itself against nature, natural perception, and the poet's circumstances. *Shelley's Mythmaking* (1959) distinguishes "Shelley's beliefs as a poet, or poetic beliefs, as opposed to his beliefs of a poet caught up in history and in an age." The unique accomplishment of strong poetry lies in creating "forms 'more real' – that is, perceived with greater imaginative intensity – than a living man himself." Mythopoeia, the distinguishing characteristic of the "visionary company" of poets at the center of the Romantic and modern tradition, signals the key poetic desire to "attain a transfiguration of the matter of common perception." This definition parallels the Transcendentalist version of poetic genius put forth by Ralph Waldo Emerson, one of Bloom's intellectual heroes; its other nineteenth-century source lies in the aestheticism of Walter Pater.

Bloom understands that the mythopoeic, or visionary, drive which characterizes such poets as William Blake, Shelley, Alfred, Lord Tennyson, William Butler Yeats, and Wallace Stevens necessarily leads to abstraction, to "visions of relationship" rather than concrete images. Such a visionary sensibility, in its strongest form, does "tend to make the visible at least a little hard to see." Again and again, Bloom's criticism finds a powerful structural order underlying poetry which has traditionally been viewed as sensual or rhapsodic, and his readings have become essential to subsequent evaluations of major Romantic and modern figures. His delight in redefining the tradition in opposition to those who prefer the more conventional humanism represented by Matthew Arnold, T. S. Eliot, and William Carlos Williams has generated as much controversy as his theories.

Bloom's other key early insight into the visionary nature of Romantic poetry is that its linguistic or vocal nature occasions "the myth's necessary defeat." Because it is, after all, meant to be read or heard rather than seen, "poetry, by being itself, actually opposes itself in its attempt to visualize reality." The desire to transcend nature necessitates a transfiguration of vision into voice, which is never as easy as traditional studies of imagery suggest. Strong poetry always gives evidence, in its underlying structure, of the struggle and conflict which are the basic conditions of its medium.

The visionary struggle at the heart of strong poetry reveals, for Bloom, the poet's "stance – rhetorical, psychological, imagistic – as he writes his poem." Thus, it provides "both a map of the mind and a profound faith that the map can be put to a saving use." The saving use of the mental patterns at the heart of strong poetry is to enable further creativity in a "belated" age – an age when innocent creative response is no longer possible, when understanding of oneself and nature is unavoidably shaped by the formulas of strong precursors. A modern poet cannot pretend that William Shakespeare, John Milton, the Romantics, Walt Whitman, and Ralph Waldo Emerson are irrelevant; instead, their works must be read in such a way that space is cleared for new accomplishment. To do this, a poet must "misread" the precursor, must find a way to believe that the precursor has somehow been wrong or missed a key point. The "visions of relationship" in a strong poem reflect strategies of misreading which permit one to feel creatively superior to the poetic wisdom of the past. Such a feeling or stance is the only antidote to the "anxiety of influence" – to the fear that one can never live up to past achievements, that one has been born too late for greatness.

Poetry, for Bloom, begins always as a reading of past poetry by means of interpretive strategies which enable the reader to imagine a seemingly greater creative vision. Because it too involves "strong" reading, criticism seeks the same wisdom as poetry, and the two activities can be equated. Weak poetry or criticism imitates or builds on the past in the manner advocated by Bloom's intellectual *bêtes noires*, Matthew Arnold and T. S. Eliot; strong poetry or criticism misreads, struggles with, and supplants the past. It is defensive and narcissistic, yet it gives the creative self a future, a voice which escapes the deadly repetition of what has already been said.

In *The Anxiety of Influence* (1973) and other key works of the 1970s and 1980s, Bloom undertook the elaboration and systematization of the ideas emergent in his earlier volumes. His gathering interest in the Gnostic tradition, profoundly influenced by his reading of Gershom Scholem, confirmed his intuition that Romantic poetry exemplifies an age-old textual tradition – a set of strategies or "revisionary ratios" available to early Greek and Hebrew writers but occulted by the Jewish and Christian traditions that eventually carried the day in the Roman world. Indeed, Bloom's criticism can be seen as a crusade on behalf of a submerged humanism, a style of reading which can redress the malaise of a belated age. His studies of Sigmund and Anna Freud led to the assertion in *Poetry and Repression* (1976) of parallels between the "revisionary ratios" of literature and psychoanalytic defense mechanisms: poet reacts against precursor as son against father in classical psychoanalysis. The influence of the theoretical climate at Yale University in the 1970s led Bloom to associate his revisionary ratios with specific rhetorical figures or tropes. The linguistically oriented critical milieu prominent after the New Criticism reinforced Bloom's contention that certain textual figures – irony, metonymy, metaphor, synecdoche, hyperbole, and metalepsis – have a privileged literary value; they are rhetorical counterparts of the misreading strategies by which creativity masters the sources of its inspiration.

The three currents in Bloom's high theoretical phase – the "revisionary ratios" underlying all forms of poetic knowledge, their corresponding Freudian defense mechanisms, and the rhetorical figures which manifest them in writing – came together in *A Map of Misreading* (1975). Here, the six "ratios" are arranged in three pairs, or "crossings." A crossing is a shift from one dominant ratio or trope to another; it may characterize either a movement within a poem or a key juncture in the career of a poet. A crossing always takes place between a "figure of limitation" – irony, metonymy, or metaphor – and a "figure of representation" – synecdoche, hyperbole, or metalepsis. Figures of limitation manifest a poet's clear confrontation with the precursor's power, and figures of representation enable the visualization of some newly discovered or recovered capacity within the creative self. In the "coda" to *Wallace Stevens* (1977) Bloom spells out his theory of poetic crossing; the three crossings permitted by his system arrange hierarchically, and the career of a strong poet must pass through all three if the struggle to supplant the precursor, to locate the origin of creative power within oneself, is to succeed.

Bloom admits at the beginning of his work that "the six revisionary movements that I will trace in the strong poet's life-cycle could as well be more, and could take quite different names than those I have employed," yet his subsequent works modify emphasis within the system rather than changing or abandoning it. In *A Map of Misreading* he allows that "what matters is not the exact order of the ratios, but the principle of substitution, in which representations and limitations perpetually answer one another." In a discussion of Freud in *Agon* (1982), he acknowledges that the precursor against whom one reacts may be one's own earlier self rather than a previous master. *The Breaking of the Vessels* (1982) focuses attention on the particular trope of metalepsis – synonymous with transumption – as a concept that contaminates every gesture of the mind. None of these or later rethinkings undermines the bedrock of the theory of influence and corresponding reading (or misreading) strategies developed by Bloom during the 1970s. His analytical system, the most ambitious and detailed since Northrop Frye's *Anatomy of Criticism* (1957), gains extraordinary depth, range, and solidity from successive elaborations.

Bloom's central theory owes its power both to inspire and to confuse to the same set of qualities. On the one hand, it glorifies the unique creative force of a limited canon of strong poems; on the other hand, it seems to turn all human life into poetry: "a poem must handle experience and emotion as if they already were rival poems." It asserts the absolute generality of figurative language: "Poetic knowledge is necessarily a knowledge by tropes, an experience of emotion as trope, and an expression of knowledge and emotion by a revisionary further troping." Yet it also privileges a specific set of six rhetorical figures culled from the hundreds available. It fathers the universally respected "practical criticism" evident in Bloom's hundreds of published book reviews and prefaces; still, it promulgates a terminology which seems deliberately strange, esoteric, and slippery.

With his 1987–88 Charles Eliot Norton Lectures at Harvard University (subsequently published as *Ruin the Sacred Truths*, 1988) and 1990 publication of *The Book of J* (a commentary on Old Testament translations by David Rosenberg), Bloom moved from his earlier technical and theoretical poetic analysis to freer and more intuitive commentary on the authors whose greatness transcends the dialectic of influence-anxiety, chiefly the Yahwist of the Hebrew Bible, Freud, and Shakespeare. To Bloom, poetry and religious belief "share the peculiarity of taking place *between* truth and meaning." Since meaning derives from "an excess, an overflow or emanation, that we call originality," ultimately poetry and prophecy share a similar force and structure. The two books mentioned above, along with *The American Religion* of 1992 and *Omens of Millennium* of 1996, form an extended meditation on the sublime poetry of religion. Since both strong poetic and religious texts evidence the creativity of spirit which reveals truth and assigns meaning to human life, it is not an error to conflate them. "I myself do not believe," Bloom writes, "that secularization is itself a literary process." Like J the Yahwist, the Shakespeare of Bloom's 1998 *Shakespeare* establishes the key terms on the basis of which we understand ourselves; without the accomplishments of such figures, we would not have access to the complex self-understanding which is our Western cultural legacy.

Argument over both Bloom's theoretical assertions and his individual readings is likely to continue for some time. Yet it is safe to say that no other modern critic matches his capacity for textual interpretation both breathtaking in intellectual grandeur and microscopic in detailed illustration, his intimacy with and fierce love for the key works of the Western tradition, and the staggering volume of his output. He has shaped our understanding of the creative spirit as no other twentieth-century critic has.

Principal criticism

Shelley's Mythmaking, 1959
The Visionary Company: A Reading of English Romantic Poetry, 1961
Blake's Apocalypse: A Study in Poetic Argument, 1963
Yeats, 1970
The Ringers in the Tower: Studies in Romantic Tradition, 1971
The Anxiety of Influence: A Theory of Poetry, 1973
A Map of Misreading, 1975
Kabbalah and Criticism, 1975
Figures of Capable Imagination, 1976
Poetry and Repression: Revisionism from Blake to Stevens, 1976
Wallace Stevens: The Poems of Our Climate, 1977
Agon: Toward a Theory of Revisionism, 1982
The Breaking of the Vessels, 1982
Freud: Transference and Authority, 1988
Ruin the Sacred Truths, 1988
The Book of J, 1990
The American Religion: The Emergence of the Post-Christian Nation, 1992
The Western Canon: The Books and School of the Ages, 1994
Omens of Millennium: The Gnosis of Angels, Dreams, and Resurrection, 1996
Shakespeare: The Invention of the Human, 1998

Other major works and literary forms

In addition to the books listed above, Harold Bloom has written countless critical essays and reviews, many for *The New York Times Book Review*. He has served as general editor for several series of critical anthologies published by Chelsea House, a task which involved writing hundreds of introductions to major works, as well as to books on writers and traditions. He has also written a novel, *The Flight to Lucifer: A Gnostic Fantasy* (1979).

Further reading

Allen, Graham. *Harold Bloom: A Poetics of Conflict*, 1994.
De Bolla, Peter. *Harold Bloom: Towards Historical Rhetorics*, 1988.
de Man, Paul. "Appendix: A Review of Harold Bloom's *Anxiety of Influence*," in *Blindness and Insight*, 1983 (second edition).
Donoghue, Denis. "Harold Bloom," in *Ferocious Alphabets*, 1981.
Fite, David. *Harold Bloom: The Rhetoric of Romantic Vision*, 1985.
Lentricchia, Frank. "Harold Bloom: The Spirit of Revenge," in *After the New Criticism*, 1980.
Moynihan, Robert. *A Recent Imagining: Interviews with Harold Bloom, Geoffrey Hartman, Paul de Man, and J. Hillis Miller*, 1986.
Short, Bryan C. *Cast by Means of Figures*, 1992.

Bryan C. Short

See also Abrams; American Literary Theory: Twentieth Century; Canon; Deconstruction

Giovanni Boccaccio

Italian writer

Born: Florence or Certaldo, Italy; June or July, 1313
Died: Certaldo, Italy; December 21, 1375

Biography

Very little is known about Giovanni Boccaccio's early years. From Petrarch's correspondence, it is known that Boccaccio was nine years his junior, which would make the year of his birth 1313. The place was probably the rustic village of Certaldo, home of his ancestors. Although Boccaccio was born out of wedlock, his father, a prosperous merchant, legitimized the youth at the age of six or seven and made provisions for his education.

In 1327 Boccaccio accompanied his father on business to Naples, where he was exposed to a world both beautiful and dissolute. In this atmosphere, Boccaccio first abandoned his business career and later the study of canon law to devote himself more fully to literary pursuits. He made many new friends and fell in love with the lady known as Fiammetta. It was under her influence that Boccaccio wrote *Il filostrato* (c. 1335; *The Filostrato*, 1873), *Il filocolo* (c. 1336; *Labor of Love*, 1566), and *Teseida* (1340–1341; *The Book of Theseus*, 1974).

Unfortunately, these happy years terminated when Boccaccio's father suffered business reverses, and by 1341 father and son were back in Tuscany. Neither financial duress nor the drab, medieval surroundings of his birthplace, however, could mute the forces which had been unleashed in Naples. It was at this time that Boccaccio penned *Il ninfale d'Ameto* (1341–1342), *L'amorosa visione* (1342–1343; English translation, 1986), and *Elegia di Madonna Fiammetta* (1343–1344; *Amorous Fiammetta*, 1587), all of which attest his unbridled love of life.

At some point between 1348 and 1351, Boccaccio wrote his masterpiece, *Decameron: O, Principe Galeotto* (1349–1351; *The Decameron*, 1620). This study of Renaissance life at the height of the Black Death in Florence would eventually win literary immortality for him. Though sometimes criticized by his contemporaries, Boccaccio was by this time an established literary figure. He was frequently called upon by the government of Florence to serve in various positions of government which brought him intermittent periods of prosperity.

In 1350 Boccaccio met Petrarch for the first time and a lasting bond was established. At Petrarch's insistence, Boccaccio undertook the study of Greek and more fully embraced the cult of Humanism. As he grew older, he turned away from the vernacular works of his youth to more scholarly endeavors. In his later years, though he became corpulent and ill, he remained very active. He was involved in a series of lectures on the life of Dante when he died on December 21, 1375.

Influence

Boccaccio was the third great poet of the fourteenth century after Dante and Petrarch. Yet, more than the others, Boccaccio broke with medieval tradition to become the spokesman for a new age. His prose and poetry, especially *The Decameron*, describe the emotions and passions, often in lurid tones, of a new age. He was severely criticized by his contemporaries, and even Boccaccio in later years may have believed that the unbridled feelings of his youth transcended acceptable bounds; nevertheless, his love of beauty, nature, women, indeed the world itself, would inspire Geoffrey Chaucer, Ludovico Ariosto, William Shakespeare, and others. He is, justifiably, called the founder of Italian prose writing.

After meeting Petrarch, Boccaccio spent less time writing in the vernacular and devoted himself more fully to classical interests. He went in search of old manuscripts and composed scholarly Latin works dealing with the gods, geography, and great men and women. Along with Petrarch, Boccaccio did much to advance the cause of Humanism.

Analysis

The antecedents of Renaissance literature are to be found within the great literary triumvirate of the fourteenth century composed of Dante, Petrarch, and Giovanni Boccaccio. Boccaccio, the junior member of this elite group, was influenced greatly by his fellow triumvirs. As Boccaccio was only a boy when the author of *La divina commedia* (c. 1320; *The Divine Comedy*) died in 1321, Dante's influence was limited to the example of his works. Petrarch, however, whom Boccaccio met in 1350, became his mentor and close friend.

Under Petrarch's guidance, Boccaccio became a disciple of Humanism, that potent force which was ultimately responsible for many of the dazzling artistic and literary accomplishments of the Renaissance. It eschewed the ethereal notions of the Middle Ages and manifested itself in a love of the Greek and Roman classics. Boccaccio was an amalgam of these elements. A product of the fourteenth century, Boccaccio preached, for much of his life, a doctrine which invited Renaissance man to enjoy the epicurean delights of this world.

Although he became enamored of Dante and Petrarch at an early age, his sojourn in Naples had a more immediate impact on his incipient literary career. In contrast to the medieval surroundings of his homeland, here he was exposed to a beautiful city, an intoxicating atmosphere, and the lady known as Fiammetta. She was to Boccaccio what Laura was to Petrarch and Beatrice to Dante. As mentioned above, he quickly lost interest in business and law and gave his life to the Muses. During the next twenty years, first in Naples and later in Tuscany, Boccaccio would compose many works dominated by a plebeian sensuality.

Many, if not most, of Boccaccio's works were composed as a result of bittersweet life experiences. They tend, therefore, to be somewhat autobiographical. The earliest works were written under the direct influence of Fiammetta and the atmosphere of the Neapolitan court. Unfortunately, these pieces betray his youth, inexperience, and devotion to earlier themes. *Labor of Love*, dedicated to Fiammetta, was derived from a simple medieval love story and transformed into something more complex with strong classical and allegorical content. With all of its deficiencies, *Labor of Love* has the distinction of being the first prose romance composed in Italian, and it would serve as a reservoir of information which many other literary figures would tap. Several of Chaucer's works, including "The Franklin's Tale" and the prologue to *The Canterbury Tales* (1387–1400), *Troilus and Criseyde* (1382), and *The Legend of Good Women* (1380–1386), were derived wholly or in part from *Labor of Love*. John Milton and John Keats were others to make use of the work. *The Book of Theseus* was the first heroic Italian epic. Reminiscent of Virgil's *Aeneid* (c. 29–19 B.C.), it might be that Boccaccio hoped to establish himself as an epic poet in this tradition. Although epic poetry was not his forte, the tale spawned a genre which became quite popular in the Renaissance. Chaucer's "The Knight's Tale" was done in imitation, while other elements of the story can be seen in Shakespeare's *A Midsummer Night's Dream* (c. 1595–1596). The most successful of Boccaccio's early works, however, was *The Filostrato*. Once again he uses classical trappings, in this case events adapted from the Trojan War; it is quite possible, however, that he is describing the contemporary court life in Naples with which he had become so familiar. Here, perhaps for the first time, the reader senses the element of future greatness in Boccaccio, the ability to tell a good story. In addition to those mentioned above, Ludovico Ariosto, John Dryden, Edmund Spenser, Lord Byron, and others were influenced by these early stories.

After his return to Florence in the 1340s, Boccaccio produced *Il ninfale d'Ameto, L'amorosa visione*, and *Amorous Fiammetta*. The first two works are significant only in that they reveal a struggling artist, one who has not yet found his style. At times he is prolix and pedantic, while the stories lack originality. As usual, however, the common denominator is love. In *Amorous Fiammetta*, however, Boccaccio was immensely successful. In all likelihood the tale was based upon a true story, possibly an incident from Boccaccio's relationship with Fiammetta. It concerns Fiammetta's complaint that she has been abandoned by her lover. Boccaccio was much more comfortable with this venue, which would provide later Renaissance writers with a wealth of romantic stories. Some years later, this theme, from which Boccaccio must have derived great pleasure, was sardonically inverted in *Corbaccio* (c. 1355; *The Corbaccio*, 1975). Like so many of his other works, this prose story was derived from a real-life experience in which Boccaccio was the spurned lover. In great pain, Boccaccio censoriously satirized the female sex.

These works, especially those which reflect Boccaccio's struggles in the arena of life, prepared the way for *The Decameron*, his magnum opus. For perhaps the first time, Boccaccio was able to write from a vantage point of something other than personal experience. Inspired by earlier works such as the fourteenth-century *Gesta Romanorum* (English translation, c. 1440), the fabliaux, and the *bestiarii, The Decameron* is a compendium of one hundred stories related by a group of young men and women who fled Florence in 1348 to a country villa to escape the ravages of the Black Death. The subject is still love, but his purpose is vastly different. In a sense, *The Decameron* was the antithesis of Dante's *The Divine Comedy*, and it had little in common with Petrarch's erudite world. It was at once a protest against the asceticism of the Middle Ages and an affirmation of the sensual pleasures of a new age. All the sacred relics are held up to ridicule – knighthood, marriage, even Christ himself. According to John Addington Symonds, it was "everything which the Church had banned, proscribed, held in abhorrence." Whereas medieval people saw this world as a vale of tears, something to be endured, Boccaccio's characters were determined to savor the temporal delights of this life. The influence of *The Decameron* on others – Chaucer, Shakespeare, Ben Jonson, Molière, to mention a few – is inestimable.

Not long after he wrote *The Decameron*, Boccaccio experienced a kind of metamorphosis, as a result of which he turned his attention to more scholarly pursuits. One of the chief reasons for the change was the Humanist influence of Petrarch. To facilitate his study of the classics, Petrarch encouraged Boccaccio to learn the Greek language, which he subsequently made a part of the curriculum at the University of Florence. Boccaccio then set about the task of translating the Homeric epics into Latin, and although he never advanced beyond a superficial understanding of the language, in the opinion of some, he became the first Greek scholar in Europe. In his quest to preserve classical learning, he also located and copied valuable manuscripts. While he greatly revered the poets of the ancient world, he did not overlook contemporary influences. Petrarch would remain a mentor and friend until he died in 1374, while Boccaccio's admiration for Dante led him to compose a biography and the commentaries which he initiated just before his death in 1375.

Most of his time in his later years was spent composing erudite Latin works which were strongly didactic and allegorical in content. Instead of contemporary love stories, his interest was now myths, legends, geography, and history. Illustrative of this period is the *De casibus virorum illustrium* (1355–1374; *The Fall of Princes*, 1431–1438) and the *De mulieribus claris* (c. 1361–1375; *Concerning Famous Women*, 1943). His most important work in this genre was probably the *Genealogia deorum gentilium* (c. 1350–1375; genealogies of the gods), in which he offered one of the first defenses of poetry. It was the purpose of the Humanists, he argued, to rescue literature from its medieval abyss and to offer it to the public in the guise of allegory and fiction. After all, Boccaccio reasoned, Christ himself used parables to reveal the truth.

Boccaccio was a very important part of Italian Renaissance literature even though the century to which he belonged was in most ways very medieval. It was the time of the Avignonese papacy, the Black Death, and learned Latin literature. Yet he espoused a doctrine which was clearly not medieval; rather, it was characterized by a plebeian sensuality unknown since the ancient world. He became the spokesperson for a new age. These feelings, often derived from bittersweet personal experiences, were expressed through a number of new literary forms. As the founder of Italian prose, Boccaccio had a tremendous impact on writers of a later age. Chaucer frequently used his themes without acknowledgment, while Ariosto, Shakespeare, and many others drew freely from his forms and stories. Nor was Boccaccio's influence limited to the vernacular. In his later years, he became more concerned with the resurrection, preservation, and composition of erudite Greek and Latin classical works. He is remembered in history, along with Petrarch, as one of the first great Humanists.

Principal criticism

Passages in *Il filostrato*, c. 1335 (*The Filostrato*, 1873), *Il filocolo*, c. 1336 (*Labor of Love*, 1566), *Teseida*, 1340–1341 (*The Book of Theseus*, 1974), *Elegia di Madonna Fiammetta*, 1343–1344 (*Amorous Fiammetta*, 1587), *Decameron: O, Principe Galeotto*, 1349–1351 (*The Decameron*, 1620), and *Genealogia deorum gentilium* (genealogies of the gods), c. 1350–1375

Trattatello in laude di Dante, 1351, 1360, 1373 (*Life of Dante*, 1898)

Esposizioni sopra la Commedia di Dante, 1373–1374

Other major works and literary forms

Most of the works listed above are not, strictly speaking, works of criticism or theory, but they proclaim – both explicitly and implicitly – Giovanni Boccaccio's beliefs concerning the nature and purpose of literature. In addition to the above works, Boccaccio wrote a variety of other works of prose and poetry. His study of the Greek language led him to translate the Homeric epics.

POETRY

Rime, c. 1330–1340
La caccia di Diana, c. 1334
Il filocolo, c. 1336
Il ninfale d'Ameto, 1341–1342 (also known as *Commedia delle ninfe*)
L'amorosa visione, 1342–1343 (English translation, 1986)
Elegia di Madonna Fiammetta, 1343–1344 (English translation, 1990)
Il ninfale fiesolano, 1344–1346 (*The Nymph of Fiesole*, 1597)
Decameron, 1348–1351 (English translation, 1978)
Buccolicum carmen, c. 1351–1366 (*Boccaccio's Olympia*, 1913)

NONFICTION

Corbaccio, c. 1355 (*The Corbaccio*, 1975)
De casibus virorum illustrium, 1355–1374 (*The Fall of Princes*, 1431–1438)
De montibus, silvis, fontibus lacubus, fluminubus, stagnis seu paludibus, et de nominbus maris, c. 1355–1374
De mulieribus claris, c. 1361–1375 (*Concerning Famous Women*, 1943)

Further reading

Bergin, Thomas G. *Boccaccio*, 1981.
Burckhardt, Jacob. *The Civilization of the Renaissance in Italy*, 1958.
Consoli, Joseph P. *Giovanni Boccaccio: An Annotated Bibliography*, 1992.
Forni, Pier Massimo. *Adventures in Speech: Rhetoric and Narration in Boccaccio's Decameron*, 1996.
Hollander, Robert. *Boccaccio's Dante and the Shaping Force of Satire*, 1997.
Krutch, Joseph Wood. "Giovanni Boccaccio," in *Five Masters*, 1959.
MacGregor, James H. *The Shades of Aeneas: The Imitation of Vergil and the History of Paganism in Boccaccio's Filostrato, Filocolo and Teseida*, 1991.
MacManus, Francis. *Boccaccio*, 1947.
Symonds, John Addington. *Renaissance in Italy*, 1935.
——. *Italian Literature*, 1964.
Wallace, David. *Chaucer and the Early Writings of Boccaccio*, 1985.

LARRY W. USILTON

See also Dante; Petrarch; Renaissance and Restoration Literary Theory

Johann Jakob Bodmer

Swiss critic, historian, and translator

Born: Greifensee, Switzerland; July 19, 1698
Died: Schönenberg, Switzerland; January 2, 1783

Biography

Johann Jakob Bodmer was born on July 19, 1698, the son of a Protestant minister in Greifensee, near Zurich, Switzerland. He first studied theology but soon turned to literature. To earn his living, he worked as a merchant's apprentice and traveled to France and Italy. When he returned to Switzerland, he became friends with Johann Jakob Breitinger, with whom he collaborated on most of his future ventures. In 1721 they edited a so-called *Moralische Wochenschriften* (moral weekly), *Die Discourse der Mahlern*, which was modeled after Joseph Addison's *The Spectator* and was published until 1723. A second, enlarged edition was published under the title *Der Mahler der Sitten* in 1746. In 1720 Bodmer became a city official (*Staatsschreiber*) in Zurich, and in 1737 he entered politics, serving as a city councillor. He finally found permanent employment as a teacher of Swiss history and politics at a Zurich grammar school. In 1775 he retired from his teaching position. Bodmer died in Schönenberg, near Zurich, on January 2, 1783.

Influence

Bodmer exerted his major influence during the mid-eighteenth century, when the Enlightenment was giving way to Romanticism. Because of Bodmer's pivotal position, his critical theories perhaps enjoy more fame than they deserve. Bodmer led the countermovement against early Enlightenment poetics and its normative rules which excluded the "supernatural" from literature. According to Enlightenment poetics, poetry was to imitate nature, and since the supernatural – angels and devils, for example – could not be observed in nature, it should not be included in poetry. Bodmer, however, thought that there was a place for the supernatural in poetry.

In his studies on the nature of poetic production, Bodmer emphasized the pleasures of imagination. Opposed to Enlightenment poetics, which contended that poetry should be a product of reason determined by the rules prescribed by the ancients, Bodmer argued in favor of feeling, enthusiasm, and imagination. He stressed the autonomy of the imagination and believed that imagination was at the center of the creative process. In this respect, he is a forerunner of Romantic aesthetics. Yet, while Bodmer considered creativity more important for poetry than imitation of nature, his didacticism in the service of Christian religion placed him squarely in the Enlightenment movement. As René Wellek has written, Bodmer's "stodgy middle-class morality constantly warps his imaginative insights." Yet, "in the context of German criticism he was a great precursor, an initiator."

Analysis

Die Discourse der Mahlern was one of the first important moral weeklies in the German-speaking countries. Through that periodical, Bodmer and Breitinger represented the Swiss opposition to Johann Christoph Gottsched, who resided in Leipzig, Germany. Friedrich Gottlieb Klopstock and Gotthold Ephraim Lessing took their cues for their opposition to Gottsched from Bodmer and Breitinger but ultimately went far beyond the Swiss critics. The Swiss opposition to Enlightenment poetics was strongly influenced by John Milton and William Shakespeare, who was hardly known in the German-speaking countries at that time. (Bodmer knew him only by a corrupted version of his name, "Saspar.") Shakespeare, nevertheless, served as a popular model against French classicism.

In his confrontation with Gottsched, Bodmer defended the role of the supernatural in literature. After he had translated Milton's *Paradise Lost* into German prose, Bodmer became a defender of the English poet against his French and German critics. Bodmer challenged the classical model established by Gottsched, who advocated imitating the style of French classicism. Bodmer's treatise *Von dem Einfluss und Gebrauche der Einbildungs-Krafft* (on the influence and usage of imagination) is, according to the scholar Steven D. Martinson, "the first in-depth study of the creative imagination in the history of German poetics and aesthetics."

For Bodmer, the primary function of the poet was to move the reader, a goal best achieved by a vivid imagination. In addition, Bodmer emphasized the importance of personal experience and observation. Finally, he stressed the need for poetic enthusiasm. In his treatise *Anklagung des verderbten Geschmackes* (indictment of corrupted taste), which consisted of a critical attack on two of the major moral weeklies in Hamburg and Halle, Bodmer continued to expound on the importance of imagination for poetry. In discussing poetic dreams and visions, he outlined the rules of imagination. Although he allowed the poetic imagination great freedom, Bodmer insisted that it have its own laws. His criteria for good poetry were that it should be "vivid," "moving," and "natural."

In his *Brief-Wechsel von der Natur des poetischen Geschmackes* (letters on the nature of poetic taste) of 1736, which is based on a real correspondence with the Italian critic Pietro dei Conti di Calepio, Bodmer offered his first defense of *Paradise Lost* and argued for the inclusion of the sublime in tragedy. In his *Critische Abhandlung von dem Wunderbaren in der Poesie und dessen Verbindung mit dem Wahrscheinlichen* (critical treatise on the supernatural in poetry and its connection to the possible), Bodmer defended the representation of the supernatural in Milton's epic poem. Granting poetry its own probability, which was not identical to that of the empirical world, Bodmer paved the way for the development of German poetry in the second half of the eighteenth century. As far as the relationship of the supernatural to probability was concerned, Bodmer was even more tolerant than Addison, whose defense of Milton is included in this treatise as an appendix. In his *Critische Briefe* (critical letters), Bodmer offered a more comprehensive account of the sublime. Following Addison's thoughts on greatness in art, Bodmer argued for the inclusion of the sublime in the work of art for the sake of its emotional impact upon the recipient; according to Bodmer, the sublime enables the reader to transcend the ordinary boundaries of the mind.

In his theory and criticism, Bodmer represented an important link between early Enlightenment poetics and Romantic aesthetics. By 1750, however, Bodmer's influence on the development of German criticism had ceased. He found no audience for his immense literary productivity after 1750. His literary output rivaled that of Johann Wolfgang von Goethe, but as a dramatist and epic poet he was imitative and exerted little influence.

Principal criticism

Die Discourse der Mahlern, 1721–1723 (expanded as *Der Mahler der Sitten*, 1746)
Von dem Einfluss und Gebrauche der Einbildungs-Krafft, 1727
Anklagung des verderbten Geschmackes, 1728
Brief-Wechsel von der Natur des poetischen Geschmackes, 1736
Critische Abhandlung von dem Wunderbaren in der Poesie und dessen Verbindung mit dem Wahrscheinlichen, 1740
Critische Betrachtungen über die poetischen Gemählde der Dichter, 1741
Critische Briefe, 1746
Neue Critische Briefe, 1749

Other major works and literary forms

As a historian, Johann Jakob Bodmer edited, together with Johann Jakob Breitinger, the *Helvetische Bibliothek* (1735–1741; Helvetian library) and wrote a number of historical monographs. Also with Breitinger, he edited texts from Middle High German literature, including *Proben der alten schwäbischen Poesie* (1748; on the minnesingers) and *Heldengedichte aus dem schwäbischen Zeitpuncte* (1757; heroic poetry of the Swabian period), the second part of *The Nibelungenlied*. In 1732 his translation of John Milton's *Paradise Lost* (1667, 1674) into German prose was published, followed by another version in verse in 1742 and a further revision in 1754. In 1778 Bodmer translated Homer's *Iliad* and *Odyssey* into German hexameters. He authored many biblical dramas and epics, classical dramas, and a historical epic (*Conradin von Schwaben*, 1771), but they were purely imitative.

PLAYS

Electra: Oder, Die gerechte Übelthat, 1760
Ulysses, Telemachs Sohn, 1760
Julius Cäser: Ein Trauerspiel, 1763
Der Tod des ersten Menschen, 1776

POETRY
Noah, 1750
Jacob und Joseph, 1751
Die Syndflut, 1751
Jacob und Rachel, 1752
Conradin von Schwabin, 1771

TRANSLATIONS
John Miltons Verlust des Paradieses, 1732, 1742, 1754 (of John Milton's *Paradise Lost*)
Iliad, 1778 (of Homer's epic poem)
Odyssey, 1778 (of Homer's epic poem)

EDITED TEXTS
Helvetische Bibliothek, 1735–1741 (with Johann Jakob Breitinger)
Proben der alten schwäbischen Poesie, 1748 (with Breitinger)
Heldengedichte aus dem schwäbischen Zeitpuncte, 1757 (with Breitinger)

Further reading

Bender, Wolfgang. *J. J. Bodmer und J. J. Breitinger*, 1973.
Bragg, Marvin. *Bodmer's and Breitinger's Main Sources, Leibniz and Addison*, 1978.
Martinson, Steven D. *On Imitation, Imagination, and Beauty: A Critical Reassessment of the Concept of the Literary Artist During the Early German "Aufklärung,"* 1977.
Robertson, John George. *Studies in the Genesis of Romantic Theory in the Eighteenth Century*, 1923.
Scenna, Anthony. *The Treatment of Ancient Legend and History in Bodmer*, 1966.
Schöffler, Herbert. *Das literarische Zürich*, 1925.
Wehrli, Max. *Johann Jakob Bodmer und die Geschichte der Literatur*, 1936.
Wellek, René. *A History of Modern Criticism: 1750–1950*. Vol. 1, *The Later Eighteenth Century*, 1955.

EHRHARD BAHR

See also Gottsched; Romanticism

Nicolas Boileau-Despréaux

French critic and poet

Born: Paris, France; November 1, 1636
Died: Paris, France; March 13, 1711

Biography

Nicolas Boileau-Despréaux was born on November 1, 1636, to an upper-middle-class family of lawyers in the very heart of Paris. He remained throughout his days the prototypical Parisian bourgeois: he was something of a cynic, a satirist, and an apostle of reason and common sense, proud of the intellectual and social rewards provided by his beloved city. He led an uneventful life, although never enjoying robust health, and was increasingly plagued by deafness, poor eyesight, chronic asthma, dropsy, and weakness.

Early in life, he opted for a church career but soon veered toward the family profession, the law. Nevertheless, though admitted to the bar in 1656, he quickly tired of his new choice. Upon his father's death in 1659, his inheritance provided a confirmed bachelor's modest needs. That same year, he discovered his true profession: man of letters. For the next fifty-two years, there flowed from his pen a stream of satirical poems, epistles, and literary criticism.

He was elected into the prestigious French Academy in 1684. His views at times proved controversial, partly for reasons religious (he favored the austere Jansenists over the more popular Jesuits), but mainly literary, notably in the "Quarrel of the Ancients and Moderns." Friends with the truly great writers of his day such as Jean Racine and Molière, he even became, with Racine, royal historiographer to Louis XIV in 1677, with an accompanying governmental pension. He rarely forsook Paris and died hardly a stone's throw from the house of his birth on March 13, 1711.

Influence

It is somewhat debatable whether Boileau influenced French, English, and European writers most as a spokesperson for the best of classical writers or through the example of his own excellence. Without doubt the finest seventeenth-century French writers – notably Racine, Molière, and Jean de La Fontaine – wrote as Boileau proposed and eschewed practices he derided. He was widely quoted, especially during the first two-thirds of the eighteenth century. During his lifetime, his works could boast of more than one hundred editions, some sixty of them professing to be complete. England's so-called Augustan Age writers sang his praises, and the rest of Europe, generally under the spell of France's literary splendor, also acknowledged his importance. Yet he was not necessarily obeyed: he lost the "Quarrel of the Ancients and Moderns." The eighteenth century was primarily modern, and many even in his own day gloried more in the luster of King Louis XIV's court writers than in the ancient Greeks or Romans. Indeed, Boileau was as often as not honored in the breach. As the eighteenth century continued the pre-Romantics increased their audience, and by the nineteenth century Romanticism and realism broke his hold on literary theory. Today he is recalled mainly as the advocate of the best of the French classic tradition, uncannily accurate in his assessment as to which of his contemporaries would withstand time's acid test. *The Art of Poetry* still speaks to questions of beauty, taste, and standards, but modern literature is scarcely inclined to heed lawgivers.

Analysis

Boileau established his literary precepts primarily in the eleven hundred or so lines and four cantos of *The Art of Poetry*, though they must be fleshed out by *Épître IX* and *Réflexions sur Longin*, along with observations gathered from the body of his work.

In one word, Boileau was an "Ancient"; that is, he believed that the best of the ancient Greek and Roman writers set standards for enduring literature which modern writers should emulate, though not necessarily expect to better. There are rules; one uses common sense and obeys the constrictions of the *bienséances* (proprieties). In addition, there are the techniques and tricks of the trade played by knowledgeable professionals.

He counsels the writer to follow reason, a path leading to truth; in so doing, one achieves beauty. Similar advice on rules and, especially, exhortations concerning common sense, can already be found in Horace's *Ars poetica* (c. 17 B.C.; *The Art of Poetry*). Indeed, whole lines of Boileau's treatise are translations from his predecessor, but much is new, or at least derived from other sources. Aristotle's *De poetica* (c. 334–323 B.C.; *Poetics*), not to mention dozens of other critical works of Boileau's day and before, such as Julius Caesar Scaliger's, inevitably left their mark on his work. Classicists of Boileau's stamp did not pride themselves on originality but rather on the fresh (ideally the better) way they found to express eternal verities enunciated by their forerunners. Horace, as has been noted, had already called upon common sense. From Aristotle virtually all the classic critics derived the credo of imitating nature.

Yet, Boileau was not a sterile theorist. He instructed himself directly from literature as well as from theory. His ability to see what constituted the greatness of the great writers of his day, to skewer the current crop of upstarts, remains one of the marvels of his career. Almost without exception, he foretold which poets, which writers of prose would retain their reputations. His taste was unsurpassed.

Was he a hidebound lawgiver as some have accused? Good classicist that he was, he wanted a theory of literature true for all ages and times. To him this necessarily demanded certain procedures, rules, suggestions, and taboos. Rules, however, were only a means for achieving a desired goal, not ropes to tie down so much as reins to guide. Basically, he calls for what is true: "Nothing is beautiful except the true." Truth can be attained only by imitating nature, thus assuring universality of appeal.

What is this "nature"? Not the outer nature of woods, streams, and wilderness so dear to the Romantics. Boileau's nature is human nature, though he did not accept everything human. Eschew the bizarre and accidental, he warns, the ephemeral and particular. Aim for the general and timeless. Yet even within this restricted realm he is selective. He writes for the cultured, metropolitan upper classes. "Study the court and understand the city," he counsels in *The Art of Poetry*. Finally, perhaps most fundamental of all, his nature is inner and psychological, not physical.

Critics may object that such an outlook is hardly realistic. One can scarcely call for truth when seeking it only in the beautiful. Actually, Boileau's "beautiful" is made of sterner stuff. It allows for the horrible and ugly, if they are not exaggerated. For example, Boileau permits the depiction of the blinded Oedipus onstage, when suitably done; Sophocles' play is not to be denied. "There is no serpent nor odious monster which will not delight, if imitated artfully," he writes, and goes on to echo Aristotle on how tragedy works through pity and terror. What he advocates may not be nineteenth-century gutter naturalism, but nature is not prettified. His art is selective, and though it does embellish, it does not falsify.

Boileau's next point is the elimination of the outer person, the inferior sensualist, in favor of the inner one who reasons. "Follow reason," he constantly advises; cultivate the most lasting, unchanging, and universal of human aspects. Reason, truth, and beauty are but one. Reason makes for beauty, but beauty is truth. What exactly is reason? Not that quality in the old, as one critic has put it, that stifles enthusiasm in the young, nor yet bourgeois utilitarianism, nor even the cold, analytical, logical reasoning of so many eighteenth-century Enlightenment philosophers. It is perhaps best expressed as that faculty which distinguishes the true from the false, the power that must rule and direct the soul.

Where will poets find reason and how can they best follow nature? According to Boileau, by imitating the ancients. Appreciated and read many centuries after their passing, they must somehow have extracted the unchanging and universal from human nature. If not all Greek and Roman writers accomplished this feat, at least the finest among them did. Unfortunately, many readers in Boileau's day had begun to be critical of the old literatures. Tastes change over time, and ancient, classical preferences were not necessarily those of seventeenth-century France. On this more modern point of view, the Ancients tended to remain silent. In any event, Boileau is not demanding servile imitations, which are hardly more than translations.

Yet even Boileau could on occasion err. For example, he condemns Christian subject matter in epics, because the ancients used mythological matter; moderns cannot do better than follow in the footsteps of such superb poets as Homer and Virgil. It does not seem to have struck him that the ancients used myths precisely because they appeared true in their eyes, much as Christianity would later. In Boileau's defense, however, it is worth mentioning that the Christian epics to which he had access were second-rate at best: he did not know John Milton's *Paradise Lost* (1667, 1674) and possibly not Dante's *La divina commedia* (c. 1320; *The Divine Comedy*). Although he allows for Christian subjects in plays such as Racine's *Athalie* (1691; *Athaliah*, 1722) and *Esther* (1689; English translation, 1715), Boileau's objections are compounded by his belief that true religion is too serious a subject for epics, in which God and angels are made to converse like human beings.

Does Boileau leave a place for originality? His doctrine might seem to laud imitation to the detriment of anything fresh or new. Indeed, his school derided originality if by that term was meant something never said before. Boileau wanted things that were not so much new or different as more perfectly expressed. Thus he talks endlessly about weighing a word or a rhyme, perfecting a figure of speech. He echoes Horace's precepts about making haste slowly, polishing and repolishing, and filing away the excess. Work and rework, compose and revise: "If I write four words I erase three." Possible subjects having long since become exhausted, invention and originality are reduced to the perfecting of style. Nevertheless, he cautions against plagiarism and especially the pastiche, that lowest type of formal imitation.

There are a few other important aspects of his doctrine. He demands that the writer strive for verisimilitude. Truth is fine, but it must sound plausible. Siamese twins, he might argue, are a proven fact, but they are unsuitable in a work of literature, for "the true can sometimes seem improbable." Historicity does not assure success. This Frenchman was a moralist. Like Horace, he conceived of literature as a noble art which should instruct as it pleases. He rejected the credo of the nineteenth-century realists, who demanded "art for art's sake." Literature must guard against the corruption of its public.

Among Boileau's numerous rules are the famous three unities of time, place, and action. The elapsed time depicted in a play must not exceed one day, the action must unfold in one place, and that action must be simple, free from plot ramifications. One must clearly observe the *bienséances*. No such bastard forms as tragicomedy are permissible; the writer should adhere to the separation of genres. Indeed, there are special rules and proprieties befitting each of the literary forms: tragedy, comedy, the novel (to him an inferior genre), epics, satires, odes, bucolic poetry, and the like. There is a place for the "marvelous" (miraculous events) but not, as has been noted, for Christian "mythology." Love makes for suitable dramatic motivation, so long as it is kept within the bounds of reason. Enjambment, the running over of one line of poetry into the next, each line failing to be an entity unto itself, is strictly forbidden. This quaint rule would remain an article of faith to French poets for some one hundred and fifty years. When Victor Hugo chose to break it in the first two lines of his drama *Hernani* (1830; English translation, 1830), it caused a riot. According to Boileau, great art not only benefits from rules, it transcends them as well.

Does Boileau conceive of poets as mere perfectionists creating masterpieces despite the constraints of regulations, or is there a place in literature for genius? Perhaps unexpectedly, yes. Boileau could appreciate inspiration, artistic sensibility, and imagination in others, even though they were not his own best suit. His commentaries discussing Longinus' first-century work *On the Sublime* and his fine translation of the treatise itself in 1674, the same year as the publication of *The Art of Poetry*, reveal a side of Boileau quite unusual in a seventeenth-century man of reason. He saw that the poetic sublime arose out of the perfect matching of word with emotion, that it represented the supreme degree to which beauty can aspire. Neither Longinus nor Boileau excludes emotion. Boileau also speaks of what he calls the "*je ne sais quoi*" (literally, the "I know not what"), by which he means that undefinable something about the beautiful that defies rational explanation.

Principal criticism

Discours sur la satire, 1668
Dissertation sur Jaconde, 1669
L'Art poétique, 1674 (*The Art of Poetry*, 1683)
Traité du sublime, 1674 (translation of Longinus' *On the Sublime*)
Épître IX, 1683 (written c. 1675)
Dialogue des héros de roman, 1688 (*The Heroes of Romance*, 1713)
Réflexions sur Longin, 1694
Preface to *Œuvres diverses*, 1701
Selected Criticism, 1965 (Ernest Dilworth, editor and translator)

Other major works and literary forms

Although Nicolas Boileau-Despréaux is remembered principally as the austere "lawgiver of Parnassus," in his own time he was almost equally famed as a polished, witty, occasionally even ruthless satirist and moralist. Possessed of a fine speaking voice and great ability as a mimic, he delighted salon audiences with readings from *Les Satires* (1666–1711; *Satires*, 1711–1713), *Les Épîtres* (1669–1698; English translation, 1711–1713), and, among others, *Le Lutrin* (1674, 1683; partial English translation, 1682), a mock epic on the foibles of the Catholic church, the title translating as a "reading desk" or "lectern." His satirical, religious, and social compositions occupied his attention off and on from 1657 almost until his death more than fifty years later. The *Satires* – indeed the satiric vein was quite typical of his view of the world – some in imitation of a Juvenal or Horace, some more original, poke spirited fun at contemporary Paris society but can become more purely religious, as in number 12. Sometimes he makes use of these other forms in matters of literary criticism as well. On occasion, his high seriousness of purpose turns overly pompous, as with his *Ode du sieur D*** sur la prise de Namur* (1693), meant to flatter Louis XIV on the event of France's military victory the year before.

POETRY

Les Satires, 1666–1711 (12 volumes; *Satires*, 1711–1713)
Les Épîtres, 1669–1698 (12 volumes; English translation, 1711–1713)
Le Lutrin, 1674, 1683 (partial English translation, 1682)
*Ode du sieur D*** sur la prise de Namur*, 1693

MISCELLANEOUS

The Works of Monsieur Boileau, Made English by Several Hands, 1711–1713 (3 volumes)

Further reading

Brady, Jules. *Boileau and Longinus*, 1958.
Clark, Alexander F. B. *Boileau and the French Classical Critics in England, 1660–1830*, 1925.

France, Peter. *Rhetoric and Truth in France: Descartes to Diderot*, 1972.
Pocock, Gordon. *Boileau and the Nature of Neo-classicism*, 1980.
White, Julian E., Jr. *Nicolas Boileau*, 1969.

ARMAND E. SINGER

See also Corneille; La Fontaine; Malherbe; Neoclassical Literary Theory; Racine

Wayne C. Booth

American critic and teacher

Born: American Fork, Utah; February 22, 1921

Biography

Wayne Clayson Booth was born in the small prairie town of American Fork, Utah, on February 22, 1921, to a staunchly Mormon family. Like most Mormon children, he was brought up to believe that "the glory of God is intelligence," and he pursued excellence in all of his scholastic endeavors. Later in his youth, Booth emerged from a period of atheism to embrace a God of reason, one who is, in his words, "the totality of Reason in Action in the world, the Power and the Law." Animated by this revitalized faith and renewed trust in the power of the human mind, Booth embarked upon the typical missionary role of young Mormon males, spending two years taking the Mormon faith door to door.

Booth received his B.A. from the intellectual center of the Mormon faith, Brigham Young University. After serving in the military from 1944 to 1946, he married Phyllis Barnes, with whom he had two children. He then entered the University of Chicago to complete his graduate education, earning an M.A. in 1947 and a Ph.D. in 1950. Booth began his teaching career at Haverford College in Pennsylvania in 1950 but moved to Earlham College in Richmond, Indiana, in 1953 and served there as professor of English and chair of the department. He remained at Earlham College until 1962, when he became George M. Pullman Professor of English at his alma mater, the University of Chicago. From 1964 to 1969 he served as dean of the college and from 1972 to 1975 was chairman of the Committee on Ideas and Methods. In 1974 he became a founding coeditor of *Critical Inquiry*, published at the University of Chicago. Booth has earned numerous awards and fellowships during his career, including Guggenheim Fellowships in 1956 and 1969.

Influence

Booth's early work, as exemplified by *The Rhetoric of Fiction* (1961), focused on updating and refining rhetorical theory and thereby almost single-handedly revived the rhetorical study of fiction. Since its publication, Booth has continued to be a stabilizing influence in contemporary criticism by mediating between extremes in warring critical camps and establishing moderating boundaries for a responsible pluralism. Refusing to align himself with any one camp, Booth attempts to articulate a holistic balance in the critical response to literary texts and has increasingly focused his attention upon issues of ethical criticism, specifically how the personal or corporate values within a culture can influence the understanding and interpretation of texts.

Analysis

Booth came to the attention of the world of literary scholarship with the publication of his landmark work, *The Rhetoric of Fiction*. This volume focused on the problematic relationships between authors and their chosen narrators in selected works. It consists of intense, painstaking readings of a variety of authors and works, including Henry James, Joseph Conrad, and Flannery O'Connor, and an analysis of the sometimes oblique and ironic relationship between what a given narrator says or does and how a narrative is to be received by the reader. It won for Booth the David H. Russell Award for Distinguished Research of the National Council of Teachers of English, establishing him at the forefront of a movement to restore rhetorical components to literary scholarship. In many ways, *The Rhetoric of Fiction* exemplifies the whole of Booth's career: his challenging of current orthodoxies while at the same time calling for the restoration of certain neglected literary values and modes of inquiry.

In the departments of literature and criticism to which Booth came in the early 1950s, dominated as they were by the New Criticism, the disciplines of rhetoric and literary criticism were seen as discrete arts and, as a result, the pursuits of rhetoricians and critics were thought to be, if not mutually exclusive, at least radically distinct. While some overlap was usually conceded, for the most part it was an unwritten assumption that literary scholars concerned themselves with different (perhaps "more important") matters than rhetoricians – specifically, the text itself and its "organic unity." It was this dichotomy between disciplines that *The Rhetoric of Fiction* tacitly attacked, and its success signaled the beginning of rhetoric's rehabilitation among literary scholars.

Booth argued that "rhetoric" as literary inquiry examined the means by which writers made known their vision to their readers and persuaded them of its validity. The concerns of the rhetorician – author, text, and audience – were not to be considered isolated or peculiar to oral discourse; the student of letters should also be committed to fleshing out the nature and impact of these relationships in the interpretation of both fiction and poetry. The effect of Booth's work was to make explicit the rhetorical nature of literary study, which formerly had been only implicit or even denied. In large measure, his work revitalized interest in the roles which reader response and authorial intention play in the process of interpreting literature. After this salvo by Booth, it became increasingly difficult to identify features of literary inquiry that would distinguish it from fields as diverse as philosophy, speech, psychology, linguistics, education, or rhetoric – a task that had been one of the prime projects of the New Critics. Researchers in other disciplines, such as Booth, realized that the network of relationships that existed between author, text, audience, and reality illuminated not only literary works but also more traditional historical and anthropological study.

Booth's early work can thus be seen as an ongoing challenge to, and even a refutation of, the excesses of the New Criticism and its infamous prohibitions against the intentional and affective "fallacies." Simply put, the New Critics had argued that authorial intention was at best irrelevant and at worst impossible to discern and that a reader's "response" to a text was not equivalent to its meaning and usually led readers to substitute their own subjective paraphrases for the "organic meaning" of the work as a whole. *The Rhetoric of Fiction* and other essays by Booth in this period specifically debated the value of these injunctions and attempted to delineate the "rhetoric" or genres of relationships between narrator and narration that an author could employ in a text to guide the reader to intended perspectives and meanings. The rhetorical view of criticism that Booth posited in some sense embraced these "fallacies" and ultimately questioned the validity of any interpretation uninformed by the respective roles the author/narrator and reader play in the reading process.

The rehabilitation of rhetoric Booth had begun in *The Rhetoric of Fiction* continued in *A Rhetoric of Irony* (1974). Building upon his previous analysis, Booth argues that irony is not a genre in itself but a device used by writers to further other effects. A stable irony demands that the reader reject the overt meaning of a statement and reconstruct a new meaning which represents the author's actual, intended meaning. This technique makes readers more active participants in the reading process, but reading remains a process in which one is assisted by the author. Unstable ironies, by contrast – those that do not bear an easily discerned and determinate message – foil the reader who is trying to recover propositional themes or meanings an author has presumably intended. Authors who deliberately make it difficult or unnatural for readers to perceive the fulcrum of their ironies not only risk undermining the privileges of the literary enterprise but also deny to critics a sense of boundary or closure to their attempted interpretations.

In the midst of an argument about particular texts, there emerges a theme that comes to dominate Booth's later critical concerns: "metacriticism," or clarifying the legitimate grounds upon which a critic can make a case for particular interpretations. He wants authors and critics to be responsible for what they say, to be respectful of common textual clues and common literary sense employed in coming to understand the craft of literary art and literary reception. An imagined critical debate over the respective merits of the world-views of Alexander Pope and William Shakespeare yields an important principle:

> I simply cannot, try as I will, claim that the total picture of man and his universe implied by Pope's couplet is as interesting, as comprehensive, as true, as important, as the picture I get from Lear. But again, if you disagree with me, where are we to turn for genuine grounds of debate? . . . Wherever we turn, then, we open up problems of value theory that some would say cannot be reasonably argued and that all would agree are not specific to "literary criticism."

Booth's response to this dilemma is to recognize that literary critical questions, that is, questions about the validity of individual interpretations, rest ultimately upon values that are outside the literary enterprise and that these values are built through the rhetorical process of consensus-building. When critics grope toward or adopt shared notions of authorial intent, reader expectation, textual reliability, and the inhabitability of fiction's evoked worlds, they can talk to one another and understand the sources of their disagreement. The alternative critical stance is an idiosyncratic, interpretive autonomy that undermines the viability of critical discourse and breeds either anarchy or a highly structured, hyper-objectivist position that regards each text as having a univocal interpretation to which all perceptive readers will or must eventually subscribe.

Booth rejects both extremes; his metacritical approach to literary criticism clearly encompasses a profound allegiance to a rhetorical pluralism whose genesis can be traced to his mentor, R. S. Crane, the Neo-Aristotelian critic and scholar who taught at the University of Chicago during the late 1940s. Informed by a view of art as imitative or representational of the world, Booth's theory of criticism posits the literary text as an object that provides the possibility for "symbolic exchange" between two minds that share both a language of criticism and the tools for distinguishing intent and effect in a text. This Aristotelian foundation for literary inquiry – tempered by Booth's commonsensical, Mormon trust in reason – is evident in this passage from his *Modern Dogma and the Rhetoric of Assent* (1974):

> We must finally ask ourselves whether a creature made through assent, a rational animal – that is, a man who can find his "self" only through his communal building of selves, who can find his life, in fact, only by losing himself back into the society of selves that made him – whether such a man can finally withhold assent to the nature of things.

Through rational reflection and inquiry the human interpreter can come to a sense of the "nature of things," both in the world and in a text. This critical pluralism incorporates Booth's view that "meaning" is a product of consensus, a "making of meaning" out of not only what is on the page but also what is within that complex of relationships that obtains between reader, writer, work, and world in the writing and reading process. The upshot is that while no one interpretation of a work can ever be exhaustively "true" – since different readers will bring different expectations and experiences to the work, all the while missing, misreading, or confusing the author's intention – there is nevertheless a range of plausible interpretations a critic can recognize and endorse. This is, thus, a "limited" pluralism that admits variant readings but not utterly or inescapably tendentious readings that can have no demonstrable basis in the text, author, or reader.

This thesis is the burden of Booth's *Critical Understanding* (1979), his major contribution to the twentieth-century understanding of the nature of textuality and interpretation. It is, in Booth's words, a "criticism of criticisms," the culmination of his attempt to articulate the criteria by which critical methods can be debated and evaluated. In a time when the hallmark of critical scholarship and theory is ambiguity, allusiveness, opacity, tentativeness, and rejection of the mimetic functions of language, Booth's work is refreshingly clear and to the point. While respectful of contemporary modes of critical thought, Booth is demonstrably drawn to the eclectic, pluralistic notion of literary criticism his own textual criticism illustrates. He is, in other words, an admirer but not the captive of many different "schools" of textual criticism.

The substance of *Critical Understanding* is an inquiry into the work of three contemporary "competing" pluralists (R. S. Crane, M. H. Abrams, and Kenneth Burke) that compares and critiques their critical methods. This analysis is extended into an examination of their relevance for understanding more recent trends, such as deconstruction and reader-response schools of criticism. Perhaps most valuable in this work is Booth's concluding synthesis that identifies the most appealing aspects of the pluralist approach to texts. The pluralism Booth endorses can embrace varying modes of inquiry in particular instances; one text may yield itself to a New Critical approach and another to a deconstructive approach. Above all, Booth's pluralism

> is committed . . . to remaining inside a mode to the last possible moment, as it were, before lapsing into heresy. It will thus at given moments appear dogmatically monistic, dogmatically committed to preserving those exemplars in criticism that can, in their integrity, best help any critic to serve the enterprise of artistic creation.

Booth's eclectic stance can extract from otherwise mutually exclusive tools and tactics important, localized reading strategies that help illuminate the text without becoming monolithic templates that rule out other possible approaches or interpretations. In a word, Booth's pluralism is calculated not so much to preclude so-called questionable readings of texts as much as it is to encourage fuller, more comprehensive ones that do justice to the complexity of human communication and human nature.

A balanced view of Booth's contribution to contemporary thinking and scholarship about literary criticism would conclude that, in fact, it far exceeds his actual scholarly output in terms of full-length volumes. As one of two founding editors of *Critical Inquiry*, the most influential contemporary journal of literary critical scholarship, Booth's editorial leadership has helped refine the art of literary debate as well as to invigorate responsible dialogue among competing camps. Booth's œuvre represents the epitome of a reasoned, nonreactionary response to trends and fads, sifting them for their insights into the relationships among authors, readers, and texts and incorporating these insights into a critical stance that leaves the interpretive task still in the hands of the informed reader – and not with the professional expert in arcane theory. In the final analysis, Booth may be credited with teaching a generation of literary theorists and critics that one need not surrender claims of validity in interpretation to either a naive relativism debilitated by its cavalier rejection of human consensus or a naive realism uninformed by the complexities of human psychology and behavior. Booth's pluralism of limits – and limits of pluralism – provides an admirably centrist outpost among extremes in critical theory at the start of the twenty-first century and continues to make literary communication possible even where literary unanimity is not possible.

Principal criticism

The Rhetoric of Fiction, 1961, 1983
Now Don't Try to Reason with Me: Essays and Ironies for a Credulous Age, 1970
Modern Dogma and the Rhetoric of Assent, 1974
A Rhetoric of Irony, 1974
"Metaphor as Rhetoric: The Problem of Evaluation," in *Critical Inquiry*. 5 (Fall, 1978), pp. 49–72
Critical Understanding: The Powers and Limits of Pluralism, 1979
"The Way I Loved George Eliot: Friendship with Books as a Neglected Critical Metaphor," in *Kenyon Review*. New series, 2 (Spring, 1981), pp. 4–27
"Freedom of Interpretation: Bakhtin and the Challenge of Feminist Criticism," in *Critical Inquiry*. 9 (September, 1982), pp. 45–75
"Between Two Generations: The Heritage of the Chicago School," in *Profession 82* (1982)
The Company We Keep: An Ethics of Fiction, 1988
The Vocation of a Teacher: Rhetorical Occasions, 1989

Other major works and literary forms

In addition to his literary criticism, Wayne C. Booth has published several works on rhetorical theory and more than one hundred articles, essays, and reviews on various rhetorical and literary topics, including the teaching of writing.

Booth has also carved out an important editorial career as founding coeditor of *Critical Inquiry*, an influential journal of literary theory and criticism.

EDITED TEXTS
The Knowledge Most Worth Having, 1967
The Harper and Row Reader, 1984 (with Marshall Gregory)

Further reading

Abrams. M. H. "The Deconstructive Angel," in *Critical Inquiry*. III (Spring, 1977), pp. 425–438.
Berrong, Richard M. "Finding Anti-Feminism in Rabelais: A Response to Wayne Booth's Call for an Ethical Criticism," in *Critical Inquiry*. XI (June, 1985), pp. 687–696.
Cain, William E. *The Crisis in Criticism*, 1984.
Killham, John "'The Second Self' in Novel Criticism," in *British Journal of Aesthetics*. VI (July, 1966), pp. 272–290.
Leitch, Vincent B. *American Literary Criticism from the Thirties to the Eighties*, 1988.
Miller, J. Hillis. "The Critic as Host," in *Critical Inquiry*. III (Spring, 1977), pp. 439–448.
Scott, Robert, and Bernard L. Brooks. *Methods of Rhetorical Criticism*, 1980.
Shaw, Peter. "Degenerate Criticism," in *Harper's Magazine*. CCLIX (October, 1979), pp. 93–99.

BRUCE L. EDWARDS

See also American Literary Theory: Twentieth Century; Rhetoric

Jorge Luis Borges

Argentine writer, poet, and critic

Born: Buenos Aires, Argentina; August 24, 1899
Died: Geneva, Switzerland; June 14, 1986

Biography

Jorge Luis Borges was born on August 24, 1899, in Buenos Aires, Argentina, to Jorge Guillermo Borges, a lawyer whose library and intellectual enthusiasms would foster his son's vocation, and Leonor Acevedo de Borges. Under the influence of his English paternal grandmother, he learned to read English before Spanish. In 1914 the family moved to Europe. Borges learned French and took his *baccalauréat* in Switzerland during World War I. In Spain from 1919 to 1921, and later in Buenos Aires, he was active in the literary avant-garde, publishing both poetry and essays. His stories appeared later, the first of his avowed mature tales only in 1939, as self-imposed therapy after a life-threatening accident.

Borges' most celebrated fiction and essays were published in the 1940s and 1950s. In 1955 he was named director of the National Library, and in 1956 he became professor of English and American literature at the University of Buenos Aires. Having inherited a disease that produces progressive blindness, Borges was sightless by the late 1950s and depended on others to read to him and take dictation.

International recognition came in full after Borges shared the Fomentor Prize with Samuel Beckett in 1961. He traveled and lectured widely abroad, receiving many honorary degrees. He published much poetry thereafter, as well as fiction, lectures, and essays. In his last years, many occasional writings were reprinted, and numerous books of interviews with him appeared. Borges' first marriage lasted from 1967 to 1970. He married his secretary, María Kodama, in Geneva, Switzerland, a month before his death from cancer on June 14, 1986.

Influence

Borges made a sharp impact on literary theory (and practice) in the Hispanic world and beyond it. Both in his critical and theoretical writings and in his fiction and poetry, the pointed stress upon artifice and literariness has provided a corrective to the emphasis of much Latin American criticism on ideological content. The Mexican novelist and critic Carlos Fuentes has referred to the Borgesian "constitution" that underlay the development of the deeply self-aware Latin American fiction of the late twentieth century.

In Europe and North America, as well as Latin America and Spain, the structuralist and poststructuralist focus on reading as a shaping element of literature was clarified by Borges' deemphasis of the notions of originality and individual authorship and his often repeated concept of the author as reader rather than creator. Borges' preference for plot structure over character energized both the practitioners and the critics of the French New Novel and other contemporary narrative forms. That criticism, poststructuralist and other, which since the 1960s has stressed the unsettling aspects of language and literature has been inspired by Borges' demonstrations of the paradoxes and the indeterminacy of philosophical and literary texts. Borges' presence and influence have extended beyond the strictly literary realm: his books of fiction and theory have appeared as visual references – emblems of contemporary culture – in several European films.

Analysis

Borges nurtured a lifelong fascination with metaphysics, both Western and Eastern. Two paternal figures encouraged his speculative bent. His father communicated his interest in Oriental culture to the young Borges and also instructed him in the idealistic philosophy of George Berkeley. Berkeley's denial of the independent existence of reality outside the mind would serve as one basis for Borges' aesthetic play with illusion and reality and his philosophical questioning of the notion of time, developed most extensively in the long essay "New Refutation of Time," included in *Other Inquisitions*. That essay is a prime example of the paradoxical nature of Borges' speculations: his writing may momentarily seem doctrinal, but any discourse of belief is undercut by skepticism and a kind of aesthetic wonder at the often-radical claims of metaphysics. "The inventions of philosophy are no less fantastic than those of art," he remarks in *Other Inquisitions*. Borges' second father figure – the eccentric Argentine novelist and metaphysical conversationalist Macedonio Fernández – specifically directed him toward such an ironic confrontation with philosophical Idealism. Always the efficient editor, Borges convinced the erratic Fernández to publish writings that otherwise might have been lost. The older man's asystematic outlook nevertheless can be seen as a model for Borges' own ironic and seemingly capricious style of critical writing.

Although Borges employed the scholarly apparatus of literary study, in his writing he comes across more as the mercurial and irreverent man of letters than as the methodical professor of literature. He did not have formal philological training, although on his own he learned medieval Germanic languages well enough to teach and write about the sagas. His early and continuing interest in literary language stemmed from the practical concerns of the avant-garde poet of the 1920s who wished to reform poetic discourse. This concern for language can be seen in the essayist Borges' diction, with its arresting etymological usages, and in his insistence on the gulf between nonverbal reality and the arbitrarily symbolic verbal medium of literature.

The typical Borges article is a brief, even fragmentary, comparative display. Often, a metaphor or a philosophical idea is presented as it appears in one author, then in others, usually from widely divergent traditions. A conclusion is derived or intimated. Complex concepts are sometimes stated with minimal elaboration. The essayist is on the one hand brilliantly erudite, ranging over vast stretches of literary time and space in his allusions, and on the other hand often dilettantish in attitude, even discussing books he professes not to have read but to know only at second hand through the reading of someone else's critical piece. One effect of this style is to underscore the precariousness, the intertextual relativity, of critical discourse; another is to achieve a singular concentration through spareness, irony, and the pose of superficiality.

It seems an easy step from the deceptive style already apparent in Borges' four essay collections, published between 1925 and 1932, to his first fantastic short story, "The Approach to al-Mu'tasim," which posed as a literary review among the essays of the book *Historia de la eternidad*. That story, inspired in part by the literary and philosophical hoaxes of Thomas Carlyle's *Sartor Resartus: The Life and Opinions of Herr Teufelsdröckh* (1835), achieves several effects similar to those of Borges' essays: the description and evaluation of a novel (in this case one that only exists in Borges' text), comparative linking of the novel to Persian and Hellenistic pantheism, and tantalizing fragments of insight into fictional technique and the vertiginous depths or heights of idealistic doctrines, which are presented more as literary artifacts than as articles of belief.

Borges' critical examples, his object-texts, include works of prestigious figures such as Dante, Gustave Flaubert, George Bernard Shaw, and Franz Kafka. He communicates his sympathy for and understanding of these texts persuasively. Kafka's nightmarish world is visible in key Borges stories such as "The Library of Babel," and Borges takes Kafka's canon as an exemplary modern text through which people of today read the literature of the past ("Kafka and His Precursors," in *Other Inquisitions*). Evaluation is one of the more traditional operations of Borgesian criticism, and Dante may be said to have been his favorite author. In one of the nine essays on Dante collected in a 1982 volume, he states flatly that *La divina commedia* (c. 1320; *The Divine Comedy*) is the best book in all literature, and his criticism points out individual elements that support this judgment. One very Borgesian contradiction in some of the Dante criticism is the critic's interest in identifying the man Dante behind the persona of Beatrice's admirer in the poem, despite his frequent questioning elsewhere of the validity of authorial projection in literary works.

Often, though, Borges highlights unheralded masterworks by writers who have been sidelined or ignored by twentieth-century critics: William Beckford, Thomas De Quincey, Rudyard Kipling, Robert Louis Stevenson. To some extent this emphasis – and the metaphysical underpinnings of his thought – recall the fact that Borges was born within the nineteenth century; many of the twentieth-century writers he studied were marginal. His only full-length book on a single modern author examines the work of a minor Buenos Aires poet of the first years of the twentieth century, Evaristo Carriego. Borges' unusual preferences demonstrate the subtle power of his critical discourse, managing to call critical attention to unfashionable topics.

Borges came to view Stevenson (a defender of the adventure novel against psychological fiction) as an honorable forerunner of those twentieth-century masters who have surpassed Stevenson and other nineteenth-century writers in the construction of fictional plots. Among those masters he counted G. K. Chesterton, Henry James, Kafka, and Adolfo Bioy Casares. In his prologue to Bioy Casares' novel *La invención de Morel* (1940; translated in *The Invention of Morel: And Other Stories from "La Trama Celeste,"* 1964), Borges frontally attacked José Ortega y Gasset's praise of the psychological novel as the twentieth-century narrative expression *par excellence*. Borges praised the "intrinsic rigor of the adventure novel . . . an artificial object that admits no unjustified part." Borges also cited detective fiction – a genre which he has studied, anthologized, and practiced – as an example of the ability of twentieth-century writers to produce captivating plots, whereas Ortega y Gasset had doubted that novelists could engage the modern sensibility with adventures. The significant body of contemporary fiction that has discarded what Borges has called "psychological simulation" has, in many cases, been directly influenced by his pronouncements and the example of his fiction.

In *Inquisiciones* – Borges' first book of essays, which he chose never to reprint – he included an article on the emptiness of personality ("La nadería de la personalidad"). Inspired by Macedonio Fernández's investigations of the void, the article introduced a recurrent theme of Borges' literary criticism: his questioning of originality, literary influence, and authorship itself. He transmuted Gnostic theories of the absent or distracted Creator and pantheist notions of the dispersion of the Creator through the universe into literary principles that have thrived in world criticism in recent decades. The author is most concrete in his text: William Shakespeare *is* his characters; he is nothing in himself ("Everything and Nothing," in *Dreamtigers*). The poetic persona of Walt Whitman is more real than the historic Whitman. Borges was one of the first contemporary critics to recognize an inverse principle which has became commonplace among the poststructuralists: the text writes its author.

In a 1934 essay Borges demonstrated that Friedrich Nietzsche's theory of eternal recurrence was itself an instance of repetition. In his literary theory, Borges held the classical, anti-Romantic view that there are no new themes, only rewritings of preexisting ones. This view is fleshed out in the incidents of many of his stories, which often appear as versions of the literary or philosophical tradition. For example, the assassination in the story "Theme of the Traitor and the Hero," arbitrarily set in Ireland by its narrator, is presented as a reprise of Julius Caesar's, Abraham Lincoln's, and other political murders. Borges' classicism is apposite to the structuralist model of literature as a system with local variants. Predictably, the Argentine writer is cited (for his *Ficciones, 1935–1944*, 1944; English translation, 1962) in Gilles Deleuze's classic philosophical study, *Différence et répétition* (1968).

The protagonist of "Pierre Menard, Author of the Quixote," the humorous story that Borges wrote in early 1939 to assure himself that septicemia had not ruined his mental faculties after his accident, rewrites chapters of Miguel de Cervantes' classic in the original words as if he were re-creating them. The ironically structured narration praises the Frenchman Menard's brilliant linguistic anachronisms in his seventeenth-century Spanish and the startling novelty of the archaic ideas of his text. The story is a striking exemplar of several of Borges' most influential ideas. Menard's work embodies the principle of repetition to an extreme, and he is a radical example of the author as reader. Menard as reader both reiterates and effaces Cervantes. His story, along with Borges' many other formulations stressing the primary role of reading in the literary process, was a key catalyst for the rich development of the theory of reading in structuralist and poststructuralist criticism, beginning with such discussions of Borges (and of Menard) as Gérard Genette's article on the Argentine critic's "literary utopia" (published in the first volume of Genette's *Figures*, 1966). Reading reproduces, rewrites, changes the text, which in this light is a continual process of signification, not a repository of meanings cast in stone by the author.

Some writers have sought to evaluate Borges' literary theory in the context of his maverick conservative (which is to say nineteenth-century liberal) politics. Borges did not often write directly about current events, but in his many published interviews he rarely hesitated to express unpopular opinions. He infuriated many Latin American intellectuals by accepting a decoration in the mid-1970s from the Chilean military dictator Augusto Pinochet. Most of the commentaries on Borges' politics have focused on externals; one exception is the Argentine critic Alicia Borinsky's "Repetitions, Museums, Libraries," which takes up the ideological elitism visible in the story of Pierre Menard and links it to a dominant ideology of repression in Argentine history. Borinsky's comparative reading, arguably itself influenced by Borges' own style of thought, does not fail to recognize the seductive qualities of that style.

Borges' deeper contribution is to the politics of literary and philosophical theory itself. With his views of the receding author and the nothingness of personality, he has contributed to the twentieth-century decline of the ideology of the subject. It is logical that the philosopher Michel Foucault should admit in *Les Mots et les choses: Une Archéologie des sciences humaines* (1966; *The Order of Things: An Archaeology of the Human Sciences*, 1970) that his study of the historical limits of the Humanist concept of mankind "first arose out of a passage in Borges."

Principal criticism

Inquisiciones, 1925
El tamaño de mi esperanza, 1926
El idioma de los argentinos, 1928
Evaristo Carriego, 1930 (English translation, 1984)
Discusión, 1932
Historia de la eternidad, 1936
Aspectos de la literatura gauchesca, 1950
Antiguas literaturas germánicas, 1951 (with Delia Ingenieros; revised as *Literaturas germánicas medievales*, 1966, with Maria Esther Vázquez)
Otras inquisiciones, 1952 (*Other Inquisitions*, 1964)
Passages in *El hacedor*, 1960 (*Dreamtigers*, 1964)
Introduction to *Macedonio Fernández*, 1961
Introdución a la literatura inglesa, 1964 (with Vázquez)
Introducción a la literatura norteamericana, 1967 (with Esther Zemborain de Torres; *An Introduction to American Literature*, 1971)
Siete noches, 1980 (*Seven Nights*, 1984)
Nueve ensayos dantescos, 1982

Other major works and literary forms

It is harder to make generic distinctions between Jorge Luis Borges' literary essays and his imaginative works than it is with most writers' canons. His first three books of poetry, all published in the 1920s, were nativist evocations of Buenos Aires, avant-garde in their language. After three decades, Borges returned to poetry in more philosophical and personal veins with *Dreamtigers* and continued publishing books of verse into the 1980s. He is most widely known for his short stories, which he began publishing in book form with the fictionalized biographies of *Historia universal de la infamia* (1935; *A Universal History of Infamy*, 1972). After establishing himself as a master of the fantastic and self-reflexive short story, he worked a slightly more realistic vein in the short fiction of *El informe de Brodie* (1970; *Doctor Brodie's Report*, 1972). He has collaborated with several other authors in writing fiction and miscellanies and in compiling anthologies. Notable among these collaborations are the witty books of fiction coauthored with Adolfo Bioy Casares, including the detective stories of *Seis problemas para don Isidro Parodi* (1942; *Six Problems for Don Isidro Parodi*, 1981). For many years Borges served numerous Buenos Aires periodicals as an editor, literary journalist, and film critic.

NOVEL
Un modelo para la muerte, 1946 (with Adolfo Bioy Casares, under joint pseudonym B. Suárez Lynch)

SHORT FICTION
Historia universal de la infamia, 1935 (*A Universal History of Infamy*, 1972)
El jardín de senderos que se bifurcan, 1941
Seis problemas para don Isidro Parodi, 1942 (with Adolfo Bioy Casares, under joint pseudonym H. Bustos Domecq; *Six Problems for Don Isidro Parodi*, 1981)
Ficciones, 1935–1944, 1944 (English translation, 1962)
Dos fantasías memorables, 1946 (with Bioy Casares, under joint pseudonym H. Bustos Domecq)
El Aleph, 1949, 1952 (translated in *The Aleph and Other Stories, 1933–1969*, 1970)
La muerte y la brújula, 1951
La hermana de Eloísa, 1955 (with Luisa Mercedes Levinson)
Cuentos, 1958
Crónicas de H. Bustos Domecq, 1967 (with Bioy Casares; *Chronicles of Bustos Domecq*, 1976)
El informe de Brodie, 1970 (*Doctor Brodie's Report*, 1972)
El matrero, 1970
El congreso, 1971 (*The Congress*, 1974)
El libro de arena, 1975 (*The Book of Sand*, 1977)
Narraciones, 1980

SCREENPLAYS
Los orilleros y El paraíso de los creyentes, 1955 (with Adolfo Bioy Casares)
Les Autres, 1974 (with Bioy Casares and Hugo Santiago)

POETRY
Fervor de Buenos Aires, 1923, 1969
Luna de enfrente, 1925
Cuaderno San Martín, 1929
Poemas, 1923–1943, 1943
Poemas, 1923–1953, 1954
Obra poética, 1923–1958, 1958
Obra poética, 1923–1964, 1964
Seis poemas escandinavos, 1966
Siete poemas, 1967
El otro, el mismo, 1969
Elogio de la sombra, 1969 (*In Praise of Darkness*, 1974)
El oro de los tigres, 1972 (translated in *The Gold of Tigers: Selected Later Poems*, 1977)
La rosa profunda, 1975 (translated in *The Gold of Tigers*)
La moneda de hierro, 1976
Historia de la noche, 1977
La cifra, 1981
Los conjurados, 1986

NONFICTION
Figari, 1930
Las Kennigar, 1933
Nueva refutación del tiempo, 1947
El "Martin Fierro," 1953 (with Margarita Guerrero)
Leopoldo Lugones, 1955 (with Betina Edelberg)
Manual de zoología fantástica, 1957 (with Guerrero; *The Imaginary Zoo*, 1969, revised as *El libro de los seres imaginarios*, 1967, *The Book of Imaginary Beings*, 1969)
La poesía gauchesca, 1960
Prólogos, 1975
¿Qué es el budismo?, 1976 (with Alicia Jurado)
Cosmogonías, 1976
Libro de sueños, 1976

ANTHOLOGIES
Antología clásica de la literatura argentina, 1937
Antología de la literatura fantástica, 1940 (with Adolfo Bioy Casares and Silvia Ocampo)
Antología poética argentina, 1941 (with Bioy Casares and Ocampo)
Poesía gauchesca, 1955 (2 volumes, with Bioy Casares)
Libro del cielo y del infierno, 1960, 1975 (with Bioy Casares)
Versos, by Evaristo Carriego, 1972
Antología poética, by Francisco de Quevedo, 1982
Antología poética, by Leopoldo Lugones, 1982
El amigo de la muerte, by Pedro Antonio de Alarcón, 1984

TRANSLATIONS
Orlando, 1937 (of Virginia Woolf's novel)
La metamórfosis, 1938 (of Franz Kafka's novel *Die Verwandlung*)
Un bárbaro en Asia, 1941 (of Henri Michaux's travel notes)
Los mejores cuentos policiales, 1943 (with Adolfo Bioy Casares, of detective stories by various authors)
Bartleby, el escribiente, 1943 (of Herman Melville's novella *Bartleby the Scrivener*)
Los mejores cuentos policiales, segunda serie, 1951 (with Bioy Casares, of detective stories by various authors)
Cuentos breves y extraordinarios, 1955, 1973 (with Bioy Casares, of short stories by various authors; *Extraordinary Tales*, 1973)
Las palmeras salvajes, 1956 (of William Faulkner's novel *The Wild Palms*)
Hojas de hierba, 1969 (of Walt Whitman's *Leaves of Grass*)

EDITED TEXT
El compadrito: Su destino, sus barrios, su música, 1945, 1968 (with Silvina Bullrich)

MISCELLANEOUS
Obras completas, 1953–1967 (10 volumes)
Antología personal, 1961 (*A Personal Anthology*, 1967)
Labyrinths: Selected Stories and Other Writings, 1962, 1964

Nueva antología personal, 1968
Selected Poems, 1923–1967, 1972 (also includes prose)
Adrogue, 1977
Obras completas en colaboración, 1979 (with others)
Atlas, 1984 (with María Kodama; English translation, 1985)

Further reading

Alazraki, Jaime, ed. *Critical Essays on Jorge Luis Borges*, 1987.
——, ed. *Borges and the Kabbalah and Other Essays on His Fiction and Poetry*, 1988.
Barrenechea, Ana María. *Borges: The Labyrinth Maker*, 1965.
Bell-Villada, Gene H. *Borges and His Fiction: A Guide to His Mind and Art*, 1981.
Bloom, Harold, ed. *Jorge Luis Borges*, 1986.
Burgin, Richard. *Conversations with Jorge Luis Borges*, 1969.
Christ, Ronald J. *The Narrow Act: Borges's Art of Allusion*, 1969.
Dunham, Lowell, and Ivar Ivask, eds. *The Cardinal Points of Borges*, 1971.
Foster, David William. *Jorge Luis Borges: An Annotated Primary and Secondary Bibliography*, 1984.
Isbister, Rob, and Peter Standish. *A Concordance to the Works of Jorge Luis Borges 1899–1986*, 1992.
Kushigan, Julia A. *Orientalism in the Hispanic Literary Tradition: In Dialogue with Borges, Paz, and Sardry*, 1991.
Lindstrom, Naomi. *Jorge Luis Borges: A Study of the Short Fiction*, 1990.
Rodríguez Monegal, Emir. *Jorge Luis Borges: A Literary Biography*, 1978.
Sarlo, Beatriz. *Jorge Luis Borges: A Writer at the Edge*, 1992.
Sorrentino, Fernando. *Seven Conversations with Jorge Luis Borges*, 1982.
Yates, Donald. *Jorge Luis Borges: Life, Work and Criticism*, 1985.

JOHN F. DEREDITA

See also Calvino

Paul Bourget

French writer and critic

Born: Amiens, France; September 2, 1852
Died: Paris, France; December 25, 1935

Biography

Paul-Charles-Joseph Bourget was born in Amiens, France, on September 2, 1852; his father was a brilliant professor of mathematics and physics, his mother a well-educated bluestocking. Unfortunately, she was neurotic and died young. Bourget himself later commented on the dichotomous analytical-emotional character he considered he owed to them. For all of his own neuroses and lifelong tendency toward hypochondria, however, he led a full literary life, with more than one hundred volumes to his credit. His private life he kept scrupulously to himself; scholars know little about it. In 1890 he married Minnie David; it was seemingly a happy, if not ideal, union. Bourget traveled extensively most of his life: England, Italy, Greece, the Near East, the United States. He was elected to the Académie Française on May 31, 1894 (a signal honor, especially for an author so young), and remained "a great man of letters" for the rest of his days. He was intimate with many of the finest authors of his time, notably Henry James, Hippolyte-Adolphe Taine, Edith Wharton, Guy de Maupassant, and Henry Bordeaux. He remained at his desk almost until the end, saddened by a sense that the world in which this former boulevardier had felt at home had long since passed him by. He died, fittingly enough for a staunch Catholic, on Christmas Day, 1935.

Influence

Bourget's *Essais de psychologie contemporaine* (essays on contemporary psychology) proved immensely popular, especially with the youth of the mid-1880s. The excesses of naturalism did not solely alarm the Catholic clergy who denounced them: the younger generation was also ready to listen to a critic who could dispassionately analyze where France had gone astray. If France was suffering from pessimism and decadence, Bourget found the cause among the writers who influenced his generation with their dilettantism, their cosmopolitan rootlessness, their nihilism, and their lack of religious faith. Yet if his message gained the allegiance of the young, he failed to hold it, as they soon lost sympathy with an outlook that was becoming more and more conservative, religious, and reactionary. Ironically, the author whose worldly, erotic novels had previously been accused of corrupting youth was increasingly (especially after World War I) viewed as an anachronistic Victorian moralist.

Even if no longer considered a leading literary critic or innovative novelist, however, Bourget remained widely read until his death. Furthermore, almost no critic or thinker today in any field can hope for the long allegiance belonging to a Plato or an Aristotle, or even to a Nicolas Boileau-Despréaux. In the modern world increasingly rapid obsolescence of literary theory is normal; a half-life of ten years or more is exceptional. Bourget's influence has proved more pervasive and lasting than most, not only through his criticism but also through the example of his popular fiction.

Analysis

Bourget turned out literary criticism, usually colored by his conservative social beliefs, throughout most of his long career. He never completely freed himself from doctrinal bias, but he neither prostituted his philosophy nor sank to abuse or invective; indeed, his pronouncements were saved by an uncommonly keen analytical perception. Some have even ventured to state that he was a better critic of literature than novelist; he was, at the very least, distinguished.

His literary baptism, years before he became either poet or novelist, was an article on Baruch Spinoza, which appeared on December 28, 1872. It was soon followed by his first important piece, "Le Roman réaliste et le roman piétiste" (the realistic and the pietist novel), published, this time under his own name, in the July 15, 1873 issue of the prestigious *Revue des Deux Mondes*. In this essay, he takes the currently popular realistic-naturalistic novel to task for its emphasis, particularly in the hands of Émile Zola, on brutality and ugliness. The pietist novel, intended for young ladies, is, Bourget admits, hardly any improvement.

Then came his first and certainly greatest success in the field of literary-social criticism, the two volumes of the *Essais de psychologie contemporaine*, in which he analyzes eleven key figures he believes deeply influenced his generation, and, by extension, himself: Charles Baudelaire, poet; Ernest Renan, religious thinker; Gustave Flaubert, author of *Madame Bovary* (1857; English translation, 1886); Hippolyte-Adolphe Taine, historian-novelist, philosopher-artist, and literature critic-social commentator (Bourget's mentor, whom he greatly resembles); Stendhal, the somewhat earlier Romanticist and realist of *Le Rouge et le noir* (1830; *The Red and the Black*, 1898); Alexandre Dumas *fils*, popular playwright; Leconte de Lisle, Parnassian poet; Edmond and Jules de Goncourt, leaders with Zola in the new naturalistic movement; Ivan Turgenev, the Russian novelist who lived in Paris for many years; and Henri-Frédéric Amiel, the remarkable Swiss diarist of the *Fragments d'un journal intime* (1883–1887; *Amiel's Journal*, 1885, also known as *Journal*). These eleven become the object of what Bourget admits to be a melancholy survey, for he finds in each of these educators of the minds and hearts of his generation the mark of a profound pessimism. Renan and the Goncourts he faults for being infected with the germ of melancholy encased in dilettantism; the latter in addition are guilty of hyperacuity of sensations, the former of understanding well a religion in which he could not believe. Stendhal, Amiel, and Turgenev are fatally flawed by the results of a cosmopolitan life. Baudelaire's poetry and Dumas' dramas depict aspects of modern love and its perversions brought on by the pressures of the analytic spirit. Flaubert, Leconte de Lisle, and Taine display the effects of the scientific outlook upon imagination and sensitivity. Bourget's penetrating analysis of the malaise of his day became the talk of all Paris. His accusations, at least to the extent it is possible to assign blame and separate cause from effect, were on target. These writers really were deeply, if not exclusively, influential, and they were neurotic – sick in the sense Johann Wolfgang von Goethe had in mind when he called classicism healthy and Romanticism unhealthy – all ten having been bitten by the germ of Romanticism in their own youth. Nevertheless, Bourget demanded no jail sentences, as it were, for their crimes, no doubt because he realized that he exhibited the very same symptoms: thus his essays were at once an indictment and a form of public confession. This fact doubtless goes far toward explaining the curious love-hate relationship he maintained with his age throughout his life, as he alternated between the urbane observer and the Victorian moralist. To be sure, his emphases changed, but he never completely metamorphosed.

He continued his psychoanalytical method in later volumes, sketching portraits of Blaise Pascal, Jean de La Fontaine, François Auguste René Chateaubriand, Alfred de Vigny, Alphonse de Lamartine, Victor Hugo, and George Sand, while penning more general articles on the theater, the novel, Parnassianism, and the writing of history. In 1906 he added a third volume of *Études et portraits* (studies and portraits), featuring perceptive studies of Honoré de Balzac, Goethe, Alfred de Musset, Guy de Maupassant, Pierre Loti, and another on Taine, among others. Four more critical volumes on literature and doctrine followed from 1912 to 1922. Most still dealt with recent figures and reflected a growing bias toward Catholic and social conservatism. His slanted treatments may not necessarily invalidate his conclusions, but if his eye remained as sharp as ever, he was nevertheless becoming predictable. The reader knew in advance how the pieces were going to end. Bourget admitted to pursuing the same method, that of analysis, his basic tenets remaining the search for hypotheses concerning causes. He would take a given fact about a novel, a philosophical system, or a political or religious figure (Bourget could not for long avoid discussions of religion and society), define and situate this fact, analyze it, probe into its origins, hunt for what his old master Taine called its "generative conditions," and, armed with these data, attach the original fact to the great body of psychological and social laws. It was a method he claimed to have followed for some forty years, if with evolving perspective.

As late as 1928, when he was seventy-five, he could still create sharply observed studies on Balzac, Louis Pasteur, Renan, and Anatole France, ending with some thoughts on Léon Daudet's *Le Stupide XIXe Siècle* (1922; *The Stupid Nineteenth Century*, 1928). He agreed with the latter's excoriation of an age that took a wrong turn but presented exceptions.

Unlike many other literary critics, Bourget was in a position to practice what he preached. The dramatists whose techniques he approved he imitated in his own plays, as even more obviously he did with the fiction writers, echoes of whose methods turn up in his twenty-five or more novels and as many collections of stories. If novels should be psychological, a form of literature in which realistic descriptions of objects and the outer appearances of people give way to inner depictions (a French specialty for at least seven hundred years), his own works fit in nicely. If the thesis novel, already deemed out of date for half a century, still had merit, as he claimed, he would resurrect and revamp it under a new name, the novel of ideas, arguing that literature without ideas is mere empty entertainment. His own examples, at their best, well illustrate his point. He did preach to excess at times; the professor's son still had to instruct. He followed Horace's precept of *utile et dulce* (the "useful with the sweet"), calling it "a moving story that at the same time makes one think." The didacticism so characteristic of the nineteenth century, the stock in trade for writers such as Balzac and Hugo, who considered themselves purveyors of truth to the masses, was carried to new heights by Bourget. In one of his novels (*Némésis*, 1918), for example, he depicted a dwarf and then noted how perfect an example of achondroplasia this character was. Elsewhere, he etymologized for his readers the English word "flirt" and explained the ceremony of dubbing knights (after having used the word "dub") – these few examples among so many. He abandoned the realistic novel of Balzac and Flaubert, confessing himself a poor observer. Actually he was not, but he had a better reason to abandon it: the abuses of the realistic method. Endlessly detailed descriptions, he argued, do not necessarily make for greater realism. Every description involves choice: which details to include, which to suppress. Thus, such descriptions are actually quite subjective and reflect each author's preferences. The professed impersonality so dear to the realistic movement is, then, an impossibility. He was lukewarm toward picturesque writing as well, offering to trade all Flaubert's 1862 novel *Salammbô* (English translation, 1886), with its exotic depiction of ancient Carthage, for one sentence of *Madame Bovary*, laid in the gray boredom of Normandy.

It should be remembered that Bourget wrote no "how-to" treatises in the manner of Horace or Boileau, not even a short manual in the form of a preface as his friend Maupassant did for novelists in *Pierre et Jean* (1888; *Pierre and Jean*, 1890). His articles psychoanalyzed; that he approved or disapproved of his subject was rarely in doubt, but he was hardly telling the reader how to start creating literature. Some of his beliefs must even be inferred or extrapolated from his novelistic practice. He favored the well-made novel, a parallel to the "well-made plays" of Eugène Scribe. The plots are tight, events occur when they best further the story, loose ends are tied up at the end, little details are given careful attention. Bourget could employ the third-person omniscient novelist form or opt for first-person narration. He favored the common nineteenth-century device, setting no precedent here, of lending a sense of reality and emphasizing the passage of time by giving dates for the start and end of his tales and locating them meticulously – in his case going so far as to name not only real cities as locales, but actual streets as well. Similarly, he sprinkled his narratives with the names of real people living at the time at which he set his plots. He used the device of recurring characters from one story to the next, often updating their biographies: the formerly struggling young poet, for example, is now the middle-aged toast of Paris. He eschewed for the most part action scenes. Often nothing much happens, perhaps because, as he said early in his career, dramas of the heart have no events. He enjoyed depicting characters afflicted with psychoses. He not only advocated such accounts, he indulged in them. Bourget haunted psychiatric clinics and became good friends with Dr. Ernest Dupré, a famous psychiatrist, dedicating one volume of his short stories to him and allowing him to append comments on the accuracy of Bourget's handling of abnormal psychology. (The doctor gave him high marks.) Enamored of science and medicine, again like so many European and American writers of the past century, Bourget described cocaine addiction, inflammatory tuberculosis, telepathy, cryptesthesia, cyclothymia, telekinesis, and the already mentioned achondroplasia, among many. In some of these practices, he merely followed or at best enlarged upon the work of others, but he also pioneered. Most of what he did he advocated openly or through implication. More often than not, his immense popularity and his residual status as the elder statesman of literature after 1918 gave his practices credibility.

Principal criticism

Essais de psychologie contemporaine, 1883
Nouveaux Essais de psychologie contemporaine, 1885
Études et portraits, 1889, 1906
Pages de critique et de doctrine, 1912 (2 volumes)
Nouvelles Pages de critique et de doctrine, 1922 (2 volumes)
Quelques témoignages, 1928, 1934

Other major works and literary forms

Paul Bourget was a critic not only of literature but also of society as a whole. Throughout his work, his growing conservatism is clearly in evidence, though he never exhibited the fascistic excesses of some fellow conservatives. Bourget showed promise with the verse novel *Edel* (1878) and two volumes of lyric poetry. He also enjoyed several stage successes, notably *La Barricade: Chronique de 1910* (1910; the barricade: 1910 chronicle) and *Le Tribun: Chronique de 1911* (1911; a tribune of the people), dealing with current social and religious problems. His travels produced *Sensations d'Italie* (1891; *Impressions of Italy*, 1892), a tribute to his love for Italian culture, and the vastly popular *Outre-mer: Notes sur l'Amérique* (1895; *Outre-mer: Impressions of America*, 1895), sympathetic but pungent observations stemming from a trip through the eastern United States, covering Boston, New York, Chicago and its stockyards, and Flagler's Florida.

He was also a dominant force among fiction writers of his day, with twenty-eight novels and almost as many short-story collections to his credit. If some are mere potboilers, most reveal remarkable psychological insight. A keen, worldly, somewhat erotic analyst in the early novels, such as *Un Crime d'amour* (1886; *A Love Crime*, 1888), he revealed almost from the start a tendency to moralize, ranging from the judgmental attitude of *Le Disciple* (1889; *The Disciple*, 1898) to the less censorious *Cosmopolis* (1893; English translation, 1893). With *L'Étape* (1902; one step at a time), he created a new form, the *roman à idées* (novel of ideas), claiming that, unlike the traditional thesis novel, which it greatly resembles, his work presented all sides of the problems depicted. His later works, such as *Le Démon de midi* (1914; midlife temptations), help preserve his role as France's literary Dutch uncle.

NOVELS
Cruelle Énigme, 1885 (*A Cruel Enigma*, 1887)
Un Crime d'amour, 1886 (*A Love Crime*, 1888)
Mensonges, 1887 (*Lies*, 1892)
Le Disciple, 1889 (*The Disciple*, 1898)
Physiologie de l'amour moderne, 1889
Un Cœur de femme, 1890 (*A Woman's Heart*, 1890)
Cosmopolis, 1893 (English translation, 1893)
L'Étape, 1902
L'Émigré, 1907 (*The Weight of the Name*, 1908)
Le Démon de midi, 1914
Le Sens de la mort, 1915 (*The Night Cometh*, 1916)
Némésis, 1918

SHORT FICTION
Pastels, 1889
Nouveaux Pastels, 1891 (*Pastels of Men*, 1891, 1892)
Recommencements, 1897
Complications sentimentales, 1898
Les Deux Sœurs, 1905
Anomalies, 1920
Conflits intimes, 1925
De Petits Faits vrais, 1930

PLAYS
La Barricade: Chronique de 1910, 1910
Un Cas de conscience, 1910 (with Serge Basset)
Le Tribun: Chronique de 1911, 1911
La Crise, 1912 (with André Beaunier)

POETRY
La Vie inquiète, 1875
Edel, 1878
Les Aveux, 1882

NONFICTION
Sensations d'Italie, 1891 (*Impressions of Italy*, 1892)
Outre-mer: Notes sur l'Amérique, 1895 (*Outre-mer: Impressions of America*, 1895)

Further reading

Austin, Lloyd James. *Paul Bourget: Sa Vie et son œuvre jusqu'en 1889*, 1940.
Feuillerat, Albert. *Paul Bourget*, 1937.
Giraud, Victor. *Paul Bourget: Essai de psychologie contemporaine*, 1934.
Martin-Gistucci, Marie-Gracieuse, ed. *Paul Bourget et l'Italie*, 1985.
Secor, Walter Todd. *Paul Bourget and the nouvelle*, 1948.
Singer, Armand E. *Paul Bourget*, 1976.
Wellek, René. *A History of Modern Criticism: 1750–1950*, 1965.

ARMAND E. SINGER

See also Brunetière; Continental Theory

Fredson Bowers

American bibliographer, editor, and critic

Born: New Haven, Connecticut; April 25, 1905
Died: Charlottesville, Virginia; April 11, 1991

Biography

Fredson Thayer Bowers was born in New Haven, Connecticut, in 1905. His father was president of a corset manufacturing company. Bowers was educated at New Haven General High School and Brown University, Providence, Rhode Island, where he took his B.A. in 1925. There followed graduate study at Harvard, where he was awarded his Ph.D. in 1934. From 1926 to 1936 he was instructor in English and tutor in the modern languages at Harvard. He held a post as instructor in English at Princeton from 1936 to 1938, before being appointed assistant professor of English at the University of Virginia in 1938. He subsequently held posts as associate professor (from 1948), alumni professor (from 1957), and Linden Kent Memorial Professor (from 1968 until his retirement in 1975). He received a great many other academic honors and held research fellowships at many institutions elsewhere in America and Europe. He was very active both as an administrator within the University of Virginia and in the wider dimensions of the academic profession, serving, for example, on the advisory board of *Shakespeare Quarterly* from 1954 to 1972, on the Modern Language Association (MLA)'s New Variorum Shakespeare Committee from 1955 to 1982, and on the executive council of the MLA from 1963 to 1966.

Influence

When, in 1973, Stanley Wells edited for Oxford University Press a volume called *Shakespeare: Select Bibliographical Guides*, the chapter on "Shakespeare's Text" was contributed by Norman Sanders. He divided his historical account into four sections called, respectively, "The Early Editions," "The Eighteenth and Nineteenth Centuries," "The New Bibliography," and "The Age of Bowers." It is an eloquent tribute to the influence and importance of Bowers' work that his should be the only personal name drawn on in this way and, indeed, that "The Age of Bowers" should seem a very natural title to give to a central area of textual and bibliographical studies in the second half of the twentieth century. Sanders went on to declare that "since the death of W. W. Greg, one name has dominated the study of Shakespeare's text – that of Fredson Bowers." But it is by no means only in the field of Shakespearean studies that Bowers' influence has been enormous. He has exerted a similarly crucial influence on the study of nineteenth-century authors; he has been a central figure in the study of such Elizabethan and Jacobean dramatists as Thomas Dekker, Beaumont and Fletcher, and

Christopher Marlowe; readers and scholars of other authors as diverse as John Dryden and Vladimir Nabokov also need to take account of Bowers' work.

Bowers' formidable output as an editor exists alongside theoretical work which has had a profound effect on the principles and working methods of textual and bibliographical scholars around the world (his death was marked by a "Fredson Bowers Commemorative Issue" of the *Bulletin of the Bibliographical Society of Australia and New Zealand*). His work has insisted upon – and demonstrated – the necessary link between textual scholarship and informed literary criticism. In the Preface to his *Textual and Literary Criticism*, the published text of four of his lectures, Bowers declares his position forthrightly: "Although the specific subjects of the four discourses present something of a mixed bag, an underlying rationale is intended to be present. Literary criticism is viewed as directly dependent upon expert textual criticism, and some horrid examples are cited to illustrate what can happen when it chooses to operate independently." When writing literary criticism Bowers himself never chose to "operate independently" of textual scholarship, though some of his work in this area, notably his early book *Elizabethan Revenge Tragedy* and his later studies of *Hamlet*, has had a considerable influence amongst readers unaware of the kinds of textual and bibliographical issues which have always been at the heart of Bowers' work.

Analysis

The proportion of Bowers' published work which falls within the boundaries of literary criticism as they are most commonly understood is not great. Much else in his work, however, has enormous importance and profound implications for any serious understanding of the disciplines of literary criticism.

Bowers' work grew, in a general sense, out of that of earlier – mostly British – scholars such as W. W. Greg. Central to all that Bowers did as a scholar and critic, as a theorist and propagandist (and not infrequently as a controversialist), was the insistence that literary works could not be understood (and therefore could not be subjected intelligently to critical discussion) without careful attention to both the status of the specific text in use and also to the history of the transmission of the work's texts. In *Textual and Literary Criticism* he wryly observed that "many a literary critic has investigated the past ownership and mechanical condition of his second-hand automobile, or the pedigree and training of his dog, more thoroughly than he has looked into the qualifications of the text on which his critical theories rest," and proceeded to provide a devastating catalogue of critical errors and misprisions occasioned by such "naiveté" (as he there called it). It is not hard to agree with Tanselle's judgment (in volume 46 of *Studies in Bibliography*) that this particular paper remains "a most effective polemic, an expert weaving together of instances – from the literature of four centuries – that show how literary critics (and editors) have been misled by failing to investigate the textual history of the works they are concerned with. It deserves to be a classic essay: it remains an ideal introduction to the need for textual criticism in the study of literature."

Bowers developed and extended the awareness he inherited from Greg and others that understanding the "qualifications" of a particular text or tracing the textual history of a work must involve exact and meticulous attention to the physical properties of the books in which such texts existed. In the five hundred pages of his *Principles of Bibliographical Description* he produced a more comprehensive and coherent methodology for recognizing and describing the physical features of printed texts than had hitherto existed. He addressed the problems of bibliographical classification involved in the use of such distinctions as those between editions, impressions, issues, and states; he suggested consistent procedures for such activities as the transcription of title-pages, the collation of signatures, and the like. The whole is a work of impressively clear-minded logic. The book sets exacting standards (something proclaimed in its very first sentence) and, for all its detail, has a clear sense of purpose – to establish a firm basis for bibliographical description, not merely as an end in itself but as an indispensable aid for textual (and thus literary) critics.

It is important to stress that everything Bowers did seems to have been informed by a genuine love of literature – though appearances may sometimes have been to the contrary. He sometimes overstated claims for the "scientific" nature of the kind of bibliographical activity he advocated (and conducted) and, relatedly, seemed to value the means more than the end, to be fascinated by the methods for their own sake rather than what could usefully (for readers and critics) be produced by the method. But his best work recognizes what he expressed clearly enough at the end of his 1958 lecture "The New Textual Criticism of Shakespeare" (printed in *Textual and Literary Criticism*): "In the history of Shakespearean editing . . . I should prefer the taste and judgment of a Kittredge (wrong as he sometimes was), and of an Alexander, to the unskilled and therefore unscientific operation of a scientific method as if it were the whole answer to the problem and automatically relieved an editor of the necessity to use his critical judgment in any way. Bibliography can only help to prepare a text for the final operation. Bibliography is a good servant but a bad master." In one of the lectures ("The Method for a Critical Edition") in his *On Editing Shakespeare and the Elizabethan Dramatists* he insisted that "it is of the nature of modern editing as against that of the past, that critical judgment must expand from a logical basis in bibliographical and linguistic fact."

Bowers' textual and bibliographical thinking focused on the restoration (or production) of an authorially intended text; so, for example, the purpose of his edition of Nathaniel Hawthorne was, he wrote, "to establish the text in as close a form, in all details, to Hawthorne's final intentions as the preserved documents of each separate work permit." For Bowers, as for most of his generation, works of literature were essentially produced by individual creators. As thinking in the larger community of literary criticism began to doubt and undermine this assumption, so challenges to Bowers' editorial stance began to grow. Some bibliographers began to place their emphasis on the idea that literary texts grew out of the complex structures of collaboration involved in the process of publication. Others challenged Bowers' position on the grounds that it was insufficiently flexible to cope with the actual phenomenon of authorial revision. Where Bowers' methods involved a degree of eclecticism (based on "scientific" principles) whereby a single "authorially intended" text might be constructed from a range of documents judged to be valid witnesses, others preferred to treat each such document as a separate text, deserving study in its own right as embodying a distinct authorial "intention." Bowers was seen as trying to fix a given work in a single "state," where some newer textual critics were ambitious, rather, to record and elucidate the essential instability of the text. We need not imagine that such a debate is one that can usefully be reduced to simple matters of right and wrong; the issues are far more complex and interesting than that, and it has to be said that many of these issues could not have been raised in quite the forms they have later taken without Bowers' original work both in theory (in setting out carefully argued rationales and principles) and in practice (as the producer of so many editions with their elaborate textual apparatuses). Without the example of Bowers many scholars would have been much slower to realize just how thoroughly the texts of literary works are the product of the material means by which they are transmitted; the recognition that, in Thomas Tanselle's words, "the study of literature in the broadest sense entails the study of books and manuscripts as physical objects," is one in large part due to the influence of Bowers' work.

Bowers' influence was felt not only through his own theoretical writings and his editing of texts. It was registered too in his founding and editing of a seminal scholarly journal. In February 1947 Bowers played a major part in the founding of the Bibliographical Society of the University of Virginia, of which he became vice-president. The society invited papers from speakers who included Bowers himself, Charlton Hinman, Giles Dawson, and James G. McManaway. Late in 1948 there was published a volume of *Papers*, under Bowers' editorship. With the second issue, one year later, the title became *Studies in Bibliography*. Bowers was to remain editor of *Studies in Bibliography* until 1991, and under his editorship it became the major journal in its field; to make even the most selective list of its contributors – they included W. W. Greg, Charlton Hinman, R. C. Bald, Harold Jenkins, and Alice Walker in the publication's early years, and many other younger scholars in later years – is to enumerate virtually all of the most important figures who worked, during this period, on the boundary between textual and literary criticism. One impressive feature of Bowers' work as editor of *Studies in Bibliography* was his openness of mind, his willingness to publish contributions by scholars and critics whose work adopted very different points of view from his own (so in the 1970s and 1980s he published articles by, amongst others, Hans Zeller, Gerhard Neumann, and Siegfried Scheibe). Leaving aside the intrinsic merits of much of the work published in *Studies in Bibliography*, Bowers' immensely successful editorship of this yearly volume can be seen as part of a prodigiously energetic personal campaign on behalf of the new movement of bibliography and textual criticism aimed, in part, at literary critics and scholars in related disciplines. Bowers' energy and stamina as a propagandist were remarkable – as a deliverer of lectures in the United States and Europe as well as through his publications.

As a "pure" literary critic, Bowers made important contributions most notably in the field of Elizabethan and Jacobean drama. His *Elizabethan Revenge Tragedy: 1587–1642* was an early work, its three hundred pages based on the 1,100 pages of his Harvard Ph.D. dissertation, "A History of Elizabethan Revengeful Drama." As a study of the background, origins, and development of Revenge tragedy it continues to be of value. Bowers examines ethical thinking on revenge and relevant literary precedents, before offering a consideration of the work of Thomas Kyd, William Shakespeare, John Webster, John Ford, and the Caroline dramatists. Many minor figures are also discussed – Bowers has things to say on over fifty plays in all. Bowers is scrupulous and often illuminating as he traces the "progress of the Kydian hero to villain-revenger." To many modern eyes he will seem too ready to see the work of the Carolines as no more than the decadence of a previous, but brief, efflorescence, as in his closing remarks: "The closing of the theaters was really a blessing in disguise. In the breathing space afforded by the Commonwealth's inhibition, the tragic drama found a relief from its dependence on empty ingenuity and worn-out tragic conventions which had lost all touch with the problems of human life and ethics, and all interest in the human soul." The picture painted is certainly too black-and-white, too ready a historical simplification. Bowers is generally more convincing in his discussion of work from the early part of the period; his discussions of Kyd and Shakespeare still have much that is perceptive and suggestive to offer. Toward the end of his life, Bowers published *Hamlet as Minister and Scourge and Other Studies in Shakespeare and Milton*, a gathering of previously published critical essays. In date they range from 1955 to 1982. There are six essays on *Hamlet*, one on *King Lear* ("The Structure of King Lear"), and one on

Henry IV ("Theme and Structure in King Henry IV, Part I"); there are four on more general Shakespearean themes ("Death in Victory: Shakespeare's Tragic Reconciliations," "Climax and Protagonist in Shakespeare's Dramatic Structure," "Shakespeare's Art: The Point of View," and "Shakespeare's Dramatic Vagueness"); there is only one essay on a non-Shakespearean subject, "Milton's *Samson Agonistes*: Justice and Reconciliation." It will be noted with what frequency the word "structure" appears in these titles – the essays on *Hamlet*, indeed, include "Dramatic Structure and Criticism: Plot in Hamlet." In a sense most of these essays can be seen as a coherent and consistent development of possibilities inherent in *Elizabethan Revenge Tragedy*, sharing as they do a central perception that in great drama structure is the resolution of ethical dilemmas. As the reader of Bowers' bibliographical and textual work would expect, his critical essays are always rigorous in their logic and precise in their definitions of terms (such a reader, it has to be said, might also have expected the occasional clumsinesses of syntax and obfuscations of expression which Bowers is, here as elsewhere, prone to). The title essay of the collection was first published in 1955 and exerted a considerable influence on critical thinking about the play, with its acute and informed analysis of Hamlet's moral predicament (and *his* analysis of that predicament) through a learned and perceptive examination of Hamlet's application to himself of the terms "scourge" and "minister."

The range of Bowers' work encompasses the quasi-scientific rigor of the *Principles of Bibliographical Description* and the traditionally humanist criticism of his best essays on *Hamlet*. What it all shares, however, is a concern for exactness and a steadfast refusal of the merely impressionistic, a capacity for sustained argument, and a passionate conviction that literature matters.

Principal criticism

Elizabethan Revenge Tragedy, 1587–1642, 1940
Principles of Bibliographical Description, 1949
On Editing Shakespeare and the Elizabethan Dramatists, 1955
Textual and Literary Criticism, 1959
The Bibliographical Way, 1959
Bibliography and Textual Criticism, 1964
Hamlet: An Outline Guide to the Play, 1965
Essays in Bibliography, Text, and Editing, 1975
Hamlet as Minister and Scourge and Other Studies in Shakespeare and Milton, 1989

Other major works and literary forms

Fredson Bowers' output as an editor was prodigious. He was responsible for scrupulously prepared editions of, amongst others, the dramatic works of Thomas Dekker (4 volumes), the works of Nathaniel Hawthorne (20 volumes), Stephen Crane (10 volumes), and William James (19 volumes), and Vladimir Nabokov's lectures (3 volumes). He also published on his chief nonacademic interests, including dogs (his *Dog Owner's Handbook* first appeared in 1936 and was reprinted in 1940), music, and stamps.

Further reading

Battestin, Martin C. "Fredson Thayers Bowers: A Checklist and Chronology," in *Studies in Bibliography*. 46 (1993), pp. 155–186.
McGann, Jerome J. *A Critique of Modern Textual Criticism*, 1983.
Parker, Hershel. *Flawed Texts and Verbal Icons*, 1984.
Tanselle, G. Thomas. "The Achievement of Fredson Bowers," in *Papers of the Bibliographical Society of America*. 79 (1985), pp. 175–190.
——. "The Life and Work of Fredson Bowers," in *Studies in Bibliography*. 46 (1993), pp. 1–154.
Thorpe, James. *Principles of Textual Criticism*, 1972.
Vander Meulen, David L. "The History and Future of Bowers' *Principles*," in *Papers of the Bibliographical Society of America*. 79 (1985), pp. 197–219.
——. "Fredson Bowers and the Editing of *Studies in Bibliography*," in *Text*. 8 (1995), pp. 31–36.

GLYN PURSGLOVE

See also Bateson; McGann

Malcolm Bradbury

English novelist and critic

Born: Sheffield, England; September 7, 1932

Biography

Malcolm Bradbury was born in the industrial city of Sheffield, in northern England, and was raised largely in Nottingham where his family moved during World War II. Bradbury's interest in books was facilitated by a heart condition that greatly limited his physical activity and that went uncorrected until he was twenty-seven. It was also facilitated by the example of D. H. Lawrence, the son of a Nottinghamshire coal miner; and by the Butler Education Act which opened academic doors that otherwise would have been closed to the son of a railroad booking clerk. Bradbury excelled academically, at the local grammar school, at the University of Leicester, where he began writing his first novel, *Eating People Is Wrong* (1959), and at Indiana University, where as a graduate student in the 1950s he first became fascinated by the idea and reality of America, including its peculiar mix of freedom and repression (McCarthyism). Upon completion of his Ph.D. at the University of Manchester and his marriage in 1959, Bradbury decided to settle in England. He held brief appointments at the universities of Hull and Birmingham; it was at the latter that he and fellow critic and novelist David Lodge began their close and, professionally speaking, mutually advantageous friendship. In 1967 he joined the American Studies faculty at the University of East Anglia.

There he and Angus Wilson founded what soon became Britain's most prestigious writing program, which he directed until his retirement in 1995 and whose graduates include two winners of the Booker Prize, Kazuo Ishiguro and Ian McEwan. Important as his work as a critic is, Bradbury is equally well known as a novelist, a witty and gently satirical master of that distinctly English form, the campus novel. Following the success of Christopher Hampton's television adaptation of *The History Man*, Bradbury began writing teleplays of his own: two *Gravy Train* series on the European Market, adaptations of John Fowles' "The Enigma," and two Tom Sharpe novels. His adaptations of Sharpe's *Porterhouse Blue* for television and Stella Gibbons' *Cold Comfort Farm* for screen were especially well received. He was awarded the CBE (Commander of the Order of the British Empire) in 1991.

Influence

The influence of others on Bradbury's work is fairly easy to determine: D. H. Lawrence, Kingsley Amis, and Angus Wilson (among novelists) and F. R. Leavis and Lionel Trilling (among critics). Bradbury's influence on others is a bit trickier to determine. One reason it is so tricky is that his influence has been as varied as Bradbury has been prolific. Another is that he has so quietly (but persistently) exerted his influence in so many ways – as professor, writing teacher, campus novelist, humorist, social satirist, adapter, script writer, literary judge, editor, reviewer, consultant, and widely traveled British Council lecturer – that he has become, in effect, a postmodern version of that seemingly extinct species, the man-of-letters. To say that he is more prolific than profound is in no way to slight either his importance or his influence and formidable achievement as a passionate advocate of the Leavis–Trilling liberal humanist line of the Great Tradition and the Liberal Imagination. "Openness of sympathy," Bradbury has professed, "is the only real justification for criticism's existence." That openness is amply evident in Bradbury's liberal humanist faith in pluralism of all kinds, critical as well as cultural; thus, for example, the wide diversity of authors and their viewpoints included in his often cited 1977 anthology *The Novel Today*: Iris Murdoch, Philip Roth, Michel Butor, Saul Bellow, John Barth, David Lodge, Frank Kermode, John Fowles, B. S. Johnson, Doris Lessing, Philip Stevick, and Gerald Graff. It also manifests itself in his interest in the literary text as a verbal construct that exists in a specific historical and cultural context, in his catholicity of taste and enormous generosity in assessing the work of other critics and novelists, and above all in his serving as a bridge between the Leavisite ethical approach and subsequent critical theories and narrative practices for which Bradbury has played the role of informed and intelligent, often sympathetic but nonetheless somewhat skeptical guide. Nowhere has Bradbury's advocacy and understanding of the new been more evident or salutary than in his chairmanship of the committee that awarded Salman Rushdie the Booker Prize for *Midnight's Children* (1981), a novel that Bradbury rightly saw would change British fiction both for good and for the better. Yet Bradbury has been equally appreciative of a writer as "formally and philosophically conservative" as Saul Bellow. Persistent rather than flamboyant, Bradbury has performed a kind of missionary work, proselytizing for both the importance of the modern novel and for a certain way of assessing that importance. Eschewing polemics, he has promoted his position through quiet pertinacity, perhaps least obviously but most influentially in those broad, well-informed but otherwise seemingly innocuous surveys of *The Modern American Novel* (1984, revised 1992) and *The Modern British Novel* (1993) that have become indispensable guides to their subjects and points of departure for all further studies.

Analysis

Bradbury's earliest critical studies were all introductory guides: a pamphlet on Evelyn Waugh (1964); a brief study, *What Is a Novel?* (1969), which grew out of an undergraduate course he taught at the University of Birmingham; and *The Social Context of Modern English Literature* (1971). His first important critical work, *Possibilities*, appeared two years later. Its title acknowledges Bradbury's debt to Leavis, who believed that the purpose of fiction is to generate a full "awareness of the possibilities of life." Although in a sense little more than a collection of previously published essays, *Possibilities* nonetheless possesses a consistency of method and perspective that makes Bradbury's otherwise scattershot history of the English novel from its beginnings to the present seem a surprisingly coherent work. The very fact that the collection's epigraph is taken from Henry James' famous essay "The Future of the Novel" implies Bradbury's enormous faith in the novel as a necessary as well as resilient form and its relation to life, which he espoused even as others were loudly declaring the death of the novel, especially the English novel, and the death of the author. This faith – in essence, a faith in the realistic novel – has been tested (but not, Bradbury claims, bested) by three developments. One is the modernist view of the author as autonomous creator rather than socially responsible and responsive reflector of his or her world. Another is the more recent contention that the history upon which realism and the realistic novel depend is itself every bit as much a human construct as the modernist novel – that history is itself a fiction. And the third is the position so persuasively argued by Bernard Bergonzi in *The Situation of the Novel* (1970), that the English novel is, quite simply, "no longer novel" – that the energy so evident in recent American and French fiction is altogether absent from contemporary English fiction and therefore proof that realism and the liberal humanist tradition from which it derives have become "formally routine and philosophically discredited." While Bradbury's defense of realism seems rather weak in the face of "the deepening distrust of both history and progressivism," *Possibilities* is noteworthy not as part of what in 1967 Rubin Rabinowitz called "the reaction against experiment in the English novel," but as an effort to understand the challenge to realism and therefore the liberal imagination while remaining committed to "the social and moral tradition of the English novel" in these changed and changing times. The goal, Bradbury believes, should be neither to be realistic in the conventional but now outmoded sense nor to transcend realism altogether but to find a way "to make realism and fictiveness coexist." This was a possibility that the Neo-Aristotelian Bradbury believed could be achieved – an achievement that would avoid having to reduce the novel, and criticism of the novel, to matters of style (as he felt his friend David Lodge had done in his 1966 study *The Language of Fiction*). Realism and fictiveness could coexist precisely because the novel is an "open form," albeit one rooted in character, plot, and questions of values.

Bradbury's second collection, *No, Not Bloomsbury* (1987), takes its title from a novel that had a profoundly liberating effect on writers of Bradbury's generation, Kingsley Amis' *Lucky Jim* (1954), a comic skewering of the staid English academic establishment which appeared at a time of enormous challenges to the social as well as literary status quo. Divided into four parts – "Writer and Critic," "Decades and Seasons," "Contemporary Writers," and "Celebrating the Occasion" – *No, Not Bloomsbury* gives the illusion of being more of a coherent whole than it actually is. In its own more random fashion, *No, Not Bloomsbury* attests Bradbury's continuing faith in the principles set forth in *Possibilities*, but principles now rethought and where necessary revised in the light of changes in the British literary climate over the intervening decade and a half. The most important themes or concerns to emerge from *No, Not Bloomsbury* are the following three. One, that while Bradbury's earlier faith in the possibilities for the British novel following a period of parochial reaction against experiment have been fully justified, much of the criticism written about "this vital period of British writing" has been "thin and patronising." Two, that literature in general and the novel in particular are now decidedly international phenomena and that nowhere is this fact more evident than in Britain where the novels of two generations of Amises, father Kingsley and son Martin, coexist with the culturally hybridized fictions and postcolonial imaginary homelands of a new and more complexly British kind of fiction by Salman Rushdie, Kazuo Ishiguro, Timothy Mo, and others. (As chair of the committee that awarded the Booker Prize to Rushdie for *Midnight's Children*, Bradbury was among the first to acknowledge not only the book's literary excellence but its marking an important and exciting turning point in the history of what had been previously and rather chauvinistically called "the English novel.") Three, and arguably most important to Bradbury's overall faith in the social importance of his chosen literary form, there is the expression of deep concern over the fate of the British novel in "an age of challenged humanism."

Admittedly, the essays on "contemporary writers" from Ivy Compton-Burnett and Evelyn Waugh through Iris Murdoch and John Fowles which take up fully half of *No, Not Bloomsbury*'s pages merely recycle the main themes from *Possibilities*, often on precisely the same terms and in the same language. Indeed, the one on Muriel Sparks recycles the very same essay. On the one hand, Bradbury's acknowledgment that F. R. Leavis was the strongest influence on him during his early years tells the reader nothing the reader could not have surmised from reading *Possibilities*. On the other hand, Bradbury's description of Leavis and his literary magazine *Scrutiny*'s "apocalyptic concerns and missionary passion" does illuminate the pronounced Arnoldian quality of Bradbury's own writing: the religion of culture which Arnold helped usher in and to which Leavis gave added urgency, an urgency that informs the work of critics of the next generation otherwise as different as Bradbury and Lodge in Britain and John Gardner in the United States. The strength and importance of *No, Not Bloomsbury* lies not in the restatement of earlier positions, however; nor does it lie in Bradbury's characteristically generous assessments of other, especially younger writers. It lies instead in two lengthy essays from the collection's opening section that were originally published in 1978–1979 and 1980, respectively. Although neither is especially original, both are as insightful as they are informed. The starting point for "'A Dog Engulfed by Sand': Character and Abstraction in Contemporary Writing and Painting" is one of Francisco Goya's "strangely abstract" "black paintings" and its relevance to "the problem, in a modern work, of putting in the person." In the painting, the figure (if it is a figure) of a dog (if it is a dog) appears to be in the process of either being engulfed in sand (if it is sand) or struggling successfully to extricate itself from its predicament, from being swallowed up. In this ambiguous scene Bradbury finds the precursor of the condition of, and the depiction of, the modern and postmodern arts in an age of challenged humanism. Drawing on a wide array of views of the contemporary arts, from Roland Barthes' "writing degree zero" to José Ortega y Gasset's "dehumanization of art," Bradbury explores modern art's (especially the modern novel's) "questioning of realism and its relation to the dissolution of character" and ways of representing the human figure in contemporary works in which "the displacement of the person may produce an intensification of form, a new pre-eminence for the text as discourse." One would expect that as a committed liberal humanist in the Leavisite mold Bradbury would deplore (as many others have) this process of displacement and dehumanization. However, rather than deplore and dismiss it out of hand, Bradbury tries to explore and understand it, in terms of its origins, practices, and above all consequences, and to do so both in his criticism and his fiction, *The History Man* (1975) in particular. As Bradbury, ever the literary historian, points out, the sense of a "capacious sense of character" was largely an invention of the mid-nineteenth century (and the mid-nineteenth-century novel). It began to break up long before the modernist and postmodern assaults, with the "double movement away from realism – toward naturalism and impressionism in the late nineteenth century." What Bradbury deplores, therefore, is not an art which has unwisely abandoned interest in the human figure and in the realism upon which the modern sense of literary and psychological character rests. What he deplores is a modern condition that makes the "forms of abstraction" – the weakened characters, the uncertain plots, the hard edges, the troubled images – all-too-accurate reflections of the dehumanized and dehumanizing way we live now. In this art, as in Goya's painting, Bradbury detects not surrender on the part of writers and artists but struggle as well as "a mood of tragic irony," and with it a "power, in the conflict between subject and form, to bring into being a sense of the strangled victim."

In "An Age of Parody: Style in the Modern Arts" (1980) Bradbury explores at length one of the central points made in "'A Dog Engulfed by Sand,'" that in many contemporary works "realism itself feels like a quotation." An age of challenged humanism is also necessarily an age of parody and of Superculture. The Superculture that seems to offer plenitude and a golden age of human universality is simultaneously haunted by a sense of emptiness, "a want of significance." In an age and art of Superculture, "Nothing seemed absent, everything seemed present, and nothing seemed there." Rather than dismissing parody as a sign of the trivializing, debunking times and the empty theatricalizing of contemporary life, or lifestyle, and style itself as nothing more than slick collage, Bradbury views parody as neither trivializing nor deconstructing but as "a form of enquiry for disorienting but also innovative times." Having made that point, however, Bradbury ends his own "enquiry" with the kind of facile remark for which he has often been faulted: "And parody is not simply a crisis of language, but a major form of creative play and artistic self-discovery which can give us a joyously experimental and comic art." It is a fault that derives less from any superficiality on Bradbury's part than from a willed optimism designed to offset the elegiac quality of a latter-day Leavisite adrift in a postmodern world he finds at once liberating and dismaying.

Bradbury's long-standing interest in the United States and its literature is especially evident in some of his most recent books: the revised edition of *The Modern American Novel* (1992), *From Puritanism to Postmodernism* (coauthored with Richard Ruland, 1992), and *Dangerous Pilgrimages* (1995). The latter brings together the many essays Bradbury has published over the years on the "highly ambiguous" literary trade, with its intriguing "mythic surplus," between England and America.

Principal criticism

Evelyn Waugh, 1964
What Is a Novel?, 1969
The Social Context of Modern English Literature, 1971
Possibilities: Essays on the State of the Novel, 1973
Saul Bellow, 1982
The Modern American Novel, 1984, revised 1992
No, Not Bloomsbury, 1987
The Modern World: Ten Great Writers, 1988
From Puritanism to Postmodernism: A History of American Literature, 1992 (with Richard Ruland)
The Modern British Novel, 1993
Dangerous Pilgrimages: Trans-Atlantic Mythologies and the Novel, 1995

Other major works and literary forms

Malcolm Bradbury's formidable reputation as a literary critic is matched by his reputation as a novelist: *Eating People Is Wrong* (1959), *Stepping Westward* (1965), *The History Man* (1975), *Rates of Exchange* (1983), *Cuts: A Very Short Novel* (1987), and *Doctor Criminale* (1992). Indeed, the fiction often reflects Bradbury's interest in critical theory, poststructuralism in particular in *Doctor Criminale* and the much shorter but equally funny *My Quest for Mensonge* (1987). The prolific Bradbury has also published poetry (*Two Poets*, 1996, with Allan Rodway), plays (*The After Dinner Game*, 1982), short stories and parodies (*Who Do You Think You Are?*, 1984, 1987), humor (*Phogey! How To Have Class in a Classless Society*, 1960, *All Dressed Up and Nowhere To Go*, 1962, *Why Come to Slaka?*, 1986, and *Unsent Letters: Irreverent Notes from a Literary Life*, 1987). He has written screenplays and teleplays and has edited numerous works, including *Modernism 1890–1930* (1976, with James McFarlane), *The Novel Today* (1977), *Introduction to American Studies* (1981, with Howard Temperley), *The Penguin Book of Modern British Short Stories* (1987), and *New Writing* (1992, with Judy Cooke).

Further reading

Boylan, Clare, ed. *The Art and Strategy of Fiction Writing Explored*, 1993.
Gray, Nigel. *Writers Talking*, 1989.
Haffenden, John. *Novelists in Interview*, 1985.
Lodge, David. *The Novelist at the Crossroads and Other Essays on Fiction and Criticism*, 1971.
Morace, Robert A. *The Dialogic Novels of Malcolm Bradbury and David Lodge*, 1989.
Widdowson, Peter. "The Anti-History Men: Malcolm Bradbury and David Lodge," in *Critical Quarterly*. 26 (1984), pp. 5–32.
Ziegler, Heide, and Christopher Bigsby, eds. *The Radical Imagination and the Liberal Tradition*, 1982.

ROBERT A. MORACE

See also British Literary Theory: Twentieth Century; Kermode; Lodge; Ricks

A. C. Bradley

English critic

Born: Cheltenham, England; March 26, 1851
Died: London, England; September 2, 1935

Biography

Andrew Cecil Bradley was the son of the Rev. Charles Bradley (1789–1871), an evangelical clergyman and autocratic father of twenty-two children by his two wives, and the younger brother of the philosopher F. H. Bradley (1846–1924). He was educated at Cheltenham College from 1864, before entering Balliol College, Oxford, in 1868. He was made a Fellow of Balliol in 1874 and in 1875 he won the chancellor's English essay prize for an essay on "Utopias, Ancient and Modern." He was a lecturer and tutor at Balliol from 1876 to 1881. In Oxford a major influence was Thomas Hill Green, the Idealist philosopher. Bradley left Balliol under circumstances which are not entirely clear, and held the post of professor of modern literature at University College, Liverpool (as it was then), from 1881 to 1889. From 1889 to 1900 he was professor of English language and literature at the University of Glasgow, where Gilbert Murray was a friend and contemporary. On leaving Glasgow he moved to London, continuing to live there while he held the post of professor of poetry at Oxford from 1901 to 1906. In 1907 he turned down the appointment to a chair at Cambridge; in 1910 he became a Fellow of the Royal Society of Literature. In 1911 he became president of the English Association. For one whose intellectual sympathies were thoroughly Germanophile, World War I was particularly disturbing and disorientating. Never particularly robust, Bradley's health became increasingly poor and a severe bout of pneumonia in 1923 seems largely to have ended his productive life.

Influence

Bradley's most substantial achievement as a critic, and his most influential work, is undoubtedly to be found in his *Shakespearean Tragedy*, ten lectures adapted from "materials used in teaching at Liverpool, Glasgow and Oxford" (to borrow the phrasing of Bradley's own Preface) and first published in 1904. Ever since its publication Bradley's *Shakespearean Tragedy* has occupied a central place in the traditions of Shakespearean criticism – a centrality implicitly recognized even by those who have most vehemently attacked it. Indeed, it is a book which has attracted extremes of both praise and denigration. For John Middleton Murry it is "surely the greatest single work of criticism in the English language" (*Katherine Mansfield and Other Literary Portraits*, 1949); D. J. Palmer places the volume "in that surprisingly small collection of Shakespeare criticism which however diverse in its assumptions is by general agreement authoritative," adding that "Bradley joins the immortals on the strength of this one book." For F. R. Leavis, on the other hand, Bradley's work was characterized by its "misdirected scrupulosity," its "comical solemnity," and its "triumphal sentimental perversity." L. B. Campbell judged that Bradley had "frequently concerned himself with problems that were irrelevant or ignored the significance of evidence important to the tracing of the moral pattern in the plays, to which tasks he had set himself." Those who dislike Bradley's work tend to complain of his insufficient appreciation of the theatricality of the plays and of his excessive speculation on character, sometimes conducted in ways which seem to treat the figures of the plays as though they were real human beings rather than dramatic constructs. Such complaints reached their height in the 1930s, in part because Bradley came to serve as a convenient exemplar of what was then seen as an outdated mode of criticism; later years, however, have seen a reevaluation of Bradley's work and the widespread recognition that *Shakespearean Tragedy* is, in the words of G. K. Hunter, "one of the classics of English criticism." (Katharine Cooke provides a general account of Bradley's influence.)

It is, though, not only Bradley's work on William Shakespeare which retains its interest. His commentary (1901) on Alfred, Lord Tennyson's *In Memoriam* is still one of the best guides to the poem, perceptive and thought-provoking in its discussion of, *inter alia*, the poem's texture of literary allusion and subtleties of meter. His *Oxford Lectures on Poetry* (1909) contain work on, amongst others, William Wordsworth and Percy Bysshe Shelley, which still has much to offer (as well as the important Shakespearean lectures on "The Rejection of Falstaff" and "Shakespeare's *Antony and Cleopatra*"), and though the material gathered in *A Miscellany* (1929) is more variable in quality, at least one essay, "English Poetry and German Philosophy in the Age of Wordsworth," offers valuable hints as to the nature of Bradley's own thinking and its significance.

In many ways Bradley can be seen as a kind of bridge between the German-influenced Romantic criticism of Samuel Taylor Coleridge, on the one hand, and the beginnings of modern criticism on the other. His own work registers the influence of Coleridge, Auguste Wilhelm Schlegel, Johann Christoph Friedrich von Schiller, and Eduard von Hartmann; but it is not merely retrospective in nature. The reader of Bradley encounters in his pages much that is, as it were, anticipatory. René Wellek observes that "Bradley stands behind John Middleton Murry, whose book on *Keats and Shakespeare* (1925) is inconceivable without Bradley's conception of both Shakespeare and Keats" and goes on to point out that "[G.] Wilson Knight came from Middleton Murry." Indeed Wilson Knight himself recognized his indebtedness to Bradley in a prefatory note to his *The Wheel of Fire* (1930). And if Bradley's analysis of character belongs in a nineteenth-century tradition, his acuteness often leads him in directions which are decidedly twentieth-century.

When he locates the cause of Hamlet's irresolution in an extreme melancholic condition caused by "the moral shock of the sudden ghastly disclosure of his mother's true nature" we are approaching ways of looking at *Hamlet* which we associate with Sigmund Freud and T. S. Eliot rather than Coleridge and F. W. J. Schelling.

Analysis

Fundamental to any understanding of Bradley's achievement as a critic is an appreciation of his early training in philosophy. Much that characterizes his approach can be traced to the influence of his years as a disciple of the British philosopher Thomas Hill Green (late in life Bradley was to say that Green had "saved his soul," and he was one of Green's close circle of admirers), through whom were mediated the examples of G. W. F. Hegel and Immanuel Kant. Such influences, as reinterpreted by Green, are everywhere evident in Bradley's 1907 Gifford Lectures, posthumously published as *Ideals of Religion* (1940). Their mark is equally clear in Bradley's literary criticism. A lecture of 1901 (printed in *Oxford Lectures on Poetry*), "Hegel's Theory of Tragedy," makes clear how powerfully formative an influence Hegel exerted on Bradley's own thinking. Following the example of Hegel, he locates the distinctive nature of tragedy in its presentation of conflict, a conflict which "appeals to the spirit [because] it is itself a conflict of the spirit. It is a conflict, that is to say, between powers that rule the world of man's will and action – his 'ethical substance.'" He paraphrases Hegel to the effect that "[i]t is the nature of the tragic hero, at once his greatness and his doom, that he knows no shrinking or half-heartedness, but identifies himself wholly with the power that moves him, and will admit the justification of no other power." The echo of such ideas is clear when, in *Shakespearean Tragedy*, we find Bradley writing of Shakespeare's tragic heroes that "[i]n almost all we observe a marked one-sidedness, a predisposition in some particular direction; a total incapacity, in certain circumstances, of resisting the force which draws in this direction; a fatal tendency to identify the whole being with one interest, object, passion, or habit of mind. This, it would seem, is for Shakespeare, the fundamental tragic trait." Given Bradley's grounding in nineteenth-century Monism, it is not surprising that he should insist that "[e]vil exhibits itself everywhere as something negative, barren, weakening, destructive, a principle of death. It isolates, disunites, and tends to annihilate not only its opposite but itself." But Bradley resists any simple antitheses of "good" and "evil" in his exposition of what he perceives to be the nature of Shakespearean tragedy; at its heart he finds the presentation of a "mystery" – "We remain confronted with the inexplicable fact, or the no less inexplicable appearance, of a world travailing for perfection, but bringing to birth, together with glorious good, an evil which it is able to overcome only by self-torture and self-waste, and this fact or appearance is tragedy."

Bradley's consequent emphasis on the meticulous examination of the moral life of Shakespeare's characters implicitly risks reading Shakespeare's plays as primarily constituting biographies or psychological profiles of their leading characters. Bradley has more than once been accused of applying to Shakespeare methods of reading and discussion better suited to the nineteenth-century novel. On the whole, such charges do not convince. Even if his answers to such questions as "Where was Hamlet at the time of his father's death?" or "When was the murder of Duncan first plotted?" now seem to us insufficiently conditioned by an awareness of dramatic and theatrical convention, and too keen to lock the "seen" events of the play into a plausible narrative of his own invention, it is absurd to talk of Bradley as though his work belonged with Mrs. Cowden Clarke's *The Girlhood of Shakespeare's Heroines* (1851–1852). Bradley's analysis of character has an intelligence and (generally) an avoidance both of inappropriate sophistication and of trivial irrelevance that enable the perception of moral and poetic significances as part of a genuine, imaginative response to Shakespeare's text. Bradley's purpose was (to quote the Introduction to *Shakespearean Tragedy*) "to learn to apprehend the action and some of the personages of each [play] with a somewhat greater truth and intensity, so that they may assume in our imaginations a shape a little less unlike the shape they wore in the imagination of their creator." This echoes a proposition Bradley made as early as 1884 (in *The Study of Poetry*) when he wrote that "we should study [poetry] in order to reproduce in ourselves more faintly that which went on in the poet's mind when he wrote."

Bradley talks mainly of "readers" of Shakespeare but this is not because he was without an interest in questions of performance – see, for example, his essay "The Locality of *King Lear* Act I scene ii" (1909) or the note on "The staging of the Scene of Lear's reunion with Cordelia" in *Shakespearean Tragedy*; indeed, he had no hesitation in declaring that "Shakespeare wrote primarily for the theatre and not for students." The work of readers is to "read a play more or less as if they were actors who had to study all the parts. They do not need, of course, to imagine whereabouts the persons are to stand, or what gestures they ought to use; but they want to realise fully and exactly the inner movements which produced these words and no other, at each particular moment. This, carried through a drama, is the right way to read the dramatist Shakespeare; and the prime requisite here is therefore a vivid and intent imagination. But this alone will hardly suffice. It is necessary also, especially to a true conception of the whole, to compare, to analyse, to dissect."

Bradley was heir to a high romantic belief in the importance and power of the imagination; to read poetry is to exercise a faculty central to a person's moral and social nature: "When a man is indifferent to the necessities of those below him, when he is unkind and selfish to those about him, even, when he commits a crime, the reason is often – nay, commonly – not that his heart is unusually hard but that he does not know what he is doing. His imagination does not act" (*The Study of Poetry*). The moral imagination is developed in the reading of poetry – "A man who has once seen the hideousness of ingratitude in *King Lear* . . . has a better chance than he had before of checking the beginnings of such things in himself" (*ibid*). His lectures on Shelley serve to endorse Shelley's proposition that "A man to be greatly good must imagine intensely and comprehensively." He values both Wordsworth and Hegel – and argues for a relationship between the two – because, in part, of their attitudes toward the imagination; he writes that "Wordsworth's doctrine, if we may use the word, is that imagination is the way to truth. By imagination he does not mean mere fancy, but a transference of the mind into the centre of the thing contemplated, and a construing of all its motions or actions from that centre outwards. Hegel would have insisted that no interpretation that is drenched with the colours of imagination can be the *final* form of truth, though he would have agreed with Wordsworth that such an interpretation may contain much more truth than a mechanical view which denies any 'active principle' and would convert Nature into 'a universe of death.'"

Far from making the naive confusion of art and reality of which he has often been accused, Bradley sees poetry's nature as "to be not a part, nor yet a copy, of the real world (as we commonly understand that phrase), but to be a world by itself, independent, complete, autonomous; and to possess it fully you must enter that world, conform to its laws, and ignore for the time the beliefs, aims and particular conditions which belong to you in the other world of reality." Life and poetry "are parallel developments which nowhere meet"; poetry "speaks only to contemplative imagination" and "the test of its poetic value for us lies simply in the question whether it satisfies our imagination." The more successful the poem, the more absolute the identity of form and content, "and the degree of purity attained may be tested by the degree in which we feel it hopeless to convey the effect of a poem or passage in any form but its own." These are not, of course, ideas unique to Bradley. But the rigorous clarity with which they are explored and the lucidity with which he articulates the results of that exploration distinguish Bradley's work as a critic, as does the constant interplay between his observations on specific poems or plays and his construction of larger syntheses. His critical work is, at its best, an eloquent elucidation of his claim (in his *Oxford Lectures on Poetry*) that "Poetry does not present to imagination our highest knowledge or belief, and much less our dreams and opinions; but it, content and form in unity, embodies in its own irreplaceable way something which embodies itself also in other irreplaceable ways, such as philosophy or religion."

Principal criticism

The Study of Poetry: A Lecture, 1884
Poetry and Life, 1889
A Commentary on Tennyson's "In Memoriam," 1901
Shakespearean Tragedy, 1904
"The Locality of *King Lear* Act I scene ii," in *Modern Language Review*. 4, (1909), pp. 238–240
Oxford Lectures on Poetry, 1909
The Uses of Poetry, 1912
Coriolanus, 1912
A Miscellany, 1929

Other major works and literary forms

A. C. Bradley edited T. H. Green's *Prologomena to Ethics* (1883), the *Philosophical Lectures and Remains of R. L. Nettleship* (1897, with G. R. Benson), and *New and Old: Literary Remains of Edith Sichel* (1917). In 1885 he published a translation of Book III of *Metaphysic* by Hermann Lotze. His Gifford Lectures, given at the University of Glasgow in 1907, were published posthumously in 1940 as *The Ideals of Religion*, in a text edited by his sister, Mrs. Ernest von Glehn.

Further reading

Blish, Mary. *Principles and Method in the Non-Shakespearean Literary Criticism of Andrew Cecil Bradley*, 1967 (unpublished dissertation).
Cooke, Katharine. *A. C. Bradley and his Influence in Twentieth-Century Shakespeare Criticism*, 1972.
Gauntlett, Mark. "The Perishable Poetry of the Unpoetical: A. C. Bradley Performs Othello," in *Shakespeare Survey*. 47 (1994), pp. 71–80.
Hunter, G. K. "Bradley's Shakespearean Tragedy," in *Essays and Studies*. 21 (1968), pp. 101–117.
Knights, L. C. *How Many Children Had Lady Macbeth? An Essay in the Theory and Practice of Shakespeare Criticism*, 1933.
Leavis, F. R. "Diabolic Intellect and the Noble Hero: or the Sentimentalist's Othello," in *Scrutiny*. 6 (1937), pp. 259–283.
Page, Adrian. "Is there a Method in his Theory? A. C. Bradley and Contemporary Criticism," in *The British Critical Tradition: A Re-evaluation*, 1993. Edited by Gary Day.
Wellek, René. "A. C. Bradley, Shakespeare, and the Infinite," in *Philological Quarterly*. 54 (1975), pp. 85–103.

GLYN PURSGLOVE

See also British Literary Theory: Twentieth Century; Knights

Bertolt Brecht

German playwright and critic

Born: Augsburg, Germany; February 10, 1898
Died: East Berlin, East Germany; August 14, 1956

Biography

Bertolt Brecht was born Eugen Berthold Friedrich Brecht on February 10, 1898, in the Bavarian town of Augsburg, where his father was an executive in a paper company. He attended primary and secondary school in Augsburg and, in 1917, matriculated at the University of Munich as a medical student. Rather than pursue his studies, Brecht devoted most of his time to reading literature, attending the theater, playing the guitar, and writing theater reviews; he never earned a degree. He was married to Marianne Zoff from 1922 to 1927. They had one daughter, Hanne, born in 1923; she became an actress under the name of Hanne Hiob. In 1929 Brecht married the famous Austrian actress Helene Weigel. They had two children: Stefan, born in 1924, who became a freelance writer, artist, and actor, and Barbara, born in 1930, who became a well-known actress with the Berliner Ensemble.

In the early 1920s Brecht worked in Munich, writing and staging his own plays as well as directing adaptations of famous classical plays. From the mid-1920s until 1933 he continued his work in Berlin, often in collaboration with the two most famous men of the theater of that time, Max Reinhardt and Erwin Piscator. During those years he devoted considerable time to the study of Marxist philosophy.

When Adolf Hitler came to power in 1933, Brecht's fifteen years in exile began. He lived in Denmark, Sweden, and Finland before he came to the United States in 1941. Living in Santa Monica, California, Brecht worked in the film industry while continuing his writing. The day following an appearance before the infamous United States House Committee on Un-American Activities in October, 1947, Brecht left the United States.

After a very successful year in Zurich, Switzerland, Brecht took up permanent residence in East Berlin. In 1949 he established, together with Helene Weigel, his own theater company – the Berliner Ensemble – for which he produced and wrote plays to conform with his philosophical views on theater. In 1954 he was given his own theater, Theater am Schiftbauerdamm, which continues to be the home of the Berliner Ensemble. During these years Brecht received many prizes and honors for his work. He died on August 14, 1956.

Influence

Since his death in 1956, Brecht has continued to be one of the most performed playwrights in Germany. His work is also performed frequently in most other countries of Europe. Even in the United States, Brecht's plays are often included in the repertoire of college and university theater companies. As a Marxist theoretician, Brecht has had a profound impact on the theater and the playwrights of Germany and other European countries. Collaborators from the Berliner Ensemble have done more than perform Brecht's work: some, such as Heiner Müller, have extended his concept and theory of the theater to the postmodern era. Elsewhere, theaters and playwrights have concentrated more on developing the didactic elements that Brecht firmly established for the modern and contemporary theater.

Analysis

In an obituary for Brecht written by an English theater critic on August 19, 1956, the playwright was described as the Shakespeare of the modern era. The article further suggested that "if one believed in the transmigration of souls, one could be tempted to think that he was Shakespeare reborn" and that through his work Brecht had created "a new style and school of theatre which today looks like [it is] saving the theatre from [a] threatening sterility." To be sure, that was not the opinion of the entire theater world. There were many who believed that he had debased and trivialized the theater with his plays and his theories. Fortunately, in the decades since his death, it has been possible to carry out a most extensive and judicious examination of all facets of Brecht's work and arrive at the conclusion that, indeed, Brecht has made a very considerable contribution to modern theater.

Brecht entered the German theater scene at a most propitious time. In the 1920s in the Weimar Republic, there existed a political atmosphere that made Socialism and Marxism attractive alternatives for many intellectuals. Furthermore, in the theater, as well as in all the other arts, a spirit of experimentation thrived. Although Brecht devoted his entire life and work to developing both the message and the medium, it is in the latter that he has had the most profound effect.

Brecht's principal theory evolves from his concept of the *Verfremdungseffekt*, or the *V-Effekt*, known in English as the "alienation effect" or the "A-effect." The A-effect was, most likely, derived from Brecht's reading and study of the German philosopher G. W. F. Hegel. The Hegelian notion of the dialectical process is that the "thesis," or something that is united and whole initially, becomes the "antithesis," which represents an opposite of that united whole, and yields to form the "synthesis," namely a new and higher form of the initial concept. In Brecht's theater, the A-effect takes the audience from its naive and sometimes incorrect perception of reality (thesis) and confronts it with an opposite, or "over-real," statement of that reality (antithesis) and thereby attains a stage in which the audience would see the truth of that reality (synthesis).

Brecht continued to develop his understanding of the dialectical process with his study of the German philosopher Karl Marx, the founder of modern Socialism and Communism. In *Das Kapital* (1867–1894; English translation 1886–1909), Marx presents his notion of dialectical materialism, a theory which sees social and economic change as the result of materialistic forces. His doctrine maintains that humans, by their economic needs, indirectly produce their own form of life, which leads to the development of classes within society. Inevitably, these classes are opposed to one another, and this conflict describes the historical process. Eventually, when the proletariat achieves power, the struggle will be resolved with the establishment of a classless society. The state, which until then will have been the oppressive tool of the ruling class, will wither away.

The theater which uses this special form of Marxist argumentation and the A-effect has a social responsibility. It is with this combination of functions that Brecht wanted to make his contribution to society and to the theater. In the decades since his death, however, Brecht's political views have become less important, while his views on the theater have had an ever-greater impact on dramatic literature and performance.

To implement the A-effect, Brecht needed a new theater. The old theater, which Brecht called the dramatic theater, failed because it emphasized the Aristotelian notion that the spectator is purged of fear and pity and, consequently, is rendered a harmless member of society. Any empathy the spectator had was totally spent while participating in the theatrical event. The new theater for Brecht was to be the epic theater. Here, the relationship between the spectator and the presentation on the stage was very different. In an essay from the mid-1930s, Brecht described the differences between the two types of theater:

> The dramatic theater's spectator says: Yes, I have felt like that too – Just like me – It's only natural – It'll never change – The sufferings of this man appal me, because they are inescapable – That's great art: it all seems the most obvious thing in the world – I weep when they weep, I laugh when they laugh.

> The epic theater's spectator says: I'd never have thought it – That's not the way – That's extraordinary, hardly believable – It's got to stop – The sufferings of this man appal me, because they are unnecessary – That's great art: nothing obvious in it – I laugh when they weep, I weep when they laugh.

Already in 1930, in his essay "The Modern Theatre Is the Epic Theatre," Brecht had drawn up a chart which illustrated the change of emphasis between the dramatic and the epic theater. This summary is the most important schema in the study of Brecht's understanding of the modern theater:

DRAMATIC THEATER	EPIC THEATER
plot	narrative
implicates the spectator in a stage situation	turns the spectator into an observer, but
wears down his capacity for action	arouses his capacity for action
provides him with sensations	forces him to take decisions
experience	picture of the world
the spectator is involved in something	he is made to face something
suggestion	argument
instinctive feelings are preserved	brought to the point of recognition
the spectator is in the thick of it, shares the experience	the spectator stands outside, studies
the human being is taken for granted	the human being is the object of the inquiry
he is unalterable	he is alterable and able to alter
eyes on the finish	eyes on the course
one scene makes another	each scene for itself
growth	montage
linear development	in curves
evolutionary determinism	jumps
man as a fixed point	man as a process
thought determines being	social being determines thought
feeling	reason

Certainly, not every play or performance will include all the elements of this statement. Furthermore, Brecht admits that the table does not set out to illustrate "absolute antithesis but [only] mere shifts of accent." It is important, however, to note the considerable change that Brecht suggests for the relationship between the theater performance and the role of the spectator. He insists that the audience must be involved intellectually and, at times, even physically in the theater event.

Brecht employed a host of theatrical devices to promote audience involvement. Not infrequently, he used very strong lighting of the stage to remind the spectators that they were simply witnesses to an event rather than emotional participants in something magical. On occasion, he went so far as to insist that the spotlights and floodlights be visible equipment on the stage.

In a variety of ways, Brecht developed techniques to break the emotional spell of dramatic theater. The action on the stage could be commented on by a narrator, by slide or film projections which might provide historical background information, by the use of signs or posters to announce the essence of the next scene or act, or by the use of curtains which were very low or almost transparent so as to allow the audience to see the actors and stagehands behind them.

In some performances, the actors appeared in extreme costumes and make-up. The use of stilts and extensive padding or hideous masks and unnatural facial make-up resulted in character images which would deny emotional association. Other costume devices might, for example, be melodramatic clichés which the spectator would recognize immediately. In the earlier plays, Brecht made a concerted effort to use nothing that might be in the slightest way beautiful, because he believed that as long as there was suffering in the world, it was mandatory that rational thought, not beauty or emotion, bring about necessary social changes.

Actors also used alienation in the epic theater. In the dramatic theater, which Brecht also referred to as the bourgeois theater, the actor would use Konstantin Stanislavsky's method of total self-identification with the part to be played. In the epic theater, however, just as the spectator was to maintain a critical distance from the performance, so the actor was to "show" rather than experience the character. This effect was accomplished in a variety of ways.

The actor, during rehearsals, might change the script in such a way that the speeches are transmitted in the third person, rather than the normal first person, or articulated in the past tense as they are performed. In addition, the actor could speak the various stage directions or might select to exchange parts with another actor. Brecht developed many practice texts for actors to use for training. One device was to have an actor play the part of two opposing characters in a play in order to understand fully the purpose that each has in the exposition of a conflict. Another device was to have the actor momentarily step out of the role being performed and use a different performance technique to illustrate the issue that had been articulated in a speech. This device results in a break of the image and leads to the consideration of the issue being articulated rather than the emotional association the spectator may have been developing with a particular character.

The clearest adaptation of the A-effect, however, can be seen in the structure and language of Brecht's plays. In numerous situations characters duplicate themselves in order to illustrate the extreme nature of different personality traits. In some plays, Brecht repeats the same narrative or situation or reenacts substantial portions of the play – an extended trial scene, for example. This second portrayal of events makes it possible to present an issue in past-tense time, allowing for more impartial examination.

One device seen frequently in all Brecht's plays is the song, the ballad, or some other poetic form. The purpose of this device is to interrupt the action of the narrative in order either to announce what will be performed subsequently or to give a summary of the events previously seen. The songs or ballads are often performed by some member of the cast who steps out of the role or by a special narrator who assures that no "fourth wall" is established in the theater.

The alienation effect, or the effect "which makes strange," does not require the use of any particular theatrical or poetic device, but it should always serve to bring about a more clearly defined apperceived reality. Brecht notes:

> The alienation effect occurs when the thing to be understood, the thing to which attention is to be drawn, is changed from an ordinary, well-known, immediately present thing into a particular, striking, unexpected thing. In a certain sense the self-evident is made incomprehensible, although this happens in order to make it all the more comprehensible.

The epic theater as developed by Brecht is a dynamic institution of teaching and learning. Some of its devices and techniques were already developed in medieval times and have been employed during other periods. Brecht's singular contribution to contemporary theater and playwriting has been to develop a new and unified theory of the theater of provocation and reason.

Principal criticism

"Das moderne Theater ist das epische Theater," 1930 ("The Modern Theatre Is the Epic Theatre," 1964)
"Literarisierung des Theaters," 1931 ("The Literarization of the Theatre," 1948)
"Über gestische Musik," written 1932, published 1957 ("On Gestic Music," 1964)
"Verfremdungseffekte in der chinesischen Schauspielkunst," written 1935, published 1949 ("Alienation Effects in Chinese Acting," 1936)
"Vergnügungstheater oder Lehrtheater?" written 1936, published 1957 ("Theatre for Pleasure or Theatre for Instruction?" 1958)
Der Messingkauf, 1937–1951 (*The Messingkauf Dialogues*, 1965)
"Die Strassenszene," written 1938, published 1950 ("The Street Scene," 1949)
"Anmerkungen zum Volksstück," written 1940, published 1950 ("Notes on the Folk Play," 1964)
"Kurze Beschreibung einer neuen Technik der Schauspielkunst," written 1940, published 1951 ("A Short Description of a New Technique of Acting," 1949)
Kleines Organon für das Theater, 1948 (*A Little Organum for the Theatre*, 1957).
The translations of essays listed above are available in *Brecht on Theatre: The Development of an Aesthetic* (1964), edited and translated by John Willett, and *The Messingkauf Dialogues*, also translated by John Willett.

Other major works and literary forms

In addition to the essays on theater, Bertolt Brecht used his own plays and many adaptations of plays by others to test his theories. There are also many notebooks and journals which he kept while preparing productions of his plays. These contain extensive commentary on acting, stage design, costuming, lighting, and – most important – ways in which the proper political attitude is created in the production of a play. There are even many poems that speak of specific aspects of theater production, for example, lighting, curtains, and the use of songs.

A new edition of Brecht's work was completed and published in 1998 in conjunction with the celebration of the one-hundredth anniversary of his birth, *Werke: Grosse kommentierte Berliner und Frankfurter Ausgabe*, 30 volumes, edited by Werner Hecht, Jan Knopf, Werner Mittenzwei, and Klaus-Detlef Müller. Brecht's entire œuvre has not been translated, but the most authoritative English edition available is *Collected Works of Bertolt Brecht: Plays, Poetry, and Prose*, 1964–1999, annotated and edited by John Willett and Ralph Manheim.

NOVELS
Der Dreigroschenroman, 1934 (*The Threepenny Novel*, 1937, 1956)
Die Geschäfte des Herrn Julius Caesar, 1956

SHORT FICTION
Geschichten vom Herrn Keuner, 1930, 1958
Kalendergeschichten, 1948 (*Tales from the Calendar*, 1961)

PLAYS

Baal, written 1918, published 1922 (English translation, 1963)
Trommeln in der Nacht, written 1918–1920, published 1922 (*Drums in the Night*, 1961)
Die Hochzeit, written 1919, published 1926 (also as *Die Kleinbürgerhochzeit*; *The Wedding*, 1970)
Im Dickicht der Städte, 1923 (*In the Jungle of Cities*, 1961)
Leben Eduards des Zweiten von England, 1924 (with Lion Feuchtwanger, based on Christopher Marlowe's play *Edward II*; *Edward II*, 1966)
Mann ist Mann, 1926 (*A Man's a Man*, 1961)
Das Elefantenkalb, 1926 (*The Elephant Calf*, 1961)
Die Dreigroschenoper, 1928 (libretto, based on John Gay's play *The Beggar's Opera*; *The Threepenny Opera*, 1949)
Aufstieg und Fall der Stadt Mahagonny, 1929 (libretto; *Rise and Fall of the City of Mahagonny*, 1957)
Das Badener Lehrstück vom Einverständnis, 1929 (*The Didactic Play of Baden: On Consent*, 1960)
Happy End, 1929 (lyrics with Elisabeth Hauptmann)
Der Ozeanflug, 1929 (radio play; *The Flight of the Lindberghs*, 1930)
Die Ausnahme und die Regel, written 1930, published 1937 (*The Exception and the Rule*, 1954)
Der Jasager, 1930 (based on the Japanese Nō play *Taniko*; *He Who Said Yes*, 1946)
Die Massnahme, 1930 (libretto; *The Measures Taken*, 1960)
Die heilige Johanna der Schlachthöfe, 1931 (*Saint Joan of the Stockyards*, 1956)
Der Neinsager, 1931 (*He Who Said No*, 1946)
Die Mutter, 1932 (based on Maxim Gorky's novel *Mat*; *The Mother*, 1965)
Die Sieben Todsünden der Kleinbürger, 1933 (cantata; *The Seven Deadly Sins*, 1961)
Die Horatier und die Kuriatier, written 1934, published 1938 (*The Horatians and the Curatians*, 1947)
Die Rundköpfe und die Spitzköpfe, 1935 (based on William Shakespeare's play *Measure for Measure*; *The Roundheads and the Peakheads*, 1937)
Die Gewehre der Frau Carrar, 1937 (*Señora Carrar's Rifles*, 1938)
Furcht und Elend des dritten Reiches, 1938 (*The Private Life of the Master Race*, 1944)
Leben des Galilei, first version written 1938–1939, second version written 1945–1947, third version published 1955–1956 (*Life of Galileo*, 1947)
Der gute Mensch von Sezuan, written 1938–1940, published 1953 (*The Good Woman of Setzuan*, 1948)
Mutter Courage und ihre Kinder, 1940 (based on Hans Jakob Christoffel von Grimmelshausen's *Der abenteuerliche Simplicissimus*; *Mother Courage and Her Children*, 1941)
Das Verhör des Lukullus, 1940 (libretto; *The Trial of Lucullus*, 1943)
Herr Puntila und sein Knecht Matti, written 1940, published 1951 (*Mr. Puntila and His Hired Man, Matti*, 1976)
Der aufhaltsame Aufstieg des Arturo Ui, written 1941, published 1957 (*The Resistible Rise of Arturo Ui*, 1972)
Die Gesichte der Simone Machard, written 1941–1943, published 1956 (with Lion Feuchtwanger; *The Visions of Simone Machard*, 1961)
Schweyk im zweiten Weltkrieg, written 1941–1943, published 1957 (based on Jaroslav Hašek's novel *Osudy dobrého vojáka Švejka ve sv[ic]etove války*; *Schweyk in the Second World War*, 1975)
Der kaukasische Kreidekreis, written 1944–1945, published 1949 (based on Li Hsing-dao's play *The Circle of Chalk*; *The Caucasian Chalk Circle*, 1948)
Die Antigone des Sophokles, 1948
Die Tage der Commune, written 1948–1949, published 1957 (based on Nordahl Grieg's *Nederlaget*; *The Days of the Commune*, 1971)
Der Hofmeister, 1950 (adaptation of Jakob Michael Reinhold Lenz's play; *The Tutor*, 1972)
Turandot: Oder, Der Kongress der Weisswäscher, written 1950–1954, published 1970
Der Prozess der Jeanne d'Arc zu Rouen, 1431, 1952 (based on Anna Seghers' radio play; *The Trial of Jeanne d'Arc at Rouen, 1431*, 1972)
Coriolan, written 1952–1953, published 1959 (adaptation of Shakespeare's play *Coriolanus*; *Coriolanus*, 1972)
Don Juan, 1953 (based on Molière's play; English translation, 1972)
Pauken und Trompeten, 1956 (adaptation of George Farquhar's *The Recruiting Officer*; *Trumpets and Drums*, 1972)

SCREENPLAYS

Kuhle Wampe, 1932 (English translation, 1933)
Hangmen Also Die, 1943
Das Lied der Ströme, 1954
Herr Puntila und sein Knecht Matti, 1955

POETRY

Hauspostille, 1927, 1951 (*Manual of Piety*, 1966)
Lieder, Gedichte, Chöre, 1934 (*Songs, Poems, Choruses*, 1976)
Svendborger Gedichte, 1939 (*Svendborg Poems*, 1976)
Hundert Gedichte, 1951 (*A Hundred Poems*, 1976)
Gedichte und Lieder, 1956 (*Poems and Songs*, 1976)

Further reading

Brooker, Peter. *Bertolt Brecht: Dialectics, Poetry, Politics*, 1988.
Esslin, Martin. *Brecht: A Choice of Evils*, 1959.
Fuegi, John. *Brecht and Company: Sex, Politics, and the Making of Modern Drama*, 1994.
Giles, Steve, and Rodney Livingstone, eds. *Bertolt Brecht: Centenary Essays*, 1998.
Gray, Ronald. *Brecht*, 1976.
Mews, Siegfried, ed. *A Bertolt Brecht Reference Companion*, 1997.
Needle, Jan, and Peter Thomson. *Brecht*, 1981.
Schoeps, Karl. *Bertolt Brecht*, 1977.
Suvin, Darko. *To Brecht and Beyond*, 1984.
Völker, Klaus. *Brecht: A Biography*, 1978.
Willett, John. *The Theatre of Bertolt Brecht*, 1959.
——. *Brecht in Context: Comparative Approaches*, 1984.

THOMAS H. FALK

See also Adorno; Benjamin; Marxist Theory and Criticism

André Breton

French poet and theorist

Born: Tinchebray, France; February 18, 1896
Died: Paris, France; September 28, 1966

Biography

André Breton was born in the small town of Tinchebray in Normandy. Almost nothing is known about his early childhood. From 1906 to 1912 Breton attended the Collège Chaptal in Paris, where he was inspired to take a keen interest in poetry.

Before being mobilized in early 1915, he had begun without enthusiasm to prepare for a career in medicine. Posted to various neuropsychiatric centers, he became interested in the work of Sigmund Freud.

In 1919 his first volume of poems was published, and with Louis Aragon and Philippe Soupault he founded the magazine called satirically *Littérature*. In it appeared the first specifically Surrealist text utilizing automatic writing.

After the war, friends helped Breton to procure a post as a proofreader for the publishing house of Gallimard and later as librarian for Jacques Doucet, an art collector. In 1921 he married Simone Kahn. That same year, Breton became the sole editor of *Littérature* and devoted his attention especially to experiments with hypnotic sleep.

In 1924 Breton edited the magazine *La Révolution Surréaliste*, the organ of the movement, and published *Manifesto of Surrealism*, which defines it and its procedures philosophically. From 1926 to 1935 Breton belonged to the Communist Party. Just before he broke away from it, he met his second wife, Jacqueline Lamba. After the birth of his daughter, he needed a more secure financial position. Eventually the Ministry of Foreign Affairs offered him a lecture mission to Mexico, where with Diego Rivera and Leon Trotsky he founded the Federation of Independent Revolutionary Art.

Recalled to service in 1939, he left France after the end of the Third Republic and made his way to the United States, where he founded the review *VVV* and organized an international exhibition of Surrealism. In 1945 he made a happy marriage with Elisa, who inspired *Arcane 17*.

Back in France in 1946 he reorganized the Surrealist group, put on a second international exposition of Surrealism, and founded several more reviews. During this period he was constantly writing and publishing poetry.

Influence

If Breton did not invent Surrealism single-handedly, he was at least its major protagonist and disseminator. Thanks largely to him, people were given a new way of looking at life and new ways of expressing their reactions to it. They were invited to explore directions in which reason places no trust; to plumb the depths of their subconscious; to revolt against civilization, society, the mental and physical order of the universe. In brief, he acted as a catalyst in the literary and artistic centers of Western culture.

The influence of Surrealism did not end with the breakup of the Surrealist group, nor with the death of Breton. It is safe to say that all Western poetry and ways of thinking about poetry and its relation to life are forever altered. Surrealism was not a literary fad but an intellectual revolution. Breton insisted that Surrealism had made a major contribution to the emancipation of humanity by demolishing old ideas and imposing new ones and by enlarging the realm of human experience.

Analysis

Breton's first idols were Stéphane Mallarmé and Paul Valéry, two Symbolists whose intellectual, recondite work was in vogue while he was a schoolboy. His army service in World War I brought him into contact with Guillaume Apollinaire, who wanted to renew poetic expression by substituting in place of the vague impressions of the Symbolists a way of writing that would correspond to the representation of objects in geometric forms proposed by the cubists; Apollinaire wanted to surprise and shock the reader and is usually credited with inventing the word "surrealism." In 1916 Breton met Jacques Vaché, whose destructive criticism and black humor turned him against traditional forms of poetry and toward total revolt. Another early influence was the work of Sigmund Freud, which led Breton to experiment with hypnosis and automatic writing.

From 1919 to 1922 he participated in the activities of the Dadaists, who, led by Tristan Tzara, were in revolt against society, civilization, and the mental and physical order of the world. It was in a review, *Dada*, that the first Surrealist text appeared, *Les Champs magnétiques*, a joint production of Breton and Philippe Soupault. These experiences with Dada helped to impel Breton toward complete poetic independence.

In contrast to most literary critics who express their views while examining the work of other writers, André Breton explained his theories in articles and books and illustrated his theories in his own poetry and prose.

In October, 1924, Breton published the first *Manifesto of Surrealism*. In it he defined Surrealism thus: "Pure psychic automatism by which one proposes to express, either verbally or in writing, or in any other way, the real functioning of thought. Dictation of thought, in the absence of any control exercised by reason, beyond any aesthetic or moral preoccupation." He rejected completely the purely realist description of the world and deemed it utterly impossible to justify everything in the world by logic.

In 1930 appeared the *Second Manifesto of Surrealism*, which contained this exhortation: "let us remember that the idea of surrealism leads simply to the total recovery of our psychic force by a means which is simply the dizzying descent into ourselves, the systematic illumination of the hidden places and the progressive blacking out of the other places, the never-ending voyage through the forbidden zone." People should not seek refuge from reality by retreating into the dream world; the dream and the real worlds are actually one and the same. Breton insisted that the imaginary is that which tends to become real.

In *Légitime Défense* (1926) Breton had announced that revolt alone is creative of light, a theme that he repeated in *Arcane 17* eighteen years later. People should be in permanent revolt against limits of all kinds; they should not accept the traditional ideas of family, religion, country any more readily than the dicta of schools of poetry. Excellence can only be the result of spontaneity, of intuition; Breton will accept no restraints of form, the care for which he considers a grievous sin. This belief did not prevent him from being an excellent prose stylist himself.

This admirable prose style is evident in *Nadja* (1928; English translation, 1960), a personal, didactic narrative camouflaged as lyric. It begins with the question "Who am I?" and then wonders if the self is not a ghost haunting a life that it thinks it is exploring but actually already knows. He proceeds to recount the curious revelations of his daily life in an apparently random sequence using the style of psychiatric observation. Finally, the reader meets Nadja, a real woman whom Breton had encountered by chance near the Opéra. She was what he termed a *trouvaille* (a find), the unexpected that adds so much to life and to art. Nadja seems to live in communication with the dynamic forces of the cosmos. She lives outside time – in the future – and escapes the ties of cause and effect which are imposed by reason. She is marvelous, and Breton believed that the marvelous is always beautiful; in fact, he believed that only the marvelous is beautiful. Nadja falls in love with Breton and finally dies in an insane asylum, but she has served to illustrate his theory of the marvelous. Its basis is the startling image that reveals unforeseen relationships between unlike objects and constitutes the highest form of human knowledge. Breton admires an image that is apparently completely self-contradictory. These images are almost always visual; he is interested in neither auditory effects nor rhythm.

Breton was convinced that the greatest weakness of contemporary thought resides in the overestimation of the known in contrast to what remains unknown. This theme he illustrated in 1937 in *L'Amour fou*. Pursuing his search for the unknown, he studied the nature of dreams and tried to show how they can solve the basic problems of life. In 1932, in *Les Vases communicants*, he had claimed that detailed analysis of a dream, proving the content derived from reality, could help the dreamer to arrive at a healthy readjustment toward the future. The next step was to assert that an examination of reality would show the presence of dream phenomena. The conclusion was that dream and reality are two communicating vessels; they continually interpenetrate. Thus Surrealism attempted to place a conductor between external reality and internal reality. In fact, Breton concluded that the world of dreams and the real world are one and the same.

During the occupation of France, Breton was in the United States, where his influence was tremendous. He advanced the cause of Surrealism in many ways, including the periodical *VVV*, an exposition which he organized in 1942, and a lecture delivered at Yale, *Situation du surréalisme entre les deux guerres* (1945). He also wrote *Arcane 17* (1944), a book-length essay that continues many of the themes of his earlier works. He talks about rebellion and freedom and evaluates humanity's situation from the point of view of Surrealism. Man desires freedom and must be able to re-create himself endlessly; thus liberty must be thought of as a force, not a state. Both poetry and love are assertions of a principle of liberty, and they will guide man to refuse respect for conventional opinions. He proposes that because man has so abysmally failed to control suffering, it is time to look to woman, to love, for the salvation of mankind. He now places love beside poetry and art as the three redemptive forces working for liberty.

In one case Breton violated his own principle of complete freedom for a poet: he wrote *Ode à Charles Fourier* (1947; *Ode to Charles Fourier*, 1970). This is a philosophical poem expressing admiration for Fourier, in which it is evident that Breton was still searching for a universal language, one that depends not on reason but on sensibility. In this work, the poet is advised to surrender him- or herself to hallucinatory experiences, abandoning the control habitually exercised by reason.

Surrealism is perhaps the most important literary movement of the twentieth century. André Breton spent his entire life promoting its theories by means of his books, his poems, his novel and essays, hundreds of articles, and many speeches and expositions. Although the movement as such is dead (in France after the war it was largely replaced by Jean-Paul Sartre's existentialism), its influence can be traced in the New Novel and in much of the poetry written since Breton's time. Gaétan Picon, a highly respected literary critic, said at the time of the poet's death that literature had been permanently enriched by André Breton.

Principal criticism

Manifeste du surréalisme, 1924 (*Manifesto of Surrealism*, 1969)
Second Manifeste du surréalisme, 1930 (*Second Manifesto of Surrealism*, 1969)
Les Vases communicants, 1932
Qu'est-ce que le surréalisme?, 1934 (*What Is Surrealism?*, 1936)
L'Amour fou, 1937
Arcane 17, 1944
Situation du surréalisme entre les deux guerres, 1945
Les Manifestes du surréalisme, 1955 (*Manifestoes of Surrealism*, 1969)

Other major works and literary forms

André Breton's theoretical work is of such worldwide significance that it has overshadowed his renown as a poet. At the time of his death the leading Paris dailies carried eulogies covering as much as a full page, filled with appreciation of Breton as a man and as a theorist, but with little or no praise for his dozen volumes of poems. Yet no anthology of twentieth-century French poetry is complete without some of his work. His masterpiece, however, is considered to be a short novel in prose, *Nadja*, published in Paris in 1928 and in translation in the United States in 1960. All of his life Breton was involved with artists as well as with writers; he believed that poetry and painting are two forms of the same language. As early as 1928, he published *Le Surréalisme et la peinture* (revised and expanded in 1965). The importance of his application of Surrealist principles to art is illustrated by the fact that this book, edited and enlarged, was republished in New York in 1945 and again with further additions in Paris in 1965.

NOVEL
Nadja, 1928 (English translation, 1960)

POETRY
Mont de piété, 1919
Clair de terre, 1923
L'Union libre, 1931 (*Free Union*, 1982)
Le Revolver à cheveux blancs, 1932
L'Air de l'eau, 1934
Fata Morgana, 1941 (English translation, 1982)
Pleine marge, 1943
Young Cherry Trees Secured Against Hares, 1946
Ode à Charles Fourier, 1947 (*Ode to Charles Fourier*, 1970)
Poèmes, 1948
Poésie et autre, 1960
Selected Poems, 1969
Poems of André Breton: A Bilingual Anthology, 1982 (includes *Free Union* and *Fata Morgana* among other selected poems)

NONFICTION
Les Champs magnétiques, 1921 (with Philippe Soupault)
Les Pas perdus, 1924
Poisson soluble, 1924
Légitime Défense, 1926
Le Surréalisme et la peinture, 1928, 1945, 1965
L'Immaculée Conception, 1930 (with Paul Éluard)
Point du jour, 1934
Perspective cavalière, 1970
What Is Surrealism? Selected Writings, 1978

Further reading

Artaud, Antonin. *Letter to André Breton*, 1974.
Aspley, Keith. *André Breton the Poet*, 1989.
Balakian, Anna Elizabeth. *André Breton: Magus of Surrealism*, 1971.
——, and Rudolf E. Kuenzli, eds. *André Breton Today*, 1989.
Bedouin, Jean-Louis. *André Breton*, 1966.
Browder, Clifford. *André Breton: Arbiter of Surrealism*, 1968.
Caws, Mary Ann. *André Breton*, 1971.
Fowlie, Wallace. *Age of Surrealism*, 1960.
Guerlac, Suzanne. *Literary Polemics: Bataille, Sartre, Valéry, Breton*, 1997.
Matthews, J. H. *André Breton*, 1967.
——. *André Breton: Sketch for an Early Portrait*, 1986.
Polizzotti, Mark. *Revolution of the Mind: The Life of André Breton*, 1995.
Rosemont, Franklin. *André Breton and the First Principles of Surrealism*, 1978.

DOROTHY B. ASPINWALL

See also French Literary Theory: Twentieth Century; Surrealism

British Literary Theory: Twentieth Century

Toward the end of the nineteenth century a number of trends were visible in British criticism, including the humanism of Matthew Arnold, the aestheticism of Walter Pater and Oscar Wilde, the socialist criticism of George Bernard Shaw, and the mainstreams of realist and naturalist criticism. The first notable group of British critics in the twentieth century were affiliated with the universities. During the nineteenth century relatively few critics were professors and wrote primarily for journals and magazines (among the few notable exceptions to this was Matthew Arnold who was elected professor of poetry at Oxford in 1857). In the last decade of the nineteenth century and the first decades of the twentieth century, with the establishment of English literature as a separate discipline, this situation changed rapidly. In 1895 the influential literary historian and critic George Saintsbury was appointed professor of rhetoric at Edinburgh, and the renowned Shakespeare scholar A. C. Bradley assumed an academic post in 1882. Walter Raleigh and Arthur Quiller-Couch took over important professorships of English literature at Oxford and Cambridge respectively. Raleigh and Quiller-Couch did not consider themselves critics as such and in fact showed considerable scorn for academic criticism. Their own approaches to texts and authors were empirical, unsystematic, impressionistic, and sometimes idealistic (in the philosophical sense). By far the most influential of this early generation of academic critics was A. C. Bradley. In *Shakespearean Tragedy* (1904), Bradley's central thesis, influenced by G. W. F. Hegel, the Hegelians T. H. Greene and F. H. Bradley (his brother), saw tragedy as a dialectic whereby the moral order and harmony of the world were threatened (by the tragic hero) and then reestablished. Shakespearean tragedy, according to Bradley, could be seen as embodying this dialectic. For all the controversy it spawned, Bradley's text remains a classic of literary criticism.

The Neo-Romantics and D. H. Lawrence

Another group of critics, who might loosely be called Neo-Romantic, included D. H. Lawrence, G. Wilson Knight, John Middleton Murry, and Herbert Read. Lawrence was an avowed irrationalist, reacting against both the mainstream rationalist tradition in Western thinking, as well as against the modern industrial world, which he saw as sexually repressive and as having stunted human potential. Lawrence's literary criticism was expressed in several reviews and in his *Studies in Classic American Literature* (1923), as well as in essays on sexuality and the unconscious. In both these works and in his fiction, Lawrence advocated a vitalism and individualism that often has parallels in the views of Friedrich Nietzsche and Sigmund Freud.

He attempted to revaluate various writers in the light of his libidinal and primitivist ideology, urging that their art achieved something contrary to their conscious and morally repressive intentions. His disposition is antidemocratic and even fascistic, reacting, like Nietzsche, against mass mediocrity and moral conventionalism, and urging hope for a "new man." In his own highly idiosyncratic way, Lawrence anticipates certain aspects of late-twentieth-century criticism, notably the stress on the unconscious, the body, and irrational motives.

Of the other Neo-Romantic critics mentioned above, John Middleton Murry (1889–1957) attempted to reinstate a Romantic belief in pantheism and the organic unity of the world. He saw as a central criterion of genuine poetry that it was not amenable to paraphrase and that it expressed truths inaccessible to reason or concepts. Herbert Read began as an advocate of imagism and classicism and eventually expressed an allegiance to Romanticism, articulating an organicist aesthetic and viewing poetry as transcending reason. G. Wilson Knight (1897–1985), a Shakespeare scholar, is best known for his *The Wheel of Fire* (1930). Drawing on the findings of anthropologists such as Sir James Frazer concerning myths, rituals, and symbols, Wilson Knight interprets William Shakespeare's plays in terms of certain recurring symbols and motifs. As a critic, he distinguishes interpretation, which aims empathetically to reconstruct an author's vision, from criticism, which he sees as evaluative. Somewhat like the New Critics, Wilson Knight wished to subordinate considerations drawn from intention or biography or morality to artistic concerns. Another significant critic in this broad Romantic-religious tradition was C. S. Lewis, whose major critical work was *The Allegory of Love* (1936) which, along with his other works, contributed to his mission of promoting understanding of the formality and didacticism of the literature of the Middle Ages and the Renaissance. Finally, mention should be made of the scholar of John Milton and Shakespeare, E. M. Tillyard (1889–1962), who engaged in a debate with C. S. Lewis in *The Personal Heresy* (1939) and whose most influential work was *The Elizabethan World Picture* (1943).

I. A. Richards and Practical Criticism

A further generation of professional critics helped both to rejuvenate the study of English literature and to pave the way for the New Criticism. The most prominent of these, associated with the new English curriculum at Cambridge University, were I. A. Richards and his student William Empson. In his *Principles of Literary Criticism* (1924) and his *Science and Poetry* (1926), Richards attempted to establish a systematic basis for the study of literature, an approach that became known as Practical Criticism. He distinguished, most fundamentally, the emotive language of poetry from the referential language of nonliterary disciplines. In 1929 he published a book, *Practical Criticism*, whose profound and pervasive influence still endures. Using samples of students' often erratic attempts to analyze poetry, he aimed to foster the skills and techniques necessary for the close reading of literature. The practice of close reading as established by Richards, at both Cambridge and Harvard (to which he later transferred), later had a profound impact on the New Critics who facilitated its academic institutionalization. While William Empson was not himself a New Critic, he produced a book, *Seven Types of Ambiguity* (1930), which had an impact on the New Criticism in virtue of the close attention it paid to literary texts and its stress on ambiguity as an essential characteristic of poetry.

Symbolism and T. S. Eliot

A convenient starting point for tracing the growth of modernistic trends in twentieth-century British criticism is the development of symbolism, as prominently manifested in the work of the Irish poet and critic William Butler Yeats. Symbolism had roots in the English-speaking world in the theory and practice of figures such as William Blake, Samuel Taylor Coleridge, William Wordsworth, Percy Bysshe Shelley, and Edgar Allan Poe. The symbolism of Yeats and subsequent writers was also influenced by French Symbolism as developed in the work of Charles Baudelaire, Stéphane Mallarmé, Paul Verlaine, and Arthur Rimbaud. French Symbolism was introduced to English and American audiences largely through Arthur Symons' book *The Symbolist Movement in Literature* (1899). In this book Symons explained the history and rationale of French Symbolism, which he saw as a reaction against nineteenth-century scientism and materialism. Recoiling from materialism and pragmatism, French Symbolism saw literature as affirming the reality of a higher, spiritual realm which could be divined not by rational thought but only in glimpses through a pure poetic language divested of any representational pretension. Symbolism is an attempt to reinvest both the world and language – stripped by much bourgeois thought and science to a utilitarian literalness – with metaphor, ambivalence, and mystery. In Symbolist poetry, concrete images are used to evoke emotions, moods, and atmospheres otherwise ineffable. Symons' book had a profound influence on major British poet-critics such as T. S. Eliot. It was actually dedicated to Yeats whom Symons saw as the chief exponent of Symbolism in Britain. Yeats' own theory and practice of symbolism drew from Blake, Shelley, Irish mythology, and magic. Yeats affirmed that external objects and scenes could express the profoundest internal states, and that the poet's task is to imbue such scenes and images with a symbolic significance transcending the time and place of their immediate origin. Symbols, for Yeats, evoke what he calls the "Great Mind" and "Great Memory." Yeats' own poetry uses numerous symbols with both private and public associations, such as the rose, the cross, the stairway, and the tower. Yeats worked out his own highly intricate cosmological symbolism in *A Vision* (1925–1937). His assessments of most poets were motivated by a search for symbolic predecessors and an attempt to explain their techniques.

The other major critic of the early twentieth century influenced by French Symbolism was T. S. Eliot. Some of the assumptions underlying his renowned critical notions, such as "tradition" (expressed in his seminal essay of 1919 "Tradition and the Individual Talent"), "dissociation of sensibility," and "objective correlative," were derived in part from French writers. Eliot's concept of "dissociation of sensibility," for example, according to which a dissociation of thought from feeling had arisen subsequent to the Metaphysical poets, was informed by his perception of some of the nineteenth-century French poets as "Metaphysical" in their attempt to harmonize these polarized faculties. Both Eliot's "dissociation of sensibility" and "objective correlative" may have had roots in the thought of French writers, especially Rémy de Gourmont. Other major influences on Eliot's criticism were Ezra Pound's Imagism and T. E. Hulme's classicism. Eliot's main critical contributions were: (1) to combat provincialism by broadening the notion of "tradition" to include Europe; (2) to advocate, as against the prevailing critical impressionism, a closely analytical and even objective criticism which situated literary works alongside one another in the larger context of tradition (in this, he contributed to the development of notions of artistic autonomy which were taken up by some of the New Critics); and (3) to foster, by his own revaluation of the literary tradition (reacting against the Romantics, for example, and highlighting the virtues of the Metaphysical poets), a dynamic notion of tradition as always in the process of change. Eliot also brought to literary criticism a sophistication drawn from his philosophical studies, which helped to display the intricate connections between literary study and other fields such as religion, philosophy, and psychology. Eliot's criticism, as he acknowledged, was motivated by a desire to explain and propagate the kind of poetry he was writing, as well as to draw attention to the various elements of literary tradition which had proved serviceable to his verse. Hence, his criticism was in part a manifesto of literary modernism, influenced by Ezra Pound and characteristically infused with political conservatism.

Bloomsbury and Virginia Woolf

Another group of artist-critics associated with modernism was the highly iconoclastic Bloomsbury Group. This circle included Virginia Woolf and her sister Vanessa, daughters of the critic and agnostic philosopher Leslie Stephen, the art critics Roger Fry and Clive Bell, the economist John Maynard Keynes, the biographer Lytton Strachey, and the novelist E. M. Forster. While each of these personalities had his or her own highly idiosyncratic artistic disposition, most members of the group fell under the influence of the Cambridge philosopher G. E. Moore's *Principia Ethica* (1903). They saw this text as affirming an "aesthetic" approach to life inasmuch as it stressed the value of allegedly timeless states of consciousness which facilitated the enjoyment of beauty. In literary-critical terms, the most influential figure in this circle was Virginia Woolf, who had read Moore's text closely.

Woolf's critical contributions spanned two broad areas: a modernistic redefinition of the novel that anticipated some of the more recent trends of literary theory, and a broadly feminist approach to literature and literary history. The nature of Woolf's critical modernism is complex, and her connections with Moore's philosophical realism and his commonsense philosophical perspective are ambivalent.

While Woolf may have taken from Moore a realist distinction between consciousness and its object, she indicts the mechanical realism of some of her contemporaries such as Arnold Bennett and John Galsworthy. In the place of this, she advocates not any form of idealism but a more refined version of realism, in line with "reality" as conceived dynamically by Henri Bergson and Marcel Proust. As many commentators have pointed out, Bloomsbury's relations with modernism are at best ambivalent. A favorite quotation cited by Woolf critics in support of her modernism comes from her famous essay "Modern Fiction" (1919):

> Life is not a series of gig lamps symetrically arranged; but a luminous halo, a semi-transparent envelope surrounding us from the beginning of consciousness to the end.
>
> . . . Let us record the atoms as they fall upon the mind in the order in which they fall, let us trace the pattern, however disconnected and incoherent in appearance, which each sight or incident scores upon the consciousness.

It has been argued by several commentators that the second paragraph suggests that the appropriate subject matter for a novelist is not that provided by "external" events but the content of consciousness itself. As against this, one can see that the paragraph accords with John Locke's theory of perception, whereby the mind receives ideas and impressions from the external world. Woolf's language, urging the novelist to "record the atoms as they fall upon the mind," could be read as a call for a refined realism, one that is not constrained by frigid imperatives pertaining to plot, character, and probability. When Woolf rejects these imperatives, she does so on the grounds that they cannot generate a "likeness to life."

However, there are passages in Woolf which gesture in the opposite direction. Reviewing Dorothy Richardson's novel *The Tunnel* (1919), Woolf insists that: "We want to be rid of realism, to penetrate without its help into the regions beneath it, and further require that Miss Richardson shall fashion this new material into something which has the shapeliness of the old accepted forms." In *A Writer's Diary* (1953) Woolf observes, after noting Arnold Bennett's charge that her characters fail: "I haven't that 'reality' gift. I insubstantise, wilfully to some extent, distrusting reality – its cheapness." But, although Woolf clearly wishes to shift novelistic attention away from the "actual event" and time-frame of conventional realism, these statements can be a little misleading. The basis of Woolf's critique of Richardson, for example, is that Richardson enables us to "find ourselves in the dentist's room, in the street, in the lodging-house bedroom frequently and convincingly; but never, or only for a tantalizing second, in the reality which underlies these appearances." It seems that Woolf does wish the novelist to engage with "reality" but this reality itself is reconceived: it is no longer in Moorean fashion an atomistic reality of independent objects but something beneath these surface appearances, something which binds them in a farther-reaching totality.

A further critical principle of Woolf's was a displacement of emphasis from moral function to the actual artistic structure of a literary text. Woolf also anticipated modern critical trends inasmuch as she wished to focus attention on texts rather than biography; moreover, she was persistently aware of the changing role and historical conditions of readers. She even saw the novel as formed by "the very process of reading . . ." Finally, she urged as a critical principle the attempt to enter a writer's mind and world.

F. R. Leavis

A central figure in English literary criticism, also associated with the new English at Cambridge, was F. R. Leavis, who might broadly be placed in the moralistic and humanistic tradition of Matthew Arnold. Leavis stood aloof from both the Bloomsbury Group (a position expressed during his editorship of the journal *Scrutiny* from 1932 to 1953) and the New Criticism, though he was influenced by I. A. Richards' Practical Criticism courses, which he attended. Leavis assumed both educational and critical roles. In the academy he attempted to foster an elite which might safeguard English culture against the technological and populist vulgarities of an industrial society. As a critic he attempted to foster rigorous intellectual standards informed by a sense of the moral and cultural importance of literature, as well as to revaluate the English literary tradition. His major works *New Bearings in English Poetry* (1932), *Revaluation* (1936), and *The Great Tradition* (1948) demoted Victorian and Georgian verse and sought to increase general appreciation of Eliot, Yeats, and Pound; he argued that the mainstream of English poetry flowed through John Donne, Alexander Pope, Samuel Johnson, and Eliot; and he traced the main tradition of fiction from Jane Austen, George Eliot, Henry James, and Joseph Conrad.

Leavis shared with Eliot and the New Critics the idea that literary criticism should be a separate and serious discipline. While he rejected any theory or system, he called for "a living critical inwardness with literature, and a mind trained in dealing analytically with it." He repeatedly insisted that literature should be approached as literature and not as a social, historical, or political document. What separated him from the New Critics, however, was an equally forceful counter-insistence that literary study cannot be confined to isolated works of art nor to a realm of purely literary values. Leavis invokes Eliot's notion of tradition as representing "a new emphasis on the social nature of artistic achievement." This social nature, for Leavis, is grounded in what he calls an "inherent human nature." Hence, the study of literature is a study of "the complexities, potentialities and essential conditions of human nature." In his essay "Sociology and Literature" (1952) he affirms that "a real literary interest is an interest in man, society and civilization, and its boundaries cannot be drawn." The apparent contradiction in Leavis' approach between viewing literature as literature and literature as inseparable from all aspects of life seems to be "resolved" by an appeal to the assimilating capacity of intuition and a maturing experience of literature, for which no conceptual or theoretical subtlety can substitute.

Left-wing criticism

The two remaining fields in which British critics have made substantial contributions are Socialist-Marxist criticism and feminist studies. The somewhat discontinuous tradition of Socialist and Marxist criticism in Britain goes back, through the nineteenth century, to the sporadic literary insights of Karl Marx's friend and collaborator Friedrich Engels and to William Morris who first applied Marxist perspectives on the theory of labor and alienation to artistic production. In 1884 the Fabian Society was formed with the aim of substituting for Marxist revolutionary action a Fabian policy of gradually introducing Socialism through influencing government policy and disseminating pamphlets to raise awareness of economic and class inequalities. The dramatist and critic George Bernard Shaw was a member of this society and produced one of its first pamphlets, *A Manifesto* (1884). Shaw edited *Fabian Essays in Socialism* (1899) and advocated women's rights, economic equality, and the abolition of private property. Despite his drawing on economic determinism, Shaw's brand of socialism has earned the scorn of some Marxists. Also in this vein might be mentioned George Orwell (1903–1950) who in his later career saw himself as a political writer and a democratic socialist, but who, however, became disillusioned with Communism as shown in his political satire *Animal Farm* (1945).

British Communists did not produce any substantial works until the mid-1930s. With the menace of Fascism and the threat of war, several writers began to engage in Marxist criticism. These included the art historian Anthony Blunt and the economist John Strachey who produced two influential books, *The Coming Struggle for Power* (1933) and *Literature and Dialectical Materialism* (1934). A group of Marxist thinkers was centered around *The Left Review* (1934–1938). The poets W. H. Auden, Stephen Spender, and C. Day Lewis at various times espoused and propagated left-wing views. The most significant Marxist theorist of this generation was Christopher Caudwell (1907–1937) who died in Spain fighting in the International Brigade. Caudwell's best-known work is his *Illusion and Reality: A Study of the Sources of Poetry* (1937). Here, Caudwell offers a Marxist analysis of the development of English poetry, somewhat crudely correlating the stages of this development with economic phases such as primitive accumulation, the Industrial Revolution, and the decline of capitalism. In this wide-ranging book, Caudwell addressed the origins of poetry, the connection of poetry to mythology and the unconscious, as well as the future role of poetry in the struggle for Socialism. Caudwell's subsequent writings included *Studies in a Dying Culture* (1938) and *Further Studies in a Dying Culture* (1949).

The theoretical vacuum in British Marxist criticism which preceded Caudwell opened up again after him and endured until the emergence of the two major British Marxist critics of the twentieth century, Raymond Williams and Terry Eagleton. The revolutionary fervor of the 1960s gave Marxist criticism a revived impetus. A group of Marxist critics was centered around the *New Left Review*, founded in 1960 and edited first by Stuart Hall and then by Perry Anderson. Its contributors included E. P. Thompson and Raymond Williams. Williams' central project, which he would later term "Cultural Materialism," was to furnish a historical and materialist rereading of the English cultural tradition, as in *Culture and Society 1780–1950* (1958), which stressed that culture was a process. *The Long Revolution* (1961) continued and refined this project using categories such as dominant, residual, and emergent cultures mediated by what Williams called "structures of feeling." Williams' work became overtly Marxist with the publication in 1977 of *Marxism and Literature*. In this work Williams undertook a critical review of earlier Marxist theories and offered his own analyses of fundamental Marxist notions such as ideology, hegemony, base, and superstructure. His own cultural materialism as set forth here attempts to integrate a Marxist conception of language and literature. *Keywords* (1976) examines the history of fundamental concepts and categories.

Terry Eagleton's work initially undertook a critique of commonplace liberal-bourgeois notions about literature as well as some of Williams' categories such as "structures of feeling." In his earlier work, enshrined most articulately in *Criticism and Ideology* (1976), Eagleton was influenced by Louis Althusser's attempt to divest Marxism of Hegelian elements and to promote its scientific status. Eagleton argued that criticism must assume a scientific position beyond the domain of ideology. In this text Eagleton formulated the fundamental categories of a Marxist criticism, and insisted that the text is a producer of ideology. Eagleton's later work turned somewhat away from Althusser and was inspired instead by Walter Benjamin's revolutionary thought. It also engaged in a sustained dialogue with many branches of recent literary theory, including feminism, deconstruction, and psychoanalysis. Eagleton skillfully situated these currents within their historical and political contexts, revealing the ways in which they were subversive of, and complicit with, liberal humanism in its manifold guises. Eagleton's *Literary Theory: An Introduction* (1983) has commanded a wide audience in both Britain and America, and he is undoubtedly the most widely read Marxist critic now living. Overall, his work has clarified the relationship of Marxism to other discourses; it has revaluated the tradition of Marxist criticism itself; and it has articulated a Marxist model of aesthetics both theoretically and in application in several studies of individual authors.

Feminism

Twentieth-century British feminist criticism might be said to begin with Virginia Woolf, who produced two works considered important in the history of feminist criticism: *A Room of One's Own* (1929) and *Three Guineas* (1938). Woolf's central concern here was to situate literature in a social and economic context, a procedure that highlighted the material, social, and psychological disadvantages suffered by female writers. In both of these texts Woolf stresses that gender is socially constructed, and deals with issues such as the viability of a female consciousness and female language. In general, she asserts, following the Bloomsbury notion of androgyny, that female writers should rise above any exclusive focus on gender and adopt a "human" perspective that embraces both female and male elements. Woolf's contributions here include an attempt to search for neglected movements of female writers, and to examine female-male relations as portrayed in the history of literature.

Much British feminist criticism has had a political orientation, insisting on situating both feminist concerns and literary texts within a material and ideological context. In her landmark work "Women: The Longest Revolution," later expanded and produced as *Women's Estate* (1971), Juliet Mitchell examined patriarchy in terms of Marxist categories of production and private property as well as psychoanalytic theories of gender. Her later works, such as *Psychoanalysis and Feminism* (1974), continue to refine her attempt to integrate the insights of Marxism and psychoanalysis. Another seminal text was Michele Barrett's *Women's Oppression Today: Problems in Marxist Feminist Analysis* (1980) which attempted to formulate a materialist aesthetics and insisted on integrating Marxist class analysis with feminism in analyzing and influencing gender representation. Other important critics have included Jacqueline

Rose and Rosalind Coward, who have integrated certain insights of Jacques Lacan into a materialist feminism; Catherine Belsey, who also has drawn upon Lacan in assessing Renaissance drama from a materialist feminist perspective; and Toril Moi, who has developed insights from Woolf and engaged in a critique of the humanism and implicit essentialism of some American feminists. Also critical of the tendency of American feminists to combat male stereotypes and to recover female traditions are Judith Newton and Deborah Rosenfelt. Finally, a number of critics such as Cora Kaplan, Mary Jacobus, and Penny Boumelha have been involved in the U.K. Marxist-Feminist Collective formed in 1976.

British literary criticism continues to embrace a wide variety of perspectives, ranging from the more traditional approaches of scholars such as John Carey through those such as Christopher Norris who have attempted to clarify and situate movements such as deconstruction to theorists of black feminism, semiotics, and film studies.

Further reading

Blamires, Harry. *A History of Literary Criticism*, 1991.
Casey, John. *The Language of Criticism*, 1966.
Goldberg, Gerald Jay, and Nancy Marmer Goldberg, eds. *The Modern Critical Spectrum*, 1962.
Needham, John. *The Completest Mode: I. A. Richards and the Continuity of English Literary Criticism*, 1982.
Smith, Harold, ed. *British Feminism in the Twentieth Century*, 1989.
Solomon, Maynard, ed. *Marxism and Art: Essays Classic and Contemporary*, 1973.
Sutton, Walter, and Richard Foster, eds. *Modern Criticism: Theory and Practice*, 1963.
Watson, George. *The Literary Critics: A Study of English Descriptive Criticism*, 1973.
Wellek, René. *A History of Modern Criticism: 1750–1950*. Vol. 2, *English Criticism, 1900–1950*, 1986.

M. A. R. Habib

See also Auden; Barfield; Bradley; Davie; Eagleton; Eliot; Empson; Forster; Graves; Hulme; Kermode; Knights; Lawrence; Leavis; Lewis; Lodge; Lubbock; Read; Richards; Ricks; Saintsbury; Shaw; Tolkien; Williams; Woolf; Yeats

Cleanth Brooks

American critic and editor

Born: Murray, Kentucky; October 16, 1906
Died: Newhaven, Connecticut; May 10, 1994

Biography

Cleanth Brooks was born on October 16, 1906, in Murray, Kentucky; his parents were Cleanth Brooks (a Methodist minister) and Bessie Lee (née Witherspoon) Brooks. At McTyeire prep school in McKenzie, Tennessee, he learned both Greek and Latin. He received a B.A. degree from Vanderbilt University, Nashville, Tennessee, in 1928, and an M.A. from Tulane University, New Orleans, in 1929. A Rhodes scholar at Exeter College, Oxford, he received a B.A. with honors in 1931 and a B.Litt. in 1932. During these years Brooks became acquainted with poets and critics involved in the New Criticism, as well as their poetry. Later he was to receive honorary doctorates from several institutions.

Brooks married Edith Amy Blanchard in 1934. His career included the post of professor of English at Louisiana State University from 1932 to 1947, and professor of English, Gray Professor of Rhetoric, and the latter emeritus at Yale. He was professor or lecturer in several institutions. With Robert Penn Warren, he was editor of the *The Southern Review* from 1935 to 1941. Other activities included Fellow, Library of Congress, from 1951 to 1962, and cultural attaché, American Embassy, London, from 1964 to 1966. A member of the American Academy of Arts and Sciences and the National Institute of Arts and Letters, he was awarded the Guggenheim Fellowship in 1953.

Influence

Brooks is regarded by many as one of the foremost American critics of the twentieth century and as the preeminent guide to the works of William Faulkner. His contribution has been varied and highly influential. He is credited with bringing about a synthesis of the ideas of the New Critics. Together with that group, he directed attention to the text of the poem and to its structure. He opposed sentimental and political as well as affective readings of poems. Though stressing the importance of matter outside the poem (biographical, social, historical), he emphasized that such is not to be confused with the poem itself. In critical works such as *Modern Poetry and the Tradition, The Well Wrought Urn*, and *A Shaping Joy*, he made a major contribution to the documents of criticism.

Perhaps his greatest influence, however, has been in the field of academic treatment of literature. A lifelong professor at two major universities and visiting professor or lecturer at numerous others, coeditor of distinguished literary journals, contributor of articles to literary journals, and keynote speaker at scholarly meetings, Brooks considered his criticism an extension of his teaching. To a limited extent in his critical works and to a great extent in his section of *Literary Criticism*, he emphasized the place of modern poetry and its criticism as a third revolutionary stage in the overall history of literature and criticism. His three long works and many articles on Faulkner are at the very heart of that criticism.

Analysis

Brooks has been called a New Critic, a formalist, an eclectic critic, and one who applies the Brooks-Warren method of criticism. In a sense all the terms are applicable, even though

Brooks expressed dissatisfaction with "New Criticism" on several occasions, stating that he preferred "formal" or "structural." Wilfred L. Guerin, in *A Handbook of Critical Approaches to Literature* (1979), devotes an entire chapter to the formalists, with special attention to Brooks and Warren; David Daiches devotes a chapter of his *Critical Approaches to Literature* (1956) to "Analysis in Action" and another to "Criticism in Scholarship": Brooks is treated in the first as an analytical critic, in the latter as a New Critic. At the 1981 Faulkner and Yoknapatawpha conference in Oxford, Mississippi, Brooks, a featured speaker, responded negatively to suggestions that he was a formalist. Later, during a private conversation, his responses to various questions implied eclecticism, an approach to literature that utilizes various methods, the one or ones most likely to give the fullest reading to the work under consideration. His detractors – R. S. Crane in "The Critical Monism of Cleanth Brooks" (1951), for one – have characterized him as too narrowly analyzing the text of a poem without sufficient attention to outside considerations. Others, including Brooks himself, tend to discount such characterizations, pointing to the fact that Brooks is much concerned with history, religion, morals, the genesis of the process of writing, and culture.

Why the contradictions? First, it should be acknowledged that Brooks is indeed a New Critic in the way that he considers poetry – in his preference for T. S. Eliot, William Butler Yeats, John Donne, and the seventeenth-century English Metaphysical poets, in his close association with the New Critics, in his collaboration with them in editing and writing, and in his valuable explications of their poems and fiction. Though there are occasional differences between his theories and theirs, he borrowed ideas from them, utilizing such in his criticism, while at the same time remaining an individual thinker. He is the one who has brought together the ideas of Eliot, I. A. Richards, Allen Tate, John Crowe Ransom, Warren, and others. It is he more than any other who popularized the New Critical ideas and methods among professors and students in academic institutions.

At the College English Association in the late 1970s, Brooks began his speech by offering two correctives: not he and Warren but Eliot and others had begun the New Criticism much earlier than had been previously suggested, and the beginning of the Brooks-Warren contribution had been not forty but forty-one years earlier, in 1938, with the publication of the first edition of *Understanding Poetry*. The term "formalist" is descriptive of one phase of Brooks' method of treating poetry, attention to form, but the term could also apply to other groups, such as the Russian Formalists.

The Brooks-Warren method is in part an assimilation of techniques and emphases of other New Critics. It began – again according to Brooks at the College English Association – with Warren's adding a section on meter to *Understanding Poetry*. What Brooks did not mention was the importance of the "Letter to the Teacher" in this text. It states the desired principles for "a satisfactory method of teaching poetry":

1. Emphasis should be kept on the poem as a poem.
2. The treatment should be concrete and inductive.
3. A poem should always be treated as an organic system of relationships, and the poetic quality should never be understood as inhering in one or more factors taken in isolation.

In a sense Brooks and Warren were reacting against criticism which focused on extraneous matters and gave little attention to the poem itself. They cautioned against substituting for the poem "paraphrase of logical and narrative content," even though such might be employed before analyzing the poem, "study of biographical and historical materials," though these may clarify interpretation, or "inspirational and didactic interpretation." The fact is that Brooks was a teacher and a very religious man, more religious than Warren or some of his other colleagues, but he made a clear distinction between religion and poetry. Elsewhere he strongly disagreed with those who would make poetry a substitute for religion and with those who would use a poem to teach a religious or sociopolitical tenet.

These principles formed the basis for many of Brooks's theories and much of his practice as a critic. He strongly disapproved of methods that turned poetry into propaganda or depended on the reader's emotional response to the poem. His close reading of the text of a poem carried over into his discussions of critical theory. One reason critics have found him difficult is that he begins treating theoretical matters but inevitably cites examples out of criticism and history and goes on to analyze others' statements as well as the texts of poems. His principal theoretical works contain excellent explications of poems. *Modern Poetry and the Tradition* treats various poems within the fabric of criticism: Eliot's *The Waste Land* (1922) is given complete analysis, for example. *The Well Wrought Urn* treats works by John Milton, Thomas Gray, William Wordsworth, John Keats, Alfred, Lord Tennyson, and William Butler Yeats. This second theoretical work, together with the introduction to the 1965 edition of *Modern Poetry and the Tradition*, indicates a change of emphasis on the part of Brooks: in the introduction, he regrets having been so narrow in his views in the first edition; the total thrust of *The Well Wrought Urn* is a relaxation of strictures while holding to basic beliefs. Can a close reading of the poem be too close? Without sacrificing the close reading, Brooks seems to agree.

One might wonder whether the careful attention to the text of the poem and the tendency to lapse into explication while discussing theory might have a common source.

It has been noted that the prep school exegesis of Greek and Latin texts could have been an influence. This is a practice not only of Greek and Latin classical scholarship but also of biblical exegesis (Greek and Hebrew). Could Brooks have also been influenced by the example of his Methodist minister father? The tendency to stop and illustrate a point or to stop and quote a scholar or another text from the primary source is clearly homiletical, whether by coincidence or by influence.

In *The Well Wrought Urn* Brooks emphasizes paradox, even the juxtaposing of violently contrasting elements, as not only desirable but also exemplary of real life. In *Modern Poetry and the Tradition* he has focused on metaphor and wit as essential elements in a successful poem. He states his preference for Metaphysical poetry because it synthesizes all these elements. Borrowing from I. A. Richards, Brooks notes that some poetry, sentimental for example, does not include the disagreeable side of life, presenting only the acceptable, whether in character, action, or thought. Brooks favors the poem that excludes neither side of life; a believer in the doctrine of the Fall, he sees both the good and the evil in real life and expects the most commendable poems to include both; the same is true of divergent views. He is also quick to differ with Marxists and others who use poetry for purposes outside the main thrust of the poem.

Moving from a consideration of Brooks as a critic of poetry to an examination of him as a critic of fiction, one notes a radical shift in approach. The difference is perhaps not one of kind but of degree, yet Brooks clearly gives more attention to philosophical, biographical, and social concerns in approaching fiction. His *The Hidden God* is, as the title suggests, of philosophical interest. *William Faulkner: The Yoknapatawpha Country* is concerned with giving the reader a cultural context within which to approach what Brooks considers Faulkner's best novels, those set in Faulkner's fictional county. The sequel, *William Faulkner: Toward Yoknapatawpha and Beyond*, treats poems, short stories, and other novels. Both works were planned from the beginning. In the former, whole chapters are given to the cultural situation from which Faulkner worked and that which he created within his novels. Since Faulkner considered himself to be writing primarily about people, Brooks gives the strongest emphasis to characterization, analyzing people as they function within the plot and setting. One chapter is given to Faulkner's philosophy of time and history in the second work. *William Faulkner: First Encounters* again reflects Brooks the teacher. It is intended for the nonspecialist in Faulkner, no doubt for the student, as it is an excellent introduction in nontechnical language. What then can be made of such attention to matter outside the literary work? It is essential to preparation for approaching the work but must not be confused with the novel or story itself.

A fit conclusion to a discussion of Brooks as critic might be attention to Monroe K. Spears' chapter in *The Possibilities of Order: Cleanth Brooks and His Work* (1976), entitled "The Responsibilities of Criticism." Spears notes that Brooks fulfills all three responsibilities: Brooks is tactful and courteous to the reader but "treats him with a certain rigor and strictness," insisting "that the reader confront *all* the work." He respects the authors who are his subjects "as serious artists," recognizing "the complexity and integrity of their work." Finally, "he respects language and historical fact." René Wellek's chapter title in the same work is a fitting description: to Wellek, "Cleanth Brooks, Critic of Critics" means one critic who studies, analyzes, and comments on the statements of other critics – one who writes analytical histories of criticism – but Wellek's title also suggests that Brooks is a theorist who stands tall among literary critics modern and ancient.

Principal criticism

An Approach to Literature: A Selection of Prose and Verse with Analyses and Discussions, 1936 (editor, with John Thibaut Purser and Robert Penn Warren)
Understanding Poetry: An Anthology for College Students, 1938 (with Warren)
Modern Poetry and the Tradition, 1939
Poetry in the Age of Anxiety, 1947
The Well Wrought Urn: Studies in the Structure of Poetry, 1947
Poems of Mr. John Milton: The 1645 Edition with Essays in Analysis, 1951 (editor, with John Edward Hardy)
Literary Criticism: A Short History, 1957 (with William K. Wimsatt)
The Hidden God: Studies in Hemingway, Faulkner, Yeats, Eliot, and Warren, 1963
William Faulkner: The Yoknapatawpha Country, 1963
The Poetry of Tension, 1971
A Shaping Joy: Studies in the Writer's Craft, 1971
William Faulkner: Toward Yoknapatawpha and Beyond, 1978
William Faulkner: First Encounters, 1983
On the Prejudices, Predilections, and Firm Beliefs of William Faulkner, 1987
Historical Evidence and the Reading of Seventeenth-Century Poetry, 1991
Community, Religion and Literature: Essays, 1995

Other major works and literary forms

In all, Cleanth Brooks published more than one hundred books and articles. In addition to those listed above are textbooks for college composition and literature courses, edited collections of letters and stories, works on dialect, and numerous articles of critical interest. Some anthologies, such as *American Literature: The Makers and the Making* (1973), contain extensive commentary. Others – *Understanding Poetry, Understanding Drama* (1945), and *Understanding Fiction* (1943) – are classic texts on the analysis of literary genres. Other works – *Tragic Themes in Western Literature: Seven Essays by Bernard Knox and Others* (1955), for example – contain excellent critical matter in introductions. Early and late, Brooks concerned himself with the dialects of the South in such works as *The Relation of the Alabama-Georgia Dialect to the Provincial*

Dialects of Great Britain (1935), the earliest published book listed herein, and *The Language of the American South*, published in 1985.

Examples of edited collections not intended as textbooks and containing relatively little critical comment are *An Anthology of Stories from "The Southern Review,"* (1953), coedited with Robert Penn Warren, and the multivolume series *The Percy Letters* (1944), coedited with David Nichol Smith and A. F. Falconer; individual volumes edited by Brooks, such as *The Correspondence of Thomas Percy and William Shenstone* (1977), however, contain much of Brooks' commentary. Composition texts include *Modern Rhetoric* (1949).

NONFICTION
The Relation of the Alabama-Georgia Dialect to the Provincial Dialects of Great Britain, 1935
The Language of the American South, 1985

EDITED TEXTS
Understanding Fiction, 1943 (with Robert Penn Warren)
The Percy Letters, 1944 (with David Nichol Smith and A. F. Falconer)
Understanding Drama, 1945 (with Warren)
Modern Rhetoric, 1949 (with Warren)
Fundamentals of Good Writing: A Handbook of Modern Rhetoric, 1950 (with Warren)
An Anthology of Stories from "The Southern Review," 1953 (with Warren)
Tragic Themes in Western Literature: Seven Essays by Bernard Knox and Others, 1955
The Scope of Fiction, 1960 (shorter version of *Understanding Fiction*, with Warren)
American Literature: The Makers and the Making, 1973 (with R. W. B. Lewis and Warren)
The Correspondence of Thomas Percy and William Shenstone, 1977

Further reading

Crane, Ronald S. "The Critical Monism of Cleanth Brooks," in *Critics and Criticism: Ancient and Modern*, 1951.
Daiches, David. *Critical Approaches to Literature*, 1956.
Geurin, Wilfred L., et al. *A Handbook of Critical Approaches to Literature*, 1979.
Havard, William C., and Walter Sullivan, eds. *A Band of Prophets: The Vanderbilt Agrarians After Fifty Years*, 1982.
Patnaik, J. N. *The Aesthetics of New Criticism*, 1983.
Rubin, Louis D., Jr., et al., eds. *The History of Southern Literature*, 1985.
Simpson, Lewis P., ed. *The Possibilities of Order: Cleanth Brooks and His Work*, 1976.
Szili, Jósef. "The New Criticism," in *Literature and Its Interpretation*, 1979.

GEORGE W. VAN DEVENDER

See also American Literary Theory: Twentieth Century; New Criticism

Van Wyck Brooks

American critic and writer

Born: Plainfield, New Jersey; February 16, 1886
Died: Bridgewater, Connecticut; May 2, 1963

Biography

Van Wyck Brooks was born on February 16, 1886, in Plainfield, New Jersey, an affluent suburb of New York City. He was the younger son of Charles Edward Brooks, a stockbroker, and a socially ambitious mother, Sarah Bailey (Ames) Brooks. Family excursions to Europe during Brooks' adolescence instilled in him a reverence for artistic tradition, augmenting his growing resentment of the American commercial bias he believed had betrayed his father. He established an early preference for a literary career while a student at Harvard University, privately publishing essays and poetry and working as an editor for the *Harvard Advocate*. Completing his degree a year early, Brooks left for England, where he worked as a journalist and wrote his first book, *The Wine of the Puritans* (1908). For financial and personal reasons he returned to New York in 1909, where he did writing chores for publishers of reference books. In 1911 he moved to California to teach English at Stanford University and marry Eleanor Stimson, his fiancée of several years.

In 1913, frustrated by the difficulty of writing while maintaining a full-time teaching schedule, Brooks and his wife returned to England, where a part-time teaching post allowed him the opportunity to write. The outbreak of World War I in 1914 forced the couple back to New York, where Brooks held editorial positions at several magazines, including *The Seven Arts* and *The Freeman*. During this time he published two volumes of essays, *America's Coming-of-Age* (1915) and *Letters and Leadership* (1918), and biographies of Mark Twain and Henry James, each biography pessimistic in its portrayal of a thwarted creative life. In 1925 financial, professional, and personal struggles brought on a severe mental breakdown (twice requiring Brooks' hospitalization) that lasted until 1931. Brooks' emergence from his "season in hell" was aided by the publication of his biography of Ralph Waldo Emerson, *The Life of Emerson* (1932). A grim note that same year, though, was the violent suicide of Brooks' older brother Charles, a quiet man whose poetic sensibilities had been stifled by his mother's insistence that at least one of the Brooks men have a successful financial life.

At his wife's suggestion, Brooks began work on his most ambitious project, a series entitled *Makers and Finders: A History of the Writer in America, 1800–1915* (1936–1952). Involving twenty years' work and the reading of more than five thousand books, the series was acclaimed for its vividness and scholarship and helped Brooks reclaim his literary reputation.

Though controversial, Brooks was respected for his wide learning and personal integrity, and he received numerous awards in his lifetime, including the Dial Award for critical excellence (1923), the Pulitzer Prize in history (1937), and the National Institute of Arts and Letters Gold Medal (1946) – as well as election to the American Academy of Arts and Letters. As an established critic in his later years, he not only continued to write but also offered support to beginning writers – answering letters, reading manuscripts, even sending money or lobbying publishers on behalf of promising talent. Brooks died in 1963, survived by his second wife, Gladys Rice (Billings) Brooks (whom he married after Eleanor's death in 1946), and two sons from his first marriage.

Influence

Brooks' major contribution as a critic lies in his chronicling of the early development of American literature. Assessing the impact of this achievement in a time not far from Brooks' own is difficult, since his critical reputation during his lifetime suffered from his unpopular and sometimes unsound aesthetic judgments. Despite his controversial ideas, Brooks was considered an influential critic by such writers as Sherwood Anderson and Sinclair Lewis and by fellow critics Randolph Bourne, Lewis Mumford, and Edmund Wilson.

Analysis

Rather than a literary critic per se, Brooks can best be described as a curious amalgam of social prophet, novelist, and cultural historian. Consistently didactic in tone and intention, he saw in the United States a social structure that was shamefully profit-oriented, that sanctioned materialism at the expense of the inner life of its people. Portraying an isolated artistic community overshadowed by economic opportunism on a national scale, Brooks declared that premature decay was the hallmark of America's aging, as opposed to the majesty and cultural richness that distinguished European society. Though concerned with all aspects of American culture, he singled out literature as its most accurate expression and was disturbed by what he believed it revealed.

To Brooks, the history of the writer in America was littered with suicides and, equally tragic, a profusion of atrophied and misused talent. Seeing this legacy as representative of the plight of the creative personality in America, he insisted that these writers failed so frequently because they were bereft of a tradition to sustain them, left without the sense of a shared vocation with which to counter the indifference that America showed its artists. It was essential, Brooks believed, that aspiring writers felt themselves part of a valuable and continuing literary community. Isolated, the creative personality was doomed, certain to be overwhelmed or seduced by America's commercialism and herd mentality. Though he later undertook to document a coherent literary tradition in the United States, Brooks' initial response was to declare such a tradition nonexistent and therefore in need of inventing, and in an essay entitled "Creating a Usable Past" he outlined a strategy for such a task.

The mold for such an impassioned literary philosophy was cast in Brooks' early years. His travels to Europe had exposed him to the grandeur of longstanding tradition, and he was awestruck not only by the magnificence of European art but also by its primacy within the cultural life. It was also in Europe that Brooks discovered the writings of the English critic John Ruskin, whose doctrine of the social and prophetic role of the artist left a deep and lasting impression. The belief that great literature had an "underlying religious intention" was an unpopular sentiment when Brooks attended Harvard, where aesthetic and formal concerns were paramount. Brooks held his ground, however, and later likened the technique-obsessed Harvard literati to Dr. Cuticle, the surgeon in Herman Melville's novel *White-Jacket: Or, The World in a Man-of-War* (1850), who, in his earnestness to demonstrate technical virtuosity, fails to observe that his patient has died on the operating table. Though he appreciated stylistic beauty and recognized the legitimacy of a necessary distance from one's subject, the idea of art and artists remote from life was abhorrent to Brooks. "Primary" literature, he maintained, was ultimately life-affirming, as opposed to the "literature of despair," with its preoccupation with technique and seeming indifference to human aspirations. As a result of this bias, he censured such significant writers as T. S. Eliot, James Joyce, and William Faulkner.

Brooks' harsh assessment of contemporary writing was dismissed as ill-conceived and extreme and was tempered somewhat as he matured. It prompted him, however, to examine American history in the hope of understanding how art could have developed such an "unreal" role. His first attempt at articulating an explanation was *The Wine of the Puritans*, a small volume in the form of a fictional dialogue. Brooks' premise was this: America suffered culturally from a schizoid temperament that had its roots in the Puritan experience. This schism was the result of an established cultural tradition (European gentility) trying to adapt to the harsh American wilderness. With the demands of physical survival necessarily sovereign, any vestiges of intellectual or cultural life came to be seen as peripheral and arbitrary. Out of piety and a Calvinistic determinism, the Puritans abandoned their spiritual concerns to God yet conducted their everyday affairs with an austere pragmatism. Spirit and matter became disparate elements, rigidly divorced. While this separation was a functional necessity for the Puritans, it resulted in a deep-seated cultural rift when conditions changed and Anglo-American society, firmly established on the continent, began to grow and take shape. In the metaphor that provided the book's title, Brooks explained that old wine had been poured into new bottles, and an "explosion" had occurred. The spilled wine became commercialism; the aroma, Transcendentalism. Brooks claimed that the two strains had evolved into "pure" types that were incompatible – a utilitarian bias that was an anachronism left from the harsh realities of settlement, and a vague idealism that, having outlived its origins and finding no new social context, had become "wholly dreamlike and vaporous."

Brooks continued and clarified this argument in his first influential book, *America's Coming-of-Age*. Once again he painted a portrait of two distinct American cultures: the "Highbrow" (aesthetic, theory-oriented, aristocratic) and the "Lowbrow" (commercial, utilitarian). Brooks lamented this cleft between theory and practice, believing that it produced art that lacked any organic connection with life and a life devoid of spiritual sustenance. He depicted America's polarization as "dessicated culture at one end and stark utility at the other," and he issued an appeal for a unifying force, a heroic figure steeped in both the ethereal and the corporeal. Such a person could use his (Brooks envisioned a male) contagious personality to bridge the cultural rift that had paralyzed America's creative life. He even offered a prototype in the person of Walt Whitman. Whitman was the vibrant, integrated personality that Brooks sought, but he had one pivotal drawback: the indiscriminate affirmation he championed had as its inevitable consequence a passive complacency toward the conventional, however mediocre. Without intensity, without some personal sense of outrage, he could not possibly have hoped to transform an entire nation, nor would he have had any such desire. On an instinctual level, Whitman's affirmation was celebratory; intellectually, it required the suspension of the critical sense and thus rendered Whitman incapable of rejecting those aspects of American society that impoverished the individual.

Brooks' portrayal of Whitman served another purpose in that it cemented his preference for approaching American literary history through the study of representative figures, analyzing how each manifested peculiar aspects of the American temperament and creative life. To do this, he developed a form of "dramatic biography," a hybrid of biography, fiction, and history that he hoped would best convey the essence of a given writer's life and work. He used this format to write his trilogy on Mark Twain, Henry James, and Ralph Waldo Emerson. The first volume, *The Ordeal of Mark Twain* (1920, revised 1933), was critical of the Missouri humorist despite his current popularity. Brooks depicted Twain as a cultural traitor who had allowed himself to be seduced by America's prevailing philistinism and money ethic. Defensively cynical from the betrayal of his own artistic ideals and talent, the Twain of Brooks' drama was doubly guilty because he had used his humor to deflate the tension produced by the repression of creativity and individualism. In doing so, he made commercialism and its accompanying spiritual sterility more viable.

Brooks was attacked, sometimes savagely, for his harsh appraisal of America's favorite humorist. Other critics accused him of oversimplifying and selectively distorting Twain's work and of superimposing his own conflicts upon a legitimate talent. Brooks, while admitting his subjectivism, defended the book as a cautionary tale of the derailed creative life, but in 1933 he issued a new edition that contained major revisions.

The Pilgrimage of Henry James (1925) also was conceived and written as a symbolic story, but it examined a different response to the American writer's dilemma. Whereas Twain had succumbed to the "baser" demands of American culture, James fled to England and wrote as an expatriate. To Brooks, this was not only an abdication of responsibility but also a turning point that marked the degeneration of James' work. James had abandoned his roots, Brooks argued, and being necessarily an outsider in European culture, was forced to dwell on formal and technical concerns for want of genuine substance. Brooks disparaged the aridity and ambiguity of James' later work but failed to see that it reflected the more complex vision of a mature artist. With his social concerns and his probing of the symbolic creative life largely ignored, Brooks' aesthetic judgments were discredited, and he was again accused, somewhat justifiably, of imposing personal conflicts onto his subject. Coinciding with his breakdown, this rupture with the literary community marked the low point of Brooks' personal and professional life. Some respite finally came with the publication in 1932 of *The Life of Emerson*, in which Brooks presented an alternative to the conformity of Twain and the escapism of Henry James. This volume offered an affirmative portrait, a personality that embodied both the masculine "Self-Reliance" and the feminine transcendental quality necessary for the successful literary life. Brooks portrayed Emerson as an example of the integrated cultural hero that America needed, a man in whom the soul of a poet was coupled with the resourcefulness and determination of an entrepreneur.

The completion of the Emerson study marked a transition in Brooks' work, born of the realization that his search for a "usable past" was destined to fail if it focused only on miscarriages of creativity and not on its triumphs. With this in mind, he began work on the project he hoped would document and affirm the American literary tradition, offering the foundation necessary for the development of young writers. The five-volume *Makers and Finders* was intended to evoke a sense of legacy and continuity among America's writers by portraying a cohesive literary fabric, one that included great creative talents (makers) as well as their followers (finders), writers who, though perhaps of lesser genius, nevertheless made valuable contributions to American cultural life. Brooks again chose a partly fictive approach, submerging his own critical voice in an attempt to render the writer's experience more accurately. The first two volumes, *The Flowering of New England* and *New*

England: Indian Summer, are considered his finest works. The remaining three volumes, though not quite as successful, were still influential.

A sixth volume intended for *Makers and Finders*, one dealing with the years after 1915, had been envisioned by Brooks but was never written. That it was not written reflects his then unstable health but also underscores what is perhaps his greatest critical limitation: the inability to see contemporary writers in perspective. This was among several inconsistencies for which Brooks was criticized. In an ironic backlash, many considered him unsympathetic to the American artist's dilemma, because while he alleged the impossibility of the creative life in America, he disparaged those who failed to achieve it. Equally troublesome was Brooks' tendency to project, often unconsciously, his own conflicts onto other lives. The same tendency toward biased selectivity also produced his idyllic portrayal of a unified European culture and the concomitant demand that America emulate that model. It was, however, for his misreading of modern writers that Brooks lost stature in the literary world. Impatient with experimentalism, Brooks often saw technical and formal complexity as mere sleight of hand, not as a means to more closely approximate the meaning a writer was trying to convey. He also mistook the naysaying of the younger generation for wanton nihilism, when in part it was merely a response to the vulgar and escapist American optimism that he himself had denounced.

In his later years Brooks published *The Writer in America* (1953), which had originally been conceived as the introductory chapter for *Makers and Finders*. In it he softened his harsh stance toward the avant-garde and even applauded its commitment to stay and speak out rather than emigrate or wallow in a cynical indifference, though these and other concessions he made to the modern temperament were often ignored. He noted the limitations, however, of any art that had to be separate from its culture in order to survive. He defended his distaste for technical concerns by insisting that since form inevitably varied with each age, it could not be the undercurrent of a literary tradition. Preoccupation with form, Brooks argued, rendered literature a merely aesthetic phenomenon and thus undermined the role it played in revealing and enriching human character. He proclaimed that great fiction always embodied a "regenerative impulse" and thereby revealed the aim implicit in his life's work – the spiritual and cultural renewal of an entire nation. For Brooks, the writer's task was not only to reflect but also to shape culture, a duty he believed had been abandoned by many moderns, whom he labeled (borrowing Arthur Miller's phrase) "mere chroniclers of disaster." Refusing to hide his disappointment, he admonished young writers to be responsible caretakers of their talent, not to rationalize their failures, and above all, not to renounce life. In documenting a sustained American tradition, Brooks had "written mainly for other writers," hoping to instill in them a sense of purpose strong enough to displace the modernist posture of despair and alienation.

Brooks' unorthodox approach was sometimes maligned as unprofessional and overly dramatic, partly because in his attempt to interpret the dilemma of the creative spirit in America, he had wandered into the stylistic domain of the fiction writer. Although his artistic gift for seeing the symbolic behind the singular had at times compromised his critical acumen and obscured the boundaries between imagination and fact, Brooks understood and could recognize spiritual suffocation. It had destroyed his father by stripping the personal resiliency from a ruined financial life, it had beckoned his brother into the path of an oncoming train, and it had scarred Brooks himself through an intense and bitter struggle for sanity.

A common complaint of Brooks' detractors was that he indulged himself in his writings, that his portraits of others were not sufficiently removed from his own life. It is a charge with some merit, but it betrays an ignorance of Brooks' deliberately fictive method and of his stated intent "to awaken feeling and imagination." More important, it disregards his motivation for writing. To Brooks, public life as a man of letters meant not opportunity alone, but the responsibility to address those societal ills that had cost him in his private life. In doing so, he illuminated significant and previously unrecognized aspects of American culture and history.

Principal criticism

America's Coming-of-Age, 1915 (also as *Three Essays on America*, 1934)
Letters and Leadership, 1918
The Ordeal of Mark Twain, 1920, revised 1933
The Pilgrimage of Henry James, 1925
The Life of Emerson, 1932
Sketches in Criticism, 1932
Makers and Finders: A History of the Writer in America, 1800–1915, 1936–1952 (5 volumes), includes *The Flowering of New England: 1815–1865*, *New England: Indian Summer, 1865–1915*, *The World of Washington Irving*, *The Times of Melville and Whitman*, and *The Confident Years: 1885–1915*
The Writer in America, 1953

Other major works and literary forms

Throughout his career, Van Wyck Brooks wrote and published numerous essays and book reviews, as well as biographies of figures as diverse as H. G. Wells, Helen Keller, and the painter John Sloan. In addition, he wrote three loosely autobiographical volumes (based on his journals) and translated from the French various works by Denys Amiel, Romain Rolland, Paul Gauguin, Georges Duhamel, and Leon Bazalgette.

NONFICTION
The Wine of the Puritans, 1908
The Malady of the Ideal: Obermann, Maurice de Guérin, and Amiel, 1913
John Addington Symonds: A Biographical Study, 1914

The World of H. G. Wells, 1915
Emerson and Others, 1927
On Literature Today, 1941
The Opinions of Oliver Allston, 1941
A Chilmark Miscellany, 1948
Scenes and Portraits: Memories of Childhood and Youth, 1954
John Sloan: A Painter's Life, 1955
Helen Keller: Sketch for a Portrait, 1956
Days of the Phoenix: The Nineteen-Twenties I Remember, 1957
From A Writer's Notebook, 1958
The Dream of Arcadia: American Writers and Artists in Italy, 1760–1915, 1958
Howells: His Life and World, 1959
From the Shadow of the Mountain: My Post-Meridian Year, 1961
Fenollosa and His Circle: With Other Essays in Biography, 1962
The Van Wyck Brooks – Lewis Mumford Letters, 1970

Further reading

Blake, Casey Nelson. *Beloved Community: The Cultural Criticism of Randolph Bourne, Van Wyck Brooks, Waldo Frank and Lewis Mumford*, 1990.
Chabot, C. Barry. *Writers for the Nation: American Literary Modernism*, 1997.
Edel, Leon. "Biographer and Subject: Lytton Strachey and Van Wyck Brooks," in *Prose Studies*. 5, no. 3 (December, 1982), pp. 281–293.
Hoopes, James. *Van Wyck Brooks: In Search of American Culture*, 1977.
Nelson, Raymond. *Van Wyck Brooks: A Writer's Life*, 1981.
Vitelli, James. *Van Wyck Brooks*, 1969.
——. *Van Wyck Brooks: A Reference Guide*, 1977.
Wasserstrom, William. *Van Wyck Brooks*, 1968.
——. *The Legacy of Van Wyck Brooks: A Study of Maladies and Motives*, 1971.
——. *Van Wyck Brooks: The Critic and His Critics*, 1979.

William LaHay

See also American Literary Theory: Twentieth Century

Ferdinand Brunetière

French critic

Born: Toulon, France; July 19, 1849
Died: Paris, France; December 9, 1906

Biography

Vincent-Paul-Marie-Ferdinand Brunetière was born on July 19, 1849, in Toulon, France, the son of Charles-Marie-Ferdinand-Emmanuel Brunetière and the former Suzanne-Delphine Hémon. His father was an officer in the navy, and it was perhaps he who instilled in Ferdinand the regard for social order and respect for authority which were always to characterize the latter's manner of judging the relationship between art and society.

While he was a brilliant student in his early years, the future critic nevertheless failed the entrance examination for the École Normale Supérieure – conceivably because he preferred his own reading lists to those prescribed by the school. Yet so omnivorously did Brunetière read on his own, especially in literature, history, and philosophy, and so vast was the erudition that he acquired, that the École Normale Supérieure hired him to teach French literature in 1886, although he possessed no advanced degree. In the meantime, Brunetière had already developed a most impressive reputation as a critic for the prestigious *Revue des deux mondes*, whose staff he had joined in 1875. He assumed the directorship of that periodical in 1894, the same year that he became a member of the French Academy and was received by Pope Leo XIII. The papal audience would be a determinative factor in Brunetière's conversion to Catholicism six years later, a conversion which would lead to the intensification of his insistence on the social and moral responsibility of art.

Before he died of tuberculosis on December 9, 1906, at the age of fifty-seven, Brunetière's renown as a literary critic had become international. A spellbinding orator, he had been invited to lecture in various European countries as well as in the United States and Canada.

Influence

During his lifetime, Brunetière was considered by many to be France's finest lecturer and most influential literary critic, and there was obviously some connection between the two distinctions. His intellectual contemporaries generally agreed that this gifted speaker and prolific writer's violent opposition to naturalism, launched at a time when the movement appeared to be well entrenched, contributed in no small measure to its decline after 1885 and heralded the resurgence of an idealistic spirit in French letters.

The subsequent waning of Brunetière's overall influence came about as the pretentiousness of his attempt to practice a totally objective literary criticism, the severe shortcomings of his theory of the evolution of literary genres, and his moralizing bias grew more and more apparent. Nevertheless, his work retained the merit of having put the scientific presumptions of naturalism in a new, if unflattering, light, and, in so doing, of having furnished by contrast a biased but provocative reappraisal of neoclassicism. Moreover, the impact of his methodology, while admittedly less extensive after his death, continued nevertheless to be felt among certain critics of the younger generation, whom he compelled, by his flawed yet exemplary pursuit of critical detachment, to reexamine constantly their subjective assumptions about criticism against the backdrop of historical patterns of organic literary development.

Analysis

At the beginning of his career as a literary critic, Brunetière appeared to be in pursuit of a critical method that would be the complete antithesis of the scientific approach to literature characteristic of his time, an approach dominated by the positivism of Auguste Comte and Ernest Renan, Charles Darwin's theory of evolution, and the determinism of Hippolyte-Adolphe Taine. Generally, Brunetière was opposed to these concepts because of their failure to recognize the limits of science, their inability to advance significantly the knowledge of human origins, nature, and destiny, and their overemphasis on environmental factors. In his first article for the *Revue des deux mondes*, published in 1875, Brunetière gave his protest a more specific literary focus by attacking Émile Zola and the naturalists. He decried their cynical view of human nature as inimical to the quest for the ideal in literature and denounced the corruption of aesthetic values which resulted from pandering to the vulgar and materialistic tastes of the masses.

In *Études critiques sur l'histoire de la littérature française* and in *Le Roman naturaliste*, Brunetière would again attack the naturalists, condemning the very notion of "scientific art," for him a contradiction in terms, and denouncing the movement for its lack of psychological depth and its neglect of what makes humans superior to nature. He would redefine true naturalism, in the process, as the faithful imitation of both internal and external human reality and would consider even Honoré de Balzac and Gustave Flaubert inferior, in this regard, to the writers of the seventeenth century.

Brunetière's early rejection of scientific literature as illustrated by the naturalists and his asserted preference for the equilibrium and universal appeal of neoclassicism seemed to portend his eventual formulation of a method of literary criticism free of the pretensions of science. Yet he remained to a significant degree a prisoner of the scientific approach. An indication of this intellectual thralldom was Brunetière's enunciation of the principle of objective criticism in his 1892 *Essais sur la littérature contemporaine*, in which he defined such criticism as involving the triple function of judging, classifying, and explaining literary works. Two years earlier, Brunetière had offered a striking example of the application of this principle with his theory of the evolution of literary genres, propounded in *L'Évolution des genres dans l'histoire de la littérature*. According to this work, ironically reminiscent of Darwin, the study of the history of literature revealed that the genres, like other worldly phenomena, had a time to be born and a time to die. They emerged, progressed to a point of perfection, then declined, with the attendant Darwinian processes of struggle for existence and natural selection, as the evolution of some genres was adversely affected by the success of others. Brunetière's analysis also sought to demonstrate that the process of evolution yielded a set of laws or rules for each genre, since the very masterpieces of a genre typified, as such, the qualities required to achieve perfection in it or to define it in absolute terms.

Brunetière's attempt to offer a concrete historical example of his theory at work nevertheless betrayed both his strictly personal – and in no way objective – preferences and the fundamental inadequacy of his system. In order to prove the viability of his theory, Brunetière chose as a testing ground the development of neoclassicism in seventeenth-century France. The aim of his ambitious work, *Histoire de la littérature française classique, 1515–1830*, was to show that certain genres (tragedy in the hands of Jean Racine, for example) reached their state of perfection in the neoclassical period. Brunetière als argued that in that same period all the prerequisites for superlative literary achievement in a broader sense were satisfied. Among these were the neoclassical writer's choice of universal themes and the perfect balance within that writer of reason and imagination, the reality of French national independence, and, most extraordinary of all, perhaps, the evolution of the French language to a state of absolute perfection. Implicit in Brunetière's argument, given this most remarkable harmony of convergent factors, was the contention that neoclassicism was not merely the product of an evolutionary process but the crystallization of a perfect literary model to be admired and emulated.

Also implicit in Brunetière's argument, because of the ideas of the perfect model, however, was the possibility of a nagging contradiction. If indeed the French language had evolved to a state of perfection in the seventeenth century, did that signify that writers of succeeding generations must necessarily resign themselves to stylistic imperfection? In his *Études critiques sur l'histoire de la littérature française*, Brunetière seemed to draw that very conclusion, claiming that the nineteenth-century Romantic poets, Victor Hugo among them, were not really capable of that earlier perfection. On the other hand, Brunetière would later contradict himself by praising a nineteenth-century novelist whom he had previously criticized harshly: his *Honoré de Balzac, 1799–1850* would emphasize that author's consummate artistry.

In all fairness to Brunetière, it must be noted that he subsequently moved away from the genre theory. He published only the first volume of *L'Évolution des genres dans l'histoire de la littérature*, whereas initially it had been his intention to produce a multivolume work; in addition, in the preface to his *Manual of the History of French Literature*, he stated his new preference for a division of literary history into periods rather than genres. As to the underlying proposition regarding the process of literary evolution, Brunetière did not abandon it entirely; rather, he began to interpret it differently. Being also a literary historian, he could not for long remain indifferent to the fact that what clearly evolved was the way in which authors and works were evaluated over the years in conjunction with changing social and economic conditions. Seen in this light, Brunetière's newfound reasons for praising Balzac, if they represented a contradiction of his genre theory as noted above, also reflected his acknowledgment that values were now manifest in that novelist's production which were not at all apparent – at least not where he, Brunetière, was concerned – at an earlier time. Furthermore, despite his unabashedly intense veneration for neoclassicism, Brunetière was eventually able to discern that the novel was a modern genre which had flourished in the nineteenth century as it had not flourished before because of patterns of socioeconomic development peculiar to that century.

The increased flexibility of Brunetière's critical method in his later years was not always sufficient, however, to offset lingering personal prejudices which, in spite of the critic's professed objectivity, often colored his judgment. Perhaps the most pervasive of these prejudices was one that grew out of Brunetière's perception of the writer's self-effacement in neoclassical literature. This bias took the form, in the socially traditionalistic Brunetière, of a deep-seated hostility to works which, instead of promoting the public good or fostering a sense of community, appeared excessively focused on the individual, whose sentimental and intellectual fantasies or rebellion against society's conventions were indulgently portrayed. Clearly reflected in the *Études critiques sur l'histoire de la littérature française*, in which Brunetière maintained that literature must deal with themes so human and so broad as to be commonplace, this aversion to the glorification of the individual also informed the *Questions de critique*, in which Brunetière inveighed against personal or confessional writings in the style of Jean-Jacques Rousseau. The critic's position on this matter caused him to be frequently unsympathetic to the Romantics, ambivalent toward the Symbolists (whose reaction against naturalism he nevertheless appreciated), and even ultimately opposed to the exponents of the "art for art's sake" movement, his early endorsement of which he recanted in a lecture at the Sorbonne in 1893.

With Brunetière's zealous conversion to Catholicism in 1900, it became difficult to determine where, in his literary judgment, formal criticism ended and religious propaganda began. Long convinced that art had a social and moral role, Brunetière had given a particularly dramatic expression to that conviction in *Art and Morality*, in which aesthetic considerations were viewed as having a definitely secondary function in literary criticism. In harmony with this outlook, Brunetière could find substantial merit in the *pièces à thèse*, or "problem plays," of Alexandre Dumas, *fils*, because of their utilitarian value.

The serious defects of Brunetière's rigid systematizations and moralizing proclivities were not apparent to many of his contemporaries, and the influence that he exerted during his lifetime was profound, especially given the abundance of his publications, his directorship of the much respected *Revue des deux mondes*, his teaching career at the École Normale Supérieure, and his innumerable public lectures, a series of which he delivered at the Sorbonne. Brunetière was commonly seen as the intellectual successor to Renan and Taine. To his students at the École Normale Supérieure particularly, because of his frontal assaults on naturalism in its heyday, he seemed to be incredibly courageous, and extraordinarily modern in his thought.

After his death, however, Brunetière's reputation diminished. The works of Gustave Lanson, the eminent critic and literary historian, reflected the change. In his *Histoire de la littérature française* (1894), Lanson lavished praise on Brunetière, but in the fourth edition of his *Manuel illustré d'histoire de la littérature française*, coauthored with Paul Tuffrau and published in 1932, Lanson replaced the praise with less flattering comments. Subsequent evaluators, with relatively few exceptions, followed suit.

Yet, however flawed his theories, Brunetière must be credited with having tried to bring the scientist's reverence for facts to the practice of literary criticism, with the aim of controlling the critic's inclination to subjectivity (although Brunetière himself objected vehemently to the scientific pretensions of naturalism). It must also be acknowledged that Brunetière provided not only enthusiastic but also penetrating studies of major figures of the neoclassical movement, such as Blaise Pascal and Jacques-Bénigne Bossuet – even if his unstinting admiration for the achievements of the movement often warped his critical perspective in other areas. Finally, it must not be forgotten that what was positive in Brunetière's approach to literature was not entirely lost on his students. Some of them, such as Joseph Bédier and Pierre Martino, applying those principles of Brunetière's method which remained valid, went on to make very distinguished contributions to literary criticism.

Principal criticism

Études critiques sur l'histoire de la littérature française, 1880–1925 (9 volumes)
Le Roman naturaliste, 1883
Histoire et littérature, 1884–1886 (3 volumes)
Questions de critique, 1889
Nouvelles Questions de critique, 1890
L'Évolution des genres dans l'histoire de la littérature, 1890
Conférences de l'Odéon: Les Époques du théâtre français, 1636–1850, 1892
Essais sur la littérature contemporaine, 1892
Essays in French Literature, 1892
L'Évolution de la poésie lyrique en France au dix-neuvième siècle, 1894 (2 volumes)
Nouveaux Essais sur la littérature contemporaine, 1895
Manuel de l'histoire de la littérature française, 1898 (*Manual of the History of French Literature*, 1898)
L'Art et la morale, 1898 (*Art and Morality*, 1899)
Discours de combat, 1900–1907 (3 volumes)
Discours académiques, 1901
Cinq Lettres sur Ernest Renan, 1904
Variétés littéraires, 1904
Histoire de la littérature française classique, 1515–1830, 1904–1917 (4 volumes)
Honoré de Balzac, 1799–1850, 1905 (English translation, 1906)
Études sur le XVIIIe siècle, 1911
Bossuet, 1913
Pages sur Ernest Renan, 1924

Other major works and literary forms

Besides books of literary criticism, Ferdinand Brunetière wrote others dealing with religious, scientific, and political questions, such as *La Science et la religion: Réponse à quelques objections* (1895). He also published scores of articles both on literature and on a wide variety of subjects ranging from Oriental history to prehistoric archaeology, from sociology to geology, from mythology and anthropology to philosophy and Assyrian epigraphy.

NONFICTION

La Science et la religion: Réponse à quelques objections, 1895
Après le procès: Réponse à quelques "intellectuels," 1898
Sur les chemins de la croyance, 1904
Questions actuelles, 1907

Further reading

Babbitt, Irving. "Brunetière," in *The Masters of Modern French Criticism*, 1912.
Compagnon, Antoine. *Connaissez-vous Brunetière? Enquête sur un antidreyfusard et ses amis*, 1997.
Gullace, Giovanni. *Taine and Brunetière on Criticism*, 1982.
Hocking, Elton. *Ferdinand Brunetière: The Evolution of a Critic*, 1936.
Klein, F. "Ferdinand Brunetière," in *The Catholic World*. LXXXV (1907), pp. 65–74.
Wellek, René. "French Literary History: Ferdinand Brunetière," in *A History of Modern Criticism: 1750–1950*. Vol. 4, *The Late Nineteenth Century*, 1965.

NORMAN ARAUJO

See also Bourget; Continental Theory; Taine; Zola

Edmund Burke

Irish-born writer and politician

Born: Dublin, Ireland; January 12, 1729
Died: Beaconsfield, England; July 9, 1797

Biography

Edmund Burke was born on January 12, 1729, in Dublin, Ireland, the second surviving son of Richard Burke and Mary Nagle. Richard was a Protestant attorney, and Mary was a Roman Catholic. As a child, Burke was delicate and sickly, finding diversion primarily in books and study. He attended a Quaker boarding school in Yorkshire, where he became a star pupil and close friend of the master's son, Dick Shackleton, with whom he later maintained a voluminous correspondence. Burke entered Trinity College, Dublin, in 1744, quickly gaining a reputation for scholarship. In 1748 he wrote, edited, and published the Dublin paper *The Reformer*. He moved to London in 1750 to begin legal studies at the Middle Temple. Almost immediately he met an English law student, Will Burke, who was to become a lifelong friend and companion. At the same time, however, Edmund Burke fell away from the study of law and therefore became estranged from his father, losing his stipend for school.

By 1757, however, Burke had resolved to be a man of public significance. He had written *A Philosophical Enquiry into the Origin of Our Ideas of the Sublime and Beautiful*, which brought him into the literary circle of Samuel Johnson, Sir Joshua Reynolds, and David Garrick. He also married Jane Nugent, the daughter of an Irish Catholic doctor, and began to seek public employment. In 1759 he became private secretary to William Hamilton, and, during the next six years of service, he began to master the world of public affairs. After breaking with Hamilton in 1765, he found employment as private secretary and adviser to the Marquess of Rockingham, the leader of a wealthy, powerful group of liberal Whigs.

Burke's association with Rockingham was to make his financial and political fortune. He received a seat in the House of Commons and, in 1766, made a large amount of money in the stock market. The former allowed him to launch a long and brilliant career in Parliament and the latter established him at a country estate in Beaconsfield, Buckinghamshire, where he lived until his death in 1797.

Influence

Burke's most original contribution to criticism was in defining and illustrating aesthetic responses to nature and art, particularly as they relate to the concepts of "the beautiful" and "the sublime." By arguing that beauty originates in pleasure and love, whereas the sublime originates in pain and fear, he was able to fashion an explanation of taste that would influence various subsequent movements in the arts. Burke's theory of the sublime contributed to thinking about landscape gardening and may have influenced such novels as Horace Walpole's *The Castle of Otranto* (1765) or the later, popular mysteries of Ann Radcliffe. More certainly, Denis Diderot, Immanuel Kant, Samuel Taylor Coleridge, and Gotthold Ephraim Lessing took his ideas into account in developing their critical theories during the later eighteenth and early nineteenth centuries.

Analysis

Burke's criticism is conditioned by his attempt to analyze human responses to any object in nature or in art, published as *A Philosophical Enquiry into the Origin of Our Ideas of the Sublime and Beautiful*. One of many eighteenth-century documents which tried to account for taste, Burke's treatise was more rigorous than its predecessors, which tended to take for granted certain traditional ideas about what is beautiful. Burke aligned himself with those who believed that responses to beauty are based on immediate perceptions of the Understanding more than on considered judgments by the faculty of Reason. Burke's goal was to discover a universal standard of taste, based on the common physical qualities of objects which seem to produce what later would be called "an aesthetic response." Burke was a behaviorist, an extreme empiricist who, like John Locke, thought carefully about his own responses to phenomena and asked others about theirs. Along with Locke, Burke argued that pleasure is a positive principle, not merely the removal or absence of pain. Burke's most original point, and his most controversial, is that the most intense aesthetic pleasure is a response to the sublime rather than to the beautiful, terms which Burke defined based on physical qualities of objects.

The sublime can consist of describable, potentially threatening qualities such as darkness, greatness of size, angularity, vastness, or profusion – qualities of a rugged mountain range, such as the Alps. Or an unfinished object such as a sketch can evoke the sublime, more so than would a finished painting, "because the imagination is entertained with the promise of something more, and does not acquiesce in the present object of the sense." Finished objects, too, that suggest ideas such as power or difficulty – Burke offered Stonehenge as an example – can also be sources of the sublime. Even certain sounds, such as the cries of wild beasts, or smells, such as stenches, or the taste of bitterness can be sources of the sublime. Burke illustrated how obscurity in literature can produce the sublime with a quotation from *Paradise Lost* (1667, 1674) in which John Milton describes death as a shape: "If shape it might be called that shape had none/ Distinguishable, in member, joint, or limb;/ Or substance might be called that shadow seemed." Burke commented, "In this description all is dark, uncertain, confused, terrible, and sublime to the last degree."

By contrast, qualities on which the beautiful depends – although they strike the mind with the same immediacy as the sublime – produce a pleasure involving sociability rather than isolation. "We love what submits to us," said Burke, so humans find beautiful what is small, smooth, and delicate such as the shape of a dove, a greyhound, or a demure woman. For an object to be beautiful its colors must be clear and, if not mild, then variegated – as in the most beautiful flowers – so as not to be bold and overpowering. Burke found William Hogarth's notion of a gradually curving "line of beauty" to be "extremely just" and went on to explain how the eye finds pain in brisk or abrupt changes of direction but pleasure in gradual variation. The opposite of beauty, he stated, is ugliness; the sublime, like beauty, is appealing, but it originates in avoidance of what is fearful rather than attraction to what is pleasurable.

Burke was at his most original when he tried to explain the psychological process of experiencing these qualities. The ruling principle of the sublime, he argued, is terror. The passion caused by the sublime is astonishment over the object's capacity for terrifying (so long as the danger is not imminent, in which case fear would supersede an aesthetic response). The beautiful, on the other hand, has its origins in pleasure – not, as many of Burke's predecessors had argued, in an object's utility, proportions, or virtue.

Responses to the sublime turn on self-preservation, then, and this basis differentiates the Burkean sublime from the Longinian sublime. The term "sublime" had become familiar in the late seventeenth century from translations of the first-century Greek critic Longinus, who used the word to describe the innate power of a rhetorical passage to lift the soul, to fill it with "a proud exaltation and a sense of vaunting joy." Writing in the mid-eighteenth century, Burke was making the term do new work, to account for experiences in any medium, through any of the senses, with an emphasis on the origins of the response in our fear of death.

Burke dedicated the last section of his treatise to issues of language. He first observed that the power words have over the passions is not the result of pictures or ideas conjured in the mind by the customary meaning of each word, for the speech or reading process is too rapid to allow that sort of word-by-word translation. Rather, he stated, humans know language-meanings by habit and respond to words immediately, as they do to perceptions of objects. Words carry associations with them, however, whose effects will arise on occasions similar to those when the word was learned; this power requires the user of language to exercise "good sense" to see that the likely associations agree with one another and the writer's purpose, so that the style will not seem "bombastic." It is this evocative power of words that enables a writer to generate particularly strong responses to the sublime or to the beautiful. Burke illustrated that point with a description of the habitation of the fallen angels in Milton's *Paradise Lost*: "Rocks, caves, lakes, fens, bogs, dens and shades of death" would carry less force if not for the last two words, "of death," which convey the terrible sublime; a painter could depict the terrain using his or her visual medium, but not the idea of death. For the very reason that poetry is more "obscure" and does not depend on the power of raising sensible images it is more evocative than painting, even if painting can describe more exactly. The business of poetry, then, according to Burke is "to affect rather by sympathy than imitation; to display rather the effect of things on the mind of the speaker, or of others, than to present a clear idea of the things themselves." The power of tragedy, he believed, similarly depends on the sympathy of an audience with those whose distresses they would like to see redressed – not merely on delight over the skill of imitation.

In this application of the concept of sympathy, Burke was following the lead of the empiricist philosopher David Hume and was anticipating the interest in sympathetic imagination by early-nineteenth-century poets such as John Keats. Burke's rejection of rational bases for decisions of taste is consistent with earlier thinkers such as Anthony Ashley Cooper, the third Earl of Shaftesbury, who also thought taste was immediate, and Frances Hutcheson, who speculated about the possible existence of a faculty or faculties which respond to beauty. Joseph Addison had extended taste to visual pleasures of the imagination, and Burke further extended the problem to include all the senses.

Burke's legacy is difficult to assess with precision. Horace Walpole's *The Castle of Otranto* can be read as a book of literary illustrations to Burke's concepts, but direct influence is uncertain. Critic J. T. Boulton comments that the later eighteenth-century vogue for graveyard poetry, ruins, mountain scenery, and Gothic novels is less the result of Burke's influence, however, than it is an evolution of the trends he helped to document and to systematize.

Certainly Burke was read by subsequent theorists of "the picturesque," when that term became a compromise, third source of aesthetic response, between the sublime and the beautiful. Late in the eighteenth century, as Immanuel Kant attempted to develop a philosophy that transcended empiricism in *Kritik der Urtheilskraft* (1790; *Critique of Judgment*, 1892), he called Burke "the foremost author" of the empirical method of aesthetic judgment. Still, it was Kant's model of the mind that helped to displace the mechanistic model adopted by Burke, where the body was assumed to be distinct from the mind, where the mind was thought to be essentially reacting to external stimuli, and where both the pleasure and the fear on which our responses were said to be based had their own origins in various a priori assumptions about nature, society, and morality.

Today Burke is remembered for having helped to fashion enthusiasm for the sublime in nature, whose images would become associated with Romanticism and would remain a staple – or cliché – of the Gothic and horror genres in popular culture even into the twenty-first century.

Principal criticism

A Philosophical Enquiry into the Origin of Our Ideas of the Sublime and Beautiful, 1757 (revised in 1759 to include an "Introduction on Taste")

Other major works and literary forms

Except for occasional poetry recorded in correspondence or journals and the work listed above, Edmund Burke published only political essays. His first foray into publishing was a satire, *A Vindication of Natural Society* (1756), directed against criticism of revealed religion and the contemporary vogue of "return to Nature." Most other essays originated as speeches for the House of Commons; they clustered around three major issues: the American colonies, the government of India, and the French Revolution. For nearly thirty years, beginning in 1758, Burke also edited the *Annual Register*, a survey of world affairs.

NONFICTION
A Vindication of Natural Society, 1756
Annual Register, 1758–1788 (editor)
Speech on American Taxation, 1775
Letters to the Sheriffs of Bristol on the Affairs of America, 1777
Speech on Mr. Fox's East India Bill, 1784
Reflections on the Revolution in France, 1790
An Appeal from the New to the Old Whigs, 1791
Letter to a Noble Lord, 1795

Further reading

Bate, Walter Jackson. *From Classic to Romantic: Premises of Taste in Eighteenth-Century England*, 1946.
Boulton, J. T. Introduction to *A Philosophical Enquiry into the Origin of Our Ideas of the Sublime and Beautiful*, 1958.
Chapman, Gerald W. *Edmund Burke: The Practical Imagination*, 1967.
Ferguson, Frances. "The Sublime of Edmund Burke, or the Bathos of Experience," in *Glyph*. 8 (1981), pp. 62–78.
McKenzie, Alan T. "'I have before me the idea of a dove': Bringing Motion to Mind in Burke's *A Philosophical Enquiry into the Origin of Our Ideas of the Sublime and Beautiful*," in *1650–1750: Ideas, Aesthetics, and Inquiries in the Early Modern Era*, 1994.
Nesbitt, Kate. "The Sublime and Modern Architecture: Unmasking (an Aesthetic of) Abstraction," in *New Literary History*. 26, pp. 95–110.
Reid, Christopher. "The Politics of Taste," in *Edmund Burke and the Practice of Political Writing*, 1985.

JAMES R. AUBREY
PERRY D. LUCKETT

See also Hume; Neoclassical Literary Theory; Romanticism

Kenneth Burke

American writer and critic

Born: Pittsburgh, Pennsylvania; May 5, 1897
Died: Andover, New Jersey; November 19, 1993

Biography

Kenneth Duva Burke was born on May 5, 1897, in Pittsburgh, Pennsylvania. He was a student at Ohio State University from 1916 to 1917 and at Columbia University the following year. Early in his career as a man of letters, he served as music critic for *The Dial* and *The Nation*.

Burke taught literary criticism and theory at the New School for Social Research, the University of Chicago, Bennington College, Princeton University, Kenyon College, Indiana University, and Pennsylvania State University. In 1928 Burke received *The Dial* Award for distinguished service to American letters, and he was a Fellow at the Princeton Institute for Advanced Study and the Stanford Center for Advanced Study in the Behavioral Sciences. He was elected to the National Institute of Arts and Letters in 1946 and won the National Medal for Literature in 1981. Burke was married twice and reared five children.

Influence

Burke's influence is most strongly felt in the field of literary criticism and theory. Never an endorser of the New Criticism, a school which flourished in the United States from the 1940s to the 1970s, Burke persistently argued against the New Critical tendency to conceive of the text as an autonomous object, as a self-enclosed universe of discourse. Throughout his writings, Burke refused to essentialize literary discourse by making it a unique kind of language and was always attuned to the dialectical relationship between literary productions and their sociohistorical contexts.

Early converts to the Burkean method were Francis Fergusson (*The Idea of a Theater*, 1949) and Stanley Edgar Hyman (*The Armed Vision: A Study of the Methods in Modern Literary Criticism*, 1948). Burke's ideas have also made an impact on sociology, most notably on Hugh Dalziel Duncan (*Language and Literature in Society*, 1953) and Erving Goffman (*The Presentation of Self in Everyday Life*, 1959). In addition, Burke has been influential in the areas of rhetoric, composition, speech criticism, and discourse theory.

Analysis

The central idea that pervades all Burke's theory and criticism is embodied in his contention that "the ultimate metaphor for discussing the universe and man's relations to it must be the poetic or dramatic metaphor." According to Burke, "dramatism" is a method of linguistic and conceptual analysis that treats language and thought primarily as modes of action rather than means of conveying information. All verbal acts are to be considered as symbolic action, and dramatism is built about the systematic view of language and literature as species of symbolic action.

Burke thinks of poetry or literature, which in his extended sense of the term comprises "any work of critical or imaginative cast," as "the adopting of various strategies for the encompassing of situations. These strategies size up the situations, name their structure and outstanding ingredients, and name them in a way that contains an attitude towards them." According to *The Philosophy of Literary Form*, "poetry, or any verbal act, is to be considered as 'symbolic action,'" and symbolic action is to be considered as having at least three levels.

First, on the level of dream ("the unconscious or subconscious factors in a poem"), symbolic action is symptomatic action and plays a compensatory or therapeutic role. It has an author-regarding element and is expressive, either directly or indirectly, of his or her psyche.

Second, on the level of prayer ("the communicative functions of a poem"), it has a rhetorical dimension or audience-regarding element, and induces attitudes and actions. This aspect of symbolic action involves the kinds of identifications and dissociations a work encourages, the structure of motives it realizes and implies. Rhetoric deals with the arousal and fulfillment of expectations, and form, Burke argues, is "the psychology of the audience," or "the creation of an appetite in the mind of the auditor, and the adequate satisfying of that appetite."

Third, on the level of chart ("the realistic sizing-up of situations that is sometimes explicit, sometimes implicit, in poetic strategies"), symbolic action has a reality-regarding element. "The Symbol is the verbal parallel to a pattern of experience" and has realistic content insofar as it encompasses the situation it represents. The encompassment is necessarily imperfect because human beings have no nonsymbolic or nonlinguistic access to the structure of reality. In later writings, Burke elaborates the dream/prayer/chart triad into a more sophisticated scheme: grammar (which corresponds to chart), rhetoric (which corresponds to prayer), and symbolic (which corresponds to dream).

Burke has a grammar in the Aristotelian sense of a set of verbal terms or categories by means of which a discourse can be analyzed. His dramatistic grammar centers on observations of this sort: for there to be an act, there must be an agent. Similarly, there must be a scene in which the agent acts. To act in a scene, the agent must employ some means or agency, and there cannot be an act, in the full sense of the term, unless there is a purpose. These five terms – act, agent, scene, agency, purpose – Burke labels the dramatistic pentad. His aim in *A Grammar of Motives* is to show how the functions which they designate operate in the imputing of motives.

The grammatical is a series of blanks to be filled out when one imputes motive to action, and any statement of motives involves the dramatistic pentad of act (what was done), agent (who did the act and under what subjective conditions), scene (the environment in which the act took place, the extrinsic factors that determined it), agency (how the act was done, what instruments were used), and purpose (why the act was done, its ultimate motive or final cause). The grammatical blanks offer opportunities for "disposition and transposition," and dialectic explores the combinatory possibilities. Different philosophical systems emphasize different parts of the pentad: realism emphasizes act, idealism emphasizes agent, materialism emphasizes scene, pragmatism emphasizes agency, and mysticism emphasizes purpose. In this view, the grammatical resources are principles and the various philosophies are casuistries in that they seek to apply these principles in and to the cases of some actual and given historical situation. The philosophies develop their distinctive characters in terms of their variant stress upon one or another of the terms of the pentad.

What Burke was doing in 1945 heralded developments in literary theory thirty years later, especially his view of the subject or agent as the function of a system. As a method of discourse analysis, *A Grammar of Motives* is protostructuralist to the extent that structure in all kinds of texts can be accounted for by five key terms. It is antistructuralist, however, to the extent that Burke recognizes that every grammar of motives implies a rhetoric of motives. Since every dialectic transposes and disposes the terms of the dramatistic pentad in a uniquely constitutive fashion with a uniquely exhortative attitude, every dialectic implies a rhetoric of action. Though a Marxist might see the historical and economic scene as determinative of the acts and attitudes that agents engage in, his "scenic" grammar implies a program of social change that urges the strategic deployment of linguistic and political agency for the purpose of revolution. "The dramatistic view of language, in terms of 'symbolic action,'" Burke writes, "is exercised about the necessarily suasive nature of even the most unemotional scientific nomenclatures."

Timothy Crusius nicely articulates the Burkean distinction between dialectic (grammar) and rhetoric:

> In contrast to dialectic's [or grammar's] exploration of verbal forms, Burke sees rhetoric's function as the overcoming of estrangement. Human beings are alienated from each other by differences of ethnic and social background, level of education, race, sex, age, economic class, etc. When language is used to overcome these differences, to foster cooperation and establish community, we are in the realm of rhetoric – and since all language use to varying degrees involves this end, all language use has a rhetorical dimension.

To the classical notion of rhetoric as persuasion, Burke adds the dramatistic notion of rhetoric as identification, by which he means the inducement to identify one's own substance with something larger and more comprehensive. He also adds the notion of unconscious factors of appeal, especially as they pertain to the suasive function of imagery. As Crusius points out, for Burke dialectic and rhetoric

> are counterparts because to identify is to share substance with something or someone, the study of substance (or motivational essence) being the affair of dialectic [or grammar], the study of tactics for achieving identification (or consubstantiality) being the affair of rhetoric.

Although rhetoric involves the formation of identity and the establishment and maintenance of affiliation and community, it is predicated upon division and difference. If identification and consubstantiality were really possible, there would be no need to induce them.

The symbolic, which Burke associates with poetics per se, is grounded in the proposition that "a work is composed of implicit or explicit 'equations' (assumptions of 'what equals what'), in any work considered as one particular structure of terms, or symbol system." Burke goes on to say that along with identifications or equations (what equals what), there are also dissociations or agons (what versus what), and that this apposition and opposition of terms unfolds in a certain way, making for dramatic resolution and dialectical transformation (what leads to what). The symbolic, then, should take at least three factors into account: associative clusters, dramatic alignments, and narrative progressions, what Burke calls elsewhere the labyrinthine internal consistency of the text.

All told, then, there is symbolic action as designation (the grammatical), as communication (the rhetorical), and as expression (the symbolical). For Burke, however, the various levels of symbolic action are interdependent. "Since the work of art is a synthesis, summing up a myriad of social and personal factors at once, an analysis of it necessarily radiates in all directions at once." This is why he admits that his

> general approach to the poem might be called "pragmatic" in this sense: it assumes that a poem's structure is to be described most accurately by thinking always of the poem's function. It assumes that the poem is designed to "do something" for the poet and his readers, and that we can make the most relevant observations about its design by considering the poem as the embodiment of this act.

A case in point is Burke's brilliant essay "The Rhetoric of Hitler's 'Battle'" (1939), an essay in which he brings his critical arsenal to bear on Adolf Hitler's *Mein Kampf* (1925–1926). Burke sees Nazism with its projective device of the scapegoat ("the 'curative' unification by a fictitious devil-function") and its ritual of rebirth (the compensatory doctrine of inborn superiority whereby Aryans are born again into the purity of their ancestral blood) as the materialization and perversion of a religious pattern. He examines Hitler's use of sexual symbolism, of the imagery of blood, pollution, and disease, and of the rhetoric of identification and dissociation, focusing on the dialectical relationship between the literary strategy and the extra-literary situation. *Mein Kampf* provides "a noneconomic interpretation of economic ills." This interpretation appeals, Burke goes on to say, because it supplies "a 'world view' for people who had previously seen the world but piecemeal" and is thus "the bad filling of a good need." Rejecting both the formalism of an intrinsic approach, which regards literature as a self-enclosed universe of discourse, and the determinism of an extrinsic approach, which regards literature as reducible to some other frame of reference such as psychoanalysis or historical materialism, Burke demonstrates how the formal unfolding and internal coherence of a work – its iterative imagery, recurrent symbolism, associative clusters, dramatic alignments, and narrative progressions – are part of its rhetorical force.

Burke's insistence on the necessity of a nonelitist point of view is an attempt to bring literary criticism back into the mainstream of social life, and his essay on Hitler gives a splendid idea of what that sort of criticism involves. "The dramatistic perspective," Burke writes, "points equally towards a concern with 'internal structure' and towards a concern with 'act-scene relationships.'" "Whatever 'free play' there may be in esthetic enterprise," Burke continues, "it is held down by the gravitational pull of historical necessities; the poetic forms are symbolic structures designed to equip us for confronting given historical or personal situations."

From *Counter-Statement* in 1931 to *A Rhetoric of Motives* in 1950, this dialectical model of the relationship between ideology, language, and sociohistorical reality predominates. From the time of *The Rhetoric of Religion* in 1961 and afterward, however, logology, a language-centered view of reality, tends to prevail.

In *The Rhetoric of Religion*, Burke's central claim is that because theology deals with ultimate terms *par excellence* it is uniquely qualified to provide the sorts of analogies which yield insight into the internal logic of symbol systems in particular and of language in general. "It is our 'logological' thesis," he writes, "that, since the theological use of language is thorough, the close study of theology and its forms will provide us with good insight into the nature of language itself as a motive." Words about the Word (theology) will bear a strong resemblance to words about words (logology). This condition results from the fact that the systematic rigor and perfectionism of theology, with its preponderance of ultimate terms, bring into relief the entelechial drive within all symbol systems, entelechy being Aristotle's term for a thing's internal principle of motivation, its incentive to attain the kind of perfection appropriate to the kind of thing it is.

The shift from dramatism to logology emerges from Burke's hypersensitivity to the nihilistic chaos that his own views about language and interpretation could engender if pushed to their extremes. Logology converts methodological priority – the heuristic method of treating communication as primary to all categories of experience and of adopting the poetic perspective of the human as communicant (a dramatistic method first developed in *Permanence and Change*) – into ontological priority: the logological view that language is the source and origin of all value because it affords the peculiar possibility of the negative, the possibility of saying "no" to "thou shalt not," a view which finds its ultimate expression in *The Rhetoric of Religion*. The problem is that such a language-centered view of reality tends toward the kind of formalism and reductionism that dramatism is designed to overcome. "Tends," however, is the operative word; in no way could it be said that dramatism is ever completely abandoned, for Burke is acutely aware that the value-bestowing "thou shalt nots" of any social order are hortatory negatives, rhetorically charged commands that play an integral role in the dialectic and drama of human relations.

Ultimately, the most important message to derive from Burke is that words are agents of power, that they are value-laden, ideologically motivated, and morally and emotionally weighted instruments of persuasion, purpose, and representation. It is at the peril of inanition that one divorces literature from the social, cultural, and political matrix that gives it life and meaning. For Burke, literature, as a form of symbolic action in the world, is inextricably linked to society – it is not a privileged form of language that exists in its own separate and autonomous sphere. As an interdisciplinary maverick in a world of specialists, Burke was for the greater part of his career relegated to the margins of serious academic discourse. In the 1980s, however, critics and theorists began to acknowledge that Burke's dramatistic theory of literature and language, which was largely developed from 1930 to 1960, is of vital interest to a wide range of disciplines.

Principal criticism

Counter-Statement, 1931
Permanence and Change: An Anatomy of Purpose, 1935
Attitudes Toward History, 1937
The Philosophy of Literary Form: Studies in Symbolic Action, 1941
A Grammar of Motives, 1945
A Rhetoric of Motives, 1950
The Rhetoric of Religion: Studies in Logology, 1961
Perspectives by Incongruity, 1964 (Stanley Edgar Hyman and Barbara Karmiller, editors)
Terms for Order, 1964 (Hyman and Karmiller, editors)
Language as Symbolic Action: Essays on Life, Literature, and Method, 1966
Dramatism and Development, 1972
On Symbols and Society, 1989 (Joseph R. Gusfield, editor)

Other major works and literary forms

In addition to the books listed above, Kenneth Burke has published numerous articles, essays, reviews, poems, stories, and translations. His novel, *Towards a Better Life: Being a Series of Epistles, or Declamations* (1932), flouts the conventions of realism and self-consciously pursues eloquence for its own sake. His collection of short fiction, *The Complete White Oxen: Collected Short Fiction of Kenneth Burke* (1969), continues this experimental trend and explores new possibilities for the genre of fiction. His poems, which have been gathered in a single volume as *Collected Poems, 1915–1967* (1968), and are more traditional in form, trenchantly capture the shifting moods, moments, and attitudes of their author. Burke is also an accomplished translator, perhaps best known in this regard for his translation of Thomas Mann's *Death in Venice*.

NOVEL
Towards a Better Life: Being a Series of Epistles, or Declamations, 1932

SHORT FICTION
The Complete White Oxen: Collected Short Fiction of Kenneth Burke, 1969

POETRY
Collected Poems, 1915–1967, 1968

TRANSLATION
Death in Venice, 1925 (of Thomas Mann's novella *Der Tod in Venedig*)

Further reading

Biesecker, Barbara. *Addressing Postmodernity: Kenneth Burke, Rhetoric, and a Theory of Social Change*, 1997.
Booth, Wayne. *Critical Understanding: The Powers and Limits of Pluralism*, 1979.
Brock, Bernard, ed. *Kenneth Burke in the Twenty-First Century*, 1998.
Brown, Merle Elliot. *Kenneth Burke*, 1969.
Bygrave, Stephen. *Kenneth Burke: Rhetoric and Ideology*, 1993.
Carter, C. Allan. *Kenneth Burke and the Scapegoat Process*, 1996.
Chesebro, James, ed. *Extensions of the Burkean System*, 1993.
Crusius, Timothy. "A Case for Kenneth Burke's Dialectic and Rhetoric," in *Philosophy and Rhetoric*. XIX, no. 2 (1986), pp. 23–37.
Frank, Armin Paul. *Kenneth Burke*, 1969.
Heath, Robert L. *Realism and Relativism: A Perspective on Kenneth Burke*, 1986.
Henderson, Greig. *Kenneth Burke: Literature and Language as Symbolic Action*, 1988.
Lentricchia, Frank. *Criticism and Social Change*, 1983.
Rueckert, William H. *Kenneth Burke and the Drama of Human Relations*, 1982.
——. *Encounters with Kenneth Burke*, 1993.
——, ed. *Critical Responses to Kenneth Burke, 1924–1966*, 1969.
Seltzer, Jack. *Kenneth Burke in Greenwich Village Conversing with the Moderns, 1915–1931*, 1996.
Southwell, Samuel B. *Kenneth Burke and Martin Heidegger: With a Note Against Deconstruction*, 1987.
Wess, Robert. *Kenneth Burke: Rhetoric, Subjectivity, Postmodernism*, 1996.
White, Hayden, and Margaret Brose, eds. *Representing Kenneth Burke*, 1982.

GREIG E. HENDERSON

See also American Literary Theory: Twentieth Century

Michel Butor

French writer and critic

Born: Mons-en-Baroeul, France; September 14, 1926

Biography

Michel Butor was born in a small village near Lille, France, in 1926. His father worked as a railroad inspector, while his mother cared for her home and seven children. In 1929 the family moved to Paris, where Butor was later to be sent to a series of Catholic elementary schools. Impressed by his studies of Percy Bysshe Shelley in an English class, Butor began writing essays and poetry while studying at the famous secular Lycée Louis-le-Grand. An interest in the arts prevailed in his bourgeois home, where young Butor learned to paint and play the violin. He soon discovered Surrealist painting and began reading philosophy and literature, exploring most of the works of Paul Claudel, Franz Kafka, James Joyce, and Marcel Proust.

While still a student at the Sorbonne, Butor began to publish. His interest in Surrealism persisted as he worked on a graduate degree in philosophy. After teaching literature and philosophy for several years in France, Egypt, and England, he published his first novel in 1954. He traveled extensively within Europe and beyond while continuing to write prolifically. In 1958 he married Marie-Josèphe Mas. They have four daughters.

Butor often accepted visiting professorships around the world, including temporary appointments in the United States at Bryn Mawr College, Middlebury College, and the University of Buffalo; in 1967 the Ford Foundation engaged him to study artistic problems in television. He continues to experiment with new forms of writing and literary structure.

Influence

Literary influence, as Henri Peyre once noted, is one of the most misleading notions encountered in literary criticism. A writer influences others when they are ready to be influenced; there are tides of fashion shared by entire generations and impulses which pervade a culture at a particular time. The writings of Butor, though indebted to the work of the Surrealists, are thoroughly original; they seem not to have been directly imitated by anyone – are, probably, inimitable. Butor's critical views, his thoughts on literary form and structure and the nature of artistic creation, have nevertheless achieved considerable popularity and are widely accepted by postwar writers. The essays expressing these views, originally published in a variety of periodicals from 1952 and collected in book form as *Répertoire I-V*, reflect ideas and attitudes which were shared by many writers after the war and which continue to interest serious authors today. Butor's reflective and interrogative essays reveal his efforts to redefine the novel so as to characterize the mood of a new era.

Analysis

The occupation of France by German forces from 1940 to 1945 shattered French life and culture in many ways, and a gulf spread to separate the first half of the century from the second. Artistic expression seemed to have been exhausted. The great writers of the 1920s and 1930s, still living and able to produce, had little more to say: André Gide published his diaries, François Mauriac contributed personal editorials to *Le Figaro littéraire*, and André Malraux wrote art criticism and moved into government administration of the arts. While their work and that of their contemporaries was interesting and significant, the flame of creative inspiration appeared to have been extinguished. In 1950 one was forced to ask what the future of literature would be.

The new generation, many of whom were teenagers during the occupation, were faced with the gigantic task of creating a new literature, a new novel. Those of this generation who wished or hoped to become artists needed to "Make it new," as Ezra Pound had said. Butor was fourteen years old, a student at the Lycée Louis-le-Grand, when the German troops advanced into Paris. As a precocious adolescent, he ignored the invaders, absorbing the intellectual currents which surrounded him by reading intensively in modern literature and frequenting avant-garde art galleries. He was delighted to meet the Surrealist André Breton and, later, the semiologist Roland Barthes.

Before the expression "New Novel" was coined in a special issue of the journal *Esprit* in 1958, these young writers were sometimes referred to as constituting an *école du regard* (school of sight) because of their preoccupation with things and their appearances. Alain Robbe-Grillet is famous for his extended descriptions of objects of all sorts – a slice of tomato on a plate, the stain left by a centipede once squashed on the wall. Butor is more dynamic and imaginative in his approach to description: through the use of fragmentation, he forces the reader to join in the imaginative re-creation of objects of enormous size – cities and buildings, Niagara Falls, even the United States. Sometimes called *chosisme* (thingism), this preoccupation minimizes the importance of plot, character, psychology, and philosophy to focus the reader's attention almost exclusively upon the reality which surrounds and impinges upon conscious awareness. The reader enters into the mind of the writer, sharing his or her consciousness, to experience with him or her, through disordered fragments of sensual perception, aspects of his or her perceived reality. Butor thinks of the reader as a coauthor participating with him in the creative process. Thus, the creation of a literary work is itself an act of criticism, and the author, through his or her example, proposes new forms and structures for art.

Butor's views on narrative literature are probably best expressed in his essay "Research on the Technique of the Novel" (1968), in which he attempts to introduce new clarity into the novel's structure, to explore and expose new obscurities. In this article Butor stresses the importance of narrative, the ever-present "news," but he rejects the importance of chronology. The reader of a novel may be as ignorant of causes and effects in the book as he is in the affairs of his private life. A complex structure requires the function of memory: flashbacks. The threads of narrative should be broken as rhythm moves it from one layer to another. Rapid juxtapositions of events far apart in time and place are possible, producing different flows and durations. Author, character, and reader are united in the process of creating the story; the reader must make the effort to collaborate with those others to create the full artistic experience of the book. This task is difficult and time consuming for the reader, but he must participate in the process in order to share in the aesthetic rewards.

According to Butor, the reader must never be a passive traveler through a tale. Books should be read like dictionaries, phone books, or cookbooks: the reader should skip around, giving attention to what interests him or her at the particular moment. A story or poem is an interior monologue, essentially documentary in nature, which presents a materialist vision of reality. Butor rejects linear construction and continuity of narration. Everyone experiences reality in a haphazard fashion, confusedly; a novel which tells a tale in an orderly fashion, then, is false to a contemporary perception of reality. Experience is chaotic and an understanding of other people impossible; a novel which implies order and continuity is therefore false and misleading.

Deceptive nonlinear narration was not new; Ford Madox Ford provided an excellent model with *The Good Soldier* (1915): the narrator is unreliable and the story folds back upon itself as he retells it. Virginia Woolf had experimented with leaps of time in *The Waves* (1931) and *The Years* (1937). Butor's view of narrative form and structure develops these earlier experiments. The problem of presentation always admits of several solutions, but the reader is always responsible for what happens in the literary work, a mirror of the human condition. Participation in the literary act will enlighten the reader about liberty.

In his essay "The Book as Object" (1968), Butor suggests numerous ways in which a writer can utilize book design, layout, and typography to encourage the reader's participation in an aesthetic experience. Contrasted with films and recordings, which are always perceived sequentially, he extols the flexibility of simultaneous exposure offered by printed words. The reader sees two pages at once, can move backward or forward through a volume at will, and can skip sections entirely or skim, as he or she wishes. Books are not commercial objects to be discarded after one use like newspapers: they should be read repeatedly over a lifetime, in different ways each time. Butor praises François Rabelais for his use of lists printed as columns, recommending the use of vertical as well as horizontal language structures. Other sorts of spacing might be devised for complex enumerations; marginal annotations, a variety of typefaces, and colored inks can also contribute to the diffusion of perception sought by an author.

In an article on the use of personal pronouns in fiction ("L'Usage des pronoms personnels dans le roman," 1964), Butor further develops this approach to reader involvement in literary creativity. He states that the most fundamental, but naive, form of narration is the third person, which simply represents a universe; use of the first person introduces a point of view which is itself a fiction, a persona of the author engaging in an enclosed interior monologue; use of the second person addresses the reader directly, instructing him or her, inviting him or her to participate personally in an unfolding literary event. When combined, the interaction of all three forms of pronouns creates a displacement of identity of character, narrator, and reader: the "I," the "you," and the "he" or "she" mingle into a complex which destroys any sort of hierarchy, creating an ambiguous pronominal architecture of superimpositions which reveals human reality.

The New Novel has sometimes been called the "anti-novel" because of its radical departures from narrative techniques of the past. It should be understood, however, that Butor in no way despises or rejects the literature of the past: he has great respect and reverence for the tradition of which he strongly feels himself to be a part. His concern for literary tradition is revealed in the many articles he has written on such figures as François Rabelais, François Auguste René Chateaubriand, Charles Baudelaire, and Marcel Proust.

Butor leans upon Honoré de Balzac as a god of literature and has written a highly perceptive article about him, "Balzac and Reality" (1968). He explains that in order to reflect reality as it is truly perceived, a writer must reveal the inherent chaos of existence through the form and structure of his or her work. He therefore admires the seventeen-volume *La Comédie humaine* (1829–1848; *The Comedy of Human Life*, 1885–1893, 1896, better known as *The Human Comedy*, 1895–1896, 1911) because Balzac did not number the volumes in consecutive order: the reader makes his or her way, haphazardly, through the tangled lives of the characters. Gustave Flaubert had offered a sustaining order; Butor reveres Balzac for his sustained disorder. This article expresses Butor's interest in oblique illuminations, the shedding of lateral lights on a subject, the use of flashbacks, and the violation of chronological order. Reading Balzac, Butor enjoys wandering at his leisure among a number of facets which are linked together, a kind of novelistic mobile, literary structures not unlike the multidimensional works of Alexander Calder. The novels can be approached by way of any trajectory which pleases the reader; it is like an enclosure with many entrances. Descriptions of places and things form concentric spheres to symbolize the relations between personal reality and the universe; their links codify internal relations within the novels. Balzac, according to Butor, provides a solid foundation upon which the New Novelists can build.

In his essay "Victor Hugo romancier" (1964), Butor praises descriptive passages which interrupt the telling of adventures in Hugo's novels. A simple linear story leads to laziness: the consciousness of the reader, having a slippery surface on which to slide, is not awakened. Yet Hugo's description of the Battle of Waterloo in *Les Misérables* (1862; English translation, 1862), for example, details a panoramic view of chaotic action which demands alert attention for comprehension. The description of the cathedral and other Parisian architecture in *Notre-Dame de Paris* (1831; *The Hunchback of Notre Dame*, 1833) vitalizes the imagination and sustains interest by immersing the reader in floods of details which he or she must strain to assimilate. Butor thinks that Hugo is at his best when he turns away from plot to meditate, to consider and dream, to explain and reflect: his parentheses contain his greatest writing, resembling psychological operatic arias, or huge waves of the ocean, which shape a book into a liberating architectural monument.

Although most of Butor's critical writings deal with the art of fiction, he has written also on poetry, music, travel, and art. His essays on Baudelaire, Stéphane Mallarmé, and Guillaume Apollinaire are particularly interesting; those describing places seem to establish a new genre, quite different from traditional travel guides. Much can be learned from Butor's essays on critical theory: difficult and demanding as they often are, these pieces offer insights to a patient and attentive reader which allow scrutiny of the aesthetic landscape through unusual, but finely focused, binoculars.

Principal criticism

Répertoire I–V: Études et conférences, 1960–1982 (partially translated in *Inventory*, 1968)
Essais sur les modernes, 1964
Essais sur "les essais," 1968
Essais sur le roman, 1969
Résistances, 1983 (with Michel Launay)
Improvisations sur Flaubert, 1984
Improvisations sur Henri Micheaux, 1985
Improvisations sur Rimbaud, 1989
Improvisations sur Michel Butor: L'Écriture en transformation, 1993 (*Improvisations on Butor: Transformation of Writing* [*Crosscurrents*], 1996)

Other major works and literary forms

In addition to the critical essays on literature listed above, Michel Butor has written novels, poetry, and radio plays, as well as books and articles on art and music. Certain of his writings are of an unclassifiable nature: in *Mobile: Étude pour une représentation des États-Unis* (1962; *Mobile: Study for a Representation of the United States*, 1963), *Description de San Marco* (1963), and *6,810,000 Litres d'eau par seconde: Étude stéréophonique* (1965; *Niagara: A Stereophonic Novel*, 1969), he attempts to create a new literary form which he calls "stereophonic studies." He has also written the libretto for an avant-garde opera, *Votre Faust: Fantaisie variable genre Opéra* (1962), with music by the serialist composer Henri Pousseur which received its world premiere at La Piccola Scala, Milan, Italy, on January 15, 1969. Butor's work, the subject of much critical controversy, interests, amazes, and puzzles the public by its unusual variety and originality. Only a small number of his writings have been translated into English.

NOVELS
Passage de Milan, 1954
L'Emploi du temps, 1957 (*Passing Time*, 1960)
La Modification, 1957 (*Second Thoughts*, 1958, better known as *A Change of Heart*, 1959)
Degrés, 1960 (*Degrees*, 1961)
6,810,000 Litres d'eau par seconde: Étude stéréophonique, 1965 (*Niagara: A Stereophonic Novel*, 1969)

PLAYS
Réseau aérien: Texte radiophonique, 1962 (radio play)
Votre Faust: Fantaisie variable genre Opéra, 1962 (with Henri Pousseur)
Elseneur: suite dramatique, 1979
La Famille Grabouillage, 1985 (with Stéphane Bastin)

POETRY
Illustrations I–IV, 1964–1976
La Rose des vents: 32 Rhumbs pour Charles Fourier, 1970
Dialogue avec 33 variations de Ludwig van Beethoven sur une valse de Diabelli, 1971
Travaux d'approche, 1972
Matière de rêves, 1975
Second sous-sol: Matière de rêves, 2, 1976
Envois, 1980
Explorations, 1981
Exprès, 1983
Herbier Lunaire: 29 illustrations de Gochka Charewicz, 1984
Chantier, 1985
La Forme Courte, 1990

NONFICTION
Le Génie du lieu, 1958 (*The Spirit of Mediterranean Places*, 1986)
Histoire extraordinaire: Essai sur un rêve de Baudelaire, 1961 (*Histoire Extraordinaire: Essay on a Dream of Baudelaire*, 1969)
Les Mots dans la peinture, 1969
Où: Le Génie du lieu 2, 1971
Intervalle, 1973
Boomerang: Le Génie du lieu 3, 1978 (*Letters from the Antipodes*, 1981)
Diego Giacometti, 1985
Adornment: Jewelry from Africa, Asia and the Pacific, 1994 (with Pierre-Alain Ferrazzini)
Gyroscope: Autrement dit Le Génie du lieu, 5 et dernier, 1996
Le Génie du lieu (translation), 1997

MISCELLANEOUS
Mobile: Étude pour une représentation des États-Unis, 1962 (*Mobile: Study for a Representation of the United States*, 1963)
Description de San Marco, 1963
Portrait de l'artiste en jeune singe: Capriccio, 1967
Matière de rêves, 1975
Second sous-sol: Matière de rêves II, 1976
Explorations, 1981
Brassée d'Avril, 1982
Avant-Goût I, 1984
Avant-Goût II, 1987
Avant-Goût III: L'Appel du large, 1989
L'Embarquement de la Reine de Saba: d'après le tableau de Claude Lorrain, 1989
Fréderic-Yves Jeannet, ed. *De La Distance: déambulation* (letters), 1990
Avant-Goût IV: En Mémoire, 1992

Further reading

Aubyn, F. C. St. "Michel Butor and the Legend of Don Juan: The Example of Don Juan dans la Manche," in *Connecticut Review*. 12, no. 2 (Summer, 1990), pp. 75–89.
Biasi, Pierre Marc de. "Michel Butor: 'Le Rêve d'une langue universelle'," in *Magazine Littéraire*. 364 (April, 1998), pp. 28–33.
Britton, Celia. "Opacity and Transparence: Conceptions of History and Cultural Difference in the Work of Michel Butor and Edouard Glissant," in *French Studies: A Quarterly Review*. 49, no. 3 (July, 1995), pp. 308–320.
Burton, Stacy. "Experience and the Genres of Travel Writing: Bakhtin and Butor," in *Romance Studies*. 21 (Winter, 1992–Spring, 1993), pp. 51–62.
Duffy, Jean H. *Butor: La Modification*, 1990.
Frohock, W. M. *Style and Temper: Studies in French Fiction, 1925–1960*, 1967.
Gaillard, G. *Butor*, 1968.
Hirsch, Marianne. *Beyond the Single Vision: Henry James, Michel Butor, Uwe Johnson*, 1981.
Jullien, Dominique. "Intertextuality as Labyrinth: The Presence of Racine in Michel Butor's *L'Emploi du temps*," in *Yale French Studies*. 76 (1989), pp. 108–124.
Lancry, Yehuda. *Michel Butor, ou La Résistance*, 1994.
Le Sage, Laurent. *The French New Novel: An Introduction and a Sampler*, 1962
Lydon, Mary. *Perpetuum Mobile: A Study of the Novels and Aesthetics of Michel Butor*, 1980.
McWilliams, Dean. *The Narratives of Michel Butor: The Writer as Janus*, 1978.
Mason, Barbara. *Michel Butor: A Checklist*, 1979.
——. "Language and Ideology in Michel Butor's *Improvisations sur Flaubert*," in *Nottingham French Studies*. 28, no. 1 (Spring, 1989), pp. 53–64.
Meakin, David. "Michel Butor and the Thomas Mann Connection," in *Forum for Modern Language Studies*. 26, no. 2 (April, 1990), pp. 109–126.
Mercier, Vivian. *The New Novel from Queneau to Pinget*, 1971.
Nadeau, Maurice. *The French Novel Since the War*, 1967.
Oppenheim, Lois. *Intentionality and Intersubjectivity: A Phenomenological Study of Butor's La Modification*, 1980.
Rahv, Betty T. *From Sartre to the New Novel*, 1974.
Rossum-Guyon, Françoise van. *Le Cœur critique: Butor, Simon, Kristeva, Cixous*, 1997.
Silk, Sally M. "When the Writer Comes Home: Narrative Failure in Butor's *La Modification*," in *Style*. 26, no. 2 (Summer, 1992), pp. 270–286.
Spencer, Michael. *Michel Butor*, 1974.
Sturrock, John. *The French New Novel: Claude Simon, Michel Butor, Alain Robbe-Grillet*, 1969.
Waelti-Walters, Jennifer. *Michel Butor: A Study of His View of the World and a Panorama of His Work, 1954–1974*, 1977.
——. *Michel Butor*, 1992.
Welch, Liliane and Cyril. *Address: Rimbaud, Mallarmé, Butor*, 1979.

RAYMOND M. ARCHER

See also French Literary Theory: Twentieth Century; Robbe-Grillet

Lord Byron

(George Gordon, sixth Baron Byron)

English poet and critic

Born: London, England; January 22, 1788
Died: Missolonghi, Greece; April 19, 1824

Biography

George Gordon was born on January 22, 1788, in London, England, the only child of Captain John ("Mad Jack") Byron and Catherine Gordon of Gight. His father, a dashing captain in a Guards regiment, who had squandered the Gordon inheritance, died when the boy was three. His mother, a Scotswoman with a penchant for drink, seems to have been alternately loving and cruel. At the age of ten, Byron succeeded to his great-uncle's title and estate, Newstead Abbey. He attended Harrow from 1801 to 1805 and Trinity College, Cambridge, from 1805 to 1807. In 1807 he published *Hours of Idleness.*

For few writers have life and work been so inextricably tied together in the public mind. In Byron's series of romantic narrative poems and plays, the heroes were taken to be the poet wearing a scanty disguise. Byron engaged in a series of love affairs with fashionable ladies, the most scandalous and tempestuous involving Lady Caroline Lamb. In 1815 he married Annabella Milbanke, a serious young woman who could scarcely have been less suited to the role of Lady Byron. The marriage, which produced one child, Augusta Ada, ended in a legal separation within a year. Lady Byron was certainly the model for the priggish Donna Inez in *Don Juan.* During his marriage, Byron had apparently continued an incestuous relationship with his half sister, Augusta. A daughter born to Augusta in 1814 is generally supposed to be Byron's. Byron, like his hero Don Juan, was driven from his homeland by the scandal and spent the rest of his life abroad.

In Switzerland, Byron continued an affair which had begun in London with Claire Clairmont, the stepsister of Mary Shelley. She gave birth to a daughter, Allegra. In Italy, Byron became the lover of Teresa Guiccioli, the young wife of an elderly count. She left her husband in 1821 and lived with Byron for the remaining years of his life.

Byron had at first refused payment for his writings because of his aristocratic scruples, but as his debts grew he was glad that his works sold well. In 1823 he abandoned literature and devoted his energy and fortune to the Greek war for liberation from the Turks. He died of a fever in 1824 at Missolonghi, attempting to unite the Greek forces.

Influence

The literary criticism of Lord Byron may strike the modern reader as being simultaneously Byronic and ironic. Byron was fearless and often acerbic in stating his literary opinions, seeming not to care – as with his social and political views – whether anyone else shared them. His first literary criticism appears in *English Bards and Scotch Reviewers*, a satirical poem begun while he was still an undergraduate, which is a scathing attack upon the leading poets and critics of his day. Then there were the literary opinions themselves. Byron, who in his own day became the incarnation of the Romantic hero, preferred the poetry of Alexander Pope to that of John Milton, favored the plays of the French classicists (at least as models) over those of William Shakespeare, and disparaged the work of William Wordsworth and Samuel Taylor Coleridge, the leaders of the Romantic movement in England. Byron's critical views often seemed eccentric in his lifetime; they often seem eccentric still. Yet it can prove profitable to study his criticism as the product of a fine mind and a courageous spirit at odds with the conventional wisdom.

Analysis

Lord Byron was a published writer from an early age. Although he would have preferred to reject the money his writings earned, he was also a professional writer whose works were popular with the general reader. He therefore tended to read as a writer. He was neither a theoretician like Coleridge nor a professional critic like William Hazlitt. His formal criticism in prose consists of only four minor reviews (one of which may not be his work alone) and four less formal letters. Many provocative comments are sprinkled throughout Byron's extensive correspondence, but to experience the best of his literary criticism one must turn to certain of the poems themselves.

As a nineteen-year-old Cambridge undergraduate, Byron was already at work on his first critical piece. He planned to satirize several contemporary poets in a work to be called "British Bards." In January, 1808, before Byron could complete his satire, the *Edinburgh Review* published a savage attack upon his *Hours of Idleness.* He responded by revising and expanding the poem, which was renamed *English Bards and Scotch Reviewers* and published anonymously in March, 1809. For the next three years Byron continued to enlarge and polish the poem, until the fifth edition extended to 1,070 lines. Pope's *The Dunciad* (1728–1743) was Byron's model and, although he would eventually change his mind about some of the victims of his satire, he would retain the neoclassical preferences implied in *English Bards and Scotch Reviewers* for the rest of his life.

In the poem, Byron not only attacks the romantic lays of Sir Walter Scott but also accuses Scott of prostituting his muse for money (Byron's debts would soon force him to do the same). Scott eventually became Byron's favorite novelist and, in a journal entry of 1821, Byron even praised Scott's poetry. He still maintained, however, that it employed an erroneous system – Romanticism. The youthful Byron also chastises Robert Southey, the author of several inferior epics, for presuming to use the poetic forms of Homer, Virgil, and Milton. (In 1822 Byron would publish *The Vision of Judgment*, a satire directed at Southey.) Byron castigates Wordsworth's simple (and, to Byron, silly) narratives of country folk and Coleridge's obscure and pixieish verses. Byron later admitted, at least to himself, that his treatment of the latter two poets had been unjust.

What of the "Scotch Reviewers" of the title? Byron voices the familiar plaint of authors everywhere – that while all other vocations require some measure of training, critics come full-blown into the world. As a study in literary criticism, the most interesting thing about *English Bards and Scotch Reviewers* is its neoclassical bias. Byron prefers the old poets to the new. He prefers the old genres and the old metrics to the new. He represents himself as the least romantic of Romantic poets.

Byron's inability to appreciate Wordsworth's talent derived essentially from two impediments. First, Byron the aristocrat agreed with Aristotle that the narrative of a great man was the proper subject matter for poetry. In Europe, the age of the common man had dawned. Wordsworth was in tune with it, Byron was not. Perhaps for purely aesthetic reasons, perhaps because of an inordinate regard for his own station, Byron simply could not understand Wordsworth's, or anyone else's, interest in the doings of the common man. Second, Wordsworth frequently wrote in blank verse, while Byron markedly favored rhyme. So great was his preference for rhyme that he once expressed the wish that Milton had chosen some sort of rhyming stanza rather than blank verse for *Paradise Lost* (1667).

Bruce Wallis, author of a two-volume study of Byron as a critic, suggests that Byron may be valued as a member of the loyal opposition of English literary criticism. Despite his numerous literary quarrels and the obvious pleasure he took in avenging real or imagined slights, he adhered to the classical dicta of moral purposiveness and clarity of thought. Furthermore, he was associated neither with the Lake Poets and their devotees nor with the Leigh Hunt circle. Therefore, Byron had a temperament and an objectivity which make him a valuable counterbalance to the prevailing literary judgments of both his and the present day.

Wallis stresses Byron's literalness of mind as the basis for his most provocative literary pronouncements. For example, Byron stated that he preferred reading prose over poetry; he went even further, to state that he actually hated reading verse and always had – a startling admission from one of England's most eminent poets. Byron's own verse reflects the classical predisposition toward narrative and didactic poetry. Prose, even fiction, is by nature more straightforward and less metaphorical than poetry, and Byron was, by his own account, a voracious reader of prose. Apparently, the very aspect of Pope's poetry which he most admired was what detractors call its prosaic quality. Pope's poetry was the standard by which Byron judged the work of others – the more it was like Pope's, the better, the less it was like Pope's, the worse.

Pope, like Horace before him, is the poet of the concrete, the commonsensical. When he is metaphorical, his figures of speech are unstrained and unambiguous. Revering Pope as his master, it is little wonder that Byron found fault with his fellow Romantics. To him, Wordsworth's primitivism was less childlike simplicity than it was childishness. Coleridge's exotic poems lacked form and purpose. The worst offender of all was John Keats.

Byron's evaluation of Keats is the best evidence of how contrary his views would be to those dominant in twentieth-century criticism. The richness, the density, the emotional engagement of the poem's persona – these qualities of Keats would eventually become almost synonymous with poetry itself. In the general reaction against Pope, his wit would come to be regarded as superficial cleverness, his restraint as a lack of feeling, his clarity as a lack of imagination, his regularity as a stuffy conservatism. Byron, however, was a poet in the spirit of Pope and a critic in the spirit of Samuel Johnson. He found Keats' poetry hyperbolic, emotionally overwrought, and unhealthy, but, most of all, infantile. Byron certainly overreacted to Keats. He was an intelligent man who should have known better than to characterize Keats' imagery as a Bedlam vision, like the product of opium. Byron somewhat modified his assessment of Keats following the young poet's death, but he continued to insist that Keats' poetry was fatally flawed, the product of an inferior poetical system. Most modern critics, however, while demurring at the severity of Byron's judgments, agree with his enumeration of the major faults of his contemporaries.

Byron's poetic tenets, although out of fashion, are defensible when not stated so baldly. He believed that poetry should be the result of experience rather than fancy (certainly, one reason for the huge sales of Byron's books was his audience's equating of the experiences of the protagonists with those of the author). Most would agree that, like any other form of writing, poetry which bears no relation to experience cannot long please the reader. Byron further believed that the principal purpose of poetry was to convey the truth rather than to achieve rhetorical or self-consciously beautiful effects. Here, his *Hints from Horace* is significant. He boasted of the literalness of his translation of Horace's Latin. Horace was a poet who, in his odes, praised the manly virtues and the simple, uncomplicated life, and in his satires, censured those poets who sought self-aggrandizement by declaiming their verses in the marketplace. Again, most readers would agree that poetry which aims primarily at the innovative manipulation of language can distort reality.

Byron's belief, inherited from his critical pedagogue, Johnson, that poetry should always have a moral purpose is the least congenial to the modern mind. This insistence upon morality in art may at first seem strange coming from a writer whose scandalous escapades and scorn for convention are so well documented. Yet, again and again, his poetry and letters make clear the distinction he drew between the true practice of virtue and cant. In the late twentieth century, other writers – foremost among them, John Gardner – took up the argument for a relinking of literature and morality but were soundly denounced by the literary establishment for doing so. *Don Juan*, Byron's mock-epic, masterfully and humorously addresses each of his basic literary concerns. Its satire and anger take aim at hypocritical uses of language which distort reality.

Throughout the nineteenth century, Byron's reputation in Europe was much greater than those of his fellow Romantics. In fact, influential critics such as Hippolyte-Adolphe Taine viewed him as the prototypical Romantic. Finally, the idea began to crystalize that, although Byron was the perfect Romantic hero for his own poems, he was in most other ways a neoclassical writer. The realization of this fact probably made the inevitable critical backlash more severe, so that in most academic circles Byron has come to be regarded as the least consequential of the major Romantic poets. Still, as a critic he owns the credentials provided by his own work. Ezra Pound, responding to what he considered incompetent criticism, once wrote that no man could judge a masterpiece who had not written one. Byron certainly meets Pound's criterion, for *Don Juan* is unquestionably a masterpiece.

A definitive evaluation of Byron as critic is no easy task. There is much that can be said against him. In 1813 he stated in writing that not only Scott but also Samuel Rogers, Thomas Moore, and Thomas Campbell ranked above Wordsworth and Coleridge in the hierarchy of poets. Byron was an inveterate reader of novels, and his taste was decidedly masculine. In 1814 he characterized the work of Maria Edgeworth, Fanny Burney, and Lady Sydney Morgan as feminine trash. Astonishingly, he nowhere mentions either Jane Austen or Ann Radcliffe. It is as if he did not know of the existence of the two best women writers of the period. Furthermore, his opinion of his own poetry was easily altered by the remarks of others. He once stated that his judgment of which of his works was the best depended upon whom he had spoken with most recently.

Such critical lapses as these must be weighed against the incisive (and entertaining) criticism to be found in *English Bards and Scotch Reviewers* and in the reflective and conversational passages of other poems. It appears that Byron the critic is as complex, contradictory, and enigmatic as Byron the poet and Byron the man.

Principal criticism

English Bards and Scotch Reviewers, 1809
Hints from Horace, 1811
Don Juan, cantos 1–16, 1819–1824, 1826
The Vision of Judgment, 1822
The Blues: A Literary Eclogue, 1823

Other major works and literary forms

George Gordon, the sixth Baron Byron, was the author of a published volume of poetry before reaching the age of twenty (this followed two volumes which had been published anonymously). Thereafter, his poetic output was continuous, prolific, varied, and financially rewarding. He wrote Oriental narrative poems (the publication in 1812 of cantos 1 and 2 of *Childe Harold's Pilgrimage*, 1812–1818, 1819, made him famous at the age of twenty-four), lyric poems, satirical poems (including the best mock-epic since Alexander Pope's *The Rape of the Lock* in 1712), and verse dramas. His Oriental romances and his plays feature characters so closely associated with himself that they have earned the sobriquet "Byronic heroes." His letters have been collected in twelve volumes.

PLAYS
Manfred, 1817
Marino Faliero, Doge of Venice, 1821
Sardanapalus: A Tragedy, 1821
The Two Foscari: A Tragedy, 1821
Cain: A Mystery, 1821
Heaven and Earth, 1822
Werner: Or, The Inheritance, 1823
The Deformed Transformed, 1824 (unfinished)

POETRY
Fugitive Pieces, 1806
Poems on Various Occasions, 1807
Hours of Idleness, 1807
Poems Original and Translated, 1808
The Curse of Minerva, 1812
Childe Harold's Pilgrimage, cantos 1–4, 1812–1818, 1819
Waltz: An Apostrophic Hymn, 1813
The Giaour, 1813
The Bride of Abydos, 1813
The Corsair, 1814
Ode to Napoleon Buonaparte, 1814
Lara, 1814
Hebrew Melodies Ancient and Modern, 1815
Monody on the Death of the Right Honourable R. B. Sheridan, 1816
Parisina, 1816
Poems, 1816
The Prisoner of Chillon, and Other Poems, 1816
The Siege of Corinth, 1816
The Lament of Tasso, 1817
Beppo: A Venetian Story, 1818
Mazeppa, 1819
The Prophecy of Dante, 1821
The Age of Bronze, 1823
The Island, 1823

NONFICTION
Letter to [John Murray] on the Rev. W. L. Bowles' Strictures on the Life and Writings of Pope, 1821
"A Letter to the Editor of *My Grandmother's Review*," 1822
The Parliamentary Speeches of Lord Byron, 1924
Byron's Letters and Journals, 1973–1982 (12 volumes; Leslie A. Marchand, editor)

MISCELLANEOUS
Byron, 1986 (Jerome J. McGann, editor)
The Complete Poetical Works of Byron, 1980–1986 (5 volumes)

Further reading

Bold, Alan, ed. *Byron: Wrath and Rhyme*, 1983.
Elledge, W. Paul. *Byron and the Dynamics of Metaphor*, 1968.
Lovell, Ernest J., Jr., ed. *His Very Self and Voice: Collected Conversations of Lord Byron*, 1954.
Manning, Peter J. *Reading Romantics: Texts and Contexts*, 1990.
Marchand, Leslie A. *Byron: A Portrait*, 1970.
Wallis, Bruce. *Byron: The Critical Voice*, 1973 (2 volumes).
West, Paul, ed. *Byron: A Collection of Critical Essays*, 1963.

PATRICK ADCOCK

See also Romanticism; Shelley

C

Callimachus

Greek scholar and poet

Born: Cyrene, a Greek colony in North Africa; c. 305 B.C.
Died: Alexandria, Egypt; c. 240 B.C.

Biography

Callimachus' life has to be reconstructed from a paucity of documentation. He was probably born around 305 B.C. in the Greek colony of Cyrene, in what is now Libya. He apparently came from a prominent family.

Cyrene must be seen in its relationship to Alexandria, the great cultural center of Egypt. In the power struggle that followed the death of Alexander the Great in 323 B.C., an Egyptian general named Ptolemy seized power, and in 322 B.C. he added Cyrene to his kingdom. In the next three decades, Ptolemy and his son, Ptolemy II, proved to be great patrons of art and learning and turned Alexandria into the cultural capital of the Mediterranean world.

Cyrenean politics under Ptolemy and his governor, Ophellas, glittered with intrigue. Ophellas revealed personal ambitions that were abruptly thwarted by his murder in 309 B.C., and he was succeeded by Ptolemy's stepson, Magas, who ruled Cyrene for more than four decades. For much of Magas' rule, Cyrene was stable and comparatively independent. Magas is supposed to have enjoyed prosperity so much that he became grossly fat and died of suffocation from his own excessive weight.

After Magas' death (c. 259 B.C.) his daughter, Berenice, became engaged to Demetrius, grandson of Ptolemy I, but Demetrius had an affair with Berenice's mother and Berenice had him killed. The strife did not end until 247 B.C., when Berenice married Ptolemy III Euergetes.

Such was the period into which Callimachus was born. At some time in his youth, Callimachus moved to Alexandria, where he studied under Praxiphanes, an Aristotelian philosopher. Alexandria had been constructed in the 330s B.C. at the behest of Alexander the Great. (There were various Alexandrias and this one was known as Alexandria-by-Egypt.) The location was felicitous, and the new city prospered under the sway of the Ptolemies. The Jews had their quarter, the Egyptians retained their original location, and the Greeks settled their own neighborhood. The city was on the island of Pharos and was connected to the mainland by a causeway, with the whole setting dominated by an impressive lighthouse.

The famous Museum (Shrine of the Muses) was begun in 294 B.C. and soon expanded into a complete university complemented by botanical and zoological gardens, as well as an observatory. Euclid wrote his *Elements* (c. 300 B.C.) at the Museum, and Apollonius of Perge developed his theory of conic sections there. There were comparable achievements in astronomy, medicine, and engineering. All these advantages must have made Alexandria an especially attractive scene for the young Callimachus. When he first arrived in Alexandria, he may have spent some time teaching, but he soon became one of the scholars attached to the Royal Library under the patronage of Ptolemy II.

Apparently Callimachus never became chief librarian but during his tenure at the library he composed many literary works, most of them, unfortunately, lost. He achieved a reputation for his poetry, his scholarship, and his pugnacious championing of his views about poetry. He is said to have died around 240 B.C. in Alexandria.

Influence

Callimachus argued for the superiority of the shorter modes of expression. He especially liked the epyllion, a brief epic that developed a single episode in detail, and he was also a successful composer of epigrams, pithy statements on many topics. A third genre that he favored was the elegy on a theme from the Greek myths. His advocacy of these types of poetry was so successful that the best surviving examples of Alexandrian poetry are in these modes.

Analysis

There is an anecdote about Callimachus that has him asserting that a big book is a big evil. Exactly what he meant by this is unclear. It may have been a librarian's judgment on the nuisance created by big scrolls. Given his frequent disparagement of the epic, however, it is consistent with his literary theory. He preferred Hesiod to Homer as a model for poetry, stating in one of his epigrams, "I hate epic poetry."

One of Callimachus' contemporaries was Apollonius of Rhodes, apparently a follower of the Homeric tradition, and it is possible that he and Callimachus were the focus of a literary squabble over the merits of epic poetry, although this view has been challenged by Alan Cameron. Whatever his relationship with Apollonius, in *Aetia* (which means "the causes of the myths"), Callimachus explodes in a tirade against the Telchines, as he calls them. The Telchines were mythological figures who came from Crete and Rhodes and were supposedly the first metalworkers. Their reputation as sorcerers lay behind Callimachus' condemnation of them as "spiteful backbiters" and his use of the name to refer to his literary antagonists. Among the Telchines were two notable Alexandrian poets, Asclepiades and Posidippus, as well as a philosopher, Praxiphanes of Mitylene.

In book I of *Aetia*, Callimachus says that

> the Telchines, who are ignorant and no friends of the Muse, grumble at my poetry, because I did not accomplish one continuous poem of many thousands of lines on . . . kings or . . . heroes, but like a child I roll forth a short tale, though the decades of my life are not few.

He adds shortly after that "poems are far sweeter for being short."

A second theme that emerges in Callimachus' writings is a kind of rebelliousness against the modish and popular. He says, also in *Aetia*, "This too I bid you: tread a path which carriages do not trample; do not drive your chariot upon the common tracks of others, nor along a wide road, but on unworn paths, though your course be more narrow."

Among the Hellenic poets who were indebted to Callimachus were the obscure Cyrene poet Philostephanus, who composed accounts of geographical wonders, and Euphorion, the author of epyllia of violent love. Moschus wrote an epyllion entitled *Europa* (c. 150 B.C.), and Parthenius also wrote epyllia. Through Parthenius, Callimachus even influenced Virgil, whose early pastorals display a characteristically Callimachean rejection of the long epic that is repented of only when he comes to write the *Aeneid* (c. 29–19 B.C.).

Among the other Augustan poets, Ovid and Propertius were notable followers of Callimachus. Propertius was even called "the Roman Callimachus." The diverse moods of Ovid's poems, especially the *Metamorphoses* (c. A.D. 8), have been described as entirely Callimachean in spirit. The poems in *Metamorphoses* are, moreover, examples of Callimachus' favored genre, the epyllion.

The only significant later poet to be influenced by Callimachus was Pierre de Ronsard, one of a group of seven French poets known collectively as the Pléiade. John Ferguson observes that although Callimachus has not directly influenced a large number of poets, "there has been from time to time across the history of poetry an assertion of Callimachean values." Ferguson cites T. S. Eliot as a particularly Callimachean poet and points out Eliot's many sympathies with Callimachean tastes and values: both make use of their learning in their poetry, both exploit mythology extensively, and both are innovators as well as traditionalists.

Ferguson calls Callimachus "the supreme exponent of Alexandrianism" and sums up that culture (about 280 to 240 B.C.) in the following features. First, even though they may have disagreed on the merits of a particular writer such as Homer, the Alexandrians were essentially traditionalists. Second, they were learned and scholarly, greatly inspired by the Alexandrian Museum and its accompanying library. Third, they were much concerned with literary technique and craft. Fourth, they seldom created new forms, except for shaped poems. Fifth, in Ferguson's words, "they were interested in pouring new wine into old bottles."

Beyond this tentative exposition of Callimachus' theory, little can be said. He emerges in vague silhouette from the past as a talented, rather prickly individual with an independent viewpoint all his own, a man still enticing to scholars.

Principal criticism

Passages in *Aetia*; *Epigrams*; *Hecale*; *Hymns*; *Iambi*

Other major work and literary form

None of the titles listed above is a work specifically of literary criticism: they are poems – some fragmentary – through which are scattered the remarks on literary criticism and theory that constitute all that is known of Callimachus' critical views. According to ancient sources, he wrote many other works in both prose and poetry, but they have not survived. Indeed, the two significant but incomplete works *Aetia* and *Hecale* were not discovered until the twentieth century.

Besides the poetical works, Callimachus also wrote scholarly tomes, his most famous being the *Pinakes* (tablets), a catalog of the books in the library of the great museum in Alexandria. He complied encyclopedias, wrote a study of Democritus, and collected notable sayings. These works were important contributions to the beginnings of Greek literary history. Altogether, his output was apparently huge, but the only surviving works that present his ideas directly are those listed above.

NONFICTION
Pinakes

Further reading

Blum, Rudolf. *Kallimachos: The Alexandrian Library and the Origins of Bibliography*, 1991.

Cameron, Alan. *Callimachus and His Critics*, 1995.

Donohue, Harold. *The Song of the Swan: Lucretius and the Influence of Callimachus*, 1993.

Ferguson, John. *Callimachus*, 1980.

Fraser, P. M. *Ptolemaic Alexandria*, 1972 (2 volumes).
George, E. *Aeneid VIII and the Aitia of Callimachus*, 1990.
Lombardo, Stanley, and Diane Rayor, eds. Notes in *Callimachus: Hymns, Epigrams, Select Fragments*, 1987.
Trypanis, C. A., ed. Notes in *Callimachus: Aetia, Iambi, Hecale, Minor Epic and Elegiac Poems, and Other Fragments*, 1958.

FRANK DAY

See also Classical Greek and Roman Literary Theory

Italo Calvino

Italian novelist, editor, and critic

Born: Santiago de las Vegas, Cuba; October 15, 1923
Died: Siena, Italy; September 19, 1985

Biography

Italo Calvino was the oldest son of two Italian scientists, Evelina Mameli, a botanist, and Mario Calvino, an agronomist, who were living in Cuba when he was born. The family returned to Italy in 1925, to San Remo on the Ligurian coast. Here a childhood of ease and serenity turned into an adolescence under Fascism. Spending three years enrolled in agrarian science in Turin and Florence, Calvino read anti-Fascist literature which determined him to join the Italian Communist Party and fight as a partisan and also to study literature following the Liberation in 1945. Before completing his undergraduate dissertation on Joseph Conrad two years later, Calvino had already won a literary prize for a short story and written his first novel, *Il sentiero dei nidi di ragno* (1947; *The Path to the Spiders' Nests*, 1998).

Calvino's critical contributions also began as early as 1945 when his first literary reviews and political journalism appeared. The writer Cesare Pavese introduced him to the publishing house Einaudi, where his novel was published and where he would work as an editor until 1983. Pavese and another writer, Elio Vittorini, both his colleagues in the left-wing intellectual climate of Einaudi, were formative models for Calvino's views on literature in the service of politics. From 1950 on Calvino fulfilled his commitments to Einaudi while at the same time writing journalism and short fiction. In 1954 he was commissioned to collect, transcribe, and edit all existing Italian folk tales, and in 1955 he began to develop and publish his own poetics of engaged literature.

With Vittorini, Calvino founded the journal *Il menabò* and began to write and lecture widely on contemporary fiction. The fantastical trilogy *I nostri antenati* (1960; *Our Ancestors*, 1980) consolidated his reputation as an author and he was in wide demand as a literary commentator. Calvino married Esther Singer in 1964 and they lived in Paris from 1967 until 1980. There Calvino attended lectures by Roland Barthes and A. J. Greimas which were reflected in both his fiction and in his theory of how fiction is generated. The French writer Raymond Queneau was another influence in this field and invited Calvino to join the Ouvroir de Littérature Potentielle, or Oulipo, an experimental literary workshop.

Calvino's novels *Le città invisibili* (1972; *Invisible Cities*, 1974) and *Se una notte d'inverno un viaggiatore* (1979; *If on a Winter's Night a Traveller*, 1981) enjoyed great acclaim and for the first time, in 1980, he published a collection of his literary criticism, *Una pietra sopra: Discorsi di letteratura e società* (*The Uses of Literature*, 1986). He was awarded the French Légion d'Honneur in 1981 and was invited to give the Norton Lectures at Harvard University in 1985. He had almost completed the lecture notes when he died in September; his drafts were published in 1988 as *Lezioni americane: Sei proposte per il prossimo millennio* (*Six Memos for the Next Millennium*).

Influence

The range, variety, and volume of Calvino's *saggistica*, his essay writing, matches that of his fiction and is destined to become equally celebrated as more translations tackle the articles that can currently be read only in Italian. In 1985 Calvino was poised to exert an international academic influence as a critic and widely expected to win the Nobel Prize for Literature. With his death that year his critical legacy was left as three main volumes, *The Uses of Literature*, *Perché leggere i classici* (1991; *Why Read the Classics?*, 1999), and *Six Memos for the Next Millennium*. These works neatly chart a poetics that evolved from political engagement to structuralism, and from structuralism to the set of abstract qualities he proposed as blueprints for the literature of the next millennium.

Calvino's discursive output mirrors the social, political, and cultural postwar history of Italy. Yet his literary critical voice speaks both of developments in contemporary Italy and also of forms and practices from outside the Italian tradition. His commentary on European classics fused with his fascination for narrative structures to produce an encyclopedic postmodern consciousness. One of the most common applications to which Calvino's theoretical writing has been put is as an analysis of his own fiction and as guidelines for contemporary authors. The first exponent of Italian metafiction, his parallel criticism can also be judged a metapoetics.

Analysis

The parabola of Calvino's criticism follows the same arc as his fictional production, reflecting his attempt to write novels for his time and to document the novel's contemporary history. His trajectory began with the Italian literary phenomenon of neorealism, a postwar explosion of texts documenting the anti-Fascist struggle in a terse, new style. Then, in the peacetime and economic prosperity of the

1950s, Calvino and his generation found themselves under pressure to bring the same vitality to a fictional representation of industrial proletarian life in Italy. In his 1964 preface added to his own Resistance novel *The Path to the Spiders' Nests*, Calvino gives one of the clearest critical accounts of neorealism and its repercussions for the next wave of writers.

As a committed Communist, Calvino created his own formulation for *letteratura engagée* (literature of [political] commitment). Like Jean-Paul Sartre, he insisted on the coexistence of ethics and poetics in literature. His 1955 essay "Il midollo del leone" ("The Lion's Marrow," 1986) states that political commitment is more than a duty, it is a necessity for today's writers, indeed for all people. By 1957 though, Calvino had broken with the Communist Party in the wake of the invasion of Hungary. In a reassessment of committed literature in Italy, "Usi politici giusti e sbagliati della letteratura" (1976; "Right and Wrong Political Uses of Literature," 1986), Calvino concludes that the impetus of engagement only lasted from 1945 to 1960, after which time Italian literature fractured into separate experimental movements which found no champions in the political upheavals of the late 1960s. The essay confirms Calvino as a writer who abandoned the didacticism and ideology of Marxist literature for a lasting commitment to make literature political through speaking the unspoken, promoting ethical values, and reminding the body politic that its power is built, like literature, on rhetoric.

As class struggle and historical destiny were replaced by fantastical, comic protagonists in *Our Ancestors*, Calvino's essays began to question the role of the novel as a mimetic and anthropocentric reflection of reality. His essay "Natura e storia nel romanzo" (1958; "Nature and History in the Novel," 1986) replays the development of the nineteenth-century European novel and marks Calvino's last attempt to provide a positivist manifesto of reason, action, and history for the novel of the late twentieth century. In his own journal *Il menabò* Calvino published two essays which heralded a new departure in his fiction. "Il mare dell'oggetività" (1959; "The Sea of Objects," 1986) impugns the French *nouveau roman* for drowning subjectivity and proposes a shift from such a "literature of objectivity" to a "literature of consciousness." "La sfida al labirinto" (1962; "The Challenge to the Labyrinth," 1986) embraces the idea of the nonanthropocentric perspective but argues that literature should not resign itself to the known map. Instead, it should dare to find a critical awareness that encompasses both the subject and the cosmos, a challenge Calvino met in *Le cosmicomiche* (1965; *Cosmicomics*, 1969). The essay "Cibernetica e fantasmi" (1967; "Cybernetics and Ghosts," 1986) acknowledges the explicit influence of Barthes' semiology and Greimas' structuralism in his fictional *Ti con zero* (1967; *Time and the Hunter*, 1993). The essay's subtitle, "notes on narrative as combinatory process," also refers to Raymond Queneau's group Oulipo, where mathematics and words meet to create infinite literary possibilities, aided also by computer technology. The novel *Il castello dei destini incrociati* (1972; *The Castle of Crossed Destinies*, 1977) was generated through this combinatoric system. All the aforementioned essays were anthologized in *Una pietra sopra*, which is partly translated in *The Uses of Literature*.

An interest in the application of structuralist principles for writing narrative can be traced directly to Calvino's work compiling and editing Italian folk tales. The critical analogue to this text is *Sulla fiaba* (1988; on the fable), a posthumously published collection of articles on fables from Italy, France, and Africa, on Formalism, and on popular tradition. Another substantial anthology of untranslated criticism is *Collezione di sabbia* (1984; collection of sand). The single literary article is one of the most important in the book. A memoir on the occasion of Roland Barthes' death, it is a disquisition on the gaze, that central Barthesian concept. It interweaves a personal account of Barthes' funeral and a review of his whole critical œuvre, all of which, concludes Calvino, was geared toward constraining the impersonality of our linguistic and cognitive mechanism to deal with the physicality of the living but mortal subject. Mostly newspaper articles on exhibitions in Paris and exotic travelogues, the modular structure of *Collezione di sabbia* is, once again, analagous to Calvino's fictional work, in this case the short stories *Palomar* (1983; *Mr Palomar*, 1985), and it also has a narrative thrust. Both texts are divided into thematic schemas and many of the observations and analyses of Parisian cultural and everyday life in *Collezione di sabbia* are narrated by a critic whose voice is interchangeable with the protagonist Palomar. Calvino's substantial contributions on nonliterary subjects are all collected in the two volumes of his *Saggi* (1995). These articles on politics, history, science, society, geography, travel, art, language, and cinema were most often composed for newspapers but nothing Calvino wrote has the ephemeral quality of journalism. When not writing literature, or writing about literature, Calvino writes a highly "literary" form of criticism.

Calvino remarked that he spent more time thinking about other people's books than about his own. The most interesting counsel and confessions he offered to writers in his capacity as an editor at Einaudi are found in selected letters he wrote to them, published in *I libri degli altri. Lettere 1947–1981* (1991; other people's books). The editorial letters shed much light on Calvino's creative and analytical processes as he exemplifies suggestions to authors with techniques he has used himself, or admires in classic texts, and tempers criticism by citing problems he has encountered in his own work. Here we see the practical critic advising a woman writer to switch her perspective from the female to the fat, male protagonist after Gustave Flaubert's example ("the fat man, *c'est moi!*"); praising a story's suffocating Hawthornesque atmosphere; and proposing to replace unsuitable titles. Most of the letters are addressed to contemporary Italian writers and document some of the forces that influenced the production of Italian fiction from 1947 to 1981. Primo Levi is advised not to rely too heavily on metaphor in the first section of *The Periodic Table* (1984); Leonardo Sciascia is warned to lose the imperturbable tone he borrows from Alessandro Manzoni.

I libri degli altri reveals to what extent Calvino's time was occupied by reading the work of his contemporaries and contextualizing them next to great works of the past. It is this tension between his love for classics and a fascination for innovative fictional forms that, perhaps more than any other dynamic, characterizes Calvino's approach to literature. "Perché leggere i classici?" ("Why Read the Classics?") asks his essay of 1981 and proceeds to give fourteen definitions of what constitutes a "classic." One example says, "6. A classic is a work which has never exhausted what it has to say to us," while another, more equivocal one suggests, "8. A classic is a work which incessantly feels the dust of critical debates on its shoulders but which is continually shaking it off." *Why Read the Classics?* is the title of a selection, preceded by the eponymous essay, of prefaces, articles, reviews, and tributes written on contemporary, classic, and classical writers.

In this critical text Calvino commemorates his canon of favorite writers and acknowledged paradigms, and in the pieces on individuals he explores the same themes that preoccupied him in his essays and fiction written during the same period. He talks, for example, of the "lion's marrow" of Conrad's prose being "the sense of an integration in the world . . . the sense of a man realising himself through what he does, in the moral implicit in his work, the ideal of knowing that he is capable to deal with the situation, on the deck of a sailing ship as on the page." An essay from the same year, 1954, on another writer as man of destiny, confesses that for Calvino's generation Ernest Hemingway, master of the laconic, paratactic, "reductive style," "was a God." Robert Louis Stevenson is admired for blending in the mechanical narrative strategy of his binary characters with both love stories and tales of pure adventure, and Stendhal for his ironic, psychological portrait of the action hero.

Writers of French nineteenth-century prose are more strongly represented in the anthology than any other group. The mythology of the Parisian metropolis as the root of Honoré de Balzac's superabundant narrative force receives the same veneration as Gustave Flaubert's spare, isolated asceticism. Calvino's French Oulipo collaborators, Raymond Queneau and Georges Perec, are also privileged in these pages. In the *Saggi* the selection of *Why Read the Classics?* has been expanded to include the enormous body of Calvino's writing devoted to single authors under the rubric "Narratori, poeti, saggisti" (prose writers, poets, and essayists), further subdivided into Classics, Italian Contemporaries, and Foreign Contemporaries. Important essays paying homage to Pavese and Vittorini can be found in *Una pietra sopra*.

The *Saggi* house an entire section of unanthologized articles under the rubric "Altri discorsi di letteratura e società" (other arguments on literature and society). These include Calvino's earliest statements about the goals of Marxist literature and his first signs of demurral faced with the constraints of socialist realism. However, it is an essay from the other end of the spectrum which deserves to be better known. "Il mondo scritto e non scritto" was written as a lecture for New York University in 1983 and was translated as "The Written and the Unwritten World" in the *New York Review of Books*. In this essay Calvino returns to the idea he first expressed in the 1950s: his duty as a writer to push at the frontiers of literature and to give a voice in language to that part of the world which is not written and lies in angry silence.

Six Memos for the Next Millennium is Calvino's best-known critical work in English and was written expressly for an American audience. There are, in fact, only five memos – "Lightness," "Quickness," "Exactitude," "Visibility," and "Multiplicity." A sixth, conclusive section called "Consistency" had been projected. The five abstractions are, by implication, what Calvino feels millennial literature should strive for. "Lightness" and "Quickness" are both qualities which can be achieved by losing the weight of excess words. "Exactitude" invokes Giacomo Leopardi and Flaubert for finding a focus that will permit only the exact term, the *mot juste*. "Visibility" explores the ability to transfer imagination to the visible image on the page. The description of a vivid visual scene can act as an epistemological instrument to discover a wider vision. Finally, "Multiplicity" is the thematics of global complexity, a fitting encapsulation of the infinite areas, forms, signs, and objects that have fascinated Calvino's mercurial and encyclopedic mind. Amongst the last words he wrote in introduction to the Harvard Norton lectures of *Six Memos for the Next Millennium* were: "My faith in the future of literature consists in knowing that there are things that only literature can accomplish through its own specific means."

Calvino's broad erudition in the classics, his omnivorous curiosity about contemporary writing, and his confidence in the postindustrial future of the book make him a fitting Janus for twentieth-century criticism, looking backward to the age of the novel and forward to the literature of a new millennium.

Principal criticism

Una pietra sopra: Discorsi di letteratura e società, 1980 (*The Uses of Literature*, 1986)
Collezione di sabbia, 1984 (collection of sand)
Lezioni americane: Sei proposte per il prossimo millennio, 1988 (*Six Memos for the Next Millennium*, 1988)
Sulla fiaba, 1988 (on the fable)
Perché leggere i classici?, 1991 (*Why Read the Classics?*, 1999)

I libri degli altri. Lettere 1947–1981, 1991 (other people's books)
Saggi, 1995 (2 volumes; essays)

Other major works and literary forms

All literary forms are represented in Italo Calvino's vast body of work from 1945 to 1985 and none more so than prose fiction.

NOVELS
Il sentiero dei nidi di ragno, 1947 (*The Path to the Spiders' Nests*, 1998)
Il visconte dimezzato, 1952 (*The Cloven Viscount*, 1962)
Il barone rampante, 1957 (*The Baron in the Trees*, 1959)
Il cavaliere inesistente, 1959 (*The Non-Existent Knight*, 1962)
I nostri antenati, 1960 (*Our Ancestors*, 1980)
La giornata d'uno scrutatore, 1963 (*The Watcher and Other Stories*, 1971)
La speculazione edilizia, 1963 (*A Plunge into Real Estate*, 1964)
Le città invisibili, 1972 (*Invisible Cities*, 1974)
Il castello dei destini incrociati, 1972 (*The Castle of Crossed Destinies*, 1977)
Se una notte d'inverno un viaggiatore, 1979 (*If on a Winter's Night a Traveler*, 1981)

SHORT FICTION
Ultimo viene il corvo, 1949 (*Adam, One Afternoon and Other Stories*, 1983)
I racconti, 1958
Marcovaldo; ovvero, Le stagioni in città, 1963 (*Marcovaldo, or, The Seasons in the City*, 1983)
Le cosmicomiche, 1965 (*Cosmicomics*, 1969)
Ti con zero, 1967 (*Time and the Hunter*, 1993)
La memoria del mondo ed altre storie cosmicomiche, 1968
Gli amori difficili, 1970 (*Difficult Loves*, 1983)
Palomar, 1983 (*Mr Palomar*, 1985)
Sotto il sole giaguaro, 1986 (*Under the Jaguar Sun*, 1992)
Prima che tu dica "Pronto," 1993 (*Numbers in the Dark and Other Stories*, 1995)
These literary works can be found in Calvino's collected fiction, *Romanzi e racconti* (novels and short stories), Volumes 1 (1991), 2 (1992), and 3 (1994). The third volume includes poetry, drama, satire, and verse translation from French, as well as some of Calvino's collaboration with Oulipo.

NONFICTION
La strada di San Giovanni, 1990 (*The Road to San Giovanni*, 1993)
Eremita a Parigi. Pagine autobiografiche, 1994
Album Calvino, 1995

EDITED TEXTS
Fiabe italiane, 1956 (*Italian Fables*, 1959, and *Italian Folk Tales*, 1975)
Racconti fantastici dell'Ottocento, 1983 (*Fantastical Tales*, 1993)

MISCELLANEOUS
Romanzi e racconti, Vol. 1, 1991, Vol. 2, 1992, Vol. 3, 1994
Fiabe italiane, 1993
Saggi, 1995 (2 volumes)

Further reading

Ajello, Nello. *Intellettuali e PCI 1944–1958*, 1979.
Barenghi, Mario. *Introduction and Notes to Saggi*, 1995.
Bonsaver, Guido. *Il mondo scritto*, 1995.
Cannon, JoAnn. *Italo Calvino: Writer and Critic*, 1981.
Clerici, Luca, and Bruno Falcetto, eds. *Calvino e l'editoria*, 1993.
Ferretti, Gian Carlo. *Le capre di Bikini*, 1989.
Hume, Kathryn. *Calvino's Fictions: Cogito and Cosmos*, 1992.
McLaughlin, Martin L. *Italo Calvino*, 1998.
Milanini, Claudio. *L'utopia discontinua*, 1990.
Weiss, Beno. *Understanding Italo Calvino*, 1993.

JOANNA STEPHENS

See also Barthes; Eco; Greimas; Narratology; Postmodernism; Structuralism

Canon

The term "canon" was applied originally to the sacred texts of Christianity in the Middle Ages, designating certain books for religious instruction, and marking all others for exclusion. It is comparatively novel to refer to a set of literary texts in such a manner. A canon in the vernacular would become widespread neither in European practice nor as an ideal until the arrival of modernity in the eighteenth century. The canon of English literature would have to await the mid-nineteenth century to achieve a level of prestige that would enable it to supplant the classics (Latin and Greek poetry and plays) in university curricula, though a canon of vernacular literature was in widespread use in secondary education long before universities took it up. Further, Gauri Viswanathan, in *Masks of Conquest: Literary Study and British Rule in India* (1989), has shown conclusively that the rise of the canon of English literature is coeval and indeed complicit with the expansion of the British Empire in India and with colonialism in general. The canon was developed, in Viswanathan's words, as an "active instrument of Western hegemony in concert with commercial expansion and military action." The same can be more generally asserted about the canons of continental European literature.

In more recent times, however, the canon has become a terrain of contention among many within literary studies, particularly in the United States. Critics ranging from Allan Bloom in *The Closing of the American Mind* (1987) to Roger Kimball in *Tenured Radicals: How Politics has Corrupted Our Higher Education* (1990) and Dinesh D'Souza in *Illiberal Education: The Politics of Race and Sex on Campus* (1991) have lined up to defend what they see as an assault upon the values represented by the canon of Western literature. In so doing they assert the value of tradition, the benefits of Western culture, and the improving effects of an education in the canon of Western literature and European humanism in general. Direct threats to the canon posed by emerging curricula associated with previously excluded groups, such as blacks, women, gays, lesbians, and working-class writers, all made such a defense of the Western canon seem necessary to Bloom and others. The canon, its opponents claimed, was structured to exclude minorities just as they had been excluded from representation in political structures outside of the academy. The charge from minorities to open the canon up to include formerly excluded writers accompanied the charge to acknowledge and generally celebrate the diversity inherent in various Western national cultures. Diversity in the canon would therefore justly reflect the diversity of cultures and identities in society at large. The debate centers around the issue of inclusion or exclusion, the preservation of Western culture versus its revision to reflect society's diversity. Launched in the late 1980s, the canon debate shows no signs of easing as conservatives and liberal pluralists line up over the issue of what to include in the canon, which authors should be thrown overboard, and who should be excluded.

The most influential critical study of the canon and the debates surrounding it, however, rejects the very terms of the controversy as described above. John Guillory's *Cultural Capital: The Problem of Literary Canon Formation* (1993) is a powerful work of scholarship and critique that displaces the arguments about the inclusion or exclusion by questioning the very assumptions upon which such arguments take place. That is, Guillory begins by asking radically different questions. Instead of "who should be represented in the canon?," he asks "why do we have a canon?" "Who benefits from the idea of an institutionalized canon?" Borrowing a concept from the French social theorist Pierre Bourdieu, he asks "how does the acquisition of 'cultural capital' – in the form of the canon – work to reinforce class distinctions in society?" While demolishing the conservatives' arguments, and accepting the crucial advances liberal pluralism has made, Guillory is not shy to point out the latter's mistakes. It is a mistake, Guillory claims, to devote so much time and critical energy to the end of getting minorities included in the canon without pressing further and asking what the social function of canonicity is, exactly. If, for example, a university system teaches women authors but continues to exclude women from tenured faculty positions, has a substantial advance been made? As he says, for example, "it is much easier to make canons representative than the university." If Zora Neale Hurston (1903–1960) now can be taught alongside Plato, while the majority of black women in society remain unable to participate in the acquisition of literary capital, what has been gained? Guillory writes: "Those who have never been taught, or have been very inadequately taught, the *practice* of reading have little occasion to rejoice at being 'represented' in the canon. Such representation does not address or compensate for the socioeconomic conditions of their existence so long as the school continues to distribute cultural capital unequally." The names change but the system remains the same: certain groups remain in positions of power and privilege while others do not, regardless of who gets put on the syllabus or included in the literary hall of fame. Furthermore, as Guillory puts it, "the formal study of cultural works produced within minority cultures is not a means of reproducing minority culture (in the ethnographic sense)." That is, formal study is a separate enterprise altogether from the transmission of culture. Formal study relies upon the act of dehistoricizing literary texts, removing them from the conditions of their production and the communities in which they arose and replacing them in the exclusive context of the university.

Guillory suggests that we understand the canon not as an actual list of great books, but as something more abstract. He says, "It would be better to say that the canon is an *imaginary* totality of works. No one has access to the canon as a totality. This fact is true in the trivial sense that no one ever reads every canonical work; no one can, because the works invoked as canonical change continually according to many different occasions of judgment or contestation. What this means is that the canon is never other than an imaginary list . . . ." It is more important for bourgeois society, in other words, that *the idea of a canon as such* be transmitted and deployed.

Guillory turns to both the writings of Antonio Gramsci and Pierre Bourdieu on the subject of education as a means to help elaborate his critique. From Gramsci, Guillory borrows an analysis of the way that school systems track students into different categories (technical and classical, for example), distributing cultural capital unequally. Gramsci proposed the idea of a "unitary school" that, as Guillory notes, was supposed to demolish the traditional educational system in which, as Gramsci says, "each group has its own type of school, intended to perpetuate a specific traditional function, ruling or subordinate." From Bourdieu, Guillory borrows the framework and assumptions of his own critique. A sociologist by training, Bourdieu elaborates his system of analysis in several places, most notably in *Distinction: A Social Critique of the Judgment of Taste*, published in French in 1979 and in English in 1989. Bourdieu's main advance, as Guillory sees it, is to elaborate a detailed critique of the distribution of cultural capital in society, explaining how educational institutions function to reinforce class divisions by bestowing knowledge upon some and not others. Within the broader framework set up by Bourdieu, Guillory intervenes in the specific terrain of the canon debate.

Further reading

Bloom, Allan. *The Closing of the American Mind*, 1987.
Bourdieu, Pierre. *Distinction: A Social Critique of the Judgment of Taste*, 1989.
D'Souza, Dinesh. *Illiberal Education: The Politics of Race and Sex on Campus*, 1991.
Gramsci, Antonio. *Further Selections from the Prison Notebooks*, 1995. Edited by Derek Boothman.
Guillory, John. *Cultural Capital: The Problem of Literary Canon Formation*, 1993.

Kimball, Roger. *Tenured Radicals: How Politics has Corrupted Our Higher Education*, 1990.
Viswanathan, Gauri. *Masks of Conquest: Literary Study and British Rule in India*, 1989.

SPURGEON THOMPSON

See also Bloom; Classic, the; Postcolonial Literature and Theory

Lodovico Castelvetro

Italian critic and playwright

Born: Modena, Italy; 1505
Died: Chiavenna, Swiss Federation; February 21, 1571

Biography

In 1505 Lodovico Castelvetro was born into a noble family in Modena, Italy. After studying at the universities of Bologna, Ferrara, and Padua, he finally received a doctorate of law from the University of Siena. He then became the Duke of Urbino's ambassador to the papal court in Rome. Dissatisfied with life in Rome, he fled to Siena to pursue studies in Greek, Latin, and Italian literature. Giving way to pressure from his father, Castelvetro returned to Modena, where he became friends with Giovanni Grilenzono. Together they established an academy for humanistic studies. Not only did they read and criticize the Greek and Latin authors, but they also encouraged the creation and study of Italian literature.

The academy had problems, however, when some of its members were accused of heresy. Also, in 1553, Castelvetro criticized one of the poems of Annibale Caro, secretary to the powerful Cardinal Alessandro Farnese. Caro attacked Castelvetro through a series of pamphlets, and Castelvetro countered his attacks until their conflict escalated into a full-scale verbal war. In collusion with one of Castelvetro's brothers, Caro had Castelvetro brought before the Inquisition on charges of heresy. Unsuccessful in defending himself, Castelvetro fled to Chiavenna, a town on the Swiss-Italian border.

Caught in the turmoil of the times, Castelvetro spent the rest of his life in flight. Moving to Lyons, he was caught in a battle between Huguenots and Catholics. His house was sacked, and he barely escaped with his life. He then went to Vienna to join one of his brothers at the court of the Emperor Maximilian II. Under the emperor's protection, he was able to publish the famous *Poetica d'Aristotele vulgarizzata et sposta*. Having fled Vienna to avoid the plague, he died in Chiavenna on February 21, 1571, at the age of sixty-six.

Influence

Castelvetro is one of the most important commentators on Aristotle. So thoroughly did he reinterpret Aristotle that he influenced the course of literary criticism for two centuries after his own death. Castelvetro offered a narrow definition of verisimilitude; fixed the concept of the three unities of time, place, and action; prescribed a series of strict rules for dramas; and led Western literature toward a rigid form of neoclassicism. In less rigid terms, the notion that a drama should contain a limited scope of action, set in a single place and played out in a narrow span of time, remains influential even today.

Analysis

Although he wrote some critical works on individual authors, Castelvetro's *Poetica d'Aristotele vulgarizatta et sposta* is his most significant work for several reasons. First, it is a summation of his thinking on literary criticism. Second, it was one of the first of many commentaries on Aristotle written in a nonclassical language, thus providing a wider audience for poetic theory. Third, since it follows the major critical commentaries of the well-known Italian Renaissance critics, it presents a synthesis of the critical philosophy of his time. Finally, Castelvetro went further than any of his contemporaries in reinterpreting, amending, and contradicting Aristotle.

Castelvetro did more than comment on Aristotle. After acknowledging the work of his predecessors, he states that he does not intend merely to follow in their footsteps; he assures his readers that he will "do more than explain" Aristotle. Unlike many previous commentators, Castelvetro did not consider Aristotle's *De poetica* (c. 334–323 B.C.; *Poetics*) sacrosanct. Believing the *Poetics* to be no more than a series of sketchy, ambiguous, and underdeveloped notes "to be used for a larger work," Castelvetro used Aristotle as a point of departure in forming his own poetics. His exhaustive analysis (seven hundred pages in quarto form) contains sections of Aristotle's Greek text, followed by a summary of the text in Italian, then an Italian translation, accompanied by voluminous commentary.

Castelvetro's commentary diverged significantly from many of the standard views of his age. At a time when literary classics were considered objects of contemplation, Castelvetro viewed poetic works (epics, tragedies, and comedies) primarily as performance pieces to be recited or acted in public. When most critics concentrated on the structural analysis of literature, Castelvetro based his poetics on an audience-response model. Unlike many of his contemporaries, who viewed the study of great literature as an elitist art directed toward a select and erudite audience, Castelvetro saw the uneducated masses as the primary audience of poetry. Contrary to most Renaissance thinking, which held moral enlightenment to be the aim of poetry, Castelvetro believed that the sole aim of poetry was delight. While others saw many possible subjects for a poem, Castelvetro sharply limited the subject matter of poetry.

Castelvetro based his poetics on three principles. First, poetry is written to be performed for the illiterate masses, whose every need must be considered. Second, the purpose of poetry is to entertain this mass audience. Third, poetry must carefully and astutely display the ingenuity of the poet. These principles inform all Castelvetro's theories.

In formulating his poetics, Castelvetro created an elaborate audience psychology for his ideal audience. Because Castelvetro's unsophisticated audience can grasp only sensory images, not universal ideas, poets must focus on the detailed actions of concrete characters. Castelvetro praises Homer's characters for being natural and individualistic, while he dismisses Virgil's characters as mere abstractions. His audience also lacks imagination; therefore, poetic works must be literal representations of life. Puzzled by actions with too many digressions, unable to absorb brief scenes, dissatisfied with dramas that are too short, uncomfortable with dramas that are too long, Castelvetro's audience puts severe restrictions on the poet and limits the range of poetry.

Unlike many of his contemporaries, Castelvetro insisted that the sole purpose of poetry is "to delight and to recreate," not to edify. Castelvetro tried to reconcile his views with those of Aristotle, holding that Aristotle saw delight as the major aim of poetry and only conceded to utility in his concept of catharsis. Aristotle had shown how, through catharsis, audience members were purged of harmful emotions; Castelvetro, however, contended that catharsis is not a means of "pleasure or delight and it ought properly to be called utility, since it is health of mind and acquired through very bitter medicine." For Castelvetro, poetry is written to give pleasure; edification in the form of catharsis is only an incidental by-product.

Shifting his emphasis away from affective criticism, Castelvetro focused on another external element in the creative process – the nature of the poet. Castelvetro refuted the prevailing notion that poets were divinely inspired. He dismissed as a misquote Aristotle's statement that the poet must be a person of excellent natural endowments or a madman, while he viewed Plato's account of a divinely possessed poet as a piece of irony. For Castelvetro, the idea of a crazed, possessed poet summoning the Muses was a myth held by the illiterate mob and perpetuated by some poets for their self-glorification. Castelvetro also contradicted Aristotle's statements that the first poets created out of intuition and that poets should identify with their characters: "It is sufficient to teach us how to fashion every part of a poem, and we need not transform ourselves into other persons. . . . It is enough that we apply the teachings of the art." Over and over again, he reiterated that the writing of poetry can be mastered by following the appropriate rules. Castelvetro measured a poet by the skill and ingenuity of his inventiveness, or, to be more exact, his ability to be innovative within the strictures and confines of a well-made artistic structure. He held Dante to be a greater poet than Petrarch, simply because Dante's poetry is more complex. In essence, Castelvetro viewed the poem as a mere vehicle for the poet to demonstrate his virtuosity. Homer's genius as a poet lay in setting difficult tasks for himself and then accomplishing them.

Given Castelvetro's construction of his ideal audience and his model poet, his rigid guidelines for the creation of a poetic text fall into place. First and foremost, there must be verisimilitude. Actions onstage or in an epic must correspond to actions which have already happened or have the possibility of happening; otherwise, the audience will not believe them. For example, Aeneas' men build a ship in several days without access to tools or building materials. For Castelvetro, this action is impossible and, thus, unbelievable. Second, poets cannot rewrite history. Actions about real kings or gods cannot be invented or distorted. In *Parere di Ludovico Castelvetro sopra ciascuna comedia di Plauto*, he censured Plautus for elaborating on historical legends: "This action involves kings and gods, but it is not known through history or through legend; hence it is not a poetic subject." Anachronisms are not to be tolerated. Aeneas was not a contemporary of Dido; therefore, they cannot meet. Reports that Orestes was killed at the chariot races in the Pythian games are inconsistent with historical circumstances because "at that time the chariot race was not among the contests at the Pythian games." Third, all actions must be probable. Homer is criticized for having Helen identify the Greek heroes for Priam; Castelvetro observes that Priam must certainly have known the Greek heroes if he had been fighting them for ten years. Fourth, all actions in a poem must concur with the customs of the times. In *Lettera del dubioso academico*, Castelvetro faulted Giovanni Boccaccio for ignoring local customs: "Everybody knows, for example, that young ladies of good family are carefully guarded by their parents; yet Boccaccio frequently has them meeting with men, and he does not tell how this surveillance had been circumvented."

Finally, Castelvetro limited the poet to reporting not only what is customary but also what is conventional. Virgil "sins against the proprieties of prophecy" by having a prophet use someone's name instead of speaking in riddles. For Castelvetro, poetry not only must be consistent within the fictional context of the poem, but also must reflect the world outside the poem. The poet must abide by the same restrictions as the historian. In fact, poetry becomes almost a subgenre of history: "If we had an art of history, we would not need an art of poetry." This statement goes beyond the bounds of Aristotle and fixes the concept of verisimilitude or resemblance as an essential criterion for judging literature.

Once Castelvetro established the need for strict verisimilitude and bound poets to the iron laws of probability, he imposed exacting prescriptions on the art of poetic composition. These restrictions are necessary to appease Castelvetro's audience and to set limits within which Castelvetro's ingenious poet can demonstrate his craftsmanship. To aid the audience in remembering certain incidents, a drama should be divided into five acts. Also, dramas must conform to the unity of time. A drama of one or two hours would not be worth the audience's time. A drama exceeding twelve hours, however, would be intolerable because this "restricted time is that during which the spectators can comfortably remain seated in the theater." The poet must be concerned with the audience's needs, such as "eating, drinking, [and] excreting the superfluous burdens of the belly and the bladder." Castelvetro's unity of time includes, however, not only the time of performance but also the method of presenting narrative time. In this area, his definition is extremely narrow: "This imagined event of the plot should occupy as much time . . . as was occupied or would be occupied by a similar event if it really happened." In other words, narrative time must correspond to actual time. If Castelvetro's rule were carried to the extreme, a character who had to wait one hour for another character would have to pace the stage for sixty minutes. Also, lapses of time between scenes are not permitted. Furthermore, narrative time must not exceed that time of performance. Thus, no dramatist is allowed to invent a story whose total actions span over twelve hours.

Attached to the unity of time is Castelvetro's own invention, the unity of place. According to Castelvetro, a drama "must be set in a place no larger than the stage on which the actors perform." Also, the action "must be restricted not only to a city or town or country place . . . but even to the view which alone can present itself to the eyes of a person." In other words, the action cannot move freely from one part of town to another, nor can one area of the stage represent different places.

As to the unity of action, the only unity which Aristotle upheld, Castelvetro, strangely enough, found it confining. Castelvetro did uphold the unity of action, however, since it would be impossible to abandon it and still maintain the unities of time and place. Thus, Castelvetro formulated the famous three unities which would haunt Western criticism for two centuries after his death. He required strict adherence to the unities only of dramas, allowing epics to break them. Still, he praised the skillful epic poet, such as Homer, who can create a powerful narrative such as the *Iliad* (c. 800 B.C.) out of one incident: the wrath of Achilles.

Given such restrictions, one might wonder how poetry delights. For this end, Castelvetro called on the marvelous. Although poetry must not contradict history, it also must not mirror history. Retelling history neither taxes the poet's skills nor creates a sense of the marvelous. If a poet picks a plot from legend, he must choose one that is very sketchy, allowing him to fill in the details without contradicting history. Then, he must create the marvelous by producing the unfamiliar and the unexpected. A drama about a man who kills his enemy produces both the familiar and the expected, but a drama about a man who kills his friend produces the unanticipated. For Castelvetro, the marvelous is no more than the ironic. It is never equated with the fantastic. Even the comic poet is not "at liberty to invent new cities or rivers [or] represent a snowfall in midsummer or a harvest in midwinter."

Castelvetro's emphasis on verisimilitude, his subjection of poetry to history, and his insistence on the complete accuracy of representation led the way to neoclassicism. So thoroughly did he rewrite Aristotle that Aristotle was lost in the process. Indeed, when those who follow Castelvetro comment on the Aristotelian unities they are, in fact, commenting on Castelvetro's unities.

Jean de La Taille's *Art de tragédie* (1572), published two years after Castelvetro's major work, almost paraphrases Castelvetro in introducing the concept of the unities into France, where they were to become the most debated critical concepts in the history of literary criticism. By 1635 Jean Chapelain, one of the founders of the Académie Française, acknowledged his debt to "the two great savants . . . Speroni and Castelvetro." Winning over Cardinal Richelieu to his point of view, Chapelain established "the rule of the three unities" as one of the guiding principles of the Académie. By the end of the controversy over Pierre Corneille's *Le Cid* (1637; *The Cid*, 1637), Castelvetro's rules had become a part of the established canon of neoclassical literature throughout Europe. Castelvetro also influenced René Rapin, another major critic of the same period. He labeled Castelvetro "the most subtle of all the commentators, and the man from whom most may be learned." Rapin influenced John Dryden, who carried the battle over the rules into England. Indirectly, Castelvetro influenced most of the major seventeenth-century critics. No less a figure than John Milton acknowledged him as the greatest commentator on Aristotle. Until the nineteenth century, whether a critic agreed or disagreed with Castelvetro's rules, he or she could not ignore them.

Principal criticism

Ragioni d'alcune cose segnate nella canzone di Annibal Caro, 1559

Lettera del dubioso academico, 1560

Poetica d'Aristotele vulgarizzata et sposta, 1570 (partially translated in *Castelvetro on the Art of Poetry*, 1984)

Opere varie critiche, 1727

Le rime del Petrarca, brevemente espote per Lodovico Castelvetro, 1756

Parere di Ludovico Castelvetro sopra ciascuna comedia di Plauto, 1868

Sposizione di Lodovico Castelvetro a XXIX canti dell' Inferno, 1886

Other major works and literary forms

Lodovico Castelvetro is known primarily for his literary criticism. An Italian comedy, *Gli'ingannati* (1550), is often attributed to him. The play's plot is borrowed from Plautus' *Menaechmi* (c. 200; *The Twin Menaechmi*) and is sometimes cited as one of the sources for William Shakespeare's *Twelfth Night: Or, What You Will* (1600–1602).

PLAY
Gli'ingannati, 1550

Further reading

Bongiorno, Andrew. Introduction to *Castelvetro on the Art of Poetry*, 1984.
Carlson, Marvin. *Theories of the Theatre*, 1984.
Charlton, H. B. *Castelvetro's Theory of Poetry*, 1913.
Hathaway, Baxter. *The Age of Criticism*, 1962.
Melzi, Robert C. Introduction to *Castelvetro's Annotations to the "Inferno,"* 1966.
Saintsbury, George. *A History of Criticism*, 1908.
Spingarn, J. E. *Literary Criticism in the Renaissance*, 1908.
Weinberg, Bernard. "Castelvetro's Theory of Poetry," in *Critics and Criticism*, 1957. Edited by R. S. Crane.
——. *History of Literary Criticism in the Italian Renaissance*, 1962.

PAUL ROSEFELDT

See also Giraldi Cinthio; Minturno; Renaissance and Restoration Literary Theory; Trissino

Geoffrey Chaucer

English poet

Born: London?, England; c. 1343
Died: London, England; October 25?, 1400

Biography

By the time Geoffrey Chaucer was born in the early 1340s, his well-to-do family had moved from the ancestral home in Ipswich to London. Beginning in 1356 – and probably after a substantial traditional education at one of the three schools near his home – Chaucer served in the household of Prince Lionel, a son of Edward III. All of his life he was to be in royal service as soldier, companion, courtier, envoy, diplomat, or minor official. These occupations provided for him a comfortable living, so that by his mature years he was financially secure. First as a soldier, later as a diplomat or messenger, he traveled to continental Europe numerous times, sometimes for extended periods; during his sojourns in Italy, France, and Spain he inevitably added to his knowledge of language and literature. Although the dates of Chaucer's royal appointments and travels are generally known from *Chaucer Life Records* (1972), dates of personal events and his literary works must often be estimated. His wife was the sister of the wife of John of Gaunt; for this royal friend he wrote *The Book of the Duchess* (c. 1370), an elegy whose subject, Blanche, was John of Gaunt's first wife. The inscription on Chaucer's tomb in Westminster Abbey, London, gives the date of his death as October 25, 1400.

Influence

As the first great poet of the English language before William Shakespeare, Chaucer has had an enormous impact on the history of literary theory. This is true in spite of the fact that he made no original critical pronouncements; his work, rather, is the supreme product of the literary artist devoted to practicing what he has learned from others: rules, theories, principles, forms, and purposes.

Analysis

Chaucer wrote very little primarily devoted to criticism, although both directly and indirectly his writings reflect his absorption of the critical theories and practices of classical Greek and Latin writers and contemporary French and Italian writers. His greatest works, *The Canterbury Tales* and *Troilus and Criseyde*, reveal again and again the consciousness of the critical thinker. Various prologues, descriptions, digressions, and epilogues within these works treat point of view and persona with critical sophistication, and numerous other structural and rhetorical devices demonstrate his dependence on, and reverence for, the critical stances of ancient and contemporary theorists. *The House of Fame* and *The Parliament of Fowls*, lesser works that normally receive little attention, examine (although incidentally and without profundity) the rules and definition of art as well as the role and character of the artist.

Of the Clerk in *The Canterbury Tales* Chaucer says, "And gladly wolde he lerne, and gladly teche." Chaucer frequently acknowledges in the text of his own work the sources of his stories and ideas. He was a lifelong student and, through his creative work, a lifelong teacher. From Aristotle's *De poetica* (c. 334–323 B.C.; *Poetics*), he must have learned about unity of time, place, and action: in his great works Chaucer shows a mastery for holding things together, for balancing by thesis and antithesis, and for introducing scenes and characters naturally and in accordance with structural reasonableness. Of the humanness of the great and mighty figure, his fatal flaw and consequent fall, Chaucer must also have learned from this greatest of ancient critics, for *Troilus and Criseyde* seems to have been written with the *Poetics* in mind. That art is an imitation of nature is another observation from Aristotle that Chaucer assimilated into his work, although often with a literal context.

Chaucer's reference to other sources is sometimes part of an ironic play on the authority of the narrator, as for example in his use of occasional (sometimes bogus) Platonic quotations to give authority to some point he wishes to make.

The Parliament of Fowls begins with a dictum from Horace's *Ars poetica* (c. 17 B.C.; *The Art of Poetry*): "Life is short, craft is long." Recognizing the enduring nature of art, Chaucer frequently refers to his own unworthiness as an artist. He calls upon the muse Cleo at the beginning of book 2 of *Troilus and Criseyde* "to ryme wel this book, til I have do; me nedeth here noon other art to use." He writes, he says, "out of Latin," and asks that it be remembered that speech has changed drastically in the thousand years that have passed since the writing of the story that is his source. He gives Pandarus, one of his characters, an education in classical rhetoric so that he may instruct Troilus in the proper way to write a letter: Pandarus calls up principles such as spontaneity (as opposed to artificiality), harmony, and form suited to function, the style to the purpose. At the end of *Troilus and Criseyde*, Chaucer expresses his indebtedness to Virgil, Ovid, Homer, Lucan, and Statius, and prays to God that no one "miswrite" his now-finished book and that the book be understood by its readers. Thus he communicates both his story and his concern for telling it well.

The conscious artistry of *Troilus and Criseyde* can be contrasted with the self-conscious artistry of *The Canterbury Tales*. In the latter, his most popular work, Chaucer is both storyteller and character. The pilgrim Chaucer appeals to his audience to relieve him of blame for presenting the other pilgrims as they were, to read past the tales that are too vulgar, and to understand that his storytelling is "base and plain" because he never slept on Mount Parnassus or studied rhetoric or Cicero. Chaucer carries over classical interest in persona into deliberate self-satire. Both directly and through other pilgrims' verbal assaults on him, Chaucer continually pokes fun at himself. He proves himself learned, intelligent, humorous, worldly-wise, and gifted, while pretending to be ignorant, stupid, humorless, innocent, and ordinary. The more he discounts his ability to give a proper account of beauty, to imitate nature, or to tell a story well, the more he persuades his audience of his genius and the more he entertains and charms. The discerning reader of Chaucer knows the value and kind of his irony: he says more than one thing at a time with it, as when he delivers "The Tale of Thopas" so as to make it appear that he is entirely indifferent to thoughtful rhyme, rhythm, or reason, delighting the audience with his skill at writing deliberately bad literature. "The Tale of Thopas" is thus an ingenious and instructive exercise in literary criticism. The Host stops Chaucer to complain of his "drasty speche" and forthwith Chaucer playfully tells a "mery tale" that is mercilessly long and dull: "The Tale of Melibeus," which is in prose as deliberately bad as the doggerel of "The Tale of Thopas."

The measure of Chaucer's originality in handling persona, or point of view, is not complete with this look at the first-person narrator of *The Canterbury Tales*. One must look still further – at the supreme creations of the Wife of Bath and the Pardoner. Each of these pilgrims achieves a roundness of character like that achieved by the pilgrim Chaucer. The Wife of Bath steps forward to tell about herself in her own words, not the words of an author; the Pardoner, equally, has an individual voice. Chaucer was centuries ahead of his time in his capacity to create living characters.

Language is the medium through which characters are given life. The other pilgrims who are given their own words to speak – principally, the Miller, the Man of Law, the Friar, the Summoner, and the Host – are, unsurprisingly, the ones who, like Chaucer, the Wife of Bath, and the Pardoner, are the most realistic characters. Chaucer gave to world literature, then, what he gave to English literature: the fruit of his long critical studies, the discovery that individuals in a story must be shown rather than merely described.

As Shakespeare was to do two hundred years later, Chaucer transformed literature, giving it energy, imagination, substance, and (therefore) interest. Like Shakespeare, he borrowed unstintingly from the past but wrought from it, out of the force of his personality and genius, the highest art. If a poet or a critic is not made by borrowing from others, at least it is true that he or she grows best of all by an awareness of what has gone before him or her.

Chaucer's literary devices are often the repositories for his theories of criticism. Dreams of various characters in Chaucer call up old tales, old authorities, old teachers, old lessons. "God turn us every dream to good!" says Chaucer at the beginning of *The House of Fame*. Consciousness of lessons learned – from dreams in this case but actually from the source of those dreams in the past – reveals the thinking critical writer. Chaucer's main borrowings were from Breton lays, fabliaux, Boethius' *The Consolation of Philosophy*, Virgil's *Georgics* (c. 37–29 B.C.) and *Aeneid* (c. 29–19 B.C.), Dante's *La divina commedia* (c. 1320; *The Divine Comedy*), Giovanni Boccaccio's *Il filostrato* (c. 1335) and, possibly, the *Decameron* (1349–1351), *The Romance of the Rose*, Petrarch, Homer, and, as often as any other source, Ovid's *Metamorphoses* (c. A.D. 8). The great poets are also instinctively the great critics. The *Metamorphoses* gave Chaucer not only the stories of gods and heroes from mythology but also the models for fusing disparate elements. *The Romance of the Rose* gave him a plan for both poetical forms and philosophical disquisition. Translation of this work and of *The Consolation of Philosophy* gave him confidence in finding his own voice and his own form. By the time he had experimented in direct translation of these works and of numerous smaller works such as French and Italian lays and legends, absorbed from the great critics and authors the best thought and literature of the past, observed human nature at home and abroad, and become well acquainted with sundry professions and the types representative of them, he was singularly equipped with a critical aesthetic preparing him for his leap into greatness.

This leap he made with *Troilus and Criseyde* and *The Canterbury Tales*. Chaucer's critical legacy is, then, without question, the same as his literary legacy. What one learns from his finished work is what he himself learned from his endless study of literature and of humanity: how to create fully human characters. To lay side by side the texts of Boccaccio's story of Troilus and Criseyde and Chaucer's story of the same is to understand how far along Chaucer had brought literature in *Troilus and Criseyde*. Boccaccio's characters are, in the medieval fashion, observed and presented from the outside; Chaucer's are seen inside and out, with all their quirks, contradictions, and nuances, to a degree that approaches the profundity and subtlety of modern psychological fiction. That which is true of *Troilus and Criseyde* in its entirety is true as well of all the prologues (especially the masterful "General Prologue") and seven or eight of *The Canterbury Tales*. Like the Parson in *The Canterbury Tales*, Chaucer may have been incapable of composing with the "rum, ram, ruf" of conventional alliteration or, indeed, with any pedestrian convention. He may have been wrong (or, perhaps, assuming an authorial persona) in denouncing much of his work on moral grounds, as he did in his famous "Retraction" at the end of *The Canterbury Tales*; at least it is admirable that he assumed ultimate responsibility for every word he composed. Thus in his final critical pronouncement, Chaucer set an example: writers are to be held accountable for their work.

Principal criticism

Passages from *The House of Fame*, 1372–1380, and *The Parliament of Fowls*, 1380

Other major works and literary forms

Geoffrey Chaucer is best known for his tales in verse, notably *Troilus and Criseyde* (1382), considered by some critics the first great novel in English, and *The Canterbury Tales* (1387–1400), a sprawling collection that draws from many sources, including several of his own earlier works. *The Legend of St. Cecilia* (1372–1380) is incorporated into *The Canterbury Tales* as "The Second Nun's Tale," *Tragedies of Fortune* (1372–1380) appears as "The Monk's Tale," and *Palamon and Arcite* (1380–1386) becomes "The Knight's Tale." Fewer than a score of his short poems have survived.

Many of the sources for Chaucer's writings, whether major or minor, were originally written in languages other than English; almost from necessity, therefore, Chaucer was a translator. His first writing efforts, it is said, were renderings of French love songs into English; not a single song of his is extant, but his mature work clearly reveals what he learned from experimentation. Although some of translations became great in their own right, *Boece* (c. 1380), his translation of Boethius' *The Consolation of Philosophy* (523), and *The Romance of the Rose* (c. 1370), a translation of part of the *Roman de la rose* (eleventh century), are pedestrian at best.

For his young son, Lewis, Chaucer wrote *A Treatise on the Astrolabe* (1387–1392). His wide knowledge of astronomy and other sciences, as well as of literature, history, and philosophy, shines forth in all of his surviving work.

POETRY
The Book of the Duchess, c. 1370
The Legend of St. Cecilia, 1372–1380
Tragedies of Fortune, 1372–1380
Anelida and Arcite, c. 1380
Palamon and Arcite, 1380–1386
The Legend of Good Women, 1380–1386
Troilus and Criseyde, 1382
The Canterbury Tales, 1387–1400

NONFICTION
A Treatise on the Astrolabe, 1387–1392

TRANSLATIONS
The Romance of the Rose, c. 1370 (of a fragment of Guillame de Lorris and Jean de Meung's *Roman de la rose*)
Boece, c. 1380 (of Boethius' *The Consolation of Philosophy*)

MISCELLANEOUS
The Works of Geoffrey Chaucer, 1987 (third edition, revised from F. N. Robinson's 1957 edition)

Further reading

Allen, Judson B. *The Friar as Critic: Literary Attitudes in the Later Middle Ages*, 1971.
Brewer, Derek S. *Toward a Chaucerian Poetic*, 1974.
De Bruyne, Edgar. *The Aesthetics of the Middle Ages*, 1969.
Evans, Ruth, and Lesley Johnson, eds. *Feminist Readings in Middle English Literature: The Wife of Bath and All Her Sect*, 1994.
Fichte, Joerg O. *Chaucer's "Art Poetical": A Study in Chaucerian Poetics*, 1980.
Howard, Donald R. *Chaucer: His Life, His Works, His World*, 1987.
Laskaya, Anne. *Chaucer's Approach to Gender in the Canterbury Tales*, 1995.
Manly, John M. *Chaucer and the Rhetoricians*, 1926.
Murphy, James J. *Rhetoric in the Middle Ages*, 1974.
Payne, Robert O. *The Key of Remembrance: A Study of Chaucer's Poetics*, 1963.
Thompson, N. S. *Chaucer, Boccaccio, and the Debate of Love: A Comparative Study of the Decameron and the Canterbury Tales*, 1996.

DAVID POWELL

See also Boccaccio; Medieval Literary Theory

Nikolai Chernyshevskii

Russian critic and writer

Born: Saratov, Russia; July 12, 1828
Died: Saratov, Russia; October 17, 1889

Biography

Nikolai Gavrilovich Chernyshevskii was born on July 12, 1828, in Saratov, a provincial city on the Volga, some four hundred and fifty miles southeast of Moscow. The son of a priest, Chernyshevskii was himself a pupil at the local seminary. He received an excellent education both at home and at school, and when, in 1846, he applied to the history and literature department at St. Petersburg University instead of continuing with his theological studies, he received an extremely high score in the entrance exams. At the university he began his intensive study of Russian literature but also read widely, most often on his own, in the fields of history, sociology, and philosophy. After completing the undergraduate program in 1850 he spent a brief interlude back in Saratov, where he taught literature at the Gymnasium. Shortly after his marriage to Ol'ga Sokratovna Vasileva in 1853, he returned to St. Petersburg in order to complete work on his master's degree. Rather than pursue a scholarly career, however, he became a key contributor to the prominent journal *Sovremennik* (the contemporary).

Prior to Chernyshevskii's time the leading figures in Russian cultural life generally came from the gentry class. By mid-century their ranks had become more diffuse and the term *raznochintsy* came into vogue: literally, people of various ranks. Specifically, like Chernyshevskii, these were individuals from the middle and lower social orders, and they eventually formed the core of the radical intelligentsia, for which *Sovremennik* became the chief forum and Chernyshevskii the acknowledged spiritual leader. Indeed, by the end of the 1850s Chernyshevskii's literary interests receded as his writing came to concentrate on social, economic, and political issues. In 1862 Chernyshevskii was arrested, ostensibly for his contacts with political émigrés, and incarcerated in the Peter and Paul Fortress. While there he completed *What Is to Be Done?* which only added to his fame. In 1864, after a less-than-fair trial, he was sent first to hard labor and then to exile in Siberia. He was to spend two decades there, living in great hardship and isolation. The little writing he could do, mostly fiction, remained unpublished in Russia during his lifetime: his voice was effectively stilled. Only in 1883, when his health was already broken, did he receive permission to return to European Russia and settle in Astrakhan, at the southern end of the Volga. In 1889 he was finally allowed to move back to his native Saratov, where he died only a few months later.

Influence

Chernyshevskii both continued and altered the direction that Vissarion Belinskii had given to a major stream of Russian critical thought in the nineteenth century. On the one hand, he followed Belinskii in advocating a literature that would be socially committed and in discussing both writers and works in terms of the degree to which they expressed the country's cultural life. He, too, wanted a "socially useful" art and often used his writings about literature to express essentially political views. In Belinskii's case, however, art remained at the forefront: Chernyshevskii established a trend in which the work of literature was less important per se than its content; works were often judged primarily according to their utility as instruments for social change. His ideas heavily influenced a number of his younger contemporaries, most notably Nikolai Dobroliubov, and also many critics and political activists over the decades to come. The degree of Chernyshevskii's influence was no doubt affected by the aura of martyrdom that surrounded him following his arrest and exile as well as by often-uncritical admiration for *What Is to Be Done?* (described by Evgenii Lampert as a "great bad novel"). Vladimir Ilich Lenin praised both the novel and Chernyshevskii's other writings, and after the Bolshevik Revolution some of Chernyshevskii's positions became entrenched in official attitudes toward literary criticism and toward literature itself.

Analysis

Of the figures who predominated in the line of what are often referred to as the social or civic critics in Russia of the nineteenth century – Belinskii, Chernyshevskii, Dobroliubov, and Dmitrii Pisarev – Chernyshevskii, despite his extensive reading and formal training in literary studies, seems to have had the least inclination toward literary criticism itself. While for a time he was the main critic for *Sovremennik*, he quickly yielded that role to his younger colleague Dobroliubov, and thus the bulk of his writings on aesthetics and literature are concentrated within a very brief period, from 1854 through 1858. During the middle of this period, in a series of essays on Gotthold Ephraim Lessing, Chernyshevskii expressed admiration for Lessing's social concerns, which often seemed to determine the directions of his scholarship. It may not be incorrect to infer that in some ways Chernyshevskii had himself in mind.

Chernyshevskii's views of Russian literature and his conception of the role that he had to play in Russian criticism both appear in his *Essays on the Gogol Period of Russian Literature*. The reference to Nikolai Gogol' in the title of this series is not accidental. Most critics, including Chernyshevskii's predecessor Belinskii, emphasized the role of Aleksandr Pushkin as Russia's first truly "national poet." Chernyshevskii's evaluation of Pushkin's role is more restrained. In an 1855 group of articles on Pushkin, Chernyshevskii gave Pushkin his due for both his talent and the role he played in moving Russian literature forward, but he asserted that Pushkin's works are distinguished primarily by their beauty, their formal perfection, rather than by the expression of profound convictions or ideas. He went on to emphasize the decline in Pushkin's popularity toward the end of his career, finding in the change proof of Pushkin's fading significance for his age. In his *Essays on the Gogol Period of Russian Literature*, he finds that Gogol' combines Pushkin's artistry with a greater social relevancy. Therefore it is Gogol' and his contemporaries who, in Chernyshevskii's view, create the first truly great Russian literature. Although Belinskii also saw Gogol''s works as a natural progression from Pushkin's, he was more evenhanded in his treatment of the two and took strong exception to the extreme conservatism that Gogol' exhibited in his later years. Chernyshevskii plays down or ignores any blemishes in Gogol'; he clearly favors literature for which it is possible to claim a sense of engagement.

Chernyshevskii was as interested in the development of criticism as in that of literature, and here the main figure was clearly Belinskii, whom Chernyshevskii places above those who came both before and after. He distinguishes between the Hegelian period of Belinskii's early writing and the greater interest in social questions that predominated after Belinskii's rejection of Hegelianism. Chernyshevskii himself had read the works of G. W. F. Hegel early but seems to have been quickly disillusioned by what he perceived as the essential conservatism of Hegel's views. Having turned, rather, to Ludwig Feuerbach's materialism, he rejected Idealism and believed that only the world of matter was of concern to humanity. A corollary of Chernyshevskii's materialism was the conviction that natural science can ultimately provide a complete knowledge of the world and of human behavior.

The rationalism that marks Chernyshevskii's approach to literature and other fields of human endeavor receives its most direct explanation in *The Anthropological Principle in Philosophy*. Here he asserts that the individual person and society as a whole act according to self-interest:

> Individuals regard as good the actions of other people that are beneficial for them; society holds as good what is good for the whole of society, or for the majority of its members. Lastly, people in general, irrespective of nation or class, describe as good that which is beneficial for mankind in general.

Since everybody wants that which will produce good for themselves, it is not necessary to try to change human nature but only to create a society in which the striving for what is beneficial will cause individuals to act for the common good. The goal of science is to discover the laws that will allow society to be arranged in the proper way. Chernyshevskii's reasoning was to be parodied mercilessly by Fedor Dostoevskii in his *Zapiski iz podpolia* (1864; *Notes from the Underground*, 1913), where a crucial point is that a person may not always behave "reasonably" and thus could well not act out of self-interest. For Chernyshevskii, though, it was but a step to assert that literature could show how a society does not yet enable individuals to live up to their full potential and could also help point the way toward a better life.

Literature, then, becomes a tool rather than an end in itself. This subservient role for literature is also evident in Chernyshevskii's well-known master's thesis, "Aesthetic Relationship of Art to Reality," where, first of all, he contends that the beauty found in art can never match that found in life:

> From the definition "beauty is life," it will follow that true, the highest, beauty, is the beauty that man meets with in the world of reality and not the beauty created by art. In conformity with this view of beauty in reality, the origin of art must be attributed to an entirely different source . . . .

The beauty found in nature is greater than that which a person can create. Hence Chernyshevskii claims that "everybody continues to prefer singing to instrumental music . . . instrumental music is imitation of singing . . . and singing as a work of art is only an imitation of and substitute for singing as a work of nature." Similarly, images in poetry, which he considers to be the highest of the arts, lack the individuality and completeness of that which is found in nature. What then is the role of art? It can attempt to reproduce reality as best it can for the sake of those who cannot experience certain things directly. More important, it can also attempt to explain reality, to use its resources to make events and relationships more intelligible. Third, and most crucial, art may also pronounce judgment on reality. To Chernyshevskii, the good artist will perforce present or solve problems of everyday life, and thus his or her works will acquire scientific value.

If the artist fails to engage current issues or at least write about the world about him or her, he or she cannot be a total success. Hence, in an 1857 review Nikolai Fedorovich Shcherbina is singled out as a poet of enormous talent whose interest in classical themes and forms have made him a less significant figure than he ought to be. At the other extreme, in "The Russian at the Rendez-vous," Chernyshevskii begins by criticizing the narrator in Ivan Turgenev's *Asia* (1858; English translation, 1877) and then launches into a broad condemnation of that type of individual in Russian society. Turgenev himself comes under attack because the nature of his talent (as opposed to that of Chernyshevskii's colleague on *Sovremennik*, the poet Nikolai Nekrasov) enables him to depict only such weak-willed figures. Chernyshevskii can, though, occasionally give pure talent its due. Thus in a discussion of Lev Tolstoi's early works, "L. N. Tolstoi's *Childhood* and *Boyhood* and *Military Tales*," he employs the term "interior monologue" for what would appear to be the first time in the history of criticism. The acumen of Tolstoi's psychological analysis and the purity of his moral feelings come in for unstinting praise. Admittedly, Tolstoi does not raise social issues. "But," says Chernyshevskii, "one must understand that not every poetic idea permits social questions to be introduced into the work. One must not forget that the first rule of art is the unity of the work . . . ."

Such statements, however, are rare in Chernyshevskii. For the most part he both insisted and concentrated on a work's social significance. His main influence on his contemporaries and on the history of Russian criticism in general lies in his contention that the literary work could provide fodder for social, political, and even economic commentary. If Chernyshevskii shared Belinskii's sense that literature ought to express something about the nation or society, he went beyond him in seeing the value of literature as primarily didactic. To Belinskii the artist had the potential to uncover truths that others did not see, and literature had a special life of its own. To Chernyshevskii the writer can only make an effort to depict as accurately as possible what is in the actual world and to educate others; art in and of itself is inferior to what the real world offers. Dobroliubov, who had a greater respect for literature than did Chernyshevskii, went on to use literary texts as realia in much the same way that Chernyshevskii discussed, for example, the figures in Mikhail Evgrafovich Saltykov-Shchedrin's *Gubernskie ocherki* (1856–1857; provincial sketches) as though they were living people. Throughout the 1860s and in the years that followed, the spiritual successors to Chernyshevskii were to continue to demand that literature respond to the burning issues of the times and to express hostility to works that were viewed as too far removed from those questions.

At the same time an important part of Chernyshevskii's influence was negative. A school of antinihilist literature arose, in which the tenets and even the personalities of the leading radicals were mocked. Although Turgenev was to deny that his *Ottsy i deti* (1862; *Fathers and Sons*, 1867) was intended as a direct attack on that generation of critics, many saw his hero Bazarov as a takeoff on either Chernyshevskii or Dobroliubov. In Dostoevskii's case, along with the direct attack on Chernyshevskii in *Notes from the Underground*, equally harsh treatment of the 1860s radicals appeared elsewhere in his fiction as well as in his journalism.

Thanks to Lenin's enthusiasm for Chernyshevskii and to the sympathy that many other Bolsheviks had toward Chernyshevskii's ideas, the approach to literature that he promulgated was revived in the twentieth century as Socialist Realism and had a great effect on postrevolutionary criticism. In some ways the demands on writers were to become even greater under Communism, but Chernyshevskii's central precepts – seeing literature as a direct reflection of reality, demanding a socially relevant art, assigning literature primarily a didactic function – provided the foundation for the Party's doctrines about literature.

Principal criticism

"Roman i povesti M. Avdeeva," 1854
"Ob iskrennosti v kritike," 1854
"O poezii: Sochinenie Aristotelia," 1854 ("The Poetics of Aristotle," 1953)
"*Bednost' ne porok*: Komediia A. Ostrovskogo," 1854
Esteticheskie otnosheniia iskusstva k deistvitel'nosti, 1855 ("Aesthetic Relationship of Art to Reality," 1953)
Sochineniia A. S. Pushkina, 1855
Ocherki gogolevskogo perioda russkoi literatury, 1855–1856 (partial translation as *Essays on the Gogol Period of Russian Literature*, 1953)
"*Detstvo i otrochestvo*: 'Voennye rasskazy' grafa L. N. Tolstogo," 1856 ("L. N. Tolstoy's *Childhood* and *Boyhood* and *Military Tales*," 1962)
"Lessing, ego vremia, ego zhizn' i deiatel'nost'," 1856–1857
"*Gubernskie ocherki* Shchedrina," 1857
"*Stikhotvoreniia* N. Shcherbiny," 1857
"Russkii chelovek na *rendez-vous*," 1858 ("The Russian at the Rendez-vous," 1962)
Antropologicheskii printsip v filosofii, 1860 (*The Anthropological Principle in Philosophy*, 1953)
"Ne nachalo li peremeny? *Rasskazy* N. V. Uspenskogo," 1861
Selected Philosophical Essays, 1953

Other major works and literary forms

Nikolai Chernyshevskii's collected works occupy some sixteen large volumes. His numerous essays and reviews treat various topics in philosophy, political science, history, sociology, and economics. After his arrest in 1862 Chernyshevskii began to write fiction; his first novel, *Chto delat'?* (1863; *What Is to Be Done?*, c. 1863), was somehow overlooked by the censor and published. It became an enormously popular work among the radical youth of his own and subsequent generations. He also wrote the semiautobiographical *Prolog* (1868, prologue), a number of novellas and stories, and several plays. Many of these works, however, survive only in a rough and sometimes incomplete form.

NOVELS
Chto delat'?, 1863 (*What Is to Be Done?*, c. 1863)
Prolog, 1868

NONFICTION
"Kritika filosofskikh predubrezhdenii protiv obshchinnogo vladeniia," 1858
"Truden li vykup zemli?" 1859
"Kapital i trud," 1860
"Pis'ma bez adresa," 1862

MISCELLANEOUS
Polnoe sobranie sochinenii, 1939–1953 (16 volumes)

Further reading

Brown, Edward J. "So Much Depends . . . Russian Critics in Search of 'Reality,'" in *The Russian Review*. 48 (1989), pp. 353–381.
Drozd, Andrew M. "Büchner and Chernyshevskii: A Century of Ideas," in *Germano-Slavica*. 9 (1995–1996), pp. 79–102.
Lampert, Evgenii. *Sons Against Fathers: Studies in Russian Radicalism and Revolution*, 1965.
Masaryk, Thomas G. *The Spirit of Russia*, 1955.
Mathewson, Rufus W., Jr. *The Positive Hero in Russian Literature*, 1975.
Moser, Charles A. *Esthetics as Nightmare: Russian Literary Theory 1855–1870*, 1989.
Paperno, Irina. *Chernyshevsky and the Age of Realism: A Study in the Semiotics of Behavior*, 1988.
Pereira, Norman G. O. *The Thought and Teachings of N. G. Chernyshevskij*, 1975.

Proctor, Thelwall. *Dostoevskij and the Belinskij School of Literary Criticism*, 1969.
Randall, Francis B. *N. G. Chernyshevskii*, 1967.
Venturi, Franco. *Roots of Revolution*, 1960.
Walicki, Andrzej. *A History of Russian Thought from the Enlightenment to Marxism*, 1979.
Woehrlin, William F. *Chernyshevskii: The Man and the Journalist*, 1971.

BARRY P. SCHERR

See also Belinskii; Dobroliubov; Dostoevskii; Pisarev; Veselovskii

Chinese Literary Theory

Traditional Chinese literary theory

Chinese literary theory had its beginnings in the Confucian classics, especially with the Confucian edition of the *Shih ching* (c. 1066–541 B.C.; *Book of Songs*). Confucius (K'ung Ch'iu), the great Chinese philosopher and teacher (551–479 B.C.), held this first monument of the Chinese imagination to be of prime importance in the education of his students. In the *Lun-yü (Analects)*, he observes that the poems selected for the *Book of Songs* are morally sound: "In the *Book of Songs* are three hundred pieces, but the design of them all may be embraced in one sentence – 'Having no depraved thoughts.'" It is said that he inquired of his son Po-yü, "Have you learned the Odes?" Receiving a negative reply, he warned the boy: "If you do not learn the Odes, you will not be fit to converse with." Confucius taught his pupils that the odes in the *Book of Songs* trained one in six different ways: they stimulated and inspired the mind, they provided insight into one's own nature, they encouraged sociability, they regulated one's feelings of resentment, they taught moral responsibility, and they acquainted one with names – of birds, beasts, plants, and trees.

The early Confucians held that aesthetics and ethos were inseparable. Such Confucian classics as the *Li chi* (English translation, 1885) and the *Tso chuan* (English translation, 1872) stress the social function of poetry. In the late Chou Dynasty, however, Confucian ideology was not yet predominant. When in 221 B.C. the state of Tsin (Ch'in) survived the downfall of the other states, its ruler declared himself First Emperor, reigning as Shih Huang-ti. Determined to unify the system of writing and the ideology, he ordered the burning of "heretical" books. Many revered classics of art and history were thus lost. Although his death in 210 was followed by a period of rebellion, imperial rule was reestablished by the Earlier Han Dynasty (206–25 B.C.).

During this period, commentaries on the *Book of Songs* began to appear in various regions of China. Eventually, that of Mao Ch'êng of Chao became the standard. Tung Chung-shu (c. 179–c. 104 B.C.) became the chief expounder of the New Text exegetical school of the classics. He succeeded in making the Confucian theory of literature official. His literary theory, expressed in a preface to the Mao edition of the *Book of Songs*, proposed that a natural language in its literary use manifests the essences of things and hence is a revelation of the will of Heaven.

Important developments that affected later literary theory took place during the Later Han Dynasty (25 B.C.–A.D. 220). Wei Hung (first century A.D.) maintained in his preface to the *Book of Songs* that literature reflects the political and social realities of its time. Pan Ku (A.D. 32–92) wrote a history of the Earlier Han Dynasty that categorized works according to the new genres of biography, bibliography, and literary history. In yet another preface to the *Book of Songs*, Chêng Hsüan (A.D. 127–200) followed Pan Ku's orderly system. Also, the study of the songs of Ch'u (an area of southern China), as well as the pictorial quality of the Han poetic form known as the *fu*, influenced later Chinese aesthetics and literary theory. During this period, Buddhism gained widespread acceptance in China; its tenets would influence later literary theory.

With the collapse of the Han and the advent of the Epoch of the Three Kingdoms (200–365), Ts'ao P'i (187–226), who ascended the throne of Wei in 220 to rule as Emperor Wên, in his *Lun-wên* (*The Art of Letters*, 1951) first proclaimed literature a worthy art in itself. Indeed, he held that as an institution it was a country's greatest possession. To him, the chief quality of literary style was *Ch'i* (vital breath), that is, a style's inner energy or vitality, whose source was within the author's personality. Ts'ao wrote: "The cleanness or muddiness" of a person's *Ch'i* "has its own embodiment,/ and it is impossible to get anywhere by main force."

Lu Chi (221–303) wrote the first genuine Chinese poetics in his prose-poem *Wên fu* (c. 302; *Essay on Literature*, 1951). Although somewhat on the order of Horace's *Ars Poetica* (c. 17 B.C.; *The Art of Poetry*), which is strictly metrical, the *Essay on Literature* is written in *p'ien-wên*, or parallel prose, with a rhyme scheme. As Horace's treatise is disguised as a *sermo*, so Lu Chi's masquerades as a *fu*.

Lu Chi believed that a text reflects the mind of its author; this mind, then, is to some degree knowable. Because the style of a text is "infinitely variable," a text demands interpretation and evaluation. Since language resists being made to conform to an author's experience, literary writing is difficult. Lu Chi maintained that a knowledge of the classics could help an author in his task by providing him with models of literary principles and thus inspiring him to follow their example. This was so even though a living author must meet the demand of his contemporaries to achieve something new. Since every literary text is made from previous texts, this demand gives rise to "artist's guilt" in the poet – fear of plagiarism. The creative process is so mysterious, however, that it is nearly impossible to analyze and describe in words.

Although he was a confirmed Confucian, Lu Chi's metaphysics was Taoist. A poet must take account of his relation to the universe, whose center is within him. From this vantage point, he surveys the universe's vast extent and contemplates its mystery. He struggles with the "Great Void," or Non-Being, challenging it to yield up Being. The poet is not interested in the physical world itself but in words as symbols. Lu held that meditation was the best means for entering into the creative process.

Two centuries after Lu Chi, Liu Hsieh (c. 465–c. 522) wrote the first book-length study of the main problems of literature. Entitled *Wên-hsin tiao-lung* (*The Literary Mind and the Carving of Dragons: A Study of Thought and Pattern in Chinese Literature*, 1959), it is a comprehensive treatise written almost entirely in *p'ien-wên*. Here Liu Hsieh explains the correspondences he believed to exist between the working of the Tao and the Great Triad of Heaven, earth, and human beings. The Tao to which he refers is not the Taoist concept, for his metaphysics is strictly Confucian. His Tao is derived from the *I Ching* (*Book of Changes*), and the commentaries appended to it are known as the "Ten Wings." In the *I Ching* it means simply "the Way of man"; Confucius gave it a polysemous meaning, connecting it with "the Way of heaven" in terms of *yin* (dark) and *yang* (light), with "the Way of earth" in terms of *kang* (hardness) and *juo* (softness), and with "the Way of man" in terms of *jên* (humanity) and *i* (righteousness). Liu Hsieh connected his Tao with Confucius' three Ways in terms of *wên*, by which he meant "pattern."

According to Liu Hsieh, the sun and moon "manifest the pattern of heaven," the mountains and rivers "display the pattern of earth," and mind and language evidence the pattern of human beings. These patterns issue from the *T'ai-chi*, or the Supreme Ultimate, whose motion produced the *Liang-i*, or the Twin Primordial Powers: *yin* and *yang*, heaven and earth, human being and intelligence. The human being alone forms with these archetypes the Great Triad, because "he alone is endowed with spirituality. He is the refined essence of the five elements – indeed, the mind of the universe." With the appearance of mind, then, language was created. When language was created, writing came into being. Liu Hsieh says, "In my opinion, oral statements are plain words, and whenever these are committed to the brush, they are literary writings." Liu Hsieh advises writers to look to the Confucian classics for the fundamental principles of literary art because they display the *wên* of the Tao.

Liu Hsieh's contemporary and opponent, Chung Jung (fl. 504), authored the first treatise that dealt exclusively with the lyric poem: *Shih-p'in* (513–517; classes of poetry). In this work, he evaluated poems according to three levels of attainment. He also took exception to the importance Liu Hsieh had attached to sounds and tones in the poetic structure. He held that the best poetry "expresses states of mind." To him, poetry is the encapsulation of a feeling induced by a particular scene, the poet's "artful reflection" on this experience. In his treatise, Chung Jung formulated the aesthetics of the new poetry that was to prevail from the third to the sixth century.

The first important critical theorist of the T'ang Dynasty (618–1227) was Wang Ch'ang-ling (c. 690–c. 756). His *Shih-kê* (rules of poetry), although lost in China, was preserved in Japan. In his treatise, Wang concerned himself with the creative process and the psychology of composition. For him, a poem is the result of a fusion of the author's mind with the world around him or her. He maintained that poetry "concentrates the sea of heaven in the inch-space of the heart." He compared the structure of a poem with the anatomy of a living creature, stating that it consists of a head, belly, and tail. These major parts must be tied together by certain kinds of words and word sequences so that the whole will be coordinated. He also believed in the infinite power of poetic language to be suggestive, advocating that a poet seek to say much in a few words.

Chiao-jan (790–799), a poet and Buddhist monk, became the most influential critic of the High T'ang period. He authored three significant works: *Shih-shih* (c. 785; models of poetry), *Shih-p'ing* (c. 785; critique of poetry), and *Shih-i* (c. 788; thoughts on poetry). Chiao-jan believed that the writing of poetry is based on the representation of scene, which is the medium for the display of the poet's personal feelings. He or she conveys his or her feelings according to the manner in which he or she pictures things in the external world. Furthermore, to Chiao-jan, ideal representation depended on the immediacy and the transparency of the poem's texture. It must be neither opaque nor translucent, such conditions being caused by adulterations: the use of allusions, affected or archaic words, and other so-called embellishments. When he condemned impurity and adulteration, he was actually condemning unnaturalness, awkwardness, and a consequent sense of strain. He maintained that the poet need not reject embellished words, yoked expressions, or hard effort so long as the representation conveyed the feelings that had prompted it and the writing gave the illusion of "effortless ease."

Chiao-jan also proposed a theory of "traces." In his view, writing in general as well as poetic writing consists merely of traces. What is truly important, however, is what lies beyond these traces. According to him, genuine poetry transcends its traces to produce in the reader a condition of enlightenment. Although this view seems strictly Ch'an (Zen) Buddhist, actually his idea of *shih Tao*, or "the Way of poetry," did not fit into any philosophical orthodoxy.

Another important critic of the High T'ang was Ssŭ-k'ung T'u (837–908), who was also a major poet. His series of twenty-four poems, *Erh-shih-ssŭ shih p'in* ("The Twenty-four Modes of Poetry," 1963), express that number of moods. These poetic microcosms also illustrate various stylistic "modes." Ssŭ-k'ung T'u proposed that the poet should escape from the mundane world of desires and get in touch with the basic processes of nature, or the working of the Tao. Only when the poet takes this step will he or she become spiritually independent. In sum, then, to Ssŭ-k'ung T'u the production of genuine poetry depended on the poet's spiritual freedom and his or her identification and harmony with the workings of the Tao.

Most Sung Dynasty (960–1275) criticism was practical rather than theoretical and figured in the debate that raged over the merits of "naturalness of tone" as opposed to "strikingness of style." Much criticism, too, addressed the work of the T'ang poet Tu Fu (712–770), perhaps China's greatest poet. Critics Yang Wan-li (1127–1206) and Ch'iang K'uei (c. 1155–1221) took steps toward developing theories of literature. In one of his prefaces, Yang Wan-li maintained that a poet could achieve originality in his or her writing only by having experienced a Ch'an-like enlightenment whereby he or she would discover his or her true "self-nature." Ch'iang K'uei made the important observation that every master poet speaks in his or her own voice, which represents his or her genuine self.

Yen Yü (fl. 1180–1235) was the most important critic of the period. In his poetics, the *Ts'ang-lang shih-hua* (poetry talk by the hermit of the Ts'ang-lang River), he attempted to fuse poetry with Ch'an Buddhism. His poetic theory is laid down mostly in his first chapter, entitled "*Shih-pien*" (on classifying poetry), wherein he applies Ch'an Buddhist terminology and metaphors to poetry. He required that a poem indicate that its author had experienced "miraculous awakening." "In general, the way of Ch'an lies in miraculous awakening alone, and so does the way of poetry. . . . Only through awakening can one 'ply one's proper trade' and 'show one's true colors.'" These stipulations indicate that "awakening" has the usual Ch'an meaning of the apprehension of one's self-nature. Yen Yü affirms: "The ultimate attainment of poetry lies in one thing: entering the spirit [*ju-shên*]. If poetry enters the spirit, it has reached perfection, the limit, and nothing can be added to it." In using the phrase *ju-shên*, which also refers to "an entrance into the realm of the marvelous," in conjunction with his "miraculous awakening," Yen apparently meant to include in the latter experience the idea of a swift, intuitive grasp of deeper reality (*shih-ju*).

The Yüan (Mongol) Dynasty (1280–1368) was an age of drama – that is, musical drama or opera. Despite the popularity of drama with the Chinese people, the literati generally looked upon plays as merely entertainment, not as literature to be taken seriously. Consequently, the period produced no dramatic theory that addressed the structure or performance of drama. Not until Li Yü's introduction to opera, *Hsien-ch'ing ou-chi* (sketches of idle pleasures), appeared during the Ming Dynasty was dramatic structure and composition treated critically.

The period of the Ming Dynasty (1368–1644) produced at least a half dozen critics who made some noteworthy contribution to literary theory. Kao-ch'i (1336–1378) considered the three elements of form, content, and interest to be central to poetry. Li Mêng-yang (1475–1529) called upon writers to imitate what he considered the highest forms of ancient literature: Chin-Han prose and High T'ang poetry. He meant the imitation not of the outward form of these styles but of the innate natural principles upon which they were based. Ho Ching-ming (1483–1521), also a member of the *fu-ku* (archaists), opposed Li's prescription. He believed that such imitation was suitable for young writers but should be abandoned by them as soon as they discovered their own personal styles. Li Tung-yang (1447–1516) shared some of the beliefs of the *fu-ku*. Although he admired Yen Yü's *Ts'ang-lang shih-hua*, the favorite textbook of this group, he was opposed to the kind of "naturalness" that depended entirely upon literary discipline and technique. He favored the "spontaneous naturalness" actually proposed by Yen Yü.

T'ang Shun-chih (1507–1560), a major essayist, stood much above these critics in importance as a literary theorist. He believed that the most important factor in prose writing was method (*fa*). Because Han prose displayed no method, he asserted, it was so esoteric in meaning that it could hardly be read. T'ang-Sung prose did show method, he said; it was so rigid and tight in structure that it supported its meaning perfectly. T'ang believed that a work of literature ought to be coherent, unified, and harmonious. Such a condition cannot exist, he held, unless the four basic elements of form, intention, inner energy, and personal voice are present. In later years, T'ang modified this position somewhat, arguing that the most important characteristic of a literary composition was "personality," which was conveyed by the author's personal voice. For an author to have a personal voice, he or she must possess the moral qualities of sincerity and truthfulness. These qualities became T'ang's criteria for both literary creation and critical evaluation.

Yen Hsieh (1627–1703) was perhaps the most important theoretical critic of the Ming period. In his main critical treatise, the *Yüan shih* (origins of poetry), he asked some of the central questions pertaining to the writing of poetry: can the writing of poetry be taught and learned? What laws govern its creation? Does its creation involve a hierarchical process?

Yen Hsieh asserted that the writing of a poem involved two sorts of regulation: the rules of prosody and the limitations of the poet's personality. The rules are partly prescriptive (determined by convention) and partly innate (already present in the human mind and employed according to the poet's talent or lack of talent). The creative process itself follows a downward course from higher to lower on three levels: abstract, semiabstract, and concrete. These levels were designated by Yen as possibility, factuality, and reality. "Possibility" in Yen's sense means "potentiality," or "the power or ability of a thing to be, an act to be done, or an event to occur without having yet been actualized"; Yen meant to suggest the power of the human mind to conceive of a poem as an abstract form. "Factuality" refers to the poet's imagining of images of universals or semiabstract forms – clouds and moonlight, grass and trees, mountains and rivers – which will fill the general outline of the poem. "Reality" refers to the poet's selecting of concrete images to represent a specific time and place which will convey his or her personal feelings. Yen Hsieh contended that the language of poetry is unique, differing from all other kinds of language, and its use constitutes an autonomous activity.

Fiction in traditional China, like drama, had little or no literary prestige. Short fiction embraced two predominant types: *ch'uan-ch'i*, which arose during the T'ang Dynasty, were written in classical Chinese, and *hua-pên*, which became prominent in written form during the Sung Dynasty, were written either in the vernacular or in very simple classical Chinese. Novels, which arose as a genre in the Ming and Ch'ing dynasties, were most commonly written in the vernacular, although some, more or less unsuccessfully, were written in classical Chinese. Confucianism had, however, rejected fiction as a literary genre, and although novels were produced on a considerable scale, they were not taken seriously by most literati. Therefore, until modern times, very little writing on theories concerning fiction was produced in China. Criticism of fiction was confined almost entirely to editing or reediting and to commentary by way of explanatory annotation. Among those critics of the Ming period who expressed some theoretical ideas in regard to fiction were Li Chih (1527–1602), Hu Ying-lin (1551–1602), and Chin Shêng-t'an (1610–1661). Li Chih's ideas were perhaps the most important.

Influenced by the T'ai-chou school of idealism, by Buddhist thought, and by his own independent spirit, Li Chih became a Confucian heretic and an enthusiastic promoter of popular literature. He provided commentaries for the novels *San kuo-chih yen-i* (1522; *Romance of the Three Kingdoms*, 1925) and *Shui-hu chuan* (c. 1589?; *Outlaws of the Marsh*, 1981). His theoretical ideas were outlined in his preface to Yüan Shu-tu's 1614 edition of the *Shui-hu chuan*, in some of his letters, and in his book of essays, the *Fên-shu* (1590; a book to be burnt).

Li Chih held the Confucian classics to be "nonliterature." They were nonliterature because, according to him, they had not been created by the "childlike heart" that originally constituted the nature of human beings. The ideal person possesses the heart of a child, from which sincere feelings and true thoughts spontaneously flow. The classical language is so far removed from the original *logos* – it had no pronunciation of its own – that the writer who uses it must lose his or her original nature in the maze of its complicated paths. Since speech came prior to writing, it is the original and true form of linguistic expression. It alone is capable, therefore, of conveying the emotions that issue from a person's childlike heart. Li Chih demanded therefore that writers abandon *wên-yen* and write in *pai hua*, or the language of the people.

Hu Ying-lin maintained that the T'ang *ch'uan-ch'i* tales were worthy of serious literary consideration. He also examined the evolution of the novels *Romance of the Three Kingdoms* and *Outlaws of the Marsh*. Chin Shêng-t'an championed literature in the colloquial language. In writing, he stressed the importance of careful planning and meticulous technique. He also proposed a theory of reading: since good literature was the result of planning and technique, readers should not be content to read for entertainment. On the contrary, they ought to examine the technical devices employed to discover their functions and thus be able to appreciate the writer's artistry. Further, readers ought not to be satisfied with understanding merely the literal meaning of a text; they ought to explore the possibility that it may contain deeper and richer meanings. Chin succeeded in raising the status of vernacular literature among the literati.

As to poetry, the last important critic of the Ming period was Wang Fu-chih (1619–1692). He edited three well-selected poetry anthologies and produced an important critical work, the *Chiang-chai shih-hua* (Chiang-chai's talks on poetry). Although it is a jumble of important assertions mixed with trivia, this book contains his theories that poetry is an autonomous activity and that a reader's interpretation of a text is not limited to the author's intention.

During the Ch'ing Dynasty (1644–1911), the most important theoretical contributions to literature were made by Wang Shih-chen (1634–1711) and Chao Chih-hsin (1662–1744). Wang Shih-chen was an important poet as well as an important critic. His critical theory is found in his *Tai-ching T'ang shih-hua* (1760; talks on poetry from Tai-ching Hall). The main feature of his theory had to do with his idea of the highest kind of poetry, which, in his view, was its permeation by the quality he called *shen-yün*. Poetry with this quality would exhibit evidence of the poet's complete control of his or her medium and of an enlightened apprehension of reality, as well as being charged with the poet's unique psychological and spiritual qualities. In short, to Wang the highest poetry exhibited the poet's spontaneous technical skill, his or her intuitive apprehension of reality, and his or her sensitive emotional response to such an experience.

Chao Chih-hsin opposed Wang Shih-chen's metaphysical view of poetry. To Chao, a poem was a technical artifact, a concrete object with an anatomy that could be studied. Chao explained his theory in a book entitled *T'an-lung lu* (talking about dragons). Here he records a conversation that took place among himself, Wang Shih-chen, and the dramatist Hung Shêng. The latter had remarked that poetry was like a dragon: if all the parts of its anatomy were not shown, it was not a poem. Wang Shih-chen responded, "Poetry is like a divine dragon, of which one can see the head but not the tail; or perhaps it may reveal a claw or a scale in the clouds, and that is all." Chao replied by acknowledging that such a dragon may indeed change "its appearance without a fixed form" and reveal merely "a scale or a claw." Nevertheless, he affirmed, "when someone who sees it dimly points only at a scale or a claw, the dragon's head and tail will have remained intact all the time."

In short, Chao's conclusion is that although one may be limited to what is directly sensible in a poem, it is important that these sensible parts suggest that the whole dragon is intact and whole. Such suggestion is what gives a poem that substance and wholeness of structure which, in his view, it ought to have. Chao's technical interest in poetry is shown by another book, *Sheng-tiao p'u* (treatise on metrics).

Chinese literary theory remained much the same throughout the remainder of the Ch'ing Dynasty. In the last decade of the nineteenth century, however, the translators Yen Fu (1853–1921) and Lin Shu (1882–1924) introduced Chinese readers to Western fiction and nonfiction, and with the turn of the century, Western ideas began to make an impact throughout China. In 1905 a momentous step was taken: the old civil service examination system that had controlled Chinese education as well as the character of Chinese literature for so many centuries was abolished.

Modern Chinese literary theory

The modern period begins with the cultural revolution associated with the May Fourth Movement of 1919, when students from Beijing University assembled in large numbers to protest that in conjunction with the Versailles Peace Conference Duan Qirui's warlord government in Beijing had consented to let Japan take over Germany's "rights" in Shandong Province in exchange for Japanese military support that would enable Duan to put down any attack upon his forces at home. The students in Beijing considered this action a "sell-out" of the Chinese nation; the Chinese delegation in Versailles refused to sign the treaty.

At the same time, this mass movement gave valuable support to the cultural movement that had begun in about 1915 when a group of literary young men had decided to publish a journal in Shanghai to be called *New Youth* (*Hsin ch'ing*), which was to be printed in the language of everyday speech. This was unprecedented in writing for any serious purpose because throughout Chinese history classical Chinese had privileged writing over speech. Written classical Chinese had no specific "voice" – no specific phonology. Its characters were the monopoly of the elite scholar-official class – the mandarins who governed China and set the standards for literary taste. Vernacular Chinese was appropriate for short stories and novels, which, however, were not taken seriously as literature. For any serious purpose – writing poetry, history, philosophy, or writing on divination, ethics, military affairs, calligraphy, or gardening – only classical Chinese, the language of the Confucian classics, had to be employed. When read aloud, the lexicon and syntax of classical Chinese was almost unintelligible to a reader unless the writing contained quotations from such works as the Confucian *Analects* or the *Book of Mencius*, which scholars had memorized in their youth. The decision to publish *New Youth* in the vernacular therefore represented both an intellectual and political break with the past.

The government examination system which determined whether contestants achieved the degrees necessary for government employment had been abolished in 1905. By 1917–1918 young Chinese intellectuals were concerned with bringing China into the twentieth century so it could compete with the Western powers and Japan. They knew that the first reform needed was language reform, so the masses could become educated in science and technology.

Leading the language reform movement were two young scholars, Hu Shih (1891–1962), who had been educated in the United States and was a Ph.D. from Columbia; and Chen Duxiu (1879–1942), Dean of the College of Letters of Beijing University, who was an editor of *New Youth*. In 1920 the Chinese Ministry of Education declared the speech of Beijing (Northern Mandarin) the official language of instruction throughout China and that its phones should be applied to the proper Chinese characters; it also declared that a romanized alphabet should be adopted to help teach pronunciation as well as to popularize the Beijing dialect. In 1918 the Chinese government had officially promulgated the National Phonetic Alphabet, and it was promoted by Hu Shih. A little earlier, in 1912, the Wade-Giles romanization had been adopted, particularly by Western scholars, and although still used, it is giving way to *pinyin*, the romanization prescribed in 1979 by the State Council of the People's Republic of China.

There are three main periods in modern Chinese literature:

1. From the cultural revolution associated with the May Fourth Movement of 1919 to the defeat of the Nationalist Government of Jiang Gaishek by the communist troops of Mao Zedong in 1949. Jiang Gaishek and his government fled to the island of Taiwan.
2. From the establishment of the People's Republic until the deaths of Premier Zhou Enlai and of Mao himself in 1976, and the removal from power of the "Gang of Four."
3. From 1976. After 1976 Deng Xiaoping was the real leader of China even though he was "depurged" for a second time in mid-1977. An ardent promoter of economic modernization, he preferred ruling from behind the scenes at this time, therefore, the third and last stage of Chinese literary production treated here is from 1977 to about the present time.

The father of modern Chinese literature, a figure who dominated the first period, was the great writer Lu Xun (pen name of Zhou Shuren, 1881–1936), who wrote his first story in classical Chinese. His main purpose was to see the China of his time realistically with a critical and satirical eye, for he had been the main spokesperson for language reform, advocating the writing of literature in vernacular Chinese. His next story was one of his masterpieces, "The Diary of a Madman" (*Kuangren riji*, 1918), whose opening section is written in classical Chinese to frame the diary format, though the narrative is told by a dramatized narrative persona who tells the story in the vernacular. A paranoic, the madman is convinced that people want to eat him because he thinks history shows that all Chinese culture of the past is based on cannibalism. In another masterpiece, "The True Story of Ah Q" (*A Q zheng zhuan*, 1921–1922), Ah Q is an itinerant village laborer living on the eve of the Revolution of 1911. He is constantly bullied by those stronger than himself, and in turn he bullies those who are weaker than himself. With the advent of the Revolution of 1911 he declares himself a revolutionary and vows to take the property of the wealthy. When the real revolutionaries enter the village, Ah Q is executed. Using an inadequate narrator, Lu Xun evidently means Ah Q to represent China and wishes to show how little was achieved by the Revolution of 1911.

Another distinguished fiction writer of the first period was Mao Dun (pen name of Shen Yanbing, 1896–1981), who received a Chinese classical education but became widely read in Western literature. He is famous for his novel *Midnight* (*Ziye*, 1933), the story of financial exploiters in decadent Shanghai. Lao She (1899–1966) was the author of the most famous novel on rickshaw men. In 1924, having studied English, he obtained a position teaching Chinese at the School of Oriental Studies at the University of London. There he read widely in English literature and became an admirer of Charles Dickens. His novel *Rickshaw Boy* (*Camel Xiangzi*, 1936) is the story of a young rickshaw puller who hopes to prosper by his hard work and ambition to better himself but is instead ground into destruction by an unrelenting all-powerful social and economic system indifferent to human welfare. Other leading writers of this period were Shen Congwen (1902–1988), a member of the Miao ethnic minority and a native of Hunan province. He is noted for *The Border Town* (*Biancheng*, 1934) and *The Long River* (*Changhe*, 1943), in which lyrical pastoralism is blended with strict realism.

During the 1920s and 1930s poetry as well as fiction flourished in the new literary movement. Of the poets who excelled may be mentioned Wen Yiduo (1899–1946). In 1922 Wen went to the United States, where he studied painting and poetry at the Art Students League in New York and the Chicago Art Institute. He returned to China in 1925, having published his first collection, *Red Candle* (*Hong zhu*, 1923); the collection *Dead Water* (*Sishui*) appeared in 1928. Another distinctive voice was Ai Qing (1910–1996), whose *Big Dike River* (*Dayan he*, 1936) was noteworthy. Two night scenes suggest "the darkness inhabited by China's masses and their future hopes," (McDougall and Louie).

The second major period in modern Chinese literature began with the Communist Party claiming literature for the cause. Although Mao Zedong and the Chinese Communists did not proclaim the founding of the People's Republic of China until October 1, 1949, in May of 1942 Mao summoned writers and artists to the Yenan Conference to affirm Communist Party authority over all spheres of life. He put forth several issues for discussion, including the writer's social position, attitude, audience, work, and education. He took the readers as workers, peasants, and soldiers, and insisted the writer must learn from them. "Socialist realism," or an optimistic depiction of socialist society, was to be the watchword.

Mao emphasized that writers needed to overcome their sense of superiority as intellectuals over manual laborers. Although himself a poet in classical Chinese, he also made it clear that art and literature were meant to serve the masses by honoring the sacrifices and the heroism of the cadres. He further reminded writers that the Party would exercise ideological control over themes, character portrayal, and language.

Censorship was carried out either by pre-publication or by command directives. Nevertheless, the woman writer Ding Ling (pen name of Jiang Bingzhi, 1904–1986), whose relationship with the Party was always uncertain, although usually orthodox, managed to write a famous novel of land-reform in north China, entitled *The Sun Shines over the Sanggan River* (*Taiyang zhao zai Sang-ganho*, 1948), which won the Stalin Prize in 1951.

By the spring of 1956, following Nikita Khrushshev's denunciation of Stalin, Mao had grown concerned by the trend in the Chinese bureaucracy toward professionalism, a trend he decried, and he took the opportunity to propose a policy of allowing criticism of Party cadres. At the same time he proposed that diversity in literature be allowed. To encourage such new policies, he proposed the motto: "Let a hundred flowers blossom, let a hundred schools contend." Despite the fact that there were misgivings among many people who saw China's real future in efficient modernization, this Hundred Flowers Campaign gathered strength through the rest of 1956 and early 1957. It seems that Mao and the Party bureaucracy did not realize the risks they were taking in allowing and even encouraging such blanket criticism. Intellectuals, students, and workers all over China launched their criticisms of basic Party policies as well as of individual cadres and soon all China was in an uproar. By mid-1957 Party conservatives forced a halt to the campaign.

This caused much bitterness, which was followed by an anti-rightest campaign that raged from 1957 to 1958 because those critics of Party policies or individual cadres were now branded as "rightists" and were exiled for indefinite periods to remote areas. By the end of 1957, it is said, over 300,000 intellectuals, especially young writers and school teachers, had met this fate, including Wang Mêng (born 1934), author of a promising novel *Long Live Youth* (*Quing-chun wan sui*, 1956). He was exiled to the countryside north of Beijing for five years of manual labor. His "rightist" label was not removed until 1961. Wang Mêng was then made Minister of Culture by Deng Xiaoping.

The third period in modern Chinese literature began with the death of Mao in 1976 at the age of eighty-two; Zhou Enlai had died two months previously. After the arrest and sentencing of the "Gang of Four," Deng Xiaoping, a man who wanted to "modernize" China, became the virtual head of state. China moved rapidly to become closer to the Western economic powers and eventually opened to the United States and the Western world. This policy received a set-back in 1989, however: in mid-April students staged massive demonstrations in Tiananmen Square in Beijing, calling on the government to end political corruption. Troops moved in and hundreds of demonstrators were wounded or killed.

Only since the 1970s and 1980s have Chinese readers finally had the opportunity to enjoy "popular literature" on a wide scale. Even before the founding of the People's Republic in 1949 most fiction was serious "critical realism" and there were few works of "popular entertainment" of the kind that now enjoy wide popularity – such as love stories, crime stories, detective stories, police procedurals, science fiction, martial-arts stories, tales of knight-errantry, Gothic romances, and criminal-case stories about wise and clever magistrates. But China's "new post-Mao literary climate," reports Jeffrey C. Kinkley, "has more than thawed . . . . Popular, romantic and even a few modernist works have appeared, along with pieces of social criticism . . . ."

Further reading

Birch, Cyril, ed. *Chinese Communist Literature*, 1963.
Bishop, J. L., ed. *Studies in Chinese Literature*, 1965.
Bush, Susan, and Christian Murck, eds. *Theories of the Arts in China*, 1983.
Ch'ên Hou-yi. *Chinese Literature: A Historical Introduction*, 1961.
Denton, Kirk A. *Modern Chinese Literary Thought: Writings on Literature 1893–1945*, 1996.
Galik, M. *Mao Tun and Modern Chinese Literary Criticism*, 1969.
Hightower, J. R. "Literary Criticism Through the Six Dynasties," in *Topics in Chinese Literature*, 1950.
Kinkley, Jeffrey C., ed. *After Mao: Chinese Literature and Society, 1978–1981*, 1985.
Knoerle, Mary Gregory. "The Poetic Theories of Lu Chi, with a Brief Comparison with Horace's *Ars Poetica*," in *Journal of Aesthetics and Art Criticism*. XXV (1966), pp. 137–143.
Lin, Julia C. *Modern Chinese Poetry: An Introduction*, 1972.
Liu, James J. Y. *The Art of Chinese Poetry*, 1962.
——. *Chinese Theories of Literature*, 1973.
Lu, Sheldon H. *From Historicity to Functionality: The Chinese Poetics of Narrative*, 1994.
McDougall, Bonnie S., and Kam Louie. *The Literature of China in the Twentieth Century*, 1997.
Martin, Helmut, and Jeffrey Kinkley, eds. *Chinese Writers: Self-Portrayals*, 1992.
Nienhauser, William H., Jr., ed. and comp. *The Indiana Companion to Traditional Literature*, 1986.
Pollard, David E. *A Chinese Look at Literature: The Literary Values of Chou Tso-jen in Relation to the Tradition*, 1973.
Wang, David Der-wei. *Fictional Realism in Twentieth-Century China: Mao Dun, Lao She, Shen Congwen*, 1992.
Zhang, Ying. *The City in Modern Chinese Literature and Film: Configurations of Space, Time, and Gender*, 1996.
Zhang, Xudong, *Chinese Modernism in the Era of Reform: Cultural Fever, Avant-Garde Fiction and the New Chinese Cinema*, 1997.
Zhao, Henry Y. H. *The Uneasy Narrator: Chinese Fiction from the Traditional to the Modern*, 1995.

RICHARD P. BENTON

See also Hu Shih; Liu Hsieh; Lu Chi

Cicero

Roman writer and rhetorician

Born: Arpinum, Latium; January 3, 106 B.C.
Died: Formiae, Latium; December 7, 43 B.C.

Biography

Marcus Tullius Cicero was born in Arpinum on January 3, 106 B.C., into a family of moderate means. As he was physically weak, he devoted himself chiefly to literary pursuits. In his youth, he came under the influence of a number of Greek and Roman scholars. His studies took him to Greece, Asia Minor, and Rhodes. Indeed, his debt to the Greeks was very great, and he would become the conduit through which much of their legacy would flow to the Roman world.

He chose law, rather than the military, as an avenue to political fortune in Rome. He first achieved success when in 70 B.C. he successfully prosecuted former governor Gaius Verres for extorting large sums of money from the Sicilians. In the years that followed, he gained even greater fame; in 64 B.C., despite his lack of political background, he was elected a consul by a wide margin. The next year, through brilliant oratory, he thwarted an attempt by Catiline (Lucius Sergius Catilina), a bankrupt aristocrat, to kill the consuls and seize the reins of government.

His uncompromising devotion to the oligarchic interests of the state, however, put him at odds with Julius Caesar and the other triumvirs. After a brief exile in Thessalonica, Cicero returned in 57 B.C. to support Pompey the Great in the Civil War. Although he was forgiven, Cicero continued to view Caesar as a tyrant and a threat to the state.

Following Caesar's assassination, he threw his support to Octavian (later Augustus) against Marc Antony, who, he believed, was a ruthless adventurer. Cicero lashed out at Antony in a series of caustic orations called the *Philippicae* (44–43 B.C.; *Philippics*). As a result, when Antony came to power as a part of the Second Triumvirate in 43 B.C., the great orator was executed.

Influence

Cicero's impact on Western civilization has been considerable. In his own day, he was a successful attorney and statesman who labored in vain to save the archaic ideals of an oligarchic Republic. Imbued with the learning of the ancient Greeks, Cicero was the most gifted representative of the senatorial aristocracy. Above all else, he was an orator, much like Demosthenes, who frequently turned his forensic wrath against those who threatened law and order. Cicero made the oration into a major literary form; many of his orations were transcribed, copied, and distributed. His diverse works profoundly influenced the development of literary theory and attitudes toward literary style in the West, particularly in the Renaissance, when a whole school of writers, dubbed Ciceronians, imitated his highly elaborate prose.

Analysis

Cicero was not a literary theorist in the modern sense of the term; he was a rhetorician. As Walter Ong notes, "Cicero used to make the point that the orator needed to know everything that could be known. Hence rhetoric, the art of oratory or public speaking, ultimately took all knowledge as its province." For Cicero, there was no sharp distinction between philosophy, literature, and political discourse. It was not his writing about literature per se but rather the entire body of his work, given unity by the principles of rhetoric, that helped to shape the development of literary theory.

Cicero's greatest ability, indeed his *raison d'être*, was oratory, a Greek bequest which he raised to its highest level of expression among the Romans. The emphasis on oratory and the proliferation of rules surrounding it can best be appreciated when one recalls that, in the Rome of Cicero's time (indeed, from the time of Aristotle well into the Renaissance), oratory – hence, the study of rhetoric – was not, as it is in this day of printed and recorded media, a mere artistic exercise but a primary means of self-advancement (in politics) and sometimes even survival (in the courts). As the path by which Cicero chose to reach the consulate, senate, and other important political offices, oratory formed the locus of virtually all of his literary activity until the last years of his life.

It is no surprise, then, that Cicero (and Quintilian after him) would place oratory at the head of the disciplines and would pay strict attention to the details of rhythm and emphasis attached to it: for Cicero, meter was as important in the orator's prose as it remains in poetry; especially at the end of a sentence (the *clasula*), the rhythm and order of elements must be precisely fitted to the orator's purpose, for they can make or break the argument. Cicero goes into great detail naming the parts of a sentence and analyzing various metrical patterns and their appropriateness or inappropriateness in particular cases. One of Cicero's strengths was his ability to vary his style according to his subject matter. Sometimes he employed the direct, austere, elevated style of the Attic school; on other occasions, possibly to conceal a weak argument, he preferred the verbosity of the Asiatic school. While borrowing from the two chief schools of Greek oratory, Cicero developed an effective style of his own which made him the finest orator of his age.

In his major works on oratory – especially *On Oratory* and *The Orator* – Cicero set forth precepts that were to shape standards of oratory in a long line of rhetoricians that had begun with Aristotle, the founder of scholastic rhetoric, and would extend through Quintilian, Longinus, the Middle Ages, the Renaissance, and into the eighteenth century. Indeed, Cicero's was one of the major classical voices that, along with Aristotle's and Horace's, had a profound effect on both the style and the thinking of Renaissance Humanism and letters. In *On Oratory*, Cicero delineates the appropriate course of study for an orator, establishes rules for the treatment of subject matter, and outlines the proper form of a speech. In *The Orator*, he focuses on the orator himself, concluding that the ideal orator must also be an ideal man (a dictum which Ben Jonson, fully conscious of his source, would echo in the seventeenth century when he proclaimed "the impossibility of any mans being the good Poet, without first being a good man"). Along with these two works, *Brutus* forms a sort of trilogy of rhetoric: it is a history of Roman oratory and orators based largely on the works of Cicero's close friend, the historian and patron of the arts Titus Pomponius Atticus.

Cicero's oratorical activity may be divided into two categories: those political speeches delivered in his capacity as defense attorney, consul, and senator, and those works dealing with the theory of the profession. Although he was a member of the senatorial aristocracy, Cicero frequently unleashed his forensic wrath against those, large or small, who threatened the Republic. In his defense of Sextus Roscius, who had been framed for murder by one of Lucius Cornelius Sulla's favorites, Cicero was animated and subdued by turns. Although this oration betrays his youth and inexperience, Sextus Roscius was acquitted, and Cicero gained a degree of renown. In the case against Gaius Verres, the evidence was so damaging that Cicero found it unnecessary to resort to histrionics. In a second set of orations composed after the fact, Cicero wrote to educate, inflame, and charm the Roman public. At other times, when the evidence was not available, Cicero had to improvise. Such was the case in the Catilinarian conspiracy. Although Cicero was aware of Catiline's machinations, there was too little evidence to bring him to trial. Cicero had to use all of his oratorical ability to arouse senatorial opinion against Catiline, a tactic which forced him to flee the city before his plans came to fruition. Cicero had the ability to arouse the patriotic fervor of some, the hatred of others.

Except for the *Philippics*, Cicero's public speeches during the last fifteen years of his life were necessarily limited by the turbulent political conditions of the age. He turned inward during this time and began to write about forensic theory. Perhaps his chief impetus, aside from the fact that he had a certain amount of leisure time, was the emergence of a younger generation of orators who had begun to question the efficacy of Cicero's flamboyant style. It was partly in his own defense, then, that Cicero wrote *On Oratory*, *Brutus*, and *The Orator*. Not only do these works delineate the educational criteria and method of delivery of the perfect orator; they are also autobiographical in nature – there can be little doubt that Cicero saw himself as that orator.

Cicero was a disciple of Greek philosophy, having studied with renowned Epicureans, Stoics, and scholars of the Academy in Athens and Rhodes; he used philosophical investigation to sharpen his oratorical skills during intervals of leisure. Most of his philosophical tracts were written during the last two years of his life, a period in which he did not hold public office. Disillusioned with politics and consumed with grief over the death of his daughter, Tullia, he plunged furiously into writing. In these works, there was little originality or attempt to synthesize, a fact of which Cicero was aware. In a letter to Atticus, he admitted to being simply the conduit through which already established ideas passed to the Roman world. Similarly, in *De finibus bonorum et malorum* (45 B.C.; *On the Definitions of Good and Evil*), he implies that his purpose was to convey the wisdom of the Greeks to his countrymen. The approach was remarkably simple – theories and opposing views set forth in Latin dialogue with illustrations from Roman history and poetry. The result was a kind of encyclopedia of Greek philosophy for Roman readers.

Cicero's work in this area may be divided into two parts: political treatises and those which were purely philosophical in nature. The political works, *De republica* (54–51 B.C.; *On the State*) and *De legibus* (52 B.C.; *On the Laws*), were written after he returned from exile in 57 B.C.. Influenced by Plato's works, they are concerned with the search for a pure, utopian form of government. He envisaged a *concordia ordinum* in which the good of the state hinged on the ability of the senatorial aristocracy to work with the wealthy equestrian class. Both treatises also reflect Cicero's Stoic and Academic affinities. Toward the end of his life, Cicero hurriedly penned several works delineating for educated Romans certain salient features of Greek philosophy. Among these were *De officiis* (44 B.C.; *On Duties*), *De finibus bonorum et malorum* (45 B.C.; *On the Definitions of Good and Evil*), *Tusculanae disputationes* (44 B.C.; *Tusculan Disputations*), *Cato maior de senectute* (44 B.C.; *On Old Age*), and *Laelius de amicitia* (44 B.C.; *On Friendship*), all of which would have a tremendous impact on later thinkers and writers – as much as his style, and perhaps even more so, after the eighteenth century.

Cicero contributed significantly to the rhetorical tradition that can be traced in unbroken continuity from antiquity to the Middle Ages. The Renaissance, however, brought a more intense interest in Cicero's works. In particular, many Humanists revered Cicero's style, holding it up as a model of classical Latin, in contrast to medieval Latin, which they regarded as debased. In C. S. Lewis' words, these Humanists "hoped to retain Latin as the living esperanto of Europe while putting back the great clock of linguistic change to the age of Cicero." Yet, as Lewis adds, the Humanists' enterprise was doomed from the start:

> Before they had ceased talking of a rebirth it became evident that they had really built a tomb. Fantastic pains and skill went to its building. Bembo's friend Longolius bound himself by oath to abstain not only from every word but from every number and case of a word that could not be found in Cicero.

Cicero's impact as a stylistic model was not limited to Latin. In sixteenth-century England, a significant number of writers, educated in Latin, sought to imitate Cicero's style in the vernacular. Ciceronian English, with its periodic constructions and other features reflecting its roots in oratory, provoked a strong counterreaction; the so-called anti-Ciceronians advocated a more direct style. This reaction anticipated a general rejection of the rhetorical tradition, which fell into increasing disfavor in subsequent centuries until the very word "rhetoric" came to have pejorative connotations.

In the late twentieth century, however, there was a marked revival of interest in rhetoric and the rhetorical tradition. Walter Ong studied Cicero's influence in terms of the residue of oral culture in literate and typographic cultures. Wesley Trimpi found in the works of Cicero and his successors a balanced approach to literary discourse that provides a much-needed corrective to the excesses of modern literary theory. These scholars and many others have demonstrated the continuing relevance of Cicero's thought.

Principal criticism

De inventione, 86 B.C.
De oratore, 55 B.C. (*On Oratory*)
De optimo genere oratorum, 52 B.C.
Orator ad M. Brutum, c. 47 B.C. (also known as *De optimo genere dicendi*)
Orator, 46 B.C. (*The Orator*)
Brutus, 46 B.C.

Other major works and literary forms

Cicero was a man of enormous literary energy, capable of writing much in a short period of time. He wrote political and philosophical treatises, many speeches which he delivered before the Roman senate, and a prodigious number of letters (especially in his later years), which carefully chronicle the political and social events of the period. He also wrote poetry, much of which has not survived.

NONFICTION
Ad Atticum, 68–44 B.C.
Ad familiares, 62–43 B.C. (*The Familiar Epistles*)
Ad Quintum fratrem, 59–54 B.C.
Oratoriae partitiones, 54? B.C.
De republica, 54–51 B.C. (*On the State*)
De legibus, 52 B.C. (*On the Laws*)
Paradoxica Stoicorum, 46 B.C.
De finibus bonorum et malorum, 45 B.C. (*On the Definitions of Good and Evil*)
De divinatione, 45–44 B.C.
De fato, 45–44 B.C.
Topica, 45–44 B.C.
Tusculanae disputationes, 44 B.C. (*Tusculan Disputations*)
De natura deorum, 44 B.C. (*On the Nature of the Gods*)
De officiis, 44 B.C. (*On Duties*)
Cato maior de senectute, 44 B.C. (*On Old Age*)
Laelius de amicitia, 44 B.C. (*On Friendship*)
Philippicae, 44–43 B.C. (*Philippics*)
Ad Brutum, 43 B.C.

Further reading

Bourne, Frank C. *A History of the Romans*, 1966.
Fuhrmann, Manfred. *Cicero and the Roman Republic*, 1992.
Heichelheim, Fritz M., et al. *A History of the Roman People*, 1984.
Lewis, C. S. *English Literature in the Sixteenth Century*, 1954.
MacKendrick, Paul. *The Philosophical Books of Cicero*, 1989.
Ong, Walter. *Rhetoric, Romance, and Technology: Studies in the Interaction of Expression and Culture*, 1971.
Petersson, Torsten. *Cicero: A Biography*, 1920.
Plutarch. "Cicero," in *Fall of the Roman Republic*, 1958.
Sinnigen, William G., and Arthur E. R. Boak. *A History of Rome to A.D. 565*, 1977.
Trimpi, Wesley. *Muses of One Mind: The Literary Analysis of Experience and Its Continuity*, 1983.
Vasaly, Ann. *Representations: Images of the World in Ciceronian Oratory*, 1993.

LARRY W. USILTON

See also Classical Greek and Roman Literary Theory; Medieval Literary Theory

Hélène Cixous

French writer, theorist, and critic

Born: Oran, Algeria; June 5, 1937

Biography

Hélène Cixous was born in Oran, Algeria, in 1937 of a French/Spanish Jewish father (a physician) and a German Jewish mother who became a midwife in widowhood. She was brought up with French and German languages but was also exposed in Algeria to Spanish and Arabic. Her father died of tuberculosis when she was eleven, an experience of loss which was to have a deep influence on her as a writer. "My writing was born in Algeria from a lost country, a dead father and a foreign mother," Cixous was to write in 1990. The mixture of languages and cultures and the experience of difference, so pregnant during her childhood in Algeria, no doubt attracted Hélène Cixous to a wide range of literature beyond natural and linguistic boundaries and made her conceive of literature as a "transnational country."

Cixous spent most of her adult life in Paris. After excelling as a student, she passed the *agrégation* in English and began teaching at Bordeaux University (1962–1965). She subsequently started a doctoral thesis on the literature of James Joyce, later published in 1968, to wide acclaim, as *L'Exil de James Joyce ou l'Art du remplacement (The Exile of James Joyce*, 1972). She was awarded her doctoral title while teaching at the University of Paris X (Nanterre) in 1968. In the same year Cixous took an active part in the Parisian events of 1968, and contributed to the creation of the Experimental University of Paris XIII (now known as Vincennes, then St. Denis). This gave her the opportunity to be appointed to a chair in English Literature. She then published a number of articles and books on both literary criticism and philosophy. In 1969 she became a cofounder of the "Revue de théorie et d'analyse littéraire,' *Poétique*, and later received the Prix Médicis for her first novel *Dedans* (1969; *Inside*, 1986). In 1974 she initiated and became director of a doctoral program in Women's Studies and of a new research center, the Centre de Recherches en Études Féminines, the first of its kind in Europe. Cixous remains the director of this center and since 1976, in her "Séminaires d'études féminines," has conducted regular fortnightly seminars throughout the academic year, open to visitors, at the University of Paris VIII.

Her teaching and research have brought her the recognition of many universities and over the years she has frequently been invited as lecturer and visiting professor, especially to the United States where in the 1990s she conducted the Wellek Lectures at the University of California at Irvine. During the 1990s she also received several honorary doctorates from universities in Canada, the United States, and England. In 1994 Cixous was awarded the national Légion d'Honneur, as well as the Prix des Critiques for best theatrical work for *La Ville parjure, ou le réveil des Érinyes* (1994). Several colloquia dedicated to her work have taken place, including one at the International Center of Cerisy-la-Salle in June 1998.

Influence

A literary critic, theorist, philosopher, novelist, playwright, and feminist, Cixous is regarded by a number of critics as one of the most important twentieth-century writers. She has produced more than forty books and well over a hundred articles. A substantial amount of her work has been translated into many languages and an impressive number of critical works and academic theses about her work are consistently produced in France and abroad.

Cixous' varied output bears the influence of her Parisian academic career, during which she became acquainted with Michel Foucault, Tzvetan Todorov, Gérard Genette, Jacques Lacan, Gilles Deleuze, and especially Jacques Derrida, with whom she keeps close connections to this day. Sigmund Freud and Martin Heidegger were also to have a significant impact on her writing. Through most of her work she praised the writing of William Shakespeare, James Joyce, Colette, Jean Genet, and Marguerite Duras, among others. In *Au bon plaisir d'Hélène Cixous* (broadcast in 1987 and translated as *At Hélène Cixous' Pleasure*) she mentioned that among her literary influences figure Friedrich Hölderlin, Franz Kafka, Heinrich von Kleist, Rainer Maria Rilke, Shakespeare, and especially the Brazilian writer Clarice Lispector. In *Vivre l'Orange/To Live the Orange* (1979) Cixous gives a first tribute to this writer who was, with Derrida, to have an exceptional place in her "sphere of references" and whose work she considers as the "most complete example to date of feminine writing."

Cixous' considerable work, which spans many genres and which addresses a wide range of issues, is still expanding; no doubt mainly because, for Cixous, writing proceeds from living: "Writing follows life like its shadow, continues it, listens to it, engraves it. It is a matter of living to the end without losing sight of life, which is a huge task." ("De la scène de l'inconscient à la scène de l'histoire," *Hélène Cixous: Chemins d'une écriture,* 1990; author's translation). Though Hélène Cixous has produced many avant-garde fictional and theatrical texts, she is mostly known – in the Anglo-Saxon world at any rate – as a literary theorist, for her project, also undertaken by Luce Irigaray and Julia Kristeva, on the poetics of social difference, and for her exploration of the links between sexuality and writing in the 1970s. Her two essays "Le Rire de la Méduse" (1975; "The Laugh of the Medusa," 1976) and "Sorties" (1980) became landmarks of the ongoing debate about feminine writing.

Analysis

Cixous' œuvre is manifold and frequently defies classification into literary categories, often effecting a cross between theory, philosophy, and poetry, a feature which makes her innovative writing, with its allusive, metaphorical, and inventive use of language, difficult to read, let alone translate. Furthermore she stresses that her work should be read conjointly:

> I have four or five forms of written expressions . . . poetic fiction, chamber theatre or theatre on a world scale, criticism, essays – without counting the notebooks that I write only to myself . . . . No one fragment carries the totality of the message, but each text (which is in itself a whole) has a particular urgency, an individual force, a necessity, and yet each text also has a force which comes to it from all the other texts.

If moments of evolution can be discerned in her work, from the literary critic to the feminist and literary theorist on the question of politics and writing and the implications of sexual difference, and to the writer of fiction and theater, it is crucial to stress that any such evolution is primarily a response to changing historical conditions and to the recognition of her subjective singularity. "My books are thus like life and history, heterogeneous chapters in a single vast book whose ending I will never know."

Cixous' literary criticism originally stemmed from her academic training in English literature and especially from her particular interest in the transgressive power of language: language conceived in the Derridean sense as exploratory rather than as striving to impose or confirm accepted meanings; a language rather evoking other possibilities which contradict, disrupt, or exceed accepted meanings. This interest led her to read other fictional writers:

> I ask of writing what I ask of desire: that it have no relation to the logic which puts desire on the side of possession, of acquisition, or even of that consumption-consummation which, when pushed to its limits with such exultation, links (false) consciousness with death.

The basis and evolution of her wider critical project was informed by her attempt to theorize the politics of writing, to deconstruct subjectivity, to denounce the hierarchies of binary oppositions, and ultimately to redefine subjectivity, textuality, and sexual difference.

Her critical reading of James Joyce in *The Exile of James Joyce* explores the context of literary creativity and examines the power of language in its relation to the unconscious. In this critical study, Cixous proceeds to read biography and literary text together. As Morag Shiach signals, however, "the drawback of this procedure is that it leads to a dissipation of Cixous' own critical voice, which often seems to be swamped by the plethora of texts with which she is engaging." In her later critical work on Joyce, "Entre l'écriture"(1986), Cixous focuses more on the representation of female subjectivity.

In *Prénoms de personne* (1974) she discusses readings of Sigmund Freud, E. T. A. Hoffmann, Heinrich von Kleist, Edgar Alan Poe, and again James Joyce, and outlines her view of literature. Cixous conceives fiction as a form of effective action: "So I have set free some texts here," she explains, "texts which I love for what they have to say about desire and the plurality which it entails."

With the discovery in 1978 of the Brazilian short-story (woman) writer Clarice Lispector, Cixous experiences a sense of recognition. Acutely aware of the limitations of Western society, in which the social script depends upon gendered binary oppositions operating in syntax, on sources of knowledge, and on our perceptions, and in which the "feminine" tends always to be the negative term in any hierarchies constructed within that society, she discovers in Lispector's writing a means of inscribing a different gender positioning which gives attention to the Other without appropriating it. The intersubjective space thus created is identified by Cixous as a feminine space *par excellence*. In "L'Approche de Clarice Lispector" (*Poétique*, 1979) and *Vivre l'Orange/To Live the Orange* Cixous examines the specificity and power of Lispector's minimalist writing. In a landmark essay "Extreme Fidelity" (1984, published 1988), Lispector's texts are viewed as "books of the right distance" in which the feminine can be expressed and in which both self and Other can coexist "as equals."

It is mostly as an influential theorist of the politics of writing and sexual difference that Cixous achieved distinction in the Anglo-Saxon world. As a theorist she was, and still is, considered as a feminist, though her relationship with the feminist movement remained complex: "Women matter to me enormously, which does not mean that I confine myself to this world. I think it must be unenclosed, as free and as broad as possible." Like Marguerite Duras, another writer whom she admired, Cixous has refused the label "feminist"; to what she viewed as its reformist demands in terms of equality, she preferred the practice of a "poetics of sexual difference."

Sexual difference for Cixous is indeed not based on the exclusion and hierarchy which she and other feminists – such as Julia Kristeva and Luce Irigaray – saw in Western systems of thought, based as they are on the subordination of the feminine to the masculine order. Her concept of feminine writing, which she repeatedly insisted could not be defined, clearly reflects this view. She intimately believes in bisexuality and, like Kristeva, she asserts that feminine writing is not necessarily linked to the gender of its author: "It could quite well be masculine writing, and conversely, the fact that a piece of writing is signed with a man's name does not in itself exclude femininity" ("Castration or Decapitation," 1981). However, in "Le Rire de la Méduse" and "La Jeune née" (1975; "The Newly Born Woman," 1986), she redefines the very notion of bisexuality away from its classical conception which erases differences; to this she opposes the concept of "the other bisexuality," which entails a recognition of plurality: "Bisexuality: that is, each one's location in self of the presence – variously manifest and insistent according to each person, male or female – of both sexes." Women however, in Cixous' conception, remain, for historico-cultural reasons, more in tune with such bisexuality, with what she called "the Realm of the Gift" as opposed to the "Realm of the proper" (in the sense of both "proper" and "property"), which she sees as a characteristic feature of masculinity.

Cixous' view of feminine writing is closely related to Derrida's concept of *différance*, and linked to the same questioning and ultimate refusal of any binary system of thought – the sign of patriarchy *par excellence* – whereby femininity becomes associated with passivity and death. Cixous' theory of writing, no doubt inspired by Derrida and Roland Barthes, advocates the free play of the signifier in an open-ended textuality. It offers a model of subjectivity based on openness to the Other, and situates sexual difference not at the level of possession, as in the masculine order, but at the level of *jouissance* – a Barthesian notion drawing, in Cixous, on the resources of the unconscious, in tune with the body's needs and pleasures and referring to the deep pleasure principle rooted in the concept of liberating love. Cixous' transgressive concept of "*l'écriture féminine*," which uses the signifying potential of language to stress the power of the feminine and to disrupt and transform the mechanisms of the masculine structure, and which encodes a different order open to the feminine, attempts to create, through subjective transformation, a framework for social and political change. Feminine writing for Cixous is a political strategy which, as she describes in "La Venue à l'écriture" (1977; *"Coming to Writing" and Other Essays*, 1991), has personal and biographical significance. The origin of such writing, which gives importance to bodily experience and is expressed through mythical and metaphorical imagery, has its source in this nameless pre-oedipal space in which the link between the (good) mother and the child is fostered. Such a concept of writing has been viewed by some critics as fundamentally contradictory and ultimately essentialist. Toril Moi, in *Sexual/Textual Politics* (1985), writes: "Cixous' theory of writing and femininity shifts back and forth from a Derridean emphasis on textuality as difference to a full-blown metaphysical account of writing as voice, presence and origin." Morag Shiach, in *Hélène Cixous: A Politics of Writing* (1991), stresses that "Cixous cannot be accused of naïveté, or epistemological ignorance. She knows the dangers of essentialism – 'if one subscribes to . . . 'anatomy is destiny,' one participates in condemning women to death' (*Sorties*) – and recognizes both 'the mother' and 'the body' as profoundly embedded in the cultural." Indeed, as the revised Irvine Lectures printed in *Three Steps on the Ladder of Writing* (1993) make clear, Cixous is undoubtedly aware of the fluctuating nature of gender.

As a fiction writer Hélène Cixous, faithful to her conception of feminine writing, produces texts which are associated, for their commitment to the "excess" of language, with the poetic rather than the novelistic mode. Her fiction texts have the same transformational force and respond to the same political impulse and sense of engagement as her theoretical writing. As she explained to Kathleen O'Grady in an interview published as "Guardian of Language: An Interview with Hélène Cixous" in 1996:

> There is not a single one of my fictional texts that does not resonate from world history . . . . I was born political, in a sense, and it was even for political reasons that I began to write poetry as a response to political tragedy.

She considers that "writers are guardians not only of the *res publica*" but also "of language . . . , above all of its freedom, its strangeness," while conceiving fiction primarily as a way of writing through the self, a way of "hearing the voices of the other in its own body."

Texts like *Inside* and *Souffles* (1975), which center on the relationship to love and death and which offer examples of feminine writing as the art of "singing the abyss," indeed address the relationship between self and others, writer and reader. From the late 1970s Cixous' fictional writing does not concentrate so much on the difficulties of self-expression but, taking love as an empowering element, investigates – for example in *Le Livre de Prométhea* (1983; *The Book of Promethea*, 1991) – different ways of relating to others while questioning the limits of language. Emma Wilson, in *Sexuality and the Reading Encounter* (1996), writes: "Cixous shows the other to be unassimilable in its very alterity and increasingly in her works shows the self to be displaced, dispossessed and perhaps even destroyed." In *Jours de l'an* (1990; *First Days of the Year*, 1998), writing has become the subject of fiction, part of an attempt to find new ways of expressing love. Words, "our antique and enemy invention," must be purged in order to rewrite the universe; in the process our relations to self, others, and the world itself are transformed.

If indeed, as Hélène Cixous suggests, "there is no decisive shift between theatre and fiction" since they are both "relative to an engagement" and respond to "something that is of the order of a responsibility of writing," theatrical writing nevertheless provided Cixous with an extra dimension for her writing project. The theater, which allows more immediacy and "a direct relation with the audience," provided her with the necessary space to feel closest to writing others. It also gave her the opportunity to link her theoretical work to the mechanisms of historical change; theater has been conceived by Cixous as a cultural space whereby history, while being written poetically, performs a historically identifiable social role.

Cixous' interest in the theater goes back to her early writing career. In a short essay "Aller à la mer" (*Le Monde*, 1977, translated in *Modern Drama*, 1984) she denounced the way women have consistently been represented in the theater as victims, objectified and silenced in order to enhance male heroism. In her conception of the theater, Cixous is deliberately modernist. Critical of popular culture, she conceives of theater as a space where the forms of subjectivity and representation which dominate contemporary life can be challenged. Echoing Antonin Artaud's "Theatre of Cruelty," in which representation avoids repetition by freeing itself from the tyranny of the text and is primarily conceived of as total presence, Cixous also believes in the specificity and nonreproducibility of any given performance. Furthermore, signals Morag Shiach, "from Freud, Cixous derives the possibility of seeing character not as something finished, the key to all actions, but rather as something structural and intersubjective." Such concepts of representation and character sustain Cixous' theatrical commitment to the will to recapture the pregnance of the present moment and to stage the bodily experience: "Where does the tragedy first of all take place?" asks Cixous. "In the body, in the stomach, in the legs, as we know since the Greek tragedies. Aeschylus' characters tell, first and foremost, a body state." Furthermore, for Cixous going to the theater constitutes a political gesture. With a view to changing, with the help of other women, its means of production and expression, she sees theater as a dialogical space which emphasizes proximity and where the audience, and especially women, can feel welcome.

In one of her first plays, *Portrait de Dora* (1976; *Portrait of Dora*, 1979) (based on Freud's case history of Dora), Cixous uses the central character to represent, through the exploration of subjectivity and desire, the embodiment of a refusal to accept the unavoidability of male economy. Two of her subsequent plays, *Le Nom d'Oedipe*, performed as an opera at the Avignon Festival in 1978, and *La Prise de l'école de Madhubaï* (1984), have also dealt with women's relation to patriarchal culture.

In the early 1980s Hélène Cixous became associated with the experimental "Théâtre du Soleil," with Ariane Mnouchkine as director. With the writing of two historical plays, *L'Histoire terrible mais inachevée de Norodom Sihanouk, roi de Cambodge* (1985; *The Terrible but Unfinished Story of Norodom Sihanouk, King of Cambodia*, 1994) and *L'Indiade ou l'Inde de leurs rêves* (1987), Cixous developed further her idea of the theater as a mirror which provides us with the opportunity "to see what we do"; such mirroring being seen as essential [illegible]der to exemplify how history is constructed through our individual struggles. The change of emphasis in her more recent plays from sexual politics to national struggle may have surprised some of Cixous' readers but again constitutes an added dimension for her versatile mode of writing. Indeed, beyond the diversity of her various writings, Hélène Cixous remains faithful to the same hermeneutic and textual strategies whereby history, the political, and the poetic remain closely associated and complementary.

Principal criticism

L'Exil de James Joyce ou l'Art du remplacement, 1968 (*The Exile of James Joyce*, 1972)
Prénoms de personne, 1974
"La Jeune née," 1975 (with Catherine Clément; "The Newly Born Woman," 1986)
Un K. incompréhensible: Pierre Goldman, 1975
"La Venue à l'écriture," 1977 (with Annie Leclerc and Madeleine Gagnon; translated in *"Coming to Writing" and Other Essays*, 1991)
"Entre l'écriture," 1986
L'Heure de Clarice Lispector, 1989
Reading with Clarice Lispector, 1990. Translated, edited, and introduced by Verena Andermatt Conley.
Readings: The Poetics of Blanchot, Joyce, Kafka, Kleist, Lispector and Tsvetaeva, 1991. Translated, edited, and introduced by V. A. Conley.
Three Steps on the Ladder of Writing (Wellek Lectures), 1993. Translated by Sarah Cornell and Susan Sellers.
Hélène Cixous, Photos de racines, 1994 (with Mireille Calle-Gruber; *Hélène Cixous, Rootprints*, 1997)
Stigmata: Escaping Texts, 1998

Other major works and literary forms

Hélène Cixous is also a contributor to numerous periodicals and the author of several dozens of articles, prefaces, and various texts, including "Le Rire de la Méduse," published in *L'Arc* no. 61 (1975), translated in *Signs* (1976) and in *New French Feminisms* (1981). She contributed to *Hélène Cixous: Chemins d'une écriture* (1990) with her article "De la scène de l'inconscient à la scène de l'histoire: chemin d'une écriture." She also wrote the preface to the *Hélène Cixous Reader* (1994).

NOVELS AND SHORT FICTION
Le Prénom de Dieu, 1967
Dedans, 1969 (*Inside*, 1986)
Le Troisième Corps, 1970
Les Commencements, 1970
Un Vrai Jardin, 1971
Neutre, 1972 (English translation, 1988)
Tombe, 1973
Portrait du soleil, 1973
Révolutions pour plus d'un Faust, 1975
Souffles, 1975
La, 1976
Partie, 1976
Angst, 1977 (English translation, 1985)
Préparatifs de noces au-delà de l'abîme, 1978
Vivre l'Orange/To Live the Orange, 1979 (bilingual edition)
An[illegible] 1979
Illa, 1980
With, ou L'Art de l'innocence, 1981
Limonade tout était si infini, 1982
Le Livre de Prométhea, 1983 (*The Book of Promethea*, 1991)
La Bataille d'Arcachon, 1986
Manne aux Mandelstams aux Mandelas, 1988 (*Manna: For the Mandelstams for the Mandelas*, 1993)
Jours de l'an, 1990 (*First Days of the Year*, 1998)
L'Ange au secret, 1991
Déluge, 1992
Beethoven à jamais, ou L'Existence de Dieu, 1993
La Fiancée juive ou de la tentation, 1995
Messie, 1996
Or: les lettres de mon père, 1997
Voiles, 1998 (with Jacques Derrida)

PLAYS
La Pupille, in *Cahiers Renaud-Barault*, 1971
Portrait de Dora, 1976 (*Portrait of Dora*, 1979)
Le Nom d'Oedipe, chant du corps interdit, 1978
La Prise de l'école de Madhubaï, 1984 (*The Conquest of the School at Madhubaï*, 1986)
L'Histoire terrible mais inachevée de Norodom Sihanouk, roi de Cambodge, 1985 (*The Terrible but Unfinished Story of Norodom Sihanouk, King of Cambodia*, 1994)
Théâtre (*Portrait de Dora, La Prise de l'école de Madhubaï*), 1986
L'Indiade ou l'Inde de leurs rêves, 1987
On ne part pas, on ne revient pas, 1991
Les Euménides d'Eschyle, 1992 (translation and introduction)
Les Atrides, 1992
La Ville parjure, ou le réveil des Érinyes, 1994
Voile noire voile blanche/Black Sail White Sail, 1994 (bilingual edition)
L'Histoire qu'on ne connaîtra jamais, 1994

Further reading

Conley, Verena Andermatt. *Hélène Cixous: Writing the Feminine*, 1984, expanded edition 1991.
——. *Hélène Cixous*, 1992.
Marks, Elaine, and Isabelle de Courtivron, eds. *New French Feminisms*, 1981.
Moi, Toril. *Sexual/Textual Politics: Feminist Literary Theory*, 1985.
Nordquist, Joan. *French Feminist Theory: Luce Irigaray and Hélène Cixous: A Bibliography*, 1990.
Rossum-Guyon, Françoise van, and Myriam Diaz-Diocaretz, eds. *Hélène Cixous: Chemins d'une écriture*, 1990.
Sellers, Susan. *Hélène Cixous Reader*, 1994.
——. *Hélène Cixous: Authorship, Autobiography and Love*, 1996.
Shiach, Morag. *Hélène Cixous: A Politics of Writing*, 1991.
Wilcox, Helen, ed. *The Body and the Text: Hélène Cixous*, 1990.
Wilson, Emma. *Sexuality and the Reading Encounter* (Chapter 4, "La Passion selon Hélène Cixous: Reading in the Feminine"), 1996.

RAYNALLE UDRIS

See also Derrida; Feminist Criticism; French Literary Theory: Twentieth Century; Gilbert and Gubar; Irigaray; Kristeva; Moi

The Classic

"Classic" is a term that is undergoing radical redefinition at the moment. However, for two thousand years critics and writers thought they understood perfectly well what a classic was: a work of literature characterized by permanent appeal, universal applicability, catholic value, metropolitan sophistication, and perfect form. Aulus Gellius, the first author to use the term, claimed in the second century: "*Classicus . . . scriptor, non proletarius*" – the classical writer is in a class all his or her own, above the mob. The idea of the classic has been linked to social class and high rank since the beginning. The notion of the classic was especially important to clerks and scribes who amassed the first great collection of ancient writings at the library of Alexandria in Egypt. These scholars forged the notion of classical culture which was in decline early in the first millennium. They sought to preserve classical texts and define the very notion of the classic. They not only identified, collected, edited, and commented on works such as *The Odyssey* and *Oedipus Rex*, they established rules for inclusion of a given work in the classical canon and for the composition of classical works in general, rules which they followed carefully in the composition of their own literary endeavors.

"Classical" is an adjective usually applied to the ancient cultures of Greece and Rome which were thought to have provided the foundation for Early Modern and contemporary Europe. The combination of these two Mediterranean cultures was fortuitous in the history of the classic because Greece was considered to represent the flowering of early, prehistoric northern European cultures (a theory now being contested by Africanists) and Rome established the reputation of Latin as the universal language for the distribution of the literary classic throughout the civilized world of the West. During the Middle Ages pagan authors were studied and their literary works allegorized and moralized to conform to Christian standards. Those pagan and Christian authors who came to be studied in the monastic and cathedral schools were known as "classical" authors. The so-called "Renaissance" of the Early Modern period referred to the rebirth of interest in classical languages and literatures, but it should be noted that Latin was the official language of medieval Europe. By the eighteenth century "neoclassicism" was fully installed as the official philosophy of art, taste, and even architecture – as the capitols of many European states attest, including the United States of America. The ideal of classical form, with its emphasis on the unities of time and place and often unreasonable demands for credibility and coherence, so put off Romantic poets like William Wordsworth and Samuel Taylor Coleridge that they abandoned the notion of the classic altogether as anachronistic, class-conscious, and stultifying.

In the late nineteenth century Matthew Arnold simplified the definition of the term in his essay "The Study of Poetry" (1880): "the true and right meaning of the word *classic* is that the work in question belongs to the class of the very best." He recommended that humanistic education should be classical, that is, it should provide students with a healthy exposure to the "best that has been thought and never so well expressed." T. S. Eliot, whose "What is a Classic?" remains itself the classic essay on the topic, characterized a literary classic by its maturity. "A classic can only occur when a civilization is mature; when a language and a literature are mature; and it must be the work of a mature mind." His example of the greatest of literary classics was Virgil's *Aeneid*, because it celebrated the accomplishments as well the origin of Roman culture. Virgil established the universal benchmark for literary accomplishment also because he wrote in Latin, the language which characterized and graced what Ernst Curtius called the Latin tradition of European culture. Eliot celebrated the metropolitan character of the *Aeneid*, the piety of its hero, and the imperial destiny of the Roman culture it was to establish in mythic form.

Frank Kermode has recently taken the notion of the term in a new direction with his book *The Classic: Literary Images of Permanence and Change* (1975), which is an extended meditation on Eliot's essay. The context for the classic is inevitably imperialistic, Kermode contends: "Eliot was . . . an imperialist; 'I am all for empires,' he once remarked." Only imperial entities can afford to disperse their cultures, their educational prerogatives, and their canons of taste and refinement across large expanses of global territory. The *imperium* imposes its own provincial religion through its armies, backs up its literary canons with real guns, imposes its language through its legal system, and administers proper taste through its state-sponsored educational system. In short, the classic is, like any literary work or philosophic discourse, a creation of its own history, an accident of the suppositions of class, gender, historical period, race, and so on that shaped it. Its claim to universality, perpetuity, urbanity, and catholicity are simply projections of the predispositions, predilections, and political agendas of the imperial culture that tautologically declared it a classic in the first place.

More interesting, perhaps, are the questions of how a classic comes to be canonized, and how it is appropriated by cultures which succeed it, often radically diverse cultures. Critics or scholars, it may be said, create classics. Teachers re-create them by including the classic, dubbed as such, in their literature and humanities courses. Literary classics such as *The Canterbury Tales* (1387–1400), *Romeo and Juliet* (1597), *Gulliver's Travels* (1726), and *Huckleberry Finn* (1884) are usually passed along to children in expurgated, abridged, and revised versions that are often mistaken for their originals by the majority culture. The Western university curriculum, which first articulated the canon of literary classics, is itself undergoing radical revision at the moment. Rival cultures and ethnic traditions are making their own legitimate claims for classics that represent what Eliot would have deemed their own "provincial" traditions. Most impressively, perhaps, is the process of appropriation and adaptation of classics that has characterized the last hundred years of literary creation. For instance, a play like William Shakespeare's *The Tempest*

(1611), a literary classic in anybody's estimation, has been effectively appropriated and revised by the African American writers Toni Morrison in *Tar Baby* (1987) and Gloria Naylor in *Mama Day* (1988). These efforts represent perhaps the most enduring characteristic of the literary classic: its continuing pertinence to radically diverse cultures as a standard to be emulated, contested, appropriated, or discarded as the needs of the time dictate.

Further reading

Arnold, Matthew. *Essays in Criticism: Second Series*, 1888.
Calder, William M., ed. *Hypatia: Essays in Classics, Comparative Literature, and Philosophy*, 1985.
Eliot, T. S. *Selected Essays*, 1972.
Kermode, Frank. *The Classic: Literary Images of Permanence and Change*, 1975.
Krieger, Murray. *The Classic Vision: The Retreat from Extremity in Modern Literature*, 1971.
Russell, D. A. *Criticism in Antiquity*, 1981.
Thomson, J. A. K. *The Classical Background of English Literature*, 1948.

JAMES R. ANDREAS, SR.

See also Canon

Classical Greek and Roman Literary Theory

Origins (Pre-Socratics and Sophists)

Greek literary theory had its unlikely beginning in the pre-Socratic philosophers of the mid-sixth century B.C. There was relatively little written literature upon which to speculate, but Greek society was remarkably sophisticated even at this early period; educated Greeks were struggling to resolve the tension between their elaborate mythology, filled with mischievous, rakish, and unethical deities, and the need to establish a more appropriate relationship between the divine and human orders. Thus it was that Xenophanes of Colophon offered a consistent way of interpreting passages in Homer (ninth century B.C.) and Hesiod (fl. c. 700 B.C.). Only about a hundred and twenty lines of Xenophanes have survived, but his criticisms are clear: the deities of Homer and Hesiod are often immoral, there is no good reason to consider the gods as having human form, and different races endow deities with their own particular characteristics. He thus posited a nonanthropomorphic notion of deity, one god neither male nor female. What Xenophanes wrote is as much theology as philosophy of literature; still, it paved the way for the Socratic view of mythic literature which would be further refined in Plato's writings.

Protagoras (fl. fifth century B.C.) went further than Xenophanes. He studied Homer's language, criticized its syntax, and developed a system for the classification of speech, which he categorized as Wish, Question, Answer (or Statement), and Command. To students of philosophy, he is best known for the statement "Man is the measure of all things." He reacted more extremely than did Xenophanes to prevailing Greek ideas about deities, revealing his agnosticism by asserting the impossibility of knowing whether the gods exist and noting the existence of certain obstacles to human knowledge, among them the brevity of life itself. Plato's dialogue *Protagoras* (c. 399 B.C.), though partly caricature, implies that Protagoras was greatly admired by his students and contemporaries for his skill with words, shared with others who could be classed as Sophists. Protagoras and Prodicus of Ceos (late fifth century B.C.), who collected synonyms and etymologies, were largely responsible for a self-consciousness about language (as well as a variety of agnosticism) that would find its artistic development in the plays of Euripides (c. 479–c. 406).

Socrates and Plato

It is neither an injustice nor an inaccuracy to classify Socrates (469–399 B.C.) as a Sophist; though he did not accept fees, give lectures, or write, his dialectical method of analysis, illustrated in the dialogues of his student Plato (c. 427–347 B.C.), reveals an original critical method. Plato took dialectic – essentially a variety of verbal polemic which he calls "eristic," or disputation, in *Sophist* (c. 365–361 B.C.), *Politeia* (c. 388–366 B.C.; *Republic*), and *Phaedrus* (c. 388–366 B.C.) – and transformed it into a formal process. A text closely examined via a series of "positions" (*hypotheses*) eventually yields its ultimate exemplar through a progressive ascent; this exemplar is the "unhypothetized principle" identified with the good in itself (*auto to agathon*). Plato thus modified Socratic dialectic in two ways. On the one hand, he formalized it and used it as a teaching tool; on the other, he applied a fundamentally philosophic procedure to literature.

There are two varieties of the dialectic process illustrated in the dialogues. The kind noted above may be described as synoptic in the sense that it aims at discerning a series of excellences. The theory of forms, as discussed in *Phaedo* (c. 388–366 B.C.), illustrates the mechanics of the process. The second variety of dialectic can be considered diacritic. Diacritic dialectic is introduced in *Phaedrus*; it relies on two procedures, "collection" (*synagogē*, that is, synthesis), and "division" (*diaeresis*), a kind of analysis.

Since both kinds of dialectic aim at attaining truth, it follows that both Socrates and Plato would echo Xenophanes in voicing strong moral objections to the traditional myths – for example, in *Euthyphro* (c. 399–390 B.C.), *Phaedrus*, and the *Republic*. One way to deal with objections to myth, short of abandoning most of Greek narrative literature, was to suggest that there were "hidden meanings" (*hyponoia*) in the ancient myths. Prodicus had used this method, but Plato rejected *hyponoia*. Instead, Plato used allegorical interpretations, either moral, physical, or cosmological, in order to extract an underlying sense. He thus eliminated mystical interpretation and applied philosophic method in an effort to extract truth from the mythic material of the poets.

Plato considered *mimēsis* (imitation) of central importance in literary as well as applied art. In *Sophist*, he divides the productive arts (*poetikai technai*) into divine craftsmanship and human craftsmanship (called *phytourgia* and *demiourgia* in *Republic*). Another type of productivity produces "copies" (*eikones*) rather than "originals," and this activity is shared by God and human creators. This is the art of poets, artists, and actors and is called *mimēsis*. The craftsman (*demiourgos*) produces either real and original objects or proximate imitations. For example, in *Republic*, the divine craftsman creates the real bed, the *eidos* of bed, and the carpenter produces its imitation (*eikon*); still, the painter produces an *eikon* of the carpenter's work, which for him is the original. In *Sophist*, the originals are natural objects as they exist in the world; artists' creations, which necessarily are based on these, are *mimēsis*. In *Timaeus*, the world is the product of divine mimetic activity, based on preexistent *eide*.

Undoubtedly, there are inconsistencies among the various dialogues in their descriptions of the creative process. Even so, it is clear that the mimetic object (the imitation of the model) is always inferior to its original. A work of literature, therefore, can never equal the natural original upon which it is based, however close the resemblance. This necessary inferiority is the basis for Plato's attack on the arts: they produce imitations and, worse, imitations of imitations (*Republic*). At best, all productions of art are untrue; in the hands of unscrupulous artists, they are deceitful and perverse.

Aristotle

Though Aristotle (384–322 B.C.) was primarily concerned with logic, metaphysics, ethics, and cosmology, his *De poetica* (c. 334–323 B.C.; *Poetics*) nevertheless provides an indication of the increased formalization of literary study. There are clear problems, however, in accepting the *Poetics* as Aristotle's definitive pronouncement on literary theory. First, the extant text is fragmentary, containing only the section on tragic drama. Should one assume that Aristotle's three unities (time, place, and action) apply as well to other literary forms, such as comedy or lyric poetry? Then, too, the *Poetics* was compiled from lecture notes and probably edited by Aristotle's students after his death. It likely was intended as a student text, never for general publication; internal evidence, mostly its unfinished style, makes this clear. Finally, to what extent does the *Poetics* represent Aristotle's own thought, and how much derives either from possible student editors or from Plato, Aristotle's own teacher? These questions indicate the difficulties in reaching definite conclusions about Aristotle's theory of criticism.

Aristotle drew his theory of *mimēsis* (that art is imitative of reality) from Plato, though in *Metaphysica* (*Metaphysics*), he states that the concept of *mimēsis* derives from the Pythagoreans, who held that things imitate numbers. He criticizes the Pythagorean view because it presents a purely mechanical reproduction of multiple imitations and eliminates the divine *demiourgos*. In the arts, *mimēsis* involves an imitation of real people engaged in plausible actions. It requires *techne* (productive skill) on the part of the artist. Here Aristotle diverges significantly from Plato, since productive skill which matches rational means to predetermined ends (a process implied in *techne*) makes poetry a rational art.

The *Poetics* also privileges the perceiver over the work itself. In other words, the effect that a drama produces on its audience is more important than the play itself. This emphasis on result makes the *Poetics* a teleological and objective treatise, since it assumes that similar effects are produced in the entire audience. If the tragic action is serious, ample, and complete, those who watch it experience collectively a *catharsis* ("purging" or "release") inspired by the aroused emotions of pity and fear. Here again is a significant departure from Plato, who in *Republic* notes that tragedy arouses emotions which ought to be kept in check.

Catharsis is essentially homeopathic; that is, it "cures" by producing the same effect that one seeks to cure. For example, the audience perceiving *hybris* (arrogant pridefulness) in a tragic character such as Oedipus will try to eliminate this *hamartia* (flaw) from themselves lest they experience its consequences in their own lives. Both Plato and Aristotle were aware of the homeopathic principle as practiced in Greek medicine (which had derived it from the "harmonizing" theory of the Pythagoreans), and neither denies its effectiveness. Plato, however, is concerned about its possible misuse by tyrants who would manipulate public morals.

Other Aristotelian terms have become familiar vocabulary in literary criticism. Tragic drama should include *peripetia* (reversal of fortune) and *anagnorisis* (eventual recognition of the circumstances which caused the reversal). In Sophocles' *Oidipous Tyrannos* (c. 429 B.C.; *Oedipus Tyrannus*), for example, the herdsman knows that Laius and Jocasta are Oedipus' parents and that Oedipus has killed Laius and lives with Jocasta as her husband. Jocasta's *anagnorisis* precedes that of Oedipus, who comes to an independent recognition of what he has done.

The Alexandrians: Callimachus

Callimachus (c. 305-c. 240 B.C.), a Greek scholar and poet, is the chief representative of the Alexandrian School of criticism. He had noble origins from the family of the Battiadae. He gave his first lectures in a suburb of Alexandria, Egypt, but Ptolemy Philadelphus, King of Egypt, quickly recognized his talents and summoned him to central Alexandria about 260 B.C., where he became curator of the great library. He held this office for about twenty years, until the time of his death.

Callimachus' greatest contribution at Alexandria was categorizing and cataloging the numerous books in the collection there. The catalog he published, called *Pinakes* (tablets), listed a hundred and twenty works in chronological order with annotations and observations on genuineness, their first and last words, and a final comment on the bulk of each. The *Pinakes* thus became the foundation for critical study of Greek literature.

Eight hundred works, in mixed prose and verse, are attributed to Callimachus; he appears to have avoided on principle the composition of long works so as to give more attention to artistic detail. The aphorism *mega biblion, mega kakon* (big book, big evil) is credited to Callimachus. The virtue of Callimachus' works, however, lies not so much in their artistry as in their erudition. The *Aetia* (causes), for example, had a specifically didactic purpose: to establish the origins of cities, of religious ceremonies, and of miscellaneous secular institutions.

Callimachus' influence extended far beyond his writing and teaching. Indeed, he set methods and parameters of study for the entire Alexandrian School. His most famous pupils included Eratosthenes of Cyrene (c. 275–194 B.C.), Aristophanes of Byzantium (c. 257–180 B.C.), and Apollonius Rhodius (c. 260-c. 190 B.C.). Each of these three had a term as chief librarian at Alexandria after Callimachus' death.

Republican Rome: Cicero

Cicero (106–43 B.C.), as a symbol of republican Rome, is a figure of undoubted historical importance, but his contributions to Roman philosophy and rhetoric are at least as significant, possibly even more so. The period through which he lived and his position in the Senate allowed him to know and converse with the tragedian Lucius Accius (170–94 B.C.). He learned aesthetics from the Greek poet Archias (fl. 100–45 B.C.). Cicero would defend his former teacher's right to citizenship in his *Pro Archia* (62 B.C.).

Versatility is the common feature of Cicero's numerous rhetorical, philosophical, and literary works. In his *De oratore* (55 B.C.; *On Oratory*), he offers the thesis that the perfect orator must have a thorough acquaintance with every art. Cicero discusses such topics as arrangement of parts of an oration in ways most likely to persuade an audience. The *Brutus* (c. 46 B.C.), originally intended as a supplementary fourth book of *De oratore*, is Cicero's enumeration and assessment of the greatest Greek and Roman orators.

De oratore is an imaginary dialogue set at the Tuscan villa of the orator Licinius Crassus. He and his rival Antonius take opposing views on what constitutes great oratory and the prerequisites of rhetorical skill. Crassus takes the Ciceronian view that a broad acquaintance with many disciplines, such as philosophy, law, and aesthetics, is essential in the formation of an orator. Antonius argues that method of delivery and arrangement of the speech itself are more important. Cicero intended in this work to construct a system of oratory and correct for his brother Quintus the rough style of *De inventione* (86 B.C.), Cicero's earliest treatise on rhetoric. *Brutus* and *De oratore*, taken together, illustrate how far the study of oratory had come in the Roman Republic. Cicero had written what was, in effect, style criticism and along the way had enumerated and assessed the achievements of the greatest orators of Greece and Rome. He no doubt envisioned as well a younger generation of speakers whose training, fostered by his outlook, would continue republican traditions in Rome.

The *Orator ad M. Brutum*, which is also called *De optimo genere dicendi* (c. 47 B.C.), is the most polished and most philosophical of Cicero's rhetorical works. Here philosophy is said to provide the best training ground for prospective rhetoricians. Cicero delineates three styles: grand, middle, and plain; the consummate orator chooses which (or which combination) to use based on the circumstances of the speech. The text of the oration should contain proof of its thesis, should give pleasure, and should persuade or move its audience. It must deal accurately with the various fields of knowledge and pay due attention to ornamentation (*sententiae*) and rhythm (*numerous oratorius*). The prospective orator learns best through criticism of models from the past rather than through textbook instruction. Cicero analyzes passages from Demosthenes and other Attic orators and pays special attention to their use of periodic sentences and rhythmic sentence endings (*clausulae*).

Literary criticism in Latin has its origins in Cicero. He drew on Roman antecedents such as Ennius (239–169 B.C.), Terence (c. 195–160 B.C.), and Lucilius (c. 180–103 B.C.) as well as Greek predecessors such as Plato and Aristotle. It is clear that Cicero did not produce any original theory of criticism; his accomplishment was to synthesize and apply Greek ideas to the Latin language and to rhetoric as he believed it should be practiced in Rome. Clearly, he paved the way for the broad and far-reaching criticism of Horace and Quintilian.

Augustan Rome: Horace

Quintus Horatius Flaccus (65–8 B.C.), more generally called Horace, was one of several poets who received the patronage of the emperor Augustus. He, like Virgil (70–19 B.C.), was also a member of the literary circle of Maecenas and was as much a man of imperial Rome as Cicero was of the Roman Republic. Horace's literary career falls into three broad periods: that of his *Epodes* and *Satires* (c. 35–30 B.C.), that of the *Odes*, books 1–3 (c. 23 B.C.), and that of the officially commissioned *Ode*, book 4 (13 B.C.).

Clearly, Horace's interests broadened in his later works. Increasingly, for example, he employed conversational phrases and even slang in his verse. He sometimes also used syncopated forms which anticipated the Romance languages and even rare words which do not appear in other extant

Latin literature. He defended such unorthodox use of language in his *Ars poetica* (c. 17 B.C.; *The Art of Poetry*).

Horace's theory of criticism, though formally stated in the *The Art of Poetry*, appears in scattered form in other writings as well. In the *Epistles* (c. 20–15 B.C.), which are essentially verse letters, Horace is both moralist and literary critic, developing a form originally used by Lucilius. Some of these letters are short, barely ten lines long, and written in a conversational style; others exceed a hundred lines and are more formal and didactic. Subjects of the short epistles include a dinner invitation to a friend on the birthday of the emperor Augustus, an announcement dispatching certain unnamed literary works to the emperor, an inquiry on various health resorts, and a general invective against fault-finding critics. The first epistle, however, is a more serious farewell to poetry. Written when the author was about forty-five, it is an announcement of Horace's intention to turn to philosophic inquiry. Criticizing the waste of energy which characterizes most human pursuits, he proclaims that wisdom is the real object of life. He prescribes a kind of philosophic calm in dealing with life's turmoil, in effect a reconciliation of Epicurean and Stoic ideas. Culture subdues the lower human nature, trains the character, and reins in the passions, which cause pain when they run to excess.

The second book of the *Epistles* deals more directly with literary theory; it was probably written a few years earlier than the first book. Horace here shows his preference for the Greek writers and rejects the general approbation, characteristic of Augustan Rome, for Quintus Ennius, Gnaeus Naevius, Lucius Accius, Plautus, Terence, and others. Though he found fault with the prevailing tastes of Augustan audiences, Horace was careful to praise generously the emperor's own discerning taste as a patron of poets. Horace believed that Roman literary genius was practical and didactic, that of Greece artistic and speculative. It is clear that he personally favored the latter, anticipating the enthusiasm for Hellenism which would reach its peak in Rome during the reign of Marcus Aurelius. Even so, Horace was happy to live in a Rome which had fostered Virgil's genius and even apologized that he himself lacked the grand style required for epic verse.

The second epistle of book 2 makes two important points: the need to acquire an ease in style and the need to be able to criticize one's own writing and delete or radically revise when necessary. The poet's language must be vigorous, clear, and rich. The habit of pruning, polishing, and rejecting lines after they have been written eventually yields the easily flowing style which the poet seeks.

The Art of Poetry, which is actually the third epistle of book 2, is neither a discrete work nor a comprehensive treatise on poetry, for it does not even consider Horace's own form of lyric. Horace thought of it simply as the *Epistula ad Pisones* (letter to the Pisos), though the identity of the Pisos to whom it is addressed remains unclear. Lucius Piso (b. 48 B.C.) was the son of the enemy against whom Cicero had directed his speeches on the Pisonian conspiracy. It appears that Lucius had two sons who would have been old enough to be addressed in the epistle, though there is no way of establishing a firm connection between them and Horace.

It is strange that *The Art of Poetry*, with drama as its main theme, should not consider Greek tragedy; unlike Aristotle's *Poetics*, however, in which the history of drama is a major consideration, *The Art of Poetry* was envisioned as a work that would help to bring about a renaissance of Latin tragic poetry. Clearly, Horace hoped that Roman drama would develop during Augustus' reign as a counterpart to Virgilian epic and Horatian lyric; this combination would create a true golden age of Latin literature. In essence then, *The Art of Poetry* addressed a developing generation of writers with the goal of fostering a national movement in literature. Its message is that obeying certain strictures, avoiding certain errors, and paying close attention to methods and stylistics will yield success.

Horace does not imply that hard work alone produces great dramatic poetry; genius must combine with art, and poetry must be crafted, not composed and recited spontaneously. In line with this, Horace offers three guidelines: write only with inspiration, submit work to a competent judge, keep it nine years, and only then publish it. Porphyrion's commentary on *The Art of Poetry* (written in the early third century A.D.), notes that Horace's major sources were Alexandrian, though clearly he had also drawn heavily on Aristotle. Precepts on the five-act division of tragedy, the *deus ex machina* (divine intervention) which halts apparently irreversible action, the number of actors, and the functions of the chorus and choral ode were certainly derived from Aristotle.

The Silver Age: Quintilian

Marcus Fabius Quintilianus, or Quintilian (c. A.D. 35–96), though born in Calagurris, Spain, and thereby a provincial, is the best known of the imperial rhetoricians and, as a teacher and writer on oratory, the best source of information on imperial education. It is generally thought that his father was a teacher of rhetoric and that Quintilian himself received his education in Rome, where he studied at first hand the techniques of the city's most famous rhetoricians. He mentions two whom he especially admired: Domitius Afer (who was his teacher) and Julius Africanus. The latter was known for lavish metaphor and a strong style. Quintilian's *Institutio oratoria* (c. A.D. 95; *On the Education of an Orator*, 1856), which is best known by its Latin title, mentions these and other orators of the day, always with descriptions and assessments of their styles. Quintilian published only one of his own declamations (an early speech defending Naevius Arpinianus). Others which have been attributed to him are probably either the works of others or transcriptions issued by admiring students.

Institutio oratoria is a carefully arranged, highly systematized treatment in twelve books of the formulation of an orator. The irony is that at this stage of Roman history, rhetoric no longer enjoyed the privileged place that it had held in the Republic; nevertheless, it was still stressed in the school curriculum, and Quintilian, though he wrote his treatise in retirement, remained an educator to the last and approached his subject as a discipline which can be studied.

Book 1 considers education from infancy, book 2 the studies pursued under supervision of a rhetor. The core of *Institutio oratoria* is its definition of rhetoric, stressing *inventio* ("invention," or the choice of subject) and *elocutio* ("elocution," or the style of speaking). Quintilian then relates *elocutio* with *memoria* (memorizing) and *pronuntiatio* ("pronunciation," or delivery). Book 12 is a summation, outlining all the qualities of a polished orator. Most noteworthy in this curriculum is Quintilian's portrait of primary education in books 1 and 2, in which he outlines his own method of teaching. The tenth book is a series of literary portraits and judgments on the relative worth of authors to be studied. Implied in Quintilian's method is that the real purpose of education is the formation of a complete human being, what in his times would have been called the education of a gentleman.

According to Quintilian, training begins in the cradle, not the schoolroom, and requires the best nursemaids, the best teachers, and a strong background in grammar (language and literature), Greek as well as Latin and Homer as well as Virgil. No student should be pushed to learn beyond his or her capacity, nor should teachers rush to display the skills of their students. Surprising, given the generally literary nature of Roman education, is Quintilian's insistence on the study of philosophy, astronomy, and geometry. Part of *inventio* involves the proper contexts for clever statements and epigrams (*sententiae*) and guarding against dry argument and self-righteous invective. Quintilian clearly hoped for a revival of rhetoric in Rome even as Horace had wished for a resurgence of Roman tragic drama. That neither happened does not diminish in the least the worth of their works.

First-century Greece: Longinus

Some confusion surrounds the authorship of *Peri hypsous* (*On the Sublime*), a work which contributed much to later literary theory. It has been attributed to Cassius Longinus, an Athenian rhetorician who studied in Alexandria in the third century, but most scholars discount the possibility of his authorship. Internal evidence suggests that *On the Sublime* is a first-century work, and for want of more precise information its author has been dubbed simply Longinus.

Longinus introduced the concept of "the sublime," the transcendent element in a piece of literature. His theory centers on the synthesis of *noesis* (intellection) and *pathos* (emotion) and the allegorical, as opposed to the literal, aspects of art. According to Longinus, the artist must avoid affectation, pedantry, and sentimentality and – in making literature – strive to inspire in the reader both objective thought and free emotion. He was one of the first theorists to consider the relationship between the artist's character and his or her work.

Written in Greek, the manuscript of *On the Sublime* was found in the tenth century. Yet Longinus' work was not printed until 1554 and received little attention until the eighteenth century, when it influenced many British authors – including Joseph Addison and Alexander Pope. Later, during the period of Romanticism, *On the Sublime* was rejected as too rigid, although many of its theses on sublime art are consistent with that movement.

Romanized Hellenes: Dionysius of Halicarnassus and Lucian

Born at Halicarnassus in southwestern Caria in Asia Minor, Dionysius came to Italy about 29 B.C. at the close of the civil war between Augustus and Antony. He remained in Rome for the last twenty-two years of his life and died there in 7 B.C. His principal work is known as *Rōmaikē archaiologia* (*The Roman Antiquities*). The first ten books of this history of the Roman people survive intact; the remaining portions, originally comprising ten additional books, are fragmentary. *The Roman Antiquities* is written in Greek and was intended to give Greek readers a more favorable view of Roman civilization than most Greeks generally had.

Dionysius also wrote a treatise on rhetoric, *Technē rhetorikē* (*On the Ancient Orators*), which contained discussion and commentary on the most celebrated orators, philosophers, and historians of the Greeks. His *Crisis Achaiōn* (criticism of the Achaeans) concentrated on the style of the historian Thucydides (c. 460–c. 401 B.C.), the orators Isocrates (436–338 B.C.), Lysias (c. 459–c. 380 B.C.), and Demosthenes (384–322 B.C.), and the philosopher Plato. Though fragmentary, enough of these works exists to assess their contents.

Dionysius argued for the independence of Demosthenes from the principles of Aristotle's rhetoric and examined the florid style of oratory practiced by the epideictic Attic orators, noting particularly word placement for rhetorical effect. He examined idiomatic language in Thucydides and commented on the authenticity of speeches by comparing the style of doubtful works to those of certain attribution. In short, he used the methods of contemporary philologists to determine the accuracy, origins, and authors of the texts he analyzed. Though not a critic of the first order, Dionysius made generally sound critical comments and possessed great erudition. His greatest limitation was that he privileged style over content. When faced with an inelegantly written text of worthwhile content, his assessment of its author was usually negative.

Though born at Samosata, Syria, Lucian (c. A.D. 120–c. 180) traveled widely in Greece, Italy, and even Gaul. His works, which reflect the breadth of his experience, are written in Greek, for grecophilic Romans living during the reign of Marcus Aurelius (121–180). Lucian is best classified as an iconoclast. He abandoned a successful teaching career at the age of forty, tired of what he considered its artifices, and turned full-time to his writing.

The irreverent character of Lucian's opinions made many enemies, and there are several apocryphal accounts of what happened to him in consequence. *Suidas* (also called *Suda*), a Greek lexicon of the late tenth century, claims that Lucian was a Christian apostate, that he was surnamed the "Blasphemer," and that he was executed – torn apart by dogs – for impiety. The dialogue offered in *Suidas* as illustration of Lucian's irreverence, *Philopatris*, was, however, probably written by Julian the Apostate (A.D. 331–363), not Lucian.

The one hundred and thirty-two extant works, as well as numerous epigrams, that bear Lucian's name fall into three general categories. The earliest group, contemporary with his career as rhetorician, comprises the rhetorical exercises; these illustrate Lucian's own strange variety of sophistry. In one of the most famous, for example, Phalaris, the infamous sixth-century B.C. tyrant of Acragas, sends the bronze bull in which he had executed countless victims to Apollo's shrine at Delphi as an offering. The shrine's officials, tempted by its monetary value, push aside ethical considerations and accept it. In another work, a defendant is forced to conduct a full-blown legal defense for having said "goodbye" instead of "good day" to an important government official. It is Lucian's irreverence, his use of satire, rather than his sophistry, which distinguishes his works from those of his predecessors.

Lucian brought unusual cleverness to his works on grammatical questions and literary topics as well. In one of these, called *Dikē phōnēentōn* (*The Consonants at Law*), the plaintiff Sigma (the Greek letter "S") accuses defendant Tau (the Greek letter "T") of having violently seized his property. The joke involves knowing that all words which were pronounced "ss" in other Greek dialects were sounded "tt" in Attic Greek. In the *Lexiphanes* (English translation, 1684), Lucian criticized purists who insisted on using Atticisms in their works even when the words had long been discarded from the vernacular language or when unnatural and forced. In *Pōs dei historian sungraphein* (*History as It Should Be Written*, 1684), Lucian is more serious, emphasizing accuracy and impartiality – the Thucydidean approach. One of the best-known works in this second group is *Alēthōn diēgēmatōn* (*A True History*, 1634), which begins by noting that everything which follows is a lie, then describes fantastic adventures such as a moon visit and an exploration of a sea monster's belly.

The greatest number of Lucian's works belong to the third group, which comprises quasi-philosophical works. Most resemble Plato's dialogues in form, though not in subject matter. *Theōn dialogoi* (*Dialogues of the Gods*) examines well-known mythic tales, but always from a jaundiced, satirical, or absurd point of view. Lucian criticizes, for example, Zeus' desire for power and introduces a Cynic philosopher who proves to Zeus that since fate controls all eventualities, the god actually has no power at all. A complementary collection, *Nekrikoi dialogoi* (*Dialogues of the Dead*), is concerned essentially with the vanity of human wishes and desires. In essence, Lucian, in nearly all of his works, used his witty, irreverent style to create a literary form which the modern world calls satire; that he managed to do this in rhetorical and literary as well as philosophical settings is one measure of his versatile originality.

Alexandrian Neo-Platonism: Plotinus

Plotinus (A.D. 205–270) and Origen (A.D. 185–254) represent the final version of Platonist interpretation. Both studied at Alexandria with the same teacher, Ammonius Saccas, about whom little is known other than that he was probably an Egyptian. The major difference between Plotinus and Origen is that Plotinus resisted a synthesis of Platonic and Aristotelian ideas, while Origen incorporated and synthesized Platonic concepts to bolster the teaching of the emerging Christian church. Both, however, are concerned with the interior life and mysticism in the pure Platonic sense.

In no sense could one consider Plotinus an iconoclast, as Lucian had been a century earlier. Plotinus believed that the highest aspiration of a human being was *homoiosis* (assimilation) with God through the highest use of *theoria* (philosophical contemplation). The route to this union is *askesis*, a rigorous intellectual and moral training. Plotinus' contribution to this fundamentally Platonic process is his method of reaching the Good. The world's activities are a series of retreats from the source of Being; thus, human beings allow their thoughts to degenerate into mere sense knowledge, falling even into *praxis* (ordinary mechanical actions). Plotinus believed that the first step toward higher forms of activity is reversing the process of distraction which seduces a person into believing that *praxis* is the essential activity of living. In this reversal, a person moves inward, past action, sensation, discursive thought, and intuition, and simultaneously moves upward toward the One. Plotinus calls this quest "the flight of the alone to the Alone." This inward and upward journey is possible because every human being carries within him- or herself a personal history of his or her descent; in the "flight," he or she retraces his or her steps.

The derivation from Plato's forms is clear; nevertheless, Plato's best hope for *nous* (intellect) was as a tool to craft (*demiourgein*), shaping the sensible universe in imitation of the higher Forms. Plotinus, at the age of fifty, systematized his interpretation of Platonism into fifty-four treatises, published after his death in a version edited by his biographer Porphyry (232/233-c. 305) as the six *Enneads* (c. 300–305; sets of nine books). His contribution is a systematic exegesis of Neo-Platonist ideas. Despite the mystical nature of his treatment, Plotinian thought remained remarkably free of the fantastic, ecstatic, and superstitious elements which characterized later Neo-Platonism.

Christian Neo-Platonism: Saint Augustine

Readers of his *Confessiones* (A.D. 397–400; *Confessions*) are familiar with the broad outline of the life of Aurelius Augustinus (354–430); Augustine carefully shaped this spiritual autobiography, however, to show a parallel between the events of his life and the intellectual progress he made. Though its central element is Augustine's conversion to Christianity, the passage which immediately follows his account of that event, his recollection of his wordless conversation with his mother, Monica, during which they seem for an instant to touch upon the Divine, is a model of Plotinian "flight."

Augustine was schooled in the classical Roman way – that is, trained in rhetoric (though apparently not receiving the equally strong grounding in Greek which Quintilian recommended). There is a double irony here: first, the world no longer required classically trained rhetoricians, and second, Augustine was a North African provincial. He was a brilliant student, though one might deduce from veiled remarks in the *Confessions* that he was less than spectacularly successful as a teacher at Rome and Milan.

Though Augustine's education conditioned him to accept traditional, mechanical analysis of texts at first, he became increasingly aware that fictive texts influence human emotions, and this disturbed him. Dido's death in Virgil's *Aeneid* (c. 800 B.C.) moved him, though he knew that the Dido described here was a literary creation rather than a real person. The *Confessions* orchestrates Augustine's increasing disenchantment with such secular texts against his increased awareness of his need for a stronger spiritual union with God. He would eventually damn the *Aeneid*, loved in his boyhood and essential in his teaching career, as a "*dulcissimum spectaculum vanitatis*" (the sweetest spectacle of vanity).

Augustine sought substitutes for seductive secular literature in Neo-Platonist ideas at first. In September, 386, he and several friends were reading Plotinus at Cassiciacum (perhaps the modern Cassiago), near Lake Como in the foothills of the Italian Alps. His works during this period show the influence of the Plotinian notion of flight toward mystical union with the Divine. Even the *De musica* (389; *On Music*), Augustine's text on meter, discusses poetry in hierarchical terms. That he never finished the "Disciplinarum libri," a collection of critical works in which *On Music* was to be a single part, shows how wholeheartedly Augustine came to espouse the Plotinus-influenced idea that *logoi* (words) must be properly directed to serve the *Logos* (God). In effect, Augustine recognized the need to replace literature which served no higher purpose than art itself with a body of material which focused upon the Lord whose imminent return the Christian community awaited. This new literature, direct and plain in style, might suffer in its art, but would have the advantage of truth.

Proof that Augustine was mindful of literature's artistic purpose is found in his *Confessions* and *De civitate dei* (413–427; *The City of God*). The *Confessions* is, in effect, autobiographical prose epic, though it is not autobiography in the modern sense. It is highly selective in the portions of Augustine's life that it presents; moreover, it portrays his life in epic terms familiar to readers of the *Aeneid*. In the *Confessions*, however, tears for Monica, Augustine's mother, at her death are tempered by faith in her salvation. *The City of God* is Augustine's extended metaphorical anticipation of the new Rome, one energized by Christianity and more powerful than its secular predecessor ever was. It is clear that both these works display, in embryonic form, elements of the technique which the Middle Ages would call allegory.

The close of Classical Antiquity: Macrobius

Inevitably, even in the fourth century, with Christianity firmly established, criticism served secular as well as sacred purposes. Macrobius Ambrosius Theodosius (c. 375–c. 422) wrote his *Saturnalia* (c. 400; *The Saturnalia*, 1969) as a series of discussions on mythology, history, criticism, and other subjects. Set during the winter holiday of Saturnalia at the house of Vettius Praetextatus, minister in the imperates of Valentinian I and Valens, *The Saturnalia* follows the form of Plato's dialogues and is particularly similar to the *Symposium* (c. 388 B.C.). Its discursive tone and miscellaneous subject matter resemble the *Noctes Atticae* (c. 143; *Attic Nights*) of Aulus Gellius (c. A.D. 123–c. 165).

Macrobius is important as a critic for several reasons. First, his broad learning is evident in frequent quotations from the first- and second-century writers Suetonius Tranquillus, Seneca, Plutarch, and Athenaeus. He provides information on religious festivals and the Roman calendar, epigrams which he attributes to various writers (not always reliably), and, most important, commentary on Virgil's works. Scholars still cite Macrobius for his comments and variant readings. Then too, Macrobius' commentary on Cicero's "Somnium Scipionis" ("Dream of Scipio") was much read during the Middle Ages. Macrobius uses Cicero's text (from the sixth book of *De republica*, 54–51 B.C.; *On the State*) to consider the tenets of Neo-Platonism on the constitution of the universe. Macrobius' treatise on Greek and Latin verbs, compiled by an otherwise unknown Ioannes, is also extant. Placed beside the works of Saint Augustine and of Fabius Planciades Fulgentius, a sixth-century North African who wrote an allegorical exposition of the *Aeneid*, *Virgiliana continentia* (*The Exposition of the Content of Virgil According to Moral Philosophy*, 1971), Macrobius' works anticipate an eventual reconciliation of criticism's sacred and secular aspects in the medieval allegory of Dante (1265–1321).

Further reading

Atkins, John William Hey. *Literary Criticism in Antiquity*, 1934 (2 volumes).
D'Alton, John F. *Roman Literary Theory and Criticism: A Study in Tendencies*, 1931.
Duff, John W. *Literary History of Rome*, 1953 (2 volumes).
Jaeger, Werner. *Paideia: The Ideals of Greek Culture*, 1936–1947 (3 volumes). Translated by Gilbert Highet.
Marrou, Henri I. *A History of Education in Antiquity*, 1954.
Pfeiffer, R. *History of Classical Scholarship from the Beginning to the End of the Hellenistic Age*, 1968.
Platnauer, Maurice, ed. *Fifty Years and Twelve of Classical Scholarship*, 1968.
Sandys, John E. *History of Classical Scholarship*, 1908 (3 volumes).

ROBERT J. FORMAN

See also Aristotle; Saint Augustine; Callimachus; Cicero; Dionysius of Halicarnassus; Horace; Longinus; Lucian; Macrobius; Plato; Plotinus; Quintilian

Samuel Taylor Coleridge

English poet and critic

Born: Ottery St. Mary, England; October 21, 1772
Died: London, England; July 25, 1834

Biography

Samuel Taylor Coleridge was born on October 21, 1772, at Ottery St. Mary, Devonshire, the tenth child (ninth son) of John Coleridge, headmaster of the King's School there and later vicar of the parish. The other children were considerably older; young Sam grew mostly alone, a situation intensified by his father's sudden death when the boy was nine years old. The following year Coleridge was admitted to the celebrated school of Christ's Hospital, where he gained a solid education and befriended Charles Lamb. In 1791 he entered Jesus College, Cambridge University, where he quickly revealed his appetite for and brilliance in conversation and distinguished himself in poetry. Here he first met William Wordsworth and formed a close friendship with Robert Southey; he also managed his private affairs so badly that he ran away to join the dragoons in order to pay his debts. Though rescued by his brothers and returned to college, he could not concentrate on his work, dropping out for good in 1794, partly to promote a utopian community he planned to found in New England with Southey.

The scheme fell through, although Coleridge lived with Southey for a year and ended up reluctantly married to Sara Fricker, the sister of Southey's fiancée. The marriage was not successful, at least partly because Coleridge at this time contracted the progressive cardiopulmonary disease which would eventually kill him and which soon drove him to experiment with opium to relieve his sufferings. He tried to support himself by publishing periodical essays and dramas, but failed; he was on the verge of accepting a position as a Unitarian minister when an annuity from the Wedgwood brothers finally gave him some financial security. At the same time, he began the remarkable literary collaboration with Wordsworth which led to the impressive publication of *Lyrical Ballads* in 1798, marking the advent of the Romantic period. Thereafter for several years he lived intermittently in continental Europe and in the English Lake District, becoming increasingly ill and increasingly addicted to opium, falling in hopeless love with Sara Hutchinson – hopeless because he did not believe in divorce – and continuing his periodical writing. He even spent a year (1805) as secretary to the governor of Malta.

From 1806 to 1816 Coleridge lived in England, separated from his wife, struggling to provide for himself – his annuity went to his wife and children – and enslaved to the twin demons of disease and opium. He even broke with Wordsworth in 1810; though they were reconciled in 1812, their friendship was never the same. Yet these years, so full of personal pain, saw some of Coleridge's most solid achievements, including his lectures on William Shakespeare and John Milton, the production and publication of *Remorse*, the beginning of *Biographia Literaria*, and the issue of *Christabel* and "Kubla Khan." Still, his addiction was literally destroying him. He saved himself only by submitting completely to the direction of a physician, James Gillman, who housed him and managed his life for the final seventeen years. During those years, the healthiest and most productive of his life, Coleridge devoted most of his attention to religious, political, and social essays, publishing *Aids to Reflection* and *On the Constitution of Church and State*, but also overseeing several editions of his poems and plays. He was also widely celebrated for his conversation. Yet he still fell short of his expectations, never completing the symposium he promised in *Biographia Literaria*, and some of his work provoked spiteful or negative reactions, notably from his former disciples William Hazlitt and Thomas De Quincey. His reputation, however, was growing at the time of his final illness and death in Highgate, London, in 1834.

Influence

As one of the primary theoreticians of the Romantic movement, Coleridge's influence on subsequent culture can hardly be overstated. His theories radically transformed the foundations of many related systems of thought, from philosophy to psychology to literary theory to theory of government. By focusing on the mind and its creative processes, he practically compelled a new understanding of mental activity; if the nineteenth century is the age of psychology, it is so largely because of Coleridge. This redefinition of the mind in turn prompted further exploration of the way it operates in interpretation as well as in creation, across the entire range of human behavior. In this way, the revolution in psychology became a revolution in philosophy, then a revolution in the criticism of all the arts. This change in orientation spread extensively, affecting even the general public concept of the arts and of artists.

Analysis

Coleridge is uniformly considered one of the half-dozen most important literary theoreticians in the history of literature; indeed, some commentators, finding in his work a synthesis of Aristotle and Plato, rank him in the top three. He was certainly uniquely constituted to carry out the compound work of the critic. He possessed prodigious talents of memory, perception, abstraction, and formulation, a rare capacity for the abstruse coupled with a fine eye for detailed empirical observation. His memory was characterized by almost uncanny power and retention. He could repeat a work verbatim after reading it once, as he more than once demonstrated in his school days. Time after time, he astonished his friends with how much he held in solution in his mind; he was never at a loss for the apposite example, and he drew examples from an unprecedented range of reading extending far beyond literature and philosophy. Further, he had unequaled powers of empathy, enabling him to identify with and enter into the spirit of a vast array of psychological states. This sensitivity allowed him to communicate with anyone; it also gave him profound insights into the contradictory aspects of his own divided being. All of these combined to produce a consciousness uniquely capable of fusing emotional feeling and intellectual understanding. It helps explain why he emphasized this fusion as the highest quality of art and the apex of artistic apprehension.

The easiest approach to Coleridge's criticism is through analysis of what he saw as the central problem in art: determining its aim and function. He begins by accepting the classical premise that art is imitation of nature, an attempt to reproduce it in some way, but he adds that art also teaches by revealing underlying truths not discernible in nature as it appears to the unmediated eye. Superficially, this formulation seems a simple expansion of the standard Horatian formula of delighting and teaching, but Coleridge was reinterpreting the classical view to allow for the newer Romantic approach to art. Whereas classical art restricted attention to classes, types, and universal forms, the modern focuses on rendering particular instances, on realizing the internal form of the individual. The modern artist works with organic form, the concrete processes of living things. This concentration on the organic individual – though anticipated in theory in German aesthetics – marks the distinctively Coleridgean position. Organicism is the integrating principle in his thought, tying together everything from comments on the practical crafting of verse to the most recondite theories of the creative imagination and its psychology. For example, it underlies his approach to Shakespeare as his ideal of the organic artist: where other dramatists have done little more than clothe and animate character types or abstractions – incarnations of a single trait – Shakespeare presents people with all the inconsistency and unpredictability of existence, yet he makes them believable. Other writers produce characters; Shakespeare creates humanity.

Coleridge did not arrive at his organic hypothesis without effort. In fact, much of his criticism can be seen as a recurrent attempt to reconcile the classical ideals of universality with the new demands of the age for vital individuality. Thus, he insists that Aristotle is correct in asserting that poetry is concerned essentially with the ideal. Further, art expresses true as opposed to hypothetical knowledge. How can this be if truth has to do with universals and art produces only particulars? Because, Coleridge asserts, the universal can be known only through the particular. Universals cannot be apprehended in themselves, only through individual instances – incarnations.

Art expresses truth, then, by modifying – "abridging" is Coleridge's term – reality. Universal and particular are not opposed but interdependent: each is understood only through the other. This concept forms a second center in Coleridge's criticism; its lens illuminates and reconciles even his most elliptical and opaque statements. Yet, as so often with Coleridge, it pulls the reader up short. For it too looks like a simple restatement of Aristotle, who had insisted that universals and particulars were inseparable in existence. To make things worse, Coleridge argues that he means something quite different, and his explanation does not at first clarify the situation. A little thought, however, reveals that what he means is indeed different. Aristotle seems to suggest that although universals and particulars cannot be perceived except in conjunction, the understanding can separate them; Coleridge, on the other hand, wants not only to assert their union but to insist that the realized and individualized universal, the felt idea, is the highest form of understanding – and of creation.

This may not seem a valid distinction. Coleridge's own discomfort with it appears in his repeated attempts to explain it. Yet it really does not matter very much whether Aristotle and Coleridge are both ultimately saying the same thing, as Jacques Maritain would argue in the mid-twentieth century. The salient point is that Aristotle was not understood in Coleridge's day to be saying what Coleridge was. The authority of Aristotle had been invoked by conservative neoclassical critics such as Samuel Johnson and Sir Joshua Reynolds to restrict art to the expression of abstract and generalized types – the representation of an idealized humanity. Coleridge needed a counter-authority to justify a criticism focused not on stuffed effigies but on living, breathing beings. With Aristotle preempted, he could only set himself up as a Platonist.

In any case, Coleridge advocated a middle position: the artist must mediate the universal and particular by fusing them. The potentiality of the universal realizes itself in the individual, fusing essence and existence. Again, Shakespeare acts as his touchstone, and in two ways. His characters can be interpreted as these realized universals – real, believable men and women – but more significantly, Shakespeare himself becomes the model of the imagination that can forge such a fusion, the vehicle for creative union of universals and particulars. Unlike other dramatists, he seized the living potentiality inherent in the individual and gave it a shape. Coleridge goes on to say in "The Statesman's Manual" that the processes of art are analogous to those of religion, which sees the divine will realizing itself in the ongoing acts of creation and duplicates this activity in the choices of the individual who puts the universal principles of virtue into practice.

In Coleridge's aesthetic theory, beauty is created when the mind perceives the assimilation of the particular and the universal. Beauty is an agent to truth, not truth itself. In this respect it is, though partly subjective, far different from pleasure, or the merely agreeable. Beauty is rooted in the objective; it leads toward the good and is distinguished from the agreeable not only in kind but also in direction. Unlike psychological subjectivists or relativists, Coleridge is emphatic on this point. "Beauty pleases because it is beautiful," he insists; pleasure is merely agreeable to the senses. No matter how pleasant scratching an itch can be, it can never be beautiful.

Art mediates between nature and humans and realizes truth; beauty makes that truth perceivable. Thus, beauty is most apparent when it discloses the fusion of many in one – that is, in symbols. This formulation is distinctively Coleridge's; in making it he not only invented a term central to his aesthetics but also introduced what would become the major tool and principle of twentieth-century criticism. The symbol in pictorial art emerges as curved lines reveal not only the image of the subject but also the inherent vitality of the thing itself – a manifestation that is more real than reality because it embodies its truth. In the verbal symbol, the two conflicting principles of the universal and the particular are balanced and harmonized as the incarnation takes place. Notably, the symbol is not fixed, but an active process: a realizing rather than a realization, an unfolding movement toward unity. In this respect, beauty accompanies symbols as they harmonize themselves in the movement of a symphony, the contours of a sculpture, or the action of a drama. All of these – and other forms of beauty – imitate or echo the unfolding harmony of the creation.

Art thus imitates the essential in nature – not by photographic duplication, which presents a copy inferior to the original, but by progressive revelation of harmonizing patterns, disclosing the true life within. Symbols work by fusing many things into one, a favorite image and paradox of Coleridge. His distinctions between symbol and allegory and between organic and mechanical form develop along similar lines. Symbols are life-giving and life-creating; allegories are lifeless equations. Organic form emerges from the material, makes the body palpable; mechanical form is superimposed, confining and distorting the life compressed within. Organic form is a symbolic equivalence to creation.

In the *Biographia Literaria*, Coleridge wrote as if his principal objective were to develop a psychology of art centered in a new theory of the imagination. Whatever his intention, that did not happen. His actual depiction of the imagination is so elliptical and piecemeal that he suggests far more than he demonstrates. What he meant about the imagination must be reconstructed from his general theory of criticism.

He begins by distinguishing between "reason" and "understanding," borrowing terms from Immanuel Kant but interpreting them in a Platonic sense. The understanding is a mechanical processor of sensory data which it interprets in terms of predetermined categories. Reason, on the other hand, sees directly into the permanent forms or patterns through which nature realizes itself. This dichotomy did help explain the difference between the two types of knowledge commonly recognized, sensory processing and intuition. Yet it violated Coleridge's unitary concept of nature, in which reality fuses both universal and particular. For Coleridge there had to be some means of reconciling these oppositions. He found one in the imagination, which integrates all mental operations.

This idea tied in neatly with his critical theories, for it posited that the created mind works analogously with that of the Creator. Nature is an unfolding realization of the universal in the particular; it is actualized, brought into act, by the Creator. Understanding and reason are fused by the imagination when this actualization is truly perceived, not simply assembled piecemeal by the understanding or fixed in still photographs by the reason. Both external reality and its mental comprehension are products of fusion. The imagination channels two streams of mind into one and transcends them. Art, moreover, is a parallel process: the artist produces an act in which the harmony of creation is further disclosed by realizing his or her ideas. The work of art thus both represents the artist's imaginative grasp of reality and guides the audience in its own imaginative reconstruction.

Coleridge viewed the imagination as a synthesizing medium; he renamed it the "esemplastic power" – coining a word from the Greek to signify "to shape into one." Yet he did not himself develop his notions. In the section of *Biographia Literaria* in which he had promised to provide a one-hundred-page explanation, he instead inserted a self-composed letter purportedly from a friend, which advises him to leave it for a separate work because it would be too difficult for unprepared readers. That work was never written, probably because he feared that it would lead logically to an affirmation of pantheism, which his conservative conscience could not accept.

He did proceed to make an often-quoted distinction between the primary and secondary imaginations. The first seems mainly a concession to common sense. Coleridge merely confirms that one's daily perceptions of reality are in fact accurate, because they are actually acts of imagination by which the perceiver enters into the ongoing creation of the universe. The secondary imagination, on the other hand, is the more conscious, creative faculty employed in art, though even here he stresses that it works in the same way as does the more basic imagination. His further distinction between imagination and fancy proves to be little more than a reinforcement of the qualities which he had already assigned to the imagination; he needed to distinguish his unifying and reconciling faculty from the mere ability to formulate "images," which can be done mechanistically by verbal manipulation and memory. This distinction, basic to the eighteenth-century associationists, was necessary for Coleridge: he was developing a new theory to support a radically different approach to poetry.

For Coleridge, the imagination is not limited to art. It becomes an actualizing force for the entire personality, informing the emotions as well as the intellect; it produces a heightened awareness, influencing behavior as well as perception. In this way he moved psychology beyond the mechanical associationism of the eighteenth century, which had been limited to fixed equations of feelings with images. In his view, the imagination synthesizes and creates truth; it then, in perceiving that truth, creates beauty, and that beauty guides the emotions. Rather than diminishing truth in this process, the artistic imagination enhances it. Coleridge saw no dichotomy of scientific truth and poetic beauty; for him they were two modes of the same essence. He would have fully appreciated and applauded the description of a mathematical theorem as "elegant."

The creative imagination organizes sensory data through intellectual energy and then projects them as symbols. In this sense, Coleridge envisions the artist as creating forms out of his or her imagination, by which he meant his or her total consciousness; he stood poles apart from the primitive subjectivists, who allowed the artist to inflict his or her self-proclaimed, instinctive "laws" on the audience. Symbols are objective constructions, rooted in the reality projected by and correspondent to the imagination. Coleridge's distinction between allegory and symbol reinforces this concept. Allegory operates on the level of sense and the abstracting power of the understanding. The symbol is like the hub radiating truth to the rim of feeling, uniting sense and understanding in its fusion of particular and universal.

As suggested earlier, this view of the symbol does not contradict Aristotle's concept of art as imitation. It is consistent with Aristotle in rejecting relativism; it also accepts the insistence of the eighteenth-century associationists that symbols had to rise beyond the level of the private and the arbitrary. The symbol in Coleridge's sense enables communication by capturing universal truth in its process of unfolding; it is simultaneously objective perception and feeling, a means of uniting humans and nature, which also contains humans. His use of the term "symbol" is an extension of Aristotelian *mimesis*, or imitation; he wanted to open up possibilities in theory and comprehension denied by the conventional uses of the term "imitation," especially since the connotation of "copy" was so closely associated with it. Symbol allowed for more flexibility of emotion. Still, Coleridge was careful to limit this flexibility by distinguishing it from allegory, thus maintaining a balance of the objective and the subjective.

The feelings that Coleridge perceived as operating in the creative imagination are only in terminology related to the primitivist insistence of the primacy of instinctive feelings. For him, art – as well as life – was a highly cultivated activity. Uninformed feelings guide with equal potency in all directions, which is no direction. Necessary and vital energies, they nevertheless require channeling; by themselves they remain passive, simple potentialities, needing ideas to set them into motion. Art is the mediator of this interaction. It is true that art must create tensions and excite sensibilities, for it operates in space and time. It arouses emotions, however, only to resolve them. For this reason, technique should not be made an end in itself, and sensibility should not be excited aimlessly. Imagination allows the artist to combine heart and intellect under the direction of nature.

The end of this process is sympathy in the fullest sense of the word: feeling all of one's natural relationships simultaneously and together. Coleridge accepts the emphasis of his time on sympathetic identification, but he carefully limits it. Feeling in its uninformed state yearns, as it were, for sympathy. Imagination allows different manifestations of feeling to merge, so that individual acts of feeling cohere in the total experience of one's being; each act is interpreted in the light of previous acts. The most fully developed sensibilities are, then, the most completely sympathetic. Coleridge again uses Shakespeare as a model of this development. Unlike lesser poets with less integrated sympathies, Shakespeare does not invest his private feelings in his matter. Rather, he fuses truth in his own being – by imagination – and then transmits this truth, which is also his created self. This process is most clearly seen in his creation of characters in his plays; there it is as if Shakespeare transforms himself into his characters, by that act becoming one with them. Coleridge probably would not mind being told that this concept transformed the practice of acting in the twentieth century.

Coleridge decreed that a similar, if less conspicuous, fusion should take place in any work of art. All art works through the fusing caldron of the imagination, heated by attendant feelings; it produces objects which compel emotional participation. In this way, art creates truth and unites artist and audience in the emergent act of creation. The imagination duplicates nature. More than this: it becomes nature by realizing nature. It is the godlike power in humans, and draws humans up to God. It is more than simply a means of realizing truth, if that is simple: it is the vessel in which humans are assimilated into nature, the vehicle by which they are drawn into the course of progressive creation.

Coleridge was indeed a primary force in the development of modern literary criticism. Of the five generally accepted divisions of literary theory – genetic or intentional, formal, affective, mimetic, and intertextual – his work provides the theoretical foundation for or is compatible with the latter four. Notably, these were the most widely practiced modes of criticism in the twentieth century. Most of the leading critics of the middle of the century – I. A. Richards, M. H. Abrams, Kenneth Burke, Cleanth Brooks, and the New Critics in general – paid lavish tribute to him. T. E. Hulme, at the outset an outspoken dissenter, in the end adopted Coleridgean positions. Though later critics, from the affectives to the intertextualists to the deconstructionists, have acknowledged their indebtedness less overtly, it remains discernible. For example, both Geoffrey Hartman and Harold Bloom began their careers with works closely derived from or focusing on Coleridgean premises.

Coleridge considered himself primarily a metaphysician. Later philosophers have found this curious, because his metaphysics – largely inspired by German Idealism – has generally been considered a failure. Still, John Stuart Mill, the person most qualified to judge, considered Coleridge one of the two seminal minds of the age, and later commentators have uniformly confirmed his judgment, though some have deplored it. The truth of the matter seems to be that, however his personal contributions are assessed, Coleridge stands at the basis of the modern consciousness. Whether later thinkers respond to him positively or negatively, they all begin with him. This necessary dependence alone accounts for the extraordinarily divergent range of assessment of Coleridge's significance: praise him or damn him, follow him or reject him, they cannot do without him.

Principal criticism

Biographia Literaria, 1817
Coleridge's Shakespearean Criticism, 1930 (Thomas Middleton Raysor, editor)
Coleridge's Miscellaneous Criticism, 1936 (Thomas Middleton Raysor, editor)
Notebooks, 1957–1986 (4 volumes) (Kathleen Coburn, editor)

Other major works and literary forms

Though Samuel Taylor Coleridge produced less than one-tenth of what he promised and ill health plagued him throughout his life, he still managed to publish an impressive amount of writing in a variety of forms: poetry, drama, translation, periodical essays, psychological self-help manuals, and political and social analysis. He also delivered several notable series of literary and political lectures. In all these genres, with the exception of drama and possibly the periodical essay, Coleridge's work was successful; some of his works have become classics of world literature. The poems include *The Rime of the Ancient Mariner* (1798), "France: An Ode," "Frost at Midnight," *Christabel* (1816), "Kubla Khan," and *Dejection: An Ode* (1802). Though his output was small, his eminence as a poet is unquestioned, his work unique: no one else has created masterpieces quite like his. The significance of his work in the analysis of church, state, and government is less well-known but equally profound. His principal text in this field is *On the Constitution of the Church and State, According to the Idea of Each: With Aids Toward a Right Judgment on the Late Catholic Bill* (1830). Finally, at a time when public speaking was still a dramatic art, he was renowned as a lecturer and conversationalist. After his death, *Specimens of the Table Talk of the Late Samuel Taylor Coleridge* (1835), *Letters, Conversations, and Recollections of S. T. Coleridge* (1836), and various lectures were still preserved and circulated. His drama *Remorse* had a successful run in 1813.

PLAYS
The Fall of Robespierre, 1794 (with Robert Southey)
Remorse, 1813
Zapolya, 1817

POETRY
Poems on Various Subjects, 1796, 1797 (with Charles Lamb and Charles Lloyd)
A Sheet of Sonnets, 1796 (with W. L. Bowles, Robert Southey, and others)
Lyrical Ballads, 1798 (with William Wordsworth)
The Rime of the Ancient Mariner, 1798
Dejection: An Ode, 1802
Christabel, 1816
Sibylline Leaves, 1817
The Complete Poetical Works of Samuel Taylor Coleridge, 1912 (2 volumes; Ernest Hartley Coleridge, editor)

NONFICTION
The Watchman, 1796
The Friend, 1809–1810, 1818
"The Statesman's Manual," 1816
"A Lay Sermon," 1817
Aids to Reflection, 1825
On the Constitution of the Church and State, According to the Idea of Each: With Aids Toward a Right Judgment on the Late Catholic Bill, 1830
Specimens of the Table Talk of the Late Samuel Taylor Coleridge, 1835
Letters, Conversations, and Recollections of S. T. Coleridge, 1836
Letters of Samuel Taylor Coleridge, 1855 (2 volumes; Ernest Hartley Coleridge, editor)

TRANSLATION
Wallenstein, 1800 (of Friedrich Schiller's plays *Die Piccolomini* and *Wallensteins Tod*)

MISCELLANEOUS
The Collected Works of Samuel Taylor Coleridge, 1961– (Kathleen Coburn, et al., editors)

Further reading

Barfield, Owen. *What Coleridge Thought*, 1971.
Bate, Walter Jackson. *Coleridge*, 1968.
Beer, John B. *Coleridge, the Visionary*, 1959.
Coburn, Kathleen, ed. *Inquiring Spirit: A New Presentation of Coleridge from His Published and Unpublished Prose Writings*, 1951.
Hanson, Lawrence. *Life of S. T. Coleridge: The Early Years*, 1938.
Holmes, Richard. *Coleridge: Early Visions*, 1989.
Lowes, John Livingston. *The Road to Xanadu: A Study in the Ways of the Imagination*, 1927.
McGann, Jerome J. "The *Biographica Literaria* and the Contentions of English Romanticism," in *Coleridge's "Biographica Literaria": Text and Meaning*, 1989. Edited by Frederick Burwick.
Nethercot, A. H. *The Road to Tryermaine*, 1939.
Potter, Stephen. *Coleridge and S. T. C.*, 1935.
Richards, I. A. *Coleridge on Imagination*, 1934.
Stallknecht, Newton P. *Strange Seas of Thought*, 1945.
Willey, Basil. *Samuel Taylor Coleridge*, 1967.

JAMES LIVINGSTON

See also Hazlitt; Romanticism; Wordsworth

Comedy

The term "comedy" derives from the Greek words *kōmos*, a festival, and *ōdos*, a singer. It originally identified any play or other literary composition with a nontragic ending.

In the sixth century B.C., or earlier, the Greeks established an annual festival to honor the god Dionysus. His festival, the City (from the Greek *keitai*, he lies, recumbent) Dionysia, was celebrated in March. Eventually, the cosmopolitan City Dionysia was succeeded by a second, domestic festival called the Lenaea (wine press), held in January. The traditional date for the appearance of tragedy as a part of the City (Great) Dionysia is 534 B.C. Tragedies appear to have been acted as a part of the festival every year thereafter. No comedy at the City Dionysia is mentioned until 486 B.C. However, the dramas at the Lenaea were solely comic in 442 B.C., and although tragedy was added in 432 B.C., comedy continued to dominate.

The very earliest comedies have not survived, but they were apparently burlesque and parodic, marked by crude clowning. The origin of comedy as the genre eventually came to be understood – any of the more or less humorous treatments of characters and their situations – dates from 425 B.C., the year in which the first surviving play by Aristophanes was produced. Although Aristophanes established many of the conventions of the genre, his brilliant combination of poetry, obscenity, farce, and wit makes him a unique comic writer. While the writers of Greek tragedy were restricted in their subject matter to myth and history, the writers of comedy were free to explore contemporary themes. Thus, Aristophanes pokes fun at the philosopher Socrates, the demagogic politician Cleon, the tragedian Euripides, and many other living contemporaries.

The characteristic which originally distinguished comedy from tragedy is usually still observed: at the conclusion of the story, play, or film, all conflicts must be resolved in some reasonably satisfactory manner, order must replace disorder. For example, in Aristophanes' best-known comedy, *Lysistrata* (411 B.C.), the Peloponnesian War between Athens and Sparta is ended by a hilarious but successful "sex strike," a withdrawal of conjugal rights, by the women of both city-states, and the play concludes with the former enemies singing and dancing their way offstage together. In actuality, the war continued for another seven years, finally ending in the total defeat of Aristophanes' Athens by the Spartans. Comedy resolves conflicts as they ought to be resolved, rather than as they so often are actually resolved.

The plays of Aristophanes point up another enduring, and somewhat paradoxical, quality of comedy. Aristophanes attacks, sometimes savagely, Socrates as a charlatan and a Sophist, and Euripides as a misogynist (historical evidence does not seem to support either charge). The reader is thus reminded that in addition to being the vehicle for satisfactory conclusions, comedy is always, to some degree, an aggressive exercise. Every joke is "on" someone, even if it is only the speaker or writer himself or herself.

It could be argued that every humorous situation, at least to some degree, involves the discomfiture of someone. In slapstick, certainly among the crudest forms of comedy, the discomfiture is obvious. If a pretty, popular student, her arms filled with books, slips and tumbles down the stairs, her skirt flying up toward her face, her books sailing through the air in all directions, the onlooker's first response is likely to be a laugh. The laugh is generally followed by feelings of guilt, but the original reaction is understandable. When she tumbles, her many virtues – her prettiness, her popularity, her studiousness – all work against her because they increase her capacity for humiliation. The pun, another basic form of humor, may appear to be victimless. However, there is a reason why a common reaction to the most inventive of puns is a groan. The punster is exhibiting a linguistic association, often quite a tortured one, that he or she has made and the hearer has not yet made. The groan that so often follows is the hearer's grudging admission that the pun has struck home. After all, the verbal fencing in Shakespeare is called "fencing" for good reason.

Aristophanes is the only writer of so-called Old Comedy (fifth century B.C.) whose work has survived. The term was coined merely to distinguish it from the comedy that developed later (New Comedy). The later playwrights eschewed the violent attacks upon living persons and wrote more of a comedy of situation. This New Comedy of the Greeks served as a model for the Latin comedies which eventually flourished in the Roman world. Bawdiness is another characteristic of Aristophanic comedy which, while certainly not absent from New Comedy, is less pervasive there. Three possible explanations may exist for the degree of this bawdiness. First, comedy originated in a fertility rite. Second, the ancient Greeks did not regard sex acts as sinful. And, third, Aristophanes may have had a personal taste for bawdiness. Sexual comedy has existed from the beginning, but it has been sometimes more, sometimes less acceptable from era to era.

A continuing literary debate concerns the equality or inferiority of comedy to tragedy as a genre. Some critics argue that tragedy travels better than comedy – that is, what is tragic to one age is tragic to every age, whereas what is humorous to one age may not be humorous to the next. For example, the comedies of William Shakespeare (even excluding the "dark" comedies of his later period), despite their many virtues, do not seem particularly humorous to later generations. (A notable exception is the rude mechanics' play of Pyramus and Thisbe in *A Midsummer Night's Dream.*) The Elizabethan delight in profuse, prolonged, and elaborate wordplay for comic effect was a taste that did not survive beyond the middle of the seventeenth century. Also, Ben Jonson's comedies of humors from the same period, while interesting in many ways, contain few scenes that could be described as really funny today.

On the other hand, Geoffrey Chaucer's comic scenes in *The Canterbury Tales* (1387–1400) clearly continue to succeed over six hundred years after they were written. Miguel de Cervantes' novel *Don Quixote* (1605, 1615), with the exception of the long pastoral passages, still delights. Molière's comedies from the late seventeenth century have been regularly produced ever since. Even the 2,500-year-old *Lysistrata* of Aristophanes, despite its many archaisms, found popular favor as an antiwar comedy during the 1970s, the period of the Vietnam War.

Throughout the eighteenth and nineteenth centuries, Oliver Goldsmith, Richard Brinsley Sheridan, Oscar Wilde, and their contemporaries wrote satirical comedies grounded in a world of shared values and of appropriate and inappropriate behavior. The inappropriate behavior was the stuff of comedy. By the twentieth century, the oft discussed angst had set in, the result of all human institutions and all religious, philosophical, and social systems having been called into question. Within this atmosphere, a new and very dark comedy emerged. Samuel Beckett, in his plays *Waiting for Godot* (1952) and *Endgame* (1957) and his novel *How It Is* (1961), presents a world which is purposeless, where the end of all effort is futility. Since human beings are cosmic accidents whose lives have no point, they are unfit subjects for tragedy. There can *be* no tragedy; therefore, Beckett's works become comedies by definition.

Though absurdity and comedy are not necessarily synonymous, the strange works of Franz Kafka have been called comic. One critic has likened Kafka's universe to an immense bureaucracy where his characters are shunted from one department to another, never getting a satisfactory answer from anyone with whom they speak (or, for that matter, never really knowing what questions to pose). And in his darkly comic novel *The Day of the Locust* (1939), Nathanael West paints a portrait of modern America almost too bleak to be borne.

This "metaphysical" or "tragic" comedy continues to be written, existing side by side with more traditional comic forms which continue to flourish in great variety.

Further reading

Bermel, Albert. *Farce: A History from Aristophanes to Woody Allen*, 1982.
Casson, Lionel. *Masters of Ancient Comedy; Selections from: Aristophanes, Menander, Plautus, Terence*, 1960.
Charney, Maurice. *Comedy High and Low: An Introduction to the Experience of Comedy*, 1978.
Jump, John Davies. *Burlesque*, 1972.
McFadden, George. *Discovering the Comic*, 1982.
Shepperson, Archibald Bolling. *The Novel in Motley; A History of the Burlesque Novel in English*, 1967.

PATRICK ADCOCK

See also Aristotle

Continental Theory

From naturalism to Symbolism and expressionism

Literary naturalism is so called because its central concern is with the basic nature, physiological and psychological, hereditary and environmental, of humankind. Its focus is on human beings in real environments. Its ideal is to set up a literary situation much as a scientist would set up an experiment, then to record accurately and dispassionately what happens to people in the situation that evolves. Its method ideally is scientific. Its outcomes ideally are objective.

Naturalism was the dominant literary movement and method of the early twentieth century, although its most significant roots could be traced to the last half of the nineteenth century. Its method has affected not only literature, most particularly the novel, the short story, and drama, but also the growth of modern critical schools, whose function it is to evaluate and interpret literature.

Between 1885 and 1905 another literary movement, Symbolism, swept France and eventually spread through much of Europe, where it had a significant influence. Although Symbolism was never the clearly focused, soundly articulated movement that naturalism became, it, along with naturalism, led to literary experimentation that resulted in the more modernist school of writing. The Symbolists were the spiritual offspring of the Romantics, who had established a powerfully influential literary movement late in the eighteenth and early in the nineteenth centuries. Although both the naturalists and the Symbolists had roots in literary Romanticism, the Symbolists were more directly influenced by it.

Whereas Romantic writers considered and represented experience in terms of their feelings, the Symbolists went a step further, emphasizing not just feelings but the psychological states of being, linking the mind with the senses in extreme ways, often enhancing the senses by the use of hallucinatory drugs and other artificial means, which caused them often to be referred to as "the Decadents." Symbolism as it developed, was a more comfortable domain for poets and playwrights than for novelists and socially-critical dramatists, who generally found a more comfortable and compatible metier in naturalism.

By the beginning of the twentieth century many literary artists who had rankled under the prescriptive constraints of naturalism began to strike out on their own into new literary territory that was derived more directly from Symbolism than from any other school. The expressionists stopped seeking the kinds of absolutes that the naturalists had pursued: their concern was emotion, not objectivity. Like the writing of the Symbolists, expressionism often was highly abstract and was more concerned with psychology, a pursuit that is necessarily focused on individuals, than with sociology, a pursuit that, in naturalism, was chiefly involved with presenting dispassionate depictions of whole societies or of major subgroups within such societies. The expressionists often found drama and poetry the most congenial forms of literature.

The roots of literary naturalism

The clearest early articulation of the tenets of literary naturalism are found in *Le Roman expérimental* (1880; *The Experimental Novel*, 1893) of Émile Zola, which essentially indicates the method of the movement and establishes its boundaries. Well before the appearance of this work, however, the spirit of naturalism was in the air, and this spirit infused much of the most significant writing in a France that had passed through a revolution to become a republic and that, like much of the Western world, was now becoming increasingly industrialized, urbanized, and scientific in its outlook. In 1866 Zola was extraordinarily affected by the scientific approach to literature that he found the brothers Edmond and Jules de Goncourt employing in their collaborative novel *Germinie Lacerteux* (1865; English translation, 1887). Zola, a writer with six novels already to his credit, reviewed the Goncourts' novel with enthusiasm and expressed his appreciation of their detached and objective presentation of character.

Zola applauded the Goncourts' ability to present the protagonist, a simple servant girl, in the light of her physiological and psychological motivations, forthrightly depicted, and their success in presenting her moral and physical illness. In doing so, they reflected accurately some of the ills of the society of which she was a part. Zola as a novelist found an artistic kinship with the Goncourts; as a critic, he welcomed the fresh and honest approach they took. In their novel, he found a credibility that was absent from much of the Romantic and realistic literature of his day.

Honoré de Balzac's attempts to record the realities of society and to interpret them honestly had early impressed Zola. Balzac, however, was a figure poised between Romanticism and realism. As Zola's theory of literary naturalism developed, it demanded a more scientific orientation than would have been possible for anyone writing before the scientific and social advances of the last half of the nineteenth century.

Charles Darwin's *On the Origin of Species* (1859) had a profound intellectual effect upon late-nineteenth-century writers, as did his later book, *The Descent of Man and Selection in Relation to Sex* (1871). Soon afterward, Karl Marx was promulgating revolutionary economic ideas in the three volumes of *Das Kapital* (1867, 1885, 1894; *Capital: A Critique of Political Economy*, 1886, 1907, 1909, better known as *Das Kapital*), completed by his collaborator, Friedrich Engels. This seminal work forced people in France and throughout Europe to rethink and reevaluate many of their fundamental beliefs about society as economy affects it. Auguste Comte in *Cours de philosophie positive* (1830–1842; *The Positive Philosophy of Auguste Comte*, 1853) called for an approach to studying society that would apply scientific principles to entities as fluid and dynamic as human social institutions. By so doing, he provided the impetus for the birth of sociology as a field of serious study.

By the end of the nineteenth century and the beginning of the twentieth, people were becoming aware of Sigmund Freud and of his pioneering work on the unconscious, which revealed aspects of human psychology that had for eons been cloaked in darkness and of which many preferred not to be made aware. Victorianism was not confined to Great Britain at that time, and the new ideas that filled the air were discomfiting to those with prudish attitudes.

Nevertheless, in this climate, literary realism flourished in France and elsewhere in Europe. With the publication of *Madame Bovary* (1857; English translation, 1886), Gustave Flaubert moved beyond the realism of his day to a new form of the novel which had yet to be given a name and whose tenets were not fully identified until the publication in 1880 of Zola's naturalistic manifesto, *The Experimental Novel*. Flaubert had imbibed the intellectual climate, scientifically based, that produced Darwin, Marx, and Freud. He was among the first to write a novel whose characters are socially, economically, and psychologically determined in the ways that naturalistic characters must be.

Émile Zola and Claude Bernard

Literary naturalism flourished in France well before the publication of Zola's *The Experimental Novel* and *Les Romanciers naturalistes* (1881). Zola himself moved toward naturalism in *Thérèse Raquin* (1867; English translation, 1881) and more completely in his contribution to *Les Soirées de Medan* (1880), a collection of stories that Zola's followers regarded as a literary manifesto. Guy de Maupassant in many of his short stories; the Goncourts in *Germinie Lacerteux, Manette Salomon* (1867), and *Madame Gervaisais* (1869); Alphonse Daudet in *Fromont jeune et Risler aîné* (1874; *Fromont the Young and Risler the Elder*, 1880) and *Jack* (1876; English translation, 1877); and Joris-Karl Huysmans in *Marthe: Histoire d'une fille* (1876; *Marthe: Story of a Prostitute*, 1927) were writing naturalistically before Zola had delineated and formalized the naturalistic method into a coherent theory in his critical writing.

The major impetus for Zola's critical writing about naturalism came from a noted French physiologist, Claude Bernard, whose *Introduction à l'étude de la médecine expérimentale* (1865; *Introduction to the Study of Experimental Medicine*, 1927) provided Zola's direct and acknowledged basis for his series of essays on the experimental novel. Zola points out that in the eyes of many, medicine, like writing, was at that time an art, not a science; Bernard, while acknowledging that medicine was in his day an art, nevertheless recognizes the need to make it as scientific as possible – not to make it less of an art necessarily, but to make it more rational and scientifically based than it had been.

Bernard's work owes much to August Comte's *Cours de philosophie positive*, which sets forth the three stages of thought as it moves toward maturity: fictitious (theological), abstract (metaphysical), and positive (scientific). The last, triumphant stage, the positive stage, is descriptive rather than explanatory, just as Bernard's experimentalism is.

Bernard seeks to redirect medicine from what he calls empiricism, which he defines as haphazard observation, to an experimental methodology that, in his mind, will bring it closer to truth than empiricism could. Bernard distinguishes between the sciences of observation, whose literary equivalent would be realism, and the sciences of experimentation, whose literary equivalent Zola considered to be naturalism.

Bernard contends that all experimentation is based upon doubt. Experimenters want to discover something and, maintaining their objectivity, they set in motion a validly designed experiment. The experiment will then produce phenomena that the experimenter must accept, regardless of personal predilections, as long as the experiment was initially valid. Although experimentation is in some ways easier with inert matter, as in chemistry, than with living matter, as in certain areas of physics, biology, and psychology, Bernard does not consider the spontaneity of living bodies to preclude experimentation grounded in scientific method. It is this element of Bernard's theory that Zola embraces most enthusiastically. He contends that when novelists select a setting and a cast of characters who act out their destinies within a given context, these novelists have set up an experiment in much the manner that scientific experimenters do.

Determinism, scientific and literary

According to Bernard, the inanimate body possesses only the external environment, whereas the living body, the higher organism, exists in an internal environment that has constant physicochemical properties like those in the external environment. From this line of reasoning, Bernard concludes that an absolute determinism exists in the conditions of natural phenomena. Those elements that determine phenomena are causes, and they are valid for animate and inanimate phenomena alike. The experimental sciences, in Bernard's view, are concerned with how things happen rather than with why things happen.

Zola, in considering whether Bernard's method is applicable to literature, concludes that it is, because authors, like experimenters, can be virtual photographers of phenomena, careful observers who set up carefully calculated situations that illustrate causes, which they present according to their own truths rather than according to their personal preferences. Writers, then, rather than being manipulators of the data their experiments yield, will be objective reporters of them, adhering strictly to both scientific principles and methods as they set up their experiments. They attempt to wrest from the situations that they have set in motion and that they observe as artists the deterministic causes of the inevitable outcomes, which Zola regards as approaches to truth. It is by such a set of principles that Zola, as critic, judged naturalistic writing, and by which he, as novelist, was guided in both his observations and his writing.

The method of literary naturalism

As Zola applies Bernard's principles to literature, the method he suggests consists of observing facts in nature and in the nature of humankind, in studying the mechanisms of these facts, in acting upon these mechanisms, and in modifying the circumstances and environment without deviating from the laws of nature. Zola admits that the results will not immediately lead to certainties like those obtained from chemical or physiological experimentation, but he asserts that when writers follow such procedures, literature will move closer to approximating scientific methodology. This will result in bringing literature closer to the discovery of truth.

Zola is adamant in his declaration that the novelist's ultimate search must be for truth, and he suggests that his proposed method will bring literature close to being an instrumentality for discovering this absolutistic verity. The artist's invention in literature is derived from producing and directing the phenomena of the true facts which Zola calls the indestructible bases of the artist's materials. In contending that observation indicates but that experimentation teaches, Zola reiterates Bernard's distinction between empiricism and experimentation.

In declaring that the literature of his day paid too much attention to form, Zola repudiated the remaining vestiges of Romanticism and the lingering echoes of neoclassicism that still pervaded some writing. Unlike the neoclassicists and the Romantics, who were concerned with the metaphysical person, Zola called for writers of the experimental novel – by which he meant the naturalistic novel – to study natural people as they are governed by natural physical and chemical laws (heredity) and as their existences are modified by the influences of their surroundings (environment). Zola accurately identified this approach as a natural outgrowth of the scientific emphasis in his century. The result would be a literature for and of an age that was becoming ever more scientific.

The social circulus

Bernard wrote of what he termed the vital circulus, by which process muscular and nervous activity preserves the organs that make blood, while the blood, in turn, nourishes the organs that are necessary for its manufacture. Zola draws another strong parallel here between medicine and literature, identifying what he calls the social circulus, which he considers identical to Bernard's vital circulus. When an organ of society becomes infected in such a way that it taints other organs, causing complicated social disorders (diseases), experimental novelists, according to Zola, must proceed just as experimental physicians do.

Zola's suggested method is to find the simple initial cause through which it is possible to understand and remedy the more complex causes from which the action results. In other words, Zola would hold a mirror up to society as it really exists in an attempt to discover the root causes of its decay. Such a method can succeed only if it remains objective, only if literary method becomes, as it were, a science. Zola's primary aim was to place literature within a controllable, scientific context, giving to it a validity that he considered necessary in a society which thought science and technology held the hope for dealing with all of life's problems.

Determinism versus fatalism

Literary naturalism has been called both an optimistic and a pessimistic approach to literary art. Although as a method for dealing with literary material in a scientific way it is really neutral, accusations that it is based on a pessimistic determinism, because they are so frequent and widespread, cannot be ignored. In order to understand these two portrayals of literary naturalism, it is necessary to realize the differences between determinism and fatalism as Zola presented these two forces.

Zola clearly states that literary naturalists are not fatalists. They are concerned with understanding the nearest determining forces of phenomena so that they can act upon these forces. Fatalism accepts as inevitable what exists, considering it, if not predestined, at least immutable; determinism seeks to understand causes, thereby enabling people to act upon them. In other words, the fatalist is powerless to change events that the determinist (naturalist), through understanding the conditions essential to the appearance of phenomena associated with those events, might be able to adjust.

Not everything can be changed. Humanity is subject, for example, to the Newtonian laws of physics. Not all the laws associated with humankind, however, are equally absolute. Economic, physiological, psychological, and environmental changes can be effected with the result that some human problems can be overcome completely or, at least, minimized.

When people can and do act on the determining causes of phenomena, they cannot be fatalists. They become naturalists in Zola's sense of the word. The moral dimension that Zola ascribes to literary naturalism, then, is that of understanding deterministic forces and through that understanding being in a position to control and, if socially desirable, to seek ways of changing those forces for the good, thereby removing both the social canker and its cause and thus preventing the spread of its disease.

It is not the purpose of the naturalists to present the smiling, upbeat side of life or to manipulate the details of their subject in order to make them more palatable to readers. Because of that, and because socially conscious writers of the time wrote about urban working people at the lower socioeconomic levels, many of their works are depressing to read and have about them an aura of pessimism. Committed naturalists, however, do not write hopelessly of the situations in which they place their characters. There are ways out, if not for their characters as individuals, then eventually for humanity, whose future will be determined by the social changes that come about in societies made aware of their ills. For some types of ills, there may be no amelioration, but such is not the case with most of the social problems about which the naturalists undertook to write.

Zola himself, in the twenty volumes of *Les Rougon-Macquart* (1871–1893; *The Rougon-Macquart Novels*, 1885–1907), writes with admirable insight about the roles of heredity and environment in the lives of people who work in banks, in coal mines, in department stores, and in such pursuits as art and prostitution. By focusing public attention on the situations, brought about deterministically, in the lives of these people, he moved his society a notch closer to being able to alter the conditions oppressing his characters. Such has been the moral impact of many naturalistic writers.

Feelings and reason

In the search for truth, humankind, which Zola labels essentially metaphysical, has to deal with feelings (intuitions) and with reason. Intuition is important because from it are born many of the ideas with which one must grapple in the search for truth. If intuition gives the ideas, reason develops them and, according to Zola, deduces their logical consequences. The personality of the writer is therefore of the utmost importance. Feeling is the wellspring of the experimental method for which Zola calls. Reason intervenes in the products of intuition and organizes the original ideas in such a way that they can lead to the experiment, which for Zola is the essence of searching for truth. He identifies the method, naturalism, as merely a tool. The genius and sensitivity of the experimenter are the *sine qua non* of successful literary naturalism.

Naturalistic novelists must test each fact with a combination of observation and experimentation and must report accurately the outcomes of the experiment if the final product – in this case the naturalistic novel – is to be valid according to the naturalistic canons. Zola warns novelists against deviating from truth because by reporting truth, they will produce great and moral works. Zola does not define fully what he means by truth, and this omission places an unfortunate limitation on his manifesto, which nevertheless provided a strong theoretical basis for literary naturalism in Europe, Great Britain, and the United States.

The decline of literary naturalism in France

Literary realism and naturalism caught on in France and succeeded so well during the half century before and the decade after the publication of Zola's seminal work defining and delineating the naturalistic movement that, by 1890, the French reading public had had an overdose of the penetrating naturalistic novels that piqued consciences and in many cases revealed personal vanities and moral corruption. The major naturalistic writers of the day – Zola, Daudet, Huysmans, Maupassant, Paul Bourget, and Edmond de Goncourt – had been enormously prolific. What they were writing had been appropriate for their times.

If the naturalists contended that human beings, rather than acting, are acted upon, at least they offered the hope that society could change in ways that would help it to overcome its inherent ills, now that these ills had been directly identified and demonstrated. Even though single individuals, particularly those from the lower economic class, might be powerless to alter their own destinies, humanity as an entity could work toward controlling those phenomena that determined the course of human existence. In such a promise, many socially concerned readers found hope and encouragement.

The day of the common man had arrived in France with the French Revolution in 1789. From early in the nineteenth century, science and industrialization offered a new hope to the masses. By the last decade of that century, however, many French people had begun to realize that the new science and the new economy could provide instant solutions neither to their own nor to society's problems. As their skepticism grew, French intellectuals became increasingly disaffected by their society, and they recoiled from the naturalistic works that now seemed to offer more pessimism than hope.

Some of the naturalistic writers themselves began to reassess what they were doing and what their society was about. Huysmans' antinaturalist novel, *À rebours* (1884; *Against the Grain*, 1922) was followed in 1887 by a strident antinaturalist manifesto written and signed by five of Zola's followers. Bourget's *Le Disciple* (1889; *The Disciple*, 1898) marked another significant defection from the ranks of the naturalistic novelists. France was now ready for the new literary forms that were soon to appear.

Naturalism in Germany

Just as France moved toward realism and then naturalism in the first seven decades of the nineteenth century, so did Germany move away from the literature of the past toward a more solidly realistic literature as the century continued. With the founding of the new German Empire under Otto Bismarck in 1871, Germans embraced vigorously new technological, economic, and industrial possibilities. Society gained an increased respect for inventors, bankers, merchants, and engineers. Modern medicine began to come of age in Germany when Wilhelm Konrad Röntgen discovered the X-ray, which brought to him a Nobel Prize in 1901, and when Robert Koch discovered bacteria, for which he received a Nobel Prize in 1905. As modern techniques were becoming an accepted part of German technology and science, Germany's literary leaders were calling stridently for a new, modern literature.

Theodor Fontane, a great admirer of the realism of his contemporary, Russian novelist Ivan Turgenev, complained that the German fiction of his time lacked credibility. He urged writers to write accurately and in detail about their times, presenting in an undistorted way the lives and the society of their age or that of the preceding generation. He scorned writing about such distant historical periods as the Middle Ages. Fontane was concerned with the question of what happens when a member of the upper class, usually male, marries someone of a lower class. His writing also focuses considerable attention on romantic mismatches and on adultery, topics that some readers found offensive.

The Germans considered naturalism, which they termed interchangeably both *Hochrealismus* and *Naturalismus*, to be closely akin to realism and a direct descendant of it. The intellectual currents that had led French novelists to naturalism were much alive in Germany's intellectual circles, where Marxism had gained a substantial foothold and where Ernst Haeckel, Darwin's foremost German follower and popularizer, was spreading Darwinism and its materialistic world-view within his not-inconsiderable sphere of intellectual influence.

Comte's theories of society found their way into Germany largely through the philosophy of John Stuart Mill, the English utilitarian philosopher whose ideas the Germans eagerly embraced. The temper of the times was scientific and materialistic. The cry for a new literature to replace the neoclassicism and Romanticism of the recent past was widespread. Zola's Rougon-Macquart series was popular in Germany at this time and provided a model for writers who wished to move toward a heightened realism just as his essays on the experimental novel provided them with a theoretical basis for their work.

Germans were also reading avidly such Russian writers as Lev Tolstoi, Ivan Turgenev, and Fedor Dostoevskii, whose vigor and whose literary formalism they much admired. They were even more affected by some of the social thinking that emanated from Scandinavia in the works of such writers as Georg Brandes, the critic; of dramatists such as Henrik Ibsen and August Strindberg; and of a broad field of novelists whose work was popular in Germany at the time, among them Jens Peter Jacobsen, Knut Hamsun, Hermann Bang, Holger Drachmann, and Ola Hansson. Most of these writers dealt directly with social and economic problems and, in so doing, developed a new kind of hero, a passive, populist hero who was in essence antiheroic.

The brothers Hart and German naturalism

Obviously influenced by Zola's work, Heinrich and Julius Hart undertook to write a huge work similar to *The Rougon-Macquart Novels*. They called their work *Das Lied der Menschheit* (1888–1896) and originally planned to write twenty-four books under this title. In actuality, they produced only three of the projected volumes. Before they embarked on this project, however, they had published their *Kritische Waffengänge* (1882–1884), six critical pieces that provided the theoretical underpinnings for German naturalism and that helped to turn Berlin into an important center of progressive literary thought. These pieces, much influenced by Zola's critical essays, call for writers to deal with real social problems and to be clinically accurate in presenting them.

Arno Holz and Johannes Schlaf had already demanded a new approach to literature that they termed *konsquenter Naturalismus* (consistent naturalism). Holz's *Die Kunst: Ihr Wesen und Gesetze* (1891–1892) was considered the manifesto of German naturalism. Holz sought to bring art and nature, science and literature, into harmony.

Literary ferment erupted throughout urban, industrialized Germany at about the same time. A number of literary societies had sprung up and met regularly to discuss the new literature; some of these societies published journals that won considerable acceptance among those who sensed the need for writing to move toward a modern scientific approach similar to that for which Zola was calling in France. Friedrich Nietzsche, much affected by Darwin's theories of evolution and of natural selection, advanced the notion that a race of supermen could be produced; his repudiation of conventional moral codes fueled the literary fires in a Germany that was already explosively energetic and whose intellectuals were at that time juggling so many iconoclastic social and economic ideologies that the stage was well set for drastic, revolutionary change.

The naturalistic novel in Germany

Although the novel had unquestionably been the most popular medium for naturalistic expression in France, such was not the case in Germany, where the most forceful expression of the new literary school occurred in the theater. Nevertheless, numerous worthwhile naturalistic novels came from the pens of German writers, among whom two of the most noteworthy transitional writers were Detlev von Liliencron and Theodor Fontane. The Germany of their day was prosperous and, because of industrial expansion, was producing a new class of citizen, a class of industrial workers who lived a hand-to-mouth existence crowded together in metropolitan slums. These workers did not share the prosperity of the class above them, a bourgeoisie much like the central characters in Thomas Mann's *Buddenbrooks* (1901; English translation, 1924), who grew rich through the labors of the people they oppressed.

Liliencron and Fontane were both conservatives, both more closely akin to the middle class than to the lower class. Their work, however, came to imbibe much of the naturalistic spirit and to focus on matters like those that the French naturalists had found enticing, even though both of them wrote critically of the working class. Liliencron, a baron without inheritance, for example, complained that its members were disrespectful. He managed in his writing, however, to capture details of the lives of working-class people and to present them much as a naturalist might have. His depiction of the loneliness, alienation, and personal isolation one feels in a large city is particularly notable; such urban alienation is a recurring and controlling theme in much naturalistic writing. Fontane's novels reflect his society with great accuracy and, because they do, they dwell on life in the large, industrialized communities that characterized Fontane's Germany. If he expressed reservations about the way Germany was changing, he at least seemed resigned to the change and was skillful in depicting his world.

Liliencron and Fontane were not the dedicated and committed naturalists that Holz was, but it must be remembered that the German naturalists as a group never felt the same spirit of reform that one finds in naturalistic writers throughout the rest of Europe or in the naturalistic literature of the United States. Germany under Bismarck had soothed the social consciences of many artists by offering them state subsidies while at the same time suggesting that they might prefer to focus on the government's "average citizen" rather than on the sick and decadent. Governmental censorship was rife throughout the country, and theater was so tightly controlled that private theaters open only to subscribers came to be the sole places in which much modern drama could be performed.

Holz set forth his definition of naturalism in *Die Kunst: Ihr Wesen und Gesetze*. With his collaborator, Johannes Schlaf, Holz called for the reproduction of an unaltered reality in writing. They transferred to literary method the idea of *Sekundenstil*, a rapid-fire style of taking photographs in which all the realities of life are caught as completely as possible. This method of capturing reality, basically a cinematographic technique, later lent itself to elements of the expressionistic theater, particularly to the productions staged by Max Reinhardt. Novelists attempted to employ this style, but the results were often quite boring because of the banality and repetitiveness of the dialogue. It was in German theater that the *Sekundenstil* had its greatest impact.

The consciously naturalistic novels of the day were largely *Grosstadt-romane*, novels about large cities, usually about Berlin. Notable among them are Max Kretzer's *Meister Timpe* (1888) and *Das Gesicht Christi* (1897); John Henry Mackay's *Die Anarchisten* (1891; *The Anarchists*, 1891); and Hermann Conradi's *Adam Mensch* (1889), which was so condemnatory of its contemporary society that German courts of law declared it immoral and banned its distribution. Karl Bleibtreu creates a protagonist in *Grössenwahn* (1887) who flees from the world and loses himself in Darwinism. Hermann Sudermann in *Frau Sorge* (1887; *Dame Care*, 1891) chooses a rustic setting in which to show how a capitalist economy grinds down good, simple people.

Among German writers, the main philosophical shift that affected the direction in which naturalism grew was the shift in emphasis from the collective social values suggested in the writings of Karl Marx to the more individualistic values that the works of Friedrich Nietzsche set forth. His idea of genetically superior people pervaded the thinking of many Germans up to and during the dictatorship of Adolf Hitler. Mackay's *The Anarchists*, Casar Flaischlen's *Jost Seyfried* (1905), and Heinrich Lilienfein's *Modernus* (1904) are among the early reflections of this tendency that survived in much German literature and thought through the first decades of the twentieth century.

Naturalism and German drama

When Silesian playwright Gerhart Hauptmann brought to the Berlin stage his naturalistic drama *Die Weber* (1892; *The Weavers*, 1899), a play about the historical revolt in 1842 of the Silesian weavers against their intolerable working conditions, audiences reacted to the point that there were fisticuffs in the theater. Hauptmann had written three earlier plays somewhat in the naturalistic tradition – *Von Sonnenaufgang* (1889; *Before Dawn*, 1909), *Das Friedensfest* (1890; *The Reconciliation*, 1910), and *Einsame Menschen* (1891; *Lonely Lives*, 1898). None of these, however, had taken Berlin by storm the way *The Weavers* did.

This play makes its dramatic impact because Hauptmann had the skill to present with great authenticity the grinding poverty and lack of leadership among the workers and to reveal simultaneously the kind of trap their employer is in because of the competitive pressures upon him from foreign industry. Finally, when the militia comes in to break up the revolt, it is clear that there are no winners. Deterministic forces act indiscriminately upon workers and employers alike. If any villain exists, it is the system that allows such forces to crush everyone who lies in their path.

Hauptmann, a Nobel laureate in literature in 1912, was the central figure in the rise of naturalism in German drama. Although he was not strictly naturalistic in all of his dramatic writing, he is generally acknowledged to be one of Germany's most significant naturalistic playwrights. His *Fuhrmann Henschel* (1898; *Drayman Henschel*, 1913), *Rose Bernd* (1903; English translation, 1913), and *Die Ratten* (1911; *The Rats*, 1929), although not so well known as *The Weavers*, are models of naturalistic drama.

In his first play, *Die Ehre* (1889; *Honor*, 1915), Hermann Sudermann presents in alternating scenes the life of the family of a Berlin factory owner and that of the family of one of the workers. Sudermann followed this play with the much more decadent *Sodoms Ende* (1890; *A Man and His Picture*, 1903), the shock of whose subject matter caused many playgoers to lose sight of how well written the play was.

Although naturalism never really developed in Austria because the country was slow to industrialize, two Austrian authors, Arthur Schnitzler and Hermann Bahr, employed naturalistic techniques in their drama. Both were far removed from the working class and wrote about encroaching industrialism more from the standpoint of management than from that of labor.

Schnitzler wrote fine dialogue, and his fidelity to realistic presentation was sustained for almost two decades in such plays as *Liebelei* (1895; *Light-o'-Love*, 1912), *Das Vermachtnis* (1898; *The Legacy*, 1911), *Der grüne Kakadu* (1899; *The Green Cockatoo*, 1913), *Der Schleier der Beatrice* (1900), *Der junge Medardus* (1910), and *Professor Bernhardi* (1912; English translation, 1913). Bahr, who was Austria's leading literary critic of the period, showed a leaning toward naturalism in his dramas, among which the best exemplars are *Das Tschaperl* (1898) and *Das Konzert* (1909), which is generally regarded as his best play.

Among the German playwrights who followed in the naturalistic tradition were Ernst von Wildenbruch, Max Halbe, Otto Erich Hartleben, and George Hirschfeld. From the collaboration of Holz and Johannes Schlaf came one of the most conspicuously naturalistic plays of the period, *Die Familie Selicke* (1890).

Naturalism's most vigorous outlet in Germany was the theater, particularly the Freie Bühne (Free Theater) in Berlin, which was organized as a private, subscription theater and thus was not subject to the repressive censorship then prevalent. But for the Freie Bühne, many of the most seminal and exciting plays of the naturalistic movement might never have been performed.

German writers of the day were more influenced by Ibsen and Strindberg – both of whose works were performed at the Freie Bühne – than by France's major naturalistic novelists, although German intellectuals around the turn of the century read widely in the works of these novelists, as they did in the works of the leading Russian writers.

The new naturalism placed significant limitations upon authors, dictating to a large extent that they concern themselves with urban settings and with characters from the working class. Naturalism had been for many a welcome relief from the sentimentality of much writing in the recent past, but it soon became apparent to those who tried to be faithful to the naturalistic credo that even the photographic realism for which they struggled fell short of revealing the absolute truth toward which they hoped they were working. No matter how faithfully and realistically recorded, all writing was subject to the impressions of those receiving it, and those impressions varied from person to person.

Literary naturalism in Scandinavia

At a time when much European literature was unabashedly Romantic, some writers in the Scandinavian countries were already rejecting the idealism and sentimentality of literature that evaded the realities of life. In *En dansk students eventyr* (written 1824; published 1843), Poul Martin Møller openly attacked the sentimentality that pervaded much of the literature of his day and made a strenuous effort to be as realistic as possible in his representations. Hans Christian Andersen, best known for his fairy tales, deals head-on with economic determinism when he writes in *Kun en Spillemand* (1837; *Only a Fiddler*, 1845) about a young musician whose poverty keeps him from his music. In his philosophical novel *At være eller ikke være* (1857; *To Be or Not to Be?*, 1857), published, quite remarkably, before Darwin and Marx had published their notable works, he condemns the materialism that he fears is encompassing his society.

Consciousness of women's rights also came to Scandinavia before it reached the rest of Europe, and numerous precursors to Ibsen and Strindberg assaulted the reading public with the kinds of social concerns that these two dramatists were to explore so fruitfully. The Norwegian novelist Camilla Collett was deeply concerned with the status of women and with determinism in her realistic novel *Amtmandens døttre* (1855). In *Det går an* (1839; *Sara Videbeck*, 1919), Carl Jonas Love Almqvist argues, with a vigor not unlike that of late-twentieth-century feminists, for a woman's right to eschew marriage and take up a profession – which is exactly what Norwegian naturalistic novelist Amalie Skram did when she left an unhappy marriage in 1877 to pursue a career in writing. In *Hellemyrsfolket* (1887–1898), a cycle of novels reminiscent of Zola's Rougon-Macquart cycle, Skram concentrates on the problems of independent-minded women who face life in a deterministic society.

Georg Brandes, a Danish critic whose pronouncements calling for a naturalistic approach to writing predate by five years the publication of Zola's *The Experimental Novel*, asked that literature examine the real problems of life, that it not isolate itself from social realities. Jens Peter Jacobsen, a biologist who had read his Darwin well, heeded Brandes' call in his novella *Mogens* (1872; English translation, 1921), in which the protagonist is viewed as a physical as well as a spiritual being, a significant departure from the Romantic writing of the past. His later novel *Fry Marie Grubbe* (1876; *Marie Grubbe*, 1914), by chronicling with meticulous accuracy the collapse of its protagonist's life through deterministic forces which are outside her control, anticipates the approaches of naturalistic writers such as Thomas Hardy and Frank Norris, even though Jacobsen was not a thoroughgoing naturalistic writer.

The Danish novelist Hermann Bang was unlike many naturalists in that he was more concerned with a realism that grew out of aesthetics than with one that was political. His *Håbløe Slægter* (1880), which is much concerned with questions of heredity that lead to the disintegration of a family, deals with the types of naturalistic problems that Eugene O'Neill would later explore in dramas such as *Desire Under the Elms* (1924) and *Long Day's Journey into Night* (1956), which are deeply concerned with genetic determinism.

Contemporaneously in Sweden, Strindberg published *Röda rummet* (1879; *The Red Room*, 1913), which, in its strident criticism of the economic and social changes brought about in Sweden by the new capitalism and industrialism, became a naturalist manifesto. Although his contributions were essentially to naturalistic drama, Strindberg continued to write novels in the same vein, among which *Hemsöborna* (1887; *The Natives of Hemsö, 1959)* and *I havsbandedt* (1890; *By the Open Sea*, 1913) are the most naturalistic. The latter is clearly an outgrowth of Nietzschean philosophy.

Strindberg became an early leader in the Swedish naturalistic movement, pointing the way to young writers of the period. He was also influential in shaping the thinking of other Scandinavian naturalists such as the Danish writer Holger Drachmann, whose *Forskrevet* (1890) deals with the ironic deterministic forces that make human beings and human existence incalculable, unpredictable, and at times seemingly randomly determined.

Naturalism in Scandinavia was distinct from naturalism elsewhere in Europe in that it dealt not only with the changes, economic and social, brought about by industrialization and capitalism but also with other social problems such as the status of women; indeed, such concerns predated by a generation the rise of industry in the Scandinavian countries. This already established tradition became especially relevant during the time that Scandinavia was moving toward industrialization, as is evident in Ibsen's *Et dukkehjem* (1879; *A Doll's House*, 1880) and *Hedda Gabler* (1890; English translation, 1891), two of the most significant naturalistic dramas ever written.

The emergence of Symbolism

The term *symbolisme* was coined in 1885 by Jean Moréas, who used it in defense of a considerable group of young poets who were generally viewed as pessimistic, nihilistic, and decadent, largely because of a life style that often included excessive drinking, indulgence in such drugs as opium and hashish, and sexual experimentation, frequently with members of their own sex, all in the name of intensifying the senses and sharpening them to the point that they could move Neo-Platonically toward understanding the essence of life.

Moréas, in a literary manifesto published in *Le Figaro* in 1886, reiterated a great deal that he had said earlier about this emerging group of writers, excusing some of the new poets' excesses by pointing out that they were questing after an ideal beauty, spiritually searching for an eternal symbol. Although his writing brought the term *symboliste* into common parlance, the movement never had a clearly articulated doctrine like that of the naturalists. Symbolism was a movement that emphasized such elements as emotion, inner feelings, high levels of abstraction, and the discovery of self, whereas naturalism adopted a scientific posture – some would call it pseudo-scientific – that focused on observing society and reporting it objectively, leaving readers to decide its effect upon humans, indeed upon the masses of humanity.

The poets who are most identified with early Symbolist writing are Arthur Rimbaud, Charles Baudelaire, Stéphane Mallarmé, and Paul Verlaine. These poets related experience to feelings that went far beyond the Romantic perception of feelings. Imbibing much of the new psychology that was in the air in the mid-nineteenth century, the Symbolists probed psychological states and human reactions to situations in which they virtually left their bodies during their hallucinatory periods. The Symbolists relied on subtle techniques involving word association that put language in a new, often nonlinear context. They dealt with the blurring of reality that occurs in hallucinatory states, with the kind of synesthesia that usually results when the mind is released from the conventional constraints of logical thought.

The Symbolists also were much concerned with the point/counterpoint of words, bringing to their writing many structures that are found more often in music than in literature. In their writing, they sought to depict inner states of mind and to project them upon the real objects that are parts of ordinary, everyday existence. The earliest Symbolist writing quite bewildered most readers, who thought in linear ways and found it all but impossible to enter the world created in the literature of such a writer as Arthur Rimbaud, who sought in his poetry to combine in extraordinary ways all of the senses: sight, sound, smell, touch, taste. His rhythms were shocking in their unconventionality. Balanced, measured cadences were not to be found in Rimbaud's poetry, which moved from reality into depictions of dreamlike states of consciousness that demanded of readers a suspension of their dependence upon rationality. Using every sensual device available to him, Rimbaud transported his readers into the world of irrationality.

In *Les Fleurs du mal* (1857), Baudelaire was moving with some certainty toward the kinds of writing that would emerge from later Symbolists. Baudelaire, in this collection, is vitally concerned with the inner turmoil of humans. He examines the causes of their despair, of their apathy, of their seeming inability to deal with the forces that make them pessimistic. In his poem "Correspondences," Baudelaire essentially states the Symbolist credo, considering especially such dichotomies as the real world versus the spiritual world, reality versus fantasy, and, in essence, body versus mind, the ideal versus the actual.

Paul Verlaine's Symbolist collection *Romances sans paroles* (1874; *Romances without Words*, 1921) makes clear his belief that poetry is a direct reflection of the poet's inner being, of each poet's individual subjectivity. As such, it strives for a harmony between sound and tone. It is not precise but is blurred in the beguiling way that makes it subject to interpretation but that also, in a sense, denies the rationality that would lead to conventional literary interpretation. Verlaine strove for musicality in his poetry and much appreciated musicality in the poetry of others, as one can see in his *Les Poètes maudits* (1884; the damned poets), in which he introduced the Symbolist poets Tristan Corbière and Auguste, Comte de Villiers de l'Isle-Adam to the reading public.

Mallarmé helped to make Paris the literary hub that it remained until World War II. Beginning in 1884, he welcomed artists and writers into his home every Tuesday to discuss the arts and their work as artists. These gatherings of intellectuals who were experimenting in their individual ways were instrumental in encouraging the work of such later Symbolists as René Ghil, Gustave Kahn, Stuart Merrill, and Francis Viele-Griffin, all of whom were moving in unique directions poetically.

Mallarmé himself sought in poetry a merging of vision and sound that would move beyond conventional logic and result in an inherent understanding based on intuition. Obviously this aim ran completely counter to what the writers of the naturalist school were trying to achieve. Mallarmé's chief focus is on apathy, hopelessness, fear, and a sense of being adrift in a world without compass or direction. He saw no place in society for poets, whom he regarded as solitary beings trapped in their own sensitive subjectivities.

Among the more daring Symbolist poets was Jules Laforgue, a highly talented writer whose aim was to purify language by overcoming in his poetry its earthly tonalities and its mysticism. In an extension of what Plato suggested in his Allegory of the Cave, Laforgue denied that words are connected with external realities – if, indeed, such realities exist. For him, philosophically, they did not.

The early Symbolists in many ways staked out artistic territory that would later be explored fruitfully by such writers as T. S. Eliot, Ezra Pound, Hart Crane, Wallace Stevens, William Butler Yeats, Edith Sitwell, Rainer Maria

Rilke, Stefan George, Gabrielle d'Annunzio, and Ugo Betti. In England, Oscar Wilde was much influenced both by the literary theories of the Symbolists and by their life styles. Arthur Symons' *The Symbolic Movement in Literature* (1899) helped to inform England about Symbolism as a major literary force.

Symbolism and drama

Symbolism lent itself more gracefully to poetry and drama than to prose fiction. Largely because of the influence of Symbolism, many playwrights began to move toward fantasy and paid particular heed to the sound and musicality of language. Among early dramatic productions that reflected some aspects of Symbolism was Villiers de l'Isle-Adams' *Axel* (1890; *Axel*, 1925). Although the play is not a thoroughgoing Symbolist drama, its leading character, Axel, is the quintessential decadent. In his every move, he epitomizes a great deal that the Symbolists represented: pessimism, apathy, concern with death, and inner turmoil.

Shortly after *Axel* was produced, the Belgian writer, Maurice Maeterlinck produced *Pelléas et Mélisande* (1892; *Pelleas and Melisande*, 1894), which went much further than *Axel* in employing Symbolist devices. The play, with its dreamlike atmosphere and its preoccupation with death, is a striking example of a Symbolist play. Similar examples were to follow in the dramas of the Austrian playwright Hugo von Hofmannsthal and the German playwright Gerhart Hauptmann, both of whom were more concerned with the tone or mood their plays achieved than with the stories they conveyed.

Symbolist influences in drama led inevitably to much of the Expressionist drama of the twentieth century. Both Hofmannsthal and Hauptmann moved with a degree of certainty into writing expressionistic plays that had their roots in their early exposure to Symbolism.

The rise of expressionism

By the early twentieth century, new aesthetic currents began to be felt in Germany's literary circles and, indeed, in literary circles throughout Europe. Those who despaired of being able to find the sorts of universals that naturalism suggested, as well as those who had never accepted the naturalistic credo in the first place, sought new literary forms. Sentimentality, which the naturalists had officially banished, came to be viewed more charitably than before. As will often happen when a countermovement occurs, the literary pendulum soon swung as far as possible from naturalism, rushing to its antithesis, expressionism.

Expressionism, elements of which were present in literature before the term was first applied to literature in 1913, was never a unified movement in the sense that naturalism and Romanticism were. It was a reaction against the past, a primal call for the shattering of old, entrenched art forms and their replacement by forms that focused on an individual instead of emphasizing a total society or segment of society. The new expressionists, particularly in Germany, first began by applauding and encouraging moves in the direction of war. After 1914 they thought that the war would destroy old institutions and methodologies and would create a world more hospitable to change than that in which they lived. They saw the war as the only hope of revitalizing a static and drab society.

As World War I progressed, however, their attitudes changed quickly. Expressionistic literature for a short while became increasingly abstract and sterile, then it turned utopian and became banal and sentimentally humanitarian. It also grew increasingly pacifist in its sympathies. The expressionists finally contented themselves with thinking that a new and better society would emerge when the smoke of World War I had cleared, but they were incorrect in this supposition. With the war over, Germany was in worse condition than it had been in the memories of the expressionists, some of whom committed suicide, some of whom joined the rising totalitarian societies that eventually spawned the Nazi Party, and some of whom left their homeland.

Expressionism is a term borrowed from art criticism. Impressionism, a term often linked to naturalism, is its opposite. Expressionism is idea-centered. Its concerns are largely abstract. Whereas naturalists and realists sought to achieve photographic realism and accuracy in their work, expressionists, reacting violently against the strictures of naturalism, thought that the real world exists all around people and that artists need to make their contributions by moving beyond the world's ubiquitous realities to create a visionary world.

Expressionists typically use external objects, situations, and occurrences that have a public referent but that are not otherwise connected to express their thoughts and feelings. In the graphic arts, this approach resulted in such art forms as cubism, in which distortion and dealing with quintessential geometric forms resulted in individualizing the expressions of human interiors rather than merely surface beings.

In literature, early manifestations of expressionism are found in Imagist poetry, which uses concrete language sparingly and consciously to express the essence of things, some abstract (silence, for example), some concrete (a red wheelbarrow), and to create sharp, simple, single images. Expressionism redefines language by eliminating its conventional logic, grammar, and syntax. Expressionists compress language and depend upon unique, unconventional imagery to reveal the inner beings of the individuals upon whom they focus.

These individuals are not presented in relation to detailed backgrounds but rather are symbolic beings defined by abstract representations – many of them as contradictory as dark and light or dead and reborn – that collectively create a collage to depict the universals the writer seeks to convey. In literature, expressionism found its best outlets in poetry and drama, although some prose fiction of the period was expressionistic and a considerable amount of it employed some notable expressionistic devices, particularly in the use of language.

Das Bettler (1912; *The Beggar*, 1963), by Reinhard Johannes Sorge, is generally looked upon as the pivotal play between the old realistic depiction of the naturalists and the new drama. The symbolic action of the play stands apart from the realities of the plot and is presented with a newly devised stage technique, cinematographic in essence, that focuses audience attention on symbols that convey the inner meanings the playwright wants to emphasize.

As early as 1893, Hauptmann felt impeded by the restrictions naturalism imposed; he bolted from the thoroughgoing naturalism achieved in *The Weavers* when he wrote *Hanneles Himmelfahrt* (1893; *The Assumption of Hannele*, 1894), in which he escapes into the fantasy of a child's delirious dreamworld. Sudermann felt equally impeded by the demands naturalism made, and in *Das Bettler von Syrakus* (1911), he escaped from it. Neither Hauptmann nor Sudermann, however, employed the techniques of Symbolism that Sorge did in *The Beggar*. Although he was not an expressionist, Carl Sternheim advanced the development of expressionism by the ironic contradictions in his dramas, particularly in his stinging satire of the bourgeoisie, *Bürger Schippel* (1913; *Paul Schippel, Esq.*, 1974). Like many plays of this period, *Paul Schippel, Esq.* was antinaturalist more than it was expressionist. It questioned the old values and, like Wassily Kandinsky's *Der Gelber Klang* (1909), called for spiritual revitalization.

In drama, expressionism is best exemplified by Ernst Toller in plays such as *Die Wandlung* (1919; *The Transfiguration*, 1935), *Masse-Mensch* (1921; *Masses and Men*, 1924), and *Die Maschinenstürmer* (1922; *The Machine-Wreckers*, 1923); by Sternheim in his trilogy, *Die Hose* (1911; *The Bloomers*, 1927), *Der Snob* (1914; *The Snob*, 1927), and *1913* (1915; English translation, 1939); by Walter Hasenclever in *Der Sohn* (1914); and by Georg Kaiser in *Von Morgens bis Mitternachts* (1916; *From Morn to Midnight*, 1920), *Die Koralle* (1917; *The Coral*, 1929), and *Gas* (1918; English translation, 1924).

Expressionistic plays, because they are so dependent for their effect on visualization, require unique staging. The theatrical producer Max Reinhardt was at the forefront of developing the startling staging innovations which the new drama demanded. In turn, many of the techniques he developed became important in the growing avant-garde field of motion pictures.

In poetry more than in theater, expressionism showed new ways to use language and its structures. The expressionist poets delved far below surface meanings to reach the metaphorical meanings of their subjects. Adjectives are used, for example, not to give attributes to the shallow surface meaning of nouns, but to reveal the metaphorical turmoil of what resides beneath the surface of words. Among the most representative expressionist poets are Georg Heym, Georg Trakl, Franz Werfel, Jakob van Hoddis, and Alfred Lichtenstein, most of them writing their early expressionistic verse when the fear of impending death during the war faced them directly.

Although no single significant expressionistic credo existed, as had been the case with the naturalistic movement, news of expressionism was widely disseminated through numerous literary journals. Among these, the most significant were *Die Aktion*, published from 1911 to 1932; *Der Sturm*, published from 1910 to 1932; and *Die weissen Blätter*, published from 1913 to 1920. Expressionism grew up in politically turbulent – often politically desperate – times. It changed with the times and, although modern writers still widely employ its techniques, by 1925, expressionism existed only in weakened and much-modified form, often as an adjunct to other literary movements.

Nevertheless, the movement is important because of the direct influence it had on writers as diverse as James Joyce, T. S. Eliot, Dylan Thomas, Gertrude Stein, Eugene O'Neill, Elmer Rice, Paul Green, Edward Albee, Sean O'Casey, and Harold Pinter. As noted above, the movement also anticipated much that was to occur in the development of the film industry, which is indebted to expressionist drama for countless techniques.

Further reading

Adams, Hazard. *Philosophy of the Literary Symbolic*, 1983.

Balakian, Anna. *The Fiction of the Poet: In the Post-Symbolic Mode*, 1992.

Bernard, Claude. *Introduction to the Study of Experimental Medicine, Introduction à l'étude de la médecine expérimentale*, 1865 (1927).

Cargill, Oscar. *Intellectual America: Ideas on the March*, 1941.

Coats, Paul. *A Comparative Study of Romanticism and Symbolism*, 1986.

Deak, Frantisek. *Symbolist Theater: The Formation of an Avant-garde*, 1993.

Friedman, Donald. *The Symbolist Dead City: A Landscape of Poets*, 1990.

Gras, Vernon W. *European Literature: Theory and Practice*, 1973.

Gray, Ronald. *The German Tradition in Literature, 1871–1945*, 1977.

Mangravite, Andrew, ed. and trans. *An Anthology of French Symbolist and Decadent Writing Based upon the* Book of Masks *by Remy de Gourmont*, 1994.

Nelson, Brian, ed. *Naturalism in the European Novel: Critical Essays*, 1992.

Newmark, Kevin. *Beyond Symbolism: Textual History and the Future of Reading*, 1991.

Osborne, J. *The Naturalist Drama in Germany*, 1971.

Pascal, Roy. *From Naturalism to Expressionism: German Literature and Society, 1880–1918*, 1973.

Praz, Mario. *The Romantic Agony*, 1933.

Pynsent, Robert B., ed. *Decadence and Innovation*, 1989.

Robertson, J. G. *A History of German Literature*, 1949.

Rose, Ernst. *A History of German Literature*, 1960.

Symons, Arthur. *The Symbolist Movement in Literature*, 1899.
Topsoe-Jensen, H. G. *Scandinavian Literature from Brandes to Our Day*, 1971.
Walcutt, Charles Child. *American Naturalism: A Divided Stream*, 1956.
Wilson, Edmund. *Axel's Castle: A Study in the Imaginative Literature of 1870–1930*, 1984.

R. Baird Shuman

See also Baudelaire; Bergson; Bourget; Brunetière; Croce; Gautier; George; Gourmont; Hofmannstahl; Holz; Mallarmé; Mann; Menéndez y Pelayo; Nietzsche; Pirandello; Proust; Symbolism; Unamuno y Jugo; Valéry; Verga; Zola

Pierre Corneille

French dramatist and critic

Born: Rouen, France; June 6, 1606
Died: Paris, France; September 30, 1684

Biography

Pierre Corneille, the first great classical French dramatist, was born in Rouen in 1606. From 1628 to 1650 he served conscientiously as king's counselor in the Rouen office of the departments of waterways and forests and of the admiralty. In 1641 he married Marie de Lampérière, with whom he had six children. Beginning in 1629, however, this good bourgeois and minor magistrate was also a successful dramatist whose plays appeared regularly on the Parisian stage. The heroic conception, novelty, and dramatic daring of *Le Cid* (1637; *The Cid;* 1637) ensured for his ninth play a resounding public success, but various criticisms touching principally on the play's regularity and its alleged indelicacy precipitated the playwright's three-year hiatus from the stage.

The second phase of his career is marked by three masterpieces – *Horace* (1640; English translation, 1656), *Cinna: Ou, La Clémence d'Auguste* (1640; *Cinna*, 1713), and *Polyeucte* (1642; English translation, 1655) – which explore different aspects of his heroic ideal. Elected to the Académie Française in 1647, he enjoyed during this period the status of premier French playwright. This success was not to last. A second absence, of five years, followed the failure of *Pertharite, roi des Lombards* (1651). Despite the success of *Œdipe* (1659) and a revival of his most acclaimed tragedies by Louis XIV in 1675 and 1676, his star was declining. His last, somewhat bitter years saw the definitive rise of the young Jean Racine, who had outdone Corneille in their respective treatments of the Bérénice theme. Corneille was sustained throughout his long, eventful career by a close relationship with his younger brother, Thomas, himself a successful playwright. Pierre Corneille died in Paris in 1684.

Influence

Corneille's conception of dramatic composition as a craft to be learned, partly from the practice and example of others, partly from the principles elaborated by the theorists, informs his entire theoretical and critical canon and led naturally to the formulation of statements intended for use by other playwrights. In the 1656 *préface* to the last part of his translation of Thomas à Kempis' *Imitatio Christi* (c. 1400; *The Imitation of Christ*, 1696), Corneille wrote that he was restudying the plays he had written up to that point with the intention of reissuing them in a collected edition. He projected a commentary on each play (the *examens*) to be based on "l'art poétique." In a letter dated August 25, 1660, he makes it clear that it is Aristotle's theories of which he is undertaking new interpretations, that the *discours* are being written in part to oppose the two most influential critics, Jean Chapelain, the writer of *Les Sentiments de l'Académie française sur "Le Cid"* (1638), and François Hédelin, Abbé d'Aubignac, the author of *La Pratique du théâtre* (1657; *The Whole Art of the Stage*, 1684), and that his writings will advance a number of ideas unknown to the ancients. The *discours* which appeared later that year sets forth Corneille's argument that Aristotle's *Poetics* is susceptible of more than one interpretation, his own being as valid as that of anyone else; that a play's merits should be measured by the degree of its success with the public in the theater, and not by the yardstick of "regularity"; and that the function of art is solely aesthetic. These theories constitute a unique literary contribution and are Corneille's critical legacy to dramatic literature.

Analysis

If differing explanations have been given as to the purposes Corneille had in writing the *discours* and the *examens*, these result – beyond the references to Chapelain and d'Aubignac noted in his correspondence – from the fact that he does not in the texts refer by name to those whose views he opposes. The appearance in 1657 of d'Aubignac's treatise *The Whole Art of the Stage* undoubtedly made Corneille undertake a more theoretical, systematic, and polemical defense of his own plays than he had originally intended. *The Whole Art of the Stage* contained judgments d'Aubignac had made verbally years earlier about Corneille's play *Horace* and those voiced by the members of the Académie Française through their spokesman, Jean Chapelain. Corneille does not take up a refutation of the treatise on a point-by-point basis, but he does allude to many of the matters taken up both there and in *Les Sentiments de l'Académie française sur "Le Cid,"* written more than twenty years earlier.

Chapelain's treatise found fault with *The Cid* on many points of detail, but the most serious criticism was that it failed to conform to the Horatian dictum that the function of art is to instruct as well as to delight. In upholding a moral purpose for art, Chapelain, Georges de Scudéry, Jules de La Mesnardière, and others could be said to follow most of the sixteenth-century Italian theorists, who in turn cited Plato. The opposing view, that the function of art is solely aesthetic, was identified with François Ogier and, above all, Corneille, who were followers of Francesco Robortello and Lodovico Castelvetro, inheritors of the pure Aristotelian doctrine. In his earliest critical writing – the *préfaces*, in 1632 and 1637, respectively, in *Clitandre* (1631) and *La Suivante* (1633) and the 1634 *au lecteur* in *La Veuve: Ou, Le Traître trahi* (1631) – Corneille made clear his view that poetry was for delight and not instruction. It was to be a constant in his critical theory.

The Latin "Excusatio" (1633) is an early attempt at poetics wherein the poet glories in the naturalness of his theatrical prowess: "Art for me consists in avoiding art; and most of the time, my verses flowing as of themselves, the rhythm comes easily to second the thought." Outside the theater, however, his genius languishes: "Torn from her great stage, my muse hardly succeeds in making herself heard; she stutters and ventures not to speak through her own mouth. Those are my limits, do not look for me outside: the theater closed, do not expect further verses from me." The later "Excuse à Ariste" calls even more strongly for freedom and again refers to the poet's successes – all arising from his own efforts and genius – with every social stratum: "I satisfy together both people and courtiers. . . . I owe to myself alone all my renown." A common theme of all these writings is Corneille's independence from the ancients. Again and again, he declares that aesthetic canons are not absolute or immutable, that they must be reexamined in the light of succeeding generations, and that "rules" cannot guarantee the perfection or success of a work of art. Most important, mere adherence to the rules cannot produce the kind of success which comes of giving delight through "*la beauté des événements*" (the beauty of the events). Corneille found a supporter for this point of view in Jean-Louis Guez de Balzac, who, in his letter of August 27, 1637, to Scudéry, claimed that *The Cid* was worthy of its great success with the public because of a kind of magic which kept the spectator spellbound: "There are perfect beauties [from the point of view of regularity] which are obliterated by other beauties which have more attractiveness and less perfection." Corneille's use of the word *beauté* is associated with the great, noble, serious subject mentioned in the *préface* to *Clitandre*. The term will evolve into "*le beau sujet*" (beautiful subject) and will eventually – in the *préface* to *Héraclius* (1647; English translation, 1664) – lead to the proposal of the *invraisemblable* (unbelievable or implausible).

While Corneille continued to experiment and to innovate, he continued also to insist that popular acclaim was a better guide than consistency with the rules. He did not change his mind on this matter even when certain of his plays (such as *Théodore, vierge et martyre*, 1645, and *Pertharite, roi des Lombards*, 1651) failed to win popular success. "La Querelle du 'Cid'" is very much alive in the 1645 *épître* that accompanied publication of *La Suite du menteur* (1644), in which the main point of contention continued to be that of *vraisemblance*. Although there are recurring themes and examinations of old arguments from new points of view, there are also critical theories about new types of plays. In the 1650 *épître* in *Don Sanche d'Aragon* (1649; *The Conflict*, 1798), Corneille proposes a new type of comedy (heroic comedy) which would treat aristocratic characters and a new type of tragedy which would treat characters other than royalty or nobility. Corneille posited that such individuals were essential only because their otherwise incredible actions needed to be justified by historical evidence, available normally only for persons of importance.

The question arises as to why Corneille did not simply disregard the rules altogether. Although he had done so several times at the beginning of his career, he had to please his audience – such was his conception of the theater – and the taste of his audience was in some measure influenced by d'Aubignac and others who were writing plays and treatises on plays. Corneille's Norman background, his schooling by the Jesuits, and his study of the law were all contributing factors in the formation of an intellect and a disposition well suited to self-examination and analysis, to polemic and argumentation.

Corneille's plays enjoyed great success in England during the seventeenth century, though his name is rarely if ever associated with their English-language presentation or publication. None of the *discours* or *examens* was translated into English until the twentieth century, nor is there much reference to them in English literary criticism. Nevertheless, in two important ways they greatly influenced John Dryden and through him exerted a significant influence on eighteenth-century England. The first influence was on Dryden the literary critic. Having read Corneille's dramatic theory, Dryden did in English what Corneille had done in French: he wrote a statement on dramatic theory, *Of Dramatic Poesy: An Essay* (1668), as well as prefaces to his plays. These writings, strongly and pervasively marked by French ideas, make up the first extended treatment of dramatic theory in English literature and thus mark the beginnings of criticism as a literary genre. Second, Dryden, like Corneille, takes into account the necessary influence of Christianity on the modern interpretation of Aristotle's dicta. He follows Corneille in valuing admiration as the chief emotion to be raised by serious drama and tends to merge two genres, heroic plays and the epic. Although imperfect and in the end unfavorable, Dryden's appreciation of learned and elaborate French tragedy was superior to that of his English contemporaries.

Principal criticism

Discours, 1660, includes "Discours de l'utilité et des parties du poème dramatique" ("On the Uses and Elements of Dramatic

Poetry," 1947), "Discours de la tragédie et des moyens de la traiter selon le vraisemblable ou le nécessaire" ("Discourse on Tragedy and of the Methods of Treating It, According to Probability and Necessity," 1950), "Discours des trois unités d'action, de jour, et de lieu" ("Of the Three Unities of Action, Time, and Place," 1960)

Examens in *Mélite: Ou, Les Fausses Lettres, Clitandre, La Veuve: Ou, Le Traître trahi, La Galerie du palais: Ou, L'Amie rivale, La Suivante, La Place royale: Ou, L'Amoureux extravagant, Médée, L'Illusion comique, Le Cid, Horace, Cinna: Ou, La Clémence d'Auguste, Polyeucte, La Mort de Pompée, Le Menteur, La Suite du menteur, Rodogune, princesse des Parthes, Théodore, vierge et martyre, Héraclius, Don Sanche d'Aragon, Andromède, Nicomède, Pertharite, roi des Lombards, Œdipe*, 1660

Examen in *La Toison d'or*, 1661

Préfaces in *Clitandre*, 1632, *La Suivante*, 1637, *Sertorius*, 1662, *Sophonisbe*, 1663, *Othon*, 1665, *Agésilas*, 1666, *Attila*, 1668

Au lecteur in *La Veuve: Ou, Le Traître trahi*, 1634, *Pompée*, 1644, *Œuvres de Corneille*, 1644, 1648, *Héraclius*, 1647, *Le Menteur*, 1648, *Pulchérie*, 1673, *Suréna*, 1675

Épîtres in *La Suivante*, 1637, *Médée*, 1639, *La Suite du menteur*, 1645, *Don Sanche d'Aragon*, 1650

"Excusatio," 1633

"Excuse à Ariste," 1637

Other major works and literary forms

Pierre Corneille's preeminence in literary history rests on his tirelessly innovative writing, from 1630 to 1675, of thirty-three dramatic works, ranging from comedy to tragedy and including heroic comedy, comedy of manners, comedy of intrigue, sacred plays, and ballet librettos. Charges of offending *vraisemblance* (verisimilitide or plausibility) and the *bienséance* (decorum), of disregarding the unities, and of misappropriation of history were leveled against *Le Cid* (1637; *The Cid*, 1637), a popular success which is probably the best-known play in French literary history. Although he made a number of changes in subsequent editions of *The Cid*, Corneille, in the formulation and interpretation of dramatic principles in the *discours*, the *examens*, and the other nondramatic texts cited above, was in fact responding on the theoretical plane to his critics and detractors; the plays written after *The Cid* constitute his practical rebuttal. Approximately one-half of Corneille's plays deal with various phases of the history of Rome. Some see in these "political" plays a running commentary not only on the classical republic and empire but also on factors of the evolving regime in seventeenth-century France. Corneille's dramatic output is almost equaled in length by his translations into poetic form of Latin religious works. The best of three lengthy texts is his free verse translation *Imitation de Jésus-Christ*, published in its entirety in 1656. Some twenty-four letters, and poetry in Latin and French, also survive, though they are of little general interest. In the last two decades of his life, Corneille's heroic, larger-than-life tragic characters gradually lost favor with a public becoming more interested in the analysis of internal psychological struggle, as exemplified in the works of Jean Racine.

PLAYS

Mélite: Ou, Les Fausses Lettres, 1630 (English translation, 1776)

Clitandre, 1631

La Veuve: Ou, Le Traître trahi, 1631

La Galerie du palais: Ou, L'Amie rivale, 1632

La Suivante, 1633

La Place royale: Ou, L'Amoureux extravagant, 1634

Médée, 1635

L'Illusion comique, 1636

Le Cid, 1637 (*The Cid*, 1637)

Horace, 1640 (English translation, 1656)

Cinna: Ou, La Clémence d'Auguste, 1640 (*Cinna*, 1713)

Polyeucte, 1642 (English translation, 1655)

La Mort de Pompée, 1643 (*The Death of Pompey*, 1663)

Le Menteur, 1643 (*The Liar*, 1671)

La Suite du menteur, 1644

Rodogune, princesse des Parthes, 1645 (*Rodogune*, 1765)

Théodore, vierge et martyre, 1645

Héraclius, 1647 (English translation, 1664)

Don Sanche d'Aragon, 1649 (*The Conflict*, 1798)

Andromède, 1650

Nicomède, 1651 (English translation, 1671)

Pertharite, roi des Lombards, 1651

Œdipe, 1659

La Toison d'or, 1660

Théâtre, 1660 (3 volumes)

Sertorius, 1662 (English translation, 1960)

Sophonisbe, 1663

Othon, 1664 (English translation, 1960)

Agésilas, 1666

Attila, 1667 (English translation, 1960)

Tite et Bérénice, 1670

Pulchérie, 1672 (English translation, 1960)

Suréna, 1674 (English translation, 1960)

Le Théâtre de P. Corneille, 1682

Chief Plays of Corneille, 1956

Moot Plays, 1960

POETRY

Imitation de Jésus-Christ, 1656

Office de la Sainte Vierge, 1670

Further reading

Barnwell, H. T., ed. Introduction to *Pierre Corneille: Writings on the Theatre*, 1965.

Bornedal, Peter. *The Interpretations of Art*, 1996.

Clarke, David. *Pierre Corneille: Poetics and Political Drama under Louis XIII*, 1992.

Harwood-Gordon, Sharon. *The Poetic Style of Corneille's Tragedies: An Aesthetic Interpretation*, 1989.

Hubert, Judd D. *Corneille's Performative Metaphors*, 1997.

Lancaster, Henry Carrington. *A History of French Dramatic Literature in the Seventeenth Century*, 1929–1942 (9 volumes).

Legouis, Pierre. "Corneille and Dryden as Dramatic Critics," in *Seventeenth Century Studies Presented to Sir Herbert Grierson*, 1938.

Lyons, John D. "Corneille's Discours and Classical Closure," in *Rethinking Classicism: Textual Explorations*, 1990, pp. 65–80. Edited by David Rubin.

——. *The Tragedy of Origins: Pierre Corneille and Historical Perspective*, 1996.

Sellstrom, A. Donald. *Corneille, Tasso, and Modern Poetics*, 1986.

Woshinsky, Barbara R. *Signs of Certainty: The Linguistic Imperative in French Classical Literature*, 1991.

MARILYN V. SCHULER

See also Boileau-Despréaux; Castelvetro; La Fontaine; Neoclassical Literary Theory; Racine

Malcolm Cowley

American editor and critic

Born: Near Belsano, Pennsylvania; August 24, 1898
Died: New Milford, Connecticut; March 28, 1989

Biography

Malcolm Cowley was born on August 24, 1898, to William and Josephine Cowley near Belsano, Pennsylvania. His father was a homeopathic physician in Pittsburgh. Cowley grew up and went to school with critic Kenneth Burke, who remained a lifelong friend. After high school, Cowley attended Harvard University, from which he graduated cum laude in 1920. During World War I he served in the American Ambulance Service in France in 1917 and in the United States Army in 1918. The following year he married his first wife, Marguerite (Peggy) Frances Baird.

After the war, Cowley, accompanied by his wife, returned to France on an American Field Service fellowship. He studied at Montpellier and received a diploma in 1922. The Cowleys returned from France in 1923 and settled in New York, where he worked as a freelance writer and translator. Hoping to become a man of letters, he served as editor and contributor on several small magazines in New York during the 1920s. In 1926 he bought an old farmhouse in Sherman, Connecticut, which he made his permanent home. In 1932 he divorced his first wife and married Muriel Maurer, with whom he had a son, Robert.

In 1930 Cowley succeeded Edmund Wilson as the literary editor of *The New Republic*. In 1935 he helped to organize the American Writers' Congress and was later active in the League of American Writers. An editor for Viking Press from 1948, Cowley served as a visiting professor at the University of Washington (1950), Stanford University (1956, 1959, 1960–1961, 1965), the University of California at Berkeley (1962), Cornell University (1964), the University of Minnesota (1971), and the University of Warwick in England (1973). He served two terms as president of the National Institute of Arts and Letters and two decades as chancellor of the American Academy of Arts and Letters.

Influence

One of America's foremost literary historians and men of letters, Cowley wrote the definitive literary account of the 1920s in *Exile's Return*. As both participant and spectator, he to a large degree influenced subsequent interpretations of the lost generation. Yet his most important single achievement may be his rescue of William Faulkner from oblivion with his brilliantly edited anthology *The Portable Faulkner*, which established Faulkner's place as a major American writer. *The Faulkner-Cowley File* records the story of that remarkable literary friendship. Another important literary history by Cowley is *A Second Flowering*, a study of eight major literary figures of the 1920s. The editor of the *Literary Times* wrote in 1965 that "Malcolm Cowley is, next to Edmund Wilson, the finest literary historian and critic alive in America today."

Analysis

Cowley belongs to a generation of American critics whose efforts and achievements may be intellectually unfashionable at the moment, but his book reviews, editing, literary histories, and wide-ranging cultural criticism may well prove as durable and significant as the work of more theoretically minded contemporary critics. Unlike his friend and fellow writer Kenneth Burke, Cowley was never theoretically oriented; he never based his critical judgments on abstract principles or ideologies. He sought for no systematic method or philosophy. Rather, his careful and considered literary judgments are based upon thorough biographical and cultural appreciation of the author and his or her milieu. Cowley attempts to select those works worthy of critical consideration and to expand the reader's appreciation of them based on careful textual understanding and a consideration of the entire range of an author's work. Cowley offers balanced judgments based on his wide knowledge of American literary and cultural history, and, in the case of his work on the 1920s, his personal experience as a young writer and his direct acquaintance with the writers whose work he discusses. His critical instincts were always those of a mediator, even during the most politically charged period of the 1930s, when his fellow critics were following a doctrinaire leftist line.

Cowley developed critical expertise in three areas, starting as a critic of French literature during the 1920s, broadening as an editor and professional book reviewer, and later becoming a scholar of the African slave trade. As a professional bookman, he has most often been compared to his contemporary Edmund Wilson, although perhaps his most important influences were the French poet and critic Paul Valéry and a fellow Connecticut writer, Van Wyck Brooks. From Brooks, Cowley learned how to write literary history by re-creating the historical and cultural milieu to form a "usable past." As a literary historian writing during the 1930s, Brooks influenced an entire generation of younger critics in his attempt, through the *Makers and Finders* series, to redefine a durable American literary past against the social chaos of the Depression years. Cowley pays tribute to Brooks' achievement in the dedication to his edition of *After the Genteel Tradition*.

Like Brooks, Cowley was primarily interested in reviving reputations of unjustly neglected American writers, rather than excluding anyone from the literary canon. His concerted efforts on Faulkner's behalf during the 1940s are a primary example. Cowley's edition of *The Portable Faulkner*, according to Robert Penn Warren, "marked the great turning point in Faulkner's reputation in the United States." Cowley deliberately set out to reestablish Faulkner's reputation and succeeded. Cowley's introduction to *The Portable Faulkner*, complete with the author's map of Yoknapatawpha County, remains one of the best introductions to Faulkner's work. In fact, Cowley's careful reading of Faulkner's novels – most of which were out of print by 1946 – and his correspondence with Faulkner while he worked on the Viking edition helped Faulkner himself realize what he had accomplished, as demonstrated by the letters in *The Faulkner-Cowley File*. The famous appendix on the Compson family which Faulkner wrote for *The Portable Faulkner* made the novel fall "into pattern like a jigsaw puzzle when the magician's wand touched it." When Faulkner received the first bound copies of the new edition, he wrote to Cowley, "The job is splendid .... By God, I didn't know myself what I had tried to do, and how much I had succeeded." Few other American critics have enjoyed such a rich and productive collaboration with a major author.

Perhaps Cowley's success can in part be ascribed to his modesty about himself and his work as a critic. For much of his career he worked within the short essay and book review form. In a 1961 essay, "Criticism: A Many-Windowed House," Cowley explains that he eschewed critical theories as partial truths. Criticism is neither a major literary art nor a science; it is writing *about* works of art. "The best of criticism," he asserts, "is inexact." The critic's primary role is to select works of art worth writing about, especially those that are new, misunderstood, or neglected. In addition, the critic should "describe, or analyze or reinterpret the chosen works as a basis for judgments which can sometimes merely be implied." Though in practice he starts and ends with the text, he rejects the assumption of textual autonomy of the New Critics, preferring instead to read the author's œuvre as a whole, taking into consideration the author's biography, notebooks, and letters as well. "Innocence is the keynote," Cowley affirms, to his critical method, which aims to avoid preconceptions in addressing internal questions of style, structure, and imagery without neglecting the "external relations of a work of art." Cowley always insisted on the social context of a literary work, denying that it is an autonomous or self-referential object; still less does it depend upon the interpretive whims of the critic or reader to affirm its validity. The consistent aim of criticism should be clarity and lucidity of expression in examining a writer's entire œuvre, which itself has a history and may be legitimately studied in the broader social and historical context.

Perhaps the best examples of Cowley's credo are *Exile's Return* and *A Second Flowering*, in which Cowley attempts to record the literary history of the 1920s, as both critic and participant. As a literary and social history of the lost generation, *Exile's Return* attempts to define a common generational identity for the American writers of the 1920s in terms of their war experience, their subsequent disillusionment and lost innocence, and their escape from the provincialism and philistinism of postwar America to the freedom of Paris, where they all hoped to write "the great American novel." He views this alienation as the condition of the American writer, breeding the myth of creativity in exile. The American writer has suffered from a threefold alienation – from the security of childhood, from regional roots, and from a mature and responsible sense of self. Fleeing from small-town America, a generation of young Americans gathered in Greenwich Village or in Paris, where they tried to live out the myth of the bohemian life. Unfortunately, their undisciplined desire for self-expression soon led, in many instances, to self-destructive acts of rebellion or dissipation. Thus the 1920s became a grand and gaudy spree in which life and art were often confused. A few writers such as Ernest Hemingway and John Dos Passos could work productively under these conditions, but for others, such as F. Scott Fitzgerald and Hart Crane, the atmosphere of the 1920s was ultimately a disaster, to be redeemed, if at all, only by the harsh reality of the stock-market crash and the Great Depression. The minor poet and wealthy dilettante Harry Crosby, whose story is told in the last chapter of *Exile's Return*, ultimately becomes a symbol for everything that was wrong with the 1920s: the irresponsibility, extravagance, and waste that ultimately led to his suicide in December, 1929.

If *Exile's Return* records the literary history of the 1920s as social history, then Cowley's sequel, *A Second Flowering*, reexamines the same period in terms of literary biography, with separate chapters on eight of the leading American writers of the 1920s. By 1973, however, the reputations of Hemingway, Faulkner, and Fitzgerald, at least, were well established in terms of the lost generation myth that Cowley himself had helped to create, and some of the material seems redundant. His appreciations of Crane, e. e. cummings, Thornton Wilder, Dos Passos, and Thomas Wolfe seem fresher, though they are not always as perceptive as his criticism of the others. Cowley's last chapter, "Taps for the Lost Generation," offers some interesting speculations on why more recent American writers have not enjoyed the same degree of adulation as did his contemporaries of the 1920s generation. His admiration even for Hemingway, Fitzgerald, and Faulkner is qualified by their lack of "the capacity for renewed growth after middle age that has marked some of the truly great writers."

Perhaps Cowley's most undervalued work is *The Dream of the Golden Mountains*, a social and cultural history of the 1930s. Originally intended as a sequel to *Exile's Return*, the manuscript was put aside for many years and not completed until late in Cowley's life, so that it takes on something of a reminiscent quality, but many of Cowley's memories of the harshness of the Depression years remain compelling. He uses the same dual perspective of onlooker and participant that was so successful in *Exile's Return*, this time depicting the social and economic chaos of the 1930s from his perspective as a staff writer on *The New Republic* and as a member of various leftist groups. He recalls the Bonus Army marches, hunger marches, bank failures, massive unemployment, corporate bewilderment, and the ineptness of the Hoover administration – that vast calculus of human misery which led many writers and intellectuals to lose faith in capitalism. Cowley is utterly plausible in his account of the appeal of Marxism during that bleak period when nothing else seemed to make sense. His narrative interweaves personal and public tragedies – the sober tale of the collapse of the American economy interspersed with vivid excerpts from personal letters recounting the events that led up to Crane's suicide. This painful story involved Cowley's first wife, Peggy, who became Crane's lover in Mexico before his death.

Just as exile to Paris and repatriation seemed to be the literary pattern of the 1920s, so commitment to leftist politics and eventual disillusionment with the Communist Party seemed to reflect the mood of the 1930s. Cowley captures the desperate idealism of the true believers – the desire to do something, anything, which led many writers to social activism, and the eventual betrayal of those hopes after the Spanish Civil War and the Hitler-Stalin Pact. Perhaps there are fewer literary celebrities in his account of the 1930s decade than in his earlier treatments of Paris of the 1920s, but Cowley mentions Theodore Dreiser, Clifford Odets, John Steinbeck, Fitzgerald, the Fugitive Group, Sinclair Lewis, and other lesser writers among the New York set. Cowley is at his best here as he reconstructs social history through the perspective of the Depression years.

An earlier and less impressive book, *The Literary Situation*, attempts to take stock of the post-World War II generation of American writers, but here Cowley's judgment seems detached and bookish. His chapters read like old book reviews, lacking the immediacy and conviction of his work on the 1920s and 1930s. "A Natural History of the American Writer," a section in which he describes writers' backgrounds and work habits, contains little more than superficial generalizations.

Cowley's strength remains in his biographical and social criticism of the lost generation, in his clear and impartial record of the writers he knew and the events through which he lived. Along with Edmund Wilson and Van Wyck Brooks, he represents the best of an older ideal of the American critic as an independent man of letters, writing from outside the academy, maintaining critical integrity uncompromised by intellectual fashions. Though *A Second Flowering* may contain Cowley's best criticism, his most important and durable work may be contained, as Henry Dan Piper points out, in *Exile's Return*, the Viking Faulkner and Hemingway anthologies, his edition of Fitzgerald's stories, and the "final" version of *Tender Is the Night* (1951; originally published in 1934). His efforts on Faulkner's behalf alone mark Cowley as one of the most perceptive and farsighted critics of his generation.

Principal criticism

Exile's Return: A Literary Odyssey of the 1920s, 1934, 1951
The Literary Situation, 1954
Think Back on Us . . . A Contemporary Chronicle of the 1930s, 1967
A Many-Windowed House: Collected Essays on American Writers and American Writing, 1970
The Lesson of the Masters, 1971
A Second Flowering: Works and Days of the Lost Generation, 1973
The Dream of the Golden Mountains: Remembering the 1930s, 1980
The Flower and the Leaf: A Contemporary Record of American Writing Since 1941, 1985
New England Writers and Writing, 1996

Other major works and literary forms

In addition to the works listed above, Malcolm Cowley published hundreds of articles, essays, and reviews. As a poet, an editor, an anthologist, a translator, and a literary historian, he has dozens of other books to his credit. Works of special importance include *After the Genteel Tradition: American Writers Since 1910* (1936, 1964), *The Portable Faulkner* (1946), *Writers at Work: The "Paris Review" Interviews* (1958), *Black Cargoes: A History of the Atlantic Slave Trade, 1518–1865* (1962; with Daniel Pratt Mannix), *The Faulkner-Cowley File: Letters and Memories, 1944–1962* (1966), *Blue Juniata* (1929, 1968), *And I Worked the Writer's Trade* (1978), and *The View from Eighty* (1980).

POETRY
Blue Juniata, 1929, revised and expanded 1968
The Dry Season, 1941

NONFICTION
Writers at Work: The "Paris Review" Interviews, 1958
Black Cargoes: A History of the Atlantic Slave Trade, 1518–1865, 1962 (with Daniel Pratt Mannix)
The Faulkner-Cowley File: Letters and Memories, 1944–1962, 1966
And I Worked the Writer's Trade, 1978
The View from Eighty, 1980

TRANSLATIONS
On Board the Morning Star, 1925 (of Pierre MacOrlan's novel *À bord de L'Étoile Matutine*)
Joan of Arc, 1926 (of Joseph Delteil's biography *La Passion de Jeanne d'Arc*)
Variety, 1927 (of volume 1 of Paul Valéry's essay collection *Variété*)
Catherine-Paris, 1928 (of Marthe Bibesco's novel)
The Green Parrot, 1929 (of Bibesco's novel *Le Perroquet vert*)

The Count's Ball, 1929 (of Raymond Radiguet's novel *Le Bal du comte d'Orgel*)
Imaginary Interviews, 1944 (of André Gide's essay collection *Interviews imaginaires*)
Leonardo, Poe, Mallarmé, 1972 (with James R. Lawler; volume 8 of *The Collected Works of Paul Valéry*)

EDITED TEXTS
After the Genteel Tradition: American Writers Since 1910, 1936, revised 1964
Books That Changed Our Minds, 1939 (with Bernard Smith)
Tender Is the Night, by F. Scott Fitzgerald, 1951
Leaves of Grass, the First (1855) Edition, by Walt Whitman, 1959
Fitzgerald and the Jazz Age, 1966 (with Robert Crowley)

ANTHOLOGIES
The Portable Hemingway, 1944
The Portable Faulkner, 1946
The Portable Hawthorne, 1948
The Complete Poetry and Prose of Walt Whitman, 1948
The Stories of F. Scott Fitzgerald, 1951
Great Tales of the Deep South, 1955
The Lessons of the Masters: An Anthology of the Novel from Cervantes to Hemingway, 1971 (with Howard E. Hugo)

Further reading

Aaron, Daniel. *Writers on the Left*, 1961.
Bak, Hans. *Malcolm Cowley: The Formative Years*, 1993.
Breit, Harvey. *The Writer Observed*, 1956.
Bulkin, Eleanor. *Malcolm Cowley: A Study of his Literary, Social, and Political Thought to 1940*, 1973.
Burke, Kenneth, ed. *The Selected Correspondence of Kenneth Burke and Malcolm Cowley*, 1988.
Eisenberg, Diane U. *Malcolm Cowley: A Checklist of His Writings, 1916–1973*, 1975.
Kempf, James Michael. *The Early Career of Malcolm Cowley: A Humanist Among the Moderns*, 1985.
Kempton, Murray. *Part of Our Time*, 1955.
Young, Philip. "For Malcolm Cowley: Critic, Poet, 1898," in *Southern Review*. New series, IX (Autumn, 1973), pp. 778–795.

ANDREW J. ANGYAL

See also American Literary Theory: Twentieth Century; Brooks, Van W.

R. S. Crane

American critic

Born: Tecumseh, Michigan; January 5, 1886
Died: Chicago, Illinois; August 27, 1967

Biography

Ronald Salmon Crane was born in Tecumseh, Michigan, on January 5, 1886. He took his B.A. from the University of Michigan in 1908 and his Ph.D. from the University of Pennsylvania in 1911. He taught at Northwestern University from 1911 to 1924. In 1917 Crane married Julia Fuller; they had two children.

In 1924 he moved to the University of Chicago, where he remained, becoming Emeritus Distinguished Professor in 1951. From 1930 to 1952 he was editor of *Modern Philology* and was noted for his high standards in editing and reviewing. The University of Chicago during this period (c. 1935) was under the influence of Robert Maynard Hutchins, and Crane enthusiastically supported innovation and reform in the humanities and particularly encouraged the study of criticism in the English department, of which he was chairman from 1935 to 1947. He was associated with the philosophers Mortimer Adler and Richard McKeon and with such English department colleagues as Elder Olson. He was Alexander Lecturer and Visiting Professor at the University of Toronto from 1951 to 1952 and received the doctor of literature degree from Northwestern University in 1963. He died in Chicago in 1967.

Influence

Crane's influence, which is also the influence of the "Neo-Aristotelians" of the Chicago School, can be seen first of all in establishing literary criticism as a respectable discipline in opposition to literary history, which had hitherto (until 1935 at least) dominated English departments. It is to his credit that he did not exclude literary history but kept it as a partner of criticism.

His influence can also be seen in his advocacy of a pluralistic conception of criticism and in his preference, within the pluralistic framework, for Aristotle. The exact extent of his influence is hard to estimate, since in some matters – in his advocacy of criticism, for example – it blends with other schools and in other matters, such as his championship of genre, it is in sharp opposition. His influence has continued to be felt in the decades since his death.

Analysis

Crane's theory, as expounded in the introduction to *Critics and Criticism* and in *The Idea of the Humanities and Other Essays Critical and Historical*, places literary criticism within the general framework of the humanities but recognizes the importance of other disciplines – "linguistics, philology, the philosophic analysis of ideas, and history" – for the study of literature. In approaching criticism, it is necessary to be aware of the bewildering diversities and oppositions of modern critics and schools. Crane rejects three possible approaches to the problem: first, a radical skepticism, which sees criticism as a vain pursuit; second, a dogmatic acceptance of one particular approach as the only valid one; and third, an attempted synthesis of all schools, taking the best elements from each. All these approaches are rendered invalid by the nature of criticism, in which the

> reference of any critic's statements, general or particular, to the things he professes to be talking about is mediated, in the first place, by the special framework

> of concepts and distinctions which, out of all others that might be, or have been, thought relevant to the things in question, he has chosen for one reason or another to employ.

One critic's framework not only may be different from another's but also may be incommensurable, so that one cannot use the one to refute the other: "There can be no genuine refutation of a critical position except within the particular framework of concepts and rules of inference in which it has been asserted."

This is not, however, a type of pluralism where "anything goes." A particular piece of criticism may be bad because the critic lacks sensitivity and knowledge or lacks tact and applies his or her theory inappropriately. Though Crane has a strong preference for Aristotle, he would admit that Samuel Taylor Coleridge can deal with some problems which find no place in Aristotle's poetics. It is not true, however, that all theories are equal; they may be compared for their scope and flexibility, for their pertinent and usable distinctions, and many modern systems will in these respects be found wanting. Crane maintains that

> critical principles are neither doctrinal absolutes nor historically necessitated beliefs but instruments of inquiry and analysis, to which a critic therefore need not commit himself dogmatically, but only hypothetically, on the ground of their appropriateness to the particular kinds of problems he is interested in solving.

All this sounds tolerant enough, but in fact Crane is anything but tolerant and spends much time exposing the errors and limitations of other critics and theories, even when he admits the value of their particular observations and general insights. Generally, he would favor a theory which takes into account the peculiar natures as well as the particular kinds of poems analyzed and would analyze the parts in relation to one another and to the definable effects which the poet was trying to attain. He condemns, on the other hand, criticism which looks for qualities characteristic of all poems or takes the "high priori" road and, having assumed such a quality, strains the evidence to fit it. The sort of critic whom Crane particularly dislikes is unscrupulous about the use of hypothesis, assuming a literary hypothesis to be true if only some scattered details in the text seem to harmonize with it.

Crane's objections do not, however, apply to Aristotle, for whose system he has an emphatic preference, though, in theory at least, he would still recognize the right of other critics to use other frameworks. With Aristotle's basic principle of mimesis, or imitation, he does some peculiar things. He persists in maintaining that only some poems "happen" to be imitations; others belong to what Crane calls the "didactic" category. Admittedly, Aristotle's system, as it is known, makes provision only for the narrative and dramatic fields, and the vast development of the lyric and related forms in the times since Aristotle certainly makes some expansion of his system necessary, but the term "didactic" is hardly a happy one as a label for all the material that Aristotle did not cover. Unlike his neoclassical predecessors, Crane does not treat imitation as representation; he prefers such terms as "analogy," "analogue," and "description."

Another basic element in Aristotle's thought, that of genre, receives more sensible treatment. The poetic kinds are "heuristic devices for discovering what are the relevant questions to be asked about the individual works"; they are not norms against which individual works are to be measured, nor can one give a definitive list of species, since new ones are constantly emerging. A possible solution to the problem of genre can be seen in Crane's concept of "power" or "dynamis" or "final cause," a power which creates the unity of the individual poem but which might be extended to cover genres or actual and possible subgenres (for example, catharsis might be considered the "power" of tragedy).

Crane's practical criticism does not follow obviously from his theory but is perfectly compatible with it and with Aristotle. Particularly impressive is "The Concept of Plot and the Plot of *Tom Jones*," which illustrates his "criticism of forms" by treating the novel as a "self-contained whole endowed with a power of affecting us in a particular way by virtue of the manner in which its internal parts are conceived and fitted together." This is something more than plot summary; it is meant to show how an artist consciously fits together the "parts" (including such elements as character) to produce a cumulative effect on the reader. Some contemporaries saw this type of criticism as not very different from the New Criticism, of which Crane was so suspicious; he could well have answered that he had analyzed Henry Fielding's *Tom Jones* (1749) in terms of its own individual power and not in terms of some form imposed a priori from without.

Any discussion of Crane's influence must recognize that he did not himself publish much practical criticism and that even if one adds the works of his fellow critics at Chicago, the volume of critical work produced by this school is modest compared to the achievements of the New Critics. Some believe that Crane's greatest service was in making criticism respectable at a time when most English programs were concentrated on literary history and philology. His own conversion to criticism, announced in 1935, could not be ignored, since he had long been a distinguished literary scholar; shortly thereafter, he became head of his department at Chicago and set about revising the program there. The New Critics were promoting criticism at the same time, but without his power and prestige.

Whatever influence Crane's pluralism had, one could only wish that it had had more; the acceptance of his conception of all conflicting theories as potentially valuable and yet incommensurable would have eliminated not only many senseless wrangles but also some vain attempts at synthesis. (In some ways Crane was tending in the same direction as Northrop Frye, but Frye did at least dream of a great synthesis of all the schools.) Some outsiders regarded the Aristotelian element as the most distinctive feature of the Chicago School; insofar as they ignored the pluralism, they misunderstood Crane's position.

Aside from these general influences, there is the more specific matter of discipleship – Crane's influence on his own students and through them on their students and on some who were never at Chicago. The Chicago School, which Crane preferred to call "a group of friends," lives on. Since the mutability of critical fashions has something cyclical about it, and Aristotle has been in and out of favor many times, common sense and flexibility may yet lead critics to rally around the theories of R. S. Crane.

Principal criticism

"History Versus Criticism in the Study of Literature," 1935
Critics and Criticism: Ancient and Modern, 1952 (editor)
The Languages of Criticism and the Structure of Poetry, 1953
The Idea of the Humanities and Other Essays Critical and Historical, 1967

Other major works and literary forms

R. S. Crane produced virtually every form of academic writing applicable to literature. He wrote literary history and the theory of literary history, he did bibliographies, he wrote and edited textbooks, he interested himself in the history of ideas, and he published innumerable reviews.

EDITED TEXTS
A Census of British Newspapers and Periodicals, 1620–1800, 1927, 1966 (with F. B. Kaye and Moody Prior)
A Collection of English Poems, 1660–1800, 1932
English Literature, 1600–1800: A Bibliography of Modern Studies Compiled for Philological Quarterly, 1952

Further reading

Bashford, Bruce W. *The Humanistic Criticism of Ronald Crane*, 1970.
Booth, Wayne C. *Critical Understanding: The Powers and Limits of Pluralism*, 1979.
——. "Criticism and the Liberal Arts: The Chicago School of Criticism," in *Profession*. 82 (1982), pp. 19–26.
Davis, Walter A. *The Act of Interpretation: A Critique of Literary Reason*, 1978.
Denham, Robert D. "R. S. Crane's Critical Method and Theory of Poetic Form," in *Connecticut Review*. 5, no. 2 (1972), pp. 46–56.
Grenander, M. E. "Evolution of an Article: The Chicago Aristotelians," in *Hypotheses: Neo-Aristotelian Analysis*. VII (Winter, 1994), pp. 2–12.
Ransom, John Crowe. "Humanism at Chicago," in *The Kenyon Review*. XIV (Autumn, 1952), pp. 647–659.
Sherwood, John C. *R. S. Crane: An Annotated Bibliography*, 1984.

JOHN C. SHERWOOD

See also American Literary Theory: Twentieth Century

Criticism

Contrary to general belief in Britain and America, literature has long been thought of from a broad theoretical perspective, rather than in critical (that is, text-specific) terms. The heyday of criticism is a brief "window" of about fifty years in the twentieth century interrupting a tradition of critical theory which had started with Aristotle's *Poetics* (c. 334–323 B.C.), and includes Longinus' *On the Sublime* (first century A.D.?) in ancient times, Sir Philip Sidney's *An Apology for Poetry* (1595) in the Renaissance, Percy Bysshe Shelley's "Defence of Poetry" (1840) in the Romantic period, and T. S. Eliot's essay "Tradition and the Individual Talent" (1920) in the twentieth century. All these are representative of a kind of writing which is best described as "literary theoretical" rather than "literary critical," since they discuss ideas about literature's purposes, effects, procedures, and status, but without primary focus on the interpretation of individual literary texts. However, in Britain and America in the period roughly from the 1920s to the 1970s literary debate was dominated (though to a greater extent in the former than the latter) by the interpretive discussion of individual literary works, in other words by literary criticism. Then from the 1970s onward, the dominance in professional discussions of literature again shifted back to the theoretical, in debates instigated by such figures as Roland Barthes, Michel Foucault, and Jacques Derrida, centered upon questions of a philosophical, historical, or linguistic nature.

The earliest precedents for the literary-critical, or text-based, approach were Samuel Johnson's Lives of the Poets and Prefaces to Shakespeare in the eighteenth century, and Samuel Taylor Coleridge's discussion of William Wordsworth's writing in *Biographia Literaria* (1817) in the early part of the nineteenth century. It is usual to distinguish two main varieties of criticism in the fifty-year "window" when criticism was dominant, these being British "close reading" (also called "practical criticism") and American New Criticism. The British practice stemmed from empirical work on the evaluation of literary texts at Cambridge in the 1920s, as described in I. A. Richards' *Practical Criticism: A Study of Literary Judgement* (1929). Richards' pupil William Empson, in his *Seven Types of Ambiguity* (1930), exemplified the practice of minute verbal scrutiny of literary texts, while T. S. Eliot's *The Varieties of Metaphysical Poetry* (the Clark Lectures at Cambridge, 1926–1927) and F. R. Leavis' *New Bearings in English Poetry* (1932) began the process of revising and supplementing the existing canon on the basis of detailed textual reassessments. The British variant, then, was characterized by three things. Firstly, a predominant interest in the evaluation of literary texts. Secondly, by its being methodologically implicit; that is, it refused to spell out as general principles the reasons for its exclusion from consideration of matters concerned with historical or biographical contexts or with the reader's response to the text. Thirdly, by its moralism; that is, it valued a literary work primarily for its embodiment of humane values, rather than for aesthetic values in the narrow sense.

The American version, known as the New Criticism, takes its name from John Crowe Ransom's book *The New Criticism* (1941), and is also seen in Cleanth Brooks' *The Well Wrought Urn: Studies in the Structure of Poetry* (1947), and in W. K. Wimsatt's *The Verbal Icon: Studies in the Meaning of Poetry* (1954). It was characterized by the opposite of the British qualities. Firstly, it was predominantly interested in the interpretation of literary texts. Secondly, it was methodologically explicit; that is, it valued explicit programmatic statements about method. These included the notions of "intentional fallacy" and the "affective fallacy" (see the essays with these titles in *The Verbal Icon*), which laid out the grounds for excluding from consideration the author's intentions and biography or the reader's reactions to the text. Thirdly, it valued a literary work primarily for formal and aesthetic reasons, such as the extent to which it maintained a fine balance of opposed qualities and brought them into a unity of synthesis.

The British interest in textual evaluation meant that key essays frequently took the form of comparisons between texts which dealt with similar subject matter, with a view to establishing grounds for ranking one as superior to the other. Well-known examples include Leavis' essay comparing Shakespeare's *Antony and Cleopatra* with John Dryden's version of the story, *All for Love* (in *The Living Principle*, 1975), and the essay "Reality and Sincerity: Notes in the Analysis of Poetry" (*Scrutiny*, XIX, no. 2, 1952–1953), in which he compares poems by Emily Brontë and Thomas Hardy on bereavement. Likewise, the original experiments recorded in I. A. Richards' *Practical Criticism* were designed to expose the uncertainty with which even well-educated readers make such comparative literary "judgements," a key word for the British practitioners of criticism.

What Leavis as a critic most valued in literature was the quality of "enactment," in which the words "embody" the sense, rather than simply indicate or describe it. In the *Antony and Cleopatra* essay he asserts that "Shakespeare's verse seems to enact its meaning . . . while Dryden's is merely descriptive eloquence," and the same distinction is used to delineate the difference between John Donne and the Romantics on the one hand and the work of the Victorian poets on the other. He praises Donne and John Keats in *Revaluation* (1936) for "the liveliness of enactment – something fairly to be called dramatic," contrasting this quality with the "decorative-descriptive" style of Alfred, Lord Tennyson. But "enactment," it should be emphasized, is a linguistic strength with a moral foundation, for it is not a matter merely of technique, but of a lived and felt life embodied in the very texture of the language. Thus, it is because Hardy has been bereaved, combined with his excellence as a poet, that his poetic language has this quality – the latter alone could not ensure it. Thus, "Hardy's poem is seen to have a great advantage in reality [which is to say] that it represents a profounder and completer sincerity" ("Reality and Sincerity"). By contrast, Emily Brontë is "dramatizing herself in a situation such as she has clearly not known in actual experience." Yet the piece also illustrates the characteristic weaknesses of the "closed" close reading approach (see below), for Leavis ignores contextualizing issues, treating the two poems as if both were personal lyrics, whereas Brontë's is actually part of a historical saga, spoken by a "character," and written in a manner appropriate to formal public declamation rather than the product of private, meditative inwardness.

The American tendency toward greater explicitness of methodological principle led to a number of useful distinctions, such as that between "intrinsic" and "extrinsic" criticism, the former being text-based, intensive, and analytical, while the latter is context-based, extensive, and discursive, making use of (for instance) historical information, knowledge of generic conventions, biographical data, and so on. F. W. Bateson's notion of "contextual reading" (in opposition to "close reading") aimed to synthesize the two modes of intrinsic and extrinsic approaches. A more recent formulation along similar lines distinguishes between "unseen close reading" (or "closed close reading," as we might call it), and "seen close reading" (or "open close reading"). The former is the textual practice that rules out of play the use of any external data, and limits the critic strictly to "the words on the page." The latter, by contrast, reads the text closely, but alongside, and open to, a range of necessary reference material. This formulation attempts to cope with the paradox that the interdict placed by dominant critical practice on the use of "external" data took root at precisely the time when the most prestigious literature (T. S. Eliot, Ezra Pound, James Joyce) increasingly required copious "external" annotation to explain the significance of allusions, proper names, historical figures, mythological parallels, and so on.

Other objections to the critical practice of minute and intense verbal scrutiny might be listed as follows. Firstly, it really only works at its best for the short lyric poem – it cannot do so even for poetry when the scale is epic and the mode primarily narrative. Secondly, for obvious reasons, it can never be a sufficient tool for the novel, given the vast scale of the text in comparison with the nature of the critical method – a close reading of the average Victorian novel would be like trying to bring in a grain harvest using only a pair of nail scissors. In practice, the main critical resource is to "poeticize" the text of the novel, giving exaggerated importance, for instance, to the novelist's use of verbal imagery. Thirdly, the method is inappropriate to drama, except verse drama, but even here the "poeticization" of the text is, again, often very marked, so that plays tend to become a static tableau of images – Leavis' praise of *Antony and Cleopatra* involves (again) treating famous speeches as if they were free-standing lyric poems, rather than moments in a drama. Fourthly, the linguistic data identified in the close reading process often remains less than convincingly integrated into the flow of critical argument – identifying a pattern of assonance in a poem is the easy part; linking this convincingly to a reading and interpretation of the poem is the real challenge.

All the same, the discipline of close reading remains the bedrock of literary study, without which it is defenseless against the appropriating territorial ambitions of history, linguistics, philosophy, politics, sociology, and cultural studies. The opposite of close reading can only be reading at a distance, and from that perspective the claims of these others will always threaten to obscure the text, to a greater or lesser extent. In a period in literary studies which is both post-critical and (allegedly) post-theoretical, that is exactly what seems to be happening.

PETER BARRY

See also Bateson; Leavis; Modern Literary Theory; New Criticism

Benedetto Croce

Italian philosopher and critic

Born: Pescassèroli, Italy; February 25, 1866
Died: Naples, Italy; November 20, 1952

Biography

Benedetto Croce was born in the small town of Pescassèroli, in the province of L'Aquila, Italy, on February 25, 1866, of a well-to-do family. He was educated in a private Catholic school in Naples, to which the family had transferred. At the age of seventeen he lost his parents and his only sister in an earthquake, and following this personal tragedy he was taken to Rome to live with a close relative. He enrolled at the law school there but showed no real interest in the study of law. In 1886 he left the university and returned to Naples, where he established himself permanently. At first he devoted himself to historical studies and antiquarian research, which he pursued for several years. He came under the influence of Marxist philosophy in 1895, but his studies on Marxism ended in 1900 with the publication of his *Materialismo storico ed economia marxistica* (*Historical Materialism and the Economics of Karl Marx*, 1914). In 1896 he began corresponding with Giovanni Gentile, and their epistolary exchange soon developed into a close intellectual collaboration and partnership lasting about thirty years, despite their philosophical differences. Together they founded the journal *La critica* to carry on the battle against positivism and to rejuvenate intellectual life. In 1910 Croce was made Senator of the Kingdom of Italy, and in 1914, at the age of forty-eight, he married Adele Rossi. They had four daughters. In 1920 Croce was appointed Minister of Education, an office he held until 1921. Although favorably inclined at first toward Benito Mussolini's government, he turned against it in 1925 and broke his ties with Gentile, who was a major supporter of the Fascist regime. Under the dictatorship, Croce was publicly ignored; the government did not, however, interfere with the publication of his works or his journal. After World War II he revamped the Liberal Party and became its leader. He was minister without portfolio in two consecutive governments. In celebration of his eightieth birthday, Croce founded the Istituto Italiano di Studi Storici in a wing of his home in Naples. He died in Naples in 1952.

Influence

Croce dominated the Italian cultural scene for half a century, exercising such a pervasive and uncontested influence that it completely transformed the intellectual climate of his country. His theory of art and criticism also had wide currency abroad: his impact on the New Critics is well known. Croce was the first in Italy to become fully aware that literary criticism cannot be based on empirical considerations, but must be founded on aesthetic principles, and that an aesthetic conception is an integral part of a philosophical system encompassing the whole of life. His main targets were positivism, intellectualism, and decadence. Through some thirty volumes of literary theory and criticism, he rid literary studies of what he considered to be "erroneous" doctrines. He asserted and demonstrated that art is a cognitive activity and that the purpose of criticism is to appreciate and judge art *qua* art, not to deal with matters external to it, such as historical and biographical erudition. His *Estetica come scienza dell'espressione e linguistica generale* (1902; *Aesthetic as Science of Expression and General Linguistic*, 1909) was a seminal work largely responsible for changing the trends in literary studies. Croce's tireless activity as a literary theorist and critic had a positive influence and produced a long line of major critics following in his footsteps; even those who opposed him could not escape his influence. His bimonthly journal, *La critica*, which he cofounded and directed and to which he was the major contributor, nourished the Italian mind for fifty years, despite the opposition of the Fascist regime.

Analysis

Croce's theory of art and criticism was born of his distaste for the trends of his times in the field of literary studies, dominated by positivistic and intellectualistic doctrines. His aesthetic marks a return to the idealistic tradition originating with Giambattista Vico. Francesco De Sanctis was his immediate predecessor and Immanuel Kant and G. W. F. Hegel his lesser influences. Croce's neo-Idealism rejects metaphysics and all presuppositions – materialistic, intellectual, theological. It is an analysis of the processes of the human mind, whose essence is freedom and to which he reduces all reality. The world of metaphysics is thus replaced by the world of history, which is the work of human thinking and action, where all begins and ends. Croce calls his philosophy a "methodology of history."

In his conception, the human mind unfolds in four distinct phases (two of them theoretical and two practical): the aesthetic and the logical, the economic and the ethical. The first produces intuitions; the second, concepts; the third, actions aimed at individual ends; the fourth, actions aimed at universal ends. The passage from one activity to the other constitutes the life of the mind, its historicity, which begins with art and ends with ethics. Yet the end coincides with the beginning, for the world of action, culminating with ethics, reverts to intuition, and the mind's life begins afresh. In this scheme, aesthetics or intuitive experience is the very foundation of knowledge, since intuition is the first source of mental life, unconditioned by metaphysical assumptions or other a priori considerations. This constitutes the basis of the autonomy of art, asserted by Croce against traditional aesthetic doctrines. Since artistic creation does not depend on any other human activity, the principles of its criticism should be drawn from its own nature, rather than from other disciplines. This concept is well reflected in Croce's theory and methodology of criticism.

Croce's artistic theory received its first formulation around the turn of the century in *Aesthetic as Science of Expression and General Linguistic*. Against naturalistic literary theory, Croce asserts the idealistic character of art; against intellectualistic theory, its alogical nature. Art, in his view, is intuitive knowledge, distinct from logical knowledge. It is the "dawn" of self-consciousness, when the mind cannot yet distinguish the real from the unreal. While logical thinking deals with the universal, intuition (art) represents the particular.

The Crocean theory rests on a few fundamental propositions, the most important being the identification of intuition with expression and, therefore, art with language. Art (or intuition) is the process by which chaotic human emotions and impressions acquire form in language. The idea of art as imitation is rejected and that of art as creation firmly established, for the human mind knows only what it creates. Artistic activity produces only images, pictures, without inquiring into their real nature. In order to gain a full understanding of reality one must move up to the sphere of logic, which lifts the haze from the world of intuitions. Croce closely follows Vico, who wrote that "Men at first feel without perceiving, then they perceive with a troubled and agitated spirit, finally, they reflect with a clear mind." This implies that imagination precedes intellect. Logic, in fact, presupposes intuition – the first degree of the cognitive process. When logic arises, art vanishes: in art there is no room for logic.

The identity of intuition with expression remains one of the cornerstones of Croce's theory. The concept of expression (or language), however, has a peculiar meaning in his theory. The term "expression" does not signify "communication" in an interpersonal sense; it designates an intrapersonal language. Expression is the inner fashioning of the image; communication (or externalization) is the physical production of the image on paper or canvas. Communication belongs not to the aesthetic but to the practical sphere. The aesthetic expression is not a conglomeration of signs and symbols; it is a constant and ever-new invention of the creative activity. The uniqueness and individuality of artistic expression render it impossible to duplicate, thus making a work of art untranslatable. Every translation is a new expression, a new work of art. In conventional language, which serves for external communication, words are labels, not living entities springing spontaneously from feeling.

Croce's distinction between expression and communication led him to deny the aesthetic existence of the arts, such as painting, sculpture, and music. In aesthetics there is only Art, with a capital A, not the arts. The distinction between the arts is simply external, based on their respective means of externalization. Their differentiation takes place on the practical rather than the aesthetic level. Consequently, for each art there is a different technique rather than a different aesthetics. Thus, all the arts are reduced to the same principle: intuition. For similar reasons, Croce denies the aesthetic existence of the literary genres.

His *Aesthetic as Science of Expression and General Linguistic* was far from being an exhaustive statement on the subject of aesthetics. In subsequent developments, Croce introduced the "lyrical" character of art (1908), the "totality" (or universality) of artistic expression (1918), the concept of art as morality (1928), and, finally, the definition of "literature" (1936). Feeling becomes the content of intuition, and lyricism is viewed by Croce as the form of the spirit shorn of any intellectual element. The term "lyric" no longer defines a particular genre, but is the very substance of all forms of artistic creation. Following De Sanctis' lead, Croce elucidates the dialectical nature of the form-content relationship. In the abstract, form and content are separate entities; concretely, they are inseparable, for there is no content without form. Feeling and image do not exist outside their aesthetic synthesis.

The growth of Croce's artistic theory from the concept of intuition of the particular to that of lyrical intuition, and to the broader notion of the "totality" of lyrical intuition, and finally to morality, resulted in a conception of art as ethical life embracing the entire human experience. Hence, his aversion to aestheticism. His last book in the field of artistic theory, *La poesia: Introduzione alla critica e storia della poesia e della letteratura* (1936; *Poetry and Literature:*

An Introduction to the Criticism and History, 1981), contains his mature statement, incorporating all of the revisions, corrections, and rethinking of thirty-five years of reflection and experience. It includes a last important integration – the concept of "literature," distinguishing it from that of "poetry." "Literature" and "poetry" designate "qualities" of expression: a work is poetic if it springs from pure intuition, be it a poem or a novel. Literature, on the contrary, indicates the rhetorical embellishments of any work, be it fiction, science, history. It is the ornate form given to any nonpoetic work.

Croce's concept of literary criticism developed alongside his aesthetic theory and was amply illustrated by his practical criticism. He followed in the footsteps of De Sanctis, but, being philosophically better endowed than his predecessor, he was able to give his own doctrine a more solid foundation. The objective of literary criticism is to express a value judgment on a work of art, that is, to determine whether a given work is art (intuition). Thus, criticism aims at distinguishing art from nonart. It must be founded on aesthetic principles inherent in the work of art, not on biographical, historical, philological, moralistic, or sociological considerations. Although history, philology, and scholarship in general are subsidiary elements, they do not accomplish the function of criticism.

This is the general principle that Croce firmly established, illustrated, and defended against positivistic and intellectualistic tendencies, the first concerned with the elucidation of facts, the second with the elucidation of ideas, but both remaining outside the true domain of art. The critic's function is to re-create the work of art, that is, to relive and reexpress it. Genius (the creative faculty) and taste (the re-creative faculty) are substantially identical. Taste is genius' discerning eye. The critic, therefore, must be endowed with an aesthetic sensibility equal to that of the artist in order to be able to penetrate the state of mind which inspired the work and so to re-create it. In *Aesthetic as Science of Expression and General Linguistic*, criticism seems to follow three distinct steps: the first consists in the historical and philological exegesis, aimed at establishing the integrity of the text; the second, in the re-creation of the work through taste; the third, in the expression of the re-creation (that is, the historical representation). The scholar, the person of taste, and the historian (Croce uses this designation for the critic) represent three successive stages of work.

Yet this approach does not carry the critic beyond the romantic formula of *artifex additus artifici*. The writing of *Logica come scienza del concetto puro* (1909; *Logic as the Science of the Pure Concept*, 1917) and *Filosofia della pratica: Economica ed etica* (1908; *Philosophy of the Practical: Economic and Ethic*, 1913) afforded Croce a better insight into the problem. As a result, critical activity was transferred to the sphere of logic, and the formula *artifex additus artifici* changed to that of *philosophus additus artifici*. Criticism is a logical operation in which a category (the concept of art) is applied to a fact (artistic intuition) in order to determine whether the fact is art or whether it is something else (moralism, indoctrination, reasoning, rhetoric) posing as art (intuition). The critical process ends with the qualification of the fact. The re-creation of the work of art is the antecedent of criticism. In *Logic as the Science of the Pure Concept*, Croce had postulated the identity of the judgment of fact with the value judgment, arriving at the conclusion that the history of a fact coincides with the evaluation of the fact itself. Therefore, all history is at the same time criticism, and all criticism, history. To ask what is that fact called *La divina commedia* (*The Divine Comedy*) is to ask what is its value, that is, to express a critical judgment. Consequently, aesthetic judgment is identical with historical judgment and criticism with history. This identity constitutes the foundation of Croce's critical methodology, which rejects any value transcending the world of history. All reality is historical reality, conceived as the activity of humankind, independent of any metaphysical, theological, or realistic objectivity conditioning human activity. Judging is no more than qualifying the nature of the fact in itself, for no values above the fact are conceivable. The historical interpretation of art and aesthetic criticism are one and the same. The full understanding of a work is achieved by placing it in the proper historical succession of its author's other works, for each poem contains the author's previous poem. To write a literary history from an aesthetic perspective is to distinguish and qualify a series of facts related to the same author. It follows that the most appropriate form of literary historiography is the monograph.

Croce's theory was a challenge to time-honored critical trends. His practical criticism proved its effectiveness. In its early period, it was mainly concerned with the individuality of lyrical intuition; it aimed at defining the distinctive traits of artistic expression, distinguishing them from other forms of mental activity and showing the individuality of each writer. This allowed Croce to single out the artistic personality and characterize it. What interested him was not the life or the practical activities of writers, but their artistic endeavors. This canon governs the essays collected in the first four volumes of *La letteratura della nuova Italia* (1914–1940), in which Croce seeks the purity and distinctness of intuitive moments. The theorization of the concept of "totality" (or universality) enhanced his critical perspective and led him to emphasize the eternal accent of poetry, above any restrictive classification. Poetry (art) is above space and time; it is the expression of "total and undivided humanity." Croce sought to demonstrate that art has no limits, that it expresses the universal *sub specie intuitionis*. To exemplify this concept, he undertook a series of monographs on major European writers, which resulted in the volumes *Goethe* (1919; English translation, 1923), *Ariosto, Shakespeare e Corneille* (1920; *Ariosto, Shakespeare and Corneille*, 1920), *La poesia di Dante* (1921; *The Poetry of*

Dante, 1922), *Poesia e non poesia* (1923; *European Literature in the Nineteenth Century*, 1924), *Poesia antica e moderna* (1941), and *Letture di poeti e riflessioni sulla teoria e la critica della poesia* (1950). Art is neither classic nor romantic, but the synthesis of both. The work of art must be not only formally perfect, but also moving. Great works express a vigorous feeling transformed into a lucid representation. Croce's doctrine of literature is felt in his later criticism, in which literary expression, though distinguished from poetry, is treated with a benevolent attitude for its positive role in civilized society.

In summary, Croce was a great innovator whose influence was widely felt. He scrutinized and discarded all previous literary theories and critical methodologies as being either faulty, insufficient, or outside the sphere of art, and he set the problem of artistic creation and criticism in its proper domain – that of philosophical aesthetics. His doctrine, before being constructive, was somewhat iconoclastic. Art is for him an autonomous cognitive activity; it is creation by the spirit, which is freedom, and it does not aim at practical, useful purposes, whether hedonistic or pedagogic. It is not a vehicle of ideas, or moral or political intentions, which the critic seeks to extract and explain: it contains only images. Art is contemplation. Croce's innovative identification of art with language, intuition with expression, and art with beauty and lyricism has been thoroughly assimilated by critical theory.

Principal criticism

Estetica come scienza dell'espressione e linguistica generale, 1902 (*Aesthetic as Science of Expression and General Linguistic*, 1909)
Problemi di estetica e contributi alla storia dell'estetica italiana, 1910
Saggi sulla letteratura italiana del seicento, 1911
Breviario di estetica, 1913 (*The Breviary of Aesthetic*, 1915)
La letteratura della nuova Italia, 1914–1940 (6 volumes)
Conversazioni critiche, 1918–1951 (5 volumes)
Goethe, 1919 (English translation, 1923)
Ariosto, Shakespeare, e Corneille, 1920 (*Ariosto, Shakespeare, and Corneille*, 1920)
Nuovi saggi di estetica, 1920
La poesia di Dante, 1921 (*The Poetry of Dante*, 1922)
Poesia e non poesia, 1923 (*European Literature in the Nineteenth Century*, 1924)
Storia dell'età barocca in Italia, 1929
Nuovi saggi sulla letteratura italiana del seicento, 1931
Poesia popolare e poesia d'arte, 1933
Ultimi saggi, 1935
La poesia: Introduzione alla critica e storia della poesia e della letteratura, 1936 (*Poetry and Literature: An Introduction to the Criticism and History*, 1981)
Poesia antica e moderna, 1941
Poeti e scrittori del pieno e del tardo rinascimento, 1945–1952 (3 volumes)
La letteratura italiana del settecento: Note critiche, 1949
Letture di poeti e riflessioni sulla teoria e la critica della poesia, 1950
Filosofia, poesia, storia, 1951 (*Philosophy, Poetry, History: An Anthology of Essays*, 1966)
Aneddoti di varia letteratura, 1953 (3 volumes)

Other major works and literary forms

Benedetto Croce was a philosopher of art and a literary critic. His complete works comprise some eighty volumes dealing with, in addition to aesthetics and literary criticism, philosophy, history, politics, and morality. *Estetica come scienza dell'espressione e linguistica generale* (1902; *Aesthetic as Science of Expression and General Linguistic*, 1909) is the first volume of his "Filosofia come scienza dello spirito" ("Philosophy of Spirit"), which includes *Filosofia della pratica: Economica ed etica* (1908; *Philosophy of the Practical: Economic and Ethic*, 1913), *Logica come scienza del concetto puro* (1909; *Logic as the Science of the Pure Concept*, 1917), and *Teoria e storia della storiografia* (1917; *Theory and History of Historiography*, 1921).

These four books encompass Croce's basic philosophical conception, which he defines as "absolute historicism." His first interest was the problem of art and criticism, but he was soon drawn to the fields of philosophy and theory of history, in order to give a philosophical foundation to his aesthetic. He was a notable historian who produced a number of valuable works in the field of history. Among his other major achievements, outside the area of literary theory per se, the following must be cited: *Ciò che è vivo e ciò che è morto della filosofia di Hegel* (1907; *What Is Living and What Is Dead of the Philosophy of Hegel*, 1915); *Etica e politica* (1931), which includes *Frammenti di etica* (1922; *The Conduct of Life*, 1924), *Elementi di politica* (1925; *Politics and Morals*, 1945), and *Contributo alla critica di me stesso* (1918; *An Autobiography*, 1927); *Storia d'Europa nel secolo decimonono* (1932; *History of Europe in the Nineteenth Century*, 1963); and *La storia come pensiero e come azione* (1938; *History as the Story of Liberty*, 1941).

NONFICTION
I teatri di Napoli dal rinascimento alla fine del secolo decimottavo, 1891
La rivoluzione napoletana del 1799, 1899
Materialismo storico ed economia marxistica, 1900 (*Historical Materialism and the Economics of Karl Marx*, 1914)
Ciò che è vivo e ciò che è morto della filosofia di Hegel, 1907 (*What Is Living and What Is Dead of the Philosophy of Hegel*, 1915)
Filosofia della pratica: Economica ed etica, 1908 (*Philosophy of the Practical: Economic and Ethic*, 1913)
Logica come scienza del concetto puro, 1909 (*Logic as the Science of the Pure Concept*, 1917)
La filosofia di Giambattista Vico, 1911 (*The Philosophy of Giambattista Vico*, 1913)
Cultura e vita morale, 1914
Teoria e storia della storiografia, 1917 (*Theory and History of Historiography*, 1921)
Contributo alla critica di me stesso, 1918 (*An Autobiography*, 1927)
Storia della storiografia italiana del secolo decimonono, 1921 (2 volumes)
Frammenti di etica, 1922 (*The Conduct of Life*, 1924)
Storia del regno di Napoli, 1925 (*History of the Kingdom of Naples*, 1970)

Elementi di politica, 1925 (*Politics and Morals*, 1945)
Storia d'Italia dal 1871 al 1915, 1928 (*History of Italy, 1871–1915*, 1929)
Etica e politica, 1931 (includes *The Conduct of Life, Politics and Morals, and An Autobiography*)
Storia d'Europa nel secolo decimonono, 1932 (*History of Europe in the Nineteenth Century*, 1963)
Varietà di storia letteraria e civile, 1935–1950 (2 volumes)
La storia come pensiero e come azione, 1938 (*History as the Story of Liberty*, 1941)
Discorsi di varia filosofia, 1945 (2 volumes)
Pensiero politico e politica attuale, 1946
Quando l'Italia era tagliata in due, 1948 (*Croce, the King, and the Allies*, 1950)
Filosofia e storiografia, 1949
Indagini sullo Hegel e schiarimenti filosofici, 1952

Further reading

Brown, Merle. *Neo-Idealistic Aesthetics: Croce, Gentile, Collingwood*, 1966.
Carr, Wildon. *The Philosophy of Benedetto Croce: The Problem of Art and History*, 1917.
Casale, Giuseppe. *Benedetto Croce Between Naples and Europe*, 1994.
Moss, M. E. *Benedetto Croce Reconsidered: Truth and Error in Theories of Art, Literature, and History*, 1987.
Orsini, Gian N. G. *Benedetto Croce, Philosopher of Art and Literary Critic*, 1961.
Palmer, L. M., and H. S. Harris, eds. *Thought, Action, and Intuition: A Symposium on the Philosophy of Benedetto Croce*, 1975.
Piccoli, R. *Benedetto Croce: An Introduction to His Philosophy*, 1922.
Roberts, David D. *Benedetto Croce and the Uses of Historicism*, 1987.
Robertson, John M. *Croce as Shakespearean Critic*, 1974.
Seerveld, Calvin G. *Benedetto Croce's Earlier Aesthetic Theories and Literary Criticism*, 1958.
Shusterman, Richard. "Croce on Interpretation: Deconstruction and Pragmatism," in *New Literary History: A Journal of Theory and Interpretation*. 20, no. 1 (Autumn, 1988), pp. 199–216.
Sprigge, Cecil. *Benedetto Croce: Man and Thinker*, 1952.
Struckmeyer, O. K. *Croce and Literary Criticism*, 1921.
Wellek, René. *Four Critics: Croce, Valéry, Lukács, and Ingarden*, 1981.

GIOVANNI GULLACE

See also De Sanctis; Hegel

Jonathan Culler

American critic

Born: Cleveland, Ohio; October 1, 1944

Biography

Jonathan Culler was born in Cleveland, Ohio, on October 1, 1944. His undergraduate degree was obtained from Harvard University, from which he graduated *summa cum laude* in 1966. From there, he moved as a Rhodes Scholar to St. John's College, Oxford University, where he gained first a B.Phil. in comparative literature and subsequently a D.Phil. in modern languages, in 1972. He had moved in 1969 to Selwyn College, Cambridge, as fellow and director of studies in modern languages, before returning to Oxford, in 1977, as fellow and tutor of Brasenose College and university lecturer in French. Having been a visiting professor of French and comparative literature at Yale University in 1975, Culler moved back to the United States more permanently in 1977, to become a professor of English and comparative literature at Cornell. He has continued to be based at Cornell ever since, having been awarded the Class of 1916 Professorship of English and Comparative Literature in 1982. He has also served as director of the Society of Humanities at Cornell, and been chair of the departments of both comparative literature and English. Culler has received many awards for his work, including the James Russell Lowell Prize of the Modern Language Association of America, for *Structuralist Poetics: Structuralism, Linguistics, and the Study of Literature* in 1975, and numerous fellowships. He has been an extremely prominent figure in American literary studies throughout his career through his affiliation, in a variety of capacities, with a range of organizations, including the English Institute, the Woodrow Wilson Foundation, the American Comparative Literature Association, the Semiotic Society of America, the Modern Language Association of America, and the International Comparative Literature Association. He has also been connected with a number of journals, including *Diacritics*, which he edited from 1994 to 1998. He lives and works in New York City.

Influence

Jonathan Culler's influence as a critic has relied on two particular talents. The first is an intellectual flexibility that has allowed him to remain at the forefront of literary theory for nearly thirty years; his career spans, and keeps pace with, some of the most crucial debates and ideas of modern literary theory and criticism, and his writing, as a consequence, is consistently fresh and relevant. Perhaps equally important is his ability to digest the complex and often impenetrable work of other writers and thinkers, and then reformulate and analyze those ideas in an accessible and inventive manner. Much of his most influential critical writing has successfully encapsulated, for students and critics alike, the main concepts of structuralism, semiotics, and deconstruction. It is perhaps in this role of interpreter that he has been most influential, bringing to ideas that are often dense and unwieldy a clarity of insight and expression that lends them renewed vigor. In fact, Culler's major works all make out a case for the very practice of literary criticism itself, quite apart from the many theories he examines. He asks the reader to confront the most fundamental and often elusive question underlying critical practices; as he puts it in the preface to *Structuralist Poetics*: "What is literary criticism for? What is its task and what is its value?". To provide satisfactory answers to these questions, Culler rejects the "orthodoxy" of the purely interpretive New Criticism, which, he says, "offers but a more thorough and perceptive version of what every reader does for himself." In turning to more experimental modes of critical inquiry, first structuralism, then deconstruction ("schools" which he firmly believes to be closely linked, despite invidious and shallow distinctions between structuralism and poststructuralism), Culler has attempted to bring to Anglo-American literary criticism their focus on the way meaning is defined, rather than on attributing to texts specific meanings. He does so guardedly, with an awareness that the issues thrown up by the work of, say, the French structuralists are often problematic:

> Not that their criticism is itself a model which could or should be directly imported and reverently imitated, but . . . through a reading of their works one may derive a sense of criticism as a coherent discipline and of the goals at which it might aim.

The creation and furtherance of this sense of coherence has been one of Culler's significant contributions to literary studies.

Analysis

Culler has developed several distinctive critical stances of his own, which echo in his writing from work to work. The first is a steadfast refutation of the principles of New Criticism, a denial of the primacy of the interpretive process as the main end of criticism. Embracing the semiotic theories of structuralists such as Roland Barthes, Culler consistently denies that the revelation of meaning in a literary text is as important as understanding how that meaning is produced, and how we as readers respond to and interpret that meaning. However, Culler's approach to semiotics is distinct from the critics of the so-called *Tel Quel* school, including Philippe Sollers, Julia Kristeva, and Stephen Heath, whose work infuses semiotics with a political agenda and utilizes a psychoanalytic methodology. Culler is more rational and less polemical – the tone of his writing, throughout his career, has been one of reasoned clarity.

Following the development of deconstructive theories of Jacques Derrida and Paul de Man, which undermine the structuralist dream of a comprehensive "science of signs," Culler has been a crucial advocate of the continuing validity of the structuralist project. He has denied what he described in *Ferdinand de Saussure* (1976) as "the facile distinction between structuralism and post-structuralism, which may caricature structuralism and transfer to post-structuralism what is most interesting in structuralist writings." As Stephen Bann has expressed it, "For Culler . . . semiotics as a critical activity involves a decisive break with New Criticism, and a salutary symbiosis with deconstruction."

Culler broadly outlines his essential beliefs about the nature and purpose of criticism in his first published book, *Flaubert: The Uses of Uncertainty* (1974). His discussion of Gustave Flaubert's works emphasizes their departure from novelistic convention, in that they seek "to invalidate the communicative contract" between author and reader, and "to make the novel an aesthetic object rather than a communictive act." The construction of Flaubert's sentences thus becomes a process more akin to sculpture than communicative writing, "more easily admired than assimilated as message." This artistic project on the part of the author, he argues, "gives the novel a new autonomy and artistic status but creates problems of interpretation, especially since it is no longer clear why it was produced." It is in response to this problem that Culler articulates his conception of the role of criticism in reading literature. On one level, the function of criticism can be explained by a psychiatric model, in which the critic attempts to make explicit the subconscious responses of the reader to the text. But Culler has reservations about basing his critical argument on the notion that an instinctive, spontaneous response to literature is in some way the most valid one. In Culler's words,

> the notion of a natural and unmediated response to literature is clearly a myth: someone who had no acquaintance with literature and the discussion of it, far from providing a "pure" response against which critics might test their corrupt and elaborated versions, would simply not know what to make of a poem or novel, because to read it *as* a poem or a novel . . . is to read it in accordance with the procedures that have been developed by a cultural tradition and are gradually assimilated during one's literary training. One cannot assume, therefore, that we have full and complete reactions to a text which criticism simply makes explicit. Reactions are likely to be awkward when we lack the formal machinery for considering them. What we cannot say we are less likely to feel. And therefore critical discourse must be recognised as a process of producing meanings and allowed to produce new meanings . . . .

Thus, for Culler, the critical project in which he is engaged is not merely interpretive of reader response; nor can it be said to have a definite aim, in the manner of traditional teleological critical approaches, which perceive all aspects of a text as contributing to an overall "unity" or "meaning." Culler wishes to avoid such critical foreclosure, arguing that "literature can be valued for qualities other than the unity or meaning it leads one to produce; one can also value the resistance to meaning and the resistance to unity." Ultimately, Culler is prepared to embrace the vaguest definitions of the aim of criticism, in order to preserve this sense of purposive openness: "One might simply say that criticism exists to make things interesting. If one thus avoids foreclosure at the cost of vacuity, that is, I believe, a necessary operating expense."

Throughout his career Culler has founded his work on an extensive knowledge of the history of ideas, as well as his engagement with contemporary theory. He has provided several useful accounts of the development of semiotics and deconstruction, and their roots in the linguistic innovations of Ferdinand de Saussure and the pragmatic philosophy of C. S. Peirce. *Ferdinand de Saussure* offers a good general survey of Saussure's main theories and his profound influence on modern semiotic theory; but perhaps the best encapsulation of the respective contributions of Saussure and Peirce (and a good example of how Culler's writing can be simultaneously provocative and explanatory) is to be found in *The Pursuit of Signs: Semiotics, Literature, Deconstruction* (1981):

> By conceiving semiotics on the model of linguistics, Saussure gave it a practical program, at the cost of begging important questions about the similarities between linguistic and non-linguistic signs . . . . But by attempting to construct an autonomous semiotics, Peirce condemned himself to taxonomic speculations that denied him any influence until semiotics was so well developed that his obsession seemed appropriate. While Saussure identified a handful of communicative practices that might benefit from a semiotic approach, and thus provided a point of departure, Peirce's insistence that everything is a sign did little to help found a discipline . . . .

The analysis of structuralism, the movement into deconstruction, and the critical consequences of this development, while they provide the backdrop for all Culler's work, are most exhaustively investigated in what are arguably his three most important books, *Structuralist Poetics*, *The Pursuit of Signs*, and *On Deconstruction*, the last being a sequel to the first. In *Structuralist Poetics*, besides providing a comprehensive survey of the work of the structuralists, Culler advances his own reformulation (via Noam Chomsky) of Saussure's distinction between *langue* and *parole*. He defines his notion of "literary competence" thus:

> Study of the linguistic system becomes theoretically coherent when we cease thinking that our goal is to specify the properties of objects in a corpus and concentrate instead on the task of formulating the internalized competence which enables objects to have the properties they do for those who have mastered the system. To discover and characterize structures one must analyze the system which assigns structural descriptions to the objects in question, and thus literary taxonomy should be grounded on a theory of reading. The relevant categories are those which are required to account for the range of acceptable meanings which works can have for readers of literature.

Implicit in this theory, which supposes we can distinguish between competent and incompetent readers, is the defence of literary criticism per se which we have already noted in *Flaubert*.

Culler himself has pointed out that when he wrote *Structuralist Poetics*, few people in academic circles were familiar with, or interested in, the application of such radical semiotic theories to literature. By the time he wrote its sequel, *On Deconstruction: Theory and Criticism After Structuralism* (1982), this climate of indifference had vanished, replaced by a bewildering multiplicity of critical approaches. In *On Deconstruction*, Culler, typically, attempts to bring a sense of coherence to what was rapidly becoming a very fragmented discipline; and although he spreads his net wide to encompass, amongst other things, recent feminist criticism, he achieves this principally by devoting his attention and exposition to the work of Jacques Derrida. Whilst skeptical about "the mythification of Derrida as an absolute presence" which had sprung up during the 1970s, he nevertheless recognizes his work, and deconstruction in general, as a "leading source of energy and innovation in recent theory."

The Pursuit of Signs was published in between the other two books, and provides a useful synthesis of their relative positions. It articulates, again, Culler's firm belief in the continuity between structuralism and deconstruction, a belief which provides a backbone to his work. As he puts it,

> deconstruction has not "refuted" structuralism and semiotics, as some "post-structuralists" would have it. If deconstructive readings give us reasons to believe that a complete and non-contradictory science of signs is impossible, that does not mean that the enterprise should be abandoned . . . . One might even say that the paradoxes which deconstructive readings identify as important insights into the nature of literary language are for semiotics the result of basic methodological distinctions – between *langue* and *parole*, system and event, synchronic and diachronic, signifier and signified, metaphor and metonymy – which are still essential to the analytical project even though they break down at certain points or yield two perspectives that cannot be synthesized.

Deconstructive criticism, and Derrida's work in particular, according to Culler, has effectively collapsed any linguistic distinction between the critical text of the critic, and the literary text which the critic is attempting to analyze, an antifoundationalism which serves to eradicate conventional boundaries between disciplines of writing:

> The discourse which attempts to analyze metaphor does not itself escape metaphor. There is a metalinguistic function – language can discuss language – but there is no metalanguage, only more language piled upon language. Deconstruction has been particularly acute in showing the uncanny involvement of theories in the domains they claim to describe, in showing how critics become engaged in a displaced reenactment of a text's scenario.

Culler asserts that the fact that the critic is caught up in the same system of signs as the text he or she is examining does not invalidate the pursuit of criticism: "On the contrary, one can continue to the pursuit of signs, the attempt to grasp, master, formulate, define, even though one knows that one is caught up in a signifying process that one cannot fully control . . . ."

In recent years Culler has remained an acute observer and commentator on the state of Anglo-American literary studies. With the publication, in 1988, of *Framing the Sign: Criticism and its Institutions*, he takes a broader view of the changes that occurred in criticism in the 1970s and 1980s, and the way many of the principles of literary theory had bled into other disciplines, such as law, anthropology, art, history, or psychoanalysis. Noting the current climate of diversity, Culler comments on the supersedence of an orthodox literary canon, of the sense of a "great tradition," by a broader analysis of language and the construction of meaning which acknowledges the impact of semiotics and deconstruction:

> If there is a unity to literary studies in this new dispensation it comes not from the canon of plays, poems and novels but from an attention to mechanisms of signification which can be studied in a wide range of texts and text-like situations.

Alongside the expansion of the field in which literary critics work, he observes the increasing politicization of literary studies. "Framing the sign" is the term Culler coins as a more accurate description of the study of context, by which he means "the institutional context of criticism" or the constraining, domesticating influence of university structures on "radical theoretical discourses"; the broader social and historical context; and "the context of other disciplines or institutions which is crucial to attempts to extend literary analysis into broader cultural or rhetorical studies." Importantly, Culler stresses that context itself is constructed, and equally shaped by interpretive strategies as the act or text to which it pertains.

Framing the Sign includes a discussion of major critics, such as William Empson, Gaston Bachelard, and Paul de Man, whose work has reached beyond the confines of literary criticism, but this is balanced by the skillful application of theory to modern life – for instance, Culler applies a semiotic analysis to tourism, arguing for its centrality in determining our conception of the world. He notes, for example, that the conflict between the authentic and inauthentic – the natural and the touristy – is a crucial issue in tourism, as it is in life and in literature; the same fallacious value is placed on "discovery" in all these fields:

> The paradox, the dilemma of authenticity, is that to be experienced as authentic it must be marked as authentic, but when it is marked as authentic it is mediated, a sign of itself, and hence lacks the authenticity of what is truly unspoiled, untouched by mediating cultural codes.

The writing in *Framing the Sign* reflects the flexibilty and inventiveness of Culler's work as a whole. His writing benefits from his ability to move effortlessly from the general to the specific, from the historical to the contemporary, and from complexity to clarity – qualities admirably on show in his recent *Literary Theory: A Very Short Introduction* (1997). Having figured prominently amongst the pioneers of semiotics in Anglo-American literary studies, Culler has also played a crucial role in overseeing its gradual introduction into university programs, ensuring that in terms of both his teaching and writing he remains in the vanguard of critical theory today.

Principal criticism

Flaubert: The Uses of Uncertainty, 1974, 1985
Structuralist Poetics: Structuralism, Linguistics, and the Study of Literature, 1975
Ferdinand de Saussure (British title: *Saussure*), 1976
The Pursuit of Signs: Semiotics, Literature, Deconstruction, 1981
On Deconstruction: Theory and Criticism After Structuralism, 1982
Roland Barthes (British title: *Barthes*), 1983
Framing the Sign: Criticism and its Institutions, 1988
Literary Theory: A Very Short Introduction, 1997

EDITED TEXT
The Call of the Phoneme: Puns and the Foundations of Letters, 1987

Further reading

Bann, Stephen. "Semiotics," in *Cambridge History of Literary Criticism*. Vol. 8, *From Formalism to Poststructuralism*, 1995. Edited by Raman Selden.
Eagleton, Terry. *The Function of Criticism: From "The Spectator" to Post-structuralism*, 1984.
——. *Literary Theory: An Introduction*, 1996 (second edition).
Eco, Umberto. *Interpretation and Overinterpretation*, 1992.
Howells, Christina. *Derrida: Deconstruction from Phenomenology to Ethics*, 1998.
Norris, Christopher. *Deconstruction: Theory and Practice*, 1982.
Wood, David. *Derrida: A Critical Reader*, 1992.

ROWLAND HUGHES

See also American Literary Theory: Twentieth Century; Barthes; British Literary Theory: Twentieth Century; Deconstruction; Derrida; Saussure; Semiotics; Structuralism

Cultural Criticism

Cultural criticism has no set topic, methodology, or politics. It does not even have a set definition or valuation of culture. What cultural critics do have in common is a conviction that the products of human thought are in a dynamic relationship with human knowledge and social practices. The field of cultural criticism, therefore, constantly changes and is often contentious. One of the most interesting results of cultural criticism is the changing perceptions it creates of what products count as culture, who participates in culture, and what mechanisms undergird the reproduction of culture. In *Keywords*, Raymond Williams identifies the "range and overlap" of the definitions of culture as signifying "a complex argument about the relations between general human development and a particular way of life, and between both and the works and practices of art and intelligence." It is precisely this complexity and questioning of relationships that defines cultural criticism.

Today cultural criticism is often recognized under the heading of cultural studies. While these two headings are interchangeable, it is worth noting that the term cultural studies has a very specific institutional history. Cultural studies in this context stems from the work of Williams and Richard Hoggart and has been further represented by the Centre for Contemporary Cultural Studies at the University of Birmingham, England. The Centre, particularly under the direction of Stuart Hall and Richard Johnson, has been influential in gaining a space for the study of popular media and movements as well as Marxist theory in the academy. Cultural studies, however, must be understood as having all of the characteristics ascribed to cultural criticism above, despite this institutional history. Lawrence Grossberg describes the history of cultural studies as "a history of political engagements and of theoretical debates in response to which alternative positions are constantly being taken into account and new positions offered," demonstrating the importance of a historical understanding of the field that makes cultural studies subject to its own critique.

It would be impossible to ascribe an origin to cultural criticism: Plato and Aristotle both wrote about the effects of art, philosophy, and religion upon society. The Enlightenment, however, does provide a theory of culture within and against which contemporary cultural criticism defines itself. Culture, understood as an amalgam of human thinking and achievements that surpasses basic human existence, was extensively theorized by Enlightenment philosophy. Within this view, culture is an abstract concept, incorporating science, history, philosophy, and art, that indicates a way of thinking about the world. It provided a critical position from which a universal perspective could be constructed. Enlightenment thinkers were concerned with finding and studying the underlying, natural principles that guided human existence as a means to bettering it. Reason, a natural faculty of the human mind that, according to René Descartes, "is the only thing which makes us men, and distinguishes us from the beasts," served as the means to this end. These writers believed that by exercising reason freely and individually, humans would progress toward a perfect society in harmony with nature. Immanuel Kant articulates the Enlightenment belief that culture is the ultimate expression of this freedom, writing that "[t]he production in a rational being of an aptitude for any ends whatever of his own choosing, consequently of the aptitude of a being in his freedom, is culture." Kant's emphasis on "aptitude" or potential helps to clarify the theorizing power culture inhabited in Enlightenment philosophy. It was important as an indicator of the future perfection of human society as well as a means to reach that future. In the first case, culture was measured according to progress in science, philosophy, and art. In the second case, culture, as distinguished from daily human practices, opened up a critique of particular social elements that were perceived to be obstacles to the progression of enlightenment because they discouraged questioning, promoted inequality, or actively repressed people.

Enlightenment ideals are incorporated into later cultural criticism in one way or another. First, it is through a distinction between life as it is normally lived and a possible future of complete freedom that culture becomes a distinct category that can be studied. Second, the moral and/or political impetus behind an exploration of the effects of culture is set by the Enlightenment – the desire for freedom. This common impetus took a number of forms, from a continuation of the universalist concept of culture, to questioning the extricability of culture from social relations to revisions of the concepts of subjects. Although the reactions can be schematized as three separate strains of cultural criticism for the purposes of clarifying social and political investments, none of these strains are pure or independent of the others. Each interacts with the others, even if in opposition, and together they form the field of cultural criticism.

One strain of cultural criticism that grew out of the Enlightenment emphasized the transcendent nature of "culture," continuing to hold out the importance of separating the future progress of human society from its quotidian products and practices. In the nineteenth century a growing industrial economy was often singled out as the particular enemy to society by writers such as Samuel Taylor Coleridge, John Ruskin, and Matthew Arnold. This body of work viewed with dismay the increasing strength and wealth of the middle class and its narrow assessments of progress. Speed, efficiency, and individual self-interest were seen to eclipse and even destroy the finer feelings essential to human development. Arnold exemplifies the rejection of industrialism and the turn to a "spiritual" alternative, asserting that culture will be the salvation of society. In

Culture and Anarchy (1869) Arnold explains that culture is a spiritual force that parallels religion, but also surpasses it by accounting for "all the voices of human experience . . . of art, science, poetry, philosophy, history, as well as religion." Arnold has often been characterized as an illiberal advocate of "high culture." Certainly his definition of the role the cultural critic plays bears out this charge. The true function of criticism, according to Arnold, is "a disinterested endeavour to learn and propagate the best that is known and thought in the world." Having said this, however, it is important to keep in mind that Arnold disapproves of the aristocracy, whom he terms "Barbarians," for their lack of ideas. While this does not absolve Arnold, he also fears the lower classes, which complicates a definition of "high culture" that sees it in direct relation to economic domination. This belief in the transformative potential of culture through its capacity to overcome material differences between people continues to resonate in contemporary cultural criticism, particularly in the United States. Some critics advocate a return to a transcendent culture much like Arnold's to counter what they see as a fragmentation of society and an ingrained inequality in education created by an overemphasis on gender, race, and class differences.

A second strain of cultural criticism rejects the liberatory role of culture, focusing on the danger inherent in the distinction between culture and the social realm. Like the transcendent strain of cultural criticism, this approach also begins in reaction to industrialism. However, rather than hold up culture as the salvation for society, it views culture as part of the complex social relations that "enslave" humanity. Karl Marx criticized Enlightenment philosophy for focusing exclusively on the development of human consciousness and thereby ignoring the actual material conditions of society. Marx's work radically altered cultural criticism by reversing the relationship between culture and daily life. Marx sums up the limits of the Enlightenment as well as his difference from it in *The German Ideology: Part 1* (1845), writing that "life is not determined by consciousness, but consciousness by life." Throughout his work, Marx insisted that true social change must happen at the "base," meaning at the level of economic exchange, and from there the changes would be expressed in the "superstructure" through art, philosophy, religion, and other intellectual productions. The relationship between base and superstructure is of course dialectic, meaning they continuously influence each other. Culture, or what Marx terms "ideology," serves as a record of the struggles to transform society as well as one of the sites of that struggle, because it is through ideology that humans recognize and theorize the economic process. For instance, Marx turns to William Shakespeare to clarify the role of money in society in *The Economic and Philosophic Manuscripts of 1844* (published 1932). Nonetheless, while Shakespeare "excellently depicts the real nature of money," this depiction alone only points to the underlying social relations that would have to be changed in order to create a free society.

The significance of Marx's work to cultural criticism can be seen in the ways it has been reinterpreted, revised, and expanded by subsequent critics. While these critics differ and often even disagree, Martin Jay points out that this work has "enriched cultural theory" through a consistent focus on the way ideology naturalizes and reinforces the dominance of the ruling class. This process, called "hegemony" by Antonio Gramsci, formed the basis of the most dominant strain of twentieth-century cultural criticism. An attention to "hegemony" arises from the need to explain the intransigence of capitalism and the changes in the structure of capital due primarily to technology and mass media. In *Dialectic of Enlightenment* Max Horkheimer and Theodor W. Adorno, both members of the Frankfurt School, explain how culture combined with technology creates a façade of individual choice that actually absorbs differences and in return churns out subjects as part of its mass production. Discussing the consumption of consumer goods from cars to Hollywood films to advertising, they explain how the escape offered by the "culture industry" is an illusion, writing that "to walk from the street into the movie theater is no longer to enter a world of dream." Technologically advanced lighting and sound reproduce the world almost exactly, and so the film exploits the audience as much as any job. While critiques such as Adorno's and Horkheimer's broaden the range of culture to include everything from television to body-piercing, they fail to offer a correspondingly complex theory of how culture creates subjects. Not all films communicate the same messages to the same people, or, to put it another way, the programming of subjectivity by culture is less predictable or controllable. In recent years monolithic, unifying theories of hegemony have come increasingly under question, because they account for neither the contradictions found within the cultural field nor the possibilities of resistance to particular messages. Paul Smith, Ernesto Laclau, and Chantal Mouffe articulate the issue in terms of moving away from a concept of a central, fixed notion of subjectivity and the social to more fluid, contingent formations.

A third strain of cultural criticism responds to both these strains, challenging the universality of a single culture as well as insisting that any description of the modes of production that excludes gender and race is incomplete. This strain of cultural criticism suggests that the theorization of one culture itself creates that culture, silencing the multiplicity of cultures which exist in a given society. Within this strain culture is aligned with dominant power structures that enforce inequality between people as well as within subjectivity itself and has been termed patriarchal, logocentric, and colonialist. However, culture is also subject to recuperation in much of this work in the form of alternative traditions, subjectivities, and institutions. In *The Madwoman in the Attic* Sandra Gilbert and Susan Gubar locate their recovery of nineteenth-century women writers between two concepts of culture. The first, tied to "an overwhelmingly male-dominated society," confined the writers, while the second, "a rich and clearly defined female literary sub-culture," enables the critic to challenge the academic literary canon and creates new spaces for women to write and relate to each other and themselves. A similar pattern of rejection and recuperation can be found in postcolonial criticism which involves a theory of the subject alienated by an enforced cultural terrorism, or what Ngugi wa Thiong'o calls "a cultural bomb." Explaining what he terms "an imperialist tradition" of economic, political, and social control over African countries, Ngugi singles out culture as the strongest imperialist weapon because it destroys "a people's belief in their names, in their languages, in their environment, in their heritage of struggle, in their unity, in their capacities and ultimately in themselves." Ngugi's contextualization of African language and literature within and against imperialist culture is an attempt to rediscover and affirm the identity that appears lost. This third strain of cultural criticism emphasizes intervention through an interactive understanding of culture and subjectivity. As Edward Said notes in *The World, the Text, and the Critic*, criticism should be "opposed to every form of tyranny, domination, and abuse; its social goals are noncoercive knowledge produced in the interests of human freedom."

Cultural criticism studies the productions and effects of culture, while at the same time reproducing culture itself. Its excursions into the cultural field are never neutral. The first cultural product with which any cultural critic must contend, therefore, is the critic him- or herself. The question of the role of the critic within criticism has been a point of debate within cultural criticism of every tradition, as one of the premises is that the critic can change culture through study. Arnold holds that culture is separate from daily life, and describes "disinterest" or a separation from practical concerns as the proper mindset for the critic. Marx assumes that the critic is immersed in ideology and first must work to escape from constitutive class conditions that narrow his perspective. Gayatri Spivak insists that the critic must understand his or her complicity with the systems he or she critiques. Ultimately it is this ethical dimension, the question of how to become conscious of the power of culture and how best to remain critical of that power that lies behind all cultural criticism.

Further reading

Berger, Arthur Asa. *Cultural Criticism: A Primer of Key Concepts*, 1995.
Curran, James, et al. *Cultural Studies and Communications*, 1996.
Gilbert, Sandra M., and Susan Gubar. *The Madwoman in the Attic: The Woman Writer and the Nineteenth-Century Literary Imagination*, 1979.
Grossberg, Lawrence. "The Formations of Cultural Studies: An American in Birmingham," in *Relocating Cultural Studies: Developments in Theory and Research*, 1993.
Horkheimer, Max, and Theodor W. Adorno. *Dialektik der Aufklärung*, 1944 (*Dialectic of Enlightenment*, 1944; John Cumming, translator).
Jameson, Fredric, and Masao Miyoshi, eds. *The Cultures of Globalization*, 1998.
Jay, Martin. *Marxism and Totality: The Adventures of a Concept from Lukács to Habermas*, 1984.
Johnson, Lesley. *The Cultural Critics: From Matthew Arnold to Raymond Williams*, 1979.
Leitch, Vincent B. *Cultural Criticism, Literary Theory, Poststructuralism*, 1992.
Ngugi wa Thiong'o. *Decolonizing the Mind*, 1986.
Said, Edward. *The World, the Text, and the Critic*, 1983.
Tucker, Robert G. *The Marx–Engels Reader*, 1972.
Williams, Raymond. *Keywords*, 1976.

DONYA SAMARA

Ernst Robert Curtius

German scholar and critic

Born: Thann, Alsace; April 14, 1886
Died: Rome, Italy; April 19, 1956

Biography

Ernst Robert Curtius was born in Thann, near Mulhouse, in German-ruled Alsace on April 14, 1886, the son of Friedrich Curtius, a civil servant who later moved to Strasbourg to become executive director of the Augsburg Confessional Church. The family came originally from the German coast of the Baltic Sea and had resided for the better part of the nineteenth century in the thriving port city of Lübeck, where they distinguished themselves for their learning and cultural patronage. Among Curtius' many distinguished ancestors is Ernst Curtius, the celebrated archaeologist and historian of Greece.

At the universities in Strasbourg, Berlin, and Heidelberg, Curtius studied Sanskrit and comparative linguistics, as well as modern literature. The great philologist Gustav Gröber at Strasbourg was influential in determining Curtius' choice of medieval literature as the focus for his research. Curtius' teaching career at Bonn, however, was interrupted almost immediately by the outbreak of World War I. After military service, Curtius taught in Marburg and Heidelberg before returning to Bonn in 1929. By the time he died in Rome in 1956, after only five years in retirement, Curtius had received numerous honors, including the Lessing Prize of the City of Hamburg, the French Order of Merit, and honorary degrees from the University of Glasgow and the Sorbonne.

Influence

Largely in response to the tumultuous effects of nationalistic extremism on European culture in the first half of the twentieth century, Curtius explored the Latin foundations of the European tradition and thus the historical interrelations of the major vernacular literatures and their shared archetypes, metaphors, and rhetorical commonplaces (*topoi*). His purpose was to remind Europe of its cultural continuity and unity. The highly influential *European Literature and the Latin Middle Ages* exhibits the qualities for which Curtius is most respected: his encyclopedic knowledge, his rigorous application of sound philological and historical methods, his synthesizing purpose in identifying and analyzing parallels, affinities, and connectionism, and finally his preeminently humanistic affirmation of the Western spiritual heritage in spite of the pessimistic outlook of the present age as he understood it.

Analysis

Romanticism in Germany is associated with the emergence of cultural and political nationalism and with the appearance of the systematic study of vernacular literatures. Not only the "folk," or national, tradition in literature was of interest to the Romantics, however, but also the culture of the Middle Ages. The growth of philology in the national literature was thus accompanied in this period by the rise of another school of scholarship and criticism that emphasized the medieval roots of the modern European literatures and the classical traditions inherited from the Latin-speaking Roman Catholic church. Curtius belongs to this latter school. He did not set out to create a new theoretical groundwork for literary criticism but to apply sound philological methods in the search for interrelations and continuity.

Romance philologists Friedrich Diez and Adolf Ebert had established the modern study of medieval literature in Germany in the first half of the nineteenth century, and Gustav Gröber continued their work on medieval documents and Latin influences on vernacular literary development. Curtius would further refine and synthesize the modern philological conception of the Middle Ages as an age of great classical erudition and universalist consciousness, with a literature both original and rich in classical themes, motifs, symbols, and – as Curtius insisted – common trains of thought, or *topoi*. The medieval period was neither the static cultural unity envisioned by some Romantics nor a "dark age" of ignorance and backwardness.

In *European Literature and the Latin Middle Ages* and elsewhere, the classical commonplace, or *topos*, functions for Curtius as the vehicle of continuity from antiquity to the present day in literary art. Some *topoi* are peculiar to certain epochs, but others (*ubi sunt, carpe diem*, and so on) seem to reappear from century to century and can represent in microcosm the spiritual and cultural integrity of Western tradition. The importance of this integrity was made clear to Curtius by crisis. Curtius believed that his contemporaries in the 1930s and 1940s had lost sight not only of the classical heritage shared by all of Europe but also of the quality and import of European achievement. In an age fraught with fragmentation and nationalism, Curtius gave criticism a humanistic mission to refresh the historical memory of the individual European nations as to the greater cultural context of the West and thus remind them of possibilities for a peaceful and spiritually enriched future. Wars and conflicting ideologies had polarized and diminished spiritual Europe, and a kind of cultural pessimism had replaced the educated European's sense of spiritual unity and intellectual progress.

European Literature and the Latin Middle Ages is Curtius' most accessible and influential book. It grew out of the moral concern for the preservation of Western culture prompted first by ominous developments in German education in the early 1930s (Curtius saw very early the damage that would be done by political extremists and Francophobe nationalists in the cultural arena). Kennard Rand's *Founders of the Middle Ages* (1928) was a great influence on Curtius as well, leading him to see a reintegration of the nearly forgotten Middle Ages as a prerequisite for cultural renewal.

Curtius' view encompasses the whole of culture, including science, religion, and politics – everything that affects the individual and collective world of which the written word is an expression. In *European Literature and the Latin Middle Ages* Curtius accounts for the necessity of discussing religious writings alongside secular poetry, for example, by applying Henri Bergson's concept of the human "fabulatory function" to suggest a common source for poetic as well as religious literature. The manifestations of the human "fabulatory function" thus make up the essential subject of literary history and criticism.

Curtius opposed the twentieth-century predeliction for theoretical abstractions about literature and called for broad reading and meticulous attention to the texts themselves in the tradition of nineteenth-century philology. He responded to this call in his critical studies not only of medieval figures but also of modern authors of international significance, such as Johann Wolfgang von Goethe, Stefan George, Hugo von Hofmannsthal, and Hermann Hesse in Germany, Paul Valéry, Jean Cocteau, and Jorge Guillén in France, Pedro Calderón de la Barca and José Ortega y Gasset in Spain, and Ralph Waldo Emerson, James Joyce, and T. S. Eliot in the English-speaking world. In fact, Curtius began his career as a critic of contemporaneous and recent French writers, such as Marcel Proust. Curtius collected many of his critical articles and republished them in 1950 as *Essays on European Literature*. In his critical discussions Curtius emphasizes artistic originality and individuality while at the same time establishing the writer's place in the larger cultural continuum by identifying and analyzing the use of traditional motifs and symbols [illegible] well as the adoption of techniques or images from the sciences or other arts.

Literary history and literary criticism share the same "mansion," as Curtius once said. Both fields have the same subject, the text, and both require the active, informed participation of the reader. Curtius instructs his reader in the very art of reading, in the appreciation of a work's textual autonomy as well as its historical and comparative relation to other works. In contrasting his method with that of the natural sciences, Curtius makes the following remarks in *European Literature and the Latin Middle Ages*:

> The advances in our knowledge of nature are verifiable .... The advance of historical knowledge, on the other hand, can be enjoyed only through voluntary participation. It has no useful economic effect, no calculably useful social effect .... The protagonists of progress in historical understanding are always isolated individuals, who are led by such historical convulsions as wars and revolutions to put new questions.

Nor does science in its explanatory apparatus grant a place to intuition, as Curtius does, recognizing the need for creative sympathy in the scholar of letters. More important, it is characteristic of Curtius that his statement expresses his humanistic conviction that the appreciation of literature and culture in general is bound up with the individual experience of the world and the search for meaning.

Curtius has no ideological program such as the sociological approaches to literature found in Marxist and feminist criticism, nor has he a philosophical agenda external to the text under consideration, as in semiotics or deconstructionism. Philology – upon which, Curtius believed, literary history and criticism must be based – can never lead to verifiable conclusions in the same sense as natural science, yet it must be empirical in method. Karl Horst has noted Curtius' affinity for Goethe's dictum "die Phänomene sind die Lehre" (the phenomena are the theory), and it is clear in his writings that Curtius saw Goethe not only as "the last universal author" after Homer but also as a genius of perceptive power and critical ability, the quintessential scientist, historian, and critic: "Rock, color, animal, man, history, the formation of the earth – everything is apprehended by the same luminous eye." The "luminous" seeing eye for the written word and the ear attuned to the spoken language – these are for Curtius the sensory requirements for the critic as he or she embarks on this most personal endeavor, the philological investigation of literary artifacts. Not through abstraction or speculation but only in the context of the empirically accessible documents can critical observations about literature arise. Accordingly, Curtius' criticism cannot be easily separated from specific discussions of specific texts. Only his guiding concerns can be summarized: the awareness of interrelations and evidence of cultural continuity in literature, aesthetic sensitivity, and sympathy for the writer behind the text. The critic's ideal task is the disclosure, through analysis of formal elements such as *topoi*, of the totality of an author's spiritual presence and significance.

Principal criticism

Die literarischen Wegbereiter des neuen Frankreich, 1919
Balzac, 1923
Französischer Geist im neuen Europa, 1925
Europäische Literatur und lateinisches Mittelalter, 1948 (*European Literature and the Latin Middle Ages*, 1953)
Kritische Essays zur europäischen Literatur, 1950 (*Essays on European Literature*, 1973)

Other major works and literary forms

In addition to the books cited above, Ernst Robert Curtius wrote polemical books and pamphlets on topical issues, specifically cultural chauvinism and the effects of nationalism on liberal education. He wrote hundreds of professional articles and essays, including numerous reviews, and he is also known as a translator of André Gide, Jorge Guillén, William Goyen, and T. S. Eliot.

NONFICTION
Maurice Barrès und die geistigen Grundlagen des französischen Nationalismus, 1921
Die französische Kultur, 1930 (*The Civilization of France: An Introduction*, 1962)
Deutscher Geist in Gefahr, 1932

Further reading

Evans, Arthur R. "Ernst Robert Curtius," in *On Four Modern Humanists*, 1970.
Gelley, Alexander. "Ernst Robert Curtius: Topology and Critical Method," in *MLN*. LXXXI (October, 1966), pp. 579–594.
Horst, Karl A. "Zur Methode von Ernst Robert Curtius," in *Merkur*. X (April, 1956), pp. 303–313.
Kowal, Michael. Introduction to *Essays on European Literature*, 1973.
Richards, Earl Jeffrey. *Modernism, Medievalism and Humanism. A Research Bibliography on The Reception of the Works of Ernst Robert Curtius*, 1983.

MARK R. MCCULLOH

See also Auerbach

D

Dante

(Durante Alighieri)

Italian poet

Born: Florence, Italy; May, 1265
Died: Ravenna, Italy; September 13 or 14, 1321

Biography

Dante (an abbreviation of Durante) Alighieri was born in May, 1265, into an aristocratic Florentine family fallen on hard times. The poet's high opinion of his noble origins and an ongoing polemic against the ideology of the increasingly influential merchant classes represent important themes in his works. Economic difficulties did not keep him from frequenting the most sophisticated Florentine intellectual circles of the period, however, particularly that circle of poets he himself would eventually canonize in *Purgatorio* (*Purgatory*), the second part of *La divina commedia* (*The Divine Comedy*), as poets of the *dolce stil nuovo*. Dante's poetic association with that school culminated in *La vita nuova* (*The New Life*), which marks the debut of the figure of Beatrice.

Little is known of his youth in Florence. He may have pursued notarial studies and studied during that time with Brunetto Latini. Between 1291 and 1295 it is believed that he attended the Florentine religious schools organized by the Franciscans and the Dominicans. Not later than 1298 he married Gemma di Manetto Donati; they had four children. Around 1297 he entered Florentine political life, eventually serving for a time as prior (one of the city's six highest magistrates) in 1300. The poet's political activities as one of the city's principal White Guelphs eventually led to his exile, upon the triumph of the Black Guelphs, in 1302.

Details concerning Dante's wanderings during exile are also sketchy, although his letters are a valuable source for information concerning his political activities. As a Florentine exile of the White Guelph party, Dante came immediately into contact with the Ghibellines of north-central Italy and obtained Ghibelline patronage in one court setting or another for the rest of his life. The failed attempt of Holy Roman Emperor Henry VII to reestablish imperial power in Italy between 1309 and 1313 disappointed Dante's hopes for the political restoration of the empire; at this same time, he may have composed *De monarchia* (*On World Government*).

He resided after 1315 at Verona under the protection of Can Grande della Scala, considered the heir of Henry's imperial mission in Italy. Dante dedicated *Paradiso* (*Paradise*) to Can Grande in the famous "Epistola X." After 1320 Dante moved to the court of Guido da Polenta at Ravenna, where he completed what remained of *Paradise*. In September of 1321, upon his return from a diplomatic mission to Venice, he fell ill, dying a few days later in Ravenna, where he was buried.

Influence

Dante's extensive critical writings have been seminal for both criticism concerned directly with the interpretation of *The Divine Comedy* and, more generally, scholarship concerned with the early history of Romance vernacular literatures. Dante's contributions, both poetic and theoretical, to the vernacular cause in its contest with Latin, have earned for him the title "father of the Italian language." Book 1 of *Il convivio* (*The Banquet*) is the first chapter in the history of the Italian language as a national vernacular, while Dante's *De vulgari eloquentia* (on the vulgar tongue) is generally acknowledged to be the magna charta of the Italian language and literature. The profound synthesis of critical and poetic faculties which characterizes Dante's genius has guaranteed the importance of his critical writings as they relate to the interpretation of *The Divine Comedy*. Throughout his works, Dante is intensely and continually engaged in various forms of self-commentary and autoexegesis. His own theoretical reflections on allegory and especially his ongoing reflection upon and revision of received canons of biblical, classical, and vernacular literature are acknowledged to be fundamental to an understanding of the nature of his achievement.

Analysis

The New Life, partly in narrative and exegetical prose, partly in verse, introduces the earliest stage of Dante's critical, theoretical reflections. The work, which relates the story of the poet's love for Beatrice, is dedicated to his "first friend" and fellow poet Guido Cavalcanti. At an important level, *The New Life* presents a theoretical statement vis-à-vis Dante's contemporaries. The work is an expression of the *dolce stil nuovo* school in polemic with Guittone d'Arezzo and his group of followers, who called themselves *guittoniani*. It also reveals Dante's poetics in the process of moving beyond its *stilnovista* origins and transcending the poetics of praise derived from the other canonical *stilnovista*, Guido Guinizelli.

Chapter 25 of *The New Life* is the most explicitly theoretical passage of the work, marking the beginning of Dante's historiography of vernacular lyric origins:

> The first poet to begin writing in the vernacular was moved to do so by a desire to make his words understandable to ladies who found Latin verses difficult to comprehend. And this is an argument against those who compose in the vernacular on a subject other than love, since composition in the vernacular was from the beginning intended for treating of love.

Dante never completely loses sight of the links between the theme of love and the courtly origins of the vernacular lyric. Following some deviation in the course of his theoretical elaborations of his mature poetics, he returns to exalting love as the source of inspiration.

In *The New Life*, Dante takes up the fight with the *guittoniani*, who had engaged in moralistic and political versifying in what Dante described as a "municipal" style. The poets of *lo stil nuovo*, according to Dante, were responsible for reinstating love as the theme for the highest lyric expression.

In the same chapter, he takes pains to justify the personification of love, basing his position upon its use by the classical authors (Virgil, Horace, Homer, Ovid). This adoption of the criteria of classic authority to regulate vernacular eloquence marks one of the founding principles in Dante's vernacular rhetorical thinking, culminating in the vernacular humanism of *The Divine Comedy*. At the same time, he criticizes those irrational and irresponsible poets who pen compositions empty of intellectual content, poets who, if asked to strip their work of rhetorical figures "in order to reveal its true meaning, would not be able to do so." Dante's developing rationalistic approach to poetry leads beyond *The New Life* to the philosophical *canzoni* and commentary of *The Banquet*. Both Dante and Cavalcanti claimed an intellectual authority for philosophically, spiritually, and intellectually engaged compositions such as Cavalcanti's "Donna me prega" ("A Lady Asks Me") or Dante's own "Donne ch' avete intelletto d'amore" ("Ladies Who Have Intelligence of Love"). The latter composition, structurally and thematically, is perhaps the most important in *The New Life*, to the degree that the poet cites its opening lines in canto 24 of *Purgatory*.

His largely implicit polemic with Cavalcantian poetics on the other hand illustrates his generally ambivalent and agonistic approach to poetic influence; a mature example of this tendency is his handling of Virgil in *The Divine Comedy*. In *The New Life*, Dante structured the story of his poetic development as a rejection of the Cavalcantian poetics exemplified in "A Lady Asks Me" with its emphasis on the irrational and negative aspects of passion in favor of the beatifying model of his love for Beatrice. The tragically ineffable object of Cavalcantian love, "Giovanna/ Primavera" is represented typologically as a John the Baptist figure who announces – "prima verrà" (she will come first) – Dante's own Christological love object. Paradoxically, Dante's initial way around Cavalcanti is to turn to the poetry of praise pioneered by the earlier *stil nuovo* master Guinizelli. By the end of *The New Life*, however, following the death of Beatrice and her ascension to Heaven, Dante concludes by stating his intention to move beyond both his predecessors and his contemporaries in his treatment of Beatrice and to write of her "that which has never been written of any other woman."

As Dante leaves behind the poetic experience of the *stilnovisti* and *The New Life*, the first problem to face him is the "question of the language." The entire first book of *The Banquet* is devoted to his justification of the use of the vernacular in a prose commentary on three *canzoni*. First, to have glossed vernacular poems with a Latin commentary would have meant an undue inversion of rhetorical order, since Latin was nobler than the vernacular. Dante based this opinion on Latin's "incorruptibility"; he believed that Latin or "grammar" had been artificially constructed for the purpose of international intellectual discourse.

Having established this premise, he then argues for the vernacular, which was better suited to satisfy the many "unlettered" persons who desire to acquire the wisdom contained in the verses, including "princes, barons, knights, and many other noble folk, not only men but women." At the same time that Dante enfranchises a non-Latinate public, he identifies that public as Italian, for in a canonical passage on the untranslatability of the poetic text, the verses of the *canzoni* are deemed inaccessible to a non-Italian public: "For nothing which hath the harmony of musical connection can be transferred from its own tongue into another without shattering all its sweetness and harmony." One of the expressed purposes of the work is therefore to demonstrate the capacity of Italian to address the highest and most arduous subject, matters normally reserved for Latin.

A corollary to his promotion of Italian is his attack on the supporters of competing vernacular tongues, especially those Italians writing in Provençal or French (as had Dante's master, Brunetto Latini). Dante's love for his mother tongue is furthered by his familiarity with it and his appreciation of the benefits he had received from it; thus he has been led to study it well and promote its preservation by providing it greater stability in his works. Although still within the linguistic hierarchy which considers Latin the "nobler" language, Dante has nevertheless come a long way when he concludes the first book of *The Banquet* with a closing vision of the apotheosis of the vernacular: "That oaten bread whereby thousands shall be sated . . . the new sun which shall rise when the wonted sun shall set, and shall give light to them who are in darkness and in shadow as to the wonted sun, which shines not for them."

The other important discourse addressed in *The Banquet* concerns the poetics of allegory. At the beginning of book 2, an account is given of the four levels of allegory, including the literal, the allegorical, the moral, and the anagogical. Dante distinguishes between the allegory of the poets and the allegory of the theologians. The theological allegory (biblical allegory) is to be taken, at the literal level, as historically true. The poetic allegory, however, is not to be taken as historically true. Instead, it is to be understood as a fiction conceived to reveal a truth beyond the literal level. Thus Ovid is allegorically, not literally, true, while the Bible can be considered historically and allegorically true.

Dante assures his reader in *The Banquet* that he is taking the allegorical sense "after the use of the poets." According to critic Maria Simonelli, this statement serves as a kind of theoretical justification for the poet's reinterpretation (or rather, rewriting) of an episode from *The New Life* involving a "lady at the window" who had pity upon him following Beatrice's death. That story is retold in book 2 of *The Banquet*, and what had represented, in *The New Life*, an infidelity and indiscretion, now represents Dante's encounter with Lady Philosophy, who provides consolation and serves as his muse. Significantly, Dante will return to a transgressional reading of the episode in *The Divine Comedy*.

Dante's theoretical discussions of allegory illustrate the dual nature of his critical interventions. His reflections consider the nature of medieval allegory in general at the same time that they illuminate his own poetic practice. The discussion of allegory in the letter to Can Grande, "Epistola X," is perhaps the best-known formulation of the medieval scheme of scriptural or theological allegory. Besides providing a lucid presentation and illustration of the four levels of theological allegory, however, the passage raises the question of the nature of *The Divine Comedy*'s allegory, since he exemplifies it not with an excerpt from the poets but rather with a passage from Exodus which must, according to his own theories, be taken as literally true. Charles Singleton has proposed that the fundamental fiction of the poem is that it is not a fiction.

The rhetorical and technical *De vulgari eloquentia* (composed in Latin and therefore addressed to the Latinate intelligentsia) directly supports the philosophical and moral poetic achieved in *The Banquet*. Begun sometime after 1303 (Dante announces its forthcoming publication in the first book of *The Banquet*), the work is unfinished, broken off abruptly in mid-chapter at the point when the length of the stanza is being considered. The interruption of work, taken together with the suspension of *The Banquet*, seems to signal a turning point, or as Pier Vincenzo Mengaldo has it, a "polarization of interests" leading to *The Divine Comedy*.

Some idea of the planned structure of the work can be derived from what Dante himself says: book 4 was to have been dedicated to the comic style and to the mediocre register. While book 3 is not mentioned, it is generally supposed that it would have dealt with the "prosa illustre," the high style in vernacular prose with which he had experimented in *The Banquet*. He opens the Latin treatise by announcing the object of study and its novelty and immediately reverses the position laid out in *The Banquet*, proclaiming this time the greater nobility of the vernacular, for three reasons: because it is one's first language, because everyone in the world has one, and finally, because it is natural as opposed to the artificial "grammar." Thereafter, book 1 is divided roughly into two parts, including a history and philosophy of language, beginning with the question of what language Adam spoke (in this work, it is Hebrew, but this position is reversed when Dante encounters Adam in *Paradise*) and proceeding diachronically down the genealogy of languages to the dialects of Italy. The second half is also in two parts. Dante first seeks to identify and locate the "illustris Ytaliae loquela," the illustrious vernacular. His recognition of the Sicilian poets at the court of Frederick II as the first Italian poetic "school" does not entail any endorsement of the Sicilian vernacular, or any other vernacular for that matter (especially not Dante's own Florentine or the Bolognese, which had the greatest pretensions). None satisfies the requirements of that illustrious vernacular sought by Dante, which reveals itself in fact to be a literary ideal of eloquence. Indeed, as Alessandro Manzoni would conclude in the nineteenth century, *De vulgari eloquentia* is essentially "a treatise on eloquence and not language." What has been termed the "pars construens" of the argument follows. There Dante illustrates the attributes of the excellent vernacular, which include its being "illustrious" (light giving), "cardinal" (like a pivot on which the other vernaculars turn), "aulic" (courtly), and "curial" (language of the highest courts of justice).

Book 2 sets out examples of this illustrious vernacular eloquence culled from the recent history of the vernacular lyric, beginning in Provence and culminating, implicitly, according to Dante's account, in the poetic of the *dolce stil nuovo* and particularly in the poetics of the author of *The Banquet*. Mengaldo notes that in the last chapters of book 2, eight of the fifteen lyrics cited are Dante's own. Mengaldo goes on to point out an aporia at the heart of *De vulgari eloquentia:* the tension between Dante's goal of establishing and outlining a general theory of rhetoric and his competing need to elaborate and develop an individual poetics.

Book 2 goes on to outline the appropriate subjects for the illustrious vernacular and in what fashion they should be treated. Dante expands his list of appropriate themes to include *salus* (war) and *virtus* (virtue) in addition to *venus* (love). While Dante has no example for martial rhetorical eloquence in Italian (he cites Bertran de Born from the Provençal) the reader understands that the *canzoni* of *The Banquet* come, presumably, at the high end of the thematic scale, under the category of *virtus*. The chapters that follow are intended to illustrate the way in which vernacular eloquence is to be achieved; this presentation consists of a formal discussion of the genre of the *canzone*, deemed to be the appropriate vehicle for the illustrious style, passing then to the ideal structure and length of verse (the hendecasyllable) and finally moving to the structure of the stanza – at which point the work is interrupted. Although the original plan of *De vulgari eloquentia* was to treat the entire spectrum of linguistic registers, from the illustrious vernacular down to the "language of a single household," Dante never goes beyond the illustrious vernacular in his treatment.

The interruption of both *De vulgari eloquentia* and *The Banquet* would seem to signal a new departure when considered in the light of the rhetorical and theoretical position which Dante implicitly assumes in *The Divine Comedy*. *De vulgari eloquentia* and *The Banquet* represent to a large extent the attempt to establish vernacular eloquence upon classical foundations, both in the adoption of the classical hierarchy of styles and in urging the imitation of "regular" poets, such as Virgil, Ovid, Statius, and Lucan for poetry and Livy, Pliny, Frontinus, and Orosius for prose. From this rhetorical perspective, Dante's "comedy" can be seen to correspond to a different rhetorical and ideological model, that is, a "Christian" comedic rhetoric whereby the low comic style of the *Inferno* (the first division of *The Divine Comedy*) can yet be part of the most sublime and ambitious of literary epics. Beyond this rhetorical discontinuity, while *The Banquet* and *De vulgari eloquentia* are explicitly seeking to move the vernacular beyond the traditional theme of love (in *The Banquet*, there is the implicit subordination of *venus* to *virtus*) and the figure of Beatrice is somewhat eclipsed (vis-à-vis Lady Philosophy), the reader witnesses the reinstatement of Beatrice and love as privileged themes in *The Divine Comedy*.

Virtually all the theoretical and critical positions of the poet are viewed and presented again poetically in *The Divine Comedy*. The unraveling of the relations between Dante's theoretical positions and their counterparts in the poem remains one of the central tasks for interpreters of *The Divine Comedy*. One of the crucial passages in this ongoing encounter with classical and vernacular literary culture is in canto 24 of *Purgatory*, in which Dante recapitulates his vernacular literary genealogy. The pilgrim's interview with one of the *guittoniani*, Bonagiunta Orbicciani, culminates in what has generally been taken to represent a statement of Dante's mature poetic: "I am one who, when Love breathes in me, takes note; what he, within, dictates, I, in that way, without, would speak and shape." These lines have been interpreted literally within their immediate textual context as a *dolce stil nuovo* manifesto reaffirming the centrality of love as the only appropriate theme for vernacular verse, a recapitulation, so to speak, of the polemic initiated in *The New Life* with the *guittoniani*. It is clear, however, that love means something more now than it did in its original *stilnovista* context. It denotes, from Dante's prophetic perspective, nothing less than the divine source of inspiration for the Christian eschatological vision of *The Divine Comedy*. Love as inspiration within the context of Dante's prophetic mission becomes God's love, and Dante assumes the role of divinely inspired vessel for the communication of God's word, placing himself and his poem at the center of sacred history leading to salvation. While Dante's theoretical-critical contributions in the so-called minor works would have guaranteed for him the highest place within the Italian tradition even had he not written *The Divine Comedy*, it is nevertheless this kind of intimate relationship between that theoretical writing and the achievement of his masterpiece which represents his most important critical-theoretical legacy.

Principal criticism

Passages in *La vita nuova*, c. 1292 (*Vita Nuova*, 1861, better known as *The New Life*, 1867)
De vulgari eloquentia, c. 1306 (English translation, 1890)
Il convivio, c. 1307 (*The Banquet*, 1903)
"Epistola X," c. 1316 (English translation, 1902)
Passages in *La divina commedia*, c. 1320 (*The Divine Comedy*, 1802)
Literary Criticism of Dante Alighieri, 1973 (Robert S. Haller, editor and translator)

Other major works and literary forms

Dante's minor compositions in the vernacular consist of eighty-nine attributed lyrics; they were never gathered by him into a unified *canzoniere* but were edited in the twentieth century by Michele Barbi in 1921, Gianfranco Contini in 1939, and Kenelm Foster and Patrick Boyd in 1967. These "extravagant" sonnets, *canzoni*, *ballate*, and *sestine* document the young poet's technical, formal, and thematic development between 1283 and 1308. Dante's minor works in Latin include approximately ten letters which reflect the Florentine exile's perspective on contemporary political developments. Two eclogues were addressed between 1319 and 1321 to Giovanni del Virgilio, a professor of grammar and rhetoric at Bologna who had urged Dante, while he was engaged in completing the third part of *The Divine Comedy*, *Paradiso* (*Paradise*), to compose poetry in Latin. *De monarchia* (English translation, 1890; better known as *On World Government*, 1957), Dante's political treatise on the relations between the Holy Roman Empire and the Papacy, is dated around 1313. *Quaestio de aqua et terra*

(English translation, 1902), the text of a public disputation held by Dante at Verona on January 20, 1320, treats the relative levels of water and land on the surface of the globe. A sonnet sequence adaptation of the thirteenth-century *Le Roman de la rose* (*The Romance of the Rose*, 1900), the *Fiore* (c. 1285–1300), has been ascribed to Dante by Gianfranco Contini, though this attribution is not universally accepted.

NONFICTION
Epistolae, c. 1300–1321 (English translation, 1902)
De monarchia, c. 1313 (English translation, 1890; also known as *Monarchy*, 1954, better known as *On World Government*, 1957)
Eclogae, 1319 (*Eclogues*, 1902)
Quaestio de aqua et terra, 1320 (English translation, 1902)
Translation of the Latin Works of Dante Alighieri, 1904

Further reading

Auerbach, Erich. *Dante, Poet of the Secular World*, 1961. Translated by Ralph Manheim.
Barolini, Teodolinda. *Dante's Poets: Textuality and Truth in the "Comedy,"* 1984.
——. *The Undivine Comedy: Detheologizing Dante*, 1992.
Freccero, John ed. *Dante: The Poetics of Conversion*, 1986. Edited and with an Introduction by Rachel Jacoff.
Hollander, John. *Allegory in Dante's "Divina Commedia,"* 1969.
Hollander, Robert. *Dante's Epistle to Cangrande*, 1993.
Mazzotta, Giuseppe. *Dante, Poet of the Desert: History and Allegory in "The Divine Comedy,"* 1979.
——. *Dante's Vision and the Circle of Knowledge*, 1993.
Migliorini, Bruno. "Dante," in *The Italian Language*, 1966, 1984.
Shapiro, Marianne. *De vulgari eloquentia: Dante's Book of Exile*, 1990.
Singleton, Charles S. *Dante's Commedia: Elements of Structure*, 1954.

THEODORE J. CACHEY, JR.

See also Boccaccio; Medieval Literary Theory; Petrarch

Donald Davie

English poet and critic

Born: Barnsley, England; July 17, 1922
Died: Exeter, England; September 18, 1995

Biography

Born in Barnsley in Yorkshire, Donald Alfred Davie had an upbringing that was strongly influenced by his family's association with nonconformist, specifically Baptist, circles. His paternal grandfather was a Baptist deacon; as a boy, Davie attended services regularly at the Sheffield Road Baptist Church in Barnsley, accompanying his father, a businessman of modest means and Tory sympathies. He was educated first at Barnsley Holgate Grammar School and then at St. Catharine's College, Cambridge. From 1941 to 1946 he served in the Royal Navy, in Russia, India, and Ceylon. (By this stage he had largely lost his religious faith, though much later in life – in 1972 – he was baptized into the American Episcopalian Church; after his retirement, on returning to England, he attended services of the Church of England.) He held academic posts at Cambridge and Trinity College, Dublin, before becoming, in 1964, professor of English at the University of Essex. In the following year he was made Pro Vice-chancellor of the university; he resigned in 1968 in the midst of student rebellion on the campus. The same year he took up an appointment as professor of English at Stanford University in California. From 1978 to 1988 he was Andrew Mellon Professor of Humanities at Vanderbilt University, Nashville, before retiring and returning to England.

Alongside his distinguished academic career, Davie wrote and published a considerable body of poetry which, if uneven in achievement, is never less than assured and intelligent, and, at its best, is both moving and formally satisfying. The interplay between his critical prose and his poetry is constant, whether in the "Movement" poetry of his early years, the more expansive ambition of *The Shires*, or the T. S. Eliot idiom of *Three for Water-Music*. Throughout his career there was cross-fertilization between criticism and his own creative writing.

Influence

Davie belongs in the line of poet-critics that runs from Philip Sidney and Ben Jonson, through John Dryden and Samuel Taylor Coleridge, to such modern figures as T. S. Eliot and Ezra Pound and such contemporaries as John Hollander and Seamus Heaney.

His first critical book, *Purity of Diction in English Verse*, was, as Davie himself recognized in a postscript written for the 1967 reissue of the book, by way of being (in part at least) an oblique manifesto for the poetry of the Movement (including his own early work – a first small collection of which was published only three years after *Purity of Diction*). It was written, Davie says, "principally so as to understand what I had been doing, or trying to do, in the poems I had been writing." *Purity of Diction* placed its stress on linguistic ideals which Davie summed up in his discussion of "The Classicism of Charles Wesley": "In the Methodist chapel, as in the drawing-room, the poet used the language spoken by his hearers. He did not try to heighten, to disrupt, or even, in the first place, to enrich that language, but to sharpen it, to make it more exact and pure, and thereby (paradoxically) more flexible. He seldom used shock-tactics. His concern was not to create a distinctive style, but to contribute to a common stock, to safeguard a heritage and to keep it bright as new." It is, though, entirely characteristic of a tension in Davie's thinking that this statement is buttressed by a quotation from an unexpected source – Ezra Pound, writing in his *A.B.C. of Reading* of Anatole France and his desire to find in his writing "the *least possible* variant that would turn the most worn-out and commonest phrases of journalism into something distinguished. Such research is sometimes termed 'classicism.'" Davie's work as critic exists between the poles of Charles Wesley and Ezra Pound and the power of his work resides, to a great extent, in his recurrent attempt to reconcile the forces exerted by both. In other ways, too, Davie's greatest influence as a critic has perhaps been as a kind of intermediary between seemingly disparate traditions and idioms – between English and American poetry, or between Slavic and English literary idioms.

Analysis

In the two-page Introduction to *Purity of Diction in English Verse* Davie offers some propositions that seem to have remained valid for him for the rest of his career as a critic. He explains his admiration for the works of some mid-eighteenth-century English poets whose work is characterized by relative sparsity of metaphor in terms of a recognition that "this economy in metaphor produces effects which I call 'poetical,' to which, it seems to me, most readers of our day are blind. The effects seem to me morally valuable; otherwise I should not care to write of them." This is poetry, Davie suggests, in which the diction is "pure" and he distinguishes the reading of it from the experience of some other kinds of poetry in which he feels "a peculiar discomfort which [he] can define only by saying that the diction is impure." Such poetry may, of course, have other "virtues (that is useful pleasures)." Clearly questions of style (and questions of pleasure) are essentially moral questions so far as Davie is concerned. That a writer's use of language is the surest guide to his or her morality – ("Synge differs from Goldsmith about diction because he has a different scheme of morality") – was a conviction that was to remain at the heart of all Davie's later work (even if there is an implicit backing-away from it in the 1967 postscript to *Purity of Diction*). It goes with a strong sense of the social purposes of art, a sense understood as, above all, a network of responsibilities:

> We are saying that the poet who undertakes to preserve or refine a poetic diction is writing in a web of responsibilities. He is responsible to past masters for conserving the genres and the decorum which they have evolved. He is responsible to the persons or the themes on which he writes, to maintain a consistent tone and point of view in his dealings with them. He is responsible to the community in which he writes, for purifying and correcting the spoken language. And of course he is responsible, as all poets are, to his readers; he has to give them pleasure, and also, deviously or directly, instructions in proper conduct.

The "chaste" diction which Davie admires is "central" – "central to the language, conversational not colloquial, poetic not poetical. The effect is a valuable urbanity, a civilized moderation and elegance." But Davie was well aware that it had its limitations too – "this is the effect attainable, I think, by Goldsmith, and not by Shakespeare," he added.

Davie's sensitivity to the language of a given poem (though he makes almost no use of the terms or methods of modern linguistics) is often manifested in brilliant close readings, but these rarely seem to be ends in themselves. Davie's attention to detail is always in the service of larger statements, larger structures of argument. But the attention itself is often full of rewards for his readers, his discriminations exact, his sensitivity to different linguistic registers often startlingly productive as, for example, in the chapter on "Shelley's Urbanity" in *Purity of Diction*, or in the excellent brief Appendix to the same volume in which he discusses "'Strength' and 'Ease' in Seventeenth-Century Criticism." In the latter his analysis of early uses of strength as a critical term discovers in it virtues that Davie himself admired – "'Strength' is not a 'loosening' but a 'tightening'; it is a matter of compression and concentration. And Johnson therefore used the word with propriety when he applied it to Denham . . . Donne achieves concentration by way of hyperbole; Denham by means of syntax. And both are 'strong.'" Davie's first substantial critical work had concentrated on diction – its closing words, quoted here, flagged up the subject of his second book – *Articulate Energy: An Inquiry Into the Syntax of English Poetry*.

Davie's concern is with the role of syntax in poetry as "a tradition central to human thought and conduct" (to borrow a phrase used of syntax in *Purity of Diction*); his account begins with an examination of what can be learnt from the influential discussions of syntax to be found in the work of T. E. Hulme, Susanne Langer, and Ernest Fenollosa and goes on to discuss what he calls "varieties of poetic syntax," which include "subjective syntax," "dramatic syntax," "objective syntax," "syntax like music," and "syntax like mathematics." It is probably fair to say that the theoretical side of Davie's book now seems rather limited and dated; what are of more enduring interest are the large questions he raises about the role (or otherwise) of logical and syntactical articulation in modern poetry and his penetrating examinations of the function of syntactical structures in work by, amongst others, Thomas Sackville, William Shakespeare, Philip Sidney, William Wordsworth, and William Butler Yeats. His awareness of how Symbolist ideas about poetry had encouraged the notion that poetry's mode of discourse was wholly distinct from that of prose raised questions which troubled him, and were to be central to much of his later work. Davie's instinct was "to agree with Yeats that the abandonment of syntax testifies to a failure of the poet's nerve, a loss of confidence in the intelligible structure of the conscious mind, and the validity of its activity."

Such sentiments are perhaps unexpected from a critic who was later to write influential work on Pound, Charles Olson, and Edward Dorn – poets whose work is very much characterized by their abandonment of traditional systems of syntax. Pound, in particular, is a recurring presence in Davie's work – the subject of two entire books, as well as many essays – and it is rewarding to watch his critical negotiations with a poet who seems to be passionately at odds with so many of Davie's fundamental principles about life and poetry and yet to whom he is, it seems, irresistibly drawn. One of Davie's virtues as a critic is that he is never a simple enthusiast; he distinguishes between parts of a writer's work (or indeed parts of a single work) with a discrimination the enthusiast is incapable of. Nowhere is this truer – and more worth the observing – than in Davie's dealings with Pound. These have been the subject of an excellent essay by Bernard Bergonzi ("Davie and Pound" in *Donald Davie and the Responsibilities of Literature* edited by George Dekker) and need not be repeated in detail here. There is much of great value in Davie's repeated critical engagements with Pound; paradoxically that value in part resides in, or is created by, Davie's failure to achieve a single, stable view of his subject. Bergonzi, indeed, characterizes Davie's work on Pound as marked by "partiality, mutability, and inconclusiveness"; these "qualities" are a measure of Davie's honesty as a critic, his refusal to write out of existence (or to look away from) the inconsistencies and contradictions of Pound and his work, his determination to register (as far as possible) the truth of his response(s) to a poet whose work produces in him (and surely Davie is not alone in this) alternating moods of exasperation and admiration. For this reason alone, as well as for his characteristic critical astuteness, Davie's writings on Pound have much to offer that is not to be found in the work of fully-committed Poundeans (they, at their best, have different virtues).

In later work, such as *Thomas Hardy and British Poetry*, Davie's argument grows from a similarly divided response to another poet. For Davie (as for Pound), Hardy stands as a poet who "registered an age" (the phrase is Pound's), and his argument here is "that in British poetry of the last fifty years (as not in America) the most far-reaching influence, for good or ill, has been not Yeats, still less Eliot or Pound, not Lawrence, but *Hardy*." Davie sees the inheritance bequeathed by Hardy as, in part, one of stylistic conservatism and relative lack of ambition. The danger – and it is one to which much in British poetry of this century can be said to have succumbed – is that such poetry may be "disablingly modest in [its] aims" – "For surely the poet, if any one, has a duty to be radical, to go to the roots. So much at least all poets have assumed through the centuries. Hardy, perhaps without knowing it, questions that assumption, and appears to reject it. Some of his successors in England, and a few out of England, seem to have agreed with him." Davie goes on, however, to elucidate the ways (and poems) in which Hardy "excels himself" and escapes from the suggested limitations. Later chapters are addressed to "Hardy's heirs" – some of them (such as Philip Larkin and John Betjeman) predictable and some (such as J. H. Prynne and Roy Fisher) very surprising. In some cases – such as Larkin – the results are illuminating, identifying Larkin's "lowered sights and patiently diminished expectations" as the poetry of "the seasons of an English soul." In others – as in the discussion of Roy Fisher – the claims for the presence of a "Hardyesque . . . sensibility" are largely unpersuasive and are sustained only by the overlooking (consciously or unconsciously) of important areas of the poet's work. The book remains very valuable both for its abundance of local insight, and for some of its larger historical suggestions – not least in its recognition that British poetry of the present is written out of "the most industrialized landscape in the world" and the associated and far-reaching observation that "it was English poetry (with Wordsworth) that in modern times first expressed ideas of elemental sanctity and natural piety; and it seems it must be English poetry which asks what to do with these ideas in a landscape where virtually all the sanctuaries have been violated, all the pieties blasphemed."

Thomas Hardy and British Poetry is a rich and suggestive book, an argument structured with characteristic cohesiveness. What is in some respects its successor, *Under Briggflatts*, lacks this larger coherence of argument (we seem rather to be reading a book that works by Poundean juxtaposition), but is similarly fecund of perception and suggestion. Its essential scrappiness makes its subtitle as a "History of Poetry in Great Britain, 1960–1988" somewhat misleading. The book's title records Davie's conviction of Basil Bunting's centrality in the poetry of this period. He admires Bunting's skill as a prosodist; he admires his devotion to "right naming"; he respects his consistent sense that "the writing and reading of [poetry] is still a *sociable* affair." He also, very significantly, insists that "all of [Bunting's] poetry can be seen as flower of dissenting Protestantism."

To see Davie's stress on this aspect of Bunting (an aspect not much discussed by earlier critics) is to be made aware of one of the abiding preoccupations of Davie's critical writing. It relates his admiration of Bunting to that insistence upon the moral significance of diction with which his first book, *Purity of Diction*, began. It enables us, too, to see something of how Davie's interest in modernism is related to another of his abiding concerns – what the subtitle of another of his books calls "the literature of the English dissenting interest." In his studies on the eighteenth-century hymn Davie returns, in effect, to the topic of poetic diction, as he himself notes in his Introduction to *The Eighteenth-Century Hymn in England*. In *A Gathered Church* he explores the ways in which "the aesthetic *and* the moral perceptions have, built into them and near to the heart of them, the perception of licence, of abandonment, of superfluity, foreseen, even invited, and yet in the end denied, fended off. Art is measure, is exclusion; is therefore simplicity (hard-earned), is sobriety, tense with the extravagances that it has been tempted by, and has denied itself." Place this by the side of his interest, more than twenty-five years previously, in *Purity of Diction* with a poetry in which he suggests one senses that "a selection has been made and is continually being made, that words are thrusting at the poem and being fended off from it," and one sees something of what gives an essential integrity to all of Davie's work.

Much of Davie's work now has, perhaps unavoidably, a certain slightly old-fashioned air to it. The last thirty years have seen a great many fresh developments in the presuppositions and methodology of criticism, and Davie's work seems altogether unmarked by such developments. Alan Durant, for example, complains that Davie's work is an "amalgam of anecdote, observation and unargued opinion," that it finds no place for the lessons of linguistics or psychoanalysis. He concludes that "the bases of Davie's views appear to be intuition and discrimination alone." One can only wish that more of Davie's successors had displayed a similar reliance upon discrimination.

Principal criticism

Purity of Diction in English Verse, 1952
Articulate Energy: An Inquiry Into the Syntax of English Poetry, 1955
The Heyday of Sir Walter Scott, 1961
The Language of Science and the Language of Literature 1700–1740, 1963
Ezra Pound: Poet as Sculptor, 1964
Thomas Hardy and British Poetry, 1972
Pound, 1975
The Poet in the Imaginary Museum: Essays of Two Decades, 1977
A Gathered Church: The Literature of the English Dissenting Interest 1700–1930, 1978
Trying to Explain: Essays, 1979
Dissentient Voice: The Ward Phillips Lectures for 1980, with Related Pieces, 1982
Czeslaw Milosz and the Insufficiency of Lyric, 1986
Under Briggflatts, 1989
Slavic Excursions: Essays on Russian and Polish Literature, 1990
Older Masters: Essays and Reflections on English and American Literature, 1992
The Eighteenth-Century Hymn in England, 1994

Other major works and literary forms

POETRY
Fantasy Poets, no. 19, 1954
Brides of Reason, 1955
A Winter Talent and Other Poems, 1957
The Forests of Lithuania, 1959
A Sequence for Francis Parkman, 1961
New and Selected Poems, 1961
Events and Wisdoms: Poems 1957–1963, 1964
Pasternak: The Poems of Doctor Zhivago, 1965 (translations with a commentary)
Essex Poems 1963–67, 1969
Poems, 1969
Six Epistles to Eva Hesse, 1970
Collected Poems 1950–1970, 1972
The Shires: Poems, 1974
In the Stopping Train and Other Poems, 1977
Three for Water-Music and The Shires, 1981
Collected Poems 1971–1983, 1983
To Scorch or Freeze, 1989
Collected Poems, 1990

NONFICTION
These the Companions: Recollections, 1982

ANTHOLOGIES
The Late Augustans: Longer Poems of the Late Eighteenth Century, 1958
Russian Literature and Modern British Fiction: A Collection of Critical Essays, 1965
Pasternak: Modern Judgements, 1969 (with Angela Livingstone)
Augustan Lyric, 1974
The New Oxford Book of Christian Verse, 1981
The Psalms in English, 1996

Further reading

Dekker, George, ed. *Donald Davie and the Responsibilities of Literature*, 1983.
Dodsworth, Martin. "Donald Davie," in *Agenda*. 14, no. 2 (1976), pp. 15–32.
Durant, Alan. "Pound, Modernism and Literary Criticism: A Reply to Donald Davie," in *Critical Quarterly*. 28 (1986), pp. 154–166.
Halberg, Robert von. "Two Poet Critics: Donald Davie's *The Poet in the Imaginary Museum* and Robert Pinsky's *The Situation of Poetry*," in *Chicago Review*. 30 (1978), pp. 108–115.
Lucas, John. "Thomas Hardy, Donald Davie, England and the English," in *Thomas Hardy Annual*. 1 (1982), pp. 134–151.
Pritchard, William H. "Davie on the Modern Poets," in *Sewanee Review*. 97 (1989), pp. 107–119.
Shelley, A. "Donald Davie and the Canon," in *Essays in Criticism*. 42 (1992), pp. 1–23.
Winter, H. "Von F. R. Leavis bis Donald Davie: Notizen zur modernen englischen Literaturkritik," in *Neue Rundschau*. 81 (1970), pp. 170–179.

GLYN PURSGLOVE

See also British Literary Theory: Twentieth Century; Empson; Kermode

Paul de Man

Belgian-born American critic

Born: Antwerp, Belgium; c. 1919
Died: New Haven, Connecticut; December 21, 1983

Biography

Paul de Man was born in Antwerp, Belgium, in about 1919. He received his undergraduate education from the

University of Brussels. De Man's political past is shadowed. In the early years of World War II, he wrote nearly one hundred pieces for the collaborationist paper *Le Soir* in support of the Nazi occupation of Belgium. The past, however, seems to have troubled de Man. Jon Wiener, in an article in *The Nation* (January 9, 1988) titled "Deconstructing de Man," quotes Frank Lentricchia of Duke University:

> Anyone who thinks that he left [his support of the Nazi occupation] behind him, that it did not motivate the life and career that followed, is crazy. He came here in 1947 at age 28 with a Belgian wife and son; he divorced his wife when he got here, and didn't speak to his son ever again. The man tried very hard to separate himself from his Belgian collaborationist past, to cut that thing out of himself. I think he suffered, he wished he never did it. He didn't start graduate school until 1952, when he was 33. What was he doing before that? Working in a bookstore, working for a publisher – a brilliant man, prepared for a literary career, who does nothing for several years.

Having obtained his advanced degrees from Harvard University, however, de Man's professional career as an educator was varied and distinguished. He taught at Harvard, Cornell, and The Johns Hopkins universities in the United States, as well as the University of Zurich in Switzerland; he had, as he pointed out in an interview, the opportunity "to compare the situation of teaching in Europe and of teaching [in the United States]: in Europe one is of course much closer to ideological and political questions, while, on the contrary, in the States, one is much closer to professional questions." Ultimately, he found the experience of teaching in the United States more satisfactory and more honest, in part, one suspects, because he was able to distance his early ideological and political affiliations. "I found bad faith involved in that ideological situation in Europe," he said, "worse than here [in the United States]." De Man married Patricia Kelly, his second wife, with whom he had a daughter and three sons, and, from 1970 until his death of cancer in December, 1983, he was the Sterling Professor of Humanities in the Department of Comparative Literature at Yale University.

Influence

De Man is principally known as an interpreter of the major British and European Romantic and post-Romantic figures, including William Wordsworth, Percy Bysshe Shelley, William Butler Yeats, Friedrich Hölderlin, Jean-Jacques Rousseau, Friedrich Nietzsche, and Marcel Proust. He is also known, through his association with such critics as Geoffrey Hartman and J. Hillis Miller, as one of the so-called Yale deconstructionists. Along with the others, he introduced the American critical audience to Jacques Derrida, the French philosopher of language, who "works very close to texts" and "reads very attentively." De Man helped renew interest in conceptually rigorous close reading of texts.

Analysis

In "Semiology and Rhetoric," the first chapter of *Allegories of Reading*, one finds the clearest exposition of Paul de Man's critical project. Kenneth Burke's distinction between grammar and rhetoric serves as a starting point. Grammar is simply the structure of rules governing the relationships of sound, syntax, and meaning. Its study in the literary text, however, is unable to account fully for rhetoric, the figurative use of language which often creates meaning in opposition to the strictly grammatical. De Man cites a particularly useful example, the rhetorical question, as "perhaps the most commonly known instance of an apparent symbiosis between a grammatical and a rhetorical structure":

> Asked by his wife whether he wants to have his bowling shoes laced over or laced under, Archie Bunker answers with a question: "What's the difference?" Being a reader of sublime simplicity, his wife replies by patiently explaining the difference between lacing over and lacing under, whatever this may be, but provokes only ire. "What's the difference?" did not ask for difference but means instead "I don't give a damn what the difference is."

De Man finds that "the same grammatical pattern engenders two meanings that are mutually exclusive," the literal and the figurative. In his critical project, he attempts not to effect a synthesis of grammar and rhetoric but to illustrate their tension, how one deconstructs the other.

The prevailing critical tendency in the United States had been the loosely labeled New Criticism. De Man acknowledges the achievements of the New Critics – particularly their insistence on close attention to figurative language. In an early article, "The Dead End of Formalist Criticism," however, he takes to task the underlying New Critical assumption that there exists "a perfect continuity between the sign and the thing signified," or, as he puts it elsewhere, "an exact correspondence between the author's originary experience and its communicated expression." The task for the New Critic is paraphrase, explication of the text, which explains the text's referentiality, the correspondence between the author's experience and expression. As de Man writes elsewhere, such explication "implies that figural discourse is always understood in contradistinction to a form of discourse that would not be figural." William Empson exposed the limits of such criticism when he discovered that "the text implies . . . significations that, against the will of their author, are mutually exclusive." Readers are often unable to decide between two mutually exclusive interpretations and, in "Criticism and Crises," de Man maintains that sign and meaning can never perfectly coincide in a "finite and single interpretation," that is, a correct interpretation.

The importation of Slavic Formalism and French semiology during the 1960s was a logical reaction to the New Criticism. Because there was no agreement on a correct interpretation of meaning, theorists put the whole question of meaning aside and instead focused their attention strictly on the language of the text. De Man acknowledged the achievements of the Formalists and the semiologists. He writes, they "demonstrated that the perception of the literary dimensions of language is largely obscured if one submits uncritically to the authority of reference." Thus, they freed "critical discourse from the debilitating burden of paraphrase."

Yet, as he goes on to insist, "it would be quite foolish to assume that one can lightheartedly move away from the constraint of referential meaning." Even if the text "engenders several meanings, some of which may even be contradictory to each other," it is nevertheless written to be read and understood. Without meaning, the text would be unreadable as a text. "To read is to understand writing," de Man writes, and "to understand primarily means to determine the referential mode of a text and we tend to take for granted that this can be done."

For de Man, the critic's task is then doubly difficult. The critic must first understand the referential, "paraphrasable" meaning the poet would communicate in his or her text. In addition, the critic must put "in question the status of referential language," carefully avoiding the "fallacy of a finite and single interpretation."

Still, one must apply a caution. De Man and the other deconstructionists have often been criticized for creating sophistic arguments to evade the question of referential meaning altogether. They ignore, or so it is asserted, the question of formal unity. By postulating a formal unity, for example, one is able to exclude, as aberrant, those interpretations that do not contribute to the unity of the text. De Man warns, however, that this unity "resides not in the poetic text as such, but in the act of interpreting the text." It is imposed on the text by the reader who, in a zeal for perfect coherence, is blind to the contradictory evidence. De Man reads with open eyes and his dual concentration on the contradictions between a figurative and a strictly grammatical reading of the text does, in fact, often disrupt formal unity.

It is not the intent of deconstructive criticism, however, to disrupt arbitrarily the formal unity of the text. The poet, in writing, reaches for "the fullest possible self-understanding," and any critical interpretation, in turn, "is oriented toward a consciousness which is itself engaged in an act of total interpretation." De Man warns that "as long as we can distinguish between literal and figural meaning, we can translate the figure back to its proper referent," and every attempt to do so must be made. Criticism becomes properly deconstructive "not when we have, on the one hand, a literal meaning and on the other hand a figural meaning, but when it is impossible to decide by grammatical or other linguistic devices which of the two meanings (that can be entirely incompatible) prevails."

One finds in de Man's criticism, as Geoffrey Hartman put it, "more of a relentless focus on certain questions, and a new rigor when it comes to the discipline of close reading." De Man relentlessly focuses on the "linguistics of literariness," the point at which "literariness, the use of language that foregrounds the rhetorical over the grammatical," disrupts the referential dimensions of language. Or, as he writes in *The Resistance to Theory*,

> Literature is a fiction not because it somehow refuses to acknowledge "reality," but because it is not a priori certain that language functions according to principles which are those, or which are like those, of the phenomenal world.

De Man goes on to point out that "what we call ideology is precisely the confusion of linguistic with natural reality, of reference with phenomenalism." His early, collaborationist essays, however, render such statements troubling. Is his focus on linguistic rather than natural realities merely an attempt to avoid difficult historical questions, including the questions raised by his own past?

De Man admits to being "oblivious to social and historical (that is to say ideological)" realities, but he insists finally that deconstructive criticism provides "a powerful and indispensable tool [for] the unmasking of ideological aberrations." He attempts to overcome "a resistance to reading," a reluctance to admit that any "text leaves a residue of indetermination that has to be, but cannot be, resolved by grammatical means." Deconstructive criticism, as de Man practices it, provides powerful, indispensable, but ultimately disturbing readings.

Principal criticism

Blindness and Insight: Essays in the Rhetoric of Contemporary Criticism, 1971, 1983
Allegories of Reading, 1979
The Rhetoric of Romanticism, 1984
The Resistance to Theory, 1986
Critical Writings, 1953–1978, 1989

Other major works and literary forms

Paul de Man has also published numerous translations, the most notable of which is *Madame Bovary: Backgrounds and Sources and Essays in Criticism* (1965), a new rendering of Gustave Flaubert's novel.

TRANSLATION
Madame Bovary: Backgrounds and Sources and Essays in Criticism, 1965 (of Gustave Flaubert's novel)

MISCELLANEOUS
Wartime Journalism, 1939–1943, 1988

Further reading

Derrida, Jacques. "Like the Sound of the Sea Deep Within a Shell: Paul de Man's War," in *Responses: On Paul de Man's Wartime Journalism*, 1989, pp. 127–164.
Eagleton, Terry. "The Emptying of a Former Self," in *Times Literary Supplement*. 4,495 (May 26–June 1, 1989), pp. 573–574.
Godzich, Wlad. Introduction to *Blindness and Insight: Essays in the Rhetoric of Contemporary Criticism*, 1983.
——. "The Tiger on the Paper Mat," in *The Resistance to Theory*, 1986.
Hartman, Geoffrey H. Preface to *Deconstruction and Criticism*, 1979. Edited by Harold Bloom, et al.
Johnson, Barbara. "Poison or Remedy? Paul de Man as Pharmakon," in *Colloquium Helveticum*. (1990), pp. 7–20.
Lehman, David. *Signs of the Times: Deconstruction and the Fall of Paul de Man*, 1991.
Loesberg, Jonathan. *Aestheticism and Deconstruction: Pater, Derrida, and de Man*, 1991.
Morrison, Paul A. *The Poetics of Fascism: Ezra Pound, T. S. Eliot, Paul de Man*, 1995.
Norris, Christopher. *Paul de Man, Deconstruction and the Critique of Aesthetic Ideology*, 1988.
Rosso, Stephano. "An Interview with Paul de Man," in *Critical Inquiry*. XII (Summer, 1986), pp. 788–795.
Wiener, Jon. "Deconstructing de Man," in *The Nation*. CCXLVI (January 9, 1988), pp. 22–24.
Yale French Studies. No. 69 (1985), pp. 3–21.

CHRISTOPHER L. PICARD

See also Deconstruction; Derrida; Hartman; Miller

Francesco De Sanctis

Italian critic, translator, and essayist

Born: Morra Irpina, Kingdom of Naples; March 28, 1817
Died: Naples, Italy; December 29, 1883

Biography

Francesco De Sanctis was born in Morra Irpina, a town in the province of Avellino, east of Naples, to a family of small landowners with liberal political traditions. At the age of nine he was sent to study under an uncle who was headmaster of a private school of letters in Naples. In 1833, at the same time that he undertook legal studies, he began to frequent the most famous private school of the time at Naples, directed by Basilio Puoti. De Sanctis began his own teaching career in his uncle's school: he eventually abandoned his legal studies in order to assume the direction of the school from his uncle, who had fallen gravely ill, supplementing his income by giving private lessons. With Puoti's help, De Sanctis obtained a position as professor of Italian at the Collegio Militare della Nunziatella. He taught nights in Puoti's school, and this period in his life, known as the "first Neapolitan school," lasted until 1848.

In a dramatic turn, De Sanctis joined the students at the barricades on May 15, 1848, and participated in the revolt against the Bourbon regime. When the reaction set in, De Sanctis was dismissed from his position at the military school and left Naples for Cosenza in Calabria in 1849. On his way to Turin at the end of 1850, by way of Naples, he was arrested and imprisoned for three years in the Castel dell'Ovo without trial. Released on July 10, 1853, De Sanctis was banished from the kingdom, and after a brief stay on Malta, he proceeded to Turin. There he taught Italian in a girls' school, where, nearly forty years old, he fell in love with a seventeen-year-old student, Teresa De Amicis. De Sanctis organized a series of public lectures on Dante's *La divina commedia* (c. 1320; *The Divine Comedy*) during this time, wrote for Florentine and Torinese journals and papers, and achieved some notoriety. He took a lectureship at the Polytechnic School of Zurich and left Turin in March, 1856. De Sanctis returned to Naples following the unification of Italy, and in August, 1860, he assumed the position of governor of the province of Avellino, and subsequently that of Director of the Ministry of Public Instruction. He was elected to the Chamber of Deputies, and soon thereafter he became Minister of Public Instruction.

Not reelected in 1865, De Sanctis returned to literature, also as a means of support (De Sanctis had married Maria Testa in 1863), and in 1868 he began work on his *Storia della letteratura italiana* (*History of Italian Literature*) under contract with the Neapolitan editor Antonio Morano. In 1872 De Sanctis accepted the nomination as professor of comparative literature at the University of Naples. This was the beginning of the "second Neapolitan school." He returned to politics in 1877, serving again in the Chamber of Deputies and as Minister of Public Instruction. He was reelected to Parliament in 1883, but his involvement in the work of that body was very limited as a result of his failing health. He returned to Naples in June of 1883 and died there on December 29.

Influence

Following De Sanctis' death in 1883, his work was eclipsed for a brief time. The positivist school had little sympathy for the author of the *History of Italian Literature*. He was viewed as a critic of ideas and therefore out of fashion from both methodological and rhetorical perspectives. The great Idealistic philosopher Benedetto Croce was responsible for the rehabilitation of De Sanctis around the turn of the century. He began in 1896 to gather together, edit, and publish the works of De Sanctis, and promoted him as a precursor of Croce's own Idealistic aesthetic theories. Croce wrote of De Sanctis in the *Estetica come scienza dell' espressione e linguistica generale* (1902; *Aesthetic as Science of Expression and General Linguistic*, 1909) that "as a critic and literary historian he has no equal." The English translations of De Sanctis' *History of Italian Literature* and the essays collected in *De Sanctis on Dante* are products of the influence in America of Croce. An appreciation of De Sanctis' importance was not diminished when Croce's own literary-critical school lost favor after World War II. In Antonio Gramsci's *Letteratura e vita nazionale* (1950), De Sanctis is identified as the precursor of the Marxist theoretician's *filosofia della prassi* (philosophy of praxis), and De Sanctis' integration of theory and practice in his approach to criticism is opposed to that of the aesthetic school of Croce. Gramsci marks the beginning of the Left's interest in De Sanctis, which would lead, for example, to the vast editorial enterprise of the Einaudi *Opere*, guided by scholars such as Carlo Muscetta and Natalino Sapegno, both of whom trace their critical lineage to Gramsci. Thus, it is no wonder if, in Italy, as René Wellek observed in *A History of Modern Criticism*, "Francesco De Sanctis is considered *the* critic, a national classic. . . ." In recognizing the problem of artistic form as an autonomous object of critical inquiry as well as the political, moral, and historical character of literature as a cultural institution, De Sanctis served as an informing source for what in the twentieth century became the two dominant critical ideologies in Italian literary culture.

Analysis

Joseph Rossi and Alfred Galpin, in the introduction to *De Sanctis on Dante*, conveniently distinguish three predominant influences on the critical thinking of De Sanctis: the formative rhetorical emphasis of Puoti's "purism," the French school of historical writing, and, finally, the influence of philosophical and dialectical Hegelian aesthetics. De Sanctis' critical writings provide ample support for this account of his intellectual origins. His profound knowledge of the Italian classical tradition as well as the frequent formal analysis of passages and precise aesthetic characterizations typical of his writings can be traced to the formative years under Puoti, whose school served De Sanctis well, long after Puoti's narrow linguistic "purism" had been discarded. De Sanctis' debt to French historical writing is clear, especially to "the good Sismondi," as he calls Jean Charles Léonard Simonde de Sismondi, author of *Histoire des républiques italiennes du moyen âge* (sixteen volumes, 1809–1818; *A History of the Italian Republics*, 1832), and to Edgar Quinet's *Les Révolutions d'Italie* (two volumes, 1848–1852). De Sanctis' Hegelianism dates to the days of his first Neapolitan school, when he studied the German philosopher's works, and from his years of imprisonment, when he learned German and translated G. W. F. Hegel's *Die Logik* (1817; *The Logic of Hegel*, 1874). De Sanctis derives from Hegel the premise that every form of art is rooted in its historical epoch: the work of art is a microcosm which expresses its period according to its own internal norms, so that the aesthetic meaning and structure of a particular form or work of art coincides with a larger historical significance. At the same time, De Sanctis rejected the Hegelian evolutionary scheme leading to an eventual "death of art" and reaffirmed, against Hegel, the autonomy of art as separable from morality and philosophy.

In discussing the development of De Sanctis' approach to literature, it is necessary to keep in mind that he was first and foremost a practical critic and never claimed to be a theoretician, much less a philosopher such as Croce. He had no systematically organized or fixed critical terminology, and he often appears to be inconsistent, as his discourse moves back and forth between the aesthetic and the moral criteria of assessment which inform his work.

In a review essay on a history of Italian literature by the Catholic conservative Cesare Cantù (written at the same time that De Sanctis was beginning work on his own *History of Italian Literature*), the critic affirmed a notion central to his own conception of literature:

> . . . the value and the importance and the morality of content [are] fine and beautiful things, but extraneous to literature which has within itself its end and value, and needs to be judged according to its own criteria which are deduced from its nature . . . .

This awareness, which would strike a responsive chord in Croce, represents a critical acquisition vis-à-vis the preceding tradition of literary historiography in Italy, including direct contemporaries such as Cantù and the liberal Luigi Settembrini. At the same time, and at another level, De Sanctis, "the defender of the autonomy of the work of art" (Wellek), conceived the role of the critic within the wider moral and political cultural context provided by the revolutionary period of the Italian Risorgimento, when issues of Italian cultural identity and conscience were paramount. In a critical essay on Giuseppe Parini, De Sanctis addressed the perspective of this other informing trend in his interpretation of literature:

> . . . that the end of art is art is very true. But the bird singing expresses his entire self. It is not enough to be an artist, one must be a man. What does he [the artist] express if his inner world is impoverished or artificial or mechanical, if there is no faith, if he has no sentiment, if he has nothing to strive for outside himself?

De Sanctis' interest in tracking the progress of the person behind the form, his concern with what Croce called "the intimate history of the Italian people," supersedes purely aesthetic criteria and provides the informing structure of his consideration of Italian literary works, which are held up as a mirror to the Italian conscience. De Sanctis' masterpiece, *History of Italian Literature*, and his critical activity in general are shaped by an overriding political and pedagogic preoccupation.

History of Italian Literature, which was originally conceived as a literary manual for the lyceum students of the newly unified Italy, is generally considered a literary masterpiece in its own right. The work has been judged by Wellek to be "the finest history of any literature ever written . . . [successfully combining] a broad historical scheme with close criticism, theory with practice, aesthetic generalization with particular analysis . . . ." The historical scheme which underlies the work, and which underlies generally the critical essays, reviews, and lectures of De Sanctis' maturity, is that the progress of the dialectic of the relationship between artistic form and religious, political, moral, and social content represents an allegory of the spiritual progress of the Italian people. The political present of the unified Italy's cultural struggle for a definition of its national culture is the ever-present filter through which the progress of this dialectic between artistic form and the content (or lack thereof) of national conscience is examined.

Contemporary and literary history intersect at the culminating point of De Sanctis' *History of Italian Literature*, in the chapter on Niccolò Machiavelli, who is heralded not only as the most profound negation of the Middle Ages and the realistic revival of a decadent literary tradition but also as the harbinger of the present age of science informed by patriotic ideals. This celebration of the resurrection of the national conscience in the writings of the Florentine Secretary coincides with the culminating act of the unification, the occupation of Rome in 1870:

> This is the true Machiavellianism, alive, rather, still young. It is the program of the modern world, developed, corrected, expanded, more or less achieved. Those nations are greatest which best approximate that ideal. We are therefore proud of our Machiavelli. The glory is his when any part of the old edifice crumbles. The glory is his when any part of the new is constructed. In this moment, as I am writing, the bells are ringing out, and they herald the entrance of the Italians into Rome. The temporal power crumbles. They are crying "Viva the Unity of Italy." The glory is Machiavelli's. . . .

At the same time that De Sanctis' militant criticism causes him to distort the "historical" sense of the tradition, however, his clear recognition of artistic form as an autonomous object of critical inquiry, coupled with his extremely fine aesthetic sensibility, leads him to treat sympathetically and characterize critically, with great precision and particularity (as it were, in spite of himself), that part of the tradition which is repugnant to his political ideals. The classic example is Ludovico Ariosto, whom De Sanctis positions, from the perspective of the national conscience, as a kind of anti-Machiavelli, at the same time that he offers an account of the unity of Ariosto's *Orlando furioso* (1516, 1521, 1532) and a description of its expressive originality, which represents the point of departure for the modern critical appreciation of that literary masterpiece of the Italian Renaissance.

De Sanctis' historical scheme is not a simple progress or decline. Its dialectic structure establishes ideal oppositions between contemporaneous authors and schools: between the Sicilian school, for example (blamed for its excessive formalism having little resonance in the "people"), and the early literary activity of Bologna and Florence, which in De Sanctis' account figure as the scientific and democratic cradles of an incipient Italian conscience. While "literature" continues even after Machiavelli, its decadent course through Torquato Tasso, Giambattista Marino, and the Arcadian poets; philosophers and scientists such as Giordano Bruno, Tommaso Campanella, Galileo Galilei, and Giambattista Vico continued on the path indicated by Machiavelli and prepared the way for the future rebirth. The eighteenth-century authors Carlo Goldoni ("the Galileo of the New Literature"), Giuseppe Parini, Vittorio Alfieri, and Ugo Foscolo were all moving with varying degrees of success in the direction of the new literature. This dialectic of form and content as it reveals the progress of a developing national consciousness is open-ended, as it projects inevitably its implications into the future. It is not surprising, then, that De Sanctis distinguishes himself by his attention to contemporary literature, particularly to the greatest of his contemporaries, Alessandro Manzoni and Giacomo Leopardi. De Sanctis' "second Neapolitan school" after 1872, at the University of Naples, addressed directly the contemporary issue of Italian political and cultural identity in courses dealing with the liberal Catholic school of writers led by Manzoni and its liberal counterpart represented by Giuseppe Mazzini and Leopardi. The course of 1876 was dedicated to Leopardi, a poet whom De Sanctis, in his role as literary critic, can be said to have virtually discovered. The radical realism of the poet whose "mind denies, but whose heart affirms" (according to one of De Sanctis' fortunate formulas) is excessive for the bourgeois realistic sensibility of the critic, so that De Sanctis focuses on the poetry and emphasizes Leopardi's affirming heart as a source for inspiration, as a striving toward ideals. While the anticlerical De Sanctis has little sympathy for the politics of Manzoni, his appreciation for Manzoni's novel is profound and extensively articulated. One observes, finally, in these critical reflections of De Sanctis' maturity, the same intimate tension between aesthetic sensibility and political and moral criteria which generally informs De Sanctis' practice as a literary critic.

Principal criticism

Saggi critici, 1866
Saggio critico sul Petrarca, 1869
Storia della letteratura italiana, 1870 (*History of Italian Literature*, 1931)
Nuovi saggi critici, 1872
Studio su Giacomo Leopardi, 1885
Scritti critici, 1885

La letteratura italiana nel secolo XIX, 1897
Scritti varii inediti o rari di Francesco De Sanctis, 1898
Esposizione critica della "Divina commedia": I corsi torinesi del 1854–1855, 1938
Lezioni zurighesi sul Petrarca e altri scritti, 1955
De Sanctis on Dante, 1957

Other major works and literary forms

The extensive critical writings of Francesco De Sanctis take a variety of literary forms ranging from the formal critical essay to the review article and the academic and public lecture. Outside the critical sphere, De Sanctis authored enough political and journalistic writing to fill two volumes of the twenty-two-volume Einaudi edition of his works, *Opere* (1951–1969), edited by Carlo Muscetta. One of the most original works in this area is an account of one of his campaigns for election to the Italian parliament, *Un viaggio elettorale* (1876). Under the title *La crisi del gusto romantico* (volume 4 of *Opere*) the editors of the Einaudi *Opere* have collected works including early literary efforts by De Sanctis including the poem "La prigione" and the play *Torquato Tasso*, both written during his imprisonment in Naples between 1850 and 1853, as well as other prose and lyric compositions, and translations from Johann Wolfgang von Goethe and G. W. F. Hegel as well as from other French and German authors. De Sanctis also wrote an autobiographical work treating his youth, *La giovinezza*, published posthumously by his student Pasquale Villari in 1889. De Sanctis' vast correspondence (gathered in *Opere*), besides its biographical interest, represents an important source for that crucial period of Italian history. It includes letters to family members, friends, students, and political and intellectual personalities, as well as his correspondence with Teresa De Amicis.

NONFICTION
Un viaggio elettorale, 1876
La giovinezza, 1889 (autobiography)
Beatrice, 1914

MISCELLANEOUS
Opere, 1951–1969 (22 volumes, Carlo Muscetta, editor)

Further reading

Borgese, G. A. *Storia della critica romantica in Italia*, 1905.
Breglio, Louis A. *Francesco De Sanctis: Life and Criticism*, 1940.
Contini, Gianfranco. Introduction to *Scelta di scritti critici di Francesco De Sanctis*, 1948.
Jachia, Paolo. *Introduzione a De Sanctis*, 1996.
Rossi, Joseph. "De Sanctis' Criticism: Its Principles and Method," in *PMLA*. LIV (1939), pp. 526–564.
Smith, Denis Mack. "Francesco de Sanctis," in *Society and Politics in the Age of the Risorgimento: Essays in Honour of Denis Mack Smith*, 1991. Edited by John A. Davis and Paul Ginsborg.
Wellek, René. *A History of Modern Criticism: 1750–1950*. Vol. 4, *The Later Nineteenth Century*, 1965.

THEODORE J. CACHEY, JR.

See also Croce; Mazzini

Deconstruction

It is tempting to begin this discussion of deconstruction with the straightforward phrase "deconstruction is . . . ." However, such a common-sense beginning relies on epistemological and linguistic assumptions that deconstruction throws into question. Deconstruction challenges the univocity of language and the logic of identity that ground such definitions and deliberately unsettles that which presents itself as "straightforward" or "common sense."

The term "deconstruction" is among those that the French philosopher Jacques Derrida has used to describe the challenge to philosophical thought that unfolds in his writings. In "Letter to a Japanese Friend," which addresses the problem of translating the word "deconstruction," Derrida remarks that it "must always be girded by an entire discourse." Derrida's work offers close readings of philosophical, literary, anthropological, and linguistic writings including works by Plato, Immanuel Kant, Jean-Jacques Rousseau, Ferdinand de Saussure, J. L. Austin, Claude Lévi-Strauss, Sigmund Freud, Stéphane Mallarmé, James Joyce, and Franz Kafka. The philosophical thought Derrida challenges through these readings is not merely a particular canon of texts or an academic discipline but fundamental assumptions about meaning, classification, communication, and authenticity that structure Western thought.

By carefully pursuing the deployment of key terms in the texts he reads, Derrida shows that philosophical thought, which he also calls "logocentric" or "metaphysical," is structured through oppositions in which a privileged term is associated with essence, origin, or immediacy and defined against a term denigrated for its latency, mediation, or contradiction. In *Of Grammatology* (1976), for instance, Derrida interrogates the privilege of speech over writing characteristic of Western philosophy. Derrida describes a pervasive tendency "to confine writing to a secondary and instrumental function: translator of a full speech that was fully present (present to itself, to its signified, to the other, the very condition of the theme of presence in general), technics in the service of language, spokesman, interpreter of an originary speech itself shielded from interpretation." The privileging of speech over writing that Derrida describes, like other instances of privileging what is considered "fully present" or originary, is important to philosophical thought because it is the possibility of full presence – absolute independence and undifferentiated identity – that grounds meaning, authorizes transcendent notions of "Truth," and assures unified subjectivity. These metaphysical assumptions are brought into question when Derrida goes on to show that these oppositions are far from stable and that the self-identity and integrity claimed for the privileged term is fundamentally undercut. In the case of writing's supposed "secondary and instrumental function" in relation to speech, Derrida shows that the valorization of speech is dependent on the denigrated qualities ascribed to writing and that the "secondarity it seemed possible to ascribe to writing alone" affects language in general. In this opposition, as in others, the privileged term can only be defined by its difference from the term with which it is paired, making its meaning dependent on its place within a relationship rather than a fully present essence. Derrida also shows that not even this difference is absolute and that the privileged term not only depends on the term to which it is opposed but is infiltrated by that term. Therefore, the privileged term's association with full presence is sustained only through suppressing both its dependence and the difference within the term itself. Thus, Derrida shows that the terms in oppositions like nature/culture, outside/inside, literal/figural, man/woman, signifier/signified, and speech/writing do not have meaning independently and do not sustain their presumed difference from each other. Insisting on these two points, Derrida makes clear that he is not simply effecting a reversal of privilege but is instead challenging the purity and unity of concept that would be necessary to sustain an opposition absolutely. The result is not to discredit the opposition in question with any sense that a demonstration of instability or infiltration permanently removes the force of that opposition.

What Derrida instead insists on is a double gesture that requires thinking contradictory ideas simultaneously. Many of his most famous terms are words which he puts in service of this impossible but necessary double gesture. The "trace," for instance, names a non-originary origin, the impossibility of origin but the continued force and allure of the originary. Other terms that take on this significance in Derrida's essays include supplement, hymen, pharmakon, writing, parergon, and so on. This double gesture is also sometimes designated by writing terms "under erasure," crossing them through as they are printed to indicate simultaneously the impossibility and inescapability of the concept they name.

An important term among those that Derrida uses to describe this simultaneous possibility and impossibility of meaning is *différance*. Derrida coins this term, exchanging the "*-ence*" ending for "*-ance*," to bring together contrary senses of the French verb "*différer*." As Derrida explains, in the essay "Différance" in *Margins of Philosophy* (1982), his "neographism" indicates differing and differentiation as well as deferral, detour, and delay. Derrida combines these senses in order to discuss the constitution of presence, and thus all that depends on presence, within the simultaneous constitution of difference and its deferral. A presence depends on its differentiation from all that it is not, its difference, but since it can never be itself absolutely, that presence is always deferred, always suspended. Thus, *différance* inhabits structures of meaning as both a condition of possibility and a denial of any absolute determination.

Derrida explains that the "movement of (the production of) *différance* without origin" could not have simply been called differentiation because "such a word, among other confusions, would have left open the possibility of an organic, original, and homogeneous unity that eventually would come to be divided, to receive difference as an event." Thus Derrida suggests that *différance* sustains alterity – radical otherness that cannot be reappropriated within a system of meaning – through the infinite deferral of difference. The simultaneous movements of *différance* make clear that absolute difference is just as dependent on notions of unity and purity as is absolute presence.

Where deconstruction happens

Deconstruction, especially in the United States, has been influential in literary criticism and literature departments. This influence is attributable in part to the work of a group of critics, including Harold Bloom, Geoffrey Hartman, Paul de Man, and J. Hillis Miller, as well as Derrida, who became known as the Yale School in the 1970s. Hartman's preface to *Deconstruction and Criticism* (1979), a collection of essays by these critics, describes their work as sharing an interest in "theory in the form of poetics and semiotics and philosophical speculation generally."

However, these critics had widely varying approaches to deconstructive thought, a point which Hartman underscores when he describes himself and Bloom as "barely deconstructionists" in contrast to Derrida, Miller, and de Man. The Yale School obviously does not form a single school of deconstructive literary criticism. Nonetheless, the influence of the Yale critics has led both proponents and detractors to describe deconstruction as a method of reading or a literary critical technique. In "Letter to a Japanese Friend," Derrida insists that "deconstruction is not a method and cannot be transformed into one." Instead, "Deconstruction takes place, it is an event that does not await the deliberation, consciousness, or organization of a subject." Thus he describes deconstruction not as the subjective deployment of a reading strategy but as something that happens in written texts and in all structures of meaning. In other words, deconstruction is not something that a reader does to a text but is a quality of textuality. In saying this, it is important to reiterate that the "text" with which deconstruction concerns itself is not simply limited to written language but includes the discursive structuring of experience, institutions, reality, subjectivity, and so on.

One of Derrida's most frequently cited and frequently misinterpreted statements is his contention, in *Of Grammatology*, that "there is nothing outside of the text" (or translated literally, "there is no outside-text"). This assertion has been read as a denial that there is anything of consequence outside a written text, and, therefore, it has been taken as a statement of disregard for what are often considered to be important extratextual factors – history and politics, for example. However, Derrida's contention that there is nothing outside the text is, instead, a challenge to the division of inside from outside, of text from some exterior "reality" to which that text refers and which anchors and authorizes textual meaning. In "Afterword: Toward an Ethic of Discussion," the final section of "Limited Inc." (1977), Derrida attempts to clarify his contention, explaining that it "does not mean that all referents are suspended, denied, or enclosed in a book, as people have claimed . . . . But it does mean that every referent, all reality has the structure of a differential trace, and that one cannot refer to this 'real' except in an interpretive experience." In other words, there is nothing outside a text that can ground its meaning absolutely, and this is precisely because there is nothing that is not subject to the movement of *différance*, nothing that is outside textuality.

Because concepts such as intentionality, consciousness, subjectivity, law, morality, and choice are produced by and subject to *différance*, they too are ungrounded and undecidable. For Derrida, the ungroundedness of such concepts urges a significant rethinking of responsibility, obligation, and other concepts important to ethical and political decision-making. In "Force of Law," Derrida contends that "any deconstruction of this network of concepts . . . in their given or dominant state may seem like a move toward irresponsibility at the very moment that, on the contrary, deconstruction calls for an increase in responsibility." To understand the connection Derrida draws between deconstruction and increased responsibility, it is important to understand how Derrida uses the term "undecidable." To say that a concept is undecidable does not mean that no decisions are possible; instead, it means that decisions must be made that cannot be determined through recourse to an absolute that would authorize and legitimize a decision. Derrida explains, again in "Force of Law," that "a decision that didn't go through the ordeal of the undecidable would not be a free decision, it would only be the programmable application or unfolding of a calculable process." In other words, for a judgment to truly be a decision, it must take place in the face of undecidability. Otherwise it is merely an application of a rule or law, a calculation for which the calculator does not take responsibility. Thus, in "Afterword," Derrida explains "there can be no moral or political responsibility without this trial and this passage by way of the undecidable." With such an understanding of responsibility, Derrida shifts the discussion of ethics away from attempting to determine in advance what answers are right and what decisions are just and toward preserving space to question the process of judgment itself.

Deconstruction in conversation

Deconstruction is both an heir and a response to continental philosophy, but as the range of Derrida's concerns makes clear, its relevance is not confined to the philosophical discipline. Because deconstruction happens everywhere, writers interested in deconstruction pursue this interest in conversation with many other concerns, including feminism and law, as well as literature and philosophy. Deconstruction reshapes the questions writers ask about their enterprises and challenges the boundaries assumed to divide those enterprises. The result of these challenges are wide-ranging and diverse critical projects that nonetheless share a concern with the function of language and representation in shaping knowledge. These deconstructive projects also often share an interest in the ethical implications of deconstruction's challenge to metaphysical thinking.

The works of Paul de Man, J. Hillis Miller, and Barbara Johnson are among many examples of deconstruction's productive engagement with literature. In *Allegories of Reading* (1979), de Man describes his approach to reading as one "in which rhetoric is a disruptive intertwining of trope and persuasion or . . . of cognitive and performative language." Pursuing this "disruptive intertwining" through particular attention to rhetorical figures, de Man contends that "a literary text simultaneously asserts and denies the authority of its own rhetorical mode." Miller, in *The Ethics of Reading* (1987), contends that "deconstruction is nothing more or less than good reading" and argues that "there is a necessary ethical moment in that act of reading as such." Taking authors reading their own texts as exemplary acts of reading, Miller locates ethical importance in deviation from rather than allegiance to a text. Barbara Johnson, in *A World of Difference* (1987), reads literary and critical works in order to address questions such as: "What are the political consequences of the fact that language is not a transparently expressive medium?" and "How can the study of suppressed, disseminated, or marginalized messages within texts equip us to intervene against oppression and injustice in the world?" Particularly concerned with issues of sexual and racial difference, Johnson shows the relevance of literary reading to such questions and also takes up questions about deconstruction's relation to feminism.

As Johnson's work suggests, feminism's sometimes troubled and troubling relationship with deconstruction can be productive for both deconstruction and feminism. While some feminists have distrusted deconstruction's challenge to identity on the basis that feminism requires a stable sense of identity to ground its politics, Judith Butler, in *Gender Trouble: Feminism and the Subversion of Identity* (1990), argues that "the radical instability of the category [of woman] sets into question the foundational restrictions on feminist political theorizing and opens up other configurations, not only of genders and bodies, but of politics itself." Similarly, Diane Elam, who takes the encounter between feminism and deconstruction as her central concern in *Feminism and Deconstruction: Ms. en Abyme* (1994), argues that feminism and deconstruction ask questions that allow a rethinking of the political. For Elam, "the ethics of deconstruction and feminism is an ethical activism which requires that judgments be made, yet which does not supply the means of legitimating those judgments. No recourse to self-present subjects, natural rights, or transcendental truths. . . ."

Deconstruction's disruption of assumptions about language, institutions, and ethics has also brought it into conversation with legal studies. Drucilla Cornell's *The Philosophy of the Limit* (1992) explores the relationship between "the philosophy of the limit" – the new name that Cornell wants to give to deconstruction – and "questions of ethics, justice and legal interpretation." Cornell attempts to show "the significance for legal interpretation of Derrida's own understanding of justice as an aporia that inevitably serves as the limit to any attempt to collapse justice into positive law." In addition to her own work on the intersection between deconstruction and the law, Cornell is coeditor of *Deconstruction and the Possibility of Justice* (1992), a collection of essays by writers in literary and legal studies addressing questions raised by this intersection.

This overview of writers interested in deconstruction is necessarily incomplete but it conveys some sense of the diversity of the conversations in which deconstruction takes part. While these conversations approach deconstruction differently, they are alike, but not identical, in that their readings of text do not take the act of interpretation for granted. They sustain the possibility or impossibility of reading as a question central to any textual engagement. They are also concerned with the inescapable implication of the critic in that which they critique, the impossibility of assuming an outside position from which to render a disinterested judgment. They also share a sense that the impossibility of disinterestedness and the simultaneous possibility and impossibility of reading open rather than foreclose ethical possibilities.

Further reading

Arac, Jonathan, Wlad Godzich, and Wallace Martin, eds. *The Yale Critics: Deconstruction in America*, 1983.

Bloom, Harold, Paul de Man, Jacques Derrida, and Geoffrey Hartman. *Deconstruction and Criticism*, 1979.

Butler, Judith. *Gender Trouble: Feminism and the Subversion of Identity*, 1990.

Caputo, John D. *Deconstruction in a Nutshell: A Conversation with Jacques Derrida*, 1997.

Cornell, Drucilla. *The Philosophy of the Limit*, 1992.

Critchley, Simon. *The Ethics of Deconstruction: Derrida and Levinas*, 1992.

Derrida, Jacques. *Writing and Difference*, 1978.

——. *Dissemination*, 1981.

——. *Positions*, 1981.

——. *The Post Card: From Socrates to Freud and Beyond*, 1987.

——. *The Truth in Painting*, 1987.

——. *Acts of Literature*, 1992. Edited by Derek Attridge.

——. "Force of Law: The Mystical Foundation of Authority," in *Deconstruction and the Possibility of Justice*, 1992. Edited by Drucilla Cornell, Michael Rosenfeld, and David Gray Carlson.

Johnson, Barbara. *A World of Difference*, 1987.

Miller, J. Hillis. *The Ethics of Reading*, 1987.

Spivak, Gayatri Chakravorty. *In Other Worlds: Essays in Cultural Politics*, 1987.

ELIZABETH KUHLMANN

See also Bloom; Culler; de Man; Derrida; French Literary Theory: Twentieth Century; Hartman; Miller; Nietzsche; Structuralism; Yale School

Gilles Deleuze

French philosopher

Born: Paris, France; January 18, 1925
Died: Paris, France; November 4, 1995

Biography

Gilles Deleuze was born on January 18, 1925, in Paris. He was a pupil at the Lycée Carnot in Paris during World War II, and he studied philosophy at the Sorbonne from 1944 to 1948, where he met François Chatelet, Michel Butor, and Michel Tournier. He was taught by some of the most influential figures in French philosophy at the time, including Georges Canguilhem, Fernand Alquié, and Jean Hippolyte. He gained his *agrégation* in philosophy in 1948, and until 1957 he taught in various lycées in France. In 1957 he moved into the university sector, working at the Sorbonne, the Centre National de la Recherche Scientifique, and Lyon. In 1962 he met Michel Foucault, with whom he maintained a friendship and intellectual exchange throughout much of his life. In 1969 Deleuze was appointed professor of philosophy at the new university of Vincennes, and in the same year he met the radical psychiatrist and psychoanalyst Félix Guattari. In 1969 Deleuze also defended his principal thesis, *Difference and Repetition*, along with his secondary thesis on Baruch Spinoza.

In the 1950s and 1960s Deleuze wrote a series of monographs on philosophers, such as David Hume, Immanuel Kant, Henri Bergson, Friedrich Nietzsche, and Spinoza, along with studies of Marcel Proust and the German novelist Leopold von Sacher-Masoch. In the 1970s Deleuze entered into a period of collaboration with Guattari. *Anti-Œdipus*, the first volume of a two-volume study of "capitalism and schizophrenia," which was published in France in 1972, constituted a practical experiment with the identity of "the author," written as it was in collaboration with Guattari. As Deleuze commented in the late 1970s, "we do not work together, we work between the two." *Anti-Œdipus* emerged from the questions posed by the events of 1968 in France, and provided the authors with temporary fame. The second volume of the capitalism and schizophrenia project, published in 1980, concentrated on the study of "rhizomatic," acentered structures. In the third phase of his career, throughout the 1980s and the early

1990s, Deleuze continued to collaborate occasionally with Guattari. He also turned increasingly to aesthetic questions, publishing a study of the painter Francis Bacon, and a well received two-volume study of cinema in the mid-1980s. Toward the end of his life Deleuze wrote on cinema, returning to Bergson in order to show how cinema has the potential to correspond to a new type of thought which resists the spatializing tendency of the intellect. In 1991 Deleuze published *What is Philosophy?*, his final collaboration with Guattari, which in many ways summarized his career. In this book Deleuze and Guattari retain a broadly Nietzschean perspective, arguing that the true objective of philosophy is neither communication nor reflection, but rather the creation of "concepts." In 1993 Deleuze published his last book, *Essays Critical and Clinical*, a collection dealing with literature and writing in general.

Deleuze retired from teaching in 1987, his seminars at Vincennes having become a weekly event in themselves (which Deleuze himself described as a sort of *Sprechgesang*). He suffered from respiratory problems for much of his adult life, and he committed suicide in 1995 by jumping from the window of his apartment in Paris.

Influence

Deleuze was, along with Michel Foucault and Jacques Derrida, one of the most celebrated poststructuralist thinkers in France. In the first part of his career he traced an alternative pathway through the history of philosophy. Deleuze challenged the importance of G. W. F. Hegel, and produced innovative readings of philosophers as diverse as Hume and Spinoza. He also began to explore the possibility of a philosophical reading of literature. For example, in *Proust and Signs* he uses Proust's *À la recherche du temps perdu* (1913–1927) to counter the idea that the mind is naturally inclined toward truth, claiming that one of the characteristics of the "sign," as it is developed by Proust, is that it can shock thought out of its habitual stupor. The figure of Nietzsche is pivotal in this period as a radically antidialectical influence, providing inspiration as a pluralist thinker who is suspicious of stable identities, along with Spinoza, whose "expressionism" challenges conventional modes of linguistic representation. Bergson was also an important influence, indicating the need to take into account the constant flux and movement which pertains to being and consciousness.

In the second period of his career, Deleuze began to develop his own philosophy of difference and multiplicity. In *Difference and Repetition* he drew upon an eclectic series of philosophical, literary, and scientific sources to produce nonlinear studies of meaning, which questioned the dominance of the category of "Sameness" and identity. Michel Foucault was sufficiently impressed with *Difference and Repetition* to claim that Deleuze was "the only philosophical mind in France," and he famously speculated that "one day, perhaps, this century will be known as Deleuzian." In *Anti-Œdipus* Deleuze and Guattari argue that desire is prior to representation, in that it constantly escapes and "deterritorializes" the Oedipal model. Deterritorialization in Deleuze's conception of aesthetics is the process by which conventional categories of representation are broken down and reconfigured in order to render visible and audible previously unseen and unheard forces. The book was subsequently criticized for idealizing the anarchic, "desiring" potential of the schizophrenic, a criticism that the authors rejected strongly.

The treatment of literature forms an important part of the work of Deleuze. In 1964 he published the first edition of *Proust and Signs*, and in 1967 a study of the work of Sacher-Masoch. *The Logic of Sense*, published in 1969, was a philosophical work which included work on Antonin Artaud, Lewis Carroll, F. Scott Fitzgerald, Pierre Klossowski, Malcolm Lowry, Michel Tournier, and Émile Zola. Together with Guattari he published *Kafka: Toward a Minor Literature* in 1975, and the two volumes of the *Capitalism and Schizophrenia* project contain important material on literature, including a long section on the concept of "becoming" in *A Thousand Plateaus*, which offers a reading of Herman Melville's *Moby-Dick*. In *Anti-Œdipus* and *A Thousand Plateaus*, works of literature are frequently cited, often from an Anglo-American canon which includes D. H. Lawrence, Henry Miller, Jack Kerouac, William Burroughs, and Melville. Deleuze and Guattari contend that much literature has a "schizophrenic vocation" and that these authors know more about schizophrenia than psychiatrists or psychoanalysts.

It is important to understand that Deleuze develops an innovative, essentially *philosophical* approach to literature. Frequently, as in his final work, *Essays Critical and Clinical*, literary writers rub shoulders with philosophers such as Kant and Spinoza. In this way, Deleuze's literary analysis draws on the inventive corpus of concepts that he created throughout his career. Two crucial concepts are those of "becoming" and "deterritorialization," both of which indicate a commitment to understanding the ways in which forces traverse the individual. In short, they are concepts which are designed to challenge stable notions of identity. This philosophical approach also means that Deleuze often talks about literature as one example of artistic production, assuming links with other forms of art such as cinema and painting. It should also be borne in mind that this philosophical approach means that Deleuze's treatment of literature often has the tenor of a manifesto, apparently setting out the components of an ideal set of literary effects.

Analysis

Although Deleuze would conventionally be located within a poststructuralist framework, his approach to literature must be distinguished from that of Derrida. Literature for Derrida is conditioned by language, linguistics, and history, whereas literature for Deleuze is geographical rather than historical, expressive rather than communicative, and is concerned with forces that are at work "in and beyond language itself" rather than a conception of literary language conditioned by the "linguistic turn." Deleuze seeks to locate literary texts within an extratextual practice, and he is concerned primarily with what he calls "vitality." By vitality Deleuze means a sort of Lucretian naturalism, according to which the literary work expresses forces and experiments with becomings, rather than entering into a process of signification. In Deleuze's own philosophy this naturalism is known as "immanence," the concept of life as an impersonal and nonorganic set of forces:

> To write is certainly not to impose a form (of expression) on the matter of lived experience. Literature rather moves in the direction of the ill-formed or the incomplete, as Gombrowicz said as well as practiced. Writing is a question of becoming, always incomplete, always in the midst of being formed, and goes beyond the matter of any livable or lived experience. It is a process, that is, a passage of Life that traverses both the livable and the lived.

The essential problem of writing does have to do with language, but it is not a textual problem. It is rather a question of creating what Deleuze calls a "foreign language" within standard, representational language. Language must be forced out of its "customary furrows" and achieve a state of delirium. In this way, he draws on the work of Maurice Blanchot in order to distinguish between a limit which is outside language, and the particular limit that he wishes to explore, which is "outside *of* language." This "outside" is made up of blocs of seeing and hearing – "visions and auditions" – which require a bold, vital use of language. Literature must attempt, to borrow Samuel Beckett's phrase, to "drill holes" in language in order to see and hear what lies behind, and to release new colors and sonorities. For Deleuze and Guattari, it is significant that Kafka's work frequently makes use of animal sounds and cries of pain. Kafka "deliberately kills all metaphor," turning language away from signification and representation toward the expression of intensities and "metamorphosis": "*Language stops being representative in order to now move toward its extremities or limits.*"

Literature for Deleuze has a vocation which is both *critical* and *clinical*. It has a critical role which is skeptical of conventional modes of representation, and a clinical role which involves assessing the potentialities of "life." The vocation of the true writer is to liberate life from the places where it is imprisoned "by and within man." Writing is inseparable from "becoming." In writing, one "becomes-woman, becomes-animal or vegetable, becomes-molecule to the point of becoming-imperceptible." A process of becoming escapes conventional categories of representation, and for this reason eschews imitation, in order to avoid the pitfalls of what Deleuze would call "State" thought which depends upon the act of assigning identities. To become is to attain a zone of indiscernibility or of indetermination. For Deleuze, the literary masterpiece of becoming is Melville's *Moby-Dick* (1851). Melville's novel is not a psychological study of Ahab's obsession with the whale, but rather an exploration of the powerful "zone of proximity" in which Ahab can no longer be distinguished from the whale: "Moby-Dick is the 'wall, shoved near' with which he merges."

Literature tends toward aformality and impersonality: "It is not the first two persons that function as the condition for literary enunciation; literature begins only when a third person is born in us that strips us of the power to say 'I' (Blanchot's 'neuter')." Literature does not recount personal experiences – memories, travels, griefs, and dreams – but rather has a "fabulating" function which does not consist in projecting an ego. The writer is ideally a "seer," a "becomer," who is more of a prophet than a psychologist. It is not a case of the writer recounting what has happened to him or her, since the writer is only a "shadow," who "returns from what he has seen and heard with bloodshot eyes and pierced eardrums." The fact that writers frequently suffer from frail personal health means that they are more likely to be open to the flow of life which passes through them.

Deleuze often expresses a preference for what he calls "Anglo-American" literature, which means American writers such as Melville, Thomas Wolfe, and Kerouac, together with English writers such as Thomas Hardy, Virginia Woolf, and D. H. Lawrence. According to Deleuze, these writers all demonstrate an approach to the individual which distinguishes them from the neurotic psychology of much French literature: "Take as an example the case of Thomas Hardy: his characters are not people or subjects, they are collections of intensive sensations, each is such a collection, a packet, a bloc of variable sensations." The essay "Bartleby; or, The Formula" uses Melville's short story *Bartleby the Scrivener* (1853) as the starting point for a general discussion of the importance of American literature. Again, Deleuze emphasizes that literature should not be thought of as psychological: "The novelist has the eye of a prophet, not the gaze of a psychologist." Melville's great characters form part of a vast *Primary Nature*, at one pole of which there are monomaniacs such as Captain Ahab, and at the other pole are angels or "saintly hypochondriacs," such as Billy Budd and the enigmatic Bartleby: "Everything sets them in opposition, and yet they are perhaps the same creature – primary, original, stubborn, seized from both sides, marked merely with a 'plus' or a 'minus' sign: Ahab and Bartleby." It is not only that the American novel is not psychological in approach: it also makes claim to a sort of higher irrationalism. To support his claim Deleuze cites Melville's reflections on the novel in *The Confidence-Man* (1857). The novel does not need to provide rational and consistent motives for characters, when the novel expresses a vitalist perspective: "It is life that justifies; it has no need of being justified." The American novel provides the reader with perplexing characters who "exist in nothingness" and who defy logic and psychology. Bartleby, the enigmatic clerk whose repetition of "I prefer not to" has a contagious quality which causes it to proliferate and creates confusion around him in the attorney's office, is a "man without qualities," who is, in all senses, not particular: "All particularity, all reference is abolished."

In *What is Philosophy?* Deleuze and Guattari argue that just as philosophers think with concepts, so artists think with *percepts* and *affects*. Percepts and affects form a bloc of sensations which mean that literature is historical and geographical, in that it expresses collective perspectives and aspirations. Deleuze distinguishes between human perception which, however complex, is always linked to a human subject, and the liberating aesthetic function of a sort of "camera-eye"; that is to say, a mode of perception which is prehuman. In short, percepts and affects are perceptions and emotions which are no longer linked to a particular consciousness:

> Percepts are no longer perceptions; they are independent of a state of those who experience them. Affects are no longer feelings or affections; they go beyond the strength of those who undergo them. Sensations, percepts, and affects are beings whose validity lies in themselves and exceeds any lived. They could be said to exist in the absence of man because man, as he is caught in stone, on the canvas, or by words, is himself a compound of percepts and affects. The work of art is a being of sensation and nothing else: it exists in itself.

When the novel works with percept – the moor as percept in Thomas Hardy, and Melville's oceanic percept – it is as if the landscape itself sees, since the perceptions have been liberated from the individual consciousness.

In *Kafka: Toward a Minor Literature* Deleuze and Guattari make one of their most important contributions to the study of literature, defining what they mean by "minor" literature. Such literature has three main characteristics: it is a language which a minority constructs within a major language; it has an unavoidably political role; and, finally, it is essentially collective. Minor literature employs a "deterritorialized" variation of a major language, such as Prague German, the "paper language" that Kafka uses. He thrives on the "withered" vocabulary and incorrect syntax of this German: "He will feed himself on abstinence; he will tear out of Prague German all the qualities of underdevelopment that it has tried to hide; he will make it cry with an extremely sober and rigorous cry." The political task of the writer is not to address a people which is already in existence, as was the case with the supposedly "democratic" art of the Soviet Union, but to invent a people who do not yet exist. Minor literature is always political, since the cramped space within which it is created means that individual concerns are forced into contact with wider political concerns. Minor literature is necessarily an "affair of the people" rather than a literature of exceptional individuals. In other words, minor literature eschews the petty concerns of the Oedipal drama. Kafka does not write Oedipal dramas, but political parables which anticipate capitalist America, bureaucratic Russia, and Nazi Germany, "the diabolical powers of the future." Minor literature is also collective, and to illustrate this Deleuze and Guattari claim that Kafka's status as a bachelor does not make him an isolated figure, but rather allows him to make collective statements: "A machine that is all the more social and collective insofar as it is solitary, a bachelor, and that, tracing the line of escape, is equivalent in itself to a community whose conditions haven't yet been established."

Similarly, *Masochism* (1967) explores the political function and significance of the work of the Marquis de Sade and Sacher-Masoch. Sade experiments with an ironic and repetitive accumulation of "reason," a technique which gives language a political significance. Similarly, Masoch's work is characterized by recurrent descriptions of suspense which imply a dialectical use of language. Sade shows his libertines striving toward a sort of "republicanism" which is far removed from the institutions of the French Revolution. Masoch, on the other hand, dreams of "a beautiful female despot, a terrible Tsarina," who will push the Slavs toward true republicanism.

In an interview from the 1980s Deleuze expresses the hope that everything he has written is "vitalistic," meaning that he strives for a philosophy of impersonality, a philosophy of forces, signs, and events which float free of human subjects. His work on literature is, by this account, vitalistic, in that he eschews individual pyschology in favor of collective enunciation, and a "free indirect discourse" which expresses intensities and becomings.

Principal criticism

Marcel Proust et les signes, 1964; second edition *Proust et les signes*, 1970 (*Proust and Signs*, 1972)
Présentation de Sacher-Masoch, 1967 (*Masochism*, 1989)
Logique du sens, 1969 (*The Logic of Sense*, 1990)
Kafka: pour une littérature mineure, 1975 (with Félix Guattari) (*Kafka: Toward a Minor Literature*, 1986)
Critique et clinique, 1993 (*Essays Critical and Clinical*, 1997)

Other major works and literary forms

Empirisme et subjectivité, 1953 (*Empiricism and Subjectivity*, 1991)
Nietzsche et la philosophie, 1962 (*Nietzsche and Philosophy*, 1983)
La Philosophie critique de Kant, 1963 (*Kant's Critical Philosophy*, 1984)
Le Bergsonisme, 1966 (*Bergsonism*, 1988)

Spinoza et le problème de l'expression, 1968 (*Expressionism in Philosophy: Spinoza*, 1990)
Différence et répétition, 1968 (*Difference and Repetition*, 1994)
L'Anti-Œdipe, 1972 (with Félix Guattari) (*Anti-Œdipus*, 1984)
Dialogues, 1977 (with Claire Parnet) (*Dialogues*, 1987)
Mille plateaux, 1980 (with F. Guattari) (*A Thousand Plateaus*, 1987)
Spinoza: Philosophie pratique, 1981 (*Spinoza: Practical Philosophy*, 1988)
Cinéma-1: L'Image-mouvement, 1983 (*Cinema 1: The Movement-Image*, 1986)
Cinéma-2: L'Image-temps, 1985 (*Cinéma 2: The Time-Image*, 1989)
Foucault, 1986 (*Foucault*, 1988)
Le Pli: Leibniz et le Baroque, 1988 (*The Fold: Leibniz and the Baroque*, 1993)
Pourparlers 1972–1990, 1990 (*Negotiations 1972–1990*, 1995)
Qu'est-ce que la philosophie?, 1991 (with F. Guattari) (*What is Philosophy?*, 1994)

Further reading

Bogue, Ronald. *Deleuze and Guattari*, 1989.
Boundas, Constantin V., and Dorothea Olkowski, eds. *Gilles Deleuze and the Theater of Philosophy*, 1994.
Goodchild, Philip. *Deleuze and Guattari: An Introduction to the Politics of Desire*, 1996.
Marks, John. *Gilles Deleuze: Vitalism and Multiplicity*, 1998.
Patton, Paul, ed. *Deleuze: A Critical Reader*, 1996.

JOHN MARKS

See also French Literary Theory: Twentieth Century; Postmodernism; Psychoanalytic Criticism

Jacques Derrida

French philosopher and critic

Born: El Biar, Algeria; July 15, 1930

Biography

Jacques Derrida was born of Jewish parents in Algeria in 1930. He was educated in France, where he first went for military service. The late 1980s saw him teaching philosophy at the École Normale Supérieure in Paris, as well as a course in the department of literature at the University of California, Irvine. For many years he taught a course in the department of comparative literature at Yale University. He also lectures frequently at other North American universities, as in the summer of 1987 when he gave a series of lectures at the annual School of Criticism and Theory at Dartmouth College.

A prolific writer, Derrida burst upon the scene of writing with two sets of major publications: first in 1967 with "Speech and Phenomena," *Writing and Difference*, and *Of Grammatology*; then in 1972 with *Dissemination*, *Margins of Philosophy*, and *Positions*. While the deconstructive theory developed in these texts has been criticized as ahistorical, Derrida has shown increasing concern for sociohistorical issues. For example, he is concerned about the role of the university in society, and about the need for the teaching of philosophy in the high schools in France. In 1975, in an attempt to fulfill this need, Derrida with some friends, colleagues, and students founded an organization called Groupe de Recherche sur l'Enseignements Philosophique. They not only wanted to ensure the continuation of the high school philosophy curriculum, which despite the government's attempt to eliminate it altogether was required in the last grade; they also wanted to restructure teaching in all disciplines through a transformation of the minds of the teachers, students, and parents. In 1983 Derrida helped to found the International College of Philosophy in Paris, an institution open to all foreign scholars regardless of title. Its purpose is to give priority to research topics not accepted in existing institutions in France or other countries.

Influence

The now famous structuralism conference at The Johns Hopkins University in 1966, where Derrida presented his paper "Structure, Sign and Play in the Discourse of the Human Sciences," marked his debut on the American intellectual scene. Structuralists argue that all meaning is produced by rule systems based on relationship and structure. The conference, intended to introduce structuralism in the United States, instead announced, principally through Derrida, the demise of structuralism and the advent of Derrida's theory of reading referred to as "deconstruction." As the main philosophical tenet of the intellectual movement known as "poststructuralism," deconstruction has had an enormous influence on the course of literary studies from the late 1960s through the 1980s. In fact, with many of his books published in English, Derrida has become an institution. He is arguably the most prominent philosopher of the second half of the twentieth century, and a controversial one at that. While some see him as a profound innovator who has instigated a radical revaluation of the basic ideas of Western humanism, others dismiss him as a nihilist who undermines the traditional values of literary study.

Both sides agree that while Derrida is obviously subversive, his attack on notions of truth, reason, and consciousness does not lead to complete meaninglessness. Derrida is a product of the deductive-analytical philosophical tradition that he criticizes, yet his work holds out the promise that by meditating on the key words of this tradition one eventually may discover important things beyond the conventional limits of ordinary consciousness. Derrida reexamines such words as "speech," "writing," and "presence," and many of his own terms – "logocentrism," "*différance*," "margin," and "deconstruction" – are now commonplace both in and out of the academy. Derrida's influence in the United States was enhanced by his colleagues at Yale University – Harold Bloom, Paul de Man,

Geoffrey Hartman, and J. Hillis Miller – who became known as the "Yale Critics," or the "hermeneutic Mafia."

Analysis

Derrida's theory of deconstruction has been praised for liberating critics from what he calls the "logocentric" tradition of Western metaphysics. The term "deconstruction" means to undo or de-construct, as in taking apart a text to analyze the conflicting forces within it responsible for the production of meaning – which according to deconstruction can never be unequivocal. "Logocentrism" is derived from "logos," the Greek word which combines in a single concept the inward rational principles of human beings, verbal texts, and the natural universe. The "logos" is identified with God, the ultimate source of truth, which has remained hidden ever since the Fall of humanity, and which Derrida claims to be a dream. In deconstructing Western metaphysics, Derrida tries to show that its theories are not universal truths but rather constructions subverted by the very texts in which they find expression. The aim of the logocentric tradition has been to return to the truth of a "metaphysics of presence." Against the logocentric idea of "presence," defined variously as transcendentality, consciousness, or God, Derrida argues that nothing is simply present, but depends for its meaning on its relation to things absent. In this negative logic, a pen is a pen mainly because it is not a pipe.

A central tenet of logocentrism, known as phonocentrism, is the notion that writing is a secondary representation of speech. This logocentric notion was supported by Aristotle, who believed that the voice, in producing the first symbols, stands in immediate relation to the mind, and that the first signs represent mental experiences in which the signifier (or sound image), the signified (or concept), and the thing itself are united by a natural bond. Thus the word "tree" consists of a unity of sound and meaning, signifier and signified, and this unity bears a natural relation to its referent, the tree itself. In deconstructing this logocentric unity, Derrida argues against the speaking subject as an immediate presence who can stand in direct relation to the unified presence of a word or thing. Any unified presence, he claims, is "always already" divided within itself.

In his general theory of writing, referred to as "graphocentrism," Derrida deconstructs the oral tradition by declaring that language is first writing and that speech, in turn, is the mirror of writing. This assertion may baffle the reader, for all historians of language agree that human beings developed speech long before they developed writing. Thomas Pyles' *The Origins and Development of the English Language* (second edition, 1971), a standard text, offers a representative treatment of the relationship between speech and writing:

> However man started to talk, he did so a breathtakingly long time ago, and it was not until much later that he devised a system of making marks in or on wood, stone, and the like to represent what he said when he talked. Compared with language, writing is a newfangled invention, although certainly none the less brilliant for being so. But it is merely symbolization of the sounds man makes in speaking or, as with ideographic writing . . ., the objects he perceives and the ideas he has, and thus not really language at all, although for convenience' sake and by long tradition we speak of written language in contrast to spoken language.

By suggesting that writing is not truly "language," that only speech merits this appellation, historians of language (so Derrida argues) have helped to sustain the metaphysics of presence.

It is precisely against this viewpoint that Derrida polemically asserts the priority of writing over speech. As Geoffrey Hartman observes, "Derrida's concept of ecriture . . ., his attack on those who privilege voice or oral perspectives, is not meant to argue that writing is primary in any literal or genetic sense." Rather, by this move Derrida insists that the process of interpretation is infinite, that there is no single meaning to be found (equivalent to the purity of speech that allegedly preceded language's representation in writing). "In this play of representation," writes Derrida in *Of Grammatology*, "the point of origin becomes ungraspable."

In building his poststructuralist theory of writing, Derrida undermines the phenomenological theory of language developed by Edmund Husserl, who proposed that any true expression is a meaning animated by the speaker's consciousness. Husserl believed the true level of language to be subjective use of voice, or a kind of heavenly inward speech for which the external signifier is a mere appendage. Derrida on the other hand, by wedging the difference of writing in the natural unity of sound and sense, undermines speech as an immediate presence. Writing for Derrida is a relational system of differences in which the sign is self-referential rather than substituting for an absent thing or concept. The word "cat," for example, gets its meaning not through a positive identification with a feline animal but through its difference from other signifiers, such as "cap" or "cab" – a system of relationships determined by convention. This difference of writing infects the very self-presence of the voice as defined by Husserl. As Derrida says in "Speech and Phenomena," "this pure difference, which constitutes the self-presence of the living present, introduces into self-presence from the beginning all the impurity putatively excluded from it." Writing, moreover, does not exist abstractly in the mind, or in airy soundwaves, but spatially in solid black marks upon a white page.

Derrida contends in *Of Grammatology* that if the written word is the only durable institution of the sign, then "writing in general covers the entire field of the linguistic sign." The relationship between the signifiers of this field and other signifiers – the graphic distribution of signs – constitutes the very basis of the language system. The result is that in graphocentrism the represented is always already a representation, not a signified. Hence, in Derrida's famous phrase, "There is nothing outside the text." Meaning is never a matter of simple intuitive evidence, absolutely present to itself. Rather, it is divided to be itself and another. Derrida uses the word "play" to refer to this absence of a transcendental signified, or truth – this dissolution of the metaphysics of presence.

One of the consequences of Derrida's theory of writing is that a sign always carries a further sense than the one intended by the author. In his criticism of Jean-Jacques Rousseau's theory of language, Derrida develops the notion of the "supplement." In *Writing and Difference* he explains that the supplemental meaning of a sign, "which seems to be added as a plenitude to a plenitude, is equally that which compensates for a lack." The supplement is added to a word because of an original lack in the signified; thus, it is not really superfluous but necessary for the word itself, which according to Derrida lacks a transcendental signified or an essential meaning. His example in *Dissemination* is the Greek word *pharmakon*, which Plato defines as "poison" and applies to writing, which he considered to be dangerous and secondary to speech. Derrida opens the word up to its alternate sense of "remedy": "The word *pharmakon* is caught up in a chain of significations – [which] is not, simply, that of the intentions of an author who goes by the name of Plato." The Greek text thus seems to say two opposite things simultaneously about writing. On this basis, Derrida claims that any single word is connected with a galaxy of other words that form a language:

> Like any text, the text of "Plato" couldn't not be involved, at least in a virtual, dynamic, lateral manner, with all the words that composed the system of the Greek language. Certain forces of association unite . . . the words "actually present" in a discourse with all the other words in the lexical system, whether or not they appear as "words."

Meaning in this way is dispersed along a chain of signifiers.

For Derrida, then, meaning does not involve a correspondence between signifier and signified, sign and thing. Indeed, he claims that the signified does not exist, except as a logocentric illusion invented to suppress the materialist play of language – the movement from signifier to signifier. If structuralism divides the sign and text from its referent, then poststructuralism divides the signifier from the signified. As a signifying chain, meaning never reaches completion but continually points away to another signifier, *ad infinitum*. This state of language, which Derrida describes as a state of dissemination, does not allow for single meanings in the writer's mind, as described by Edmund Husserl, or even for multiple meanings, since both univocity and polysemy involve meanings based on the signified, which for Derrida does not exist. Dissemination is a state of play in language through which meaning as a finite concept remains perpetually unfulfilled – leaving the mind in a state of openness and freedom. Without the opposition between the sensible and the intelligible, the sign theoretically cannot exist. Yet Derrida finds the concept of the sign indispensable, for his own critique of logocentrism depends on his using language as a function of correspondence, not as a self-referential system of differences.

At the heart of Derrida's theory of writing as dissemination is the notion of *différance*, an invented word derived from the French verb *différer*, which combines the verb "to differ" and the verb "to defer." A signifier differs from its meaning or signified, which in turn is infinitely deferred by the signifying chain. On the one hand, *différance* indicates the movement of differing, of spacing, of not being identical, while on the other hand it indicates a movement of deferring, of temporalizing, of putting off until later. This deferral in the signifying chain is what causes meaning to flow from one signifier to another, always different yet always the same insofar as the same force of signification responsible for the production of meaning flows between them. *Différance* precludes a transcendental signified or truth from existing outside the sphere of writing and thereby controlling the field of play. Furthermore, the play of *différance*, which eludes vision and hearing, produces an order that resists the opposition in philosophy between the sensible and the intelligible, an order that exists "between" writing and speech, beyond the logocentric idea that they are separate things.

By thus questioning a series of philosophical oppositions that cancel each other out – such as the oppositions between signifier/signified, speech/writing, inside/outside – Derrida tries to illustrate that logocentric notions of a central presence must be treated as if under erasure, as if having methodological importance but theoretical nonvalue. Since presence for Derrida depends on a hierarchic opposition in which one term is thought superior, such as speech over writing, then once the opposition is undermined the notion of presence becomes invalid. Derrida treats his own terms, such as "play" and *différance*, as if under erasure in the attempt to prevent them from being taken for transcendental signifieds.

Derrida decenters the self, or subject, as the origin of meaning and thus separates it from writing, which spontaneously disseminates meaning under its own centrifugal force. He also replaces the transcendental signified with play. As a result, the signified, as understood in logocentric terms, loses its immediate relationship with the divine logos and can no longer be considered a meaning independent of all signifiers. Rather, the concept becomes the signifier; meaning unites with its graphic manifestation. While the phonocentric transcendental signified has its form in the voice, an intangible psychic image, Derrida's grammatology shows that to become an object of knowledge the signified must have a material form that can open it to the process of knowing. Derrida materializes subjectivity by collapsing the opposition between abstract/concrete, inside/outside. In this way he brings the "thing-ish-ness" of meaning into the subjective world, almost as if he were uniting sound and meaning in a way characteristic of the unity of language in the logocentric model.

For Derrida the difference of writing, in the form of the "arche-gram," is prior to the unity of speech. This theory of original writing, or "arche-writing," is derived from Sigmund Freud, especially his essay "Note on the Mystic Writing Pad." The Mystic (or Magic) Writing Pad, a toy for children, consists of a transparent sheet of celluloid over a waxed base upon which a child using a stylus can produce marks in the wax below. These marks appear dark, as though made with a pen, on the celluloid but are erased when the sheet is pulled up, leaving only their traces on the waxed pad beneath. According to Freud, the unconscious memory is analogous to the Magic Writing Pad in that it retains traces from past impressions, which need not have been consciously perceived. For Derrida, the Mystic Writing Pad becomes an analogy for arche-writing, which has the form of a trace, an incised channel made by the force of the signifying chain, or the sentence as a flow of signifiers. Just as the trace is a sign of something having gone before, not an origin or presence, so writing is a sign, not a presence or an absolute signified. This substitution of the sign for the thing seems to make it secondary to a missing presence. Since, however, the two faces of the sign (the signifier and signified) and the idea of presence have both been deconstructed, writing cannot be construed in terms of substance, either present or absent, but only in terms of difference. As Derrida says in "Speech and Phenomena":

> *Différance* is what makes the movement of signification possible only if each element that is said to be "present," appearing on the stage of presence, is related to something other than itself but retains the mark of a past element and already lets itself be hollowed out by the mark of its relation to a future element.

It is not that a sign conceived as a trace breaks up the present, but that the present never existed except as a synthesis of past and future, a synthesis of traces.

The key point in the idea of difference as the source of meaning is not merely that two words differ but also that each word differs from itself. As Derrida says in *Positions*, "Nothing – no present and in-*different* being – thus precedes *différance* and spacing." The two words "cat" and "dog" are alternately present and absent in the two sentences "the cat is on the mat" and "the dog is on the mat," but while the word "cat" is present in the first sentence and not the second (in which the word "dog" is present), the referent "cat" nevertheless remains absent. This absence of the referent is what makes a word differ from itself and opens discourse to the play of consciousness, a play that deconstruction tries to understand.

Derrida concludes that one can never perceive things in themselves because one never has direct sensory contact with the phenomenal world, which is always already an interpretation, a trace of an infinitely deferred presence. The same applies to signifiers, which signify before they are things, pointing to other signifiers before being themselves. As Derrida says in *Of Grammatology*, the property of the signifier "is to be itself and another . . . to be separated from itself." Derrida's materialism is therefore qualified by what he calls a "radical alterity," which renders his materialism paradoxically metaphysical.

Derrida sees the history of critical theory as leading to a new status of critical discourse through the abandonment of all human principles: center, presence, essence, substance, referent, transcendentality, consciousness, foundation, human, and God. Yet the Derridean trace has been criticized for being a type of transcendental signified. The fact that Derrida uses a logic beyond the usual kind of reason has often been observed. In *Derrida on the Mend* (1984), Robert Magliola analyzes the parallels between Derrida's grammatology and Eastern philosophy. Magliola observes that in spite of Derrida's attack on metaphysics and "mysticism," his own reasoning suggests a lived experience that is not in the world of ordinary waking consciousness.

Derrida's glimmer of another way of knowing is also remarked by Richard Harland, who in *Superstructuralism* (1987) draws an analogy between Derrida's theory of the trace and "meditation," a word that Derrida often uses in describing his writings. Meditation, in which a sound, or "mantra," is used to go beyond the ordinary waking state of consciousness into the state of transcendental consciousness, is analogous to the theory of the trace in four ways: they both use words as mere signifiers; they involve a signifying process expanding toward infinity; they work by absence or negativity, that is, by negating appearances; and they operate spontaneously without activity on the part of the subject, as if motivated by natural law. Moreover, the logic of sameness and difference with which Derrida deconstructs Western logocentrism is also analogous to the quantum mechanical logic with which modern physicists deconstruct the classical Newtonian model of the universe. For this mechanistic billiard-ball model, modern physicists substitute the model of the unified field, the unmanifest foundation or ground state of natural law. The notion of difference, then, seems both to undermine and to uphold metaphysics, just as Plato's *pharmakon* seems both to praise and to condemn writing.

Largely because of Derrida, poststructuralism in the United States has broadened the scope of literary criticism and has led to a general questioning of the conventions that underlie the supposedly natural structures in modern society. The disciplines affected by poststructuralism include a movement in law known as critical legal studies, and a new kind of analytical theology, both of which involve reading texts in a manner similar to that of deconstructive critics. Feminists have also benefited from poststructuralism in their efforts to show how gender distinctions are culturally constructed. As a theoretical enterprise, poststructuralism involves a movement away from blindly accepting universals on the basis of a finite level of consciousness. In his brilliant way of expanding the reader's awareness through the graphic signifier, of deconstructing the opposition between the subject and the object, Derrida may indeed be considered a metaphysical materialist.

In recent work, Derrida examines the way social processes are constituted and simultaneously undermined by the structures of meaning. Of particular concern is the relation between deconstruction and religion. In *The Prayers and Tears of Jacques Derrida* (1997), John D. Caputo explores the religious motifs of Derrida's later writing, with its "deep, messianic, apocalyptic and prophetic tones." Caputo argues that, while Derrida has broken his covenant with Judaism, he remains a man of faith in his "impossible religion." Caputo says of Derrida's writing that it "is more performative than constative, that it is religious without a theology, that it hangs on by a prayer." Similarly, in *Derrida and Negative Theology* (1992), Harold Coward and Toby Foshay argue that, while Derrida's thought may not constitute a negative theology or philosophy, it follows in a tradition (both Western and Eastern) that culminates in modern negativity. Hence, the negative formula of the Upanishads, *neti, neti* (not this, not this), which points to pure consciousness (*atman*) beyond the mind's empirical phenomenological content, resembles Derrida's deconstruction (negation) of concepts such as the transcendental signified – part of the mental content transcended in the experience of pure consciousness.

Principal criticism

La Voix et le phénomène: Introduction au problème du signe dans la phénoménologie de Husserl, 1967 (*"Speech and Phenomena," and Other Essays on Husserl's Theory of Signs*, 1973)
L'Écriture et la différence, 1967 (*Writing and Difference*, 1978)
De la grammatologie, 1967 (*Of Grammatology*, 1976)
La Dissémination, 1972 (*Dissemination*, 1981)
Marges de la philosophie, 1972 (*Margins of Philosophy*, 1982)
Positions: Entretiens avec Henri Ronse, Julia Kristeva, Jean-Louis Houdebine, Guy Scarpetta, 1972 (*Positions*, 1981)
L'Archéologie du frivole, 1973 (*The Archeology of the Frivolous*, 1980)
Glas, 1974 (English translation, 1986)
Éperons: Les Styles de Nietzsche, 1976 (*Spurs: Nietzsche's Styles*, 1979)
Fors, 1976
"Signature Event Context," 1977
"Limited Inc.," 1977
Titus-Carmel, 1978
La Vérité en peinture, 1978 (*The Truth in Painting*, 1987)
"Living On: Border Lines," 1979
La Carte postale: De Socrate à Freud et au-delà, 1980 (*The Post Card: From Socrates to Freud and Beyond*, 1987)
Scribble, 1980
D'un ton apocalyptique adopté naguère en philosophie, 1983
Oreille de l'autre, 1984 (*The Ear of the Other: Autobiography, Transference, Translation*, 1985)
Otobiographies: L'Enseignement de Nietzsche et la politique du nom propre, 1984
Signéponge, 1984 (*Signéponge-Signsponge*, 1984)
Taking Chances: Derrida, Psychoanalysis, and Literature, 1984
La Faculté de juger, 1985
De l'esprit: Heidegger et la question, 1987 (*Of Spirit: Heidegger and the Question*, 1989)
Mémoires d'aveugle: L'Autobiographie et autres ruines, 1990 (*Memoirs of the Blind: The Self-Portrait and other Ruins*, 1993)
Acts of Literature, 1992 (Derek Attridge, editor)
Donner la mort, 1992 (*The Gift of Death*, 1995)
Aporias, 1993 (*Apories: Mourir—s'attendre aux limites de la vérité*, 1994)
Spectres de Marx: État de la dette, le travail du deuil, et la nouvelle Internationale, 1993 (*Specters of Marx: The State of the Debt, the Work of Mourning, and the New International*, 1994)
Given Time: The Time of the King. Vol. I: Counterfeit Money, 1993
Passions, 1993
Word Traces: Readings of Paul Celan, 1994
"Adieu," in *Philosophy Today*. 40, no. 3 (1996), pp. 33–40
Résistance à la psychanalyse, 1996
Politics of Friendship, 1997

Other major works and literary forms

Although most of Jacques Derrida's works concern themselves, at least in a broad sense, with literary theory, many of his books also focus on a wide range of philosophical topics. Trained in philosophy and not in literary criticism, Derrida is considered unique among his French contemporaries for his ability to "read" texts rather than merely generalizing about them. His questioning approach to texts resembles the close reading developed by the New Critics, an approach that he applies not only to philosophy, literature, and semiotics but also to sociology, history, psychoanalysis, archeology, politics, and painting. Explaining his interest in literature (in an interview with Irme Salusinszky published in *Criticism and Society*, 1987), Derrida says that his deepest desire is "to write literature, to write fictions," that he thought that he could write differently, as he believes that he did in *Glas* and in *The Post Card*. Philosophy was a detour to bring him back to literature. In *Memoires for Paul de Man* (1986), Derrida laments, "I have never known how to tell a story," and he then proceeds brilliantly to tell the story of his intellectual friendship with the critic Paul de Man.

NONFICTION
L'Origine de la géometrie, 1962 (*The Origin of Geometry*, 1974)
Memoires for Paul de Man, 1986
For Nelson Mandela, 1987 (editor, with Mustapha Tlili)

Further reading

Caputo, John D. *The Prayers and Tears of Jacques Derrida: Religion without Religion*, 1997.
Coward, Harold, and Toby Foshay, eds. *Derrida and Negative Theology*, 1992.
Culler, Jonathan. *On Deconstruction: Theory and Criticism After Structuralism*, 1982.
Esch, Deborah, and Thomas Keenan. *Institutions of Philosophy*, 1997.
Gasché, Rodolphe. *The Tain of the Mirror: Derrida and the Philosophy of Reflection*, 1986.
Hartman, Geoffrey. *Saving the Text: Literature / Derrida / Philosophy*, 1981.
Leavey, John P. *Glassary*, 1987.
Magliola, Robert. *Derrida on the Mend*, 1984.
Norris, Christopher. *Derrida*, 1987.
Schultz, William R., and Lewis L. B. Fried. *Jacques Derrida: An Annotated Primary and Secondary Bibliography*, 1992.
Staten, Henry. *Wittgenstein and Derrida*, 1984.

WILLIAM S. HANEY II

See also Barthes; Culler; Deconstruction; French Literary Theory: Twentieth Century; Postmodernism

Dialogic Criticism

Critical theory

Dialogic criticism, or dialogism, involves the application of the theories of the Russian scholar, philosopher, and philologist, Mikhail Bakhtin – and a host of his disciples and interpreters including Michael Holquist, Caryl Emerson, and Gary Saul Morson – to the literature of the West and, increasingly, to world literature. Generated in the early twentieth century by a scholar who worked in obscurity most of his life only to be lionized in the last thirty years of the twentieth century, dialogism was very much ahead of its time as a critique of Russian Formalism and what was called New Criticism in the United States. Both Russian Formalism and New Criticism were varieties of modernism, and Bakhtin and his dialogic approach to literature were to play a major role in the shaping of what has now come to be known as postmodernism. Whereas modernism was influenced very much by visual aesthetic influences such as cubism and linguistic theories derived from writing and the assumptions of a script and print culture, dialogism is predicated on what Jacques Derrida called the "parent of writing," oral speech and the aural culture it generates. Very basically, readers are passive spectators of the written page, whereas language – a word derived from *lingua* meaning tongue in Latin – demands a speaker and a listener and is by its very nature participatory, interactive, and auditory. Speech, in fact, defines our very being and existence as a species. Script is a mere four thousand years old and has been used since its invention almost exclusively, in terms of pure volume, for bureaucratic purposes. And yet, the greatest literature – a term derived from *littera*, meaning written letter – frequently emulates speech and its structures. It records, as William Wordsworth said somewhat chauvinistically of true lyric, a man speaking to men.

Artistically, in most worthwhile poetry, in all dramatic texts, and in many of the great novels written by the likes of Petronius, François Rabelais, Miguel de Cervantes, Henry Fielding, Mark Twain, James Joyce, Louis-Ferdinand Céline, J. D. Salinger, and Kurt Vonnegut, dialogue assumes primary importance in the construction, style, and impact of the text, not just in the direct quotation of the characters. Readers in these texts are treated like auditors, confidantes, participants, coaxed here into alliance, teased there into opposition. In short, dialogic criticism is a mode of investigation which is bearing more and more fruit in elucidating the performative and participatory nature of many great literary and dramatic texts. Of course Bakhtin was not alone in inventing or, as he might say, reinventing an oral poetics: Walter Ong, Marshall McLuhan, Eric Havelock, and Paul Zumthor were going about the same business shortly after him. What Bakhtin did was articulate a methodological terminology that identified the oral/aural foundation for and function of literary discourse, and he did it by grounding the higher literary forms in the "vulgar," that is the "folk" notion of language, laughter, and what he called the "carnivalesque" sensibility. Dialogic criticism, in short, is a bottom-up enterprise beginning with ordinary language, the folk who speak it, and the subversive populist laughter that often accompanies it.

The basic unit of dialogic criticism for Bakhtin is the utterance, a "speech act" which presupposes a speaker, addressee, and a "super-addressee." The super-addressee is the idealized listener who might apprehend the utterance perfectly. To be understood, a speaker frames his or her utterance by appealing to a generic context which is conditioned by the historical moment and the conventions of speech within that genre, a code every speaker understands implicitly when delivering a joke, expressing fear, or celebrating an event or person. The primary genres of speech condition their derivatives, the broad "secondary" genres of literary composition and reception. In *The Formal Method in Literary Scholarship* (1928; English translation, 1978) Bakhtin insisted early in his career that "poetics should really begin with genre not end with it. For genre is the typical form of the whole work, the whole utterance." Literary or secondary genres, as Bakhtin labeled them, are forms that foster the illusion of finality, encourage the inclusion and participation of the listener/reader, and license the verbal shortcuts in literary form that characterize speech.

Every utterance also includes within itself anticipation of a rejoinder. The utterance is, in fact, itself a conjunction of prior utterances and responses that necessitate and expect rejoinder. In opposition to dialogue stands monologue, the utterance that assumes no response as a sort of "rhetorical question," or, worse, impedes or forbids "answerability," another important corollary of dialogism. Such monologic utterance can take many narrative or dramatic forms, but may also become "official" – that is, the "party line" adopted in most governmental proclamations, legal briefs, and state-sanctioned historical narratives. Bakhtin and his successors often characterize so-called omniscient narratives such as historical novels and certain scripted genres such as scientific reports as highly monologic and monotonous.

The notion of dialogue may recall the Hegelian notion of dialectic, so crucial to Marxist ideology, but is in fact Bakhtin's controversial refutation of dialectic. As the party line of Soviet Marxism, dialectical materialism had developed into an "official" philosophic methodology even by the time of G. W. F. Hegel, whose *Phenomenology of the Spirit* (1807) Bakhtin declared "monologic." In one of his final essays, "Toward a Methodology of the Human Sciences," Bakhtin pronounced that "(d)ialectics was born of dialogue so as to return again to dialogue on a higher level." By this he means that dialectic – with its theory that a thesis generates an antithesis which produces a finalized synthesis – had obviously grown out of the vocal exchange we call dialogue in the first place. But in dialogue there is no final synthesis precluding subsequent utterance on the subject, only one utterance producing another in an endless chain of dialogue. As he explained in "The Problems of Speech Genres," "(e)ach individual utterance is a link in the chain of speech communication." To make the leap to literature, each text operates as an utterance within a chain of literary works in that genre or on the given theme. "The text lives only by coming into contact with another text (with context). Only at the point of this contact between texts does a light flash, illuminating both the posterior and anterior, joining a given text to a dialogue" ("Toward a Methodology of the Human Sciences").

Practical application

Bakhtin's theory of dialogism became known to the West initially only in its later, applied stages, with the publication of *Rabelais and His World* (1965; English translation, 1968), *The Problems of Dostoevsky's Poetics* (1929, 1963; English translations, 1973, 1984), and the series of literary essays entitled *The Dialogic Imagination* (1975; English translation, 1981). His first major contribution to Western aesthetic theory was to reunite literary criticism with its parent discipline, rhetoric. In a desperate attempt to distinguish *belles lettres* from the "mere rhetoric" of vulgar political discourse, Russian Formalism and New Criticism severed what was in the ancient world called *grammatica*, the study of ancient literary texts as declamatory exercises, from *rhetorica*, the practice of the verbal arts of persuasion in oratorical delivery. However, rhetoricians, dealing primarily in oratory, have assumed for over two thousand years that oral speech was the primary datum of language and its perfection in oral discourse, the major objective of rhetoric.

Bakhtin himself tried to provide the outline for a history of dialogical literature by way of contextualizing the novels of Fedor Dostoevskii in *The Problems of Dostoevsky's Poetics*. What he offered was a strange and startling genetic and generic outline for the rise of the novel as a chapter in the history of literary realism, an outline other critics have been busily detailing since the mid-twentieth century. Dialogic criticism continues to trace the development of the realistic style in poetry, drama, and fiction out of the eruption of what Bakhtin and other of his contemporaries like Eric Auerbach and Ernst Curtius called "dialogue" – speech conceived and articulated in the context of actual social experience – into the loftier monologue of the pseudo-objective modes of history, romance, homily, saints' legends and the other "official" genres of the upper strata of European culture.

Bakhtin cites Homer frequently as the parent of dialogical writing, often lamenting the loss of Homer's apparently scurrilous parody of the epic about the fool Margit, *The Margites*, and pointing out that the Greeks shamelessly attributed the epic poem "War Between the Mice and the Frogs" to Homer himself. For Bakhtin, Odysseus is the archetypal trickster – a descendant of the rogue Autolycus on his mother's side – and was represented as such on Greek vases along with the comic Hercules. Obviously, we are speaking here of the Homer who provides us with the archetype for all subsequent fabliaux in Demodokos' titillating tale of Ares and Aphrodite recited at Phaiakia, the same Homer who was banned by Plato as an illicit curriculum for Greek youth and who continued to scandalize authors like Voltaire nearly two thousand years later. The dialogues of Plato, particularly those with Socrates as the chief spokesperson, are crucial in Bakhtin's literary genealogy for dialogical writing. The Socratic dialogue is not simply a rhetorical-philosophical genre. Situated in the marketplace, eliciting polyphonic responses, and subversive enough to put Socrates on trial, dialogues like the occasionally scatological, highly eroticized *Symposium*, which pose queries that demand response, grow, says Bakhtin in *Dostoevsky's Poetics*, "out of the folk-carnivalistic base and (are) thoroughly saturated with a carnival sense of the world."

Bakhtin was at his most radical in his examination of the stylistic revolution represented by the "carnivalization" of the Christian gospels, the Acts of the apostles, apocalypses, and the lives of the saints and martyrs which become prototypes for the "gay" *symposia* of *The Cena Cypriani* ("Cyprian's Supper," a satire written between the fifth and eighth centuries A.D., that parodies Christian themes, including the Last Supper), Geoffrey Chaucer, Desiderius Erasmus, Rabelais, Cervantes, and Denis Diderot. The Christian genres beginning with the gospels recall the ancient Menippean satires of Lucian and Petronius in which ideas and their representative characters are tested by means of temptation and martyrdom, particularly in the saints' legends. As in the Menippea (a group of Greek satires attributed to the philosopher Menippus of Gadara, third century B.C.), rulers, aristocrats, thieves, and beggars meet in these narratives on equal terms in a single, fundamentally dialogized plane. Christian literature in the early centuries of the first millennium absorbed other related genres including the classical symposium in the feasts of the New Testament.

Meta-concepts in Bakhtinian dialogism include "polyglossia," a polyphonic discourse that is multivocal like musical counterpoint, and "heteroglossia," where two or more languages are incorporated into the discourse. Chaucer's *Canterbury Tales* (1387–1400) provides a near perfect example of the polyphonic exchange of extended narratives that represent competing utterances in a contest to determine the best tale, an example that Bakhtin never pursued but which has provided Chaucerians with the major new approach to the poem for the last twenty years. Examples of heteroglossia occur in the plays of William Shakespeare like *Titus Andronicus*, where English and Latin are conjoined often with grotesque effects, or in *Henry V*, where English and French are presented as competing frames of national reference. Polyphony, of course, characterizes drama, particularly the dramatic discourse of the Elizabethan period where styles and vocal dialects are mixed in a given passage such as the Porter scene interposed between the murder and the discovery of the dead king in *Macbeth*, or in Francis Beaumont's *Knight of the Burning Pestle* (1606–1613) where vocal actors seated in the audience compete for attention with the scripted performance of the play throughout the text. It is interesting to note that Bakhtin planned an extension of *Rabelais and His World* which would have included projected chapters dealing with carnivalesque episodes of *Hamlet*, *King Lear*, *Macbeth*, and other Shakespearean plays that mingle the serious and the comic, the high and the low, and the tragic and the grotesque.

The first and still the favorite discoveries of Bakhtin in the West remain his examination of the revolutionary frames of subversive laughter and the carnivalesque, although he actually discovered these dialogic ideas later in his career, after composing texts that dealt extensively with the philosophy of the act, art, and answerability, and the nature and function of speech genres. As Charles Darwin noted, laughter is a visceral, oral response that we share most probably with animals. It is dialogical because it responds to the unexpected clash of what is assumed, such as an imagined form of behavior, and what actually is. Closely tied to laughter is the ancient and medieval festival known as carnival where laughter is elicited, indulged, and celebrated. In the Middle Ages the officially sanctioned aesthetic form was the romance and its variants, including saints' legends. It was responded to dialogically by the "vulgar" or folk form of the "carnivalesque." Just as Aristotle locates the sources for tragedy and comedy in Dionysian and phallic rituals respectively, Bakhtin looks to ancient and medieval carnival for the fullest expression of comic popular culture. Although carnival has been reduced in most localities to an annual street fair or church bazaar, it was a vital activity in the Middle Ages and Renaissance, dominating up to three months of the secular and liturgical calendar. Such carnivalesque activities as open-air spectacles and parodies of church and state rituals were joyously cataclysmic events devoid of mysticism and piety: anarchy was the disorder of the day.

The literary form of the carnivalesque or grotesque has several identifying features, all of which are well represented in the fabliaux of Chaucer's *Canterbury Tales* such as the scatological narratives of the Miller and Summoner, or in the routine obscenities of Rabelais' *Gargantua and Pantagruel* (1532–1564), and even Jonathan Swift's *Gulliver's Travels* (1726), written during the eighteenth century when the carnivalesque was officially challenged as vulgar and illicit. Carnival is a form radically rooted in the here and now. Its mimes and skits may purport to occur elsewhere, but dialogical cues about then and now are given to indicate that the activity has been radically contemporized. The settings for the Chester or Wakefield miracle plays were undoubtedly the market place or the cathedral squares of the English medieval towns where the plays were being performed. Those highly specific, actual locales were featured in the representations of sacred time recaptured in the dramatic productions, just as Chaucer's pilgrimage to the "new Jerusalem" is marked by real, historic landmarks all the way from the Tabard Inn in Southwark, London, to Canterbury. In short, anachronism – the past dialogically rendered as contemporaneous with the present – is the essence of carnival activity and of the comic narrative or drama it inspires. The reaction to this "collapsing" or deflation of space and time in the carnivalized event or its literary rendering is, of course, laughter.

Dialogic criticism is proliferating exponentially at the present moment. Bakhtin himself initiated the critical revaluation of nineteenth-century fiction in his book on Dostoevskii's dialogic poetics. Books by Ruth Coates and Walter Reed have applied Bakhtinian methods to an analysis of the Bible and to Christian exegesis and theology. The works of twentieth-century polyglossic and occasionally heteroglossic writers like James Joyce, D. H. Lawrence, William Faulkner, and Henry Miller have been scrutinized along dialogical lines by David Lodge and R. B. Kershner. Even film and the visual arts – particularly those by artists of the "grotesque" like Pieter Brueghel the Younger and Hieronymus Bosch – have been approached as works that elicit carnivalesque responses, revolutionary awareness, and laughter in studies by Robert Stam and Deborah Haynes. Wayne Booth, Karen Hohne, and Helen Wussow have identified Bakthin as a protofeminist and deployed his dialogical methods to recover the marginalized voices of female characters and writers long ignored in the Western literary tradition. Such dialogical analyses are bound to continue given the broad categories of linguistic, philosophic, and philological methodologies touched on by Mikhail Bakhtin whom Tzvetan Todorov has declared "the greatest theoretician of literature in the twentieth century."

Related developments

Bakhtin was not alone in developing the theory and application of dialogic criticism in the twentieth century. A group of German scholars known as the *Romanisten* were investigating the emergence of the novel from the tradition of literary realism, notably Erich Auerbach, whose *Mimesis: The Representation of Reality in Western Literature* was first published in 1945 and translated in 1968. In the meantime Ernst Curtius' *European Literature in the Latin Middle Ages* (1973) was mapping out much of the same ground. About the time Bakhtin's theory was being rediscovered in the West, literature was being reevaluated along oral lines in Marshall McLuhan's *The Gutenberg Galaxy: The Making of Typographic Man* (1962) and *Understanding Media: The Extensions of Man* (1968), Walter J. Ong's *The Interface of the Word* (1977), Ruth Finnegan's *Oral Poetry: Its Nature, Significance, and Social Context* (1977), Eric Havelock's *The Literate Revolution in Greece and Its Cultural Consequences* (1982), Sylvia Huot's *From Song to Book: The Poetics of Writing in the Old French Lyric and Lyrical Narrative Poetry* (1987), and, most recently, Paul Zumthor's *Oral Poetry: An Introduction* (1990).

Further reading

Andreas, James R. "'Newe Science' from 'Olde Bokes': A Bakhtinian Approach to The Summoner's Tale," in *Chaucer Review*. 23 (1990).

Booth, Wayne. "Freedom of Interpretation: Bakhtin and the Challenge of Feminist Criticism," in *Critical Inquiry*. 9 (1982).

Coates, Ruth. *Christianity in Bakhtin: God and the Exiled Author*, 1999.

Farrell, Thomas, ed. *Bakhtin and Medieval Voices*, 1996.

Haynes, Deborah. *Bakhtin and the Visual Arts*, 1995.

Hohne, Karen, and Helen Wussow, eds. *A Dialogue of Voices: Feminist Literary Theory and Bakhtin*, 1994.

Kershner, R. B. *Joyce, Bakhtin, and Popular Literature: Chronicles of Disorder*, 1992.

Kinser, Samuel. *Rabelais' Carnival: Text, Context, Metatext*, 1990.

Lodge, David. *After Bakhtin: Essays on Fiction and Criticism*, 1990.

Reed, Walter L. *Dialogues of the Word: The Bible as Literature According to Bakhtin*, 1993.

Stam, Robert. *Subversive Pleasures: Bakhtin, Cultural Criticism, and Film*, 1992.

JAMES R. ANDREAS, SR.

See also Bakhtin

Denis Diderot

French editor, writer, and theorist

Born: Langres, France; October 5, 1713
Died: Paris, France; July 31, 1784

Biography

Born on October 5, 1713, in the country town of Langres, the son of a skilled cutler, Denis Diderot soon displayed a keen intelligence and a penchant for heterodoxy. Although tonsured, taught in a local Jesuit college, and later sent to Paris to further his religious education (where he was granted a master's degree by the age of nineteen), he gradually veered from a possible career in the priesthood. A flippant book of philosophical observations written by the young Diderot was officially burned in 1746. The even more daring *An Essay on Blindness* (also known as *Letter on the Blind*) resulted in his being imprisoned for three months. By this time, he was already immersed in the momentous *Encyclopedia*, not to be completed until 1772, a work that attracted the most brilliant minds of the day. These collaborators were drawn from among a loose association of argumentative, unconventional, Deistic rationalists, the so-called *philosophes*, who between them forever changed the face of Europe.

For the next third of a century, Diderot not only edited and supervised the twenty-eight volumes of his *Encyclopedia* but also produced a steady stream of art and literary criticism, several novels, three plays, many brilliant philosophical tales, and ethical, historical, political, educational, and scientific tracts, eventually becoming, with Voltaire, Jean-Jacques Rousseau, and Charles-Louis de Secondat (known by his title, Montesquieu), one of the four truly great men of letters during the brilliant French Enlightenment.

At the age of thirty he married a practical woman who brought stability to his errant life but could not restrain his lifelong illicit relationships with women. He died peacefully at dinner, beside his long-suffering wife, in Paris on July 31, 1784.

Influence

Although already a strong force in his own day because of his unorthodox ideas, his editorship of the *Encyclopedia*, his correspondence with people from all over Europe, and his readiness to fight for freedom's cause on almost any battlefield, Diderot was nevertheless not fully appreciated until well after his death. Some of his most original works could not be printed during his lifetime. *Rameau's Nephew*, for example, first appeared in German, translated by Johann Wolfgang von Goethe in 1805, whence it was retranslated into French in 1821; the first authentic edition from the original manuscript was not published until 1891.

Diderot's literary theories greatly influenced Gotthold Ephraim Lessing, himself a most influential theorist. These theories, such as his concept of the paradox of the actor, helped to establish many of what are today's commonplaces. His writings on drama are not only echoed in nineteenth-century practice but in such disparate areas as Hollywood, Broadway, and television as well. Other Germans, from Johann Gottfried Herder, Goethe, Friedrich Schiller, and August Wilhelm Schlegel to Bertolt Brecht, have admitted their indebtedness. He established a lasting tie with Russia, thanks to his correspondence with Catherine the Great and a long visit to that country. His influence on Italy's Luigi Pirandello, Brazil's Joaquim Maria Machado de Assis, and dramatists from England, Portugal, and Spain is provable. Diderot may well qualify as the most enduringly influential of all eighteenth-century French critics. His best works, many still in print and translated into other languages, if anything are growing in importance.

Analysis

Diderot, insofar as he took cognizance of the famous "Quarrel of the Ancients and Moderns," was a modern. At issue was the possibility of modern writers surpassing the ancient Greek and Roman masters: the Moderns believed that they could; the Ancients, refusing to equate progress in science with progress in the arts, denied it. The seventeenth-century writers at Louis XIV's brilliant court were ambivalent, but almost all of their successors, especially after 1750, either were aggressively modern or else considered the argument a dead issue; Diderot was of their number. Nevertheless, at times he still spoke the language of the past, echoing older critics such as Nicolas Boileau-Despréaux on matters of good taste, the proprieties, and the need for verisimilitude, citing Aristotle and Horace, praising the beauties of Homer's epics. As such he could sound like a typical neoclassical theorist of the old school. He defended the use of Christian subjects in epics against the stricter Boileau, who had allowed only classical myths; other critics had also done so, however, and after John Milton's *Paradise Lost* had been published in 1667 and revised in 1674, the fight had long since become academic. In any case, such comments, whatever their point of view, reflect the conservative Diderot, a modern who was nevertheless no shatterer of tradition.

Yet there is another Diderot, one who was both liberal critic trying to break neoclassical bonds and visionary actually escaping into the present. No other writer of his day approaches his fascinating mix of the two. This Diderot was truly an early Romantic. Some of his ideas were seemingly his own, some were borrowed from England, whose climate proved more favorable to Romanticism. He was one of the first to appreciate William Shakespeare, showing a much better understanding than did, for example, Voltaire, whose translation of Hamlet's soliloquy is almost a travesty, however much intended as flattery. Diderot's fondness for sentimentality suggests Laurence Sterne, another of his favorites. He imitated the bourgeois figures in George Lillo's tragedies such as *The London Merchant: Or, The History of George Barnwell* (1731). His praise for the moral qualities of Samuel Richardson's novel *Clarissa: Or, The History of a Young Lady* (1747–1748), its complexity, its occasional ambiguities, and its masterful artistry may appear exaggerated to modern readers, but at that time they sounded a new note in French criticism. This Romantic terrain he was destined to plough in two seminal works, the *Entretiens sur "Le Fils naturel"* and the *Discours sur la poésie dramatique*. The first was published as part of the play itself, the second in conjunction with *The Father of the Family*. Between them (with occasional help from other, minor pronouncements), they define Diderot's concept of literary art, especially as it pertains to drama.

There are several useful criteria for judging an eighteenth-century writer's literary theories: his concept of the beautiful, of nature, of the role of genius, along with his adherence to rules. Diderot denied absolute beauty. According to him, it exists, to be sure, externally, but one interprets it subjectively. Poets insist on imitating *belle nature* (beautiful nature) but cannot define it. Beauty in all ages depends upon the relation between the object and the individual perceiver, something based on different talents, facts, interests, passions, prejudices, customs, climates, governments, and forms of worship. Diderot, then, echoed the relativism that distinguished much of the eighteenth century from its predecessor. In any case, his concept of nature was far different from that of the earlier theorists, such as Boileau, who by "nature" meant human nature (often further limited to a depiction of superior beings imitated from the ancient classic models of royalty or great heroes). Diderot's hero in the *Entretiens sur "Le Fils naturel,"* Dorval (really his alter ego), is described as standing at the foot of a solitary hill facing a backdrop of mountains. Dorval abandons himself to the spectacle before him. Here, he says, breathing heavily, is the sacred spot for enthusiasm. Here one can shed tears in the crystal-clear waters of some pool, tread the meadow grass, flee to the depths of the woods, or welcome their secret horror. The poet will seek out a cave for inspiration. He will blend his voice with the roar of the torrent descending off the mountains. This beneficent world is the source of all truths. Enthusiasm (a word dear to Diderot's heart) is born of nature itself. The poet's passion, once aroused, gives birth to his art. Dorval, somewhat recovered from his outburst, later claims not to remember what he has said. This somewhat naive, even faintly ridiculous, description of the wellsprings of poetry and beauty would later be repeated by an even more famous pre-Romantic, Jean-Jacques Rousseau.

Diderot demanded for such a concept of art that genius be unfettered by rules. Taste is often separate from genius, a pure gift from nature. Rules and the laws of taste would shackle genius, which it must break to rise to the sublime, the pathetic, the great. Poets such as Milton violate the rules of their language at every step, he concluded. Poetry needs something of the enormous, the barbaric, and the wild. Reason, common sense, order, clarity, those watchwords of French poets past, seem to be ignored.

Some, at least, of these new concepts anchored Diderot's theories about the nature of dramatic art. He admitted to having observed the three unities of time, place, and action, but should he need to change the setting, he would do so. He objected to the use of valets as confidants in drama (a widespread practice all through the neoclassical period), because they are scarcely the people to whom one would tell one's troubles. The young soubrette as confidante is allowable, but Diderot wished that someday children would confide in their own parents. He attacked other theatrical conventions as well: settings, he said, should reflect the surroundings of ordinary people. If something is suitable for one's own home, it can be depicted onstage. What is needed is fine, truthful tableaux to draw tears from the audience. He insisted that actors strike attitudes as artists do in paintings and thus achieve verisimilitude. True dignity is showing the truth. The tableau is truer than the *coup de théâtre* (sudden, striking change), according to his theories, though the latter is permissible if it deals with facts and tells the whole truth. Pantomime, a then-neglected art, should be revived. Since setting is so important to drama, the play should reproduce actual home life exactly. To be sure, a play can show only one action at a time, but in the real world, there are almost always simultaneous actions. To remedy the lack, Diderot suggested that the stage could use two sets, alternating pantomime with speech. Thus the audience would view two actions but would be spared the confusion of hearing two sets of dialogue voiced concurrently. Diderot also wanted alternating speech and pantomime to replace the use of asides. It might be pointed out how many of his recommendations rule the modern stage.

Dialogue, he continued, is not natural enough: some speeches demand interludes of silence, monosyllables, exclamations, broken phrases. (It should be recalled that French plays traditionally were written in strictly managed, rather artificial twelve-syllabled Alexandrine couplets, declaimed rather than spoken. In being couched in prose, Diderot's drama was already innovative.) Onstage he would show a bed, a sleeping father, a crucifix, a corpse, scenes alternately silent and spoken. When Dorval's interlocutor objects that the proprieties are being ignored, Dorval, still speaking for Diderot, answers, "Cruel proprieties, how decent and petty you make a work!" In short, Diderot called for a new genre, the domestic, bourgeois tragedy, a "serious genre," somewhere between comedy and tragedy, but not tragicomedy, which is a mixture. The new genre would be very moral and would employ events in everyday life with everyday people, things that affect the audience more than Greco-Roman subjects do. Drama must "inspire in men a love of virtue and a horror of vice," and the more horror, the better the play.

Diderot also noted that there are at most only some dozen different dramatic characters (the depiction of which was basic to the whole of neoclassic theater); instead of these limited subjects, he recommended that dramatists should depict occupations as the principal aim of the new drama. Social stations affect the audience more closely than do characters, which do not always elicit empathy. Therefore depict the man of letters, the judge, the lawyer, the financier, the family father, the sister – subjects suitable not only for this new, serious genre but for tragedy and comedy as well.

The object of serious drama is to preach virtue and human duty. Here Diderot went beyond the classic doctrine of mixing the pleasant with the useful (*utile et dulce*). In any case, he demanded that his new genre be judged on its own merits and not in relation to any other – thus rejecting the neoclassical adherence to models. In fact, he came close to the modern concept of judging a work only by how well it does what it proposes to do.

One of the most incisive and prophetic examples of Diderot's observations is discussed in what is perhaps his best-known literary treatise, *The Paradox of Acting*. Diderot was smitten with a love for the stage. As friend and admirer of the great English actor David Garrick, he had noted how superbly the latter interpreted his roles, and therein lay a paradox. The best actors, such as Garrick, perfectly simulate emotions they do not actually feel, whereas those who actually do feel what they are portraying give very uneven performances. If true, and many modern actors would agree, Diderot's contention flies in the face of so-called Method acting as taught by the Russian Konstantin Stanislavsky, who asked performers to attempt complete identification with the character portrayed. In this perception, as in so many others, Diderot was ahead of his time. Small wonder that many critics have seen in his theory and practice the beginnings of modern stage realism.

Principal criticism

Articles in *Encyclopédie: Ou, Dictionnaire raisonné des sciences, des arts, et des métiers*, 1751–1772 (editor, 17 volumes of texts, 11 volumes of plates; partial translation as *Select Essays from the Encyclopedy*, 1772, full translation as *Encyclopedia*, 1965)

Entretiens sur "Le Fils naturel," 1757

Discours sur la poésie dramatique, 1758

Parodoxe sur le comédien, 1830 (written c. 1773; *The Paradox of Acting*, 1883)

Other major works and literary forms

In an age when specialists were the exception, Denis Diderot was still exceptional. His best novels – *La Religieuse* (1796; *The Nun*, 1797), with its complicated hoax of a plot and psychological probings, *Le Neveu de Rameau* (1821; *Rameau's Nephew*, 1897), multifaceted and enigmatic, and *Jacques le fataliste et son maître* (1796; *Jacques the Fatalist and His Master*, 1797), its philosophy ambivalent, its use of a proletarian hero something quite new – if somewhat typical of his own age, nevertheless just as clearly look ahead to twentieth-century practices. His three plays, *Le Fils naturel* (1757; *Dorval: Or, The Test of Virtue*, 1767), *Le Père de famille* (1758; *The Father*, 1770, better known as *The Father of the Family*, 1927), and *Est-il bon? Est-il méchant?* (1781) are equally innovative, though somewhat spoiled by Victorian moralizing. Diderot excelled not only in literary criticism, understandable enough in a novelist, voluminous spinner of tales, and playwright, but in art criticism as well. He also wrote essays on blindness and deafness and a major treatise, *Pensées sur l'interprétation de la nature* (1754); philosophical and ethical works, such as *Pensées philosophiques* (1746; English translation, 1819) and *Le Rêve de d'Alembert* (1830; *D'Alembert's Dream*, 1927); historical studies, for example, *Essai sur Sénèque le philosophe* (1779), a proposal for a university to be constructed in Russia, done at the request of Catherine the Great; and charming lesser pieces, such as the late 1760s piece, *Regrets sur ma vieille robe de chambre* (regrets over my old dressing gown, discarded in favor of a splendid new one). Yet this huge production still had to make room for the monumental *Encyclopedia*, for which he served as a driving force, tireless editor, and frequent contributor for more than twenty years.

NOVELS

Les Bijoux indiscrets, 1748 (*The Indiscreet Toys*, 1749)
Jacques le fataliste et son maître, 1796 (written c. 1773; *Jacques the Fatalist and His Master*, 1797)
La Religieuse, 1796 (*The Nun*, 1797)
Le Neveu de Rameau, in German 1805, in French 1821 (*Rameau's Nephew*, 1897)

SHORT FICTION

Supplément au voyage de Bougainville, 1796 (*Supplement to Bougainville's Voyage*, 1927)
Rameau's Nephew and Other Works, 1964

PLAYS

Le Fils naturel, 1757 (*Dorval: Or, The Test of Virtue*, 1767)
Le Père de famille, 1758 (*The Father*, 1770; better known as *The Father of the Family*, 1927)
Est-il bon? Est-il méchant?, 1781

NONFICTION

Pensées philosophiques, 1746 (English translation, 1819; also as *Philosophic Thoughts*)
Lettre sur les aveugles à l'usage de ceux qui voient, 1749 (*An Essay on Blindness*, 1750; also as *Letter on the Blind*)
Notes et commentaires, 1749
Lettre sur les sourds et muets à l'usage de ceux qui entendent et qui parlent, 1751
Pensées sur l'interprétation de la nature, 1754
Les Salons, 1759–1781 (9 volumes)
De la suffisance de la religion naturelle, 1770 (written 1747)
Entretien d'un père avec ses enfants, 1773 (*Conversation between Father and Children*, 1964)
Essai sur Sénèque le philosophe, 1779 (revised and expanded as *Essai sur les règnes de Claude et Néron*, 1782)
Essais sur la peinture, 1796 (written c. 1765)
Pensées détachées sur la peinture, 1798
Plan d'une université pour le gouvernement de Russie, 1813–1814 (written c. 1775–1776)
La Promenade du sceptique, 1830 (written 1747)
Le Rêve de d'Alembert, 1830 (written 1769; *D'Alembert's Dream*, 1927)
Diderot's Early Philosophic Works, 1916 (includes *Letter on the Blind, Letter on the Deaf and Dumb, Philosophic Thoughts*)
Concerning the Education of a Prince, 1941 (written 1758)
Correspondence, 1955–1970 (16 volumes)
Œuvres philosophiques, 1956
Œuvres esthétiques, 1959
Œuvres politiques, 1962

TRANSLATIONS

L'Histoire de Grèce, 1743 (of Temple Stanyan's *Grecian History*)
Essai sur le mérite et la vertu de Shaftesbury, 1745 (of the Earl of Shaftesbury's *An Inquiry Concerning Virtue and Merit*)
Dictionnaire universel de médecine, 1746–1748 (of Robert James' *A Medical Dictionary*)

MISCELLANEOUS

Œuvres, 1798 (15 volumes)
Œuvres complètes, 1875–1877 (20 volumes)
Diderot, Interpreter of Nature: Selected Writings, 1937 (includes short fiction)
Selected Writings, 1966 (Lester G. Crocker, editor, and Derek Coltman, translator)

Further reading

Crocker, Lester G. *The Embattled Philosopher: A Biography of Denis Diderot*, 1954.
——. *Diderot's Chaotic Order: Approach to Synthesis*, 1974.
Fellows, Otis. *Diderot*, 1977.
France, Peter. *Diderot*, 1983.
Furbank, Philip Nicholas. *Diderot: A Critical Biography*, 1993.
Green, Frederick C., ed. *Diderot's Writings on the Theatre*, 1936.
Havens, George R. *The Age of Ideas: From Reaction to Revolution in Eighteenth Century France*, 1955.
Mayoux, J. J. "Diderot and the Technique of Modern Literature," in *The Modern Language Review*. XXXI (1936), pp. 518–531.
O'Gorman, Donal. *Diderot the Satirist: "Le Neveu de Rameau" and Related Works, an Analysis*, 1971.
Wilson, Arthur M. *Diderot*, 1972.

ARMAND E. SINGER

See also Johnson; Rousseau; Voltaire

Dionysius of Halicarnassus

Greek teacher and rhetorician

Born: Halicarnassus, Asia Minor; between 78 and 54 B.C.
Died: Rome, Italy; 7 B.C.

Biography

Very little is known about the life of Dionysius of Halicarnassus, but some reasonable assumptions can be made based on what was common to the lives of teachers and scholars of his day and what he writes about himself. The facts he reveals include his arrival at Rome in 29 B.C. and his residence there for the next twenty-two years while he researched and wrote *The Roman Antiquities*. His departure from Halicarnassus was presumably motivated by either the desire to write the history in Rome or the desire to live and work in Rome as a teacher of Greek and rhetoric. The latter occupation would have been reasonable for a man trained as Dionysius was (education in the Greek language was part of the training of young men of Rome). It has also been suggested that Dionysius must have enjoyed considerable success as a teacher and writer at Halicarnassus prior to his departure, a situation which would have made his voluntary relocation less of a risk. He died in Rome in 7 B.C., the same year that his most substantial work was published.

Influence

Dionysius was the most important of the Atticists. In the era that commenced with the ascendance of Alexander the Great and ended with the final efforts of classical Greek literature, he insisted that the best models for writers and orators were the classic ones. He examined the classic rhetoricians for the purposes of attacking the "Asiatic" style that he considered inferior. More important, he compared the classic writers, and in the process he created what is arguably the first literary history. In addition, his more theoretical writing, *On the Arrangement of Words*, provides a tantalizing glimpse of lost beauty: the sounds of a literature that cannot be duplicated.

Analysis

Dionysius can at once be considered several different critics. He is the sometimes hypercritical, but always practical, assessor of the skills of the ancient orators. He is the literary historian, concerned with the accuracy of dates and times as well as the identifying traits of writers. He is the firm believer in the ultimate importance of style. He is also the theorist of the word, dedicated to the idea that rhetoric is crafted as much as it is written. These positions are not in any sense mutually exclusive. At the core of them all is the notion that comparison of various writers is more than an expression of a vague preference: it is a rigorous determination of the critic's ability to join with the reader or the student to judge a writer's ability to withstand comparison against an ideal. Finally, Dionysius' criticism is rhetorical, not only in the sense that it has rhetorical works as its subject but also because it seeks a rhetorical purpose itself.

There was, however, a purpose to this process beyond its benefits as a tool for instruction. Dionysius was trying to defend the works and efforts of the classical theorists and orators against what, in the view of many, was the destructive and undisciplined efforts of the Asiatic style. His efforts as an Atticist were directed at the maintenance of tradition and excellence in the face of those whose experimentations in rhetoric led them to uncontrolled, unrestrained change. Dionysius describes the Asiatics and their rise: "Thus was wisdom driven out by ignorance, and sanity by madness." This motive, the persuasive effort, was the first factor that made Dionysius' criticism essentially rhetorical.

The ideals against which Dionysius measured the writers about whom he wrote constituted the other factor. These yardsticks were his inheritance from two earlier theorists. Aristotle and Theophrastus provided, respectively, the fundamental, systematic rules of rhetoric and the appreciation for the power and effects of style. While the system of Aristotle is assumed in Dionysius' writings, it is not the area on which he chooses to concentrate. Instead of an examination of the orators based on the classification and taxonomic division of Aristotle, Dionysius concentrates on style. In particular, the "middle" style, that arrangement of words that most closely resembled the common speech of an educated person, is his interest and the basis upon which he judges the skill of an orator or writer.

The skills of orators are the subjects of the three essays contained in Dionysius' *On the Ancient Orators*. (Lysias, Isaeus, and Isocrates are the three; examination of six was planned.) Dionysius' purpose is to note the worthwhile and clearly superior points of each orator but, where necessary, to expose ruthlessly their shortcomings. This is practical, didactic "criticism," conducted as much for the elucidation of students as to propose, exemplify, and support a theory. It is also almost hypercritical.

Yet Dionysius refutes this charge in the very construction and purpose of his critical essays. His observations form the framework of a system of judgment. Clearly, the job of the critic in forming a judgment, and supporting it to a reader, makes the critic's job essentially rhetorical: to argue the case for the subject using, in essence, all three of Aristotle's types of rhetoric. First, does the reader or critic find fault with the work? If so, the work is examined forensically, to determine its guilt or innocence. Is the issue at hand the writer, as opposed to the work itself? The work is praised or blamed as if the critic were ceremonially assessing the writer. Finally, is the reader to accept and admire the skill of the writer? The critic ultimately argues that it is expedient or inexpedient to agree with the writer. The critic's effort is then deliberative; he or she must convince the reader of the worth of the work. Given this knowledge, the reader can then not only appreciate the passages in question but use the convincing arguments of the critic as well.

Stephen Usher, in the introduction to *The Critical Essays* (1974), calls the contribution of Dionysius' technique as it relates to the Asiatic controversy "eclectic imitation" and notes that Dionysius was the first to use it. The technique is repeated, and expanded upon, in Dionysius' critical essays on Demosthenes and Thucydides. The essay on

Demosthenes leaves the subject of the orator himself to examine in some detail the methods that make him, and presumably any orator who follows his example, so attractive.

The chapters of the essay on Demosthenes that discuss the types of style and the theories of superiority are similar to *On the Arrangement of Words*. Together, the two works offer the practical and theoretical aspects of Dionysius' critical thinking with regard to style. Various styles are examined in detail, and examples of each are put forth for appreciation. Dionysius emphasizes the arrangement of words over figures of speech and gives much strength to the rhythm of prose. It is, he writes, "the most potent device of all for bewitching and beguiling the ear." The overall effect is to make the reader understand that the construction of prose is, like the creation of poetry, a craft. The techniques are different – the rhythm of prose is not to be mistaken for the meter of poetry – but they are analogous. They are the building blocks of different houses. Rhythm reinforces reason, while meter reinforces emotion.

Dionysius' immediate influence as a critic is difficult to discern, and perhaps equally difficult to appreciate. The Asiatic controversy to which he devoted so much effort seems insignificant. He was not the sole voice of the Atticists or the critics who taught from the Greek model. The by-products of his efforts, however, are the real and lasting contribution. They consist of the maintenance of a standard, the technique of comparison, and the close reading of texts to develop examples for instruction.

The approaches he used, the techniques he explored, lack the self-consciousness that characterizes modern criticism. Dionysius did not have a critical theory, per se. A vigorous critic, he compared his subjects to an ideal and made a "theory" in that his objectivity and independence are evident in his heavily documented work. His appreciation for the lucidity, rhythm, and beauty of the ancients distinguishes his writing. He is an example of the value of example.

Dionysius attempted to preserve what was, in his day, the most fundamental study, the most important area of investigation in society. Hypercritical, resistant to change, limited in scope, he remains, nevertheless, a fascinating example of the very beginnings of literary criticism.

Principal criticism

The following works of Dionysius were written c. 20 B.C.:
On the Ancient Orators, "First Letter to Ammaeus," *On the Arrangement of Words*, *On Imitation* (first two books), "On the Style of Demosthenes," "Letter to Cn. Pompeius," "On Thucydides," "Second Letter to Ammaeus," "On Dinarchus," and *On Imitation* (third book)
The Three Literary Letters, 1901
The Literary Treatises of Dionysius of Halicarnassus, 1939

Other major works and literary forms

As the early part of his life was devoted to teaching and the production of rhetorical criticism, Dionysius of Halicarnassus devoted much of the later part of his life to the creation of a comprehensive history of the Roman people. *The Roman Antiquities* (7 B.C.) begins with the earliest mythical tales of the origins of the Roman people and ends with the First Punic War, in 264 B.C. It is an extensive – though sometimes inaccurate – account of Roman civilization and an honest effort to justify the notion that the Romans were not a barbarian race.

Dionysius was a historian with a rhetorical purpose. He desired that his minute investigation of every part of Roman law, custom, religion, and political organization would serve to convince readers of the complexity and maturity of the Roman world. His intention was to support the idea that the inheritors of the Greek world were not only conquerors but also sophisticated people who were worthy of the traditions and precepts of classical Greek life. Aside from the question of the work's success, the method of Dionysius is clear: to make frequent use of rhetorical efforts to present the history of a people through the voices of the people. His reliance on speeches indicates more than his faith in the study of rhetoric as an indicator of the state of a civilization; the technique also demonstrates that even as a historian Dionysius never strayed far from rhetoric, the primary interest of his life.

NONFICTION
The Roman Antiquities, 7 B.C.

Further reading

Gabba, Emilio. *Dionysius and the History of Archaic Rome*, 1991.
Grube, G. M. A. *The Greek and Roman Critics*, 1965.
Hadas, Moses. *A History of Greek Literature*, 1950.
Lesky, Albin. *A History of Greek Literature*, 1963.
Murray, Gilbert. *A History of Ancient Greek Literature*, 1900.
Roberts, W. Rhys. *Greek Rhetoric and Literary Criticism*, 1928.
Usher, Stephen. Introduction to *The Critical Essay*, 1974.

DAVID P. SMITH

Discourse

Discourse is an invaluable term for critical theorists but it is also extremely difficult to define. Because of the very varied history of its use, it is used to refer to a number of different theoretical entities. The major proponent of what is now termed "discourse theory" is Michel Foucault, the French philosopher, who expanded the usage of the word discourse from its original meaning in French (a treatise or speech on a subject) to mean the general domain of the production and circulation of statements. This wider definition of discourse encompasses not only all that is written or said, but also the unwritten rules and structures according to which those utterances and texts are produced. Foucault sees discourse as produced by rules which are not formulated by any one individual or group of people, but which are integral to discourse itself. Implicit in this definition of discourse is the notion that the production of statements is constrained by rules. Thus, when Foucault describes the production of statements which are considered by a particular society to be true, he suggests that true statements are maintained by a system of knowledge which treats true and false statements very differently. False statements are those which are not circulated throughout society and which are not given institutional support of any kind; those which are considered to be true are placed in a position of some power by being repeated, and through being commented on by those in positions of authority. Thus, Foucault is trying to move the discussion of truth away from the notion that there is anything inherently true or factual about a statement or text toward an analysis which focuses on the rules which societies develop to keep certain statements in powerful positions in relation to other texts and statements.

The notion of constraint is important in this definition of discourse, since although it is theoretically possible to say anything, since there are no limits as such on what it is possible to express, in fact, we tend to speak and write within a very narrowly limited set of topics, using a limited vocabulary. This theoretical stance feels counterintuitive, since we generally feel as if we are expressing our innermost self when, for example, we are telling someone that we love them. However, Foucault would argue that in fact there are very strict limits on what it is possible to say within such an interaction. Within each particular historical period and culture, individuals tend to discuss ideas in very similar ways. For Foucault, this is because constraint is part of the very nature of discourse.

Foucault's analysis of discourse is concerned with the way in which knowledge, those statements which we take to be factual, are kept in place by rules of exclusion. He suggests that this process of exclusion constitutes knowledge. Thus reason is kept in place because insanity is constructed as a zone where other threatening unruly knowledges can be hived off. Again, Foucault is concerned to look less at the seeming substance of what is classified as insanity, but rather at the procedures which have been developed to separate off insanity from reason and sanity.

Many of the theorists who have worked on the term discourse have defined it in relation to the term ideology. Some theorists, such as Norman Fairclough, have felt able to use the two terms almost interchangeably while others, such as Foucault, have defined discourse as in opposition to ideology. We might define ideology, as Louis Althusser has, as those statements which disguise the real relations of production by giving us an imaginary representation of the way things are. Individuals are thus kept in their place by a false view of their own position, and these ideological views are invented by those in positions of authority and power in order to subjugate others. Thus, we might consider that in the West we live in democracies because most people have the right to vote for an elected government. However, this view can be seen to be ideological because although we can elect a representative, we cannot make any decisions about the allocation of resources and taxes or about how the government acts in our name. Implicit in this definition of ideology is the sense that ideological statements and views work to the benefit of those in power and to the disadvantage of others. Whilst discourse theorists also see many statements working to the advantage of those in power, Foucault's formulation and those of other theorists, such as Michel Pecheux, do not see discourse operating in such an intentionalist way. That is, whilst Marxist theorists working on ideology might wish to identify the State as the origin of ideological statements, discourse theorists do not feel that there is a "will" or intention which produces these statements. Rather, the production of discourse is always more haphazard and contested than theorists of ideology would allow. Implicit in the notion of discourse is the sense of resistance, which is in marked contrast to those theories of ideology where individuals are represented as passive victims of false knowledge foisted upon them by the State.

Thus, those theorists who work on discourse are interested in the way that power relations affect the production of utterances and texts and the way that knowledge is produced and maintained in positions of authority.

Further reading

Althusser, Louis. *Essays on Ideology*, 1984.
Fairclough, Norman. *Language and Power*, 1989.
——. *Discourse and Social Change*, 1992.
Foucault, Michel. *The Order of Discourse*, 1970.
——. *The Archaeology of Knowledge*, 1972.
——. *Power/Knowledge: Selected Interviews*, 1980. Edited by Colin Gordon.
Mills, Sara. *Discourse*, 1997.
Pecheux, Michel. *Language, Semantics and Ideology*, 1982.

SARA MILLS

See also Foucault

Nikolai Dobroliubov

Russian critic and poet

Born: Nizhnii Novgorod, Russia; February 6, 1836
Died: St. Petersburg, Russia; November 30, 1861

Biography

Nikolai Dobroliubov was born in the Volga river port city of Nizhnii Novgorod on February 6, 1836. His early life bears an almost uncanny resemblance to that of his friend and mentor, Nikolai Chernyshevskii. Both were sons of priests, both received their early education at a seminary, both were excellent students and extremely well-read in literature, philosophy, and social thought, and both left home cities on the Volga to pursue secular education and then a career in St. Petersburg. Dobroliubov came to the Russian capital in 1853 and entered the department of history and literature at the Main Teachers' College. The following year, when he was only eighteen, first his mother and then his father died; their deaths hastened the process of his turning away from religion and toward social activism. Dobroliubov met Chernyshevskii in 1856 and at about the same time began to publish articles and reviews in various journals, including *Sovremennik* (the contemporary), where Chernyshevskii was literary editor. After his graduation in 1857, Dobroliubov devoted himself to journalism, taking over Chernyshevskii's position on *Sovremennik* in 1858; there he published virtually all of his significant work. His background and political views made him a prominent figure among the *raznochintsy*, the "people of various ranks," who formed the core of the radical intelligentsia. He entered wholeheartedly into the heated polemics of the day, attacking not only conservative opponents but also liberals, who were regarded as too timid. One result was a break with Ivan Turgenev, a one-time contributor to *Sovremennik*, who went on to castigate the radicals in his novel *Ottsy i deti* (1862; *Fathers and Sons*, 1867), which appeared the year after Dobroliubov's death. The first signs of Dobroliubov's tuberculosis had already appeared in 1858; weakened by illness and overwork, he went to Europe for rest and treatment in May, 1860. While he continued to write, his health deteriorated steadily. He returned to Russia in June of 1861 and died a few months later, only twenty-five years old but already the most widely read critic of his generation.

Influence

Dobroliubov, along with his older colleague on *Sovremennik*, Chernyshevskii, was instrumental in advocating a social and political role for literary critics over aesthetic considerations. His strong positions led to breaks with writers who were former allies, such as Turgenev and to polemics with others, such as Fedor Dostoevskii, but he was highly influential on other critics and to some extent on writers as well. The most important aspects of his legacy include the great importance assigned to both the writer and the critic in the development of social and political institutions, a belief that the analysis of literature can lead to the discovery of real-life "types" found in society, and an insistence that good literature must always be true to life.

Analysis

During his brief career as a literary critic Dobroliubov did not write any purely theoretical articles, nor did he at any one point elaborate his aesthetic views fully. Nevertheless, various comments embedded in his practical criticism suggest both a consistent and a carefully worked out position. Dobroliubov was indebted to the German philosopher Ludwig Feuerbach for much of his overall outlook, and he was influenced as well by Vissarion Belinskii and Aleksandr Ivanovich Herzen. The most important figure for his development as a critic was no doubt Chernyshevskii, his close associate on *Sovremennik*. Since the two men read many of the same works, it is sometimes difficult to be sure how much Dobroliubov borrowed and how much he arrived at on his own. Still, his strongly rationalist views owe at least something to Chernyshevskii. Both talk of history and of human nature as phenomena that are completely knowable. It is possible to discern a logical development in history, and it is also possible to order society in a way that will be beneficial to people; hence, human failings are frequently blamed on imperfections in both the social and political orders. A key difference, though, is that Chernyshevskii had a particularly high regard for science, while literature was seen as primarily an instrument for enlightenment and instruction. Dobroliubov is closer to Belinskii in that he reserves a major role for the writer. He regards literature, or at least significant literature, as seeing deeply into the individual and into society as a whole. As a result it can present both ideas and movements that are just coming into being, and it has a leading role to play in social developments. Dobroliubov is as insistent as Chernyshevskii in his claims that art deals only with what is real: literature takes its lead from what occurs in society; life does not follow literature. Yet in granting the artist a primal knowledge that is still hidden from others, Dobroliubov places a greater responsibility, and hence a greater importance, on the writer.

In his article "O stepeni uchastiia narodnosti v razvitii russkoi literatury" (1858; on the role of popular aspirations in the development of Russian literature), Dobroliubov asserts that the natural progression of Russian literature is toward a greater expression of the needs and desires of the people. In this sense literature over the years has become more relevant and also more "Russian." Dobroliubov is cool toward Aleksandr Pushkin, generally regarded as the founder of modern Russian literature, both here and in reviews of his works. He admits that Pushkin was the first to create a truly national literature, but he believes that Pushkin himself did not share in the aspirations of the people; instead, he assigns a higher role to both Nikolai Gogol' and Mikhail Lermontov, though they too fall short in some ways.

For the most part, though, Dobroliubov pays less attention to historical surveys and prefers to concentrate on the current literary scene. In a review of Aleksandr Ostrovskii's plays, *Temnoe tsarstvo* (1859; *The Kingdom of Darkness*, 1948), he offers one of his most concise formulations of literature's significance and the artist's responsibility:

> By concentrating the facts of real life, by focussing them, as it were, the images created by the artist

> greatly facilitate the formulation of correct ideas about things and the dissemination of these ideas among men.

Hence it is clear that the principal merit of the author-artist lies in the *truth* of the images he creates; if they were not true, false conclusions would be drawn from them and false ideas would result.

Dobroliubov goes on to admit that some artists do create falsehoods because they focus on what is irrelevant or unimportant and thus their works cannot be used to "formulate correct ideas." This line of reasoning leads to the implication that the more talented the artist the more truthful the work and the more that it will deal with significant themes. Conversely, as Dobroliubov notes in "Literaturnye melochi proshlogo goda" (last year's literary trifles), literature that fails to engage the crucial concerns of the time cannot be regarded highly.

Interestingly, Dobroliubov does not demand that the writer take a position. Since the work of art reflects reality, so long as the author is simply objective and sufficiently talented to provide an accurate and full picture, it is up to the reader to do the rest:

> He [Goncharov] gives you no deductions, and evidently does not set out to do so. The life that he depicts serves him not as a subject for abstract philosophy, but as a direct object in itself. He is not concerned about the reader, or about the deduction that you draw from his novel: that is your business. . . . He presents you with a living image and guarantees only that it resembles reality; the task of defining the merit of the objects depicted is yours: it is of complete indifference to him.

Thus all that Dobroliubov asks is for art to be concerned with the larger questions and to be true to life. In his review of Ivan Aleksandrovich Goncharov's *Oblomov* (1859; English translation, 1963), from which this quotation is taken, he also stresses the artistic perfection of the work, but that is not a necessity for him. To be sure, the very best works combine artistry and social significance, but if a choice must be made, then he sides with the latter. Thus in "Features for Characterizing the Russian Common People," he admits that Marko Vovchok (pseudonym of Maria Aleksandrovna Vilinskaia-Markovich, 1834–1907) is not the most skillful of writers, yet Dobroliubov places a high value on her works for revealing much about contemporary society. In the last of his purely literary articles, "Zabitye liudi" (downtrodden people), he continues a polemic with Fedor Dostoevskii, who talked of the need to deal with "eternal themes" and to place aesthetic considerations at the forefront. Interestingly, Dobroliubov offers a positive review of what was then Dostoevskii's latest novel, *Unizhennye i oskorblennye* (1861; *The Insulted and the Injured*, 1887), but he goes on to claim that it is good precisely because it deals with contemporary social themes – considered on purely aesthetic grounds it would, says Dobroliubov, be found wanting.

Not surprisingly, Dobroliubov displays a particular interest in satire, which by its very nature must engage social themes. During the last years of his life much of his energy was devoted to the satirical section within *Sovremennik* and in his essay on "Russkaia satira v vek Ekateriny" (Russian satire during the age of Catherine the Great) he deals with the limitations of earlier satirists, using the occasion to point out that the social ills against which they had protested were still in existence. Like Chernyshevskii, he singled out Mikhail Evgrafovich Saltykov-Shchedrin's *Gubernskie ocherki* (1856–1857; provincial sketches) for praise, finding that the caustic depictions of rural figures provided a profoundly realistic picture of Russian life.

Dobroliubov's importance for the history of Russian criticism lies, first of all, in the manner in which he used literature as the source for defining broad social types. The very title of what remains perhaps his most famous essay, "What Is Oblomovism?," is indicative: he sees in literary figures realistic types of individuals who either already play an important role in society or perhaps are just coming into being. Thus in this essay he defines "Oblomovism" as a kind of social illness, associated with the figure of the "superfluous man" in nineteenth-century Russian literature. Ostrovskii, in *The Kingdom of Darkness*, presents the boorish yet powerful provincial merchant; Aleksei Nikolaevich Pleshcheev, in "Blagonamerennost' i deiatel'nost'" (1860; "Good Intentions and Good Deeds," 1948), depicts still more weak figures of the Oblomov type. Dobroliubov is impatient for the appearance of more active people in Russian life, but the male characters are always lacking in some way. Thus in "When Will the Real Day Come?" he finds a possible hero in Turgenev's Insarov in the novel *Nakanune* (1860; *On the Eve*, 1871), but the character turns out to be Bulgarian, not Russian. Curiously, the most positive figures are women. They include Ol'ga in *Oblomov*, Katerina in Ostrovskii's play *Groza* (1859; *The Storm*, 1899), and the main female figure in *On the Eve*:

> The point is that, bad as our present way of life is, the appearance of types like Helena has proved to be possible. And not only have such creatures become possible in life, they have already been grasped by the artists' mind, they have been introduced into literature, they have been elevated to a type.

Dobroliubov's effort to define social types through literature influenced more than his contemporaries; particularly after the Bolshevik Revolution, critics often contended that literary figures bear a direct resemblance to types found in society. Yet this last quotation also points to another way in which Dobroliubov's example was to prove important in the years following the Revolution. He hints that literature depicts not only what is evident to everybody (the Oblomovs) but also types that are just about to emerge. Thus literature may also point to the future – much in the way that the post-revolutionary doctrine of Socialist Realism was to call for a literature that would show society and people not as they are, but as they develop toward a more perfect and more nearly Communist existence.

Finally, Dobroliubov makes the critic particularly important:

> The realistic critic must say what impression these persons make upon him, and he can indict the author, only if this impression is incomplete, vague and ambiguous . . . . Then the critic goes on to investigate whether such a type of person is possible, and whether it exists; on finding that it is true to reality the critic will go on to express his own views as to the causes which engendered such a type.

Thus the critic, like the author, is supposedly objective, but the critic is also the judge and the interpreter of what the writer has produced. In this way the critic's significance becomes hardly less than that of the artist – an assumption that would appear to be reflected in the close attention that is given to literary criticism within the former Soviet Union.

Principal criticism

"*Sochineniia* grafa V. A. Solloguba," 1857
"*Gubernskie ocherki* Shchedrina," 1857 ("*Provincial Sketches* by M. E. Saltykov [-Shchedrin]," 1948)
"*Sochineniia* Pushkina," 1858
"O stepeni uchastiia narodnosti v razvitii russkoi literatury," 1858
"Literaturnye melochi proshlogo goda," 1859
"Chto takoe oblomovshchina?," 1859 ("What Is Oblomovism?" 1903)
"Temnoe tsarstvo," 1859 ("The Kingdom of Darkness," 1948)
"Russkaia satira v vek Ekateriny," 1859
"Kogda zhe pridet nastoiashchii den'?," 1860 ("When Will the Real Day Come?" 1948)
"Blagonamerennost' i deiatel'nost'," 1860 ("Good Intentions and Good Deeds," 1948)
"Luch sveta v temnom tsarstve," 1860 ("A Ray of Light in the Kingdom of Darkness," 1948)
"Cherty dlia kharakteristiki russkogo prostonarod'ia," 1860 ("Features for Characterizing the Russian Common People," 1948)
"Zabitye liudi," 1861
Selected Philosophical Essays, 1948 (J. Fineberg, translator)

Other major works and literary forms

During his lifetime Nikolai Dobroliubov was known almost exclusively as a literary critic. Yet, while still a student at the seminary in his native Nizhnii Novgorod, he began to write poetry; the earliest surviving poems date from 1849, when he was only thirteen years old. The more than three hundred poems that survive can be roughly grouped into three categories: lyrical poems, which he continued to write throughout his life and which remained largely unpublished until after his death; political poems, which were circulated in manuscript but could not be published because of the censorship; and satirical poems, most of which were written for a section of the journal *Sovremennik* (the contemporary) called "Svistok" (the whistle), which was established by Dobroliubov and devoted to satire. Dobroliubov also made a few attempts at prose, which he does not appear to have taken very seriously. Two tales written during his student years, however, were eventually published: "Donos" (1857; the denunciation) and "Delets" (1858; the operator).

SHORT FICTION
"Donos," 1857
"Delets," 1858

POETRY
Polnoe sobranie stikhotvorenii, 1969

NONFICTION
"O znachenii avtoriteta v vospitanii (Mysli po povodu *Voprosov zhizni* g. Pirogova)," 1857 ("The Importance of Authority in Education [Reflections on Mr. Pirogov's *Problems of Life*]," 1948)
"Pervye gody tsarstvovaniia Petra Velikogo," 1858 ("The First Years of Peter the Great's Reign," 1948)
"Robert Oven i ego popytki obshchestvennykh reform," 1859

MISCELLANEOUS
Sobranie sochinenii, 1961–1964 (9 volumes)

Further reading

Kuhn, Alfred. "Dobroliubov's Critique of *Oblomov*: Polemics and Psychology," in *Slavic Review*. XXX (1971), pp. 93–109.
Kuyakin, Valery A., ed. *A History of Russian Philosophy from the Tenth through the Twentieth Centuries*, 1994, Vol. 1.
Lampert, Evgenii. *Sons Against Fathers: Studies in Russian Radicalism and Revolution*, 1965.
Mathewson, Rufus W., Jr. *The Positive Hero in Russian Literature*, 1975.
Matlaw, Ralph E., ed. *Belinskii, Chernyshevskii, and Dobroliubov: Selected Criticism*, 1962.
Moser, Charles A. *Esthetics as Nightmare: Russian Literary Theory, 1855–1870*, 1989.
Proctor, Thelwall. *Dostoevskij and the Belinskij School of Literary Criticism*, 1969.
Stacy, Robert H. *Russian Literary Criticism: A Short History*, 1974.
Terras, Victor. *Belinskij and Russian Literary Criticism: The Heritage of Organic Aesthetics*, 1974.
Walicki, Andrzej. *A History of Russian Thought from the Enlightenment to Marxism*, 1979.
Wellek, René. "Social and Aesthetic Values in Russian Nineteenth-Century Literary Criticism (Belinskii, Chernyshevskii, Dobroliubov, Pisarev)," in *Continuity and Change in Russian and Soviet Thought*, 1955. Edited by Ernest J. Simmons.

BARRY P. SCHERR

See also Belinskii; Chernyshevskii; Dostoevskii; Pisarev; Veselovskii

Fedor Dostoevskii

Russian novelist

Born: Moscow, Russia; November 11, 1821
Died: St. Petersburg, Russia; February 9, 1881

Biography

The second of eight children, Fedor Dostoevskii was born on November 11, 1821, in Moscow. His father at that time was a practicing physician; his ancestors included landowners from northwestern Russia. His mother was from a family of Moscow merchants. Dostoevskii was educated in local schools and in St. Petersburg, where in 1843 he completed course work at the Military Engineering School. He fell rather early under the spell of literature; in 1844 he resigned his commission as a lieutenant of engineers, and during the next several years his first published works appeared. He also translated works of some of his favorite French authors. He became involved as well in meetings at the house of Mikhail Petrashevskii, where utopian socialist ideas were discussed. Other allegedly subversive works, including some by Russians, were also circulated. In 1849 Dostoevskii, along with many of his associates, was arrested on criminal charges and condemned to death. After a dramatic reprieve shortly before the scheduled execution, he was sentenced to four years of hard labor in Siberia. Dostoevskii later served as a private and then a lieutenant in the army. In 1859 he was permitted to return to European Russia; in St. Petersburg, he recommenced his literary career on a higher plane than before and many of his later masterpieces vividly recaptured the events he had experienced. His first marriage, to Mar'ia Dmitrievna Konstant Isaeva, was troubled by discord and ended with her death from illness in 1864. In 1867 he remarried, to his secretary Anna Grigor'evna Snitkina; she became the mother of his four children. Lengthy periods of travel, when Dostoevskii visited many parts of Western Europe, provided some material for his writing but also produced in him a deepening conviction that Russia's national destiny had diverged from those of other countries. He suffered from a number of illnesses; indeed, the epileptic condition which affected him for many years was depicted in some moving and memorable passages from his novels. He was beset as well by other complaints even as his literary career seemingly reached new heights. He died in St. Petersburg on February 9, 1881.

Influence

Dostoevskii's major fiction has been an example and a source of inspiration for many later writers, leading to a number of similar efforts in the later nineteenth and early twentieth centuries. His efforts subsequently had a clear impact upon the early Soviet novelist Leonid Leonov; affinities were also acknowledged by the dissident, and later émigré, writer Aleksandr Solzhenitsyn. Among Western authors who studied Dostoevskii's works with care were André Gide, Hermann Hesse, and Thomas Mann. Dostoevskii's literary conceptions also were vital to the ideas and situations created by French writers such as Albert Camus, André Malraux, and Jean-Paul Sartre; he has been regarded as a precursor of those identified with an existentialist persuasion. Specifically critical writings, however, had somewhat narrower effects: his views on literature were overshadowed by the wide reception and extraordinary impact of his fictional works. Nevertheless, reflections of his literary conceptions may be found in the writings of Vladimir Solovev, the philosopher; other writers who found Dostoevskii's theories useful included Vasilii Rozanov and Dmitrii Merezhkovskii. Comparative studies by Lev Shestov sought to elucidate the philosophical bases of Dostoevskii's works. Dostoevskii's critical ideas in the main have concerned literary scholars, who have found them important in tracing the development of his major fiction.

Analysis

At the outset of his career, Dostoevskii was particularly concerned with the success of his fictional works, and his first articles having some critical intent were written at intervals between his other efforts. A brief announcement for a humorous work, in 1845, was followed by a series of newspaper articles published in 1847, in which he contrasted the superficial forms of European manners that had crept into life in the Russian capital with the genuinely Russian ethos he believed should be preserved. On another front, his outlook was deeply affected by controversies arising from the reception of his own works. Vissarion Belinskii, the most widely known Russian critic of that time, praised Dostoevskii's first novel, *Poor Folk*, and, with some reservations, rendered a favorable judgment of *The Double*, his second major work; Dostoevskii was embittered, indeed personally stung, however, when Belinskii dismissed the stories "Gospodin Prokharchin" (1846; "Mr. Prohartchin," 1918) and "Khoziaika" (1847; "The Landlady," 1913) as monstrous and poorly developed. Although he had taken some interest in Belinskii's ideas – ironically enough, the charges the government brought against Dostoevskii cited his reading Belinskii's open letter to Nikolai Gogol', which had been suppressed for political reasons – during his interrogation, Dostoevskii disavowed any serious commitment to sweeping social change. Much later, when his views as a writer had taken more definite forms, Dostoevskii castigated Belinskii for his lack of spiritual and religious understanding.

After his return from penal servitude and exile, the thematic elements of Dostoevskii's novels had begun to take shape; some statements of his standpoint as an author came during his association with the journal *Vremia* (time), of which his brother Mikhail was the editor. To some extent as well, the views of Apollon Grigor'ev, a prominent critic and frequent contributor to the journal, were important in the evolution of Dostoevskii's conception of national culture. Grigor'ev, and others of like mind, espoused an organic theory of criticism which also upheld the virtues of *pochvennichestvo*, or attachment to the native land; this conception rebuffed the ideas of liberal and radical publicists while avoiding the more narrowly national preconceptions that others applied to art, literature, and social questions. In an article from 1861, Dostoevskii contended that Russian civilization in some respects could achieve a synthesis of Western ideas while exemplifying qualities universally sought by humanity.

Other essays from this time, notably his review of an exhibition at the Academy of Arts in St. Petersburg, showed Dostoevskii wrestling with aesthetic problems that recurrently troubled him. He posed questions such as whether human suffering could be portrayed in a beautiful manner or whether the moral concerns of art required the affirmation of positive human values. A review of stories by Nikolai Uspenskii raised another problem. Uspenskii claimed in effect to apply the principles of photography to his depictions of peasant life. To Dostoevskii, however, the result was by no means realistic; it seemed a mechanical approach that ignored the observer's point of view and left open issues of human perception and consciousness.

In "Gospodin -bov i vopros ob iskusstve" (1861; "Mr. -bov and the Question of Art," 1963), one of the more widely known of his critical articles, Dostoevskii contrasted images of beauty and suffering while declaiming against purely aesthetic criteria as applied to literary functions. Indeed, he declared point-blank that art should not be valued merely for its own sake; such notions were shallow and frivolous. Nevertheless, he launched a particularly severe attack upon those he derided as utilitarians; in so doing, he seized upon one element of his opponents' beliefs as a focal point for his criticism. Ostensibly this essay was meant as a commentary on stories by Marko Vovchok, who had written about the condition of the peasantry under serfdom; it generally has been taken as aimed at Nikolai Dobroliubov, whom Dostoevskii regarded as a representative of new and potentially pernicious ideological trends. It would appear that, because Dobroliubov died at about the time the article appeared, his name in the title was deleted in part. Specifically, Dostoevskii contended that the new generation of literary critics had not found ways by which the usefulness of art could be determined. For that matter, it seemed a vain hope to seek a scientific standard that could measure its utility. In so doing, he decried the tendency among some literary figures to subsume problems of character and individual morality in much broader quests for the resolution of social problems.

Elsewhere, Dostoevskii advanced some implied criticism of the utilitarian ideas expressed by another writer, Nikolai Chernyshevskii. For example, in the novel *Notes from the Underground*, the narrator's, and presumably the author's, disparaging comments about the Crystal Palace, which had been built for the London World's Fair of 1851, suggested a contrast with Chernyshevskii's treatment of this matter in *Chto delat'?* (1863; *What Is to Be Done?*, c. 1863), in which the great exhibition hall was taken as an example of the advances that might be achieved through scientific rationalism. Although at that time, probably because Chernyshevskii had been sentenced to exile and a term of forced labor, Dostoevskii refrained from mentioning him by name, his narrator goes to great lengths to denounce any groundless faith in the improvement of the human condition. Dostoevskii also had some acerbic comments to make in an article for *Epokha* (the epoch), in which he maintained that the writings of the noted satirist Mikhail Saltykov-Shchedrin provided evidence of disarray and confusion among literary partisans of nihilism.

Other issues were considered in an essay from this period that was published as "Poslednye literaturnye iavleniia: Gazeta 'Den','" (1861; "The Latest Literary Controversies," 1963). In this work, he reproached those of a Slavophile persuasion and cited the views of Ivan Sergeevich Aksakov and others whose work was featured in another journal. Dostoevskii upbraided the Slavophiles for an insensate intolerance of other points of view; their rejection of Western ways had, he contended, proceeded well beyond the bounds of reason and good sense. The wholesale elimination of European influence would actually diminish the vitality of Russian culture. The balance achieved at this stage in Dostoevskii's views on national culture eventually was to give way to a renewed emphasis on the distinctions that separated Russia from the West.

During the middle period of his career, Dostoevskii was preoccupied with work on the novels that established his literary reputation; his position with respect to other controversies could be inferred largely from the standpoint of his major fiction. In a certain sense as well, the issues raised in *Crime and Punishment* and *The Idiot* mirror the concerns that also figured in his later critical writings. Problems of crime and morality are raised alongside speculation about beauty and realism; these issues also were discussed, sometimes in sharp, arresting terms, in the author's notebooks and letters. The work most closely related to Dostoevskii's journalism, however, was *The Possessed*, in which political ideals to support revolutionary action are discussed against a background of violent death. In some ways, the novel was taken as an indictment both of liberalism and of more radical creeds. The work is also notable for its specific mention of certain literary thinkers; Belinskii, for example, is invoked by some self-important advocates of social change.

While in some of his letters Dostoevskii had proposed devoting more of his energies to criticism, the main outcome of his interest in this area was the commencement, in 1873, of a series of columns which appeared in the journal *Grazhdanin* (the citizen) under the title "Dnevnik pisatelia";

three years later, and sporadically thereafter, it became available separately by subscription under the same title. (It was compiled in part and translated as *Pages from the Journal of an Author* in 1916, and a complete edition was published in 1949 as *The Diary of a Writer.*) Although this endeavor also contained observations on political events, commentary on other news, and some short fictional works, taken in its entirety it represented Dostoevskii's most sustained effort to explore the ideas underlying his fictional efforts. For that matter, though it has been common to cite his notebooks and his correspondence in this connection, many of the statements published during his lifetime, when taken together, suggest the attempts to resolve issues which are central to any theory of literature and criticism.

The conception of realism that emerges from the critical writings of this time illustrate a concern for artistic truth which Dostoevskii believed transcended the mundane details that could be recaptured, as it were, by a camera; this principle applied to painting and the visual arts in much the same way as it did to any literary production. Comparisons of this sort, which were drawn from his articles about well-known paintings on display, were developed further in his discussions of the relationship between literature and ordinary life. He insisted upon the need for a guiding idea to unify the clutter of detail and impressions that presented themselves to the observer. Where literary resources were concerned, he thought that the raw material of actual experience should be used at first hand. Many of his journalistic writings dealt with famous criminal trials, which he followed avidly and which he discussed at length for his readers; nevertheless, he maintained as well that the social and moral significance of such events was necessarily implicit in any effort to describe them. Although his detractors, beginning with Belinskii, had found fault with Dostoevskii's fantastic, seemingly unreal situations, he insisted that his works had depicted the human concerns underlying actual occurrences. It was this interaction between commentary on events of the day and the exercise of artistic insight that attracted many readers to Dostoevskii's literary diary.

The moral element that figured so prominently in his fiction also was expressed in his musings on the events that were reported in his literary columns. Religious themes, particularly in shocking or seemingly unexpected contexts, fascinated him; such issues presented two concerns to which he returned repeatedly. He often speculated about whether beauty could be found in the grim and sordid aspects of life he noticed. In his comments on stories about murder, suicide, and the wilful mistreatment of children, the presence of devotional objects was noted ironically. At junctures, he raised questions about the Christian beliefs of the Russian people, pointing out extraordinary manifestations of religious commitment that appeared alongside acts of outrageous indifference to moral precepts. The tension between realism, as he conceived it, and aesthetic functions was intensified by his quest for principles of religious truth that would distinguish the elements of good and evil in the occurrences he reported. These issues, which were posed for the consideration of the reading public, were also raised frequently in his notebooks; such questions were discussed at length in his last novel, *The Brothers Karamazov.*

To be sure, reflections of this sort appeared intermittently in Dostoevskii's later writings; nevertheless, many columns were devoted to journalism in a narrower sense. His discussion of political issues, which preoccupied him at times, revealed a stern conception of Russia's mission in the world that some people, including later foreign readers, found unsettling. In many places as well, Dostoevskii dealt with specific literary controversies, occasionally in a whimsical spirit and sometimes more combatively. In 1873 he published a brief sketch, drawn from memory, of one of his meetings with Belinskii; he suggested that the great critic's political preoccupations distorted his conception of Christian ideals. Shortly thereafter, he discussed his recollections of a meeting with Chernyshevskii and insisted that personal antipathy had not motivated his seeming caricatures of the other man's ideas. Somewhat later, however, Dostoevskii again referred to problems arising from Belinskii's thought and influence.

Concerns of another sort, closely related to Dostoevskii's critical standpoint, were raised in his review of Nikolai Leskov's novel *Soboriane* (1872; *The Cathedral Folk*, 1924). Although he had some sympathy for works of this sort, Dostoevskii commented that the author's depiction of a thaumaturgical icon left disquieting doubts about his commitment to truthfulness in literature. In spite of difficult personal relations, Dostoevskii had some words of praise for the works of Ivan Turgenev, which he thought exhibited talent in abundance. Dostoevskii also had great respect for the fiction of Lev Tolstoi; upon its first appearance in print, he reviewed *Anna Karenina* (1875–1877; English translation, 1886), which in some ways he seems to have read according to his own views. Dostoevskii maintained that Tolstoi had created a fictional setting in which culpability and abnormal situations could not be dealt with in a manner common to European writing. Indeed, Dostoevskii contended that by his treatment of problems affecting individual morality and the human spirit Tolstoi had portrayed the distinctive traits characteristic of Russians and their destiny.

Dostoevskii had often referred to the importance of Aleksandr Pushkin, whom he regarded as a major creative influence for subsequent writers. One of his most famous pronouncements on literature was a speech in Pushkin's honor, delivered in June, 1880; it was published two months later in his literary diary. Dostoevskii maintained that Pushkin's works exemplified the universal qualities of literary art in a way that had not been approached by anyone else in the world of letters. Pushkin's extraordinary ability to depict foreign settings and situations was strikingly complemented by his evocation of typically Russian ways; this capacity was the more remarkable in view of his consummate mastery of the literary language and its uses. In many ways Dostoevskii believed that Pushkin's contributions to literature remained a positive active force among his later readers. By opening new paths for creative work, his writings stood as a prophecy and a revelation.

Although Dostoevskii's critical writings might seem disjointed, it should be recalled that often such works were composed in response to specific controversies that arose during his creative lifetime. Moreover, his literary theories were formulated primarily with a view toward the composition of his major fiction; thus the ideas expressed in his critical essays sometimes had an inchoate or a tentative appearance. Nevertheless, the depth and vitality of his thought are revealed at many turns in his critical works; in many respects such views have warranted the consideration of those interested in the concerns raised in his fiction.

Principal criticism

Articles appearing in *Vremia* (1861–1863) and *Epokha* (1864–1865)
Dnevnik pisatelia, 1876–1877, 1880–1881 (2 volumes, *A Writer's Diary 1873–1876*, and *1877–1881*, 1997)
Dostoevsky's Occasional Writings, 1963
F. M. Dostoevskii ob iskusstve, 1973

Other major works and literary forms

Fedor Dostoevskii is known primarily for his novels and short stories, which combine penetrating psychological insight with intense and searching philosophical speculation. Among his early works, *Bednye liudi* (1846; *Poor Folk*, 1887) and *Dvoinik* (1846; *The Double*, 1917) are of some interest. *Zapiski iz mertvogo doma* (1861–1862; *Buried Alive: Or, Ten Years of Penal Servitude in Siberia*, 1881, better known as *The House of the Dead*, 1915) was based upon his own experiences during a period of punishment in exile. *Zapiski iz podpol'ia* (1864; *Letters from the Underworld*, 1913, better known as *Notes from the Underground*, 1918) aroused attention for its withering treatment of materialism and rationalism as applied to social issues of the time. Dostoevskii's four great novels, *Prestuplenie i nakazanie* (1866; *Crime and Punishment*, 1886), *Idiot* (1868; *The Idiot*, 1887), *Besy* (1871–1872; *The Possessed*, 1913), and *Brat'ia Karamazovy* (1879–1880; *The Brothers Karamazov*, 1912), demonstrate his thorough and profound treatment of major themes involving crime, penitence, and the quest for salvation in the context of basic concerns with religious truth and problems of good and evil. Although Dostoevskii's other novels were not quite so significant, shorter works such as "Belye nochi" (1848; "White Nights," 1918), "Krotkaia" (1876; "The Gentle Maiden," 1913), and "Son smeshnogo cheloveka" (1877; "The Dream of a Queer Fellow," 1916, better known as "The Dream of a Ridiculous Man," 1919) also took up the enduring issues developed in his longer fiction.

Other writings deal more directly with the personal concerns and creative struggles that affected his life. Travel impressions from a visit to Europe were recorded in "Zimnie zametki o letnikh vpechatleniiakh" (1863; "Winter Notes on Summer Impressions," 1955). The most important collection of his correspondence appeared as his four-volume *Pis'ma* (1928–1959); a broad but judicious English compilation is *Selected Letters of Fyodor Dostoyevsky* (1987). Sources demonstrating the means by which his works were composed appeared as fragments after his death and were published in more complete editions as *Iz arkhiva F. M. Dostoevskogo: "Prestuplenie i nakazanie"* (1931; *The Notebooks for "Crime and Punishment,"* 1967), *Iz arkhiva F. M. Dostoevskogo: "Idiot"* (1931; *The Notebooks for "The Idiot,"* 1967), *Zapisnye tetradi F. M. Dostoevskogo* (1935; *The Notebooks for "The Possessed,"* 1968), *F. M. Dostoevskii: Materialy i issledovaniia* (1935; *The Notebooks for "The Brothers Karamazov,"* 1971), and *F. M. Dostoevskii v rabote nad romanom "Podrostok"* (1965; *The Notebooks for "A Raw Youth,"* 1969). Further materials appeared as *Neizdannyi Dostoevskii: Zapisnye knizhki i tetradi, 1860–1881 gg.* (1971; *The Unpublished Dostoevsky: Diaries and Notebooks, 1860–1881*, 1973–1976, three volumes).

NOVELS
Bednye liudi, 1846 (*Poor Folk*, 1887)
Dvoinik, 1846 (*The Double*, 1917)
Netochka Nezvanova, 1849 (English translation, 1920)
Unizhennye i oskorblennye, 1861 (*Injury and Insult*, 1886; better known as *The Insulted and Injured*, 1887)
Zapiski iz mertvogo doma, 1861–1862 (*Buried Alive: Or, Ten Years of Penal Servitude in Siberia*, 1881; better known as *The House of the Dead*, 1915)
Zapiski iz podpol'ia, 1864 (*Letters from the Underworld*, 1913; better known as *Notes from the Underground*, 1918)
Igrok, 1866 (*The Gambler*, 1887)
Prestuplenie i nakazanie, 1866 (*Crime and Punishment*, 1886)
Idiot, 1868 (*The Idiot*, 1887)
Vechnyi muzh, 1870 (*The Permanent Husband*, 1888; better known as *The Eternal Husband*, 1917)
Besy, 1871–1872 (*The Possessed*, 1913; also as *The Devils*, 1953)
Podrostok, 1875 (*A Raw Youth*, 1916)
Brat'ia Karamazovy, 1879–1880 (*The Brothers Karamazov*, 1912)
The Novels, 1912 (12 volumes)

SHORT FICTION
Sochineniia, 1860 (2 volumes)
Polnoe sobranie sochinenii, 1865–1870 (4 volumes)
Povesti i rasskazy, 1882
A Christmas Tree and a Wedding, and an Honest Thief, 1917
White Nights and Other Stories, 1918
An Honest Thief and Other Stories, 1919
The Short Novels of Dostoevsky, 1945

NONFICTION
"Zimnie zametki o letnikh vpechatleniiakh," 1863 ("Winter Notes on Summer Impressions," 1955)
Pis'ma, 1928–1959 (4 volumes)
Iz arkhiva F. M. Dostoevskogo: "Prestuplenie i nakazanie," 1931 (*The Notebooks for "Crime and Punishment,"* 1967)

Iz arkhiva F. M. Dostoevskogo: "Idiot," 1931 (*The Notebooks for "The Idiot,"* 1967)
Zapisnye tetradi F. M. Dostoevskogo, 1935 (*The Notebooks for "The Possessed,"* 1968)
F. M. Dostoevskii: Materialy i issledovaniia, 1935 (*The Notebooks for "The Brothers Karamazov,"* 1971)
F. M. Dostoevskii v rabote nad romanom "Podrostok," 1965 (*The Notebooks for "A Raw Youth,"* 1969)
Neizdannyi Dostoevskii: Zapisnye knizhki i tetradi 1860–1881 gg., 1971 (3 volumes; *The Unpublished Dostoevsky: Diaries and Notebooks, 1860–1881*, 1973–1976)
Fyodor Dostoyevsky: Complete Letters, 1991 (5 volumes)

TRANSLATION
Evgeniia Grande, 1844 (of Honoré de Balzac's novel *Eugénie Grandet*)

MISCELLANEOUS
Polnoe sobranie sochinenii v tridtsati tomakh, 1972–1990 (30 volumes)

Further reading

Conradi, Peter. *Fyodor Dostoevsky*, 1988.
Dolenc, Ivan. *Dostoevsky and Christ: A Study of Dostoevsky's Rebellion Against Belinskii*, 1978.
Dowler, Wayne. *Dostoevsky, Grigor'ev, and Native Soil Conservatism*, 1982.
Jackson, Robert Louis. *Dostoevsky's Quest for Form: A Study of His Philosophy of Art*, 1966.
Jones, Malcolm V. *Dostoyevsky After Bakhtin: Readings in Dostoyevsky's Fantastic Realism*, 1990.
Kabat, Geoffrey C. *Ideology and Imagination: The Image of Society in Dostoevsky*, 1978.
Kjetsaa, G. *Fyodor Dostoevsky*, 1987.
Lary, N. M. *Dostoevsky and Soviet Film: Visions of Demonic Realism*, 1986.
Leatherbarrow, W. J. *Fedor Dostoevsky: A Reference Guide*, 1990.
Leonard, Linda Schierse. *Witness to the Fire: Creativity and the Veil of Addiction*, 1989.
Linnér, Sven. *Dostoevskij on Realism*, 1967.
Morson, Gary Saul. *The Boundaries of Genre: Dostoevsky's "Diary of a Writer" and the Traditions of Literary Utopia*, 1981.
Moser, Charles A. "Dostoevsky and the Aesthetics of Journalism," in *Dostoevsky Studies*. III (1982), pp. 27–41.
Proctor, Thelwall. *Dostoevskij and the Belinskij School of Literary Criticism*, 1969.
Sekirin, Peter, and Igor Volgin, eds. *The Dostoevsky Archive: Firsthand Accounts of the Novelist from Contemporaries' Memoirs and Rare Periodicals*, 1997.
Straus, Nina Pelikan. *Dostoevsky and the Woman Question: Rereadings at the End of a Century*, 1994.

J. R. Broadus

See also Belinskii; Chernyshevskii; Dobroliubov; Pisarev; Veselovskii

Drama: Theory and Criticism

"Drama" and "theater," the two words used to describe this genre, are both Greek in origin and emphasize the focus of this literary form upon live performance. *Drama*, which means "thing done," refers especially to the actions of the actors, while *theater*, derived from the Greek verb "to see," deals with the audience which witnesses these actions. While attempts have been made to write plays to be read rather than performed, such so-called "closet dramas" are really derivatives of a genre founded upon the concept of live actors speaking before a live audience. Indeed, conversational mode is central to this genre in which the author "speaks" to the audience through the second-person voices of the actors, while in lyric the writer uses the first-person and, in narrative, the third-person voice. While the Greek vocabulary stresses drama as performance, the English word "play" and its German equivalent "Schauspiel" add to performance the idea of "amusement," "jest," or even "joke." Etymologically, then, "drama" is just "play"; it is not real; it is a reenactment or re-creation of life, but it is not life itself.

While the specific origin of the genre is shrouded in the mists of time and remains controversial, it is clear that the two broad types of Western drama, tragedy and comedy, go back to Greek models developed especially for the worship of the god Dionysus at Athens in the sixth and fifth centuries B.C. The Greeks generally viewed tragedy as serious drama based upon plots and characters from the mythic past, and comedy as light drama with more contemporary characters and themes. Gradually, however, these Greek distinctions were replaced by a general view of tragedy as a play with a sad ending and comedy as one with a great deal of humor and/or a happy ending.

Dramatic criticism was incorporated into actual performance in Aristophanes' *Frogs* (405 B.C.), in which a competition between the deceased tragedians Aeschylus and Euripides takes place in Hades. While Euripides stressed drama as a portrayal of reality, Aeschylus looked more to the didactic possibilities of the genre and therefore won the contest because his dramas were judged to be more serious and politically useful.

Formal dramatic theory begins in the West with the *Poetics* (c. 334–323 B.C.) of Aristotle, a treatise which survives in two books, one devoted to epic and a second to tragedy. A third book on comedy is lost. Central to Aristotle's theory of drama is the concept of mimesis, of literature as an imitation of life. Aristotle argued that the ideal tragedy depicts an essentially good person who experiences a downfall (*peripeteia*). In the best tragedies, this *peripeteia* occurs at a moment of recognition, or *anagnorisis*, when the central character finally sees the true nature of his or her situation. Aristotle cited Sophocles' *Oedipus Tyrannus* (c. 420 B.C.) as an example of a tragedy combining *peripeteia* and *anagnorisis* and suggested that the character's downfall was due to *hamartia*, a Greek word which can mean anything from "a mistake or error" to "a grievous sin." Another controversial term in the *Poetics* is *katharsis*, or "purification." While Aristotle said that the spectator of a tragedy experiences a catharsis of pity and fear, it is unclear whether an immediate emotional purgation or a more metaphorical one is meant. Despite the ambiguities of Aristotle's dramatic theory in the *Poetics*, his terminology and his approach have essentially established the basic direction of dramatic criticism in the West.

In *The Art of Poetry* (c. 17 B.C.) the Roman poet Horace devoted considerable portions of his poem on literary theory and criticism to drama. For Horace decorum and propriety were central features of good literature and good drama and the goal of a poet or dramatist was *utile* ("the useful") and *dulce* ("the sweet or pleasing"). Horace's reference to the five-act drama became a rule in later periods and his emphasis on coherence of time was eventually expanded into the three unities of time, place, and plot.

During the medieval period in Europe, mystery and morality plays emphasized edification by employing drama to illustrate and encourage Christian morals and values. In the Renaissance, drama returned to its Greco-Roman origins and to a renewed emphasis on Aristotelian and Horatian standards. Neoclassic theory, which dominated various parts of Europe from the early seventeenth through the late eighteenth centuries, encouraged playwrights to follow the three unities as well as classical standards of *decorum* and *vraisemblance* (verisimilitude), that is, the creation of characters and plot which were true-to-life.

Only in the late eighteenth century did the rules of neoclassicism begin to yield to dramas which emphasized more contemporary middle-class plots and characters, and dramatic theory became more focused on Romantic themes of nature, medievalism, individual freedom, and the dignity of the emotions. By the end of the nineteenth century, Romantic theory was replaced by theories like naturalism, with its realistic dialogue and character development, the conflict of social forces, and an emphasis on the "well-made play." Also popular in this period was the concept of the play of ideas, in which psychological or inner truth was more important than superficial realism.

In the twentieth century dramatic theory moved even further away from realism as playwrights and critics experimented with the Theater of the Absurd, Symbolism, expressionism, and Surrealism.

Further reading

Atkins, J. W. *Literary Criticism in Antiquity*, 1934 (2 volumes).
Butcher, Samuel Henry. *Aristotle's Theory of Poetry and Fine Art*, 1951 (fourth edition).
Carlson, Marvin. *Theories of the Theater*, 1984.
Cooper, Lane. *The Poetics of Aristotle. Its Meaning and Influence*, 1963.
Else, Gerald F. *Aristotle's "Poetics": The Argument*, 1957.
Hall, Vernon, Jr. *Renaissance Literary Criticism*, 1945.
Spingarn, Joel. *History of Literary Criticism in the Renaissance*, 1963 (second edition).

THOMAS J. SIENKEWICZ

See also Aristotle; Bentley; Brecht; Esslin; Shaw

John Dryden

English poet, critic, and translator

Born: Aldwinckle, England; August 19, 1631
Died: London, England; May 1, 1700

Biography

John Dryden, the oldest of fourteen children in a landed family of modest means whose sympathies were Puritan on both sides, was born in Aldwinckle, Northamptonshire, on August 19, 1631. Little is known of his youth, for Dryden, though seldom hesitant about his opinions, was reticent about his personal life. At about the age of fifteen, he enrolled in Westminster School, notable for its production of poets and bishops. Having attained at Westminster a thorough grounding in Latin, he proceeded to Trinity College, University of Cambridge, taking the B.A. in 1654. After the death of his father brought him a modest inheritance in the form of rents from family land, he left the university and settled in London, serving briefly in Oliver Cromwell's government in a minor position. He produced an elegy on the death of Cromwell, yet when Charles II ascended the throne Dryden greeted the new ruler with a congratulatory poem, *Astraea Redux* (1660). After the Restoration he turned his main interest to drama, collaborating with Sir Robert Howard on one heroic play. He married Lady Elizabeth Howard, Sir Robert's sister, in 1663, a marriage which brought him a generous dowry and eventually three sons.

Determining to become a professional man of letters, Dryden devoted most of his energy to writing plays for the London stage. In 1668 he was appointed poet laureate, a position he held for twenty years, until after the Glorious Revolution of 1688. During this term he received a two-hundred-pound annual stipend, later increased to three hundred when he became historiographer royal, but irregularly paid. His greatest efforts remained with drama until the late 1670s, when he turned his efforts to poetic satire. With events surrounding the Popish Plot posing a threat to the government of Charles II, Dryden wielded his pen in the Tory cause, writing satires, translations, and religious poems. Initially he carried the field for the king, but after the fall of James II and the loss of his political cause, he also lost the laureateship and its accompanying pension.

During the final period of his life, 1688 to 1700, he made a brief return to the theater but devoted most of his considerable energy and talent to translation, achieving success with his patrons and public. Although his unpopular political and religious positions kept him out of official favor, in his final decade he produced some of his best verses. He died in London on May 1, 1700.

Influence

Grounded in the classics by education and thoroughly knowledgeable about French literature of his time, Dryden sought to apply the principles of neoclassicism to English literature of the Elizabethan period and the Restoration. Accepting the assumptions about literature inherent in neoclassicism, he applied its terms and rules to the practices of English authors. Yet as a moderate neoclassicist, he often found it necessary to question the extent to which rules apply to literary composition. Dryden's most influential criticism arises from his efforts to evaluate earlier poets and dramatists, to define genres, or to break new critical ground as in providing, for example, definitions of "wit" or a theory of translation.

Analysis

In his eighteenth-century biography of John Dryden, Samuel Johnson wrote, "Dryden may be properly considered as the father of English criticism, as the writer who first taught us to determine upon principles the merit of composition." By this he meant, among other things, that Dryden was the first Englishman to produce a cohesive body of literary criticism applying neoclassic principles to literary works. Although writers such as Sir Philip Sidney and Ben Jonson had previously left significant critical works, Dryden was the first to write criticism as a matter of course over a long career. From the French dramatist Pierre Corneille, he derived the precedent of attaching critical prefaces to his published plays, and he expanded the practice to poetry and translations as well. Yet, as George Watson has noted, whereas Corneille wrote his prefaces for a collected edition long after the plays were written, Dryden produced his critical prefaces to accompany the initial publication of the plays. Among English critics before the twentieth century, literary historians rank him as one of the five greatest, along with Ben Jonson, who preceded him, and Samuel Johnson, Samuel Taylor Coleridge, and Matthew Arnold, who followed him.

Dryden's range of critical topics is extensive, reflecting his own varied literary practice. In the early criticism, until about 1680, he concerned himself almost exclusively with drama. After 1680 the emphasis gradually shifts to subjects such as satire, biography, translation, the epic, and forms of lyric poetry. Essentially, his critical writings are occasional, intended to explain to the reader the work that he was engaged in at the time. Except for *Of Dramatic Poesy: An Essay* (1668), the only critical work he issued as a separate publication, all of his major criticism takes the form of dedications, prefaces, or addenda to other literary productions. In addition to these, Dryden's letters and poetry, notably the prologues and epilogues, contain significant critical commentary and reflection. The occasional nature of the criticism results in a central focus of the essays upon practical purposes – to explain to the reader his current objectives, to point out strengths, to acknowledge weaknesses, and to anticipate and answer objections from literary adversaries.

Yet the thrust and content of the essays are influenced by more than Dryden's purpose of informing the reader. A major element is the critical controversies which surface with regularity throughout his long career and are reflected in the criticism. Among the more significant are those with his brother-in-law Sir Robert Howard over the desirability of rhymed verse in heroic tragedy, with Thomas Shadwell over the Jonsonian comedy of humors, with the Duke of Buckingham over heroic plays, and with Jeremy Collier over the dramatist's ethical responsibility. To a considerable extent, Dryden's critical views developed through adversarial relationships with patrons, fellow dramatists, and poets; the essays reflect Dryden's efforts to defend his point of view and to discredit those of his adversaries.

Yet the most pervasive influence on Dryden's critical theory and practice was neoclassicism. Like other neoclassic writers of the seventeenth century, he accepted certain basic assumptions about literature. He believed that classical authors had established the important literary genres and had brought them, if not to perfection, at least to a level of excellence that assured their survival over time. Thus, in the view of Dryden and his contemporaries, study of ancient practice offered the best guidance to those who sought to re-create these genres in the vernacular literature of modern nations. Further, through study one might formulate the rules which guided classical writers and apply them to the production and evaluation of modern works. Neoclassic critics attempted to derive rules of composition from early Greek and Roman authorities such as Aristotle and Horace. Like the other neoclassicists, Dryden was heavily influenced by Horace's *Ars poetica* (c. 17 B.C.; *The Art of Poetry*), a work brimming with useful advice to practicing poets. It is the most frequently quoted critical source in Dryden's essays. Yet he was also well versed in the writing of such French neoclassic critics of the seventeenth century as René Rapin, René Le Bossu, *père*, Pierre Corneille, and Charles de Saint-Évremond.

Neoclassic influence is most apparent in Dryden's use of literary terms and in his firm sense of genre. Throughout his criticism, one encounters the familiar neoclassical terminology, derived largely from Horace – "nature," "art," "delight," "instruction," "decorum," and "dramatic unities" of time, place, and action, and numerous others. His sense of genre was derived in part from his assumption that modern literature should reproduce the classical genres. Thus it was to be expected that he would seek to define each genre, and in fact he produced numerous definitions, some of them highly tentative. Biography is "a history of particular men's lives"; satire is "undoubtedly a species" of heroic poetry; a play "ought to be a just and lively image of human nature, representing its passions and humours, and the changes of fortune to which it is subject, for the delight and instruction of mankind." From the definition of a genre, Dryden often proceeded to discuss, formally or informally, its parts and conventions and to measure his own performance in the light of these, somewhat in the manner of Corneille. He sometimes included a formal extended analysis of a work, as he did with Ben Jonson's *Epicoene: Or, The Silent Woman* (1609) in *Of Dramatic Poesy* and his own *Troilus and Cressida: Or, Truth Found Too Late* (1679) in "The Grounds of Criticism in Tragedy," (1679).

Among the neoclassic critics of his time, however, Dryden was a moderate. While he acknowledged the primacy of the classics, he thought it possible that modern writers might surpass the Greeks and Romans. Although he upheld the efficacy of rules, he often defended modern writers who disregarded them. The Elizabethan dramatists, as Dryden observed, had produced works that pleased over a long period of time, works that violated rules such as the dramatic unities. Except for Ben Jonson, most Elizabethan playwrights had composed as if the rules did not exist. In defense of the Elizabethans' departure from precedent, Dryden argued that the rules, rather than representing indispensable guides, were additional ornaments or beauties in a drama. The writer who ignored them yet succeeded with the audience might well have discovered a new way of pleasing. (John Fletcher, for example, while violating the dramatic unities, pleased the audience by developing the theme of romantic love more effectively than the ancients had done.) When faced with departures from rules, Dryden was inclined to seek offsetting merit in order to explain a work's appeal. He followed the same inclination when he ignored the rules in his dramas. An alternative tactic was to argue that genius cannot be bound by rules, that some touches of art transcend the rules – a concession found in Horace's *The Art of Poetry*. While Dryden rarely challenged the validity of neoclassic rules, he did on one occasion point out that the unity of place is not to be found in Aristotle's *De poetica* (c. 334–323 B.C.; *Poetics*), and in the later criticism he became increasingly flexible in the application of rules.

Where rules and theories did not exist, Dryden sought to discover and establish them, often extending neoclassic principles to genres that critics had previously ignored. An excellent case in point is the art of translation, which received much of Dryden's attention late in his career. Dryden classified translations as "metaphrase" (literal), "paraphrase" (close to the original but implying liberties), and "imitation" (a loose, free translation). He preferred paraphrase, arguing that a translator's main objective should be to convey the author's tone and meaning to a modern audience – to achieve the same effect with the translation that the poet achieved with the original.

Through his defense of English poets and dramatists who wrote irregularly and through his championing of modern literature in the vernacular, Dryden discerned the outlines of British literary history, though they are dimly perceived at best. Long accustomed to seeing parallels or analogies, he found a close analogy between royal and poetic successions, the political kingdom being analogous to the kingdom of letters. As Edmund Spenser succeeded Geoffrey Chaucer, Lord Edward Fairfax, Edmund Waller, and Sir John Denham succeeded Spenser. Chaucer, according to Dryden, fathered English verse, Spenser refined it, and Denham and Waller brought it to perfection. When he considered the long history of drama, Dryden preferred an analogy to mythical ages. The Elizabethan dramatists are compared to the giant race before the Flood, while Dryden's own age usually is viewed less favorably. Dryden's sense of history represents more a mode of perceiving reality than a settled literary history; decades would pass before a clear sense of English literary history began to take shape.

In spite of his previous emphasis upon rules and conventions, the tone of Dryden's criticism is tentative, as if he were unwilling to speak with authority. His most significant critical work, *Of Dramatic Poesy*, was called an "essay," as Dryden notes, to stress its tentative, skeptical nature. Written in the form of a Socratic dialogue, it introduces four speakers, each an advocate for the drama of a different age or nation: Crites, arguing for classical drama; Lisideius, for French; Eugenius, for Elizabethan; and Neander, for contemporary English. Although there are no clear winners in the debate, Dryden's spokesman, Neander, is represented somewhat more favorably than the others. The tentative and exploratory tone of the work adumbrates an important element in Dryden's criticism, his receptivity to change, a quality consistent with his concern with practical matters rather than a systematic theory. When Dryden uses terms such as "wit," "fancy," and "decorum," their meanings are not always consistent; they vary depending upon the context.

Dryden also altered his views on larger issues. On the use of rhymed verse in drama, he initially supported it as an additional ornament that heightens style, then opposed it as tedious and artificial. He vacillated about instruction or pleasure (delight) as the primary end of literature and about whether the epic or tragedy is the greater literary form. When translating Virgil, he assured the reader that Virgil's genius is most suitable to his own, only to discover later that Homer's fiery imagination was more in accord with his own spirit. Dryden's enthusiasm for the project at hand contributed to such changes, yet his criticism lacks the rigor of a well-ordered theoretical approach.

If theoretical consistency is not among his strongest points, the reason is that Dryden did not accord it the highest priority. Among his definitions of genres and terms, there is one of criticism, "a standard of judging well; the chiefest part of which is, to observe those excellencies which should delight a reasonable reader." It was Dryden's special gift as a critic that he could identify an author's unique characteristics and describe them clearly, so as to convey a sense of individual merit. The most memorable passages in the critical writings are those which evaluate the strengths of eminent writers – Homer, Virgil, Lucretius, Ovid, Horace, Juvenal, and Persius among the ancients and Geoffrey Chaucer, William Shakespeare, Ben Jonson, and John Fletcher among the moderns. In these passages, rejecting analysis of single works, Dryden seeks to clarify the essence of a writer's genius, often treating poets in pairs for the sake of comparison and contrast. In his preface to *The Fables* he included a lengthy tribute to Chaucer, the "father of English poetry," "a perpetual fountain of good sense," a writer whose greatest strength lay in his creation of character:

> He must have been a man of a most wonderful comprehensive nature, because . . . he has taken into the compass of his *Canterbury Tales* the various manners and humours . . . of the whole English nation in his age. Not a single character has escaped him. All his pilgrims are severally distinguished from each other; and not only in their inclinations, but in their very physiognomies and persons. . . . The matter and manner of their tales, and of their telling, are so suited to their different educations, humours, and callings, that each of them would be improper in any other mouth. Even the grave and serious characters are distinguished by their several sorts of gravity: their discourses are such as belong to their age, their calling, and their breeding; such as are becoming of them, and of them only. Some of his persons are vicious, and some virtuous; some are unlearned, or (as Chaucer calls them) *lewd*, and some are learned. Even the ribaldry of the low characters is different: the Reeve, the Miller, and the Cook, are several men, and distinguished from each other as much as the mincing Lady Prioress and the broad-speaking, gap-toothed Wife of Bath.

Insightful and generous evaluations such as this are a hallmark of Dryden's criticism, and he was the first Englishman to produce memorable and well-phrased tributes to Chaucer and Shakespeare in a critical context.

Yet the most enduring value of Dryden's criticism may lie in his own prose style, appearing at its best in critical essays such as the preface to *The Fables* (1700). Informal but not familiar, personal but never embarrassing, Dryden takes the reader into his confidence and candidly explains the work that follows his preface or dedication. Even in the essays written in old age, he gives the impression of a mind that is supple, tolerant, engaging, and growing. The prose is rhythmic, fluent, idiomatic, digressive, and adorned with images, metaphors, and similes. Even though the emotional range is limited, the style rewards the reader with its richness and variety.

Principal criticism

Epistle dedicatory of *The Rival Ladies*, 1664
Preface to *Annus Mirabilis*, 1667
Of Dramatic Poesy: An Essay, 1668
"Defence of *An Essay of Dramatic Poesy*," 1668
Prologue to *Secret Love: Or, The Maiden Queen*, 1668
Preface to *An Evening's Love: Or, The Mock Astrologer*, 1671
Epilogue to *The Second Part of "The Conquest of Granada,"* 1672
"Defence of the Epilogue," 1672
"Of Heroic Plays: An Essay," 1672
"The Author's Apology for Heroic Poetry and Poetic Licence," 1677
Preface to *All for Love*, 1678
Preface to *Troilus and Cressida*, 1679
"The Grounds of Criticism in Tragedy," 1679
Preface to Ovid's *Epistles*, 1680
Dedication of *The Spanish Friar*, 1681
Preface to *Albion and Albanius*, 1685
Preface to *Sylvae*, 1685
Dedication of *Examen Poeticum*, 1693
A Discourse Concerning the Original and Progress of Satire, 1693
"A Parallel of Poetry and Painting," 1695
Dedication of *The Aeneis*, 1697
Preface to *The Fables*, 1700
"Heads of an Answer to Rymer," 1711

Other major works and literary forms

If one follows the practice of literary historians and assigns John Milton to an earlier age, then John Dryden stands as the greatest literary artist in England between 1660 and 1700, a period sometimes designated "the Age of Dryden." In addition to his literary criticism, he excelled in poetry, drama, and translation. He wrote or coauthored more than twenty-five plays, including tragedies, heroic plays, tragicomedies, comedies of manners, and operas.

Among his approximately two hundred English poems, Dryden produced significant satires such as *MacFlecknoe* (1682) and *Absalom and Achitophel* (1681–1682), memorable odes such as the two St. Cecilia's Day odes, "A Song for St. Cecilia's Day" (1687) and *Alexander's Feast: Or, the Power of Music* (1697), and many popular prologues and epilogues. He often achieves his best poetic effects, marked by deliberative reasoning in heroic couplets, in passages from panegyric poetry, verse epistles, and verse essays.

For every verse of original poetry Dryden wrote, he translated two from another poet. In addition, he translated two long volumes of prose from French originals – Louis Maimbourg's *Histoire de la Ligue* and Dominique Bouhours' *La Vie de Saint François Xavier* – and had a hand in the translation of Plutarch's *Lives* published by Jacob Tonson in 1683. The translations were usually well received, especially the editions of Juvenal and Persius (1693) and of Virgil (1697).

PLAYS
The Wild Gallant, 1663
The Indian Queen, 1664 (with Sir Robert Howard)
The Rival Ladies, 1664
The Indian Emperor: Or, The Conquest of Mexico by the Spaniards, 1665
Secret Love: Or, The Maiden Queen, 1667
Sir Martin Mar-All: Or, The Feign'd Innocence, 1667 (with William Cavendish, Duke of Newcastle; adaptation of Molière's *L'Étourdi*)

The Tempest: Or, The Enchanted Island, 1667 (with Sir William Davenant; adaptation of William Shakespeare's play)
An Evening's Love: Or, The Mock Astrologer, 1668 (adaptation of Thomas Corneille's *Le Feint Astrologue*)
Tyrannic Love: Or, The Royal Martyr, 1669
The Conquest of Granada by the Spaniards, Part I, 1670
The Conquest of Granada by the Spaniards, Part II, 1671
Marriage à la Mode, 1672
The Assignation: Or, Love in a Nunnery, 1672
Amboyna: Or, The Cruelties of the Dutch to the English Merchants, 1673
Aureng-Zebe, 1675
The State of Innocence, and Fall of Man, 1677 (libretto; dramatic version of John Milton's *Paradise Lost*)
All for Love: Or, The World Well Lost, 1677
The Kind Keeper: Or, Mr. Limberham, 1678
Oedipus, 1678 (with Nathaniel Lee)
Troilus and Cressida: Or, Truth Found Too Late, 1679
The Spanish Friar: Or, The Double Discovery, 1680
The Duke of Guise, 1682 (with Lee)
Albion and Albanius, 1685 (libretto; music by Louis Grabu)
Don Sebastion, King of Portugal, 1689
Amphitryon: Or, The Two Socia's, 1690
King Arthur: Or, The British Worthy, 1691 (libretto; music by Henry Purcell)
Cleomenes, the Spartan Hero, 1692
Love Triumphant: Or, Nature Will Prevail, 1694
The Secular Masque, 1700 (masque)
Dramatick Works, 1717
The Works of John Dryden, 1808 (18 volumes)

POETRY
Heroic Stanzas, 1659
Astraea Redux, 1660
"To My Lord Chancellor," 1662
Prologues and Epilogues, 1664–1700
Annus Mirabilis, 1667
Absalom and Achitophel, Part I, 1681
Absalom and Achitophel, Part II, 1682 (with Nahum Tate)
MacFlecknoe, 1682
Religio Laici, 1682
Threnodia Augustalis, 1685
The Hind and the Panther, 1687
"A Song for St. Cecilia's Day," 1687
Britannia Rediviva, 1688
Eleonora, 1692
"To My Dear Friend Mr. Congreve," 1693
Alexander's Feast: Or, The Power of Music, 1697
"To My Honour'd Kinsman, John Driden," 1700

TRANSLATIONS
Ovid's Epistles, 1680
The History of the League, 1684 (of Louis Maimbourg's *Histoire de la Ligue*)
The Life of St. Francis Xavier, 1688 (of Dominique Bouhours' *La Vie de Saint François Xavier*)
The Satires of Juvenal and Persius, 1693
The Works of Virgil, 1697

Further reading

Ade[illegible]hn M. *The Critical Opinions of John Dryden*, 1963.
Frost, William. *John Dryden: Dramatist, Satirist, Translator*, 1988.
Hammond, Paul. *John Dryden: A Literary Life*, 1991.
Hume, Robert D. *Dryden's Criticism*, 1970.
Huntley, Frank L. *On Dryden's "Essay of Dramatic Poesy,"* 1951.
Ker, W. P., ed. *Essays of John Dryden*, 1961 (2 volumes).
Miner, Earl Ray. *John Dryden*, 1972.
Pechter, Edward. *Dryden's Classical Theory of Literature*, 1975.
Wasserman, George Russell. *John Dryden*, 1964.
Watson, George, ed. *Dryden: "Of Dramatic Poesy" and Other Critical Essays*, 1962 (2 volumes).
Winn, James A. *John Dryden and His World*, 1987.

STANLEY ARCHER

See also Addison; Neoclassical Literary Theory; Pope

Joachim du Bellay

French critic, poet, and translator

Born: Château de la Turmelière, Anjou, France; 1522
Died: Paris, France; January 1, 1560

Biography

Joachim du Bellay was born in the Château de la Turmelière in the French province of Anjou; modern research suggests that he was born in 1522. His was an ancient if not wealthy noble family. Both of his parents died when he was nine or ten years old, and his older brother René was entrusted with his upbringing. Joachim would later complain that his brother had not taken the responsibility of giving him a solid education very seriously. Sometime in his early twenties, however, Joachim enrolled at the University of Poitiers, where he studied Latin and the law and developed a deep admiration for classical culture.

In 1547 he met the poet Pierre de Ronsard and also began to study Latin and Greek literature at the Parisian Collège de Coqueret. The college's principal was the eminent Humanist Jean Dorat, to whom du Bellay would dedicate *La Deffence et illustration de la langue françoyse* (1549; *The Defence and Illustration of the French Language*, 1939). During his two years of intensive study in Paris, du Bellay learned both Italian and Greek and read Latin and Greek masterpieces from the classical period to the late medieval period. Although his relationship with his brother René was never very positive, he did have three cousins whose influence on his career was significant; these cousins were all important prelates. One, the Cardinal de Langey, who died in 1543, was also a Latin poet. Cardinal Jean du Bellay was a learned classicist, who invited Joachim in 1553 to serve as his French and Latin translator at the Vatican. For four years, Joachim du Bellay worked in Rome, saw the surviving architectural monuments from imperial Rome, and experienced at first hand the presence of Latin culture in his world. In October, 1557, he returned to Paris, where he obtained a position with yet another cousin, Eustache du Bellay, then the Archbishop of Paris. Unfortunately, Joachim's health worsened during 1558, and by 1559 he had become almost completely deaf. He was already in very poor health when he suffered a fatal stroke and died in Paris on January 1, 1560.

Influence

Although du Bellay wrote only one work of literary criticism, it is difficult to overestimate the importance and influence of *The Defence and Illustration of the French Language*. In this short but thoughtful book, du Bellay argued that the systematic study of the classics should enable French writers to enrich both the language and the cultural life of France. He described eloquently the values of French civilization and presented practical suggestions for those seeking to develop a rich and pleasing style of writing. He explained in great detail how the creative imitation of the classics should enable his compatriots to produce literary and philosophical works in French as significant as those composed in Latin during the classical era and by such early Christian writers as Saint Jerome and Saint Augustine. Du Bellay encouraged the French to be justly proud of their native culture and of their subtle and complex language.

Analysis

Du Bellay's *The Defence and Illustration of the French Language* has remained a problematic work since it was published in 1549. Certain scholars cannot reconcile in their own minds du Bellay's ardent defense of classical learning with his insistence that French authors write in their own tongue. Other critics are surprised that du Bellay, an apologist for the French language, composed so many original poems in Latin and Greek. Some believe that du Bellay chose not to implement in his own poetry the basic arguments developed in his only theoretical work.

Many commentators have interpreted *The Defence and Illustration of the French Language* very narrowly. In 1904, for example, the eminent Renaissance specialist Pierre Villey demonstrated that du Bellay had translated into French selected passages from a 1542 book in which Italian writer Sperone Speroni had encouraged his countrymen to compose their creative works in Italian and not in Latin. Villey may have correctly identified a previously unknown source for *The Defence and Illustration of the French Language*, but he underestimated the profound significance and meaning of du Bellay's book.

Although du Bellay did make use of many contemporary sources, his book is original. He analyzed systematically two interrelated elements of literary composition and described both proven techniques for developing a mature style in any language and imaginative ways of imitating respected authors in order to produce thoroughly creative and personal literary works. There is a definite unity in du Bellay's *The Defence and Illustration of the French Language*. As its very title suggests, this theoretical book "defends" and "illustrates" the value and relevance of classical culture for du Bellay's compatriots.

Numerous eloquent apologies for classical learning were written during the sixteenth century both in Latin and in the vernacular languages throughout Europe. Du Bellay's *The Defence and Illustration of the French Language* contains several direct references to two influential defenses of classical learning by Desiderius Erasmus. These works were Erasmus' 1512 textbook of rhetoric *De duplici copia verborum ac rerum* (*On the Twofold Abundance of Words and Things*, 1978) and his 1528 dialogue *Dialogus, cui titulus Ciceronianus, sive, de optimo dicendi genere* (*The Ciceronian*, 1986). In the earlier work, Erasmus showed that the careful study of the Latin language and culture could enable students to expand their vocabulary, refine their style, and learn how to present moral arguments persuasively and elegantly. In *The Ciceronian*, Erasmus examined correct and inappropriate ways of imitating respected authors. Like Erasmus, du Bellay criticized Christophe de Longueil, a fanatical Ciceronian who strove to exclude from his Latin style all words not recorded in Cicero's extant works. Du Bellay agreed with Erasmus that such servile imitation is unworthy of a mature person; one should rather rely on a vast understanding of classical literature in order to develop an eloquent personal style.

Du Bellay divided his defense into two books. The first half of this work is theoretical in nature, while the second deals with the art of composing French verse. He begins this work by affirming that all languages are inherently equal and attributes the greater richness of certain languages to the "industry" and "diligence" of the native speakers of these languages. In addition, he encourages his compatriots to imitate the classical Romans, who enriched the Latin language and literary traditions by transforming the best elements of Greek culture into the Roman view of the world.

The seventh and eighth chapters in the first book express succinctly du Bellay's belief in the importance of Latin culture for any attempt to enrich the French language and literary traditions. Du Bellay affirmed that learned Roman authors such as Cicero and Virgil had "digested the rarest and most exquisite virtues" of Greek philosophy and literature and then had "converted" these Greek models into a literary style which was "fitting and appropriate" for each writer's personality and for the subject matter which the writer wished to present to his or her readers. Greek pastoral poetry inspired Virgil to give a new and eloquent meaning to this conventional poetry in his *Georgics* (c. 37–29 B.C.) and *Eclogues* (43–37 B.C.; also known as *Bucolics*). The study of Greek oratory taught Cicero how to develop effective arguments in his speeches before the Roman Senate and tribunals. Virgil and Cicero interpreted Greek literature in ways that had never occurred to the poets and orators whom they imitated.

Du Bellay hoped that his compatriots would imitate Latin writers as imaginatively as Virgil and Cicero had imitated the Greeks. Profound social and religious changes had taken place between the first century B.C. in Rome and the European Renaissance. It would be foolish to write like the fanatical Longueil, who believed that nothing worthwhile had been produced in European literature since Cicero's death. Cicero and Virgil were, after all, pagans, while Renaissance societies in Europe adhered to the Judeo-Christian religious and ethical value systems. Thus it was necessary to adapt respected works from classical Rome to the sensibilities and beliefs of the modern world. Du Bellay believed that the creative imitation of classical literature would help his compatriots to enrich the cultural life of Renaissance France.

Near the end of the first book of *The Defence and Illustration of the French Language*, du Bellay presents two cogent arguments. He affirms that it is haughty to believe that one can equal or surpass classical Roman authors by writing in Latin. He also states that one can write naturally and eloquently only in one's mother tongue. Although the rare genius such as Joseph Conrad is able to write extremely well in a language he first learns as an adult, du Bellay's contention remains true for most writers.

Regretting that many French Renaissance thinkers felt compelled to compose their philosophical treatises in Latin and not in French because of their conviction that French lacked many abstract terms essential for philosophical discussions, he admits the partial validity of this attitude. Nevertheless, he advises French thinkers to create French equivalents for Latin philosophical and technical terms so that no Frenchman will feel ill at ease while writing in French. Du Bellay desired to enrich his country's language so that all ideas could be expressed eloquently and naturally in it.

In the second book, du Bellay reaffirms his conviction that natural talent by itself "does not suffice for a poet wishing to create a work worthy of immortality." A genius who lacks solid erudition may well produce sentimental and ephemeral literary works which will not interest and challenge readers from other cultures. Du Bellay believes that an effective French poet must combine a solid understanding of classical poetry with a mastery of the techniques of French poetry. He cites approvingly Cicero's belief that new ideas and inventions require the creation of new words, arguing that the gradual increase of the French vocabulary will enable writers to describe fully the complexity of ever-changing society. Several chapters in the second half of du Bellay's work illustrate how a learned poet can compose poems of true originality within the apparently restrictive French poetic conventions. Du Bellay ends his defense first by exhorting the French to write in their mother tongue and then by praising several contemporary French poets whose verses illustrated the excellence and rich potential of their language.

Du Bellay's *The Defence and Illustration of the French Language* was the most influential theoretical book written on poetry in sixteenth-century France. This work is much more than an important document in the history of French literary criticism; with an eloquence matched only by Erasmus during the sixteenth century, du Bellay described both the profound importance of classical learning for the modern world and the very nature of poetic creativity and originality within an established poetic tradition.

Principal criticism

La Deffence et illustration de la langue françoyse, 1549 (*The Defence and Illustration of the French Language*, 1939)

Other major works and literary forms

Although Joachim du Bellay died at the age of thirty-seven, he was an extremely prolific lyric poet, translator, and literary critic. Like his eminent contemporary, and close friend, the poet Pierre de Ronsard, du Bellay sought inspiration in the literary traditions of both classical Greece and Rome. Du Bellay's mastery of Greek and Latin was so thorough that he composed original poems in both of those languages. During his short life, he wrote three significant sonnet sequences. Although the well-crafted sonnets in *L'Olive* (1549; the olive) are stylistically impressive, they are primarily refined imitations and often elegant translations of love poems by Petrarch and Ludovico Ariosto.

During his four-year residence in Rome as the French and Latin secretary for his cousin, Cardinal Jean du Bellay, he developed into an original and creative poet. In 1557 he returned to Paris, and his sonnet sequences *Les Regrets* (*The Regrets*, 1984) and *Les Antiquitez de Rome* (the antiquities of Rome) were published in 1558. In *The Regrets*, du Bellay expressed keen insight into an exile's feelings as he longs for his homeland and its cultural life. In *Les Antiquitez de Rome*, du Bellay reflected on the profound meaning of classical culture for modern writers and poets.

POETRY

L'Olive, 1549
Les Regrets, 1558 (*The Regrets*, 1984)
Les Antiquitez de Rome, 1558
Les Divers Jeux rustiques, 1558

TRANSLATION

Le Quatrième Livre de l'Eneide traduict en vers françoys, 1552 (partial translation of Virgil's *Aeneid*).

Further reading

Chamard, Henri. *Joachim du Bellay: 1522–1560*, 1900.
Clements, Robert J. *Critical Theory and Practice of the Pléiade*, 1942.
Coleman, Dorothy Gabe. *The Chaste Muse: A Study of Joachim du Bellay's Poetry*, 1980.
Demerson, Geneviève. *Joachim du Bellay et la belle romaine*, 1996.
Keating, L. Clark. *Joachim du Bellay*, 1971.
Langer, Ullrich. *Divine and Poetic Freedom in the Renaissance*, 1990.
Meerhoff, Kees. *Rhétorique et poétique au seizième siècle en France: Du Bellay, Ramus et les autres*, 1986.
Merrill, Robert. *The Platonism of Joachim du Bellay*, 1970.
Tucker, George H. *The Poet's Odyssey: Du Bellay and the Antiquitez de Rome*, 1990.

Edmund J. Campion

See also Malherbe; Renaissance and Restoration Literary Theory

E

Terry Eagleton

English critic, writer, and editor

Born: Salford, England; February 22, 1943

Biography

Terry Eagleton was born on February 22, 1943, in Salford, England. His father, Francis Eagleton, was an engineer on what was then the largest factory shop floor in England. Eagleton was educated at local schools and at the University of Cambridge, where he worked with Raymond Williams and became a Fellow in English. He was married for ten years, between 1966 and 1976. In 1969 he became Fellow in English at Wadham College, Oxford. Since 1992 he has been Thomas Warton Professor of English at Oxford. He has been a visiting professor at several universities throughout the world and has lectured at a variety of public institutions, including schools and working men's clubs.

Influence

Eagleton has effectively renovated what was a vestigial Marxist critical tradition in Britain. He influenced Marxist theorists such as Fredric Jameson (for example, in the latter's concept of the "political unconscious") and kindled reaction from liberal humanist antitheorists, Marxist and non-Marxist critics alike. Throughout his canon he has entered, in a strikingly broad and persistent manner, into a critical dialogue with both past and contemporary literary and cultural criticism. He has launched powerful arguments for the necessity of both literary theory and socialist criticism.

Analysis

Eagleton ranks among the major Marxist cultural theorists of the twentieth century. His intellectual and political development falls into three, or perhaps four, phases. His journey toward historical materialism effectively began at Cambridge University in the 1960s. Here, under the influence of Williams, he reacted against the prevailing critical orthodoxies of the New Criticism (with its treatment of the literary text as autonomous, dissevered from moral, historical, and political elements) and especially those inspired by F. R. Leavis' liberal humanism. This reaction is evident in Eagleton's first book, *The New Left Church*, which attempts to reconcile Roman Catholicism with socialist humanism; the feasibility of such a synthesis was in part given ideological sanction by the ecumenical and modernistic spirit of the Vatican Council of the 1960s. Again, Eagleton's subsequent *Shakespeare and Society* treats William Shakespeare's work not as autonomous but as inseparable from fundamental social issues. In this first phase of his activity, Eagleton became for a short time the editor of the left-wing Christian journal *Slant*.

Eagleton's next phase, announced by the publication of *Criticism and Ideology* and the expository work *Marxism and Literary Criticism* in 1976, marked both his abandonment of his Catholic socialist humanism and the formulation of an approach that would have a broad impact on the practice of literary criticism. In this approach, even the expository text is subjected to a resolute contextualization and demystification of "liberal bourgeois humanist" notions: that art somehow "transcends" its time, that it can be "explained" by individual psychology, that the artist is a "creator," and that aesthetics is merely a question of "style." Eagleton shows how a Marxist criticism tries to grasp "forms, styles and meanings as the products of a particular history" and even individual psychology as a social product. The artist, moreover, does not "create" from nothing, but rather "produces": his or her starting materials are to a large extent given, and he or she participates in the production of forms that are determined ultimately by their historical and ideological content. At this stage, Eagleton viewed artistic form, itself "a way of perceiving social reality," as comprising a complex unity of three elements: a "relatively autonomous" literary history of forms, certain dominant ideological structures, and a specific set of relations between author and audience. "Ideology," which elsewhere in Eagleton's work is treated in an extraordinarily complex and subtle manner, he defined in these years as "the way men live out their roles in class society, the values, ideas and images which tie them to their social functions and so prevent them from a true knowledge of society as a whole."

Having examined the diversity of Marxist criticism, Eagleton rejected the Hegelian Marxist tradition, of which Georg Lukács is the major representative. Lukács' ideological demand that a literary text be properly "realist," that it re-create a totality shattered by the configurations of capitalism (with its separation of general and particular, conceptual and sensuous, social and individual), is, in Eagleton's eyes, more Hegelian than Marxist. It is a demand which led Lukács dogmatically to denounce what he himself had termed the fragmented, alienated "ontological image" of humanity in modernist texts. Eagleton prefers Pierre Macherey's view of the text as "decentered" form, exposing ideological contradictions through what it fails to say (its "absences") and its incompleteness of structure. Eagleton also expresses sympathy with Walter Benjamin's assertion of the need for a "revolutionary" art, as exemplified in the openness and fragmentedness of Brechtian theater, which, by its "alienation effect," defamiliarizes experience previously accepted as "natural" by the audience.

In this second phase, Eagleton accomplished the major task of articulating with immense subtlety the foundational categories of a materialist aesthetics. During this period, Eagleton was influenced (though by no means uncritically) by Louis Althusser, particularly with regard to the epistemological break between the earlier "humanistic" and later "scientific" attitudes which Althusser claimed to have found in Karl Marx's work — hence Eagleton's view that "criticism must break with its ideological prehistory, situating itself outside the space of the text on the alternative terrain of scientific knowledge." He launched a sustained critique of that prehistory, especially of Leavis' liberal humanist project as enshrined in his journal *Scrutiny*, as well as of Williams' achievements and deficiencies in the light of the absence of a revolutionary critical tradition in England.

Eagleton formulated materialist categories (such as general and literary modes of production and general, authorial, and textual ideologies) out of his detailed scrutiny of the relations between literary text and ideology. His notion of ideology is derived from Macherey (cited as "the first Althusserian critic"): the text produces ideology rather than reproducing or reflecting it. For Eagleton, the object of the text is not history but ideology. So, as with the performance of a play, the text is effectively the production of a production: it "produces" already produced ideological representations of reality into an imaginary object. Fiction, for example, does not represent imaginary history, but an ideological experience of real history. Its ultimate signifier and signified is history, but this fact is only apparent to criticism, not in the text itself. Eagleton rejects both Althusser's view of ideology as homogenous and Macherey's characterization of ideology as somehow "illusory": what the text, through criticism, "reveals" depends on the character of the ideology in conjunction with the transmutative operations of the literary form. There subsists, moreover, an internal relation between text and ideology; the text's "truth" is not an essence, but the practice of its relation to ideology and ideology's relation to history.

Eagleton's Althusserian phase in the 1970s was inspired, as he himself was to reflect, by "a major revival of radical political activity in Western society as a whole." Within such a political milieu, Althusser's work had yielded key theoretical concepts such as the relative autonomy of superstructures; in its "scientific" antihumanism, it appeared politically revolutionary. The third phase of Eagleton's writing, however, was marked by a break with, or at least a far more critical attitude toward, Althusserian Marxism. That this change corresponds with a new focus on Benjamin's work is itself symptomatic of a shift in Eagleton's stance toward the relatively autonomous possibility of Marxist theory. Inspired by the antihistoricism inherent in Benjamin's attitude toward bourgeois history, an approach which advocates "blasting open" and demystifying the bourgeois continuum so as to redeem the past for revolutionary purposes, Eagleton seems no longer to be searching for a unity or coherence internal to theory; instead, coherence must be a function of the very internality of relation between theory and political practice. As Eagleton has it, in "altered political conditions" offering dwindling opportunities for radical politics, trapped between "essentialistic notions of social totality" and "an equally ineffectual politics of the fragment or conjuncture" (both of these being variants of bourgeois ideology), critics cannot hope to resolve theoretical dilemmas without further developments in political history. This view is reminiscent of Marx's own analyses of German ideology. Yet Eagleton in this phase produced a series of intricate, if avowedly provisional, dialogues between his own Marxism and other contemporary movements in literary-cultural theory.

There are those, such as Richard Aczel, who view Eagleton's engagement with non-Marxist literary theory as entailing a compromising "strategic" relativism and pluralism. "Strategic," in the spirit of Benjamin, is an acceptable (and desirable) descriptor. The charge of compromise, however, is unjustified. Eagleton has embraced only those aspects of deconstructionist, psychoanalytic, or structuralist theory which either already overlap with Marxist theory or can subserve the extrapolation of Marxist analysis into traditionally unexplored realms. The unconscious, for example, can itself be a site of ideological struggle; the "always already written" of Jacques Derrida, or Jacques Lacan's "Other," can be translated into the "historical conditions of possibility," since historical (including unconscious and linguistic) determination is already an implicit deconstruction of the self-identity of any entity, as shown by G. W. F. Hegel. Eagleton, it should be said, has little sympathy with those of Derrida's acolytes who indulge in an unbridled play of the signifier, an unrestrained dance of semantic plurality; what he does share is Derrida's own view that "truth" is institutional. Eagleton distinguishes, moreover, between the "right" and "left" interpretations or uses of deconstruction.

Eagleton's brilliantly argued *Literary Theory* offers a coherent statement of his own theoretical position regarding non-Marxist theory. His invaluable achievement here, as in other works, has been to show from a balanced and sane perspective how the historical and ideological conditions of such theory yield an understanding of its significance and its limitations. A strategic integration of perspectives informs Eagleton's penetrating studies of individual writers such as Samuel Richardson and Shakespeare. In his second study of the latter, Shakespearean intimations of the vulnerable arbitrariness of human order and of personal values made ironic by cosmic indifference are placed within a poststructuralist paradigm of general signifying systems being subverted by particular utterances. Characterizing Shakespeare as a "conservative patriarch," Eagleton sees his political ideology as productively disrupted by the subversive energies of his language.

Eagleton's treatment of recent critical trends places them in the context of the entire history of modern criticism. In *The Function of Criticism*, he argues that modern bourgeois criticism emerged through a "public sphere" of rational consensus. This sphere gradually disintegrated and criticism finally committed "political suicide" when it was institutionalized in the nineteenth-century universities. Leavis' *Scrutiny* and other projects attempted belatedly to re-create the public sphere. The New Criticism's "disinterested" objectivism "mimed the reifying habits of industrial capitalism even as it resisted them." Reacting against that literary autonomy, modern literary theory has nevertheless merely continued to displace attention from criticism's social function. Deconstruction, for example, abolishes the classical liberal hypostatization of the subject, but only at the expense of abolishing that subject as a political agent. In fact, a truly socialist criticism cannot even exist until a counter public sphere has been created. The most striking contemporary possibility of such a sphere, according to Eagleton, is contained in feminist discourse and practice, the women's movement having reformulated the connection between public and "intimate" (family) spheres. For Eagleton, the critic's role is a traditional one: to move beyond an isolated concern with the text and to reconnect signifying practices (in literature and culture at large) with political practice, in a struggle against the bourgeois state.

If there can be said to be a fourth phase of Eagleton's work, this is marked perhaps by a dual impetus: to refocus critical attention on Marxist categories and concepts which have been rapidly slipping into disuse, abuse, and oblivion; and to continue his insistence on the genuinely radical power of Marxist thinking as opposed to the more fashionable critical trends which are often accommodated and domesticated by the academic establishment, trends whose radicalism remains largely gestural. Eagleton has addressed this dual concern in a number of ways: by revisiting the history of aesthetics; by intervening in the historiography of a particular culture; and by reclaiming for Marxist analysis central concepts such as ideology. What emerges in Eagleton's later work is the urgency of the task of dissociating Marxist discourse from other discourses whose surface radicalism threatens to drown it as just one other, and almost silent, voice among the endless liberal cacophony of ideological voices. Perhaps his broadest aim here is to reinstate the meaning and value of the category of the political, by reaffirming the pervasively overridden connections between what is called "theory" and political context or agency.

In *The Ideology of the Aesthetic*, which is in theoretical terms the most substantial of his later works, Eagleton examines the history of the aesthetic from the Earl of Shaftesbury, David Hume, and Edmund Burke through a German tradition including Immanuel Kant, Friedrich Schiller, G. W. F. Hegel, Friedrich Nietzsche, and Sigmund Freud to Martin Heidegger, Walter Benjamin, Theodor Adorno, and postmodernism. Affirming in general that the emergence of the aesthetic as a theoretical category occupies an increasingly central position in the dominant discourses at the heart of bourgeois hegemony, he argues specifically that this emergence is closely interwoven with material processes whereby cultural and artistic production becomes autonomous. This newly emergent discourse was centrally concerned with elaborating such autonomy and provided the middle class with an ideological model of subjectivity for its material operations. The aesthetic effectively furnished a prototype of subjectivity in early capitalist society. The same process, however, laid the foundation for various forms of opposition to bourgeois utility and rationalism, enabling a creative turn to the sensuous body.

The theme of ideology is subjected to a more sustained rigorous examination in *Ideology: An Introduction*. Eagleton suggests that postmodernism's anti-representationalism, epistemological skepticism, and neo-Nietzschean realignment of the relations between rationality, influence, and power have conspired to discredit the classical concept of ideology. His own book aims to clarify the notion of ideology via a historical examination of its modern history; it also aims thereby to make a political intervention. Eagleton concludes by insisting on the complexity and historical variability of ideology; he resists essentialist accounts, both Marxist and non-Marxist, which reduce ideology through rationalism, psychologism, historicism, or objectivism to any kind of determinate structure or effect with invariable characteristics. In even more polemical vein, Eagleton's *The Illusions of Postmodernism* examines critically the genesis, assumptions, and contradictions of postmodernism, especially in relation to rationality, human subjectivity, epistemology, and history.

Within Eagleton's broad-fronted challenge to both conservative thought and pseudo-radical dispositions, two further kinds of contribution are particularly worth mentioning. The first is exemplified by Eagleton's *Heathcliff and the Great Irish Hunger*, which marks an attempt to intervene in Irish historiography on the premise that Irish history needs to be inserted into the discourse of cultural theory, a procedure for which it is peculiarly and dialectically appropriate given that the realities of class, state, revolution, and material production, so often glided over in modern cultural theory, have been central to Irish experience. The second type of contribution is contained in Eagleton's persistent endeavor not only to rewrite literary and cultural history from a left-wing perspective, but to encourage such rewriting as a concerted political endeavor by editing texts which treat a broad range of authors and themes.

As charted above, Eagleton's influence and contribution span five broad areas: the establishment of Marxist categories of literary-cultural analysis; a critical engagement with, and historical contextualization of, other recent critical trends; a persuasive argument for the need for theory; a revaluation of critical tradition and a redefinition of the critic's function; and the analysis of specific authors from a Marxist standpoint. The subtlety, range, and courage of Eagleton's enterprise may, through increasing recognition, elevate him to that distinction which he himself reserved for Raymond Williams: the single most important critic of postwar Great Britain.

Principal criticism

The New Left Church, 1966
Shakespeare and Society: Critical Studies in Shakespearean Drama, 1967
Exiles and Émigrés: Studies in Modern Literature, 1970
Myths of Power: A Marxist Study of the Brontës, 1975
Criticism and Ideology: A Study in Marxist Literary Theory, 1976
Marxism and Literary Criticism, 1976
Walter Benjamin: Or, Towards a Revolutionary Criticism, 1981
The Rape of Clarissa: Writing, Sexuality, and Class Struggle in Samuel Richardson, 1982
Literary Theory: An Introduction, 1983
The Function of Criticism: From "The Spectator" to Post-structuralism, 1984
Against the Grain: Essays, 1975–1985, 1986
William Shakespeare, 1986
Nationalism, Colonialism, and Literature, 1990 (with Fredric Jameson and Edward Said)
The Ideology of the Aesthetic, 1990
Ideology: An Introduction, 1991
The Crisis of Contemporary Culture, 1993
Heathcliff and the Great Hunger: Studies in Irish Culture, 1995
The Illusions of Postmodernism, 1996
Crazy John and the Bishop and Other Essays on Irish Culture, 1998

Other major works and literary forms

In addition to the works cited above, Terry Eagleton has written numerous essays and reviews on topics ranging from literary criticism through modern art to philosophy. A writer and performer of political and satirical songs, Eagleton also wrote a musical drama, *Brecht and Company*, performed at the Edinburgh Festival in 1979, as well as a novel, *Saints and Scholars*, published in 1987. Further accomplishments include a volume entitled *St. Oscar and Other Plays* (1997), and a television play commissioned by British television, filmed by Derek Jarman, and published as *Wittgenstein: The Terry Eagleton Script: The Derek Jarman Film* in 1993. Like his other creative works, these plays are rich in intellectual content, transgressing what Eagleton calls "the jealously patrolled frontiers between 'art' and 'ideas.'"

NOVEL
Saints and Scholars, 1987

PLAYS
Brecht and Company, 1979
St. Oscar and Other Plays, 1997

FILM
Wittgenstein: The Terry Eagleton Script: The Derek Jarman Film, 1993

NONFICTION
The Body as Language: Outline of a "New Left" Theology, 1968

EDITED TEXTS
From Culture to Revolution: The Slant Symposium, 1968 (with Brian Wicker)
Directions: Pointers for the Post-Conciliar Church, 1968
Hard Times, by Charles Dickens, Methuen English Texts, 1988
Raymond Williams: Critical Perspectives, 1989
Plays, Prose Writings and Poems, by Oscar Wilde, Everyman's Library Series, Vol. 42, 1991
Marxist Literary Theory: A Reader, 1996 (with Drew Milne)

MISCELLANEOUS
Regan, Stephen, ed. *The Eagleton Reader*, 1998

Further reading

Aczel, Richard. "Eagleton and English," in *New Left Review*. CLIV (November/December, 1985), pp. 113–123.
Anderson, Perry. *English Questions*, 1992.
Bennett, Tony. *Formalism and Marxism*, 1979.
Kimball, Roger. "The Contradictions of Terry Eagleton," in *The New Criterion*. 9, no. 1 (September, 1990), pp. 17–23.
Nakano, Yukito. "Terry Eagleton as Critic," in *Studies in English Language and Literature*. 37 (March, 1987), pp. 27–51.
Selden, Raman. *A Reader's Guide to Contemporary Literary Theory*, 1985.
Slaughter, Cliff. *Marxism, Ideology, and Literature*, 1980.
Wood, James. "Terry Eagleton in Conversation," in *Poetry Review*. 82, no. 1 (Spring, 1992), pp. 2–7.

M. A. R. Habib

See also Althusser; Benjamin; Gramsci; Jameson; Lukács; Marxist Theory and Criticism; Williams

Umberto Eco

Italian writer, semiotician, and critic

Born: Alessandria, Italy; January 5, 1932

Biography

Umberto Eco began his career as the cultural editor for Italian Radio-Television and an assistant lecturer at the University of Turin. Following the publication of his first two books on medieval aesthetics and his marriage to Renate Ramge on September 24, 1962, Eco held faculty appointments at a number of Italian universities, lecturing first in aesthetics, then in architecture and visual communications, and, since the late 1960s, semiotics. In addition to founding a journal, *VS*, devoted to semiotics, Eco has held visiting professorships in the field at a number of European and American colleges and universities and has lectured on the subject throughout the world. The publication of his novel *The Name of the Rose* in 1980 brought Eco unexpected fame outside the community of semioticians and James Joyce scholars and, in addition to a host of literary prizes, an even wider platform from which to make his case for semiotics.

Influence

Eco's voice has proved to be one of the most influential in the rapidly growing field of semiotics – the interpretation, or "decoding," of signs and symbols – and as a result in those areas, such as literary and cultural studies, in which semiotics has begun to exert its importance. Eco's influence has, however, been a rather complex matter. Within the field of semiotics as a scholarly discipline, his has been a double achievement. On the one hand he has managed to summarize much of what has gone before and on the other hand to build upon that summary, to advance the field by a process of fine-tuning. Further, Eco manages to be comprehensive without pretending to be definitive; he leaves semiotics replenished but still incomplete, still in search of its final word. His considerable achievement derives from these characteristics as well as from his willingness to advance the study of semiotics on several fronts simultaneously: the theoretical and the practical (especially in his semiotic studies of literary works), and the academic and the popular, where he has sought to make his highly specialized field both accessible and understandable to nonspecialists.

Analysis

Eco began his academic career as a medievalist, but interesting and important as his early studies *The Aesthetics of Thomas Aquinas* and *Art and Beauty in the Middle Ages* may be, his most significant and influential work has been in the field of semiotics. As a semiotician, Eco has devoted much of his work to formulating a theory of general semiotics and, therefore, to answering those questions that the very idea of such a theory immediately raises: can so many diverse phenomena as are present in a culture in fact be approached and understood semiotically? Does semiotics constitute a unified discipline or, rather, a field of studies having similar interests but not amenable to consolidation under one theoretical banner? Can the study of semiotics be considered truly scientific?

Eco answers the first two questions in the affirmative and supports his position with a detailed theory of codes and sign production. For all the closeness of his argument, he nevertheless rejects the claim that semiotics is an exact science, for semiotics is not and cannot be objective. Semiotic analysis contaminates its subject in that semiotics and the semiotician do not stand outside, objectively detached, observing what occurs within the semiotic field but instead stand within the field itself, caught in the same web. The semiotician cannot hope to be scientifically detached, but he can become pragmatically aware of his own limitations. Eco's pragmatic approach leads him to posit two additional limitations, one at each end of the semiotic spectrum. The first is that although the aim of semiotics is to study the whole of culture, not everything in a culture is a sign (everything in a culture can, however, be taken as a sign). The second limitation is that although the reasons behind the human urge to produce signs may be tremendously important and may eventually become the subject of semiotic inquiry, such reasons lie outside the field as Eco defines it, for the subject of semiotics is not metaphysics but, instead, semiosis: the production and interpretation of signs.

The semiotician's first problem is how to define the sign. The linguist Ferdinand de Saussure's bifurcation of the sign into two parts, the signifier (the word "red," for example) and the signified (the color red), constitutes a more precise formulation of the classical philosophers' *aliquid stat pro aliquo* (this stands for that), but it has the unfortunate result of reducing the sign to a matter of simple correspondence open to recognition, rather than interpretation, on the part of the sign user. Louis Hjelmslev's division of the sign into expression and content planes is less precise but more useful in defining the sign's complexity. Better still is Charles Sanders Peirce's triadic definition of the sign as "something which stands to somebody for something in some respect or capacity" or, alternately, "something by knowing which we know something more."

Whereas Saussure's sign implies the existence of an actual antecedent object (a word, thing, idea, or person), Peirce's does not, for the "sign" as such is replaced by the "sign function." Instead of the recognition of meaning dependent upon the sign user's ability to isolate discrete semiotic units (signifier and signified), there is for Peirce and for Eco a sequentially irreducible and theoretically limitless process of interpretation, in which (to put the matter as simply as possible) a sign includes the idea (interpretant) to which it gives rise, an idea that in turn becomes a sign, open to the same interpretive process of "unlimited semiosis" of which the final sign, theoretically speaking, would be the entire semantic field.

Semiosis – that is, the interpretive process of "decoding" – is not, however, a matter of simple, linear causality. It entails a process of recognition and invention operating according to a semiotic version of Werner Heisenberg's uncertainty principle, in which every semiotic act alters the semiotic universe in some unforeseen way. The interpreter may understand, or decode, the word "red" by drawing from a storehouse of correlated decodings ("red" equals fire, danger, passion). The process is not nearly so mechanical, however, for the interpreter not only draws from the semantic storehouse, but also adds to it. The decoding process does not involve a system of eternally fixed rules or correlations so much as it resembles a field of play, or associations, in which the rules may be observed, revised, combined, or even disregarded. Against this rather open, even chaotic prospect, Eco posits his "pragmatic perspective": unlimited semiosis is enacted within the context of the social world of real speech acts, of culturally produced and culturally interpreted signs whose meanings are at once fixed, open, and arbitrary.

The meaning of a sign is not a matter of simple correlation; nor is it a matter of some essential but inexpressible connection between sign and meaning that can only be intuitively grasped. For Eco, there are not inherent essences in the world of semiotics, only transitory couplings within the semantic field of interpretive possibilities. Meaning is, therefore, nothing more (and nothing less) than "the site of a combinatorial interplay" which results from the imposition of a rule, or code, "upon the indeterminacy of the source." The word/sign "red," for example, may be fixed, but its meaning is plural – the result of a potentially infinite number of inferential interpretive acts. The code is a set of arbitrary and often vague rules used to make possible the inferences which constitute a sign's meaning. Inference, not correlation, is at the center of semiotics. Any decoding "x is y" either falsifies or metaphorizes the semiotic process unless one understands that the coupling verb "is" serves not to equate but as "a metalinguistic device." It is a shorthand way of identifying the entire interpretive process of disambiguation in which "to decode" means "to interpret," that is, to infer, to hypothesize. Peirce termed such an interpretive hypothesis an abduction, which Eco explains as "the tentative and hazardous tracing of a system of signification rules which will allow the sign to acquire its meaning."

Just as no sign (and no code) exists in isolation, no message is either simple, or simply itself, but instead is "a network of different messages depending on different codes and working at different levels of signification." In other words, a sign vehicle conveys a message that is in semiotic fact a text, a maze of intertwined meanings, or of possible meanings. A sign as simple as "He follows Marx" requires that the interpreter perform a number of decodings. If "Marx" equals (is decoded as) "Karl Marx," then "follows" equals "is a disciple of" rather than "walks behind." Such a sign nevertheless includes its own punning ambiguities. "Marx" may be "Karl" or "Groucho" (or Harpo or Zeppo). In the case of this particular example, context will very likely pragmatically determine the sign's, and the sentence's, "correct" meaning.

Yet most (perhaps all) signs, Eco believes, remain ambiguous and therefore open to interpretation. They invite, even require the interpreter's active participation in the decoding process. Unlike signals, signs do not send instructions to be followed (the smoke which activates a smoke detector) but messages to be interpreted, and interpretation necessitates the making of choices.

Eco's semiotic maze resembles the intertextuality that Julia Kristeva identified in her seminal essay on Mikhail Bakhtin and that has since become a fact of life in poststructuralist critical theory. Disambiguation of the sign occurs within the theoretical frame of intertextuality, within, that is to say, the entire semantic universe of the sign user, a universe that itself resembles an encyclopedic labyrinth of meanings rather than a regulative dictionary of precisely coded correlations. The coexistence of and necessity for both correlations and inferences leads to the conclusion that codes involve a double action, simultaneously narrowing and broadening the semiotic search for a sign's meaning.

Eco's metaphoric conceptualizing of the semiotic field as a labyrinthine encyclopedia – or as an encyclopedic labyrinth – leads as if inevitably to his peculiar but convincing analysis of metaphor as a cognitive instrument which, contrary to the common view, develops by means of metonymic additions to a sign's interpretive possibilities that are invented as the poet (the metaphor-maker) scans the entire semantic field for useful material, rather than metaphoric substitutions which are the result of the poet's heightened perception of (essential) correlational similarities. Thus, Robert Burns' love is like a red, red rose as the result of a fortuitous coupling which the poetic code of Burns' day made possible but did not foresee. As Eco explains, metaphor as a cognitive tool involves the invention of "combinatory possibilities or semantic couplings not anticipated by the code." The inventing as well as the interpreting of metaphors epitomizes the entire – and entirely arbitrary – semiotic process and thus undermines the poetic definition of the metaphor as an intuitive leap of the imagination, which imagination Eco defines not as the evidence of romantic genius but instead as "nothing other than a ratiocination that traverses the paths of the semantic labyrinth in a hurry and, in its haste, loses the sense of their rigid structure." By violating the code, the imagination enriches the code's possibilities.

The semiotic process that metaphor epitomizes exists in a similarly foregrounded, though much more extensive, form in those texts which Eco terms aesthetic and which serve as "the structured model for an unstructured process of communicative interplay." Useful as Eco's discussions of such texts are for the clarification of his semiotic theory, these discussions serve another and perhaps more important purpose. They serve to clarify the ways in which such texts – especially, though not exclusively, prose narratives – affect the reader and are affected by (or perhaps effected by) the reader, whose role in the interpretive, and therefore creative, process has been one of Eco's most significant subjects of inquiry, the results of which have proved far more penetrating than those found in much of the reader-response literary criticism produced since the 1960s. "The maze-like structure" of James Joyce's *Finnegans Wake* (1939) serves as the most extreme and therefore the most apparent instance of the underlying structure of every aesthetic text and indeed of every sign (itself a micro-text), in that the purpose of the one and the effect produced by the other are in fact identical: to "stimulate reactions" rather than to "communicate contents." Such a generalization requires some refinement, however, for not all texts are created equal. "Closed" texts – Superman comics, for example, and James Bond novels – attempt to elicit a fairly specific response from the reader. (Paradoxically, the mind-deadening redundancy of closed texts opens them to any number of readings, that is, decodings, that may be considered "aberrant" insofar as they are neither planned nor foreseen by the author of the text, that is, the sender of the message.) Ian Fleming's 007 novels, for example, constitute a kind of aesthetic "machine," which produces a set of precise narrative units whose manufacture is governed by rigorous combinatorial rules which allow the permutation and interaction of a limited number of fairly simple oppositions (such as Bond-villain, Bond-woman).

At the opposite extreme of the aesthetic spectrum lie those texts that Eco terms "open" and in which the reader's interpretation is made a significant part of the author's compositional and narrative strategy, a strategy that exploits the very principle which governs both the generation and interpretation of any text, aesthetic or not. (This includes deconstruction, which Eco faults for paying insufficient attention to the ways a given text both invites *and* limits interpretation.) Open texts are indeterminate, discontinuous, inexhaustible in movement, and without any one privileged point of view (least of all the "author's") from which the message may be decoded. Most important, open texts require the reader's participation (as does any sign) in order that they may be completed, though such completion must be understood as being at best provisional in the reading of a truly open work. Paradoxically, the openness of the open text is itself closed in that these texts invite only a certain kind of response, or interpretive insertion, from the reader. Open texts leave no room for the aberrant readings that closed texts so unwittingly and promiscuously invite.

Eco also confidently believes that "it is possible to distinguish between the free interpretive choices elicited by a purposeful strategy of openness and the freedom taken by a reader with a text assumed as a mere stimulus." His demonstration of this hypothesis in *The Role of the Reader* is convincing, but whether it can be applied so readily to more ambiguously open texts – as Roland Barthes demonstrates in his semiotic reading of a seemingly closed (or what Barthes calls a "readerly") text – remains to be seen. Much more certain is the fact that Eco's open text is an expanded sign to be disambiguated by a reader whose cooperation is, as Jonathan Culler has pointed out, provoked by "the manipulative strategy of a scheming author." The author is, as the reader is, a textual strategy rather than an actual person; each exists in order to achieve the role of the semiotic other.

Eco's own role as scheming author manipulating his hapless but nevertheless happy reader is especially evident in *The Name of the Rose* and *Postille a "Il nome della rosa"* (1983; *Postscript to "The Name of the Rose,"* 1984), which he wrote as if to explain the novel, but in effect to mock all such efforts to impose the closure of correlation on so open a text. The result is a postscript that takes the form of a Peircean interpretant, which in turn becomes a sign in need of an interpretant, and so on, in precisely the kind of semiotic daisy chain in which Eco the novelist and Eco the theorist take such delight. The playfulness that marks the novel, its postscript, and the numerous articles he has written for Italian newspapers and magazines evidences itself in his more scholarly critical writings as well. His sense of play has, however, its own serious purpose: to undermine the high seriousness of both abstract theory and of all final interpretive solutions. His sense of play thus supports his pragmatic approach to the paradoxical openness of the semiotic world, cheerfully trapped in its own semiotic workings ("semiosis explains itself by itself") and closed off from the consolations of metaphysical speculation.

Against the immense breadth of his learning and the scope of his semiotic theory, Eco posits a sense of not only his own limitations but those of semiotics itself. Together they form the beginnings of what will likely prove his most lasting legacy as a critic: a paradoxical sense of boundless limitations, a world theory – and a theoretical world – each open to its own incompletion and to Eco's own brand of rigorous semiotic play.

Principal criticism

Il problema estetico in San Tommaso, 1956 (*The Aesthetics of Thomas Aquinas*, 1988)
Sviluppo dell'estetico medievale, 1959 (*Art and Beauty in the Middle Ages*, 1986)
Opera aperta, 1962
Opera aperta, la definizione dell'arte, 1968
La struttura assente, 1968
Le forme del contenuto, 1971

A Theory of Semiotics, 1976
The Role of the Reader: Explorations in the Semiotics of Texts, 1979
Semiotics and the Philosophy of Language, 1984
The Limits of Interpretation, 1990
Interpretation and Overinterpretation, 1992 (with Richard Rorty and Jonathan Culler)
La ricerca della lingua perfetta nella cultura europea, 1993 (*The Search for the Perfect Language*, 1995)
Sei passeggiate nei boschi narrativi, 1994 (*Six Walks in the Narrative Woods*, 1994)

Other major works and literary forms

Umberto Eco has written extensively for Italian newspapers and magazines on a wide variety of subjects which, in one way or another, deal with his semiotic approach to culture and his cultural approach to semiotics. Several book-length selections of these short pieces have been translated into English, beginning with *Travels in Hyper Reality* (1986). Eco has also written three novels which, despite their complexity and erudition, have proved enormously popular. The first of these, the critically acclaimed *Il nome della rosa* (1980; *The Name of the Rose*, 1983), was translated into more than twenty languages, became an international best-seller, and has been made into a major motion picture (1986). In addition to writing his own books, this prolific author and polymath has edited many others, including a pictorial history of inventions, a collection of Chinese comics, and a book on Agent 007, James Bond.

NOVELS
Il nome della rosa, 1980 (*The Name of the Rose*), 1983)
Il pendolo di Foucault, 1988 (*Foucault's Pendulum*, 1989)
L'isola del giorno prima, 1994 (*The Island of the Day Before*, 1995)

FICTION FOR YOUNG READERS
La bomba e il generale, 1966 (*The Bomb and the General*, 1989)
I tre cosmonauti, 1966 (*The Three Cosmonauts*, 1989)

NONFICTION
Diario minimo, 1963 (*Misreadings*, 1993)
Le poetiche di Joyce: Dalla "Summa" al "Finnegans Wake," 1966 (*The Aesthetic of Chaosmos: The Middle Ages of James Joyce*, 1982)
Postille a "Il nome della rosa," 1983 (*Postscript to "The Name of the Rose,"* 1984)
Sette anni di desiderio: Chronache 1977–1983, 1983
Travels in Hyper Reality: Essays, 1986
Faith in Fakes, 1986
Le isole del tesoro, 1988
Le dimensioni dell'infinito = Les Dimensions de l'infini, 1989
Apocalypse Postponed, 1994
Il secondo diario minimo, 1992 (*How to Travel with a Salmon and Other Essays*, 1994)
Serendipities: Language and Lunacy, 1998

EDITED TEXTS
Storia figurata delle invenzioni: Dalla selce scheggiata al volo spaziali, 1961 (with G. Zorzoli; *The Picture History of Inventions from Ploughs to Polaris*, 1963)
Il caso Bond, 1965 (with Oreste del Buono; *The Bond Affair*, 1966)
The People's Comic Book: Red Women's Detachment, Hot on the Trail, and Other Chinese Comics, 1973 (with J. Chesneaux and G. Nebiolo)
A Semiotic Landscape, 1979 (with Seymour Châtman and Jean-Marie Klinkenberg)
Sign of the Three: Dupin, Holmes, Peirce, 1984 (with Thomas A. Sebeok)
Bologna 1088–1988, 1988
Meaning and Mental Representations, 1988 (with Marco Santabroglio and Patrizia Violi)
On the Medieval Theory of Signs, 1989 (with Constantino Marmo)

Further reading

Cannon, JoAnn. *Postmodern Italian Fiction: The Crisis of Reason in Calvino, Eco, Sciascia, Malerba*, 1989.
Coletti, Theresa. *Naming the Rose: Eco, Medieval Signs, and Modern Theory*, 1988.
Culler, Jonathan D. *On Deconstruction: Theory and Criticism After Structuralism*, 1982.
Hawkes, Terence. *Structuralism and Semiotics*, 1977.
Inge, M. Thomas, ed. *Naming the Rose: Essays on Eco's "The Name of the Rose,"* 1988.
Innis, Robert E. *Semiotics: An Introductory Anthology*, 1985.
Martin, Jorge Hernandez. *Readers and Labyrinths: Detective Fiction in Borges, Bustos, Domecq, and Eco*, 1988.

ROBERT A. MORACE

See also Calvino; Narratology; Semiotics

Leon Edel

American biographer, critic, and editor

Born: Pittsburgh, Pennsylvania; September 9, 1907
Died: Honolulu, Hawaii; September 5, 1997

Biography

Leon Edel was born on September 9, 1907, in Pittsburgh, Pennsylvania. In 1927 and 1928 he received his B.A. and M.A. degrees from McGill University in Montreal, Canada. In 1932 he received a Litt.D. degree from the University of Paris. He served with the United States Army in France and Germany from 1943 to 1947 and was decorated with the Bronze Star. He was also Chief of Information Control, News Agency, in the United States Zone from 1946 to 1947.

Edel's academic career began in 1932 as an assistant professor at Sir George Williams College in Montreal, but after two years he turned to a career as a journalist. After his years in the army, he assumed a series of distinguished academic positions at Princeton University, New York University, Indiana University, the University of Hawaii, Harvard University, Purdue University, and Dartmouth College.

Edel was the recipient of major academic and literary awards, including a Guggenheim Fellowship and a Bollingen Fellowship. In addition to numerous honorary degrees, he was awarded several distinguished literary prizes, including the National Institute of Arts and Letters Award (1959), the National Book Award for nonfiction (1963), the Pulitzer Prize in biography (1963), and the National Arts Club Medal for Literature (1981).

Influence

Edel is regarded as one of the foremost literary biographers of the twentieth century. He earned his reputation through his innovative multivolume biography of Henry James and his consistent arguments over many years for a sophisticated biographical method. He was an ardent advocate for applying the insights of modern psychology to the study of literature and of writers' lives. No critical account of modern biographical writing would be complete without a discussion of Edel's theory and practice of literary biography, and many recent studies and collections of essays on the nature of biography contain contributions by him or about his impact on what he called "the writing of lives."

Analysis

Throughout his career as a biographer and biographical theorist, Edel maintained that biographers must strive for excellence of literary form. A fine biography must have a pleasing aesthetic shape, a concrete delineation of human character, and an economical approach to the biographical subject that reveals the most telling details of a life. In short, modern literary biography must model itself after the novel in order to achieve a vivid and deeply penetrating study of the subject's life.

The biographer should aspire to be an artist, Edel insists. What is most important is that the "central myth" of the writer's life be revealed. Edel's contention is that there is a unified shaping vision by which the creative artist lived, and the biographer must discover and dramatize that vision. As a literary critic, Edel showed that the themes of a writer's life and writing are inevitably intertwined. This does not mean that all creative work is autobiographical, but it does mean, according to Edel, that all art arises from deeply personal feelings: "We know that all literature is a form of disguise, a mask, a fable, a mystery: and behind the mask is the author," he writes in the foreword to *Stuff of Sleep and Dreams*.

Edel's theory of literary biography is best understood by considering an example from his work on Henry James. In his condensed and revised version of the biography, *Henry James: A Life*, Edel provides a remarkably succinct and insightful summary of one of James' finest and most intricate novels, *The Ambassadors* (1903), that at the same time is a profound revelation of James' own psyche. The novel is told from the point of view of Lambert Strether – in Edel's words, "a middle-aged 'ambassador' sent out" to Europe to retrieve a young American male who has apparently been seduced by the Old World charms of a mature woman. The novel is as much about Strether's acculturation as it is about the young man's presumed debauchery. Edel focuses on two key scenes that reveal Strether's developing realization that in Europe the young man has had the opportunity to grow and to fulfill himself. Concomitantly, Strether recognizes that he has not himself managed to live life to the fullest. Insulated from the choices Europe has offered this young man, Strether has to admit that he has never pursued his own desires or developed his own talents. In sum, he has never been free, and his decision is to allow this young man – in many ways Strether's younger self – the liberty to choose his own life.

At the conclusion of his remarks on *The Ambassadors*, Edel notes that "beyond 'technique' and its resourceful experiments, beyond its near symmetrical design, the care with which it is 'composed' . . . spoke for the central myth of Henry James's life." That myth has to do with leaving the United States as a young man for the richer life of Europe, not an easy choice for James, who had to struggle with what Edel calls the "authority figures" of his Puritan past. James, in other words, had to reverse the very direction of his family history, the movement from Europe to America, and contend that a return to Europe was, in fact, a liberating decision. All the terror, the uncertainty, and the anguish – and also the charm, the boldness, and the creativity – of James' commitment to a life in Europe are dramatized in the character of Lambert Strether. Edel's own artistry as a biographer is revealed in his emphasis on the word "composed" to speak for both James' novel and his life. The novel is not autobiography in the sense of reproducing the events of James' life, but it is his life in the most profound, psychological sense.

In all of his writing on biographical theory, Edel was careful to point out that he was not psychoanalyzing the writer; that is, Edel was not claiming to know James' innermost thoughts or to be engaging in a scientific analysis of the writer's maladies. Edel was no doctrinaire follower of Sigmund Freud, the founder of modern psychoanalysis. Still, he was impressed with Freud's analyses of the patterns of people's lives and of those crucial moments in which truths about their lives are revealed.

In *Stuff of Sleep and Dreams*, Edel defines his terms. He favors the phrase "literary psychology" to distinguish his method from "other psychologies that are concerned with treating the neuroses and pathological conditions of mental health. In other words, literary psychology is criticism and biography divorced from psychotherapy." In the same book, in a chapter entitled "The Nature of Psychological Evidence," Edel enumerates the "three postulates" he has taken from psychoanalysis. First, he believes that there is such a thing as the unconscious that manifests itself in human behavior, "in dreams, in imaginings, thoughts." Second, within this unconscious are "certain suppressed feelings and states of being which sometimes emerge into awareness in the consciously created forms of literature." Finally, "by the process of induction – that is, by examining the mental representation in words of things not present to the senses – we can detect deeper intentions and meanings, valuable both to the biographer and the critic."

Edel insists that the biographer work with facts and with evidence. His biography of James is the distillation of a massive amount of material on the writer's life and work that includes diaries, journals, notebooks, letters, and various accounts of James' life by himself and by others. As Edel often said, the biographer is not free to imagine facts, but he is charged with inventing a form that makes the most profound sense of his subject's life.

It was perhaps inevitable with a great writer such as James, who lived a long, productive life, and whose archive continues to grow with newly discovered letters and many other materials, that Edel was forced to write a lengthy, multivolume biography. Nevertheless, the size of the James biography would seem to contradict Edel's strictures about precision and economy in the writing of lives. Edel tacitly acknowledged this discrepancy between his theory and practice by revising and rewriting his biography twice – in two volumes in 1977, and then in one volume in 1985. Each time he did more than cut wordage: he added newly discovered material and, with the aid of editors, reshaped the entire biography.

In the latest edition of the James biography, Edel also responded to "the changes that have occurred in biographical writing and in social attitudes toward privacy and our sexual lives." It is not that he went in search of James' "sex life," Edel pointed out, but rather that he abandoned "former reticences" and "proprieties" of an earlier age. He also acknowledged the fact that his earlier edition of the biography was written "out of respect for surviving members of the James family, and the children of William James."

All these changes that occurred during the course of three decades in Edel's work on Henry James make a fascinating study of how the writing and the discussion of biography have changed. Edel is one of several biographers who have taken bolder positions as literary writers, not merely as compilers of facts. Edel led the way in speculating on the pattern of James' life and in refusing to be bound by conventions that other biographers have treated as sacrosanct. For example, although his life of James is told in chronological fashion, he availed himself of novelistic devices, such as the flashback to earlier events and flashforward to the later events in James' life. The implication of such techniques is that "the facts do not speak for themselves," that the biographer must be an interpreter of evidence and create a structure for it.

While Edel has enormous prestige as a biographer, he has not been immune to criticism. He has been accused of adopting the theories of modern psychology too readily and of shifting the emphasis in biography too far toward novelistic forms of literature. Other theorists of biography have insisted on a strictly chronological approach to biography and have eschewed the use of psychological theory, since the employment of fictional techniques and of psychological speculation reveals, in their view, more about the biographer than the subject of the biography. In the main, however, Edel has remained the principal theorist of biography, whose arguments have been open to challenge but not to significant refutation.

In *Writing Lives*, Edel discusses many of his fellow biographers, especially predecessors such as Lytton Strachey and André Maurois. His chief criticism of them has been their tendency to allow their own personalities to distort the lives about which they have written. In a way, Edel's studies of his precursors constitute a reply to his critics. By studying how Strachey, Maurois, and others have been heir to this tendency, Edel was surely trying to critique his own practice.

The single most important influence on Edel was Strachey. In *Eminent Victorians* (1918), Strachey wrote pithy and provocative studies of Thomas Arnold, Florence Nightingale, General Charles George Gordon, and Cardinal Henry Edward Manning in order to debunk their "eminence." At the same time, Strachey was hailed as an artist for his turns of phrase, his economical use of biographical evidence, and his ability to dramatize human personality and history in essay-length form. Edel did not adopt Strachey's satirical style, but he emulated Strachey's compression of human lives into deft, self-sufficient essays on human character. Indeed, all Edel's work after the James biography, including his study of the Bloomsbury Group, was predicated on the essay form. In this way, he sought to vindicate his view that biography should be to the point; it should be the crystallization of a life, not a long and tedious, if faithful, chronicle of it.

Principal criticism

Henry James, Volume I: The Untried Years, 1843–1870, 1953
The Psychological Novel: 1900–1950, 1955, revised 1964 (as *The Modern Psychological Novel*)
Henry James, Volume II: The Conquest of London, 1870–1881, 1962
Henry James, Volume III: The Middle Years, 1882–1895, 1962
Literary History and Literary Criticism, 1965 (editor)
Henry James, Volume IV: The Treacherous Years, 1895–1901, 1969
Henry James, Volume V: The Master, 1901–1916, 1972
The Life of Henry James, 1977 (2 volumes, revision of the five-volume biography)
Bloomsbury: A House of Lions, 1979
Stuff of Sleep and Dreams: Experiments in Literary Psychology, 1982
Writing Lives: Principia Biographica, 1984
Henry James: A Life, 1985 (revision)

Other major works and literary forms

Leon Edel published several hundred articles, essays, and reviews, primarily in the fields of biographical and literary criticism. Some of his shorter pieces are collected in *Literary Biography* (1957). His concern with the psychological interpretation of lives is reflected not only in his biographies but also in his critical study *The Psychological Novel* (1955, revised 1964).

NONFICTION
James Joyce: The Last Journey, 1947
Willa Cather, 1953
Literary Biography, 1957
Henry D. Thoreau, 1970

EDITED TEXTS
The Complete Plays of Henry James, 1949
Selected Letters of Henry James, 1956
The Complete Tales of Henry James, 1962–1965 (12 volumes)
The Diary of Alice James, 1964
Stories of the Supernatural, 1971
Alphabet of the Imagination, 1975
Henry James: Letters, 1843–1875, 1975
The Twenties: From Notebooks and Diaries of the Period, 1975 (with Edmund Wilson)
The Thirties: From Notebooks and Diaries of the Period, 1980 (with Wilson)
Henry James: Letters, 1875–1883, 1980
Henry James: Letters, 1883–1895, 1981
The Forties: From Notebooks and Diaries of the Period, 1983 (with Wilson)
Henry James: Letters, 1895–1916, 1984
The Fifties: From Notebooks and Diaries of the Period, 1986 (with Wilson)

Further reading

Altick, Richard. *Lives and Letters: A History of Literary Biography in England and America*, 1965.
Petrie, Dennis W. *Ultimately Fiction: Design in Modern American Literary Biography*, 1981.
Powers, Lyall H., ed. *Leon Edel and Literary Art*, 1988.
Rollyson, Carl. *Biography: An Annotated Bibliography*, 1992.

CARL ROLLYSON

See also Ellman; Psychoanalytic Criticism; Wilson

Joseph von Eichendorff

German poet, writer, and critic

Born: Lubowitz Castle, near Ratibor, Silesia; March 10, 1788
Died: Neisse, Silesia; November 26, 1857

Biography

Joseph Freiherr von Eichendorff was born on March 10, 1788, at Lubowitz Castle, the Silesian estate of his parents, as the second child and second son of Adolf von Eichendorff and Karoline von Kloch. Of his five siblings, only his brother Wilhelm, eighteen months older than he, and his younger sister Luise, in her later years a good friend of Adalbert Stifter, survived. Eichendorff's studies at the Gymnasium in Breslau and at the Universities of Halle and Heidelberg were shared by Wilhelm, with whom he practically lost touch after their university years. Eichendorff went into law when it became clear that the family's Silesian estates were floundering economically, and he passed his bar examinations in Vienna with highest honors.

In Heidelberg, Eichendorff associated with a group of Romantic poets and began to publish his own poetry, which changed in tenor and form after he had been exposed to the poetry of Achim von Arnim and Clemens Brentano and their edition of *Des Knaben Wunderhorn* (1805; the boy's magic horn). With the encouragement of Friedrich and Dorothea von Schlegel, Eichendorff finished his first novel, *Ahnung und Gegenwart*, in 1812 in Vienna. His output of both poetry and prose was steady, but, since he was one of the later adherents of a waning literary movement, scant attention was paid to his work.

After a brief time of service in the Prussian army against Napoleon Bonaparte, Eichendorff married Luise von Larisch, with whom he had five children; two died at a very early age. Eichendorff tried to make a career in the civil service, first in Danzig, then in Breslau, and finally in Berlin. There, he belonged to the Mittwochsgesellschaft (Wednesday society), a group of literati which met once a week; its membership included Arnim, Brentano, Adam Müller, and Heinrich von Kleist.

Because he never advanced very far in the hierarchy of the civil service, and because of a lung ailment, Eichendorff was granted an early retirement in 1844. After his retirement he devoted his energies to literary criticism, mainly for the *Historisch-politische Blätter* and other journals. In 1857 Eichendorff died at the age of sixty-nine in the Silesian town of Neisse, where he had made his home for the last two years of his life with his daughter Therese and where his wife had died in 1855.

Influence

Eichendorff's literary criticism was mainly influenced by four prominent poets and thinkers of his time. His profound admiration for Clemens Brentano not only led him to experiment with the same literary forms Brentano used but also confirmed Eichendorff's own adherence to religious tenets, which he then employed as the basis of his literary value judgments. The lectures given at the University of Heidelberg by the philosopher Joseph von Görres and in Vienna by Friedrich Schlegel deepened Eichendorff's understanding of the aesthetics and ethics of literature. Eichendorff began to give expression to his critical opinions on literature after retiring from government service in 1844, at the urging of Karl Ernst Jarcke, a professor in Vienna, whom he had met during his brief visit there in 1838.

Analysis

With the exception of the rather brief early article *Zur Kunstliteratur* (about artful literature), Eichendorff's literary criticism was produced during the period from his retirement in 1844 to his death in 1857. There had already been manifestations of his specific literary judgments in his earlier novelistic writings; one need only point to the ironic mentions of August Lafontaine and Otto von Kotzebue in the early novel *Ahnung und Gegenwart*, the frequent allusions to Johann Wolfgang von Goethe and other contemporary poets in the novel, and the rather abstract thoughts about the nature of poetry that surface in the plot. Friedrich, the young protagonist, is a poet who, after a long worldly quest, enters a monastic order to dedicate his life to religious service. The same course is followed by Victor, the poet in Eichendorff's novel of 1834, *Dichter und ihre Gesellen*, written twenty-two years after *Ahnung und Gegenwart*. Not only is such a development not a contradiction for Eichendorff, it is the only logical possibility in both novels, since the author makes it abundantly clear that he believes religious dedication to be the highest form of poetic sensibility.

When applying for the position of censor in Berlin in 1832, Eichendorff also advertised his broad literary knowledge, apparently unusual for a civil servant. He must have voiced his opinions about contemporary writing unabashedly during the meetings of the literary societies he frequented, in Berlin as well as in Vienna, because it was there that his critical views came to the attention of Karl Ernst Jarcke, an eminent advocate of Catholic journals and publications. It was at the urging of this Viennese professor that Eichendorff began to apply himself seriously to writing down his critical opinions. His first sizable publication, *Zur Geschichte der neueren romantischen Poesie in Deutschland* (history of contemporary Romantic poetry in Germany) consists of three separate articles which had appeared in succession in the journal *Historisch-politische Blätter*, where most of his subsequent shorter pieces were also published. Not only was Eichendorff flattered to have his views taken seriously, but he also found the honorarium paid by the journal "positively brilliant," as he confided in a letter to his son Hermann, who after Eichendorff's death was instrumental in publishing all those works the poet had not let be published in his own lifetime.

Whereas most German poets of the Romantic movement seem to have adopted Catholicism because they saw in it the embodiment of the unity of all life which had existed at its high point, the Middle Ages, Eichendorff was born into this faith. Eichendorff's family was, however, what one would call in German *gut katholisch*, that is, Catholic in a rather conventional sense, content with ritual observations of the teachings of the Church. Eichendorff's own intellectual and emotional adherence to the tenets of Catholicism, however, was rooted in personal experience. The poet and his brother were schooled by a private tutor in their younger years, and the tutor had the habit of reading to them from the Bible. As Eichendorff related in the diary he kept intermittently between 1788 and 1815, after the tutor began to read the story of Christ's Passion the young Eichendorff demanded to be allowed to continue reading it on his own. He was profoundly shaken by the experience, acquiring a deep sense of being implicated in Christ's life, the consequences of which he saw permeating all life on earth. When he began writing, it was only one more deductive step to the conviction that poetry is, not the "sensuous appearance of an idea," as Friedrich Theodor Vischer explicated Eduard Mörike's poem "Auf eine Lampe" ("On a Lamp"), but the "sensuous appearance of the eternal." Eichendorff summarized this view in the introduction to his two-volume work *Geschichte der poetischen Literatur Deutschlands* (history of literature in Germany):

> Poetry is therefore rather the indirect, i.e. sensuous appearance of that which is eternal, always and everywhere significant, while at the same time it is the beautiful as well, shining through a veil of earthly matters. This eternal, significant matter is quite simply religion, and the artistic sense is therefore the indestructible religious sense dwelling in the human breast.

Eichendorff's religious disposition gave him his ethical code and his feeling for the eternal in art, but this disposition went beyond that also to a veritably nationalistic love for home and country. In 1841 Johann Heinrich Gelzer had published *Die deutsche poetische Literatur seit Klopstock und Lessing* (German literature since Klopstock and Lessing), in which poetry is judged from a strictly Protestant and rationalistic point of view, and from 1835 to 1842 Georg Gottfried Gervinus had published the five-volume *Geschichte der poetischen National-Literatur der Deutschen* (History of the national literature of the Germans), in which political views are deemed the most important criteria by which to judge literary value. To a great extent, Eichendorff's writings countered both of these works, since his Catholic viewpoint was strongly antirationalist. Eichendorff took these men to task for their lack of veneration of tradition, flattening out of values, demystification of life, propensity to stress fact over feeling, and passive acknowledgment of a destruction of ethics, in general and within the family and state in particular.

It is not surprising that such a didactic stance did not produce scholarly works of great exactitude; in fact, critics have found many factual errors in Eichendorff's theoretical writings. His temperament and the personal engagement with which he dealt with religious and political problems turned many of his projects into polemical treatises. Eichendorff himself made no claim to impeccable scholarship: he wanted, so he said, to describe "the soul" of Romanticism, noting that the "details" had already been written about by others. Eichendorff's achievement does not lie in new ideas, but rather in the authorial brilliance of his statements and their inner cohesiveness. Some of his greatest work can be seen in his personal readings of his contemporary poets.

In the introduction to *Geschichte der poetischen Literatur Deutschlands* Eichendorff calls religion the "inner history of a nation," distinguishing it from factual historical happenings, which are the "outer or surface history." According to him, only both together can provide a nation with a healthy existence. Poetry, then, is the expression of the inner history of a people. Because of such a view, Eichendorff can, in the first of the three essays which make up this work, call poetic matters of the year 1795 "desperate": he saw the "outer" historical situation in revolutionary disarray and the "inner" as suffering from the effects of the *Sturm und Drang* (literally, "Storm and Stress") movement in German poetry. He gives Gotthold Ephraim Lessing, Johann Georg Hamann, and Johann Gottfried Herder credit for having provided the seeds to a better future, and he excepts Johann Wolfgang von Goethe and Friedrich Schiller from all of this as standing above the general chaos. The second essay delineates the first stirrings of the Romantic movement as a new beginning, dwelling on the dictum by Novalis that only religion can reawaken Europe and on Wilhelm Heinrich Wackenroder's new-found enthusiasm for religious art, while he gives Friedrich Schlegel his due for having proclaimed that faith and knowledge, rent asunder in the eighteenth century, can be reunited again through religion. Finally, the third essay addresses those figures in the Romantic movement who were problematic and, as such, were already moving away from Romanticism proper: Ludwig Tieck ("in his paradisical flowers death is already lurking"), Heinrich von Kleist ("one of the best, but faltering between arrogance and despair"), and Heinrich Heine. Only Adalbert Stifter, although also a figure of waning Romanticism, is praised for his "devout truth of nature."

The most refreshing of Eichendorff's critical works, the one with the least derivative ideas, is *Der deutsche Roman des achtzehnten Jahrhunderts in seinem Verhältnis zum Christentum* (the German novel of the eighteenth century in its relationship to Christianity). To underscore the importance of this genre, Eichendorff juxtaposed the novel with the epic and described them in the following way: "The epic is man in the world, the novel is the world in man." What he wished to extract from the novels, then, was a description of the inner historical changes of his country: "Our task will be the attempt to briefly delineate the history of the ethical and religious changes in the Germany of the last century, as they are hinted at hieroglyphically in our novel." Conversely, *Zur Geschichte des Dramas* (history of the drama) is Eichendorff's most derivative work. Although he knew much about Spanish drama from having translated Pedro Calderón de la Barca's work, he adopted general Romantic notions and treated the history of this genre as *Geistesgeschichte* (intellectual history), not as that of a literary genre.

The work that was Eichendorff's final statement, *Geschichte der poetischen Literatur Deutschlands*, subsumes a reprinting of the earlier monograph, *Über die ethische und religiöse Bedeutung der neueren romantischen Poesie in Deutschland* (the ethical and religious meaning of contemporary Romantic poetry in Germany), and can be seen as the final summation of his literary-critical endeavors. Eichendorff's later critical writings include many personal judgments on his fellow poets, ultimately providing more of a picture of Eichendorff than of the authors about whom he wrote. Eichendorff wrote of Christoph Martin Wieland that he "was the first to free poetics of religion and morals," of Tieck that he had a "secretly demoralizing irony," of Novalis that he adhered to a "certain pantheism," of Ludwig Uhland that his poetry showed his "open return to Protestantism," of Kleist that his was a "poetics of hatred," and of Adalbert von Chamisso that he was "indifferent in religious matters." Only Arnim remained unscathed: "Even though he was and has remained of the Protestant faith, [his work is] much more Catholic in content than that of most of his catholicizing colleagues."

Eichendorff was certainly a well-informed reader and an astute observer of his times. His critical voice, although it cannot be trusted as that of an objective and scholarly observer, adds much to what is known of the heated intellectual discussions during the middle of the nineteenth century in Germany.

Principal criticism

Zur Kunstliteratur, 1835
Zur Geschichte der neueren romantischen Poesie in Deutschland, 1846
Über die ethische und religiöse Bedeutung der neueren romantischen Poesie in Deutschland, 1847
Brentano und seine Märchen, 1847
Die deutsche Salonpoesie der Frauen, 1847
Novellen von Ernst Ritter, 1847
Die neue Poesie Österreichs, 1847
Die geistliche Poesie in Deutschland, 1847
Die deutschen Volksschriftsteller, 1848
Zu den Gedichten von Lebrecht Dreves, 1849
Der deutsche Roman des achtzehnten Jahrhunderts in seinem Verhältnis zum Christentum, 1851
Zur Geschichte des Dramas, 1854
Geschichte der poetischen Literatur Deutschlands, 1857 (2 volumes)

Other major works and literary forms

Joseph von Eichendorff was one of the foremost poets of the Romantic movement in Germany. His lyrics have been set to music by Franz Schubert and Robert Schumann. Eichendorff is counted among the later Romanticists, and his poetry embodies the quintessential traits of that literary movement: he makes a highly symbolic use of the forces of nature and their beneficent and demoniac traits, expressed in forms based on folk song and fairy tale. The term *Waldeinsamkeit* (forest solitude) seems to be synonymous with Eichendorff's name. Eichendorff also wrote two novels, *Ahnung und Gegenwart* (1815; presentiment and the present) and *Dichter und ihre Gesellen* (1834; poets and their companions), the form of which follows Friedrich von Schlegel's desiderata for the novel: a loose structure interspersed by poems and stories connected or unconnected to the plot. Eichendorff wrote many short stories and novellas as well, of which the best known is *Aus dem Leben eines Taugenichts* (1826; *Memoirs of a Good-for-Nothing*, 1866). All Eichendorff's prose writings center on some form of quest: the search for the spiritual essence of the protagonist.

NOVELS
Ahnung und Gegenwart, 1815
Dichter und ihre Gesellen, 1834

SHORT FICTION
Das Marmorbild, 1819 (novella *The Marble Statue*, 1927)
Aus dem Leben eines Taugenichts, 1826 (novella; *Memoirs of a Good-for-Nothing*, 1866)
Viel Lärmen um nichts, 1833 (novella)
Eine Meerfahrt, 1835
Das Schloss Dürande, 1837 (novella)
Die Entführung, 1839
Die Glücksritter, 1841
Das Incognito: Ein Puppenspiel, 1841
Libertas und ihre Freier, 1849
Julian, 1853

PLAYS
Krieg den Philistern, 1824
Ezelin von Romano, 1828
Der letzte Held von Marienburg, 1830
Die Freier, 1833
Robert und Guiscard, 1855 (verse)

POETRY
Gedichte, 1837 (*Happy Wanderer and Other Poems*, 1925)

NONFICTION
Die Wiederherstellung des Schlosses der deutschen Ordensritter zu Marienburg, 1844
Erlebtes, 1857

MISCELLANEOUS
Neue Gesamtausgabe der Werke und Schriften in vier Bänden, 1957–1958

Further reading

Brown, Marshall. "Eichendorff's Times of Day," in *The German Quarterly*. L (1977), pp. 485–503.
Flores, Angel, ed. *An Anthology of German Poetry from Hölderlin to Rilke in English*, 1965.
Forster, Leonard, ed. *The Penguin Book of German Verse*, 1972.
Hillach, Ansgar, and Klaus-Dieter Krabiel. *Eichendorff Kommentar zu den Dichtungen*, 1971.
Niggl, Günter, and Irmgard Niggl. *Joseph von Eichendorff im Urteil seiner Zeit*, 1975.
Peucker, Brigitte. *Lyric Descent in the German Romantic Tradition*, 1986.
Radner, Lawrence. *Eichendorff: The Spiritual Geometer*, 1970.
Schindler, Robert. *Eichendorff als Literaturhistoriker*, 1926.
Schwarz, Egon. *Joseph von Eichendorff*, 1972.

LISELOTTE M. DAVIS

See also Romanticism; Schlegel, F.

Boris Eikhenbaum

Russian theorist

Born: Krasnyi, Russia; October 16, 1886
Died: Leningrad, U.S.S.R.; November 24, 1959

Biography

Boris Eikhenbaum was born on October 16, 1886, in Krasnyi, in the Smolensk region of Russia. He graduated from the University of St. Petersburg in 1912 with a degree in history and philology and taught at that institution, renamed Leningrad State University after the Revolution, intermittently from 1918 to 1949. He also lectured periodically at the Leningrad Institute of the History of Arts from 1920 to 1931.

Eikhenbaum was attracted early in his career to the emerging formal method of literary criticism. In 1918 he joined and became a major contributor to the Society for the Study of Poetic Language, an important organization of the Russian Formalist movement. Marxist challenges to Formalist doctrine in the later 1920s persuaded Eikhenbaum to shift his focus to literary biography. After 1930 the censorial strictures of the Joseph Stalin period forced him to pursue his studies in private, while publicly he was engaged in editorial work.

The World War II blockade of Leningrad affected Eikhenbaum's health and in 1942 caused his evacuation, during which he lost a major manuscript on the subject of Lev Tolstoi. His subsequent scholarly activity also proceeded in the face of much adversity. He suffered especially severe harassment during Stalin's postwar purge of writers, but after the dictator's death in 1953 he resumed his critical work and remained active in Leningrad until his death in that city on November 24, 1959.

Influence

Eikhenbaum's work on the importance of sound patterns and phrase melody, as well as his descriptive analyses of short prose, served as the basis for further investigation by structuralist theoreticians of both the Prague and the Polish schools. His Formalist contributions influenced the development of semiotic approaches to literature, especially those of Mikhail Bakhtin and Iurii Lotman. By his meticulous attention to stylistic development he fostered scholarly interest in the formal elements of literary constructs.

Analysis

Eikhenbaum's development as a literary theorist consists of several stages, each characterized by changes in his own thinking and by external, political factors. During the first phase of his career Eikhenbaum was one of the most influential and prolific contributors to Russian Formalist literary theory. Formalist activity – spanning roughly the years from 1914 to 1928 – was concerned with examining literature from a descriptive point of view, concentrating on literary devices, language, structure, and technique, and with making literary scholarship independent of other disciplines. As a Formalist, Eikhenbaum refuted traditional approaches such as analyzing works in terms of the author's personal experience and world-view or as documents of a given time and, instead, proposed a new understanding of the nature of literature by limiting analysis to its form.

Of particular interest to Eikhenbaum was the notion that literary language is a form of expression radically different from language as a whole and must be delineated as such. He preferred to see the language of literature as a creative deformation of practical, communicative speech and defined the finished literary piece as the sum of the specific artistic devices employed in it. It was his firm conviction that a literary work was an artificial construct, creatively arranged, and in order to understand its significance one had to explain how it was assembled. By focusing on the descriptive side of his subject matter, on style, verse structure, and prose technique, Eikhenbaum gave his studies a decidedly scientific flavor, partially utilizing the tools of the science of linguistics.

An important contribution to Russian Formalist theory was Eikhenbaum's insistence that there exist one or more dominant artistic devices in each work which deform and mute all other elements. In applying this principle to poetic texts, Eikhenbaum identified dominant intonation patterns in certain types of poetry. This examination of the impact of phrase melody on verse, presented in *Melodika russkogo liricheskogo stikha* (1922; the melodics of Russian lyric verse), led him to classify Russian lyrical poetry into a declamatory, conversational, and melodic style, according to the importance played by intonation in each category. His most noted finding was that in the melodic group the verbal or semantic component is entirely subordinated to the phonic element, that sound rather than meaning becomes the formative principle of the composition. Though Eikhenbaum's method of classification and choice of texts engendered disagreement among the Russian Formalists, he is credited with isolating distinct, poetic intonation patterns in which the gliding quality of sounds peculiar to nonartistic, practical speech is significantly reduced, demonstrating a conscious effort by poets to superimpose melodic phrasing onto their lyrics in an effort to mimic musical melody.

In "Poet-Zhurnalist" (1928), Eikhenbaum also presented the popular civic poet Nikolai Nekrasov in a new light. Until Eikhenbaum's analysis, Nekrasov had not been regarded as a competent literary craftsman because of his unpolished, often-uncouth style and content. Eikhenbaum, through his descriptive method, demonstrated that Nekrasov deliberately chose an innovatively shocking style, incorporating folk material, slogans, and vaudeville elements, in order to advance beyond the conventional, smooth, but shop-worn norms of earlier Russian poets and to forge a new mode of poetic expression. In like manner, many famous Russian poets were subjected to re-interpretation by Eikhenbaum. For example, Aleksandr Pushkin, who had long been accepted as the creator of a uniquely Russian Romantic poetics, was found to have followed traditional classical norms after Eikhenbaum had scrutinized his compositional style and other formal elements. Mikhail Lermontov's and Anna Akhmatova's verse also emerged redefined from Eikhenbaum's investigation, and only Eikhenbaum's erudition and scholarly objectivity somewhat balanced the unpopularity with which his novel theories were received by non-Formalist literary scholars.

Eikhenbaum utilized his narrow focus of examination in the analysis of prose also, favoring parody and highly stylized works, in which formal technique was an obvious component. Thus in "Kak sdelana 'Shinel'' Gogolia" (1919) he reinterpreted Nikolai Gogol''s revered classic "Shinel'" (1842; "The Overcoat," 1886) solely in terms of sound and facial gestures, by tracing wordplay, grotesque articulations, and, in particular, expressive phonetic combinations. Disdaining all reference to the plot of this beloved tale, whose unfortunate, pitiful hero had touched the hearts of millions, Eikhenbaum stripped the work of its sentimental heritage and defined it wholly as a clever juxtaposition of diverse narrative styles. Stylistic considerations played an equally prominent role in Eikhenbaum's first of many analyses of Tolstoi's creative method. In *Molodoi Tolstoi* (1922; *The Young Tolstoi*, 1972) Eikhenbaum proposed that Tolstoi's penchant for psychological self-examination was not a result of private circumstances, as was widely believed, but represented a new narrative form aimed at overcoming prevailing stereotypical Romantic prose.

A thorough familiarity with Western culture and literature permitted Eikhenbaum to extend his descriptive investigation beyond Russian borders and to evaluate O. Henry's craftsmanship from a different point of view. In "O. Genri i teoriia novelly" (1925; "O. Henry and the Theory of the Short Story," 1971) Eikhenbaum identifies the stylistic devices through which the author achieves parody and shows exactly how the illusion of reality is destroyed. He values O. Henry highly for his skill in laying bare and distorting conventional authorial technique and considers his style a turning point in the evolution of the American short story. Through much of Slavic scholarship rejected Eikhenbaum's attempt to reduce literary masterpieces to a set of devices as soulless and one-sided, his analytic approach and many acute insights eventually became an accepted part of Russian prose analysis. His term "skaz" (spoken tale), used to denote a narrative mode in which oral delivery is dominant, has entered standard literary vocabulary.

Eikhenbaum's insistence on the autonomy of literary scholarship and his focus on purely formal aspects generated criticism, especially from Marxist theorists, for whom literature was inextricably linked to social causes.

Eikhenbaum defended his position very eloquently in "Teoriia 'formal'nogo metoda'" (1926; "The Theory of the 'Formal Method,'" 1965), which serves as an excellent summary of the entire Russian Formalist movement. Quite aware that political exigency, exacerbated by tightened censorship after Stalin's rise to power, demanded diplomatic adjustment, Eikhenbaum carefully identified the formal method with scientific inquiry, hoping thereby to render it compatible with Marxism. The Marxists, however, rejected any such notion, and their opposition soon led to dissolution of the Formalist movement, whereupon several of its theorists, Eikhenbaum among them, moved to more inclusive theories.

There is some indication that Eikhenbaum himself came to see the inadequacy of limiting inquiry to formal elements of a literary text, for he labored conscientiously to incorporate what he termed "literary mores" into his theory. His new thinking is most clearly formulated in "Literaturnyi byt" (1929; "Literary Environment," 1971). This shift in methodology – more literary history than analysis of text – involved investigating the social factors influential in shaping a new literary style. Eikhenbaum endeavored to establish how writers are fashioned by their cultural surroundings, such as existing genres, prevailing philosophical outlook, political atmosphere, and public expectations. Though inclusion of these sociological elements, more in line with the Marxist position, represented a drastic departure from his earlier theories, Eikhenbaum felt confident that he had not compromised his insistence on the autonomy of literature, and he devoted the remainder of his career to developing his new type of literary biography.

In tracing how writers evolve new forms of literary expression under pressure of a changing social environment, Eikhenbaum reflected the writer's changed situation under revolutionary Communism. Yet he wisely abstained from treating contemporary subjects or materials. Instead, he applied his theory to the evolution of nineteenth-century literature, focusing especially on the influences acting upon Tolstoi. True to his earlier convictions, he did not let his subject's personal life intrude on the analysis. Tolstoi is described in discourse with important individuals and groups of a given period, in correspondence with literary colleagues, and in search of novel narrative techniques. Eikhenbaum examines Tolstoi's letters, writings, diaries, and notebooks only insofar as they nudge the writer toward a new style and thus chronicle the evolution of literature. The personality of the subject rarely emerges from these monographs, and the literary biography does not come across as biographical. Eikhenbaum tended to overload these post-Formalist studies with extensive verbatim passages, many of them peripheral to the literary environment under discussion. By their inclusion he hoped to minimize Marxist criticism of conclusions so abundantly backed by factual material. Even so, some of his more substantial efforts, such as *Lev Tolstoi, semidesiatye gody* (1960; *Tolstoi in the Seventies*, 1982), were long suppressed and were published only posthumously.

Eikhenbaum's genre of literary biography has not replaced customary biography, because the exclusion of the subject's personality, coupled with the presence of a wealth of diverse environmental minutiae, deprives the works of a unifying center. On the other hand, Eikhenbaum's meticulously researched, detached, intellectual observations and collections of related facts provide an abundant source of useful material for literary historians. Moreover, his many stimulating Formalist studies, seminal to later structuralist endeavors, represent an important contribution to twentieth-century literary theory.

Principal criticism

Melodika russkogo liricheskogo stikha, 1922
Molodoi Tolstoi, 1922 (*The Young Tolstoi*, 1972)
Anna Akhmatova: Opyt analiza, 1923
Lermontov, 1924 (*Lermontov: A Study in Literary-Historical Evaluation*, 1981)
Skvoz literaturu, 1924
Literatura: Teoriia, kritika, polemika, 1927
Lev Tolstoi, 1928
Lev Tolstoi, 1931 (*Tolstoi in the Sixties*, 1982)
Lev Tolstoi, semidesiatye gody, 1960 (*Tolstoi in the Seventies*, 1982)
Stat'i o Lermontove, 1961

Other major works and literary forms

Many of Boris Eikhenbaum's analyses of short, individual literary works are in essay form, often in coauthorship with other Russian Formalist theoreticians. In addition, he wrote innumerable polemical articles, defending his scholarly points of view to Marxist challengers. Much of his Formalist writing was done during the hectic, lean postrevolutionary years, when publishing in book form was difficult. As a result, may of his essays remain uncollected into larger forms. Subsequent censorial suppression of his output further prevented collection of hundreds of pieces into books. His literary endeavors rarely strayed from the field of criticism.

NONFICTION
Russkaia proza, 1926 (*Russian Prose*, 1985)
Moi vremennik, 1929

Further reading

Any, Carol Joyce. *Boris Eikhenbaum: Voices of a Russian Formalist*, 1994.
Erlich, Victor. *Russian Formalism: History – Doctrine*, 1965 (second edition).
——, ed. *Modernism and Revolution: Russian Literature in Transition*, 1974.
——, ed. *Twentieth Century Russian Literary Criticism*, 1975.
Jackson, Robert Louis, and Stephen Rudy, eds. *Russian Formalism: A Retrospective Glance*, 1985.
Lemon, Lee, and Marion Reis, eds. *Russian Formalist Criticism: Four Essays*, 1965.
Matejka, Ladislav. *Readings in Russian Poetics: Formalist and Structuralist Views*, 1971.

Pike, Christopher, ed. *The Futurists, the Formalists, and the Marxist Critique*, 1979.
Pomorska, Krystyna. *Russian Formalist Theory and Its Poetic Ambiance*, 1968.
Stacy, Robert H. *Russian Literary Criticism: A Short History*, 1974.
Steiner, Peter. *Russian Formalism: A Metapoetics*, 1984.

MARGOT FRANK

See also Bakhtin; Lotman; Prague School; Russian Formalism; Tynianov

T. S. Eliot

American-born English poet, dramatist, and critic

Born: St. Louis, Missouri; September 26, 1888
Died: London, England; January 4, 1965

Biography

Thomas Stearns Eliot was born in St. Louis, Missouri, into a branch of the famous Eliot family of Boston. He followed family tradition by enrolling at Harvard University, where he studied philosophy as an undergraduate and graduate student; his work on the philosophy of F. H. Bradley is especially important since it had a great influence on his criticism and his poetry. He studied at the Sorbonne from 1910 to 1911 and at Oxford University in 1914. Eliot taught and worked in Lloyds Bank for eight years. While working at the bank, he wrote the poems that very quickly made him famous, including "The Love Song of J. Alfred Prufrock" in 1917 and *The Waste Land* in 1922.

In 1922 Eliot founded and became editor of *Criterion*, a critical journal that propagated his critical ideas. The journal lasted until 1939 and was very influential. Eliot's financial difficulties were alleviated by his becoming an editor and later a director of the publishing house Faber and Faber, where he worked from 1925 until his death. Eliot married first Vivian Haigh-Wood in 1915 from whom he was separated in 1932–33. In 1957 he married Valerie Fletcher. He was received into the Anglican church in 1927. To cap a long and productive life as poet, dramatist, and literary critic, he received the Nobel Prize for Literature in 1948. He died in London in 1965 and was buried at East Coker in Somerset.

Influence

Eliot led the fight in the early twentieth century against Romantic literature and impressionistic criticism. He wished to redirect attention from the poet to the poem. In doing so, he created the critical perspective that led to the elaborate rhetorical analyses of the New Criticism and redefined the nature of literary tradition, thereby changing some methods and assumptions of historical criticism. Eliot created this revolution in criticism by his own example as a poet as well as by his persuasive essays; his reputation as the preeminent poet of his age gave the essays an authority and power that helped to change critical attitudes toward movements in literature, such as Romanticism, and toward particular writers such as John Milton and Percy Bysshe Shelley. He achieved a position in English letters that can only be compared to those of Samuel Johnson and Matthew Arnold; he was the arbiter of taste and definer of the age. Because he is so rooted in his time and the then current controversies about poetic modernism and dramatic structures and language, however, his criticism is of little influence in a postmodern literary scene. The revolution that Eliot led fell victim to new rebels and new critical ideas such as poststructuralism, reader criticism, and feminist criticism; thus the New Criticism that followed Eliot's precepts has had little influence since the 1960s.

Analysis

Eliot was not, in general, a theoretical critic; much of his criticism is occasional and consists of prefaces to books as well as reviews in such journals as *The Egoist*, *The Times Literary Supplement*, and *Criterion*. The major exception is an essay that appears in *The Sacred Wood*, "Tradition and the Individual Talent," a landmark in Eliot's critical thought and a seminal work in twentieth-century criticism; it attempts to displace Romantic criticism and to provide a theoretical base for modern criticism. From this essay, it is possible to extract the critical principles that permeate Eliot's critical writing. The first of these principles is "tradition."

Eliot attempted to resuscitate the concept of tradition in literature in order to restructure the then current view of literary history. In contrast to Romantic theory and practice, which emphasized the "individual talent" and denied tradition, Eliot suggests that the best part of a poet's work will be found in those aspects that are traditional. Therefore, any great writer must have a developed sense of tradition, "the historical sense." In order to possess this sense, however, he or she must have knowledge of where the tradition can be found. It is not found in all the works written, nor is it evidenced by popularity. It is, instead, to be discovered in what Eliot calls the "main current," an idea that is more fully defined in later essays on specific writers or works.

One important aspect of Eliot's view is that the tradition can be found in the "ideal order" formed by the works of the past. Furthermore, a new work alters the nature and shape of the previously established tradition. It is, then, not a static concept, but an organism that is constantly being reshaped and reformed. An example of Eliot's own reshaping and defining of tradition can be found in "The Metaphysical Poets," an essay written in 1923.

Eliot first sets out to define metaphysical poetry in a less negative way than Johnson did in his "Life of Cowley."

Eliot cites Johnson's famous definition, which characterizes Metaphysical poetry as that in which "the most heterogeneous ideas are yoked by violence together." Where Johnson saw ideas "yoked but not united," Eliot finds both a "new unity" and a model for modern poetry. Eliot wished to redraw the tradition so that twentieth-century poetry would follow the example and tradition of the poets of the seventeenth century. Eliot states his position clearly: "In the seventeenth century a dissociation of sensibility set in, from which we have never recovered." The two parts of sensibility – thought and feeling – were one in the "heterogeneous" structures of Metaphysical poetry, but became separated in the eighteenth and nineteenth centuries. According to Eliot, the feelings in the poetry of these centuries became "coarse" and the poets fled from "thought." The breach might, however, be healed in the twentieth century if poets were willing to imitate the complexity and difficulty of Metaphysical poets such as John Donne. It hardly needs saying that Eliot's own poetry by this time was complex and united very heterogeneous materials, so that Eliot is both redefiner and representative example of the "main current" of the new literary tradition.

Another anti-Romantic aspect of Eliot's critical theory is the demand that the poet be "impersonal," extinguishing his or her personality. Eliot even describes the poetic process in scientific terms. "When a bit of finely filiated platinum is introduced into a chamber containing oxygen and sulphur dioxide, it acts as a catalyst and produces a new combination, leaving no trace of itself." So for Eliot the poet is a catalyst who transforms the materials of experience into a new work of art, but leaves no trace of his or her personality. The best poet is, for Eliot, not one who expresses his or her personality by such processes as William Wordsworth's "emotion recollected in tranquillity," but one who acts as a "medium" to fuse emotions, thought, and experience. In addition, Eliot sees the best part of a person's work, as he does with the concept of "tradition," in this "continual self-sacrifice, a continual extinction of personality." This critical concept is, once more, an attempt to expose Romantic doctrine and replace it with a classical distance between the poet's experience and the final product which is the poem. It is not, however, a prescription for a lack of feeling in the work, but for a transformation by the poet of raw experience into an ordered poem. Furthermore, Eliot does warn the reader that "only those who have personality and emotions know what it means to want to escape from these things."

It is necessary to add to these general principles a few related ideas. One is the concept of the "objective correlative," which is found in the essay "Hamlet and His Problems" (1920). It is a famous formulation that demands that "a set of objects, a situation, a chain of events . . . be the formula of that *particular* emotion," so that emotion is not stated but embodied in an image or a scene. The concept was later used by critics and poets such as William Carlos Williams, who insisted that there be "no ideas but in things" in all literature, although Eliot applied it only to drama. The second concept, found in "'Rhetoric' and Poetic Drama," is related to the "objective correlative." Eliot declares that "the really fine rhetoric of Shakespeare occurs in situations where a character in the play *sees himself* in a dramatic light." Such a self-dramatization is another version of "expressing one's personality," condemned in "Tradition and the Individual Talent," and a clear violation of the equivalency of imagery demanded by the "objective correlative." Eliot was to make a poetic career out of exposing speakers such as J. Alfred Prufrock seeing themselves "in a dramatic light."

These principles are applied again and again to essays on a variety of literary works, authors, and types. Eliot uses the method of comparison and analysis in discussing these authors and works and finds them commendable or deficient according to the principles of "tradition" as well as the "individual talent." For example, Eliot finds Dante to be a safer model for a writer than is William Shakespeare, since Dante's language is more "universal" and less individual, arising from a more settled and central tradition; Dante "employed a method which was common and commonly understood throughout Europe," while Shakespeare was "*inimitable*" and therefore individual. Eliot makes another important distinction between the belief systems of Dante and Shakespeare. What is important is how that "private belief" became "a different thing in becoming poetry." Therefore, the reader does not have to believe in Dante's theology, but he has to understand it and "enter the world of thirteenth-century Catholicism."

In contrast to Eliot's commendation of Dante as an essentially traditional poet, William Blake's private system-making and style are criticized, in a 1936 essay, as not fitting into the main current. Eliot does praise Blake for his honesty and his early, more traditional efforts; when Blake creates and puts into poetic form his own philosophy, however, Eliot accuses him of being eccentric and "inclined to formlessness." The contrast between Eliot's approval of Dante's use of St. Thomas Aquinas' system in *La divina commedia* (c. 1320; *The Divine Comedy*) and his disapproval of Blake's personal and jerry-built system could not be stronger. What Blake needed, according to Eliot, was a "framework of accepted and traditional ideas which would have prevented him from indulging in a philosophy of his own." The final judgment is that "Dante is a classic, and Blake only a poet of genius." In a later essay, "What Is a Classic?" Eliot defines a classic as possessing "maturity," a concept that was used by Eliot, and by many of the New Critics who followed his precepts, to evaluate and dismiss such writers as Shelley and Milton.

Dante and Blake form opposite poles in the criticism of Eliot: the traditional, impersonal poet is celebrated, while the "eccentric," personal poet is placed lower on the scale. In Eliot's two essays on Milton, however, the categories begin to waver. The first essay on Milton, written in 1936, uses the familiar Eliotic strategy of beginning with praise and ending with censure. Milton is first described as a "very great poet," but soon he is rejected as a "bad influence." The primary problem for Eliot is that Milton's language is almost completely auditory and lacking in the visual. Making "no attempt to follow actual speech or thought," Milton was consumed with the sound of the poem. Eliot contrasts the individual style of Milton with the "tradition of conversational language in poetry" in John Dryden and finds Dryden to be a safer and "healthier" example. In a startling comparison, Eliot links Milton's style to that of James Joyce in *Finnegans Wake* (1939), finding both to be quirky and unrepresentative, although Joyce does retain "the conversational tone."

In 1947 Eliot wrote a very different evaluation of Milton. He now finds that his certainty that Milton was a "bad influence" has weakened, since he has come to believe that it is never certain how one poet influences another. In addition, he suggests that the use by critics of his term "dissociation of sensibility" to dismiss Milton is probably inappropriate: the concept is too "complex and too profound" to use as a critical term. Above all, he places his attack upon Milton in the context of his own earlier struggle to change attitudes and to create a new type of poetry in the period after World War I; that revolutionary period is now over, however, and one cannot "live in a perpetual state of revolution." The aim, now, is for *all* poetry to help "refine the language of the time" and "to prevent it from changing too rapidly." The change is quite significant. Eliot tries to blunt the attempt to use such critical concepts as "dissociation of sensibility" as weapons against certain poets, and he has come to see himself not as a critic trying to alter the accepted view, but as one who tries to preserve and defend the revolutionary changes he had brought about earlier. The confident ranking of poets within the newly created "tradition" has been replaced by a more conservative tolerance for a variety of writers.

In addition to writing on poets and poetry, Eliot wrote numerous essays on Elizabethan and Jacobean drama. The most notorious essay in this group is "Hamlet and His Problems," in which Eliot declares that *Hamlet* (c. 1600) is an "artistic failure" because the emotion displayed by Hamlet is disproportionate to his problems, thereby violating the principle of the "objective correlative." Ascribing this "failure" to Shakespeare's inability to "express the inexpressibly horrible," Eliot wonders "under what compulsion of what experience" Shakespeare attempted such an impossible task. In asking this question, Eliot seems to fall into what he had earlier described as the error of concentrating on the poet and not the poem, but by the end of the essay he states that it is impossible to discover such biographical information.

"Shakespeare and the Stoicism of Seneca" (1927) is concerned more with what the artist does with his material and ideas than with any close investigation of Senecan influence upon Shakespeare. Eliot does contrast the belief system available to Dante with that of Shakespeare and finds that Dante has superior materials upon which to draw. He does not, however, as he does in the later essay on Blake, rank Shakespeare lower because he drew upon inferior sources. What is important here for Eliot is the transformation of sources and material into a work of art. So while "neither Shakespeare nor Dante did any real thinking, . . . each expresses in perfect language, some permanent human impulse." Eliot's primary concern in this essay seems to be not the tradition or ideas the poet uses, but the quality of the emotion produced by each writer in his poem. The end of a work of art, then, is in the feelings that the artist has transformed into a work; how he transformed that material or what sources he drew upon for it is less important.

The other essays on Elizabethan and Jacobean drama are concerned with adjusting the reputations of various dramatists; Eliot wishes to promote Ben Jonson and Cyril Tourneur and demote Philip Massinger. The essay on Jonson is primarily an attempt to place him in a proper generic context, so that Jonson becomes, not a mere satirist or comic writer who used "humours," but one who "projects a new world into a new orbit." Eliot sees Jonson as a "traditional" playwright who is not appreciated by critics or the public. Eliot's defense of the tradition is less effective and less revolutionary in this essay, however, than in the earlier one "The Metaphysical Poets."

In the essay on Tourneur, Eliot finds the author of *The Revenger's Tragedy* (1606–1607) to have many deficiencies that are nevertheless overcome by the virtues of style, stagecraft, and plot. The most interesting essay of this group is the one on Massinger. Massinger's work is seen by Eliot as reflecting the decay of a once-great tradition. His failure is not only in style and characterization but also in the incapacity for "perceiving, registering, and digesting impressions." Furthermore, Massinger is accused of lacking a personality. "Massinger is not simply a smaller personality: his personality hardly exists." At first glance, Eliot seems to be exhibiting an excessive concern with the individual talent rather than with the tradition. Eliot makes it clear, however, that a personality is a necessary starting point and not an end in itself; the artist must "build a world of art" out of that personality. If the personality is deficient, then it is impossible to create great or even good art.

Eliot's later criticism is primarily cultural and religious; his conversion and entrance into the Anglican church changed the focus and subject matter of his criticism. Many of his followers were dismayed when he declared himself to be "classicist in literature, royalist in politics, and Anglo-Catholic in religion." In "Religion and Literature," Eliot takes a stand concerning the ethical and moral effects of literature on an audience. He even suggests that contemporary literature is "degrading" and that his own earlier works may have had some "pernicious influence."

"Tradition" is no longer a sufficient concept for criticism, since "literary criticism should be completed by criticism from a definite ethical and theological standpoint." This Eliot is virtually unrecognizable as the author of "Tradition and the Individual Talent," who insisted on the integrity of a work of art within a literary tradition.

T. S. Eliot was the most important critic of the first half of the twentieth century. His influence can still be seen in the now accepted view of the "main current" of English literary tradition. His promotion of the Metaphysical poets and his negative judgments on many nineteenth-century writers still constitute accepted doctrine in textbooks and classrooms. In addition, Eliot's critical method of comparison and analysis, as well as his urbane style, set a standard for other critics to follow. His influence was diminished, however, by his insistence on an ethical dimension in the criticism of literature and by his Christian polemics. In addition, critics who followed Eliot tended to use critical concepts such as the "objective correlative" and the "dissociation of sensibility" with much less tact and subtlety than Eliot did, thereby further decreasing their effectiveness. The change in critical modes in the second half of the twentieth century also diminished his influence. Eliot's critical works will be of permanent interest and value, however, because of the excellence of their style and their perfect evocation of the critical milieu of the early twentieth century.

Principal criticism

The Sacred Wood, 1920
Shakespeare and the Stoicism of Seneca, 1927
Selected Essays, 1917–1932, 1932
The Use of Poetry and the Use of Criticism: Studies in the Relation of Criticism to Poetry in England, 1933
After Strange God: A Primer of Modern Heresy, 1934
Elizabethan Essays, 1934
Essays Ancient and Modern, 1936
The Idea of a Christian Society, 1939
What Is a Classic?, 1944
Notes Towards the Definition of Culture, 1949
The Three Voices of Poetry, 1953
On Poetry and Poets, 1957

Other major works and literary forms

T. S. Eliot was not only a major critic, but also one of the most important poets of the twentieth century and an important dramatist. His early poems, such as "The Love Song of J. Alfred Prufrock," changed the style and structure of the poetry of the period, and *The Waste Land* (1922) is perhaps the most important poem of the century. It defined the lack of sustaining values after World War I and became a literary model because of its complexity, allusiveness, and mixture of past and present, the ordinary and the sublime.

Eliot's poetry changed and assumed a more Christian attitude after "Gerontion" (1919). The great monument of this period is the *Four Quartets* (1943). In this sequence of poems, Eliot is more assertive about the possibility of Christian belief opposing or even overcoming the terrors of time. In contrast to *The Waste Land*, here Eliot envisions a "still point" of "timeless moments" that can redeem history.

Eliot's plays were less influential than the poems. The most important one is *Murder in the Cathedral* (1935), based on the murder of Thomas à Becket by hired assassins of Henry II. The use of verse and a chorus in the play harks back to the Elizabethan and Jacobean drama about which Eliot had written so often.

PLAYS
The Rock: A Pageant Play, 1934
Murder in the Cathedral, 1935
The Family Reunion, 1939
The Cocktail Party, 1949
The Confidential Clerk, 1953
The Elder Statesman, 1958
Collected Plays, 1962

POETRY
Prufrock and Other Observations, 1917
Poems, 1919
Ara Vos Prec, 1920
The Waste Land, 1922
Poems, 1909–1925, 1925
The Journey of the Magi, 1927
A Song for Simeon, 1928
Animula, 1929
Ash Wednesday, 1930
Marina, 1930
Triumphal March, 1931
Sweeney Agonistes, 1932
Words for Music, 1934
Collected Poems, 1909–1935, 1936
Old Possum's Book of Practical Cats, 1939
Four Quartets, 1943
The Cultivation of Christmas Trees, 1954
Collected Poems, 1909–1962, 1963
Poems Written in Early Youth, 1967

NONFICTION
Ezra Pound: His Metric and Poetry, 1917
Homage to John Dryden, 1924
For Lancelot Andrewes, 1928
Dante, 1929
Thoughts After Lambeth, 1931
Charles Whibley: A Memoir, 1931
John Dryden: The Poet, the Dramatist, the Critic, 1932
The Music of Poetry, 1942
The Classics and the Man of Letters, 1942
Poetry and Drama, 1951
Knowledge and Experience in the Philosophy of F. H. Bradley, 1964
To Criticize the Critic, 1965

MISCELLANEOUS
The Complete Poems and Plays, 1969

Further reading

Ackroyd, Peter. *T. S. Eliot*, 1984.
Asher, Kenneth. *T. S. Eliot and Ideology*, 1995.

Freed, Lewis. *T. S. Eliot: Aesthetics and History*, 1962.
——. *T. S. Eliot: The Critic as Philosopher*, 1979.
Jay, Gregory. *T. S. Eliot and the Poetics of Literary History*, 1983.
Kenner, Hugh. *The Invisible Poet: T. S. Eliot*, 1959.
——. *T. S. Eliot: A Collection of Critical Essays*, 1962.
Lucy, Sean. *T. S. Eliot and the Idea of Tradition*, 1960.
Newton-de Molina, David, ed. *The Literary Criticism of T. S. Eliot: New Essays*, 1977.
Ricks, Christopher. *T. S. Eliot and Prejudice*, 1988.
Shusterman, Richard. *T. S. Eliot and the Philosophy of Criticism*, 1988.
Tamplin, Ronald. *A Preface to T. S. Eliot*, 1988.

JAMES SULLIVAN

See also Auden; British Literary Theory: Twentieth Century; Pound

Richard Ellmann

American biographer and critic

Born: Detroit, Michigan; March 15, 1918
Died: Oxford, England; May 13, 1987

Biography

Richard David Ellmann was born in Highland Park, Detroit, Michigan, the son of James Isaac Ellmann, a lawyer and Jewish Romanian immigrant to the United States, and Jeannette Barsook, an immigrant from Kiev, Ukraine. After his years of secondary schooling in Detroit, he was admitted to Yale, where he took a B.A. degree with distinction in English in 1939, and completed an M.A. thesis on "The Social Philosophy of Thomas Carlyle" in 1941. In 1943 he joined the United States Navy, and was eventually seconded to the Office of Strategic Services in London, England, in 1945. While military service did not appeal to Ellmann, he soon turned his stationing in London to his advantage. In September of 1945 he visited and befriended Georgie Yeats, the widow of William Butler Yeats, in Dublin, Ireland, who gave him unrestricted access to her substantial archive of Yeats' library, letters, drafts, and papers. Immediately after the war, Ellmann returned to Dublin to take a Litt.B. degree at Trinity College, Dublin, while simultaneously working on his doctoral dissertation at Yale. Ellmann's 1947 dissertation at Yale, "Triton Among the Streams: A Study of the Life and Writings of William Butler Yeats," was the first Yale Ph.D. dissertation written on a twentieth-century writer, and one of the first on a modernist writer in the Anglophone world. It was revised and published in 1949 as *Yeats: The Man and the Masks*, the foundational study of Yeats' poetry. In 1947 Ellmann began a teaching career at Harvard, where he met the Irish-American feminist critic Mary Donaghue, whom he shortly thereafter married. Two years afterwards he was appointed professor of English at Northwestern University in Evanston, Illinois, where he stayed until 1968, when, after several visiting appointments, he moved to New College, Oxford, England. In 1970 he was elected Goldsmiths' Professor of English Literature, where he remained until his retirement from Oxford in 1984 and his move to fill the Woodruff chair at Emory University in Atlanta, Georgia. He died of a debilitating motor neurone disease on May 13, 1987, in Oxford.

Influence

Ellmann's biography *James Joyce*, published in 1959, almost single-handedly elevated Joyce to the status of international modernist and is responsible for the creation of what is today euphemistically called "the Joyce Industry." The massive quantity of critical writings about James Joyce, which is second only in bulk to those on William Shakespeare (according to the Modern Language Association bibliography), would not be possible without Ellmann's foundational and magisterial study. No biography of Joyce has superseded it in the forty years since its publication. Aside from his status as the (perhaps accidental) founder of modern Joyce studies, Ellmann also contributed substantively to the study of Yeats and Oscar Wilde. His 1949 book *Yeats: The Man and the Masks* is still the best introduction to the poetry of Yeats and remains widely cited in Yeats criticism. As Roy Foster, the author of the definitive 1997 two-volume biography of Yeats wrote in his introduction, Ellmann's works "still hold the critical field." Ellmann's *Oscar Wilde*, which he crafted until just a few weeks before his death, is regarded as a masterful and authoritative biography of a difficult and elusive subject. Consistent with Ellmann's disposition toward popular art and his cooperation in radio and TV adaptations of Joyce and Yeats, the biography was used as the basis for the award-winning Brian Gilbert film *Wilde* in 1997 starring Stephen Fry.

Aside from his direct influence in criticism and popular culture, Ellmann has exerted his influence in more subtle ways. A roster of his students reads like a *Who's Who* of contemporary literary critics: Jonathan Culler, Frank Kermode, Elizabeth Cullingford, Vivian Mercer, Daniel Albright, Declan Kiberd, and others all studied with Ellmann. Many of them have followed Ellmann's interests, with Daniel Albright, for example, editing the Everyman edition of Yeats' poetry, containing the most detailed notes available in any edition. Elizabeth Cullingford has written two foundational books on Yeats: the now classic study of Yeats and politics *Yeats, Ireland, and Fascism* (1981) and the first book-length feminist study of Yeats, *Gender and History in Yeats's Love Poetry* (1993). Declan Kiberd went on from his work with Ellmann to become one of the most important Irish literary critics, as is manifested in his comprehensive *Inventing Ireland* (1995). In their works, his former students all share with Ellmann a commitment to a clear style and a willingness to meet complexity without reduction but with lucid explanation. As one of them put it, "His words were always simple, his thought invariably sophisticated, and the more complex his syntax became, the more straightforward the diction." In their homage to Ellmann, *Essays for Richard Ellmann* (1988), forty-one of his former students expressed their appreciation by contributing essays on modern literature, all of which, in various ways, show Ellmann's mark on their work. In the volume's introduction, its editors summarize Ellmann's influence thus: "He established, for two generations, the contexts of modern writing, and his own works have become a fundamental part of the context of modern criticism."

Analysis

Ellmann's approach to literary biography "shrewdly fused," as one critic puts it, "the celebratory techniques of Victorian biography with the close analytic methods of the New Criticism, essentially advancing an inclusive approach to literature, quite innovative when he began, and comprising a synthesis in a dialectical process." While it may sound archaic now and liable to be attacked outright for its simplicity, Ellmann stuck to a single conviction from his dissertation onward: that it is necessary to study literary texts in their biographical, historical, and political contexts. Context was a word at the height of New Criticism that was heresy. Though Ellmann took on board many, if not most, of the analytic methods of New Criticism and would likely number himself a sometime practitioner, he met literature with honest questions rather than critical, programmatic agendas. When asked once whether he followed any methodology for literary biography, his response was that "half the job of the biographer is to devise a new method for each subject." Indeed, this philosophy is demonstrated in his biographical studies of Yeats, Joyce, and Wilde. The same can be seen in Ellmann's methods of literary analysis.

In his first and enduring book, *Yeats: The Man and the Masks*, Ellmann displays what could be roughly characterized as biographical criticism. Though where it differs from its nineteenth-century antecedent, this brand of criticism incorporates the attempt at "objectivity" prevalent in the school of New Criticism. For example, in his analysis of Yeats' poem "Sailing to Byzantium" (*The Tower*, 1928), Ellmann's argument moves in a zig-zag fashion between biography and formal analysis. First he weaves in the direction of New Criticism: "The protagonist of the poem," he says, "is not Yeats but may be described as a symbol of Yeats and of the artist and of man. In his apostrophe to the sages, 'O sages standing in God's holy fire/ As in the gold mosaic of a wall,' the use of the connective 'as in' prevents our knowing whether the sages are primarily images in the mosaic and secondarily sages in God's holy fire or the reverse. . . ." After this formal interpretive consideration, Ellmann takes us immediately in another direction, saying that the poem "is full of echoes of Yeats's other works, of his reading, and of his experiences. In a sense he had been writing it all his life." And then Ellmann cites eight examples that support this claim, including one about Yeats as a child: "As a boy in London, Yeats had stared for hours at Turner's picture of 'The Golden Bough' in the National Gallery." This is where his image of a form "set upon a golden bough to sing" arrives from. Yeats' biography, for Ellmann, is a source of his poetry and of the meaning it should invoke in the reader.

In *James Joyce*, Ellmann moves even further in the direction of biographical analysis. The opening sentences declare the method he has devised in the case of Joyce: "The life of the artist, but particularly that of Joyce, differs from the lives of other persons in that its events are becoming artistic sources even as they command his present attention. Instead of allowing each day, pushed back by the next, to lapse into imprecise memory, he shapes again the experiences which have shaped him. He is at once the captive and the liberator." The biographer's job, Ellmann says, is to trace out these two separate processes: the living and the making of life into art. In this way, it is impossible to understand art as something capable of being divorced from biographical context – from life – and abstracted into a vacuum of objective analysis. The crucial thing in any analysis of Ellmann's methodology, however, is to ask just what Ellmann means by "life." Ellmann is a humanist who believes in the Enlightenment ideal of the individual. He remained untouched by structuralism or poststructuralism. And his idea of the individual is distinctly Freudian (at least in the 1950s, when Ellmann was writing this biography). He or she participates in life-dramas such as the Oedipus complex, has an unconscious, and works out traumas or fantasies via artistic expression. The individual develops, grows from child to adult, and carries with him- or herself all of the experiences of childhood. To explain his approach, Ellmann refers famously to the best-known literary biography in English literature. He cites James Boswell's biography of Samuel Johnson as an example of what modern literary biography is not: "No doubt it was hard for Boswell to conceive of Dr. Johnson as a small boy in short trousers, at least until that short-trousered boy began to translate Virgil and Homer." For Ellmann, the boy is as important as the fully developed artist. Indeed, the boy is not only in the man but in the man's works. For understanding the emotional life of the artist is perhaps most important to understanding his or her work, particularly in the case of James Joyce, asserts Ellmann.

Take for example his interpretation of the short story "The Dead" (*Dubliners*, 1914) in his biography of Joyce. While occasionally turning toward formal analysis, Ellmann explains almost everything in the story in terms of what Joyce experienced, who Joyce knew, what jealousies Joyce harbored, what songs he had recently heard and who sang them to him, and so on. Ellmann does a spectacular job tracing out the sources of characters, symbols, situations, and themes in Joyce's own life. For Ellmann knew that of all the modernist writers it was Joyce who most fully drew upon the materials of his own life to create his art. Because he is so comprehensive or even encyclopedic in his approach to Joyce, however, sometimes such a matching exercise is pushed to an extreme. For example, Ellmann was unable to discover where the idea of snow came from for the concluding lines of "The Dead" ("snow was general all over Ireland"). He says, "No one can know how Joyce conceived the joining of Gabriel's final experience with snow." The obvious response to this is: perhaps Joyce simply made it up. Perhaps it had nothing at all to do with anything in his life, and he just imagined the idea of snow for the ending of the story. But Ellmann's approach in this case has been dictated by his subject. Joyce's work demands a biographical interpretation, demands the return to context to make meaning possible.

Ellmann's method of reading T. S. Eliot's *The Waste Land* (1922) follows closely his method of reading Joyce. In the often overlooked collection of essays *Golden Codgers: Biographical Speculations*, published in 1973, Ellmann includes an essay on *The Waste Land* that violated all the tenets of New Criticism, even while looking to one of the school's principle texts. Of Eliot, he says, "*The Waste Land* compiled many of the nightmarish feelings he had suffered during the seven years from 1914 to 1921, that is, from his coming to England to his temporary collapse." The idea of the central poem of high modernism being a "compilation" of Eliot's own personal feelings from a specific period in his life is a challenging and heretical one for the time. He proceeds in that analysis to detail Eliot's biography and disclose the situation and events Eliot endured while writing the poem, while at the same time discussing the merits of the decisions Eliot made in his revisions. His essay puts Eliot's poem in a context that enriches its meaning in ways that would have been missed by more programmatic approaches. Yet Ellmann did not see the kind of biographical interpretation he was engaged in with Joyce and Eliot as at all a method that could be universally and programmatically applied. Ellmann's biography of Wilde practices very little of the "text to life" matching exercise we see in his other biographical criticism. Different literary subjects demand different methodologies. Ellmann's works teach us the humility of his approach.

Aside from his biographical approaches to literature, Ellmann also gave to modern literary criticism the idea of "eminent domain," in a 1967 book of the same title. His theory of literary "influence" was ingenious for its time and anticipates Harold Bloom's *The Anxiety of Influence* (1973). "'Influence,'" he says, "is a term which conceals and mitigates the guilty acquisitiveness of talent. That writers flow into each other like waves, gently rather than tidally, is one of those decorous myths we impose upon high-handed, even brutal procedure. . . . Writers move upon other writers not as genial successors but as violent expropriators, knocking down established boundaries to seize by the force of youth, or of age, what they require." Ellmann concludes, "They do not borrow, they override." For Ellmann, it is the language an artist uses that is the marker of these expropriations and literary coups d'état. The words in a book, he says, "are coded records of successive impositions of eminent domain. The best writers expropriate best, they disdain petty debts in favor of grand, authoritative larcenies." *Eminent Domain: Yeats Among Wilde, Joyce, Pound, Eliot, and Auden* (1967), is a brilliant exercise in mapping these larcenies.

Principal criticism

Yeats: The Man and the Masks, 1949
James Joyce: Letters, 1957
James Joyce, 1959
The Identity of Yeats, 1964
Eminent Domain: Yeats Among Wilde, Joyce, Pound, Eliot, and Auden, 1967
Oscar Wilde; A Collection of Critical Essays, 1969
Literary Biography, 1971
Golden Codgers: Biographical Speculations, 1973
Four Dubliners: Wilde, Yeats, Joyce, and Beckett, 1987
Norton Anthology of Modern Poetry, 1988 (editor)
Oscar Wilde, 1988

Other major works and literary forms

Richard Ellmann was not only an academic but a popular intellectual who contributed to TV and radio adaptations of Joyce and Yeats, as well as writing countless articles for *The Times Literary Supplement* and various American publications, ranging from the *New York Review of Books* to the *New Republic* and *Critical Inquiry*.

Further reading

Donoghue, Denis. *Being Modern Together*, 1991.
Horden, Peregrine. *Freud and the Humanities*, 1985.
Kelly, John. *Dictionary of National Biography Supplement*, 1990.
Kiberd, Declan, ed. *Essays for Richard Ellmann: Omnium Gatherum*, 1988.

SPURGEON THOMPSON

See also American Literary Theory of the Twentieth Century; Edel

Ralph Waldo Emerson

American essayist and critic

Born: Boston, Massachusetts; May 25, 1803
Died: Concord, Massachusetts; April 27, 1882

Biography

Born on May 25, 1803, in Boston, Ralph Waldo Emerson was only eight years old when his father, a Unitarian minister and chaplain of the state senate, died. His mother boarded guests to support her four children – Ralph, William, Edward, and Charles. Ralph attended Boston Latin School and Harvard University, keeping journals, winning prizes for his essays, and reading extensively. He became familiar with the works of Sir Walter Scott, Benjamin Franklin, Cicero, William Shakespeare, numerous English essayists, Miguel de Cervantes, Dante, Euripides, Michel Eyquem de Montaigne, Blaise Pascal, and Plato. After teaching at his brother William's school for young women, Ralph studied for the ministry at Harvard University and was ordained pastor of Second Church in Boston in 1829.

The next several years were tumultuous for Emerson. His marriage to Ellen Tucker ended after only three years when she died in 1831 of tuberculosis, a disease that had infected Emerson and other members of his family as well. The next year, Emerson informed his church that he had become skeptical of the validity of the Lord's Supper and could no longer administer it. A few months later, in 1832, he resigned his pastorate and left for the first of three trips to England.

In 1834 he moved to Concord, Massachusetts, and received the first installment of his wife's legacy. With the assurance that he would receive more than one thousand dollars annually, he realized that he would not have to hold a steady job again; thus he entered into a life that included occasional preaching, frequent lecturing, and even more frequent meetings of the Transcendental Club, a group composed mainly of intellectuals who came to Emerson's home to discuss literary, theological, and philosophical ideas. Among the members were the educator Bronson Alcott, the abolitionist and Unitarian minister Theodore Parker, and the Unitarian minister Orestes A. Brownson. With his marriage to Lydia Jackson and the publication of *Nature* in 1836, Emerson's life at Concord with his circle of friends and admirers was established.

Emerson's reputation as an American prophet and literary liberator was assured with the publication of *Essays: First Series* in 1841. These pieces, most of which had been presented earlier as lectures, heralded the establishment of a new literature and a new vision for the new land called America. Honored by his readership, Emerson spent the last half of his life dealing with both fame and suffering. His first son, Waldo, died at the age of five in 1842, a loss that severely pained Emerson. His son Edward was born in 1844, the same year that his *Essays: Second Series* was published.

Continuing to write essays, poetry, and journals until his last years, Emerson enjoyed the admiration and adulation of his contemporaries even during the last decade of his life, when he declined into senility. He died in Concord on April 27, 1882.

Influence

Emerson's influence upon his contemporaries and upon American literary history was, and is, monumental. During the mid-nineteenth century he was one of the most influential figures in the literary world, inspiring other writers by his call for a new American literature and by his explicit encouragement of new voices. Emerson's fellow writers in his own country, such as Walt Whitman, and writers in Europe, such as Friedrich Nietzsche, learned innovative techniques from a master of aesthetic experimentation. In the twentieth century the Emersonian influence continued as writers looked back at the master who invited Americans to look forward.

Analysis

In nineteenth-century America, Emerson was the hub around which intellectual life revolved. His background of extensive reading and traveling prepared him to be the spokesperson for his generation, the man who formulated the theory and set down the generalizations that his contemporaries adopted. His theory of Transcendentalism was used by all the Romantics of the period and has been continually adapted by subsequent writers.

For Emerson and his followers, Transcendentalism was a religious, philosophical, and literary movement. In religion, it was post-Unitarian and freethinking and was articulated in Emerson's *Divinity School Address*. In philosophy, it was Kantian and idealistic. In fact, the name was derived from writings of Immanuel Kant: "I call all knowledge *transcendental* which is concerned, not with objects, but with our mode of knowing objects so far as this is possible *a priori*." Emerson's works *Nature* and "The Transcendentalist" demonstrate this philosophical thrust. In literature, Transcendentalism was Romantic and individualistic, impulses explained by Emerson in "Self-Reliance" and *The American Scholar*. Although American Transcendentalism was eclectic rather than systematic, it did have a single focus: a concern with knowing and seeing. Emerson and his followers explored the ways in which the human being can intuitively go beyond or transcend the limits of the senses and of logic and receive higher truths.

Transcendentalism as a religious movement offered a new approach to God. By the 1830s Unitarianism had lost its emotional appeal. Unitarians believed in God as a single personality, in liberal rationalism, and in the excellence of humanity, but these, according to Emerson, had become largely verbal constructs and did not address the emotional needs of people. As Emerson struggled with his own religious questions, leaving the ministry in 1832, he began to formulate his ideas about Transcendentalism as a response to the vacuum left by his rejection of Unitarianism. He made his ideas public in the *Divinity School Address*, delivered to the Harvard Divinity School seniors in 1838.

In this controversial address, Emerson asserted that the Christian Church had erred in two serious ways: it had exaggerated the personal and miraculous authority of Jesus Christ, and it had viewed revelation as something past and dead, confined to biblical terms and interpretation. Emerson explained that these erroneous views of miracles and revelation were responsible for the decaying Church and the waning faith among Christians. His solution was bold: "Let me admonish you, first of all, to go alone; to refuse the good models, even those which are sacred in the imagination of men, and dare to love God without mediator or veil."

This religious aspect of Transcendentalism, with its call to reject past ways of knowing and to discover new, intuitive approaches to God, was reinforced by the philosophical concepts of the movement, articulated by Emerson in his first, perhaps most important, work, *Nature*, and in his essay "The Transcendentalist." In the latter, he explained the term which originally had pejorative meanings. Charles Dickens, for example, said scoffingly that "whatever was unintelligible would be certainly transcendental." Emerson attempts in the first lines of the essay to correct such misconceptions: "What is popularly called Transcendentalism among us, is Idealism; Idealism as it appears in 1842." In fact, that Idealism had been first articulated in 1836, when Emerson published *Nature*.

Nature captured and spoke to its historical time. Emerson understood the spirit of his age when he structured his essay to move from a consideration of the past – "Our age is retrospective" – to its last section, entitled "Prospects," with its call for a vision that looked toward the future – "Build therefore your own world." The essay celebrates "I," "Eye," and "Aye," as the critic Kenneth Burke has pointed out: beliefs in the power of the individual, a new way of seeing, and an affirmative, positive attitude toward the universe. In this celebration of I, Eye, and Aye, Emerson articulated and shaped American philosophy.

The essay begins with a call for solitude, that state in which the human being is truly an individual and completely self-reliant: "If a man would be alone, let him look at the stars." For Emerson, the state of solitude is important, not simply because it separates one from society, but also because it offers the opportunity to see clearly, to become "a transparent eyeball." Emerson described this state of solitariness as an experience in which one is connected with the universe: "I am nothing; I see all; the currents of the Universal Being circulate through me; I am part or parcel of God."

When one enters into this new way of seeing and becoming connected with what Emerson called the Over-Soul, one reads nature for its moral meanings and learns that nature has its own methods, which Emerson called flux, polarity, and correspondence. Emerson finds meaning in the perpetual movement and ceaseless change everywhere in the natural world: "Who looks upon a river in a meditative hour and is not reminded of the flux of all things? Throw a stone into the stream, and the circles that propagate themselves are the beautiful type of all influence." Related to this notion of flux is the concept of polarity, the belief that south attracts and north repels, the movement being constant and necessary between the two poles. And finally, nature works through correspondence, so that there is a connection between what is seen and what is unseen, between natural law and moral law. To understand the ways of nature – the flux, polarity, and correspondence – is to read nature as if it were a book:

> A life in harmony with Nature, the love of truth and of virtue, will purge the eyes to understand her text. By degrees we may come to know the primitive sense of the permanent objects of nature, so that the world shall be to us an open book, and every form significant of its hidden life and final cause.

The true reader will then affirm the unity of the universe and will proclaim "Aye" with the "Eye" as a literate self, an "I."

Transcendentalism was clearly a literary movement as well as a religious and philosophical one. Emerson's works *The American Scholar* and "Self-Reliance" articulate the ways in which a new America demanded and deserved a new literature that would speak to and of the American people. The earlier work, published in 1837, defined the American scholar as "Man Thinking," with an emphasis upon process, an idea embraced by Emerson and other writers who preferred ongoing change to static existence. The essay explores the three influences upon the American scholar: nature, the past, and action.

Echoing the message of his earlier work *Nature*, Emerson admonishes Man Thinking to combine the ancient adage, "Know thyself," with what he called "the modern precept, 'Study nature,'" to produce one fundamental maxim. The scholar would thus arrive at a unifying experience and understand the connections between the self and the Self, an idea Emerson emphasizes in his essay "Self-Reliance." This process of comprehending the relationships within oneself and the universe is central to Emerson's view of transcendental vision. He points out the way in which the young, searching mind becomes mature as it begins to see unity where it had earlier seen only discrete entities:

> To the young mind every thing is individual, stands by itself. By and by, it finds how to join two things and see in them one nature; then three, then three thousand; and so, tyrannized over by its own unifying instinct, it goes on tying things together, diminishing anomalies, discovering roots running under ground whereby contrary and remote things cohere and flower out from one stem.

In addition to the influence of nature, the American scholar must be shaped by the mind of the past, especially the books of the past. Emerson warns, however, about the use of books – they are not simply excuses to return to some earlier period, to escape from the demands of the day. Rather, books exist to inspire the scholar to act and to create. "Each age . . . must write its own books," Emerson proclaims, reminding the scholar that the past is useful insofar as it helps shape the future.

The final influence upon Man Thinking is action, an idea that Emerson qualified by saying that it was subordinate but essential to the scholar. Emerson's inclusion of this influence is yet another example of his effort to help Americans see that there was a new way of defining all things, including the concept of scholar and scholarship. Whereas the traditional European idea of scholarly endeavor emphasized the distance between the scholar and the world, Emerson's contribution was to show the way in which the speculative thinker could also be a practical person, engaged in the daily activities of life. In Emerson's view, the scholar was compelled to be actively involved in the world: "Life is our dictionary. . . . Life lies behind us as the quarry from whence we get tiles and copestones for the masonry of today." Just as the scholar needs books for inspiration, so Man Thinking needs action as a resource for creativity.

While *The American Scholar* spoke to individuals about nature, the past, and action, it was also a message with national implications. Individualism and nationalism were parallel beliefs for Emerson and his colleagues, who were committed to awakening both the person and the nation to a new vision. Thus *The American Scholar* concludes with famous words aimed at galvanizing American men and women of letters as individuals and as a nation:

> We have listened too long to the courtly muses of Europe . . . . We will walk on our own feet; we will work with our own hands; we will speak with our own minds. The study of letters shall be no longer a name for pity, for doubt, and for sensual indulgence. The dread of man and the love of man shall be a wall of defence and a wreath of joy around all. A nation of men will for the first time exist, because each believes himself inspired by the Divine Soul which also inspires all men.

If *The American Scholar* ultimately called America as a nation to develop its own culture, "Self-Reliance," published in 1841, beckoned individuals to develop themselves as independent, self-determining units who would rely upon intuition to guide them:

> To believe your own thought, to believe that what is true for you in your private heart is true for all men, – that is genius. Speak your latent conviction, and it shall be the universal sense; for the inmost in due time becomes the outmost, and our first thought is rendered back to us by the trumpets of the Last Judgment.

The essay is filled with Emersonian aphorisms:

> Whoso would be a man, must be a nonconformist. . . . Nothing is at last sacred but the integrity of your own mind . . . . A foolish consistency is the hobgoblin of small minds, adored by little statesmen and philosophers and divines . . . . To be great is to be misunderstood.

Yet the heart of this essay is not its quotable quotes; the core of "Self-Reliance" is Emerson's message that the self – both the individual and the nation – must rely upon itself, look within itself, and create itself.

This message shaped literary history during and after Emerson's time. Emerson articulated and proclaimed the strengths of Transcendentalism for a period that was searching to define itself and its literature. His voice of optimism, even when it qualified its sound in an essay such as "Experience," inspired nineteenth-century Americans to discover themselves and their language. Whitman, for example, wrote that he had been "simmering, simmering, simmering" until Emerson brought him to a boil. Emerson saw in Whitman the embodiment of an American approach to literature and encouraged the poet when he read an early version of *Leaves of Grass* (1855–1892). Similarly, he fortified Henry David Thoreau, assuming the role of patron for the young nonconformist who, like many others in Concord, sat at Emerson's feet, listening to the man whose vision of American literature demanded a new voice, a new language, a new way of seeing.

This early influence was not confined to the United States. Nietzsche copied dozens of passages from Emerson into a notebook, borrowed the phrase "the gay science" from him, and was almost certainly influenced by Emerson's concept of the Over-Soul. Thomas Carlyle sponsored Emerson, and Matthew Arnold once said that no prose had been more influential in the nineteenth century than Emerson's. During three trips to England, Emerson mingled with British literati and had an enormous impact, especially on young writers who, like their American counterparts, were searching for innovative ways to speak, write, create.

Emerson continues to be a significant influence today. Modern writers continue to acknowledge their debts to him, as Robert Frost did in his essay "On Emerson," pointing out that some of his first thinking about language "was certainly Emersonian." Less specific but no less important is the general sense that Emerson's voice, perhaps even more than his particular words, has made a lasting impression upon American literature. As orator and preacher, Emerson spoke from Delphic heights, mesmerizing his audiences by his poetic, sweeping rhetoric that captured the hearts and imaginations of people whose own voices sounded tinny and provincial by contrast. That same Emersonian voice – meditative, oratorical, poetic – continues to influence writers who are concerned with the sound of their words and the shape of their language.

Principal criticism

Nature, 1836
An Oration Delivered Before the Phi Beta Kappa Society, Cambridge, 1837 (better known as *The American Scholar*)
An Address Delivered Before the Senior Class in Divinity College, Cambridge, 1838 (better known as *Divinity School Address*)
"Circles," 1840
"Self-Reliance," 1841
"The Transcendentalist," 1841
"Experience," 1844
"The Poet," 1844
"Politics," 1844
Representative Men: Seven Lectures, 1850
"Fate," 1860
Works and Days, 1870
"Thoreau," 1884

Other major works and literary forms

While the essay was clearly the most significant genre for Ralph Waldo Emerson, two other forms were important to him. Like most of his contemporaries, he admired poetry as the greatest literary art. Although in a letter to his future wife, Lydia Jackson, he wrote that he was "born a poet" and that poetry was his "nature and vocation," he went on to note that his singing was "husky" and that it was "for the most part in prose," a point of agreement between Emerson and most of his critics. Nevertheless, Emerson's *Poems*, published in 1847, demonstrate his commitment to this genre and his contribution to poetic theory, particularly since his essay "The Poet" and his verse reveal his emphasis upon the poet's symbol-making power.

Another genre important to Emerson was the journal. Not published in full until the 1960s through the 1980s under the title *The Journals and Miscellaneous Notebooks* (1960–1982), his journal writings are perhaps the most important revelation of the man, his artistic and philosophical musings, and his spiritual life. The journal entries indicate Emerson's continual quest to explore and make meaning of many ideas, particularly the notion of soul, a concern that is central in all Emerson's writings.

POETRY
Poems, 1847
May-Day and Other Pieces, 1867

NONFICTION
Essays: First Series, 1841
Essays: Second Series, 1844
Addresses and Lectures, 1849
English Traits, 1856
The Conduct of Life, 1860
Society and Solitude, 1870
Lectures and Biographical Sketches, 1884
The Journals and Miscellaneous Notebooks, 1960–1982 (16 volumes; William H. Gilman, et al., editors)

Further reading

Baker, Carlos. *Emerson Among the Eccentrics: A Group Portrait*, 1996.
Bercovich, Sacvan. *The Puritan Origins of the American Self*, 1975.
Gelpi, Donald L. *Endless Seeker: The Religious Quest of Ralph Waldo Emerson*, 1991.
Paul, Sherman. *Emerson's Angle of Vision*, 1952.
Poirier, Richard. *Poetry and Pragmatism*, 1992.
Porte, Joel. *Representative Man: Ralph Waldo Emerson in His Time*, 1979.
Robinson, David. *Apostle of Culture: Emerson as Preacher and Lecturer*, 1982.
——. *Emerson and the Conduct of Life: Pragmatism and Ethical Purpose in the Later Work*, 1993.
Rusk, Ralph L. *The Life of Ralph Waldo Emerson*, 1949.
Sealts, Merton M. *Emerson on the Scholar*, 1992.
Stovall, Floyd. "Ralph Waldo Emerson," in *Eight American Authors*, 1971. Edited by James Woodress.
Waggoner, Hyatt H. *Emerson as Poet*, 1974.
Whicher, Stephen E. *Freedom and Fate: An Inner Life of Ralph Waldo Emerson*, 1953.
Zwarg, Christina. *Feminist Conversations: Fuller, Emerson, and the Play of Reading*, 1995.

MARJORIE SMELSTOR

See also American Literary Theory to 1900; Fuller; Poe

William Empson

English critic and poet

Born: Yokefleet, England; September 27, 1906
Died: London, England; April 15, 1984

Biography

William Empson was born into the landed gentry of Yorkshire on September 27, 1906, the son of Arthur Reginald Empson and Laura Mickelthwait Empson. He was the youngest of five children. Empson went to preparatory school in Folkestone and entered Winchester College in 1920. In 1924 he won a mathematics scholarship to Magdalene College, at the University of Cambridge, where he earned a first in part 1 of the mathematics tripos, followed in 1929 by a starred first in part 1 of the English tripos. He was the literary editor of *Granta*, the Cambridge undergraduate journal, for which he also reviewed books and wrote poems; in addition, he coedited *Experiment*, another Cambridge literary magazine, to which he contributed poems.

Empson published *Seven Types of Ambiguity* in 1930, and the next year he took a post on the faculty of Tokyo University of Literature and Science. He returned to England in 1934, published *Poems* and *Some Versions of Pastoral* in 1935, and in 1937 left to accept an appointment at Peking National University. By the time he arrived in China, however, the university had moved 1,000 miles to the southwest under the pressure of war; Empson had to catch up with the students and teach them from memory. He returned to England in 1940 to work for the British Broadcasting Corporation, and in 1941 he married Hester Henrietta Crouse, a South African. According to Empson, their two sons, William Hendrick Mogador and Jacobus Arthur Calais, "each had to have an English name, an Afrikaans name, and the name of a town captured by the Allies on the day he was born."

Empson went back to Peking in 1947, participated in the Kenyon summer school programs in 1948 and 1950, and returned to England in 1952 to become professor of English literature at Sheffield University. He retired from Sheffield in 1971, was knighted in 1978, and died on April 15, 1984.

Influence

With *Seven Types of Ambiguity*, Empson became the first critic to treat ambiguity as a useful tool in the analysis of literary texts. In *Some Versions of Pastoral*, he introduced an understanding of pastoral that praised its presentation of the complex in the simple, an interpretation now called on frequently by other critics. *Milton's God* and many of his essays provoked critical controversy with their lacerating assaults on the conventional Christian readings of such works as *Paradise Lost* (1669, 1674) and Samuel Taylor Coleridge's *The Rime of the Ancient Mariner* (1798). Empson's writings were usually original, often obscure, and frequently polemical.

Analysis

Empson was still a student when he wrote the famous *Seven Types of Ambiguity*, one of the seminal texts of twentieth-century criticism. Inspired by Laura Riding and Robert Graves' analysis of William Shakespeare's sonnet 129 in *A Survey of Modernist Poetry* (1927), Empson proceeded to write the bulk of his book in two weeks. Admitting that the seven types were "merely a convenient framework," he explained that he would discuss only poems he admired, an explanation which nevertheless failed to ward off criticism that his system was purely descriptive and offered no criteria for judging the aesthetic merit of a work.

Other objections were raised: critics claimed that Empson's close analysis of short passages slights the complete works from which they are extracted; that his formal analyses ignore the relations among poetry, history, and ideology; and that the human needs satisfied by poetry are dismissed in a welter of formalist explication. Furthermore, many critics thought that Empson's approach valued ambiguity too highly as a measure of quality and that Empson was too quick to find ambiguities which fueled his method. Much of this criticism implies that in Empson's practice the meaning of a work derives too much from the imagination of the critic, leaving the text itself a mere inkblot open to irresponsible exploitation. The supporters of *Seven Types of Ambiguity* praised the work's invitation to play, which opens poetry up to fresh explication. Herein lies the central question behind the critical method: do works of literature have fixed, objective meaning, or are all readings simply the product of the play of mind?

Empson has argued in "My Credo: Verbal Analysis" (1950) that his analytical approach is a valid – and valuable – aspect of criticism and that although assessing value is part of the critic's task, it is not everything. He explains that he begins with an intuitive sense of the worth of a work and proceeds to study its complexities, but that a lack of complexity is not necessarily a bad thing in a text.

As for the irresponsibility of his method, Empson maintains a steady defense of the authority of the author's mind, asserting that whenever he fails to make sense of a text which he intuitively knows to be good, it is his fault and not the author's. This insistence on the firm presence of the author's mind provokes Empson to scorn the intentional fallacy because, as he notes in "The Intentional Fallacy, Again" (1972), "the students are denied any spontaneous contact with an author's mind."

In sum, *Seven Types of Ambiguity*, although burdened by a too intricate theoretical apparatus, encourages the close analysis of poems and therefore contributes to the complex of ideas embodied in the New Criticism. It repudiates that school's dissociation of the poem from its origins and its accompanying elevation of the poem to its status as "verbal icon."

The seven essays in *Some Versions of Pastoral* depart significantly from the method of *Seven Types of Ambiguity*. They analyze whole works, such as *The Beggar's Opera* (1728) and *Alice's Adventures in Wonderland* (1865), in a broad context; they discuss topics of class and society (such as proletarian literature); and they employ insights from cultural anthropology and Freudian psychology. Unfortunately, they are often bafflingly oblique and they reveal no clear-cut thematic progression. Empson provides no direct definition of pastoral, but the mode seems to dissolve the complex into the simple and to mitigate the differences between social classes. Thus, the pastoral isolates in the comparatively simple lives of rural people those features common to all social classes and in so doing, emphasizes the human virtues and brings people together. Empson's approach is demonstrated brilliantly in the essay "*Alice in Wonderland*: The Child as Swain," in which "the obscure tradition of pastoral" is transferred to the child, exploiting the insight that a child's intuition "contains what poetry and philosophy must spend their time laboring to discover."

The intent of the essays collected in *The Structure of Complex Words* is explained this way by Empson: "Roughly, the moral is that a developing society decides practical questions more by the way it interprets words it thinks obvious and traditional than by its official statements of current dogma." Behind this view of the social function of language lies Empson's preoccupation with the emotive theory of language taught by his Cambridge mentor, I. A. Richards. Empson does not deny that words carry feeling but argues that in Richards' formulation, the feelings conveyed by words get separated from their sense.

As is common with Empson, the excellent essays in *The Structure of Complex Words* are crippled by an unnecessarily formidable critical apparatus. The main idea – that a word is a "complex molecule which must not be unpacked in ordinary use" – is reasonable enough, but the "bits of machinery" that Empson contrives for the unpacking are too algebraic in conception and lie inert on the pages of his explications. Many of the individual essays are stimulating, however, despite the cumbersome theory. In "Honest in *Othello*," Empson concludes from the fifty-two uses of "honest" and "honesty" in *Othello, the Moor of Venice* (1604) that Shakespeare hated the "hearty and individualist" use of the word in his day. In a sparkling essay on "The English Dog," Empson studies "dog" as one of several words (including "fool," "rogue," "honest") that in the sixteenth through the eighteenth centuries accumulated both patronizing and hearty meanings.

Throughout his career, Empson was intent on de-Christianizing and desymbolizing the classics of British literature, and that impulse is revealed most strongly in *Milton's God*. Empson often appears as an old-fashioned Enlightenment rationalist, and his hatred of the Christian deity invigorates *Milton's God* at the same time that it shapes what most critics view as a perverse argument: "the startling irreducible confusions" in *Paradise Lost* "so far from proving that the poem is bad, explain *why* it is so great."

Despite the eccentricity of his central theme, Empson as always makes some good points in *Milton's God*. He observes, for example, that "a parent who 'foresaw' that the children would fall and then insisted upon exposing them to the temptation in view would be considered neurotic, if nothing worse; and this is what we must ascribe to Milton's God." Empson's basic decency and fairness shine through in such passages, but apologists for Christianity have worked for centuries to erect defenses against such common-sense arguments.

Of the eleven essays in the posthumous *Using Biography*, only three are original. The title expresses Empson's affirmation of the value of biography and authorial intention in criticism. One essay treats "Joyce's Intentions" in *Ulysses* (1922) directly, and the brilliant essay "*Tom Jones*," although it posits a dubious irony in *The History of Tom Jones, a Foundling* (1749), is an inspired reading of Tom's noble nature. Empson also finds in the novel support for his claim that "the central purpose of reading imaginative literature is to accustom yourself" to the basic fact that different moral codes exist in the world. In the piece on James Joyce's intentions, Empson rejects all arguments that Joyce ever relented in his antipathy to the Church, and he lambasts one of his favorite whipping boys, the neo-Christian "majority of Eng. Lit. criticism, especially in America," who pretend they have "never heard of the opinions of the Enlightenment."

A similar pugnaciousness informs the pieces collected in *Essays on Shakespeare*. In "*Macbeth*," for example, Empson rebuts Dover Wilson's thesis that Shakespeare shortened *Macbeth* (1606) in an early revision and that the hypothetical longer version presented a longer struggle between Macbeth and his wife. Empson again takes on Wilson in "Falstaff," sneering at him for "preaching at us about his Medieval Vice and his Ideal King" and finding in Wilson's arguments a need to explain away the "pathetic description" of Falstaff's death and thereby justify the "modern royalist" in his respect for Hal. The Shakespeare essays are among Empson's best, prickly and original.

In *Faustus and the Censor*, Empson contends that both the A and the B versions of Christopher Marlowe's play show evidence of ecclesiastical censorship. Empson believes that the A text is closer to the original and superior to the B text. The crux of Empson's argument comes back to his aversion to Christianity; for the censor, Faustus would have had to suffer for his overreaching, and Empson asserts that the original play held out the possibility of Faustus' escape. It is a bold argument, shot through with Empson's prejudices but well informed and cannily reasoned.

A final judgment on Empson's influence is problematic. He began in *Seven Types of Ambiguity* the critical opening up of literary texts to an exploration of their polysemy, and his explication of the social ramifications of pastoral has been fruitful. His eccentric approach to linguistic analysis, however, and his assault on Christian "Eng. Lit. criticism" seem to have made little impression on the academic critical establishment. Despite the enthusiasm with which the New Critics exploited ambiguity in their formalist analyses, Empson remained ill at ease with that school's touting of such tenets as the intentional fallacy and the minimal importance of historical background. He has never really been identified with a particular school of criticism or supported by a family of satellite critics. In his most powerful criticism, he was often alienated from the academic mainstream, especially when he fought against Christian and Symbolist readings of such standard works as *The Rime of the Ancient Mariner*. The seven types of ambiguity that he postulated are largely unmanageable, and the typology remains an odd, elaborate fossil half submerged in the shifting sands of literary theory. In his attempt in *The Structure of Complex Words* to repudiate I. A. Richards' emotive theory of meaning, Empson devised "an apparatus for breaking down words into their subatomic components" that is too intricate for general use. Commonly with Empson, the theory has proved overly subtle, but in his own hands, the results have often been striking. He is perhaps best judged as a critic who is impossible to imitate but whose spirited and intelligent commentaries will enliven literary criticism for some time.

Principal criticism

Seven Types of Ambiguity: A Study of Its Effects on English Verse, 1930
Some Versions of Pastoral, 1935 (also known as *English Pastoral Poetry*, 1938)
The Structure of Complex Words, 1951
Milton's God, 1961, 1965
Using Biography, 1984
Essays on Shakespeare, 1986
Faustus and the Censor, 1987
Argufying: Essays on Literature and Culture, 1987
Essays on Renaissance Literature, Vol. 1: Donne and the New Philosophy, 1993 (John Haffenden, editor)

Other major works and literary forms

Although better known as a critic of the first rank, William Empson was also a poet; his work is often anthologized. His characteristically gnarled and difficult poems are collected in *Poems* (1935), *The Gathering Storm* (1940), and *Collected Poems* (1949, 1962); the 1962 edition of *Collected Poems* is the most complete. Most of his verse was written before 1942; after that time, he devoted himself mainly to criticism. In addition to his poetry and criticism, he coedited *Coleridge's Verse: A Selection* (1972) with David Pirie. *The Royal Beasts and Other Works* (1986), edited by John Haffenden, collects various early pieces of prose, poetry, and drama.

PLAY
Three Stories, 1927

POETRY
Poems, 1935
The Gathering Storm, 1940
Collected Poems, 1949, 1962

EDITED TEXT
Coleridge's Verse: A Selection, 1972 (with David Pirie)

Further reading

Brooks, Cleanth. "Empson's Criticism," in *"Accent" Anthology: Selections from "Accent," A Quarterly of New Literature, 1940–1945*, 1946. Edited by Kerker Quinn and Charles Shattuck.
Constable, John, ed. *Critical Essays on William Empson*, 1993.
Day, Frank. *Sir William Empson: An Annotated Bibliography*, 1984.
Donoghue, Denis. *Ferocious Alphabets*, 1981.
Fry, Paul H. *William Empson: Prophet Against Sacrifice*, 1991.
Gill, Roma, ed. *William Empson: The Man and His Work*, 1974.
Hough, Graham. *Style and Stylistics*, 1969.
Hyman, Stanley Edgar. "William Empson and Categorical Criticism," in *The Armed Vision: A Study in the Methods of Modern Literary Criticism*, 1955.
Kenner, Hugh. "Alice in Empsonland," in *The Hudson Review*. V (1952), pp. 137–144.
Kermode, Frank. "On a Chinese Mountain," in *London Review of Books*. (November 20, 1986), pp. 8–10.
Norris, Christopher. *William Empson and the Philosophy of Literary Criticism*, 1978.
Ransom, John Crowe. "Mr. Empson's Muddles," in *The Southern Review*. IV (July, 1938–April, 1939), pp. 322–339.
Richardson, D. E. "Cheering Up with Empson," in *Sewanee Review*. (Spring 1996), pp. 305–311.
Sale, Roger. "The Achievement of William Empson," in *Modern Heroism: Essays on D. H. Lawrence, William Empson, and J. R. R. Tolkien*, 1973.

FRANK DAY

See also British Literary Theory: Twentieth Century; New Criticism; Richards

Epic

The genre of epic poetry springs from traditional societies, in which narratives about great events and individuals associated with a distant past are told and retold from generation to generation. Indeed, the word "epic," derived from the Greek word *epos*, meaning "word, tale, or story," emphasizes the oral act of telling such a story.

At the beginning of the Western epic tradition stands Homer's *Iliad* and *Odyssey*, the only epics surviving from a rich ancient Greek tradition of poetic narratives connected with a Heroic Age and the Trojan War. While traditionally attributed to a blind, unlettered poet named Homer who lived in about 750 B.C., the question of authorship of these epics, as well as the oral epics of other cultures, is complicated by the contribution of earlier storytellers and oral poets. This so-called "Homeric question" takes us to the heart of the oral epic genre, in which singers use a rigid, stylized language based upon epithets, formulas, and themes often set in specific metrical contexts in order to preserve the narrative and facilitate its retelling and re-creation. The process of oral composition during the performance of a traditional epic was illuminated in the mid-twentieth century by scholars like Milman Parry and Albert Lord who compared the structure of the ancient Homeric epics to that of a living tradition of epic performance in Yugoslavia. More recently, study of the West African epic tradition associated with the hero Sunjata not only reinforced these oral features of epic but emphasized the tendency of oral epic to be multigeneric, that is, to incorporate a variety of literary forms including praise poetry, genealogy, and narrative in order to celebrate the culture of the people by linking them with the heroic accomplishments of their distant ancestors.

Such traditional epics suggest the following definition of the genre: a long, serious, and complex poem about a hero who lived in the distant past and whose story reflects the cultural values and identity of succeeding generations. Certain features of the Homeric epics have come, in the West, to be considered standard elements of the epic genre. These include the use of dactylic hexameter meter, an introductory invocation or prayer for inspiration, starting in the middle of the narrative (*in medias res*), elaborate description (*ekphrasis*) of significant objects such as weapons and other tools, assemblies of gods and of humans, and the direct involvement of the gods or the supernatural in the narrative.

Once the Homeric epics were written down, perhaps in the sixth century B.C., they continued to be performed by professional reciters called *rhapsodes*, but they were no longer a living tradition. The transition from the fluid composition of epic in performance to the fixed nature of a written text leads eventually to a new form of epic, often called "literary" as opposed to "oral," in which an individual, literate poet combines the techniques of written composition with features of oral epic. An important Greek example of such a literary epic is the *Argonautica* by Apollonius of Rhodes (born c. 295 B.C.), in which the multigeneric features of the Homeric epics are expanded to include elements of other dramas, for example drama and lyric poetry. Apollonius' epic about Jason and the Argonauts is intentionally much shorter than either of the Homeric epics and focuses more directly on the amorous relationship between the hero Jason and the witch Medea. The *Argonautica* is also a much more learned epic than the Homeric epics and lacks the cultural centrality of traditional oral epics. In the first century B.C. Lucretius, a Roman philosopher and poet, adapted many of the features of oral epic to *De Rerum Nature* (*On the Nature of Things*), a treatise on the atomic theory of Democritus and the philosophy of Epicurus.

The masterpiece of the ancient literary epic is unquestionably Virgil's *Aeneid*, in which the plots of the Homeric epics are used as models to tell the story of the Trojan Aeneas, who travels to Italy after the fall of Troy and founds a dynasty from which spring the Roman state in general and the family of Julius Caesar in particular. Virgil revitalizes the cultural centrality of epic by celebrating the political destiny and superiority of Rome, while describing a highly humanized hero and his doomed love for the Carthaginian queen Dido. More than any other epic, the *Aeneid* establishes the genre in the West with its blend of epic conventions with history, political propaganda, and religion.

Later Romans tried less successfully to move the epic form in new directions. In his *Metamorphoses*, Ovid (43 B.C.–A.D. 18) offered a catalogue of myths about change of form beginning with cosmic creation and ending with the apotheosis of Julius Caesar. In *Pharsalia*, Lucan (A.D. 39–65) used the political clash between Julius Caesar and Pompey the Great to immortalize republican ideals during the reign of the emperor Nero. Neither poem, however, has rivaled Virgil's *Aeneid* as an epic model.

During the medieval period several surviving epics sprang from the European oral tradition. These include the Anglo-Saxon *Beowulf* and the French *Chanson de Roland*, both celebrating the value system of warrior societies like those in the Homeric epics and the *Aeneid*.

In *La divina commedia* (c. 1320; *The Divine Comedy*), the Italian poet Dante Alighieri intensified the personal and religious aspects of the epic form, as he described his own journey through Hell and Purgatory with the epic poet Virgil as his guide, and then into Heaven with the help of his dead beloved Beatrice. Dante wrote in the vernacular Italian instead of Latin and used terza rima, a meter more suitable to Italian than the dactylic hexameter of the Greco-Roman tradition.

During the Renaissance the literary epic was revitalized throughout Europe, especially in the works of Ludovico Ariosto (1474–1533) and Torquato Tasso (1544–1595) in Italy and of Edmund Spenser (1552/3–1599) and John Milton (1608–1674) in England. Milton's *Paradise Lost*, in particular, illustrates the adaptability of the epic genre. Writing in iambic pentameter, Milton combines the structure and techniques of Homer and of Virgil with the Christian emphasis of Dante to tell the biblical story of the fall of Adam and Eve.

In the nineteenth century archaeological finds in Mesopotamia revealed that a rich epic tradition had reached a literary stage of development by the fourteenth century B.C., especially in the *Epic of Gilgamesh*. The use of epithets, divine involvement, and poetic language in both *Gilgamesh* and the Greco-Roman epics emphasizes that the genre must be seen in a broad cultural context.

A subform of the epic is the mock epic in which epic conventions are used to create a narrative about much less serious themes, such as *Batrachomyomachia* ("The Battle of Frogs and Mice"), which survives in the Homeric corpus, and "The Rape of the Lock" by Alexander Pope.

Since the Renaissance few poets have aspired successfully to the epic genre, which has been supplanted in large part by the prose form of the novel, especially the historical novel with sweeping scope and powerful political implications. The term "epic" has now broadened to include such major prose narratives as *Les Misérables* by Victor Hugo (1802–1885) and *War and Peace* by Lev Tolstoi (1828–1910) or even cinematic sagas such as *Gone With the Wind* and *Star Wars*.

Further reading

Johnson, John W. *The Epic of Son-jara*, 1992.
Lewis, C. S. *A Preface to "Paradise Lost,"* 1942.
Lord, Albert. *The Singer of Tales*, 1965.
Merchant, Paul. *The Epic*, 1971.
Okpewho, Isidore. *The Epic in Africa*, 1979.
Parry, Milman. "The Traditional Poetic Language of Oral Poetry," in *Homer*, 1986. Edited by Harold Bloom.

THOMAS J. SIENKEWICZ

Desiderius Erasmus

Dutch theologian, scholar, and critic

Born: Rotterdam, the Netherlands; October 27, 1466?
Died: Basel, Swiss Confederation; July 12, 1536

Biography

Desiderius Erasmus was born in Rotterdam, the Netherlands, probably in 1466. In 1488 he entered an Augustinian monastery in Steyn, the Netherlands; he was ordained a priest in 1492. One year later, he received permission to leave his monastery so that he could serve as the Latin secretary for the Bishop of Cambrai. He would never again live in a monastery. He studied classical letters, first at the University of Paris and then at the University of Turin, where in 1506 he received his doctorate in theology.

Erasmus traveled extensively during his long life. During three extended visits to England, he worked closely with such eminent British humanists as John Colet, John Fisher, and especially his close friend Thomas More. Erasmus always remained a Catholic. Some Catholic theologians, however, resented his criticism of certain abuses such as the sale of indulgences, and many Protestant writers could not understand his refusal to side with Martin Luther and leave Catholicism. Many Catholics and Protestants became suspicious of his intentions, and their overt intolerance caused him to move several times during the last two decades of his life. In 1521 opposition from conservative Catholic theologians convinced him to leave the University of Louvain in Flanders for the Swiss city of Basel, where his main publisher, Johann Froben, worked. After eight years in Basel, he left for the German city of Freiburg because a religious civil war had broken out in the Swiss Confederation. When relative calm was reestablished in Basel, he returned there in 1535. Unfortunately, his health deteriorated very rapidly, and he died in Basel on July 12, 1536.

Influence

Erasmus was the most eloquent Renaissance apologist for classical learning. His writings illustrate classical Humanism, the Renaissance literary and intellectual movement that encouraged the systematic and imaginative use of the classics in order to rejuvenate contemporary letters. He argued quite persuasively that the creative imitation and adaptation of respected classical authors would lead to the production of lasting literary works of true originality, either in Latin or in the vernacular languages. He convinced his contemporaries that an admiration for classical literature was perfectly compatible with a belief in Christian dogma. He explained that practising Christians could discover many important moral truths in the works of pagan writers and philosophers from the classical era.

Erasmus consistently stressed the ethical and social implications of Christ's teaching. For Erasmus, such moral values and the need to respect the dignity and freedom of each individual were more significant than theological discussions on doctrinal matters. He encouraged his contemporaries to be tolerant of those who did not share their religious beliefs. During the last fifteen years of his life, he lamented that the intolerance of both Catholics and Protestants had caused so much unintended suffering and strife among Christians. For many generations after his death in 1536, Erasmus was admired not only for the excellent quality of his scholarship but also – and especially – for his eloquent call to respect the intellectual and religious beliefs of each individual.

Analysis

There is a definite unity in Erasmus' literary criticism. Throughout his lengthy career, Erasmus expressed his firm conviction that the systematic study and creative imitation of classical writers would enable his contemporaries to enrich the cultural life of Europe and to create literary works of lasting beauty. Erasmus had a fine sense of humor. His wit and elegant style create a favourable impression on his readers and thus make them more willing to accept his views on topics as diverse as classical scholarship, the art of letter-writing, biblical exegesis, and social injustices. His Latin style is complex but never awkward or artificial; his long sentences are at once elegant and natural. Erasmus was a master of the art of dialogue. This style of argument, combined with his skillful use of paradox and irony, encourages his readers to reflect on the true significance of the literary, philosophical, and social problems discussed in his works.

Erasmus' most frequently translated work is *The Praise of Folly*, which describes with much wit and wisdom the pleasures and importance of intellectual pursuits. A lengthy declamation by the character Folly constitutes this entire book. Its ambiguous title, *Moriœ encomium*, which can be translated as either "speech in praise of folly" or "speech in praise of (Thomas) More," indicates the need to interpret this paradoxical book at several levels. Folly points out that the world generally admires wealth and high social standing more than spiritual meditation and intellectual accomplishments. Folly encourages her listeners to heed Saint Paul's admonition to become fools in the eyes of the world in order to acquire true wisdom. Moral virtue has nothing to do with our material possessions. Financial wealth may disappear very quickly, but spiritual growth and the life of the mind bring personal joy and satisfaction which social changes can never destroy. Folly praises scholars and writers by stating that their writings can enrich the experiences of sensitive readers for generations and even for centuries to come.

Only one year after *The Praise of Folly* was first published, Erasmus completed his influential textbook of rhetoric entitled *On the Twofold Abundance of Words and Things*. This is a cumbersome title, and most scholars refer to this work as the *De copia*, a shortened form of its original Latin title. Erasmus dedicated *De copia* to John Colet, an eminent English educator who had just founded St. Paul's School in London. The *De copia* illustrates the relevance of classical learning for the modern world. Erasmus demonstrates how the systematic imitation of classical writers enables the writer to express his or her ideas persuasively in a variety of styles and in many different situations. Reading the classics is helpful for learning to think and to write clearly. Erasmus linked the study of classical literature with the development of moral values. He did not admire literary texts merely for their stylistic brilliance; like many other Renaissance writers, he believed that a literary work should praise virtue and condemn vice. For Erasmus, an important work of literature had to express some significant moral or religious truth. Within ten years of its first publication in 1512, the *De copia* became the standard Latin textbook of rhetoric in schools throughout Europe. Its influence, however, extended well beyond Latin classes and Renaissance works composed in Latin. Erasmus' thoughtful comments on the nature and process of artistic creativity inspired many sixteenth-century authors, who wrote mostly in vernacular languages, to create works of true originality.

The Book Against the Barbarians, Erasmus' third major work of literary criticism, was first published in 1520, although he had begun writing it almost thirty years earlier. In this work, Erasmus dismissed as "barbarians" those intolerant individuals who denied the relevance of the classical tradition for believing Christians. Erasmus agreed with Saint Augustine, who had utilized the best elements of classical philosophy and rhetoric in order to teach more effectively the revealed truths of Christianity.

Both Erasmus and Augustine used the same paradoxical argument in order to encourage Christians to study classical works written by pagans. They both referred to the comment in Exodus 12:35–36 that God had approved of the Jews' theft of Egyptian gold at the time of their flight from slavery in Egypt. Theft is normally considered to be morally wrong, but the Jews acted with God's approval in this situation. Both Erasmus and Augustine affirmed that this theft represented the symbolic and proper transfer of "heathen wisdom to the adornment and use of our faith." Imitating respected pagan writers from antiquity does not require acceptance of their religious beliefs. Their moral insights and techniques of persuasion can be creatively adapted in a way that is meaningful for contemporary believers. Both Erasmus and Augustine were convinced that an admiration for classical literature was perfectly compatible with a belief in Christianity.

In *The Book Against the Barbarians*, Erasmus presented an eloquent apology for classical learning. In his very witty 1528 dialogue, *The Ciceronian*, he discussed correct and inappropriate methods for imitating classical authors. The three participants in this dialogue are Nosoponus, Bulephorus, and Hypologus. All three express sincere admiration for the Roman orator Cicero, whom Erasmus once called "the parent of all eloquence." Nosoponus, however, lacks aesthetic judgment. He wishes to include in his writings only those words and stylistic devices to be found in Cicero's extant works. In order to ensure his absolute fidelity to a Ciceronian style, Nosoponus has prepared for his own use a massive concordance of Cicero's works. Nosoponus composes so artificially that it takes him more than a week to complete a brief letter requesting that a friend return some books to him. Because of his fanaticism and lack of sound reasoning, Nosoponus believes that it is preferable to be a Ciceronian in this life than to spend eternity in Heaven. Hypologus and Bulephorus eventually cure Nosoponus of his strange malady.

In this refined dialogue, Erasmus demonstrated the need to imitate classical authors in a creative rather than servile manner. Bulephorus realizes that the classical tradition should be adapted to the reality of the modern world. Major social and religious changes had occurred since the end of the Roman republic. It would be foolish for a modern preacher to deliver speeches exactly like those given by Cicero before the Roman Senate. Erasmus points out that a modern orator must make sure that every imitation of a classical source is "fitting and appropriate" for the style and subject matter of his or her speech. Erasmus argues persuasively that the imaginative imitation of classical works can result in truly original and profound works of modern literature.

Erasmus' literary criticism influenced generations of scholars and demonstrated clearly the relevance of classical learning for the modern world. His reflections in *The Ciceronian* indicated that literary criticism must combine creativity with solid scholarship. He argued persuasively that literary critics should not merely identify the classical sources for a poem or a play. The role of a literary critic is to analyze thoughtfully and imaginatively how and why gifted writers utilized classical sources in order to create elegant and original works of literature.

His *De copia, The Book Against the Barbarians*, and *The Praise of Folly* had a lasting influence on European literary criticism. He showed that the classical rhetorical tradition enables scholars to describe with great precision both the art of writing and the art of conveying significant ideas to others in a pleasant and eloquent style. A modern scholar, Marc Fumaroli, has referred to the sixteenth and seventeenth centuries in Europe as "the age of eloquence." Like his contemporaries, Erasmus did not admire eloquence for its own sake; he argued for the inseparability of eloquence from the expression of significant moral values. In a celebrated 1532 letter to Erasmus, the French writer François Rabelais called Erasmus both "the protector of letters and the invincible fighter for truth." Rabelais understood well the dual nature of literary criticism for classical Humanist Desiderius Erasmus.

Principal criticism

Moriæ encomium, 1511 (*The Praise of Folly*, 1549)
De duplici copia verborum ac rerum, 1512 (*On the Twofold Abundance of Words and Things*, 1978; better known as *De copia*)
Antibarbarum, 1520 (*The Book Against the Barbarians*, 1930)
Dialogus, cui titulus Ciceronianus sive, de optimo dicendi genere, 1528 (*The Ciceronian*, 1900)

Other major works and literary forms

It is difficult and perhaps artificial to divide Desiderius Erasmus' works into specific categories. He was a Catholic theologian, an editor of and commentator on classical texts and the Bible, a historical philologist, a prolific letter-writer, an essayist, a social critic, and an educator. Though he was Dutch by birth, he chose to write exclusively in Latin, the language understood by almost all well-educated Europeans of his day. During the first three decades of the sixteenth century, he was the most influential and admired scholar in Europe.

The quality and variety of his works are still impressive today. In 1516 he published the first serious critical edition of the Bible since that prepared by Saint Jerome more than a millennium earlier. His learned commentaries on specific books of the Bible were largely responsible for the rise of modern techniques of biblical exegesis. In his commentary and paraphrases of the New Testament, Erasmus made creative use of historical linguistics and writings of Church Fathers to demonstate the many different levels of meaning in the New Testament. Erasmus did not know Hebrew and thus could not translate the Old Testament into Latin. As a social critic, he consistently denounced the many European wars fought during his lifetime; many readers even today consider his 1517 *Querela pacis* (*The Complaint of Peace*, 1559) to be the most eloquent Christian defense of pacifism ever written. During the last forty years of his life, Erasmus corresponded with the most important thinkers of his age. His elegant letters are both profound and aesthetically pleasing. In many books, such as his 1516 *Institutio principis Christiani* (*The Education of a Christian Prince*, 1936), he advocated reforms in educational systems throughout Europe. In all of his works, Erasmus strove to demonstrate and illustrate the continued value and relevance of the classical literary and philosophical traditions for Christians.

NONFICTION
Adagia, 1500 (*Proverbs or Adages*, 1622)
Enchiridion militis christiani, 1503 (*The Manual of the Christian Knight*, 1533)
De rationae studii, 1512 (*A Method of Study*, 1978)
Institutio principis christiani, 1516 (*The Education of a Christian Prince*, 1936)
Querela pacis, 1517 (*The Complaint of Peace*, 1559)
Colloquia familiaria, 1518 (*The Colloquies of Erasmus*, 1671)
De libero arbitrio, 1524 (*Discourse on the Freedom of the Will*, 1961)
Opus epistolarum, 1529 (partially translated in *The Epistles*, 1901, 3 volumes)

TRANSLATION
Novum Instrumentum, 1516 (of the New Testament)

Further reading

Allen, Percy S. *The Age of Erasmus*, 1914.
Bainton, Roland H. *Erasmus of Christendom*, 1970.
Campion, Edmund J. *Montaigne, Rabelais, and Marot as Readers of Erasmus*, 1995.
Halkin, Léon F. *Erasmus: A Critical Biography*, 1993. Translated by John Tonkin.
Huizinga, Johann. *Erasmus of Rotterdam*, 1924.
Margolin, Jean-Claude. *Erasme par lui-même*, 1965.
——. *Erasme: Précepteur de l'Europe*, 1995.
Schoeck, R. J. *Erasmus of Europe*, 1990–1993 (2 volumes).
Tracy, James D. *Erasmus: The Growth of a Mind*, 1972.

EDMUND J. CAMPION

See also Renaissance and Restoration Literary Theory

The Erotic

World literature abounds in examples of writing frequently termed "erotic." One thinks, for example, of the *Kamasutra* from fourth-century India, or the Arabic *One Thousand and One Nights*, originating in the eighth century, or the much older *Song of Songs* in the Hebrew Bible, attributed to Solomon but dating back to the fourth/third centuries B.C. In the Western tradition, however, the term "erotic" derives from the name of the Greek god Eros, the god of love. In Hesiod's *Theogony* (eighth century B.C.), Eros is a primeval force preceding the creation of all things, described as "the most handsome among the gods, dissolver of flesh, who overcomes the reason and purpose in the breasts of all gods and men." According to later versions, however, Eros is the son of Aphrodite, the Greek goddess of love (for the Romans, Venus). (By contrast, Priapus, the son of Dionysos and Aphrodite, was a mere fertility god – of gardens, flocks, and herds.) Depicted in Hellenistic times as a winged archer, Eros was known in this form by the Romans as Cupid, whence he has persisted down to more modern times, in the popular cultural imagination, on chocolate boxes and St. Valentine's day cards.

For Plato, it was important to distinguish between Uranian and Pandemic Eros, a heavenly and a common love – related, but distinct. In the *Symposium*, Socrates recounts how Diotima, the wise woman of Mantineia, told him that love, rightly understood, could lead to Beauty itself. Thus we find in Greek philosophy not only the notion of "Platonic love" but an essential link between Eros and art.

In Greek literature of the seventh and sixth centuries B.C., love forms the explicit theme of lyric poetry, most famously perhaps with Sappho of Lesbos; and Camille Paglia has written of the role of the erotic in constituting identity, arguing that "Sappho shows that love poetry is how Western personality defines itself." In the tradition of Roman literature, erotic poetry treated of the so-called *quinque lineae amoris*, or five stages of love, namely *visus* (seeing), *allocutio* (addressing), *tactus* (touching), *basium* (kissing), and, finally, *coitus* (physical union). Description of the final stage is, however, chiefly the preserve of more modern literature. In Ovid's *Amores* 2. iv, the poet emphasizes the vast extent of his sexual appetite, and *Amores* 1. v provides a classic example of late Roman erotic writing. The influence of Catullus, Tibullus, Propertius, Martial, and Ovid on the Western erotic tradition is immense; for example, Ovid's *Ars amatoria* (c. 1 B.C.; *The Art of Love*) offered a blueprint for the classic textbook of twelfth-century Western European "courtly love," *De arte honeste amandi* (c. 1185; *The Art of Courtly Love*) by Andreas Capellanus.

To be sure, the medieval love lyric, performed by *trouvères* (in old French), *troubadours* (in Provençal), and *Minnesänger* (in German), represents the persistence of Platonic conceptions in their depiction of an attractive but unattainable Beloved. Yet medieval literature is also full of descriptions of more physical sexual appetites. Gottfried von Strassburg (fl. 1210), for example, describes at length the mutual attraction and desire of Tristan and Isolde (early thirteenth century). Equally, the humorous side of the erotic is evident in such works of the Renaissance period as *The Decameron* (1349–1351) by Giovanni Boccaccio, who was almost certainly an influence on Geoffrey Chaucer, some of whose *Canterbury Tales* (c. 1387) feature erotic, and predominantly bawdy, elements. So whereas Dante Alighieri's love for Beatrice in *La vita nuova* (c. 1292; *The New Life*) becomes, in *La divina commedia* (c. 1320; *The Divine Comedy*), a mystical experience focused on an idealization of the same woman, and whereas Petrarch's Laura, hymned in the *Canzoniere*, is physically present for the poet, yet even more unreachable, there is a contrast between these writers and the celebration of the more earthly aspects of Eros in other literature, especially of later centuries. In France, in particular, the eighteenth century, known as the age of the *galant*, produced numerous works of erotic literature; see, for example, the tales and dialogues of Claude-Prosper Jolyot Crébillon (Crébillon *fils*), the novel *Les Liaisons dangereuses* (1782; *Dangerous Liaisons*) by Pierre Choderlos de Laclos, the novels of Nicolas Restif de la Bretonne, and, above all, the works of the Marquis de Sade.

Perhaps the most successful attempt in the eighteenth century to revive, yet modernize, the erotic traditions of antiquity was undertaken by Johann Wolfgang von Goethe, a great admirer of the influential erotic poet of the Dutch Renaissance, Johannes Secundus, and who recommended reading *Daphnis and Chloé*, an erotic tale by the third-century writer Longus, every year. Goethe's *Römische Elegien* (1789; *Roman Elegies*) explicitly refer to the "triumvirate" (presumably, Catullus, Tibullus, Propertius), while the poem "Das Tagebuch" (1810; "The Diary") demonstrates a decidedly modern erotic sensibility. Friedrich Schiller pointed to a link between the erotic and the aesthetic in *Über die ästhetische Erziehung des Menschen* (1795; *On the Aesthetic Education of Man*) (see III. 2, XV. 9, XXVII. 7), and in *Über naive und sentimentalische Dichtung* (1796; *On Naive and Sentimental Poetry*) he distinguished between erotic poetry that was objectionable and vulgar, and another kind that was beautiful and noble. And in the nineteenth century, erotic elements became *de rigueur* in the literature of *décadence*, the writings of Leopold von Sacher-Masoch (1836–1895) deserving special mention.

In critical discourse, there is nearly always a need to distinguish the erotic from, for example, bawdiness, smut, pornography, or the obscene. But for more recent theorists, the importance of the erotic has become totemic. In *Götzen-Dämmerung* (1889; *Twilight of the Idols*), Friedrich Nietzsche had pointed out that "the sexual symbol was to the Greeks the symbol venerable as such, the intrinsic profound meaning of all antique piety." And, building on the insights of psychoanalysis, which were extremely important for the Surrealists, various theorists have averred its centrality. These include René Girard, who offered a masterly analysis of the "triangulation" of desire in Stendhal, Fedor Dostoevskii, and Marcel Proust (1961); Roland Barthes, who wrote two major essays on the Marquis of Sade (1967, 1971); and, beyond literary theory as such, Gilles Deleuze and Félix Guattari, who viewed the unconscious as a "desiring machine" (1972), and Jacques Lacan, whose blend of structuralism and psychoanalysis ("Desire is the essence of man"; *The Four Fundamental Concepts of Psycho-Analysis*, 1973) has proved immensely influential on literary criticism, feminist theory, and, above all, cinema studies. Equally, Georges Bataille ("It is possible to say of eroticism that it is the commendation of life to the point of death") and Michel Foucault ("In the *ars erotica*, truth is drawn from pleasure itself, understood as a practice, and accumulated as experience") are to be counted among others, rediscovering in the erotic a transgressive moment of great liberating potential.

Further reading

Barthes, Roland. *Sade, Fourier, Loyola*, 1971 (English translation, 1976).
Bataille, Georges. *L'Érotisme*, 1957 (*Eroticism*, 1987).
Brusendorff, Ove. *A History of Eroticism*, 1963–1967.
Carter, Angela. *The Sadeian Woman and the Ideology of Pornography*, 1978.
Deleuze, Gilles, and Félix Guattari. *Anti-Oedipus: Capitalism and Schizophrenia*, 1977.
Foucault, Michel. *Histoire de la sexualité*, 1976–1984 (*The History of Sexuality*, 1978–1985).
Girard, René. *Deceit, Desire and the Novel*, 1965.

Helm, Karl. "Quinque lineae amoris," in *Germanisch-romanische Monatsschrift*. 29, 1941, pp. 236–247.
Klossowski, Pierre. *Sade mon prochain*, 1947 (*Sade My Neighbor*, 1991).
Loth, David Goldsmith. *The Erotic in Literature: A Historical Survey of Pornography as Delightful as it is Indiscreet*, 1961.
Paglia, Camille. "Love Poetry" [Western], in *The New Princeton Encyclopedia of Poetry and Poetics*, 1993. Edited by Alex Preminger and Terry V. F. Brogan.
Praz, Mario. *The Romantic Agony*, 1933.
Wedeck, Harry Ezekiel. *Dictionary of Erotic Literature*, 1962.

PAUL BISHOP

See also Bataille; Foucault

Martin Esslin

Hungarian-born English drama critic

Born: Budapest, Hungary; June 8, 1918

Biography

Martin Julius Esslin was born to Paul Pereszlenyi and Charlotte Pereszlenyi (née Schiffer) in Budapest, Hungary, on June 8, 1918. Esslin's family moved to Vienna as political refugees before their son was two. From 1936 to 1938 he attended the Gymnasium in Vienna, then the University of Vienna, studying philosophy and English, and next the Max Reinhardt Seminar of Dramatic Art from which he graduated as a producer. In 1938 Esslin became a refugee for a second time when he left Austria to escape Adolf Hitler's occupation. He went to Britain and joined the BBC in 1940, producing, writing, and broadcasting for radio. He married Renate Gerstenberg in 1947 and they have one daughter. It was in 1947 also that Esslin saw a production of Jean Genet's *The Maids in Paris* and was captivated by the Theater of the Absurd.

From 1941 to 1955 Esslin was a producer and scriptwriter for BBC European Services using his German to broadcast Allied propaganda into Germany. Appointed assistant head of BBC European Productions in 1955, his career at the BBC was divided into two halves. The first was devoted to political broadcast journalism which also took him to Africa. Due to the success of his 1959 book on Bertolt Brecht, *Brecht: A Choice of Evils*, Esslin was made assistant head of radio drama in 1961, the year he published *The Theatre of the Absurd*, and the second half of his BBC career began. Appointed head of radio drama from 1963 to 1977, he presided over what he called "the largest theatre" and "dramaturgical department in the world" and came into frequent contact with Samuel Beckett.

Esslin participated in all aspects of British dramatic life – criticism, production, dramaturgy, and administration. In addition to his publications on the theater and work for BBC Radio, he was a member of the British Arts Council, chairman of its drama panel from 1976 to 1977, and advisory dramaturg to the Royal Shakespeare Theatre. As a visiting professor of theater at Florida State University from 1969 to 1976 he began to divide his life between Britain and America, later taking up the post of professor of drama for two quarters annually at Stanford University, California, from 1977 to 1988. In the United States he was advisory editor to the *Tulane Drama Review* and became the dramaturg of the Magic Theater in San Francisco from 1978 to 1989, during which period several plays by Sam Shepard were premiered and Beckett pieces were revived. In 1967 the president of Austria conferred upon Martin Esslin the title of professor; in 1978 he received an Hon. D.Litt. from Kenyon College, Ohio; in 1972 he was awarded the OBE; and he is currently professor emeritus of Stanford University.

Influence

Martin Esslin's name is synonymous with the Theater of the Absurd. His definition, in *The Theatre of the Absurd*, of a form of drama that was absurd, "out of harmony" with reason, logic, and propriety, fixed a new term in the critical vocabulary of the theater. Thanks to the influence of Esslin's book, furthermore, the group of dramatists on whom it is focused – Samuel Beckett, Jean Genet, Eugène Ionesco, Arthur Adamov, and Harold Pinter – continue to enjoy the acclaim and attention of both academics and theatergoers. Students of drama acknowledge the formative impact the text has had on perspectives on twentieth-century theater, giving intellectual order to the chaos portrayed in postwar drama, and furnishing an introduction to pre-absurdist drama, Dada, and German expressionism. The Theater of the Absurd prepares all readers for the experimental theater and new, nonrealist aesthetic to which most contemporary theater owes its freedom.

Esslin is an avant-garde critic who is also, notably, in the vanguard of criticism. First to analyze the trend of absurdist theater, first to write a full-length book in English on Brecht and to attract the interest in Brecht of the British directors Peter Brook and Peter Hall, he was also among the first to write in English about the French writer Raymond Queneau and the first to publish a monograph on Harold Pinter. He continues to give extempore lectures drawing on an impressive knowledge of European theatrical contexts and his intellectual and artistic presence remains invaluable to old and new students of twentieth-century drama.

Analysis

Three influential texts in theater criticism of the twentieth century were published in 1961. J. L. Styan's *The Dark Comedy* and George Steiner's *The Death of Tragedy* argued that the two principal genres of theater, tragedy and comedy, had been redefined in modern drama. It was Esslin's *The Theatre of the Absurd*, however, which gave a new name to the tragicomic, nonrealistic plays. Esslin's work was intended as a polemical contribution to the debate on an "aberrant and abased" form of drama. Esslin coined the less censorious term "absurd" to describe the new antirational form of theater in postwar Europe, especially the avant-garde theater of 1950s Paris. Keen from the outset to dispel the notion of Theater of the Absurd as a school or doctrine, Esslin called it a "working hypothesis." Instead, a new aesthetic category was created and Esslin's critical cornerstone, twice updated, grew into a history of absurdist plays.

He bases his observations on the work of four major playwrights, Beckett, Genet, Ionesco, and Adamov (Pinter was included in 1980). The new drama shared the same metaphysical concerns as the existentialist theater of Albert Camus and Jean-Paul Sartre, which underscored the futility of human life. Those dramatists had used traditional theatercraft to convey their ideas, but the Theater of the Absurd, argues Esslin, "has renounced arguing *about* the absurdity of the human condition; it merely *presents* it in being – that is, in terms of concrete stage images." The meaningless, illogical nature of existence is reflected in language that is radically devalued as a conveyer of truths. Equally, this absurd, nonsense language becomes beautiful and poetic when uprooted from a context of meaning. Absurdist theater also abandons a rational plot structure to produce "a theatre of situation as against a theatre of events in sequence." So an absurdist play, like Beckett's *En attendant Godot* (1952; *Waiting for Godot*, 1955), has no story, no delineated characters, no overall thematic or philosophical meaning, makes no attempt to reflect reality, and has babbling non sequiturs for dialogue.

Esslin also isolates four techniques used in absurdist theater which derive directly from age-old theatrical practices. These are: "'Pure' theater; i.e. scenic effects ... jugglers, acrobats, bullfighters or mimes, Clowning, fooling and mad-scenes, Verbal nonsense [and] The literature of dream and fantasy which has a strong allegorical component." Esslin has traced origins for the Theater of the Absurd far beyond its turn-of-the-century predecessors, Alfred Jarry and Guillaume Apollinaire, and Surrealism, and lays a strong emphasis on the effects achieved by nonverbal imagery and spectacle. He concludes by suggesting that the "dethronement of language and logic forms part of an essentially mystical attitude toward the basis of reality," so rescuing the Theater of the Absurd from a dark, nihilist interpretation and thanking it for the vitality and innovation it has offered to the drama in its wake.

In 1959 Esslin had published *Brecht: A Choice of Evils*, in which he explained to an English-speaking audience the theory of "epic theater" Brecht imagined would replace the illusionist model based on the theories of the Russian director Konstantin Stanislavsky to become the leading form of Communist theater. Brecht's theater used the *verfremdungseffekt* (distantiation), a style of production designed not only to prevent the audience from identifying with characters, but specifically to alienate them from the events and to awaken their critical faculties. Brecht reckoned that a play which allowed spectators to keep a rational, critical distance from the social conflicts portrayed would inevitably lead them to arrive at Marxist conclusions about how to resolve enduring social problems. In reality, the East German Communist authorities preferred propagandist theater in a naturalist style that gave no latitude for interpretation.

Esslin's Brecht is an "unorthodox Communist poet," committed to the rationalism of Marxism as a check to instinctive behavior, and a tragic genius who created complex art when he sought to create cold, persuasive logic. The book met with some controversy and the attacks which challenged Esslin's deviation from a standard hagiography of the great man and suggestions that his biographical approach to Brecht used a crypto-Marxist methodology are answered in the preface to the third edition of his *Brecht*.

A collection of essays from the 1960s, *Reflections* (1969; UK title: *Brief Chronicles: Essays on Modern Theatre*, 1970), looks at the making of contemporary theater and contemporary European playwrights as well providing an interesting document of debates on the theater and media in Britain, reflected in "Violence in Modern Drama" and "Nudity: Barely the Beginning." It also contains a short piece about Harold Pinter who was the subject of a major monograph by Esslin first published in 1970.

Pinter: The Playwright, originally published as *The Peopled Wound: The Plays of Harold Pinter* (1970), was then revised as *Pinter: A Study of his Plays* (1970) and again in a fourth edition in 1982. The text offers a psychoanalytic approach to explain the impact and effect of Pinter plays on the audience but not, significantly, to impute meaning to the author. Esslin's criticism locates Pinter's tendency to build plays on three levels of interpretation – social, existential, and archetypal – in order to create several strata of meaning and thus deliberate ambiguity. The original title, *The Peopled Wound*, referred to the open wound representing the unexplained meaning of Pinter's ambiguous plays, which Esslin interprets with a view to leaving their mystery unchallenged. The chapter "Language and Silence" is particularly valuable for its investigation of what makes the economy, suspense, and pathos of a phrase or a pause tellingly "Pinteresque." All editions offer a growing chronology of Pinter's career in collaboration with the author who also allowed Esslin to preview new written material to include in new editions before it was staged.

While he did not write a monograph work on Beckett, *Waiting for Godot* is the exemplary, cardinal text of *The Theatre of the Absurd*. As early as 1965 Esslin edited and wrote the introduction to *Samuel Beckett: A Collection of Critical Essays* and later he published an anthology, *Mediations: Essays on Brecht, Beckett and the Media* (1980), containing six of his own essays on Beckett. In "A Theatre of Stasis" he states that the innovative strength of all Beckett's drama goes beyond the rejection of a narrative, linear plot and use of poetic language. Rather the power of "these dramatic metaphors is precisely the overall impact of a single over-whelmingly powerful image, composed of the startling visual element." Esslin details the endeavor of producing a stage play for nonvisual radio in "Beckett and the Art of Broadcasting," a very detailed history of Beckett and the BBC, including Esslin's own collaboration with him. "Beckett and his Interpreters" charts the critical approaches to Beckett's multilayered œuvre and responses to the intellectual and emotional courage of one who can enclose nothingness in words.

Artaud (1976) sets Antonin Artaud's theatrical contribution in the framework of his broader vision and psychological case history. Esslin reconstructs Artaud's untheorized views on language calling it his "conviction that it is a profound mistake to equate all human consciousness with that part of it capable of verbal expression." Theater, of course, permits more readily the expression of emotion and Artaud's "Theater of Cruelty" proposed an instrument of communication which would break down barriers so spectators could share the experience of great horrors communally.

Esslin is concerned with Artaud's medical history because it forms part of his greatest œuvre, "himself as his supreme subject matter." Esslin notes the irony that after being expelled from the Surrealist movement Artaud realized the aims of the group more honestly than any member in his furious, "mad" writing unmediated by conscious thought and became a living example of the attainment of Surrealist goals. In "incarnating his experience," suggests Esslin, Artaud's suffering became the inspiration for many thinkers of the twentieth century in the fields of psychiatry and mental health – R. D. Laing, Michel Foucault (*Folie et déraison: Histoire de la folie à l'âge classique*, 1961; *Madness and Civilization: A History of Insanity in the Age of Reason*, 1965), Gilles Deleuze and Félix Guattari (*L'Anti-Oedipe*, 1972; *Anti-Oedipus*, 1984) – and theater. Esslin traces Artaud's influence in European and American theater noting that mass media, radio and television, more than any other dramatic forms, use the Artaudian principle of "reality as raw material for a dramatically structured presentation of life," a vindication of the double of Artaud's "Life as Theater" and vice versa.

Esslin's experience in broadcast media, theater, and dramatic literature formed the background to what might be seen as his trilogy on the nature of drama. The first of these, *An Anatomy of Drama* (1976), seeks to extend the narrow definition of drama as a realistic performance of dialogue on a stage with costume and scenery to embrace all the types of performance made possible by audiovisual media, film, television, radio, and animation. Driven by his desire to show the common denominators shared by "low" and "high" culture, Esslin attempts to go beyond a vision of drama as mimetic entertainment to explore why it is the best expression of human communication. The postwar successor to A. R. Thompson's *The Anatomy of Drama* (1942), Esslin's text distills the nature of drama to the expression of human thought and behavior which creates conditions for measuring the consequences of a situation, "a cognitive process, a method by which we can translate abstract concepts into concrete human terms."

Demonstrating the unity of the dramatic form in all mechanical media (television, film, radio, and the stage) in *An Anatomy*, Esslin took his perceptions about one form in particular as the starting point for his next book. Nearly forty years spent working within the ethos of a public broadcasting system had made Esslin acutely sensitive to its advantages when he began to experience American television on his regular visits to the United States. *The Age of Television* (1982) is a persuasively argued plea for a revitalization of public broadcasting in the United States and a reduction of its pernicious commercial influence in the rest of the world.

A critique of US television and its global impact, Esslin's study finds Marshall McLuhan's axiom "the medium is the message" useful but overstated since, he says, McLuhan dismisses the information transmitted by the medium as negligible. Esslin wants to retreat from the broad concept that television abolishes time and space and instead to concentrate on the mode of televisual communication – in structuralist terms, the language system which conveys the messages that television delivers.

Esslin contends that the language in question is the language of drama and that the tools of dramatic criticism can be used to understand it. For example, because of its underlying dramatic structure television turns everything, even news, into entertainment. Added to the market forces controlling editorial decisions, this leads to a false consciousness being created through commercial television networking that does not represent reality. The book sounds a clarion call for a functional nationwide public television service in the United States where its absence is a "national tragedy" and whose current "wasteland of television" threatens to have the same deadening, homogenizing effect on world culture. (See also five essays on the media in *Mediations: Essays on Brecht, Beckett and the Media*.)

Esslin's final book on the nature of drama develops the insight of the previous book about a universal language of drama in every visual medium. *The Field of Drama* (1987) submits a semiotic reading of what unites and what differentiates the drama of stage, film, and television, "examining the signs that are used to achieve the desired communication." The sign-system is a useful way of looking at elements that create meaning in a performance and Esslin is impressed by the practicality of the semiotic approach but dismayed by its abstract language. Thus, avoiding jargon and using his experience as critic, director, and dramaturg, he tests the theories of Roland Barthes, Patrice Pavis, Umberto Eco, and some German semioticians against his own results.

The principal signs of drama are the icon (picture), the index (a deictic, pointing-showing sign, like arrows or pronouns), and the symbol (the category that includes words which have no visual relation to their "signified"). Esslin takes all the elements of drama and relates them to these categories. The actor or actress, for example, is an iconic sign. In him or her we see a human being who represents a human being. The actor or actress is also capable of making signs with his or her facial expression, body gestures, movement within dramatic space, make-up, and costume before even uttering a word.

Different sign genres and registers form various discrete signifying structures built on separate sign systems which then fuse to create the macrostructure of spectacle. Thus form (set, theater, costumes, staging), content (text, linguistic style, delivery), and atmosphere (music, lighting, audience response) are strands, built respectively of constituent strands of signifiers which, when entwined, create one overall interpretation of a performance from innumerable individual others. Drama, then, according to this system, is an accumulation of perceived signifiers synthesized, filtered, and coalesced into complex structures. Esslin characterizes such a structure as a pyramid of meaning, with many foundations but only one apex.

Esslin's critical perspective is the product of repeated cultural displacement that nevertheless had a happy outcome in his disposition to try a broad range of methodological and theoretical lenses in his writing and to see himself not as a disadvantaged exile, but as a privileged mediator. Esslin has called his approach to literary criticism a "search for subjective truth" and he has devoted much of his criticism to communicating the work of writers whose literature is the rare expression of intense subjective experience. The rest he has given to the literary and performing art which he describes as the "best expression of human communication" and the best way to share subjective, emotional experience – drama.

Principal criticism

Brecht: A Choice of Evils, 1959, 1980 (third edition)
The Theatre of the Absurd, 1961, 1980 (third edition)
Reflections, 1969 (UK title: *Brief Chronicles: Essays on Modern Theatre*, 1970)
Pinter: The Playwright (originally published as *The Peopled Wound: The Plays of Harold Pinter*, 1970; revised as *Pinter: A Study of his Plays*, 1970), 1982 (fourth edition)
Artaud, 1976
An Anatomy of Drama, 1976
Mediations: Essays on Brecht, Beckett and the Media, 1980
The Age of Television, 1982
The Field of Drama, 1987

Other major works and literary forms

Martin Esslin has contributed scores of papers and articles to books and journals on Samuel Beckett, Bertolt Brecht, Eugène Ionesco, Henrik Ibsen, Luigi Pirandello, Harold Pinter, Anton Chekhov, Max Frisch, Friedrich Dürrenmatt, Joe Orton, Edward Albee, radio and television drama, and British, European, and American contemporary theater and dramaturgy. Some titles the critic considers particularly important are his articles on Brecht and Beckett for the *Encyclopaedia Britannica*; the chapter "Modern Drama 1890–1920" in the *Oxford Illustrated History of Theatre* (1995); his essays on Beckett and Raymond Queneau in *The Novelist As Philosopher* (1962), edited by John Cruickshank; the essay "Romantic Cosmic Drama" in *Romantic Drama* (1994), edited by Gerald Gillespie; "Goethe's Faust: Pre-modern, Post-modern, Proto-Postmodern" in *Interpreting Goethe's Faust Today* (1994), edited by Jane K. Brown, Meredith Lee, and Thomas P. Saine; "Towards an American Dramaturg –: Adapting the Function of Dramaturg to US Conditions" in *Dramaturgy in American Theater. A Source Book* (1997), edited by Susan Jonas and Geoffrey S. Proell; "Modern Drama – Wedekind to Brecht" in *Modernism 1890–1930* (1976), edited by Malcolm Bradbury and James McFarlane; and "Hugo von Hofmannsthal" in *Die Grossen Oesterreicher, Salzburg* (1998). He is the editor of *Samuel Beckett: A Collection of Critical Essays* (1965), *The Genius of German Theater* (1968), *The New Theatre of Europe* (1970), and *The Illustrated Encyclopaedia of World Theatre* (1977). Esslin has also written many introductions to anthologies of European theater and drama criticism.

TRANSLATIONS AND RADIO FEATURES

Writing in more than one language extends Esslin's range beyond that of many other critics. It has also allowed him to exercise a different literary skill as a bilingual translator of, from German into English, plays by Heinrich von Kleist, Frank Wedekind, Oedoen von Horváth, and Wolfgang Bauer, and, from English into German, many plays by Harold Pinter, Peter Barnes, Peter Nicholls, and others. Hundreds of radio features mark Esslin's years as a writer, producer, and director at the BBC.

Further reading

Brater, Enoch, and Ruby Cohn, eds. *Around the Absurd: Essays on Modern and Postmodern Drama*, 1990 (dedicated to Martin Esslin).
Dace, Letitia. "On Jean Genet and Martin Esslin, or Here Absurdist, There Absurdist, Everywhere . . .," in *Kansas Quarterly*. 3, no. 2 (1971), pp. 110–116.
Esslin, Martin. "A Search for Subjective Truth," in *What is Criticism?*, 1981. Edited by Paul Hernadi.
——. *"Refugee-gemass"; Osterreicher in der BBC wahrend des Krieges*, 1996.
Hernadi, Paul, ed. "On Being Reviewed," in "Re-Viewing Reviews," in *Bulletin of the Midwest MLA*. 11, no. 1 (1978), pp. 19–24.
Hollis Merrit, Susan. *Pinter in Play: Critical Strategies and the Plays of Harold Pinter*, 1990.
Kott, Jan. "The Icon of the Absurd," in his *The Theatre of Essence*, 1984.

JOANNA STEPHENS

See also Absurd; Artaud; Bentley; Brecht; British Literary Theory: Twentieth Century; Drama: Theory and Criticism; McLuhan

Existentialism

Existentialism as a literary critical term is derived from twentieth-century European existential philosophy (primarily in the works of Martin Heidegger and Jean-Paul Sartre) and its nineteenth-century roots (in the works of Friedrich Nietzsche and Søren Kierkegaard), and its prominence in literature is in many respects concomitant with the rise of modernist art. Existential philosophy holds the position that the individual and his or her unique perception supersedes any abstract conceptual or transcendentally-grounded designation of what is "real," that is, the nature of reality and human life. The well-known logical syllogism "All human beings are mortal. Socrates is a human being. Therefore Socrates is mortal" may well be true from a strictly logical point of view but when it is seen from the experiential viewpoint of the individual person who is going to die a very real and very solitary death, the quality and experience of this "truth" changes radically. Thus, in this prospect, the nature of rational truth is never absolute as such, that is, valid for any and all circumstances, but rather is relative, that is, based on individual perspective or point of view. It is a question of rational or conceptual truth versus experiential or existential truth. The issue of death or human finiteness – and by implication the pivotal question of time as defining human existence – is also central to existential thought. Human consciousness is in essence infinite, that is, our minds can always conceive of another possibility beyond the present (for example, situation x + 1) or we can always transcend ourselves, can always envision a future. Our physical body is, however, finite. The problem of an infinitely self-transcending consciousness trapped in a finite physical world – the existential fundamentals of finiteness and time – constitutes the defining existential dilemma of human life.

It can be argued that the roots of existentialism lie in the nineteenth-century questioning of religion and the meaning/existence of God, especially in the writings of the Danish thinker Kierkegaard and the German philosopher Nietzsche. The former was a devout believer but realized most acutely – as he described in his book *Fear and Trembling* (1843) – that the divinity and its will are ultimately unknowable to human consciousness and that the Christian must therefore make an irrational (and frightening) choice – a "leap of faith" – in order to maintain his or her belief. Kierkegaard's ideas put the burden of the creation of meaning upon individual human existence and not on a transcendent deity whose will is incomprehensible. Furthermore, the nature of individual human experience remains incommunicable to others; the individual is absolutely alone. The atheist Nietzsche questions religion in a more radical manner in his *Also sprach Zarathustra* (1883–1885; *Thus Spake Zarathustra*, 1896) when he declares that "God is dead" for modern humanity. He rejects all belief in any metaphysical realities – God and Heaven – in favor of an unconditional and joyous affirmation of human existence in this earthly life despite the abyss of nihilism which becomes apparent when the idea of a transcendent divinity is taken away. As in Kierkegaard, Nietzsche places the burden of the creation of meaning squarely upon the individual. The Russian writer Fedor Dostoevskii also broached many of these existential questions in his fictional works. All describe a modern view in which the traditional divinity that had provided a transcendent and absolute meaning for existence is either completely unknowable to or totally absent from the human sphere. As the later existential Irish writer Samuel Beckett playfully alludes in the title of his well-known French-language play *En attendant Godot* (1952; *Waiting for Godot*, 1955), the modern individual is now (vainly) waiting for God.

A major theme in existential thought – especially in Heidegger and Sartre – is whether the individual lives an "authentic" existence or not. This means that the person does not live in a state of denial – an "inauthentic" mode of being – concerning the existential fundamentals of human life (death, time, finiteness), that is, one does not escape to some imaginary metaphysical ideal, God and religion for example, nor does one succumb to some kind of addictive behavior which diverts attention from reality. To live an authentic existence, as Sartre maintains, is indeed a great burden (of a great yet frightening freedom) and most people choose to live "in bad faith," in a state of denial. We can see here that existential themes in literature are closely related to issues of individual psychology in that both relate directly to the experiential dimension. As a method of literary criticism, then, existentialism tends to treat texts in which the characters experience some kind of mental/spiritual breakdown in which they begin to question the meaning of reality and existence. Sartre's own fictional writings, for example the novel *La Nausée* (1938; *Nausea*, 1959), deal with his characters' personal crises or "metaphysical problems," as does the French existential writer Albert Camus in his well-known essay on the "absurdity" of the human situation, *Le Mythe de Sisyphe* (1942; *The Myth of Sisyphus*, 1955). Simone de Beauvoir, Sartre's intellectual colleague, also wrote novels that directly confront existential subjects. The Czech-born German writer Franz Kafka, whose texts revolve around the complex psychological states of the characters, is also, in many significant respects, to be considered an existential author as is the complex philosophical poetry of the German Rainer Maria Rilke who was influenced by Nietzschean thought. The Spaniard Miguel de Unamuno must also be considered an existential writer.

Samuel Beckett is undoubtedly the best-known author whose works involve existential themes and fictional techniques. Well-versed in European thought from René Descartes and Arthur Schopenhauer to Nietzsche, Ludwig

Wittgenstein, and Sartre, he is a thoroughly modernist and philosophically astute writer of fiction with a highly refined sense of the surreal and the absurd. His novels and plays revolve around the phenomenological themes of the elusive nature of human consciousness – the self/ego – and its perception/construction of "reality," the very real existential suffering prompted by the absurd situation of an infinite mind trapped in a finite body, and the essential incommunicability of individual human experience (and the associated idea of the insufficiency of language to convey – and conversely the capacity of language to falsify – this existential experience). His style utilizes modernist techniques of multiple perspectives, abstraction, as well as a terse and cutting sense of the nihilistic irony implicit in the human dilemma in order to realize the existential themes that preoccupy him.

Further reading

Barrett, William. *Irrational Man. A Study in Existential Philosophy*, 1958.
——. *What is Existentialism?*, 1964.
——. *Time of Need. Forms of the Imagination in the Twentieth Century*, 1972.
Cooper, David E. *Existentialism: A Reconstruction*, 1990.
Heller, Erich. *The Artist's Journey into the Interior and Other Essays*, 1965.
——. *The Disinherited Mind*, 1975.
——. *In the Age of Prose. Literary and Philosophical Essays*, 1984.
Hubben, William. *Dostoevsky, Kierkegaard, Nietzsche, and Kafka*, 1952.
Kaufmann, Walter. *Existentialism: From Dostoevsky to Sartre*, 1988.
Kern, Edith. *Existential Thought and Fictional Technique. Kierkegaard, Sartre, Beckett*, 1972.
Koenig, Thomas R. *Existentialism and Human Existence: An Account of Five Major Philosophers*, 1992.
Macquarrie, John. *Existentialism: An Introduction, Guide and Assessment*, 1973.
Oaklander, L. Nathan, ed. *Existentialist Philosophy: An Introduction*, 1995.
Raymond, Diane Barsoum. *Existentialism and the Philosophical Tradition*, 1990.
Sartre, Jean-Paul. *Essays in Existentialism*, 1993.
Wahl, Jean. *Philosophies of Existence*, 1969.
Warnock, Mary. *Existentialism*, 1970.

Thomas F. Barry

See also Absurd; Heidegger; Sartre

F

Benito Jerónimo Feijóo y Montenegro

Spanish writer and critic

Born: Casdemiro, Spain; October 8, 1676
Died: Oviedo, Spain; September 26, 1764

Biography

Benito Jerónimo Feijóo y Montenegro was born in the town of Casdemiro, a part of the northern Spanish region of Galicia, where his family had a vacation estate. He was the eldest son of the noble and cultured Antonio Feijóo y Sanjurjo and María de Puga Sandoval Nova. He was educated in the town of Allarís, where his family had its permanent residence, and also in the Colegio Real de San Esteban de Ribas de Sil. At the age of twelve Feijóo entered the Benedictine monastery of San Julián de Samos, where he joined the order in 1690. After attending several Benedictine colleges and the University College at Salamanca, Feijóo received a bachelor's degree in theology in 1709. He continued doctoral studies, eventually earning the title of *padre maestro* (father master). Feijóo taught theology at the monastery of San Vicente, in the city of Oviedo, and at the Universidad de Oviedo, where he occupied three different theology chairs of increasing seniority until his retirement in 1734. From 1710 to 1721 Feijóo was in charge of students in his monastery, and in 1721 he was elected abbot, a position which he held until 1723 and again from 1729 to 1731.

Feijóo's first published pieces appeared in 1725, and already by 1727 his accomplishments were recognized with an honorary membership in the Real Sociedad de Medicina in Seville. His tireless efforts to introduce modern science and thought to Spain gave rise to innumerable disputes among the intellectuals of the time. In 1748 Feijóo received further recognition when he was honored by Fernando VI with the title of *conciliar* (councillor). The impact of his forward-thinking works created such controversy and provoked so much hostility from the conservative intellectual establishment of the time that in 1750 a royal decree forbade further attacks on Feijóo's works. He died at his monastery on September 26, 1764.

Influence

Feijóo should be credited above all with interpreting and introducing many Enlightenment ideas to Spain. His work served as the basis for much learning and controversy among intellectuals and influenced profoundly the thought of two Spanish monarchs, Fernando VI and Carlos III. Feijóo's concept of style, language, literary themes, and literature as a vehicle for education had a tremendous impact upon the culture of his day. His thoughts, reasoning methods, and literary style were echoed by many learned journals such as the *Memorial Literario* (literary memorandum), the *Diario de los Literatos de España* (journal of Spanish men of letters), and the *Diario Extranjero* (foreign journal). Another journal that followed Feijóo's example of social and intellectual criticism was the renowned *Correo de Madrid* (Madrid courier), which was widely circulated in literary circles of the capital. Feijóo's influence also can be seen in the work of writers such as José Isla de la Torre y Rojo, whose best-selling novel *Fray Gerundio de Campazas* (1757–1768; Friar Gerund of Campazas) ridiculed the inflated language in vogue in the Catholic church, and José Cadalso y Vázquez, whose epistolary novel *Cartas marruecas* (1793; Moroccan letters) reflects the style of the *Cartas eruditas y curiosas* (intellectual letters). The emphasis on didacticism in Spanish theater and poetry in the second half of the eighteenth century is also evidence of Feijóo's impact, and even today his literary achievements command respect in intellectual circles.

Analysis

The critical intelligence of Feijóo was not focused solely on literature. In order to understand this extraordinary figure, it is necessary to remember that the first half of the eighteenth century in Spain and most of Europe was a time of intense, profound change. The philosophical and scientific ideas of past centuries began to give way to modern science and technology, and the empirical method was rapidly replacing scholastic thought. As knowledge became more specialized, the sciences came to be seen as separate from religion and theology. The Age of Reason was afoot, and Feijóo is the supreme example of the enlightened humanist in Spain. It is in this context that the concept of "critic" needs to be interpreted. A critic is an intellectual who looks at a society and social ideals, applies reason to discover the nature of that society's flaws, and suggests remedies for them. This type of criticism is precisely what Feijóo accomplished.

Both the *Teatro crítico universal* (universal theater of criticism), published in nine volumes between the years 1726 and 1740, and the *Cartas eruditas y curiosas* (intellectual letters), published in five volumes from 1742 to 1760, present a picture of Feijóo's society and represent a veritable compendium of the knowledge of that era. Feijóo read about and commented upon scientific, social, political, theological, historical, and artistic matters, foreign and national, for more than thirty years, always with the same purpose: to educate the reading public, to modernize university teaching and learning, and to employ reason and scientific knowledge in the betterment of society. His literary criticism was guided by this spirit of modernization and education.

The discourses and letters that address literary topics are scattered throughout the *Teatro crítico universal* and the *Cartas eruditas y curiosas*. One topic that surfaces on several occasions is the question of style. In "Reflexiones sobre la historia" (reflections on history), "La razón del gusto" (the reason of taste), and "El no sé qué" (I know not what), Feijóo advocates freedom for those of creative genius and underlines the importance of writing without the fetters of prescribed style. In *Cartas eruditas y curiosas*, he goes as far as to declare that style is a question of each author's personal choice. These were revolutionary concepts in an era still dominated by scholastic methods. Feijóo rejected the bombastic, inflated language prevalent in the pulpit and in academia, choosing instead to use a natural, uncluttered prose style that was accessible to the reading public. His only concession to an established style was to allow for the existence of three levels of writing: the "sublime," to be used in the expression of affection, the "medium," best suited to didactic matters, and the "low," used solely in comical situations. Thus, style was to be accommodated to material.

Three other linguistic themes are important in Feijóo's thought: the validity of vernacular languages as instruments of expression, the richness and suitability of the Spanish language in particular as a medium for learned discourse, and the necessity of introducing terms from other languages in order to express new ideas. These themes, repeated throughout his work, are fully enunciated in three pivotal pieces. In one of the *Cartas eruditas y curiosas*, Feijóo discusses the suitability of the modern languages for intellectual writing, going so far as to declare that the Romance languages are the legitimate heirs of the classical languages, which he considers dead. This assertion naturally caused enormous controversy, for many scientists as well as churchmen still held firmly to the Renaissance notion that Latin was the only appropriate medium for learned communications. Feijóo did not stop here with his linguistic innovations; in "Paralelo de las lenguas castellana y francesa" (parallel of the Spanish and French languages), he declared that Spanish was superior to French in richness of vocabulary and suppleness of expression. This bold encomium for Spanish, issued at a time in which all things French were viewed in Europe as superior, reveals Feijóo's independence of thought and his ability to see beyond the wisdom of the day.

The third important piece dealing with linguistic themes appears in the first volume of the *Cartas eruditas y curiosas*. "Defensa de la introducción de algunas voces peregrinas o nuevas en el idioma castellano" (in favor of the introduction of new words into the Spanish language) touches upon a much-debated issue: the use of neologisms to express new concepts and ideas. This question surfaces again in Feijóo's discussion of the craft of translation. Together these pieces clarify the critic's view of language: he sees language as a living instrument, changing with time and adapting itself to the material and ideas to be expressed, rather than as a mold into which every concept must fit. This liberation of language, together with his idea of stylistic individuality and freedom and the concept of the artist as born and not trained, constituted a definite step toward the modern concept of literary creation.

Feijóo discusses the theater early in the *Teatro crítico universal*. In "Las glorias de España" (glories of Spain), he credits Spain with initiating modern dramatic art and affirms that the work of dramatist Lope de Vega Carpio, admirable for its thematic and stylistic freedom, constitutes the foundation for European theater.

"Los bailes y las comedias" (dances and comedies) and "El teatro como espectáculo" (theater as a spectacle) set forth additional ideas about theater. Contrary to neoclassical dramatic precepts, Feijóo does not advocate rigid adherence to the Aristotelian unities of drama or the division of genres. His stance toward theater is similar to his ideas on style, allowing freedom of creation to the dramatist and respecting individual style. Concerned as always with the betterment of society, however, he warns that the spectacle can be of detriment to the masses and advocates a carefully controlled schedule of representations.

Feijóo considered other genres and authors as well. In "Paralelo de las lenguas castellana y francesa," he praises several figures of Spanish and European letters: Teresa de Ávila for her clarity of diction and mystical inspiration, the poet Garcilaso de la Vega, and the writers Luis de Góngora and Francisco de Quevedo y Villegas for their purity and naturalness. Another essay that touches upon literary criticism is "Defensa de las mujeres" (defense of women), in which Feijóo commends women authors in the course of his apology for women. He mentions the novels of Madeleine de Scudéry, whose talent he compares to that of Sappho, and refers to the work of other writers. The qualities that Feijóo recognizes in these and other authors accord with his concepts of learning and art. He applauds creativity, forthright reasoning, innovation, clarity, individualism, and rectitude of character. For Feijóo, literature, like the natural sciences and philosophy, has a high goal: the education of the people and the betterment of society.

Principal criticism

Teatro crítico universal, 1726–1740 (9 volumes; volumes 1–4 translated as *Essays or Discourses Selected from the Works of Feijóo*, 1780)
Cartas eruditas y curiosas, 1742–1760 (5 volumes)
Adiciones a las obras del muy ilustre y reverendísimo padre maestro D. Fr. Benito Jerónimo Feijóo y Montenegro, 1783

Other major works and literary forms

Benito Jerónimo Feijóo y Montenegro was a prolific writer and thinker of a stature comparable to that of his English contemporary Samuel Johnson. He reviewed and commented on a wide range of the intellectual questions of his time. In addition to the encyclopedic *Teatro crítico universal* (universal theater of criticism) and *Cartas eruditas y curiosas* (intellectual letters), Feijóo published other works on such diverse topics as medicine, education, earthquakes, superstition, physics, and women. He also wrote poetry and maintained a voluminous correspondence with scholars and intellectuals throughout Europe.

POETRY
Poesías inéditas del P. Feijóo, 1881

NONFICTION
Aprobación apologética del escepticismo médico del doctor Martínez, 1725
Respuesta al discurso fisiológico-médico del doctor don Francisco Dorado, 1727
Justa repulsa de iniquas acusaciones, 1749
El terremoto y su uso, 1756
El pecador convertido, romance, y la conciencia, décimas, 1759

Further reading

Cerra Suárez, Silverio. *Doscientos cincuenta años de bibliografía feijoniana*, 1976.
Cook, John A. *Neo-classic Drama in Spain: Theory and Practice*, 1959.
Cox, R. Merritt. *Eighteenth-Century Spanish Literature*, 1979.
Eguiagaray, Francisco. *El padre Feijóo y la cultura de su época*, 1964.
Glendinning, Nigel. *A Literary History of Spain: The Eighteenth Century*, 1972.
Lázaro Carreter, Fernando. *Significación cultural de Feijóo*, 1965.
McClelland, I. L. *Benito Jerónimo Feijóo*, 1969.
Marañón, Gregorio. *Las ideas biológicas del padre Feijóo*, 1934.
Otero Pedrayo, Ramón. *El padre Feijóo: Su vida, doctrina, e influencias*, 1972.
Vila Selma, José. *Feijóo: Ideas literarias*, 1963.

LINA L. COFRESI

See also Luzán y Claramunt

Feminist Criticism

Introduction

Feminist literary criticism is an interdisciplinary approach which focuses on gender politics. It rarely confines itself to merely textual analysis; rather, it looks at the text within the society in which it was produced in order to discover what this tells us about what gender means in that particular context. It emphasizes the ways in which discrimination against women is manifested and how this can be resisted and countered. Unlike many other academic approaches, therefore, feminist criticism is not simply a theoretical approach; it also has political aims.

Feminist criticism developed from the women's movement in Europe and North America in the 1960s, the so-called second wave of feminism. This movement was characterized by the founding of a number of consciousness-raising groups whose fundamental beliefs can be summarized by the slogan "The personal is political," meaning that personal experience is neither individual nor isolated, rather it is social, political, and systematic. First-wave feminism, which began around 1860 and started to decline in 1918, secured rights that were previously denied women, such as the right to education and the right to vote. Various works of feminist literary criticism came out of and followed on from the first wave, such as Virginia Woolf's *A Room of One's Own* (1929), and many such writings share a number of concerns apparent in more recent work. However, such early works were relatively isolated and it was not until the early 1970s that feminist criticism began to constitute a body of study with its own distinct identity. This identity has never been homogeneous: it has varied according to the identity and political perspective of the individual critic; moreover, it has changed through time as critics have responded to and developed the work of their predecessors.

The 1970s

Initially, Anglo-American feminist criticism was primarily concerned with challenging the notion of the canon in two main ways. First, critics noted that the texts which constituted the canon were mainly male-authored and that their representations of female characters tended to be largely negative and stereotyped. For example, Kate Millett (1970) documented the ways in which many canonical authors represented women as sexual objects whose needs were subservient to those of the text's male protagonists. Second, in a shift that has been termed "gynocriticism," critics sought an alternative tradition to the male canon believing that this would offer examples of more positive representations of women. For example, Elaine Showalter (1977) drew attention to a tradition of neglected women novelists from the nineteenth and twentieth centuries. Furthermore, Showalter highlighted the pressures that inhibited women's writing, including material circumstances, such as economic dependence; and social pressures, most significantly the pressure to conform to the dominant definition of femininity, which did not incorporate the notion of woman-as-writer. Any women's writing produced in these circumstances could thus be regarded as a significant achievement.

Many gynocritics saw femininity as a social construct, that is, something created through social conditioning. Additionally, they believed that it hindered women's creativity. However, Sandra Gilbert and Susan Gubar (1979) took a more complex position. They combined a social constructionist perspective with a psychoanalytical approach to suggest that femininity was not only a constraint on women's creativity but also, simultaneously, a source of creative tension. They argued that women writers of the nineteenth century had a set of fears and anxieties about their identities as creators since, at that time, childbearing was considered the only natural form of female creativity. All other forms of creativity were considered as harmful to women's physical and mental health – leading to infertility, on the one hand, and madness, on the other. Additionally, an unlicensed female imagination was seen as an indication of unlicensed female sexuality. Thus, in Charlotte Brontë's *Jane Eyre* (1847), Bertha Rochester is interpreted as a mirror image of the eponymous heroine, able to express what both Jane and Brontë are unable to articulate: their anger at women's confinement within the domestic context and within their bodies. Although gynocriticism was an important stage in feminist criticism, it has been criticized: in creating an alternative "women's" tradition, it constructed a canon that was just as exclusive, in its own way, as the male tradition had been, since most of the writers it privileged were middle-class, white, and (ostensibly, anyway) heterosexual.

A final significant strand of 1970s' Anglo-American feminist criticism was a body of work that has come to be known as the "female aesthetic." This uses literary styles and forms that are seen as coming from a specifically female experience, and much of this work blurs the distinction between critical and creative writing. For example, Alice Walker's essay "In Search of Our Mothers' Gardens" (1977) is a feminist exploration of both the expression and the suppression of black women's creativity. Whilst this draws on *A Room of One's Own*, it also makes use of biography and personal testimony, prose fiction, and poetry. Adrienne Rich (1979) advocated a similar search for an avant-garde form of writing; however, she saw this as deriving from lesbianism, which she saw as present in all women. During this same period in France, a strand of feminist criticism which bore some similarities to the female aesthetic was developing. Building on the work of Jacques Lacan and poststructuralists, a number of scholars, chiefly, Hélène Cixous, Luce Irigaray, and Julia Kristeva, described a style of writing which they termed *l'écriture féminine*. This undermines the linguistic, syntactical, and metaphysical conventions of Western writing since it is characterized by absences, ruptures, the irrational, the chaotic, and sexual pleasure or *jouissance*. Many French feminist critics have attempted to create a critical form of *l'écriture féminine* by emphasizing textual pleasure, and using devices such as puns and neologisms. Although some critics maintained that *l'écriture féminine* can be written by either women or men, many argued that it was more likely to be produced by women; further, women had an interest in writing it because of its subversive qualities which could counter their oppression. Despite some similarities between the female aesthetic and *l'écriture féminine*, many observers saw the Anglo-American and French feminist critical traditions as oppositional, with the former concerned with the analysis of experience and issues such as the canon, whilst the latter focused on overtly theoretical issues.

As a result of the 1970s' debates about feminist literary criticism, in many European and North American countries women's writing became accepted into the academy as part of the curriculum, both within mainstream literature courses and separately as part of women's studies. This move was facilitated by the publication of a number of women-authored texts that had previously gone out of print. Many such works were reprinted by the new feminist publishing houses, such as Virago which was launched in Britain in 1978 with the republication of Antonia White's *Frost in May* (first published in 1933). The growth of both feminist publishing houses and academic courses ensured the proliferation of feminist criticism into the 1980s.

The 1980s

The 1980s can be characterized as a decade in which feminist literary critics looked both backward, to earlier feminist critical work, and outward, to the work of feminists in other disciplines. Sometimes the earlier work was developed relatively uncritically; sometimes it was rigorously attacked and found to be lacking. The work in other disciplines often forced literary critics to adapt their own approaches in order to incorporate the most interesting and effective aspects of these alternative approaches.

One of the critics who reviewed some of the earlier work was Toril Moi (1985). She broke down the perceived opposition between the Anglo-American and French traditions through a summary and analysis of the main kinds of these criticisms, albeit with the notable exclusion of black studies. Moreover, she introduced the possibility of incorporating the two traditions. Subsequently, others, including Sara Mills and her coeditors (1989), have drawn on her work to bring a combined approach to a number of well-known literary texts. However, at the same time, other critics still worked mainly in one of these two traditions. Following on from Showalter's exploration of nineteenth- and twentieth-century novelists, Jane Spencer (1986) explored the work of a number of neglected women writers of the seventeenth and eighteenth centuries. This exploration of an earlier period enabled her to claim that women writers played a much more important role in the development of the novel than had been allowed by other (male) historians of the genre.

However, whilst others found it useful to develop some of the 1970s' gynocriticism, Showalter (1989) herself was questioning the very premises upon which her own earlier work was based. In a move which situates her close to the earlier position taken up by Millett, Showalter argued against a gynocritical approach, suggesting instead that feminist critics now needed to focus on gender and sexual difference in texts by men as much as by women. Other critics also challenged some of the earlier gynocriticism. Looking back to the work of Gilbert and Gubar, Terry Lovell (1987) argued that texts that they identified as subversive were often more complicit with existing power structures than they allowed since such works privileged heterosexual romance and marriage. Whilst Showalter and Lovell can be seen as reacting against one specific theoretical approach, Audre Lorde's (1984) attack on earlier feminist criticism was much broader. She argued that most of such work was flawed since it drew upon the methods and language inherited from a male critical tradition: "the master's house." Additionally, Lorde, along with a number of other lesbian critics, attacked the heterosexism of much existing literary criticism, both feminist and nonfeminist. As part of this attack they challenged male-defined concepts of femininity and examined lesbian images and strategies.

Another significant reaction to earlier work, both feminist and nonfeminist, came from postcolonial feminist literary theory. This reacted against two main tendencies: the lack of address to gender issues in mainstream postcolonial theory, and universalizing within feminist work. For example, Gayatri Spivak (1985), in her reading of *Jane Eyre* and Jean Rhys' *Wide Sargasso Sea* (1966), critiqued feminists' tendency to focus on the white central female characters in such texts arguing that this kind of reading ignores both the production and marginalization of other characters. In her own interpretation of *Wide Sargasso Sea* she argued that even as Rhys attempted a rewriting of *Jane Eyre*, the constraints of the genre she adopted, the novel, meant that she could not avoid rewriting from the perspective of the colonizer. Thus Christophine the Martiniquan maid, whilst treated sympathetically to some extent, is still, ultimately, marginalized within the novel. However, whilst some feminists were developing and reacting against existing feminist criticism, others were questioning the definition of theory itself. Barbara Christian (1987) argued that defining theory as abstract logic privileged a Western philosophical tradition and excluded the theorizing of people of color which is found in story-making and telling, riddles, and proverbs.

Despite such debates, many other feminist critics still found the use of theory effective. However, the theories within the discipline of literature, even those which were feminist, were increasingly perceived as less than adequate and many feminist critics looked to work being written by feminists in other disciplines to compensate for this inadequacy. Whilst feminist criticism has traditionally been interdisciplinary, combining textual analysis with an interest in the social construction of gender, during the 1980s this interdisciplinary approach broadened to incorporate work in disciplines previously ignored. For example, feminist critics looked to gender theory in science, such as Evelyn Fox Keller's (1992) feminist critiques of the construction of science; history, including Joan Scott's (1992) discussions of an approach which is both feminist and poststructuralist; and queer theory, which identifies and reverses homophobic categories to link sexuality with race and political activism, as in Eve Kosofsky Sedgewick's (1985) study which identifies the links between homophobia and misogyny. The legacy of such incorporations plus the revisions of the earlier feminist criticism meant that feminist literary critics writing in the 1990s inherited a rich legacy on which they could base their work.

The 1990s

The combining of existing feminist criticism with feminist theory from other disciplines proved to be a productive dynamic in the 1990s. Important influences on feminist literary criticism in the 1990s included Liesbet van Zoonen's (1994) work in media studies. The close relationship between some media study approaches, which consider the visual and narrative characteristics of texts and genres through semiotic and structural analysis, and traditional literary criticism has meant that this relationship has been a comfortable one and conducive to the production of much interesting work. A number of important feminist studies in the 1990s were anthologies which placed explorations of literary texts alongside examinations of media texts or popular cultural forms. For example, Frances Bonner and her coeditors (1992) juxtaposed essays on gender and genre and the short story with essays on science fiction, blockbuster novels, TV soap operas, and stand-up comedy. Similar multimedia, interdisciplinary approaches can be found in the work of Sara Mills (1994) and Beverley Skeggs (1995).

Additionally, such approaches have often mirrored the definition of femininity used by many feminists working in the areas of media and cultural studies: Angela McRobbie (1996) notes that women's and girls' magazines contain a series of different female subjectivities which may complement or contradict each other, and Ien Ang (1996) sees this as influential, positing femininity as a shifting identity which women may continually construct and reconstruct. Such a conceptualization of femininity, which has effectively deconstructed the term "woman," is believed by many to have proved to be more conducive to inclusive forms of feminism than the monolithic femininity privileged in much of the early feminist criticism. For example, Maggie Humm

(1998) has observed that 1990s' feminist literary criticism has been, positively, characterized by the crossing of borders, both disciplinary and geographical. However, other feminists are concerned that the deconstruction of woman undermines the possibility of a united politics.

Conclusion

Since the late 1960s, the term feminist literary criticism has been used to discuss a number of diverse and dynamic approaches to literature. Initially these approaches focused on challenging the androcentricism of the canon, rediscovering women writers previously "lost in history," and creating an alternative female tradition. However, over subsequent decades this work has been both developed and challenged and a more complex range of approaches has evolved. Such approaches tend to eschew the notion of a monolithic femininity and acknowledge that the term "woman" incorporates a number of diverse groups of women. However, whilst doing so, they still seek to retain ways of revealing and resisting discrimination against women. The tension between, on the one hand, the politics of feminism, which assumes women's shared oppression, and, on the other, the realization that woman can no longer be discussed as a homogeneous term, has resulted in the production of much complex and exciting work. Feminist literary criticism thus continues to be an important area of study in its own right and to also influence other areas of literary criticism and study.

Further reading

Ang, Ien. *Living Room Wars*, 1996.
Bonner, Frances, et al., eds. *Imagining Women: Cultural Representations and Gender*, 1992.
Brontë, Charlotte. *Jane Eyre*, 1847.
Christian, Barbara. "The Race for Theory," in *Cultural Critique*. 6 (Spring, 1987), pp. 51–63.
Cixous, Hélène, and Catherine Clément. *The Newly Born Woman*, 1986.
Fox Keller, Evelyn. "How Gender Matters, Or, Why It's So Hard For Us To Count Past Two," in *Inventing Women: Science, Technology and Gender*, 1992. Edited by Gill Kirkup and Laurie Smith Keller.
Gilbert, Sandra M., and Susan Gubar. *The Madwoman in the Attic: The Woman Writer and the Nineteenth-Century Literary Imagination*, 1979.
Humm, Maggie. "Feminist Literary Theory," in *Contemporary Feminist Theories*, 1998. Edited by Stevie Jackson and Jackie Jones.
Irigaray, Luce. *Spéculum de l'autre femme*, 1974 (*Speculum of the Other Woman*, 1985).
Jackson, Stevie, and Jackie Jones. *Contemporary Feminist Theories*, 1998.
Kristeva, Julia. *About Chinese Women*, 1977. Translated by H. Ranous.
Lorde, Audre. *Sister Outside*, 1984.
Lovell, Terry. *Consuming Fiction*, 1987.
McRobbie, Angela. "More!: New Sexualities in Girls' and Women's Magazines," in *Cultural Studies and Communications*, 1996. Edited by James Curran, David Morley, and Valerie Walkerdine.
Millett, Kate. *Sexual Politics*, 1970.
Mills, Sara, et al., eds. *Feminist Readings/Feminists Reading*, 1989.
——, ed. *Gendering the Reader*, 1994.
Moi, Toril. *Sexual/Textual Politics: Feminist Literary Theory*, 1985.
Morris, Pam. "Women and the Novel," in *The Realist Novel*, 1995. Edited by Dennis Walder.
Rhys, Jean. *Wide Sargasso Sea*, 1966.
Rich, Adrienne. *On Lies, Secrets and Silence*, 1979.
Scott, Joan. "Deconstructing Equality-Versus-Difference: Or, the Uses of Poststructuralist Theory for Feminism," in *Defining Women: Social Institutions and Gender Divisions*, 1992. Edited by Linda McDowell and Rosemary Pringle.
Sedgewick, Eve Kosofsky. *Between Men*, 1985.
Showalter, Elaine. *A Literature of Their Own: British Novelists from Brontë to Lessing*, 1977.
——, ed. *Speaking of Gender*, 1989.
Skeggs, Beverley, ed. *Feminist Cultural Theory: Process and Production*, 1995.
Spencer, Jane. *The Rise of the Woman Novelist: From Aphra Benn to Jane Austen*, 1986.
Spivak, Gayatri. "Three Women's Texts and a Critique of Imperialism," in *Critical Inquiry*. 12, no. 1 (Autumn, 1985), pp. 243–261.
Walker, Alice. "In Search of Our Mothers' Gardens," in *Working It Out*, 1977. Edited by S. Ruddick and P. Daniels.
White, Antonia. *Frost in May*, 1933.
Woolf, Virginia. *A Room of One's Own*, 1929.
Zoonen, Liesbet van. *Feminist Media Studies*, 1994.

JANINE LILADHAR

See also Cixous; Fuller; Gilbert and Gubar; Irigaray; Kristeva; Moi; Woolf

François de Salignac de La Mothe-Fénelon

French theologian and writer

Born: Château de Fénelon, Perigord, France; August 6, 1651
Died: Cambrai, France; January 7, 1715

Biography

Born of an aristocratic family, François de Salignac de La Mothe-Fénelon followed his uncle into an ecclesiastical career. He was ordained after completing his theological studies in 1677 at the University of Cahors. Fénelon's gifts as a preacher and his family connections gained for him in 1679 his appointment as superior of Nouvelles Catholiques, the institute for recently converted women, in Paris. As an adviser to Françoise de Maintenon, the second wife of Louis XIV, Fénelon was associated with the school for young noblewomen at Saint-Cyr. His success within the religious and political establishment peaked between 1689, when he was named preceptor to the duke of Burgundy, Louis XIV's grandson and potential heir to the throne, and 1695, when he was consecrated archbishop of Cambrai.

When he became embroiled in the controversy surrounding the Quietist heresy, however, Fénelon found himself the loser in a dispute with the influential prelate Jacques-Bénigne Bossuet. Exiled in 1697 by royal command to Cambrai, Fénelon lost his preceptorship. During the last fifteen years of his life he devoted himself with energy and integrity to the administration of his archdiocese. For a while it seemed possible that the succession of his princely pupil to the throne would bring him back to Paris as a major political power, but the death of the duke in 1712 ended such hopes. His last major public statement was made in 1714, when he responded to the French Academy's public inquiry as to what project the Academy should undertake upon completion of its dictionary. Fénelon proposed eight projects, including a poetics and treatises on tragedy, comedy, and history. He concluded his response with a discussion of the "Quarrel of the Ancients and the Moderns," which then divided the Academy.

Influence

Fénelon's criticism marks the transition between the French classicism of the reign of Louis XIV and the incipient Romanticism of the eighteenth century. Much of his thought anticipates the historical relativism of Charles de Secondat, Baron de la Brède et de Montesquieu in France and Giambattista Vico in Italy with the insistence that all human creations be judged in their original context. He undertook a demystification of the great writers of the seventeenth century from François de Malherbe to Jean Racine, thus providing the basis for Victor Hugo's remarks in the nineteenth century; like Fénelon, Hugo deplored the impoverishment of literary language in the epoch of classical "politeness."

Analysis

Fénelon saw all discourse as the object of interlocking disciplines and did not entirely separate literary criticism from grammar, rhetoric, and history. Although he divided his *Letter to the French Academy* into eight separate disciplinary projects, these projects are interdependent. The rhetoric is illustrated with quotations from poets and framed by a historical consideration of the kinds of rhetoric appropriate for specific periods and forms of civilization. In the proposed project for a poetics, the books of the Old Testament are described as a form of poetry because they contain figures of speech. Poetic language is therefore recognizable as such through the application of a subdivision of rhetoric, the study of figures and tropes. The proposal for a treatise on history in turn deals with the kind of sentence structure that will lead to the moral improvement of the reader. Fénelon begins his suggestion for a new poetics by stating that "poetry is more useful and more serious than common people believe." Bland as they are, these terms contain in a nutshell a whole theory of literature and place the author on the side of a semantically weighted view of literature as opposed to a predominantly stylistic view. To move readers deeply and to change them, rather than to entertain them, is his overarching poetic principle. This emphasis alone seems to many readers of Fénelon to place him squarely among the partisans of the Ancients in the notorious controversy which erupted in 1697 between the Moderns, supporters of Charles Perrault, and the Ancients, followers of Nicolas Boileau-Despréaux. Yet Perrault was pleased by Fénelon's letter, as were the Ancients. Fénelon's success with both sides shows that he had managed to transcend the sterile dichotomy of Greco-Roman classical literature and modern European literature, specifically the literature of seventeenth-century France, to articulate a theory that is historicist, utilitarian, and mimetic.

Fénelon's whole approach to discourse is based on the awareness of history. Just as the decay of deliberative bodies led to a decline in rhetorical arts, so poetry is part of an evolving system; only an understanding of the relationship between an author and his or her predecessors and between the work and its social context can provide the basis for critical evaluation. This historical relativism permitted Fénelon to view Virgil as a modern in relation to Homer, with whom Virgil contended by rewriting such *topoi* as the theme of the descent into the underworld. At the same time, Fénelon noted the linguistic limits faced by modern French poets, even as he applauded their intentions. For example, after expounding at length on the value of the Latin periodic sentence, Fénelon argued that Pierre de Ronsard attempted too brutally to impose such constructions on sixteenth-century French verse. The poet can only work within the linguistic system as it exists at the time of writing.

On this historicist basis, Fénelon superimposed his two basic critical tenets, which are themselves transtemporal and apply to all periods. Despite the different means of achieving those goals, he insisted first on the need for the faithful representation of reality, or nature, and second on the need to move the reader's profoundest emotions. The first of these is a reworking of the seventeenth-century French insistence on verisimilitude (the *vraisemblable*) as it had appeared in other celebrated critical disputes of the preceding century, notably the quarrel of Pierre Corneille's *Le Cid* (1637; *The Cid*, 1637) and Madame de La Fayette's *La Princesse de Clèves* (1678; *The Princess of Clèves*, 1679). Fénelon's use of the term seems to stress less the reader's own limits of belief, typical of earlier usage, and more the objective reality of what is being represented. He uses it interchangeably with terms such as "nature," "le naturel," and "naïve." These are all positive terms. The depiction of nature, that is, the "painting" of reality, is a critical metaphor illustrated with parallels in the painting of Titian and Raphael. The modern critics of Homer, who censure him for the uncouth manners and the religious and philosophical primitivism of the society he represents, are attacking the Greek author for one of his principal strengths, since he has given a true record of the state of civilization in Greece and Asia Minor in antiquity. Anything standing between the apprehension of reality and the reader is a defect. The reader's consciousness of style and of cleverness in selection or arrangement of detail is a sign of decadence in art and in literature. Choosing his examples from Virgil and Homer, Fénelon disregards felicities of phrasing to argue that the emotions of the characters of classical epic are true in their context: "Wit unfortunately weakens the great passions it pretends to adorn." Virgil, in Fénelon's *Dialogues des morts* (1719; *Dialogues of the Dead*, 1723), is himself said to be inferior to Homer because the *Aeneid* yields too much to the stylistic demands of the Latin public. Literature always declines, according to Fénelon, when authors think more about the readers' reception of the work than about plain representation.

Attention to the ornamental detail of language is not compatible, in Fénelon's view, with deep emotion. The Moderns' attention to style and politeness is incompatible with great tragedy because such attention prevents the reader from concentrating on the events of the plot and prohibits the writer from expressing the characters' feelings. Fénelon, following the lead of Boileau, who had translated Longinus' first-century treatise *On the Sublime*, points toward the sublime as the goal of all poetry, and indeed, of all elevated discourse. The sublime results from the effect of the whole text upon the reader, with the result that the reader loses the awareness of the text's objective status as art and artifice. In the sublime, art and nature fuse or art reaches its goal of a naive depiction of nature. The experience of the sublime raises the reader above the activity of consuming and criticizing the products of wit and permits his or her integration into the experience of nature.

The conception of eloquence, lyric, and tragedy as oriented toward moving and improving its audience links Fénelon backward with the Pléiade poetics of the sixteenth century and forward with Jean-Jacques Rousseau, François Auguste René Chateaubriand, and the other Romantics. Despite the kinship between his concept of a fully mimetic discourse and the seventeenth-century verisimilitude, however, Fénelon's views depart from the consensus of the seventeenth century on other points as well. His desire to see the French lexicon enlarged so that the language could more fully represent nature also linked him to Joachim du Bellay's *La Deffence et illustration de la langue françoyse* (1549; *The Defence and Illustration of the French Language*, 1939), a view distinctly opposed to the "refinement" of the French vocabulary which culminated in the dictionary of the Academy itself. His moral and utilitarian poetic varied from the predominantly aesthetic purposes of the seventeenth century. Significantly, he spoke highly of the fabulist Jean de La Fontaine, in whose work he saw a breaking down of the formal restraints of meter and rhyme and a movement toward the kind of representational emphasis which favors contact with nature.

Nature, however, is somewhat ambiguous in Fénelon's theory, since it is both a historically relative concept, referring to the way things were at the time the work was composed, and a transcendent, absolute one. This second view is a virtual return to the Golden Age, as he lauds the natural truth and simplicity of pastoral. This contradiction can be resolved by taking seriously Fénelon's historical relativism in conjunction with his representational emphasis. If beauty is in what is represented and not in the manner of its representation, then only certain states of society would both furnish beauty worthy of depiction and permit its honest, immediate expression. Fénelon's theory of discourse thus opens onto the kind of engaged political literature that appealed to many of the Romantics.

The opposite of nature, wit or *bel esprit*, is oddly linked to gender and thus reveals a more conservative side of his theory. If he was not frankly misogynist, Fénelon was at least disdainful of women's influence on literature, for he saw them as responsible for the fashion of witty expression. This view, not without historical justification, sets Fénelon against the important *précieux* current in which women played a major role as authors and arbiters of taste in seventeenth-century France. In his discussion of tragedy he sees wit as weakening the genre: "Fine wit put profane love everywhere." If nature, represented in language, provokes deep feeling in the reader, how can wit, which blocks the depiction of nature by stressing superficial style, provoke a feeling of profane love? This idea seems a weak point in Fénelon's mimetic theory of literature, yet it may actually be a consequence of mimetism rather than its contradiction. Words take the place of nature but delude the reader into thinking that he or she is beholding nature. Witty language therefore creates a synthetic emotion which blocks a "truer" emotion. This truer emotion may well be synonymous in Fénelon's doctrine with violent masculine emotion, which he sees as kept in check by the politer exchange encouraged by the women of the salons. While Fénelon is connected with the rise of Romanticism because of some of his views, this refusal to take women's taste into account involves him in a rearguard action against historical trends and seriously limits the applicability of his concept of nature. Nevertheless, his theory as a whole has the important virtue of rising above an isolated stylistics to achieve a vision of the relationship between literature and the structure of society as a whole.

Principal criticism

Lettre à l'Académie française, 1714 (*Letter to the French Academy*, 1984)

Dialogues sur l'éloquence en général et sur celle de la chaire en particulier, 1718 (*Dialogues Concerning Eloquence in General and Particularly That Kind Which Is Fit for the Pulpit*, 1951)

Other major works and literary forms

François de Salignac de La Mothe-Fénelon's lasting work, besides his works on poetics and rhetoric, consists of his texts of educational theory, didactic fables, stories, and a novel. In addition, Fénelon published more than a score of pamphlets on religious controversy and numerous pious works.

NOVEL
Les Aventures de Télémaque, 1699 (*Adventures of Telemachus*, 1699)

SHORT FICTION
Les Aventures d'Aristonüs, 1699
Fables, 1718

NONFICTION
De l'éducation des filles, 1687 (*The Education of Girls*, 1966)
Explication des maximes des saints sur la vie intérieure, 1697
Réponse à la Relation sur le quiétisme, 1698 (*Report on Quietism*)
Recueil de sermons, 1706
Sermons choisis, 1718
Dialogues des morts, 1719 (*Dialogues of the Dead*, 1723)
Lettre à Louis XIV, 1785

Further reading

Davis, James H. *Fénelon*, 1979.
Dedeyan, Charles. *Télémaque ou La Liberté de l'esprit*, 1991.
Leduc-Lafayette, Denise, ed. *Fénelon, philosophie et spiritualité. Actes du Colloque du Centre d'Étude des Philosophes français*, 1996.
Orcibal, Jean. "L'Influence de Fénelon dans les pays Anglo-Saxons au XVIIe siècle," in *Dix-septième siècle*. XII–XIV (1951–1952), pp. 276–287.
Pizzorusso, Arnaldo. *La poetica di Fénelon*, 1959.
Ronzeaud, Pierre, ed. *Fénelon, "Télémaque". Actes de la Journée Fénelon*, 1995.
Warnick, Barbara. *Fénelon's "Letter to the French Academy" with an Introduction and Commentary*, 1984.

JOHN D. LYONS

See also Boileau-Despréaux; La Bruyère; Neoclassical Literary Theory

Leslie Fiedler

American critic and writer

Born: Newark, New Jersey; March 8, 1917

Biography

Born in the same year as the Russian Revolution, Leslie Aaron Fiedler came of age during the 1930s. Although he went through the Newark, New Jersey, public school system, his real education came from reading books at the public library and attending radical political meetings. After completing his B.A. in English at New York University in 1938, he began what he calls his "flight from the East." It led him first to the University of Wisconsin, where he took his M.A. in 1939 and his Ph.D. in 1941, and later to Montana State University, where he taught intermittently from 1941 to 1964. Fiedler's years in Montana were interrupted by service in the navy during World War II and by fellowships at various other universities. He left the state permanently in 1965 to become Samuel Clemens Professor of English at the State University of New York at Buffalo.

In addition to being a widely published critic, Fiedler is a popular lecturer who seems to thrive on controversy. During the 1960s he was identified with the counterculture and agreed to sponsor a campus organization seeking to repeal laws against the possession and use of marijuana. This association resulted in considerable police harassment and an arrest that brought him national publicity. As Fiedler himself has noted, "I have graduated, in the view of my critics, from the status of *enfant terrible* to that of 'dirty old man' without passing through a decent maturity."

Influence

Probably no other American critic of the postwar era has had as varied and as controversial a career as that of Leslie Fiedler. From the late 1940s to the late 1950s he was known as an original and provocative myth critic. Three major volumes of the 1960s – *Love and Death in the American Novel*, *Waiting for the End*, and *The Return of the Vanishing American* – constitute what Fiedler has described as his "venture in literary anthropology." Since the late 1960s he has been increasingly concerned with challenging traditional distinctions between "high art" and "popular culture." This iconoclastic stance has infuriated keepers of the literary canon, while endearing Fiedler to students, cultural rebels, and freethinkers of every stripe.

Although Fiedler has tried to disavow his early theoretical work as pompous and excessively academic, his essays "Archetype and Signature" and "In the Beginning Was the Word" (first published in *The Sewanee Review* in the 1950s) were seminal works in the backlash against aesthetic formalism (the so-called New Criticism). His most enduring legacy, however, has probably been as an interpreter of American culture. *Love and Death in the American Novel* is one of a handful of studies to earn a permanent place on Ph.D. reading lists.

Analysis

Fiedler first drew attention in academic circles as a champion of myth criticism, one of several approaches challenging the dominance of aesthetic formalism, or New Criticism, in the 1950s. In his essay "In the Beginning Was the Word," he gives a new twist to the old notion that poetry and science constitute different modes of knowledge. This split, according to Fiedler, is simply a variation on the more fundamental dichotomy between *logos* and *mythos*. Fiedler sees *mythos* as the source of poetry and *logos* as the language of philosophy (understood in its older, inclusive sense). Put another way, "philosophy invented *logos*, but *mythos* created poetry." Something of a mystic at heart, Fiedler regards the artist as neither copyist nor maker, but as priest – the shaman who sacramentalizes in song and story pure essences that (be they Platonic forms or Jungian archetypes) exist prior to experience.

Fiedler's most important treatment of the essences that constitute literature can be found in his essay "Archetype and Signature." Although much of this essay is a polemical indictment of the antibiographical excesses of aesthetic formalism, Fiedler also establishes a firm theoretical footing for his own alternative position. He accuses the formalists of an extreme nominalism (the philosophical position that only individual entities exist and that universal concepts are merely "names" for groups of individuals). Fiedler believes that it is more important to develop an appreciation for the *mythos* of literature than to lose oneself in the close reading of individual texts.

When he uses the word "Archetype" (which he later replaced with the more inclusive *mythos*), Fiedler means "the immemorial patterns of response to the human situation in its most permanent aspects: death, love, the biological family, the relationship with the Unknown." By "Signature," he means "the sum total of individuating factors in a work, the sign of the persona or personality through which an archetype is rendered, and which itself tends to become a subject as well as a means of the poem." Consequently, literature "can be said to come into existence at the moment a Signature is imposed upon an Archetype."

Because Fiedler does not share the formalists' obsession with staying inside the poem, his critical stance is enriched by an openness to history, including the personal history of the poet's own life. Because archetypes are not bound by time, however, he is also free of the temporal provincialism of traditional literary scholars; Fiedler speaks not of "influences" but of "confluences." Whereas conventional academicians would reject a Freudian reading of William Shakespeare on the grounds that Shakespeare preceded Sigmund Freud, Fiedler would say that the poet has simply intuited that which the psychoanalyst would later explicate. The biographical fact that Freud drew much of his imagery and vocabulary from literature would tend to strengthen the notion that he was simply putting his personal signature on immortal archetypes.

If "Archetype and Signature" is Fiedler's most respected theoretical essay, his best-known and most controversial foray into practical criticism is "Come Back to the Raft Ag'in, Huck Honey!" Originally published in the June, 1948, issue of *Partisan Review*, this essay has been reprinted countless times and is known by reputation to large numbers of people who have never read it. Fiedler's thesis here is that the central concern of classic American fiction is not the European preoccupation with adult heterosexual passion, but rather a flight from heterosexual bonding (what Washington Irving referred to as "petticoat government"). The great novels of American literature are boys' books because American men are to a large extent boys at heart. An essential aspect of the sentimental life of American men is "the camaraderie of the locker room and ball park, the good fellowship of the poker game and the fishing trip."

Although the refugee from matriarchal civilization is occasionally isolated (as was Henry David Thoreau at Walden), more often there is a wilderness bonding between males. The most enduring relationship in American literature, this bonding is a pure antimarriage, because it is freed of the complications of sexual passion and of the responsibilities of domestic life. In a world without women, it is possible to enjoy both freedom and community – even if it is only the community of a boy and a runaway slave floating downriver on a raft.

What makes this theme of male bonding more complex (and seemingly at odds with the official mores of American society) is that it frequently joins a white man and a man of color. The most famous examples are to be found in James Fenimore Cooper's Leatherstocking Tales (1823–1841), Herman Melville's *Moby Dick: Or, The Whale* (1851), and Mark Twain's *Adventures of Huckleberry Finn* (1884). When the white man (or boy) dreams himself a renegade from society, he is symbolically joined to that alien other who has always (as if by definition) been a renegade. It should not be surprising, then, that that dream finds its embodiment in the most mythically resonant American literature.

Fiedler's views on the broad spectrum of that literature are most fully developed in his magnum opus, *Love and Death in the American Novel.* Here he argues that at its beginning American fiction could avail itself of three eighteenth-century British prototypes: the sentimental love novels of Samuel Richardson (featuring a comic face in *Pamela: Or, Virtue Rewarded*, 1740–1741, and a tragic one in *Clarissa: Or, The History of a Young Lady*, 1747–1748), the pseudo-Shakespearean epic of Henry Fielding, and the Gothic romance of "Monk" Lewis. Although the Fielding epic has fallen on largely barren soil, the sentimental novel has been preserved in popular literature from soap opera to pornography, and the Gothic romance has been so thoroughly Americanized as to become the main tradition in canonical American fiction. This transformation was begun by the first major novelist of the New World, Charles Brockden Brown, and continued by the first classic novelist of the American nation, Cooper. By combining the more recent historical romance of Sir Walter Scott with the Gothic mode, Cooper – like Brown – adapted European prototypes to the vastly different American landscape.

If the first half of *Love and Death in the American Novel* is concerned with the adaptation of European models to an American environment, the second half is devoted to the later transmutations that have given American classic literature a tradition of its own. Fiedler begins by discussing the very different uses of Richardson's suffering maiden prototype in the work of Nathaniel Hawthorne, Stephen Crane, and Theodore Dreiser. Anticipating the later commentary of feminist critics, Fiedler traces a misogynist theme in the works of American novelists, beginning with Washington Irving and Mark Twain and extending through such twentieth-century giants as Ernest Hemingway, F. Scott Fitzgerald, and William Faulkner. After expatiating at great length on *eros*, Fiedler concludes his study with a nod to *thanatos* – first in a chapter on Edgar Allan Poe's contribution to American Gothicism and then with a jaunty, if not entirely successful, discussion of the American Faust.

Having completed his massive study of the American novel, Fiedler began to notice at some point in the 1960s that the genre itself was nearly dead. The novel had come into being in the eighteenth century, when the Industrial Revolution made the mass production of books possible and the rise of capitalism created a middle-class audience to read those books. By the early 1960s, however, the mass audience was abandoning the mainstream realistic novel for more technologically advanced storytelling media – principally films and television – and for various forms of popular literature – romance novels, detective fiction, soft-core pornography, and the like. At the same time, highbrow readers and critics had renounced mimetic fiction for neofabulist art novels that were increasingly divorced from the concerns of everyday life. (According to the *Oxford English Dictionary*, Fiedler is responsible for contributing the term "postmodernism" to the English language.) In *Waiting for the End*, Fiedler declared the death of the novel as "the last narrative art form invented, or capable of being invented, for *literates*." This phenomenon and its implications for American culture remained important themes in his criticism for the next two decades, as can be seen in *Cross the Border, Close the Gap* and *What Was Literature?*

Fiedler's growing interest in and respect for popular culture eventually caused him to redefine his notion of myth criticism. In *What Was Literature?* he argues that the critic should focus on those subconscious and unarticulated sources of appeal that cause certain works of art to please many and please long. Because these sources exist irrespective of the formal excellence of the works in which they are embodied, critics will find themselves "speaking less of theme and purport, structure and texture, signified and signifier, metaphor and metonymy, and more of myth, fable, archetype, fantasy, magic and wonder."

In the second half of *What Was Literature?* Fiedler proceeds from theoretical to practical criticism in an attempt to open up the American canon to a sequence of works that have moved the majority audience without gaining favor with elitist critics. He contends that this sequence of works, written by many hands over a period of more than a century, constitutes an "inadvertent epic." This epic consists of Harriet Beecher Stowe's *Uncle Tom's Cabin: Or, Life Among the Lowly* (1852) and the various "Tom" plays it spawned, Thomas Dixon, Jr.'s *The Clansman: An Historical Romance of the Ku Klux Klan* (1905) and its cinematic re-creation as D. W. Griffith's *The Birth of a Nation* (1915), Margaret Mitchell's *Gone with the Wind* as both novel (1936) and motion picture (1939), and the various incarnations of Alex Haley's *Roots* (1976) – from *Reader's Digest* condensation through television miniseries.

Formally, these works are similar in their ability to survive transformation from one genre to another without loss of mythic power. Substantively, they present a version of the American experience diametrically opposite to what is found in the stories discussed in "Come Back to the Raft Ag'in, Huck Honey!" The inadvertent epic reverences home and hearth rather than the flight into the wilderness. Instead of celebrating interethnic male bonding, with its homoerotic overtones, the epic is a continuous denunciation of heterosexual miscegenetic rape – the salient difference being that in *Uncle Tom's Cabin* and *Roots* the attackers are white and the victims black, while in the mythic projections of Dixon, Griffith, and Mitchell, it is the other way around. In a sense, the concept of the inadvertent epic completes the examination of American literature begun in "Come Back to the Raft." As Fiedler writes in *What Was Literature?* (a book he dedicated "to Sam and Hattie"), "If Sam Clemens is a literary father to us all, Hattie Stowe is our mother."

Principal criticism

An End to Innocence: Essays on Culture and Politics, 1955
No! In Thunder: Essays on Myth in Literature, 1960
Love and Death in the American Novel, 1960, 1966
Waiting for the End, 1964
The Return of the Vanishing American, 1968
The Stranger in Shakespeare, 1972
Cross the Border, Close the Gap, 1972
To the Gentiles, 1972
Unfinished Business, 1972
The Inadvertent Epic: From "Uncle Tom's Cabin" to "Roots," 1980
What Was Literature? Class Culture and Mass Society, 1982
Olaf Stapledon: A Man Divided, 1983
Fiedler on the Roof: Essays on Literature and Jewish Identity, 1991

Other major works and literary forms

In addition to his prolific output in the area of literary criticism, Leslie Fiedler has published four novels, two collections of short stories, and a small but interesting body of poetry. His arrest in 1967 on dubious drug charges (for which he was later acquitted) resulted in the autobiographical book *Being Busted* (1969). In 1978 he achieved considerable popular success with an interdisciplinary meditation on human oddities entitled *Freaks: Myths and Images of the Secret Self*. In addition, Fiedler has published numerous essays on various aspects of American popular culture.

NOVELS
The Second Stone: A Love Story, 1963
Back to China, 1965
The Last Jew in America, 1966
The Messengers Will Come No More, 1974

SHORT FICTION
Pull Down Vanity and Other Stories, 1962
Nude Croquet and Other Stories, 1969

NONFICTION
Being Busted, 1969
A Fiedler Reader, 1977
Freaks: Myths and Images of the Secret Self, 1978
Tyranny of the Normal: Essays on Bioethics, Theology and Myth, 1996

ANTHOLOGIES
The Art of the Essay, 1958
In Dreams Awake: A Historical Critical Anthology of Science Fiction, 1975

Further reading

Larson, Charles R. "Leslie Fiedler: The Critic and the Myth, the Critic as Myth," in *Literary Review*. XIV (Winter, 1970/1971), pp. 133–143.
Webster, Grant. "Leslie Fiedler: Adolescent and Jew as Critic," in *Denver Quarterly*. I (Winter, 1967), pp. 44–53.
Winchell, Mark Royden. *Leslie Fiedler*, 1985.

MARK ROYDEN WINCHELL

See also American Literary Theory: Twentieth Century; Archetypal Criticism

Film Criticism

Relying on the supposed superiority of literature over popular culture (including film), literary study has traditionally been able to wield a considerable amount of academic authority. This authority, however, has been somewhat eroded as critics have come to appreciate that literature and film are simply two different kinds of signifying practice, producing meaning in different ways, and that neither should be considered superior to the other.

The literary genre generally considered closest to film is the novel. Indeed, Morris Beja has argued that films and novels are "two forms of a single art: the art of narrative literature." This claim, however, places too much emphasis on narrative at the expense of other elements. As a primarily visual medium, films have a distinctive grammar stemming from the use of physical equipment unavailable to the literary artist. Martin Esslin has divided this grammar into two parts: "signs derived from the camera" (including different kinds of shot – static, panning, tracking . . .) and "signs derived from the linking of shots" (including dissolves, fades, sharp cuts . . .). This film grammar clearly helps to distinguish film criticism from other types of criticism and theory. In turn, film criticism may best be understood in relation to the evolution of film theory.

The first phase of film theory, which held sway until about the mid-1930s, was formalist, and the principal practitioners were Rudolf Arnheim, Sergei Eisenstein, and Hugo Musterberg. Arguing that film did not simply copy but interpreted and molded material, Arnheim, in particular, anticipated and rejected the phase that would follow which came to be known as "the classical realist phase." The most celebrated theorists in this later phase, which lasted until about the 1960s, were André Bazin and Siegfried Kracauer. Classical realism for film theorists shares some of the conventions of literary realism and naturalism prevalent especially in novels of the nineteenth and early twentieth centuries. This involves a privileging of content as opposed to form, and the belief that the medium can accurately present historical and social reality. Film theorists in this phase of film theory, especially Bazin, emphasized the way that certain films tried to conceal the fact that they were films by making sure that the viewer was always given enough information to follow the plot and by ensuring that shot transitions were as inconspicuous as possible.

In spite of the rebellious ethos of the 1960s in terms of a general opposition to the academic establishment, the more liberal mood of the decade coincided with film criticism's burgeoning acceptance as an academic discipline. The 1960s saw the emergence of semiology, soon to be called semiotics. Some of the most innovative work in film semiotics was carried out by Christian Metz. In the course of his long career, Metz was able to incorporate into the field of film semiotics work from other disciplines, including linguistics (relying briefly on concepts derived from the American philosopher C. S. Peirce and more substantially on the work of Ferdinand de Saussure) and psychoanalysis (relying on the work of Sigmund Freud and Jacques Lacan's rewriting of Freudian theory).

Metz is perhaps best remembered, though, for his articulation of his *grande syntagmatique*, in which he divided filmic narrative into eight autonomous units or syntagmas, including the autonomous shot (a syntagma consisting of one shot), the descriptive syntagma (in which objects are shown successively to suggest spatial coexistence), the scene (similar to the theatrical scene although conveyed through diverse shots), and the ordinary sequence (which relies on ellipses in order to leave out unimportant details). Although Metz's work has given rise to a good deal of film criticism within the domain of semiotics, it has been criticized by some for being too politically neutral.

Some thinkers have located the pivotal moment in film theory as the widespread political demonstrations of 1968, after which the social role of cinema could hardly be ignored. At this time film critics also looked back to the work of thinkers like Theodor Adorno and Walter Benjamin. The latter has been particularly influential. His optimistic view of the cinema's ability to transform people's consciousness in a positive way was an important counter to Adorno's apprehensive view of cinema as part of the fantasy culture industry, a breeder of mass conformity, and paralyzer of independent thought. Benjamin's influence was especially felt in England where film study was gaining respectability despite the opposition of the Leavisite school of thought, which sought to defend the study of English literature with its canon against the barbarism of "mass culture."

The late 1960s and early 1970s saw the emergence of major film journals with a theoretical slant, notably *Cahiers du Cinéma* and *Cinétique* in France, and *Screen* in Britain. Film theory increasingly subscribed to the notion that all film was political. Contributors to *Cahiers du Cinéma*, in particular, were inclined to evaluate films in terms of their ability to depict or stand up against prevailing social attitudes or ideology. *Screen* was initially heavily influenced by structuralism and theories about the position of the spectator or the subject indebted to Louis Althusser's notion of "interpellation" (the view that ideology constructs individuals as subjects). First Claude Lévi-Strauss' structural anthropology, and then Roland Barthes' structuralist or mythological critique and Michel Foucault's analysis became increasingly influential. Following Foucault, films came to be seen as "discursive formations" depicting relations between power, knowledge, and the body.

In the 1970s film criticism also coalesced with feminist criticism, as could be seen in the first feminist film journals, for example *Camera Obscura*. Critics began to question the ways in which women, and particularly women's sexuality, had been represented in films. By the 1980s feminist theory, often supported by Freudian or Lacanian psychoanalytic theory, was flourishing. It is worth noting here the work of Claire Johnston, E. Ann Kaplan, Teresa de Lauretis, and Laura Mulvey. Mulvey's 1975 essay "Visual Pleasure and Narrative Cinema," which analyzes the male gaze and attempts to pave the way for "a new language of desire," stands out as a landmark in film theory and has produced an important and substantial body of film criticism.

At about the same time, the male theorists Stephen Heath, Colin MacCabe, and Peter Wollen were also carrying out important initiatives in film criticism. In their early work, Heath and MacCabe seemed to share Althusser's optimism in terms of cinema's potential to bring about revolutionary change. These thinkers became wary of structuralism – Wollen, for example, in "Godard and Counter-Cinema: *Vent d'Est*" reflects on the limitations of trying to understand film in terms of straightforward binary oppositions. Then, with the turn toward poststructuralism, these theorists became more skeptical about links between film and society and the possibilities of "worlds of plenitude," a concept undercut by the theories of Jacques Lacan. For Lacan our existence is constructed around a gap or hole, and we spend our lives trying to make up for this by trying to recapture the moments of plenitude which as babies we are said to have experienced with our mother. Some film critics have connected this to film's deployment of the ideology of romantic love, and especially the notion that love will make us whole.

As for film criticism in the 1990s, the decade can perhaps best be described, in Susan Hayward's words, as one of "postmodern pluralism," a time when the door that started to be opened in the 1960s stood wide open. Contemporary film criticism seems to be able to incorporate a plurality of approaches; none of the familiar approaches have been discarded but instead tend to resurface in different forms – like neoformalism and poststructuralist semiotics. As for the future, academic film criticism will have to face up to and come to terms with digitalized technology: there is a danger, for example, that we will have at our fingertips a surfeit of information, but as Jean Baudrillard says, "not enough meaning." In other words, if insufficient attention is paid to earlier film theories or the history of the discipline, film criticism may run the risk of becoming too open-ended and losing its autonomy or distinctive space.

Further reading

Andrew, Dudley. *Concepts in Film Theory*, 1984.
Arnheim, Rudolf. *Film as Art*, 1957.
Beja, Morris. *Film and Literature*, 1976.
Carson, Diane, Linda Dattimar, and Janice R. Welsch. *Multiple Voices in Feminist Film Criticism*, 1994.
Cavell, Stanley. *The World Viewed: Reflections on the Ontology of Film*, 1979.
De Lauretis, Teresa. *Alice Doesn't: Feminism, Semiotics, Cinema*, 1984.
Deleuze, Gilles. *Cinéma-1. L'Image-mouvement*, 1983 (*Cinema 1: The Movement-Image*, 1986).
——. *Cinéma-2. L'Image-temps*, 1985 (*Cinema 2: The Time-Image*, 1989).
Eberwein, Robert T. *A Viewer's Guide to Film Theory and Criticism*, 1979.
Eisenstein, Sergei. *Film Form*, 1949.
Heath, Stephen. *Questions of Cinema*, 1981.
Jameson, Fredric. *Signatures of the Visible*, 1990.
Johnston, Claire, ed. *Notes on Women's Cinema*, 1973.
Kaplan, E. Ann. *Women and Film: Both Sides of the Camera*, 1983.
——, ed. *Psychoanalysis and Cinema: Both Sides of the Camera*, 1983.
Kracauer, Siegfried. *Theory of Film: The Redemption of Physical Reality*, 1960.
MacCabe, Colin. *Theoretical Essays*, 1985.
Mast, Gerald, Marshal Cohen, and Leo Braudy. *Film Theory and Criticism: Introductory Readings*, 1974, 1992.
Metz, Christian. *Film Language: A Semiotics of Cinema*, 1974.
——. *The Imaginary Signifier: Psychoanalysis and the Cinema*, 1982.
Mitry, Jean. *Esthétique et psychologie du cinéma*, Vol. 1, 1963, Vol. 2, 1965 (*The Aesthetics and Psychology of the Cinema*, 1997).
Mulvey, Laura. *Visual and Other Pleasures*, 1989.
Musterberg, Hugo. *The Film: A Psychological Study*, 1916.
Stam, Robert, Robert Burgoyne, and Sandy Flitterman-Lewis. *New Vocabularies in Film Semiotics: Structuralism, Post-Structuralism, and Beyond*, 1992, 1996.
Wollen, Peter. *Signs and Meaning in the Cinema*, 1976.

NICHOLAS O. PAGAN

Stanley Fish

American critic

Born: Providence, Rhode Island; April 19, 1938

Biography

Stanley Eugene Fish was born on April 19, 1938, in Providence, Rhode Island. His parents, Max and Ida Fish, ran a plumbing, heating, and contracting business. Although neither had a formal education, Max Fish was a Talmudic scholar in Poland before emigrating in 1923, and Ida Fish has for many years written novels and poems she has shown no one.

Stanley Fish received his bachelor's degree from the University of Pennsylvania in 1959, and his master's degree and doctorate from Yale in 1960 and 1962, respectively. In 1962 he began teaching at the University of California at Berkeley. He remained at Berkeley until 1974, when he joined the English department at The Johns Hopkins University. From 1985 to early 1999 he was the English department chair and Arts and Sciences Distinguished Professor of English and Law at Duke University. Later in 1999 Fish was appointed Dean of the College of Liberal Arts and Sciences at the University of Illinois at Chicago. Throughout his career he has received numerous research grants and fellowships, including the Berkeley Humanities Research Professorship in 1966 and 1970, an American Council of Learned Societies Fellowship in 1966, and a Guggenheim Fellowship in 1969.

From 1959 until their divorce in 1980, he was married to Adrienne Aaron, with whom he had one daughter, Susan. In 1982 he married Jane P. Tompkins. Fish has included among his nonliterary interests playing basketball, watching television, and purchasing automobiles.

Influence

Fish is a perceptive and thoughtful critic of seventeenth-century English poetry, but he is best known as the proponent of a particular style of reader-oriented literary theory. His reader-oriented theory is not at all interested in the psychologies or processes of individual readers, but focuses instead on the processes of literary interpretation and on how interpretation is constrained by the situations in which readers read literary texts.

Analysis

One of the dominant metaphors in Fish's work is expressed in the title of his third book: *Self-Consuming Artifacts: The Experience of Seventeenth-Century Literature*, published in 1972. Self-consuming artifacts, argues Fish, are artifacts that self-destruct, entangling their readers along the way and undermining the positions with which they began, so that what starts out as certain and stable is, by the end of the reading, questioned, unsettled, and undermined. Reading, says Fish, is a temporal process of "progressive decertainizing" in which the reader is asked to believe something and then forced to call that belief into question.

Although Fish would not hold to some of the views he offered in 1972, his interest in self-consuming artifacts has remained strong. With the publication of *The Living Temple: George Herbert and Catechizing* in 1978 and *Is There a Text in This Class? The Authority of Interpretive Communities* in 1980, however, what is under scrutiny and what is being unsettled are not seventeenth-century poems and their readers, but Fish's own earlier positions, his own texts, and his own readings of them.

The Living Temple ends with what has become a characteristic Fish move, that of taking back what he has just said, of consuming his own artifact. In "A Conclusion in Which It May Appear That Everything Is Taken Back," Fish argues that he has not, in *The Living Temple*, demonstrated anything, in the sense of having found factual, objective evidence to "prove" his interpretation, even though that is what it seems he has been doing. Rather, he says, he was able to find those facts because of his interpretation, and if he has been convincing, it may be attributed to the fact that he has "initiated [his reader] into a way of seeing as a consequence of which the facts could not be otherwise" than the way he presents them. This admission, he says, "might seem to risk undermining the . . . confidence" of his reader, but then again, he says, there is no reason to believe that that confidence might not survive the admission that what has occurred is persuasion, not demonstration.

The move at the end of *The Living Temple* is a foreshortened version of what Fish does in *Is There a Text in This Class?* where he again explores his own progressive decertainizing. *Is There a Text in This Class?* collects Fish's major theoretical pieces to that point, linking them with revisions and with a narrative that explains how he no longer believes what he used to believe. Then, on the last two pages, Fish seems to take back the new theory he has just proposed by saying that it has absolutely no practical consequence. He consumes his own artifact and then consumes his consuming.

Several "artifacts" have been "consumed" in Fish's theoretical journeys since 1972. The first artifact to go was the text, which became subsumed in the reader's experience of the text. Next to go was the reader, who, in *Is There a Text in This Class?* became consumed and subsumed in the activity of "interpretive communities." "Interpretive community" is the most crucial concept in this book. Both terms of the formulation are important. "Interpretation," Fish says, is "the only game in town," by which he means that all human activity is interpretive; that is, there is never some state – in perception, in description, in knowing, in reading, or in any other human activity – that exists prior to interpretation. To describe or understand or read is to interpret. Textual features do not exist as objective facts; rather, they come into view as a result of the interpretations held by their perceivers. This leads Fish to one of his major premises: texts are not found, but made. They are not made by authors but by readers (authors being among these readers), who approach these texts with interpretive frameworks that cause them to see certain features that will accord with their already-held interpretive frameworks.

This is why rhetoric – the art of persuasion – becomes so important to Fish. "The whole of critical activity [is] an attempt on the part of one party to alter the beliefs of another so that the evidence cited by the first will be seen *as* evidence by the second." Fish is somewhat unclear about how this change occurs. Roughly, it seems to involve locating that set of assumptions that his readers and he share and then using that shared understanding to convince them of the inevitability of a new set of assumptions.

Despite his contention that literature is what a reader chooses to see as literature, Fish is not a relativist; literary discussion, he says, does not dissolve into a chaos of solipsism and conflicting and infinite interpretations. That is prevented by the second term in his formulation: community. The interpretive frameworks directing readers' perceptions are not unique to individual readers. Readers have assumptions not because they choose them or invent them, but because they are members of communities which share these assumptions. One never perceives, reads, knows, or interprets in the abstract; one is always in a situation or a context – a community. To be in a situation is "to be in possession of (or to be possessed by) a structure of assumptions, of practices understood to be relevant in relation to purposes and goals that are already in place; and it is within the assumption of these purposes and goals that any utterance is *immediately* heard." Readers, in other words, are not free agents. The "mental operations" they perform are "limited by the institutions in which [they] are *already* embedded." Thus, if there is stability in interpretation, it exists because of the stability of the interpretive communities that authorize that interpretation, not because of any intrinsic stability in the text.

Since *Is There a Text in This Class?* Fish has continued along many of the same paths, modifying and clarifying earlier positions and striking out in some new directions. One of the threads running through this work is his concern to defend the "particular" against the "general," where what is particular is what is tied to a context, or context-specific, and what is general is abstract or universal, or devoid of context. This concern comes into play in his essays on antiprofessionalism in literary studies, where Fish argues that the discipline of literary studies runs the risk of eviscerating itself by undermining its own strength. Responding to contemporary complaints (from both within and without the literary community) that current literary study is too "specialized" and is not looking at how texts transcend culture and history, Fish points out that to accept these complaints is to deny professional status to literary studies, for, in fact, to be a "professional" is to have a specialization others lack. By insisting on a criticism of generality (as did New Criticism), people in literary studies end by denying the validity and value of what they do. Thus, Fish calls for a renewed sense of professionalism in literary studies through a new historicism.

Perhaps this concern for professionalism derives from Fish's growing interest in a profession with less self-doubt about its status and value than the English profession, that is the legal profession. Not only has Fish studied and taught law, but he has also become a frequent contributor to journals such as the *Stanford Law Review* and to symposia on the role of interpretation in the law. In these debates he extends his position to the legal context, specifically that of constitutional interpretation, arguing that it is impossible to determine the meaning of a law by recourse to a literal meaning or intention available prior to interpretation. Rather, when a law is intended or read, it is intended and read within a context which specifies possible meanings. Both interpretation and intention are constrained by institutional beliefs and practices which establish available possibilities. In other words, laws have no general, always-applicable meaning; they only have meaning within a particular, specific context.

A third area with which Fish has been concerned is an elaboration of the point raised in the final chapter of *Is There a Text in This Class?* – the non-consequences of his theory, or indeed of any theory, for literary practice. Here, again, Fish reveals an interest in the particular rather than the general. He argues that the implications of his theory for the practice of literary criticism are "none whatsoever. That is, it does not follow from what I have been saying that you should go out and do literary criticism in a certain way or refrain from doing it in other ways." Indeed, Fish's own critical works since 1980 seem to confirm this. Except for the fact that readers are often seen as themes in the works he interprets, his interpretations proceed as though he believes that texts say something, that authors create them, and that meaning is something one can confidently identify. In *Is There a Text in This Class?* he explains the fact that his theory has no consequences for practice by the fact that his theory simply explains a process "we are all living out."

In later discussions of this point, Fish argues that no theory has practical consequences. Theory, as he characterizes it, is abstraction, the process of specifying immutable, universal rules that are always true; therefore, because nothing can ever be specified divorced from a particular context or situation, theory cannot exist. In other words, Fish has returned to his earlier point: no description, including theoretical description, is neutral; it is always embedded in a context. Theory, therefore, is practice. That is why Fish continues to write theory – not because it has consequences for how people practice literary criticism, but because, at this juncture in the institution of literary studies, doing theory is one of the institution's accepted practices.

All of these issues reveal Fish's increasing interest in the problems of history and change. In rejecting the general for the specific in literary studies, legal studies, and theoretical studies, Fish is arguing for an increased awareness of the situation of an utterance or artifact or text, especially of the historical situation. In so doing, he appears to be responding to some of the criticisms levied against *Is There a Text in This Class?* Many of Fish's reviewers criticized him (and rightly so) for the vagueness of his concept of interpretive communities and for his consequent inability to account for how interpretive communities change or how individuals change their memberships in interpretive communities. As Catherine Gallagher has pointed out, Fish uses the notion of interpretive communities "as a way of escaping from the hermeneutic circle," dispensing with the problem of explaining the sources of interpretive agreement by "relocating them in an epistemological promised land."

Robert Scholes, although he misreads Fish as saying that people can only be members of one interpretive community at a time, nevertheless aptly notes another problem in Fish's analysis of interpretive communities. Fish, he says, uses "interpretive community" to cover too wide a variety of groupings of individuals – from a particular classroom situation to people who speak the same language. Scholes points out that these groupings may all function in different ways, which Fish's single term, "interpretive community," tends to obscure.

As Fish's critics note, to say that what people assume, know, and believe is a function of their interpretive communities, and then to say that interpretive communities are groups of people who share the same assumptions, ways of knowing, and beliefs, is a tautology that begs the question of how interpretation occurs. Fish, over the years, has argued that it is not texts that constrain interpretation but readers, and then he has said that it is not readers who constrain interpretation, but interpretive communities who, through constraining readers, constrain interpretation. What, one might ask, constrains interpretive communities? How does it happen? Why are some assumptions acceptable to a community and others not? Why do some communities have power while others do not? How does a person gain entry into a community? How does the community recognize membership and how do people's affiliations change? What, in short, are the processes, politics, and history of these interpretive communities? These are some of the questions Fish must answer if he hopes to "persuade" others to join his particular interpretive community. Fish's 1986 exploration of a (partial) history of the interpretation of the last two books of John Milton's *Paradise Lost* gets much closer to exploring this issue of how interpretive communities change. All of his work after *Is There a Text in This Class?* can be seen as an attempt to address these issues. Since Fish has no fear of changing his mind and indeed relishes the opportunity to engage in dialogue with other theorists, it seems likely that some of these questions will eventually be answered more satisfactorily.

As *Doing What Comes Naturally* (1989) shows, during the 1980s Fish's ability to develop his ideas in unexpected ways remained undiminished. Among his project, for example, was the attempt to establish a link between literary theory and criticism and what may at first sight seem an unlikely partner, namely legal studies. He insisted that in both disciplines theory (the attempt to provide a general theory of interpretation) was doomed to failure for it is not, and cannot be, independent of a theoretical and institutional / professional context. This controversial emphasis on "practice rather than theory" made him a leading figure in what became known as "neo-pragmatism," an approach notably advocated by Steven Knapp and Walter Benn Michaels in "Against Theory," an essay first published in 1982.

Fish, as so many of his critics have mentioned, is slippery – and changeable, outrageous, and argumentative. Those in the profession who wish to be able to locate meaning at least partially in the text find Fish's perspective profoundly disturbing. In an essay entitled "Let's Hope There *Is* a Text in the Class: Stanley Fish and the Profession of English," Keith Wilson argues, for example, that Fish's "retreat from judgment and discretion" and his "kaleidoscopic permutations" may be "dangerous" for the profession. Regardless of whether people agree with Fish, certainly no one would disagree that – in the interpretive community of American literary theory of the last two decades of the twentieth century – Stanley Fish has been one of its most creative leaders, one of its most brilliant thinkers, and one of its most provocative polemicists.

Principal criticism

John Skelton's Poetry, 1965
Surprised by Sin: The Reader in Paradise Lost, 1967
"Literature in the Reader: Affective Stylistics," 1970
Self-Consuming Artifacts: The Experience of Seventeenth-Century Literature, 1972
The Living Temple: George Herbert and Catechizing, 1978
Is There a Text in This Class? The Authority of Interpretive Communities, 1980
"Working on the Chain Gang: Interpretation in the Law and in Literary Criticism," 1982
"Interpretation and the Pluralist Vision," 1982
"Profession Despise Thyself: Fear and Self-Loathing in Literary Studies," 1983
"Authors-Readers: Jonson's Community of the Same," 1984
"Anti-Professionalism," 1985
"Pragmatism and Literary Theory: Consequences," 1985
"Transmuting the Lump: *Paradise Lost* 1942–1982," 1986
Doing What Comes Naturally: Change, Rhetoric, and the Practice of Theory in Literary and Legal Studies, 1989

Other literary forms

Stanley Fish is known primarily as a literary critic and theorist, although his interest in interpretation has expanded to include a concern with legal interpretation as well as literary interpretation.

Further reading

Bagwell, J. Timothy. "Who's Afraid of Stanley Fish?," in *Poetics Today*. IV (1983), pp. 127–133.

Cain, William E. *The Crisis in Criticism*, 1984.

Culler, Jonathan. *The Pursuit of Signs: Semiotics, Literature, Deconstruction*, 1981.

Graff, Gerald. "Interpretation on Tlon: A Response to Stanley Fish," in *New Literary History*. 17 (1985).

Knapp, Steven, and Walter Benn Michaels. "Against Theory," in *Against Theory: Literary Studies and the New Pragmatism*. Edited by W. J. T. Michaels.

Mailloux, Steven. *Interpretive Conventions: The Reader in the Study of American Fiction*, 1982.

Ray, William. "Stanley Fish: Supersession and Transcendence," in *Literary Meaning: From Phenomenology to Deconstruction*, 1984.

Scholes, Robert. "Who Cares About the Text?," in *Textual Power: Literary Theory and the Teaching of English*, 1985.

Suleiman, Susan R. "Introduction: Varieties of Audience-Oriented Criticism," in *The Reader in the Text: Essays on Audience and Interpretation*, 1980. Edited by Susan R. Suleiman and Inge Crosman.

Tompkins, Jane P., ed. *Reader-Response Criticism: From Formalism to Post-structuralism*, 1980.

JoAnne Liebman Matson

See also American Literary Theory: Twentieth Century; Reader-Response Criticism

E. M. Forster

English novelist and critic

Born: London, England; January 1, 1879
Died: Coventry, England; June 7, 1970

Biography

Edward Morgan Forster was born on January 1, 1879, in London, the only surviving child of a London architect (Edward Morgan Llewellyn Forster, who died of tuberculosis when the child was two years old) and his wife, Alice Clara (Lily), née Whichelo, a descendant of the Clapham sect of wealthy evangelicals. His years at King's College, Cambridge, where he studied classics and history (he received a degree in 1901), were decisive in his intellectual development. There he met the exponent of Greek classicism Goldsworthy Lowes Dickinson, and there he encountered G. E. Moore and his *Principia Ethica* (1903), whose ideas enormously influenced Forster and other members of what later became Forster's social circle, the Bloomsbury Group (which included Virginia and Leonard Woolf, Vanessa and Clive Bell, J. M. Keynes, Lytton Strachey, Roger Fry, Duncan Grant, and other prominent artists and intellectuals). Moore stressed that "'the truth' is not an esoteric pursuit requiring special powers of the intellect and a specific language for its expression, but that it necessitated complete honesty in rigorous thinking." According to Moore, one experiences the Good and the True primarily by experiencing good states of mind which are induced by "admiration of things of beauty" and by right personal relationships.

While establishing himself as a major writer of fiction, Forster worked as tutor, teacher, lecturer, editor, columnist, and radio broadcaster. His extensive travels in India, Greece, Italy, and Egypt made Forster increasingly skeptical of the adequacy of British middle-class values and intensified his awareness of injustice in the world. He saw clearly the need for and the difficulty of communication across barriers of race, class, and nationality. He was twice elected a president of the National Council for Civil Liberties. In 1945 he was elected Honorary Fellow at King's College, Cambridge, where he spent most of the last years of his life. He declined an offer of knighthood in 1949, but accepted nomination to the Order of Companions of Honor by Queen Elizabeth in 1953. In 1969 he was awarded the Order of Merit. He died the next year.

Influence

Although a preeminently tolerant man, Forster would undoubtedly scoff at any attempt to trace his "influence" in modern letters ("criticism adores influence" studies, he once mockingly noted), and, his reputation for tolerance notwithstanding, he would undoubtedly scorn the turn of literary criticism toward the quasi-scientific theories of structuralism and poststructuralism, particularly in their academic tendencies to separate literature from life. (Tolerance, he believed, does not mean giving in.) Forster's own passion was not to analyze, categorize, and divide but to integrate, to "connect," as he put it in the epigraph to *Howards End*. In his vision, the modern world is in a "muddle" (one of his favorite words); it is becoming increasingly chaotic and may disintegrate entirely, because of a failure to make connections – between art and life, intellect and emotion, body and spirit, the moral and the practical, the earthly and the eternal.

Forster regarded himself as an amateur in literary criticism. As teacher and writer, he was a spiritual mentor of younger left-leaning English writers of the 1930s, such as W. H. Auden, Christopher Isherwood, C. Day Lewis, Louis MacNeice, and George Orwell. Whoever believes in the moral intelligence of literature, whoever believes that literature is indeed connected with life, and whoever rejects the idea that the world is too complicated to try to understand, these are Forster's spiritual kindred.

Analysis

Amid the late-twentieth-century vogue for structuralist and poststructuralist criticism, the critical writings of E. M. Forster seem particularly anachronistic. Most of his assumptions and interests run counter to those of critics who are his contemporaries. He does not believe that literature is a self-referring or a self-consuming artifact. He also does not believe that a critic's concern is with codes and strategies or that criticism is in any way superior (or even equal) to imaginative literature, which is to say that his intellectual mentors are not Jacques Derrida and Roland Barthes and Roman Jakobson but Desiderius Erasmus and Michel Eyquem de Montaigne. By his own confession, Forster belongs "to the fag-end of Victorian liberalism," and as critic he seems allied with Matthew Arnold (the Victorian author whom he most admires) in his belief that literature is a criticism of life and that literature may help one to see life both steadily and as a whole.

In "The Raison d'Être of Criticism in the Arts" (1947), an address delivered at Harvard University, Forster identifies the two principal aims of criticism:

> The first and the more important is esthetic. It considers the object in itself, as an entity, and tells us what it can about its life. The second aim is subsidiary: the relation of the object to the rest of the world. Problems of less relevance are considered, such as the conditions under which the work of art was composed, the influences which formed it, . . . the artists' life, . . . and so on, straying this way into psychology and that way into history.

Criticism has educational and cultural value: it can expose fraud and pretentiousness and check conceit, and it can form theories and build standards. Yet Forster remains skeptical that criticism necessarily results in better art. He concedes that in theory "good standards may lead to good work," but as a practical matter criticism usually is of value to the artist in trifling rather than in great matters. Possibly he would believe (with John Bayley and others) that literary criticism is responsible for a decline in the quality of modern literature. Forster states that the artist generally does well to ignore the critic. Forster clearly does not believe criticism is of the same order of importance as the work of art, nor is "the claim of criticism to take us to the heart of the Arts" justified. Criticism cannot help a reader with the private, subjective encounter with the work of art which is the center of the aesthetic experience – what he calls "infection," the feeling of being caught up, transported, the "sense of cooperation with a creator," which for Forster is one of the hall-marks of great literature. Forster finds the creative and the critical faculties to be distinctly different from each other. Art comes from the depths, from the unconscious, while criticism comes from a shallower realm. After creating, the artist wonders "how on earth he did it. And indeed he did not do it on earth." The difference in the two kinds of writing is succinctly stated: "Think before you speak is criticism's motto; speak before you think creation's."

Given Forster's assertion that aesthetic concerns are the most important aspect of criticism and that "the relation of the object to the rest of the world" is of only secondary importance, one might expect to find a formalist bent in his writings. In fact, Forster's criticism and novels both reveal a persistent concern with the sociomoral aspects of literature. In "Art for Art's Sake" (1949), Forster asserts that the primary, unique value of art is that art has order. Percy Bysshe Shelley was correct in stating that "poets are the unacknowledged legislators of the world," because, according to Forster, the artist "legislates through creating. And he creates through his sensitiveness and his power to impose form. Without form the sensitiveness vanishes." Forster believes that "form of some kind is imperative," a human necessity for sanity, but it is not to be found in the social, political, astronomical, or religious realms. He writes, "Works of art . . . are the only objects in the material universe to possess internal order, and that is why, though I don't believe that only art matters, I do believe in Art for Art's Sake." As an outward sign of "internal harmony," even as an outward sign or evidence of humanity's ability eventually to create a sane social order, art is desperately needed in an increasingly chaotic, disintegrating world.

Aspects of the Novel (originally the Clark lectures at Trinity College, Cambridge) has become a minor classic on techniques of fiction. Some of Forster's famous distinctions between "flat" and "round" characters or between "story" and "plot" ("'the King died and then the Queen died' is a story. 'The King died, and then the Queen died of grief' is a plot") may now seem rudimentary, but at the time these lectures were delivered, there was a paucity of critical theorizing about the novel. Forster's appropriation of musical concepts, such as leitmotif and rhythm (rhythm's function is "not to be there all the time like a pattern, but by its lovely waxing and waning to fill us with surprise and freshness and hope"), inspired new approaches to criticism of the novel and provided an important key to Forster's own novelistic techniques, particularly in *A Passage to India*. Yet Forster remains the least theoretical and least academic of critics. His remarks on "pseudo-scholars" (among whom in typical self-deprecation he counts himself) are revealing:

> This constant reference to genius is another characteristic of the pseudo-scholar. He loves mentioning genius, because the sound of the word exempts him from trying to discover its meaning. Literature is written by geniuses. Novelists are geniuses. There we are; now let us classify them. Which he does. Everything he says may be accurate but all is useless because he is moving round books instead of through them, he either has not read them or cannot read them properly. Books have to be read (worse luck, for it takes a long time); it is the only way of discovering what they contain. A few savage tribes eat them, but reading is the only method of assimilation revealed to the west. The reader must sit down alone and struggle with the writer, and this the pseudo-scholar will not do. He would rather relate a book

to the history of its time, to events in the life of its author, to the events it describes, above all to some tendency. As soon as he can use the word "tendency" his spirits rise, and though those of his audience may sink, they often pull out their pencils at this point and make a note, under the belief that a tendency is portable.

The conversational style, the urbane wit, and the skeptical and irreverent tone are characteristic of Forster's critical writings, but these are not qualities which have been universally admired. Lionel Trilling in *E. M. Foster* (1943) maintains that Forster's "seriousness . . . of intellectual enterprise is too often reduced by the unbuttoned manner he affects. The quaint, the facetious and the chatty sink his literary criticism below its proper level." Although Trilling is warmly appreciative of Forster's fiction and acknowledges that *Aspects of the Novel* contains many important insights, he finds an "excessive relaxation" in Forster's critical writings which at times even vitiates his critical discernment, particularly in Forster's evaluations of Sir Walter Scott, James Joyce, and, especially, Henry James.

In an era in which literary criticism has attained an eminence based on an appearance of intellectual rigor, Forster's critical writings do seem relaxed, impressionistic, and personal. Yet Forster is allied with an intellectual tradition of liberal humanism which he takes seriously and which imposes its own kind of discipline. His essay titled "What I Believe" (published in *Two Cheers for Democracy*) paradoxically begins with the statement "I do not believe in Belief" – by which he means dogmas, doctrines, or other intellectual rigidities. He does, however, have beliefs – in tolerance, good temper, sympathy, individualism (the best defense against totalitarianism), and particularly in personal relationships. According to Forster,

> personal relations are despised today . . . we are urged to get rid of them, and to dedicate ourselves to some movement or cause instead. I hate the idea of causes, and if I had to choose between betraying my country and betraying my friend, I hope I should have the guts to betray my country.

Forster distrusts Hero worship and the idea of the Great Man, but he does believe in an aristocracy – "not an aristocracy of power, based upon rank and influence, but an aristocracy of the sensitive, the considerate and the plucky. Its members are to be found in all nations and classes, and all through the ages. . . . They represent the true human tradition, the one permanent victory . . . over cruelty and chaos." Because democracy allows a variety of human beings and because it allows criticism, Forster gives it two cheers. He writes, "Two cheers are quite enough; there is no occasion to give three. Only Love the Beloved Republic deserves that."

Forster, then, is a liberal humanist critic who can use words such as "tolerance," "love," and "true human tradition" in an unapologetic if at times ambiguous way. Foster once defined humanism as having four characteristics: curiosity, a free mind, aesthetic taste, and a belief in humanity, all of which are evident in his writings. Forster's connection with liberalism has been debated. Trilling argues that actually Forster is "at war with the liberal imagination," because liberalism requires "ideals" and "absolutes." It requires the idea of good and evil as separate, antagonistic forces. It does not accept the idea of good and evil inextricably bound up with each other, an idea Trilling consistently finds in Forster's writings.

Trilling directs attention to the fact that Forster is a more complex, subtle thinker than may at first appear, one who resists being safely fenced behind secure classifications. As the critic Austin Warren remarked, "He has ideas but no 'idea.'" Considering the evils to which ideology has contributed in the modern world, the way in which belief solidifies into dogma and fanaticism, Forster's skepticism of movements and causes is not surprising. Forster praised George Orwell for being a "true liberal," because he "hoped to help through small things. Programmes mean pogroms." Forster's most unqualified faith remains with the small, with individuals, and with the personal relationships among those who have "developed hearts."

Principal criticism

Aspects of the Novel, 1927
Abinger Harvest, 1936
Two Cheers for Democracy, 1951

Other major works and literary forms

E. M. Forster is best known as a major writer of English fiction, principally novels. Of the six that he wrote, two of them, *Howards End* (1910) and *A Passage to India* (1924), have attained the status of classics. The others are *Where Angels Fear to Tread* (1905), *The Longest Journey* (1907), *A Room with a View* (1908), and *Maurice*, which was written in 1913 but published posthumously in 1971. He is also the author of four collections of short stories, of which the best known are *The Celestial Omnibus and Other Stories* (1911) and *The Eternal Moment and Other Stories* (1928). Forster also wrote two biographies, one a tribute to his mentor and friend at the University of Cambridge, *Goldsworthy Lowes Dickinson* (1934), and one as a memorial to a great-aunt whose generous bequest of a private income enabled Forster to attend Cambridge, to travel, and to become a professional writer, *Marianne Thornton, 1797–1887: A Domestic Biography* (1956).

Forster's extensive travels were frequently the inspiration for his writing, both fiction and nonfiction. During three years in Alexandria with the Red Cross during World War I, Forster wrote two historical guidebooks: *Alexandria: A History and a Guide* (1922) and *Pharos and Pharillon*

(1923). *The Hill of Devi* (1953) records reminiscences of Forster's second visit to India in 1921. Forster's collaborations with composers are one indication of his serious interest in music. He wrote a libretto (with Eric Crozier) for an opera with music by Benjamin Britten, *Billy Budd* (1951), and he collaborated on two pageants with Ralph Vaughan Williams. At his death, Forster left numerous uncollected letters, articles, reviews, and pamphlets.

NOVELS
Where Angels Fear to Tread, 1905
The Longest Journey, 1907
A Room with a View, 1908
Howards End, 1910
A Passage to India, 1924
Maurice, 1971

SHORT FICTION
The Celestial Omnibus and Other Stories, 1911
The Eternal Moment and Other Stories, 1928
The Collected Tales of E. M. Forster, 1947
The Life to Come and Other Stories, 1972
Arctic Summer and Other Fiction, 1980

PLAY
Billy Budd, 1951 (libretto; with Eric Crozier, music by Benjamin Britten)

NONFICTION
Alexandria: A History and a Guide, 1922
Pharos and Pharillon, 1923
Goldsworthy Lowes Dickinson, 1934
Virginia Woolf, 1942
The Development of English Prose Between 1918 and 1939, 1945
The Hill of Devi, 1953
Marianne Thornton, 1797–1887: A Domestic Biography, 1956

MISCELLANEOUS
The Abinger Edition of E. M. Forster, 1972 (Oliver Stallybrass, editor)

Further reading

Cox, C. B. *The Free Spirit: A Study of Liberal Humanism in the Novels of George Eliot, Henry James, E. M. Forster, Virginia Woolf, Angus Wilson*, 1963.
Crews, F. C. *E. M. Forster: The Perils of Humanism*, 1962.
Gillie, Christopher. *A Preface to Forster*, 1983.
Page, Norman. *E. M. Forster*, 1988.
Stape, J. H., ed. *E. M. Forster: Interviews and Recollections*, 1993.
Trilling, Lionel. *E. M. Forster*, 1943 (revised 1967).
Wilde, Alan. *Art and Order: A Study of E. M. Forster*, 1964.
——, ed. *Critical Essays on E. M. Forster*, 1988.

KAREN A. KILDAHL

See also British Literary Theory: Twentieth Century; Woolf

Michel Foucault

French philosopher and writer

Born: Poitiers, France; October 15, 1926
Died: Paris, France; June 25, 1984

Biography

Michel Foucault was born on October 15, 1926, in Poitiers, France, into the middle-class family of Dr. Paul Foucault and his wife, Anne Malapert. After attending the local Catholic school, in 1944 the promising young scholar was sent to the Lycée Henri IV in Paris, where he prepared for the entrance examinations to the prestigious École Normale Supérieure. There and at the Sorbonne, he studied under Jean Hippolyte, a philosopher specializing in G. W. F. Hegel; Georges Canguilhem, a historian of science; and Louis Althusser, a Marxist theoretician interested in structuralist thought. Foucault received his undergraduate degrees in philosophy in 1948 and in psychology in 1950.

Perhaps as a result of Althusser's influence, Foucault became a member of the Communist Party, but he soon found its ideological rigidity too confining and resigned in 1951. He received his diploma in psychopathology from the University of Paris in 1952, and then – an unusual step for a French intellectual of his time – embarked upon a period of teaching at foreign institutions. From 1953 to 1957 he was a member of the French department at the University of Uppsala in Sweden, then spent a year as director of the Warsaw Institut Français, and from 1959 to 1960 he occupied the same position at the Institut Français in Hamburg.

Foucault returned to France in 1960, taking up a professorship at the University of Clermont-Ferrand in Auvergne. He remained there until 1968, when he accepted a post at the University of Paris at Vincennes; this position led to a 1970 appointment to the chair in the history of systems of thought at the Collège de France in Paris. Foucault now began to become something of a public figure, forming the Groupe d'Information sur les Prisons as a spur to penal reform and campaigning vigorously for the rights of women and homosexuals. He also criticized the repressive nature of the East European bloc countries and became associated with the general wave of disillusionment with Communism so characteristic of French intellectual life in the 1970s and 1980s.

Foucault was for a time in the early 1970s the editor of the political weekly *Liberation*, and he served on the editorial boards of the intellectual reviews *Critique* and *Zone des tempêtes*. As a scholar whose views were in demand all over the world, he lectured at universities in Copenhagen, Oslo, Madrid, Lisbon, Istanbul, and Buffalo, among others. On June 25, 1984, he died of a rare neurological disorder, whose ravages he had kept a secret from all but his closest friends.

Influence

Foucault has had a profound effect upon postmodern literary theory, even though most of his writings have nothing to do with literary criticism per se. His probes into the historical archaeology of human culture place great emphasis on the forces operating behind the concepts of "discourse" and "the word," and these have been eagerly taken up by scholars unhappy with the New Criticism's often uncritical focus on the text alone. Frank Lentricchia, Timothy Reiss, Michel Serres, and Edward Said are among the numerous critics who have acknowledged Foucault as a source of fruitful ideas and suggestions, and his well-publicized disagreements with Jacques Derrida have served as the jumping-off point for many a book and article. Along with Derrida, Claude Lévi-Strauss, Jacques Lacan, and Roland Barthes, Foucault is a member of that group of French thinkers who – whether classified as structuralists, poststructuralists, or deconstructionists – have sparked the development of what has become known as the postmodern school of literary criticism.

Analysis

There are two points which should be made before considering Foucault's contributions to literary theory and criticism. The first of these concerns the central focus of his work, which takes the nature of language – rather than the nature of literature – as the crucial question: unlike many literary critics, Foucault does not differentiate between literature and nonliterature in ways that exalt the status of the former, and indeed his writings tend to subvert traditional notions of literature's distinctive qualities. Secondly, his researches are almost always carried out in a spirit of open-ended inquiry rather than one of seeking absolute truths. He accepts paradox as a source of potentially valuable insights and is never ashamed to admit that he has changed his mind. At the time of his death, he was engaged in making major revisions to the first volume of *The History of Sexuality*, a fact that underlines his commitment to projects which would in a sense always remain unfinished.

Foucault's initial interest in the nature of language arose out of his investigations into the history of how those classified as social or psychological deviants had been perceived by their peers. In books such as *Madness and Civilization* and *The Birth of the Clinic*, he conceptualized this understanding primarily in terms of power relationships similar to those hypothesized in Louis Althusser's epistemological Marxism and stressed the use of such institutions as agents of control and repression that exclude their inmates from meaningful participation in society. The obvious political implications of such views made Foucault one of the heroes of France's would-be revolutionaries of 1968; they are also evident in his prominence as a defender of the rights of women, homosexuals, and other oppressed groups.

Yet Foucault's subsequent development took him well beyond the orthodoxies of the kind of Marxist social science so popular in Western culture during the 1950s and 1960s. Instead of simply accepting the idea that language was nothing more than a function of one class's dominance over another, Foucault went on to consider how the strategies with which language was employed – those specific modes of discourse that appropriate words into highly technical vocabularies – were in fact the means of exercising power upon its subjects. *Discipline and Punish* came to the conclusion that power was a set of techniques for organizing human knowledge; while not inconsistent with Marxist ideology, it was such an essentially intellectual construct that Foucault ceased to be considered a reliable friend of the Left.

The key word in this reorientation of Foucault's thinking is "discourse," which he uses in the sense of language as rhetorical persuasion, as the determinant of the boundaries within which it speaks, and as the hidden workings of operations obscured by the superficial objectivity of its constituent words and sentences. It is when one tries to think about the concept of discourse – to discourse upon discourse, as it were – that one starts to break through to levels of meaning denied to those who take language at its face value. As Foucault puts it in his most important theoretical statement, *The Archaeology of Knowledge*:

> The question posed by language analysis of some discursive fact or other is always: according to what rules has a particular statement been made, and consequently according to what rules would other similar statements be made? The description of the events of discourse poses a quite different question: how is it that one particular statement appeared rather than another?

In undertaking such examinations, Foucault usually begins with paradoxes aimed at breaking down the conventional formulations of thinking on particular subjects. In *The Archaeology of Knowledge*, it is the supposed unity of the concepts of the book, the body of the author's work, and the author's character which he demolishes before proceeding onward; in volume 1 of *The History of Sexuality*, it is the detestation of sex attributed to the Victorians that attracts his subversive attentions. What he wants to do for any given branch of knowledge is

> to account for the fact that it is spoken about, to discover who does the speaking, the positions and viewpoints from which they speak, the institutions which prompt people to speak about it and which store and distribute the things that are said. . . . The essential aim will not be to determine whether these discursive productions and these effects of power lead one to formulate the truth, . . . but rather to bring out the "will to knowledge" that serves as both their support and their instrument.

Foucault sees such assaults upon traditional modes of thought as a necessary prelude to those investigations of "positivity," of the material realities of history, which constitute the middle sections of his books. These typically range over an extraordinarily wide panorama of empirical evidence, display an erudition that reflects his extensive studies in philosophy and the social sciences, and make illuminating connections among phenomena that at first sight seem completely disparate. Since Foucault considers inherited notions about the need for logical coherence and linear organization as obstacles, and not aids, to knowledge, he presents his researches in an allusive, unrestrained manner that seems simply to break off rather than come to manifest conclusions. Although this method can be maddening for the reader expecting to be told what to think, it can also spark the kind of creative reordering of experience that results in genuinely fresh insights.

The problematic aspects of such a methodology are obvious and are squarely faced by Foucault himself. The possibility of an infinite regress of discourses – of discourses that merely recede into ever-murkier depths of disguised assumptions – certainly threatens his work, and he does his best to avoid it by striving for a discourse that

> is trying to operate a decentering that leaves no privilege to any centre ... it does not set out to be a recollection of the original or a memory of the truth. On the contrary, its task is to *make* differences ... it is continually making *differentiations*, it is a *diagnosis*.

Foucault's selection of specific pieces of evidence, which he wishes to be random and unrestrained, is also open to question: his belief that he is working outside conventional discourse may in fact simply mean that he is operating within an unconventional – but nevertheless constraining – discourse of his own, and he tends to assume that materials from the same historical period must exhibit the same fundamental characteristics. The openness of Foucault's approach ensures that he is always cognizant of these problems, although much of the debate about his work centers on the extent to which he has actually managed to transcend them.

In fact, Foucault's explorations of the history of madness, of prisons, and of sexuality – his probes into the subject matter of particular intellectual disciplines – have had relatively little influence on the disciplines themselves: it is not the world's psychiatrists, criminologists, and sexologists who have made Foucault's writings a basic unit of modern intellectual currency. It is in the humanities, and especially in literary studies, that his ideas have been adopted as important sources of critical insight. In the field of postmodern literary theory, in particular, they have become extremely influential.

Foucault's interest in history and his use of historical materials as a means of examining an era's normative characteristics have strongly appealed to those postmodern critics who resist Jacques Derrida's call for the complete reconstruction of the text. Books such as Frank Lentricchia's *Criticism and Social Change* (1983) and Timothy J. Reiss' *The Discourse of Modernism* (1982) apply Foucault's conceptions of discourse and language to the creation of works of literature and call for a literary criticism that is vigilantly aware of its provisional and constantly changing character. One of his most ardent disciples, Edward Said, has in books such as *The World, the Text, and the Critic* (1983) argued that literary critics should emulate Foucault's openness to historical evidence of every variety and cease restricting themselves to an elitist canon.

It is in his public disagreements with Derrida, however, that Foucault has probably exercised his greatest degree of influence upon the course of postmodern literary criticism. These conflicts between Derrida's efforts to reconstruct history in order to set free its hidden possibilities and Foucault's attempts to experience history as a means of making explicit its latent structures have generated numerous scholarly commentaries, many of which seek either to reconcile or selectively choose from the work of these two French thinkers. Some notable examples are Wesley Morris' *Friday's Footprint: Structuralism and the Articulated Text* (1979), which tries to integrate Derrida's textuality with Foucault's historical interpretations, and David Carroll's *The Subject in Question: The Languages of Theory and the Strategies of Fiction* (1982), which is highly critical of Foucault's concrete historical methods but accepts his broader theories as a necessary component of serious literary criticism. Whatever the specific weight given to Foucault's writings in these books, the significant fact is that he is constantly cited as the foremost spokesperson for an important intellectual position.

The difficulty of Foucault's style and the sheer complexity of his thought have tended to limit his direct influence to the realm of the university, and even here his work has often been dismissed as chaotic or useless by more traditional scholars. His ideas have nevertheless become an integral part of postmodern literary theory. Foucault disclaimed any intention of leading his readers to a promised land of absolute certainties, but it is certain that he is an absolutely essential figure in the development of alternatives to the New Criticism's once-dominant critical methodologies.

Principal criticism

Folie et déraison: Histoire de la folie à l'âge classique, 1961 (*Madness and Civilization: A History of Insanity in the Age of Reason*, 1965)

Naissance de la clinique: Une archéologie du regard médical, 1963 (*The Birth of the Clinic: An Archaeology of Medical Perception*, 1973)

Les Mots et les choses: Une archéologie des sciences humaines, 1966 (*The Order of Things: An Archaeology of the Human Sciences*, 1970)

L'Archéologie du savoir, 1969 (*The Archaeology of Knowledge*, 1972)
L'Ordre du discours, 1971 (*The Discourse on Language*, 1971)
Surveiller et punir: Naissance de la prison, 1975 (*Discipline and Punish: The Birth of the Prison*, 1977)
Histoire de la sexualité, 1976–1984 (3 volumes; *The History of Sexuality*, 1978–1987), includes *La Volonté de savoir (An Introduction)*, *L'Usage des plaisirs (The Use of Pleasure)*, and *Souci de soi (The Care of the Self)*

Other major works and literary forms

As well as the major works of philosophical social science listed above, Foucault has produced one critical study of literature, *Raymond Roussel* (1963; English translation, 1978). Appropriately enough for a thinker who believes in the value of paradox, it is among his least-known and least-influential works. Foucault's first book, *Maladie mentale et personnalité* (1954), revised and expanded in 1962 as *Maladie mentale et psychologie* (*Mental Illness and Psychology*, 1976), reflects his interest in psychopathology, also evident in his short monograph *Moi, Pierre Rivière, ayant égorgé ma mère, ma sœur et mon frère . . .: Un Cas de parricide au XIXe siècle*, 1973 (*I, Pierre Rivière, Having Slaughtered My Mother, My Sister, and My Brother. . .: A Case of Parricide in the Nineteenth Century*, 1975). Two collections of interviews and essays, *Language, Counter-Memory, Practice: Selected Essays and Interviews* (1977) and *Power/Knowledge: Selected Interviews and Other Writings, 1972–1975* (1980), offer an accessible introduction for English-speaking readers to a sometimes esoteric thinker.

NONFICTION
Maladie mentale et personnalité, 1954 (revised and expanded as *Maladie mentale et psychologie*, 1962; *Mental Illness and Psychology*, 1976)
Raymond Roussel, 1963 (English translation, 1978)
Moi, Pierre Rivière, ayant égorgé ma mère, ma sœur et mon frère . . .: Un Cas de parricide au XIXe siècle, 1973 (*I, Pierre Rivière, Having Slaughtered My Mother, My Sister, and My Brother . . .: A Case of Parricide in the Nineteenth Century*, 1975)
Language, Counter-Memory, Practice: Selected Essays and Interviews, 1977
Power/Knowledge: Selected Interviews and Other Writings, 1972–1975, 1980

Further reading

Burke, Sean. *The Death and Return of the Author: Criticism and Subjectivity in Barthes, Foucault and Derrida*, 1998.
Clark, Michael. *Michel Foucault: An Annotated Bibliography. Toolkit for a New Age*, 1983.
Cooper, Barry. *Michel Foucault: An Introduction to the Study of His Thought*, 1982.
Cousins, Mark, and Athar Hussain. *Michel Foucault*, 1984.
Dean, Mitchell. *Critical and Effective Histories: Foucault's Methods and Historical Sociology*, 1994.
Dreyfus, Hubert L., and Paul Rabinov. *Michel Foucault: Beyond Structuralism and Hermeneutics*, 1982.
Gutting, Gary. *Michel Foucault's Archaeology of Scientific Reason*, 1989.
——, ed. *The Cambridge Companion to Foucault*, 1994.
Halperin, David M. *Saint Foucault: Towards a Gay Hagiography*, 1995.
Macey, David. *The Lives of Michel Foucault*, 1993.
Merquior, J. G. *Foucault*, 1985.
Rajchman, John. *Michel Foucault: The Freedom of Philosophy*, 1985.
Sheridan, Alan. *Michel Foucault: The Will to Truth*, 1980.
Smart, Barry. *Foucault, Marxism and Critique*, 1983.

PAUL STUEWE

See also Discourse; French Literary Theory: Twentieth Century

The Frankfurt School

The Frankfurt School is the label applied to a group of German intellectuals attached to the Institut für Sozialforschung (Institute for Social Research), founded in Frankfurt in 1923. In particular, the term refers to the work of Theodor W. Adorno, Walter Benjamin, Max Horkheimer, and Herbert Marcuse, called the first generation, while the most famous member of the second generation is Jürgen Habermas. The approach of the Institute, known as "critical theory," represents a major tributory in that flow of ideas known as "Western Marxism," to which such thinkers as Georg Lukács, Louis Althusser, Ernst Bloch, and Jean-Paul Sartre also belong.

The Institute

The first director of the Institute was Carl Grünberg, a key figure in "Austro-Marxism," a revisionist version of Marxism that emerged between 1904 and 1910. Yet the main contours of the so-called Frankfurt School took shape when Horkheimer assumed the directorship of the Institute in 1930. The work of the Institute was published largely in its journal, the *Zeitschrift für Sozialforschung*, as well as such studies as *Studien über Autorität und Familie* (1936). Following the rise of National Socialism in Germany in the 1930s, the members of the Institute emigrated to Geneva in 1933 and thence to America, where the Institute was located, from 1935, in New York and, from 1941, in California. After World War II, some members (Horkheimer, Adorno, Friedrich Pollock) returned to the Federal Republic of Germany, whilst others (Marcuse, Leo Lowenthal, Otto Kirchheimer) remained in the United States. From 1958 until his death in 1969, the Institute's director was Adorno. Between them, Adorno and Horkheimer lent the Institute's work its characteristic tone and shifted it firmly away from empirical analysis toward a variety of *Kulturkritik* (the analysis of culture).

Philosophical sources

In order to appreciate the work of the Frankfurt School, it is essential to understand its theoretical grounding in the thinking of Karl Marx, who in turn saw himself as reworking the philosophy of G. W. F. Hegel or, as Marx put it, turning Hegel upside down and putting him back on his feet (*Capital*, afterword to second edition, 1873). In his philosophical writings, Hegel argued that the state was an inevitable expression in history of *Geist* (spirit, or mind – wherever there is human activity, there is *Geist*). In his introduction to *The Philosophy of History* (1822), Hegel declared: "The history of the world is the progress of the consciousness of freedom." In other words, history embodied human progress. And at the beginning of the *Philosophy of Right* (1821), he claimed: "The rational is actual, and the actual is rational." By this, Hegel meant that the human world structured itself according to the dictates of reason: reality followed thought, and thought real-ized (*verwirklicht*) itself in reality (*Wirklichkeit*). Thus, according to Hegel, history represents the working-out of a suprahuman *Geist* or Idea, which comes to know itself in history through the activities of human minds. So not only is all history the product of the self-productive Idea, but all aspects of history are aspects of that Idea. Convinced by Ludwig Feuerbach's critique of Hegel, Marx replaced Hegel's idealist dialect with its opposite, dialectical materialism (although Marx himself never used the term). In his 1873 afterword to *Capital*, Marx wrote:

> My dialectical method is not only different from the Hegelian, but is its direct opposite. To Hegel, the life-process of the human brain, i.e. the process of thinking, which, under the name of 'the Idea,' he even transforms into an independent subject, is the demiurge of the real world, and the real world is only the external, phenomenal form of 'the Idea.' With me, on the contrary, the Ideal is nothing else than the material reflected by the human mind, and translated into forms of thought.

Or, as Marx and Engels put it in *The German Ideology* (1845): "It is not consciousness that determines life, but life that determines consciousness." The Frankfurt School took this principle of Marx, only applied it not to political economy, but to culture in general and aesthetics in particular (areas extensively discussed by Hegel, although not Marx). And there is another important difference. Whereas Marx believed in the necessity of revolution, the Frankfurt School hoped merely to sustain the "critical potential" of thought. Of the resultant mix of Hegel and Marx, Adorno wrote: "What distinguishes dialectical criticism from cultural criticism is that it heightens cultural criticism until the notion of culture is itself negated, fulfilled and surmounted in one [*dasß sie diese bis zur Aufhebung des Begriffs der Kultur selber steigert*]."

Reification

In particular, the Frankfurt School drew on Marxian notions of "reification," "commodity fetishism," "alienation," and "false consciousness." According to Marx, value does not reside in the natural properties of a commodity (its use-value) but in its exchange-value. So where does profit come from? From the difference between exchange-value and use-value, or surplus-value, which is "added" to the object by the labor of the workers in producing it. By being denied those profits, the workers are not just denied the fruits of their labors but are "alienated" from the object produced and, more important, themselves. That the workers do not understand this is due to "false consciousness" (see Engel's letter to Franz Mehring of July 14, 1893) and the effects of "commodity fetishism." As Marx put it in *Capital*, "a commodity appears at first sight a very trivial thing, and easily understood. Its analysis shows that it is, in reality, a very strange thing, abounding in metaphysical subtleties and theological niceties." By fetishism, Marx meant the mystification accompanying its production by the exploitation of the workers or, as he put it, "a definite social relation between men . . . assumes, in their eyes, the fantastic form [*die phantasmagorische Form*] of a relation between things." What for Marx was a social phenomenon was, as far as Adorno was concerned, primarily a mode of consciousness (as the account by Gillian Rose, 1978, shows). For Hegel, and also for Adorno, a concept (*Begriff*) is not simply a universal but also the attributes or properties which the object described by the concept notionally possesses. In "identity thinking," a concept can be applied to an object, even if the object in fact lacks those properties; indeed, that very lack may thereby be veiled. In *Negative Dialectics* (1966), Adorno wrote: "Identity thinking says under what [concept] something falls, of what it is an exemplar or representative, what it is thus not itself." By contrast, "non-identity thinking" or "negative dialectics," Adorno claimed, "also identifies, but to a greater extent and in a different way from identity thinking. It seeks to say what something is." He offers the following example:

> The judgment that somebody is a free man refers . . . to the concept of freedom; but that concept is itself much more than what is predicated of the man, just as that man, because of other determinations, is more than the concept of his freedom. The concept of freedom does not only say that it can be applied to all men defined as free; it is nourished by the idea of a condition in which individuals have qualities that cannot be ascribed to anyone here and now. In a fallen world, and especially a capitalist one, the object will never be completely identical with the concept.

To put it another way, "identity thinking" is the thinking of reification (*Verdinglichung*). Marx himself never used this term, although it is a favorite of Marxist thinkers. Lukács understood reification to mean that the social relation between people appears in the form of a relation between things, and in a manuscript of 1935 Walter Benjamin declared his work aimed "to show how reference to the reified representation of culture, to new creations and forms of life especially determined by the production of commodities . . . is a reference to the ensemble of a phantasmagoria." But Adorno's point was that the reified object does not fulfill the concept. As Adorno and Horkheimer put it in *Dialectic of Enlightenment*: "All reification is a forgetting." It is perhaps no surprise that, speaking of his collection of aphorisms *Minima Moralia* (1951), Adorno described his work as "the melancholy science" (an inverted form of the "joyful science" of Friedrich Nietzsche, also a major philosophical source for the Frankfurt School). Indeed, Lukács spoke of the members of the Frankfurt School as living in "Grand Hotel Abyss." And Leszek Kolakowksi's verdict on *Negative Dialectics* was: "There can be few works of philosophy that give such an overpowering impresssion of sterility."

Art

Were our consciousness completely reified, as Adorno sometimes claims, then no criticism would be possible. Yet the possibility of dialectical *Kulturkritik*, based on the principle that the concept is not identical with the object, was demonstrated by the substantial critical output of the Frankfurt School. Adorno was especially prodigious, discussing a wide range of literature and, in particular, music (he was an accomplished pianist). In *The Philosophy of New Music* (1949), he argued against what he regarded as the reactionary primitivism of Stravinsky and in favor of the progressive tonality of Schoenberg (described by Adorno as "the surviving message of despair from the shipwrecked"). For Adorno, writing in *Introduction to the Sociology of Music* (1962), the relationship between art (especially music) and society was "comparable to Leibniz's monad. Windowless – that is to say, without being conscious of society, and in any event without being constantly and necessarily accompanied by this consciousness – the works of art, and notably of music which is far removed from concepts, represent society."

Hence Adorno argued that the aesthetic structures of the culmination of Viennese classicism, the music of Beethoven, could yield sociological insights. Implicitly, Adorno is thinking of the Hegelian dialectic in such remarks as this: "The developing variation, an image of social labor, is definite negation: from what has been once posited it ceaselessly brings forth the new and enhanced by destroying it in its immediacy, its quasi-natural form." By contrast, his contempt for popular music knew no bounds. In "On the Fetish-Character in Music and the Regression of Listening" (1938), he wrote "Where [the consumers of hit songs] react at all, it no longer makes any difference whether it is to Beethoven's Seventh Symphony or to a bikini," and an earlier essay "On Jazz" (1936) was first published under the pseudonym Hektor Rottweiler. But although Adorno famously wrote, in "Cultural Criticism and Society," that "to write poetry after Auschwitz is barbaric," his final, uncompleted work was a theory of art, *Aesthetic Theory* (1970). And for the Frankfurt School there remained the possibility of escaping not just reification but the "dialectic of enlightenment," which meant that for every step forward, "instrumental reason" took ten steps back, because it reified reality by conceptualizing it in terms of purpose. That way of escape from reification was art, particularly avant-garde, which spoke of its own illusory nature (or "semblance"):

> Art is semblance even at its highest peaks; but its semblance, the irresistible part of it, is given to it by what is not semblance. What art, notably the art decried as nihilistic, says in refraining from judgments is that everything is not just nothing. If it were, whatever is would be pale, colorless, indifferent. No light falls on men and things without reflecting transcendence. Indelible from the resistance to the fungible world of exchange is the resistance of the eye that does not want the colors of the world to fade. Semblance is a promise of nonsemblance.

Redemptive criticism

For the Frankfurt School, in the words of Adorno, "the greatness of works of art lies solely in their power to let those things be heard which ideology conceals." But for the Frankfurt School, criticism itself comes almost to replace the function of art, and Walter Benjamin offered (in the words of Habermas) a "redemptive criticism" (*rettende Kritik*). For Benjamin in particular, the "immanent criticism" of the Frankfurt School took a theological twist. In his unfinished *Passagen-Werk*, Benjamin invoked the un-Hegelian notion of "dialectics at stand-still":

> Where thought comes to a standstill in a constellation saturated with tensions, there appears the dialectical image. . . . It is to be sought at the point where the tension between the dialectical oppositions is the greatest. The dialectical image . . . is identical to the historical object; it justifies blasting the latter out of the continuum of history's course.

In his correspondence with Benjamin, Adorno regarded such ideas as "insufficiently dialectical." Moreover, it is easy to see how close Benjamin's notion of the "Now-Time" (*Jetztzeit*) was to the *Augenblick* (moment) of Ludwig Klages and the archetype of C. G. Jung, even though both men were, to the Frankfurt School, politically suspect. In Benjamin's terms, art had lost the "aura" (another Klagesian expression) of its early cultic origins, but in "The Work of Art in the Age of Mechanical Reproduction" (1936), Benjamin welcomed this loss inasmuch as it resisted "the aestheticization of politics" under Fascism.

As typical Frankfurt School thinkers, Adorno and Benjamin agreed on the task of culture but also on the difficulty in fulfilling this task. For Horkheimer, the choice was stark: "There is nothing left but barbarism or freedom." In Benjamin's words, however, "there is no document of culture which is not at the same time a document of barbarism." We have come a long way from Hegel's view of history as progress, and Marx's belief in revolution: "The philosophers have only *interpreted* the world in different ways, the point is to *change it.*" In *Negative Dialectics*, Adorno gloomily observed: "No universal history leads from savagery to humanitarianism, but there is one that leads from the slingshot to the megaton bomb." And in the ninth of his historico-philosophical theses, referring to Paul Klee's painting *Angelus Novus*, Benjamin imagines the "angel of history," whose face is "turned towards the past. Where we see a chain of events, he sees one single catastrophe, piling wreckage upon wreckage before his feet. . . . A storm blows from paradise so violently that he cannot close his wings . . . and propels him inexorably towards the future to which his back is turned . . . . That storm is what we call progress."

The 1960s

Of the entire Frankfurt School, the thinker who came the closest to taking any action was Herbert Marcuse. Following work on Husserl and Heidegger, Marcuse produced a fusion of Marx and Freud in *Eros and Civilization* (1955), where he advanced the notion of "surplus repression." In *One-Dimensional Man* (1964), Marcuse argued social control was dominant to the point of totalitarianism. But in *An Essay on Liberation* (1969) and *The Aesthetic Dimension* (1978), art was once again envisaged as a potential escape from the repression of modern society. There can be no doubt that the heyday of the Frankfurt School was the 1960s, when Marcuse became a supporter of the anti-Establishment student movement and a founder of the "counterculture," while Adorno's lectures were packed out. But the students turned against their professor, and in April 1969 Adorno's lecture was interrupted by a militant action group as three female students rushed up to him and bared their breasts. Shortly afterwards, he died of a heart attack. As Peter Sloterdijk has remarked: "It was not naked violence (*nackte Gewalt*) that silenced the philosopher but the power of nakedness (*die Gewalt des Nackten*)." Apparently the object exceeded the concept.

Further reading

Arato, Andrew, and Eike Gebhardt, eds. *The Essential Frankfurt School Reader*, 1978.
Buck-Morss, Susan. *The Origin of Negative Dialectics: Theodor W. Adorno, Walter Benjamin, and the Frankfurt Institute*, 1977.
Connerton, Paul. *The Tragedy of Enlightenment: An Essay on the Frankfurt School*, 1980.
Geuss, Raymond. *The Idea of a Critical History: Habermas and the Frankfurt School*, 1981.
Held, David. *Introduction to Critical Theory: Horkheimer to Habermas*, 1980.
Jay, Martin. *The Dialectical Imagination: A History of the Frankfurt School and the Institute of Social Research, 1923–1950*, 1973.
Kolakowski, Leszek. *Main Currents of Marxism*, 1978.
Lunn, Eugene. *Marxism and Modernism: A Historical Study of Lukács, Brecht, Benjamin, and Adorno*, 1982.
Merquior, J. G. *Western Marxism*, 1986.
Rose, Gillian. *The Melancholy Science: An Introduction to the Thought of Theodor W. Adorno*, 1978.
Taylor, Ronald, ed. *Aesthetics and Politics*, 1977.
Wiggershaus, Rolf. *Die Frankfurter Schule: Geschichte, theoretische Entwicklung, politische Bedeutung*, 1986 (*The Frankfurt School: Its History, Theories, and Political Significance*, 1994).

PAUL BISHOP

See also Adorno; Benjamin; Gramsci; Marxist Theory and Criticism

French Literary Theory: Twentieth Century

The twentieth century in France saw an unparalleled expansion in the growth of literary theory. It was a period marked by a series of radical changes in the way we look at literature and at its relationship to society, with French literary theory showing a remarkable ability to respond to developments in philosophy, linguistics, psychoanalysis, sociology, and political philosophy. The impact of these developments – not only on literary studies but also on a wide range of intellectual disciplines – has been enormous. Their influence has also been felt on literary theory and criticism abroad, notably in the United States, where since the end of World War II successive generations of students and scholars have welcomed French literary approaches influenced by existentialism, Marxism, psychoanalysis, structuralism, or deconstruction. Their impact in Britain, however, has been less marked.

French literary theory before World War II

The nineteenth-century legacy

At the end of the nineteenth century three approaches to literature dominated in Europe. The first of these was a purely impressionistic approach, centered on the critic's intuitions. Particular importance was attached to moral and psychological features of the text. The second was a strictly scientific approach where works of art were seen as reflections of general laws of behavior. The principal advocate of this view was the French historian Hippolyte-Adolphe Taine, for whom the individual was strictly determined by factors of race, period, and social milieu. Literary texts were regarded, therefore, as a direct reflection of social reality. This positivist approach was also adopted by Ferdinand Brunetière who attempted to apply Darwinian theories of evolution to the literary genres. The third approach was a biographical approach where works of art were studied predominantly in terms of the life of the author. This approach was widespread throughout Western Europe, Britain, and America.

At the turn of the century these traditional attitudes came under attack from the French critic and academic Gustave Lanson (1857–1934). Lanson is generally regarded as the founder of the branch of criticism known as literary history and one of the first proponents of what we now term genetic criticism, an approach that was to enjoy a new wave of popularity at the end of the twentieth century.

Literary history and genetic criticism

Unlike his predecessors, Lanson considered that the primary focus of the critic's attention should be the text itself. This switch in emphasis would become a characteristic feature of twentieth-century critical theory in France. Lanson's contribution to critical thinking was twofold. First, he was one of the first to stress the importance of historic context and historic detail in our understanding of texts. He produced two seminal critical editions, one on Voltaire, *Lettres philosophiques* (1909), and one on Alphonse Lamartine, *Méditations* (1915). Second, he was also one of the first to focus critical attention on the genesis of a text, that is on the different versions or manuscripts that make up the process of composition. An excellent example of this approach is his essay "Un manuscript de *Paul et Virginie*" (*Revue du mois*, 1908).

Lanson's theories were extremely influential, dominating the teaching of literature in French universities for almost half a century. They gave rise to a form of textual commentary known as the *explication de texte* with which every French schoolchild became familiar. Needless to say, however, these theories did not receive universal acclaim. Among the first to voice their objections were the writers themselves.

The writer as critic

In his critical texts, such as *L'Argent* (1913; money), the poet Charles Péguy (1873–1914) attacked Lanson, violently objecting to any attempt to explain a literary work in terms of cultural or social influence. Similarly, the novelist Marcel Proust, in his essay "Contre Sainte-Beuve" (written c. 1908–1909), advocated a complete divorce between art and social reality, arguing that the social self (*le moi social*) has nothing in common with the creative self (*le moi profond*). And in a series of lectures at the Collège de France (1937–1945) the poet Paul Valéry urged a return to poetics, to the study of the nature of literary language and of the creative process. Foreshadowing the early Roland Barthes (*Critique et vérité*, 1966), he made a sharp distinction between the literary and everyday uses of language.

Of special interest during this period are the critical writings of the short-story writer Jean Paulhan (1884–1968). In a collection of essays on language and criticism, *Les Fleurs de Tarbes* (1941; the flowers of Tarbes) he argued that there exist certain codes and laws of language to which every writer must submit. Anticipating the theories of structuralism, he challenged what he called "the Terror," the Romantic notion of originality.

In the immediate prewar years and after, many critics of the Lansonian approach drew their inspiration from contemporary developments in philosophy. Of particular importance were the findings of phenomenology, epistemology, and existentialism.

Literature and philosophy before 1968

The Geneva School

The Geneva School was the name loosely given to a group of critics – many of whom lived in Paris – who, influenced by phenomenology, shared a similar outlook on literature. Often referred to as "critics of consciousness," their critical approach was more personal than either that of Lanson or of the writer-critics. Members of this group viewed the literary text as the expression of a writer's consciousness rather than as the expression of an objective set of meanings. The critical process was described as one of empathy, an existential encounter between the consciousness of the reader and that of the writer. Early exponents of this approach include Marcel Raymond (1897–1984) and Albert Béguin (1901–1957).

After World War II some members chose to focus their attention on the study of a number of recurrent themes or leitmotifs which were seen to be the privileged expression of the author's consciousness. This approach has been termed *thematic criticism*. Under the influence of Maurice Merleau-Ponty's *Phénoménologie de la perception* (1945; *Phenomenology of Perception*, 1962), the themes that were selected related in particular to the body and its perceptions/sensations. Critics whose work reflect these preoccupations include Georges Poulet, who produced, among other texts, seminal works on time, *Études sur le temps humain* (1949; studies on human time), and on space, *L'Espace proustien* (1963; space in Proust), and Jean-Pierre Richard (1922–) who focused on the link between verbal structures and the structures of perception. His works include *Poésie et profondeur* (1956; poetry and depth) and *Onze études sur la poésie moderne* (1964; eleven studies on modern poetry). This phenomenological approach was also adopted by the critic Jean Starobinski (1920–), in his *Jean-Jacques Rousseau, la transparence et l'obstacle* (1957; *Jean-Jacques Rousseau: Transparency and Obstruction*, 1988) and *Montaigne en mouvement* (1982; *Montaigne in Motion*, 1985). It further inspired the works of the philosopher Paul Ricœur who, developing the findings of the Geneva School, focused on the role of the reader in the process of interpretation and of understanding. His substantial writings contributed to the development of reception theory from the 1970s onward.

Gaston Bachelard

Instrumental to the growth of new critical theories during this period was the work of the philosopher of science and epistemologist Gaston Bachelard (1884–1962). One of Bachelard's principal concerns was with a psychology of the imagination. In his critical works he focused on a study of images and on the process of creative reverie from which they spring. In texts such as *La Psychanalyse du feu* (1938; *The Psychoanalysis of Fire*, 1964), *L'Air et les songes* (1943; *Air and Dreams*, 1988), and *La Terre et les rêveries du repos* (1948; earth and dreams of rest) he accorded particular attention to elemental images (*l'imagination matérielle*) such as those of fire, water, and air, examining their structural role within the literary text. Adopting a Jungian perspective, he considered the meanings associated with these images to be archetypal, arising from a collective preconscious rather than from an individual unconscious.

Bachelard's approach to literature had a profound impact on the development of French literary theory in the twentieth century. He not only exerted an immediate influence on the "critics of consciousness" but was also a precursor of structuralism. At the same time, his theory of knowledge stimulated Marxist philosophers and critics to rethink their notions of time and of subjectivity.

Maurice Blanchot

Another important figure during the immediate postwar years was the writer and philosopher Maurice Blanchot (1907–), the author of a number of brilliant studies of European writers. In his seminal texts *L'Espace littéraire* (1955; *The Space of Literature*, 1982), *Le Livre à venir* (1959; the book to come), and *L'Entretien infini* (1969; *The Infinite Conversation*, 1992) he advocated the complete divorce of literary language from everyday language, of literature from social reality. Clearly influenced by the German philosopher G. W. F. Hegel, he argued that the central preoccupation of literature should be a quest for its own origins, for the wellspring of artistic creation. It should not concern itself, therefore, with ideology or ethics. In this context, the role of the critic should be one of complete effacement before the text. Indeed the function of both criticism and literature is to destroy any link with the real, to create a space of absence, of "the Outside" (*le Dehors*), and of death.

Jean-Paul Sartre

The critical writings of the philosopher Jean-Paul Sartre were clearly influenced by his philosophy of existentialism. Indeed, his primary concern was with literature as the expression of the subject's quest for meaning or as the reflection of a metaphysical standpoint. In his study of Albert Camus' novel *L'Étranger* (1942; US *The Stranger*, UK *The Outsider*, 1946) for example, a study which appeared in his series of articles *Situations 1* (1947), he focused on Camus' philosophy of the absurd showing how it is manifested in the choice of style, narrative technique, and thematic content. Sartre's critical works also include studies (mainly biographical) of Charles Baudelaire, Gustave Flaubert, and Jean Genet in which he illustrated his concept of an existential psychoanalysis.

A landmark in the development of literary theory after World War II is Sartre's *Qu'est-ce que la littérature?* (1948; *What is Literature?*, 1978) in which he drew attention to the relationship between literature and social reality. In contrast to critics such as Blanchot, Sartre expressed the need for social and political commitment on the part of the artist. He maintained that literature can have a liberating function, helping to dissolve "bad faith" and to promote greater self-awareness in the reader. This book was to have a profound impact on literary studies, fueling a debate on the relationship between literature and ideology and on the role of literature in contemporary society. It was, for instance, pivotal to the emergence of the *Tel Quel* group in the 1960s and to the development of Marxist theories of literature in the 1950s.

Literature and society before 1968

The 1950s saw an upsurge in sociological criticism, mainly of Marxist inspiration. A leading role was played by Lucien Goldmann (1913–1970) who in 1955 published his seminal study of Jean Racine's tragedies, *Le Dieu caché* (*The Hidden God*, 1964). Under the influence of the Marxist Hungarian philosopher Georg Lukács, Goldmann saw literary works not as the product of an individual genius but as the expression of a collective social awareness or world-view (*vision du monde*), thus anticipating the "death of the author" announced ten years later by Roland Barthes. This relationship between text and social reality is expressed in terms of "structural homologies": in *Le Dieu caché* a recurrent structure of categories (those of God, World, and Man) are seen to reflect the structure of ideas or world vision of the French religious movement Jansenism. This approach was developed in Goldmann's later work *Pour une sociologie du roman* (1964; *Towards a Sociology of the Novel*, 1975) where he presented a homology between the structure of the modern novel and the market economy. He was to exert a strong influence on the critic Jacques Leenhardt who is best known, perhaps, for his *Lecture politique du roman:* La Jalousie *d'Alain Robbe-Grillet* (1973; a political reading of Alain Robbe-Grillet's *La Jalousie*).

An important figure to emerge in the 1960s was the critic Pierre Macherey (1938–), the author of the highly influential *Pour une théorie de la production littéraire* (1966; *A Theory of Literary Production*, 1978). In this book

Macherey saw writers as necessarily working within preexisting literary genres, conventions, and ideological structures. These undergo a process of transformation in the literary text. Echoing Marxist thinking, he also argued that texts are essentially incomplete and communicate contradictory ideological messages. In the 1970s he moved away from this production model to stress the political role of literature and of criticism as a means of propping up the state and strengthening the status quo. Eventually Macherey began to question the values society ascribes to literature, and started to see literary criticism as part of a political criticism of culture.

The impact of structuralism

The 1960s saw the arrival of the literary movement known as structuralism. This brought with it a number of revolutionary changes in the way we approach literature. Heavily indebted to the theories of the Swiss linguist Ferdinand de Saussure, and undoubtedly influenced by the writings of the "new novelists," in particular by Alain Robbe-Grillet's manifesto *Pour un nouveau roman* (1956; *For a New Novel*, 1965), this mode of criticism rests on two principles: (1) language is essentially nonreferential – there is no content without form; (2) meaning is a product of difference – there is no meaning without structure (here understood as essentially binary).

These principles were developed by the critic Roland Barthes in his text *Critique et vérité* (1966; *Criticism and Truth*, 1987), a defense of literary structuralism against an attack by the academic and traditionalist Raymond Picard. Barthes stressed the productive nature of language as the means whereby we construct reality. It is language rather than the individual author that is the source of meaning. Like Paul Valéry and Maurice Blanchot, he argued for the complete divorce of literary from everyday language: literary language is polysemic, hence literary texts can never be reduced to one meaning. The aim of structuralist criticism is to reveal the signifying systems at work in a text; like poetics (also called stylistics), it is concerned with how meaning is produced rather than with the meanings themselves.

Early proponents of this mode of criticism include Tzvetan Todorov who in his *Grammaire du Décaméron* (1969; a grammar of the *Decameron*) used Giovanni Boccaccio's *Decameron* stories to illustrate the structure of narrative in general; and Barthes himself in his *Introduction à l'analyse structurale des récits* (1966; introduction to the structural analysis of narrative). One of the key exponents of narratology – the name given to this branch of criticism – was the linguist A. J. Greimas who in his *Sémantique structurale* (1966; *Structural Semantics*, 1983) presented a number of fundamental narrative models that have since become the indispensable tools of critical practice. Of particular significance during this period was the work of the narratologist Gérard Genette. His book *Figures III* (1972; *Narrative Discourse*, 1980) is a remarkable contribution to structuralist theory. With his analysis of Proust's novel cycle *À la recherche du temps perdu* (1913–1927; *Remembrance of Things Past*, 1922–1931, 1981) he illustrated the practical purpose narrative theory may have for the reading of an individual text.

The structuralist movement in France is generally associated with the early and mid-1960s. The 1968 May Revolution represents an intellectual landmark contributing to the growth of what has come to be known as poststructuralism. The term is applied very loosely to mean both a continuation of structuralism and a contestation of its principles. One of its strongest contesters was Barthes himself who in his *S/Z* (1970; English translation, 1975), a commentary on a short story by Honoré de Balzac, rejects any notion of a structure, viewing the text as an endless play of signifiers, and as an interaction of codes where meaning is constantly dispersed. This notion of codes was developed by the critic Julia Kristeva who in the early 1970s further elaborated the concept of intertextuality, that is, the reading of texts in the light of other texts. This phenomenon became a fundamental characteristic of poststructuralism.

Critical theories after 1968

Semiotics

In 1965 a group was formed in Paris, the *Groupe de recherches sémio-linguistiques*, under the leadership of the linguist A. J. Greimas, which later came to be known as the Paris School of Semiotics. Semiotics can be seen initially as a development of structuralism and of Barthes' research in the field of semiology. Greimas' early work was concerned with the elaboration of narrative models which were subsequently refined in the 1970s. With the introduction of the concept of levels of meaning and in particular of the deep level, the relationship between form and content was tightened. Indeed, semiotic analysis can be described as both a description of how meanings are produced and an interpretation of these meanings.

At the same time, a number of differences began to emerge. In the 1970s semioticians began to dispute the structuralist divide between literary and nonliterary language, arguing that there are structures of meaning common to all language and to all signifying practices. They also opened new areas of investigation moving from an original preoccupation with narrative to an exploration of surface effects of meaning, of elements relating to space and time, for example. The notion of the subject was reintroduced – this time the subject constructed by the text – and the pragmatic, or persuasive function of literature was stressed, highlighting its role, for example, in the communication of an ideology.

In the 1980s and 1990s a "semiotics of the emotions" was also developed, and preoccupations at the end of the twentieth century included a concern with the body, with movement, and with the sense of smell.

Jacques Derrida and deconstruction

The work of Jacques Derrida presents both a development and a critique of structuralist theories. Like Roland Barthes in *Critique et vérité*, he attacked all forms of thought which base themselves on some external point of reference such as the notion of truth – these are termed *logocentric*. Arguing against the notion of transparency in language, he deplored the tendency in Western culture to privilege speech over writing. In his books *De la Grammatologie* (*On Grammatology*, 1976), *L'Écriture et la différence* (*Writing and Difference*, 1978), and *La Voix et le phénomène* (*Speech and Phenomena*, 1973), all published in 1967, Derrida presented a science of the written sign called grammatology. He introduced the concept of *différance* describing the free play of signifiers, of differences, where meaning is being constantly deferred. He rejected totally the notion of structure on the grounds that the parts are subservient to a closed totality, replacing it with that of *signification*, a more open-ended nonteleological process. For Derrida, then, the meanings of a literary text are limitless: there can be no ultimate meaning. The critical method he employed is frequently termed deconstruction, the process whereby the critic tries to elicit contradictions. In his reading of Jean-Jacques Rousseau in *On Grammatology*, for example, he showed that what Rousseau actually writes is quite different from what he means to say. Derrida's approach provoked controversy from many quarters. Semioticians, for instance, dispute the belief that a text can have limitless meanings, one of the main goals of semiotic analysis being to arrive at the fundamental value-systems underlying a text. Like Maurice Blanchot, Derrida has been accused of nihilism and political conservatism – unjustifiably no doubt – on the grounds that if a text can mean anything then it can have no critical impact on society. In this context, it is interesting to note the sympathy Derrida shows in his later works for Karl Marx.

Jacques Lacan and the unconscious

During the 1970s and 1980s the writings of Jacques Lacan, heavily influenced by structuralism, became the source of inspiration for new psychoanalytical readings of the text. Lacan called into question the theory of classical Freudian psychoanalysis and its practice of using texts as clues to the author's psychology or to the psychology of the characters. Instead he focused on the central role of language, maintaining that the unconscious is structured like a language. It manifests itself for example in metaphor and metonymy.

Particularly influential in the development of this new mode of psychoanalytical criticism was Lacan's own reading of Edgar Allen Poe's story "The Purloined Letter" in *Écrits* (1966; *Écrits: A Selection*, 1977). Here the purloined letter becomes a metaphor for the unconscious and a signifier of unconscious desire. The story's development is shaped not by the character of individuals or the contents of the letter but by the position of the letter in relationship to the trio of persons in each episode.

This approach to the text inspired a number of seminal readings of contemporary writers. An example would be studies of Marguerite Duras' novel *Le Ravissement de Lol V. Stein* (1964; *The Ravishing of Lol V. Stein*, 1986), where the narrative structure is seen to mirror the Lacanian themes of the gap, the gaze, and repetition.

Feminist critical theory

The post-1968 period is also characterized by an upsurge in feminist theoretical writings inspired by the works of Lacan, Derrida, and the philosopher and writer Simone de Beauvoir (1908–1986). Of central importance was de Beauvoir's book *Le Deuxième Sexe* (1949; *The Second Sex*, 1961), which stimulated debate on the nature of the female subject. Significant figures in this field include Julia Kristeva, Hélène Cixous, and Luce Irigaray.

In her work on literary meaning *La Révolution du langage poétique* (1974; *Revolution in Poetic Language*, 1984) Kristeva drew upon Lacanian psychoanalysis to show how what is ordered and rationally accepted – the symbolic order of language – is continually being threatened by the "irrational" and "unorganized" – the "semiotic" prelinguistic material. The symbolic she associates with the male, the Law of the Father, and the semiotic with the female. The semiotic material is manifest in poetry, in a language and syntax that disrupts Western Cartesian logic. It is through this disruption of authoritarian discourses that a radical social change can be effected. Kristeva does, however, reject the notion of a specifically female writing, preferring to see the female in terms of position, that is as occupying a position that has always been marginal in relationship to the dominant male. Kristeva was also one of the original members of the *Tel Quel* group (1966), named after the journal they founded (later to become *L'Infini*). Combining Marxism and structural linguistics, these writers drew attention to the political role of language – of polysemy – as a vehicle for social revolution.

In her essay "Le Rire de la Méduse" (1975; "The Laugh of the Medusa," 1976), Hélène Cixous called for women to liberate themselves by putting their bodies into their writing and letting their unconscious speak. Women who have always operated within male-dominated discourse must now invent their own language. Influenced by Derrida, Cixous attacked and deconstructed binary oppositions which, in her view, are imbricated in the patriarchal value system. The opposition male/female, for example, is used to construct a positive/negative evaluation in which the female occupies the negative position. She called for a new feminine language (*l'écriture féminine*) which would subvert these binary schemes.

Luce Irigaray, likewise, saw patriarchal discourse as a force of repression of the feminine. In her book *Spéculum de l'autre femme* (1974; *Speculum of the Other Woman*, 1985) she argued that throughout history the feminine has been repressed by and excluded from Western philosophical discourse. There is therefore no language in which the female can express itself except in the blanks and silences of the text. Later, in *Ce Sexe que n'en est pas un* (1977; *This Sex Which is Not One*, 1985), Irigaray described female discourse as a multiple, fluid, and heterogeneous force analogous to the female genitals. This stress on the anatomy led some to accuse her of falling into the trap of female essentialism.

Literature and society after 1968

Claude Duchet

A significant development in sociological criticism in the 1970s was the growth of what is known as sociocriticism. Central to this process was the work of Claude Duchet who in his *Sociocritique* (1970) argued the structuralist position that the focus of sociological readings should be the language and structures of the text itself. An excellent example of this approach is Henri Mitterand's *Le Discours du roman* (1980; the discourse of the novel) where he gives an ideological reading of Émile Zola's novel *Germinal* (1885) based on the three functions of language: the mimetic, the narrative, and the symbolic. Sociocriticism influenced the critical writings of the sociologist Pierre Bourdieu as well as more recent developments in semiotics. The Paris School semiotician Denis Bertrand produced in 1985 a seminal study of space in Zola's *Germinal*, *L'Espace et le sens* (space and meaning), which is a theoretical development of Mitterand's approach.

Michel Foucault

Of central importance to the growth of new approaches to the text during this period was the work of the philosopher Michel Foucault who focused on the relationship between language and power. In his books, such as *Folie et déraison. Histoire de la folie à l'âge classique* (1961; *Madness and Civilisation. A History of Insanity in the Age of Reason*, 1973), *Naissance de la clinique: une archéologie du regard médical* (1963; *The Birth of the Clinic: An Archaeology of Medical Perception*, 1975), and *Les Mots et les choses* (1966; *The Order of Things*, 1970), he showed the relationship between various forms of "knowledge" and the sociopolitical, stressing how these forms of knowledge change throughout history. His approach influenced, among others, the American critic Edward Said who in his book *The World, the Text, and the Critic* (1983), for example, argues for the need to relate texts to their historic context and challenges Derrida's view that interpretation can be limitless. Foucault also drew attention to literature as a powerful cultural institution whose status is historically relative. This leads to a shift in emphasis away from the dominant literary canon to a privileging of those writers who have hitherto been excluded, such as women, Third-World writers, and ethnic minorities. Indeed, during the 1980s and 1990s French critics were to focus their attention, in particular, on literature from North Africa, the Caribbean, and the suburbs of Paris.

Pierre Bourdieu

Another major critical voice during the 1980s and 1990s was the sociologist Pierre Bourdieu (1930–). Bourdieu's aim was to reveal the underlying modes of class domination in capitalist societies as these appear in all aspects of education and art. In *La Distinction* (1980; *Distinction*, 1984) and *Les Règles de l'art* (1992; *The Rules of Art*, 1996) – which contains a very interesting study of Gustave Flaubert's novel *L'Éducation sentimentale* (1869; *Sentimental Education*, 1989) – Bourdieu related taste and aesthetic criteria of judgment to social class and social expectations. Studies by his pupils have linked literary movements such as naturalism as well as the content of art to "strategies" for the acquisition of what he terms symbolic capital on the part of the artists themselves.

Jean-François Lyotard

An important contribution to critical theory was also made by the philosopher Jean-François Lyotard (1924–). In his seminal works *La Condition postmoderne* (1979; *The Postmodern Condition*, 1984) and *Le Différend* (1983; *The Differend*, 1986) Lyotard saw society as essentially fragmented. Privatization and decentralization had produced a number of unidentifiable "microcenters of power." In this situation it was no longer possible to speak of "grand narratives" or metanarratives such as the idea that knowledge is produced for its own sake or for the purpose of liberating humanity – the theories of Sigmund Freud and Karl Marx were among the grand narratives Lyotard rejected. Instead the grand narrative was replaced by a number of often contending micronarratives. Lyotard's thought can be seen as defining postmodernity.

Jean Baudrillard

Frequently linked with the name of Lyotard is that of Jean Baudrillard. In his works, such as *À l'ombre des majorités silencieuses ou la fin du social* (1982; *In the Shadow of the Silent Majorities or The End of the Social*, 1983), he deplored the disappearance in the modern world of the distinction between the artificial and the real, the simulated and the actual. He condemned the media, where even terrorist acts may be staged for the benefit of the viewer. The notion of truth had completely disappeared; traditional oppositions such as that between good and evil had been eroded. In his later work *L'Illusion de la fin* (1992; *The Illusion of the End*, 1994) he saw history as an unending recycling and derealizing of itself. He attacked the theory of the "end of history" presented by the US historian Francis Fukuyama (*The End of History and the Last Man*, 1992), seeing the downfall of historical Communism in the late 1980s not as an "end" but as a "selling-off," as an aspect of the recessional market economy "under whose sign the tawdry beginning of the end of the twentieth century is playing itself out" (in the words of Keith Reader).

Literature and philosophy after 1968

Gilles Deleuze and Félix Guattari

Significant figures to emerge in the early 1970s were the philosopher Gilles Deleuze and the radical psychiatrist Félix Guattari who in their seminal text *L'Anti-Oedipe: Capitalisme et schizophrénie* (1972; *Anti-Oedipus: Capitalism and Schizophrenia*, 1977) rejected the Freudian unconscious as a capitalist construction, an internalized set of power relations whose goal is to repress desire. Instead, they advocated the liberation of desire through a method known as "schizoanalysis." This method constructs an unconscious seeing the libido as still fluid rather than already stabilized by Freudian constraints. An example of the application of this theory is their study *Kafka: pour une littérature mineure* (1975; *Kafka: Toward a Minor Literature*, 1986). The 1990s witnessed a revival of interest in the philosophy of Gilles Deleuze.

Emmanuel Levinas

From the 1980s onward critics drew inspiration from the works of the Lithuanian-born French philosopher Emmanuel Levinas (1906–1995). Also strongly influenced by phenomenology, Levinas' thought revolved around the concept of the Other, otherness being seen as at the core of human identity. His primary concern, therefore, was with the ethical dimension of human experience. His works include *Totalité et infini* (1961; *Totality and Infinity*, 1969) and *Sur Maurice Blanchot* (1975; on Maurice Blanchot). His writings contested the Western tradition of reducing the Other to the same and of imposing our own values on other people. They inspired the critic Edward Said and contributed to the development of a postcolonial criticism.

Michel Serres

The end of the twentieth century saw an upsurge of interest in the works of the philosopher and writer Michel Serres (1930–). Serres was concerned with making links between literature and science, drawing our attention to the contemporary relevance of the thought of the Roman poet and philosopher Lucretius and of chaos theory. Focusing on concepts of time and space and on the role of the senses, he saw literary texts as characterized by complexity and by a multiplicity of meanings. The primary metaphor in his work is that of the crossroads. In his analysis of Guy de Maupassant's short story "Le Horla" (1887), for example, he rejected traditional notions of spatial and temporal linearity describing the narrative instead as a multiple proliferation of intersecting spaces. His works include the *Hermès* series I–V (1969–1980; *Hermes: Literature, Science, Philosophy*, 1999) and a stimulating study of a text of Émile Zola. His thought marks a fundamental challenge to the more nihilistic trends associated with postmodernism: in its focus on matter and on a world outside language, it could herald a new era in literary criticism.

Further reading

Barry, Peter. *Beginning Theory: An Introduction to Literary and Cultural Theory*, 1995.
Culler, Jonathan. *Structuralist Poetics: Structuralism, Linguistics, and the Study of Literature*, 1975.
Eagleton, Terry. *Literary Theory: An Introduction*, 1983.
Hawkes, Terence. *Structuralism and Semiotics*, 1977.
Jarrety, Michel. *La Critique littéraire française du XXe siècle*, 1998.
Jefferson, Ann, and David Robey, eds. *Modern Literary Theory: A Comparative Introduction*, 1982.
Ryan, Michael. *Literary Theory: A Practical Introduction*, 1999.
Seldon, Raman. *A Reader's Guide to Contemporary Literary Theory*, 1985.
Simon, John K., ed. *Modern French Criticism: From Proust and Valéry to Structuralism*, 1972.
Sturrock, John. *The Word from Paris: Essays on Modern French Thinkers and Writers*, 1998.
Tadié, Jean-Yves. *La Critique littéraire au XXe siècle*, 1987.
Todorov, Tzvetan, ed. *French Literary Theory Today*, 1982.
Wright, Elizabeth. *Psychoanalytic Criticism: Theory in Practice*, 1984.

BRONWEN MARTIN

See also Althusser; Artaud; Barthes; Bataille; Baudrillard; Bergson; Breton; Butor; Cixous; Deleuze; Derrida; Foucault; Genette; Girard; Greimas; Irigaray; Kristeva; Lacan; Lévi-Strauss; Maritain; Poulet; Proust; Ricœur; Robbe-Grillet; Sartre; Valéry

Northrop Frye

Canadian critic and theorist

Born: Sherbrooke, Quebec, Canada; July 14, 1912
Died: Toronto, Canada; January 23, 1991

Biography

Herman Northrop Frye was born on July 14, 1912, in Sherbrooke, Province of Quebec, Canada. He received a B.A. in 1933 from the University of Toronto, an institution with which he was to be associated throughout his life. He later studied at Oxford University and received an M.A. in literature in 1940. Just before that, in 1939, Frye took up his lifetime work as a lecturer at Victoria College, University of Toronto. A professor at Victoria College for many years, he was named chancellor in 1978.

Another side of Frye's life can be seen in his church work. He was ordained a minister of the United Church of Canada in 1936, and the Christian perspective has informed his work from beginning to end, although he is hardly dogmatic about his religious beliefs or affiliation.

Frye's first important book was *Fearful Symmetry: A Study of William Blake*. Ten years later, at the age of forty-five, he published his most important book, *Anatomy of Criticism*. The books and essays that followed represent attempts to illustrate or expand the critical system enunciated in *Anatomy of Criticism*.

Influence

Frye's influence on modern criticism has been substantial; those who agree with him have incorporated his ideas into such areas as genre criticism and archetypal criticism, and even those who disagree with him have used his criticism or have had to deal with it as a first step before establishing alternatives. Perhaps the most important effect Frye has had on other critics is his tolerant spirit and inclusive critical view. The battles between New Critics and historical critics in the 1950s were lessened when Frye showed how both approaches could be included in a critical system.

Moreover, Frye's work on comedy and romance remains critically important. His essay on comedy in *Anatomy of Criticism* is the best available description of that genre, and the essay on romance in the same book, as well as his later study, *The Secular Scripture*, gave critics a helpful tool for explaining and understanding that type of literature. Frye's critical system as well as his urbane and tolerant attitude are out of fashion in a period of poststructuralism and feminist criticism, but his work remains as a critical monument that others will continue to draw on and, perhaps, complete.

Analysis

Frye has often been called a "myth critic" or an "archetypal critic" – that is, one who finds the structures of literary works in myths or archetypal images. That type of analysis is prominent in Frye's criticism, from his first major book, *Fearful Symmetry*, to his later studies of William Shakespeare. At one point, Frye declared that the mythic approach could help reveal the structure of all literature, not simply works that consciously use myth. The concept of "displacement," which he elaborated in "Myth, Fiction, and Displacement," holds that even works that are realistic on the surface contain hidden traces of original myths. The label of "myth critic," however, does not do justice to Frye's work as a whole, and it fails to explain his critical vision fully. He described himself in his most influential book, *Anatomy of Criticism*, as a "synoptic" critic who is attempting to provide the basis for a unified structure of knowledge about literature which can then be implemented and extended by future literary critics. It is true that the center of this proposed synoptic criticism would be archetypal criticism, but it would not be the only or exclusive method in this unified theory. Frye does suggest that one must get rid of "meaningless criticism," which he associates with social value judgments masquerading as literary ones, and "antithetical criticism," or the answering of a critical theory by its opposite. All other forms of criticism, however, are to be welcomed in this new synthesis.

The first element Frye addresses in his synoptic criticism is the "historical modes." Classifying literature by historical periods or movements is an ancient critical method. Frye constructs his "modes," however, according to the "power the hero has over his environment" rather than by one-hundred-year periods or by the reigns of kings. Frye's five categories are mythic, romance, high mimetic, low mimetic, and ironic, regressing from the power of a god to less power than the ordinary person or the reader. This codification roughly conforms to the standard scheme of classical, medieval, Renaissance, Romantic, and modern. What use can this scheme have? First of all, it is an attempt to give equal value to each phase rather than to demand that all literature be realistic or conform to what Frye terms "low mimetic prejudices." Each work must be seen as coming from particular concepts about the nature of the hero and read within that context. Frye's work has been very useful in calling readers' attention to the values of the form and period of "romance," in which the hero is a demigod rather than an ordinary person. In addition, the modal concept is not a rigidly structured straitjacket for readers or writers. Frye suggests that there is a modal "counterpoint" in many works, a conscious mixture of high and low modes. The works of Geoffrey Chaucer, for example, reveal this type of counterpoint. Finally, Frye's vision of literary history is literary: its classifications come from literary developments, not from the accidents of history, the restrictions of periods to one hundred years, or the lengths of monarchs' reigns. The arbitrariness of literary periods as set forth in basic textbooks needs rethinking, and Frye's work on the historical modes is a first step.

The next element of Frye's critical synthesis deals with the formal features of a literary work. His theory of symbols is an adaptation of Dante's fourfold method. For Frye, the five phases are literal, descriptive, formal, archetypal, and anagogic. Like that of Dante, Frye's system moves from a literal description of the linguistic elements of a work and expands to the individual work as the center of all literature.

Archetypal criticism is central to any systematic criticism, in Frye's view. Without a sense of how one work relates to another, literature would be nothing more than a heap of discrete works. Furthermore, the vision of the critic expands from the individual work to society: "The archetypal critic studies the poem as part of poetry, and poetry as part of the total imitation of nature that we call civilization." Frye's description of the "anagogical phase" is somewhat mystical; he seems to have borrowed the concept from William Blake. In this phase, any work can become the center of the whole "order of words" which now exists independently from any other world. Anagogy is "universal meaning," although it is difficult to see how it can be used as a critical concept. It seems an unnecessary or confusing addition. Frye himself has suggested that readers take whatever is useful in his criticism and leave what is not. His concept of anagogy may be the least useful part of his critical theory.

The most successful part of synoptic criticism is the theory of "mythos." Frye redefines and redescribes the traditional genres of Western literature and provides an outline of the central archetypal images. For Frye, archetypal imagery comes out of the natural elements of life: divine, human, animal, vegetable, mineral, fire, and water. In addition, he sees these images divided into the "apocalyptic" and the "demonic," the positive and negative sides always working against each other. To privilege one or the other is to deprive literature of its mission, which is to provide an alternative or opposing vision. The classification is fascinating, but the archetypal images remain, as Frye says, "static" until they are seen within the context of a specific work. To bring the imagery together with the work, Frye constructs a theory of "mythos," or archetypal plot patterns.

The plot patterns conform to the distinctions of the seasons: spring (comedy), summer (romance), autumn (tragedy), and winter (irony and satire). Frye is especially good on comedy, describing it as the attempt to create a new or "free society." Comedy is not a static genre in Frye's system but has five phases which define various sorts of plot patterns, including the traditional comedy of marriage found in Shakespeare and the ironic comedy of Ben Jonson, in which the society is not freed but remains "undefeated." Frye also classifies the character types in comedy, as he does in each genre. Typical comic characters are impostors, self-deprecators, and buffoons. In addition, Frye was one of the first to describe a type he calls "churls" or "refusers of the comic society" in Shakespearean and other comedy. Their function is to warn the reader that the synthesis of the new comic society is only provisional.

Frye's description of romance is centered on the concept of the quest. He offers one of the first and fullest descriptions of one of the most repeated plot patterns in literature. The form, for Frye, is not complex, but it can take on infinite variations. It has three parts: a journey, minor adventures, and a climactic battle. Characters are described in black-and-white terms and are evaluated by whether they are for or against the quest.

Frye is less successful with the genres of tragedy and irony and satire. His attempt to define tragedy by using the Adam and Eve myth is not very useful, and works that most readers would consider tragedies, such as *King Lear* (1605–1606), spill over into irony. Perhaps Frye's natural sympathies are with comedy and romance, so that he finds it difficult to represent or describe their opposites. His description of two character types in tragedy is more useful; he calls the friends of the tragic hero "plain dealers" and the young women whose death intensifies the tragedy "suppliants." Anyone who has read a Shakespearean tragedy will recognize these types.

The final component of synoptic criticism is Frye's theory of genres. Here he attempts to describe the relationship between the speaker and his or her audience in four types of presentation: drama, epos, fiction, and lyric. Here again Frye describes a range of differences rather than polar opposites: if drama is enacted by characters on stage, epos is the oral recitation of the ancient epic, fiction is presented on the printed page, and lyric is "over-heard" speech. Each of these presentations has its typical "melos," or sound pattern, and "opsis," or visual pattern. Perhaps most useful is his subdivision of the loose category of prose fiction into four aspects: novel, romance, anatomy, and confession. A novel emphasizes the social world, while romance stresses character and is less realistic; confession is found in the fictional autobiography or the so-called novel of education, while anatomy is identified by Frye as a "Menippean satire" such as *Gulliver's Travels* (1726), in which intellectual problems are the focus. The "radicals of presentation," like other elements in Frye's system, are meant to be flexible, so that a novel by Charles Dickens can be seen as fiction on the page, but epos when Dickens read it aloud. A work such as James Joyce's *Ulysses* (1922) is at once novel, confession, romance, and anatomy. Frye's suggestions regarding the differences between musical and visual poets are also illuminating. Most would think that Alfred, Lord Tennyson, is a musical poet, but Frye shows that his poems are very static and lack the musical devices that can be found in the poetry of Robert Browning. Frye speaks of the "discontinuous epic" in reference to works such as *In Memoriam* (1850), *The Waste Land* (1922), and *The Cantos of Ezra Pound* (1925–1970). The old epic continuity has been lost, and Frye shows how the fragmentary form arose as a modern solution to the problem of how to write the long poem.

Frye exemplified and extended these critical ideas in the many books that followed the *Anatomy of Criticism*. *A Natural Perspective* is a study of Shakespearean comedy that uses more fully and in greater detail the principles of "The Mythos of Spring: Comedy," and *Fools of Time* is a study of Shakespearean tragedy using and refining the principles of "The Mythos of Autumn: Tragedy." *Fools of Time* does seem to correct some of the terminological confusion of *Anatomy of Criticism*. Tragedy is now described more clearly as "the tragedy of order, the tragedy of passion, and the tragedy of isolation." Within these categories, Frye analyzes and classifies a number of the tragedies of Shakespeare with special attention to *King Lear, Macbeth* (1606), *Hamlet* (c. 1600–1601), and *Othello* (1604).

In a similar manner, Frye has extended the observations on romance in "The Mythos of Summer" into a book, *The*

Secular Scripture. The most important part of the book is the two chapters "Themes of Descent" and "Themes of Ascent," describing and discussing the opposite movements of romance. The themes of descent are associated with such patterns as metamorphosis or a change from an earlier idyllic world, while those of ascent stress a growth of identity. In addition, Frye expands his analysis of character in romance.

There is no doubt that Northrop Frye is one of the most important and influential critics of the twentieth century. His influence can be seen nearly everywhere in twentieth-century criticism, including the works of those who reject his critical philosophy. Certain persistent questions about Frye's criticism have recurred throughout his career: for example, numerous critics have been concerned by his rejection of value judgments in literature. Frye believes, however, that apparently objective value judgments often are concealed social judgments and that a criticism that is systematic needs to do without these divisive and unjustified evaluations. What he has done better than any twentieth-century critic is to begin the process of establishing literary criticism as a progressive and systematic discipline.

Principal criticism

Fearful Symmetry: A Study of William Blake, 1947
Anatomy of Criticism: Four Essays, 1957
The Well-Tempered Critic, 1963
Fables of Identity: Studies in Poetic Mythology, 1963
A Natural Perspective: The Development of Shakespearean Comedy and Romance, 1965
The Return of Eden: Five Essays on Milton's Epics, 1965
Fools of Time: Studies in Shakespearean Tragedy, 1967
The Modern Century, 1967
A Study of English Romanticism, 1968
The Stubborn Structure: Essays on Criticism and Society, 1970
The Secular Scripture: A Study of the Structure of Romance, 1976
Spiritus Mundi: Essays on Literature, Myth, and Society, 1976
Northrop Frye on Culture and Literature: A Collection of Review Essays, 1978
The Great Code, 1983
Northrop Frye on Shakespeare, 1986
Words with Power: Being a Second Study of the Bible and Literature, 1990

Other major works and literary forms

Northrop Frye was a professional literary theorist and critic throughout his career, and his other writings are distinctly less weighty or significant. Nevertheless, a few patterns of interest do emerge. Frye wrote articles on Christianity, education, the other arts, and Canadian culture. For example, he contributed an essay, "The Church: Its Relation to Society," in *The Living Church* (1949) and wrote extensively on education in Canada. His most important work on education is *The Educated Imagination* (1963), which applies some of his critical principles to the problem of teaching literature to young people. In addition, he wrote numerous essays and reviews on Canadian poetry.

NONFICTION
The Educated Imagination, 1963
T. S. Eliot, 1963
The Bush Garden: Essays on the Canadian Imagination, 1971
On Teaching Literature, 1972
Creation and Recreation, 1980

Further reading

Abrams, M. H. "Anatomy of Criticism," in *University of Toronto Quarterly*. XXVIII, no. 2 (1958 / 1959), pp. 190–197.
Crews, Frederick. *Out of My System*, 1975.
Culver, Jonathan. *Structuralist Poetics*, 1975.
Denham, Robert D. *Northrop Frye and Critical Method*, 1978.
Feder, Lillian. "Myth, Poetry, and Critical Theory," in *Theories of Myth*. Edited by Robert A. Segal, 1996.
Fraser, John. "Northrop Frye and Evaluation," in *The Cambridge Quarterly*. II, no. 2 (Spring, 1967), pp. 97–116.
Hamilton, A. C. *Northrop Frye: Anatomy of His Criticism*, 1990.
Krieger, Murray, ed. *Northrop Frye in Modern Criticism*, 1966.
Lee, Alvin, and Robert D. Denham, eds. *The Legacy of Frye*, 1994.

JAMES SULLIVAN

See also American Literary Theory: Twentieth Century; Archetypal Criticism

Fulgentius

Christian Latin writer

Born and died: Africa; c. A.D. 500–600

Biography

No records survive containing biographical information on Fulgentius, but some knowledge about his life may be gleaned from references in his works. He was probably a cleric, and he was familiar with the Bible and early Christian histories, and with Latin and Greek texts. The extent of his Latin and Greek, the identities of writers he refers to and borrows from, his interests in Africa, his knowledge of stories and legends known in Egypt, and the fact that several surviving copies of his works are addressed to a priest in Carthage, indicate that he lived and was educated in colonial North Africa during the fifth or sixth century. If indeed he lived and wrote in that region, it was before A.D. 632, when much of North Africa began to be conquered by the Muslims.

In the *Content of Virgil*, Fulgentius refers to Romans in a manner that indicates he does not consider himself Roman. He appears by his attitudes to have been an orthodox Christian. *On the Ages of the World and of Man* reveals strong anti-Jewish prejudice.

Influence

Although little-read today (there were no translations of Fulgentius into English – perhaps into any modern language

– until Leslie Whitbread's in 1971), Fulgentius' works were very important to writers and critics during the Middle Ages and Renaissance. *The Mythologies* introduced the allegorical interpretation of classical myths which was popular for many centuries after his death. Borrowers range from the seventh-century compiler known as the Vatican Mythographer I; to Petrarch, Giovanni Boccaccio, and Geoffrey Chaucer in the fourteenth century; to Robert Burton in the seventeenth century. Fulgentius' *Content of Virgil* is the earliest sustained allegorical reading of a Latin poetic classic to have survived. This exploration of the allegorical nature of epic influenced epic poets (including Torquato Tasso and Edmund Spenser) and theories of epic poetry (most notably the *Aeneid* commentaries of Bernardus Silvestris and Cristoforo Landino) from the sixth century to the sixteenth.

Analysis

Fulgentius' most significant work is arguably the *Content of Virgil*. This work follows by two hundred years a series of *Aeneid* commentaries which includes the work of Marius Servius Honoratus, Ambrosius Theodosius Macrobius, and Tiberius Claudius Donatus. The earlier works, largely collections of footnotes to difficult passages in the *Aeneid* and rhetorical analyses of Virgil's style, contain almost none of the allegorical interpretation to which the *Aeneid* is subjected in the *Content of Virgil*. Even so, Fulgentius draws on the wisdom of his predecessors, following Servius' lead in tracing (or inventing) etymology to determine allegorical significance, and following Donatus in reading the *Aeneid* as an encomium (song of praise) as well as epic.

Just as epic and tragedy were clearly defined and prescribed by classical commentators, so also was the encomium, a poem which existed to teach virtue through the example of the life of one virtuous man. The story begins at or just before birth, and presents a chronological accounting of episodes which demonstrate the acquiring, nurturing, and perfecting of wisdom. The *Content of Virgil* takes this prescription seriously, and this leads Fulgentius to a remarkable reading of the poem. For example, the *Aeneid* opens with the story of the storm and shipwreck in book 1. This episode is usually read as a classic example of the epic's beginning *in medias res*. For Fulgentius, however, the *Aeneid* is an ecomium, and the encomium begins *ab ovo*, at the beginning. This tempest and shipwreck, then, is for Fulgentius an allegorical representation of the soul's birth into the dangers and pains of this world. What appears superficially to be the middle of things is actually the beginning of the life of the encomium hero.

As the poem continues, Fulgentius unwaveringly fits the poem into a chronological pattern and provides the allegorical interpretation of the acquiring, nurturing, and perfection of wisdom in three stages of life: birth, learning, and happiness. Aeneas' wanderings in the early books of the poem represent the various confusions and innocences of infancy and childhood: "As soon as Aeneas touches land, he sees his mother, Venus, but does not recognize her, indicating complete infancy in that it is given to newborn babes to see their mother from birth, but the ability to recognize her is not immediately added." At the end of a series of episodes in which Aeneas is entertained and diverted as a young boy, his father, Anchises, is buried, and Aeneas the adolescent is no longer under parental control. His affair with Dido, his hunting, and the storms he encounters are allegorical representations of the adolescent's control by his passions; under the influence of intellect (Mercury), his evil, lustful deeds are brought to ashes. Having learned from his mistakes, Aeneas engages in more appropriately "manly" exercises – the funeral games.

In book 6, Aeneas approaches the temple of Apollo, that is, he begins the pursuit of wisdom. At this point he buries Misenus, whose name means "vain praise," for vainglory must be set aside before wisdom can be acquired. In the underworld, Aeneas obtains the golden bough of learning and witnesses the punishments and rewards of evil and good. He sees many souls in punishment for the sin of pride. At the end of his journey through the underworld, Aeneas plants the golden bough in Elysium, because learning, once acquired, must be planted forever in memory.

The last six books of the *Aeneid* show the virtuous man in struggle against evil. Aeneas visits Ausonia, increase of good. He marries Lavinia, showing that he knows the value of labor; he seeks the help of Evander, the good man, demonstrating that the virtuous man seeks the company of virtue; he wears the armor of Vulcan, the protection of the ardent mind, and fights Turnus, or fury. So clad, he conquers Turnus (furious rage), Mezantius (the spirit which despises good), and Messapus (defying speech). In book 12, Juturna, who stands for destruction, is forced to quit the war.

In the *Content of Virgil*, Fulgentius has two purposes: to establish that the *Aeneid* is indeed an allegorical representation of the soul's passage through life, and to demonstrate episode by episode how this allegory works. Within a fictional framework, no lesser guide than Virgil himself takes Fulgentius through the fable to reveal the message at its core. Throughout the *Content of Virgil*, Fulgentius assumes the posture of abject student relying on the wisdom of Virgil the schoolmaster. After Fulgentius has proven himself a worthy pupil by reciting the first book of the *Aeneid*, Virgil conducts what is essentially a dialogue between teacher and pupil, very much in the manner of Plato, Cicero, and Saint Augustine.

The idea that the *Aeneid* might be examined in terms of moral philosophy was not new to Fulgentius; the poet as the source of wisdom was a major theme of late classical writers. In the fourth or fifth century, Ambrosius Theodosius Macrobius' *Saturnalia* had already compared Virgil with Nature herself, and compared his poem with the universe, divinely crafted and including everything.

Servius also finds in Virgil an omniscient source of wisdom, a revelation of the truths of Plato and Cicero. By Fulgentius' time, Christian readers assumed that Virgil was something of a pagan prophet and that Christian truths could be easily extracted from his works. A large body of interpretive commentary already existed for certain passages of the *Aeneid*. Fulgentius, however, was the first to take on the entire poem and to find in the overall structure of the work an allegory for Christian life.

To the modern reader, Fulgentius' reading of the *Aeneid* is primitive and illogical; attempting to make his allegorical reading "fit," Fulgentius avoids the possibility that an event in the poem may be caused by an action that precedes it, and in treating each book as a self-contained unit he strays far from what is now assumed to be Virgil's intention and meaning. Yet in his reading of the epic as an essentially moral treatise, revealing Christian truth through pagan legend, Fulgentius set up a framework for what an epic poem might be expected to accomplish. On this framework, Tasso hung his *Gerusalemme liberata* (1575) and Spenser *The Faerie Queene* (1590, 1596). Literary criticism of the Middle Ages and Renaissance, including the *Aeneid* commentaries of Bernardus Silvestris in the twelfth century and Cristoforo Landino in the fifteenth, agreed with Fulgentius that Platonic truth could be extracted from Virgil and that Christian truth was reflected in pagan art. For these commentators, the *Aeneid* described the soul's progress from birth to knowledge, or wisdom, or grace.

Other scholars and poets of the Middle Ages and Renaissance, including Dante (who also is guided by a fictional Virgil in his great work, although this can hardly be credited to Fulgentius), expect to find in the *Aeneid* a model of the proper progress through life; in his own commentary on Dante, Boccaccio draws a parallel between the invocations to the Muses in Fulgentius and in Dante. Manuscripts of the *Content of Virgil* were still circulated in the sixteenth century, and the text was printed in the early part of the century. Compilers of myth respected Fulgentius into the seventeenth and eighteenth centuries, but nineteenth-century readers were more likely to see his work as exaggerated and irrelevant.

Fulgentius was influential also in his treatment of some of the building blocks of epic: mythical tales and individual words. Since the poet is a divine revealer of secrets, conveying truths through the instrument of words, Fulgentius looks for secrets in etymology. He uses this technique liberally in both the *Content of Virgil* and *The Mythologies*; some of the etymological evidence Fulgentius presents is sound, but much of it is far-fetched. Discussing book 7 of the *Aeneid* in the *Content of Virgil*, for example, Fulgentius' fictional guide Virgil explains:

> Then he seeks to marry Lavinia, that is, the road of toil, for at this stage of life Everyman learns the value of toil in furthering his worldly possessions. She is also called the daughter of Latinus and the descendent of Caunus. Now Latinus is from *latitando*, being concealed, because toil is always concealed in various places; wherefore Latona is also called *luna*, moon, because now she hides her upper parts, now her lower, and now is entirely concealed. And Caunus is *cannonus*, that is, toiling mind. Moreover, Caunus marries the nymph Marica, for *merica*, that is, thought.

The sentences are long and convoluted, the Latin is notoriously inflated and crude, the erudition is unreliable. Yet in his reaching ever further for etymological evidence for an allegorical interpretation, Fulgentius is perhaps less to blame than are the excesses of his times. Fulgentius derived much of his pompous, convoluted style, and many of his interpretations of *The Mythologies*, from earlier works.

Although discussions of Greek myth were available from several sources, it is to him that the Middle Ages and Renaissance most often turned for allegorical interpretation. In the seventh century, Fulgentius' influence is apparent in Vatican compilations of mythic material and perhaps in the anonymous *Liber monstrorum*, a possible source for *Beowulf*.

In the eighth through tenth centuries, *The Mythologies* had a remarkable influence on major and minor poets and compilers of learning. M. L. W. Laistner's *The Intellectual History of the Early Middle Ages* (1957) documents extensive borrowings of Fulgentius' interpretation and style in writings of this period; several copies of *The Mythologies* are listed in library catalogs of these centuries, and it appears that a copy of the manuscript may have reached England by the ninth or tenth century. Throughout the Middle Ages, new compilations of interpretations of myths and fables were produced and declared to be Fulgentius' work. Borrowings from *The Mythologies* continued well into the thirteenth century; in the twelfth century a thousand-line versification of parts of the text was produced.

In the fourteenth century, writers including Chaucer, Boccaccio, and Petrarch still looked to Fulgentius, or to his tradition. In minor details in the descriptions of classical figures, Chaucer at least echoes Fulgentius, although direct borrowing cannot be established. Boccaccio's fourteenth-century collection of myths, *Genealogia deorum gentilium* (*Genealogy of the Gentile Gods*, 1930), borrows Fulgentius' versions of several stories and even accepts with high praise his etymologies, allegorical interpretations, and literary style. Petrarch, who had a copy of *The Mythologies* in his own library, agreed with Fulgentius that one of the purposes of poetry is to present veiled moral truths.

In the fifteenth and sixteenth centuries, writers who may not have known Fulgentius' name or texts were still following him in seeking allegorical interpretation for classical myths; some even used bits of Fulgentius that had been handed down intact. The sixteenth century saw continued circulation of Fulgentius' texts. By the end of the seventeenth century, his four extant texts had been printed. They remained in print through most of the century. John Lydgate, Samuel Daniel, John Milton, and Robert Burton are among the most important late borrowers from Fulgentius' *The Mythologies*, or receivers of its tradition.

Principal criticism

Expositio Virgilianae continentiae secundum philosophos moralis, early sixth century (*The Exposition of the Content of Virgil According to Moral Philosophy*, 1971, commonly known as the *Content of Virgil*)

Mythologia, sixth century (*The Mythologies*, 1971). Fulgentius is sometimes also credited with the authorship of the *Super Thebiaden* (*On the Thebiad*, 1971), assigned in the one extant copy to *sanctus Fulgentius episcopus*. This was almost certainly written at a later time, perhaps by the sixth-century saint Fulgentius, bishop of Ruspe

Fulgentius: Selected Works, 1997 (Robert B. Eno, translator)

Other major works and literary forms

In addition to the works listed above, Fulgentius is the author of *Fulgentii expositio sermonum antiquorum* (sixth century; *The Explanation of Obsolete Words*, 1971), consisting of sixty-two brief glosses for difficult Latin words, and *De aetatibus mundi et hominis* (sixth century; *On the Ages of the World and of Man*, 1971), a biblical and classical history.

In the prologue to *The Mythologies* Fulgentius refers to his earlier satiric poems. In the *Content of Virgil* he mentions former writings on physiology. These works have not survived.

NONFICTION

Fulgentii expositio sermonum antiquorum, sixth century (*The Explanation of Obsolete Words*, 1971)

De aetatibus mundi et hominis, sixth century (*On the Ages of the World and of Man*, 1971)

Further reading

Bush, Douglas. *Mythology and the Renaissance Tradition in English Poetry*, 1963.

Comparetti, Domenico. *Virgil in the Middle Ages*, 1929. Translated by E. F. M. Benske.

Irvine, Martin. *The Making of Textual Culture: "Grammatica" and Literary Theory, 350–1100*, 1994.

Laistner, M. L. W. "Fulgentius in the Carolingian Age," in *The Intellectual Heritage of the Early Middle Ages*, 1957.

Preminger, Alex, O. B. Hardison, Jr., and Kevin Kerrane, eds. "Fulgentius," in *Classical and Medieval Literary Criticism*, 1974.

Silvestris, Bernardus. *Commentary on the First Six Books of Virgil's "Aeneid,"* 1979. Translated by Earl G. Schreiber and Thomas E. Maresca.

Whitbread, Leslie. *Fulgentius the Mythographer*, 1971.

CYNTHIA A. BILY

See also Medieval Literary Theory; Saint Isidore of Seville

Margaret Fuller

American critic and social reformer

Born: Cambridgeport, Massachusetts; May 23, 1810
Died: Off the coast of Fire Island, New York; July 19, 1850

Biography

Sarah Margaret Fuller was born on May 23, 1810, in Cambridgeport, Massachusetts, the first of nine children of Timothy and Margaret Crane Fuller. Disappointed that his first child was female, lawyer Timothy Fuller determined that he would bring up the child as though she were a boy, and to this vow Margaret's exceptional education can be attributed. From the age of six she studied English and Latin grammar and began to read Latin authors, a practice she continued daily throughout her youth. For the most part alone, Margaret was encouraged to find companionship in the books of the house. By the time she was thirteen, it became clear to her father that Margaret needed companionship with young people her own age, so he sent her away to the school run by Susan Prescott and her sister in Groton, Massachusetts (1823–1824).

Upon her return, Margaret engaged in rigorous days of study, beginning before five in the morning and not ending until midnight. In 1826 her father moved the family closer to Harvard Yard, where Margaret was quick to become an associate of several Harvard youths. In her early twenties, Margaret began to learn German in a kind of partnership with James Clarke. At the end of the day, they would get together to share ideas and translations from the German. Her lifelong attachment to Johann Wolfgang von Goethe had begun.

In 1833 family finances forced the family to move to a farm in Groton. Margaret sorely missed being in the intellectual center of a city. Yet her predicament was soon to become even worse: her father died in 1835, and Margaret became virtual head of the household. Saying a temporary good-bye to her family, she left the farm in Groton and rented rooms from an uncle in Boston, from where she could walk easily to the Temple School, where she taught from 1836 to 1837. When the Temple School closed, she taught at Hiram Fuller's Greene Street School in Providence, Rhode Island (1837–1839), and in 1839 she translated *Eckermann's Conversations with Goethe*. In this year, too, she moved the family from Groton to Jamaica Plain and began the "conversations" in Boston and Cambridge which enhanced her reputation.

Margaret Fuller's work in journalism began in earnest when she agreed to edit *The Dial* (1840–1842). Also in 1842, she published her translation of the *Correspondence of Fraülein Günderode and Bettina von Arnim*. In 1844 she published *Summer on the Lakes, in 1843*, an account of a trip west with James and Sarah Clarke. This work attracted the attention of Horace Greeley, who subsequently offered her the position of literary critic for the New York *Daily-Tribune*. After the publication of *Woman in the Nineteenth Century* (1845) and *Papers on Literature and Art* (1846) Fuller sailed to Europe, and the final chapter of her life.

In Rome in 1847, Fuller met and married a young Italian nobleman, the Marchese Ossoli. Their son Angelo was born on September 5, 1848. After the fall of the Roman Republic, the nobleman lost all claim to family fortune. In May of 1850, all three sailed for America. On July 19, off the shore of Fire Island, the entire family died as the result of a shipwreck. Many Americans, including Henry David Thoreau, hastened to New York to search the beach for Fuller's body, but it was never found.

Influence

Fuller was a woman to be reckoned with among the intellectual circles of her time. A leading figure in the Transcendentalist movement, she countered the movement's male domination and New England insularity with both her powerful personality and the intensity of her intellectualism. Furthermore, as teacher, journalist, editor, critic, translator, and historian (at the time of her death, she was bringing home with her a manuscript history of the Italian revolution, for which she had already asked Ralph Waldo Emerson to arrange a publisher), Fuller worked consistently to lessen American parochialism and to develop an international awareness in the arts and in ideas. She should also be credited with broadening the critic's role by addressing the concerns of visual art, music, and theater as well as of literature. She influenced American criticism by beginning the process of separating American artistic taste from a sense of morality. That is, she tried to measure art by principles other than moral ones.

Her greatest influence, however, was through her early feminism. She insisted that women should have the same freedoms as men, that women should not be restricted by the conventions of their gender and the institutions of their society. Her comment, "Let them be Sea-Captains, if you will," is often quoted, and it proclaims the spirit of her *Woman in the Nineteenth Century*. Many leaders of the women's rights conventions of the early 1850s attributed their newborn courage to Fuller, and while Fuller herself never focused specifically on gaining political rights for women, as the women's movement soon did, it was Fuller's philosophical support that provided the foundation for the advances American women made during the nineteenth and twentieth centuries.

Analysis

Fuller wrote criticism at a time when the United States was still quite unsophisticated in its appreciation of art and its understanding of the function of criticism. Indeed, most Americans were more interested in the growth and development of the country through towns and cities and in the construction of public and private buildings than in the arts. When Americans thought of art, they thought of Europe, home to an established audience and strong traditions. Many American artists chose to study and sometimes to live in Europe because they found the environment so much more conducive to artistic endeavor than America. Americans interested in art inevitably preferred the European artist to the home-grown variety; a nationalist movement in American art was only in its infancy. Fuller tried to help the United States develop its artistic taste both by appreciating European artists and by recognizing American talent. She encouraged artistic standards that would be universal rather than parochial.

It is important to remember, too, the function and place of women during the first half of the nineteenth century. Women were not educated in the leading colleges and universities. Women were not allowed to vote in public elections. Women had few vocational opportunities open to them besides teaching, which was low-paying. Few women dared to engage in criticism during the nineteenth century in America because few had the broad educational background necessary to make critical judgments. Fuller was an exception: she knew languages and literatures, she had a background in history, and she was sensitive in several areas of the arts. She was therefore unusually qualified to assume the critic's role. That she did so at a time when such a profession was generally closed to women highlights her accomplishments.

Fuller recognized early that she herself was not talented as a literary artist. She had had tremendous success with her "conversations," informal discussions with friends and associates on the leading ideas of the day. When she tried to write, her work came out stilted and sometimes confused by the metaphors she used. As a result, she turned to criticism, accepting it as the handmaiden to art. Yet she always believed that skill in conversation was her special gift, in a time when the ability to conduct good conversation was considered an art.

Fuller understood the function of criticism to be as an assistant to art. The critic was not an antagonist, as is perhaps the case now, but a friend to the artist. Through the critic, the work of the artist could be interpreted or filtered to the artist's audience. When the critic saw the work of a genius, the mission was to make that genius apparent to all people. The critic's function was also to recognize talent, to bring it to the attention of a wider audience than it might otherwise have. Finally, the critic was to support less talented writers, to encourage all who might have some inclination and some talent rather than restrict art to the few creators with true genius.

In the first volume of *The Dial* (July, 1840), which she edited, Fuller divided critics into three categories. "A Short Essay on Critics" claims that the first kind of critic is the "subjective" critic. This critic uses criticism primarily as an excuse to vent his or her own opinions on any number of tangentially related subjects. This critic gives his or her own impressions of a work of art, not bothering to check his or her notions against any wider measures of history or context than his or her own personal background. Fuller insists that this kind of criticism is quite worthless and should not be given credence. The second kind of critic is the "apprehensive" critic. This critic enters into the spirit and philosophy of the artist studied, empathizes with the artist, and enters imaginatively into the spirit of the work. There is no distance between this critic and the work which is criticized. The apprehensive critic is preferable to the subjective critic, but the best is the third kind: the "comprehensive" critic. This critic is apprehensive in that he or she enters the work imaginatively and gives each artistic artifact his or her full response and genuine engagement, but at the same time the comprehensive critic measures the work against absolute and universal principles and sees the relationships between a particular work and the universe. Only this third kind of critic should venture to judge a work of art, according to Fuller. The ability to say what a work is not, which is one of the functions of the comprehensive critic, is as important as the ability to say what a work is, for it presupposes a universal criterion, a measure that can be taken as absolute. Fuller insists that the purpose of criticism is never to degrade but merely to classify.

There were two negatives in Fuller's theory of criticism. One was that the critic should not set himself or herself up as a dictator of what people should and should not read. The critic's function was not to restrict or discourage access to an artist, but always to encourage it. Another significant aspect of Fuller's criticism is her belief that art should be judged on aesthetic grounds, not on moral grounds. Edgar Allan Poe's disdain for the "heresy of the didactic" is well known, but in fact Fuller made moves in the same direction even before Poe did. Art for art's sake was a long time in coming to America, but Fuller did her best to bring the philosophy to some fruition.

Fuller's work on behalf of art in general in her criticism was important and influential, but her work on behalf of particular artists was also significant, for the major writers of the day as well as many who have now been lost to fame suffered her perusal. Fuller's first assignment for Greeley's *Daily-Tribune* was to review her friend Emerson's second series of *Essays* (1844). She clearly admired the volume and encouraged her readers to make the essays "the companions of our lives." Nevertheless, she performed her critical function in recording also some of the less positive views of Emerson's writings, and she seemed to affirm that in Emerson's works single sentences or short passages often engage the attention more than the whole. In like manner, she objected to Emerson's poems as too philosophical. Yet on the whole, she recognized in Emerson a sincere and honest man dedicated to the pursuit of truth. Her judgments of Emerson have come to be accepted as the critical consensus.

Concerning Poe, Fuller noted an original writer whose imaginative capabilities penetrated into "the causes of things," a far deeper and more constructive use of the imagination than most of the clever tales being published about the same time. Poe was not a man generous of spirit, and Fuller did not escape his acerbity. All the more to her credit, then, is the positive tone of her criticism. She recognized even in his failures "an intellect of strong fiber and well-chosen aim." One comment in a *Daily-Tribune* piece, however, strikes an odd note: Fuller urged Poe to devote his genius to writing long works – the metaphysical novel, for example – rather than limiting himself to stories. Poe's novel, *The Narrative of Arthur Gordon Pym* (1838), suggests that Poe understood, or learned, at any rate, that his genius was best suited to the short tale.

Fuller praised other writers, too, whose work has also stood the test of time. Nathaniel Hawthorne, for example, she admired freely, believing him to be the best American writer of the day, even before his great classic *The Scarlet Letter* (1850). She regarded highly Charles Brockden Brown's work because Brown refused to imitate European writers, and Fuller was ever on the lookout for the makings of an American national literature, although never at the expense of artistic merit. Fuller also appreciated Brown's depiction of forceful women in his novels, and she approved of his great respect for intellectual companionship as fictionally played out in his novels. Fuller anticipated that Robert Browning would be esteemed one of Great Britain's major poets, and she encouraged an audience for Browning in the US. In "American Literature: Its Position in the Present Time, and Prospects for the Future," Fuller also praised Washington Irving, William Cullen Bryant, and the society poet Fitz-Greene Halleck. For these men, it is the vicissitudes of literary taste and fashion rather than artistic merit that have shaded their reputations.

More treacherous for Fuller was the task of guiding Americans to judge fairly some of the artists who had become most popular. The praise generally given to both Henry Wadsworth Longfellow and James Russell Lowell was inflated, Fuller believed. Although these men had talent, they were not the creative geniuses many readers claimed. Fuller objected to the superficiality of James Fenimore Cooper's characters and the obvious contrivance of his plots despite the fact that his novels were in great demand. Fuller saw Longfellow, Lowell, and Cooper for what they were, and her judgments rather than the popular opinions of the time have come to be the accepted view.

Fuller did, however, misjudge some writers. She rated the works of Ellery Channing and Cornelius Mathews far more positively than they are rated today. She underestimated Honoré de Balzac, largely because she could not tolerate the heavy dose of realism in his work. Try as she might to extricate herself from the burden of moral criteria in criticism, sometimes she succumbed to the disease of the time and ceased to be the comprehensive critic she aspired to being. Yet, given the deadlines under which she worked and the volume and breadth of material for which she was responsible, her occasional lapses are certainly understandable. For the roughly two years that she worked as literary critic of Greeley's *Daily-Tribune*, Fuller distinguished both herself and that publication. After she sailed to Europe in 1846, she continued to send articles back to New York, and some of them continued to comment on art, but her great period of literary criticism had passed.

Whether abroad or at home, Fuller was always dedicated to improving and sustaining American art and artists. Not nationalistic in a narrow or parochial sense, she nevertheless looked forward to a day when American art would stand on its own, or to be more specific, when America would show literary genius the match of continental Europe's greatest work, which demonstrated both strength and expansiveness, both national and individual greatness. In Emerson, Fuller saw a "harbinger of the better day." Yet she realized that in 1846 that better day was still a good way off. Indeed, Fuller believed that American literature would not come into its own until three conditions were met in American society. First was that the plenitude of races in America would have to come together more fully. The tragedy of the Civil War lay in America's future, but even that most horrific of wars would not overcome the great hindrance to American art that Fuller saw in racial bigotry. Second, Fuller claimed that it would be necessary for the country to prize moral and intellectual freedom as much as political freedom if art were to achieve the dignity to which it aspired. The third condition was that the physical extent of the country must be fully tamed, fully domesticated, before Americans would have the leisure to turn to art over material prosperity.

Given her "conditions," perhaps Fuller would find American art today still in its swaddling clothes. At any rate, it is unfortunate that she died before the remarkable fruition of what has been called the American Renaissance, for she would surely have appreciated its glory. On the other hand, Fuller left a legacy of optimism and hope that American art would ultimately blossom.

Principal criticism

Articles in *The Dial*, 1840–1842
Articles in the New York *Daily-Tribune*, 1844–1846
Papers on Literature and Art, 1846
The Dial: A Magazine for Literature, Philosophy, and Religion, 1961 (4 volumes)

Other major works and literary forms

In her extensive writings for *The Dial* and the *Daily-Tribune*, Margaret Fuller was responsible for writing on all aspects of art, although she was best when writing about literature – reviews, appreciative pieces, and essays introducing foreign writers to American audiences. In addition to these essays, she translated works written in German: *Eckermann's Conversations with Goethe* (1839) and the *Correspondence of Fräulein Günderode and Bettina von Arnim* (1842). *Summer on the Lakes, in 1843* (1844) is an account of Fuller's trip out West with James and Sarah Clarke. Her most famous work is *Woman in the Nineteenth Century* (1845), a greatly expanded version of a July, 1843, article in *The Dial* entitled "The Great Lawsuit: Man *versus* Men, Woman *versus* Women." *Woman in the Nineteenth Century* is widely accepted as the earliest formal declaration of feminism to be written by an American; it defends basic human rights and celebrates both the history and the potential of women.

The publication of a scholarly edition of Fuller's letters from 1983 to 1993, edited by Robert Hudspeth, has further enhanced her literary reputation.

NONFICTION
Summer on the Lakes, in 1843, 1844
Woman in the Nineteenth Century, 1845
At Home and Abroad: Or, Things and Thoughts in America and Europe, 1856
Life Without and Life Within, 1859
Love-Letters of Margaret Fuller, 1845–1846, 1903

TRANSLATIONS
Eckermann's Conversations with Goethe, 1839
Correspondence of Fräulein Günderode and Bettina von Arnim, 1842

Further reading

Allen, Margaret Vanderhaar. *The Achievement of Margaret Fuller*, 1979.
Blanchard, Paula. *Margaret Fuller: From Transcendentalism to Revolution*, 1978.
Brown, Arthur W. *Margaret Fuller*, 1964.
Dickenson, Donna. *Margaret Fuller: Writing a Woman's Life*, 1993.
Durning, Russell E. *Margaret Fuller: Citizen of the World*, 1969.
Ebbitt, Wilma R. "Margaret Fuller's Ideas on Criticism," in *Boston Public Library Quarterly*. III (July, 1951), pp. 171–187.
Mitchell, Catherine C., ed. *Margaret Fuller's New York Journalism: A Biographical Essay and Key Writings*, 1995.
Myerson, Joel, ed. *Critical Essays on Margaret Fuller*, 1980.
Urbanski, Marie Mitchell Olesen, ed. *Margaret Fuller: Visionary of the New Age*, 1994.

PAULA KOPACZ

See also American Literary Theory to 1900; Emerson; Feminist Criticism

G

Hans-Georg Gadamer

German philosopher and critic

Born: Breslau, Germany; February 11, 1900

Biography

Hans-Georg Gadamer was born on February 11, 1900, in the Silesian city of Breslau, now Wroçlaw, Poland. His father, Johann Gadamer, was a professor of pharmaceutical chemistry at the local university. Against the wishes of his father, Gadamer began to study philosophy in 1918, as he was "anything but mature – a bashful, clumsy, inwardly turned kid." In 1919 he moved to Marburg, home of the neo-Kantian philosophers Hermann Cohen and Paul Natorp. Gadamer was to stay in Marburg until 1938. At Marburg University he studied philosophy, German literature, art history, and classical philology.

After writing a doctoral thesis under Natorp in 1922, Gadamer became interested in the work of Martin Heidegger, who taught in Marburg from 1923 to 1927 and by whose personality and work Gadamer "was immediately spellbound." In 1928 he wrote his thesis for Heidegger on Plato's dialectical ethics. Gadamer taught at Marburg University from 1923 to 1938, first as an assistant and, from 1928, as a private docent. However, under the rising power of Adolf Hitler's Nazism, he was denied a full professorship. Finally, he was given the professorship in 1937 and received an offer from the University of Leipzig a year later. He stayed in Leipzig until 1948. In 1946 Gadamer was appointed rector of the university and worked for its reconstruction after World War II, but he decided to leave Leipzig after becoming disillusioned by the interference of the East German Communist Party, which was seizing power in the Russian-occupied East German zone.

After a brief stint at the University of Frankfurt (from 1948 to 1949), Gadamer became Karl Jasper's successor as chair of the philosophy department at the University of Heidelberg, where he worked until his retirement in 1968. It was during his Heidelberg years that Gadamer completed his magnum opus, *Truth and Method*. After retiring, he remained active in the scholarly world by participating in and presiding over various learned societies, writing, and teaching at Boston College, a task which Gadamer regarded as "a second youth." Among the many awards which Gadamer received are the Grand Federal Cross of Merit and Star and honorary doctorates from universities in Ottawa and Washington, D.C.

Influence

Gadamer's contribution to literary criticism is the concept of "philosophical hermeneutics," which has been adopted and applied by numerous scholars. Philosophical hermeneutics and the stress on meaning and truth in a literary text, as opposed to the epistemological knowledge of the natural sciences, are often compared to Jacques Derrida's method of deconstruction, which runs counter to hermeneutics. Deconstructionists have rejected the theory of hermeneutics as the last bastion of "the metaphysics of presence." In the 1970s and 1980s Gadamer's work became a major force in literary criticism in the United States; almost all Gadamer's writings are available in English translation, and many secondary studies on philosophical hermeneutics have been written by American scholars.

Analysis

Although Gadamer's work expands into literary criticism, he is first and foremost a philosopher. Philosophical hermeneutics, his primary legacy, has had a great impact on literary criticism, since its main purpose is to analyze the problems that arise when the reader tries to understand a text. The main questions with which Gadamer is concerned could be formulated as follows: how can one understand tradition as it is provided in texts? Is there such a thing as a truth which goes beyond the truth the "exact" sciences offer? How do the answers to these questions affect humanity's understanding of itself?

The sciences, in Gadamer's view, only provide an explanation (*Erklärung*) of the world, not an understanding (*Verständnis*) – an opposition first used by Wilhelm Dilthey. Gadamer writes in *Truth and Method* that it is his intention "to seek that experience of truth that transcends the sphere of the control of scientific method wherever it is to be found and to inquire into its legitimacy."

Gadamer wants to overcome the hubris of the natural sciences, which for him is the hubris of modern times: the belief that an objective, clear truth which is apparent to everyone can be assured by scientific methodology. His evaluation of the sciences does not acknowledge that a critique of the unquestioned obviousness of scientific methodology and its results was opened up in the 1920s from within the sciences and that since then every responsible scientist would admit that the scientific perspective is only one out of many possible outlooks. Gadamer attempts to hold up the notion that meaning and understanding, and ultimately truth, can be found only in the process of communication (*Verständigung*), either between individuals or, more important for hermeneutics, between a text and its reader. One of his strongest arguments is that each person is part of a tradition (for Gadamer always the philosophical tradition of the Western world) which is responsible for values and prejudices (*Vorurteile*) and therefore influences one's understanding of texts and of the world in general.

In order to understand Gadamer's position, one must consider the tradition of which Gadamer himself is a part: Platonic philosophy and the principles of hermeneutics, from Friedrich Schleiermacher and G. W. F. Hegel to Heidegger. Scholarship on Plato up to the 1920s had been mainly concerned with revealing a systematic philosophy in Plato's dialogues, which were seen as containing a hidden truth beneath the Socratic method of dialogical questioning and answering. The scholars of that period took Plato's ironic approach as a disguise for this truth. For this philosophical school, Aristotle's ethical writings were the first major step toward an "empirical," "objective" way of thinking.

Gadamer, however, believes that Plato's dialogues constitute the paradigmatic hermeneutical attitude in which a human being seeks to understand its world and that truth lies in the Platonic model itself. It must be stressed that Gadamer, rooted in this Platonic background and unlike his opponent Derrida, believes firmly in a truth which is present in the texts of the human tradition. Gadamer does not take part in "the great project of hermeneutic troublemaking," instigated by Friedrich Nietzsche and Søren Kierkegaard. He assumes that texts speak to their readers in a meaningful way about meaningful matters and that each reader has only to obey the hermeneutic rules of understanding in order to engage in a fruitful dialogue with these texts.

Yet what exactly is hermeneutics, and in which way does Gadamer further its theory and practice? The word "hermeneutics" was derived from the Greek god Hermes, who served as messenger for the other gods. Until the nineteenth century, hermeneutics was defined as the art of understanding and interpreting texts. In the Middle Ages the preferred text for hermeneutic exercises was the Bible, and the hermeneut's task was to restore the Bible's original contents and intentions, thus reestablishing its normative authority for the pious reader. Hermeneutics basically dealt with erasing the uncertainties, inconsistencies, and ambiguities of a text. Understanding a text was understanding its contents, an apparently unproblematic venture.

With the advent of secular rationalism in the seventeenth century a variety of texts were explicated. Since rationalistic thinking holds that what can be said can be said clearly, all unexplainable ambiguities in a given text had to be a result of its author's inability to make him- or herself understood.

Hermeneutics' leap into modernity took place in the nineteenth century, with the arrival of both the Romantic and the historicist movements. The Romantic philosopher Friedrich Schleiermacher was the first to stress an author's individual creativity and the problems this poses for the interpreter. For Schleiermacher, a text does not necessarily reveal an everlasting truth; instead, it is simply a particular utterance of a particular author at a particular time. In order to understand fully the author's intention, the hermeneut has to reconstruct the historical circumstances of the author's time period and to delve into this period. A text's meaning is not at all self-evident but has to be explored in the context of its historical conditions. Schleiermacher's concept remained the hermeneutic model well into the twentieth century and was elaborated by Wilhelm Dilthey.

Gadamer, in *Truth and Method*, made Schleiermacher's concept a subject of criticism from a hermeneutic standpoint. For Gadamer, the reconstruction of a certain historical moment is "a pointless undertaking in view of the historicity of our being." He claims that, instead, one must follow Hegel's ideas. For Hegel, historicity is overcome by the self-revelation of the absolute spirit in history, because – according to Gadamer – Hegel posits "the most extreme counter-position to the self-forgetfulness of historical consciousness." Truth is not merely revealed in history; it is experienced as a higher knowledge beyond history. Gadamer's foremost goal is to attain this knowledge.

By adopting Hegel's principle, Gadamer was able to offer a solution to one of the main problems of all hermeneutic efforts since Schleiermacher: the hermeneutic circle. Romantic and historicist hermeneutics had always pointed out that the parts of a literary work (sentences, paragraphs, chapters, and so on) can only be understood in the context of the whole work. Yet this notion clearly rests on circular reasoning: the interpreter is supposed to understand the whole of a text if he or she wants to understand its parts, but the understanding of the whole is precisely what he or she wants to gain by the interpretation of the parts. The problems which the hermeneutic circle necessarily poses are exacerbated by the prejudices of the interpreter, for which mostly his or her historical situation is responsible. The role of these prejudices becomes larger when the hermeneut tries to understand a text which was written under completely different historical conditions.

Like Heidegger and the phenomenological philosopher Edmund Husserl, Gadamer perceives the hermeneutic circle and the prejudices of the interpreter as positive forces. The importance of Heidegger's philosophy is based on Heidegger's insight into the historicity of human life, a historicity which is ruled by "a past [the human being] did not create and a future over which it has no control." Historicity, which Heidegger called "thrownness into the world," cannot be escaped, not even by the exact sciences that derive their claim of objectivity from the denial of this historicity. It is to Gadamer's credit to have placed the historicity of understanding at the center of his hermeneutics as the condition for any understanding. With his theory, the humanities again emerge as the field in which humankind tries to define itself.

To understand history and to learn from it no longer means to bury it under historistic falsifications, but to claim and presuppose the truth, which can be found in history and in the human tradition. Still, the truth in history must be considered with the truth the historian or the interpreter of literature knows already, leading to a higher truth. Gadamer calls this process the "fusion of horizons" of the interpreter and of the author of the text in question.

For Gadamer, the privileged experience of truth is the experience of art, an experience which exceeds any truth methodological or epistemological knowledge can provide. At this point Gadamer becomes especially important for literary criticism: "That truth is experienced through a work of art that we cannot attain in any other way constitutes the philosophic importance of art. . . . The experience of art issues the most pressing challenge to the scientific consciousness to acknowledge its own limits."

In adherence to this concept, Gadamer commences *Truth and Method* with a systematic critique of idealistic aesthetics, which had placed the experience of art within the subject and had understood itself, in the tradition of Immanuel Kant, as a science of art "that would produce the truth *about* art but could not acknowledge the truth *of* art." It is this truth *of* art, as a means in the process of understanding humanity, with which Gadamer is concerned.

The proper mode of being in which one can experience the truth of art is the mode of play. Yet, unlike Kant or Friedrich Schiller, Gadamer does not see play as a subjective activity opposed to the objective attitude of science; he sees it as a mode in which one can "lose" oneself in a literary text, thus allowing the text to "speak" about its truth, an "objectivistic" enterprise in Gadamer's opinion: when "we speak of play, this refers neither to the attitude nor even to the state of mind of the creator or of those enjoying art, nor to the freedom of a subjectivity expressed in play, but to the mode of being of the work of art itself."

After criticizing both traditional aesthetics and hermeneutics and claiming as fundamental for understanding the search for and acceptance of truth in art and literature, Gadamer widens his view by stressing the importance of the medium in which truth, as Gadamer conceives it, reveals itself: language. He reduces his standpoint to the simple Heideggerian statement: "Being that can be understood is language." To interpret a text and to understand it means always to "translate" it from one language into another, from the one of the original text into the one of the interpreter, a proceeding, which, as shown, ultimately leads to the "fusion of horizons."

By rooting the hermeneutic process in the dialogical situation of language, Gadamer returns to his own beginnings: truth lies in the dialogues of Plato and in all the texts of the human tradition. Being a philosophical hermeneut means to take part in a dialogue with this tradition and to listen to its truth.

Principal criticism

Plato und die Dichter, 1934 (*Plato and the Poets*, 1976)
Wahrheit und Methode, 1960 (*Truth and Method*, 1975)
Kleine Schriften I–IV, 1967–1977
Philosophical Hermeneutics, 1976
Die Aktualität des Schönen, 1977 (*The Relevance of the Beautiful*, 1986)
Gesammelte Werke, 1985
Literature and Philosophy in Dialogue. Essays in German Literary Theory, 1994

Other major works and literary forms

Hans-Georg Gadamer's only published work outside the realm of philosophical or hermeneutical study is his autobiography, *Philosophische Lehrjahre* (1977; *Philosophical Apprenticeships*, 1985). In this work Gadamer gives an account of his intellectual development from his early Breslau and Marburg years to the 1970s. Included are vignettes of some of his teachers, colleagues, and friends, many ranking among the most influential German philosophers of the twentieth century: Paul Natorp, Max Scheler, Rudolf Bultmann, Karl Jaspers, and above all, Martin Heidegger, whom Gadamer admired and whose influence is evident throughout Gadamer's work.

NONFICTION

Platos dialektische Ethik, 1931
Hegels Dialektik: Fünf hermeneutische Studien, 1971 (*Hegel's Dialectic: Five Hermeneutical Studies*, 1976)
Philosophische Lehrjahre, 1977 (autobiography; *Philosophical Apprenticeships*, 1985)
Die Idee des Guten zwischen Plato und Aristotle, 1978 (*The Idea of the Good in Platonic-Aristotelian Philosophy*, 1986)
Dialogue and Dialectic: Eight Hermeneutical Studies on Plato, 1980
Reason in the Age of Science, 1981

Further reading

Bleicher, Josef, ed. *Contemporary Hermeneutics: Hermeneutics as Method, Philosophy, and Critique*, 1980.
Hahn, Lewis Edwin, ed. *The Philosophy of Hans-Georg Gadamer* (The Library of Living Philosophers XXIV), 1997.
Hollinger, Robert, ed. *Hermeneutics and Praxis*, 1985.

Shapiro, Gary, and Alan Sica, eds. *Hermeneutics: Questions and Prospects*, 1984.
Silverman, Hugh D. *Gadamer and Hermeneutics*, 1991.
Wachtershauser, Brice R., ed. *Hermeneutics and Modern Philosophy*, 1986.
Warnke, Georgia. *Gadamer: Hermeneutics, Tradition, and Reason*, 1987.
Weinsheimer, Joel C. *Gadamer's Hermeneutics: A Reading of "Truth and Method,"* 1985.
——. *Philosophical Hermeneutics and Literary Theory*, 1991.

MICHAEL J. BÜSGES

See also Heidegger; Hermeneutics

John Gardner

American novelist, translator, and critic

Born: Batavia, New York; July 21, 1933
Died: Susquehanna, Pennsylvania; September 14, 1982

Biography

John Champlin Gardner, Jr., was born on July 21, 1933, in the dairy farming community of Batavia in western New York. Strongly influenced by his father, a dairy farmer and lay preacher, and his mother, a teacher of English, Gardner, nicknamed Bud (Welsh for "poet"), took an early interest in storytelling. The death of his younger brother, Gilbert, in a farm accident on April 4, 1945, became the single most formative event in his life and the subject of one his finest and most illuminating short stories, "Redemption" (1977).

Gardner attended DePauw University for two years, where he majored in chemistry. After marrying Joan Patterson, a cousin, on June 6, 1953, he transferred to Washington University in St. Louis where he began his writing career in earnest under the tutelage of Jarvis Thurston. The doubleness of his career first became noticeable during his graduate studies at the University of Iowa, where Gardner studied medieval English literature under John C. McGalliard while attending classes at the university's Writer's Workshop, writing a surprisingly good novel that was accepted as his Ph.D. dissertation. Gardner began teaching at Oberlin College, the first of his many academic appointments.

The publication of his third novel, *Grendel*, in 1971, brought Gardner to international literary prominence. His rise to fame continued with the publication of three best-selling novels, including *October Light* (1976), which won the National Book Critics Circle award for fiction. Gardner's life then took a number of turns for the worse: the breakup of his marriage, colon cancer, troubles with the Internal Revenue Service, a dismaying plagiarism charge that *Newsweek* thought fit to publicize, and finally the uproar which followed the publication of *On Moral Fiction* in 1978. Like one of his own characters, he somehow continued, becoming director of the writing program at the State University of New York at Binghamton, marrying the poet Liz Rosenberg (they divorced amicably in 1982), and continuing to write and devote himself to his moral fiction cause until his death in a motorcycle accident on September 14, 1982.

Influence

The sudden and dramatic shift that occurred in American fiction from the innovative postmodernist "texts" that seemed to dominate the literary scene in the 1960s and 1970s to the more realistic and more "conventional" stories and novels of the 1980s is far too complex a phenomenon to be attributed to any single cause, but certainly of the various factors that contributed to this shift Gardner's tireless efforts in promoting his theory of "moral fiction" must be ranked among the most important. Those who had grown weary of aesthetic experimentation or who had been disturbed by the postmodernist challenge applauded Gardner's critique, while those who had embraced innovation indiscriminately and who had come to accept wholeheartedly what art critic Harold Rosenberg termed "the tradition of the new" derided Gardner's efforts to turn the aesthetic clock back. Although Gardner cannot be judged a "major" twentieth-century critic, the proof of his importance is to be found in the fact that even those who derided his views felt compelled to address themselves to the issues Gardner raised. A less fortunate result of Gardner's nearly messianic desire to save the contemporary novel has been the way in which his most hostile as well as his most sympathetic reviewers and critics have applied his moral fiction theory rather reductively to his own later works in an attempt either to undermine or to buttress both his credibility as a critic and his reputation as a novelist.

Analysis

Although his interests, aims, and methods remained virtually the same over the course of his career as a literary critic, Gardner's criticism is best understood as falling into two unequal parts. The first begins with the publication of *The Forms of Fiction*, edited with Lennis Dunlap, in 1962, and ends with the appearance of *The Poetry of Chaucer* and *The Life and Times of Chaucer* in 1977. Aside from a number of reviews of contemporary fiction, the bulk of Gardner's critical writings during this period involve more or less academic articles and books published in scholarly journals, such as *PMLA*, or by university presses. The seemingly academic aim of and audience for these writings is rather misleading, however, for throughout this period, and indeed throughout his entire career, Gardner considered his role as scholar-critic to be identical with his role as teacher-mentor. It is significant that his first book was *The Forms of Fiction*, an anthology designed for use in undergraduate literature classes and successful enough for the publisher, Random House, to reprint at least five times over the next five years. The works which followed, modernized versions of the complete works of the Gawain-Poet and a number of other Middle English poems, fully attest Gardner's teacherly side, making these works both available and accessible to a much wider and less narrowly academic audience than that of academic specialists.

Their titles notwithstanding, *The Construction of the Wakefield Cycle* and *The Construction of Christian Poetry in Old English* are intended for a similar reader – the interested student – and like so many of Gardner's writings, both fictional and critical, manage to appeal to two essentially distinct audiences simultaneously. In these works it is Gardner's enthusiasm that evidences itself most forcefully, reclaiming scholarship from the hermeticism of mere pedantry. Another and no less important feature of these writings is Gardner's habitual deference to the literary artist, no matter how anonymous that artist may be: the Gawain-Poet, for example, or the Wakefield Master. For Gardner, as for James Joyce's Stephen Dedalus, the artist makes no mistakes. Thus his critical writings evidence Gardner's belief in the aesthetic wholeness of not only individual works but also entire cycles of poems and plays.

These critical assumptions and interests come to special fruition in the two books on Chaucer. Gardner's reputation as at once a serious and a popular novelist helps to explain the widespread attention that these books received, but it was largely Gardner's characteristically enthusiastic approach that gained for them – the biography in particular – a similarly enthusiastic response from newspaper and magazine reviewers. Academic reviewers tended to be much more guarded in approving books that are less studies than celebrations, in which Gardner's analysis of themes, techniques, and historical and intellectual currents manages to entertain as well as illuminate. Gardner relies more on broad synthesis and plausible assertion than on scholarly objectivity and narrow specialization of approach, all of which is especially noticeable in his mingling of fact and fiction in the biography.

The Chaucer volumes also clarify one aspect of Gardner's critical method that is for the most part only implicit in the earlier critical works – though fully obvious in the novels *Grendel* and *The Wreckage of Agathon* (1970) – namely, Gardner's reading of the past in terms of the present, and vice versa. In his reading of Chaucer, Gardner emphasizes the ways in which uncertainty, that most contemporary of fixations – typified in Werner Heisenberg's principle of indeterminacy – also characterized the age of Chaucer. It did not, however, exert the same debilitating effect on Chaucer's art that, Gardner believed, it has on contemporary writers, for whom it has become, in Donald Barthelme's judgment, the age's Song of Songs.

Although their ostensible subjects may be separated by some six centuries, the one year which separates the publication of the Chaucer books from Gardner's most controversial work, *On Moral Fiction*, serves to gauge more accurately the closeness of Gardner's approach to both criticism and the literary arts. *On Moral Fiction* became the focus of an international debate on the contemporary arts. Yet the book must be understood as only the most visible manifestation of Gardner's participation in that debate – a participation that began in the late 1960s when he began work on his "moral fiction" manuscript and that has continued after his death with the publication of *On Becoming a Novelist* and *The Art of Fiction. On Moral Fiction* summarizes Gardner's critique of what had gone wrong in both the contemporary arts (fiction in particular) and contemporary criticism and of what both fiction and criticism should be. No doubt Gardner would have run less risk of having his views misunderstood had he given his book another title. His moral fiction theory made its first appearance just as Jerry Falwell's religiously fundamental and politically reactionary organization, the Moral Majority, was making its presence felt in American life. The surprising fact is not that an avant-garde writer such as John Barth should have attacked Gardner's polemic as "a shrill pitch to the literary right," but that the polemic should have come from a writer who had himself often been discussed as a major postmodernist writer.

What Gardner means when he says that fiction is, or should be, "moral" requires some explanation, especially given the fact that many of his opponents seem to have seized on the word "moral" without taking the trouble to understand Gardner's particular use of it. Moral fiction is that which affirms life, preserving what is best:

> presenting valid models for imitation, eternal verities worth keeping in mind, and a benevolent vision of the possible which can inspire human beings toward virtue, toward life affirmation as opposed to destruction or indifference.

Gardner's vision is not of what is – which is chaos – but of what should be – which is the realism of true, or moral, art.

The function of art is, then, to instruct, not didactically as some of Gardner's critics have charged, but instead by its very process: by creating in the reader's mind a vivid and continuous dream which duplicates for the reader the same process of discovery by which the artist has discovered a moral, or a truth, that cannot be explained but only felt – understood intuitively rather than known rationally. Writing is, therefore, a mode or process of thought, a way of testing ideas and values that is at once linguistic, aesthetic, and ethical.

Gardner conceives of the artist in similarly exalted terms, as the poet-priest whose task it is to discover, record, and affirm the truth; the artist is, in short, Percy Bysshe Shelley's poet as legislator for all humankind. Not surprisingly, against such a high standard, virtually all contemporary writers fail. While it is true that Gardner may be loading the dice by holding up Homer, Dante, and (in part) Leo Tolstoi as his literary heroes, his critique of the contemporary novelist's shortcomings merits attention, for the contemporary writer does indeed seem to be, as Gardner claims, "short on significant belief."

In his fiction as in his criticism, Gardner makes clear his beliefs, especially in characterization. (Plot, he contends, gives the character something to do, and setting somewhere to do it.) Thus he takes to task those writers who either reduce their characters to mere vehicles for espousing preformed ideas, especially ones involving some melodramatic opposition between good and evil (E. L. Doctorow), or who resort to caricature (Stanley Elkin) and cartoon (Kurt Vonnegut), or substitute style for substance, linguistic surface for moral depth (William Gass, for example, who, like Roland Barthes, contends that a character is nothing more than the repetition or intersection of certain verbal patterns or markers). What Gardner objects to is not actually the fiction of Doctorow, Elkin, Gass, and others like them, but the failure on the part of these writers and of critics to distinguish trivial art from true art. Their failure to do so is a sign of the democratically pluralistic times, a general leveling downward in art as in life, and a corresponding cynical denial of all tradition, including that of morality as well as of moral fiction. The task of the true critic is not to succumb to the age by merely describing and analyzing a work but instead to explain and evaluate it: to say not merely what the work does but what it ought to do, morally as well as aesthetically.

Gardner's theory of moral fiction is part of a more widespread if often less vociferous dissatisfaction with the state of the arts, of criticism, and of American political, social, and cultural life in general in the second half of the 1970s; witness the publication of two widely discussed and similarly controversial, if more rigorously argued, works: Christopher Lasch's *The Culture of Narcissism* (1978) and Gerald Graff's *Literature Against Itself: Literary Ideas in Modern Society* (1979). Although short on intellectual rigor and scholarly substance, Gardner's position gained strength from the sheer audacity of his sweeping polemic, from his unflagging efforts to promote what was less a position than a cause on campuses across the country, and from the attention he received in newspapers, magazines, scholarly journals and forums, and even on television, including an appearance on *The Dick Cavett Show*.

The immediate and overwhelming impact of Gardner's criticism on literature and on literary criticism is a fairly simple matter to assess. Its long-range effect is another and more difficult matter altogether. His efforts to save contemporary fiction from self-destructing by trivializing itself and thus making fiction culturally marginal brought about a counterattack that successfully undermined his reputation and his credibility both as a novelist and as a critic. As a result, he turned to effecting a change in that literary climate by devoting himself more fully to teaching young writers at SUNY-Binghamton and at Bread Loaf, to preparing his notes for these writing workshops into books (*On Becoming a Novelist* and *The Art of Fiction*), and to publishing his students' work in *MSS*, the literary magazine he had founded and revitalized and in which, ironically, he had published one of William Gass' earliest stories. As for Gardner's efforts to effect a change in the course of literary criticism – to make it less an academic specialization and more a means for cultural as well as literary evaluation – that has largely come to nothing, as the rise of semiotic and poststructuralist theories and methods eloquently, though at times obscurely, attests.

Principal criticism

The Complete Works of the Gawain-Poet, 1965
The Alliterative "Morte Arthure," "The Owl and the Nightingale," and Five Other Middle English Poems, 1971
The Construction of the Wakefield Cycle, 1974
The Construction of Christian Poetry in Old English, 1975
The Poetry of Chaucer, 1977
The Life and Times of Chaucer, 1977
On Moral Fiction, 1978
On Becoming a Novelist, 1983
The Art of Fiction, 1984
On Writers and Writing, 1994

Other major works and literary forms

John Gardner was as versatile as he was prolific. Best known for his novels and most notorious for his critique of the contemporary arts, *On Moral Fiction*, Gardner also published two collections of short fiction, an epic poem, four books for children, a volume of poems, a radio play, opera libretti, and translations of *Gilgamesh* and a number of Middle English poems – all of this in addition to a steady stream of academic books and articles as well as numerous reviews and essays in mainstream publications such as *The New York Times Book Review* and the *Saturday Review*. Since Gardner's death in 1982, the outpouring has slowed but hardly stopped. There have been two more novels, two books of advice to aspiring young writers, a translation, a collection of literary reviews and essays, and the promise of more to come from novelist Nicholas Delbanco, executor of Gardner's literary estate.

NOVELS
The Resurrection, 1966
The Wreckage of Agathon, 1970
Grendel, 1971
The Sunlight Dialogues, 1972
Nickel Mountain: A Pastoral Novel, 1973
October Light, 1976
In the Suicide Mountains, 1977
Freddy's Book, 1980
Mickelsson's Ghosts, 1982
"Stillness" and "Shadows," 1986 (with Nicholas Delbanco)

SHORT FICTION
The King's Indian: Stories and Tales, 1974
The Art of Living and Other Stories, 1981

PLAYS
Death and the Maiden, 1979
Frankenstein, 1979 (libretto)
Rumpelstiltskin, 1979 (libretto)
William Wilson, 1979 (libretto)

RADIO PLAY
The Temptation Game, 1977

POETRY
Jason and Medeia, 1973
Poems, 1978

CHILDREN'S LITERATURE
Dragon, Dragon and Other Tales, 1975
Gudgekin the Thistle Girl and Other Tales, 1976
A Child's Bestiary, 1977
The King of the Hummingbirds and Other Tales, 1977

ANTHOLOGY
The Forms of Fiction, 1962 (edited with Lennis Dunlap)

Further reading

Cowart, David. *Arches and Light: The Fiction of John Gardner*, 1983.
Ekelund, Bo G. *In the Pathless Forest: John Gardner's Literary Project*, 1995.
Henderson, Jeff, and Robert E. Lowrey, eds. *Thor's Hammer: Essays on John Gardner*, 1985.
Howell, John. *John Gardner: A Bibliographical Profile*, 1980.
——. *Understanding John Gardner*, 1993.
McWilliams, Dean. *John Gardner*, 1990.
Morace, Robert A. *John Gardner: An Annotated Secondary Bibliography*, 1984.
——, and Kathryn VanSpanckeren, eds. *John Gardner: Critical Perspectives*, 1982.
Morris, Gregory L. *A World of Order and Light: The Fiction of John Gardner*, 1983.

ROBERT A. MORACE

See also American Literary Theory: Twentieth Century

George Gascoigne

English writer and critic

Born: Cardington, Bedfordshire, England; c. 1525
Died: Stamford, Lincolnshire, England; October 7, 1577

Biography

The connection between George Gascoigne's life and his literature and criticism was unusually close: much of his œuvre is notable for its conspicuous autobiographical elements. Contrapuntal themes of pride and humility appear repeatedly. Associated with the pride Gascoigne felt in his education – youthful studies under a fine tutor, attendance at Trinity College, Cambridge University, and two periods a decade apart at Gray's Inn – is Gascoigne's exposure to classical and contemporary literature. (Both *Jocasta* and *Supposes* were produced at Gray's Inn.) In his criticism, he expressed admiration for intellectual prowess: invention, originality, ingenuity in handling literary conventions and genres, and what was variously called *euphues*, "copy" (for *copia verborum*, or ready copiousness of words), or *sprezzatura* (quickness and facility in literary composition).

Gascoigne's regret and sense of humility are apparent in his references to his misspent youth, his failure to pursue the legal profession, his frustration (as well as near bankruptcy) in attempting to succeed as courtier, and the hard lessons of his military career. His active service as captain in the Low Countries was not devoid of honor, as intimated in the motto concluding many of his literary works (*Tam Marti quam Mercurio*, "as much by Mars or war as by Mercury or the Arts"). Nevertheless, the deception, betrayal, defeat, capture, and inhumanity he experienced in campaigns were chastening, as was Gascoigne's reason for enlistment in the first place (to escape creditors and a pending legal charge). Consequently, his war poems "The Fruites of Warre" and "Gascoigne's Voyage into Holland" emphasize moral uprightness and plain speaking. Indeed, these concepts recur in his nonmilitary works also, particularly in works dealing with the falsities in court life.

Influence

Ultimately, Gascoigne's importance in the history of literary criticism lies in the impetus he helped provide in the beginnings of the English Renaissance. The range and acuity of the critical comment scattered throughout his literary corpus is remarkable. Poet Michael Drayton's disparagement in 1627 aside, Gascoigne was admired widely in his era; his criticism was especially influential in treatises by John Grange, King James VI of Scotland (later James I), and William Webbe. Gascoigne's literary works were mentioned approvingly in prefaces, letters, or disquisitions by Edmund Spenser, Gabriel Harvey, Thomas Nashe, George Puttenham, and Francis Meres. Apparently, Gascoigne's literary criticism, explicit and implicit, had a wide and influential circulation among educated readers and writers of the time.

Like many critical theorists (particularly those who are also creative writers or authors of practical criticism), Gascoigne is not altogether consistent in his ideas, shifting stances and even contradicting himself throughout his œuvre. This variety, as well as the fact that his concepts provide a distillation of Renaissance views of literature, lends Gascoigne's criticism much of its interest.

Analysis

Probably Gascoigne's foremost concern as a critic is literature's capacity for moral didacticism. Reflecting an affective theory of literature, Gascoigne's didacticism is conveyed even in the subtitle of the first edition of his collected works, *A Hundreth Sundrie Flowres* . . ., "Yielding Sundrie Sweet Savors of Tragical, Comical, and Moral Discourses, Both

Pleasant and Profitable to the Well-Smelling Noses of Learned Readers." The Horatian concept of blended "pleasant and profitable" recurs in the third preface to the first edition of *The Discourse of the Adventures Passed by Master F.J.*, and again in his praise of "pleasant" and "pithy" aspects of a work by Saint Augustine which he translated for inclusion in his late tract *A Delicate Diet for Daintiemouthde Droonkardes*. To the accusation that autobiographical accounts of misdeeds in literature may allure rather than warn, Gascoigne replied in numerous prefaces, explaining that the spider may derive its nourishment and poison from the flower, while the bee its sustenance and honey from the weed or thistle. Further, Gascoigne appealed to authority and tradition, citing the verse in Romans 15 in which Saint Paul says that "all that is written is written for our instruction."

By 1575, however, Gascoigne had begun moving toward a moral repudiation of his early courtly poetry and toward the elevation of satire to the highest literary rank. In his prefaces to the 1575 works, Gascoigne not only concedes the existence of some "wanton words" in his poetry and fiction but also divides his works into the three categories of flowers, herbs, and weeds, corresponding to their appeal, medicinal value, or dangerousness. A long allegorical passage in *The Steele Glas, a Satyre* differentiates between court poetry and straightforward speech: after rape and lingualectomy by the courtier Vain Delight and his entourage, Satyra, sister of Poesis, aims to reveal truth. "With the stumps of my reproved tongue,/ I may sometimes Reprovers' deeds reprove,/ and sing a verse to make them see themselves." In the prefaces to *The Droome of Doomes Day*, *A Delicate Diet for Daintie-mouthde Droonkardes*, and *The Tale of Hemetes the Hermit*, Gascoigne rejects his former "*thriftless book of Posies*" in favor of satire and the literature of divinity or moral philosophy. In song 1 of *The Griefe of Joye*, Gascoigne complains that the skill and style needed to do justice to his difficult subject have been weakened by his youthful misbehavior and early "wanton rhymes," while in song 2 he makes a refutational roll call of the ladies from his encomiastic courtly poems.

Vivid imagery and actions, as well as explicit statements, in Gascoigne's works constantly refer to literature's active moral function. For example, he summarizes his aim in "The Fruites of Warre" as "I meant no more, but modestly/ To warn the wise." Pervading Gascoigne's œuvre (not only *The Steele Glas* and *The Glasse of Governement*) are scores of references to looking glasses or mirrors, not so much suggestive of accurate representation of nature as of the medieval notion of a reflection of mankind's moral state. Further, Gascoigne uses the martial imagery of pen as spear, lance, or sword in witty allusions to his military service. At other times, he envisions his poetry as a goshawk attacking vermin in a field or as a thorn being used as a toothpick to clean people's mouths. In *The Glasse of Governement*, the contrast between proper and improper uses of literature is embodied in two younger brothers who obey their teacher's request to make his precepts memorable and palatable by adapting them to verse and their two elder disobedient brothers who indulge in the composition of amorous and grandiose verse.

"Certayne Notes of Instruction Concerning the Making of Verse or Rhyme in English" focuses on the concept of invention and its correlatives. Discovering a sound, ingenious, and original idea on which to base one's literary work for Gascoigne takes precedence even over style and meter. The tension between inventiveness and didacticism is acknowledged in one of the prefaces to *The Posies of George Gascoigne Esquire*. Here Gascoigne remarks that he allowed the first publication of his works "only to the end men might see my Method and manner of writing" and that in the new edition he is "desirous" of showing "all men . . . the reformation of my mind." However, in the following preface, he proudly designates one category of his works "Flowers because . . . they have . . . in them . . . some rare invention and Method before not commonly used." Similarly, the fictitious editor of *The Discourse of the Adventures Passed by Master F.J.* repeatedly commends "the quickness of invention" and "good store of deep invention" of the title character's poems.

Repeatedly, Gascoigne extols originality, directing especially pointed barbs at those who adhere slavishly to Petrarchan conventions. Though in several works Gascoigne acknowledges the authority and traditions represented by the Bible, Lucilius, Cicero ("Tully"), Geoffrey Chaucer, and Petrarch, dull imitation is reproved. The title character of *The Discourse of the Adventures Passed by Master F.J.* is praised by editor G. T. because the former "is no borrower of inventions," while Mistress Elinor, another character, is obliquely condemned for insincerity, deception, and wickedness. Her lack of originality is shown by her dependence on her male secretary to write letters for her.

Invention's link with style and poetic diction is suggested in "Certayne Notes of Instruction Concerning the Making of Verse or Rhyme in English" by the observation that the poet's subject matter needs to be "finely handled," with study and care devoted to "some depth of device . . . and some figures in the handling thereof." Similarly, in *The Complaynt of Phylomene*, Nemesis enjoins the poet to "remember all my words,/ And bear them well in mind,/ And make thereof a metaphor." Besides avoiding mindless imitation of Petrarchan clichés, good style includes "proper vocables," "apt epithets," "pleasant words," "store of monosyllables," and appropriate figures and tropes. Excessive ornamentation, however, is to be avoided.

Gascoigne repeatedly advocates, explicitly or implicitly, plainness in language, though not to the complete exclusion of wit. The words "rough," "ragged," "plain," "witless words," and "plainsong" are used in associating ornateness with deception, and plainness with honesty, truth, and virtue. Gascoigne employs homely images to convey his convictions; for example, an old-fashioned steel mirror is better than a fancy crystal one (*The Steele Glas*). In another piece, he says, "Plain dealing biddeth me to cast/ This bone [plain advice] amid my doggerel rhyme." The cleverness of Gascoigne's pun on "bone" and "doggerel" demonstrates how the plain style need not be barren.

The concept of literary purity – basing the subjects and language of literary works on native language and national myths – is incipient in Gascoigne's criticism. Monosyllabic native English words (in contrast to "ink-horn" or polysyllabic Latinate terms) and idiomatic English syntax (the adjective before, not after, the noun it modifies) are to be preferred; strange, obsolete, archaic, and obscure words are to be eschewed as much as possible. These are not rigid rules, however, for at times the pragmatic Gascoigne allows exceptions – and confesses some of his own. Indeed, Gascoigne often supplies a marginal annotation or translation in his literary works of the occasional Latin, Italian, French, Dutch, or archaic English word he uses.

In "Certayne Notes of Instruction Concerning the Making of Verse or Rhyme in English," Gascoigne promotes monosyllabic words not only for their purity but also for their metrical convenience in creating regular accentual patterns in poetic lines. While Gascoigne's comments on prosody are not as comprehensive as those in later treatises and sometimes fail to account for meaningful irregularities, they form a solid foundation, by a skilled poet, on which to build. Significantly omitted in the treatise is a treatment of blank verse, though paradoxically in the rhymed preface to *The Steele Glas*, Gascoigne discusses it, asserting that only it is powerful enough to breach the enemy tower of vice.

Gascoigne advocated the concept of accentual rather than classical syllabic or quantitative verse, a position that later English poets would come to take for granted. His definition of the sonnet as a fourteen-line form also eventually gained acceptance. His practice sometimes contradicted his theory, for Gascoigne in his poetry often borders on excessive alliteration. Arguably, however, his "rumbling rhyme in raffe and ruff" or "thundering in Rym, Ram, Ruff by letter" (his own satiric characterizations) aims at ethopoeia: the depiction of character in a heightened, especially mournful, emotional state.

A final set of critical topics broached in several of Gascoigne's works includes matters of decorum, genre, and unity. Decorum has to do with a work's suitability to its occasion and subject. Hence, in "The Fruites of Warre" the "verse is rough" since "it treateth of rough matters"; again, "a doleful speech becomes a dumpish man" ("The Fruite of Fetters"). Sonnets, Gascoigne asserts, are to be "pleasant" or "sweet" and are suited for love or "discourse." Gascoigne warns against indecorum – intermixing different styles or losing sight of the literary work's founding concept.

Ultimately, while his didacticism has fallen out of favor, in his formalist emphasis on style and unity, Gascoigne's critical heritage extends to the New Criticism of the mid-twentieth century and beyond, in critics' attention (in American poet-critic John Ciardi's memorable phrase) to "how a poem means."

Principal criticism

Preface to *A Hundreth Sundrie Flowres Bounde up in One Small Poesie*, 1573

Passages in "The Passion of a Lover," 1573, "Epitaph upon Captain Bourcher," 1573, "The Delectable History of Dan Bartholmew of Bath," 1573, "The Fruites of Warre: Dulce Bellum Inexpertis," 1573, "In Praise of a Countess," 1573, "The Lover Declareth His Affection," 1573, "Gascoigne's Counsel to Duglasse Dive," 1573, "Gascoigne's Counsel to Master Bartholmew Withipoll," 1573, "Gascoigne's Voyage into Holland," 1573, *The Discourse of the Adventures Passed by Master F.J.*, 1573, and *The Glasse of Governement*, 1575

Prefaces to *The Posies of George Gascoigne Esquire*, 1575

"Certayne Notes of Instruction Concerning the Making of Verse or Rhyme in English," 1575

Passages in *The Steele Glas, a Satyre*, 1576, and *The Griefe of Joye*, 1576

Prefaces to *The Tale of Hemetes the Hermit*, 1579

Other major works and literary forms

Known primarily as a pioneer in English literature, George Gascoigne produced firsts in all four main literary genres. He wrote prototypes of the sonnet sequence ("The Looks of a Lover Forsaken," "The Fruit of Reconciliation," "David Saluteth Bersabe"). *The Steele Glas, a Satyre* (1576) represented the first original nondramatic blank verse and one of the earliest satires in English. Gascoigne also experimented with Ovidian narrative verse in *The Complaynt of Phylomene* (1576). *The Discourse of the Adventures Passed by Master F.J.* (1573) is an unusual early novella. His dramatic works include the Greek tragedy *Jocasta*, coauthored with Francis Kinwelmershe (1566; based on works by Euripides and Lodovico Dolce), the prose comedy *Supposes* (1566; based on Ludovico Ariosto's *I suppositi*), and *The Glasse of Governement* (1575). His nonfiction war correspondence was published in *The Spoyle of Antwerpe* (1576).

NOVEL

The Discourse of the Adventures Passed by Master F.J., 1573 (revised as *The Pleasant Fable of Ferdinando Jeronimi and Leonora de Valasco*, 1575)

PLAYS

Jocasta, 1566 (with Francis Kinwelmershe; based on Lodovico Dolce's play *Giocasta*)

Supposes, 1566 (based on Ludovico Ariosto's play *I suppositi*)

A Devise of a Maske for the Right Honorable Viscount Mountacute, 1572

The Glasse of Governement, 1575

The Princelye Pleasures at Kenelworth Castle, 1575 (with others)

POETRY
"The Fruites of Warre: Dulce Bellum Inexpertis," 1573
The Complaynt of Phylomene, 1576
The Griefe of Joye, 1576
The Steele Glas, a Satyre, 1576

NONFICTION
A Delicate Diet for Daintiemouthde Droonkardes, 1576
The Spoyle of Antwerpe, 1576

TRANSLATIONS
The Droome of Doomes Day, 1576 (of Pope Innocent III's theological treatise *De contemptu mundi* and two other unidentified works)
The Tale of Hemetes the Hermit, 1579 (Latin, Italian, and French renderings of an anonymous English romance)

MISCELLANEOUS
A Hundreth Sundrie Flowers Bounde up in One Small Poesie, 1573 (poetry and prose; revised as *The Posies of George Gascoigne Esquire*, 1575)

Further reading

Atkins, J. W. H. *English Literary Criticism: The Renasence*, 1947.
Cave, T. *The Cornucopian Text*, 1979.
Ing, Elizabeth. *Elizabethan Lyrics: A Study in the Development of English Metres and Their Relation to Poetic Effect*, 1951.
Johnson, Ronald C. *George Gascoigne*, 1972.
Kinney, A. F. *Humanist Poetics: Thought, Rhetoric and Fiction in Sixteenth-Century England*, 1986.
Prouty, C. T. *George Gascoigne: Elizabethan Courtier, Soldier, and Poet*, 1942.
Schelling, Felix. *The Life and Writings of George Gascoigne*, 1892.
Schott, Penelope S. "The Narrative Stance in 'The Adventures of Master F.J.': Gascoigne as Critic of His Own Poems," in *Renaissance Quarterly*. XXIX (1976), pp. 369–377.
Thompson, John. *The Founding of English Metre*, 1961.

NORMAN PRINSKY

Henry Louis Gates, Jr.

American critic and editor

Born: Keyser, West Virginia; September 16, 1950

Biography

Henry Louis Gates, Jr., was born in the hospital at Keyser, West Virginia, on September 16, 1950, and grew up in nearby Piedmont, West Virginia. The two small towns are located on the Potomac River across from western Maryland in the picturesque Appalachian Mountains. His mother was a housewife and his father a union official for the United Papermakers and Paperworkers of America. As a young man, Gates served in the Anglican Mission Hospital in Kilimatinde, Tanzania, and in the West Virginia gubernatorial campaign of John D. Rockefeller IV. Gates graduated *summa cum laude* from Yale University in 1973, with a B.A. in American political history; he spent the next two years studying literature at Cambridge University, where he came under the influence of Wole Soyinka, there as a Fellow for one year. During vacations Gates was a staff correspondent for the London bureau of *Time* magazine. He received his M.A. from Cambridge in 1974 and his Ph.D. in 1979, with a dissertation entitled "History and Theory of Afro-American Literary Criticism, 1773–1831."

Gates returned to Yale in 1976 as a lecturer and became an assistant professor of English and director of undergraduate Afro-American studies in 1979. That same year he married Sharon Adams, a potter, and they have since had two daughters, Maude and Elizabeth. In January, 1985, Gates moved to Cornell University, where he became professor of English, comparative literature, and African studies, and in January, 1988, he was appointed to an endowed chair, becoming the W. E. B. Du Bois Professor of Literature.

Gates has received numerous other honors, including early fellowships to go to Africa and to study at Yale and Cambridge. He has also received grants from the National Endowment for the Humanities, an A. Whitney Griswold Fellowship, a Rockefeller Foundation Fellowship, a Whitney Humanities Center Fellowship, and the much-desired, five-year MacArthur Foundation Prize Fellowship (1981–1986). The award of which Gates is most proud, however, is the Zora Neale Hurston Award for Creative Scholarship (1986), named after the influential Harlem Renaissance writer.

Influence

Gates is perhaps the leading black literary theorist in the United States, although a friendly contender for this honor is Houston A. Baker, Jr., the author of *Blues, Ideology, and Afro-American Literature: A Vernacular Theory* (1984) and other works. Indeed, Gates acknowledges Baker as an important influence on his thinking. Both are spokesmen for black American literature, upon which their literary theorizing is centered. Their respective theories, however, have interesting contrasting origins: whereas Baker began with what is called the Black Aesthetic, based on black consciousness and rejection of white culture, Gates began with an academic immersion in the fashionable critical movements coming out of Europe, notably formalism, structuralism, and deconstruction. Gradually their work has grown closer, with both emphasizing the importance of the black vernacular, analogies to black music, and the sometimes painful symbiotic relationship of black American literature and the white literary tradition.

Analysis

After studying history as an undergraduate at Yale, Gates was introduced to literary theory by his Cambridge tutor, John Holloway, who encouraged Gates to use contemporary literary theory as a means of analyzing Afro-American literature. In the introduction to *Figures in Black: Words, Signs, and the "Racial" Self*, Gates attaches considerable significance to these facts: using contemporary literary theory to analyze black American literature enabled Gates to distance himself suitably from both the theory and the literature. He found it difficult to identify with theories – "Russian Formalism, French Structuralism, Anglo-American Practical Criticism, among others" – that treated black literature as noncanonical; thus, he avoided "the embarrassment of conversion (full baptismal immersion, new language and all)" to any of the vociferous competing schools. At the same time, the "prism" of literary theory enabled Gates to overcome the problem of analyzing black literature only for its content, its trueness to the black experience, which Gates identifies as a prominent fallacy in much black literary criticism and particularly in the Black Aesthetic.

Gates saw his switch from history to literary theory as another problem at the time, but in the long run, his background in history has proved to be a tremendous advantage. His literary theory is distinguished by its historical perspective, its setting within the context of history and change. As Gates himself says in the preface to *The Signifying Monkey: A Theory of Afro-American Literary Criticism*, he is "concerned to register a theory of criticism, and more precisely, a theory of literary history." He has, in effect, written the *Roots* of Afro-American literary theory.

In Gates' theory, Afro-American literary history stretches back sadly, on the one hand, to the racist attitudes coming out of the European Enlightenment. Synonymous with rationalism and the search for freedom, producing among other things the American and French revolutions, the "Enlightenment" has a hypocritical and ironic sound to the Afro-American ear. That may be explained by the fact that the Enlightenment also equated civilization with literacy and a written tradition; people who lacked such a tradition, who could not even read or write, were considered savages. In fact, there was some question whether blacks were closer to humans or to apes. Their presumed inferiority was used to justify their enslavement. For captured blacks, the literacy test was epitomized in the trope of the Talking Book, which spoke to white readers but not to them.

Afro-American literary history begins, then, with the efforts of blacks to write themselves into the human race. The first black writings were presented as evidence and greeted by abolitionists as positive proof. An early black literary form was the slave narrative, an autobiographical, propagandistic work documenting the cruelty of slavery and attacking it. These beginnings, in Gates' view, account for a number of trends in Afro-American literary history that in some cases continued all the way up to, and even into, the twentieth century. For example, black American writing tended to be painfully imitative of the white literary tradition: Gates places most black American writers from the Reconstruction through the end of the nineteenth century into what is called the Mockingbird School. The early emphasis on content over form (or content poured into form) has continued until fairly recently. Gates tends to see even the Black Aesthetic as, in some ways, merely the obverse of the tradition's beginnings, with emphasis on content and proof positive of blackness.

On the other hand, there is a happier side of Afro-American literary history, with roots stretching all the way back to Africa. Gates finds these roots in the Hermes-like god known as Esu-Elegbara among the Yoruba in Nigeria and as Legba among the Fon in Benin. This "divine trickster figure" survived the passage to the New World as Exu in Brazil, Echu-Elegua in Cuba, Papa Legba in Haiti, and Papa Las Bas in the United States. Like Hermes, Esu is a mediator between the other gods and humans, presenting his messages in the configurations of sixteen palm nuts that priests must "read" through divination. As this description indicates, Esu is associated not only with language but also with the principles of uncertainty and indeterminacy. In some versions of the myth, monkeys supply the palm nuts or a monkey accompanies Esu, and this monkey, too, survived the passage to the New World, where he took on the associations of Esu and in folklore became a less-than-divine trickster figure known as the Signifying Monkey. The Signifying Monkey embodies the play with language called "signifying" that, in Gates' literary theory, distinguishes Afro-American literature.

The word "signifying" is also an important term in Ferdinand de Saussure's linguistic theory, which forms the basis of much of contemporary literary theory, but Gates is careful to show that the use of the term in the black American vernacular is different and in fact predates Saussure. To indicate this difference, Gates spells the word with a capital *S* and as it might be pronounced in the vernacular: "Signifyin(g)." In the black American vernacular, one does not so much "signify" a meaning as one "signifies upon" a previous meaning, much as a jazz musician plays a riff on a previous tune. Indeed, Signifyin(g) has strong parallels to jazz. One may also "signify upon" the person who expressed the previous meaning (or, as the vernacular has it, "trope a dope"). Gates calls Signifyin(g) "the trope of tropes" or master trope because it encompasses all the others (as well as play with sound and structure). Utilizing indirection, Signifyin(g) was developed as a means of survival over the centuries of slavery and segregation and exists today most notably in the vernacular (for example, in street talk and rapping).

Gates identifies Signifyin(g) as the leading characteristic of black American literature, noting its close relationship to the vernacular. Examples of subtle and not-so-subtle Signifyin(g) abound – for example, in the titles of works: Harriet E. Wilson's *Our Nig* (written 1859, published 1983), Richard Wright's *Black Boy* (1945) and *Native Son* (1940), Ralph Ellison's *Invisible Man* (1952), H. Rap

Brown's *Die, Nigger, Die!* (1969), Ishmael Reed's *Mumbo Jumbo* (1978), and Alice Walker's *The Color Purple* (1982). In Gates' theory, however, Signifyin(g) occurs not only as individual examples but also as a rhetorical strategy and structural principle in black American literature: the writers signify upon one another through tropological revision and intertextuality. For example, Zora Neale Hurston's "speakerly text" (shifting levels of voice incorporating the vernacular) in *Their Eyes Were Watching God* (1937) signifies upon her contemporaries and their debate about using dialect; Ralph Ellison's modernism signifies upon Richard Wright's naturalism; Alice Walker's epistolary form in *The Color Purple* signifies upon Hurston's "speakerly text"; and Ishmael Reed's use of parody and pastiche in *Mumbo Jumbo* signifies upon the whole black literary tradition. In other words, black American writers find their respective voices by "talking with" one another, and the voice of the black American literary tradition is appropriately symbolized by the trope of the Talking Book.

Intertextuality and something akin to Signifyin(g) exist in all literary traditions; Gates' point is not that these features are exclusive to black American literature but that they are its distinguishing characteristics. In articles first appearing in *Critical Inquiry* and then collected by Gates in *"Race," Writing, and Difference*, Tzvetan Todorov attacked Gates' earlier theorizing for its "racialism," and Houston A. Baker, Jr., criticized Gates for "ideological" inconsistency; in *The Signifying Monkey*, however, Gates elaborates his theory fully, carefully, and convincingly. *Figures in Black* and *The Signifying Monkey* compose two parts of a trilogy of literary theory; the third part, *Black Letters and the Enlightenment*, is forthcoming.

Principal criticism

Black Literature and Literary Theory, 1984 (editor)
"Race," Writing, and Difference, 1986 (editor)
Figures in Black: Words, Signs, and the "Racial" Self, 1987
The Signifying Monkey: A Theory of Afro-American Literary Criticism, 1988
Loose Canons: Notes on the Culture Wars, 1992
Colored People: A Memoir, 1994
The Future of the Race, 1996 (with Cornel West)

Other major works and literary forms

The writings of Henry Louis Gates, Jr., also include a number of critical articles and introductions, the most important of which have been revised and incorporated into the books listed above. Even more extensive than his own writings, however, is the amount of material that Gates has edited. He began by paying respect to his two mentors, Charles T. Davis at Yale University and Wole Soyinka at the University of Cambridge. Gates edited and introduced Davis' 1982 *Black Is the Color of the Cosmos: Essays on Afro-American Literature and Culture, 1941–1981* after the older scholar died. For Soyinka, the 1986 Nobel Prize winner from Nigeria, Gates edited *Critical Essays on Wole Soyinka* (1985) and coedited *Wole Soyinka: A Bibliography of Primary and Secondary Sources* (1986). Mainly, however, Gates has been concerned with reviving black American literary texts. To that end he started and has guided the extensive Black Periodical Literature Project, dealing with material published in periodicals between 1827 and 1940. With Davis he edited *The Slave's Narrative* (1985) and by himself *The Classic Slave Narratives* (1987). His editing of Harriet E. Wilson's 1859 autobiographical novel, *Our Nig: Sketches from the Life of a Free Black* (1983), drew considerable praise, and he is also series editor of the monumental thirty-volume *The Schomburg Library of Nineteenth-century Black Women Writers* (1987).

NONFICTION

Introduction to *Black Is the Color of the Cosmos: Essays on Afro-American Literature and Culture, 1941–1981*, by Charles T. Davis, 1982

EDITED TEXTS

Our Nig: Sketches from the Life of a Free Black, by Harriet E. Wilson, 1983 (written 1859)
Critical Essays on Wole Soyinka, 1985
The Slave's Narrative, 1985 (with Charles T. Davis)
Wole Soyinka: A Bibliography of Primary and Secondary Sources, 1986
The Classic Slave Narratives, 1987
The Schomburg Library of Nineteenth-century Black Women Writers, 1987 (30 volumes)
Reading Black, Reading Feminist: A Critical Anthology, 1990
Mule Bone: A Comedy of Negro Life, by Langston Hughes and Zora Neale Hurston, 1991 (with George Houston Bass)
Bearing Witness: Selections from African-American Autobiography in the Twentieth Century, 1991
Langston Hughes: Critical Perspectives Past and Present, 1993 (with Kwame Anthony Appiah)
Richard Wright: Critical Perspectives Past and Present, 1993 (with Appiah)
The Dictionary of Global Culture, 1996 (with Appiah)
The Norton Anthology of African American Literature, 1997 (general editor, with Nellie Y. McKay)

Further reading

Abrahams, Roger D. *Deep Down in the Jungle: Negro Narrative Folklore from the Streets of Philadelphia*, 1970.
Baker, Houston A., Jr. *Blues, Ideology, and Afro-American Literature: A Vernacular Theory*, 1984.
Mitchell-Kernan, Claudia. "Signifying as a Form of Verbal Art," in *Mother Wit from the Laughing Barrel: Readings in the Interpretation of Afro-American Folklore*, 1973. Edited by Alan Dundes.
Todorov, Tzvetan. "'Race,' Writing, and Culture," in *"Race," Writing, and Difference*, 1986. Edited by Henry Louis Gates, Jr.

HAROLD BRANAM

See also American Literary Theory: Twentieth Century; Black Literary Theory and Criticism; Postcolonial Literature and Theory

Théophile Gautier

French writer and critic

Born: Tarbes, France; August 31, 1811
Died: Neuilly-sur-Seine, France; October 23, 1872

Biography

Pierre Jules Théophile Gautier was born on August 31, 1811, in Tarbes, France. He was the son of Pierre Gautier, a minor civil servant, and his wife, Antoinette-Adélaïde Cocard. In 1814 the family moved to Paris, where Gautier later enrolled in the Collège Charlemagne, having there as a classmate another future poet, Gérard de Nerval. While at the school, Gautier frequented the studio of the painter Louis Édouard Rioult, but his involvement in the Romantic movement drew him from painting to poetry, and in 1830 he published his first book of verse, *Poésies*.

In 1836 Gautier began what was to become a lifelong career in journalism, joining the staff of *La Presse* to write criticism in the fields of art, music, and literature. He would leave *La Presse* in 1855 to assume the same responsibilities for *Le Moniteur universel*, and in 1856, he would become an editor of the influential periodical, *L'Artiste*, his position enabling him to disseminate widely the credo of art for art's sake. Gautier's eminence and influence as a poet and critic were reflected by the company that he kept: his dinner companions were Victor Hugo, Honoré de Balzac, Gustave Flaubert, and Charles Baudelaire, among others. During the Second Empire he was invited to the Tuileries by the emperor and was a frequent guest in the salon of Princess Mathilde.

Despite the acclaim that he received as a poet, and the great impact of his massive critical output, Gautier remained convinced throughout his life that he had squandered his creative talents in the alien and absorptive world of journalism. He died of heart trouble on October 23, 1872, in Neuilly-sur-Seine, a suburb of Paris.

Influence

As a highly respected critic – whose expertise encompassed art and music as well as literature – and as a widely acclaimed poet, Gautier exerted an immense influence on the literary climate of his time. For Charles Baudelaire, he was a revered mentor; for the demanding Stéphane Mallarmé, his poetic achievement was worthy of acknowledgment. Nor was Gautier's influence limited to the theory and practice of his poetry: his insistence on the artistic polish of fictional prose and his emphasis on precise detail and vivid color affected the writing of realists such as Gustave Flaubert. Moreover, the idealism which inspired Gautier's dramatic criticism had a definite impact on the Symbolist theater.

Before his death, Gautier had already won fervent disciples abroad, such as the English poet Algernon Charles Swinburne. In the early twentieth century Gautier's standards of poetic achievement were endorsed not only by his fellow countryman Paul Valéry, but by American and English poets, such as Ezra Pound and T. S. Eliot, as well. Afterward, however, his reputation declined, as a new age developed different notions about the writing of poetry and more rigorous criteria for the practice of literary criticism.

Analysis

A high point of Gautier's literary life was his colorful support of Victor Hugo at the premiere of *Hernani* (1830; English translation, 1830), on February 25, 1830: Gautier came attired in a scarlet doublet, pale gray pants, and a broad-brimmed hat. Only a few years later, however, in the preface to his novel *Mademoiselle de Maupin* (1835–1836), Gautier formulated a view of art which, while remaining idealistic, rejected the lyrical and utilitarian aspects of Romanticism. He suggested that art should have beauty as its sole objective and should not pursue moral or political goals. In the text of *Mademoiselle de Maupin* itself, Gautier appeared to divinize beauty, to the degree that it was characterized as the visible manifestation of God.

What form should literary beauty take? In a celebrated remark recorded by Edmond de Goncourt in *Journal: Mémoires de la vie littéraire* (1887–1896, 1956–1959), and translated by Lewis Galantière in *The Goncourt Journals (1851–1870)* (1937), Gautier provided a possible answer to that question when he said, "Nobody has ever remarked that all my value lies in the fact that *I am a man for whom the visible world exists.*" If Gautier's comment indicated a fascination with material beauty, and if his own illustrative poetry, such as *Émaux et camées* (1852; *Enamels and Cameos*, 1900), betokened a preoccupation with the sculptural description of that beauty, he did not believe, nor did his poetry demonstrate, that art was the mere photographic reproduction of the visible, however attractive it might be. Even when natural beauty was involved, Gautier did not share either the rhapsodic adoration characteristic of the Romantics or their desire to capture that beauty "naturally," whether what was meant by "natural beauty" was the beauty of nature or the beauty of the human body. Significant, in this regard, was Gautier's recollection, in *Souvenirs romantiques* (1929), of his disenchantment when he contemplated, for the first time, a studio nude. The impression that he conveyed was that even when nature itself was beautiful, art was still able to enhance that beauty.

According to Gautier, rather than attempt an exact imitation of the object that he was describing, the great artist created from an inner vision, from a microcosm or self-sufficient universe within him or herself. This inner vision enabled the artist to transform the very reality that he or she was depicting, not only converting that reality into something beautiful by exquisite craftsmanship, but also investing it with spiritual meaning. With specific respect to poetic creation, Gautier thought that the virtues of this inner vision were admirably illustrated in the poetry of Baudelaire. In his *Souvenirs romantiques*, Gautier noted approvingly Baudelaire's requirement that the object of the poet's contemplation be transformed before passing into his verse. Gautier appreciated the notion implicit in this requirement – namely, that, through artistic metamorphosis, the unpalatable or the ugly could enter into the domain of poetic expression.

Yet Gautier was sufficiently flexible in his thinking to understand that the relationship between inner vision and formal craftsmanship might vary somewhat from poet to poet. Consequently, he could apprize the work of poets whose manner differed noticeably from Baudelaire's. Gautier was able to recognize the exceptional talent of a Charles Marie Leconte de Lisle with his Parnassian brand of poetry, just as he was able to evaluate favorably the poems of his former classmate, Gérard de Nerval, whose arcanely subjective style he discussed in *Portraits et souvenirs littéraires* (1875), commenting on the fact that Nerval's vision was steeped in mythology and governed by a symbolism which affected every word.

Nor did Gautier's critical flexibility vanish when he considered the representatives of the novel's realistic school, despite his declared opposition to their endeavor to reproduce the social and economic reality of their times. To be sure, there were realists whom Gautier could not abide, such as the theorist of the movement, Champfleury, or Stendhal, whom Gautier virtually ignored. Nevertheless, in *Portraits contemporains* (1874; *Portraits of the Day*, 1900), Gautier commended Balzac for having discarded the abstractions cultivated by previous novelists, whose total absorption with the theme of love had caused them to create characters who functioned in an unreal world, one bereft of material concerns. Gautier saw Balzac, on the other hand, as placing his characters in the real world, and as highlighting, in so doing, the overriding importance of money. Yet Balzac's principal merit, in Gautier's opinion, came from his possession of an inner eye, a visionary quality which permitted him to plumb the very depths of the material world that he detailed so carefully in his novels. In *Souvenirs romantiques*, Gautier did not hesitate to stress this visionary quality by using the word *voyant* to characterize Balzac the observer. Another realist who found favor with Gautier was Flaubert. When the latter published *Salammbô* (1862; English translation, 1886), Gautier, sensitive to Flaubert's masterful descriptive technique, reviewed the novel with praise.

In his dramatic criticism, Gautier applied the same standards which governed his assessment of poetry and fictional prose: he was still in search of artistic beauty, preferably untrammeled by utilitarian pursuits. Indeed, his quest was all the more ardent in this area since he viewed the theater as the inevitable focus of modern civilization, as an incomparable setting for the wondrous materialization of the ideal. For Gautier, characteristically, beauty in the theater began with the physical aspect, with the scenery as well as the costumes. He also stressed that the theater must be a refuge from the bleakness of everyday existence. Through his emphasis on the importance of the physical aspect of the theater, Gautier appeared to echo the point of view of certain Romantic theoreticians of the stage, such as Victor Hugo, who had objected to the poverty of the scenery and the costumes in the classical and neoclassical theater. With Gautier, however, the beauty of such accessories was not secondary to characterization or plot: the accent here was on the aesthetic rather than on the functional. If Gautier insisted on the visual appeal of the purely material dimension of the theater, he also underscored the need for beauty of language. His thought was that the language of the theater, far from duplicating the prosaic utterances of real life, should have a poetic charm and constitute a study in verbal idealization. To this effect, he reminded his readers that art was not life but its embellishment.

Since his regular fare in the theater was, for the most part, the bourgeois comedies, vaudevilles, and melodramas which dominated the French stage during a large segment of his life – with the extraordinarily successful Eugène Scribe being the bourgeois dramatist *par excellence* – Gautier's criticism only rarely reflected the type of aesthetic joy that he derived from a poem by Baudelaire or a novel by Balzac. Nevertheless, there were occasional compensations. Gautier delighted in the gorgeous pageantry of certain Romantic historical dramas, such as those of Alexandre Dumas, *père*. The drama critic also enjoyed the wit and beauty of language displayed in the fundamentally different Romantic theater of Alfred de Musset, and in that of the eighteenth-century dramatist, Pierre Marivaux.

Whether Gautier was evaluating Baudelaire's poetry, Balzac's prose, or the plays of Dumas, *père*, his critical method remained the same. Betraying the lasting imprint of his earlier interest in painting, Gautier almost invariably attempted a transposition of art, seeking to create a verbal picture in order to communicate vividly the effect that the work being reviewed had had on him. Nor did this technique go unnoticed among Gautier's contemporaries: the celebrated critic Charles-Augustin Sainte-Beuve observed that Gautier's critical approach involved in fact a system of transposition. However defined, Gautier's method yielded neither an analysis nor a dissection of the work being appreciated, but a prose poem, often most exquisitely fashioned, and, in the case of Gautier's dramatic criticism, not infrequently of greater literary value than the play that he had been called upon to review.

Amplified by the example of his personal achievement as a poet and as a writer of fiction, the impact of Gautier's criticism was considerable during his lifetime. The significance of this impact became evident when Baudelaire, who also regarded Gautier as an incomparable and indispensable critic, dedicated to him *Les Fleurs du mal* (1857; *Flowers of Evil*, 1909), recognizing his mentorship as well as his mastery of poetic language. Of the many other comparable tributes paid to Gautier, perhaps the most striking, because of the exacting standards of its author, was that of Mallarmé, who acknowledged Gautier's remarkable craftsmanship in *L'Artiste*. As for the novelists, they honored Gautier simply by imitating him – a case in point being that of Flaubert, whose novel *Salammbô* was in all likelihood inspired by Gautier's *Le Roman de la momie* (1857; *Romance of the Mummy*, 1863). While dramatists writing for the bourgeoisie were less inclined to follow Gautier's theories or dramatic example, the Symbolist theater did reflect his influence. The same Mallarmé who saluted Gautier the poet was extremely sensitive to the appeal of the latter's advocacy of a poetic theater, one freed from the shackles of bourgeois conventions and animated by a pursuit of the ideal. Through Mallarmé's disciples, such as Camille Mauclair – who was, with Aurélien-François Lugné-Poë, the cofounder of the Théâtre de l'Œuvre – Gautier's ideas became part of the doctrine of the Symbolist theater.

It is clear that Gautier's influence was bounded neither by national frontiers nor by the writer's life span. Among his English admirers, Algernon Charles Swinburne manifested a particular reverence by composing pastiches of Gautier's poems and including them in his *Poems and Ballads* (1866). After Gautier's death, aspects of his aestheticism lived on in the works of Paul Valéry, a twentieth-century French poet who in his early years was greatly impressed by Gautier's artistry. Once again, however, it was in the English-speaking world that Gautier's aesthetic principles and their application in his own writings appeared to have their most conspicuous impact. In his *French Poets and Novelists* (1878), Henry James had gone so far as to venture the view that Gautier was superior to Baudelaire. That view was shared by T. S. Eliot, who, with Ezra Pound, also praised Gautier for curbing the excesses of Romantic lyricism.

Later, however, both Gautier the poet and Gautier the critic fell out of favor. Poetic aestheticism lost its attractiveness, especially when suspected of being devoid of any meaningful spiritual or emotional components; Gautier's critical method – descriptive and impressionistic, lacking in strict analysis and documentation – gave way to techniques featuring a closer structural scrutiny of the text.

Yet the shift in poetic fashions did not diminish, in an objective sense, the intrinsic value of Gautier's poetry as the admirable expression of an artistic temperament concerned primarily with the beauty of language and the perfection of form. Nor did the objections to his critical methodology alter the fact that his insightful judgments regarding many of his contemporaries, such as Baudelaire and Balzac, were ratified by posterity, as were his assessments, in *Les Grotesques* (1844; *The Grotesques*, 1900) of preclassical writers who had previously been largely ignored, such as the medieval poet François Villon and the seventeenth-century poet Théophile de Viau. In the final analysis, even Gautier's dramatic criticism, despite obvious shortcomings, was not entirely without merit: by his criterion of beauty and by his repugnance against the mediocre and the commonplace, he succeeded in elevating such criticism to an artistic level and in investing it with a certain dignity.

Principal criticism

Preface to *Mademoiselle de Maupin*, 1835–1836
Les Grotesques, 1844 (2 volumes; *The Grotesques*, 1900)
Honoré de Balzac: Sa Vie et ses œuvres, 1858
Histoire de l'art dramatique en France depuis vingt-cinq ans, 1858–1859 (6 volumes)
"Les Progrès de la poésie française depuis 1830," 1868 ("The Progress of French Poetry," 1900)
Histoire du romantisme, 1872 (*A History of Romanticism*, 1900)
Portraits contemporains, 1874 (*Portraits of the Day*, 1900)
Portraits et souvenirs littéraires, 1875
Fusains et eaux-fortes, 1880
Souvenirs de théâtre, d'art, et de critique, 1883
Victor Hugo, 1902
Critique artistique et littéraire, 1929
Les Maîtres du théâtre français de Rotrou à Dumas fils, 1929
Souvenirs romantiques, 1929

Other major works and literary forms

In addition to his voluminous output as a literary critic, Théophile Gautier published an abundant amount of art and music criticism. His eclectic interests embraced virtually all the arts and their leading exponents, however, and he did not restrict himself to the works of the nineteenth century or to those of his native land. One of the most distinguished poets and writers of fiction of his time, Gautier also produced a significant body of true literature: several books of poetry, two novels, novellas, and numerous short stories. He also composed plays and wrote a series of ballet librettos, the most celebrated of which was *Giselle: Ou, Les Wilis* (1841; *Giselle: Or, The Wilis*, 1970).

NOVELS
Mademoiselle de Maupin, 1835–1836 (2 volumes; *Mademoiselle de Maupin: A Romance of Love and Passion*, 1887)
Fortunio, 1838 (novella; English translation, 1915)
Le Roman de la momie, 1857 (*Romance of the Mummy*, 1863)
Le Capitaine Fracasse, 1863 (*Captain Fracasse*, 1898)
Spirite: Nouvelle fantastique, 1866 (*Spirite*, 1900)

SHORT FICTION
Les Jeunes-France: Romans goguenards, 1833
Nouvelles, 1845
Un Trio de romans, 1852
Jettatura, 1857 (English translation, 1888)
Romans et contes, 1863

PLAYS
Une Larme de diable, 1839
Tra los montes, 1843
Le Tricorne enchanté, 1845

La Fausse Conversion, 1846
Pierrot posthume, 1847
Théâtre de poche, 1855

BALLET SCENARIOS
Giselle: Ou, Les Wilis, 1841 (*Giselle: Or, The Wilis*, 1970)
La Péri, 1843
Pâquerette, 1851
Gemma, 1854
Sacountala, 1858
Yanko le bandit, 1858

POETRY
Poésies, 1830
Albertus: Ou, L'Âme et le péché, 1833 (*Albertus*, 1909)
La Comédie de la mort, 1838 (*The Comedy of Death*, 1909)
Poésies complètes, 1845
Émaux et camées, 1852 (*Enamels and Cameos*, 1900)
Dernières Poésies, 1872

NONFICTION
Voyage en Espagne, 1843 (*Wanderings in Spain*, 1853)
Salon de 1847, 1847
Caprices et zigzags, 1852
Italia, 1852 (*Travels in Italy*, 1900)
Constantinople, 1853 (*Constantinople of To-Day*, 1854)
Les Beaux-Arts en Europe, 1855, 1855–1856 (2 volumes)
L'Art moderne, 1856
Abécédaire du Salon de 1861, 1861
Trésors d'art de la Russie ancienne et moderne, 1861
Loin de Paris, 1865
Quand on voyage, 1865
Voyage en Russie, 1867 (*A Winter in Russia*, 1874)
Ménagerie intime, 1869 (*My Household of Pets*, 1882)
Tableaux de siège, 1871 (*Paris Besieged*, 1900)
L'Orient, 1877
Tableaux à la plume, 1880
Les Vacances du lundi, 1881
Guide de l'amateur au Musée du Louvre, 1882 (*The Louvre*, 1900)
La Musique, 1911

MISCELLANEOUS
The Works of Théophile Gautier, 1900–1903 (24 volumes; S. C. De Surnichrast, editor and translator)

Further reading

Gosselin Schick, Constance. *Seductive Resistance: The Poetry of Théophile Gautier*, 1994.
Grant, Richard. *Théophile Gautier*, 1975.
Patch, Helen E. *The Dramatic Criticism of Théophile Gautier*, 1922.
Richardson, Joanna. *Théophile Gautier: His Life and Times*, 1958.
Tennant, P. E. *Théophile Gautier*, 1975.
Ubersfeld, Anne. *Théophile Gautier*, 1992.
Wellek, René. *A History of Modern Criticism: 1750–1950*. Vol. 4, *The Later Nineteenth Century*, 1965.

NORMAN ARAUJO

See also Baudelaire; Continental Theory; Sainte-Beuve

Gay Theory and Criticism

The late-nineteenth-century emergence of homosexuality as a distinct feature (and shaper) of personal identity, and the late-twentieth-century development of gayness as a "lifestyle" demanding equal recognition with the various modes of heterosexual life, have been accompanied by cultural changes which have continuously been monitored and encouraged by cultural historians and critics who themselves identified as lesbian or gay. Fresh modes of criticism have developed alongside new ways of being homosexual, for gay literary theory has always depended on current theories of homosexuality itself. Gay literary critics operate with a closer eye on gayness than on literary criticism. This has always tended to infuriate the "universalists" among critics who identify as heterosexual.

Just as there is no such single entity as "feminist criticism," the concept of "gay theory" – merely a convenient phrase – has to be broken down by period, by culture, and by politics. For the purposes of the present essay, "gay theory" is to be taken to cover a range of tendencies which have emerged since the late nineteenth century. Of these, one might most straightforwardly distinguish between "homosexual," "gay," "lesbian," and "queer" patterns of thought. All are overlapping and none is so definitive as ever to have been set in stone (although certain "party lines" have, at various moments in history, tended to prevail). Their concerns, despite the apparent exclusiveness of these convenient labels, should be understood to overlap with bisexual, transsexual, and transvestite issues, and ultimately to reflect back on our understanding of heterosexuality.

Many of the men who were first involved in the shaping of a homosexual identity at the end of the nineteenth century believed that it was also necessary to identify and help further to mold a homosexual culture. They had distinctly bookish interests. The German-Swiss historian of homosexuality Heinrich Hoessli anthologized the literature as a way of advocating homosexual rights. Karl Heinrich Ulrichs, the lawyer turned sexual-liberationist pioneer, wrote poetry and planned to compile an anthology of classic homosexual literature; he saw the need for a homosexual publishing house. John Addington Symonds wrote poetry and literary criticism, expressing in both his homoerotic interests. Marc-André Raffalovich's *Uranisme et unisexualité* (1896) is replete with literary and bibliographical materials. Edward Carpenter was a poet and an anthologist of homosexual literature. The Dutch criminal anthropologist Arnold Aletrino, who argued in 1897 that homosexuality could occur in otherwise normal, healthy individuals, was also a creative writer. Xavier Mayne, the American author of *The Intersexes* (1908), was a novelist as well as a sexologist. The multidisciplinarity of the work of men like Magnus Hirschfeld, the great theorist of sexuality and campaigner for sexual law reform, and Iwan Bloch, the physician and reputed inventor of sexology

(*Sexualwissenschaft*), was routinely inclusive of literary scholarship. Moreover, many major gay literary figures of the twentieth century were also theorists of homosexuality. To take only French examples: Marcel Proust, André Gide, Marcel Jouhandeau, Tony Duvert, and Guy Hocquenghem were all theorists of their own sexualities.

Almost all of these men had received a classical education of some sort. They were intensely aware of the ancient Greeks; and although they were attempting to classify the sexualities with new names, those names were invariably derived from Greek or Latin etymological roots and bastardized into modern German, French, English, or whatever. (Remember, too, Sigmund Freud's reuse of classical mythology: Oedipus, Narcissus, and so on.) For virtually all homosexual theorists of the second half of the nineteenth century and the first half of the twentieth century, the Ur-theorist was Plato (or Plato's Socrates) and his key text the *Symposium*. What Plato offered, in an era of criminalized and newly pathologized homosexualities, was an incomparably positive endorsement and celebration of male–male love.

The fact that there was little significant "homosexual criticism" published between World War I and the Vietnam War can be explained, not only by the fact that male homosexual acts were illegal and homosexual men were lying relatively low, but also by the dominance of critical orthodoxies such as Practical Criticism and the New Criticism, which effectively outlawed attention to authorial biography and even to social context. Attempts at lesbian or gay readings tended to be dismissed as irrelevant to the universal integrity of the text itself. For universal, of course, read "heterosexual."

However, some conspicuous critical interventions helped to undermine these fixed ideas. In *Love and Death in the American Novel* (1960), Leslie Fiedler pointed out the extent to which classic American fiction keeps returning to the intimate relationship between two men, usually a white refugee from the conformity and domesticity of society and a dark-skinned man of nature, either black or native American. While Fiedler's brilliant readings of the texts in question – by the likes of James Fenimore Cooper, Mark Twain, Herman Melville, and Nathaniel Hawthorne – prefigured the ways in which gay critics would later seek to identify "gay themes" in canonical texts, his book is not gay criticism. The main problem with his analysis is that, by adhering to a standard psychoanalytic assessment of homoeroticism as being both puerile and narcissistic, he rather grandly characterizes American writers' failure to come to terms with mature heterosexual relationships as a sign of arrested cultural development. After the Stonewall Riots of 1969 and the subsequent flowering of the gay liberation movement, such approaches to gay literature would look prejudicial and old-fashioned.

Much of the first wave of gay liberationist critical groundwork concentrated on the following necessary tasks: the identification of homosexual or bisexual authors and of themes in their works which are attributable to their sexual orientations; the quasi-archaeological resurrection of "gay texts"; critical reading of antigay texts; and the identification of representations of homosexual or bisexual people in texts by authors of any sexual orientation from any culture or period. Gay texts whose reputations had suffered at the hands of antigay critics because of their subject matter were reassessed according to gay liberationist principles. (It should be noted that these principles were often applied anachronistically and inappropriately.) Much of this work involved the establishing of a field of study. Often the precise mode of study was of secondary importance.

In 1974 a special issue of *College English*, the official journal of the United States National Council of Teachers of English, gave an impression of what gay and lesbian literary studies would strive to become. At this stage, the locating and naming of homophobia in both the academy and the wider arena of literary discourse was still an important priority. To the extent that they had been distorted by antigay prejudice, matters such as employment practices and curriculum development had to be addressed. Early accounts of some of the first gay and lesbian literature courses in the United States demonstrate how closely the defining of a canon relates to the shaping of a curriculum acceptable to conservative course-validation processes. In the following year the poet Ian Young, who had already published an influential anthology of gay poetry, produced his bibliography of *The Male Homosexual in Literature*, a major resource for those scholars who needed to discover *where* gay literature was before they could go on to try defining *what* it was.

The historian John Boswell's use of literary evidence in his influential tour de force *Christianity, Social Tolerance, and Homosexuality* (1980) had the doubly beneficial effect of illuminating history with poetry and poetry with history. Although this book has been criticized by social constructionists for its eagerness to call man-loving men in the medieval period "gay," it remains an effective challenge to orthodox versions of that period as having been consistently hostile to male–male relationships. On the contrary, in the context of monasticism, same-sex relationships, even when verging on physicality, were regarded as being infinitely purer and more spiritual than the earthbound relation between man and woman.

Lesbian criticism's close relationship with feminist criticism has been to both its advantage and its disadvantage. The relationship mirrors that which has existed between lesbian politics and the women's liberation movement itself: what is gained in strength of numbers and by cross identification may be lost by assimilation into the concerns of the greater number and consequent loss of identity. The bulk of Anglophone feminist critical work of the 1970s concentrated on gender difference at the expense of sexual difference. Critiques of patriarchy tended to assume that women were living, as wives or lovers, with the patriarchs. In this respect, lesbian scholars had to work against the grain, not only of male-centered gay critical writing, but also of feminist heterocentricity. The American poet Adrienne Rich reacted against the erasure of the lesbian in her now classic essay "Compulsory Heterosexuality and Lesbian Existence" (1980), arguing that the presumption of heterosexuality obliterates a range of types of lesbian desire between friendship and sexual passion. She values the possibilities of lesbianism as capable of disrupting masculinist systems and of uniting women in alternative networks of feeling and meaning.

Lesbian theory has been heavily influenced by French women theorists' and practitioners' celebration of *l'écriture féminine*, a creative response to the erasure of women's experience from patriarchal calculations of value. Hélène Cixous' concept of "phallogocentrism" (splicing phallocentrism, the symbolic primacy of the phallus, with Jacques Derrida's logocentrism, the privileging of the spoken word above the written) has proved a useful tool in the shaping of a coherent critique of the verbose masculinism of Western culture. However, Anglophone lesbians have been less comfortable with Cixous' inclination to include among the achievements of *l'écriture féminine* the work of writers as conspicuously unfeminine as James Joyce.

Lesbian literary criticism has had to pay close attention to cultural "ephemera" such as the letters, diaries, and commonplace books in which "mere" female friendships have traditionally been recorded (if at all). Reevaluating the status and meanings of such texts has enabled lesbian critics to reconstruct a textual history of lesbian love. Doing so has involved far-reaching explorations of Western culture's rigid distinctions between friendship and love, and between spirit and physique. Lillian Faderman's *Surpassing the Love of Men* (1981) was the pioneering contribution to this field.

When Michel Foucault's *Le Volonté de savoir* (1976), the introductory volume to his history of sexuality, was published in English in 1978, many scholars in lesbian and gay studies – as elsewhere – were forced to rethink their categories. Foucault's theorization of the construction of sexualities as a dimension of the exercise of power in social relations argued against the previous assumption that sexual matters had been censoriously erased from public discourse ever since the Middle Ages. On the contrary, he argued, Western culture had presided over an explosion of discourse about sexual pleasure even while categorizing certain sexual acts as being unspeakable; and such discourses had generated "reverse discourses" whereby (as one example) homosexual people were able to speak on their own behalf. This argument had especially resonant implications for the analysis of pre-gay liberationist, oblique, metaphorical texts about same-sex desire.

The main distinction between lesbian or gay theory, based in the identity politics of the women's and gay liberation movements, and queer theory is that the latter seeks to call identity itself into question. Given such ambitious aims, it follows that the compass of queer theory is not restricted to homosexuality itself – indeed, *hetero*sexuality becomes one of its central topics – nor even to sexuality in general. By analyzing the institutionalized homophobia of all cultural institutions from the strategic advantage of a marginalized position, it calls into question the fondest assumptions of culture itself.

Eve Kosofsky Sedgwick's ground-breaking work has its origins in her doctoral research on the gothic novel. But it was in her book *Between Men* (1985), a study of literary representations of the intermale relationships on which society relies, that she set out a number of the key propositions of what came to be known as queer theory. Looking at a range of canonical authors and texts from William Shakespeare's *Sonnets* to Charles Dickens' *Edwin Drood*, Sedgwick delineates the "homosocial" bonds which are established between men, and often mediated through women, to negotiate exchanges and transfers of property and social status. She demonstrates that although society makes a point of emphatically drawing clear distinctions between the homosocial and the homosexual, nevertheless the two categories are too unstable and too close to resist not only overlapping but even collapsing into each other. Misogyny and homophobia are the oppressive instruments with which the boundaries of the homosocial are policed; but as with the Iron Curtain, the more the line is policed the more it fosters the conditions in which it is liable to be breached. In *Epistemology of the Closet* (1991) Sedgwick went on to apply her project of systematic antihomophobic analysis to the likes of Herman Melville, Oscar Wilde, Henry James, and Marcel Proust.

Judith Butler's work constitutes a radical departure from mainstream feminist work in the United States. Her bold assertion that feminine identity (and masculine identity correspondingly) is less a matter of being than of doing, not so much essence as performance, opens up intriguing possibilities in our understanding not only of gender but of a range of sexualities, and even of identity itself. Her perception that the individual's conformity to the culturally given norms of gender is only ever approximate has generated a welcome self-recognition in many of her queer readers. Once "being" a woman or a man is redefined as a sequence of acts of becoming, failures to conform to fixed, normative patterns of behavior may rematerialize as performative variations on a range of possibilities. Butler's work is an especially useful tool in the notoriously difficult task of theorizing camp.

A number of critics and theorists have recently been reassessed by queer theorists in the light of what we now know about their own homosexuality. These include F. O. Matthiessen, best known for his work establishing the canon of the American Renaissance, and Roland Barthes.

According to a growing number of gay academics, chief among them those working in sociology, the downside of the widespread espousal of Michel Foucault's work on discourse has been a downgrading of the importance of empirical research along with a general reduction of sexual questions to "mere" discourse. An anticonstructionist reaction in literary studies has been initiated by such cultural historians as Rictor Norton, who questions the accuracy of the historical assertions on which constructionist theory is based. While not taking this line, the cultural materialist Alan Sinfield and the sociologist Kenneth Plummer have recently suggested, albeit from different standpoints, that an excessive concentration on discourse theory may have the inadvertent effect of placing career academics who call themselves queer theorists at a distant remove from the empirical concerns of ordinary lesbians and gay men.

Further reading

Boswell, John. *Christianity, Social Tolerance, and Homosexuality: Gay People in Western Europe from the Beginning of the Christian Era to the Fourteenth Century*, 1980.

Butler, Judith. *Gender Trouble: Feminism and the Subversion of Identity*, 1990.

Crew, Louie, and Rictor Norton, eds. *The Homosexual Imagination–in Literature–in the Classroom–in Criticism*, special issue of *College English*. Vol. 36, no. 3 (November, 1974).

Faderman, Lillian. *Surpassing the Love of Men: Romantic Friendship and Love Between Women, from the Renaissance to the Present*, 1981.

Fiedler, Leslie A. *Love and Death in the American Novel*, 1960.

Foucault, Michel. *The History of Sexuality, Volume 1: An Introduction*, 1978.

Norton, Rictor. *The Myth of the Modern Homosexual: Queer History and the Search for Cultural Unity*, 1997.

Rich, Adrienne. "Compulsory Heterosexuality and Lesbian Existence," 1980, reprinted in *Adrienne Rich's Poetry and Prose*, 1993.

Sedgwick, Eve Kosofsy. *Between Men: English Literature and Male Homosocial Desire*, 1985.

Sinfield, Alan. *Cultural Politics – Queer Reading*, 1994.

Summers, Claude J., ed. *The Gay and Lesbian Literary Heritage: A Reader's Companion to the Writers and their Works, from Antiquity to the Present*, 1995.

Woods, Gregory. *A History of Gay Literature: The Male Tradition*, 1998.

Young, Ian. *The Male Homosexual in Literature: A Bibliography*, 1975, second edition 1982.

GREGORY WOODS

Clifford Geertz

American cultural anthropologist and critic

Born: San Francisco, California; August 23, 1926

Biography

Clifford James Geertz was born in San Francisco in 1926. After World War II he studied English and philosophy at Antioch College in Ohio, graduating with an A.B. in 1950. He moved to Harvard for his doctoral work, shifting from his undergraduate discipline to anthropology. However Geertz's ethnography is celebrated for its literary approach and its philosophical reflections. He is, at heart, a literary critic and a philosopher still.

Geertz was part of an American research team in Java from 1952 to 1954; he also worked in Bali from 1957 to 1958. This was the source of his much quoted and much anthologized essay "Deep Play: Notes on the Balinese Cock Fight" (1971). His Indonesian fieldwork formed the basis of his early books *The Religion of Java* and *The Social History of an Indonesian Town*, as well as the more literary and historical account of *Negara: The Theatre State in Nineteenth Century Bali*. In the 1960s and 1970s Geertz also researched in Morocco, the other end of the Islamic world. His experiences in both places, and their effect on his intellectual trajectory, are elegantly recounted in his autobiographical work *After the Fact: Two Countries, Four Decades, One Anthropologist*. Between them, Java, Bali, and Morocco form the basis of the searching adventures in ethnography which shaped the essays in his two most influential books, *The Interpretation of Cultures: Selected Essays* and *Local Knowledge: Further Essays in Interpretive Anthropology*.

Geertz taught at Harvard (1956–1957), the Massachusetts Institute of Technology (1957–1958), Stanford (1958–1959), and Berkeley (1958–1960) before joining the Anthropology Department at the University of Chicago in 1960. He taught there for ten years before joining the Institute of Advanced Study at Princeton, to which he is still affiliated. He has lectured all over the Western world and been granted many honorary doctorates. He is clearly seen as one of the most influential anthropologists of his generation.

Influence

Geertz has exercised an enormous influence on his home discipline, permanently reshaping the way cultural anthropology is written. Appreciations and critiques of that influence may be found in the collection of essays *Writing Culture: The Poetics and Politics of Ethnography* (1986), edited by James Clifford and George E. Marcus. As the special 1997 issue of *Representations* ("The Fate of Culture: Geertz and Beyond") also shows, Geertz holds a special status as the "ambassador from anthropology," exercising an influence on historians, sociologists, media analysts, and literary critics. In particular, New Historicist critics of the 1970s and 1980s, chief among them Stephen Greenblatt, found Geertz's writing a powerful stimulus to their own poetic and imaginative evocations of the cultures and texts of the English Renaissance.

Two Geertz essays have been seminal for his literary followers: "Deep Play" and "Centers, Kings and Charisma: Reflections on the Symbolics of Power" (1983). In turn these exemplify the two central aspects of Geertzian ethnography: "thick description" and the "local reading." As Geertz himself puts it: "The aim is to draw large conclusions from small, but very densely textured facts; to support broad assertions about the role of culture in the constructions of collective life by engaging with complex specifics." Geertz thus attempted a close reading of a cockfight, a royal procession, or a Moroccan bazaar, attending to local details, metaphors, and images the way, as an undergraduate during the peak years of the influence of New Criticism, he had been taught to read *King Lear* or *Macbeth*. At a time when, in the late 1960s, literary criticism had seemed to lose its way, Geertz offered reassurance, as Greenblatt puts it: "returning my own professional skills to me as more important, more vital and illuminating, than I had myself grasped . . . I was excited to find a sophisticated, intellectually powerful, and wonderfully eloquent anthropologist who could make use of the tools in my disciplinary kit and in so doing renew in me a sense of their value."

Close reading, then, was once more acceptable. Moreover, since Geertz's close readings were ethnographic and not literary, one could take license from his example and read any artifact any given society had produced. With Geertz as their great exemplar, New Historicists felt free to roam through the textual archives of Renaissance England, and were just as liable to read a travel account, a witch trial, or a triumphal entry as a poem or a play. They attended also to nontextual remnants of culture: jewelry, costume, architecture. The powerful readings which resulted offered densely written depictions of the "symbolics of power" in the reigns of Queen Elizabeth I and her successor James I. Like Geertz, they were transfixed by the yoking of art and power, the placing of art, very broadly interpreted, at the service of power. Geertz's rhetoric led them into this energizing new territory. His summation of the art of power in Elizabeth's court was proven to be true over and over again:

> In sixteenth-century England, the political center of society was the point at which the tension between the passions that power excited and the ideals it was supposed to serve was screwed to its highest pitch; and the symbolism of the progress, consequently, admonitory and covenantal: the subjects warned, and the queen promised.

Analysis

Geertz did not originate the term "thick description." Rather, he borrowed it from Gilbert Ryle, the Oxford philosopher, who juxtaposed thick and thin descriptions of the same physical event. An eye might be seen to twitch involuntarily. If so, one could thinly describe the mere physical action. If, however, the eye was deliberately winking, one could devise multiple layers of scenarios which might account for this winking, embedding the wink in contexts of human meanings and intentions. The wink's effect would differ radically from context to context, and from culture to culture. Geertz and his followers attempt thus to "thickly" describe all manner of human events, all traces of human culture. They embed those events or texts in layer upon layer of significance. In his essay "Thick Description" (1973) which opens his collection *The Interpretation of Cultures: Selected Essays*, Geertz describes his method thus: "Cultural analysis is (or should be) guessing at meanings, assessing the guesses, and drawing explanatory conclusions from the better guesses." Once having thickly described a social event, poetically mining its local and specific meanings (for its time, its place, its participants), you could then generalize about the society which framed that event. As an ethnographer Geertz had, of course, been trained to make such generalizations and return to the American heartland with news of the lands beyond.

In his single most famous essay on the Balinese cockfight, "Deep Play," Geertz thus describes in great detail the particular cockfight he witnessed. Beyond that he describes the general behavior during cockfights; beyond that again he evokes the whole swathe of Balinese society: the cockfight becomes a central part of the expression of Balinese masculinity. A brutal sport becomes in effect a work of art; one which functions, Geertz claims, much like the kind of "high" art with which, he assumes, his American readers are familiar:

> What [the cockfight] does is what, for other peoples with other temperaments and other conventions, *Lear* and *Crime and Punishment* do; it catches up these themes – death, masculinity, rage, pride, loss, beneficence, chance – and ordering them into an encompassing structure, presents them in such a way as to throw into relief a particular view of their essential nature . . . . An image, fiction, a model, a metaphor, the cockfight is a means of expression.

The cockfight, then, was a work of art, a key to Balinese society. Literary critics have seized on the excitement Geertz betrays here, both at witnessing these extraordinary occasions, as well as witnessing his own power in celebrating them. He depicts a collective fiction, not, he would insist, in the sense that the cockfight was invented: as an ethnographer he is constrained to report only events which actually happened. Rather, they are fictions in the sense of being events made and crafted, told and retold. Cocks fight, the loser bleeds to death. What attracts Geertz is not so much the blood lust of the sport, though his account resonates with his excitement at that. What excites him further, and has empowered his New Historicist followers, are the kinds of critical fictions you might describe around events. The fictions include the Balinese readings of the fight, as well as Geertz's own "made," "crafted" responses to it. Here he deploys another strategy crucial to his ethnographic, historical, and literary followers: he puts himself in the picture.

Geertz's philosophizing of ethnography gained attention during the 1960s, as part of the "linguistic" turn which marked the debates over structuralism, poststructuralism, and deconstruction. Geertz denied the vulgar reading of Jacques Derrida's mantra: "il n'y a pas d'hors texte" (there is nothing outside the text), which at its boldest insisted that the world was entirely constructed of text; there was nothing in the world but what we would now call cyber text. Geertz insists rather on describing the "real" in his ethnography. But he insists also that our only access to the real is through the mediation of texts. With this consciousness of the ethnography as "written," Geertz disavows the empirical accuracy of science. For him, rather, ethnography becomes an art; an art, moreover, supremely conscious of the nature of its creator. The thickly described anecdotes which comprise Geertz's repertoire frequently feature himself: he never lets us forget that he is an observer observing, screening data, constructing hypotheses: we see darkly through lenses he has provided.

Geertz thus feeds into another obsessive preoccupation of critics in the 1970s, 1980s, and 1990s: the nature of the self, the self understood as constructed from texts; subject, moreover, to the constraints of a specific time and place, and bound thereby by specific prejudices and ideologies. For Geertz's literary followers, this obsession leads to the confessional mode; the helpless critic trapped in realms of ideology he understands but cannot escape. There is subversion, endless subversion, Greenblatt famously remarks, only not for us. Such critics cannot escape the symbolics of power which they describe so well.

The concern with self-fashioning the critic led also to a concern with the critic/ethnographer as writer, crafter of elaborate, beguiling sentences. Geertz, as David Richards aptly puts it, is a "master of the subordinate clause and the dash." The model here is the mocking tone of the learned mandarin, part pedant, part dandy, adopted by Roland Barthes, especially in his late writings *Roland Barthes by Roland Barthes* (1977) and *The Pleasure of the Text* (1975). Geertz and Greenblatt remain committed themselves to producing texts which, like the elaborate social fictions they evoke, may be read for pleasure.

Geertz of course has his detractors as well as his adherents: samples of each are gathered in the two collections *Writing Culture* and "The Fate of Culture: Geertz and Beyond." Geertz's thick descriptions are seen to have distinct drawbacks. Geertz raises the apparently trivial to the status of art: a symbolic construct frozen in time. This makes for densely textured reading of social situations. Yet it becomes difficult using Geertz's strategies to convey the dynamism of particular situations: frozen and formalized they cannot change in time. Thus, although Geertz often describes situations with complex political backgrounds, such as the welter of imperial, colonial, and nationalist energies in the Indonesian archipelago, his method prevents him from portraying the way, through time, those differing political situations might effect the social rituals and their participants. The societies evoked thus tend to seem unchanging and rigid: they may be poetically described, but they may not alter.

The problem is exacerbated by Geertz's status as an eminent American ethnographer, describing "Third World" societies very different from his own. However subtle his descriptions, they still run the risk of acquiring a patronizing, "First World" air, a series of intellectual postcards sent back to the West. His insistence on presenting the autobiographical eye of the observer raises the question also of the knowledge that eye offers. His crafting of motive and action suggests a deep and secret knowledge of the locals he describes, as if he knows them better than they know themselves. This, of course, is the privilege of the novelist, especially the realist novelists of the nineteenth century whom Geertz frequently cites. To tell a Moroccan or Balinese villager, though, that the visiting expert knows them better than they know themselves is to dismiss their role in their own lives. Geertz's tactics were taken up in the 1990s by a range of postcolonial historians and literary critics; yet they were at pains to distance their own local knowledges from the apparent Western elitism Geertz has sometimes been accused of practising.

Principal criticism

The Religion of Java, 1960
Agricultural Involution, the Processes of Ecological Change in Indonesia, 1963
Peddlers and Princes, 1963
The Social History of an Indonesian Town, 1965
Person, Time and Conduct in Bali: An Essay in Cultural Analysis, 1966
Islam Observed: Religious Development in Morocco and Indonesia, 1968
The Interpretation of Cultures: Selected Essays, 1973
Kinship in Bali, 1975 (with Hildred Geertz)
Meaning and Order in Moroccan Society, 1979 (with Hildred Geertz and Lawrence Rosen)
Negara: The Theatre State in Nineteenth Century Bali, 1980
Local Knowledge: Further Essays in Interpretive Anthropology, 1983
Works and Lives: The Anthropologist as Author, 1988
After the Fact: Two Countries, Four Decades, One Anthropologist, 1995

Other major works and literary forms

For Clifford Geertz, this heading is paradoxical, for his other "forms" are the more literary: the autobiographical *After the Fact: Two Countries, Four Decades, One Anthropologist* (1995) and the intellectual critique of *Works and Lives: The Anthropologist as Author* (1988). His criticism as such can be found in his many ethnographies, the thick descriptions for which he is so celebrated. *Works and Lives*, in contrast, can be considered a more orthodox work of literary criticism, though the works critiqued are those by the famous ethnographers Claude Lévi-Strauss, Bronislaw Malinowski, Edward Evans-Pritchard, and Ruth Benedict. The subtitle of *Works and Lives – The Anthropologist as Author* – indicates the approach, an evaluation of their work through their writing strategies. Geertz shows that these ethnographers, like himself, derive their power not just from the originality of their fieldwork but also through their command of a powerful writing style. Like Geertz they do not disavow the real, but their sentences embellish and adorn it.

After the Fact depicts Geertz's own adventures in the real. It is at once an autobiography and an intellectual history. He describes his experiences in the two countries, Indonesia and Morocco, which formed the basis of his fieldwork archive. He charts his professional career: from Harvard through Chicago to Princeton. More importantly, he charts his own shifting positions within the fast-moving field of modern ethnography, as it responded to the wider energies of postmodern criticism over the last thirty years. He surveys his path through these changes, avoiding abstract theorizing and describing his own constructs as "stories about stories, views about views." Reviewing his own stories he becomes yet again a graceful and powerful storyteller himself. For critics in all disciplines, that looks likely to be his major legacy.

Further reading

Clifford, James, and George E. Marcus, eds. *Writing Culture: The Poetics and Politics of Ethnography*, 1986.
Davis, Natalie Zemon. *The Return of Martin Guerre*, 1983.
Greenblatt, Stephen. *Renaissance Self-Fashioning: From More to Shakespeare*, 1980.
Hunt, Lynn, ed. *The New Cultural History*, 1989.
Ortner, Sherry B., ed. "The Fate of Culture: Geertz and Beyond," in *Representations*. 59 (Summer, 1997).
Richards, David. *Masks of Difference: Cultural Representations in Literature, Anthropology and Art*, 1994.
Sahlins, Marshall. *Islands of History*, 1985.

MARK HOULAHAN

See also New Historicism

Gérard Genette

French critic and editor

Born: Paris, France; 1930

Biography

Gérard Genette was born in Paris, France, in 1930. He graduated from the École Normale Supérieure in 1955 and then taught secondary school from 1955 to 1963 before taking a position as a lecturer in French literature at the Sorbonne. In 1967 he left the Sorbonne for a position as assistant professor at the École des Hautes Études en Sciences Sociales, thereafter assuming the post of director of studies. Genette's reputation became international after the publication of his first two books, and after 1969 he was in high demand as a visiting professor, particularly in the United States. The American universities where he has taught as a visiting scholar include Yale, Johns Hopkins, Wisconsin, Berkeley, and New York University. When not working abroad, Genette lives in Paris with his wife and children.

Influence

Genette is one of the leading theoreticians of structuralist poetics, particularly in that domain of narrative theory that Tzvetan Todorov has named narratology. His influence can be most clearly seen in the work of such writers as Mieke Bal, Seymour Chatman, Gerald Prince, and Shlomith Rimmon-Kenan, all of whom derive much of their theoretical framework and terminology directly from Genette, but his ideas have also been influential for a wide range of other theorists, not only of literature but also of film. It may safely be said that no study of narratological theory can now be written without frequent reference to Genette's writings. His work is of comparable importance for specialists in the works of Marcel Proust, his favorite subject for examples and applications. Genette's most widely known critical study, *Narrative Discourse*, is at once comprehensive development of his model for narrative analysis and a close reading of Proust's *À la recherche du temps perdu* (1913–1927; *Remembrance of Things Past*, 1922–1931, 1981).

Analysis

Genette's work may be generally located within the field of structuralist poetics, a field which finds its antecedents in the structuralist linguistics of Ferdinand de Saussure. Saussure's structuralism, extended to studies of folk literature by Vladimir Propp and to literary analysis by Roman Jakobson and the Russian Formalists, laid the groundwork for a broader structuralism which includes the anthropology of Claude Lévi-Strauss, the linguistics of Noam Chomsky, and, most important here, the structuralist studies of literature by such writers as Roland Barthes, Todorov, and Genette himself, who have attempted to develop a poetics of literature which would play something like the role that linguistics plays for language.

Genette has traced the evolution of literary theory as a structuralist activity in "Structuralism and Literary Criticism" in *Figures of Literary Discourse*, assessing the contributions of such seminal figures as those listed above and adding to the movement the critical writings of Proust, T. S. Eliot, and Paul Valéry, and also of Anglo-American New Criticism. Indeed, Genette argues that "the notion of structural analysis can be regarded as a simple equivalent of what Americans call 'close reading,'" to the extent that such "criticism abandons the search for the conditions of existence or the external determinations – psychological, social, or other – of the literary work, in order to concentrate its attention on that work itself, regarded no longer as an effect, but as an absolute being." While this approach would thus reject such transcendent explanations as psychoanalytic or Marxist readings, Genette does not follow this formalist orientation at the expense of ignoring content or thematic analysis.

As he explains in "Principles of Pure Criticism," in *Figures of Literary Discourse*, his formalism "is not opposed to a criticism of meaning . . . but to a criticism that would confuse meaning and substance, and neglect the role of form in the *work of meaning*." Genette's emphasis is on the forms in which themes are embodied, "those two-sided structures in which the concerns of language and the concerns of existence are articulated together." Such a study of the particular forms of language as they relate to particular functions has affinities with traditional rhetoric, and Genette sees his theory in part as a new rhetoric (Wayne Booth's *The Rhetoric of Fiction*, 1961, is an obvious parallel), though one closely tied to linguistics. His concern with rhetorical models includes extending the concerns of poetics beyond the metaphor and metonym, which are only two figures among many, but which nevertheless have come to be inordinately privileged by modern theorists.

The dual emphasis on the letter and the meaning is fundamental to Genette's analysis of the "figure," a term borrowed from rhetoric that provides the titles of his first three books and is defined most explicitly in his essay "Figures" in *Figures of Literary Discourse*. The figure is the form of the gap or space between what an author has written and what he or she has thought. Every phrase, however common or simple (as Genette explains, these are not the same thing), has a form. Rhetorical analysis is the comparison of the form of a given word or sentence to that of another which might have been used in its place. The figure encloses the space between this unmarked virtual signifier and the curve traced by the real signifier used by the author. The existence of the figure thus depends on the reader's awareness of the literary expression as a deviation from the virtual sign to which it is translatable. This admission of the reader's response into the equation is characteristic of Genette's open-ended structuralism. Rather than emphasizing the objective status of textual components – the practice of most earlier structuralist studies – his analyses are always aware that "no study is innocent and without prejudice, the strongest of which is the belief that one is exempt from it." His concentration on the exceptional and aberrant in texts allies him in some respects with poststructuralist criticism, as his analysis of the figure illustrates. While rhetoric is a "system of figures," an apparently structuralist claim, "every figure is translatable, and bears its translation, transparently visible, like a watermark, or a palimpsest, beneath its apparent text. Rhetoric is bound up with this duplicity of language" and thus "bears presence and absence *simultaneously*," an analysis sharing affinities with poststructuralist thought.

Genette's emphasis on the interdependence of form and meaning is related to his emphasis on the close relation between criticism and theory. He sees the two as linked by a similar relation of complementarity and argues that "the future of literary studies is essentially in the necessary exchange and give-and-take between criticism and poetics." This poetics, or "theory of forms" can be arrived at only by working from the particular text to the general principle, an approach exemplified by what has thus far been the most influential of Genette's writings, *Narrative Discourse*. Though several of the key terms developed in this piece were introduced in earlier essays, it is here that Genette gives them their fullest treatment, describing a comprehensive model that has proved useful in the analysis of narrative in film as well as in fiction. This text is also, paradoxically, his fullest examination of the work of Proust, a writer whose work provides a focus of interest to which Genette returns in many of his writings. This dual focus is justified in the preface to the essay:

> Like every work, like every organism, the *Recherche* is made up of elements that are universal, or at least transindividual, which it assembles into a specific synthesis, into a particular totality. To analyze it is to go not from the general to the particular, but indeed from the particular to the general. . . . What I propose here is essentially a method of analysis; I must therefore recognize that by seeking the specific I find the universal, and that by wishing to put theory at the service of criticism I put criticism, against my will, at the service of theory.

Genette's focus on the narrative as "a linguistic production undertaking to tell of one or several events," as the expansion of a verbal statement, leads him to organize his analysis of narrative discourse according to three categories borrowed from the grammar of verbs: tense, dealing with temporal relations between the verbal discourse and the events it recounts; mood, dealing with the modalities of narrative representation; and voice, treating the narrator and his or her audience. This grammatical analogy recalls Genette's interest in paralleling poetics to linguistics.

The treatment of tense analyzes the dual nature of time in narrative. On the one hand is the time of the narrative as it is embodied in the written text, on the other is the time of the events recounted by this narrative discourse. Genette divides tense into three categories: order, duration, and frequency.

The study of order compares the order in which events are arranged in the discourse with the order of events in the story, the order in which the discourse indicates that they occur. It would be possible, at least in a very simple narrative, to have a kind of zero degree here, a perfect correspondence in which the events of the story are narrated in straightforward chronological order. Yet this is seldom the case in literature. Most narratives exhibit what Genette calls anachronies, discordances between these two orders. The beginning of the classical epic (and most novels) *in medias res*, followed by an exposition of earlier events, provides a familiar example. An anachrony of this type, the narrating of an event which took place earlier than the present point of the story, is an analepsis; the narrating in advance of an event that will take place later is a prolepsis. The temporal distance between the events of the anachrony and the moment of the story when the narrative was interrupted is the anachrony's reach. The duration of the events of the anachrony is its extent.

Comparing the duration of a discourse to that of the story it tells is a bit trickier. While one can determine, for example, that the events of a story take place over a ten-year period, the discourse narrating the action has a length, measured in pages, rather than a duration, measured in time (time of reading being too variable to use as a standard). Nevertheless, the variations in speed, the rhythm, may be measured for a given narrative by taking narrative units and considering the ratio of story time to discourse length. The theoretical limits would be the ellipsis, in which nothing is narrated about a certain period of story time, and the pause, in which no story time passes during a section of discourse (as in many descriptions). Intermediate forms would be the scene, usually in dialogue, which conventionally takes about as much time to read as to occur, and the summary, a form with variable tempo, covering narrative rhythms between scene and ellipsis.

While order and duration had been discussed, though not so comprehensively, by other writers, frequency was very little studied until Genette's treatment of it. A system of relations between the frequency of occurrences, the repetitions, of events in the story and narrative statements about them may be established. Three major possibilities are presented: narrating once what happened once, the singulative form of narrative ("Yesterday I went to bed early"); narrating *n* times what happened once, the repetitive form ("Yesterday I went to bed early, yesterday I went to bed early, . . ."); and narrating once what happened *n* times, the iterative form ("Every day I went to bed early"). While iterative and, especially, repetitive narrative might seem at first glance to be more hypothetical possibilities than options really used by writers, Genette shows that they in fact occur much more frequently than might be supposed.

After tense, the second of Genette's three categories is mood, under which he discusses much of what is frequently called "point of view." Under mood he distinguishes distance and perspective. Distance treats the differences between the narrative of events, the transcription of the nonverbal (actions, descriptions) into the verbal, and the narrative of words, the transcription of characters' speech. The narrative of words may take three forms: narrated speech, which summarizes characters' speech; transposed speech, in indirect style; and reported speech, which directly quotes characters. Under perspective Genette distinguishes three possibilities of narrative point of view: nonfocalized narrative, or narrative with zero focalization, in which the narrator tells the audience more than any character knows; internal focalization, in which the narrator is limited to telling what a given character knows (fixed) or what a series of characters know (variable or multiple); and external focalization, in which the narrator does not reveal what any characters know or think. These categories refine and systematize the relations between such traditional categories as "omniscient" and "objective" narration and free them from the misleading concepts carried by such terms as "first-person" and "third-person," which attempt to describe characteristics not necessarily related to mood.

These considerations are classified under the category of voice, which replaces the imprecise first- and third-person categories (all narrators refer to themselves in the first person and other characters in the third) with a system for describing narrators according to their relation to the time of the events narrated, the level at which they narrate, and their degree of participation in the events narrated. Genette also integrates the narratee, the character to whom the events are narrated, into his scheme.

Narrative Discourse proved to be so influential and controversial that Genette was obliged to return to the subject a decade later with his *Narrative Discourse Revisited*, in which he systematically surveys the responses of dozens of critics to his model, defending it and adjusting it as necessary. Genette has since continued to map out his general theory of structuralist poetics in a series of increasingly ambitious studies.

Mimologics traces through history the belief that he calls "Cratylism," first expounded by Cratylus in one of Plato's dialogues, which holds that words are not merely arbitrary signs agreed upon by convention but have a natural relation to the things for which they stand. The form of words is related to the form or essence of the real objects they represent. Genette had touched upon this topic in several early essays, including "Le Jour, le nuit," "Poetic Language, Poetics of Language," "Proust and Indirect Language," and "Rhetoric Restrained," and, at greater length, in a series of articles in the journal *Poétique* appearing in 1972 and 1973.

Three other works, *The Architexte*, *Palimpsestes*, and *Seuils*, form a unit aimed at surveying the field of transtextuality, by which Genette means to indicate "all that which puts one text in relation, manifestly or secretly, with other texts." These relations may take five distinct forms: intertextuality, the presence of one text within another; metatextuality, present when one text speaks of another; architextuality, the relation of text to genre; hypertextuality, any relation between a text B (hypertext) and an anterior text A (hypotext) which is not a citation of (intertext) or commentary on (metatext) but a transformation of that text; and paratextuality, the relation between a text proper and the paratext which accompanies it, including such elements as titles, prefaces, advertisements, epigraphs, and illustrations. Considering that the intertext has been treated sufficiently by Michael Riffaterre and Julia Kristeva, and that the time is not yet ripe for a work on the metatext, which would have to be a universal history of literary criticism and commentary, Genette set himself the task of writing books on the other three elements: *The Architext* on the architext, *Palimpsestes* on the hypertext, and *Seuils* on the paratext. The latter two are especially sweeping and yet closely analytical works, along the lines of *Narrative Discourse*, whose influence on other theorists began almost immediately: a special issue of *Poétique* devoted to essays by various writers on the concept of the paratext accompanied the publication of *Seuils*.

Genette's next triad of books, *Fiction and Diction* and the two volumes of *The Work of Art*, also form something of a coherent unit, collectively addressing perhaps the broadest of the questions literary theory can be posed: What is literature? and What is art? *Fiction and Diction* offers a model for determining the conditions of literariness itself, the aesthetic aspect of literature, while *The Work of Art* extends the investigation well beyond the usual field of poetics into the more general realm of aesthetics, traditionally the province of philosophers rather than literary critics. In the first volume, *Immanence and Transcendence*, Genette postulates the existence of two modes of art, immanence (the type of object the work consists in) and transcendence (the different ways in which the work of art exceeds this physical object in different versions or functions). Immanence is further divided into two regimes, which Genette christens (following the American philosopher Nelson Goodman) the autographic regime, in which the work of art is a physical object (paintings, sculptures), and the allographic regime, in which the work itself is an ideal object not uniquely represented in any one physical manifestation (literary texts, musical compositions). In the second volume, *La Relation esthétique* (the aesthetic relation), Genette builds upon this classification of the status of the production and reception of artistic objects.

Henri Mitterand has remarked that "Barthes being gone, there remains only Genette," and his point would seem to reflect a consensus that Genette is one of the most important and influential of contemporary literary structuralists. His achievement has been at the same time ambitious in its scope and meticulously grounded in detail, erecting a comprehensive theoretical framework on the foundation of careful readings of specific texts. His influence has been the most significant among American theorists, for whom his writings have the distinct merit of having brought together Anglo-American and Continental theories of narrative in his model. He uses English and American theory and literature as freely and authoritatively as French or other European traditions. The question becomes, as Mitterand poses it, not "What books has Genette read?" but "Is there a book that he has not read?"

Principal criticism

Figures, 1966–1972 (3 volumes; partial translation as *Figures of Literary Discourse*, 1982)
"Discours de récit," 1972 (*Narrative Discourse*, 1979)
Mimologiques: Voyage en Cratylie, 1976 (*Mimologics*, 1995)
Introduction à l'architexte, 1979 (*The Architext*, 1992)
Palimpsestes: La Littérature au second degré, 1982
Nouveau Discours du récit, 1983 (*Narrative Discourse Revisited*, 1988)
Seuils, 1987
Fiction et diction, 1991 (*Fiction and Diction*, 1993)
L'Œuvre de l'art: Immanence et transcendance, 1994 (*The Work of Art: Immanence and Transcendence*, 1997)
L'Œuvre de l'art: La Relation esthétique, 1997

Other major works and literary forms

In addition to the books listed above and many essays on narrative theory published in journals, Gérard Genette has had an impact on critical theory through his work as an editor. In 1970 Genette, with Tzvetan Todorov and, through 1973, Hélène Cixous, founded and directed the journal *Poétique*, which became almost from the first issue the most prominent French-language forum for recent critical theory. He and Todorov directed the journal until 1979, when they turned it over to Michel Charles. Genette and Todorov also directed the influential series of books on critical theory published by Éditions de Seuil, also under the rubric *Poétique*, until June of 1987, at which time Genette became sole director of the series. He and Todorov have also edited volumes of essays on Marcel Proust and on Gustave Flaubert, for which Genette wrote the introductions. He has also introduced an edition of Pierre Fontanier's *Les Figures du discours* (1968).

EDITED TEXTS

Les Figures du discours, by Pierre Fontanier, 1968
Sémantique de la poésie, 1979
Recherche de Proust, 1980
Littérature et réalité, 1982
Travail de Flaubert, 1983
Pensée de Rousseau, 1984
Théorie des genres, 1986
Esthétique et poétique, 1992

Further reading

Chatman, Seymour. *Story and Discourse: Narrative Structure in Fiction and Film*, 1978.
Culler, Jonathan. *Structuralist Poetics*, 1975.
Henderson, Brian. "Tense, Mood, and Voice in Film," in *Film Quarterly*. XXXVI, no. 4 (1983), pp. 4–17.
Martin, Wallace. *Recent Theories of Narrative*, 1986.
Mosher, Harold F., Jr. "The Structuralism of Gérard Genette," in *Poetics*. V (1976), pp. 75–86.
Nelles, William. *Frameworks*, 1997.
Rimmon, Shlomith. "A Comprehensive Theory of Narrative," in *PTL: A Journal for Descriptive Poetics and Theory of Literature*. I (1976), pp. 33–62.

Rimmon-Kenan, Shlomith. *Narrative Fiction: Contemporary Poetics*, 1983.
Scholes, Robert. *Structuralism in Literature*, 1974.

WILLIAM NELLES

See also French Literary Theory: Twentieth Century; Intertextuality; Narratology; Structuralism

The Geneva School

The Geneva School of literary criticism is so called because several of its leading members were associated with the University of Geneva, although some of the critics included under the broad umbrella of the school were not Swiss. Sarah Lawall has suggested that a less misleading title for the group would be "critics of consciousness," a more accurate description of their common theoretical ground. The school can be roughly divided into an early and a late period, the former encompassing the work of Marcel Raymond (1897–1981), Albert Béguin (1901–1957), and Georges Poulet, and the latter featuring Jean Rousset (1910–), Jean-Pierre Richard (1922–), and Jean Starobinski (1920–). All these critics share an intuitive approach to literature, stressing the need to eliminate the distinction between the critic and the author, and viewing the text as an expression of the author's consciousness in which the critic can immerse him- or herself. A common theme in their work is the paradoxical idea that the most pure form of poetry is silence, as language cannot encapsulate the absolute, which is the aim of poetry. The school, on this level, preempts deconstruction in its recognition of the inadequacy of language for expressing the "*monde imaginaire*" of the poet – Poulet, in particular, was a strong formative influence on the American critic J. Hillis Miller, who later became a prominent deconstructionist. Indeed, the Geneva critics have had a peripheral impact on several major critical movements of the twentieth century. In their rejection of the principal tenet of New Criticism – that an individual literary text is in effect an independent verbal artifact – and the refocusing of critical attention on the authorial consciousness behind the text, the Geneva School paved the way for later reader-response theorists to emphasize the role of the reader in the delicate process of attributing meaning to a literary text.

Phenomenology

The roots of the Geneva School's approach to literature lie in the phenomenological philosophy propounded by Edmund Husserl (1859–1938) and his followers, but other powerful influences include the strain of Romanticism descending from Jean-Jacques Rousseau and the theory of intellectual history, or *Geistesgeschichte*, proposed by the nineteenth-century German philosopher Wilhelm Dilthey (1833–1911), which focused upon the spirit of an age or epoch rather than specific events. The term "phenomenology" was initially coined by the German philosopher Johann Heinrich Lambert (1728–1777) in 1764, to mean "the science of illusions." Immanuel Kant subsequently drew a distinction between "phenomena" – the realm of appearances – and "noumena" – the realm of essences, or things as they really are. Hegel rejected Kant's division, characterizing phenomenology as the study of different stages of the human consciousness as it becomes aware of itself. As the nineteenth century progressed, the term came to be associated with the study of things in their essences, as they "really are." It owes its modern sense to Husserl, for whom phenomenology was a rigorous mode of thought seeking to arrive at absolute truth. Rejecting both naturalism and psychologism, Husserl believed phenomenology could achieve positive truth, basing this belief on the theory of intentionality derived from his former teacher Franz Brentano (1838–1917). According to Brentano and Husserl, consciousness is necessarily intentional, always possessing a goal or moving toward an object. It does not merely passively receive sense impressions from the world around us. This intentionality allows us to perceive meaning in the sensory perceptions with which our consciousness is continually bombarded, extracting from this current of impressions not the object itself, nor a representation of an object, but an awareness of the intentional act.

The second fundamental component of phenomenology is Husserl's notion of *Anschauung*, or intuition, by which he denotes the faculty of human understanding which allows us to understand abstract concepts, and hence to perceive "essences" – for if we relied solely on our sensory apparatus we could comprehend only the empirical features of our experience, which are necessarily contingent. The application of phenomenological intuition, according to Husserl, requires the suspension or "bracketing" of all presuppositions – historical, existential, eidetic, and transcendental. It must be applied in isolation to reach authentic, uncontaminated knowledge of the world.

In response to criticism from Martin Heidegger, Husserl adapted his conception to accept the notion of an unsuspendable "life-world," by which he denoted the universally held set of presuppositions – beliefs, values, feelings – deriving from our immediate sensory perception, without which we would be unable to make sense of our everyday experience. In this refined form, phenomenology began to be applied to aesthetic questions, most significantly by Roman Ingarden, a Polish student of Husserl. As he explains in *The Literary Work of Art* (1931), a work of literature, as an object whose intentional structure is a predicate, presents the phenomenologist with a valuable theoretical testing-ground. His work outlines what he sees as the inherent structure of a literary work of art, consisting of four strata: firstly, the "word-sounds" (*Wortlaute*), including such effects as rhyme and rhythm; secondly, the "meaning units" (*Bedeutungseinheiten*), incorporating words, sentences, and longer units such as stanzas; thirdly, what he terms the "schematized aspects" (*schematizierte Ansichten*) of the work, by which he means the consistent perceptual features outlined by the meaning units; and fourthly, the represented objects (*dargestellte Gegenstände*) in the work, such as people, trees, or houses, which possess, Ingarden posits, a character similar to ideal objects, and exist in "represented time and space." Ingarden's other major theoretical contribution was his analysis of how we relate aesthetically to a work of literature, particularly in his *The Cognition of the Literary Work of Art* (1968). He highlights the presence of "indeterminacies" (*Unbestimmheitstellen*) in literature, cognitive gaps, which the reader intuitively fills in a process he calls "concretization." The necessarily subjective, personal nature of concretization means that no two experiences of a work of literary art are ever identical, although the work itself is stable, as defined in its strata. Ingarden's approach to literature, however, remains intrinsically conservative, leaning toward a classical definition of literary art – he fails to address the application of his theory to more experimental, modernist works.

Heidegger, wedding these ideas with his own existential approach, introduced a more ontological aspect into aesthetic phenomenology. For Heidegger, art, and particularly poetry, is a process of revealing the Being of things, disclosing truth, which does not reside in an adherence to reality, but in this "closeness to Being." It was through Heidegger's work that phenomenology came to exert an intellectual influence in France, and this explains the existential and ontological preoccupation of French thinkers, such as Emmanuel Levinas (1905–1995), Gabriel Marcel (1889–1973), and Jean-Paul Sartre. As far as the Geneva School is concerned, however, the most significant interpreter of phenomenological tradition in France was Maurice Merleau-Ponty (1908–1961). Merleau-Ponty affirms the centrality of perception for all forms of consciousness, the subject and the object defining and determining each other. Art gives form to that which is perceived, but its meaning derives not only from the perception of the artist, but from those who participate in its experience.

The Geneva School

The members of the Geneva School absorbed these various phenomenological views of art and incorporated them into a more conventional approach to literary criticism. They are bound by their shared conviction that literary criticism can itself be a form of literature. As J. Hillis Miller has expressed it, for the Geneva critics,

> Literary criticism is literature at a second degree. It reaches the subject matter of literature by way of the intercession of poems, novels, plays, journals, and letters which others have written . . . . It therefore makes the same use of language as literature does, and it expresses the same kind of reality.

Marcel Raymond is often considered the founder of the school. A Protestant Genevan by birth, he had an orthodox education in classic French literature, particularly specializing in poetry of the late sixteenth century. In 1926 he married and moved from Paris, where he had studied, to the University of Leipzig. Here he was exposed to the *Geistesgeschichte* of Dilthey, and actually met Husserl. Returning to Switzerland as professor of French literature at the University of Basel, Raymond wrote his first major work, *De Baudelaire au surréalisme* (1933; *From Baudelaire to Surrealism*, 1950), which marks his move from literary history to criticism, and exerted a profound influence over subsequent critics of the Geneva School. In it, Raymond identifies two incompatible traditions in French poetry: realism, which attempts to describe the concrete, essential reality of things, and draws on myth; and a second tradition which tries to establish a transcendental world relating to the condition of humanity, in life and after death. Both traditions struggle equally with the incapacity of language to express the absolute. This observation leads Raymond toward a mysticism that emerges with increasing force in his later work. He cites with admiration Stéphane Mallarmé's notion of the "orphic" – the primal or mystical – and the romantic yearning to be absorbed into nature, and thus eradicate the distinction between human beings and the universe, between subject and object. Raymond's œuvre is essentially a reinterpretation of the French canon with these concerns in mind. In *Génies de France* (1942; the geniuses of France), for instance, he attempts to define French literary genius, by surveying great writers throughout French history – perhaps most characteristically in essays on Victor Hugo and Charles Baudelaire which isolate their primitivistic and mystical leanings and relate these to their entire literary output. Raymond takes issue with the influential view (derived from the Swiss linguist Ferdinand de Saussure) that language is arbitrary and limited, arguing for the ability of the poet to impart meaning to words, thus displaying a great, though somewhat vague, faith in the unifying potential of poetry. For Raymond, as René Wellek comments, "poetry means participation in the world, identification of subject and object, and thus an all-embracing sympathy. The universal and the particular must both be emphasized, and in this is implied the unity of mankind."

Albert Béguin was a direct contemporary of Raymond, and his work has many common features. Béguin came from a Protestant family in the Swiss Jura, and claimed in later life that he first became interested in literature, particularly German, when working in a book shop in 1926. He went on to study in Geneva, before gaining a French lectureship at the University of Halle in 1930, where he stayed for five years studying German. Resigning in 1934 because of the Nazi regime, which he had denounced in a series of polemical articles, Béguin returned to Geneva and composed his doctoral thesis. He then developed this into his first major work, *L'Âme romantique et le rêve* (1937; the romantic soul and the dream), which he published in 1937 in a very limited edition of two volumes. The success of this secured him a professorship at the University of Basel. With the onset of war, Béguin increasingly turned away from his focus on German. In 1940 he converted to Catholicism, and the following year helped to found and run the anti-Nazi journal *Les Cahiers du Rhône*, which published articles by Resistance writers in France. Following the Liberation, Béguin moved to Paris, established the literary magazine *Esprit*, and his final decade was a period of great literary activity.

Béguin's approach to literature, by his own admission, is extremely subjective, even nonacademic, based as it is on the belief that the only means of judging poetry, particularly Romantic poetry, is through sympathy with the poet. *L'Âme romantique et le rêve* offers an extensive discussion of German Romantic authors and their relation to the development of French literature (Proust, to Béguin, is "one of the greatest mystics of modern times"). He concentrates on the importance of the dream world, and emphasizes, again, the inherent problem that we can only experience dreams through language, in the form of a text. He followed the German Romantics in their belief that dreams offer us a glimpse of "the golden age" and are an expression of the soul in its purest state. Poetry is the closest we can come to a deliberate removal of the barrier between our individual consciousness and the elemental, mystical realm of universal consciousness; and thus the dream is the model of aesthetic experience. In Béguin's vision, people are essentially dualistic, split between the psychological and the mystical, an account of consciousness which has been criticized for being resolutely nonphilosophical. His influences and sources are literary, and his interpretation of them extremely personal and religious.

Georges Poulet, a Belgian by birth, was educated at the University of Liège. He is the writer most responsible for the Geneva School's ideas filtering into Anglo-American, partly through teaching positions held at the University of Edinburgh (1927–1951) and Johns Hopkins University (1952–1957). Although never associated with the University of Geneva, he was strongly influenced by both Raymond and Béguin. His critical approach, however, eschews their leanings toward mysticism and religion, adopting instead a thematic approach to the consciousness of individual authors, from all literary periods, which he termed "genetic criticism." Despite sharing the common belief of the Geneva School that criticism involves the total submergence of the mind of the critic in the mind of the author, for Poulet, this "criticism of pure identification" is an end in itself. He takes up the notion, previously borrowed by Raymond from René Descartes, of the *cogito* (the "thinking I"), arguing that the purest form of consciousness is awareness of the self, consciousness divorced from any exterior influences or sensations. Thus, for Poulet, the aim of criticism is to connect with the mind of the author at this original moment of self-consciousness, "in the surging forth and genetic action of its power . . . not yet invaded and, as it were, masked by the thick mass of its objective contents." Whereas, for all the other members of the Geneva School, in line with the theories of Husserl and his followers, consciousness entails consciousness of something, Poulet's approach to literature keeps the traditional dualism of mind and body firmly in place.

The classic Cartesian formulation of the *cogito* saw it as the seat of pure consciousness, the one certainty in a world of subjective sensory data. Poulet's interpretation is more phenomenological – he believes individual consciousnesses function in unison with a temporally defined universal *cogito*, of which all consciousnesses of a particular period partake. This *cogito*, although subject to historical change, and allowing for individual fluctuations, accounts for thematic unity in works from a common era. Poulet's approach to literary criticism was to locate one particular aspect of the *cogito* and trace its articulation and development over the course of literary history. His multivolume *Études sur le temps humain* (1949–1968; studies in human time) concentrates on the temporal and spatial awareness of French authors from the Renaissance to the modern era; *Les Métamorphoses du cercle* (1961; *The Metamorphoses of the Circle*, 1966) conceives of consciousness as a series of concentric circles emanating from a single point, and strives to locate this pattern of thought in a similar selection of literary works. The idea is to use these aspects of the *cogito* as a means of accessing the whole, thus bridging the gap between subject (critic) and object (literary work). What Poulet calls "the phenomenology of reading" occurs when this division is overcome, and readers exchange their own subjectivity for that of the author. Thus his theory of criticism is not really concerned with the individual work at all, but with the consciousness of the author, with whom he seeks a complete identification. Poulet expresses it thus:

> The annexation of my consciousness by another (the other which is in the work) in no way implies that I am the victim of any deprivation of consciousness. Everything happens, on the contrary, as though from the moment I become prey to what I read, I begin to share the use of my consciousness with this being whom I have tried to define and who is the conscious subject ensconced at the heart of the work.

Of the critics of the later Geneva School, Jean-Pierre Richard follows Poulet in his belief that the author should be the focus for literary criticism, coupled with Merleau-Ponty's emphasis on the primacy of perception. Having been educated at the École Normale Supérieure and the Sorbonne in Paris, he also studied under Poulet at the University of Edinburgh, but his own critical output differs markedly from his teacher's in that it rejects the notion of the *cogito*, of a single originating moment in which the consciousness is aware only of itself. Richard remains convinced, like Merleau-Ponty, that the forms and ideas of literature derive from a basic physical experience. As he boldly declares, "It is in sensation that everything begins." In his first two books, *Littérature et sensation* (1954; literature and feeling) and *Poésie et profondeur* (1955; poetry and profundity), Richard examines the work of a range of nineteenth-century French writers – novelists in the former, poets in the latter – and consistently stresses, in line with much phenomenological thought, that consciousness entails content, and thus depends on perception and sensation. For Richard, ideas are less fundamental than material images. Like Béguin, Richard believes that dreams, particularly daydreams (*rêveries*), are patterns of images that reveal the consciousness; and similarly his criticism patiently highlights to the reader how recurring physical images impart meaning and order to the work of his subject authors, including Gérard de Nerval, Gustave Flaubert, Charles Baudelaire, Arthur Rimbaud, and Stéphane Mallarmé.

Jean Starobinski, another Genevan by birth, studied literature at the University of Geneva under Raymond, and was also trained in medicine and psychiatry. He has continued to write on medical and psychological subjects throughout his career, and to explore their points of crossover with other disciplines. In particular, Starobinski has maintained a particular fascination for melancholy, and its various connections to medicine, literature, philosophy, and visual art – in 1988 he published a series of lectures on this theme entitled *La Mélancolie au miroir: Trois Lectures de Baudelaire* (the melancholy of the mirror: three lectures on Baudelaire). Certainly, his background in psychology informs his literary criticism, which exhibits a marked concentration on mental phenomena. Like Poulet, he tries to convey in his criticism a sense of the inner world of his subject author, although, unlike Poulet, he highlights the dependence of consciousness on the body and the sensible world, in the manner of Merleau-Ponty. Despite acknowledging the force of the phenomenological insistence on the interdependence of the mind and the body, Starobinski harbors in his criticism an ideal notion of "the perfect intellectualization of the body," to use Miller's phrase – an approach very evident in his most famous work, *Jean-Jacques Rousseau, la transparence et l'obstacle* (1957; *Jean-Jacques Rousseau: Transparency and Obstruction*, 1988). In this study, Starobinski examines Rousseau's theoretical and autobiographical writing and identifies a twofold movement in his life and work: an initial withdrawal from society and the trappings of civilization – "to escape from his carnal condition and make himself an angel" – and a subsequent attempt at social reintegration through the process of writing, which he characterizes as the effort to rediscover lost purity (*la transparence*). In a familiar echo of other critics of the Geneva School, however, Starobinski argues that Rousseau's attempt to recover and express the lost purity of humankind is doomed to fail because of the inherent fallibility of language. This book also exemplifies Starobinski's belief that the most productive way of understanding an author is to take into account the whole of his or her output – letters, journals, fragments, as well as published texts – and apply to them a detailed close reading technique that draws on a comprehensive knowledge of the period in which they were written (Starobinski's own field of particular expertise, on which he exerted considerable influence, was the eighteenth century). In this way, one might achieve the greatest possible proximity to the writer's inner world. He also borrows from the existentialist phenomenology of Sartre, in his presentation of criticism as a process of intersubjective connection between critic and writer. Starobinski's articulation of what he terms "*le regard critique*" (critical gaze) is, in fact, a useful distillation of phenomenological criticism in general, with its dual emphasis on the critic's reconstructive analysis of the text, in search of the authorial consciousness, on the one hand, and a parallel subjective vision emanating from the consciousness behind the text. It is the crossover of these two related visions, Starobinski argues, that criticism attempts to define and express.

For Richard and Starobinski, in common with most phenomenological critics, the essence of a work resides not in its form, but in the consciousness of the author. The one member of the Geneva School who bucks this trend is Jean Rousset, in whose work the form of the individual piece of literature occupies a central position. Another native Genevan, he studied at the University of Geneva, and taught at several German universities before returning to his alma mater, where he became professor of literature. Richard was first a student, then a colleague of Raymond, and a close friend of Poulet. His essays tend to concentrate on individual works of literature, a practice which has led to somewhat misleading comparisons with American New Criticism. His first book, *La Littérature de l'âge baroque en France* (1953; the literature of the Baroque age in France) studies the Baroque imagination by looking at its manifestation in literary form. But it is in the introduction to *Forme et signification* (1962; *Form and Meaning*, 1962) that Rousset gives the fullest explication of his critical credo – the form of a literary work is not distinct from the consciousness of the author, as New Criticism would have it, but is rather the means by which it is expressed. Where Poulet had dismissed form as "a matter of indifference," for Rousset it is the means by which the mind becomes fully aware of itself. Far from seeing form as an artificial construct imposed upon a piece of literature, Rousset refers to the "interior form" of a work, which emerges naturally as the author discovers him- or herself in the process of writing. This notion is succinctly expressed in *Form and Meaning*, in which he defines a work of literature as "the simultaneous development of a structure and of a way of thinking, the amalgamation of a form and of an experience which are interdependent in their genesis and growth."

Rousset does not dispute the opinion, espoused by other critics of the school, that the goal of criticism is to access the consciousness of the author (what Rousset calls the foyer, which dictates the formal structure of a work); he merely disagrees as to the means by which this is achieved. However, his acknowledgment of the importance of form was at least a step in the direction of the structuralist theories that ultimately displaced the phenomenological approach of the Geneva School in French critical circles.

Further reading

de Man, Paul. "The Literary Self as Origin: The Work of Georges Poulet," in *Blindness and Insight: Essays in the Rhetoric of Contemporary Criticism*, 1971, 1983.

Derrida, Jacques. "The Linguistic Circle of Geneva," in *Critical Inquiry*. 8, no. 4 (Summer, 1982), pp. 675–691. Translated by Alan Bass.

Lawall, Sarah N. *Critics of Consciousness: The Existential Structures of Literature*, 1968.

Macksey, Richard. "The Consciousness of the Critic: Georges Poulet and the Reader's Share," in *Velocities of Change*, 1974.

——, and Eugenio Donato, eds. *The Languages of Criticism and the Sciences of Man: The Structuralist Controversy*, 1970.

Magliola, Robert R. *Phenomenology and Literature: An Introduction*, 1977.

Miller, J. Hillis. "The Geneva School: The Criticism of Marcel Raymond, Albert Béguin, Georges Poulet, Jean Rousset, Jean-Pierre Richard, and Jean Starobinski," in *Critical Quarterly*. VIII (1966), pp. 305–321; reprinted in *Theory Now and Then*, 1991.

Poulet, Georges, Jean Rousset, Jean Starobinski, and Pierre Grotzer, eds. *Albert Béguin et Marcel Raymond: Colloque de Cartigny*, 1979.

ROWLAND HUGHES

See also Heidegger; Miller; Phenomenological Criticism; Poulet

Geoffrey of Vinsauf

English scholar

Born: Place unknown; c. 1200
Died: Place unknown; date unknown

Biography

Nothing much is known about the life of Geoffrey of Vinsauf, except what he writes in the dedications to his work. The only information known with certitude is that Geoffrey was English and that at one time during his career he went to or possibly lived in Rome. The *Poetria nova* was written sometime around the year 1210. It may also be gleaned from the work that he studied in Paris and taught at Hampton in England. Two patrons are mentioned in the dedications to the *Poetria nova*, one at the beginning and one at the end of the poem. The first is Innocent III, with whom Geoffrey may have had an audience during his stay in Rome, and the second is one William, identified in two early manuscripts as either William of Wrotham, an administrator of the navy, or William, Bishop of London. It is true, however, that the mention of patrons in medieval poems does not guarantee or even imply acquaintance. A treatise on the cultivation of wines was attributed to Geoffrey, *De vino et vitibus conservandis*, from which his surname was probably derived, *de vino salvo*, or, in French, *vinsauf*.

Influence

Geoffrey was a key figure in the transmission of ancient linguistic, grammatical, and rhetorical theory to the Middle Ages and the Renaissance. Some fifty manuscripts of the *Poetria nova* alone survive, making it a poem statistically as popular as Geoffrey Chaucer's *The Canterbury Tales* (1387–1400) in its own time. Geoffrey was part of a school of "new rhetoric" that sought to adapt the ancient precepts of Aristotle, Isocrates, Cicero, and Quintilian to the needs of medieval preachers, writers, scribes, and students. Other writers associated with the new school, many of whom were influenced by Geoffrey, include Matthew of Vendôme, Gervase of Melkley, John of Garland, and Eberhard the German.

Although there are traces of Saint Augustine's "Christianization" of the study of language in the works of these new rhetors, the objective of the treatises seems largely secular and practical. Much of what is said by these literary scholars derives from an astute analysis of available classical and contemporary texts; still, the tone of the tracts is clearly prescriptive. The purpose is to teach the "communication skills" of writing and speaking, much like modern prescriptive grammatical and rhetorical texts for college students. For this reason, the impression of Geoffrey that survives in the practicing poets of the High Middle Ages is condescending. His theory, however, has become increasingly important in terms of the analysis of medieval literary texts and as a precursor of modern critical theories based on linguistic approaches to literature.

Analysis

Geoffrey announced that he was doing something new for his poetic era, the thirteenth century, in the very title of his major work, *Poetria nova*. Medieval literary scholars distinguished between the old rhetoric and the new rhetoric – much like modern critics continually celebrate "new" critical or literary theories – and Geoffrey was following their lead. The old rhetoric was derived from the ancient theories of Cicero, Quintilian, and Horace, which were civically oriented; the rhetor was a speaker and the exemplar of the good citizen. The new rhetoric was developed from the pseudo-Ciceronian text called the *Rhetorica ad herennium* (c. 86–82 B.C.), which emphasized a more linguistically and artistically directed analysis of literature than the oratorical texts of the old school. To be sure, poetry was still conceived of as an oral art, as the title to the *Documentum* suggests – "on the mode and art of speaking and composing verses" – but the emphasis was now decidedly aesthetic and analytical.

"New" is a word which reappears throughout the *Poetria nova*, the *Documentum*, and the *Summa de coloribus rhetoricis*, the major surviving texts of Geoffrey. The function of the poet is to remake, or "rejuvenate," archaic poetic "fables." The material for poetry was assumed to be a given; it was derived from the existing texts of the ancient or the medieval world. Geoffrey never talks about imitation in his treatises, imitation of either nature or of literary models in the revered classical and neoclassical sense. Nor does he discuss invention in the modern or Romantic sense, as discovery of original ideas. "Nothing is new under the sun," as Aristotle said. The artist is not imaginative or spontaneously creative; he or she is merely skilled in manipulating old tales.

The first of the five major categories of the discipline of rhetoric, invention, comes from the Latin word *invenio*, meaning "to find" or, more literally still, "to come upon." Literary material exists in the *mythos*, the plots inherited from the ancient world, or in tales from the oral tradition, such as the fabliaux, which were circulating as elaborate jokes during Geoffrey's time. Originality consists in the innovative ordering of those existing materials. Chaucer, aware of these theories, like all the great poets of his generation, states this notion as a poetic axiom at the beginning of *The Parliament of Fowls* (1380):

For out of olde feldes, as men seyth,
Cometh al this newe corn from yer to yere,
And out of olde bokes, in good feyth,
Cometh al this newe science that men lere.

Since, however, the raw material of literature is verbal, as opposed to tonal or visual, the burden of the artistic work is internally conceived and carried out. The writer is a craftsman, but the verbal medium is immaterial, even spiritual. Most of Geoffrey's elaborate metaphors for the poetic process, therefore, are Platonic: they depict an internal workshop where poetic decisions are made and carried out before pen is ever set to paper. He writes: "As a prudent workman, construct the whole fabric within the mind's citadel; let it exist in the mind before it is on the lips."

Geoffrey's assumption about the exclusively verbal nature of the poetic process provides the key to the syncretic, eclectic poetics of the Middle Ages, where old poems are "finished" in a sort of open-ended, editorial process. Guillaume de Lorris and Jean de Meung's *Le Roman de la rose* (thirteenth century; *The Romance of the Rose*) and Chaucer's *The Canterbury Tales* come to mind. An existing work is finished by improvising a conclusion or providing transitions or variations – or by beginning again in a version which may grow to many times the size of the original, as in the case of the *The Romance of the Rose*. In *The Canterbury Tales*, one story generates its successor; a pilgrim "requites" another in an endless chain. The fabliaux, a third example, were being written down for the first time in the thirteenth century; in that tradition, one joke "tops the topper."

Language is thought by the medieval *grammatici* to be generative by nature; it precipitates more of itself out of itself as a response. Geoffrey suggests in the *Documentum* that a discourse may even be spun out of a single word: "The meaning of a single verb is sufficient for extending material endlessly." The "Word" stands at the "beginning" of the poetic discourse, just as it does in religious mystery, for the Word contains, grammatically and semantically, all the elements of discourse within it: the ideas of place, context, duration, action, agency, and so on.

The word Geoffrey advances significantly is *lego*, meaning "I read." Where does one read? What does one read, and how does one read? How is reading depicted in prior texts? The topics generated by the word are methodological, not substantive. They provide modes or categories within which any verbal idea may be manipulated, expanded, or abbreviated. "Language is the House of Being," as Martin Heidegger says, the source of all ideas and their derivations. Old language generates new language; old fields bring forth new corn.

The second major category of traditional rhetoric is arrangement, or the disposition (*ordo*), of the given material. Geoffrey begins by distinguishing between the natural, or what one might call chronological, order in a given tale and the artificial, or artful (*artificale*), order that the poet might conceive for it. Artful order is preferred, because the poet is limited to a single alternative in the inflexible ordering of, say, the story of Troilus and Cressida, as told in Giovanni Boccaccio's *Il filostrato* (c. 1335; *The Filostrato*, 1873). Yet, as fixed as the fable might be, the story may be unfolded or revealed to an audience in any number of different, artful ways. For example, the poet might begin by revealing the ending (Diomede gets Cressida) or he or she might take up the story *in medias res*, in the middle of the action (Cressida, after professing her love for Troilus, is exchanged for Anteonor as a hostage). Clearly, one may begin at the beginning with the love affair of Troilus and Cressida, but that is the least interesting alternative and represents the "natural order."

Getting started, as anyone who has tried to write knows, is the trick. One needs to grab the reader's attention, and Geoffrey notes that the great writers who serve as his inspiration – Cicero, Virgil, Horace, Ovid, Sidonius, Statius – often begin with proverbs or with *exempla* (illustrative anecdotes). In short, one may use a proverb or *exemplum* at the beginning, middle, or end of the story. Eight ways of beginning are explored by Geoffrey – and eight ways of continuing and concluding. The poetic *materia* may be likened to a melody or a harmonic structure that a jazz musician takes as the form on which he or she will improvise. The alternatives chosen, the variations pursued (not the beauty of the original melodic or harmonic motif), constitute the art of the performance.

The freedom of the artist is one of Geoffrey's recurrent themes. Beauty is a function of choice – the choice, for example, of whether to follow the natural or the artistic order. A second choice, conditioned by context, genre, intent, and audience, is whether to amplify and extend or abbreviate and compress the given material. Polonius is echoing Geoffrey when, for example, he dilates on the theme that "brevity is the soul of wit" in *Hamlet, Prince of Denmark* (c. 1600–1601). There are figures appropriate for each method – amplification and abbreviation, which might be likened to fission and fusion in the physical sciences. Fission proliferates, fusion distills. For amplification, the range of pertinent figures or rhetorical "colors," as Geoffrey calls them, include repetition, circumlocution, interpretation, and so on. For fusion, or compression, emphasis, implication, and the fusion of clauses are the requisite figures. The point here is that rhetorical figures are not merely ornaments for the "clothes" of discourse which adorn the crucial idea of the text (although they do assume that function, too); the figures of rhetoric constitute the very methodology for developing or contracting the seminal idea. The figures, or tropes, are the author's palette, the rhetorical colors which will provide the shadow and light, the line and mass, and the composition of the finished picture as well as its verbal flourishes.

Since poetic theory in the Middle Ages was derived from rhetoric, much of the *Poetria nova* is devoted to a catalog of the figures of speech, verbal "ornaments," as they were called, that were deployed to "clothe" the idea in a beautiful verbal garment. If the word was "old," the writer should play the tailor and redesign it – or the physician, and rejuvenate it. There are two major varieties of ornament: "difficult" and "easy." Difficult ornaments or figures are those which derive their meaning from their purely figurative implications, easy, from their literal, aural beauty. Examples of difficult ornaments include metaphor, metonymy (an attributive or suggestive word is substituted for the thing signified), hyperbole (exaggeration, to enlarge or diminish the meaning), synecdoche (indicating the whole by naming the part or the part by naming the whole), and allegory (when a hidden meaning is intended throughout a given narrative). The easy ornaments, designed to appeal to the ear and to the eye in the case of written manuscripts, include repetition (the repetition of a word or phrase at the beginning of succeeding lines of verse), interrogation (rhetorical question asked for effect, not response), and the sentence (the expression of a truth in the compressed form of a maxim).

Poetic theory in the Middle Ages was also derived from grammar. Classic texts were read, translated, and commented on much the same way they are in modern Latin classes. Ovid's story of Theseus is translated, grammatical choices are noted, rhetorical figures in the text are elucidated, structural strategies are discussed, and general meaning, finally, is examined. Geoffrey's theories of "conversion" and "determination" have to do with literary nuance in the case structure of Latin; he discusses whether, for example, to deploy a noun in an ablative absolute or in the accusative or genitive case. The point of this elaborate doctrine is that the minutest detail of the literary text is of semantic and thematic value.

There are three final matters in Geoffrey's literary scheme to be discussed, the three remaining areas of the old rhetoric: style, memory, and delivery. Style must be decorous, that is, appropriate to its subject. From Horace and Quintilian, Geoffrey has learned the notion of the "levels of discourse": high, middle, and low. Certain genres call for dilation or abbreviation and a given range of rhetorical figures. Comedy, for example, demands abbreviation, colloquial diction, straightforward grammatical constructions, and breezy, lighthearted figures. Serious material, on the other hand, should be laced with difficult ornaments as well as pithy *exempla* and proverbs.

Memory and delivery are disposed of quickly, because they concern orally delivered discourse – oratory – with which Geoffrey seems to be only tangentially concerned. Material should be memorized in small, manageable pieces, and delivery should be mellifluous and accompanied by appropriate gestures and facial expressions. Geoffrey reminds the reader that traditional literary discourse was a total performance: a dance of text, song, gesture, expression, and tone.

To be sure, much of the poetic theory of Geoffrey seems archaic and oddly academic for modern tastes, but several of his ideas strike the postmodern sensibility as provocative and up-to-date, namely the linguistic approach to poetry, the concern with an orally delivered and aurally received poetic discourse, and the seminal, generative power of poetic language. The dialogism of Mikhail Bakhtin, for instance, focues on the generative power of language, the crucial importance of context and genre, intertextuality, linguistic reflexivity, and the interrelationship of the oral and scribal transmission of texts, all anticipated by the "new" rhetorical theories of Geoffrey and his contemporaries. Perhaps we might speak finally, after years of deprecation, of Geoffrey of Vinsauf's now fashionable *postmodernitas* — his attention to the importance of the signifier as well as the signified, the verbal surface as well as thematic depth, and to aesthetic as well as theological consciousness. Both Geoffrey and Bakhtin envision language as primarily oral and as therefore a social process whereby speakers, and even authors of different eras, are in constant "dialogue" with one another to refashion discourse or to re-present the great texts of the past in exciting new ways. In many ways, contemporary literary scholars are just beginning to "catch up" with their medieval predecessors in such sophisticated analyses of poetic reflexivity and literary structure.

Principal criticism

Documentum de modo et arte dictandi et versificandi, c. 1208–1216 (*Instruction in the Art and Method of Speaking and Versifying*, 1968; better known as *Documentum*)

Summa de coloribus rhetoricis, c. 1208–1216 (dictionary of the rhetorical colors)

Poetria nova, c. 1210 (*The New Poetics*, 1967; better known as *Poetria nova*)

Other major works and literary forms

The *Poetria nova*, while primarily a treatise on the composition of rhetoric and poetry, like the *Documentum*, is also a poem in hexameters written to exemplify the various theories it propounds and to include the rhetorical figures it explains.

NONFICTION

Causa magistri gaufredi vinesauf, c. 1208–1216

Further reading

Andreas, James R. "'Wordes Betwene': The Rhetoric of the Canterbury Links," in *Chaucer Review*, 1994.

Baldwin, Charles S. *Medieval Rhetoric and Poetic*, 1928.

Curtius, Ernst Robert. *European Literature in the Latin Middle Ages*, 1953. Translated by Willard R. Trask.

Gallo, Ernest. *The "Poetria nova" and Its Sources in Early Rhetorical Doctrine*, 1971.

Hardison, O. B., Jr., et al. *Medieval Literary Criticism: Translations and Interpretations*, 1974.

Jordan, Robert. *Chaucer's Poetics and the Modern Reader*, 1987.

Leupin, Alexander. "Absolute Reflexivity: Geoffroi de Vinsauf," in *Medieval Texts and Contemporary Readers*, 1987.

Murphy, James J. *Rhetoric in the Middle Ages: A History of Rhetorical Theory from Saint Augustine to the Renaissance*, 1974.

Nims, Margaret, trans. *Poetria Nova of Geoffrey of Vinsauf*, 1967.

Parr, Roger, trans. *Documentum de modo et arte dictandi et versificandi*, 1968.

JAMES R. ANDREAS, SR.

See also Alan of Lille; Medieval Literary Theory

Stefan George

German poet, critic, and theorist

Born: Büdesheim, Germany; July 12, 1868
Died: Locarno, Switzerland; December 4, 1933

Biography

Stefan Anton George, the second of three children, was born on July 12, 1868, in Büdesheim to middle-class, Catholic parents. His vintner father and his mother, Eva Schmitt, acknowledged George's intellectual promise by giving him a classical preparatory education and by then supporting him in his initial and formative travels. These included extended stays in the cultural and literary capitals of London and Paris. In Great Britain he improved the language skills he would later use in translating William Shakespeare and Algernon Swinburne. Bilingual in French and German in the manner of many Rhinelanders, he began translating Charles Baudelaire's *Les Fleurs du mal* (1857, 1861, 1868; *Flowers of Evil*, 1909) soon after arriving in Paris in March, 1889. This predisposition, and the chance acquaintance with the young French poet Albert Saint-Paul, led to the most important formative encounter of these early years, with Stéphane Mallarmé and his circle.

The influence of Paris was extraordinary in the way it affirmed in George a sense of the supreme importance of poetry, a sense of vocation modeled after the example of the "master" Mallarmé, and a sense that he, George, might contribute in his own fashion to a poetic, spiritual, and cultural renewal in Germany. After only three semesters at the University of Berlin, George devoted himself entirely to this vocation, publishing the first volume of his own poetry in 1890, *Hymnen* (*Odes*, 1949). In 1892 he founded the journal *Blätter für die Kunst* (leaves for art) with his friend Carl August Klein.

A somewhat fluid but constantly devoted circle of friends, fellow poets, and disciples became a singular feature of George's life and literary theory. These included poets such as Albert Verwey, Karl Wolfskehl, and Hugo von Hofmannsthal, artists such as Melchior Lechter, and literary scholars such as Friedrich Gundolf. This group also included the only woman with whom biographers establish a romantic link, Ida Coblenz, and the youth Maximilian Kronberger, known as Maximin. Although his fame and influence grew steadily, George refused all public honors save the Goethe Prize of the city of Frankfurt on the double occasion of his sixtieth birthday and the publication of his Collected Works. In frail health, and under pressure from the National Socialists to dignify their cultural policies by accepting honors and public office, George left Germany for Switzerland in 1933. He died in Locarno on December 4, 1933, and was buried in the adjacent village of Minusio, according to his own wishes.

Influence

Although not the first to introduce Charles Baudelaire, Paul Verlaine, and Stéphane Mallarmé to the German-speaking world, George is generally regarded as the seminal force in creating and educating a German public for the French Symbolists. He accomplished that by his skillful and remarkably sensitive translations, by featuring these and other modern poets in his influential journal *Blätter für die Kunst*, and by adapting the ideas and style of Mallarmé's circle in Paris to his own aesthetic mission in

Germany. In the latter sense he moved far beyond the role of mere interpreter of Symbolism to become one of the most articulate voices in defining and creating modern German poetry.

George's influence was threatened for several decades during and directly following the period of National Socialism, initially because his austere insistence upon a new and higher cultural order was misappropriated by the National Socialists for political purposes and because that very misappropriation dampened for a time continued critical resonance of his ideas and much of his poetry. A revival of interest in George since the late 1960s suggests that while the extent of his influence has yet to be measured, his place in the constellation of highly significant theoreticians in the twentieth century is as firm as his stature as a poet.

Analysis

While a certain sense of George's critical starting point may be gleaned from the prose included in the Collected Works, George wrote no single, comprehensive statement of literary theory. By far the most productive interpretive commentary is that offered by the aphoristic notes appearing in the *Blätter für die Kunst*, a journal for the arts. Since these were often joint statements, George's contribution cannot be separated from that of his collaborators, and for this reason these notes have not been included in his Collected Works. Like George's poetry, however, the notes in the journal remain indispensable to an elucidation of his critical theory.

In the absence of a notable manifesto, readers interested in George's theoretical position will find in *Tage und Taten* (1903; *Days and Deeds*) a scant page and a half entitled "Über Dichtung" ("On Poetry"). The penultimate aphorism might be rendered as follows in English: "Beauty exists neither as a beginning, nor as an end, but rather as climax. . . . Art is most compelling at the instant one perceives the stirring of new, still sleeping spirits." Contained within that succinct credo are two key words, "beauty," evoking the Platonic triad of the Good, the True, and the Beautiful, and "new." Until fairly recently, most critics have regarded George primarily as an apostle of beauty, dwelling on his affinity with the French Symbolists, on his insistence upon formal elegance, and on his unabashed elitism. Critics focus on his predilection for exotic settings, ritual, and a level of exclusiveness that carried over to vocabulary, orthography, and many other details of the craft of literature usually ignored or accepted as convention by poets and literary theorists.

George's first three volumes of poetry, *Odes*, *Pilgerfahrten* (1890; *Pilgrimages*, 1949), and *Algabal* (1890; English translation, 1949), actually function as the early critical treatise he deigned not to write, indeed could not have written until some of his ideas had resonated among trusted friends back in Germany after his travels through the cultural centers of Europe. It is significant, for example, that *Odes* was first published in an exclusive edition of only one hundred copies, that George penned, arranged, and bound his volumes exactly as he wished and then supervised the printing in the minutest detail, including the selection of the correct paper. A new typeface was created in imitation of George's meticulous hand, ornamental frontispieces by Jugendstil artist Melchior Lechter graced each volume, and a unique system of punctuation (minimalizing punctuation in general and substituting a raised period for comma and semicolon) sent clear signals that these early poems were celebrations of form. They were a direct challenge to the competing aesthetic of naturalism.

Naturalism, as formulated in Germany by Arno Holz, issued from a positivistic belief that reality could be adequately described by scientific means. An entire theory of art could be expressed by a simple "scientific" formula: "Art = Nature - X," according to which art is distinguished from reality only by the manipulations of the artist, the "X." In their efforts to be new, modern, and scientific, proponents of naturalism sought to reduce this "X" to a minimum and tended to depict dark and gritty themes which were good vehicles for the theories of social determinism popular at the close of the nineteenth century. The naturalists perceived art as a tool to approach, and change, social reality; art that avoided the ugly to celebrate beauty, poetry that appealed to the few rather than concerned itself with the masses, an aesthetic rooted in an ideal rather than in the real were sharply criticized in the naturalist manifestos.

George was equally sharp in his repudiation of naturalism. The introduction to the first issue of *Blätter für die Kunst* issued a clear challenge:

> The name of this publication contains in part its purpose: to serve the arts, in particular poetry and literature, excluding all things political and social. This journal seeks to promote a SPIRITUAL ART on the basis of contemporary sensibilities and craft – an art for the sake of art – and is therefore opposed to that impoverished and inferior school which sprang from a false concept of reality. Neither can it concern itself with utopian dreams for improving the world, dreams construed currently as the core of all things modern, dreams which although perfectly lovely belong to a domain other than poetry.

The poems published by the time of this challenge to naturalism in 1892, particularly the *Algabal* cycle, elaborate on these aesthetic premises. In *Algabal* George draws on the sensuality associated with the Roman emperor Elagabalus and upon all he has learned from the Symbolists to create a luxurious, exotic vision whose rarefied beauty is as mysterious as it is compelling. The sensuality of the youthful emperor Algabal's subterranean realm has a hard, cold quality. His garden "needs neither light nor warmth," his rooms are filled with glittering jewels, burnished metal, crystal, and ivory. Even the royal peacocks have feathers "white as swans" and tails that glisten like ice.

What softens the severity of the *Algabal* cycle is the remarkable music of George's language, what C. M. Bowra has called "the slow and loaded movement" of his verse. Unlike the French Symbolists from whom he learned and used much, George preserves in his own verse great formal regularity, compactness, and metrical simplicity. This musicality, the formal elegance, and the transparent desire to create ideal worlds filled with objects of unparalleled beauty, such as his now famous clasp of fire-red gold ("Die Spange") and Algabal's mysterious "dark great black flower," are as clear a repudiation of the naturalists' position as any of the notes in the *Blätter für die Kunst*. The poems of the *Algabal* cycle, together with the other early cycles and *Die Bücher der Hirten- und Preisgedichte, der Sagen und Sänge, und der hängenden Gärten* (1895; *The Books of Eclogues and Eulogies, of Legends and Lays, and of the Hanging Gardens*, 1949), are peopled with richly robed rulers of magical kingdoms, with shepherds who crown themselves with holy garlands, with noble knights, and with a solitary, majestic, and legendary bird, all testifying to George's rejection of the drab world of the naturalists, but also to his avoidance of even the aestheticized ugliness of Baudelaire. These figures also hint at the ethical and increasingly didactic role of the poetry to come, as George, for all of his early renunciation of direct involvement in social issues, focuses ever more on the aesthetic revitalization of a higher, nobler Germany.

Running throughout the anonymous comments during the twenty-seven-year span of the *Blätter für die Kunst* is a constant motif:

> A higher level of culture can be attained only when the vital rhythms of one or more primeval spirits are perceived and embraced, first by a small community, then by a larger layer of society. Such a primeval spirit affects others not through his teachings, but through his rhythm: the teaching is accomplished by his disciples.

According to George and those he influenced, literary criticism is inseparable from cultural criticism. Literature, especially poetry, is the center of culture and thus a means to revitalize, shape, and transform a confused, hollow, debased culture into a noble one. The poet, as primeval spirit (*Urgeist*), manifests through his or her insistence on beauty that ideal gesture which a chosen few will understand, emulate, and eventually transmit to later generations.

George's poetry of the turn of the century is emblematic of the critical insistence on the poet as crafter of a higher spiritual and aesthetic order. His most popular collection, *Das Jahr der Seele* (1897; *The Year of the Soul*, 1949), begins with an invitation to the reader to enter an autumnal park where quiet moments of surprising and elegant beauty await those of sensibility. For the masses, the park is already dead. In soft and resonant measures the poet leads his intimate companion to discovery after discovery, finally to urge the crafting of a wreath, an object of still greater beauty, from among the simple treasures of a cultivated nature. The next collection, *Der Teppich des Lebens und die Lieder von Traum und Tod, mit einem Vorspiel* (1899; *Prelude, The Tapestry of Life, The Songs of Dream and Death*, 1949), marks a subtle change, as the subjective, intimate, and still personal voice of the early poems gives way to a more complex presence, one concerned, as Erika and Michael Metzger have pointed out, with specifically German cultural and poetic traditions, rather than the pan-European orientation prominent in the early issues of George's journal.

The significance of this shift around 1900 is seen in the increasingly prophetic tone of the later poetry, in the heightened didacticism of the final issues of the *Blätter für die Kunst*, in the collaboration with Karl Wolfskehl on a three-volume anthology of German poetry, *Deutsche Dichtung* (1900–1902), and in the remarkable influence of George's circle of friends and disciples, known as the *Georgekreis*. The changes represented by these years also go far to explain the pivotal "Maximin" experience (George's relationship with his young disciple who died of meningitis), as well as the ultimate silence of George's closing years.

George's loss, in 1904, of the youthful poet named Maximilian Kronberger is understood by most critics today as the climactic moment in George's aesthetic development. In venerating Maximin as a god of youth and beauty, George affirms a Hellenistic expression of divinity immanent in this world and manifest in poetry. The Maximin experience forms the center of George's *Der siebente Ring* (1907; *The Seventh Ring*, 1949); perhaps more significant, it confirmed for George the possibility of aesthetic and national renewal, preparing the way for those works of poetry and criticism to follow.

More poetry is contained in one additional cycle, *Der Stern des Bundes* (1914; *The Star of the Covenant*, 1949), and in the final collection of poems, *Das neue Reich* (1928; *The Kingdom Come*, 1949). In *The Star of the Covenant* George completes the shift from his early but unfocused concentration on beauty to a powerful vision of a new aesthetic state. This vision was latent in the earliest formulations of his critical theory, but it was reinforced and given extraordinary emphasis by the Maximin experience. George's biographers relate that at this point George split with several of his contemporaries to put most of his hopes and energies in the next generation, a reorientation that changed the nature of his circle and emphasized the disciple character of those who remained loyal to him.

As "poet-king," George sets forth his aesthetic and moral principles for those who will follow in realizing the ideal of a transformed nation. The temptation is strong to interpret some of these poems in political terms as a call for the catharsis of war. Some of George's circle undoubtedly did, a small number even banded together to publish, between 1910 and 1911, a few issues of a companion journal, *Jahrbuch für die geistige Bewegung* (yearbook for the renewal of the spirit), with sometimes strident political positions. It is more accurate to see in George nothing more politically sinister than the elitism conspicuous in even his earliest pronouncements, coupled with the apocalyptic overtones characteristic of the times (and found, for example, in the poetry of German expressionism, where George's influence was remarkable). What distinguished his voice was his vision of a higher order, one to which he remained still dedicated after World War I. In the last issue of the *Blätter für die Kunst*, published in 1919, readers are directed to look "beyond the great swamp" of the recent chaos, while still cautioned that "the final fate of a people will manifest itself in poetry."

George wrote no poetry during his final few years, devoting himself instead to encouraging others, especially the poets of the younger generation who he believed would carry on with the aesthetic revitalization of Germany, which he had accepted as his mission. The poems in the last collection, *The Kingdom Come*, do not have the same formal relationship to one another characteristic of his other cycles; they represent those individual poems written between 1908 and 1928. Texts of consummate grace and spare beauty ("The Dancer," "You pure and slender as a flame") coexist with cryptic poems on the limitations of language ("The Word") and longer, darker, even despairing allegories ("The Destruction of the Temple," "The Man and the Faun").

These final poems, many already published in the closing issues of the journal, affirm George's lifelong commitment to an aesthetic ideal which became very vulnerable to the grossest kind of distortion under National Socialism. Because of George's prestige and the prestige of his influential circle, attempts were made to interpret *The Kingdom Come* as a prophecy of Adolf Hitler's Third Reich. Like Johann Wolfgang von Goethe and Friedrich Nietzsche, George was appropriated for narrow political purposes, his ideas debased in an uncomprehending parody of the cultural and aesthetic renewal to which he aspired. Neither his silence from 1928 onward nor his departure for Switzerland in 1933 insulated his ideas and works from bitter criticism after World War II. When it was discovered, however, that one of his disciples was the young count Claus Schenk von Stauffenberg, who attempted to assassinate Hitler on July 20, 1944, many believed that George's influence had been restored to respectability. His vision of a great national renewal may never be fulfilled as he imagined. It remains intact as a vision, however, and continues to anchor the antipositivist position in historical discussions of aesthetic issues in German literature. As enduring manifestations of that vision, his poems have been of keen influence in the development of contemporary German poetry, from the radical experiments of the expressionists to the careful constellations of the concrete movement.

Principal criticism

Blätter für die Kunst, 1892–1919 (12 volumes)
Tage und Taten, 1903 (*Days and Deeds*, 1951)

Other major works and literary forms

Stefan George's importance as a literary theorist is inseparable from his importance as a poet and cultural critic. To a degree perhaps unsurpassed in contemporary German letters he developed a consistent and highly influential aesthetic almost exclusively through his own poems and the force of his personality. The two-volume collection *Werke* (1958, 1968) contains a scant fifty pages of prose, but five hundred pages of translations and six hundred pages of poetry.

POETRY

Hymnen, 1890 (*Odes*, 1949)
Pilgerfahrten, 1890 (*Pilgrimages*, 1949)
Algabal, 1890 (English translation, 1949)
Die Bücher der Hirten-und Preisgedichte, der Sagen und Sänge, und der hängenden Gärten, 1895 (*The Books of Eclogues and Eulogies, of Legends and Lays, and of the Hanging Gardens*, 1949)
Das Jahr der Seele, 1897 (*The Year of the Soul*, 1949)
Der Teppich des Lebens und die Lieder von Traum und Tod, mit einem Vorspiel, 1899 (*Prelude, The Tapestry of Life, The Songs of Dream and Death*, 1949)
Die Fibel, 1901 (*The Primer*, 1949)
Der siebente Ring, 1907 (*The Seventh Ring*, 1949)
Der Stern des Bundes, 1914 (*The Star of the Covenant*, 1949)
Das neue Reich, 1928 (*The Kingdom Come*, 1949)
The Works of Stefan George, 1949 (includes the English translation of all titles listed above)

ANTHOLOGY

Deutsche Dichtung, 1900–1902 (3 volumes; with Karl Wolfskehl)

TRANSLATIONS

Baudelaire, die Blumen des Bösen, 1901 (of Charles Baudelaire's *Flowers of Evil*)
Übertragungen aus den Werken von Albert Verwey, 1904
Zeitgenössische Dichter, 1905 (2 volumes)
Shakespeare, Sonette, 1909
Dante, Göttliche Komödie, 1912 (of *The Divine Comedy*)

MISCELLANEOUS

Werke, 1958, 1968 (2 volumes)
The Works of Stefan George, 1974 (includes *Days and Deeds*)
Sämtliche Werke: in 18 Bänden, Band XVII Tage und Taten: Aufzeichnungen und Skizzen, 1998

Further reading

Ahn, Bang-Soon. *Dekadenz in der Dichtung des fin de siècle*, 1996.
Bowra, C. M. *The Heritage of Symbolism*, 1943.
Braungart, Wolfgang. *Ästhetischer Katholizismus: Stefan Georges Ritvale der Literatur*, 1997.
Breuer, Stefan. *Ästhetischer Fundamentalismus: Stefan George und der deutsche Antimodernismus*, 1996.

Durzak, Manfred. *Der junge Stefan George: Kunsttheorie und Dichtung*, 1968.
Goldsmith, Ulrich K. *Stefan George*, 1970.
Metzger, Michael M., and Erika A. Metzger. *Stefan George*, 1972.
Petrow, Michael. *Der Dichter als Führer? zur Wirkung Stefan Georges im "Dritten Reich,"* 1995.
Weber, Frank. *Die Bedentung Nietzsches für Stefan George und seinen Kreis*, 1989.

MARK E. CORY

See also Gundolf; Symbolism

Sandra M. Gilbert and Susan Gubar

American critics

Sandra M. Gilbert
Born: New York, New York; December 27, 1936

Susan Gubar
Born: New York, New York; November 30, 1944

Biography

Sandra Mortola Gilbert was born in New York City on December 27, 1936, the daughter of Alexis Mortola and Angela Caruso. She attended Cornell University, where she earned her bachelor of arts degree in 1957. She received her master of arts from New York University in 1961 and her doctor of philosophy from Columbia University in 1968. Gilbert's career includes teaching posts at Queens College of the City University of New York, from 1964 to 1966, California State University at Sacramento and Hayward, from 1967 to 1971, St. Mary's College at Moraga, California, 1972, Indiana University at Bloomington, from 1973 to 1975, and the University of California, Davis, from 1975 to 1985. In 1985 Gilbert took up the C. Barnwell Straut Chair of English at Princeton University, returning to Davis in 1989. She served as president of the Modern Language Association in 1996, and was recently named to the American Academy of Arts and Sciences. She was married to Elliot Gilbert and has three children. *Wrongful Death: A Medical Tragedy* (1996) is a personal account of her husband's death.

Susan David Gubar was born in Brooklyn, New York City, on November 30, 1944, the daughter of Frank David and Luise Dreyfus. She attended City College of New York, earning a bachelor of arts degree in 1965. She received a master of arts in 1967 from the University of Michigan and her doctor of philosophy from the University of Iowa in 1971. Gubar's teaching career started in 1971 at the University of Illinois, Chicago Circle. Since 1973 she has taught at Indiana University at Bloomington where she is professor of English and Women's Studies. She is married to Edward Gubar and has two daughters.

Influence

The work of Sandra M. Gilbert and Susan Gubar constitutes a bold departure from traditional literary criticism. Following the early efforts by Kate Millett, Mary Ellmann, and others to establish a school of feminist literary criticism in the United States and the English-speaking world, Gilbert and Gubar have reinterpreted the concepts of literary creation, characters, and themes found in works by women writers. Their view of the production of women authors has brought a new appreciation to previously neglected writers and helped to expand the literary canon. The impact of their critical theories transcends the limits of national literatures; their work has become a model for feminist critics of other countries and languages.

Analysis

Gilbert and Gubar's collaboration began when they taught a course in literature by women at Indiana University at Bloomington. Their first book-length effort, *The Madwoman in the Attic* (1979), caused a tremendous furor in literary circles and has become a standard text. The book, which takes its title from Charlotte Brontë's *Jane Eyre* (1847), consists of criticism and close readings of important writers from the period. Departing from the traditional view of women writers as minor and isolated talents in the literary world, *The Madwoman in the Attic* sets out to prove the existence of a female literary tradition and show how it is expressed in the production of the nineteenth century in Great Britain and the United States.

The book's premise is simple and revolutionary. It assumes that the coherence found in the themes, landscapes, and shapes in works by women of the period stems from a conscious effort by the writers to redefine themselves, their art, and the society in which they lived. This theoretical base opens the door to fresh readings of the books and writers treated. The works of Jane Austen, Emily Dickinson, George Eliot, and others are interpreted against the background of their society. These women are viewed not as less talented imitators of male models, but as rebellious creators expressing their own reality. This reading forms the basis for a new theory of women's literary creativity.

The Madwoman in the Attic sees the woman writer as a challenger to a domain considered exclusively male. The woman author, in her search for self-expression, reaches for authority, the right to create and possess an identity of her own. Critics and male authors, deeming those qualities masculine, find fault with the work of the women who assume them, accusing them of presumptuousness and lack of femininity. Therefore, Gilbert and Gubar assert, the woman writer is caught in the dilemma of conforming to patriarchal literary standards, in order for her production to be accepted by the critical establishment, or rejecting these rules which oppress and deny her talents. The rage and instability created by such a conflict inform much of the work of the women of the time and explain the relative scarcity of works by women in the literary canon.

Almost a companion piece to *The Madwoman in the Attic*, the collection *Shakespeare's Sisters*, also published in 1979, deals with the relationship of gender, genre, and production in literature. The title of this volume echoes the famous 1928 article by Virginia Woolf in which she reflects on the fact that women have always been denied access to literature. Gilbert and Gubar examine the factors that have kept women from literature and search for answers to the questions of authorship and the relative value of different literary genres. They claim that most readers and critics have ascribed more intellectual value to poetry than to fiction, and that both are considered the sole realm of men because inspiration and the creative spirit are seen as emerging from the male sexual impulses. Under these circumstances, the woman writer, especially the woman poet, is an outsider, lacking the necessary physical characteristics for creation and denied the education deemed indispensable to produce competent works.

Even if women did overcome these obstacles and produce a body of poetry, their works were judged as trivial and feminine if they dealt with domestic subjects, sententious and masculine if they touched on philosophical or serious themes, too broad if they treated a variety of topics, and limited if they concentrated on selected matters. They never excelled enough in the eyes of the critics to reach the level of the most mediocre of the male poets. The bias of the critic against women is uncovered time and again in these essays, which examine the works of women poets in relation to their social mores, expose the effort of the patriarchal establishment to suppress women's writing, and chronicle the success of those women who were able, in the face of such odds, to write poetry and to achieve a lasting place in the history of literature.

In 1985 W. W. Norton and Company published *The Norton Anthology of Literature by Women*, edited and prefaced by Gilbert and Gubar. This anthology, produced by one of the most respected and conservative printing houses of the English-speaking world, marks a momentous achievement for women writers and feminist criticism. The fact that the material in the anthology was chosen and edited by Gilbert and Gubar, known for their nontraditional view of literature, is no less significant than the publication of the anthology itself. Here is tangible evidence of the growing importance of women's literature in the academic world, where women's writing has routinely been viewed as marginal or, at best, minor.

In order to reflect better the reality of women's literary history, Gilbert and Gubar depart from the usual division into artistic ages or periods and divide the anthology into six broad parts, corresponding to the Middle Ages and the Renaissance, the seventeenth and eighteenth centuries, the nineteenth century, the turn of the century, and contemporary literature, eliminating some literary epochs not relevant to women. Also departing from the customary showpiecing of well-known works, the editors seek to avoid the use of excerpts from famous works, choosing instead shorter, less-known works in order to provide a better sampling of the authors represented. Another significant characteristic of this anthology is that it gathers, perhaps for the first time, material that is not bound by country, class, or themes. Included in this volume are women writers from all the countries that constitute the English-speaking world, emphasizing the unity and diversity of their literary tradition and the importance of seeing women's writing not as a separate and sporadic manifestation of talent but as a coherent part of a literary tradition. Another major contribution to the better understanding of women's literary history is that many of the texts chosen had been out of print or nearly inaccessible before the publication of the anthology. These, together with the illuminating essays written by Gilbert and Gubar about periods and authors, make this work a vital part of the contemporary critical canon.

The Female Imagination and the Modernist Aesthetic (1986) contains essays that deal mainly with the early twentieth century and the role of women artists in the development of the so-called modernistic period in literature, exploring the connections of gender and historic, artistic, social, and economic events. The disruption and reshaping of society caused by war, which usually causes change and expansion of traditional roles, allowed, during this time, an opening of doors to feminist concerns and an assertion on the part of women of their right to artistic and economic freedom.

These topics are central to the three-volume work *No Man's Land: The Place of the Woman Writer in the Twentieth Century* (1988–1994). Among the most significant products of Gilbert and Gubar's collaboration, this work continues and expands their critical reassessment of the literary canon, examining the writings of women in the twentieth century and also the writing and criticism of men whose work is considered to be important in the period.

No Man's Land takes its title from the space between two warring armies and reflects the existing conflict between men and women and their different aesthetic priorities, their ideas about society and the world, and the resulting gulf of understanding between them. The first volume of the work, subtitled *The War of the Words* is a social, literary, and linguistic overview from the middle of the nineteenth century to the late twentieth century, studying how different factors affected the work of male and female writers. Gilbert and Gubar affirm that modernism and avant-garde literature in the early twentieth century were products of the sexual battle that takes place in society and in artistic circles, in which women struggle to attain a position in the world and men try to hold on to their privileges, attempting to keep women out of the spheres of political and artistic eminence. This struggle causes society to undergo radical changes, and these changes in turn are reflected in the literary production of the era. The concluding volumes, *Sexchanges* and *Letters from the Front*, contain detailed readings and criticism of literary works of the period.

The work is based on the premises that it is possible to know history, and that literature is produced by people affected by the material conditions of their time. Thus the authors consider works of art as integral parts of the period in which they are produced and believe that an understanding of that period aids in the understanding of the work. This understanding of the period demands the detailed study of the masculinist and feminist ideologies in vogue and the way in which they determined society – an exegesis of twentieth-century literature as pivotal to an understanding of the modern era as *The Madwoman in the Attic* was to the comprehension of the nineteenth century. The critical work of Sandra M. Gilbert and Susan Gubar is essential reading for anyone interested in understanding the development of literature in the English language.

Principal criticism

The Madwoman in the Attic: The Woman Writer and the Nineteenth-Century Literary Imagination, 1979
Shakespeare's Sisters: Feminist Essays on Women Poets, 1979 (editors)
The Norton Anthology of Literature by Women: The Tradition in English, 1985 (editors)
The Female Imagination and the Modernist Aesthetic, 1986 (editors)
No Man's Land: The Place of the Woman Writer in the Twentieth Century, Vol. 1: The War of the Words, 1988
——, *Vol. 2: Sexchanges*, 1989
——, *Vol. 3: Letters from the Front*, 1994

Other major works and literary forms

Sandra M. Gilbert and Susan Gubar have written much independently from their collaborative work. Gilbert has edited works by Virginia Woolf, D. H. Lawrence, and others, and has published articles, book reviews, and several collections of poetry. Susan Gubar has published book reviews, articles on literary theory, and criticism on fiction and literary history.

POETRY (by Gilbert)
In the Fourth World, 1973
The Summer Kitchen, 1983
Emily's Bread: Poems, 1984
Blood Pressure, 1987

NONFICTION (by Gilbert)
Acts of Attention: The Poems of D. H. Lawrence, 1973
Wrongful Death – A Medical Tragedy, 1996

EDITED TEXTS (by Gilbert)
Shakespeare's "Twelfth Night," 1964
Two Novels by E. M. Forster, 1965
D. H. Lawrence's "Sons and Lovers," 1965
Two Novels by Virginia Woolf, 1966
"The Awakening" and Other Stories: Selections from Kate Chopin, 1984

EDITED TEXTS (by Gubar)
For Adult Users Only: The Dilemma of Violent Pornography (with Joan Hoff), 1989
English Inside and Out: The Places of Literary Criticism (with Jonathan Kamholtz), 1993

Further reading

Benstock, Shari. *Feminist Issues in Literary Scholarship*, 1987.
Cain, William E., ed. *Making Feminist History: The Literary Scholarship of Sandra M. Gilbert and Susan Gubar*, 1994.
Heilbrun, Carolyn G. "*The Madwoman in the Attic*," in *The Washington Post Book World*. IX (November 25, 1979), p. 4.
Moi, Toril. *Sexual/Textual Politics: Feminist Literary Theory*, 1985.
Schreiber, LeAnne. Review of *The Madwoman in the Attic* in *The New York Times Book Review*. LXXXIV (December 9, 1979), p. 11.
Speck, Patricia. "*The Madwoman in the Attic*," in *Yale Review*. LXIX (Winter, 1980), pp. 266–270.
Watts, E. S. "*Shakespeare's Sisters*," in *Journal of English and German Philology*. LXXIX (April, 1980), pp. 265–266.

LINA L. COFRESI

See also American Literary Theory: Twentieth Century; Feminist Criticism; Fuller; Moi

Giambattista Giraldi Cinthio

Italian playwright and theorist

Born: Ferrara, Italy; November, 1504
Died: Ferrara, Italy; December 29, 1573

Biography

Giambattista Giraldi Cinthio lived and worked in Ferrara for much of his life. Named to the university chair in rhetoric in 1541, he lectured on Horatian and Aristotelian literary theory. At the same time, as ducal secretary to Ercole II d'Este, he undertook ambassadorial missions to France and Venice. Between 1541 and 1563 he presented his plays at court, obtaining renown in Ferrara but generating envy elsewhere. He published his theoretical works in 1554. That same year a former student, Giovambattista Nicolucci, known as Pigna, published his own *Libro dei romanzi*, in which he denied ever having been Giraldi Cinthio's student and accused his former teacher of plagiarism. Giraldi Cinthio then published three letters written by Pigna wherein the young man exhorted his master to compose a theoretical work in defense of Ludovico Ariosto's *Orlando furioso* (1516, 1521, 1532; English translation, 1591). Pigna acknowledged having written one of them, but claimed that it was a fictional piece intended for a collection Giraldi Cinthio was compiling. No such collection was ever published.

Pigna was most likely motivated by ambition, not by any claim to real injustice. Giraldi Cinthio suffered greatly from the affront, as Pigna redoubled his efforts to supplant his former master. In 1561 he succeeded, and Giraldi Cinthio eventually moved to Mondoví to teach humanities. From there he went to Turin, and in 1568 he moved to Pavia. Because of failing health he returned to Ferrara in 1571, where he died in 1573.

Influence

Giraldi Cinthio was among the first to relate Aristotelian criticism to contemporary literary theory, and his own theories were often the subject of controversy. His influence extended through much of Europe until early in the seventeenth century. His short stories were sources for plays by William Shakespeare (*Measure for Measure*, 1604; *Othello, the Moor of Venice*, 1604) and Lope de Vega Carpio (among others, *El piadoso veneciano*, 1638, and *Servir a señor discreto*, 1618). Works by Miguel de Cervantes in Spain, François Ogier and Jacques Peletier in France, and Sir Philip Sidney in England also reflect Giraldi Cinthio's theories.

Analysis

Giraldi Cinthio's theoretical writings are evidence of the controversy and uncertainty of his age. The growing influence of Aristotle's *De poetica* (334–323 B.C.; *Poetics*) in the sixteenth century led to conflicts over the propriety of certain genres which did not conform to his theory. Chief among these disputed genres was the romance, exemplified by Ariosto's *Orlando furioso*. Its plot involved multiple actions by many characters and did not therefore reflect Aristotle's definition of unity, according to which the removal of any part would cause the entire structure to collapse. In his treatise on romance, Giraldi Cinthio defended Ariosto, arguing that epic and romance are two different genres. In the treatise on comedy and tragedy, as well, he considered Aristotle respectfully but differs from him on certain questions.

Many of Giraldi Cinthio's modifications to Aristotle reflect his adherence to the Horatian principle that works of art must be both delightful and useful. While moral instruction is the end of poetry, delight is its means. The romance plot, for example, must imitate illustrious actions in order to instruct people to lead an honest life. Giraldi Cinthio defended Ariosto's interweaving of multiple plots, noting that although such a structure violates Aristotelian unity, its use of suspense produces greater delight, making it potentially more edifying. Tragedy, although it presents miserable and terrible things, contains the hidden pleasure of catharsis and by arousing pity and fear shows people what actions to avoid. Comedy, on the other hand, enlightens through more direct pleasure. While Giraldi Cinthio generally preferred flat verse for drama, he favored rhyme in the tragic chorus or at moments of particular thematic or affective purpose: the more pleasant the passage, the more persuasive it is.

Giraldi Cinthio acknowledged that his sensitivity to reader/audience reaction distinguished him from Aristotle, but he persisted nevertheless. While his position is in part Horatian, it also reflects his understanding of contemporary taste. He knew of the enormous success of *Orlando furioso* and of the dismal failure of Giangiorgio Trissino's attempt at an authentic Aristotelian epic, *La Italia liberata dai Goti* (1547–1548; Italy liberated from the Goths). From his own experience with the highly successful *Orbecche* (1541), Giraldi Cinthio understood what made tragedy pleasing to an audience. The conflict over epic was especially vexing, however, since it involved the seeming irreconcilability of theory and practice. In his treatise on romance, Giraldi Cinthio sought to resolve these conflicts.

In *Discorso intorno dei romanzi, delle commedie, e delle tragedie e di altre maniere di poesia* (1554; *On Romances*, 1968) Giraldi Cinthio labels romance a genre distinct from epic, thus exempting it from many of Aristotle's rules. He traces the origins of romance to France, where it had supplanted the heroic compositions of Greek and Latin poets. Unlike epic, which narrated the single action of a single person, romance from the outset treated the multiple actions of many people. From France it had moved into Spain and finally Italy, where it assumed a unique verse form, the Italian hendecasyllable. Italian poetic forms, Giraldi Cinthio points out, are not those of other languages and nations and therefore are not subject to others' rules; slavish adherence to Aristotle and Horace would be inappropriate since neither knew Italian or the Italian tradition.

Having eliminated the issue of genre, Giraldi Cinthio then elaborates more fully his theory of proper romance content and form, following the Aristotelian categories of invention, disposition, and elocution. Choice of the story itself is the poet's primary task; the subject must be credible and have the potential for ornamentation and splendor, which will increase the reader's pleasure. Following Aristotle, who found fictive material more pleasing in tragedy, Giraldi Cinthio recommends its use in romance as well, instead of old histories. Tales of Christian wars make good choices because a Christian audience would take pleasure in divine retribution against the infidels. Matteo Maria Boiardo's *Orlando innamorato* (1495; English translation, 1598) and Ariosto's *Orlando furioso* provide the best models to follow; Luigi Pulci's *Il Morgante* (1483; partial English translation, 1823) is inadequate as it is too comical and lacks heroic gravity.

In considering disposition, the believable order of events, Giraldi Cinthio distinguishes the poet's role from that of the historian. While the historian should recount events in chronological order, the poet, as Horace instructs, should begin his or her tale *in medias res*, introducing earlier history through later digressions. These must be interdependent, well linked to the story, proportionate to the rest of the poem, and within the realm of poetic fictions – believable even if not absolutely realistic. In general, the poet should shorten the tale when possible, particularly through expedients such as predictions, narrative paintings, and intercalated stories. If following the Italian tradition of multiple actions, the poet should begin with the most important, upon which all others will depend. In all these aspects, the poet should learn from his or her teachers or from reading other poems, though in both cases he or she must rely on his or her native ability to distinguish virtues from vices. Trissino failed in this aspect, Giraldi Cinthio explains, because he took only the "dung" from Virgil, erroneously deeming it pure gold.

His treatise on tragedy and comedy, *Discorso intorno al comporre delle commedie e delle tragedie*, considers similar questions of genre, story, and form. As in the treatise on romance, Giraldi Cinthio begins by asserting that he will not be summarizing Aristotle, though often he does. He follows Aristotle in discussing the same six aspects of theater: plot, song, diction, character, thought, and spectacle. His definitions of comedy and tragedy are Aristotelian as well: tragedy moves from fortune to misfortune, comedy from misfortune to fortune. In addition to describing these two standard forms, Giraldi Cinthio discusses the tragicomedy, which is a tragedy with a happy ending. His own *Altile* (c. 1545), *Selene* (c. 1554), and *Gli antivalomeni* (1548) take this form, which he justifies as pleasing to the audience and in conformity with contemporary trends. He warns, however, that the poet must keep the audience in suspense until the very end; the audience must see the end approaching but not guess it. Both comedy and tragedy should use verse and not prose. Tragedy has a chorus; comedy does not. Dramatic action should occupy the space of one day, though some works represent longer action. The story is again of central concern; all parts of the work should depend on it, so that if anything were removed the entire structure would collapse. While some would argue that a historical plot is proper to tragedy and a fictive one to comedy, Giraldi Cinthio agreed with Aristotle that both can be fictive: one need not use history to achieve verisimilitude.

Giraldi Cinthio preferred the five-act structure of Latin comedy for both comedy and tragedy. Like Aristotle, he found the core of dramatic plot to lie in reversals (a movement from a good to a bad state or vice versa) and recognitions (the discovery of something a character did not previously know). For comedy or tragedy to succeed, the poet must carefully construct the intrigue and its solution, avoiding the *deus ex machina* at all costs, since it does not arise spontaneously from the plot and is not satisfying to the spectator. Nor should the tragic effects of pity and fear depend entirely upon the spectacle; they should grow from language and composition as well, so that both the reader and the audience may experience them. Good examples for the poet to follow are Sophocles' *Oidipous Tyrannos* (c. 429 B.C.; *Oedipus Tyrannus*) for tragedy, Terence's *Andria* (166 B.C.) and Ariosto's *La cassaria* (1508; *The Coffer*, 1975) for comedy.

Giraldi Cinthio also discusses whether theatrical works should have single or double plots, and on this point he differs from Aristotle. Aristotle objected to double plots precisely because they were the stuff of tragicomedy, which he thought merely pandered to public taste. Giraldi Cinthio endorses them for comedy and tragicomedy, but in pure tragedy only if handled carefully. He agrees with Aristotle that the characters of tragedy should be midway between good and evil, as the spectator will see their misfortune as deserved but believe that it should not have been so grave. Comedy, on the other hand, admits a much wider range of character types.

The treatise on satyr plays is far briefer than the other two. In it, Giraldi Cinthio attempts to formulate a coherent theory of their form and nature, since no previous theory had been written. He traces their origins to attempts to appease angry gods and discusses their relationship to comedy and tragedy, concluding that each form probably developed independently of the others. The satyr play fuses aspects of both comedy and tragedy: at the outset it should be light and ribald, but it should end unhappily in order to provoke fear and pity. Like tragedy, the satyr play may have a chorus, since satyrs, while rough and lewd, have divine aspects; the satyr chorus should not, however, be as majestic as its tragic counterpart, and it must always be mobile, while the tragic chorus is primarily stable. The language of the play should follow a middle road between comic and tragic and should always be appropriate to the characters. The setting should be wooded, and the set should make use of machinery capable of creating wonders, such as the appearance of gods and the effects of lightning and thunder. Giraldi Cinthio's model for the satyr play is Euripides' *Cyclops* (c. 421 B.C.).

Throughout these works, Giraldi Cinthio's discussion of representation and elocution is ruled by the principle of decorum, which he describes as that which is proper to the place, the time, and the characters. He warns the poet to avoid descriptions that are annoying, graceless, or unworthy of the hero. He labels indecorous the introduction of the Christian God in romance action as a substitute for the pagan gods of classical epic, endorsing instead the use of fates, infernal spirits, and incantations. He prefers these figures to celestial angels, since the latter are perfect and thus not interesting. Tragic language should be grand, royal, and magnificent; characters should make long speeches. Comedic language should be familiar and popular, the speeches brief. The comic poet should avoid tropes, but the tragic poet may use them, as they lend gravity to the discourse. Comedic humor must not be dirty or obscene but must arise from the situation, appearing thus to be natural and civil. This use of humor is characteristic of Terence, Giraldi Cinthio argues, but not of Plautus; Plautus used a lower form of comedy, thinking that it would better reach his plebeian audience. Tragic speeches must also appear natural; they should not seem so inappropriate as to induce laughter. Moreover, while the poet does not necessarily direct his or her work, he or she should take care that decorum is maintained in set design, acting, and costumes.

Thus, while Giraldi Cinthio differed from Aristotle in many ways, especially in his sensitivity to reader / audience response, he was ultimately loyal to many of Aristotle's tenets. The significance of his work lies in his sensitivity to classical models of imitation and his effort to modify those models to account for contemporary taste. Later theorists such as Torquato Tasso would undertake similar endeavors, as writers of the later sixteenth century continued to grapple with fundamental conflicts over the nature of poetry.

Principal criticism

Giuditio sopra la tragedia di Canace et Macario, 1550
Discorso intorno dei romanzi, delle commedie, e delle tragedie e di altre maniere di poesia, 1554, includes *Discorso intorno al comporre dei romanzi* (*On Romances*, 1968), *Discorso intorno al comporre delle commedie e delle tragedie*, and *Discorso sopra il comporre le satire atte alla scena*

Other major works and literary forms

In addition to his theoretical work, Giambattista Giraldi Cinthio wrote plays, Latin and Italian poetry, moral treatises, and short stories. His plays include the successful tragedy *Orbecche* (1541); the comedy *Eudemoni* (1549); a satyr play, *Egle* (1545); and the so-called tragicomedy *Altile* (c. 1545). Other works are the epic poem *Hercole* (written in 1557 but not published until 1864) and a collection of a hundred and twelve short stories, *Hecatommithi* (1565), stylistically in the tradition of Giovanni Boccaccio's *The Decameron* (1353) but ideologically akin to the moralism of the Counter-Reformation.

SHORT FICTION
Hecatommithi, 1565

PLAYS
Orbecche, 1541
Didone, 1541
Cleopatra, c. 1543
Altile, c. 1545
Egle, 1545
Gli antivalomeni, 1548
Eudemoni, 1549
Selene, c. 1554
Euphimia, 1554
Arrenopia, 1563
Epitia, 1583
Le tragedie di Giambattista Cinthio, 1583

POETRY
Poemata, 1540
Fiamme, 1548
Hercole, written 1557, published 1864

Further reading

Bruscagli, Riccardo. "G. B. Giraldi: Comico, satirico, tragico," in *Stagioni della civiltà estense*, 1983.
Guerrieri-Crocetti, Camillo. *G. B. Giraldi ed il pensiero critico del sec XVI*, 1932.
Herrick, M. T. *Italian Tragedy in the Renaissance*, 1965.
Horne, P. R. *The Tragedies of Giambattista Cinthio Giraldi*, 1962.
Spingarn, Joel. *A History of Literary Criticism in the Renaissance*, 1938.
Toffanin, Giuseppe. *Il cinquecento*, 1927.
Weinberg, Bernard. *A History of Literary Criticism in the Italian Renaissance*. Vol. 1, 1961.

MICHAEL SHERBERG

See also Castelvetro; Minturno; Renaissance and Restoration Literary Theory; Trissino

René Girard

French cultural critic

Born: Avignon, France; December 25, 1923

Biography

René Noël Girard was born on December 25, 1923, in Avignon, France, and attended the University of Paris, from which he graduated in 1947. He was an instructor in the French department at Indiana University from 1947 to 1952, finishing his Ph.D. in 1950. The following year he married Martha V. McCullough, with whom he had three children.

Girard has taught in the French department of several major universities in the United States, including Duke University, Bryn Mawr College, The Johns Hopkins University, and the State University of New York at Buffalo. An active participant in academic circles, Girard has served as general editor of *Modern Language Notes* for two terms and has twice been a Guggenheim Fellow. He is professor emeritus at Stanford University and since 1962 has been a professor at the Institut d'Études Françaises d'Avignon.

Influence

As a cultural critic, Girard brings back to the intellectual realm a sense of excitement with his belief that answers to large social problems can be found or should at least be attempted without apology. His interdisciplinary approach, reassessing hitherto unquestioned assumptions in several fields of inquiry, challenges literary critics to look beyond specific ideologies and engage in the search for a unifying system of thought.

Though he tends to turn to the traditional canon of literature for his study of the mimetic, he confidently believes that literature, far from sinking into an "empty and dying cult," has aesthetic, intellectual, and indeed ethical value. His work is described by one commentator as a "daring, nostalgic return to a criticism of ultimate explanations unlocked by a simple theory." His work provides an important hypothesis about culture and serves as the basis for perceiving the similarity of patterns not only in literary texts but also in the political, social, and psychological behavior of human beings.

Analysis

Girard's critical approach stands out as one that reaches ambitiously beyond literature to offer a theory of culture which combines several normally disparate fields of study: anthropology, psychology, sociology, philosophy, and religion. Put simply, his studies originate with the hypothesis that societal patterns of behavior are reflected in written texts; these structures, however, have to be recovered for their true meaning to be understood. The critic's privilege and responsibility is to discover these universal structures.

In his first major study, *Deceit, Desire, and the Novel*, Girard sets forth his method of studying literary works, which seeks to show their essential similarity of approach, an approach which reflects larger social truths. In the first chapter of this study, Girard firmly defends the need for a systematic, even scientific approach to literary criticism:

> A basic contention of this essay is that the great writers apprehend intuitively and concretely, through the medium of their art, if not formally, the system in which they were first imprisoned together with their contemporaries. Literary interpretation must be systematic because it is the continuation of literature. It should formalize implicit or already half-explicit systems. To maintain that criticism will never be systematic is to maintain that it will never be real knowledge. The value of a critical thought depends not on how cleverly it manages to disguise its own systematic nature or on how many fundamental issues it manages to shirk or to dissolve but on how much literary substance it really embraces, comprehends, and makes articulate.

The ambitiousness of this goal may result in failure, Girard continues, but the attempt must nevertheless be undertaken, for it is the "very essence of literary criticism." In all of his major studies, then, the methodology he offers is one which encompasses the literary text, the novelists, the critics, and culture in general; the cast of his net widens considerably after his first major study, but the key concept throughout his work is that of mimesis, or imitation.

Girard's distinctive but controversial contribution to the many meanings of this age-old term is his perception that imitation leads to rivalry and thus to violence. In *Deceit, Desire, and the Novel*, for example, Girard traces the ways in which writers reflect the life of illusion fostered by the romantic imagination. Instead of the dichotomy of the Self and the Other in the novel, Girard proposes that there is instead a triangle, of the Self, the Other, and the desire to be the Other. Because the Self in the novel always imitates the desire of the Other, rivalry results over the object of desire.

The duality of the title in French (translated as the "romantic lie and the novelistic truth") refers to two kinds of literature: one which maintains the triangular desire, thus the "lie" of romantic desire, and a superior one, which strips the illusion and reveals the falsity of the romance-fed desire.

The scope of Girard's theory here foreshadows the even wider cultural implications in his later works. Girard not only explains how each of the main characters in the novels of Miguel de Cervantes, Stendhal, Gustave Flaubert, Marcel Proust, and Fedor Dostoevskii comes to realize that he or she has been motivated by a false desire, but he also postulates that this stripping-away process occurs with each novelist. The great novelists, according to Girard's system, share one victory: "This victory over a self-centeredness which is other-centered, this renunciation of fascination and hatred, is the crowning moment of novelistic creation."

The critical act itself, Girard maintains, either recognizes this novelistic truth or reinforces the romantic lie. Rather than condemning novelistic conclusions, "the primary location of truth," for being banal, Girard argues, critics should celebrate the banality, for it is the "absolute banality of what is essential in Western civilization."

These seminal ideas, which spring from his analysis of selected literary texts, are developed in Girard's succeeding works, which increasingly focus on religion; the break between his initial studies and his later ones results from Girard's shift in interest from an analysis of mimetic desire in literature to his interest in mimetic phenomena in general.

Starting with a recapitulation of the mimetic desire which leads to rivalry between the self and the other and thus to violence, Girard develops his hypothesis of one all-encompassing cultural structure – the unanimous victimage mechanism – in several books. Though the idea of the scapegoat has been elaborated by many other critics taking the anthropological approach, Girard's distinctive contribution is his argument that first, there was a real historical crisis which precipitated the need for scapegoats; second, that it is society itself, not a vengeful or bloodthirsty god, which requires the sacrifice of a victim; third, that the selection of an arbitrary victim enables society to rid itself of its own violence; and fourth, that this deflected violence of the community then enables the foundation of religion and the social order.

With his theory of the surrogate victim Girard claims, in *Violence and the Sacred*, the validity of a scientific approach to the relationship between literature, specifically tragedy, and society. The sacrificial victim in Greek tragedy, Oedipus being the classic case, cannot be understood in terms of guilt and innocence but rather must be seen as the scapegoat of society, the one who succumbs to violence and thus deflects it from the society as a whole. To interpret Sophocles' tragedy as a debate over a moral or psychological problem is to miss the underlying pattern of substitution for violence.

In Girard's system, however, the scapegoat is not merely a symbol. One of his more controversial assertions is that the scapegoat paradigm results from real historical events and is pervasive in historical and religious texts, assertions developed in *The Scapegoat* and in *Things Hidden Since the Foundation of the World*. Most texts, written by the persecutors of the chosen victim, do not reflect any awareness of the real purpose or mythic nature of the scapegoating process. Here analogous to Suzanne Langer's application of the biological rhythm of life in her analysis of the comic rhythm in *Feeling and Form* (1977), Girard points out that the scapegoating mechanism applies to the animal kingdom as well, reinforcing his point that the pattern he describes is not only literary symbolization but also a literal pattern of communal behavior to be found in nature, a pattern that becomes mythologized.

Nevertheless, the Bible, in Girard's estimation, is a prime source of demystification, a theme developed at length in both *The Scapegoat* and *Job, the Victim of His People*. In this pattern of hiding the real purpose of violence, Job stands out as the scapegoat who refuses the ceremonial accusation of his friends, who speak on behalf of the community; Job protests his innocence, thereby revealing the pattern that is otherwise hidden in such texts as *Oidipous Tyrannos* (c. 429 B.C.; *Oedipus Tyrannus*), in which Oedipus accepts, as royalty is designed to accept, the role of the martyr to rid his people of the plague. According to Girard, religion, far from being parasitic, is "really the generative force behind human culture." Thus he defines as religious any phenomenon which is "associated with the acts of remembering, commemorating and perpetuating a unanimity that springs from the murder of a surrogate victim." Hence the connection between violence and the sacred found in many religions.

If religious systems are characterized by their diversity rather than by their coherence, it is, Girard reasons, because myths and rituals around the world try to recall what has been never completely understood. Literature, which takes over the function of ritual in the later stages of culture, reproduces the mystifications; only certain great texts give a glimpse of the original historical truth. As in *Deceit, Desire, and the Novel*, Girard divides literary texts into those that unconsciously incorporate this structure and the great ones, like those of William Shakespeare, which allow a glimpse of the hidden pattern of scapegoating.

Girard argues that those who have previously studied the theme of the scapegoat have not appreciated the power of religious texts to show the true significance of the victimage mechanism and have instead made religion the "scapegoat for human thought." Then, in a demonstration of the breadth of his hypothesis, Girard states that critics who insist on bankrupt modes of traditional interpretation participate in another sacrificial crisis, bowing to the myths of modernism.

The extent to which Girard sweeps together a literary text, the writer of the text, the critic, and the history and the society in which the text is produced into one unified scheme of thought is both the strength and the weakness of his hypothesis. As a system which is unified, coherent, and self-contained, and one which attempts to propose an explanation for the way the world functions, Girard's is impressively stimulating. As a thinker, Girard stands out as one who refuses to be intimidated by the overwhelming skepticism about language, indeed the overwhelming skepticism about anything except uncertainty, that characterizes his contemporaries. His is a clear voice, maintaining with conviction that a theory not only of literature but also of culture is possible.

Such a reach for an all-encompassing theory leads to some confusion about Girard's single-minded categorization and, inevitably, to the criticism that it is sometimes obvious and excessively generalized. Because it is meant to be so generally applicable, Girard's hypothesis, while internally coherent, loses some of its impact in the complexity of the categorization. Furthermore, Girard's hope for an "elaboration of a real science of man" leads him to reject a "theory of literature" approach. His interest in literature, he himself says, is limited to certain exceptional works as "agents of a very special demystification that bears on the hidden role of mimetic effects in human interaction." It is left to other critics to apply the framework he posits to a practical analysis of literature.

Nevertheless, in the very breadth of his approach, Girard, like the other great thinkers to whom he is often compared, such as Sigmund Freud, G. W. F. Hegel, Jean-Paul Sartre, Émile Durkheim, and James Frazer, lifts the discussion of literature from the quagmire of obfuscating theorizing to which excessive concern for the purely literary quality of a text has led and restores a sense of vitality to literary studies.

Principal criticism

Mensonge romantique et vérité romanesque, 1961 (*Deceit, Desire, and the Novel*, 1965)
Dostoievsky: Du double à l'unité, 1963
La Violence et le sacré, 1972 (*Violence and the Sacred*, 1977)
Critique dans un souterrain, 1976
Des choses cachées depuis la fondation du monde, 1978 (*Things Hidden Since the Foundation of the World*, 1987)
"To Double Business Bound" Essays on Literature, Mimesis, and Anthropology, 1978

Le Bouc émissaire, 1982 (*The Scapegoat*, 1986)
La Route antique des hommes pervers, 1985 (*Job, the Victim of His People*, 1987)
Violent Origins: On Ritual Killing and Cultural Formation, 1987 (with Walter Burkert and Jonathan Z. Smith)
The Theatre of Envy: William Shakespeare, 1991

Other major works and literary forms

In addition to several book-length studies, René Girard has contributed articles to numerous scholarly journals and written introductory matter for studies by other scholars.

EDITED TEXTS
Proust: A Collection of Critical Essays, 1962
Alphonse Juilland: D'une passion à l'autre, 1987

Further reading

Brooks, Peter. "The Modern Element," in *Partisan Review*. XXXV (1968), pp. 630–638.
DeGuy, Michel, and Jean-Pierre Dupuy. *René Girard et le problème du mal*, 1982.
Dumouchel, Paul, ed. *Violence et vérité: Autour de René Girard*, 1985 (*Violence and Truth: On the Works of René Girard*, 1988).
Farenga, Vincent. Review of *Violence and the Sacred in Comparative Literature Studies*. XXXII (Fall, 1980), pp. 419–424.
Hamerton-Kelly, Robert G., ed. *Violent Origins: Walter Burket, René Girard, and Jonathan Z. Smith on Ritual Killing and Cultural Formation*, 1987.
Livingstone, Paisley. *Models of Desire: René Girard and the Psychology of Mimesis*, 1992.
McKenna, Andrew. *Violence and Difference: Girard, Derrida, and Deconstruction*, 1992.
Orsini, Christine. *La Pensée de René Girard*, 1986.
"An Interview with René Girard," in *Diacritics*. VIII (1978), pp. 31–54.

SHAKUNTALA JAYASWAL

See also Bataille; French Literary Theory: Twentieth Century

Johann Wolfgang von Goethe

German poet, novelist, playwright, and critic

Born: Frankfurt am Main, Germany; August 28, 1749
Died: Weimar, Germany; March 22, 1832

Biography

Johann Wolfgang von Goethe was born in Frankfurt am Main in 1749. His parents were well-to-do and interested in education and the arts. He received an excellent education in his youth and at sixteen commenced the study of law at the University of Leipzig. When ill health forced him to return home, he took up studies in the natural sciences, a field that was to become a life-long interest. He finished his studies at the University of Strasbourg and practiced law for a few years in Frankfurt. It was in Strasbourg that he came under the influence of Johann Gottfried Herder and the *Sturm und Drang* movement. As one of these "angry young men," Goethe penned works that brought him instant fame: *Götz von Berlichingen mit der eisernen Hand* (1773; *Gotz von Berlichingen with the Iron Hand*, 1799) and *Die Leiden des jungen werthers* (1774; *The Sorrows of Young Werther*, 1779).

In 1775 Goethe received an invitation to come to the court of Duke Karl August of Weimar, a ruler interested in science and letters. Goethe did so and remained until his death in 1832. During the first decade of residence, Goethe bore a heavy load of administrative tasks; any spare time was devoted to scientific investigations. He was given the status of nobility in 1782. A sojourn in Italy from 1786 to 1788 returned Goethe's attention to literature, specifically to neoclassical literature. In 1794 he met Friedrich Schiller, who shared many of his literary values. Goethe offered suggestions during the writing of several of Schiller's best-known plays, while Schiller urged Goethe to take up once more a long-abandoned project, which became *Faust*. In 1807 Goethe married Christine Vulpius, the woman with whom he had been living for some time. His last years were spent in splendid isolation; contemporary writers tended to view him as an Olympian and themselves as epigones.

Influence

Goethe's influence as a literary theoretician rests on his status as Germany's greatest writer. Aside from their intrinsic merit, his observations have commanded attention simply because they are Goethe's observations. The single thread that unites his criticism is the concept of organic totality developed during the *Sturm und Drang* (literally, "Storm and Stress") period. That concept, as well as his analysis of symbol in literature, had a direct impact on Romanticism. He began a revival of interest in Shakespeare and English literature that continued into Germany's nineteenth century. His attitude that the artist is a sovereign creator and that the audience is of secondary importance provided a precedent for the posture of literary and artistic Impressionism of the *fin de siècle*. Finally, he offered a concept of "world literature" that accents the unique role of each nation as a contributor to the culture of humankind.

Analysis

Goethe did not write a single comprehensive statement of his literary theory and critical practice. Yet the abstractions that he developed in order to understand his own literary productivity, that of his contemporaries, and the literary expressions of other cultures can be gleaned from several sources: *Aus meinem Leben: Dichtung und Wahrheit* (1811–1814; *Poetry and Truth from My Own Life*, 1908), his essays and reviews for literary journals, his letters and recorded conversations, and statements made about art and literature by his literary creations – foremost among them, Wilhelm Meister.

In the course of a long and active life, Goethe continually altered and refined his literary theories. The stages of development parallel the stages of a complex literary career: the remarkably productive association with Johann Gottfried Herder and the other writers and theoreticians of the *Sturm und Drang*; the first years at the court of the Duke of Weimar, from 1775 to 1786; the Italian sojourn from 1786 to 1788; the resumption of literary activity and the collaboration with Friedrich Schiller until the latter's death in 1805; and the final twenty-five years as the universally acknowledged master of German letters. It is particularly important to discriminate between beliefs held by the young Goethe before the seminal Italian sojourn and those held by the mature Goethe of German classicism.

Goethe's first impressions of literature and literary life were colored by the Rococo tradition dominant in Germany during the 1760s. This sophisticated, stylized, and form-conscious literature is best represented by the works of Christoph Martin Wieland. Goethe's first theoretical statements arose from the confrontation of his modish, postadolescent attitudes with the contrasting, if not antagonistic, theories of the genial and charismatic Herder. During the winter of 1770–1771, Goethe was drawn into the *Sturm und Drang* movement. In print, he extolled the virtues of simple, even primitive, folk literature; he worshipped at the altars of Homer and the fictive Celtic bard Ossian. Of contemporary commentators on art and culture, Goethe most admired Jean-Jacques Rousseau and the famous "return to nature" injunction.

Herder's intellectual enthusiasm, however, is reflected most clearly in Goethe's passion for Shakespeare. In Shakespeare's characters, Goethe found exact representations of nature, nature in the broadest sense. The young Goethe rejected French classicism with its careful attention to dramatic conventions; still, he also rejected the campaign against form waged by the more radical members of the *Sturm und Drang* group. He found that each Shakespeare piece holds to an "inner form" that brings the diverse phenomena of nature into sharp focus. Shakespeare's reputation had suffered since the late-seventeenth-century advent of the German Enlightenment, with its insistence on strict rationality and order in art. Goethe's approbation effectively rehabilitated Shakespeare for the German-speaking world.

Goethe's analysis of literature proceeds from great writer to great writer rather than from movement to movement. This results from his acceptance of the *Sturm und Drang* concept of the artist as genius, as the sovereign creator of a new, that is, fictional, world. The shape of that world does not depend on the writer's audience. In fact, one function of theorizing about literature is the emancipation of the writer from the demands, stated or implied, of the reading public. Goethe's perduring advocacy of the "genius concept" made him an early proponent of what French Impressionism called *l'art pour l'art*. His standing as a theorist and a writer has risen and fallen according to the responses of successive generations of critics and scholars to the Olympian principle of art for art's sake.

As Goethe grew away from the *Sturm und Drang*, he refined his standards for evaluating literature. The individual elements of a particular work – linguistic, structural, or thematic – should be woven together so that each becomes an essential part of the whole. The standard of wholeness or totality was developed as an analogy to or even an extension of nature. Goethe employs it in the famous discussion of Shakespeare's *Hamlet* led by the title character of *Wilhelm Meisters Lehrjahre* (1795–1796; *Wilhelm Meister's Apprenticeship*, 1824). Meister, who is to play the character onstage, vigorously rejects suggestions for change in the text offered by the company members and their director. Each component of the work, however insignificant or offensive it may appear in isolation, must be retained. Meister draws a comparison with a tree, which maintains its natural integrity only when all components are present, from the trunk to the smallest bud. Goethe consistently sought totality in literature; he assumed, however, that each writer offers a personal approach to artistic wholeness. Therefore, Goethe usually focused on authorial intent and tended to be a sympathetic, even relativistic, critic.

The period of German classicism, in large part including the mature writings of Goethe and Friedrich Schiller, dates from Goethe's conversion to classicism as articulated by the art historian and theoretician Johann Winckelmann. Neoclassicism had been a frequently recurring phenomenon in German literature since the High Middle Ages. The hostility of the *Sturm und Drang* to neoclassicism was rooted in animosity to the highly normative, supposedly rule-bound nature of classicist art, that is, latter-day art that consciously followed the principles embodied in the art of ancient Greece and Rome. For a number of years after his Italian sojourn, Goethe recommended rigorous neoclassicism in theoretical statements that the Goethe of 1771 would have found abhorrent. The conversion to neoclassicism, however, was tempered by Goethe's lasting commitment to the sovereignty of the artist as creator and to the autonomy of the art created.

Throughout his career, Goethe asserted that literary production is above all an act of self-expression. His famous statement that each of his works is a fragment of a great confession is supported by frequent mention of the psychological release he experienced through writing. The creative process is described as semiconscious, as the act of a sleepwalker. This is not to say that he advocated solipsism in art: true art had to be based on perceptions of external reality. Goethe redefined "occasional poetry" to mean poetry occasioned by the ever-changing environment of the poet. In the art of classical antiquity, Goethe saw a convergence of objective nature and subjective creativity. Hence, he could assert that order in art should follow order in nature so closely that art and nature fuse.

In his theoretical statements about art and nature, Goethe used the concept of totality to develop a new approach to the term "symbol." In 1797 he visited his childhood home of Frankfurt am Main and was struck by his own response to familiar sights in the city. He found that imagination expanded his sensory impressions to create a larger totality, a larger order that contained both objective and subjective elements. Goethe theorized that symbols are produced by a reconciliation of subject and object, human and nature. Before Goethe, the terms "symbol" and "allegory" had been virtually synonymous. Goethe separated them by describing allegory as further from nature and closer to reason. Through images drawn from objective reality, symbols suggest that larger totality. The symbol operates indirectly, whereas allegory employs imagery as a vehicle for initiating a direct communication through the common faculty of the understanding. Allegory soon abandons nature.

Although Goethe's initial meditations on the symbol-making faculty were expressed in slippery generalities, they found an immediate audience among the leading figures of German Romanticism. The theories of metaphor and symbol developed by Friedrich and August Wilhelm Schlegel and by the philosopher Friedrich Wilhelm Schelling were derived from Goethe. Goethe viewed myth as a particularly fruitful type of symbol and used it throughout his career. He commented that legends and ancient traditions had been forever present in his mind and that such myths had been distilled over the years.

The significance of myth to Goethe is nowhere more evident than in the second part of *Faust*, where classical and medieval mythology are woven together. The balancing of apparent opposites is typical of Goethe's aesthetic theory and literary practice. He asserts that art blends nature and reason in such a way that each is still readily identifiable. The symbol is a metaphor for true poetry, since both bring the particular and the general together in a state of productive tension.

Of particular concern to Goethe as a theoretician was the classification of literature into genres. Enlightenment poetics had focused on the theory of genres since the pioneering work of Johann Christoph Gottsched in the 1730s and 1740s. Goethe distinguished the three "natural" genres from the perspective of the genial creator: the creator is emotionally involved (lyric), dispassionately narrating (epic), or demonstrating (drama). Goethe realized that no clear boundaries separate the three: a particular work may well evince elements of each. One of the three will usually dominate. Goethe was less interested in the origins of the three than he was in their present form and in their relationships to one another.

Much of Goethe's speculation about natural genres arose from dialogues with Friedrich Schiller about the distinction between tragedy and the epic. Goethe finally determined that the epic confronts the audience with historical activity, whereas tragedy offers its audience current human anguish, suffering in the spectators' time. The epic requires unrestricted space because its characters develop through interaction with a procession of sets of circumstances, new acquaintances, foreign cultures, and other determinants beyond the control of the individual. Tragedy, in contrast, requires the closely limited space of a stage because it examines the internal, psychological fiber of its characters. Like Aristotle, Goethe demanded the willing suspension of disbelief of a theater audience. The spectator must respond emotionally, not critically, as the action unfolds. Goethe found that the literature of his own age was drawn to drama because of its penchant for naturalism. Of the three genres, drama is related to the present time most clearly.

Despite that contemporary preference, Goethe distrusted drama because of its dependence on an audience. Art should be understood in its relation to its producer, not its consumer. To the extent that drama strives for effect, it is of questionable value. Goethe doubted that catharsis has any lasting value for the spectator: everyday concerns, he believed, will soon overshadow responses to a dramatic performance. He therefore harbored few hopes concerning the efficacy of the stage as a pedagogical instrument. Any didacticism in literature should be suggestive; the reader should infer a lesson from literature as he or she infers it from nature, that is, from life.

A final contribution to the theory of literature was Goethe's coinage of the term *Weltliteratur* (world literature). A literature of all nations that would form a common cultural heritage was not Goethe's intent. He first suggested the phrase in 1827 in the hope that literary exchange among nations would increase during what he considered a time of peace and recuperation after the Napoleonic era. Such intercourse supposedly was preparing the way for the merger of all national traditions into one great literature. Goethe had in mind a distant goal, a mosaic to which each national tradition would bring its own distinctive and essential color.

Goethe's cosmopolitanism developed fully in the years after Schiller's death in 1805. Not only did he express interest in and knowledge of other literary traditions, such as those of the Czechs, Greeks, Arabs, and Persians, but he also praised the German Romantics for their study of regional German folk art. Great tolerance characterizes the critical writings of Goethe's old age; his hope was that the contribution of each nation or region would further, however modestly, the development of civilization. Thus, even the concept of *Weltliteratur* partakes of the fertile notion of organic totality. Indeed, if Goethe is to be remembered as a theoretician of literature, it will be for the treasure trove of critical insight brought forth from that one naive precept of the *Sturm und Drang*.

Principal criticism

Aus meinem Leben: Dichtung und Wahrheit, 1811–1814 (6 volumes)

Memoirs of Goethe, 1924, also known as *The Autobiography of Goethe*, 1848–1849; best known as *Poetry and Truth from My Own Life*, 1908)
Goethe's Literary Essays, 1921 (arranged by J. E. Spingarn)

Other major works and literary forms

Johann Wolfgang von Goethe is to German literature what William Shakespeare is to English literature: the standard by which other writers are measured. His lifework is both large and diverse. His lyric poetry is possibly the finest in German. His prose works include one of the more important examples of the *Bildungsroman, Wilhelm Meisters Lehrjahre* (1795–1796; *Wilhelm Meister's Apprenticeship*, 1824), one of the better-known literary autobiographies, *Aus meinem Leben: Dichtung und Wahrheit* (1811–1814; *Poetry and Truth from My Own Life*, 1908), and the first international best-seller in the history of modern German literature, *Die Leiden des jungen Werthers* (1774; *The Sorrows of Young Werther*, 1779). Goethe's dramas include the ultimate statement of German neoclassicism, *Iphigenie auf Tauris* (1779, 1787; *Iphigenia in Tauris*, 1793), and the best-known work of German literature, the two-part *Faust: Eine Tragödie* (1808, 1833; *The Tragedy of Faust*, 1823, 1838).

NOVELS
Die Leiden des jungen Werthers, 1774 (*The Sorrows of Young Werther*, 1779)
Wilhelm Meisters Lehrjahre, 1795–1796 (4 volumes; *Wilhelm Meister's Apprenticeship*, 1824)
Die Wahlverwandtschaften, 1809 (*Elective Affinities*, 1849)
Wilhelm Meisters Wanderjahre: Oder, Die Entsagenden, 1821, 1829 (2 volumes; *Wilhelm Meister's Travels: Or, The Renunciants*, 1827)

SHORT FICTION
Unterhaltungen deutscher Ausgewanderten, 1795 (*Conversations of German Emigrants*, 1854)
Novelle, 1826 (*Novel*, 1837)

PLAYS
Die Laune des Verliebten, written 1767, published 1806 (*The Wayward Lover*, 1879)
Die Mitschuldigen, first version written 1768, published 1787, second version written 1769, published 1777 (*The Fellow-Culprits*, 1879)
Götz von Berlichingen mit der eisernen Hand, 1773 (*Götz von Berlichingen with the Iron Hand*, 1799)
Götter, Helden und Wieland, 1774
Clavigo, 1774 (English translation, 1798, 1897)
Erwin und Elmire, 1775 (libretto; music by Duchess Anna Amalia of Saxe-Weimar)
Stella, first version 1776, second version 1806 (English translation, 1798)
Claudine von Villa Bella, first version 1776, second version 1788 (libretto)
Die Geschwister, 1776
Iphigenie auf Tauris, first version 1779, second version 1787 (*Iphigenia in Tauris*, 1793)
Jery und Bätely, 1780 (libretto)
Die Fischerinn, 1782 (libretto; music by Corona Schröter; *The Fisherwoman*, 1899)
Scherz, List, und Rache, 1784 (libretto)
Der Triumph der Empfindsamkeit, 1787
Egmont, 1788 (English translation, 1837)
Torquato Tasso, 1790 (English translation, 1827)
Faust: Ein Fragment, 1790 (*Faust: A Fragment*, 1980)
Der Gross-Cophta, 1792
Der Bürgergeneral, 1793
Was wir bringen, 1802
Die natürliche Tochter, 1803 (*The Natural Daughter*, 1885)
Faust: Eine Tragödie, 1808 (*The Tragedy of Faust*, 1823)
Pandora, 1808
Die Wette, written 1812, published 1837
Des Epimenides Erwachen, 1814
Faust: Eine Tragödie, zweiter Teil, 1833 (*The Tragedy of Faust, Part Two*, 1838)

POETRY
Neue Lieder, 1770 (*New Poems*, 1853)
Sesenheimer Liederbuch, 1775–1789, 1854 (*Sesenheim Songs*, 1853)
Römische Elegien, 1793 (*Roman Elegies*, 1876)
Reinecke Fuchs, 1794 (*Reynard the Fox*, 1840)
Epigramme: Venedig 1790, 1796 (*Venetian Epigrams*, 1853)
Xenien, 1796 (with Friedrich Schiller; *Epigrams*, 1853)
Hermann und Dorothea, 1797 (*Herman and Dorothea*, 1801)
Balladen, 1798 (with Schiller; *Ballads*, 1853)
Neueste Gedichte, 1800 (*Newest Poems*, 1853)
Gedichte, 1812, 1815 (2 volumes; *The Poems of Goethe*, 1853)
Sonette, 1819 (*Sonnets*, 1853)
West-östlicher Divan, 1819 (*West-Eastern Divan*, 1877)

NONFICTION
Von deutscher Baukunst, 1773 (*On German Architecture*, 1921)
Versuch die Metamorphose der Pflanzen zu erklären, 1790 (*Essays on the Metamorphosis of Plants*, 1863)
Beyträge zur Optik, 1791, 1792 (2 volumes)
Winckelmann und sein Jahrhundert, 1805
Zur Farbenlehre, 1810 (*Theory of Colors*, 1840)
Italienische Reise, 1816, 1817 (2 volumes; *Travels in Italy*, 1883)
Zur Naturwissenschaft überhaupt, besonders zur Morphologie, 1817, 1824 (2 volumes)
Campagne in Frankreich, 1792, 1822 (*Campaign in France in the Year 1792*, 1849)
Die Belagerung von Mainz, 1793, 1822 (*The Siege of Mainz in the Year 1793*, 1849)
Essays on Art, 1845
Goethe on Art, 1980

MISCELLANEOUS
Works, 1848–1890 (14 volumes)
Goethes Werke, 1887–1919 (133 volumes)

Further reading

Bruford, W. H. *Theater, Drama, and Audience in Goethe's Germany*, 1950.
Burgard, Peter J. *Idioms of Uncertainty: Goethe and the Essay*, 1992.
Carlson, Marvin. *Goethe and the Weimar Theatre*, 1978.
Curtius, Ernst Robert. "Goethe as Critic," in *Essays on European Literature*, 1973.
Fink, Karl J., and Max Baeumer. *Goethe as a Critic of Literature*, 1984.
Strich, Fritz. *Goethe and World Literature*, 1949.
Wellek, René. *A History of Modern Criticism: 1750–1950*. Vol. 1, *The Later Eighteenth Century*, 1955.

JOHN VAN CLEVE

See also Heine; Herder; Lessing; Romanticism; Schiller

Witold Gombrowicz

Polish critic and writer

Born: Małoszyce, Poland; August 4, 1904
Died: Vence, France; July 24, 1969

Biography

Witold Gombrowicz was born on August 4, 1904, in Małoszyce, on the landholdings of his father near Warsaw. He was the fourth and youngest son of Jan Gombrowicz and Antonina Kotkowska. His father was a landowner who also occupied high positions in industrial firms. It was, however, Witold's relationship to his mother that had a decided influence on his development as an artist. Speaking of this influence during conversations with Dominique deRoux (recorded in *A Kind of Testament*), he stated: "I am an artist, and in this take after my mother. . . . She was for me a school of values. . . . From her I derive my cult of reality."

In 1922 Gombrowicz graduated from a Catholic lycée, and four years later he obtained his master's degree in law from the University of Warsaw. Soon afterward, he left for Paris to continue his studies, but after various vagaries in the French capital, he soon returned to his native Poland. There he began to work in a modest legal capacity (law was a profession which he always loathed); during this period he wrote his first short stories.

The next few years were dedicated to the composition of the novel *Ferdydurke*, which brought Gombrowicz instant fame in Poland and abroad, and which remains to this day his most popular and most discussed book. In 1939 he sailed to Argentina in the company of other Polish literati on the maiden voyage of the transatlantic liner *Stefan Batory*. While Gombrowicz was abroad, the political situation of Central Europe boiled over into World War II. Although many of the Poles who had accompanied him on the trip elected to travel to England, Gombrowicz decided to remain in South America and take no active part in the struggle. Fond of pointing out that writers do not make good soldiers, he later countered various attacks on his patriotism with the egotistical assertion that, had he taken up arms and been killed in the war, the loss to Polish literature would have been devastating. Even his foes acknowledge the objective truth of this brash statement. The twenty-four years which Gombrowicz spent in Argentina had a decided influence on his creative output. One of the most highly prized fruits of this period is the picaresque semiautobiographical novel *Trans-Atlantyk*.

At the start of Gombrowicz's residence in Argentina, extreme penury prevented him from devoting much time to literary composition. During these years he came close to starvation on several occasions; he often attended the funerals of strangers in order to partake of the luncheon following the interment – a practice that he called "eating the corpse." In 1947, however, he obtained a position at the Banco Polacco in Buenos Aires. Now he had more time to pursue his literary vocation. He was soon surrounded by a circle of young, admiring Argentinian writers, whose help he enlisted in translating his works into Spanish. In 1963 the Ford Foundation invited him to Berlin, where he thereafter made a living as an internationally acclaimed writer, lending his brilliance to the cultural scene of the divided city by giving talks on his work and dedicating more time to composition.

The writer's last years were plagued by a continually worsening illness. In 1968, one year before his death, Gombrowicz married his longtime companion, the young Canadian student Marie-Rita Labrosse, who would later manage her husband's literary estate after his death.

Influence

In the case of Gombrowicz, who was above all a creative artist, it is more fitting to speak of his influence in the field of creative literature than of his legacy to literary criticism. As a sensitive and talented writer, however, he was aware of various trends in literature and criticism, reacting to and exerting some influence of his own upon them. Without a doubt, he developed a very individual method for the study of literature, one to which contemporary Polish critics often refer. Yet Gombrowicz belittled the importance of literary criticism, preferring to see critics as hindrances rather than aids to the correct reception of the artist's work by his reading public. His own program was built around what he termed the "discovery of the individual man," for him the most crucial goal of thought and research.

Analysis

Gombrowicz is best known as a writer of fiction and drama. His literary activity, however, was not confined to these two genres. Throughout his creative life, he carried out a two-pronged literary program: in his novels and stage pieces he dedicated himself to art, while in his diaries and other journalistic writings he warred with literary theorists and critics. Most of his specific critical commentary centers on the literature of his native land. His general statements concerning the writer's craft, however, have a universal significance. Gombrowicz had much to say regarding the vocation of the writer, the relation of the literary work to its audience, the redundancy of professional critics, and the Polish literary tradition.

The one work which contains the great bulk of Gombrowicz's critical commentary is his three-volume journal, written between 1953 and 1966. During his long sojourn in Argentina, far from Poland and the "literary mechanisms" and atmosphere of Europe, he gave vent to his desire to criticize European culture and literature. "Criticize" is used here in both its literary and popular senses, for Gombrowicz's critical commentary usually took the form of an attack on some individual or institution.

Indeed, he once remarked that his entire philosophy was to be "in spite of, against, and contrary to." This rather belligerent statement is not too difficult to decipher. Gombrowicz bowed to no sacred cows. An iconoclast, he stubbornly resisted the literary status quo and scorned the conventional wisdom of his day. This attitude, though it motivated his vociferous attacks on the classics of Polish literature, did not weaken his lifelong reverence for one writer of classics, the Romantic poet Juliusz Słowacki.

Such a combination of pugnacity and veneration does not in itself make Gombrowicz's literary criticism interesting. What does attract one's attention is the fact that, because he is not so much critic as creative artist, he speaks of the artist's problems from the artist's point of view. The complaints with which he assailed conventional literary judgment do not spring from abstract theories; they represent concrete postulates which he employed in his own literary œuvre.

Who, in Gombrowicz's opinion, is a writer? It is not one who "comes to the pen by vocation." The true writer, or poet, is one whose works serve as a mirror for reality. "Whatever type of literature one is speaking about, be it realistic, fantastic, romantic, it must ever be linked to reality with the tightest bonds."

Linking literature to reality with the tightest bonds means writing from oneself, about oneself. He continues in his diary: "Of all my characters, I am the most important and only unique hero, the only one with whom I am really concerned." The literary work must have a constant relationship with the individual human being who creates it. It was important for Gombrowicz that people understand him, which, however, does not mean that he was to present them with a shallow, easily understandable self-portrait in his work. Indeed, Gombrowicz's idea of his readership betrays an elitist attitude: according to him, there existed only very few people in the world of the same "high mental caliber" as himself. Further, in accordance with his desire to make literature reflect reality, he strove to keep his works from being facile; instead, they were to mirror the difficult, complex nature of life.

As to the reception of the writer's particular brand of reality by an audience, though Gombrowicz asserted the authority and independence of the author, he spoke with scorn of what he considered the excessive isolation in which many contemporary writers produced their works. He was especially concerned about the tendency among poets to write for their own tight cliques and for no one else. "It is not a bad thing that contemporary verse is not easily understandable by the mob, but it is bad that it is created in an atmosphere of the narrow give-and-take of identical worlds." When attacked with the claim that it was inconsistent for an elitist author to demand that art be more widely accessible, he answered, "But I am not demanding that art be 'popularized' at all. . . . I only claim that literature works itself out otherwise than we expect."

This quick shrug of the shoulders hardly constitutes a theory of literature. It does, however, underscore Gombrowicz's view of artistic creation. The writer, though immersed in and working with the stuff of reality, cannot create with one eye on the literary modes of the day and the other eye on the book-buying habits of the "mob." He or she is obligated solely to him- or herself. The reader must be prepared to confront the author on the author's terms, and not vice versa. If the reader is not up to the task before him or her, the author cannot be held accountable.

Yet Gombrowicz also asserted that there are too many writers who are venerated and far too many books which, though they go unread, are considered classics. In *A Kind of Testament* he singles out James Joyce and Franz Kafka as examples of this phenomenon. "The greatness of their works," he says, "is begotten in a vacuum." Such works, according to Gombrowicz, were not written with the reader in mind, but rather with abstraction as their goal. Clearly, this curious judgment is open to debate, as there are no doubt legions of Joyceans and Kafka enthusiasts who can claim that they find the realities presented by these two authors compelling, regardless of the writers' intent. This facet of the literary theories of Gombrowicz is perhaps the most difficult to defend without resorting to the "philosophy of contrariness."

In line with his cult of the individual, Gombrowicz stressed the idea that each artist should create his or her own theory of literature, his or her own approach to the problems and essence of writing. "Create an image of a world, a human being, a culture, which would be in agreement with you," he counsels fellow writers. Theory is left to the practitioners.

As for critics, they are a breed for whom Gombrowicz had no great love. He thought of them as a block standing between the writer and his or her audience. "The critic catalogs, levels, melts down metal into little ingots," he writes, meaning that the endless dissection of a literary text into smaller and smaller particles not only obscures a view of the work's totality but also can lead the reader astray from the artist's real intent by emphasizing the curious instead of the important. The jettisoning of professional critics and the creation of personal worlds by the author permit the artist to find a road to authentic, serious literature. The looseness of this stream of thought prevented Gombrowicz from leaving behind any unified legacy of critical methodology. His forays into the world of criticism may be considered as one more example of this creative writer's need to find and explain himself, creating his own mirror image of reality.

Gombrowicz was not, however, a sloppy thinker, and the looseness of his aesthetic enabled him to strike out in every possible direction in the pursuit of progress and novelty in literature. His desire to move ever forward may be seen clearly in his relationship to the Polish literary tradition. Gombrowicz insisted that Polish literature needed to be reevaluated and renewed. There had been far too much uncritical homage paid to such Polish writers as Adam

Mickiewicz, Juliusz Słowacki, and Stanisław Wyspiański. Poles, he contended, must be weaned away from their past in order that they may create a future. This future would be possible only if Polish authors determined to throw from their shoulders the weight of their inheritance and to cease the childish return to the womb of the past. Only then would they be free to create "real, serious works." Literature, asserted Gombrowicz, must become the "raw literature of naked people, full of authenticity and openness."

In his fight for "naked, open literature," Gombrowicz was at times taken to task for his vehement attacks and seeming contradictions. Such opposition did not dishearten him; rather, he saw it as an integral part of his crusade: "For me, the essence of literature is provocation. I understand literature to be a fight for spiritual life – and just as ruthless a fight as any other struggle for survival. The word which cannot wound is worthless."

In sum, it cannot be said that Gombrowicz created a specific critical direction or methodology. He was far too opposed to cataloging of any type, asserting that he was too concrete and individual to be amenable even to self-description: "No, I am neither yesterday's individualist, nor am I an existentialist, nor am I a surrealist. . . . I am simply someone who strives to extract consequence from the time allotted him." Time has shown, and will continue to show, that Witold Gombrowicz, individual, artist, and critic, succeeded in doing just that.

Principal criticism

Dziennik, 1953–1956, 1957 (*Diary: Volume 1*, 1988)
Dziennik, 1957–1961, 1962
Dziennik, 1961–1966, 1967
Rozmowy z Gombrowiczem, 1969 (*A Kind of Testament*, 1973)
Varia, 1973
Wspomnienia polskie: Wędrówki po Argentynie, 1977 (11 volumes)

Other major works and literary forms

Besides the above-mentioned volumes, in which Witold Gombrowicz most clearly presents his critical perspective, it is helpful to note certain other works which shed some light on his critical outlook. The novel *Ferdydurke* (1937; English translation, 1961), the play *Iwona, księżniczka Burgunda* (1938; *Princess Ivona*, 1969), the novel *Trans-Atlantyk* (1953), the play *Ślub* (1953; *The Marriage*, 1969), the novels *Pornografia* (1960; English translation, 1966) and *Kosmos* (1965; *Cosmos*, 1966), and the play *Operetka* (1966; *Operetta*, 1971) all contain "critical asides," as it were, which give the reader some inkling of Gombrowicz's thoughts about literature and about those persons who create it.

NOVELS
Ferdydurke, 1937 (English translation, 1961)
Opętani, 1939 (*Possessed: Or, The Secret of Myslotch*, 1981)
Trans-Atlantyk, 1953
Pornografia, 1960 (English translation, 1966)
Kosmos, 1965 (*Cosmos*, 1966)

SHORT FICTION
Pamiętnik z okresu dojrzewania, 1933
Bakakaj, 1957

PLAYS
Iwona, księżniczka Burgunda, 1938 (*Princess Ivona*, 1969)
Ślub, 1953 (*The Marriage*, 1969)
Operetka, 1966 (*Operetta*, 1971)

NONFICTION
Sur Dante: Glose, 1968

MISCELLANEOUS
Dzieła zebrane, 1969–1977 (11 volumes)

Further reading

Anders, Jarosław. "Unsentimental Journey," in *The New Republic*. 211, no. 24 (1994).
Barańczak, Stanisław. "Witold Gombrowicz: Culture and Chaos," in *Partisan Review*. 56, no. 1 (Winter, 1989).
Berressem, Hanjo. "Witold Gombrowicz: Cosmos. The Case of the Hanged Sparrow," in *The Polish Review*. 36, no. 2 (1991).
——, and Ulrich Prill. " 'Die entbrannten Degenspitzen/Von macht'gen Gegnern'—Witold Gombrowicz' Lectura Dantis," in *Arcadia*. 28, no. 1 (1993).
Bolecki, Włodzimierz. "Gombrowicz avait-il des yeux? (La Problématique de la description dans *Ferdydurke*)," in *Revue des sciences humaines*. 239 (1995).
Decottignies, Jean. " 'Mes Aventures avec la forme' Witold Gombrowicz entre théorie et poésie," in *Revue des sciences humaines*. 239 (1995).
Farasse, Gerard. "Gombrowicz énergumène," in *Revue des sciences humaines*. 239 (1995).
Grzegorczyk, Marzena. "Discursos desde el margen: Gombrowicz, Piglia y la estética del basurero," in *Hispamerica*. 25, no. 73 (1996).
Holmgren, Beth. "Witold Gombrowicz in the United States," in *The Polish Review*. 33, no. 4 (1988).
——. "Witold Gombrowicz within the Wieszcz Tradition," in *Slavic and East European Journal*. 33, no. 4 (Winter, 1989).
Kalicki, Rajmund. *Tango: Gombrowicz*, 1984.
Kępiński, Tadeusz. *Witold Gombrowicz i świat jego młodości*, 1974.
Kuharski, Allen. "Gombrowicz and Faust," in *New Theatre Quarterly*. X, no. 40 (1994).
Łapiński, Zdzisław. *Gombrowicz i krytycy*, 1984.
——. *Ja Ferdydurke*, 1985.
Thompson, Ewa M. *Witold Gombrowicz*, 1979.

CHARLES S. KRASZEWSKI

Stephen Gosson

English critic and writer

Born: Canterbury, England; April 17, 1554 (baptized)
Died: London, England; February 13, 1624

Biography

Stephen Gosson was born in April, 1554; the precise date is unknown, but he was christened on April 17. The eldest son of Cornelius Gosson, a joiner, young Gosson was a king's scholar at the cathedral school in Canterbury, and later a scholarship student at Corpus Christi College, Oxford; these facts suggest that the family was probably lower-middle-class.

Gosson entered Oxford in April of 1572. His teachers at Corpus Christi included such eminent men as Richard Hooker and John Rainolds; the first undoubtedly influenced Gosson's religious beliefs, while the second helped shape his prose style. Gosson left Oxford in 1576 without completing the requirements for his degree; the reason is not known.

Gosson next attempted to make his living as a writer in London. Neither poetry nor playwriting proved successful, and his one attempt at prose romance was also disappointing. Only his attacks on the theater and poetry won readers.

From 1579 to 1584 Gosson was absent from London, part of the time apparently as a tutor in a nobleman's house, part of it traveling in Europe, perhaps as an agent for the English government.

In 1584 he took holy orders in the Church of England and began a steady rise. Within two years he was presented with his own vicarage in Hertfordshire and was able to marry Elizabeth Acton; they had two sons and a daughter. In 1591 Queen Elizabeth I appointed him parson at Great Wigborough in Essex, and as a preacher he made such a reputation that several times he preached before the mayor and the alderman of London. In his sermons Gosson strongly attacked enemies of the ecclesiastical and political establishment. In 1600 he was made rector of St. Botolph's in London, one of the richest churches in England. He served there for twenty-four years, until his death.

Influence

Gosson's attack on the stage – and, by extension, on poetry and fiction – had two major effects. The first was that it provoked both immediate and lasting counterblasts. Thomas Lodge, a contemporary author of considerably greater ability than Gosson, quickly produced *A Reply to Gosson's Schoole of Abuse, in Defence of Poetry, Musick, and Stage Plays*, sometimes cited as *Honest Excuses* (1579–1580). Although the book was soon suppressed because it had been published without a license, it is highly important as the first English-language defense of drama and poetry during the Renaissance. It also anticipates many of the arguments later developed, in much more classic shape, in Sir Philip Sidney's *Defence of Poesie* (1595). Gosson had dedicated his attack on the stage to Sidney – without permission – but his views found little favor with one of the premier poets and prose authors of his time (Sidney produced the sonnet sequence *Astrophel and Stella*, 1591, and the romance *The New Arcadia*, 1590). The fact that men of Sidney's character could be sterling courtiers and stalwart champions of the Protestant cause yet also devotees of the arts did much to undercut Gosson's attacks.

On the other hand, the rising Puritan movement in England gained intellectual ammunition from Gosson's criticisms. An intelligent and highly learned man, Gosson was able to construct attacks on drama and poetry that carried substantial weight in his day, particularly since he made extensive use of appeal to scriptural and patristic authority. In the end, however, the arguments of Lodge and Sidney have come to prevail – although not without considerable struggle.

Analysis

Gosson and his contemporaries were primarily concerned with the practical effects of art, whether dramatic, literary, or musical. Arguments both for and against plays centered on their effects on viewers; in essence, did drama make people behave better or worse for having watched it? Such an emphasis meant that works of the period discussing literature were mainly moral rather than critical. Questions of theme, subject, technique, and craftsmanship were distinctly subordinate to topics of morality, conduct, and religious scruples.

Both defenders and opponents of the drama and fiction of the Elizabethan Renaissance agreed on this essential point. Both sides firmly believed that art has an immediate, lasting, and practical effect on the reader or spectator. Poetry, as Sidney would argue in his *Defence of Poesie*, is superior to history because it not only presents facts but also moves readers to emulate noble actions and scorn base ones. Gosson would have agreed that poetry had the power to move its audience, but he insisted that it provoked bad rather than good conduct.

Gosson's underlying argument is consistently developed throughout his three published works on plays and poetry. He claims that drama is basically immoral in three fundamental respects: its basis, its presentation, and its effect. The major shift in his criticism of plays (and, by extension, all fictional art, including music) is to increase his attacks and strengthen his condemnation. As a corollary, his arguments against plays come to rely more on moral and religious foundations than on literary or philosophical ones.

Gosson's arguments reveal an underlying tension that pervaded the entire Elizabethan milieu: the age was caught between medieval and Renaissance thought, suspended in so many ways between scholasticism and Humanism. The essentially religious and moral concerns of an earlier time were forced into repeated contact and combat with more secular, worldly viewpoints. While Humanists such as Sidney might claim a positive, instructive role for fiction, Gosson and other conservative thinkers came to deny any possible good to a craft which was, they would claim, based on falsehoods and lies.

There are four main points which Gosson develops throughout his critical works. As noted, the major shift in his thought is the developing intensity and moral fervor of his presentation.

First, he considers whether art might be used to instruct people in good behavior. In his first two works he admits this as a possibility, but later he denies it. Even when he allows a potential salutary effect of good art, he insists that bad art is much more prevalent in the contemporary world and likely to remain so.

Second, Gosson points to the fact that art, by its very nature, must appeal to the emotions, rather than to reason. This sort of appeal is doubly dangerous, since emotions are easily misled, especially into sinful error, and because reason is the special, God-given character of humans. To prefer emotion over reason is therefore to reject the most distinctive gift bestowed upon humans – a rejection that is itself sinful, according to Gosson and other conservative religious thinkers of the time.

Third, literary fiction, especially the stage, requires mimicry and impersonation. To Gosson, such mimicry, or imitation, presents serious problems of an essentially religious nature. Three points which he develops in his works are particularly notable. He argues that representation of immoral persons is not only itself bad, but provokes evil in spectators; that the practice of having men play women's roles – and thus wear their garments – is specifically condemned in the Bible; and that to mimic God's creation is to usurp God's role and is therefore blasphemous.

Gosson's fourth and concluding argument is, again, basically religious. Having presented the evil foundations and effects of fiction and drama, he maintains that this corruption must be the work of the Devil, designed as a snare for the foolish and a trap for the unwary.

These views are presented first in Gosson's most famous work, *The Schoole of Abuse, Conteining a pleasaunt inuectiue against Poets, Pipers, Plaiers, Iesters, and such like Caterpillers of a Comonwelth; Setting vp the Flagge of Defiance to their mischieuous exercise, & ouerthrowing their Bulwarkes, by Prophane Writers, Naturall reason, and common experience: A discourse as pleasaunt for Gentlemen that fauour learning, as profitable for all that wyll follow vertue*. In this work, Gosson remains at least partially favorable to drama. It should be remembered that he himself had recently written plays; he even cites one of them as proof that good art can instruct people in proper behavior. In discussing the positive benefits of drama, he mentions

> The *Blacke Smiths daughter, & Catilins* conspiracies vsually brought in to the Theater: The firste contayning the trechery of *Turkes*, the honourable bountye of a noble minde, & the shining of vertue in distresse: The last, bicause it is knowen too be a Pig of myne owne Sowe, I will speake the lesse of it; onely giuing you to vnderstand, that the whole marke which I shot at in that woorke, was too showe the rewarde of traytors in *Catilin*, and the necessary gouernment of learned men, in the person of *Cicero*, which forsees euery dager that is likely to happen, and forstalles it continually ere it take effect.

Gosson is thus willing to admit, in *The Schoole of Abuse*, that good drama may exist, and might produce beneficial effects in the audience. He steadfastly maintains, however, that such plays are in the minority at the time and that it is much more likely that bad art will corrupt by presenting imitations of evil actions.

Gosson subscribes to the belief, which he supports with quotes from Plutarch and other ancient authors (the "Prophane Writers" of his title), that older ways are better ways and that the world and society have degenerated from earlier, more moral times. Such being the case, Gosson argues, honest men and women should avoid the theaters in order to avoid temptation.

Finally, *The Schoole of Abuse* attacks theaters themselves and their spectators, as well as the plots and the actors. The sudden and enormous popularity of the playhouses presented problems for public authority: large numbers of people were gathering together, providing an opportunity for prostitutes, thieves, and other criminals. Disturbances and riots were common, and there seemed to be a real threat to public order. The emphasis on this undesirable nature of the theater in Gosson's first work has prompted speculation that he was actually commissioned by London authorities to write his attack. The fact that his book was printed in an unusually large first edition and was widely distributed supports this suspicion.

If Gosson was supported by the civil authorities, he was certainly attacked by the theatrical community. Even before *The Schoole of Abuse* had been through the press, an intense verbal attack was launched on the work and the author. Thomas Lodge, another aspiring writer of the time, was moved to pen *A Reply to Gosson's Schoole of Abuse, in Defence of Poetry, Musick, and Stage Plays*, which, being unlicensed, was quickly suppressed. Still, enough of a counterattack had been made to cause Gosson to rephrase his original points in a second work, *An Apologie of the Schoole of Abuse, against Poets, Pipers, Players, and Their Excusers*. It was appended to Gosson's prose romance, *The Ephemerides of Phialo*.

Essentially, Gosson had to meet three thrusts of Lodge's *Reply*: that poets and the arts in general are the source of all civilization; that poetry is of ancient and honorable ancestry, being found both in pagan and biblical writings; and that there are numerous authorities, profane and sacred, who have endorsed poetry and the stage.

Gosson's response moved him further away from the emerging Humanist thought and closer to the conservative, religious opposition to the stage and art in general. Plays might have once been laudable, he says, but currently they pervert their rightful purpose; in addition, they offend reason; finally, the temptation of the playwright is to please the audience in base ways, and the inclination of the playgoer is to imitate that baseness. Gosson is firm on the point that people are especially vulnerable to the sort of deception practiced onstage; here again is the belief in the practical effect of art, which so colored literary discussion during the period.

Gosson's most developed and sustained attack is found in his final work on the stage, *Playes Confuted in Fiue Actions Prouing that they are not to be suffred in a Christian common weale, by the waye both the Cauils of Thomas Lodge, and the Play of Playes, Written in their defence, and other obiections of Players frendes, are truely set downe and directlye aunsweared.* This piece has been termed the "single most significant attack on plays during Elizabeth's reign"; it is a thorough summary of all the possible arguments against drama. Gosson uses Aristotle's four causes, as set forth in *Physica*, as the scaffolding for his work. Each of these causes, he maintains, is another reason for rejecting drama and its baleful effects.

The *efficient* cause of plays is their origin, which, according to Gosson, is the Devil. This evil origin can be proved by their sinful mimicry of God's creation, which is a diabolical act in itself.

The *material* cause involved is the content of the plays and the character of the actors. Both of these involve the counterfeiting of real actions, usually immoral. The incitement to sin is bad, but the counterfeiting itself, by its very nature, is even worse. Once again, Gosson argues that this mimicry is actually a blasphemous mockery of the Lord's creation.

The *formal* cause is the presentation of plays, yet another counterfeit. Gosson terms plays and fictions lies, rejecting the claim by Sidney and Lodge that they are really fables or allegories.

The *final* cause of plays, according to Gosson, is that they have as their main purpose the overflow of emotions in the spectators. With this attack, Gosson returns to one of the original objections he presented in his first work, *The Schoole of Abuse*, and also reveals how his attacks on the stage and fiction are essentially moral, rather than artistic, arguments.

Principal criticism

The Schoole of Abuse, 1579
An Apologie of the Schoole of Abuse, 1579
Playes Confuted in Fiue Actions, 1582

Other major works and literary forms

Stephen Gosson, whose name endures in English literary history as one of the earliest and harshest critics of the new drama of the Elizabethan Renaissance, began his own career as a playwright and writer of romances in the vein of John Lyly's *Euphues, the Anatomy of Wit* (1578). The fact that his own original compositions met with little success may have contributed to the vehemence of his later attacks.

Of Gosson's three known plays, only one, *Catilins Conspiracies* (1577), seems to have been produced before his attack on the theater. The other two works, *Captaine Mario* and *Praise at Parting* (both 1577), were most likely staged after the publication of his first work against drama, *The Schoole of Abuse*; the productions were intended to embarrass the author and discredit his arguments. No copies of these works remain; they survive only as titles.

In 1579 Gosson published *The Ephemerides of Phialo*, which was written in the highly rhetorical and elaborately artificial style made popular by Lyly's *Euphues*. In place of Lyly's romance, however, Gosson presented a didactic tract only lightly covered by a narrative. The characters in the work present various points of view, and their lengthy set speeches make up most of *The Ephemerides of Phialo*. The most telling comment that can be made about this work is that it fits well into Gosson's later views: those of a serious, middle-class, pragmatic citizen, suspicious of art and its effects.

LONG FICTION
The Ephemerides of Phialo, 1579 (romance)

PLAYS
Captaine Mario, 1577
Praise at Parting, 1577
Catilins Conspiracies, 1577

NONFICTION
The Trumpet of Warre, 1598 (sermon)

Further reading

Hardison, O. B. *English Literary Criticism: The Renaissance*, 1963.
Kinney, Arthur. *Markets of Bawdrie: The Dramatic Criticism of Stephen Gosson*, 1974.
Lee, Sir Sidney. "Stephen Gosson," in *Dictionary of National Biography*, Vol. 7, 1921–1922. Edited by Leslie Stephen and Sir Sidney Lee.
Lewis, C. S. *English Literature in the Sixteenth Century Excluding Drama*, 1954.
Ringler, William. *Stephen Gosson: A Biographical and Critical Study*, 1942.

MICHAEL WITKOSKI

See also Gascoigne; Puttenham; Renaissance and Restoration Literary Theory; Sidney

Gothic

"Gothic" as a genre term entered the literary vocabulary in the eighteenth century as a means of describing tales of murder, terror, and suspense. The novel *The Castle of Otranto* (1764) by Horace Walpole signals the beginning of what we now recognize as a genre frequently set in gloomy locations and populated by ghosts, monsters, ghouls, and other emblems of our fear of the supernatural. A precise literary definition of Gothic literature would refer to the period between Walpole's work and the appearance of Mary Shelley's *Frankenstein, or, The Modern Prometheus* (1818), Jane Austen's Gothic parody *Northanger Abbey* (1818), and Charles Maturin's *Melmoth the Wanderer* (1820), considered the last great Gothic text. However, Gothic as a connotative term continues to make spectral returns, ceaselessly mutating as a pronounced element in both popular and alternative forms of entertainment. As such, it enjoys a burgeoning cultural currency that shows no sign of abating.

The term Gothic derives from a style of medieval architecture popular in Europe between the twelfth and sixteenth centuries of which Notre Dame in Paris is perhaps the best-known example and the cathedrals at Rheims, Chartres, and Amiens the most spectacular. Essentially, it is the decayed and atmospheric ruins of original Gothic medieval buildings that function as settings for the genre's exploration into our fears of the unknown. Ann Radcliffe's *The Mysteries of Udolpho* (1794) makes full use of this decaying Gothic mood with tales of ghosts and ghouls inhabiting desolate castles and cathedrals. Crucially, the sheer variety of grotesque gargoyle figures and other supernatural creatures that populate the curtained walls of these cathedrals suggest an alternative mode of expression to the aesthetic rules of clarity and symmetry that had governed neoclassical eighteenth-century thought. In other words, these grotesques served the Gothic writer as symbols for the type of psychic disturbances that the neoclassical desire for order repressed. As a result, some Gothic explorations into the collective unconscious became extremely dark in both tone and subject matter; M. G. Lewis' *The Monk* (1796), for example, combines ghosts and demons with shocking cruelty and horror in what many critics believe to be the articulation of unconscious reactions against eighteenth-century rationality.

The *dramatis personae* of Gothic literature also expanded as the genre developed. Ghosts, monsters, living skeletons, undead corpses, demons, monks and nuns were joined by mad scientists and vampires in the nineteenth century. In Mary Shelley's *Frankenstein* the preceding era's preoccupation with rationality was fundamentally challenged by the last, despairing laments of the Romantic imagination. Moreover, Enlightenment certainty was radically challenged by the sympathy Shelley evoked for her murderous creature against the backdrop of an ill-advised human attempt to play God. As an indication of the degree to which *Frankenstein* succeeded in reflecting internalized cultural anxieties, the more traditional Gothic gloom of Victor Frankenstein's laboratory shares the novel's geographical setting with the North Pole, the unexplored land of perpetual light replacing Gothic stereotypes as the scene of the darkest story yet.

These psychological and geographical shifts in *Frankenstein*, which reflect the movement and metamorphoses of our own unconscious repository of fluctuating uncertainties and fears, help to illuminate the sheer versatility of the modern Gothic impulse, and particularly its representations in popular culture. For example, Ridley Scott's film *Blade Runner* (1980) retells the Frankenstein/Prometheus myth, articulating our unresolved fears both of technology and the specter of genetic engineering for cinema audiences. The welding of traditionally gloomy and decayed Gothic landscape, science fiction, and horror is nowhere better exemplified than in the *Alien* series of films (1979–), in which decaying space stations litter the horizon of deserted planets and where the horror comes, literally, from within.

The original cinematic cross-fertilization of Gothic with science fiction, Fritz Lang's *Metropolis* (1926), remains among the most influential along with such Gothic essentials as Friedrich Murnau's *Nosferatu* (1922) and Robert Wiene's *The Cabinet of Dr. Caligari* (1920). Indeed, these three films inspired James Whale's *Frankenstein* (1931) and Tod Browning's *Dracula* (1932), which in turn led to the explosion of Hammer Horror technicolor Gothic. The contradictory repellent/attractive nature of the latter two Gothic stalwarts featured as a direct influence on Alan Moore's novel *The Dark Night Returns* (1987), a revisionist treatment of Batman as a dark vigilante which was in turn sanitized for the big screen by Tim Burton in *Batman* (1990). Nonetheless, the increasing menace with which contemporary DC graphic artists have invested Bob Kane's original creation makes Batman the quintessential late-twentieth-century Gothic figure in the quintessential post-modern, Gothic landscape.

Another, similar cross-fertilization of genre takes place in the film *Angel Heart* (1986), in David Lynch's TV series *Twin Peaks* (1990–1992), and in *Seven* (1997). In these examples, Edgar Allen Poe is resurrected in postmodern, detective Gothic. Interestingly, the internalized anxiety that reduced the necessity of external, physical gloom in *Frankenstein* is nowhere better illustrated than in the shift from perpetual rain to sun in *Seven* at the point where a medieval murderer turns himself over to the police and so sets in train the film's black and macabre conclusion.

Elsewhere, in less calculated representations, the relation of modern Gothic to the unconscious is difficult to assess. *The Munsters* (1962) and *The Addams Family* (1964) may well be compromise formations allowing for the displacement of the more unpalatable aspects of Gothic through laughter, while the rock musical *The Rocky Horror Show* (1975) would also appear to facilitate the release of unconscious repressions in its celebration of comically diverse sexuality; a valuable antidote to a proliferation of Gothic Heavy Metal bands crooning about the apocalyptic fate of Mordor (the Kingdom of the Dark Lord in J. R. R. Tolkien's trilogy *The Lord of the Rings*, 1954–1955). Indeed, a more inclusive, polymorphous sexuality would appear to have arisen in the 1980s in the style-conscious Gothicism of musicians such as Robert Smith and The Cure and in the extremely successful DC comic Vertigo/Neil Gaiman *Sandman* series

(1988). Conversely, other recent Gothic explorations such as Francis Ford Coppola's film *Dracula* (1992) and Neil Jordan's interpretation of Anna Rice's *Interview With A Vampire* (1994) attempt to work through blood-sucking in a reasoned, self-conscious fashion that debilitates much of the unconscious dynamism of the original vampire myth. Yet such notable failures serve only to indicate the sheer variety of modern and postmodern Gothic representations and confirm the vitality and authentic cultural significance of this ceaselessly mutating and innovative genre.

Further reading

Bayer-Berenbaum, Linda. *The Gothic Imagination: Expansion in Gothic Literature and Art*, 1982.
Botting, Fred. *Gothic*, 1996.
Punter, D. G. *The Literature of Terror*, 1980.
Summers, Montague. *The Gothic Quest; a History of the Gothic Novel*, 1938.
Todorov, T. *The Fantastic*, 1973.
Tracy, Ann. *The Gothic Novel 1790–1830: Plot Summaries and Index to Motifs*, 1981.

RODNEY SHARKEY

Johann Christoph Gottsched

German critic and philosopher

Born: Judittenkirchen, Prussia; February 2, 1700
Died: Leipzig, Saxony; December 12, 1766

Biography

Johann Christoph Gottsched was born in the small town of Judittenkirchen, near Königsberg (now Kaliningrad), Prussia. The son of a pastor, he began his university studies in theology, philosophy, and philology at the University of Königsberg. In 1730 he became professor of poetics and in 1734 professor of logic and metaphysics in Leipzig. In 1727 Gottsched's involvement with the improvement of the German language led to the transformation of the regional language society Deutschübende Poetische Gesellschaft into a national organization modeled after the Académie Française. He then attempted to implement his reform efforts by convincing the theater troupe of Karoline Neuber to adopt his new ideas and realize them onstage.

In 1735 he married Luise Adelgunde Victoria Kulmus, the gifted and extremely well-educated daughter of a scholar. Together they collaborated on writing plays and translating foreign, mostly French, plays as ideal examples for a new German theater. Gottsched's initial success – the Neuber troupe with its new, purified theater productions was able to perform at the court – was, however, short-lived. Already in 1739 differences arose between Gottsched and the theater company, and a first blow against his dominance as the leading theater critic was dealt by two Swiss critics, Johann Jakob Breitinger and Johann Jakob Bodmer.

Since his influence over the acting company had waned and his plays were no longer performed, Gottsched became active as the editor of *Die deutsche Schaubühne*. The period of rationalistic theater reform he had implemented came to an end with the seventeenth installment of Gotthold Ephraim Lessing's periodical *Briefe, die neueste Litteratur betreffend* (1759–1760; letters on current literature), in which he dismissed Gottsched's attempts to introduce a classicist theater, based on French models, as no longer appropriate for the emerging German theater. Gottsched died in 1766, and the elaborate funeral for him demonstrated that, regardless of his literary adversaries, his contemporaries recognized the importance of his reforms.

Influence

Gottsched was the preeminent disseminator of Enlightenment thought and its influence on literature, especially drama, in Germany. His theater reform raised the standards of the plays and the performances on the German stage and paved the way for a classicist theater. As a philosopher, Gottsched was interested in improving the morals of the audience, and the theater he envisioned was to have a moral purpose. He was the first consciously to couch this didactic purpose in dramatic action, an approach which held sway in Germany until Lessing's celebrated attack on Gottsched in 1759.

Analysis

Gottsched's literary criticism cannot be fully understood without some background concerning his philosophical writings. Gottsched condensed the work of the first systematic German Enlightenment philosopher, Christian von Wolff, into two volumes, making it available to a broader audience. This philosophy, informed by discoveries in the natural sciences, popularized the idea that the cosmos was a machine which was rationally explicable; it liberated people from a strictly religious interpretation of the world and particularly from the fear of eternal damnation. Gottsched propagated the view that when people understand their environment and allow this knowledge to guide their conduct they will experience the "best of all worlds."

In his weekly *Die vernünftigen Tadlerinnen*, Gottsched intended to improve the conduct of his readers, freeing them from their slavish adherence to the mores of the courts, which he found unacceptable for the educated bourgeoisie to which he was addressing his works. At the same time, Gottsched criticized the inferior German linguistic abilities of his audience, and he protested against the exclusive usage of French in educated circles.

In his next editorial endeavor, *Der Biedermann*, he invented an exemplary bourgeois family with a new rational and independent life-style. Reason became the guiding principle for this reform. The most natural expression in language, the most natural conduct in everyday life, is the most reasonable – and the most reasonable is the best possible behavior. Before Gottsched could fully establish his literary reform he had to institute a substantial linguistic improvement. He hoped to achieve this by laying a theoretical and practical foundation with his reorganized Deutsche Gesellschaft in 1727. His hope was to implement a linguistic reform which would establish a single dominant dialect based on Saxon usage.

In his major critical work *Versuch einer kritischen Dichtkunst vor die Deutschen* (1730) he offered a systematic overview of all genres of literature. It provided general rules of poetics and gave examples for the writer and the critic. Gottsched utilized previous works of the philosophy of art from Aristotle, Horace, Martin Opitz, and, above all, Nicolas Boileau-Despréaux. His major statement of literary criticism can therefore be regarded as a compilation of important statements on poetics from antiquity to neoclassicism. At the core of his investigation are several concerns: the qualifications of a true poet, the nature of poetry, and how one writes a good poem. At the center of all literature, according to Gottsched, is the imitation of nature. The poet has a natural ability for imitation which, nevertheless, must be cultivated by proper training; such training Gottsched intends to offer in his works.

Gottsched's form of literary criticism differs from earlier works in its pronounced moral and didactic intent. Each work of art should have a fixed moral message couched in a fable. For this reason, he considered drama the most useful genre. Yet the theater, as it existed in Germany at the beginning of the eighteenth century, was not suitable for this didactic purpose. It consisted of pompous baroque drama, the elaborate, Italian-inspired opera at the courts, and the theater for the common people. The latter was composed of mostly improvisational comedies dominated by the *Hanswurst*, the buffo, with his crude sense of humor. If plays were to have a message, the ad-lib character of theater performance had to be abolished. Therefore Gottsched established fixed roles for the actors; the "unreasonable" entertainment of the *Hanswurst* was removed from the plays; and the language was elevated to a more acceptable level in order to address a more educated audience and improve the tastes of the common people.

Since the fable, or plot, was the most important element to convey the underlying message, Gottsched paid particular attention to this feature to assure its plausibility. Since action was produced by characters, he demanded that the dramatist, or poet, be a good judge of human nature. After choosing the moral statement he or she wished to make, the poet should find a plot line which serves his or her purpose in an exemplary fashion; he or she then should look for characters in history who have experienced a similar fate. The poet must outline the characters in such a manner that their actions and reactions seem natural and in keeping with their particular character traits; according to Gottsched, nothing is more repulsive than an inconsistent character.

The poet's next step is to add circumstances to render the main plot probable. This includes adding an intrigue to weave into the plot and make it more interesting for the spectators. He or she should then divide the fable into five equally long pieces and arrange them according to their natural logic, not necessarily according to their actual historical sequence. Since the plot has only one underlying message it should have only one main sequence of events – in other words, unity of action. Gottsched also maintained the importance of the unity of time and place, because the best and most probable fables are the ones which take as long on the stage as they would in reality. The reason given is also that of plausibility; since the spectators remain in one place, so should the characters onstage. In addition, Gottsched gave instructions on the stylistic qualities of the language used in a tragedy: his general rule is to observe the true nature of a particular emotion in everyday life and to imitate it, in verse, as closely as possible.

Gottsched also carefully outlined the technical details of the stage. Elaborate machinery used to create special effects was banned, because it was deemed unnatural. The costumes of the actor or actress should be true to each particular character. Finally, Gottsched also gave specific instruction about the manner of acting: the actor or actress must realistically reenact the emotion he or she is supposed to experience.

As noted above, in order to demonstrate fully the way he wanted the reformed drama to look, he wrote, translated, and edited exemplary pieces. His own tragedies, *Der sterbende Cato* (1732; the dying Cato), *Agis, König zu Sparta* (1745; Agis, King of Sparta), and *Die parisische Bluthochzeit* (1745; the Parisian blood wedding), were performed quite frequently in their time but are, beyond their documentary function, of little lasting artistic value.

Gottsched demonstrated that literary reform, linguistic reform, and social reform are intrinsically connected. Furthermore, he realized that an improvement could not be achieved by theoretical criticism alone, and therefore he supplied the theater with an improved repertory and tried to influence the leading theater troupe to implement his reforms. Before Gottsched there was no respectable drama criticism. He managed to rid the stage of the "Haupt- und Staatsaktionen," which customarily dealt with historical subjects laced with sensationalism, improvised comedy, and overly confusing intrigues. By banishing the *Hanswurst*, who was even an integral part of plays with serious intent, he removed the comical interruption of the plays and a source of bawdy entertainment. The use of metered elevated language forced the actors to depart from the traditional extemporaneous style of performing.

Admittedly, Gottsched was a reformer of the externals of literature. His overtly moralistic and rationalistic view of literature and his mechanistic approach to the creation of art failed to recognize the powers of imagination and the more complicated aesthetic aspects of art. Although his criticism was neither original nor particularly insightful, it nevertheless laid the basis for more sophisticated approaches to literature.

Principal criticism

Ausführliche Redekunst, 1728
Versuch einer kritischen Dichtkunst vor die Deutschen, 1730
Grundlegung einer deutschen Sprachkunst, 1748
Nötiger Vorrat zur Geschichte der deutschen dramatischen Dichtkunst, 1757–1765

Other major works and literary forms

Johann Christoph Gottsched was known not only as a literary critic but also as a philosopher. The most important document of his philosophy is *Erste Gründe der gesamten Weltweisheit* (1733–1734). With that work he became the principal representative of Christian von Wolff's Enlightenment thought in Germany. In addition, he translated into German Pierre Bayle's *Dictionnaire historique et critique*, which was to become a seminal work for German Enlightenment ideas. As editor of two important *moralische Wochenschriften* (moral weeklies), *Die vernünftigen Tadlerinnen* (1725–1726) and *Der Biedermann* (1727–1729), modeled after the English periodicals *The Spectator* and *The Tatler* edited by Joseph Addison and Richard Steele, he popularized his philosophy.

Gottsched exercised his influence on one of the most important theater companies of the day, the company of Karoline Neuber, reforming their acting style. In addition, he wrote tragedies – including *Der sterbende Cato* (1732; the dying Cato) and *Agis, König zu Sparta* (1745; Agis, King of Sparta) – for them to perform. He collected his own dramatic works, those of his wife Luise Adelgunde Gottsched, translations, and other plays which he believed improved theater in Germany in a six-volume collection *Die deutsche Schaubühne* (1740–1745; the German stage).

PLAYS
Der sterbende Cato, 1732
Agis, König zu Sparta, 1745
Die parisische Bluthochzeit, 1745

NONFICTION
Die vernünftigen Tadlerinnen, 1725–1726 (editor)
Der Biedermann, 1727–1729 (editor)
Erste Gründe der gesamten Weltweisheit, 1733–1734

TRANSLATION
Historisches und kritisches Wörterbuch, 1741–1744 (of Pierre Bayle's *Dictionnaire historique et critique*)

MISCELLANEOUS
Die deutsche Schaubühne, 1740–1745 (6 volumes)

Further reading

Bragg, Marvin. *From Gottsched to Goethe: Changes in the Social Function of the Poet and Poetry*, 1984.
Gostwick, Joseph, and Robert Harrison, eds. "Sixth Period, 1725–70," in *Outlines of German Literature*, 1873.
McGormick, Allen. "The Eighteenth Century: Foundation and Development of Literary Criticism," in *The Challenge of German Literature*, 1971. Edited by Horst S. Daemmrich and Diether H. Haenicke.
Mitchell, Philip Marshall. *Johann Christoph Gottsched (1700–1766): Harbinger of German Classicism*, 1995.

KARIN WURST

See also Bodmer; Lessing

Rémy de Gourmont

French writer and critic

Born: Bazoches-en-Houlme, France; April 4, 1858
Died: Paris, France; September 27, 1915

Biography

Rémy de Gourmont was born on April 4, 1858, in Bazoches-en-Houlme, Orne, France, the first of two sons born to Auguste and Marie (née de Montfort) de Gourmont. On his father's side, Gourmont was descended from a family of established printers and engravers. His mother's ancestors were related to the seventeenth-century poet François de Malherbe. Gourmont was educated at the Coutances Lycée and the University of Caen in Normandy. He received his *diplôme* in 1883 and went to Paris, where he was an assistant librarian at the Bibliothèque Nationale. He held this post until 1891, when he was dismissed for writing a seemingly unpatriotic, pro-German article for *Le Mercure de France*. At this same time, he became afflicted with chronic lupus, a disease that disfigured him. He was known as a contemplative writer who shunned society; he maintained a productive literary life, however, and enjoyed considerable prestige among the poets of the Symbolist school. He never married but was disposed to a series of infatuations, which provided him with material for his novels, short stories, and poems.

Gourmont's career is distinguished by his contributions to numerous periodicals. By 1886 he was familiar with the work of Stéphane Mallarmé and other Symbolists. He also met Joris-Karl Huysmans, who was associated with the Decadent movement of the early 1880s. Gourmont and Huysmans collaborated with Henri de Régnier and Alfred Vallette in founding *Le Mercure de France*. Many of Gourmont's essays were later collected in the fourteen volumes that constitute his *Épilogues* (1903–1913), *Promenades littéraires* (1904–1927), and *Promenades philosophiques* (1905–1909; *Philosophic Nights in Paris*, 1920). This achievement compares favorably to the works of other well-known French critics, notably Charles-Augustin Sainte-Beuve, Hippolyte-Adolphe Taine, and Ferdinand Brunetière.

The publication in 1896 of *Le Livre des masques* (*The Book of Masks*, 1921) marked the beginning of Gourmont's rise to the upper ranks of the most influential critics in Europe. In this work he established a philosophical justification for Symbolism, and in later critical works he articulated important propositions regarding the aesthetics of language. At the time of his death, in 1915, he was writing an article protesting the German bombing of the cathedral at Rheims.

Influence

Gourmont refined the nineteenth-century concept of subjective idealism and offered compelling literary models for its application. He clarified the intentions of "Decadent" writers and removed much of the misunderstanding that surrounded this term. In the 1890s he emerged as the spokesperson and codifier of the Symbolist movement. His doctrine of "dissociation of ideas" prepared the ground for T. S. Eliot's theory of art. Gourmont extolled poetry as the only viable genre and he repeatedly argued that content and form are inseparable.

Gourmont was one of the first writers to validate the function of criticism by regarding it as autonomous discipline, thus pointing to the conceptions of J. Middleton Murry and I. A. Richards. The literary values that Gourmont endorsed – intelligent sensibility, affirmation of personality, analysis, and comparison – became the cornerstones of twentieth-century applied criticism. Gourmont's study of linguistics and the natural sciences led him to believe that perception is the basis of literary art. For this reason, many of Ezra Pound's ideas concerning aesthetics can be seen as corollaries of Gourmont's theories. Furthermore, Gourmont's principles of individualism, freedom from classification, and self-differentiation galvanized the thinking of André Gide. Gourmont's ideas concerning the process of literary absorption (fusion of author, protagonist, and reader) and subconscious creation are essential to the understanding of the stream-of-consciousness technique.

Analysis

Gourmont's lasting influence is best perceived in those writers who forged a link between the Symbolist movement of the 1880s and the Surrealists of the 1920s. Léon-Paul Fargue and Alfred Jarry acknowledged that it was Gourmont who opened new possibilities for writers of the first generation of the twentieth century. Jarry found in Gourmont's theories all the necessary ingredients (idealism, imagery, iconography) for an artistic break with the past.

As a habitual enemy of received ideas, Gourmont rose to prominence as the critic who rescued the Symbolist movement from its detractors and from those who attempted to transform its original purposes. By 1890 the Symbolists were generally regarded as poets concerned with the expression of their own inner sensations. Thus, they were often criticized for being obscure or incomprehensible. This view was compounded by critical perceptions that linked Symbolism with classical Greek tragedy because it was centered in a cosmic void and because it relied on purely objective images for its artistic expression.

Writing in *La Revue des revues* (from January to September, 1896), in a section entitled "Les Nouveaux Venus," Gourmont began to assimilate the accomplishments and delineate the individuality of the Symbolist poets. These essays constitute more than half the contents of *The Book of Masks*, and the preface to this work contains his often-cited definition of Symbolism:

> What does Symbolism mean? If one keeps to its narrow and etymological sense, almost nothing; if one goes beyond that, it means: individualism in literature, liberty of art, abandonment of existing forms, tending toward what is new, strange, and even bizarre; it also may mean idealism, disdain of social anecdote, anti-naturalism, a tendency to take only the characteristic detail from life, to pay attention only to the act by which a person distinguishes himself, and to desire to realize results, essentials. . . . Symbolism is, even though excessive, tempestuous, and pretentious, the expression of individualism in art.

Gourmont envisioned Symbolism as a mental attitude, not as an academic system. He understood that literature is like yeast that expands in response to its environment; its form, texture, and disposition record the process of change. This principle of the ideality of the world derives its inspiration from the metaphysical speculation of the German Idealists, primarily Johann Gottlieb Fichte and Arthur Schopenhauer. For Gourmont, the true expression of the Absolute Ego is the process of striving toward a unique vision that is, in turn, manifested in art. He reinforced the Symbolist ideal that reality is fundamentally unknowable, but it is revealed by contemplating a delicate world of nuance and intuition.

Gourmont perceived Symbolism as a reaction against naturalism, which attempted to depict in a journalistic style the external, ordinary, and vulgar existence of people. Hence, Gourmont classified the Symbolists according to a theory of emotional sensation, by which the *sensoriel* artist transforms visions into words. The Symbolists distinguished themselves by their imaginative powers, through which thoughts and feelings were transmuted as symbols or verbal icons. Gourmont contrasted the *sensoriel* poets with *idéo-émotif* writers who associate emotion and memory with common abstractions, who are unable to translate these emotions and memories into unique images.

Gourmont wrote one of his most ambitious and provocative studies in memory of Mallarmé, who died in 1898. In this essay, "Mallarmé et l'idée de décadence," he extended the legacy of Symbolism into new domains and endowed the concept of decadence with fresh vigor. He regarded Mallarmé as a poet who practiced alchemy with words and who cast a diaphanous mist over nature. Thus, Mallarmé successfully presented emotion through the musical arrangement of words as he mastered the art of grasping the images and sensations produced by the interrelationship of words.

Gourmont maintained that style cannot be learned and that mediocre stylists had caused writing to become depreciated as an art form. He distinguished between two literatures: that created by writers with style and that which lacked invention. In order to realize the utmost beauty, words must be used that are analogous to the impression caused by the object of contemplation. The world of sensations and the world of words are infinitely apart – that is, parallel.

Decadence, for Gourmont, was a form of imitation, a "natural death" that was not necessarily counterproductive. He argued against the idea that France was socially and artistically decadent by tracing the term to its source in the waning years of the Roman Empire when the purest of Greco-Roman ideals were emulated. Thus he declared that political decadence creates favorable conditions for intellectual and cultural growth. This statement must have seemed like balm for the wounds of France's deeply divided Third Republic during the Dreyfus affair.

La Culture des idées (1900; *The Cultivation of Ideas*, 1921) contains a frequently mentioned essay about the "dissociation of ideas," in which Gourmont reasserts the need to abolish the unquestioning acceptance of predetermined ideas and stereotypes (for example, "pleasure" should be dissociated from "procreation," "political liberty" from "individual freedom," "virtue" from "self-abnegation," "rectitude" from "respectability"). Words are organisms that should be cultivated; without new ideas, literature liquefies into an amorphous mass of common phrases. "Dissociation," then, implies the methodology of scientific rationalism, by which false associations are dismantled and reclassified. Gourmont admitted the complexity involved in demolishing absolute truths: "To explain a straw, the entire universe must be pulled apart." He refused to accept the notion that ideas were immutable and he saw in this lucid interrogation of thought a method of deliverance.

Gourmont's belief in the power of words led to the composition of several works on linguistics. In *Le Latin mystique* (1892) and *Esthétique de la langue française* (1899; *What Is Pure French?*, 1922), he continued to explore the complex process by which sensation and idea become language. The translations of and commentaries on medieval Latin poetry in *Le Latin mystique* reveal his attraction to the symbolism of the Catholic religion. He examined revelation objectively in an effort to understand the connection between sexual passion and mystical experience. What he sought to uncover was the pagan, carnal residue of Christianity, which disappeared after the sixteenth-century Counter-Reformation.

In *What Is Pure French?*, he set the stage for *Le Problème du style* (1902) by denouncing clichés as logically incoherent and trite. Books that abound in clichés are the product of an "anonymous brain, of perfect intellectual servitude." The true poet, on the contrary, does not allow his or her perception to be simplified by practical considerations. He or she comprehends the universal in the particular because his or her intellect is dissociated from his or her sensibility. This is why Gourmont praised Émile Verhaeren and other *vers libristes* who suggested an intuitive grasp of concrete reality behind their elusive symbols. In addition, he commended Gustave Kahn for drawing attention to the accentuated verse pattern of the French language and for exploring new metrical combinations to arrive at *le beau inédit* (unprecedented beauty).

Gourmont's modernity presupposed the classical tradition in French literature. He admired the formal eloquence of Jacques-Bénigne Bossuet and the Comte de Buffon, the relativism of Pierre Bayle and Michel Eyquem de Montaigne, and the wit and precision of Voltaire and Jean Le Rond d'Alembert. His relentless curiosity and versatility, however, bring him closer to Denis Diderot, who enjoyed the same spontaneous mixture of aesthetics, myth, and paradox. Like Diderot, Gourmont attempted to test his theories in his own fiction. Each writer examined sexual instinct in the light of rational control in order to comprehend what Gourmont called "the complete anatomy of intelligence."

Gourmont advocated an alliance of body and brain by stating that humans think with their bodies – intelligence being a form of sensibility. Gourmont's numerous allegories and fantasies reflect his deterministic belief that human behavior is rooted in biology. Novels such as *Sixtine: Roman de la vie cérébrale* (1890; *Very Woman: A Cerebral Novel*, 1922) and *Les Chevaux de Diomède* (1897; *The Horses of Diomedes*, 1923) and the drama *Lilith* (1892; English translation, 1946) reveal astute psychoanalytic insight and point toward Gourmont's scientific study *Physique d'amour: Essai sur l'instinct sexuel* (1903; *The Natural Philosophy of Love*, 1926), which analyzed complex mental states from the perspective of sensualist philosophy. The erotic atmosphere of Gourmont's novels is reminiscent of the Marquis de Sade, while the lassitude of his cerebral heroes evokes the tenuous world of introverted reflection and insubstantiality found in the writings of Huysmans and other Decadent novelists.

Gourmont's interest in the psychology of sexual behavior was stimulated by the pioneering work of Havelock Ellis. In 1890 he wrote a favorable review of Ellis' *The New Spirit* in *Le Mercure de France* and made arrangements for its translation into French. Late in life he entertained the notion of a psychic androgyny in his *Lettres à l'Amazone* (1914; *Letters to the Amazon*, 1931), written to an American admirer of his theories, Nathalie Clifford Barney. This work contains one of his most significant pronouncements regarding impressionist criticism. He affirmed that the principal aim of the scrupulous critic is "to build his personal impressions into laws." This is achieved through honesty of feeling and intellectual rigor. Gourmont regarded criticism as a subjective genre because it relies on the vitality of the critic's mind.

Such a view accounts for the genial skepticism of Gourmont's critical temperament. His rationalist-Symbolist fusion allowed for the development of a literary conscience that distrusted an overzealous intellect. He strove to contain the extreme individualism of the Symbolists within the province of reason; in doing so, it is clear that he was not timid about raising contradictions that could not be resolved. This accounts for the fluidity of his ideas, what he called "the immense diversity of aptitudes." With his encyclopedic mind, Gourmont represents the ultimate flowering of nineteenth-century philology: an all-embracing, protean form of scholarship. He gave a new direction to modern criticism by adding to it an aesthetic dimension consistent with the traditional values of insight and intuition.

Principal criticism

Le Latin mystique, 1892
Le Livre des masques, 1896 (*The Book of Masks*, 1921)
Le Deuxième Livre des masques, 1898
La Culture des idées, 1900 (*The Cultivation of Ideas*, 1921)
Le Problème du style, 1902
Le Chemin de velours, 1902 (*Path of Velvet*, 1921)
Épilogues, 1903–1913 (4 volumes)
Promenades littéraires, 1904–1927 (7 volumes)
Promenades philosophiques, 1905–1909 (7 volumes; *Philosophic Nights in Paris*, 1920)
Dialogues des amateurs sur les choses du temps, 1905–1907, 1907
Nouveaux Dialogues des amateurs sur les choses du temps, 1907–1910, 1910
Lettres à l'Amazone, 1914 (*Letters to the Amazon*, 1931)
Lettres intimes à l'Amazone, 1928

Other major works and literary forms

For twenty-five years, from 1890 to 1915, Rémy de Gourmont regularly contributed articles to *Le Mercure de France* under the heading "Actualité." The range of topics is prodigious and indicates the breadth of his scholarship. Gourmont was also a celebrated poet whose influence contributed to the formation of the Imagist movement. In addition, he was a prolific novelist and short-story writer whose primary concern was to develop the contrast between intellectual heroes and the sexual instincts of the women who captivate them. In like manner, his five dramas portray an intuitive grasp of feminine psychology; these plays were conceived as theoretical works not intended for the stage. Gourmont also retained a lifelong fascination for the scientific study of sexuality. He combined this interest with a philosophical inquiry into the hierarchy of living organisms. The result was a widely read and controversial treatise entitled *Physique d'amour: Essai sur l'instinct sexuel* (1903; *The Natural Philosophy of Love*, 1926), which reflects Freudian psychology and anticipates the sexual theories of D. H. Lawrence.

In the years before his death, with Europe on the verge of war, Gourmont examined the relationship of social forces to political apathy in a series of studies on militarism and morality. These works reveal his constant growth and development as a Nietzschean moralist. Despite the brooding quality of some of his wartime commentaries, it is the same discursive and observational spirit which informed his major critical works that prevailed, along with the detached irony of a modern François, Duc de La Rochefoucauld.

NOVELS
Merlette, 1886
Sixtine: Roman de la vie cérébrale, 1890 (*Very Woman: A Cerebral Novel*, 1922)
Le Fantôme, 1893
Les Chevaux de Diomède, 1897 (*The Horses of Diomedes*, 1923)
Le Songe d'une femme, 1899 (*The Dream of a Woman*, 1927)
Une Nuit au Luxembourg, 1906 (*A Night in the Luxembourg*, 1912)
Un Cœur virginal, 1907 (*A Virgin Heart*, 1921)
Lettres d'un satyre, 1913 (*Mr. Antiphilos, Satyr*, 1922)

SHORT FICTION
Proses moroses, 1894
Histoires magiques, 1894
Le Pèlerin du silence, 1896
D'un pays lointain, 1898
Couleurs, 1908 (*Colors*, 1929)
La Patience de Griseldis, 1921

PLAYS
Lilith, 1892 (English translation, 1946)
Théodat, 1893
La Princesse Phénissa, 1895
Le Vieux Roi, 1897 (*The Old King*, 1916)
L'Ombre d'une femme, 1924

POETRY
Divertissements, 1912 (*Poems: Selections from the Works of Rémy de Gourmont*, 1928)

NONFICTION
Esthétique de la langue française, 1899 (*What Is Pure French?*, 1922)
Physique d'amour: Essai sur l'instinct sexuel, 1903 (*The Natural Philosophy of Love*, 1926)
Pendant l'orage, 1915
Dans la tourmente, 1916
Pendant la guerre, 1917

Further reading

Burke, Kenneth. "Three Adepts of 'Pure' Literature," in *Counter-Statement*, 1953.
Burne, Glenn S. *Rémy de Gourmont: His Ideas and Influence in England and America*, 1963.
Cornell, Kenneth. *The Symbolist Movement*, 1951.
Lowell, Amy. "Rémy de Gourmont," in *Six French Poets*, 1967.
Pondrom, Cyrena N. *The Road from Paris*, 1974.

Pound, Ezra. "Rémy de Gourmont: A Distinction," in *Literary Essays of Ezra Pound*, 1968.
Sieburth, Richard. *Instigations: Ezra Pound and Rémy de Gourmont*, 1978.
Turnell, Martin. *Critiques and Essays in Criticism, 1920–1948*, 1949.
Uitti, Karl. *The Concept of the Self in the Symbolist Novel*, 1961.

ROBERT J. FRAIL

See also Bourget; Brunetière; Continental Theory; Symbolism

Antonio Gramsci

Italian writer and political theorist

Born: Ales, Sardinia, Italy; January 23, 1891
Died: Rome, Italy; April 27, 1937

Biography

Antonio Gramsci, born on January 23, 1891, in the small town of Ales on the island of Sardinia, Italy, was the fourth of seven children. His father, Francesco Gramsci, came to Sardinia from the Italian mainland as a minor civil servant; his mother, Giuseppina Marcias, was a native Sardinian. Frail since birth, Gramsci suffered a serious illness at the age of four, as a result of which he was hunchbacked and always remained small in stature. Because of his family's straitened circumstances, Gramsci had to work for two years upon completion of his elementary education. He returned to school in 1905 and, in spite of daunting financial and physical problems, succeeded not only in completing grammar school but also in winning a scholarship to attend the University of Turin. He moved to Turin in 1911, and before long he met and befriended several young Socialists, among them Palmiro Togliatti and Angelo Tasca, both of whom would later figure most prominently in the Italian Socialist and Communist movements.

While making his mark as an unusually promising student of linguistics at the university, Gramsci became increasingly involved in politics. In 1913 he joined the Italian Socialist Party (PSI), and within two years he had abandoned his studies and was a regular contributor to Socialist newspapers and periodicals. As a young journalist, Gramsci wrote numerous theater reviews, polemical articles, and brief commentaries on sociocultural and political issues. At the same time, his political activity kept him in contact with industrial workers and revealed his leadership abilities. In 1919 he helped found the periodical *L'ordine nuovo* (the new order), which became the organ of a very energetic faction that sought to renew the PSI and its relations with the proletariat. During a national Socialist congress held in 1921, Gramsci was among the core members of a group that seceded from the PSI and formed the Italian Communist Party (PCI), of which he became general secretary in 1924. Gramsci's relentless opposition to the Fascist regime led to his arrest in 1926, notwithstanding the immunity from prosecution to which he was constitutionally entitled as a parliamentary deputy. Gramsci was held in prison until 1935, when his wretched physical condition required that he be transferred to a clinic. The years of mistreatment, however, had exacted a fatal toll, and he died on April 27, 1937, only a week after regaining his freedom.

In 1922 Gramsci had met Giulia Schucht in Moscow. They had two children, Delio and Giuliano. Since Giuliano was born in Moscow only three months before his father's arrest and imprisonment, Gramsci died without ever having set eyes on his younger son.

Influence

When Gramsci's prison notebooks were first published in Italy after World War II, they had a profound effect in cultural and intellectual circles. In the field of literary studies specifically, Gramsci's work pointed to the serious deficiencies of the dominant critical attitude, which, under Benedetto Croce's exceedingly powerful influence, legitimated a strict separation between aesthetic considerations and sociopolitical concerns. Gramsci's writings have special relevance for those critics who seek to integrate the study of literature within the larger context of cultural and social analysis. His ideas are an indispensable point of reference for Western Marxist literary criticism and cultural study.

Analysis

Gramsci never produced a systematic study of aesthetics, literary theory, or criticism. Nevertheless, scattered throughout his writings there is a large body of material that not only is of considerable intrinsic literary and critical interest but also contains all the elements necessary for a thorough and sophisticated formulation of a Marxist approach to literature and criticism. It is virtually impossible to separate without grave distortion Gramsci's reflections on culture in general or on literary issues in particular from his life's work in political organization, revolutionary activity, and the elaboration of Marxist theory. Indeed, it is precisely this close intertwining of culture and politics in Gramsci's theory and practice that gives his writing on literature its unique character and its special value.

From his earliest years as an active Socialist Party member, Gramsci vigorously opposed all positivistic and economistic versions of Marxism. He firmly believed that the goal of a socialist revolution is not only the radical change of the economic order but indeed the establishment of a totally new "integral conception of the world . . . a total integral civilization." In order to achieve this goal, one had, first of all, to liberate the masses from the thrall of the hegemonic bourgeois world-view and then to foster the emergence and growth of a proletarian consciousness and culture. "Every revolution," he pointed out, "has been preceded by an intense labor of criticism, of cultural penetration, of the permeation of ideas." For Gramsci, then, cultural and political activity were so intimately related as to be practically inseparable.

Whether he was writing on labor relations or philosophy, economic policy or literature, Gramsci never adopted the posture of a detached spectator. Indeed, he went to great lengths to demonstrate how the privileged position of objectivity and disinterest so carefully cultivated by traditional intellectuals actually conceals or camouflages the class interests which they serve, sustain, and legitimate. At the same time, though, Gramsci was a fierce opponent of politically reductive criticism. He would never judge the merits of a work of art solely on the basis of the sociopolitical position it represented or embodied. He considered the dogmatism that produces such vulgar criticism a politically regressive perversion of Marxism.

Gramsci believed that there need be no conflict between literary criticism and cultural politics. To put it another way, for Gramsci a good critic remains cognizant of and appreciates the literary merits of a given work even when his or her critical practice is informed by a political interest – and the reverse is true, as well. Even if one were to uphold the principle that in examining a work of art the critic should be concerned with its aesthetic quality, one need not suppose that this same principle "prohibits a search for the mass of sentiments, the attitude towards life which circulates in the work of art itself. . . . What is prohibited is the notion that a work of art is beautiful because of its political and moral content rather than because of its form in which the abstract content is fused and modified." What must be kept in mind at all times, however, is that every work of art is grounded in history and that, therefore, its form as much as its content manifests or embodies a worldview, an attitude toward life.

Gramsci is very cautious when dealing with the issue of form versus content. Recognizing that the historical and politicized criticism which he favors tends to focus primarily on the content of a literary work, he still does not wish to minimize the importance of the formal element in literature. "Can one talk of a priority of content over form? One can talk about it in this sense, that the work of art is a process and the changes in content are also changes in form, but it is 'easier' to talk about content than form because content can be 'recapitulated' logically." Ultimately, the question of privileging content over form or vice versa should not arise for the Marxist critic who remains faithful to historical materialism, because both content and form "besides having an 'aesthetic' meaning have also a 'historical' meaning." The distinguishing feature of Gramsci's literary criticism is its rootedness in a historical and material view of culture; for him, "literary history is a part and an aspect of a much larger history of culture."

In the opening pages of the prison notebook devoted to literary and critical issues, Gramsci sets up a comparison between two preeminent figures in the history of Italian literary criticism – Francesco De Sanctis and Benedetto Croce. Through this comparison, Gramsci articulates more directly and explicitly than anywhere else in his writing two basic features of his own critical theory and practice. First of all, the criticism of De Sanctis attests the presence within the Italian tradition of a militant, engaged, and historically grounded approach to literature. It stands in sharp contrast to Croce's uncompromising demands for detachment and aesthetic distance in the analysis and assessment of literary works. Croce's strict, ahistorical formalism and his assertion of the autonomy of the work of art had attained the status of fundamental dogma among the vast majority of Italian literati; Gramsci invoked the authoritative figure of De Sanctis in order to draw attention to a different critical tradition that does not sever literary criticism from the sociopolitical concerns of worldly existence. De Sanctis' work represents "the kind of literary criticism proper to the philosophy of praxis," meaning Marxism.

Gramsci does not, however, propose a simplistic return to De Sanctis' aesthetic theories or a straightforward retrieval of De Sanctis' specific views and speculations on the nature of literature and literary history. Rather, Gramsci offers De Sanctis as an example of militant criticism, a criticism which stems from a profound sense of civic and political responsibility – that is, a criticism which does not seek to establish itself as a completely autonomous sphere of knowledge. For this reason, when Gramsci contrasts De Sanctis to Croce he does not do so by juxtaposing and evaluating their general aesthetic theories. Instead, he declares his preference for the militancy of De Sanctis, his "passionate fervor" as opposed to Croce's "elevated serenity." This is not to say that Gramsci has no interest in theoretical issues. Far from it; in numerous notes Gramsci criticizes and rebuts Croce's key concepts and procedures, such as the categorical separation of "poetry" from "non-poetry," the idea of criticism as a transcendental act of universal subjective value, and the distinction between poetry and structure. Yet, Gramsci does not offer De Sanctis' aesthetics as an alternative to Croce's; he does not suggest that Crocean criticism be surpassed or displaced simply by taking a jump backward into De Sanctis' world. Gramsci invokes De Sanctis as an exemplary man in whose life and work one could observe how aesthetic theory, cultural criticism, and political militancy were fused so as to inform and transform one another.

Gramsci, therefore, focuses on those features of De Sanctis which most closely parallel his own view of the ideal critic: an intellectual who is deeply committed to the establishment of a new culture, who participates fully in the struggle it would entail, and who is willing to abandon his or her privileged position within the elite class and within the academic sanctuary in order "to go to the people." Gramsci sees in De Sanctis a critic with a political program; the cultural struggle is an essential part of that program, and the technical and speculative study of aesthetics, literature, philosophy, history, and so on is an important element of the cultural struggle. The primary interest of such a critic, according to Gramsci, is not the "refinement of culture," as it is for Croce, but the cultural-political struggle for a new order.

In all of his writings on literature, Gramsci was participating directly in the revolutionary struggle for a new culture. Whether he was writing on theatrical performances, popular literature, or the masterpieces of the Italian literary canon, Gramsci sought to lay bare the sociopolitical and institutional interests at play in the works themselves and in the various cultural and academic operations through which these works are interpreted, evaluated, and transmitted. Gramsci's literary criticism was, in fact, a historical-materialist critique of culture aimed at clearing the ground and preparing for the emergence of a nonelitist, nonsectarian, classless civilization.

Principal criticism

Letteratura e vita nazionale, 1950

Selections from Cultural Writings, 1985 (David Forgacs and Geoffrey Nowell-Smith, editors. William Boelhower, translator)

Other major works and literary forms

The books listed above contain almost all those items of literary and drama criticism that are scattered throughout Antonio Gramsci's writings. Nevertheless, these books represent only a fraction of Gramsci's œuvre. Although he did not publish any books during his lifetime, Gramsci wrote voluminously on an enormous range of political, social, historical, and cultural topics. Until his imprisonment in 1926, Gramsci's essays, articles, and reviews appeared in Italian Socialist and Communist newspapers and periodicals. While in prison, he recorded and collected his ideas in a series of notebooks which were published posthumously and established his widespread reputation as a major figure in Marxist thought. Gramsci's letters from prison, another important vehicle for his reflections on a broad variety of subjects, including literature, were published in a collection that in 1947 was honored with the Viareggio Prize for Literature.

NONFICTION

Lettere dal carcere, 1947 (*Letters from Prison*, 1973)

Quaderni del carcere, 1948–1951 (6 volumes; partial translation as *Selections from the Prison Notebooks of Antonio Gramsci*, 1971)

Quaderni del Carcere, 1975 (4 volumes; Valentine Gerratana, editor)

Antonio Gramsci: Selections from His Political Writings, 1910–1920, 1977

Selections from Political Writings: 1910–1920, 1977 (Quintin Hoare, editor. John Matthews, translator)

Selections from Political Writings: 1921–1926, 1978 (Quintin Hoare, editor and translator)

An Antonio Gramsci Reader. Selected Writings, 1916–1935, 1988 (David Forgacs, editor)

Prison Notebooks, 1992–1996 (5 volumes; Joseph A. Buttigieg, editor and translator)

Letters from Prison, 1994 (2 volumes; Frank Rosengarten, . editor. Raymond Rosenthal, translator)

Further reading

Bove, Paul. "Dante, Gramsci, and Cultural Criticism," in *Rethinking Marxism*. 4, no. 1 (Spring, 1991), pp. 74–86.

Buttigieg, Joseph A. "The Exemplary Worldliness of Antonio Gramsci's Literary Criticism," in *boundary* 2. XI (Winter, 1982–1983), pp. 21–39.

Davidson, Alastair. "The Literary Criticism of Antonio Gramsci," in *The Radical Reader*, 1977. Edited by S. Knight and M. Wilding.

——. Antonio Gramsci: *Towards an Intellectual Biography*, 1977.

Dombrowski, Robert. "On Gramsci's Theatre Criticism," in *boundary* 2. XIV (Spring, 1986), pp. 91–117.

——. *Antonio Gramsci*, 1989.

Holub, Renate. *Antonio Gramsci: Beyond Marxism and Postmodernism*, 1992.

Landy, Marcia. "Culture and Politics in the Work of Antonio Gramsci," in *boundary* 2. XIV (Spring, 1986), pp. 49–70.

——. *Film, Politics and Gramsci*, 1994.

Rosengarten, Frank. "Gramsci's 'Little Discovery': Gramsci's Interpretation of Canto X of Dante's *Inferno*," in *boundary* 2. XIV (Spring, 1986), pp. 71–90.

Watkins, Evan. "Conflict and Consensus in the History of Recent Criticism," in *New Literary History*. XII (1981), pp. 345–365.

——. "Gramsci's Anti-Croce," in *boundary* 2. XIV (Spring, 1986), pp. 121–135.

Williams, Raymond. *Marxism and Literature*, 1977.

JOSEPH A. BUTTIGIEG

See also Althusser; Benjamin; Eagleton; Frankfurt School; Lukács; Marxist Theory and Criticism

Robert Graves

English poet, writer, and critic

Born: Wimbledon, England; July 24, 1895
Died: Deya, Mallorca; December 7, 1985

Biography

Robert Graves came from a distinguished family on both sides of the cradle. He was the grandson of an Anglican Bishop of Limerick, whose passion for Irish folklore and especially the ancient Ogham alphabet was to find a distant, elaborate echo in Graves' pioneering (some would say cranky) mythological studies. His mother was of the von Rankes of Prussia, and one of Graves' direct antecedents was Leopold von Ranke, one of the most influential historians of the modern era. In his adolescence Graves was enrolled at the Charterhouse School, Surrey. It was during this time that he became enamored of poetry, determining to some day know more about poetry than any living person. He was helped on in his pursuits by a literary father, who assigned him poetic exercises in Latin.

The first important experience of Graves' mature life was service during World War I as an officer of the Royal Welsh Fusiliers. He was wounded twice – once severely at the Battle of the Somme – and the horrors of the bloody conflagration were to remain with him for many years. Upon returning to England, the twenty-two-year-old Graves married Nancy Nicholson, four years his junior, with whom he had four children, and finally took up residence at St. John's College, Oxford, from where he had been awarded a scholarship before the war. His matter-of-fact martial autobiography, *Goodbye to All That* (1929), had the cathartic effect on him of an exorcism. Finally, he was able to face the pain of the war to end all wars which he had seen at such close quarters and suffered, literally, on his own skin. Just as importantly, perhaps, the financial success of the book enabled Graves to settle in his beloved Mallorca, where he was to remain until the end of his life save for the nine years of the Spanish Civil War and World War II (1936–1945).

In 1929 the decade-long close collaboration with the American poet Laura Riding began. Riding became his mistress after the break-up of his first marriage. Always deferring to her as "the better poet," Graves credited to her influence a new sharpness and directness of style and ironic expression that were lacking from the first three volumes of his poetry, which were published during World War I and are markedly Georgian in feel. Riding left Graves in 1939. Soon thereafter he met Beryl Hodge, with whom he was to have a further four children. He lived with Beryl until his death in 1985.

Graves' romantic association with Riding is a concretization, of sorts, of the poet's obsession with womankind in general. More than just cavalier or sexual, Graves' interest in woman is of a spiritual, religious nature. During his years with Riding, he worked on his masterpiece of mythological scholarship, *The White Goddess: A Historical Grammar of Poetic Myth*, which was finally published in 1948. In this closely argued, labyrinthine text, Graves argues that the matriarchal religion of the Near East and Europe before the great migration of the peoples, which brought in its train the continuing dominance of patriarchal Indo-Aryan tribes with their male divinity, is still the true religion of all real poets. According to Graves, every poet worthy of the name is a devotee of the "white goddess" or muse, who is for Graves not an idea or a personified mental state (like inspiration), but very real indeed.

Together with Riding, Graves established the small but influential Seizin Press (1927–1938) and published a journal (*Epilogue*, 1935–1938) and the influential book *A Survey of Modernist Poetry* (1927). For many people, however, Graves is above all the author of immensely popular (and lucrative) historical novels, chief among which are *I, Claudius* and *Claudius the God* – serialized in a BBC dramatization in the 1970s. Except for a short stint as professor of poetry at the University of Oxford, from 1961 to 1966, it was the popularity of these novels that supplied the income to keep him and his large family in financial comfort, though Graves considered his novels less artistically significant than his poetry.

Graves was a hard-working writer. His prodigious output in prose and verse, and the meticulous care he took with his critical and mythological writings, may have exhausted him. It is said that the last ten years of his life or so were spent in a quiet senility.

Influence

Graves was a poet above all else; the historical novels he wrote were a lucrative, if diverting, job, and the criticism he wrote was composed solely out of a love for poetry, or, in his idiom, out of love for the "white goddess." As he was to say in the essay "These Be Your Gods, O Israel!" (1954–1955), "Waste no money on books *about* poetry; not even on mine." Although as a poet he was even more "out of step with his time" than Ezra Pound's Hugh Selwyn Mauberly (for he insisted on traditional poetic forms and despised the victorious trends of modernism), he was considered enough of a poetic heavyweight to enthrall the young Dylan Thomas, and imposing enough to garner accolades as "the greatest living English poet" from W. H. Auden, one of the "living idols" at whom Graves had wagged the finger in an earlier essay.

As a critic, the influence of Graves is more widespread than is generally realized. The techniques of textual analysis developed by Graves and Riding during their long sojourn together in Mallorca had a great impact upon the development of New Criticism. As the New Critics wished to focus on the literary work itself as an exclusive object of critical attention, paying no regard to historical or biographical material in the critical handling of a poem, it is instructive to consider this paragraph from the spirited denunciation of modernism "These Be Your Gods, O Israel!":

> The poet who pleads his case before Dame Ocupacyon is expected to present a plain, unannotated text of his own poems, with no supporting documents or testimonials whatsoever. I am here to remind you that poets are not idols, nor are idols poets; and that the Muse alone deserves your love.

This incisive approach to the text, aimed at cutting out pseudoscholarly mystification from the poetic text (and quite obviously directed at *The Waste Land*), is elaborated by Graves into something of an *apologia pro obscuritate* in the related article "Dame Ocupacyon" (1954–1955):

> About obscurity. Obscurity is often charged against a poem by readers for whom it was not intended, because they are outside the poet's natural circle of friends. They feel aggrieved at having wasted their money or time. This is foolish. Since I am neither scientist nor philosopher, I should not venture to call any scientific or philosophical treatise obscure. If for some reason or other I find myself bogged down in a technical passage which someone has pressed into my hands, I assume that the terms are beyond me, and make no complaints; unless the fault lies clearly in the careless or illogical use of English prose, which has certain agreed semantic principles.

Behind this can be seen the New Critics' insistence on the nature of poetry as a type of communication essentially different from the philosophical and scientific; one that must be approached on its own terms, without the crutches of extra-textual matter. If this results in one reader getting less out of a particular poem than another, the fault does not necessarily lie with the poet. Graves returns to this theme in Chapter XIII of *The White Goddess*, where he insists that the poet's "function is truth, whereas the scholar's is fact."

As well as his influence on the New Critics, Robert Graves made a mark on mythological studies with *The White Goddess*. While it might be argued that Graves should not be included in the company of the great names of mythology and anthropological criticism such as Joseph Campbell and Sir James Frazer, Graves' unwieldy, arcane masterpiece has at the very least established him as a commentator on myth who cannot be ignored. Campbell himself pays the poet the ultimate critical honor by quoting him in his own works.

Analysis

Graves did not consider himself a scholar. Despite his obvious erudition, talent for close and sustained critical argumentation, as well as his brushes with the academy, "I make no claim to be a scholar," he wrote in "The Two Births of Dionysus" (1973), an essay on the role of hallucinogens in ancient culture, "I get, record and pass on news and intuitions; but any mention of my work in academic books is so suspect as to detract from their sales value and general acceptance."

The composition of poetry is, for him, a quasi-mystical process. As he explains in "Speaking Freely," a 1970 radio interview with Edwin Newman, "If you're writing a poem and you want to have any effect on your readers . . . though you should not really be thinking of your readers, but only of yourself as your own reader – you've got to put them under the hypnotic trance in which you yourself write poems. And you impose this trance by certain hidden technical aids in the use of words and language; but to find this out takes years and years." Although this may sound reductionist, nothing could be further from the truth. Graves is here referring to the modern equivalent of the rigorous instruction that went into the creation of the ancient Irish *ollave*, or master poet, and which he describes in the opening chapters of *The White Goddess*. This training is much more than mastery of apparatus such as vowel length and syllabic versus quantitative meter – which would suffice for rhymers and "anti-poets," as he described Virgil. Graves is aiming for a more comprehensive knowledge of the poet's craft, which includes a thorough mastery of ancient symbols, of the roots of art in magic and ritual, and an unswerving, disinterested devotion to the muse, the "white goddess," who, as he expresses it in "The Crowning Privilege" (1954–1955), "has a real existence – as real, for her devotees, as Karl Marx's existence, or Freud's, or Aquinas's, to theirs."

Graves' poetics can be introduced by two basic statements. First, the poet is inspired when he or she creates. In a way that echoes Plato's electric ring allegory of the "possession" of the poet by the god, Graves makes a distinction "between Muse poetry, which is the real sort, and literary or academic poetry [and this is] whether the poet becomes truly entranced or whether he merely plays at being entranced. In my own view Homer is a true poet, whereas Virgil is a literary pretender to poetry" ("Address to the Poets of Hungary," 1970). Second, inspiration and devotion to the muse do not result in spontaneous poetic utterance; the poet is also a craftsman. One of the clearest and most finely elaborated examples of what Graves means may be found in "Harp, Anvil, Oar" (1954–1955):

> The religious connexion between poetry, smithcraft, and medicine is a close one. Medicine presupposes a knowledge of times, seasons, and the sovereign properties of plants, trees, beasts, birds, fish, earths, minerals. Poetry presupposes an inspired knowledge of man's sensuous and spiritual nature. Smithcraft – for the smith was also carpenter, mason, shipwright, and toolmaker – presupposes an inspired knowledge of how to transform lifeless material into active forms.

Thus Graves the poet approached his *métier*; thus Graves the critic expected other poets to approach it also. He was sharp in attacking those critics who lost track of the purpose and significance of the task before them. In "These Be Your Gods, O Israel!" he wrote:

> An anonymous leader-writer in *The Times Literary Supplement*, discussing the poetry of today, has described ours as an "Age of Consolidation." I find "Consolidation" too active a word, and should prefer "Age of Acquiescence" or "Age of Acceptance". . . . The education emphasis is now on appreciation of contemporary as well as ancient literature, and since to appreciate no longer means "to evaluate," as it did

> in earlier days, but has become a synonym for "to admire," there must be recognized objects of official appreciation – namely idols.

The "five living idols" that Graves goes on to discuss in the essay are William Butler Yeats, Ezra Pound, T. S. Eliot, W. H. Auden, and Dylan Thomas. Earlier, we mentioned his criterion that a poem should be able to stand on its own, without extra-poetic apparatus. In "Dame Ocupacyon" Graves applauds the primacy of directness to which Laura Riding had years earlier converted him:

> Some readers, with theatrical rather than poetic interests, are entranced by tricks of rhetoric, and expect from the poem a wide range of fantasies, irrelevant to its central statement. Personally, I expect poems to say what they mean in the simplest and most economical way; even if the thought they contain is complex. I do not mind exalted language in poetry any more than I mind low language, but rhetoric disgusts me. . . . I don't at all mind what are called dull books, so long as they are factual, accurate, and unpretentious: Brazilian politics, the digestive apparatus of sea-urchins, the art of wig-making – all is reading matter to me.

The significance of Graves' insistence on directness and disdain for "rhetoric" for textual criticism can be best exemplified by an entertaining excerpt from "Legitimate Criticism of Poetry" (1958), a talk he once gave to undergraduates at Mount Holyoke College. Returning to his familiar insistence upon the correct meaning of "appreciation" as "judicious examination" rather than "admiration," he turned his attention to William Wordsworth's "Solitary Reaper," a poem he found hopelessly overburdened with rhetoric and meaningless repetition:

> Have you ever seen a squirrel "appreciating" hickory nuts? It weighs them in its little paws and flings away the light ones. Well, a good habit which I recommend to all you young squirrels as a test of your own poems, is to weigh them. You can turn it into a game called "Cables." Imagine yourselves badly off for cash and having to cable the sense of this first verse [of the "Solitary Reaper"], at your own expense, to a friend in New Zealand. By the rules, you must use Wordsworth's own vocabulary, and leave out no word of importance. What about this? Solitary Highland Lass Reaping Binding Grain Stop Melancholy Song Overflows Profound Vale. Twelve words instead of forty-three!

Predictably, Graves has little patience with those "appreciators" of poetry who never "get beyond the jingle-loving, or, at best, the music-loving stage, of poetic appreciation." As he says in the same "Legitimate Criticism of Poetry," "Poetry (need I say?) is more than words musically arranged. It is sense, good sense; penetrating, often heart-rending sense . . . [Yet] how few give any thought to the sense of a poem, though it often has layer after layer of meaning concealed in it!" An exaggerated attention to "music" at the expense of meaning-communication is what Graves took Dylan Thomas to task for, despite the fact that Thomas is the one poet among the "living idols" for whom Graves expresses the most grudging approbation.

By the same token, this paragon of poetic common sense in an age of the neglecting of traditions retained the highest regard for meter. Seeing the cause of the abandonment of strict meter on the part of the modernists and their followers in the triumph of nonrepresentational painting and sculpture, he pointed out the faults of *vers libre*:

> Everyone can make what experiments he pleases, but poetry is necessarily linked with metrical forms designed to create in the listener, or reader, a hypersensitive awareness of the meaning. Personal rhythmic variations can be, and should be, made on the metrical norm . . . just as one expresses one's personality by an individual variation of copperplate handwriting. ("Legitimate Criticism of Poetry")

Metrical variations that do not derive their meaning from the metrical norm of the poem he described as being "like a jaunt in the family car after mixing a little water with the gasoline to make it go by fits and starts."

One of the most appealing characteristics of the textual criticism of Robert Graves is its humor. An excellent classicist, who precociously pointed out contradictions and lazinesses in Virgil's Latin at school, Graves gently irritated his master T. E. Page with his irreverence (see "The Anti-Poet," 1961); he also took exception to Ezra Pound's free adaptations of Sextus Propertius. What others were lauding as a "deliberate distortion of the strict sense in order to bring out vividly Propertius's latent irony" (*Times Literary Supplement*, September 18, 1953), Graves saw as inexcusable sloppiness or, what is worse, the poet's incompetence in Latin. His response to the overcommendatory article took the form of a grammar-school dialogue:

> DR SYNTAX: Talking of Dog-Latin, my boys, you all doubtless recall Virgil's immortal lines beginning *Vere novo gelidus canis sub montibus umor/ Liquitur* . . . ["When spring is young, cold mist runs to water below the hoary mountains."] Unlike good Citizen Pound, I claim no talent for free verse, but I think I can knock up a pretty fair Shakespearean line: *Vere novo*, Strange yet how true, *gelidus canis*, the dog with chills and fevers, *sub montibus liquitur*, Makes water at the lofty mountain's foot, *umor*. ("Dr. Syntax and Mr. Pound," 1953)

In *The White Goddess*, Graves makes his famous assertion that all "true" poets – that is "muse" and not "academic" poets – deal with one theme and one theme alone. Citing Alun Lewis, this "single poetic theme" is that of "Life and Death . . . the question of what survives of the beloved." Two pages later on, this poetic theme is broadened. The structure of *The White Goddess* itself is that theme's exemplification:

> The Theme, briefly, is the antique story . . . of the birth, life, death and resurrection of the God of the Waxing Year . . . the God's losing battle with the God of the Waning Year for love of the capricious and allpowerful Threefold Goddess, their mother, bride and layer out. The poet identifies himself with the God of the Waxing Year and his Muse with the Goddess; the rival is his blood-brother, his other self, his weird. All true poetry – true by Housman's practical test – celebrates some incident or scene in this very ancient story, and the three main characters are so much a part of our racial inheritance that they not only assert themselves in poetry but recur on occasions of emotional stress in the form of dreams, paranoic visions, and delusions.

This is very similar to Joseph Campbell's theory of the "monomyth" which he explained at length in his Jungian anthropological study of literature *The Hero with A Thousand Faces*, published in 1949, the year after *The White Goddess*. To give just one example of the type of argumentation to be found in *The White Goddess*, a short section dealing with what Graves terms "the masculinization of the Holy Spirit" is cited:

> It is possible that the Apostles' Creed, the earliest Latin version of which is quoted by the second-century Tertullian, was originally composed by some Gnostic Christian in Egypt and syncretically modelled on the Hercules formula. For "conceived by the Holy Ghost," when read in the Gnostic light, has a direct reference to the Flood . . . . The masculinization of the Holy Spirit was assisted by a remark in the First Epistle of St. John, that Jesus would act as a paraclete or advocate for man with God the Father; in the Gospel of St. John the same figure is put in Jesus's own mouth in a promise that God will send them a paraclete (usually translated "comforter") after he has gone; and this paraclete, a masculine noun, understood as a mystical emanation of Jesus, was wrongly identified with the archaic Spirit that moved on the face of the waters. The Gnostics, whose language was Greek, identified the Holy Spirit with Sophia, Wisdom; and Wisdom was female.

It is difficult for the reader not to feel like Graves here in the earlier quote from "Dame Ocupacyon" about obscurity, and assume that the obscurity of *The White Goddess* is due to the fact of the subject's being "beyond him." After all, it is hard going indeed for the noninitiate in the sacred trees of Europe, who neither has any knowledge of the secret hand-language of the Druids. The careful reader of the above-cited passage will wonder just how the Gnostics, "whose language was Greek," would suddenly associate the word spirit (*pneuma*), which is of neuter gender in Greek, with *sophia*, the eternal Feminine, and where Graves receives the authority to rededicate the ancient cathedral of Constantinople, the Hagia Sophia, to the Virgin Mary (a Christian localization of the White Goddess, as Graves would have it in the essay "Goddesses and Obosoms," 1973), when history tells us that the anti-Gnostic Orthodox Church named the cathedral the Church of the Divine Wisdom in honor of the indubitably male Christ – the Word, the Wisdom of the Father. Graves explains neither of these anomalies, and the ungenerous reader will wonder whether or not the mythologist/critic is twisting the data a bit so as to fit in with his preconceived thesis.

Earlier on in the text, Graves tells us that "the scholar is a quarryman, not a builder, and all that is required of him is that he should quarry cleanly. He is the poet's insurance against factual error." Thus, we are perhaps not out of line in questioning some of the more inexplicable statements found in *The White Goddess*, for we would be doing nothing but quarrying a little deeper, and wider, than Graves himself. It must be pointed out that in this towering monument of mythological criticism, Graves' perhaps most visible critical text, he never really ceases to be a poet – which fact should keep us on our guard.

Principal criticism

The White Goddess: A Historical Grammar of Poetic Myth, 1948
The Crowning Privilege: Collected Essays on Poetry, 1956
On Poetry: Collected Talks and Essays, 1969
Difficult Questions, Easy Answers, 1973

Other major works and literary forms

The poetry of Robert Graves can most easily be consulted in his *Collected Poems*, the last edition of which was published by Cassell in 1975 (reprinted by Oxford University Press, 1988). It is also instructive to ponder his earlier *Collected Poems* (1926, 1938, 1947, 1959, 1965) in order to trace the process by which he discarded poems from the new editions in his relentless, honest editing of his poetic corpus.

The historical novels are perennial favorites. Chief among them are *I, Claudius* (1934), *Claudius the God* (1935), *Count Belisarius* (1939), *Wife to Mr Milton* (1943), *Hercules, my Shipmate* (1945), and *King Jesus* (1946). The reader interested in autobiography will find *Goodbye to All That* (1929) one of the two greatest first-hand accounts of World War I, along with e. e. cummings' *The Enormous*

Room (1922). Graves also penned several translations, a grammar of English prose (*Occupation: Writer*, 1950), and studies in religious and mythological subjects, *The Greek Myths* (1955) and *The Nazarene Gospels Restored* (1945, with Joshua Podro).

Further reading

Canary, Robert H. *Robert Graves*, 1980.
Day, Douglas. *Swifter than Reason: The Poetry and Criticism of Robert Graves*, 1963.
Enright, D. J. *Robert Graves and the Decline of Modernism*, 1974.
Graves, Richard Perceval. *Robert Graves*, 1986.
——. *Robert Graves: The Years with Laura, 1926–1940*, 1990.
——. *Robert Graves and The White Goddess, 1940–85*, 1998.
Hoffman, Daniel G. *Barbarous Knowledge: Myth in the Poetry of Yeats, Graves, and Muir*, 1967.
Keane, Patrick J. *A Wild Civility: Interactions in the Poetry and Thought of Robert Graves*, 1980.
Sabater, Gaspar. *Robert Graves: de Wimbledon à Deya*, 1986.
Seymour-Smith, Martin. *Robert Graves, His Life and Work*, 1982.
Smeds, John. *Statement and Story: Robert Graves's Myth-making*, 1997.
Snipes, Katherine. *Robert Graves*, 1979.
Vickery, John B. *Robert Graves and the White Goddess*, 1972.
Weinzinger, Anita. *Graves as a Critic*, 1982.

CHARLES S. KRASZEWSKI

See also Archetypal Criticism; British Literary Theory: Twentieth Century

A. J. Greimas

Lithuanian-born French semiotician

Born: Tula, Lithuania; March 9, 1917
Died: Paris, France; February 27, 1992

Biography

Algirdas Julien Greimas was born in Tula in Lithuania in 1917. After commencing his law studies at Kaunas, he was awarded a grant in 1936 to study the French language at the University of Grenoble in France. The completion of his degree in 1939 led to further research in the franco-provençale dialect. In 1939 he returned to Lithuania to undertake his military service. He subsequently took up the post of geography teacher for four years. In 1944 Greimas' parents were deported to Siberia where his father died of hypothermia. This precipitated Greimas' own departure for France where he settled permanently. Pursuing his interest in lexicology, he immediately embarked on a thesis on vestimentary vocabulary in the fashion magazines of 1830 (*La Mode en 1830: Essai de description du vocabulaire vestimentaire d'après les journaux de mode de l'époque*) and was awarded a doctorate in 1948 by the University of Paris. It was during this period that Greimas met the celebrated linguists Georges Matoré and Bernard Quemada and, influenced by their reading of Ferdinand de Saussure, the three embarked on a radical reassessment of the basic principles of lexicology.

In 1949 Greimas was appointed lecturer (*maître de conférences*) at the University of Alexandria, Egypt, where he taught the history of the French language. A year later he was joined by Roland Barthes and Charles Singevin and the group collaborated in their research projects, coming under the influence of, amongst others, Roman Jacobson, Louis Hjelmslev, Claude Lévi-Strauss, Jacques Lacan, and Maurice Merleau-Ponty. In 1956 Greimas published an important article on Saussure in which he acknowledged the importance of a number of key theoretical concepts which were later to influence the development of semiotics. Amongst these were the couple *signifier/signified*. In this same article Greimas advocated the extension of the structuralist method to all branches of social activity whether it be the visual arts, architecture, politics, or music, and so on, thus anticipating a future program for semiotic activity.

In 1960 Greimas made the acquaintance at Besançon of the British linguist Michael Halliday. It was during this period that he also came under the influence of the works of the Russian folklorist Vladimir Propp which were to have such a powerful impact on his intellectual development. From 1962 to 1965 Greimas taught French linguistics at the University of Poitiers and from 1963 to 1964 he also gave lectures in structural semantics at the Institut Henri-Poincaré in Paris which were later to form the basis of his seminal work *Sémantique structurale* (*Structural Semantics*), published in 1966. In this book he outlined a narrative grammar which was later to become one of the basic working tools of French semiotic practice. In 1965 Greimas was appointed director of studies at the École Pratique des Hautes Études in Paris. In the following year and together with Barthes, Jacques Dubois, and Quemada, he founded the journal *Langages*. A research group was also formed under his leadership (*Groupe de recherches sémio-linguistiques*) which subsequently came to be known as the Paris School.

The 1970s saw a period of development and consolidation of Greimas' thought. He broadened the sphere of his preoccupations to include not only the literary text and myth but also the social sciences, producing, for example, studies of urban space and of legal discourse. In 1979 a first volume of a dictionary of semiotics (*Sémiotique, dictionnaire raisonné de la théorie du langage*) was published in collaboration with his colleague Joseph Courtés to be followed in 1986 by a second volume. Together with the journal *Actes sémiotiques* (begun in 1978), later to become the *Nouveaux Actes sémiotiques* (from 1989 onward), these dictionaries present the fundamental concepts or working tools of European semiotics. In the 1980s Greimas further widened the scope of his interests to develop a semiotics of passion. This included studies relating to the concept of the aesthetic, some of which appeared in his book *De L'Imperfection* (1987). Greimas died in Paris on February 27, 1992. His ashes are buried in Lithuania.

Influence

Greimas is now widely recognized as one of the greatest intellectuals and critics of the twentieth century. The author of numerous theoretical works, he is the founder of European semiotics and of the Paris School. His contribution to the development of literary theory has, therefore, been immense. His critical approach has two principal aims: (1) to elaborate theories and models describing how meaning is produced, and (2) to apply these theories to texts in an attempt to unravel the multiplicity of meanings that underlie the "surface" of a text. By text is meant any manifestation of meaning (signifying activity) – the line between text and context, literary and nonliterary is thus frequently blurred.

When Greimas' work first came to the attention of critics outside France, it was, generally speaking, unfavorably received. In the main, critics expressed a distrust of theory together with an aversion to a more scientific approach to literature. It was also argued by some – wrongly, as it turned out – that the application of models to a literary text must necessarily be reductionist. These views, however, were not universally held – either in England or elsewhere. Indeed, Greimassian semiotics is currently taught at a wide range of institutions and the value of semiotic analysis as a method for uncovering layers of textual meaning is widely appreciated. Moreover, semiotic research itself has progressed considerably since the formulation of its original models. Following the example of Greimas, semioticians are continually refining their concepts to produce ever more sophisticated and precise tools of analysis. At the same time, the whole field of semiotic research is constantly being broadened and new areas of investigation – such as, for example, a semiotics of the body – are being opened up.

Analysis

Greimas' fundamental concern is with the nature of meaning. What is meaning? How does it originate? In contrast to the American linguist Charles Sanders Peirce, Greimas does not see meaning as residing in individual phenomena but rather in a network of relationships or structures. These structures underpin all forms of communication – written, oral, gestural, and so on – and are susceptible to representation in the form of models.

The first of these models was presented in his 1966 book *Sémantique structurale* (*Structural Semantics*, 1976). In this work Greimas formulates a narrative grammar based on the theoretical principles elaborated by Vladimir Propp forty years previously. After studying a large quantity of folk tales, Propp concluded that there are thirty-one functions common to all these stories. These functions he distributed amongst seven *spheres of action*, which include those of villain, donor, helper, hero and false hero, dispatcher, a princess, and her father. Greimas reformulated and simplified these spheres of action to produce his own narrative model known as the *actantial narrative schema*. This schema presents six actantial or narrative roles arranged in three sets of binary oppositions: subject/object, sender/receiver, helper/opponent. Together the six actants (narrative roles) and their organization account for all possible relationships within a story and indeed within human action in general.

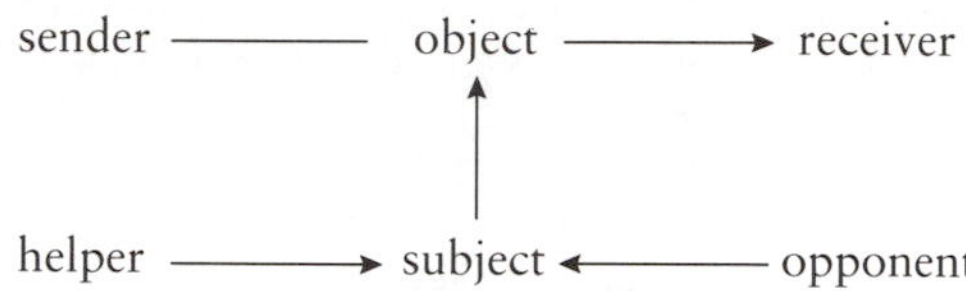

These narrative roles may be held by people, places, objects, emotions, or abstract ideas. Let us now briefly define our terms.

subject/object
The *subject* – usually the main character in a story – is an agent who performs an action and who is in pursuit of a goal or *object*. The positions *subject/object* are mutually interdependent. In semiotic terms we do not exist as subjects, as autonomous human beings, unless we possess a goal. The *object*, therefore, is the goal of the subject's quest. It could, of course, be concrete or abstract. In the story of *Treasure Island*, Jim Hawkins is the *subject* and his *object* or goal is the finding of the treasure.

sender/receiver
The *sender* is the motivating force behind an action. The *sender* communicates to a *receiver* the desire or need to do something. Once the *receiver* decides to act, it is transformed into a subject ready to embark upon a quest. The *sender* could naturally be internal, such as a sense of duty which might impel me to act.

helper/opponent
The subject could be helped or hindered in its quest. If my goal is to climb Mount Everest, then courage and good weather could be my *helpers*. My *opponents* could be the slippery rocks or bad weather. An opponent with a strong quest of its own that is in opposition to that of the subject is known as the *anti-subject*. If I am competing with someone else in climbing Mount Everest, then that other person is the *anti-subject*.

This actantial narrative schema has become a basic working tool of semiotic practice. It represents the starting point in any analysis of narrativity bringing to light the more general patterns underlying what could be a very complex textual surface. It has certainly proved itself an indispensable tool in the unraveling of "difficult" writers such as Italo Calvino or Samuel Beckett.

Propp's influence, however, does not stop here. In *Structural Semantics* Greimas also discusses a more comprehensive schema outlining the logical stages through which any action or quest must necessarily unfold. This schema, based on Propp's division into narrative sequences, takes the form of three types of event or *tests*:

a) The *qualifying test* where the subject/hero acquires the necessary means to carry out the principal action. In the story of *Aladdin*, acquiring the magic lamp makes it possible for Aladdin to succeed in the quest. The qualifying test will later be equated with the stage of competence (see presentation of the *canonical narrative schema*).
b) The *principal test*, also known as the *decisive test*, where the hero accomplishes the mission. In the story of *George and the Dragon*, the slaying of the dragon is the principal test. It can be equated with the stage of *performance*.
c) The *glorifying test* where the performance is evaluated and where the hero is frequently rewarded or punished. In the story of *The Luck Child*, the prince is rewarded for his actions when the father gives him his daughter's hand in marriage. The glorifying test is equivalent to the stage of *sanction*.

These three tests are preceded by the *contract*, the stage at which the subject accepts to embark on the mission.

The mid-1960s saw not only the development of a narrative grammar. In *Structural Semantics* Greimas also presents a fundamental model – perhaps the cornerstone of semiotic theory – known as the *elementary structure of meaning*. This model, mirroring the Saussurian conviction that there can be no meaning without difference, is essentially based on the structure of binary opposition. There can be no "up" without "down," no "hot" without "cold," no "good" without "evil." In other words, meaning is generated by the oppositions that we perceive between two semes (the smallest units of meaning). To constitute true oppositions or *contraries*, the contrasting semes must share a common element of meaning, a common denominator. For instance, the semes "up" and "down" have *verticality* in common, "hot" and "cold" have *temperature* in common. Greimas then develops this basic structure to include negating or *contradictory* terms. If "freedom" and "imprisonment" are *contrary* terms, then "non-freedom" and "non-imprisonment" are the *contradictory* or negating terms. In the late 1960s this elementary structure of meaning was further developed to produce a visual representation known as the *semiotic square*. This square presents three kinds of relationships:

- *contrariety* or opposition (the symbols S1 and S2 are frequently employed to illustrate this relationship);
- *contradiction* (-S1 is the contrary of S1, and -S2 the contrary of S2);
- *implication* or complementarity (-S1 implies S2 and -S2 implies S1). Good and evil, for example, can be analyzed as follows:

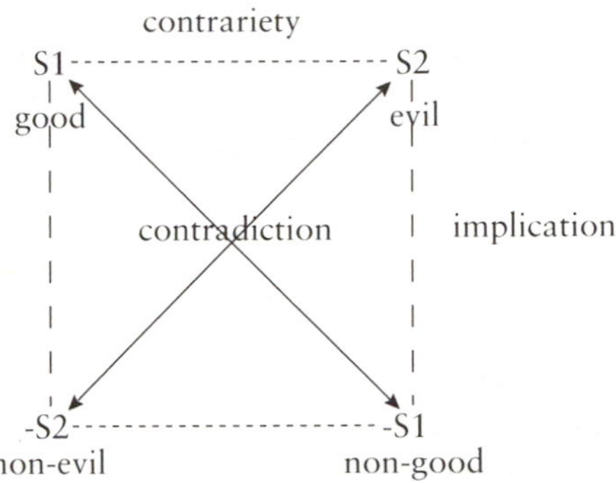

The elaboration of the elementary structure of meaning and of the semiotic square led Greimas to formulate what is known as the *generative trajectory* describing the overall process whereby meaning is produced, and bringing together in a cohesive whole hitherto seemingly disparate elements. The trajectory is based on the notion of a hierarchy of meaning reflecting the fundamental division between deep and surface structures and between concrete and abstract. The starting point of this generative trajectory is the *deep abstract level* associated with the semiotic square. This is the level at which the fundamental values of a text are articulated. It is from this abstract level that the *narrative level* (associated with the unfolding of the quest) is generated, which in turn gives rise to a surface level known as the *discursive level* (associated with the concrete evocation of time, place, and character).

In the 1970s Greimas' theories were further enriched through the introduction of the concept of *modalization* and of the *modalities*. Modalities are terms such as *wanting*, *having to*, *ought to*, *being able to*, which modify basic statements. A statement such as "Mary is rich" could, for example, be modified to "Mary wants to be rich." The application of modal theory to the unfolding of narrative sequences (the three tests) led to the production by Greimas of a *canonical narrative schema*, a more comprehensive and more precise description of plot structure. The qualifying test, for example, can now be divided into episodes where the subject acquires the values of *being-able-to-do* or *knowing-how-to-do*, necessary prerequisites to establish competence. The stage of contract or manipulation preceding the three tests marks the point at which the modalities of a *wanting-to-do* and/or of a *having-to-do* are communicated by the sender to a receiver who is thereby transformed into the subject of a quest. The canonical narrative schema can be presented thus:

contract	**competence** *qualifying test*	**performance** *decisive test*	**sanction** *glorifying test*
acquisition of a wanting-to-do and/or a having-to-do	acquisition of a being-able-to-do and/or a knowing-how-to-do	primary event where object of quest is at stake	action of subject is evaluated praise/ blame success/ failure

These modals, both narrative and deep-level (the semiotic square), were successfully applied by Greimas to an analysis of Guy de Maupassant's short story *Deux amis* (*Two Friends*). Indeed, they have subsequently proved extremely useful in eliciting the core values on which a particular text is based and in the construction of an overall semantic framework.

The greater sophistication of the semiotic models led to their wider application to all kinds of text whether it be verbal, visual, musical, or gestural. Greimas himself wrote extensively on the discourse of the social sciences, of law, and of urban space. Indeed, the canonical narrative schema was now felt to represent the prototype of all human action and thus to be responsible for our sense of a meaning in life.

After the publication of the semiotics dictionary in 1979, attention was focused on the surface or discursive level of meaning. Greimas' efforts were now directed toward the examination of enunciative strategies – the presence of the speaker in the text – with particular emphasis on spatial and temporal organization. Here the concept of *aspectualization* proved to be of particular significance. By aspectualization is meant the process whereby the implied presence of an observer is established in the discourse. In spatial terms, for example, reference to objects placed on the right or on the left is only meaningful in relation to an implied point of observation. Temporal aspectualization, on the other hand, makes itself felt in the stopping or starting of an event or in the duration of a process.

This focus on aspectualization led Greimas to undertake a semiotic study of the passions and to the development of the concept of an affective subject (*le sujet passionné*). In his study of Paul Éluard's poem *Capitale de la douleur*, for instance, the stress is on the subject's experience of inchoateness (that is, the beginning of love) rather than on love as a semantic value. In 1991 Greimas and his colleague Jacques Fontanille published the book *Sémiotique des passions* (*The Semiotics of Passion*, 1991) which includes studies of jealousy and avarice.

An interest in precognitive states also led Greimas to an exploration of the concept of beauty and of the aesthetic. In his book *De L'Imperfection* (1987) he links the experience of beauty with the aspectual moment of the finished or perfect: it is the moment at which subject and object of value fuse in a state of ecstatic indifferenciation. The experience is frequently marked by a process of synaesthesia. Greimas examines these privileged moments as they appear in passages from writers such as Italo Calvino, Rainer Maria Rilke, and Michel Tournier. He shows how they constitute a sudden rupture or break with the everyday and thus share much in common with the experience of the sacred.

A humanist at heart, Greimas always attached great importance to intellectual rigor in his lifelong pursuit of meaning. His work will undoubtedly remain a source of inspiration for generations to come.

Principal criticism

Sémantique structurale, 1966 (*Structural Semantics*, 1976)
Du Sens: Essais sémiotiques, 1970
Maupassant, la sémiotique du texte: exercices pratiques, 1976 (*Maupassant, The Semiotics of Texts*, 1988)
Sémiotique et sciences sociales, 1976 (*The Social Sciences: A Semiotic View*, 1990)
Sémiotique, dictionnaire raisonné de la théorie du langage, 1979, 1986 (2 volumes, with Joseph Courtés) (*Semiotics and Language. An Analytical Dictionary*, 1982, first volume)
Du Sens II: Essais sémiotiques, 1983 (*On Meaning: Selected Writings in Semiotic Theory*, 1987)
De L'Imperfection, 1987
Sémiotique des passions: des états de choses aux états d'âme, 1991 (*The Semiotics of Passion*, 1991)

Other major works and literary forms

A. J. Greimas was the author of numerous essays and contributed to a wide range of journals including *Langages* and *Langue française*. Many of his literary analyses appear in the series *Actes sémiotiques* (1978–1987) which later became *Nouveaux Actes sémiotiques* (1989 onward). He was always interested in myths, producing a study of Lithuanian mythology, *Des Dieux et des hommes. Études de mythologies lithuanienne* (*Of Gods and Men: Studies in Lithuanian Mythology*), in 1985. He also devoted considerable energy to an examination of biblical discourse, making an important contribution to two books, *Signes et paraboles* (1977) and *Parabole-Figure-Parabole* (1987), both edited by Jean Delorme. He collaborated with the Centre pour l'Analyse du Discours Religieux, which was particularly indebted to his more recent research on surface effects of meaning (relating to the construction of time, space, and characters).

Although Greimas is known principally as a semiotician, it must not be forgotten that he was also an outstanding lexicologist. In 1969 he published the *Dictionnaire de l'ancien français*, to be followed in 1992 by the *Dictionnaire du moyen français* (with Teresa Keane).

Further reading

Arrivé, Michel, and Jean-Claude Coquet. *Sémiotique en jeu: à partir et autour de l'œuvre de A. J. Greimas*, 1987.

Bertrand, Denis. *L'Espace et le sens.* Germinal *d'Émile Zola*, 1985.

Landowski, Eric, ed. *Lire Greimas*, 1997.

Martin, Bronwen. *Semiotics and Storytelling: An Introduction to Semiotic Analysis*, 1997.

——. *The Search for Gold: Space and Meaning in J. M. G. Le Clézio*, 1998.

——, and Felizitas Ringham. *Cassell Dictionary of Semiotics*, 1999.

Schleifer, Ronald. *A. J. Greimas and the Nature of Meaning: Linguistic Semiotics and Discourse Theory*, 1987.

BRONWEN MARTIN

See also French Literary Theory: Twentieth Century; Genette; Narratology; Propp

Franz Grillparzer

Austrian dramatist and critic

Born: Vienna, Austria; January 15, 1791
Died: Vienna, Austria; January 21, 1872

Biography

Franz Grillparzer was born in Vienna on January 15, 1791, to a middle-class family. His father was a lawyer, and his mother, a musician, fostered Grillparzer's artistic talent. He began law studies at the University of Vienna in 1807 and two years later wrote his first tragedy, *Blanca von Kastilien* (1912; Blanca of Castile), which was rejected by the Burgtheater. While continuing his literary studies and beginning his study of Spanish, Grillparzer began his career in the civil service in 1814. With the encouragement of Joseph Schreyvogel, artistic director of the Burgtheater, he eventually wrote *Die Ahnfrau* (1817; *The Ancestress*, 1938), which was well received at first but later heavily criticized as a *Schiksalstragödie*, or "fate-tragedy." His next play, *Sappho* (1818; English translation, 1928), was well received.

In 1819, while in Italy, Grillparzer wrote a poem, "Campo Vaccino," which the Pope considered an attack on the Church and which resulted in a reprimand by the authorities. During the 1820s he had an extraordinarily creative period when he wrote or planned many of his dramas. Still, he continued to be plagued by a lack of confidence in himself and difficulties with censorship.

In the early 1830s he was promoted to Archivdirektor (director of the archives) of the Burgtheater and had a successful play in *Der Traum ein Leben* (1834; *A Dream Is Life*, 1946) and a failure in *Des Meeres und der Liebe Wellen* (1831; *Hero and Leander*, 1938). With the death of Schreyvogel, Grillparzer felt isolated from theater circles and decided to travel abroad, including a journey to Paris and London. His new play, *Weh' dem, der lügt* (1838; *Thou Shalt Not Lie!*, 1939) was jeered by the audience when it opened in 1838. This experience caused Grillparzer to withhold publication of his subsequent works.

During the 1840s Grillparzer withdrew from social life more and more but still maintained some contact with other artists, and in 1847 he became a founding member of the Academy of Sciences. When the revolution of 1848 started, Grillparzer welcomed it, but as more radical elements took control, he opposed their actions. In 1861 he became a member of the upper house of the Austrian parliament and received recognition as some of his plays were revived at the Burgtheater. His last play, *Die Jüdin von Toledo* (1872; *The Jewess of Toledo*, 1913–1914), was completed in 1851 and marked the end of his writing career. He died in Vienna in January, 1872.

Influence

Grillparzer was concerned with ideas of art and the process by which a work of art comes into being. He distrusted, however, aesthetic theories which propose to explain the process comprehensively. In the last analysis, Grillparzer believed that it is the dramatist's natural talent which produces a successful play, and it was his own talent as a dramatist, not as a literary theorist, which established his literary reputation. Nevertheless, as nineteenth-century German writers became interested in Golden Age Spanish dramatists such as Pedro Calderón de la Barca, they discovered the merits of Lope de Vega Carpio's work as well through Grillparzer's studies of Spanish drama and his descriptions of Lope de Vega's individual works.

As a literary critic, Grillparzer has not received much recognition. Yet his background as a cultured citizen of nineteenth-century Austria made him as keen an observer of his literary times as Johann Wolfgang von Goethe was of his. As an admirer of ancient literature, of Spanish drama, and of William Shakespeare, Grillparzer's observations transcend the boundaries of German-speaking countries. In fact, his ideas and commentaries on literature and aesthetics have been compared to Goethe's, even though he has not been as readily recognized for his contributions, probably because of the fragmented form in which they appear.

Analysis

Although Grillparzer was preoccupied throughout his life with ideas and reflections on aesthetic problems and literary criticism, he never organized this material into a systematic account. His ideas appear as entries in his journals, essays, and critical commentary – as well as in letters, autobiographical writing, and conversations with contemporaries which have been reconstructed. He apparently used his journal in particular to record and work out his thoughts, freed from the pressure of publication. Topics range from the nature of writing and its forms (for example, parody, poetry, and drama) to consideration of other literatures, including Greek, Roman, Italian, French, English, and Spanish. Most important are his reflections on drama, including a series of studies on Lope de Vega with summaries of many of his individual plays. He also specifically comments on the plays of Shakespeare and on the work of Goethe and Friedrich Schiller. His wide range of literary interests seems geared to a critical view of the German and Austrian literature of his time, which was the focus of his essay "Über den gegenwärtigen Zustand der dramatischen Kunst in Deutschland" (on the present state of drama in Germany).

Grillparzer was, on principle, opposed to placing art forms into a system. He made his observations as they occurred to him and was not concerned about possible contradictions, since these would resolve themselves or, if this were impossible, would prove the "impossibility of a system." In spite of the lack of a system in his observations, Grillparzer's aesthetic writings do have a broad unity and an affinity with the classical ideals of Goethe and Schiller.

According to Grillparzer's aesthetic principles, a work of art is essentially an object of beauty: the ultimate aim of any work of art is to allow the spectator to experience this beauty in such a way that both the sensual and spiritual sides of human nature are satisfied. He defines beauty as "the complete harmony of the sensual and the spiritual." The pleasure that is experienced allows a feeling of wholeness or unity within the person and is not to be understood as a pleasure of the senses only. How this occurs is not clearly analyzed, but certainly the form must contribute to this effect. A drama, for example, combines the spoken language and the visual component of the stage action and the props to produce a totality. The ability to do this corresponds to the talent of the individual dramatist.

Grillparzer's view of genius and talent clarifies an important difference for him; genius is originality in thought or interpretation, whereas talent is the ability to express it. Talent can put an event into artistic form so that an audience can share the experience. Genius is a personal gift with no particular worth to others. Grillparzer's major criticism of his contemporaries was that there was genius but no talent.

In his fiction as well as in his theatrical work Grillparzer considered the problem of the writer in society, a popular classical theme. In his poetry, he wrote of the elusiveness of artistic inspiration, which often troubled him during his artistic career. The isolation of the poet torn between the claims of life and art is the theme of his drama *Sappho*. The theme of art and life is treated with irony in the case of Jacob the fiddler, the main character of *Der arme Spielmann* (1847; *The Poor Fiddler*, 1946), who is inept at solving the problems of life and, at the same time, horrifies his listeners with his music. With his intense interest in human beings and their motivating passions, Grillparzer often used the central concern of his own life as a writer for his dramas, and his theoretical writings can be seen as his attempt to understand the process of artistic creation, which he so greatly valued.

In line with classical ideals, Grillparzer believed that beauty is important for its own sake, and he also followed classical dramatic form and many of the classical themes, such as the fate of the artist in society, mentioned above. He admired Goethe's and Schiller's work, particularly their formal qualities, but found them lacking in naturalness of expression. Here Lope de Vega was his ideal.

The second guiding principle of Grillparzer's theories concerns theatrical presentation. Grillparzer insisted on the relationship between art and reality in the sense that drama represents a subjective version of the truth. A work of art must create an illusion of the truth or the real word, producing its effect on the audience as an "aesthetic or artistic truth." Works of art must not be untrue, but at the same time they are not a simple reproduction of nature. They have their own subjective truth, true on its own terms, even though it is not objective reality. This essential element is referred to as the *Täuschung der Kunst*, art's deception or illusion. Because the drama must represent truth, Grillparzer demanded the internal logic of causality or a convincing motivation based on cause and effect, which he called *strenge Kausalität*, strict causality, in his essay "Über das Wesen des Dramas" (on the essence of drama).

Within the illusion of a drama, each element of human nature must be addressed: intellect, imagination, feelings, and senses. Grillparzer's theories oppose a strictly intellectual appeal within a work of art. In fact, he very strongly opposes any kind of a didactic aim as hostile to dramatic or artistic effect. A drama should, in his view, never be a medium for expressing philosophical ideas, and he refers to "the so-called moral purpose" as the greatest enemy of true art. He separates two ways of viewing the world into scientific (*wissenschaftliche*) and contemplative (*beschauliche* or *kontemplative*), a distinction which may have been the result of Arthur Schopenhauer's influence on his thinking. Philosophy is inimical to art because it analyzes or divides a thing into parts in a scientific way to find understanding, while art is of its nature contemplative and depends on its wholeness for effect.

Grillparzer's demand that the action on the stage carry the force of something actually occurring in real life is the key to his admiration of Shakespeare and Lope de Vega, as well as to his criticism of many of his German contemporaries. The immediacy and strong visual quality in both dramatists' work drew Grillparzer's attention. Shakespeare's work puts as much action as possible on the stage, and Lope de Vega's drama reveals an emphasis on the playlike aspect of theater rather than on reflection. In its spontaneity and visual elements, Grillparzer finds the strength of Spanish Golden Age drama. It is for this reason that he champions Lope de Vega over Calderón de la Barca, who was so admired by the Romantics during the first part of the nineteenth century. The naive (as opposed to the "sentimental" in Schiller's theory), or natural, quality of these two dramatists provided the theatricality Grillparzer so desired and missed in much of German drama.

Grillparzer viewed drama as an art to be performed, not read, which puts him very much in the tradition of the popular Viennese stage. The reaction of the public is the only judgment that matters – thus Grillparzer's own depression when his work was rejected. His view of the critics of his day was notably hostile. In *The Poor Fiddler* he has his dramatist-narrator say that audience response is the measure of his work rather than the flawed judgment of "some literary matador, crippled in body and soul and bloated like a spider with the blood sucked from authors."

Grillparzer's theoretical writings contain ideas and influences which appear in his own drama: for example, he draws on Shakespearean tragedy, German classicism, the comedy of popular Viennese theater, and Spanish Golden Age drama. In the history of German literature, Grillparzer is a transitional figure, showing aspects of the German classical period in the framework of his dramas and a tendency toward the German realism of the second half of the nineteenth century in his treatment of unconscious motivation in his characters. In his critical work, his emphasis on creating the illusion of reality unfolding on the stage is probably his greatest contribution. In his essays and comments, he was harshly critical of German dramatists in particular for degenerating into philosophical speculation and failing to develop the necessary theatrical component in their work. In turn, he praised some Austrian writers for following in the popular tradition of Viennese theater. In the aftermath of Goethe's overwhelming presence, Grillparzer criticized a decline in the quality of German literature. His attempt, as both a dramatist and a theorist, was to maintain the positive aspects of classical form and ideals while adding a naturalness and vitality to the theater.

Principal criticism

Articles in *Tagebücher und literarische Skizzenhefte* (written 1804–1871), collected in volumes 7 through 10 (1914–1916) of *Sämtliche Werke: Historischkritische Gesamtausgabe*, 1909–1948 (42 volumes), and in *Sämtliche Werke, Ausgewählte Briefe, Gespräche, und Berichte*, 1960–1964 (4 volumes)

Other major works and literary forms

Franz Grillparzer is best known as a major Austrian dramatist. His plays include twelve completed tragedies, one comedy, and several fragmentary works. He also wrote a considerable amount of poetry, epigrams, and the prose work *Der arme Spielmann* (1847; *The Poor Fiddler*, 1946). Grillparzer's drama is noted for its successful use of the visual possibilities of the stage and for its portrayal of the psychology of his protagonists. The conflict between the demands of art and life (the contemplative life versus the active life) is a recurring theme in his work. Among his collected works are also autobiographical writings, letters, observations about other languages, and fragments of translations.

LONG FICTION
Das Kloster bei Sendomir, 1827
Der arme Spielmann, 1847 (*The Poor Fiddler*, 1946)

PLAYS
Blanca von Kastilien, written 1809, published 1912
Die Ahnfrau, 1817 (*The Ancestress*, 1938)
Sappho, 1818 (English translation, 1928)
Das goldene Vliessa, 1821 (*The Golden Fleece*, 1942), includes *Das Gastfreund (The Guest)*, *Die Argonauten (The Argonauts)*, and *Medea* (English translation)
König Ottokars Glück und Ende, 1824 (*King Otokar's Rise and Fall*, 1930)
Ein treuer Diener seines Herrn, 1828 (*A Faithful Servant of His Master*, 1941)
Des Meeres und der Liebe Wellen, 1831 (*Hero and Leander*, 1938)
Der Traum ein Leben, 1834 (*A Dream Is Life*, 1946)
Weh dem, der lügt, 1838 (*Thou Shalt Not Lie!*, 1939)
Ein Bruderzwist in Habsburg, 1872 (*Family Strife in Habsburg*, 1949)
Libussa, 1872 (English translation, 1941)
Die Jüdin von Toledo, 1872 (*The Jewess of Toledo*, 1913–1914)
Sämtliche Werke, 1892–1894

POETRY
Tristia ex Ponto, 1835
Gedichte, 1872

Further reading

Field, George Wallis. "Drama in the Nineteenth Century," in *A Literary History of Germany: The Nineteenth Century 1830–1890*, 1975.
Horvay, Frank D. "Grillparzer as a Critic of European Literature," in *Studies in Germanic Languages and Literatures*, 1963.
Mullan, W. N. B. *Grillparzer's Aesthetic Theory: A Study with Special Reference to His Conception of the Drama as "Eine Gegenwart,"* 1979.
Papst, E. E. "Franz Grillparzer," in *German Men of Letters: Twelve Literary Essays*, 1961. Edited by Alex Natan.
Roe, Ian F. *An Introduction to the Major Works of Franz Grillparzer, 1791–1872, Austrian Dramatist*, 1991.
——. *Franz Grillparzer: A Century of Criticism*, 1995.
Thompson, Bruce. *Franz Grillparzer*, 1981.
Wagner, Eva. *An Analysis of Franz Grillparzer's Dramas: Fate, Guilt, and Tragedy*, 1992.
Ward, Mark G. "The Structure of Grillparzer's Thought," in *German Life and Letters*. 44, no. 3 (April, 1991), pp. 236–252.
Yates, W. E. *Grillparzer: A Critical Introduction*, 1972.

SUSAN L. PIEPKE

See also Goethe; Kleist; Schiller

Grotesque

The term "grotesque" was first used in the sixteenth century to describe paintings found in Roman ruins from the time of the emperor Nero. Excavations revealed rooms – *grotte* – decorated with bizarre depictions of humans becoming animals or transforming into inanimate objects. The term for the room came to stand for the art found within. The term seems to have first been used to describe a style of verbal art by the sixteenth-century French essayist Michel Eyquem de Montaigne when, in his essay "On Friendship," he describes his essays as "monstrous bodies, patched and hudled up together of divers members, without any certaine or well ordered figure, having neither order, dependence, or proportion. But causall and framed by chance" (John Florio's translation of 1603).

Texts can then be considered grotesque in two key ways. They may deal with grotesque subject matter, bizarre, macabre, extravagant, and animalistic. Or they may assume a grotesque form, deliberately avoiding a classical form or shape, breaking boundaries of genre and rhetoric. Frequently, of course, works will seek to do both: grotesque characters and incidents may be found within grotesque forms. One of the most celebrated examples of grotesque in modern literature is James Joyce's novel *Ulysses* (1922), which in this light can be seen as the depiction of "the bodies" of several Dubliners, and the immersion of those bodies in birth, death, sex, and food. Joyce grotesquely manipulates also the forms of realist fiction: each chapter invents a new style and form, climaxing with the apparently formless embodiment of Molly Bloom's final monologue.

Joyce's grotesque is celebratory, a modern descendant of the triumphant grotesque of Renaissance carnival as depicted by the Russian theorist Mikhail Bakhtin in his seminal work *Rabelais and His World* (1968). The carnivals celebrated what Bakhtin calls the "material lower bodily stratum," immersing human beings in the communal and earthly processes of eating and defecating, birth and death, connecting humans with the rest of creation. Humans become matter. This intersection between humans and matter is the natural home of the grotesque, and was the frequent subject of Renaissance painters, most notably Giuseppe Arcimboldo, Hieronymus Bosch, and Pieter Brueghel the Elder, and many Renaissance authors – it can be seen for example, in William Shakespeare's depiction of the gravediggers in *Hamlet*, or Ben Jonson's vision of the lower orders of London in his comedy *Bartholomew Fair* (1614).

Bakhtin anticipates also a darker age of grotesque, where imagery of animality and matter has become internalized and psychological. He calls these "chamber grotesques," which register not the joyousness of matter, but rather the painful physical reality of being human: the body as a trap and a tomb. These modern grotesques are still comic, but they have an uneasy, painful edge to them, registering the ambivalence of humans in a world comprised largely of inanimate and uncaring matter. This is the world of Samuel Beckett's tragic clowns, imprisoned on stages and country roads, in funeral urns and mounds of dirt. Their grotesque lot is to suffer, as gaily as they can.

The jubilant grotesque has become a fixation in much postmodern fiction. Women writers, postcolonialists, and magic realists have all taken up Montaigne's invitation, embedding "monstrous" (grotesque) characters in monstrous texts "patched and hudled up together of divers members." The bird woman Fevvers in Angela Carter's *Nights at the Circus* (1984) is a classic instance, as is the rapidly aging Moraes Zogoiby in Salman Rushdie's *The Moor's Last Sigh* (1995). As they break from patriarchal and metropolitan norms, such writers find the grotesque distorting of form as well as figure a site of ecstatic release. Where earlier writers such as Beckett found the grotesque to resonate with pain and unease, these later writers reject such anguish, returning instead to the liberation of the "carnival grotesque" described by Bakhtin. In a world growing increasingly random and distorted, writers find the grotesque a useful ally, whether they wish to weep like Beckett or chortle like Rushdie. The ambivalence of the grotesque makes it possible for grotesque writers to do both, as they have always done.

Further reading

Bakhtin, Mikhail. *Rabelais and His World*, 1968. Translated by Helene Iswolsky.
Clayborough, Arthur. *The Grotesque in English Literature*, 1965.
Kayser, Wolfgang. *The Grotesque in Art and Literature*, 1963. Translated by Ulrich Weisstein.
Rhodes, Neil. *Elizabethan Grotesque*, 1980.
Russo, Mary. *Female Grotesques: Risk, Excess and Modernity*, 1994.
Stallybrass, Peter, and Allon White. *The Politics and Poetics of Transgression*, 1986.
Thomson, Phillip J. *The Grotesque*, 1972.

MARK HOULAHAN

See also Bakhtin; Bataille; Gothic

Friedrich Gundolf

(Friedrich Gundelfinger)

German writer and critic

Born: Darmstadt, Germany; June 6, 1880
Died: Heidelberg, Germany; July 12, 1931

Biography

Friedrich Gundolf was born Friedrich Gundelfinger on June 6, 1880, in Darmstadt, Germany. Rejecting his father's name as well as his profession (professor of mathematics at the University of Darmstadt), he changed his name to

Gundolf at the age of eighteen when he was admitted into Stefan George's circle of poets and artists. Gundolf was among the first young men to declare George to be his "master" and himself to be his "disciple" in the sense that Jesus and Meister Eckehart in the Christian tradition and Buddha and Confucius in the non-Christian traditions were spiritual masters. This spiritually torrid relationship lasted well into the 1920s. As George grew older, however, he became more tyrannical. The inevitable separation of disciple and master was as agonizingly emotional as the marriage had been exhilaratingly spiritual.

Gundolf spent his entire professional life at the University of Heidelberg, first as docent in 1911 and then as professor of the history of literature from 1920 to his unexpected death in 1931. He was a typical German university professor of his era, which meant that he was not an inspiring teacher in the classroom but was respected by his colleagues. He was elected to the Heidelberg Academy of Sciences in 1929, and he received the city of Hamburg's first Lessing Prize in 1930. Yet academe never replaced allegiance to Stefan George.

The break between master and disciple came in 1927. Gundolf's literary ideals were not heretical, but his affections strayed. There was first a Swedish woman whom George would not permit him to marry, and then, decisively, there was Elisabeth Salomon, whom he did marry in 1926. George never really recovered, dying in 1933, but he was preceded in death by his younger disciple, who died on the master's sixty-third birthday, July 12, 1931.

Elisabeth, known as "Elli," would spend her long widowhood defending her husband's legacy. Directly after his death, she struggled in vain against the Nazi charges that Gundolf's Jewishness contaminated his writings. At the same time she began her longer war to fight the anti-Nazi accusations that the George circle and Gundolf in particular paved the way for the rise of Nazi culture. After the fall of the Third Reich, she fought these accusations throughout Europe and the United States until her death in 1958.

Influence

Gundolf's reputation as a critic and man of letters will live and die with Stefan George and his circle (known as *Der Kreis*, literally "the circle"), which set an indelible mark on the German literary scene in the fifteen years before World War I. Under George's authoritarian, charismatic leadership, dozens of German novelists and poets formed a self-dramatizing, public cult to celebrate the artist as genius. Disdaining ordinary human experience as dross, despising economic activity and political aspiration as materialistic, scorning academic research and teaching as pedantic, and abhorring science as enslaving the spirit, George's circle believed in pursuing art for art's sake. The ideals of nineteenth-century Romanticism in literature and art were pushed to their egoistic, spiritualized extreme.

Gundolf's particular contribution lay in his literary biographies of those figures who were considered to be the greatest geniuses of all time: Johann Wolfgang von Goethe, Heinrich von Kleist – the purest, most spiritual of the geniuses who wrote poetry in German – and William Shakespeare and Julius Caesar, the supreme non-German geniuses of thought and action, respectively.

Analysis

Gundolf approached literature as an experience rather than a task. Drawing on the principles of Goethe and the subsequent Romantic movement, he argued that the reader must immerse him- or herself in the written word in order to experience it fully. Drawing from the German Idealist historical tradition as propounded by Leopold von Ranke, who demanded immersion in the archives to study the raw documents, and Wilhelm Dilthey, who articulated a method of empathizing with historical characters and reliving events, Gundolf turned to the writings of great poets and writers to experience them. Before the terms "existentialist" and "engaged" (*engagé*, in French) were invented by Jean-Paul Sartre, Gundolf coined the words *Urerlebnis* (experience from the origin of things) and *Bildungserlebnis* (conceptually elaborated experience) to describe his encounters with the geniuses of the past.

This approach merged the great work and the author. While one must surrender oneself completely to the original work of the great human being (*Gesamtmensch*, literally "the whole human being"), one must nevertheless remember that the work is greater than the person. In fact, the work defines the artist. As Gundolf put it many times, the two-part *Faust: Eine Tragödie* (1808, 1833; *The Tragedy of Faust*, 1923, 1938) told the authentic story of Goethe's life much better than Goethe's own letters and anecdotes. Therefore, the critic makes contact with the greatest geniuses of history when he or she immerses him- or herself in their greatest works of art.

The shadow of Goethe loomed large over the George circle, and the shadow of Stefan George loomed large over Gundolf. In the German sphere, where young artists had been pursuing beauty and practicing art for art's sake for almost a century, Goethe was the master of them all. George had become the master in person for many disciples. It was in this context that Gundolf developed the theme of "master-disciple" in an early essay entitled "Gefolgschaft und Jüngertum" (in issue 7 of *Blätter für die Kunst*, 1908–1909; discipleship and youth). In this essay Gundolf defines discipleship as an archetypal mode of existence, exemplified in the Western world by Pythagoras, Socrates, Jesus, and Eckehart, among others, and in the non-Western world by Confucius, Buddha, Zen Buddhist masters, and others. He insists, however, that disciples need not be slavish or fanatical advocates of their master; in fact, they serve their masters more truly by becoming independent and indeed masters themselves. Yet discipleship is essential to being a literary critic, for only through this kind of diciplined and obedient study of the master's works of art can the critic truly engage and experience the genius him- or herself.

Gundolf expressed himself in poetry and in literary biography. Most of his poems have not survived, and there is reason to believe that he came to see them as unworthy. He chose, instead, to engage other geniuses by immersing himself in their works. In doing this, and in settling for a secure academic appointment at Heidelberg, he gave up his youthful dream of becoming another Goethe or George. Thus, it was in transmitting the heritage of his beloved geniuses of language, rather than in becoming one himself, that Gundolf staked his own hopes for immortality. Besides, according to the George circle, which echoed Goethe's apodictic pronouncement on the subject, genius was natural (inborn) not acquired (achieved).

Gundolf was most attracted to Shakespeare and Goethe. His study of the latter yielded the most academically respectable of all the popular biographies of Goethe. Furthermore, Goethe's greatest work, *Faust*, provoked and inspired Gundolf to study the writings and life of Paracelsus, the Swiss alchemist whose original name was Theophrastus Bombastus von Hohenheim and who was considered by many to be the prototype for Faust.

Shakespeare, however, was Gundolf's greatest love. As he often stated it, while he was touched by Goethe, he was embraced by Shakespeare. Perhaps Gundolf was drawn to Shakespeare because Shakespeare set greater prize on poems but was remembered primarily for his plays; more likely it was Shakespeare's gritty, common quality that attracted Gundolf, in contrast to Goethe's unrelenting intellectual arrogance. Although Gundolf himself was considered to be an idealistic pursuer of beauty who never hardened into a mature, practical adult when compared to the power-wielding George, who manipulated his followers, Gundolf ventured to follow his book on Kleist, who was unworldly, with one on Julius Caesar. Gundolf's treatment of Caesar focused on his writings and resembled his analyses of Goethe, George, and the others.

Shakespeare had already been admitted to the pantheon of German genius by the early-nineteenth-century translation and criticism of August Wilhelm Schlegel. Assisted by his brother Friedrich, who was a philosopher and more interested in French culture, August Wilhelm Schlegel performed one of Western Europe's major transcultural feats as he elevated Shakespeare in German translation to the same level of reverence that the Bard enjoyed in his native land. Building on this foundation, Gundolf began his literary career by connecting Shakespeare's "genius" with the Goethe "spirit" (*Geist*), and he closed his academic life with a two-volume edition of and commentary on Shakespeare's works. Gundolf believed that as he interpreted Shakespeare he turned himself into a better and wiser man.

Canons of criticism have changed. In fact, they are almost entirely opposite. Where Gundolf sought intimacy and even identification with the object of his study, the modern critic seeks distance. Where Gundolf sought to isolate the particular genius of the author, the modern critic seeks to recover the context of nonartistic aspects of the author's life. Gundolf ignored the political and social setting: he despised the psychological orientation composed of internal drives and external pressures. Gundolf considered the economic circumstances to be irrelevant. Even in the area of literary components, Gundolf preferred to examine the finished product instead of the components, for he insisted that the sum was greater than the parts.

About the literary components, however, Gundolf's position was not simple. On the one hand, Gundolf did subscribe to the Romantic view that genius existed. Genius was the element which made the sum greater than the parts. Genius made the whole poem, story, critique, or any artistic creation worthy of study. Genius was reached when the critic could overcome the distance between him- or herself and the work of art. In fact, genius was reached when the critic identified with the author of the work through examination of and immersion in the work itself.

Still, Gundolf the scholar needed to know about the ingredients which constituted the whole. He wanted to understand the historical setting, using the Diltheyian method of empathizing with and getting into the subjects who acted in the past. He demanded to know the intellectual customs and conventions, the words in their contexts of denotation and connotation, the personalities of the people surrounding the creator, and so on. In sum, Gundolf ignored the nonliterary aspects of the creator's life and the nonliterary circumstances surrounding the creation, but he tried to know and describe all the intellectual and spiritual factors and facets of both creation and creator, which in essence were one and the same.

Principal criticism

Shakespeare und der deutsche Geist, 1911
Goethe, 1916
George, 1920
Heinrich von Kleist, 1922
Cäsar: Geschichte seines Ruhms, 1924 (*The Mantle of Caesar*, 1928)
Paracelsus, 1927
Shakespeare: Sein Wesen und Werke, 1928 (2 volumes)
Romantiker, 1930–1931 (2 volumes)

Other major works and literary forms

In addition to the books listed above, Friedrich Gundolf wrote many essays, articles, book reviews, poems, and private letters which have been published. Many of his shorter prose pieces first appeared in Stefan George's journal *Blätter für die Kunst* (leaves for art), which flourished from 1892 to 1919 and was published as a book in 1968.

POETRY
Gedichte, 1930

NONFICTION
Caesar in der deutschen Literatur, 1904
Dichter und Helden, 1921
Martin Opitz, 1923
Hutten, Klopstock, Arndt, 1924
Cäsar im Neunzehnten Jahrhundert, 1926
Andreas Gryphius, 1927
Adalbert Stifter, 1931
Rainer Maria Rilke, 1937
Anfänge deutscher Geschichtschreibung, 1938
Frank Wedekind, 1954
Stefan George–Friedrich Gundolf: Briefwechsel, 1962
Friedrich Gundolf: Briefwechsel mit Herbert Steiner und Ernst Robert Curtius, 1962–1963
Blätter für die Kunst, 1968 (written 1892–1919; 6 volumes)

Further reading

Bock, C. V. "First Report on The Gundolf Papers," in *German Life and Letters*. XV (October, 1961), pp. 16–20.
Helbing, Lothar, and C. V. Bock. "Friedrich Gundolf," in *On Four Modern Humanists*, 1970. Edited by Arthur R. Evans, Jr.
Hohendahl, Peter Uwe, ed. *A History of German Literary Criticism, 1730–1980*, 1988.
Urban, G. R. "The Idea of the Significant Form in the Work of Friedrich Gundolf," in *Anglica Germanica*. II, 1962.

DAVID R. STEVENSON

See also George

H

Geoffrey H. Hartman

German-born American critic and editor

Born: Frankfurt, Germany; August 11, 1929

Biography

Geoffrey H. Hartman was born on August 11, 1929, in Frankfurt, Germany. After living for a time in England, he emigrated to the United States in 1946. He received his B.A. in 1949 from Queens College in New York and his Ph.D. in 1953 from Yale University, where his dissertation, *The Unmeditated Vision*, was directed by René Wellek. After serving in the United States Army from 1953 to 1955, Hartman taught at Yale until 1962. He taught at the University of Chicago, the University of Iowa, and Cornell University before returning, in 1967, to Yale, where he is Karl Young Professor of English and Comparative Literature. Hartman served as director of the School of Criticism and Theory at Dartmouth College from 1986 to 1987 and is faculty adviser to Yale's Video Archive of Holocaust Testimonies, which he helped found in 1982.

Influence

Hartman has played an important role in the reassessment of Romanticism. His *Wordsworth's Poetry, 1787–1814*, says Donald Marshall, marked an epoch in Wordsworth studies and in studies of Romanticism, shifting attention from an opposition between imagination and reason in Wordsworth to a dialectic or antagonism between nature and imagination. He has also been influential in overturning the Arnoldian hierarchy that places criticism in a secondary role vis-à-vis "creative" literature. His works show a concern for a hermeneutics of indeterminacy and an openness to Continental influences, including German philosophy and the "deconstructive" writing of Jacques Derrida. With the critics of the Yale School, Hartman has questioned the temporal and genealogical structure of history while calling for a creative criticism that avoids the dangers of language-centeredness by analyzing the relations among literature, philosophy, politics, history, and religion.

Analysis

The history of Hartman's criticism, if such a thing were, in all rigor, possible, would have to recognize a double attitude toward theory. On the one hand, one sees in Hartman's work an openness to and sympathy with many varieties of "theory." He has acknowledged, for example, the force that semiotic theories of language have had on his thinking; psychoanalytic theories, both Freudian and Lacanian, find their place in his writings; and, especially in *Saving the Text*, Hartman seeks not to explain but to describe deconstruction, in this case that master text, Jacques Derrida's *Glas* (1974; English translation, 1986). German philosophical criticism and theory, especially that of Martin Heidegger and G. W. F. Hegel, made important contributions to Hartman's writing. In his continuing desire to move "beyond formalism" – a project which Hartman admits is not without its difficulties – he has not, however, been one simply to take up the most recent theory as the last word. Nor has his engagement with theory necessarily been a pluralistic one, as it might appear, because accompanying Hartman's openness to Continental influences, in philosophy as well as in literature and literary criticism, has been a certain vigilant questioning of "theory." Like Paul de Man and J. Hillis Miller, Hartman insists on the possibility that literature is always capable of undoing theory, and that theories of structuralism and semiotics carry with them the dangers of "formalistic devaluation" and "ideological appropriation" when they are used to establish relations between literature and other disciplines. In his view, literary theory is based on the experience of a limited canon and results from a generalizing from particular texts. This opinion makes him resistant to comprehensive literary theory and literary history.

Criticism in the Wilderness, Hartman's most influential and in some ways most accessible assessment of the critical scene, is part of his continuing critique of "practical criticism." He sees a movement from the "Arnoldian Concordat," which delimits criticism and separates it from the creative, to what he calls the "New-Critical Reduction," as influenced by T. S. Eliot. Besides playing down analogies between literary-critical and philosophical or religious discourse, the New Criticism for Hartman limited the powers of criticism by "reducing its sphere of competence to specific, formal or evaluative, remarks on art." Although liberated in some ways, criticism was denied autonomy because its focus was to be exclusively on the literary work.

Along with the critics of what he calls the "Revisionist Reversal," Hartman challenges this inherited attitude, accepted as natural, which condemns criticism to nonliterary status. Choosing instead to reinvest criticism with creative potential, even while questioning such loaded words as "creative" or "power," Hartman shifts the emphasis to criticism and the critical essay and to issues of language – the language of criticism as well as that of art – and proposes that texts of criticism and philosophy be read as closely as "literary" texts are.

One would be mistaken to see Hartman's engagement with the "Revisionist Reversal" as a complete acceptance of Derridean deconstruction, since even this most advanced of critical writing is not immune to Hartman's questioning; nevertheless, his willingness to put pressure on the language-centeredness he sees in some deconstructive writing and to challenge some of deconstruction's assumptions should not be mistaken for a refutation. Rather than opposing, or even explaining (much less explaining away) Derrida, Hartman sees his own project as a way of taking "a different turn in how to state the matter," and he proposes a "counterstatement" that might offer a "restored" theory of representation.

Hartman's relation to Derrida and deconstruction is thus not a simple one of influence or refutation. Wallace Martin (in *The Yale Critics: Deconstruction in America*, 1983) sees Hartman "incorporating deconstruction in order to overcome it," and J. Hillis Miller, in an interview with Robert Moynihan, has stated that he is "sure that [Harold] Bloom talked about and emphasized that he was not a deconstructionist. Geoffrey [Hartman] may have said the same thing." Those too concerned with whether Hartman goes by the name of deconstruction and those anxious to oppose Hartman and Derrida risk overlooking the fact that, since 1968, Hartman has been a careful, serious, and for the most part sympathetic reader of Derrida, especially since the appearance of *Glas* in 1974. Further, while de Man and Miller are generally seen to have wholeheartedly embraced deconstruction (and even this perception is not entirely true, given de Man's critique of Derrida's reading of Jean-Jacques Rousseau, for example), Hartman is the only member of the "Yale Critics" who has written a book-length study of Derrida.

Perhaps most interesting in Hartman's work, and possibly most influential, is his critical reassessment of Romanticism and ideas about literary history, since for Hartman, as for Miller and de Man, literary history cannot adequately be viewed in temporal or genealogical terms. Theories of loss or gain and concepts of fall, restoration, or secularization, for example, are falsely progressive and run the risk of monumentalizing, and therefore deadening, the past. Such theories of art need to be rethought and subjected to rhetorical analysis. Hartman thus figures with de Man and Bloom as one of those chiefly responsible for the revaluation of Romanticism.

Influential, too, has been Hartman's call for criticism to break away from the restraints of practical criticism and the Arnoldian Concordat and to allow for play in and of language – for a truly creative critical style. Hartman's own style, what Christopher Norris calls "deconstruction on the wild side," is for Norris and others "undoubtedly . . . the guise in which deconstruction has made its greatest impact on American literary studies"; it has been referred to as "beguiling," "speculative," and as an "exuberant, virtuoso style" (*The Contest of Faculties: Deconstruction, Philosophy, and Theory*, 1985). In spite of other, less positive, assessments of Hartman's "skywriting," his style continues to be influential – dizzying to some, exhilarating to others – and has certainly made deconstruction more easily accessible for many English and American readers who are resistant to the difficult and demanding work of de Man and Derrida.

Finally, Geoffrey Hartman has been willing to respond in his writing to the increased demand for a criticism which addresses the relation of literature to other disciplines, considering relations between literature, law, economics, and the process of institutionalization. Such relations may be far from certain or determinable, yet the questions posed by Hartman – questions of ethics, religion, and politics – are questions that must be asked if criticism is to move "beyond formalism."

Principal criticism

The Unmediated Vision: An Interpretation of Wordsworth, Hopkins, Rilke, and Valéry, 1954
André Malraux, 1960
Wordsworth's Poetry, 1787–1814, 1964
Beyond Formalism: Literary Essays, 1958–1970, 1970
The Fate of Reading and Other Essays, 1975
Criticism in the Wilderness: The Study of Literature Today, 1980
Saving the Text: Literature/Derrida/Philosophy, 1981
Easy Pieces, 1985
The Unremarkable Wordsworth, 1986
Minor Prophecies: The Literary Essay in the Culture Wars, 1991
The Sympathy Paradox: Poetry, Feeling, and Modern Cultural Morality, 1996
The Fateful Question of Culture, 1997

Other major works and literary forms

In addition to the books listed above, Geoffrey Hartman has written many articles, essays, and reviews on a variety of subjects, including film, religion, psychoanalysis, and history. Among his prefaces are those to *Deconstruction and Criticism* (1979) and to Maurice Blanchot's *The Gaze of Orpheus and Other Literary Essays* (1981). Since 1969 Hartman has contributed to *The New York Times Book Review*, including "How Creative Should Literary Criticism Be?" His essay "On the Jewish Imagination" appeared in *Prooftexts* in September of 1985, and his essays on psychoanalysis and literature have appeared in *The Literary Freud:*

Mechanisms of Defense and the Poetic Will (1980) and in *Psychoanalysis and the Question of the Text* (1978).

POETRY
Akiba's Children, 1978

NONFICTION
Preface to *Deconstruction and Criticism*, 1979
Essays in *The Literary Freud: Mechanisms of Defense and the Poetic Will*, 1980
Preface to *The Gaze of Orpheus and Other Literary Essays*, 1981, by Maurice Blanchot
"How Creative Should Literary Criticism Be?," 1981
"On the Jewish Imagination," 1985

EDITED TEXTS
Hopkins: A Collection of Critical Essays, 1966
Selected Poetry and Prose of William Wordsworth, 1970
New Perspectives on Coleridge and Wordsworth, 1972
Romanticism: Vistas, Instances, Continuities, 1973 (with David Thorburn)
Psychoanalysis and the Question of the Text, 1978
Shakespeare and the Question of Theory, 1985 (with Patricia Parker)
Bitburg in Moral and Political Perspective, 1986
Midrash and Literature, 1986 (with Sanford Budick)
Holocaust Remembrance: The Shapes of Memory, 1994

Further reading

Arac, Jonathan, Wlad Godzich, and Wallace Martin, eds. *The Yale Critics: Deconstruction in America*, 1983.
Atkins, G. Douglas. "Dehellenizing Literary Criticism," in *College English*. XLI (March, 1980), pp. 769–779.
Gasché, Rodolphe. "Deconstruction as Criticism," in *Glyph*. VI (1979), pp. 177–215.
Lewis, Philip E. "Athletic Criticism," in *Diacritics*. I, no. 2 (1971), pp. 2–6.
Marshall, Donald G. "Geoffrey Hartman, Wordsworth, and the Interpretation of Modernity," in *Romantic Revolutions: Criticism and Theory*, 1990, pp. 78–97. Edited by Kenneth R. Johnston et al.
Moynihan, Robert. *A Recent Imagining: Interviews with Harold Bloom, Geoffrey Hartman, Paul de Man, J. Hillis Miller*, 1986.
Norris, Christopher. *Deconstruction: Theory and Practice*, 1982.
Saluinszky, Imre. *Criticism in Society: Interviews with Jacques Derrida, Northrop Frye, Harold Bloom, Geoffrey Hartman, Frank Kermode, Edward Said, Barbara Johnson, Frank Lentricchia, and J. Hillis Miller*, 1987.

ROBERT F. DENTON

See also American Literary Theory: Twentieth Century; Deconstruction; The Yale School

Hāzim al-Qartājannī

Arabic theorist, grammarian, and poet

Born: Cartagena (Spain); 1211
Died: Tunis (Tunisia); November 23, 1285

Biography

Abūl-Hasan Hāzim Ibn Muhammad al-Qartājannī was born in Cartagena (Spain), one year before the disastrous defeat of the reigning Almohad dynasty by the Christians at Las Navas de Tolosa (1212), which led to the fragmentation of their empire. From his father Hāzim received an education in Arabic grammar and Islamic jurisprudence, before moving to Murcia, Granada, and then Seville, where he was introduced to *falsafa*, Greek philosophy as it had been developed by Muslim scholars, particularly Ibn Sīnā (Avicenna). In 1235, shortly before the fall of Cordoba, he moved to North Africa, where he spent the rest of his life. After a few years in the Almohad capital, Marrakesh, he finally moved, not yet thirty years old, to Tunis, the capital of the Hafsid dynasty under its founder Abū Zakariyyā Yahyā (ruled 1228–1249) and his successors. He acquired some fame as a grammarian, rhetorician, and poet.

Influence

Hāzim wrote some interesting poetry, including odes on the Hafsid rulers and an unfinished didactic poem on grammar. His masterpiece is a very long ode of 1,006 lines in monorhyme (no mean feat even by Arabic standards). Dedicated to al-Mustansir (ruled 1249–1277), it is full of historical and geographical references; a commentary on it was written in the fourteenth century. It is on his work on poetics, however, an isolated and to some extent successful attempt at a synthesis between Arabic and Greek theory, that his fame must rest, even though it had virtually no influence on the course of Arabic literary theory and has been rediscovered only in the last few decades.

Analysis

As pointed out in the entry on Arabic literary theory, there were several reasons why Greek poetics and rhetoric failed to make much of an impact on the indigenous Arabic tradition, in spite of the very great influence of Greek thought in almost every field of learning written in Arabic. Ibn Sīnā (Avicenna, died 1037), although himself a poet, did not attempt to reconcile Aristotle and the Arabic tradition when he wrote his commentaries or paraphrases of the *Poetics* and *Rhetoric*. When Ibn Rushd (Averroës, died 1198) did the same, he at least attempted to provide examples taken from Arabic poetry or to find Arabic equivalents. The results are not always convincing – replacing "comedy" with "invective poetry," or "dénouement" (Greek *lysis*) with "transition," in a polythematic ode, from the amorous introduction to the panegyric, to give some examples. Ibn al-Haytham (Alhazen, died 1039), the great physicist, had written a *Risāla fī sināʿat ash-shiʿr mumtazija min al-yūnānī wa-l-ʿarabī* (treatise on poetics, mixed from the Greek and the Arabic), but nothing is known of it.

The title of Hāzim al-Qartājannī's *Minhāj al-bulaghā' wa-sirāj al-udabā'* (the path of the eloquent and the lamp of the lettered) suggests that it deals with eloquence, like countless other works in Arabic literary criticism. It is, however, exclusively concerned with poetry and, refreshingly, does not even pay lip service to the eloquence of the

Koran or the sayings of the Prophet. The book is divided into four parts, on *alfāz* (words, wording, expression), *maʿānī* (meanings, motifs), *nazm* (composition), and *turuq shiʿriyya* ("poetic paths, or methods") or *asālīb* ("models, modes"). The first part is unfortunately lost, and with it any introduction that might have shed light on his reasons for writing his highly original synthesis. It seems that he knew the Greek tradition only through Avicenna and not through Averroës, who was chronologically and geographically closer to him. He integrates ideas from the *Poetics* and *Rhetoric*, since eloquence is concerned not only with evoking images (*takhyīl*) and "imitating" (*muhākāh*, compare Greek mimesis) but also with persuasion. The two cooperate closely, sometimes in one line, as when Abū Tammām says, "You made him act out of character: fire may sometimes be drawn from fresh mimosa wood"; here a poetic image is used rhetorically, in order to make something likely. They may also cooperate in giving structure to passages and whole poems, in which imaginative lines are often effectively rounded off with a persuasive line. This technique is discussed in the third part, on *nazm*, which shows that to Hāzim this term comprises far more than to other writers on eloquence: *nazm* is not merely sentence syntax, but the composition of lines into passages and of passages into whole poems.

In the four parts of the book Hāzim moves from small, concrete units to large and more abstract ones. This order is reversed, however, in a few passages on the poetic process, where he enumerates the various phases through which the poet moves, or the powers that are required from him (or her; at least one famous poetess is quoted), and where Hāzim moves from a kind of poetic deep structure to the surface structure. Thus the poet moves from a general "purpose" to a "path" for this, with its various motifs; then he imagines their arrangement, with proper transitions. Next, he selects the wording, together with a suitable meter and rhyme. It is not certain that the suggested chronological order of these phases is to be taken literally; and even if we are supposed to do so, there may be no reason to rely on his words in every respect: in the *Minhāj al-bulaghāʾ* it is the systematic scholar rather than the poet Hāzim who speaks.

The second part, on "meanings," includes not only discussions of the relationship of poetical, mimetic elements and rhetorical, persuasive elements in poetry but also sections on figures of speech that are familiar from traditional criticism, on clarity versus obscurity and original motifs versus commonplace motifs. The third part, concerned with "composition," contains an interesting theory of meter that differs from the traditional ideas. Possibly following Greek theory, he attempts to connect certain meters with particular themes or modes, although a predecessor, the philosopher al-Fārābī (Alfarabius, died 950), had denied that Greek theory could be transposed to Arabic in this case. Since he deems the gap between the concept "mode" ("purpose") and its constituent "motifs" too great, Hāzim posits an intermediate concept, *jiha*, "subtheme" (literally "direction"); similarly, between a poem and its constituent verses he puts the "passage" (*fasl*), which has its own structure. The part ends with a characterization of two different kinds of poet, the maker of long odes and that of short poems. The fourth part, on poetic modes and themes, opens with an interesting basic distinction between serious style and jesting. Hāzim's classification of modes and themes is thoroughly utilitarian. The aim of poetry is either to bring about something useful or to eliminate something harmful; further subdivision depends on whether the useful or harmful things have already occurred or are expected, and whether they are brought about by fate or human action. This is elaborated in some detail. The goal-directed concept of poetry is rubbed in also by the terminology employed throughout: *gharad* and *maqsid* (both "purpose"), *tarīq* and *uslūb* (both "path"), *jiha* ("direction") as well as the title of the book (*minhāj*, "path") and the terms for chapters and subsections: *manhaj* ("path" again), *maʿraf* and *maʿlam* (both "road sign"), while short paragraphs are alternately called *idāʾa* and *tanwīr* (both "lighting, illumination").

All this is worked out by Hāzim with a passion for classification and subdivision that borders on the excessive. The reader, moreover, is not rarely frustrated by his dauntingly long sentences and general dryness of style, disappointing when one thinks that he was no mean poet. But the work's merits far outweigh these defects. More than any other Arabic critic since Qudāma Ibn Jaʿfar, he attempted to present a coherent and comprehensive theory (meaning, as usual in Arabic criticism, a mixture of description and prescription), in which many observations, loosely made by his predecessors, find a proper place, and to which he added a number of original observations of his own. It is the presentation, however, rather than the content, of his poetics that is different: his concept of poetry is essentially identical with the traditional Arabic one. He does not advocate the writing of new kinds of verse, certainly not, for instance, poetry that follows Greek genres or modes. He knew, through Avicenna's paraphrase of Aristotle, that Greek poetry mostly "turns around fables (*khurāfāt*) made up by them," and that they had "parables" (*amthāl*) like the stories of *Kalīla and Dimna* (animal fables, originally Indian and translated from Persian into Arabic in the eighth century). The word *khurāfa* reflects, of course, Greek *mythos*; in Arabic, it has a rather negative connotation (superstition, trumped-up story). The Arabs were undoubtedly great storytellers, yet Arabic literary theorists, perhaps because they took this ability almost for granted, did not attach much importance to the telling of stories and the production of fiction. Not surprisingly, Hāzim, at the same time berating and pitying Aristotle, goes on to say that "if Aristū the philosopher had found in Greek poetry all the splendid adages, proverbs, argumentations, and the various original ways of expression and ideas . . . of Arabic poetry, he would have said more about this when writing down his laws of poetry."

In spite of its impressive synthesis, *Minhāj al-bulaghā' wa-sirāj al-udabā'*, that often arduous path and obscure lamp, was largely ignored by later critics. Only a few short quotations are found in subsequent centuries; presumably, its style formed a barrier. That Ibn Khaldūn (died 1406), the great historian of culture, does not mention Ḥāzim in his chapter on the history of literary criticism in his *Muqaddima* (introduction), even though both were active in Tunis, is almost as remarkable as Ḥāzim's silence on the popular work on poetry and poetics *al-'Umda* (the support) by Ibn Rashīq from Cairouan, in present-day Tunisia. Writing on Ḥāzim, a modern scholar, Muhammad Ridwān ad-Dāya, deplores the neglect of a work "that might have changed literary studies after him and would even have affected the course of Arabic poetry itself." This last clause is, of course, a gross overestimation of the role of criticism.

Principal criticism

Minhāj al-bulaghā' wa-sirāj al-udabā' (the path of the eloquent and the lamp of the lettered), 1966 (Mohamed Habib Belkhodja, editor; partially translated in the works by Vicente Cantarino, Wolfhart Heinrichs, and Gregor Schoeler)

Other major works and literary forms

POETRY

Dīwān (collected poetry), 1979 ('Uthmā al-Ka''āk, editor)

Further reading

Averroës. *Averroës' Middle Commentary on Aristotle's Poetics*, 1986. Translation with introduction and notes by Charles E. Butterworth.

Cantarino, Vicente. *Arabic Poetics in the Golden Age*, 1975 (see pp. 206–220).

Dahiyat, Ismail M. *Avicenna's Commentary on the Poetics of Aristotle: A Critical Study with an Annotated Translation of the Text*, 1974.

Fārābī, al-. "Le Kitāb al-ḫaṭāba [Rhetoric] d'al-Fārābī," in *Mélanges de l'Université S.-Joseph*. 42, no. 3 (1968), pp. 61–177.

Heinrichs, Wolfhart. *Arabische Dichtung und griechische Poetik: Ḥāzim al-Qarṭāğannīs Grundlegung der Poetik mit Hilfe aristotelische Begriffe*, 1969.

Schoeler, Gregor. *Einige Grundprobleme der autochthonen und der aristotelischen arabischen Literaturtheorie: Ḥāzim al-Qarṭāğannī's Kapitel über die Zielsetzungen der Dichtung und die Vorgeschichte der in ihm dargelegten Gedanken*, 1975.

Van Gelder, G. J. H. *Beyond the Line*, 1975, pp. 171–190.

——. "Critic and Craftsman: al-Qarṭājannī and the Structure of the Poem," in *Journal of Arabic Literature*. 10 (1979), pp. 26–48.

GEERT JAN VAN GELDER

See also 'Abd al-Qāhir al-Jurjānī; Arabic Literary Theory; Qudāma Ibn Ja'far

William Hazlitt

English critic and essayist

Born: Maidstone, England; April 10, 1778
Died: London, England; September 18, 1830

Biography

William Hazlitt was born on April 10, 1778, at Maidstone in Kent, England. He was the fourth child and third son born to William Hazlitt the Elder, a Unitarian minister, and his wife, Grace Loftus. The growing family moved to the elder Hazlitt's native Ireland in 1780 and, three years later, to the United States. In 1787 the peripatetic clan returned to England, where William lived for the rest of his life. He was, like his father, radical in his politics, and, unlike so many of his fellow Romantics, he remained so to his death.

Hazlitt zealously studied philosophy at Hackney College, London, from the age of fifteen to eighteen. John, the eldest Hazlitt child, became a successful miniaturist, and William sporadically pursued a career as a painter himself until as late as 1812. He finally turned to journalism in his mid-thirties. He was often in financial straits, and his domestic life was untidy. He divorced his first wife, from whom he had long been separated, so that he might marry his landlord's daughter. After toying with him for a time, however, she jilted him. He later married a well-to-do widow, who left him within three years.

Hazlitt met, made friends with, and eventually quarreled bitterly with most of the leading Romantic writers of the time. Only with the tolerant Charles Lamb was he able to maintain a lasting friendship. In his fifty-third year he died in near poverty of a lingering illness which his physician characterized, perhaps inexactly, as cholera.

Influence

Hazlitt stands as the quintessential Romantic critic. He immediately recognized the greatness of William Wordsworth. His work shows a penetrating understanding of Samuel Taylor Coleridge's virtues and vices, both as poet and as critic. Although Hazlitt's drama reviews and lectures lack Coleridge's theoretical approach to literature, they evince an impressive self-confidence in the critic's taste and perceptiveness. Perhaps the dominant trait of this impressionistic criticism, however, is its *gusto* (to use the Italian term in the sense which Hazlitt introduced into his own writings). Hazlitt felt and communicates a zest for the objects of his criticism which appeals even to the reader who may question his conclusions.

Analysis

Hazlitt once observed that he had started his life with the French Revolution. He spent his last year of life completing his multivolume biography of Napoleon I. The work was a failure. These three facts combine to make an almost metaphorical statement about Hazlitt's literary career. He was born into a Dissenting and activist family (his father preached in favor of both the American and the French revolutions), and he never lost the republican enthusiasm he had imbibed as a boy. He watched as Wordsworth, Coleridge, and Robert Southey became disillusioned with the French Revolution and went over to the Tories. Yet, although deeply depressed by the failure of the Revolution, he remained faithful to it and its symbol, Napoleon, to the end. Unfortunately, as regards his work *The Life of Napoleon Buonaparte*, the very fervor and passion that made him a great Romantic critic made him a bad historian.

Hazlitt serves as one of the best specific examples in support of the generalizations most often made about Romanticism. In "On Reason and Imagination," one of the essays from *Table-Talk*, he argues the merits of experience against those of arid speculation, of living against mere thinking. Hazlitt uses the term "reason" to mean the analytical sense, that faculty which determines the nominal differences between the things perceived. By "imagination," he seems to mean the apprehension of things in their given circumstances, in their particularity. Although he cites dialogue from John Webster's *The Duchess of Malfi* (1613–1614) in the essay, Hazlitt makes moral as well as literary claims for the imagination. The excellence or the shoddiness of a thing, its truth or falsity, even its goodness or its evilness are judged more reliably by the emotions than by Benthamite rationality.

In his essay "On Gusto," written in 1816, Hazlitt discusses the sense of power emanating from certain paintings and literary works. The critic who trusted his emotional response far more than his intellectual response would, understandably, praise a quality so passionately rendered in the work that it would immediately stir the reader's feelings. The judgments pronounced in "On Gusto," however, might well surprise the reader who views its author as the stereotypical Romantic. John Milton's poetry has great gusto, says Hazlitt; William Shakespeare's drama has little. The reader would expect Hazlitt to feel the gusto in the prose of Giovanni Boccaccio and François Rabelais, but he also finds it in some neoclassical works, notably those of John Dryden, Alexander Pope, and Matthew Prior. He concludes the essay by declaring that if John Gay's *The Beggar's Opera* (1728) is not permeated with this zest, he has altogether mistaken the nature of gusto.

Hazlitt's style is plain and straightforward, in an era still dominated by the elaborate prose models of the early seventeenth century. His organization, on the other hand, is loose – on the surface, it is frequently nonexistent. A partial explanation is the pressures of daily journalism, since most of the material in his books was first written for periodicals or to be delivered as public lectures. Writing rapidly, though, was probably congenial to his temperament. He is said to have turned out ten or more printed pages at a sitting – like Shakespeare, scarcely blotting a line. He would introduce a subject, then proceed from one to another associated idea as his background of wide reading and his fertile imagination would lead him. His criticism usually states or implies a thesis, but he does not feel obliged to argue it closely throughout. Unlike the New Critic of the next century, with a pseudoscientific approach, Hazlitt fills his essays with literary allusions cited from memory. He is an essayist in the tradition that stretches from Michel de Montaigne to Aldous Huxley.

Since Hazlitt's criticism is more impressionistic than rigorous, he is vulnerable to the New Critic's charge that his essays often treat his own sensibilities more than the alleged subject matter. It has been observed, for example, that Hazlitt sheds more heat than light upon Shakespeare. A turn-of-the-century biographer, Augustine Birrell, complains that in *Characters of Shakespeare's Plays* Hazlitt seldom compares a character in one play with a character in another. Birrell accounts for this lapse by noting the origins of *Characters*: the material comes largely from Hazlitt's newspaper reviews of specific performances. Hence, the critic is bound too closely to the text of each play he treats.

Hazlitt came of age as a literary critic with the lectures he delivered between 1818 and 1820. The structure of the three sets of lectures is identical. The first lecture is a general introduction to the subject; it is followed by seven more, arranged in chronological order. Hazlitt does not, however, allow himself to be too constrained by chronology. Nor, for that matter, do the title and purported subject of an essay discommode him much if he decides to roam. For Hazlitt, there were four categories of English literature which had attained the greatest degree of excellence: Elizabethan and Jacobean tragedy, Restoration comedy, the periodical essay, and the eighteenth-century novel. The poets to whom he was most attracted were Geoffrey Chaucer, Edmund Spenser, and Milton. To this subject matter he would return, even if doing so meant giving historical short shrift elsewhere. Hazlitt biographer Herschel Baker points up the frequently roundabout nature of the lectures by means of two examples. Sir Philip Sidney's *Arcadia* (1590) infiltrates and eventually captures a lecture nominally about eighteenth-century poetry, and a long disquisition on Rabelais and Voltaire becomes the focal point in an essay supposedly dealing with Jonathan Swift.

Hazlitt is at his best as an appreciative critic, when he is extolling the beauties of a piece rather than enumerating its flaws. He regards most scholarship as pedantry and delights in celebrating genius. Thus, his lectures are largely a rather unsystematic record of his enthusiasms. He adopts a conversational style and fosters the pretense that his audience is a friend with whom he is chatting about his favorite books. He announces that pointing up the author's minor errors and trifling oversights is not his job. Nor is it his job to enumerate the requirements for literary greatness, then check them off as the particular writer meets each one. Having faith that he can feel what is good, he attempts to substantiate his emotional response only when it is absolutely necessary and within his power to do so. His literary opinions are closely related to his metaphysical and political opinions. The originality – occasionally, the eccentricity – of his observations on a particular author or work has made them, quite apart from the object which occasioned them, pleasurable reading for later generations. The observations have themselves become literature. It is precisely this quality of Romantic criticism which later writers have praised or blamed, sometimes both simultaneously.

The strength of Hazlitt's opinions, his fearlessness in stating them, and his prolific output combine for predictable results: he is frequently rash, ill-informed, and intemperate. When a subject has proved sufficiently arresting to engage his full attention, however, his criticism can be penetrating. His lecture 8 on the English poets, "On the Living Poets," contains assessments of Lord Byron, Sir Walter Scott, Wordsworth, and Coleridge that have well stood the test of time. He vividly describes the spellbinding but essentially ephemeral impact of Coleridge's conversation. In "My First Acquaintance with Poets," written for the April, 1823, number of the *Liberal*, Hazlitt again discusses Coleridge, recounting a walk that he took with the poet in 1798, when he, Hazlitt, was only twenty years of age. He describes Coleridge as talking every step of the way on their six-mile journey, and as constantly crossing from one side of the footpath to the other, apparently incapable of proceeding in a straight line. Hazlitt would later interpret his companion's erratic progress along the footpath as symptomatic of his weaknesses as man, philosopher, and poet. This fortuitous memory from his youth is exactly the sort of apt detail which Hazlitt, at his best, seizes upon to illuminate an author's character or work.

Hazlitt's three courses of lectures were delivered before the general public at the Surrey Institution in London. His contemporary Sir Thomas Noon Talfourd described the audiences as being far from ideal. They were made up of Dissenters, Quakers, ordinary Londoners seeking self-improvement, a few admirers, and a few enemies hoping to see him fail. The audiences were sometimes so inert that they would provoke Hazlitt into a remark designed solely to shock them, even if it meant departing entirely from his subject. On the other hand, a comment slightly critical of Voltaire brought a cheer from the Francophobes in attendance, while a disparaging reference to Hannah Moore elicited a shouted objection from a defender. According to Talfourd, Hazlitt persevered doggedly to the end. It must be noted, however, that one regular and receptive auditor of the lectures was a young man named John Keats. Moreover, as the lectures were published, Hazlitt's influence spread. His views on the merits of the major poets by no means accorded with the popular wisdom of his day, but within a hundred years they had become the popular wisdom.

In the introductory lecture to each series, Hazlitt makes his most systematic arguments. "On Poetry in General" defines poetry in terms far too encompassing to be very useful but also argues, in brilliant and oft-quoted language, the superiority of the imagination and of passion to the rigid rules of the neoclassicists. In "On Wit and Humour," Hazlitt undertakes the daunting task of differentiating the witty, the humorous, the comic, the ludicrous, and the ridiculous. Humor is a product of the head, not the heart, and, true to his temperament, Hazlitt asserts that it is inferior to serious and impassioned literature. His introduction to *Lectures Chiefly on the Dramatic Literature of the Age of Elizabeth* is a tour de force in which he stirringly synthesizes the diverse elements that produced Britain's golden age.

Ten years later, Hazlitt met his end with all of his Romantic instincts intact. Despite his history of virulent literary feuds, broken friendships, marital disharmony, ill health, and financial distress, Hazlitt said on his deathbed, "Well, I've had a happy life." It is a suitably romantic exit for the most Romantic of critics.

Principal criticism

Characters of Shakespeare's Plays, 1817
A View of the English Stage, 1818
Lectures on the English Poets, 1818
Lectures on the English Comic Writers, 1819
Lectures Chiefly on the Dramatic Literature of the Age of Elizabeth, 1820

Other major works and literary forms

A man of wide interests and firm opinions, William Hazlitt also wrote on philosophy, ethics, economics, and politics. He gave a series of public lectures on philosophy in 1812. He entered journalism as parliamentary reporter for *The Morning Chronicle* and eventually became its drama critic. In addition to his drama criticism, Hazlitt contributed miscellaneous essays to Leigh Hunt's *Examiner*, the *Edinburgh Review*, and other periodicals.

Hazlitt showed his mastery of the familiar essay in the two volumes of *Table-Talk: Or, Original Essays* (1821–1822). In 1823 he published *Liber Amoris: Or, The New Pygmalion*, a thinly fictionalized account of his unsuccessful courtship of his landlord's daughter. He wrote a series of sketches of the eminent figures of his day, which was published under the title *The Spirit of the Age: Or, Contemporary Portraits* (1825). A tireless workman, Hazlitt labored almost to the very end of his life on the fourth and final volume of *The Life of Napoleon Buonaparte* (1828–1830).

NONFICTION
On the Principles of Human Action, 1805
Free Thoughts on Public Affairs, 1806
Light of Nature Pursued, 1807 (editor)

The Eloquence of the British Senate, 1807 (editor)
Reply to Malthus, 1807
New and Improved Grammar of the English Tongue, 1810
Memoirs of the Late Thomas Holcroft, 1816 (editor)
The Round Table, 1817 (with Leigh Hunt)
Political Essays, 1819
Table-Talk: Or, Original Essays, 1821–1822
Liber Amoris: Or, The New Pygmalion, 1823
The Spirit of the Age: Or, Contemporary Portraits, 1825
The Life of Napoleon Buonaparte, 1828–1830 (4 volumes)

Further reading

Baker, Herschel. *William Hazlitt*, 1962.
Birrell, Augustine. *William Hazlitt*, 1926.
Bromwich, David. *Hazlitt: The Mind of a Critic*, 1983.
Kinnaird, John. *William Hazlitt: Critic of Power*, 1978.
Law, Marie Hamilton. *The English Familiar Essay in the Early Nineteenth Century: The Elements, Old and New, Which Went into Its Making, as Exemplified in the Writings of Hunt, Hazlitt, and Lamb*, 1965.
Maclean, Catherine Macdonald. *Born Under Saturn: A Biography of William Hazlitt*, 1944.
Mahoney, John L. *The Logic of Passion: The Literary Criticism of William Hazlitt*, 1978.
Park, Roy. *Hazlitt and the Spirit of the Age: Abstraction and Literary Theory*, 1971.
Wardle, Ralph M. *Hazlitt*, 1971.

PATRICK ADCOCK

See also Coleridge; Keats; Romanticism; Shelley; Wordsworth

Stephen Heath

English critic, editor, and translator

Born: London, England; March 31, 1946

Biography

Stephen Heath was born in 1946 in Haringay, North London. His family background was not academic in any way, but he attended Enfield Grammar School and succeeded (in his own words, "by the skin of my teeth") in gaining a place at Jesus College, Cambridge University. Whilst there he was taught by Raymond Williams and Terry Eagleton, and in his final year as an undergraduate, partly at the prompting of Williams, he began the study of contemporary French novel-writing and criticism that would give shape to his subsequent career. After graduation he went to live, work, and study in Paris, attending seminars at the École Pratique des Hautes Études. It was here that he came into contact with Roland Barthes, whose work and teaching have been probably the greatest influence on Heath's own critical output. Through Barthes, too, he became a friend and associate of the critic Julia Kristeva and novelist Philippe Sollers. He held a research fellowship at Downing College, Cambridge, became a Cambridge University lecturer at Jesus College in 1969, and a fellow of the same college in 1973. From 1973 he was a regular contributor to the British film journal *Screen*, and a member of its editorial board. In 1975 he became a member of the Corps Enseignant Littéraire at the École Normale Supérieure in Paris. He has also been a visiting lecturer in the Department of Fine Arts, University of Wisconsin-Milwaukee. In 1991 he became a reader in the faculty of English at Cambridge, where he continues to live and work.

Influence

Heath was one of the first British academics to import the structuralist ideas that had gained a footing in France in the 1960s. His efforts to bring these new theories to an English-speaking audience, through his translations, for example of Barthes, and through his own critical writing and teaching, made him, in the words of Frank Kermode, "the virtual leader of the English group" of young, avant-garde theorists in the early 1970s. A friend of Kristeva and Sollers, Heath had been a contributor, whilst in Paris, to the avant-garde journal *Tel Quel*, which attempted to combine the idea of political revolution with the notion of revolution in language – a premise, in Heath's words, that "offered urgency and value to a cultural work of critique and opposition in the politically confused post-1968 moment when the old versions of politics were deadeningly reasserting themselves." Bringing these influences back with him, he acted as a conduit for European ideas to reach the mainstream academic culture in the United Kingdom, and the presence of critical theory in British university syllabuses can, to a large extent, be traced back to the championing of such an approach by Heath and his contemporaries some thirty years ago. In the early 1970s he was a prominent participator in a series of seminars organized at University College London by Kermode, which became an influential forum for the discussion and dissemination of structuralist and poststructuralist ideas in England. Whilst still a young tutor at Cambridge, Heath taught and collaborated with Colin MacCabe on their first publication. Then, in the mid-1970s Heath was instrumental in pushing for a change in the undergraduate English syllabus at Cambridge, to incorporate contemporary thinking about critical theory, gender, minority, and colonial discourses. A ensuing ideological dispute within the Cambridge faculty culminated in 1981 with the decision by traditionalist dons not to confirm MacCabe's tenure as a lecturer. Ironically, the furor generated by this decision in academic circles, which also became a controversial *cause célèbre* in the national press, brought structuralism (a reductive term used to denote all "foreign theory" by its opponents) a greater exposure, and provoked many critics into a vocal support of its tenets.

Heath's contributions to the journal *Screen* in the 1970s were crucial in the introduction of semiotics to film theory in the English-speaking world, particularly his analysis of the French theorist Christian Metz. Since then, his critical output has remained diverse, encompassing both the sociological analysis of sexuality of *The Sexual Fix* (1982), and an ongoing interest in literary and film theory.

Analysis

Heath's early criticism focused on the introduction of French structuralist semiotics, as articulated by Barthes, Kristeva, and Sollers in particular, into the far more traditional British academic arena. As Barthes has defined it, structuralism entails a concentration on the system of language, rather than the meaning of individual words or sentences. Borrowing Ferdinand de Saussure's distinction between *langue* and *parole* (that is, between the system and the units that comprise that system), Barthes sought "less to assign completed meanings to the objects . . . than to know how meaning is possible." Thus, the emphasis of structuralist literary study moves away from the interpretation of intrinsic meaning in texts and asserts, firstly, that the reader is central to the meaning of a text, rather than the author, and, secondly, that *all* texts, from a novel by Henry James to a restaurant menu, are equally valid linguistic signifiers. Such a position was radical enough in its challenge to conventional criticism, but its practitioners, especially Barthes, also had a flair for memorably inflammatory phraseology – such as Barthes' famous pronouncement of "the death of the author."

Heath's exposure to structuralist theory and the teaching of Barthes exerted a profound influence on his career, as he recalls:

> The impact for me was immediately, and always thereafter first and foremost, Barthes. I went to the seminar he was then giving, the seminar that subsequently became *S/Z*, and was held by the sheer intelligence in play, the intellectual fineness of the particular analyses and the general developments coming out of his reading of the Balzac story . . . nothing had prepared me for this relation of cultural-ideological analysis to linguistic and textual analysis that Barthes was inventing week by week.

His early work shows him to have imbibed a somewhat polemical attitude toward the literary establishment alongside the critical tenets of French theory. The preface to *Signs of the Times: Introductory Readings in Textual Semiotics* (1971), to which Heath contributed the article "Toward Textual Semiotics" and an interview with Barthes, as well as being coeditor, makes clear both the adulatory attitude toward French theory, and the hostility toward British conservatism:

> here, the explosive force of modernism has not been permitted to fracture the transparent sufficiency of the window of traditional humanism, generally resisted (or, perhaps worse, recuperated). In this situation, we can only begin to try to read and question the texts of Barthes, Kristeva, Sollers and so on by retracing (inscribing ourselves along) the paths they have already opened in the wake of that force of modernism in the hope of reaching, within the limits of our ignorance, the vital growing point of contemporary research at which they are working.

Although the fiery rhetoric was quickly left behind by Heath, this small, early publication, with a very limited circulation ("a vilely printed book," Kermode recalls in his memoirs), is important for several reasons. As one of the first English-language publications to attempt a definition, explanation, and exploration of structuralist semiotics, it located its editors, Heath in particular, at the cutting edge of radical literary theory. Furthermore, it established a self-consciously "difficult" critical style for Heath which has persisted throughout his career (with the possible exception of the much lighter work *The Sexual Fix*). The same preface acknowledges and justifies "the difficulty of these texts, of that work carried through in the development of semiotics. The difficulty is not to be hidden – we ourselves have no right to hide it. Nor, however, is it to be submitted [sic] to the terrorism of plain language, that mythical weapon of those who prefer the comforting reception of the ideological caress; who do not want to READ. The difficulties are real: it is up to us to master them."

This is a stance Heath seems to have retained. Barthes had identified two distinct kinds of texts – the *lisible* or "readerly" text, accessible, predictable, and traditional, asking little of the reader; and the *scriptible* or "writerly" text, which forces the reader to play an active part in constructing meaning, to participate in the creative process. Heath's writing provides a kind of critical counterpart to the writerly text, in its consistent refusal to make concessions to the reader. This approach to language and to the constructive elevation of reader above writer is exemplified in literature by the writers of the French "new novel," the *nouveau roman*, who compel the reader to take an active part in the reading process by their deliberate obscurity, a conscious avoidance of "the terrorism of plain language." The publication in 1972 (although it had been substantially completed in 1969) of *The Nouveau Roman: A Study in the Practice of Writing* was, then, a natural project for Heath, as the writers on whom he centers his discussion – Michel Butor, Philippe Sollers, Alain Robbe-Grillet, Nathalie Saraute, and others – carried into practice, to a large extent, the structuralist credo. The book attempts to explore, in Heath's words,

> the radical shift in emphasis in the novel from this monologistic realism to what I shall term *the practice of writing* . . . . Its foundation is a profound experience of language and form and the demonstration of that experience in the writing of the novel which, transgressed, is no longer repetition and

> self-effacement but work and self-presentation as text. Its "realism" is not the mirroring of some "Reality" but an attention to the forms of the intelligibility in which the real is produced, a dramatization of possibilities of language, forms of articulation, limitations, of its own horizon.

The example of James Joyce, particularly *Finnegans Wake* (1939), Heath argues, is key to much of the experimentation with language undertaken in the *nouveau roman*, just as the realist Balzacian novel is its antithesis. Honoré de Balzac's work is "not a process of composition but of representation"; but Heath identifies a problem with literary criticism's conventional preoccupation with the role of the author in the construction of a text. "The task of criticism," he argues, "has been precisely the construction of the author. It must read the author in the texts grouped under his name .... Criticism, in short, is the modern hermeneutics: the passage from God to Author." Heath attempts to question the very idea of the author as the source of the discourse, to redefine the notion of realism: "far from being the unique creation of the author as originating source, every text is always (an)other text(s) that it remakes, comments, displaces, prolongs, reassumes. A text opens in and from that complex formation of modes of articulation that gives, as it were, the theatre of its activity ...." From this point of view, the author becomes "an effect of the text, held in an empire of signs ...."

Finnegans Wake is held up as a contrary example, a text which is virtually "unreadable." Heath had produced an extensive analysis and interpretation of this text in his earlier essay "Ambiviolences," written in French and published in *Tel Quel* in 1972, in which he argues that it presents "the working of language in which the limits of communication come undone, are set out and fractured in the play of the signifier ...." Its unreadability is not meant to be deciphered or solved by translation into a familiar language; rather it is the very intention of the work, an exercise in the "practice of writing," in which the drama is enacted not at the level of narrative but at the level of the sentence, in the play of meaning and association between words. A similar approach animates the writers of the *nouveau roman*, although, as Jonathan Culler has argued, these works are not as divorced from the Balzacian emphasis on "real life" as is often assumed. Heath cites Butor's assertion that in a *nouveau roman*, "the system of signification within the book will be an image of the system of meanings within which the reader is caught in his daily life" – but this claim, Culler points out, could be made equally of the realist novel: "For all its opposition to models of intelligibility and coherence, the radical novel relies on the link between text and ordinary experience just as traditional novels did."

As well as further disseminating French theory by translating some of Barthes' key essays in *Image, Music, Text* (1977), much of Heath's important critical work in the 1970s derived from his association with *Screen*, and the pursuit of an interest in film theory "towards the development of a critical and theoretical account of cinema and film able to engage cultural and political issues." He was instrumental in introducing the semiotic approach to film advocated by the French scholar Christian Metz, whose wide-ranging and influential articles had been collected in 1967 as *Film Language – A Semiotics of Cinema*. In a special issue of *Screen* in 1973, entitled "Cinema Semiotics and the Work of Christian Metz," Heath provides an introduction to Metz's work, but also imposes a crucial caveat. Whereas Metz believed that film semiology should be "the *total* study of the filmic act," Heath argues that it must progress beyond the simple analysis of cinematic language, and instead engage in "the general enterprise of semiology as analysis of forms of social practice grasped as signifying systems."

Screen became an influential forum for the circulation of these new ideas about semiotics and film, and in an attempt to understand "how film and television functioned to produce meaning," many of its contributors, including Heath, explored the position of the viewer as subject, and the psychological devices employed by film. To quote Heath: "There was no political value to be got out of some formalist structural analysis ... what had to be looked at was the subjectivity the film invokes, how it sets the viewer up as a viewer, positions you, moves you along." Heath himself produced perhaps the best example of this technique in his two-part essay "Film and System: Terms of Analysis" (1975), in which he marries Metz's idea of "the large syntagmatic category" (defined in *Film Language* as "the organization of the major actual relationships among units of relation in a given semiological system") with an examination of the film's psychological impact on the subject. Film, he argues, begins with the psychoanalytic construction of the subject, and proceeds to the replacement of that construction by a system of signifiers; the critic must therefore blend psychoanalysis and semiotics.

Heath's involvement with *Screen* continued throughout the 1970s, and some of his articles from the journal, together with other writings on film, were collected in the book *Questions of Cinema* in 1981. It was around this time that he embarked on a somewhat different project, resulting in *The Sexual Fix*. Heath's own claims for the book were restrained – "a small contribution to sexual politics, that's all" – but, despite its often almost flippant tone, it provides a searching analysis of the contemporary sexual "democracy." Heath encapsulates his main argument thus:

> sexuality is without the importance ascribed to it in our contemporary society (Western capitalist); it is without that importance because it does not exist as such, because there is no such thing as sexuality; what we have experienced and are experiencing is the

> fabrication of "sexuality", the construction of something called "sexuality" through a set of representations – images, discourses, ways of picturing and describing – that propose and confirm, that make up this sexuality to which we are then referred and held in our lives, a whole *sexual fix* precisely.

For Heath, the two cultural poles of sexuality are "the nineteenth century," with its tendency toward the repression of sexual freedom, and the overblown psychobabble (principally, but not exclusively, American) of modern sexology. Both of these stances contribute to contrary but equally powerful sexual myths that stigmatize those they exclude. Although the bulk of the work is not really literary criticism, it does turn its attention toward certain writers – for instance, D. H. Lawrence – and demonstrates how they reinforce stereotypical sexual roles and entrench sexual differences. More importantly, Heath mounts a defense of writing even as he condemns its contribution to "the sexual fix." For if it has, along with other modern phenomena such as psychoanalysis, "generalized the pornographic," it has also revealed an awareness of how it does so, and thereby provided the opportunity for self-criticism.

The Sexual Fix displays the range over which Heath's critical work extends. In the 1980s and 1990s his critical concerns remained determinedly modern, encompassing gender and mass media studies. Heath had opened "A Conversation with Roland Barthes" in *Signs of the Times* by commenting on the Frenchman's flexibility and diversity of output: "You have talked of a certain distance which now separates you from your early works, and indeed you have stated that the writer 'must look upon his former texts as other texts, to be taken up again by him, cited or deformed just as he would a multitude of other signs.'"

Although Heath's own critical output does not partake of this dialectic quality to quite the same degree as Barthes' œuvre, there is nevertheless a deliberate expansiveness and unpredictability to his work that owes something to the desire to avoid what Barthes terms *doxa*, or orthodoxy. The influence of Barthes provides a firm backbone to his work, and though Heath is perhaps best known for his pioneering work in the early 1970s, the frequency with which that work is reprinted shows the currency and importance of his ideas today.

Principal criticism

"Roland Barthes and Semiology," in *Cambridge Opinion/Circuit* special publication entitled *Language*, 1969, pp. 9–12
"The Structuralist Adventure," in *Cambridge Review*. May, 1970, pp. 183–189
"Ambiviolences: Notes pour la lecture de Joyce," in *Tel Quel*. Part 1 in no. 50 (Summer, 1972), pp. 22–43; Part 2 in no. 51 (Autumn, 1972), pp. 64–76. English translation in *Post-structuralist Joyce*, 1984 (Derek Attridge and Daniel Ferrer, editors)
The Nouveau Roman: A Study in the Practice of Writing, 1972
"The Work of Christian Metz," in *Screen*. 14, no. 3 (Autumn, 1973), pp. 5–28
Vertige du déplacement. Lecture de Barthes, 1974
"Film and System: Terms of Analysis," in *Screen*. 16, nos. 1 and 2 (Spring and Summer, 1975). Sections reprinted in *Touch of Evil*, 1984 (Terry Comito, editor)
Questions of Cinema, 1981
Madame Bovary, 1992

Other major works and literary forms

TRANSLATIONS
"The Semiotic Activity," by Julia Kristeva, in *Screen*. 14, nos. 1 and 2 (Spring and Summer, 1973)
"Joyce & Co," by Philippe Sollers, in *Tel Quel*. 64 (Winter, 1975)
Roland Barthes – Image, Music, Text: Essays Selected and Translated, 1977

EDITED TEXTS
Signs of the Times: Introductory Readings in Textual Semiotics, 1971 (with Colin MacCabe and Christopher Prendergast)
The Cinematic Apparatus, 1980 (with Teresa de Lauretis)
Cinema and Language, 1983 (with Patricia Mellencamp)

MISCELLANEOUS
The Sexual Fix, 1982

Further reading

Culler, Jonathan. *Structuralist Poetics: Structuralism, Linguistics and the Study of Literature*, 1975.
Tredell, Nicolas. "Stephen Heath in Conversation," in *PN Review*. 18, no. 3 (January/February, 1992). Reprinted in *Conversations with Critics*, 1994 (Nicolas Tredell, editor).

ROWLAND HUGHES

See also Bradbury; British Literary Theory: Twentieth Century; Lodge; Ricks

Georg Wilhelm Friedrich Hegel

German philosopher

Born: Stuttgart, Württemberg, Germany; August 27, 1770
Died: Berlin, Prussia; November 14, 1831

Biography

Georg Wilhelm Friedrich Hegel was born in Stuttgart, Württemburg, on August 27, 1770. His father was a civil servant. During his early school years the young Hegel became fascinated with the religion and literature of ancient Greece. In 1788 he enrolled as a student in the famous Protestant theological foundation at the University of Túbingen, where he became close friends with the later Romantic philosopher Friedrich Schelling and the poet Friedrich Hölderlin, with whom he engaged in heated political debates over the French Revolution. He graduated in 1793. In 1801 he obtained a teaching position at the University of Jena. He also taught in the cities of Nuremberg and Heidelberg, and in 1818 he accepted a professorship at the University of Berlin, where he lectured extensively until his death, during a cholera epidemic, in 1831. During the later part of his life, he was considered Germany's premier philosopher and intellectual.

Influence

Hegel's influence on subsequent thinkers and writers was pervasive. It was particularly important for those of the nineteenth century who maintained a leftist or revolutionary orientation toward society and its institutions, thinkers such as David Friedrich Strauss, the author of a celebrated early-nineteenth-century critical study of Christianity, and Karl Marx, whose concept of dialectical materialism (and its corollary aesthetic views) owes much to the thought of Hegel. The plays of Friedrich Hebbel are also deeply indebted to Hegel's aesthetics, as is the thought of the late-nineteenth-century philosopher and aesthetician Wilhelm Dilthey. The work of such major modern Italian aesthetic philosophers as Benedetto Croce and Giovanni Gentile also reflects the influence of Hegel. The well-known Hungarian Marxist critic Georg Lukács was a devout Hegelian in his youth. The philosopher Herbert Marcuse wrote an important volume on Hegel and modern social theory. Modern French thinkers such as Jacques Derrida and Jean Lyotard have also written on Hegelian concepts.

Analysis

Because Hegel's aesthetics is an integral part of his overall intellectual system, it is necessary to comment on the philosophical context in which his ideas on art and literary criticism are to be found. As a post-Kantian Idealist thinker, Hegel sees all being as divided into the finite and transitory, or sensuous (comparable but not identical to the Kantian notion of the phenomenal), which he termed Nature, and the absolute and infinite, or eternal (comparable but also not identical to the Kantian notion of the noumenal), which he termed *Geist*, or Spirit – the One that unites the Many (or what those who are religiously inclined might call God). This infinite force is quintessentially rational and is also termed the logical, or the Absolute Idea. Hence, Hegel's philosophy is often designated Logical Idealism. The Absolute Idea as Spirit realizes itself through the multitudinous phenomena of being: hence, Hegel's major work is called *The Phenomenology of Spirit*, that is, a study of the various manifestations of the Absolute.

The end point or goal of the universe is for the ultimate and absolute realization of Spirit, its self-consciousness, in Nature, specifically through humankind and the human capacity for reflection and contemplation. The rational discipline of philosophy is the highest human activity for Hegel because here the Absolute becomes self-knowledge. Religion is the second highest activity because faith, although illogical and irrational, also presents a vision of the Absolute as God. Art is the third highest activity, since it presents the Absolute not through logic or faith but through the senses in the form of Beauty. This progressive manifestation of Spirit through phenomena makes up the dynamic course of history.

For Hegel, this process of self-realization is a dialectical one, thesis generating its antithesis and the two merging into a higher synthesis. The process involves the *Aufhebung*, or simultaneous cancellation/negation of thesis and antithesis and their preservation/sublimation as synthesis. This synthesis in turn will constitute a new thesis. The development continues until the end of history, when the Idea is fully realized and Nature and Spirit are one. Hegel's view of history is a progressive one in which each stage leads to a higher level of being.

The historical development of religious faith or the irrational vision of the Absolute, for example, illustrates this progress of the Spirit. Religion first made its appearance in human civilization as polytheism (thesis) in the worship of a multitude of spirits thought to be the cause of natural phenomena. This was the source of early Greek religions with their numerous gods. Eventually, a belief in a single deity, monotheism (antithesis), developed among the Hebrews and then through the early Christians and the later institution of Christianity and the Church (synthesis). The vision of the Absolute thus evolved from one of faith in a multiplicity to faith in a unity. Yet religion, being illogical, was not a perfected form for the self-realization of the Idea. During the Renaissance, faith (thesis) came to confront another, more logical vision of the Absolute in science (antithesis), which explained natural events through rational means. Philosophy (synthesis), through logical argument and proof, comes to subsume even the theories of science and thus places them within a broader context or vision of the Ideal. That is the endpoint at which Hegel believed his philosophical thought had arrived. The Spirit had reached a state of self-reflection through his own philosophy.

All Nature, including human society and its institutions (its legal, religious, political, cultural, or educational systems, for example), is a sensuous manifestation of Spirit. Art presents the Idea as Beauty, a vision of physical perfection and harmony, to the senses. It allows the Absolute to appear (*scheinen*) in a concrete or tangible form and as such instructs or uplifts human consciousness. The perfect work of art represents the harmonious union of subjectivity and objectivity, Spirit and Matter, in the physical manifestation of Beauty.

Hegel goes on to distinguish among three types or modes of aesthetic creation: symbolic art, classical art, and romantic art. Symbolic art occurs when the sensuous or material elements predominate. The spiritual content of the work is not as apparent as it should be, and this type of creation is perceived as mysterious and ambiguous. The art of ancient Egypt is cited as a major example, and architecture is its most obvious expression. Classical art, on the other hand, is found when the spiritual content is clearly present and expressed in sensuous or concrete form, namely that of the human figure. Greek art, especially sculpture, is given as an example of this kind of creation, a perfect union of Spirit and Matter. Romantic art occurs when the spiritual is perceived as dominant and infinite and therefore tends to overcome or transcend its sensuous or finite representation. This is a dynamic art form which reflects the movement or activity of the Spirit and is found in painting, music, and poetry. Hegel's preference is for classical art, because it presents the most harmonious vision of the Absolute.

The more evolved and refined the societal institution is, the more it presents with clarity the achieved stage of the Spirit's self-realization. As stated, philosophy and religion are the most developed forms in Hegel's view. The institution of art, because it operates through the senses, which are a less reliable source of knowledge, is a lesser means through which a society, and ultimately the Spirit, contemplates itself. Therefore, art maintains an important, if less privileged, position as a mode of reflection upon the Spirit. Literary criticism, because it involves philosophical reflection about the meaning of aesthetic creation, also represents a significant genre.

The most famous example of Hegel's literary criticism – the application of his view of art – is to be found in his *The Phenomenology of Spirit*. Here he presents an extended interpretation of the Greek tragedian Sophocles' *Antigonē* (441 B.C.; *Antigone*). Hegel considers the play to be an excellent illustration of the way in which art depicts the progression of the Spirit through history. Greek art in general represents for him the highest development of Beauty because its themes were so firmly rooted in their religious world-view. Subsequent periods of art have become divorced (as distinct secular institutions) from the totality of such a view and are thus less revealing of the Absolute.

The plot of the Sophocles play involves the conflict between Antigone, daughter of the banished Oedipus, and Kreon, Oedipus' brother-in-law and present King of Thebes. Polyneices, the elder son of Oedipus, had raised an army against his native city-state and was killed in battle before the city walls by Eteocles, Oedipus' other son, still pledged to Thebes, who also perished. When Antigone sought for her brother Polyneices a proper ritual burial, Kreon forbade it, since the son had been a traitor to his homeland. Anyone who touched his body would also be considered a traitor to the state and would be executed. Antigone, who is secretly in love with Kreon's son Haimon, disobeys the king's orders and is sentenced to death. In his stubborn pride, Kreon refuses to take back his sentence. Antigone hangs herself, and in bitterness against his father, Haimon also kills himself. Kreon, inwardly desolate, is left behind to survey the ruins of his world.

For Hegel, the play presents a crucial point in the Spirit's dialectical evolution through history, a moment when thesis and antithesis are in clear conflict. The position of Antigone represents the demands of the centuries-old pagan religion: that the dead must receive proper ritual burial so that their souls may gain entrance to the underworld (thesis). This is a pious though antiquated point of view based upon irrational custom and superstition. Kreon, as King of Thebes, stands for the demands of the newly emerging political state: that the authority of the leader must be obeyed under all circumstances, especially those during wartime (antithesis). This is a position based upon the logical and rational structure of the political state. Two very different and opposed views of the world stand here in sharp contrast.

The play, as a drama which is based upon action and conflict, depicts the dynamic movement of the Spirit and hence does not reveal the ultimate synthesis of the characters' viewpoints. The evolution of the Absolute as synthesis here would presumably be the transformation of religious faith into political loyalty to a rational and benevolent nation-state and its representative ruler. Antigone and Kreon are world-historical individuals in that their human dilemma objectifies the movement of the Spirit and their unavoidable but necessary sacrifice serves the progress of history.

The overall idea of Hegel's aesthetics – that art depicts the essential elements or the world-view (*Weltanschauung*) of a civilization and its culture – has been the most influential aspect of his writings on subsequent thinkers. Marxist aesthetics, for example, derives from a Hegelian foundation, namely, the idea that art reveals in symbolic form the fundamental class and economic conflicts which propel the movement of history.

Principal criticism

Phänomenologie des Geistes, 1807 (*The Phenomenology of Spirit*, 1872, also known as *The Phenomenology of Mind*, 1910)

Vorlesungen über die Aesthetik, 1835–1838 (*Lectures on Fine Art*, 1886, also known as *The Philosophy of Fine Art*, 1920)

Other major works and literary forms

Georg Wilhelm Friedrich Hegel was a systematic philosopher whose writings and transcribed lectures covered the various traditional subfields of the discipline: ontology, logic, epistemology, and aesthetics. He also wrote several treatises on religion. Hegel did not write in any other genres.

NONFICTION

Wissenschaft der Logik, 1812–1816 (*Science of Logic*, 1929)

Encyclopädie der philosophischen Wissenschaften im Grundrisse, 1817, includes *Die Logik* (*The Logic of Hegel*, 1874), *Naturphilosophie* (*Philosophy of Nature*, 1970), and *Die Philosophie des Geistes* (*Philosophy of Mind*, 1894)

Grundlinien der Philosophie des Rechts, 1821 (*Philosophy of Right*, 1875)

Further reading

Beiser, Frederick C., ed. *The Cambridge Companion to Hegel*, 1993.

Copleston, Frederick C. "Hegel," in *A History of Philosophy*. Vol. 7, 1965.

Kainz, Howard P. *An Introduction to Hegel: The Stages of Modern Philosophy*, 1996.
Kaminsky, Jack. *Hegel on Art: An Interpretation of Hegel's Aesthetics*, 1962.
Karelis, Charles. *Hegel's Introduction to Aesthetics*, 1979.
Knox, Israel. *The Aesthetic Theories of Kant, Hegel, and Schopenhauer*, 1936.
Mills, Patricia Jagentowicz, ed. *Feminist Interpretations of G. W. F. Hegel*, 1996.
Scruton, Roger, ed. *German Philosophers: Kant, Hegel, Schopenhauer, Nietzsche*, 1997.
Singer, Peter. *Hegel*, 1983.
Solomon, Robert C. *From Hegel to Existentialism*, 1987.
Spencer, Lloyd, et al. *Introducing Hegel*, 1996.
Stewart, John, ed. *The Hegel Myths and Legends*, 1996.
Taylor, Charles. *Hegel*, 1975.
Wellek, René. "Hegel," in *A History of Modern Criticism: 1750–1950*. Vol. 2, *The Romantic Age*, 1955.

THOMAS F. BARRY

See also Croce; Kant; Lukács; Romanticism; Schelling

Martin Heidegger

German philosopher

Born: Messkirch, Baden, Germany; September 26, 1889
Died: Freiburg im Breisgau, West Germany; May 26, 1976

Biography

Martin Heidegger was born in the small southwestern German town of Messkirch on September 26, 1889. His father, Friedrich Heidegger, was a local barrel maker and a Catholic sexton. His mother was Johanna Kempf. Young Martin's parents sent him to the Gymnasium in Konstanz from 1903 to 1906, then to another college preparatory school in Freiburg im Breisgau from 1906 to 1909. Heidegger was a religiously motivated youth who at one time joined the Jesuits as a novice. One of his formative influences was the "descriptive psychology" of the Catholic philosopher Franz Brentano. Heidegger enrolled as a student of Catholic theology at the University of Freiburg in 1909. However, he changed to philosophy in 1911, in large measure due to the influence of the writings of Edmund Husserl, a pupil of Brentano's who would himself later accept a position at Freiburg. Heidegger received his doctorate in 1913 and was promoted to full professor in 1915, but World War I led to his conscription in 1915 and he served three years in the army.

Heidegger married Elfride Petri in 1917. She bore him two sons, Jörg in 1919 and Hermann in 1920. In the year following the birth of Hermann, the family began construction of a cottage in the Black Forest, at Todtnauberg, where Heidegger was able to concentrate almost solely on thinking and writing. He spent part of every year there in the remote woods. In 1923 he accepted a position at the University of Marburg, but returned to Freiburg five years later to accept Husserl's position upon the latter's retirement. While in Marburg he and the influential Protestant theologian Rudolf Bultmann became friends.

Heidegger became rector of the University of Freiburg in May of 1933 under the auspices of the National Socialists. He was elected unanimously by the faculty after the previous rector resigned in protest when a Jewish professor was pressured by the Nazis to quit. Heidegger in turn left office less than a year later, having allied himself with the wing of the party that lost influence after the "Night of the Long Knives" in 1934, when Adolf Hitler had many leading Nazis assassinated. He seems to have remained a supporter of the Nazi cause, renewing his party membership annually and proudly sporting a swastika lapel pin. Though he criticized "Hitlerism" after the war, even in his last interview before his death he declined to gratify those who had hoped he would one day speak out against Fascist ideology.

After the war Heidegger was prohibited from teaching by the French occupation authorities because of his association with the Nazi movement. He returned to the classroom in 1951, and retired a year later, but his tireless lecturing and writing continued for another twenty years. Heidegger died on May 26, 1976, and was buried in his hometown of Messkirch.

Influence

Heidegger's thought, like that of the Danish theologian Søren Kierkegaard (1813–1855) before him, represents a rejection of the highly (self-)reflective philosophizing in the tradition of Immanuel Kant and the German Idealists, and a return to the fundamental questions of human existence. What does it mean to be human, alive in this world? What does it mean to "be"? Kierkegaard and Heidegger are both often seen as forerunners of the school that would come to be called *Existenzphilosophie* in German-speaking Europe, and existentialism elsewhere. Heidegger's writings had a tremendous impact in France, where his ideas influenced Jean-Paul Sartre, Albert Camus, and others in the 1940s and 1950s. French existentialism, with its Heideggerian contention that we *create* the meaning of our lives through our acts in the world, had a tremendous influence in Western intellectual circles, especially on novelists, philosophers, and theologians. Another wave of influence was felt in France in the 1970s and 1980s with the rise of deconstructionism (Heidegger had early on called for the "destruction of metaphysics"). This movement gained a large following on university campuses, primarily in the United States. However, Heidegger was otherwise slow to attract a following in the English-speaking world, as evinced by the fact that his magnum opus *Sein und Zeit*, first published in 1927, did not appear in the form of a complete English translation ("Being and Time") until 1962.

Hans-Georg Gadamer is the best-known proponent of Heidegger's line of thought in German philosophy. Gadamer's writings explore the nature of being and the understanding of being as "dialogue"; all meaning can be described as dialogic at base. The other major philosopher of postwar Germany, Jürgen Habermas, stands in strict opposition to the Heideggerian rejection of Kantian rationality. Aside from Heidegger's influence, via deconstructionism, on literary theory in the English-speaking world in the last quarter of the twentieth century, the American philosopher Richard Rorty is the most important respondent to Heidegger's impact.

In the light of Heidegger's controversial comparison of mechanized agriculture to the holocaust, it is ironic that one of his most influential (and loyal) students was the German Jew Hannah Arendt, who wrote several of the standard works on the lessons of the Nazi concentration camps, including a study of the Adolf Eichmann trial in Jerusalem, a book with the telling subtitle *A Report on the Banality of Evil* (1963). Regardless of the problem posed by Heidegger's silence on the salient and pressing question of the moral status of the Nazi past for himself and for German and Austrian history (that is, in light of his existentialist assertions about authenticity and truth), Heidegger's works continue to be read and reread for their striking philosophical originality, literary sensitivity, and evocative power. His ideas have found application in psychology, hermeneutics, pedagogy, theology, literary criticism, and even jurisprudence. Next to Ludwig Wittgenstein (1889–1951) he is by many accounts the most important German-speaking philosopher of the twentieth century.

Analysis

In what is generally conceded to be his most important work, *Sein und Zeit*, Heidegger sets out to accomplish the destruction of traditional ontology, that is, to peel back all the layers of previous reasoning that obscure the truth about the nature of being and our presence in the world. He seeks his answers in phenomenology, the study of human consciousness and its awareness of objects, not in psychology.

The deepest ontological meaning of being is *Zeitlichkeit*, temporality. The knowledge of death endows life with creative urgency and admits the possibility of authenticity (*Eigentlichkeit*); it does not empty life of meaning or render it absurd. *Dasein* (individual being) does not in and of itself escape inauthenticity, but is "being ahead of itself," and as such distinctly human. The Greek word *aletheia* is a key concept in *Sein und Zeit*, and refers (according to Heidegger) to what he calls *Unverborgenheit*, "non-hiddenness." To us as human beings, the temporal, historical features of life and the world, specifically transience, are openly revealed. But how are we to shape our lives in light of this knowledge? Anxiety (*Angst*) is a natural feature of our condition, but its counterpart is conscious freedom to act authentically in the world. Technology is alien to this authenticity; in fact, it contributes to alienation (*Entfremdung*). Heidegger's *Sein und Zeit* is a lengthy, step-by-step explication of the possibilities and limitations of being.

The intellectual project Heidegger labored on throughout his career was predicated on the search for a new way of speaking about philosophy. He often employs the German language in an emphatically final way, as if its shades of meaning and etymological associations, when examined in depth, held in themselves the key to ultimate answers. And while he cannot be accused of failing to define his terms, his diction is tightly bound to distinctively German present and past participles, compound nouns formed from various Teutonic roots, and adjectives used as abstract nouns. Heidegger emphasizes not only word roots (in both Greek and German, sometimes Latin), but in some cases even prefixes, set off by hyphens to demonstrate new semantic possibilities. Direct correspondences are rare or awkward in English. Thus, translators are often hard-pressed to reflect, through their own native languages, Heidegger's German usage in a meaningful, unstilted way. And occasionally liberties have been taken that have led to outright misrepresentations or have allowed non-German-speaking scholars to make false assumptions that have been in turn perpetuated. Even some of the titles of Heidegger's works have been imprecisely translated, as in the case of *Was heisst Denken?* (1954), which has gone into the literature as the unnatural sounding "What is Called Thinking?" (1968). In the original, Heidegger's language may be idiosyncratic (there have been many parodies), but it is absolutely clear that academic philosophy is being conducted in a new and forcefully questioning way.

Heidegger placed philosophy and poetry very close to one another in origins, and he considered literary and other artistic subjects within his provenance as a thinker. Indeed, even with his intentional dismantling of the edifice of Western metaphysics, or more precisely, because of it, he was often occupied with textual questions, especially in ancient Greek. His philosophical methodology in large part has much in common with hermeneutics, the science of textual interpretation. Ever present in Heidegger's approach is the consciousness of a certain circularity: the one who asks the questions is also the one who answers them. Still, Heidegger's avoidance of traditional philosophical terminology makes his thinking highly referential, in that he turns to the immediately accessible natural world for his analogies and examples. This use of nature as a source of a new vocabulary is often seen as part of Heidegger's "romanticism" (along with his backward-looking disdain for technology), but it gives many readers the sense they are walking on solid ground in the company of a great thinker, pursuing answers independently of disputes among familiar philosophical schools.

In postulating memory as the wellspring for poetry, for instance, he uses the concrete metaphor of water to describe the poetic process. Water in time flows back down into its source, the groundwater, "remembering" its way (and leaving its mark); similarly the act of poetic creation is predicated on a journey back to its own source, memory. By the same token, this act is like the process of thinking itself, which begins with the search for the object of thought, ever drawn toward the receding "that which is to be thought."

Heidegger does not pretend to solve, but to expose and describe the puzzling elusiveness of the meaning of thinking, and more specifically, poetic thinking. In the end, the truth reached by thinking is, however, different from that arrived at by poetic thinking. Poetic thinking manifests itself in beauty – not necessarily in "pleasing" beauty, but in that "destiny of the essence of truth" which is met when the eternally imperceptible merges with the immediately perceptible. In water we encounter a symbolically rich metaphor pointing to the centrality of time in Heidegger's attempt to understand phenomena, as water is in constant motion over time. The apparent paradox at the heart of poetry – the union of the eternally imperceptible and the immediately perceptible in poetic expression – is best expressed for Heidegger in the words of an obscure fragment of German poetry on memory, "Ein Zeichen sind wir, deutungslos . . ." ("A sign are we, indecipherable . . .").

Heidegger first turned his attention to aesthetics in general in 1935 with "Der Ursprung des Kunstwerks" ("The Origin of the Work of Art," 1964). Here he is not concerned with the act of poetic thinking, but with the ontology of the work of art. In contrast to "thingness" of utilitarian technology, the truth of art's "being" as human endeavor is bound up with its emergence out of the earth, in Greek, its *physis* ("The work [of art] lets the earth be the earth"). For Heidegger, the salient characteristic of all art is its "opening up" (*Eröffnung*), its coming to light out of "hiddenness" (*Verborgenheit*). Poetry or, in German, *Dichtung* – literary art in all its forms – is regarded by Heidegger as the most primal, original expression of being. Some of Heidegger's best-known literary criticism concerns the works of the poet whose "obscure" fragment is mentioned above, Friedrich Hölderlin (1770–1843). In the poetry of Hölderlin, Heidegger finds, as with the ancient Greeks, the essential tension of aesthetics, between the world that "is" (*Welt*) and the *physis*, or earth, in which art has its origins. In Heidegger's "anti-metaphysical" aesthetic theory, works of art, generally speaking, do not so much point to ideas or themes, or make statements, as exist after their own fashion as art. They uncover or reveal the hidden "doing" that something does, such as the sky's "sky-ish doing," or, to use Heidegger's example, a river's "river-ish doing."

Related to this aesthetic effect of uncovering is the mood that is evoked by a poem (or any work of art). The special nature of a poem's mode of existing is manifested temporally in the basic mood awakened by the artist – in the case of the poet Hölderlin, the mood is often one of "holy, mournful, compliant tribulation." Hölderlin also delivers the kind of imagery that lends itself well to Heidegger's explication through references to the meaning of natural phenomena – Hölderlin's poems on rivers (*Ströme*) offered especially rich ground for Heidegger's method. Time, like the river, is always "here," but that "here" is in constant movement. From afar the river appears static within in its banks, but its water is always passing, disappearing both into our past and its own future, the sea from whence it came. Again, Heidegger leaves the reader with a circularity which is frustrating for some, liberating for others in the apparent truthfulness of its insight.

In an epistolary exchange with the literary theorist Emil Staiger, Heidegger states what is perhaps the essence of his ontological aesthetics, revealing at the same time his debt to the early-nineteenth-century philosopher G. W. F. Hegel. Heidegger's comments concern a poem by Eduard Mörike (1804–1875), in which the poet elegiacally describes an old lamp hanging from the ceiling in a room no longer lived in. In interpreting the final line of the poem, Heidegger draws at length on the Hegelian notion of the Ideal, according to which the work of art (in this case, both the Mörike poem and the lamp to which it refers) exists as an entity, the outward form and the inner being of which are merged into a unity that is entirely the object's own. Again, the Heideggerian viewpoint presumes a rejection of traditional metaphysics; the lamp (and indeed the poem) does not point or refer to something else, either symbolically, thematically, or allegorically, but reveals itself as its essential self in its own external form. While the argument between Heidegger and Staiger centers around the ambiguity of the verb *scheinen* in German, an ambiguity that cannot be resolved by "proving" what Mörike meant from external sources such as diaries, notes, or interviews with contemporaries, but by exploring hermeneutically the use and function of the work within the poem itself. Important is understanding what is said in a poem, but Heidegger also recognizes the significance of what is left unsaid. (One may of course disagree, and many critics do, with his characterization of that which is left unsaid by a given poem.) For Heidegger, the richest meaning derived from reading arises in an interplay of the said and the unsaid, the revealed and the hidden.

Whether analyzing the works of Sophocles and other ancient Greeks, or his beloved Hölderlin, or a more modern poet like Georg Trakl, Heidegger stays close to the text, and his criticism consists largely in determining just what the poet can be said, in existential terms, to have revealed, or, conversely, to have left unexpressed.

Principle criticism

"Der Ursprung des Kunstwerks," 1935 ("The Origin of the Work of Art," 1964)

"Der Wille zur Macht als Kunst," 1936 ("The Will to Power as Art," 1979)

Erlauterungen zu Hölderlins Dichtung, 1944 (includes the 1936 article "Hölderlin und das Wesen der Dichtung," translated as "Hölderlin and the Essence of Poetry" in *Existence and Being*, 1949; William Brock, editor)
"Aus der Erfahrung des Denkens," 1947 ("The Thinker as Poet," 1971)
"Zu einem Vers von Mörike," 1951
"Bauen Wohnen Denken," 1951 ("Building Dwelling Thinking," 1971)
Unterwegs zur Sprache, 1959 (*On the Way to Language*, 1971)
Nietzsche, Vols. 1 and 2, 1961; *Nietzsche: der Wille zur Macht als Kunst*, 1985 (translated as Vol. 3, 1987)
"Hölderlins Hymne 'Der Ister,'" 1981 ("Hölderlin's Hymn 'The Ister,'" 1996)
Heidegger's seminal essays on literary subjects, including some of those above, can be found in Albert Hofstadter's edition *Poetry, Language, Thought* (1971).

Other major works and literary forms

Many of Martin Heidegger's essays began as classroom or occasional lectures. Heidegger was also known as a great correspondent, and there are several collections of his letters (to and from the novelist Erich Kästner, the philosopher Karl Jaspers, and others). Among Heidegger's major philosophical writings, the following are frequently cited: *Sein und Zeit*, 1927 (*Being and Time*, 1962), *Hegels Phänomenologie des Geistes*, 1930 (*Hegel's Phenomenology of the Spirit*, 1988), *Einführung in die Metaphysik*, 1953 (*An Introduction to Metaphysics*, 1959), *Was heisst Denken?*, 1954 (*What is Called Thinking?*, 1968), and *Zur Seinsfrage*, 1956 (*The Question of Being*, 1958).

Further reading

Ettinger, Elzbieta. *Hannah Arendt/Martin Heidegger*, 1995.
Guignon, Charles, ed. *The Cambridge Companion to Heidegger*, 1993.
Hallburton, David. *Poetic Thinking: An Approach to Heidegger*, 1981.
Kockelmans, Josef. *On Heidegger and Language*, 1972 (3 volumes).
McNeill, William, and Julia Davis. *Hölderlin's Hymn "The Ister,"* 1996.
Sluga, Hans. *Heidegger's Crisis: Philosophy and Politics in Nazi Germany*, 1993.

MARK R. MCCULLOH

See also Gadamer; Hermeneutics; Nietzsche; Phenomenological Criticism

Heinrich Heine

German poet and writer

Born: Düsseldorf, Germany; December 13, 1797
Died: Paris, France; February 17, 1856

Biography

Born into a Jewish family as Chaim Harry Heine, Heine adopted the name Heinrich when he converted to Christianity in 1825. His youth was marked above all by the French presence in his hometown of Düsseldorf; Napoleon Bonaparte's entry into Düsseldorf in 1811 left an indelible impression on the boy. While studying law in Bonn, Berlin, and Göttingen, Heine began publishing poetry in the Romantic style. Unable to secure a profession in the later 1820s, he turned to writing prose works critical of the political situation in Germany.

Attracted by the July Revolution in France and under increasing political pressure in Germany, Heine went to Paris in 1831, where he was to remain in exile. During the 1830s Heine was occupied with journalistic writings; he saw his role as that of intermediary between French and German culture and thought. In 1835 Prussia issued a ban against the writings of the so-called Young Germans, including Heine, intensifying his lifelong battle with the censors. The 1840s mark the period of Heine's most radical writings and his brief association with Karl Marx.

Heine, who suffered most of his adult life from a disease of the spinal cord, collapsed physically in 1848, spending the remaining eight years of his life in the "mattress grave." Some of his best poetry stems from this period, which also saw a waning of his revolutionary hopes and a resurgence of his Jewish faith. Heine died on February 17, 1856, and was buried in Paris' Montmartre Cemetery.

Influence

Heine's reception in Germany has been controversial. Conservative critics tend to minimize the influence of his literary theory, claiming that he left no cohesive body of thought, only fragmentary, subjective reactions to a variety of literary events. Leftist critics, on the other hand, have seen Heine as one of the founders of neo-Marxist criticism and a precursor to such later theorists as Theodor Adorno and Walter Benjamin. Liberals take the somewhat uncomfortable middle position of interpreting Heine as "modern" in his perception of literature in crisis and in his emphasis on sociopolitical realities; they point to his unmistakable influence on such figures as Bertolt Brecht, Kurt Tucholsky, and Wolf Biermann. There can be no doubt, however, that Heine marks a watershed in the history of literary theory in Germany, representing as he does the transition between the unified aesthetic theories of German classicism and idealism and the fragmented views of literature propagated since the middle of the nineteenth century.

Analysis

Strictly speaking, Heine was neither a literary critic nor a systematic literary theorist. It was not in his nature to distinguish carefully genres or prose forms in his writing. He assimilated a wealth of literary experience, primarily through avid reading but also through acquaintance with leading writers of the day. Heine did not leave a body of writings that can be neatly labeled literary criticism, so the listing below is approximate. These are works in which discussion of literary matters occupies a central but not necessarily exclusive place; conversely, in many other writings Heine touches on literature but does not give the subject primacy. For example, *Die Romantische Schule* (1820; *The Romantic School* 1876) not only represents Heine's major assessment of German classicism and Romanticism but also sheds light on political, philosophical, and religious questions; its sister work, *Zur Geschichte der Religion und Philosophie in Deutschland* (1835; *On the History of Religion and Philosophy in Germany*, 1876), though focusing on the intellectual history of Europe, includes significant commentary on Gotthold Ephraim Lessing and Johann Wolfgang von Goethe. The two works are complementary and were, in fact, first published together in France. In a similar manner, the two mock epics, *Deutschland. Ein Wintermärchen* (1844; *Germany: A Winter's Tale*, 1892) and *Atta Troll* (1847; English translation, 1876), take issue with the literary scene in Germany, although the former is generally considered a political work and the latter an aesthetic work. Even the lyric poetry contains numerous pronouncements which complement the theoretical commentary in prose.

Heine was one of the first writers to make a living as an independent poet, essayist, and journalist, which means that his writings were at times determined by market factors. The often-bitter correspondence with his Hamburg publisher, Julius Campe, testifies to Heine's persistent difficulties in maintaining his intellectual and artistic freedom while continuing to publish. Concomitantly, Heine well understood that the right blend of gossip, scandal, and provocation would sell books. Thus, from the early *Briefe aus Berlin* (1822; letters from Berlin) to the late collection of articles on Paris, *Lutetia* 1854; English translation, 1891–1905), commentary on contemporary authors and works, as well as insights into the momentous changes occurring in literature, are woven into the rich fabric of Heine's provocative observations on the state of modern life. Heine's literary theory must be gleaned from the sum of his writing and seen in the context of his wider concern with the emancipatory struggle on the social, political, and religious fronts.

The axis around which Heine's commentary on literature turns is the fundamental question of whether autonomous, enduring art is reconcilable with sociopolitical concerns. Repeatedly, Heine addressed the problem of the poet's relationship to reality, and for the first time in Germany his criticism applied the yardstick of liberal and democratic, even revolutionary, values to literature. In doing so, however, Heine suffered from nagging doubts about the acceptability of both the artist as soldier and the artwork as tendentious. This discrepancy lends Heine's criticism its distinctive paradoxical flavor and has been the focus of virtually all studies of Heine's aesthetics. In a famous passage in *The Romantic School*, Heine projects a vision of the writer as artist, tribune, and apostle, one who does not differentiate between science, art, and religion. This vision can be viewed as Heine's ideal for the future; neither in his own work nor in the writings of the Young Germans (to whom the epithet is attributed) was the goal fully realized.

The tension in Heine's literary criticism is related to the struggle with Romantic lyricism which occupied him on the creative level. As a student, he was heavily influenced by the Romantic theories of Novalis, Friedrich Schlegel, and, in particular, August Wilhelm Schlegel, who was for a time his mentor in poetic matters. If the early essay "Die Romantik" still defends Romanticism as the modern synthesis of expressive feeling and plasticity of form, subsequent commentary becomes increasingly critical of the Romantic movement, primarily as a result of what Heine saw as its fatal link to the Christian mysticism of the Middle Ages. *The Romantic School* represents Heine's scintillating, if self-willed, dismissal of Romanticism in favor of the Enlightenment tradition, which is linked, in his thinking, to the revolutionary spirit of Martin Luther's Reformation and has Gotthold Ephraim Lessing and the lesser-known Johann Heinrich Voss as its literary leaders. In this work, Heine discusses the major figures of the German Romantic movement, including Ludwig Tieck, E. T. A. Hoffmann, Clemens Brentano, and Ludwig Uhland.

For Heine, the positive antithesis to the spiritual elements of Romanticism is not, however, the Enlightenment but the healthy sensualism of pre-Christian antiquity; his reception of German Grecophilia played a central part in his aesthetic thinking. Though present from the beginning, this duality, Hellenism-Nazarenism, as Heine also called it, becomes dominant in the writings on Germany, and in *Ludwig Börne* (1840; English translation, 1881), after Heine had participated briefly in the Saint-Simonist movement in Paris.

It was in the figure of Goethe that Heine saw the Hellenic tradition incarnate, and in *The Romantic School*, he paints a glorified picture of Goethe as a modern Jupiter. Goethe's enduring literary masterpieces are consummate works of realistic art. Yet at the same time, Heine sees their beauty as sterile and condemns Goethe for propagating a school of literature indifferent to contemporary social and political issues. In this respect, he leans toward the other great German classicist, Friedrich Schiller, whose tragedies have greater relevance to the revolutionary struggle. In his vehement insistence that the independent "age of art" had ceased and was about to be replaced by literature espousing the cause of emancipation, Heine shares in aesthetic ideas put forward by the philosopher G. W. F. Hegel, whom Heine had known personally in Berlin.

Yet when faced with the actual writings of liberal and radical poets in the pre-1848 period, Heine's sense of artistic integrity once more asserts itself; he satirizes the bad verse and misguided nationalistic zeal of his revolutionary colleagues in *Atta Troll*, a work which he calls "the last/ Free forest song of Romanticism." When he adds that his song is "purposeless," "Yes, purposeless/ Like love, like life,/ Like the Creator with the Creation," Heine leaves himself open to the charge of espousing a view of art for art's sake. While the body of Heine's writing refutes such a theory, the insistence on aesthetic autonomy remains a counterbalance to Heine's call for engaged literature.

With *Germany: A Winter's Tale*, Heine comes closest to his ideal of a fusion of poetry and politics on a high aesthetic level. It is significant that in one scene the poet imagines that he is being shadowed by a lictor who immediately transforms the poetic word into the radical deed. The failure in Germany of the revolution of 1848, however, seemed to confirm Heine's skepticism about the poet's role as tribune. In the developing Communist movement, he recognized promise for the oppressed masses on the one hand and the demise of artistic autonomy on the other.

Heine's reception in the critical world has split along ideological lines and been affected by anti-Semitism. In the nineteenth century the rise of German nationalism brought with it an attempt to trivialize Heine's importance; reactionary critics branded him as a Jewish Francophile and ignored or belittled his literary theory. With the emergence, toward the end of the century, of Goethe as Germany's greatest literary figure, Heine came under increasing attack as his antipode. Positive voices, such as that of Friedrich Nietzsche and Thomas Mann, were drowned out by the criticism of such influential figures as Heinrich von Treitschke and Karl Kraus.

Neo-Marxist critics, such as Georg Lukács, have long championed Heine as the first antibourgeois literary critic, and after 1945 East Germany attempted to appropriate Heine as the spokesman for its socialist view of art. In the West, there has been an astonishingly broad range of reception, covering the political spectrum from left to right: Heine as champion of sociopolitical criticism to Heine as champion of aestheticism. The situation has prompted one keen observer of Heine's fortunes, Jeffrey L. Sammons, to conclude that the tendency in the West has been for critics to fashion him into what they want him to have been. Thus, Heine remains one of Germany's most fiercely debated literary figures.

Principal criticism

"Die Romantik," 1820
Briefe aus Berlin, 1822
"*Die deutsche Literatur* von Wolfgang Menzel," 1828
Die Bäder von Lucca, 1829 (*The Baths of Lucca*, 1855)
Die Romantische Schule, 1836 (*The Romantic School*, 1876)
"Einleitung zu *Don Quixote*," 1837
Über die französische Bühne, 1837 (*Concerning the French Stage*, 1891–1905)
Shakespeares Mädchen und Frauen, 1838 (*Shakespeare's Maidens and Ladies*, 1891)
Ludwig Börne: Eine Denkschrift von H. Heine, 1840 (*Ludwig Börne: Recollections of a Revolutionist*, 1881)
"Erläuterungen zu *Der Doktor Faust*," 1851 ("Commentary to *Doctor Faust*," 1891–1905)
Lutetia: Berichte über Politik, Kunst, und Volksleben, 1854 (*Lutetia: Reports on Politics, Art, and Popular Life*, 1891–1905)

Other major works and literary forms

Heinrich Heine produced work in a variety of literary forms. He is best known as a lyric poet, having published three major cycles of poems, including many short love poems, ballads, elegies, and romances. Numerous poems became popular when used as lyrics by composers such as Robert Schumann and Franz Schubert. Heine excelled at writing verse and also left two important longer mock epic poems. In prose he was less secure, experimenting with various fictional styles ranging from the novella to fictionalized biography. These works leave a fragmentary impression; indeed, he was unable to finish his only attempted novel.

Heine also produced a large body of journalistic and essayistic prose, largely newspaper articles, reports, and reviews, which he then collected and published in separate volumes. Heine revealed himself as an astute, critical observer of contemporary society and politics. One literary form in particular appealed to Heine's wide-ranging interests and versatility as a narrator: the travel sketch. He has left his mark on this protean genre, producing a number of works which are stylistic masterpieces. The same cannot be said of his verse tragedies, which are generally considered failures.

NOVEL
Der Rabbi von Bacherach, 1840 (*The Rabbi of Bacherach*, 1891)

SHORT FICTION
Aus den Memoiren des Herrn von Schnabelewopski, 1834 (*The Memoirs of Herr von Schnabelewopski*, 1876)

PLAYS
Tragödien, nebst einem lyrischen Intermezzo, 1823 (*Tragedies, Together with Lyric Intermezzo*, 1905)

POETRY
Gedichte, 1822 (*Poems*, 1937)
Tragödien, nebst einem lyrischen Intermezzo, 1823 (*Tragedies, Together with Lyric Intermezzo*, 1905)
Buch der Lieder, 1827 (*Book of Songs*, 1856)
Neue Gediehte, 1844 (8 volumes; *New Poems*, 1858)
Deutschland: Ein Wintermärchen, 1844 (*Germany: A Winter's Tale*, 1892)
Atta Troll. Ein Sommernachtstraum, 1847 (*Atta Troll. A Midsummer Night's Dream*, 1876)
Romanzero, 1851 (English translation, 1859)
Gedichte, 1851–1857 (4 volumes; *Poems*, 1937)
Letzte Gedichte und Gedanken, 1869 (*Last Poems and Thoughts*, 1937)
Atta Troll and Other Poems, 1876
Heinrich Heine: The Poems, 1937
The Complete Poems of Heinrich Heine, 1982 (Hal Draper, editor)

NONFICTION

Reisebilder, 1826–1831 (4 volumes; *Pictures of Travel*, 1855)
Zur Geschichte der neueren schönen Literatur in Deutschland, 1833 (*Letters Auxiliary to the History of Modern Polite Literature in Germany*, 1836)
Französische Zustände, 1833 (*French Affairs*, 1889)
Der Salon, 1834–1840 (4 volumes; *The Salon*, 1893)
Zur Geschichte der Religion und Philosophie in Deutschland, 1835 (*On the History of Religion and Philosophy in Germany*, 1876)
Vermischte Schriften, 1854 (3 volumes)
De l'Allemagne, 1855 (2 volumes)

MISCELLANEOUS

The Works of Heinrich Heine, 1891–1905 (12 volumes)
Heinrich Heine: Selected Works, 1973 (Helen M. Mustard, editor and translator)

Further reading

Brod, Max. *Heinrich Heine: The Artist in Revolt*, 1956.
Hofrichter, Laura. *Heinrich Heine*, 1963.
Holub, Robert C. *Heinrich Heine's Reception of German Grecophilia*, 1981.
Prawer, Siegbert. *Heine the Tragic Satirist. A Study of the Later Poetry, 1827–1856*, 1961.
Reeves, Nigel. *Heinrich Heine: Poetry and Politics*, 1974.
Sammons, Jeffrey L. *Heinrich Heine: The Elusive Poet*, 1969.
——. *Heinrich Heine: A Modern Biography*, 1979.
Spencer, Hanna. *Heinrich Heine*, 1982.

GEORGE F. PETERS

See also Goethe; Hegel; Lessing; Romanticism; Schlegel, F.

Johann Gottfried Herder

German writer

Born: Mohrungen, East Prussia; August 25, 1744
Died: Weimar, Germany; December 18, 1803

Biography

Johann Gottfried Herder was born on August 25, 1744, in the East Prussian town of Mohrungen to Gottfried Herder, a pietistic teacher and church warden, and his wife, Anna Elisabeth. Young Herder attended the local Latin school and received a strict and vigorous education. In 1760 he moved into the house of the vicar Trescho, who owned a large library from which Herder industriously read.

In 1762 Herder went to nearby Königsberg, the home of Immanuel Kant, and enrolled in the university, first for medicine and then for theology. He supported himself by tutoring and teaching at a boarding school. In Königsberg, Herder met the philosopher Johann Georg Hamann, whose ideas influenced Herder throughout his life.

In 1764 Herder was appointed to teach at the cathedral school in Riga, the capital of Latvia. Soon disenchanted, he left the town in the summer of 1769 for an extensive journey through France, including Paris, which he disliked. Still restless, Herder accepted an offer to accompany the prince-bishop of Oldenburg-Eutin's son on a three-year tour through Europe.

Herder and the prince first went to Darmstadt, where Herder met Karoline Flachsland, his future wife. Dismayed with his post, he decided to quit and proceeded to Strasbourg for a long overdue eye operation. There, he met the young Johann Wolfgang von Goethe in the fall of 1770 and thus began their lifelong, yet problematic, friendship.

In 1771 Herder became court preacher in Bückeburg, the capital of the small state Schaumburg-Lippe. He held this position until 1775, when, prompted by Goethe, Herder moved to Weimar and was appointed superintendent of church affairs. Although Herder's union with Goethe seemed promising, it was disrupted by the arrival of Friedrich Schiller in nearby Jena in 1789; the close collaboration between Goethe and Schiller excluded Herder.

Herder spent the last years of his life writing and preaching, often in isolation. He was to leave Germany only once more, for a one-year journey to Italy in 1788. He further isolated himself by opposing the celebrated philosophy of Kant. Herder died on December 18, 1803.

Influence

Herder's influence on German literary criticism between 1770 and 1810 is paramount. His early writings, especially his articles on William Shakespeare and Ossian, are generally considered the beginning of the literary movement of the *Sturm und Drang* (storm and stress). Herder rebelled against contemporary criticism, which, patterned after French criticism, favored copies of Greek tragedies as a literary paradigm. Herder stressed that each poet had his own genius and originality, rooted in the tradition of his own nation. Also, Herder strongly influenced Weimar classicism, mainly by his concept of humanity, expressed in his ten-volume work *Briefe zu Beförderung der Humanität* (1793–1797; *Letters for the Advancement of Humanity*, 1800).

The notion of the importance and specificity of each nation's cultural heritage is reflected in Herder's collection of *Volkslieder* (1778–1779; folk songs), which contains poems and tales from England, Germany, France, Denmark, and Spain, as well as translations of Estonian, Latvian, Old Norse, Indian, and Latin literature. In Herder's view, each nation makes its very own contribution to the development of humankind; hence, there are no superior or inferior nations, a principle that was adopted by the historicist school and that earned for Herder the title "gatekeeper of the nineteenth century." Although Herder is foremost remembered for his collaboration with Goethe, the intricacy of his literary theory has been explored by many scholars, and he is regarded as one of the early proponents of Romanticism and historicism.

Analysis

The beginning of Herder's career as a writer and critic is inherently contradictory. On the one hand, he was certainly a child of the intellectual mainstream of his time, the Enlightenment. On the other hand, he tried to overcome its restraints and narrow-minded adherence to reason. The Enlightenment gave birth to a school of critics – including Johann Christoph Gottsched and his disciples – which focused mainly on the didactic function of literature, where literature had to serve the goal of leading the reader to higher virtue through the use of his reason. According to these theorists, each poet has to strive for the ideal – first achieved by the Greeks of antiquity, and at Herder's time aimed for by French classicism – by adopting a set of rules formulated by Aristotle. Herder rejected all the main claims of rationalistic criticism: clarity of style, decorum, and imitation.

In following some of the arguments of Gotthold Ephraim Lessing, who had already sharply criticized Gottsched in the *Briefe, die neueste Litteratur betreffend* (1759–1760; letters concerning the newest literature), Herder rejected direct imitation of Greek art and literature. He conceived his first, anonymously published, works – from *Über die neuere deutsche Literatur* (1767; on recent German literature), which was actually a response to the "*Litteratur briefe*," to the *Kritische Wälder* (1769; critical forests) – as a critique as well as a further elaboration of the program of the Enlightenment. In these works, he surmises that a poet has to look to his own nation for his roots and that the literature of each nation grows organically: "Like a tree from its roots, the development and blooming of art must be deducted from its origin." Herder's interest in folk art originated with this idea; he considered folk art to be the expression of the native genius of a nation, a *Volk*: "Let us return to the oldest human nature, and everything will be found and put in order."

Herder's historical approach and his reevaluation of literary history focuses on "forgotten," or neglected, authors and on literary traditions outside the contemporary canon in order to vitalize hidden qualities in these works that could bear fruit for the epoch. Although each poet is part of a *Volk* and should always be aware of his heritage, it is mainly the critic's task to preserve and study this heritage. A true poet does not need a set of rules for his art, as was required by Gottsched; a poet's creation will be intuitive.

Two of Herder's main contributions to literary criticism are his article on Shakespeare, "Über Shakespeare," and his fictitious correspondence on James Macpherson's spurious "translations" of the works of the Gaelic warrior Ossian, both published in 1773 in the collection *Von deutscher Art und Kunst* (of German nature and art). This collection is considered by many to be the first utterance of the *Sturm und Drang* movement and its cult of the genius.

Shakespeare's tragedies and comedies had been denounced by French and German critics for their alleged lack of consistency and their crudeness, manifested in Shakespeare's obvious disregard of the three Aristotelian unities. The favored dramas of eighteenth-century German critics were the neoclassical French court plays of Jean Racine and Pierre Corneille. Herder – again, following in Lessing's footsteps – rejected the canonization of the French and stated that Germans should look to the English literature of the seventeenth century, epitomized in Shakespeare, since the German dramatic art arose, like the English form, from the medieval Passion and puppet plays and not from the Greek choir and dithyrambs.

For Herder, and for most critics that would follow him, Shakespeare represented the ideal of a pure poet who does not need to comply with any rules, since his genius always assured that he intuitively created great art. Shakespeare "speaks the language of all ages, all human beings, he is interpreter of nature in all its tongues." According to Herder, Shakespeare created his own world and explored the continents of the human soul; he did not imitate nature, he was himself nature.

Herder combined this image of Shakespeare as a lone genius, which was perpetuated in Germany up to the twentieth century, with his ideas of the essence of poetry, which were drawn to a large extent from Johann Georg Hamann's rhapsodic work *Aesthetica in Nuce* (1762). According to Hamann's antirationalistic thinking, nature and poetic language are one. A poem's utterances reflect nature by way of their symbolic means and point toward God. Thus, a poem is "the mother tongue of the human race," and the poet becomes a second creator.

By adopting Hamann's views, Herder stood in the middle of a dispute involving all critics of the eighteenth century: the question of the constituencies of poetry and its relation to the visual arts. Johann Joachim Winckelmann, in his highly influential study *Geschichte der Kunst des Alterthums* (1764; *History of Ancient Art*, 1849–1873), stated that Greek art in its "noble simplicity and quiet greatness" should be regarded as the highest ideal on which all modern art should be modeled. In his *Kritische Wälder* Herder analyzes Lessing's critique of Winckelmann in his famous study of the Hellenistic sculpture *Laokoon: Oder, Über Die Grenzen der Mahlerei und Poesie* (1766; *Laocoön: An Essay on the Limits of Painting and Poetry*, 1836). Lessing maintained that poetry functions as a succession of signs, whereas painting and sculpture work as a simultaneity of signs; therefore, the two are inherently different from each other.

In showing that Lessing was only partially correct, and by substantiating his own theory by referring to some of Winckelmann's arguments, Herder developed his own concept of the nature of poetry. Poetry, in its usage of language – which humankind from its very beginnings had used to create its myths and fables – touches directly on the soul and hence does not function as a mere succession of sounds but as pure, divine energy. Therefore, poetry is the privileged medium for artistic expression. In Herder's words, "the arts that deliver works" (such as painting or sculpture) "take effect in space, the arts that take effect in succession, . . . poetry, . . . function through energy." It is not easy to understand what Herder actually means by using the term "energy" (*Kraft*). René Wellek suggests that Herder meant an "organizing power, a coherence of imaginative ideas" that enables the poet, who is rooted in the symbolic reference system of his nation, to express images that can be interpreted by his readers as metaphors of divine nature.

Of Herder's contemporaries, the poet closest to this ideal was, in Herder's opinion, Friedrich Gottlieb Klopstock. Herder wrote in his *Journal meiner Reise im Jahre 1769* (1769; *Journal of My Travels in the Year 1769*, 1953) that he wished "to be given one spark of [Klopstock's] fire," and in *Über die neuere deutsche Literatur* he exclaims, "Maybe his great talent to depict the soul is of higher value than everything in the old Greek." With his definition of the poetic imagination, Herder left the realm of rationalistic literary criticism and opened the field for both Goethe's and the Romantics' concepts of poetry and nature.

The true expression of poetic symbols and metaphors, however, can be found not only in individual poets but also in the rich history of folk poetry. Herder's prime example for such poetry are Ossian's songs, published between 1760 and 1763 by Macpherson, which Herder at the time he wrote his "Auszug aus einem Briefwechsel über Ossian und die Lieder alter Völker" (extract of a correspondence on Ossian and the songs of ancient peoples), published in 1773, believed to be authentic third-century Scottish folk poetry. Herder claims that "the wilder and freer . . . a people, the wilder . . . and freer are its songs." Ancient folk art in its spontaneity, originality, and simplicity describes an ideal condition, and Herder believed that if man could overcome the restraints of rationalism, this condition could be reinstated. Friedrich Schiller, who otherwise opposed Herder's views, called for a similar goal in his *Über naïve und sentimantalische Dichtung* (1795–1796; *On Naïve and Sentimental Poetry*, 1845), without giving credit to Herder.

Yet Herder's examination of the Ossian songs reveals one of the weaknesses of his approach: the lack of a profound philological and systematic method, which was to be developed by the positivists of the nineteenth century. Such a method would have provided him with a tool to see through Macpherson's forgery. Instead, Herder relied on intuitive insight into the essence of poetry and subsequently projected his own concept of a future literature onto Ossian, finding only what he wanted to find.

For Herder, the development of a nation is connected and mirrored by the state of its literature, a standpoint not very surprising in light of Herder's concept of history, which is always allied with the history of literature.

Herder's many considerations in the area of aesthetics, from *Über die neuere deutsche Literatur* to *Adrastea* (1801–1804), unfold in three different directions: as philosophy, as history, and as literary criticism. "It is thoroughly impossible to have a theory of beauty . . . without history," he wrote. Ultimately, these three directions shape a unity in Herder's mind; therefore, one should consider the full range of Herder's writings in order to understand his literary theory. It is possible to find literary criticism embedded in one of his philosophical works or to find a lengthy elaboration on the nature of language in a sermon. Herder was by no means a systematic thinker, and he does not give easy access to his thoughts. Nevertheless, after a century ruled by pedantic reason, Herder's voice was well received.

Principal criticism

Über die neuere deutsche Literatur, 1767 (3 volumes)
Über Thomas Abbts Schriften, 1768
Kritische Wälder, 1769 (3 volumes)
Von deutscher Art und Kunst, 1773
Vom Erkennen und Empfinden der menschlichen Seele, 1778
Vom Geist der hebräischen Poesie, 1782 (*Spirit of Hebrew Poetry*, 1832)
Zerstreute Blätter, 1785–1797 (6 volumes)
Briefe zu Beförderung der Humanität, 1793–1797 (10 volumes; *Letters for the Advancement of Humanity*, 1800)
Kaligone, 1800
Adrastea, 1801–1804 (6 volumes)

Other major works and literary forms

Johann Gottfried Herder's voluminous work includes only a small section of literary criticism. He has written on such diverse subjects as theology – Herder was a preacher – philosophy, anthropology, language, folk art, history, and geography.

Herder's most famous work is the *Abhandlung über den Ursprung der Sprache* (1772; *Treatise upon the Origin of Language*, 1827), in which he rejects the assumptions that human language is acquired by imitating nature and is of divine origin. Herder theorizes that human beings develop language by means of their ability to reason, and this differentiates them from all other beings. Furthermore, each individual, as well as the human race as a whole, possesses this ability. Hence, the individual learns language as a child, and a nation develops language throughout the process of history.

This genealogical approach toward a wide range of topics can be traced in Herder's complete œuvre, most notably in his philosophical writings, from *Auch eine Philosophie der Geschichte zur Bildung der Menschheit* (1774; *Yet Another Philosophy of History*, 1968) to *Metakritik* (1799; metacritique). He was convinced that man is moving toward a final goal: humanity (*Humanität*). The earlier stages of history serve as necessary intermediate stages.

Aside from studying and interpreting literature, Herder was a poet in his own right. He wrote many inspirational poems and a lengthy ballad, *Der Cid* (1805; *The Cid*, 1828), based on the Spanish romance *El Cid Campeador*. Since the exploration of neglected authors is central to Herder's literary theory, his work also includes numerous translations, many of them contained in Herder's two-volume collection *Volkslieder* (1778–1779; folk songs).

POETRY
Volkslieder, 1778–1779 (2 volumes)
Der Cid, 1805 (*The Cid*, 1828)

NONFICTION
"Auszug aus einem Briefwechsel über Ossian und die Lieder alter Völker," 1773
Journal meiner Reise *im Jahre 1769*, 1769 (*Journal of My Travels in the Year 1769*, 1953)
Abhandlung über den Ursprung der Sprache, 1772 (*Treatise upon the Origin of Language*, 1827)
Auch eine Philosophie der Geschichte zur Bildung der Menschheit, 1774 (*Yet Another Philosophy of History*, 1968)
Älteste Urkunde des Menschengeschlechts, 1774–1776 (2 volumes)
Plastik, 1778
Ideen zur Philosophie der Geschichte der Menschheit, 1784–1791 (*Outlines of a Philosophy of the History of Man*, 1800)
Christliche Schriften, 1794–1798 (5 volumes)
Metakritik, 1799

Further reading

Clark, Robert T., Jr. *Herder: His Life and Thought*, 1955.
Fugate, Joe K. *The Psychological Basis of Herder's Aesthetics*, 1966.
Gillies, Alexander. *Herder*, 1945.
Koepke, Wulf, ed. *Johann Gottfried Herder: Innovator Through the Ages*, 1982.
——. *Johann Gottfried Herder*, 1987.
——. *Johann Gottfried Herder: Language, History and the Enlightenment*, 1990.
Leventhal, Robert Scott. *The Disciplines of Interpretation: Lessing, Herder, Schlegel, and Hermeneutics in Germany, 1750–1800*, 1994.
Mayo, Robert S. *Herder and the Beginnings of Comparative Literature*, 1969.
Wellek, René. "Storm and Stress, and Herder," in *A History of Modern Criticism: 1750–1950*. Vol. 1, *The Later Eighteenth Century*, 1955, pp. 176–200.

MICHAEL J. BÜSGES

See also Goethe; Hegel; Kant; Lessing; Romanticism; Schiller; Winckelmann

Hermeneutics

Hermeneutics is a term for any formal methodology for the interpretation of texts. Often used almost exclusively to refer to scriptural exegesis, hermeneutics since the nineteenth century has been increasingly applied to texts other than the Bible, especially to modern poetry. Hermeneutics depends to such an extent on the erudition, sensitivity, and skill of the interpreter, that it has often been called an art rather than a science, although in the nineteenth century considerable efforts were made to establish objectifying, "scientific" principles. A line of thinking in modern philosophy has also adopted a hermeneutical approach, beginning with Martin Heidegger in Germany in the 1920s and carried forward by his student Hans-Georg Gadamer. Traditionally the field of hermeneutics has been dominated by European, mostly German theologians, philologists, and philosophers.

Hermeneutics in Antiquity and the Middle Ages

The word "hermeneutics" is derived from Hermes, the name for the messenger of the gods in Greek mythology (from Greek *hermeneuein,* "to announce," "to explain," "to translate"). The first reference to the art of hermeneutics occurs in Aristotle's *Organon* (335–323 B.C.), in the famous passage "On Interpretation" (*Peri hermeneias*). Validity was Aristotle's concern – the veracity or falsity of original statements to be interpreted. In Aristotle's scheme, poetry strives to move the emotions, rhetoric to encourage political action, but hermeneutics has a higher, more theoretical aim – to determine truth or falsity. This determination of a text's validity, or lack thereof, is the first step in the hermeneutical process, followed by interpretation (logical analysis).

Borrowing from Aristotle and other classical authorities, the early Christian commentators on scripture, especially Tertullian (c. A.D. 160–after 220), developed hermeneutical standards for biblical exegesis. Their critical interpretation of the scriptures relied on concepts familiar to them from classical rhetoric. It was Saint Augustine who combined rhetorical hermeneutics and Christian dogma in a systematic approach to scripture that served as the model for textual interpretation throughout the Middle Ages.

Modern hermeneutics

Modern hermeneutics begins with Martin Luther, whose major contribution to the field's further development is his uncompromising insistence on the primacy of the text itself in providing the concepts and principles to guide exegesis. His New Testament translation, which gave inestimable momentum to the Protestant Reformation, is the product of his method, combining faithfulness to the ancient texts with careful attention to authenticity of expression in the present. Humanism during the same period also generally held up original texts as sources of the keys to interpretation, and developed a secular hermeneutics. René Descartes, Baruch de Spinoza, Christian Wolff, and many others in the seventeenth and eighteenth centuries occupied themselves with questions of "profane," that is, rationalistic hermeneutics. The next generally recognized breakthrough was brought about by the German theologian Friedrich Schleiermacher (1768–1834). Beginning in 1799, Schleiermacher developed a new approach to textual interpretation that emphasized not rational or moral principles but the experience of the human being in relation to the text (as well as the experience of the author of that text). Language is the precondition for everything – speech, thought, comprehension. Schleiermacher thus placed hermeneutics in the foreground of all analytical and speculative thought by pointing to the linguistic nature, not only of speaking and hearing, but of thinking and understanding. Much of Schleiermacher's theory has to do with the question of the nature of the act of understanding (*Verstehen*) as a kind of dialogue between the word of the author and the mind of the reader/hearer/thinker. Hermeneutics for Schleiermacher is a reconstructive process with the ultimate goal of "re-experiencing" what has already been experienced (*Nacherleben*), as in the case of the authors of the Gospel. While the later Schleiermacher delved into areas more properly deemed psychological in his search for the essence of individuality revealed in the text, his original insights concerning the language-based communicative act are considered to have established hermeneutics as a science in and of itself. Schleiermacher raised hermeneutics above the level of a mere disciplinary methodology confined to the fields of theology and philology.

It was the German philosopher Wilhelm Dilthey (1833–1911) who in fact applied the science of hermeneutics to all humanistic disciplines or *Geisteswissenschaften*. He believed hermeneutics could provide a common methodological basis for all the humanities, including everything from literary criticism to art history to sociology. He rejected the psychological focus of the later Schleiermacher and sought the truth of the communicative act in its temporality, and thus, its historicality. Hermeneutical understanding, or *Verstehen*, was conceived by Dilthey as the mind's attempt to understand the mind (*Geist*) of the other person who speaks in the text. This understanding occurs within and is thus part of a frame of reference – our own contemporary context influences the way we approach the context in which a given text can be said to exist. While attempting to "objectify" by standing outside our subject-object relationship with signs and symbols from the past, and at the same time identifying influencing contextual factors, hermeneutics confronts an inevitable circularity. This "hermeneutic circle" had already been articulated by Schleiermacher, but for Dilthey the hermeneutical circle refers to the historicality of meaning as it arises in the act of understanding. In simple terms, knowledge of the whole is needed to understand the meaning of the parts; the parts possess different meaning for us before we gain knowledge of the whole (as in completing a novel by Lev Tolstoi). Indeed, the meaning of the whole is itself historically defined and can change. But since all meaning is historical, this circularity does not undermine objective validity.

Dilthey paved the way for Martin Heidegger's expansion of the provenance of hermeneutics beyond the *Geisteswissenschaften* to phenomenology. Heidegger made the hermeneutic method a tool of analysis for understanding not just texts and the experiences they relate, but also our basic relation to the world of phenomena. Thus, in his magnum opus *Sein und Zeit*, 1927 (*Being and Time*, 1962), Heidegger applied hermeneutics to the nature of being itself, and to the existential significance of understanding. Heidegger's book, which avoids in large measure traditional philosophical jargon, manages to find a new way to talk about what can be revealed, or "brought to light," through language about the phenomena about us, even the very phenomenon of our own existence. As with Dilthey, a fundamental truth of being is its temporality. But in Heidegger's hands, hermeneutics is no longer an interpretation of an interpretation (text), but a primary act of grasping reality, of understanding "being-in-the-world" (*Dasein*). The premise of this "universal" hermeneutics or, as Heidegger called it, "hermeneutics of facticity," is the idea, increasingly dominant in German philosophy and linguistics since at least the last decade of the eighteenth century, that language constitutes the horizons of our world. In short, language is our world and thus the world is the subject of hermeneutical investigation.

Contemporary hermeneutics

Deeply rooted in Heidegger's thinking is that of Hans-Georg Gadamer, the most important figure in hermeneutics in the latter half of the twentieth century. Gadamer is more concerned than Heidegger with the act of understanding and explores systematically the "dialectics" or historical growth of knowledge, but shares Heidegger's rejection of the subject-object dichotomy implicit in scientific or technological thinking. Both view science as having taken subjectivity and built a putative objectivity on its foundations. Gadamer arrives at his conclusions about aesthetic consciousness, the noninstrumental nature of language, and historical understanding through detailed analysis of previous thought, beginning with the ancient Greeks. He takes the linguistic definition of the phenomenal world one step further than had previously been done, emphasizing that language is not primarily a system of signs pointing to things, but first and foremost a medium of expression that is "always already meaningful" on its own terms. Thus, it cannot fully be made into an object of thought by any language-based methodology, as Gadamer is fully aware in mapping out the dialectics of the hermeneutical experience of literary and historical texts as well as philosophy. Language occurs, as Gadamer reminds us, as dialogue, and his philosophical hermeneutics explores the way meaning arises out of this dialogue.

Yet theories of the Heideggerian school have serious weaknesses – critics point out that the theories provide no objective norms for determining the validity of interpretation, and that the hermeneutical effort to understand is itself historical, and at best part of a dialectical progress. Emilio Betti in Italy attacked Gadamer's ontological approach to hermeneutics as offering no normative direction. More recently, Jürgen Habermas in Germany has argued for a return to confidence in the "structure of communicative rationality." He appeals to Kantian enlightened reason and stresses the validity of "transpersonal" agreement in his conception of the ideal communicative act. Similarly, E. D. Hirsch, Jr., in the United States has written that a realm of objective validity exists, and that the praxis of interpretation should reveal that realm, not obscure it. Hirsch is an enemy of the "indeterminacy" of the text; he decries the notion that any given text offers the potential for virtually infinite possible readings. The well-known American philosopher Richard Rorty, on the other hand, has responded to issues raised in European hermeneutics by taking an "antifoundationalist" or "pragmatic" view that rejects the possibility of the normative, that is, "truth." The salient division between schools of hermeneutics is still marked by disciplinary boundaries, with theologians and literary scholars on one side practicing textual interpretation, and phenomenological philosophers on the other, applying interpretive theory to broader theoretical questions of being and understanding.

Further reading

Bruns, Gerald L. *Inventions, Writing, Textuality, and Understanding in Literary History*, 1982.
——. *Hermeneutics Ancient and Modern*, 1993.
Dilthey, Wilhelm. *Selected Works of Wilhelm Dilthey*. Vol. 4, *Hermeneutics and the Study of History*, 1996.
Gadamer, Hans-Georg. *Wahrheit und Methode*, 1960 (*Truth and Method*, 1975).
Hay, David Couzens. *The Critical Circle: Literature, History, and Philosophical Hermeneutics*, 1978.
Heidegger, Martin. *Sein und Zeit*, 1927 (*Being and Time*, 1962).
Hirsch, E. D., Jr. *Validity in Interpretation*, 1967.
Mueller-Vollmer, Kurt, ed. *The Hermeneutics Reader: Texts of the German Tradition from the Enlightenment to the Present*, 1988.
Palmer, Richard E. *Hermeneutics: Interpretation Theory in Schleiermacher, Dilthey, Heidegger and Gadamer*, 1979.
Rorty, Richard. *The Mirror of Nature*, 1979.
——. *Philosophical Papers. Objectivity, Relativism, and Truth. Essays on Heidegger and Other Philosophical Papers*, 1991 (2 volumes).
Wachterhauser, Brice R. *Beyond Being: Gadamer's Post-Platonic Hermeneutic Ontology*, 1999.

Mark R. McCulloh

See also Gadamer; Heidegger

Hugo von Hofmannsthal

Austrian poet, dramatist, and critic

Born: Vienna, Austria; February 1, 1874
Died: Rodaun, Austria; July 15, 1929

Biography

Hugo Laurenz August Hofmann Elder von Hofmannsthal was born in Vienna, Austria, on February 1, 1874, the only child of German-Jewish and Lombard parents. He had private tutors until the age of ten, when he entered Wiener Akademisches Gymnasium. He showed early genius: when he was only sixteen years old he published his first lyric poems and literary essays. A year later, in 1891, he began a relationship with the German poet Stefan George, who published many of Hofmannsthal's poems. Already famous as a poet under the pseudonym of "Loris Melikow," Hofmannsthal entered the University of Vienna to study law in 1892, but never practiced it. He earned a Ph.D. in Romance philology, and wrote his dissertation on Victor Hugo. He planned to become a teacher, but, upon suffering a psychological crisis, he turned to other interests. He married Gertrud Schelesinger in 1901 and settled in Rodaun just outside Vienna, using a small inheritance as financial support.

In addition to Stefan George, two other acquaintances were particularly important to Hofmannsthal. In 1903 he met Max Reinhardt, who introduced him to the theater. Hofmannsthal began to compose plays, and in 1904 his play *Elektra* (1903; *Electra*, 1908) was produced by Reinhardt. In 1906 he met Richard Strauss, with whom he collaborated on six operas; he was to continue working with Reinhardt and Strauss through the rest of his life.

Hofmannsthal served in the Austrian army in World War I and, thereafter, with the Austrian War Ministry on secret missions. By the end of the war his inheritance was depleted, and he was faced with supporting his wife and three children.

In 1917 he became the principal founder of the Salzburg Festival, which opened with the performance of his own adaptation of the medieval morality play *Jedermann* (1911; *Everyman*, 1917).

On July 13, 1929, his oldest son committed suicide, and only two days later, just before his son's funeral, Hofmannsthal himself died of a cerebral hemorrhage. They were buried in the same grave.

Influence

Hofmannsthal's aesthetics developed in three stages: first as a Pre-Raphaelite and advocate of naturalism, second as a Symbolist under the influence of Stefan George, and finally as one of the foremost promoters for the preservation of cultures and traditions of modern humanity. His basic premise was that a writer ought to be a living force of his or her time, offering the ordinary person opportunities for cultural and ethical growth by providing a variety of mediums and styles of expression. In this manner each person is free to develop in an independent and open atmosphere. Hofmannsthal wanted to bridge the gap between the elite and the commoner, the poet and his or her audience, prehistory and modern history, preexistence and self-consciousness.

Analysis

"There is something in us which is above and behind all ages and plays with all ages," wrote Hofmannsthal in *Buch der Freunde* (1922; *The Book of Friends*, 1952). This statement provides the answer both to formative questions concerning his writing creed and to critical misunderstandings about the change in direction he undertook when he began writing librettos for Strauss operas.

In his early years, Hofmannsthal was a Symbolist of the school of Charles Baudelaire, Stéphane Mallarmé, and Paul Verlaine, and, briefly, an aesthete under the dominating influence of Stefan George. Hofmannsthal's humanism, however, was at such odds with George's ideal of the artistic elite that in a matter of months he broke with George and wrote seven short dramolets (between 1891 and 1897) which were all direct rejections of the decadent way of life of the aesthete as espoused by George. While a student at the University of Vienna, he read the works of Henri Bergson and attended the lectures of Ernst Mach, from whom he learned the philosophy that human consciousness is the sum total of sensory impressions. This concept, coupled with his belief in the preexistence of the soul and his strong reliance on the folk elements in human culture, formed the basis for his critical theory.

Hofmannsthal's literary development has three major phases. His early lyrical works (poems and verse plays written from 1890 to 1899) gave way to the prose works of a later period, which in turn were replaced by his dramatic works. The critical essays and letters, however, were written across all three of these periods and became his best medium for analysis and pronouncements of literary direction.

In his essay *Der Dichter und diese Zeit* (1907; *The Poet and His Time*, 1955), Hofmannsthal makes it clear that the poet, rather than being one endowed with a higher sense, a blessing only bestowed on a few, is more appropriately seen as a spokesperson for his or her age, in close contact with his or her audience and preaching to them the doctrine of common experience. In Hofmannsthal's view, a poet is anyone who uses normal imaginative powers to heighten his or her sensibility, gather information, assimilate the various "intersecting vibrations" of reality, and reconstruct them into recognizable images or symbols. The purpose of the poet, then, is to open up all periods of history to the present, including meta-languages, prehistory, pristine culture, and preconsciousness. It is a radical change from William Wordsworth's "priest-poet" to Hofmannsthal's generic poet.

In *Die Briefe des Zurückgekehrten* (1907), he also claims no exclusive poetic diction or universal language for the poet. Each age can find its own poetic form, and each poet can borrow from past works to help recapture the essence of preexistence. Hence, Hofmannsthal contrasts the civilized nations of Europe with the "primitive" nations of Asia to show that those untarnished by modern consciousness have an advantage over the educated elite.

An essay written in 1902, "Brief des Lord Chandos" ("The Letter of Lord Chandos," 1952, in *Selected Prose*), is Hofmannsthal's single most influential critical statement. Chandos describes a desperate search for a way to express the intrinsic rather than the ephemeral nature of the universe. Hermann Broch makes the point perhaps better than most in his introduction to *Selected Prose* (1952). When the "I" becomes isolated from the rest of phenomena and when the world of tangible objects becomes meaningless, Chandos loses his orientation. In a state of preexistence there was no separation between the tangible and the intangible, the empirical and the essential. Now, however, the "I" finds itself walled off from the inner "truth" of things. What is new here is a predicament of total disintegration in the existential sense. Having moved from a preexistence state to a material world, the "I" is threatened by an unstable perspective, by a disoriented relation between self and object, between inner and outer realities, and Hofmannsthal comes to realize that the problem, though stated in a personal manner, is a modern, universal dilemma.

The underlying assumption in all Hofmannsthal's criticism is the rejection of a writer as mimetic, which is tantamount to a denial of the naturalism/realism movement at the time. This idea can be found, for example, in an essay entitled "Balzac," in which he rejects the theory of "true-to-life" characterization in favor of the spirit found beyond the empirical. The artist is not to imitate nature but to forge the work of art from the stuff of his or her preexistent self. The problem is in bridging that gap between the pure/spiritual being and the impure/materialistic world. One has only two avenues of approach: one can attempt to reach back to preexistent memory, or one can, like Johann Wolfgang von Goethe, bypass one's value-laden language to touch directly the pure essence of things in the present. Hofmannsthal relates one such mystical experience in the Chandos letter. Chandos had recently ordered that the rats in his milk cellar be poisoned, and as he rode off that evening he described a miraculous transformation of the mental event into an actual physical sensation: ". . . there suddenly loomed up before me the vision of that cellar, resounding with the death-struggle of a mob of rats. I felt everything within me." There is in this experience "something entirely unnamed, even barely nameable which, at such moments, reveals itself to me, filling like a vessel any casual object of my daily surroundings with an overflowing flood of higher life." That the experience is likely the highest form of consciousness attainable can be seen in terms used to characterize it – such as "exultation" and "revelation" – but he despairs at trying to find the words to encapsulate this transformation. This was the crisis addressed, but left unresolved, in the Chandos letter.

One final question needs to be addressed concerning Hofmannsthal's poetics: wherein lies the impetus for the creative act? The Chandos letter describes the extreme case of alienation born out of a despair at the loss of identification of self, a loss of linkage between the perceived and the perceiver. This split inside the psyche came to be seen as an identity crisis by the Freudian school. Yet Hofmannsthal saw that it is precisely because of this psychic split between the conscious and the nonconscious, between perception and object, that poetic inspiration is conceived. This dialectic engenders a creative tension: the work of art is not a rejection of material substance but a "transformation" (a key word in Hofmannsthal's critical theory) to higher levels of understanding. A poet's job, then, is to synthesize opposing elements and show unity and harmony in the whole.

Again and again, Hofmannsthal charges that a writer's obligation is to evoke in the reader a deeper, inner harmony that may not be observable in external reality. The writer should strive to trace the interrelation of the whole down to its very core, not embrace the disintegration of parts found on the surface of things. In "Balzac," he speaks of

> transitions everywhere, nothing but transitions, in the moral as well as in the social world. The transitions between vice and virtue . . . are as finely graded and as continuous as those between rich and poor. Hidden in the most far-removed and most contradictory things lie certain secret relationships through which everything is connected with everything.

Although this "relationship to the Whole" is a difficult concept to grasp, it is basic to a full understanding of Hofmannsthal's metaphysical theory. What Hofmannsthal envisions is a vast underground spirit moving in and through all things, connecting all things to all things – "an invisible co-ordinating system by which I can orientate myself." If all the myriad Balzac characters "are really nothing but the transitory embodiments of one nameless power" (what Hofmannsthal calls "infinite relativities" of an "Absolute"), then it follows that "all mythology, even the last, the most tenacious, that of words, is here dissolved." Thus, Hofmannsthal sought to reveal a different order of reality above and beyond life as it is normally perceived.

In the eyes of some critics, Hofmannsthal's influence has waned because of his neglect of the purely creative, his abandonment of lyrical poetry, and his dependence on other sources for the content of his works. Nor was Hofmannsthal the kind of person to command a large following, such as the school of writers found around Jacques Derrida and the deconstructionists or, in Hofmannsthal's time, around Émile Zola and the naturalists. Rather, he appealed to the spiritual function of literature in welding a nation, or a culture, or a humanitarian group focused on a certain principle. His career paralleled an enormous growth in Austrian literature, and his works added a unique contribution to music, folk stories, and classical works for his nation which no other Austrian writer approached. His reflections on the disintegration of European civilizations after World War I, as recorded in his political drama *Der Turm* (1925; *The Tower*, 1963) and in several essays dealing with the future of Western culture, show his great interest in finding a bonding agent for the whole of Europe.

No discussions of Hofmannsthal's achievements is complete which omits his analysis of language as a tool of perception. His search for the "deep structure" of language and his passion for peeling away the exterior layers of words to get at essences led to his crisis in writing, but it also paved the way for word scrutiny by such writers of the twentieth-century theater of the absurd as Eugène Ionesco and Samuel Beckett.

Hofmannsthal's greatest degree of influence, consequently, is in his attempt to unify all genres, all nations, all time frames, all language, all perception under a single, underlying current that moves through nature. Thus Aether, Bacchus, and Christ can all coalesce in the same spirit of love. It was to the influence of this spirit that W. H. Auden and Chester Kallman dedicated their libretto for Han Werner Henze's *Elegy for Young Lovers* (1961). It is indeed fitting, then, that the medieval play *Everyman* is performed regularly at the Salzburg Festival in Hofmannsthal's honor.

Principal criticism

"Brief des Lord Chandos," 1902 ("The Letter of Lord Chandos," 1952)
Gespräch über Gedichte, 1904
Unterhaltungen über literarische Gegenstände, 1904
Die Briefe des Zurückgekehrten, 1907
Der Dichter und diese Zeit, 1907 (*The Poet and His Time*, 1955)
Wege und die Begegnungen, 1913
Reden und Aufsätze, 1921
Buch der Freunde, 1922 (*The Book of Friends*, 1952)
Augenblicke in Griechenland, 1924 (*Moments in Greece*, 1952)
Früheste Prosastücke, 1926
Ad me ipsum, 1930
Loris: Die Prosa des jungen Hugo von Hofmannsthal, 1930
Die Berührung der Sphären, 1931
Festspiele in Salzburg, 1938
Selected Prose, 1952
Selected Essays, 1955

Other major works and literary forms

Hugo von Hofmannsthal is known for his breadth of literary forms as well as his breadth of subject matter. His essay topics range from Eugene O'Neill to Maria Teresai, from Ludwig van Beethoven to Victor Hugo, from Czechoslovakia to Africa, from classical Greece to Buddhism, from writing poetry to theater staging. He wrote plays based on the works of Sophocles, Molière, and Pedro Calderón de la Barca, mystery plays, a collection of aphorisms, collections of short stories, collections of poems, ballet scenarios, librettos for the operas of Richard Strauss, and an unfinished novel.

NOVEL

Andreas: Oder, Die Vereinigten, 1932 (*Andreas: Or, The United*, 1936)

SHORT FICTION
Reitergeschichte, 1899 (*Cavalry Patrol*, 1939)
Erlebnis des Marschalls von Bassompierre, 1900 (*An Episode in the Life of the Marshal de Bassompierre*, 1952)
Das Märchen 672: Nacht, und andere Erzählungen, 1905 (*Tale of the Merchant's Son and His Servants*, 1969)
Lucidor, 1910 (English translation, 1922)

PLAYS
Gestern, 1891
Der Tod des Tizian, 1892
Der Tor und der Tod, 1894 (*Death and the Fool*, 1913)
Alkestis, 1895
Das kleine Welttheater, 1897 (*The Little Theater of the World*, 1936)
Die Frau im Fenster, 1898 (*Madonna Dianora*, 1916)
Der Abenteurer und die Sängerin, 1899 (*The Adventurer and the Singer*, 1917)
Die Hochzeit der Sobeide, 1899 (*The Marriage of Sobeide*, 1913)
Der Kaiser und die Hexe, 1900 (*The Emperor and the Witch*, 1961)
Elektra, 1903 (*Electra*, 1908)
Das gerettete Venedig, 1905 (*Venice Preserved*, 1915)
Ödipus und die Sphinx, 1906 (*Oedipus and the Sphinx*, 1968)
Christinas Heimreise, 1910 (*Christina's Journey Home*, 1916)
Der Rosenkavalier, 1911 (libretto; *The Rose Bearer*, 1912)
Jedermann, 1911 (*Everyman*, 1917)
Ariadne auf Naxos, 1912 (libretto; *Ariadne on Naxos*, 1922)
Josephslegende, 1914 (libretto; *The Legend of Joseph*, 1914)
Die Frau ohne Schatten, 1919 (libretto; *The Woman Without Shadow*, 1957)
Der Schwierige, 1920 (*The Difficult Man*, 1963)
Florindo und die Unbekannte, 1921
Das Salzburger Grosse Welttheater, 1922 (*The Salzburg Great Theater of the World*, 1958)
Die grüne Flöte, 1923 (libretto)
Prima Ballerina, 1923 (libretto)
Der Unbestechliche, 1923
Achilles auf Skyros, 1925 (libretto)
Der Turm, 1925 (*The Tower*, 1963)
Die ägyptische Helena, 1928 (libretto; *Helen in Egypt*, 1963)
Das Bergwerk zu Falun, 1932 (written 1899; *The Mine at Falun*, 1933)
Arabella, 1933 (libretto; English translation, 1955)
Selected Plays and Libretti, 1963
Three Plays, 1966

POETRY
Ausgewählte Gedichte, 1903
Gesammelte Gedichte, 1907 (*The Lyrical Poems of Hugo von Hofmannsthal*, 1918)
Loris, 1930
Nachlese der Gedichte, 1934
Gedichte und lyriche Dramen, 1946 (*Poems and Verse Plays*, 1961)

NONFICTION
Richard Strauss und Hugo von Hofmannsthal: Briefwechsel, 1926 (*Correspondence of Richard Strauss and Hugo von Hofmannsthal*, 1927)
Briefwechsel zwischen George und Hofmannsthal, 1938 (letters)

ANTHOLOGY
Die österreichische Bibliothek, 1915–1917 (26 volumes)

EDITED TEXTS
Deutsche Erzähler, 1912 (4 volumes)
Deutsches Epigramme, 1923 (2 volumes)
Schillers Selbstcharakteristik, 1926

MISCELLANEOUS
Gesammelte Werke in Einzelausgaben, 1945–1959 (15 volumes)
Selected Writings of Hugo von Hofmannsthal, 1952–1963 (3 volumes)
Hofmannsthal: Gesammelte Werke, 1979 (10 volumes)

Further reading

Bangerter, Lowell A. *Schiller and Hofmannsthal*, 1974.
——. *Hugo von Hofmannsthal*, 1977.
Bennett, Benjamin. *Hugo von Hofmannsthal: The Theatres of Consciousness*, 1988.
Broch, Hermann. Introduction to *Selected Prose*, 1952.
——. *Hugo von Hofmannsthal and His Time: The European Imagination, 1860–1920*, 1984.
Day, Leroy T. *Narrative Transgression and the Foregrounding of Language in Selected Prose Works of Poe, Valéry, and Hofmannsthal*, 1988.
Frink, Helen. *Animal Symbolism in Hofmannsthal's Works*, 1987.
Gilbert, Mary E. Introduction to *Selected Essays*, 1955.
Guidry, Glenn A. *Language, Morality, and Society: An Ethical Model of Communication in Fontane and Hofmannsthal*, 1989.
Hamburger, Michael. Introduction to *Poems and Verse Plays*, 1961.
——. *Hofmannsthal: Three Essays*, 1972.
Hammelmann, Hanns. *Hugo von Hofmannsthal*, 1957.
Kovach, Thomas A. *Hofmannsthal and Symbolism: Art and Life in the Work of a Modern Poet*, 1986.
Norman, Frederick, ed. *Hofmannsthal: Studies in Commemoration*, 1963.
Wood, Frank. "Hugo von Hofmannsthal's Aesthetics: A Survey Based on the Prose Works," in *PMLA*. LV (March, 1940), pp. 253–265.

ERNEST R. PINSON

See also George; Symbolism

Norman N. Holland

American critic

Born: New York, New York; September 19, 1927

Biography

Norman Norwood Holland was born on September 19, 1927, in New York City, the son of a lawyer, Norman Norwood Holland, and Hariette (née Breder) Holland. On December 17, 1955, he married Jane Kelley, with whom he has had two children. He received his B.S. degree at the Massachusetts Institute of Technology (MIT) in 1947, his LL.B. from Harvard University in 1950, and his Ph.D. from Harvard in 1956.

While teaching at MIT from 1956 until 1966, Holland studied psychoanalysis at the Boston Psychoanalytic

Institute, where he was a resident candidate; he continued this affiliation throughout his professional career. He became a professor and chairman of the Department of English at the State University of New York at Buffalo (SUNY-Buffalo) in 1966; there he began the Center for the Psychological Study of the Arts in 1970. Until 1979 he served as director of the center and in that position influenced numerous students and critics to use a Freudian model to study the reader's response to literature.

Holland has received numerous honors because of his work, including appointments as visiting professor at the University of Paris in 1971 and 1972 and American Council of Learned Society Fellow in 1974 and 1975. In 1979 he was named McNulty Professor at SUNY-Buffalo. After the publication of his influential studies of literary response, Holland broadened the focus of his work, producing books on more general topics such as laughter and identity.

Influence

Holland's *The Dynamics of Literary Response* came at a time when the explication of individual texts by means of the New Criticism was beginning to weaken its hold on literature teachers and critics and when psychoanalytic criticism was beginning to degenerate into a quest for phallic and vaginal symbols in every pillar and pothole in literature. His emphasis on psychoanalysis as a means of understanding the dynamic relationship between the reader and the literary work is therefore largely responsible for the revival of psychoanalytic criticism in the United States. More than any other American literary critic, he has encouraged a return to the origins of psychoanalysis, and he has made the study of the reader's interaction with the text an important element in the study of literature. He is the undisputed leader of the "Buffalo school" of literary criticism, more properly termed "transactive criticism," and has influenced studies by other critics of the same school such as David Bleich and Murray Schwartz.

Analysis

After thirty years of embracing the critical methods of such English and American formalist critics as T. S. Eliot, I. A. Richards, John Crowe Ransom, Cleanth Brooks, and Robert Penn Warren, literary critics and teachers in both Europe and America were ready for a new approach. Thus, in the latter part of the 1960s, scholars proposed fresh models for approaching literature in terms of the response of the reader. In Europe, Hans Robert Jauss and Wolfgang Iser put forth the "reception aesthetic" approach (later championed by American critic Stanley Fish as "affective stylistics"). In the United States, Norman Holland offered his transactive theory in *The Dynamics of Literary Response*.

Whereas the approach of the European reception theorists was based on the phenomenological philosophy and psychology of Edmund Husserl and focused on gaps of indeterminacy in a work and the idea of an implicit reader concealed within the text, Holland's study urged a return to the often discredited and frequently reductionist psychoanalytical approach to literature, especially Sigmund Freud's ego psychology. Instead of using Freud's theories of dreams as a justification for ferreting out sexual symbolism in literary works, Holland turned to the psychoanalyst's theories of humor, suggesting a dynamic transaction between reader and text in which the themes inherent in a reader's personality or identity constructed the themes or meaning of the text.

The three central works in Holland's attempt to establish his transactive theory are *The Dynamics of Literary Response*, in which he used his own personality as the model of a responding reader to establish the groundwork of his theory, *Poems in Persons*, a brief introductory book of three chapters which focuses on one poet, H. D. (Hilda Doolittle), one poem by H. D., and the identity patterns of two student readers, and *5 Readers Reading*, which, as the title suggests, focuses on five readers and their dynamic interaction with a small group of short stories, particularly William Faulkner's "A Rose for Emily." After 1975 Holland reemphasized and defended his theories in various essays in the major American literary journals. Since all Holland's studies focus ultimately on the mysterious concept of the ego, the individual identity of the reader, it is not surprising that his 1985 book, a broad-based study that moves away from literary criticism toward a more inclusive consideration of identity, is entitled *The I*.

The central premise underlying Holland's approach is that literary criticism should not take a literary text as its subject matter, but rather that its proper subject matter is the transaction between a reader and a text. By his own account, Holland was drawn to psychoanalytic criticism because of his early interest in comedy; Freud's emphasis on details in his study of jokes, Holland believed, fitted in well with his own early training in the New Criticism. Holland soon realized, however, that he did not agree with the sense of objectivity or certainty of interpretation that motivated the formalists. Instead, he began trying to generalize into a theory of literary response Freud's theory that certain details in jokes released forbidden impulses.

The theory that resulted, published in *The Dynamics of Literary Response*, urged that literature be studied not as a static object, but as a dynamic process. By means of form, which functions much like a human defense mechanism, and meaning, which functions much as sublimation does in human beings, literature transforms unconscious desires or repressed wishes in the reader, integrating them into a higher aesthetic, intellectual, and moral unity: it is this unity, a unity not inherent in the work but created by the needs of the reader, that the formalist critic is always seeking.

Almost as soon as Holland's theories were published, however, for various reasons he began to rethink them.

First, there was the difficulty he met in trying to follow up on his own suggestion that his theories could be empirically tested. He gathered a group of subjects (English majors at SUNY-Buffalo), had them take Rorschach and Thematic Apperception tests, interviewed them extensively, and then had them read a group of stories to determine if he could predict their responses based on what he knew about them.

His uneven success with these attempts at prediction, as well as suggestions from colleague David Bleich, who had been doing his own research in reader response, prompted Holland to move beyond the ego psychology of what he has termed the "second phase" of psychoanalysis to Freud's "third phase." Instead of a "bi-active" model of literary response that treats a literary text as an objective absolute to which a reader provides a subject variation, Holland developed what he considers to be a more truly transactive model along the lines of psychoanalytic "objects-relations" theories developed by such British thinkers as W. R. D. Fairbairn and David W. Winnicott. His revised assumption about the literary work was that it functioned somewhat analogously to Winnicott's "transitional object." Thus, when readers read a text they bring to it their own particular set of fantasies, defenses, and meanings, that is, their own personal style or identity.

The major shift is that, instead of looking for a sameness in the text and a difference in the reader, Holland began to look for a difference in the text and a sameness in the reader. Holland's frequently acknowledged theoretical source for this revision of his theory is Heinz Lichtenstein's 1961 essay, "Sexuality and Identity," later included in his 1977 book *The Dilemma of Human Identity*. According to Holland, the means by which Lichtenstein determined human identity themes – synthesizing an individual's various actions, thoughts, and statements – is very similar to the means by which formalists or New Critics formulated a theme of a literary work – focusing on the relationship of its various parts, themes, or motifs. The result is not so much the identification of the theme in a pure form, either in the individual or in the text, but rather, to use the musical analogy often employed by formalists, a variation on the theme.

Holland argues that a reader brings to a literary text a set of expectations that are consistent with his or her identity theme. The reader then shapes the text according to his or her own defense mechanisms, attributes to the text his or her own fantasies, and finally transforms the text into a unified formal experience which has become the literary work for that reader. Holland has developed an acronym for this fourfold process of expectation, defense, fantasy, and transformation: DEFT. He says that readers apply these four steps to the literary work so as to re-create their own identity in the work.

In his book *Five Readers Reading*, he systematically exemplifies and supports this model through his extensive study of his student readers and their responses to the works they read. At SUNY-Buffalo, he and his colleague Murray Schwartz developed the "Delphi Seminar," in which the model is used as a teaching device. Students and faculty share free associations of their responses to literature and then respond to the free associations as the texts.

Holland has summarized, expanded, and refined his model in various essays since *Five Readers Reading*. In one of the most concise and commonly cited of these articles, published in 1975, he identifies the four key terms of his theory in its title, "UNITY IDENTITY TEXT SELF." After summarizing briefly the history of unity, text, and self, he spends much more time defining the most crucial word in his fourfold title – the term he borrows from Lichtenstein – "identity." Because unity resembles identity and text resembles self in the way Holland is using the terms, he develops the formula "unity is to identity as text is to self." His basic point is that identity is the unity which a reader finds in a self if he or she looks at that self as if it were a text. The difference between the two sets of terms is that whereas text and self are terms that correspond to actual experience and therefore are variable, unity and identity are terms that result from abstracting from that experience and are therefore relatively fixed.

Another important twist of this model, however, is that when an individual reader attempts to develop a sense of unity from a literary text or a sense of identity from another self, he or she does it in accordance with his or her own identity theme or pattern. Thus when literary critics say that they have determined the unity or theme of a text, they have actually created a unity or theme that is characteristic of their own identity. Everyone who reads a literary work, then, makes use of the text to re-create his or her own style or identity.

Readers interact with the work and make it part of their own psychic makeup in three basic ways, according to Holland. First of all, since they will find in the work those fantasies that they most fear and desire, they will also create in the work the means by which they defend themselves against those fantasies. According to Holland, readers will accept the work to the extent that they can re-create within it their individual patterns of coping with the world. Once this has been managed, the reader is then free to give the self up to the literary work to enjoy through it his or her preferred fantasies. Finally, the reader transforms this fantasy material into a unified and significant formal experience which *is* the literary work, that is, it is the experience of the literary work for the reader.

As is the case with much modern literary theory, Holland's studies have given birth to a school of criticism, this one centered at SUNY-Buffalo, as well as a group of followers and critics. Perhaps his most important critic and colleague is Bleich, who, in his 1978 study, *Subjective Criticism*, has done more than anyone else to try to integrate reader-oriented criticism with the more rigorously philosophical theories deriving from structuralist and deconstructionist approaches originating in Europe.

Whereas Bleich very early critiqued Holland's theory for its misplaced emphasis on the objectiveness of the text, Holland has critiqued Stanley Fish, the best-known representative of another important line of reader-oriented criticism, for his failure to allow for the subjectivity of the reader. Perhaps the difference between the reader-response theories of Holland and the reader-oriented theories of Fish could best be summed thus: whereas Holland focuses on the radical subjectivity of the reader – that is, all the reader's unique likes, dislikes, fantasies, and wishes, as they are applied to the literary text – Fish is more interested in how the trained reader applies more formalized and internalized literary competencies to the text. Consequently, it can be said that Holland's approach focuses more on the psychological, whereas Fish focuses more on the literary.

In the 1990s Holland was busy as usual promoting his own version of reader response. In 1995 he published a detective novel entitled *A Death in a Delphi Seminar*, in which his theories are used to solve a crime in one of his own university courses. Holland has also placed a number of his recent articles and academic conference presentations on-line on his own Internet web page to, as he says, "enlighten and delight readers." In some of these, he recants his earlier interpretations of such films as Federico Fellini's *8½*, Alfred Hitchcock's *Vertigo*, and Ingmar Bergman's *The Seventh Seal*, to argue that although our perceptual styles never really change, our value systems do. In addition, he has explored the implications of reading in hypertext and communicating on the Internet, and has criticized influential psychoanalytic theorist Jacques Lacan by insisting that his whole theoretical structure of signifier/signified is based on the faulty behaviorist theories of Ferdinand de Saussure, challenged by Noam Chomsky in the 1960s, and that Lacan's key concept of the child's "mirror stage" is contradicted by all empirical research in child development. His response to the postmodern literary theory of Lacan is best seen in his essay "Recovering 'The Purloined Letter': Reading as a Personal Transaction." Always blunt and self-assured, Norman Holland continues to be an important gadfly in contemporary psychoanalytic literary theory.

Principal criticism

The First Modern Comedies: The Significance of Etherege, Wycherley, and Congreve, 1959
The Shakespearean Imagination, 1964
Psychoanalysis and Shakespeare, 1966
The Dynamics of Literary Response, 1968
Poems in Persons, 1973
5 Readers Reading, 1975
Laughing: A Psychology of Humor, 1982
The I, 1985
"Recovering 'The Purloined Letter': Reading as a Personal Transaction," in *The Purloined Poe: Lacan, Derrida, and Psychoanalytical Reading*, 1988 (John P. Muller and William J. Richardson, editors)
The Critical I, 1992

Other major works and literary forms

Although Norman N. Holland's major contributions have been his booklength studies of William Shakespeare and his theoretical and empirical studies of the literary transaction between reader and text, he is also the author of more than one hundred articles, reviews, and occasional pieces on a variety of psychological and popular-culture subjects such as laughter, human defense mechanisms, human identity, film, and pornography. He has also published a detective novel, *A Death in a Delphi Seminar* (1995).

NOVEL
A Death in a Delphi Seminar, 1995

Further reading

Berg, Temma F. "Psychologies of Reading," in *Tracing Literary Theory*, 1987. Edited by Joseph Natoli.
Bleich, David. *Subjective Criticism*, 1978.
Leitch, Vincent B. "A Primer of Recent Critical Theories," in *College English*. XXXIX (October, 1977), pp. 138–152.
Ray, William. "Norman Holland: Reading as Self-Creation," in *Literary Meaning*, 1984.
Schwartz, Murray. "Introduction: The Space of Psychological Criticism," in *Metapsychological Literary Criticism – Theory and Practice: Essays in Honor of Leonard Falk Manheim*, 1973. Edited by Melvin Goldstein.
——. "Where Is Literature?," in *College English*. XXXVI (1975), pp. 756–765.
Suleiman, Susan R., and Inge Crossman, eds. *The Reader in the Text: Essays on Audience and Interpretation*, 1980.
Wright, Elizabeth. "Modern Psychoanalytic Criticism," in *Modern Literary Theory*, 1982. Edited by Ann Jefferson and David Robey.

CHARLES E. MAY

See also American Literary Theory: Twentieth Century; Psychoanalytic Criticism; Reader-Response Criticism

Arno Holz

German critic and poet

Born: Rastenburg, East Prussia; March 26, 1863
Died: Berlin, Germany; October 26, 1929

Biography

Arno Holz, the son of a druggist, was born in Rastenburg, East Prussia, on March 26, 1863. At the age of twelve, he moved with his family to Berlin, his residence for the rest of his life. There, he attended the Gymnasium (high school) but, in the wake of his parents' divorce, never graduated.

From 1881 onward he had to earn his own living and, after an unsuccessful career as a journalist, managed to eke out a meager existence as a freelance writer and an inventor of children's toys. During the years 1888 and 1889 Holz shared his dingy garret apartment with Johannes Schlaf, who became a partner in his naturalism by contributing to *Papa Hamlet* (1889) and *Die Familie Selicke* (1890; the Selicke Family). Later, Holz broke with Schlaf as it became apparent that the two no longer shared a common view on the future direction of naturalistic art.

Although most of his works – and especially his dramas – were quite well received by the public, Holz was, compared to his famous and much more prolific rival Gerhart Hauptmann, never able to turn a real profit from them. Consequently, he lived out his life as a poor and extremely bitter man, even after witnessing the publication of his complete works, *Das Werk von Arno Holz* (1924–1925). Holz died in Berlin on October 26, 1929.

Influence

Holz was the founder and first significant author and theorist of German "consistent naturalism," which, inspired by Émile Zola's portrayals of lower-class Parisian society, was dedicated to the unidealized documentation of daily life at the lower and exploited levels of society. Holz's works, both literary and theoretical, had a profound influence on the German literary scene of the late nineteenth century, leading many authors, among them the famed dramatist Hauptmann, to adopt naturalism. More important, however, Holz's writings thrust German literature into the modern age by rejecting all traditional idealizations of the human condition and, in poetry, all artificial devices such as rhyme, meter, and strophic form. In this sense, Holz's influence extends well beyond the naturalistic generation, the so-called *Jüngstdeutschen*, to include many authors of the twentieth century. Indeed, several twentieth-century critics praise Holz as the father of the social drama and concrete poetry, acknowledging his major influence in the development of modern and even postmodern literature in Germany.

Analysis

It is surprising to many that Holz, the social-minded founder of German naturalism and a revolutionary force in modern poetry, did not begin his literary career with very progressive aspirations at all. In fact, he was, as a young man, completely entrenched in literary tradition. His early poetry collections, *Klinginsherz* (1883) and *Das Buch der Zeit* (1885; the book of time), used time-honored poetic devices (rhyme, meter, and strophic form) and adhered to the dominant aesthetic values of nineteenth-century Germany – values which dictated that literature portray its subjects in an ideal and poetic manner consonant with "enlightened" society's general disdain for all things ugly, banal, and overly realistic. Only after these early collections failed to attract attention in the extremely competitive literary marketplace of the 1880s did Holz divorce himself from the formal and aesthetic encumbrances of tradition.

Holz took his first significant step toward modernism when he proposed that literature shift its emphasis from an idealistic, and hence utterly subjective, perception of reality to one that is eminently objective and verifiable. To his mind, this project entailed viewing the world as it actually exists, namely as an often bleak and merciless place characterized by overcrowded cities, where the hungry, the poor, and the mentally and physically disabled fall prey to ruthless exploitation by greedy slumlords and unscrupulous sweatshop owners.

Holz's newfound view of reality is most clearly manifest in *Papa Hamlet* and *Die Familie Selicke* – works which were meant not only to salvage Holz's ailing literary career but also to motivate society to reassess its mostly nonexistent social welfare policies. In these writings, various victims of society – a deranged, unemployed Shakespearean actor and his penniless family in the first work and the malnourished family of a chronic alcoholic in the second – are allowed, in their own seemingly unedited dialect, to give accounts of the inhumane living and working conditions faced by the lower classes in Berlin, a major European industrial center during the late nineteenth century. So detailed are these accounts, which attain a high degree of credibility because they are not phrased in the contrived, polished language of traditional literature, that the audience is able to "live through" the poverty of Holz's characters and the many real-life people whose tragic fate they share. The audience can, for example, see the anguish on a poor mother's face as she coddles her sick and starving infant, smell the rank odor of death hovering over the victims of a psychotic father's murderous rage, and hear and feel the incessant rumbling of trains as they pass by the dilapidated tenements of the poor.

The extremely lifelike portrayal of social reality in *Papa Hamlet* and *Die Familie Selicke* became the foundation of what Holz coined consistent naturalism, the art of depicting nature and the world in a painstakingly honest and objective manner. It is significant that Holz's concept of naturalism was not limited to literature. Indeed, it included all possible art forms – music, painting, sculpture, and so on – as outlined in *Die Kunst* (1891–1892; art), a theoretical treatise containing Holz's now-famous naturalistic maxim: "All art has the tendency to become nature again." Holz asserts in his *Die Kunst*, however, that the desired perfect correspondence between art and nature can only be achieved if the artist predicates his work on a thorough, firsthand study of his intended subject. Here, Holz is clearly drawing upon his own experience, for he had invested much time and effort in observing and analyzing the working-class inhabitants of Berlin before depicting them in his various writings.

It is not by chance that the direct and objective observation of artistic subjects, as discussed in *Die Kunst*, so closely resembles the empirical methods of analysis employed by the natural sciences. After all, it was Holz's ultimate aim to raise art, especially his own literary creations, to the high level of objectivity and general credibility enjoyed by the sciences. Holz wanted art to have a lasting impact on society, the type of impact Charles Darwin's theories on evolution and natural selection had, for example, when they were first made public in 1859.

Ever the realist, Holz admits toward the end of *Die Kunst*, that a perfect correspondence between art and nature, as postulated in his naturalistic maxim, could never be achieved. He attributed this to the natural bias inherent in all human thought and observation – a bias which he defines as the discrepancy between the artist's intent, the actual reality he wishes to portray, and the version of reality he ultimately ends up portraying. This discrepancy represents the factor "X" in Holz's final, and this time formulaic, statement of his naturalistic maxim: "Art = Nature – X."

As a further step toward modernism, Holz later expanded his theory of consistent naturalism, which thus far had focused primarily on the basic content of art, to include the very complex issue of artistic form as well. Generally speaking, he rejected all formal requirements traditionally imposed on art as contrived, artificial, and hence completely antinaturalistic and maintained that the form of an artwork, like its content, must arise entirely out of nature itself. In this way, he reasoned, form can actually contribute to the realistic portrayal of life and can thereby transcend that which is merely ornamental and thus completely foreign to naturalistic aesthetics.

Much of what Holz wrote about artistic form pertains especially to poetry, his own literary medium of choice since about 1898. In his *Revolution der Lyrik* (1899; revolution of poetry), for example, he states that poetry must abandon such traditional structuring devices as rhyme and meter, the artificial products of a poet's imagination, and instead base its flow on the natural rhythm inherent in the individual words and phrases of which it is composed. Lines of poetry are thus to read like ordinary spoken prose, complete with interjections, strings of nouns and adjectives, and language- and dialect-specific intonation patterns. According to Holz, this allows each line of poetry to convey its content – a description of some aspect of reality – in a much more convincing fashion than if it were cloaked in the highly stylized, unworldly garb of traditional lyrical form. Holz also specifies that all lines of poetry, regardless of their length, are to revolve around a common midpoint (or central axis) on the printed page. Here, his obvious intention is to remove strophic organization, yet another stratagem traditionally deployed by poets in their never-ending struggle to artificially structure language.

Holz pioneered this rhythmically based central-axis poetry in his mammoth poem cycle *Phantasus*, which, in its various editions dating from 1898 to 1961, presented a total naturalistic picture of the universe, encompassing everything from an exact description of the birth of new stars to a detailed portrayal of Holz's most intimate feelings of sexual desire, love, hate, fear, and insecurity. This cycle, which grew to a length of more than sixteen hundred pages in its final version, has been hailed as the crowning achievement of German naturalism.

At first glance, Holz's theories on literature and art may appear somewhat limited in scope. After all, Holz intended them primarily as a legitimation of his unconventional literary style. A closer look reveals, however, that these theories went far beyond their original legitimative purpose to become the foundation of an entire literary movement, namely German naturalism. This phenomenon, which Holz almost single-handedly put on the literary map, represents the first significant departure from traditional (idealistic and formalistic) literature in Germany. It opened the door to a plethora of literary innovations that would have been largely unthinkable to most authors of the nineteenth century: concrete and working-class poetry, the social drama, impressionistic and expressionistic literature, and the like. Indeed, the prominent West German poet Helmut Heissenbüttel went so far as to suggest that there is hardly a modern German author who cannot in some way trace his or her roots to Holz's literary and theoretical works. This statement summarizes Holz's enduring influence on German literature as a whole.

Principal criticism

Die Dichtkunst der Jetztzeit, 1883
Die Kunst: Ihr Wesen und Gesetze, 1891–1892 (2 volumes)
Revolution der Lyrik, 1899
Die befreite deutsche Wortkunst, 1921

Other major works and literary forms

In addition to the critical and theoretical works listed above, Arno Holz, the founder of German naturalism, published a variety of literary works encompassing all major genres. As a poet, he authored four principal collections: *Klinginsherz* (1883), *Das Buch der Zeit* (1885; the book of time), *Dafnis* (1904), and *Phantasus* (1898–1961). The best known of these collections, *Phantasus*, which was revised and expanded during a period of more than thirty years, ultimately burgeoned from two fifty-page booklets to a monumental sixteen-hundred-page model of Holz's controversial *Mittelachsendichtung* (central-axis poetry), as outlined in his *Revolution der Lyrik* (revolution of poetry).

In the area of prose, Holz – using his Norwegian pseudonym Bjarne P. Holmsen – coauthored the novella *Papa Hamlet* (1889) with Johannes Schlaf. This novella tells the story of an unemployed Shakespearean actor who, together with his poverty-stricken family, must endure the most inhumane living conditions imaginable. Finally, as a dramatist, Holz wrote five major plays: *Die Familie Selicke* (1890; the Selicke family), written with Schlaf, a heart-wrenching portrayal of the misery faced by a penniless family awaiting the arrival home of the drunken father on Christmas Eve; *Sozialaristokraten* (1896; social aristocrats), one of only a few successful naturalistic comedies; *Die Blechschmiede* (1902; the sheet metal workshop), a complex verse drama incorporating more than three thousand different characters; *Sonnenfinsternis* (1908; eclipse of the sun), the tragedy of an artist who learns to master his craft only after sacrificing his marriage; and *Ignorabimus, Tragödie* (1913), an epistemological work stressing the differences between natural-scientific positivism and the cosmic monism of Ernst Haeckel.

SHORT FICTION

Papa Hamlet, 1889 (as Bjarne P. Holmsen, with Johannes Schlaf)

PLAYS

Die Familie Selicke, 1890 (with Schlaf)
Sozialaristokraten, 1896
Die Blechschmiede, 1902
Sonnenfinsternis, 1908
Ignorabimus, Tragödie, 1913

POETRY

Klinginsherz, 1883
Das Buch der Zeit, 1885
Phantasus, 1898, 1916, 1925, 1929, 1961
Dafnis, 1904

MISCELLANEOUS

Das Werk von Arno Holz, 1924–1925 (10 volumes)

Further reading

Domandi, Agnes, ed. "Arno Holz," in *Modern German Literature*, 1972.
Heissenbüttel, Helmut. "Ästhetik und Wortkunst: Arno Holz und sein Phantasus," in *Text und Kritik*. 121 (1994), pp. 64–75.
Hermand, Jost, ed. "Einleitung," in *Phantasus*, 1968.
Mattenklott, Gert, and Klaus R. Scherpe, eds. "Der Fall Arno Holz," in *Positionen der literarischen Intelligenz zwischen bürgerlicher Reaktion und Imperialismus*, 1973.
Motekat, Helmut. *Arno Holz: Persönlichkeit und Werk*, 1953.
Scheuer, Helmut. *Arno Holz im literarischen Leben des ausgehenden 19. Jahrhunderts (1883–1896): Eine biographische Studie*, 1971.
Schulz, Gerhard. *Arno Holz: Dilemma eines bürgerlichen Dichterlebens*, 1974.
Soergel, Albert, and Curt Hohoff. *Dichtung und Dichter der Zeit*, 1927.
Wende, Waltraut. "Modern sei der Poet, modern vom Scheitel bis zur Sohle . . .: Zum Verhältnis von Kunsttheorie und literarischer Praxis bei Arno Holz," in *Text und Kritik*. 121 (1994), pp. 43–52.

DWIGHT A. KLETT

See also Continental Theory; Zola

Gerard Manley Hopkins

English poet and Jesuit priest

Born: Stratford, Essex, England; July 28, 1844
Died: Dublin, Ireland; June 8, 1889

Biography

Gerard Manley Hopkins was the eldest of nine children of Manley Hopkins, a minor English poet and government official, who had in his time been British Consul General to Hawaii. He attended Highgate Grammar School, matriculating in 1863 to Balliol College, Oxford, where he went on to have a very successful career (the great classical scholar Benjamin Jowett was to call him the "star of Balliol"). He took his degree in 1867. Hopkins' Oxford years had a profound religious effect on him. It was during this time that High-Church Anglicans such as John Henry Newman, John Keble, and Richard Hurrell Froude coalesced into the Oxford Movement, a grouping of learned Anglican ecclesiastics whose common interest was the Catholicity of the Church of England, and, to some extent, *rapprochement* with Rome. Although many of the "Tractarians," as they were also known, were to remain Anglicans, Newman, the most famous of them, eventually converted to Catholicism. Young Hopkins too felt compelled to become a Catholic, which he did in 1866 (being accepted into the Roman Catholic Church by Newman himself).

Not long after, Hopkins, who had always possessed a strong religious bent, felt a vocation to the priesthood. In 1868 he entered the Jesuit novitiate after burning the verses of his youth as "not belonging to my profession," and in 1877, after theological studies at St. Beuno's College in North Wales, he was ordained to the priesthood. His new duties saw him as preacher and parish priest in London, Oxford, Liverpool, Glasgow, and Chesterfield, often among the poorer segments of the populace, whose cries for social justice did not leave him untouched. In a famous letter to his friend the poet Robert Bridges, he confessed to being startled and disturbed by the sympathy he felt toward the young socialist movements just then sweeping Europe. He was born a scholar, however, and this was recognized. He was appointed professor of classics at Stonyhurst College in Lancashire, and, later, professor of Greek at University College in Dublin, where he missed crossing paths with the young James Joyce by a few years.

Overworked and ill, at times spiritually tormented (experiences which are reflected in the so-called "dark sonnets" written at this time), he died of typhoid fever in 1889, with his parents at his bedside. His last words were "I am so happy." Hopkins is buried in Glasnevin Cemetery, Dublin.

Influence

Hopkins again took up writing poetry in 1875, prompted by the tragic death of five Franciscan nuns exiled from

Germany, whose last hours are recorded in the triumphant and structurally brilliant *Wreck of the Deutschland*. Although the poem was rejected by the Jesuit magazine *The Month*, the fact that his superior had suggested that he resume his poetry (and had thus in Hopkins' mind blessed the endeavor) released his creative urge from his self-imposed restraints. Over the next decade and a half Hopkins composed the marvellous sonnets and lyrics in his inimitable sprung rhythm for which he is justly famous.

Thus, Gerard Manley Hopkins is first and foremost an artist. As far as criticism goes, he extrapolated his own poetic practice into a cogent theory of art as representation and explication of nature ("inescape," "instress," *haecceitas*), which can be applied to artworks other than his own (as he himself often did in his letters and personal writings). Secondarily, his letters offer us occasional, specific criticism of the poetry of his friends Robert Bridges, Coventry Patmore, and R. W. Dixon, as well as certain glimpses of his personal predictions as far as other poets (notably John Milton, Robert Browning, and Alfred, Lord Tennyson) are concerned.

We consider Hopkins a poet; he considered himself, above all, a priest; one would be hard put to find a person who would primarily associate "critic" with the name Gerard Manley Hopkins. Therefore, his primary sphere of influence would be among poets themselves. His extant letters reflect the fact that the writing of his intimate circle of poet-friends (all of whom, including the Poet Laureate Bridges, are considered quite minor poets by most scholars today) was influenced by the careful reading he gave to the works they sent him. Although he was an assiduous student of expression, allusion, and the logic of the poetic image, Hopkins was most sensitive to meter and the sound of poetry. He applied his bafflingly expert grasp of the rules of meter, both Anglo-Saxon and classical, to the poems of his friends and the great poets of the past in ways that opened up to his correspondents the great possibilities of the musicality of verse, especially what he called "counterpoint," in other words, a secondary, contrastive meter running counter to the established meter – not to overpower it, but perceptively, regularly enough to make itself felt.

Like his contemporary the great Polish romantic Cyprian Kamil Norwid (1821–1883), whose modern rhythms and delight for wordplay kept him an enigma among his contemporaries, but who rocketed into preeminence in the early twentieth century, Hopkins was unknown as a poet during his lifetime. His reputation grew, however, among younger poets during the first decades of the twentieth century. His first posthumous volume of poetry was published by Bridges in 1918. In the 1930s Hopkins took the poetic world by storm. He influenced a number of important British poets such as T. S. Eliot, Stephen Spender, and C. Day Lewis. However, as W. H. Auden, another young writer upon whom Hopkins made a great impression, was to write in later years, Hopkins' style is so original and idiosyncratic that it is quite inimitable – one cannot write like Hopkins, with his word-compounds, pregnant, multileveled puns, and looping sprung rhythms, without immediately being branded a second-rate imitator. Perhaps the only poet of note who was able to emulate the master's style in an original way was Dylan Thomas, in his early poem "This day winding down now." It is significant that Thomas took what he could of Hopkins only in this poem, and set out on his own crooked road of genius thereafter, recognizing that his spirit brooked no long apprenticeship. At any rate, among poets it is Thomas who most resembles Hopkins in his originality, his use of idiosyncratic meter, and word-bending power.

Analysis

If this were an analysis of Hopkins' achievements as a poet, one would expect a discussion of his quiet revolution in poetics: the development of his "sprung rhythm," according to which a single metrical foot can by constituted by one stressed and virtually any number of unstressed syllables. As we are to analyze his contributions to criticism, this is a more complicated task, for his ideas on criticism and poetics in general take the shape of brief comments enclosed in his informal correspondence to friends. On the other hand, Hopkins had a very clear and consistent manner of looking at the world as an object to be "re-presented" in art, and his theory of poetics implicit therein can be and has been applied to the work of other poets. Key to this "theory" are the ideas of *haecceitas* ("thisness"), "inscape," and "instress."

Hopkins is indebted for the first of these terms to the medieval theologian Duns Scotus, whom he discovered in about 1872 and went on to praise in one of his most famous and exuberant sonnets ("Duns Scotus's Oxford") as "realty's rarest-veinèd unraveller." The core concept of Scotus' anthropology, indeed of his ideas concerning reality in general, is the "principle of individuation," which asserts that individuality, or what he termed *haecceitas*, is the "final perfection" of any being. It should not be surprising that so original a poet, so careful an observer as Hopkins, should be swept off his feet by this confirmation of his own strong love for "all things counter, original, spare, strange." Although mentioned only three times in his *Journal*, the entry from early August 1872 is eminently interesting: "At this time [August 3] I had just begun to get hold of the copy of Scotus on the Sentences in the Baddely library and was flush with a new stroke of enthusiasm. It may come to nothing or it may be a mercy of God. But just then when I took in any inscape of the sea or sky I thought of Scotus."

This last-named term, "inscape," predates his discovery of Scotus by at least four years. It appears in his writings in an early essay on Parmenides composed shortly after his graduation from Oxford. In it, he states "His [Parmenides'] feeling for instress, for the flush and foredrawn, and for inscape is most striking." In the most simple terms, inscape is the innermost essence of a being, or event: that which "unmistakably distinguishes and individualises things" (*Journal*, September 14, 1871). It allows the beholder an infallible, almost mystical understanding of reality, and it is both the poet's duty and great joyful privilege to communicate that inner essence through his art.

Most, if not all, of Hopkins' poetry is built upon the idea of inscape. For example, the inscape of a soldier, ready to die for his fellow man, is Christ Himself (see his poem "The Soldier"). Likewise, the beauty of the bluebell in some way indicates the divine beauty of God: "I do not think I have ever seen anything more beautiful than the bluebell I have been looking at. I know the beauty of the Lord by it. It[s inscape] is [mixed of] strength and grace, like an ash [tree]" (*Journal*, May 18, 1870; the brackets are Hopkins').

One comes to know inscape by instress. This term is sometimes understood as the conscious, meditative effort on the part of the beholder to arrive at the inscape of a being or event, but more often Hopkins speaks of it as the nearly irrepressible power which beats from the particular object and makes us aware of the individual beauty before us. Of the ornamentation in the Norman tower at Ely, he writes: "the all-powerfulness of instress in mode and the immediateness of its effect are very remarkable" (*Journal*, September 1, 1868). At the very least, whether a conscious effort on the part of the beholder is necessary or not, he felt that one need certainly be open to the inflowing of this essential, individual power, and that the least distraction might impede the process. As he writes in his *Journal* of an outing of about December 12, 1872: "I saw the inscape . . . freshly, as if my eye were still growing, though with a companion the eye and the ear are for the most part shut and instress cannot come." Inscape and instress, then, are above all intimate whispers to the individual, not shouts, all the same "Crying *What I do is me: for that I came*" ("As kingfishers catch fire, dragonflies draw flame," line 8). It can be shared – and here is the mission of art. To do so, the poem must become as it were a channel of the inscape described, and must itself act as an instressing charge to trigger the experience in the reader. To end with just one example, the above-cited poem translates the poet's original impression of the individualized scene via strongly evocative alliteration: "As kingfishers catch fire, dragonflies draw flame."

Scotus aside, it is difficult to say just how Hopkins developed his theories of inscape and instress. One can note distant foreshadowings of the emphasis he was to put on individual beauty in the writings of Walter Pater. In his preface to *The Renaissance* (1873), the celebrated Victorian aesthete, who served as Hopkins' tutor at Balliol College, spoke of the proper critical attitude in a way that recalls Hopkins strongly: "What is important, then, is not that the critic should possess a correct abstract definition of beauty for the intellect, but a certain kind of temperament, the power of being deeply moved by the presence of beautiful objects." What is this but that openness to individual instress that Hopkins was to make the cornerstone of his poetic theory?

Earlier in the same essay, Pater refers to the critic's approach to the "pleasurable sensations . . . each of a more or less peculiar or unique kind" exerted by the aesthetic object, and again locates the same largely in the unrepeatable nature of the object, or person, in question. But how different the *end* of the critical process is for tutor and student! Pater writes: "The function of the aesthetic critic is to distinguish, to analyse, and separate from its adjuncts, the virtue by which a picture, a landscape, a fair personality in life or in a book, produces this special impression of beauty or pleasure, to indicate what the source of the impression is, and under what conditions it is experienced. His end is reached when he has disengaged that virtue, and noted it, as a chemist notes some natural element." Whereas Pater, whom the Oxford Movement had left untouched, who viewed the pursuit of absolute truth as a futile task, is satisfied to keep the beauties he has culled from the arts and nature in separate glass vials, as it were, like so many violets and flowers of the wild, content to sniff at each now and then and replace it on its dusty shelf, for Hopkins, inscape is revelatory: it is an outward sign, sacramental in a way, of God's own beauty, toward which it points. God, and God's love for humanity, are the truths toward which we are drawn upward through the beauty and joys that a merciful Creator has showered around us in abundance, perceptible to those with eyes to see them. Unlike the case of Pater, for Hopkins beauty is never an end in itself (that "dangerous mortal beauty" of which he speaks in the poem "To what serves mortal beauty?"), but rather a means toward an eternal end. As he puts it himself in that often anthologized favorite, "Pied Beauty": "All things counter, original, spare, strange;/ Whatever is fickle, freckled (who knows how?)/ With swift, slow; sweet, sour; adazzle, dim;/ He fathers-forth whose beauty is past change:/ Praise him."

Principle criticism

Hopkins' critical ideas may be delved for in the following titles:

The Correspondence of Gerard Manley Hopkins and Richard Watson Dixon, 1935 (Claude Colleer Abbott, editor)

The Letters of Gerard Manley Hopkins to Robert Bridges, 1935 (C. C. Abbott, editor)

Further Letters of Gerard Manley Hopkins, 1938 (C. C. Abbott, editor)

The Journals and Papers of Gerard Manley Hopkins, 1959 (Humphry House and Graham Storey, editors)

Besides allowing the reader a glimpse at Hopkins' creative processes (the *Journal* itself is almost exclusively concerned with art, poetry, their limitations and possibilities), the reader will find in Hopkins' letters to Bridges, Dixon, and Patmore a refreshingly intimate and sincere body of particular criticism. After all, Hopkins did not intend these letters to be published, and did not need to keep his guard up with one eye on the amorphous audience, as is the case with most critics.

As said above, stray, enlightening critical comments on the great writers of the past will be mined from these sources. The reader may be surprised by Hopkins' great esteem for the nineteenth-century novelists, which went so far as to prompt him to compare the glories of Victorian prose with the golden age of drama during the reign of Elizabeth I. Also of interest are the theses written during his undergraduate years, collected in the *Journals and Papers*, most especially his "On the Origin of Beauty: A Platonic Dialogue."

Other major works and literary forms

Of course, and above all, the reader wishing to understand Gerard Manley Hopkins intimately is directed toward *The Poems of Gerard Manley Hopkins*, now in its fourth edition under the editorship of N. H. MacKenzie, to whom W. H. Gardner passed on the torch in 1967. This fourth Oxford edition, which has changed the numeration of Hopkins' poetry to a small extent, is the most comprehensive volume available of the main legacy of Gerard Manley Hopkins: his finished and unfinished poems, his dramatic fragments, translations, and original poetry in Latin, Greek, and Welsh, as well as English.

Further reading

Boggs, R. M. C. "Poetic Genesis, the Self, and Nature's Things in Hopkins," in *Studies in English Literature*. 37, no. 4 (Autumn, 1997), pp. 831–856.

Coogan, M. "Inscape, Instress. Further Analogies with Duns Scotus," in *PMLA*. LXV (1950).

Erzgräber, W. "Zu Hopkins' Sonettkunst," in *Literaturwissenschaftliches Jahrbuch*. 38 (1997), pp. 281–306.

Gardner, W. H. *G. M. Hopkins. A Study of Poetic Idiosyncrasy in Relation to Poetic Tradition*, Vol. 1, 1944, Vol. 2, 1949.

Heuser, A. *The Shaping Vision of G. M. Hopkins*, 1958.

Lichtman, M. R. "The Incarnational Aesthetic of Gerard Manley Hopkins," in *Religion and Literature*. 23 (1991), pp. 37–50.

Lloyd Thomas, M. G. "Hopkins as Critic," in *Essays and Studies*. Vol. XXXII (1946). Edited by Basil Willey.

Mathison, J. K. "Poetic Theory of G. M. Hopkins," in *Philosophical Quarterly*. XXVI (1947).

Molloy, S. "The Ardour of Gerard Manley Hopkins," in *Kwartalnik neofilologiczny*. 33, no. 2 (1986), pp. 149–153.

Moulin, J. "L'Élan voulu: Une Problématique du mouvement chez Gerard Manley Hopkins," in *Études anglaises*. 49 (1996), pp. 40–52.

Ward, B. W. "Philosophy and Inscape: Hopkins and the *Formalitas* of Duns Scotus," in *Texas Studies in Literature and Language*. 32 (1990), p. 214.

Weyand, Norman. *Immortal Diamond. Studies in G. M. Hopkins*, 1949.

CHARLES S. KRASZEWSKI

See also Literary Theory in the Age of Victoria; Pater

Horace

(Quintus Horatius Flaccus)

Roman poet and writer

Born: Venusia, Italy; December 8, 65 B.C.
Died: Rome, Italy; November 27, 8 B.C.

Biography

Quintus Horatius Flaccus (Horace) was born on December 8, 65 B.C., in Venusia (now Venosa), Italy, of a humble freedman. His father arranged for him to study in Rome with an established *grammaticus* and to complete his studies in Athens. Following Julius Caesar's assassination (44 B.C.), he briefly accepted a post as a tribune with Brutus; after the latter's defeat in 42 B.C. at Philippi, he returned to Italy to find that his family's property had been confiscated. Horace obtained a treasury clerkship and at this time began work on the earliest *Satires* and *Epodes*. These efforts, and friendships with Virgil and Varius Rufus, led to an introduction to Maecenas, a literary patron close to the powerful Augustus (known as Octavian until 27 B.C.). Maecenas, a lifelong friend, eventually provided Horace with his beloved Sabine farm soon after the first book of *Satires* was published in 35 B.C.; it was followed by book 2 of the *Satires* and the *Epodes*, in about 30 B.C. From this time until 23 B.C., Horace wrote the first three books of the *Odes*; he then turned away from lyric poetry with the first book of his literary *Epistles*, published in 20 B.C., followed by *The Art of Poetry* in about 17 B.C. He resumed the lyric form at this time when he accepted Augustus' commission to write the choral *Carmen saeculare* for the *ludi saeculares*. The date of book 2 of the *Epistles* is somewhat uncertain, perhaps 15 or 14 B.C., and book 4 of the *Odes* followed soon after, probably in 13 B.C. Horace died in 8 B.C., only a few months after the death of his great friend and patron, Maecenas.

Influence

The influence of Horace's literary criticism on world literature has been enormous, in many eras unexpectedly outweighing the importance of his lyric poetry. Horace's groundbreaking work concerning the genre of satire was followed in antiquity by the more biting works of Persius and Juvenal. Under the reign of Nero, the first critical edition of Horace was produced, and under Hadrian an edition was published of the *Satires, Epistles*, and *The Art of Poetry*.

In the Middle Ages, the *Satires* and *Epistles* were considered to be far more important than the lyric poems, in part because this was an era during which satire was in vogue; the commentary on *The Art of Poetry* in the Scholia Vindobonensia is often attributed to the famous Alcuin. During and after the Renaissance, while the lyrics went in and out of fashion, the didactic works, especially *The Art of Poetry*, retained a strong influence on the literatures of individual national cultures. In Italy, Dante and Petrarch both had knowledge of *The Art of Poetry*, and the first printed edition of Horace (1470) was followed by various translations of the literary critical works; also of interest are Giovanni Antonio Volpi's treatise on satire, which deals with Lucilius and Horace, Ludovico Ariosto's Horatian-style satires, and Giacomo Leopardi's parody of *The Art of Poetry*.

The Art of Poetry had considerable influence in France, where important translations were produced in the sixteenth century, and soon after Joachim du Bellay based his treatise on the Pléiade heavily on this work. In the next century, Nicolas Boileau-Despréaux's own *The Art of Poetry* (1674) secured the hold of Horace's critical guidelines on subsequent French drama. The first English translation of Horace was of the *Satires*, in 1565, and in 1567 Thomas Drant translated the *Satires, Epistles*, and *The Art of Poetry*; in 1640, Ben Jonson's translation of *The Art of Poetry*, the first translation of Horace by a major British poet, was published posthumously. John Dryden, William Temple, Richard Hurd, and Samuel Johnson all invoke *The Art of Poetry*, and Alexander Pope's *An Essay on Criticism* (1711) discusses the pervasive influence of this work on English writers. Overall, Horace's literary criticism, especially *The Art of Poetry*, has exerted enormous authority over the discipline of letters in Western culture.

Analysis

Horace's *Satires* represent a genre that originated with the Romans, and he had very few genuine predecessors. It is, therefore, not surprising that Horace devotes several of his *Satires* to explaining and defending this relatively new type of poetry. The *Satires* that self-consciously discuss satire are 1.4, 1.10, and 2.1, and from a careful scrutiny of these works it is possible to extrapolate Horace's literary-critical view of the genre. It should first be noted that all three of these *Satires* seem to be responses to specific criticism, perhaps following preliminary readings of other *Satires*; it should further be observed that Horace's attitude toward such criticism appears to evolve and mature within this series of *Satires*, moving from the serious, defensive tone of 1.4 to the less serious, more playful poses of 1.10 and 2.1.

Although the Greeks did not write satire per se, Horace finds the roots of his genre in the Greek Old Comedy of Aristophanes, Eupolis, and their contemporaries, because these writers engaged in personal lampoon. Horace's most important Roman model was Lucilius, but Horace perceives Lucilius' works as suffering from the faults of negligence and copiousness (1.4). He himself would like to preserve the spirit of satire but avoid Lucilius' faults and also avoid giving personal offense through any maliciousness. Horace later tempers his criticism of his predecessor (1.10) by noting his urbanity, wit, and good temper (Lucilius is praised for the way he "rubs down the city with salt" – that is, wit), although he is more critical of Lucilius' intermingling of Greek words with Latin and finds Lucilius' work to be somewhat unpolished by the standards of his own day. Horace expresses doubt over whether Lucilius' satires or his own should be considered true poetry, or for that matter whether Greek New Comedy qualifies, since all three modes closely approximate everyday human speech.

By way of defending himself more personally, Horace reminds the reader that he recites his work only privately and by invitation, that the human foibles he holds up for ridicule are intended to instruct and not to cause hurt, that he wishes to be appreciated by a knowledgeable audience, and that individual writers must make their own choices of genre, and he has opted for satire. *Satire* 2.1 contains a very lighthearted continuation of these same themes within the fictional structure of a dialogue between Horace and his legal adviser, Trebatius. The attorney finds legalistic reasons for Horace to abandon satire, but Horace playfully suggests that he will take his chances; Lucilius, too, had prominent friends, yet they were not offended by his lampoon.

Satires 1.4, 1.10, and 2.1, then, help to define the genre of satire, then in its infancy, and Horace therein establishes that his own choice of satiric tone will be gently mocking. Later writers of satire moved back to the sharper attacks of the Old Comic playwrights invoked by Horace at the beginning of *Satire* 1.4.

In his *Satires* "on satire," Horace touches briefly on a topic which he treats in greater depth in several of his *Epistles*: the use of literary models, especially Greek models, and the proper relationship between a poet and his mentors. Horace's interest in literary history stems, in part, from an organic view of literary tradition in which one borrows carefully chosen elements from an earlier writer, but also forges ahead and improves upon the model; he especially decries the "older is better" dictum that had induced some of his contemporaries to offer unmerited praise for earlier, awkward Roman poetry (*Epistle* 2.1). Good poets, he adds (*Epistle* 2.2), make use of new inventions of language and style, though in *The Art of Poetry* he urges caution in the coinage of new words. In his *Satires*, Horace followed Lucilius; in his lyric poems, Sappho and Alcaeus were the major models, and they in turn followed the earlier Archilochus. *Epistle* 1.19, in which Horace's lyric predecessors are discussed, defends against accusations by Horace's critics that his lyric poems lacked originality. Here Horace also points out that one should imitate only very carefully, avoiding imitation of eccentricities.

Horace readily acknowledges the Roman debt to Greek letters in the famous phrases of *Epistle* 2.1, 156–157: "*Graecia capta ferum victorem cepit et artes/ intulit agresti Latio*" (Greece, having been captured, seized her savage victor and brought the arts to rustic Latium), but he quickly adds that only very recently have Roman writers learned to make good use of Greek technique. In general, then, Horace never questions the practice of employing literary models; he asks only that it be done prudently and well.

The area of Latin literature where the Greek had the greatest influence was probably dramatic poetry. Although not himself a dramatist, Horace is clearly interested in dramatic genres from his viewpoint as a literary critic. In *Epistle* 2.1, addressed to Augustus, Horace discusses Fescennine verse. As a satirist, Horace is most interested in the invective aspect of this native Italic predramatic form, and he describes the descent from witty attack to malicious slander, culminating in the imposition of sanctions for libel. He also describes the first translations of Greek plays into Latin and criticizes Plautus for overall negligence and inattention to detail. Speaking more generally, Horace impugns the practice of pandering to the audience through excessive use of spectacle and praises the playwright who creates magical illusions merely by the skill of his words.

Much of Horace's theory of drama is found in *Epistle* 2.3, addressed to the Pisones and often referred to by Quintilian's designation, *Ars poetica*. Porphyrion, an ancient commentator, states that Horace relies rather heavily here on Neoptolemus, a third-century B.C. rhetorician, as a source, but this statement has been challenged by modern scholars. *The Art of Poetry* does not follow a formal structure, and its words of advice often seem to be ordered randomly; moreover, it is not always entirely clear which lines are addressed specifically to the playwright and which to the larger group of poets in general.

The Art of Poetry warns the playwright to consider what words are appropriate to the ages and fortunes of his characters, to conform to established tradition in dealing with characters from ancient myth and legend, and to exercise discretion in choosing which actions will be shown onstage and which will be narrated by messengers (long tradition precluded the dramatization of violent acts). The canonical number of acts in a play is five, and of actors, three. Horace frowns on the use of a *deus ex machina* (literally, "god from the machine") to unravel complex plots; he suggests that the chorus be accorded the importance of an actor, appear between episodes, offer morally sound advice, praise plain living, and keep the secrets with which it is entrusted.

Horace also discusses aspects of the history of drama, accounting for the increasingly broad gestures of ancient drama's accompanist, the flutist, considering at length the proper use of meter, and describing the rise of the satyr play, a burlesque genre which often followed tragic presentations in classical Greece. Horace describes the beginnings of Greek drama with the performer-playwright Thespis, whose face was smeared with wine-lees in lieu of a mask, and the improvements initiated by Aeschylus: masks, costumes, a stage area, and stylized acting. He describes Greek Old Comedy, whose freedom degenerated into license, producing legal restrictions and, ultimately, silence. Roman writers can succeed at both imitation of the Greeks and original creation, but Horace urges care, diligence, and a willingness to revise.

The Art of Poetry also dispenses more general advice to all poets, regardless of specific genre. A poem should be a coherent composition with no disharmonious elements; the "purple patch" (*purpureus pannus*) must be avoided, and the final product is to be "*simplex . . . et unum*" (consistent and one in the same). Urgency to avoid one kind of error can lead the unwitting writer to the opposite extreme; writers must choose their words carefully, use the appropriate poetic meter, and avoid incongruous lines. Wisdom is the principal source of all good writing, which reflects accurate observation of human speech and behavior, but the writer must exercise care to balance didacticism with entertainment. Genius joins with training to produce good writing, and poets must submit their work to accurate, impartial critics for help. Second-rate writers and "mad poets" must be avoided.

The Art of Poetry also takes up the old Platonic question of the function of the poet in society. Beginning with the legendary feats of Orpheus, whose music tamed the savage, and Amphīon, whose chords moved stone, Horace notes the uplifting, masculine spirit of Homer and Tyrtaeus and the broader functions of poems: to reveal words of the oracles, express human joy, and praise the gods. *Epistle* 2.1 also discusses the poet's contributions to society, in avoiding materialism, offering friendly advice, pointing to noble examples, and comforting those in despair.

Very early in *The Art of Poetry*, Horace warns the poet to choose a subject equal to his own strength and abilities. These are words with very special meaning for Horace, who often struggled against external pressures, perhaps from Maecenas and Augustus, to write more lyric poetry and even to try his hand at epic. The theme of *recusatio*, "demurral, refusal" to write a grander type of poem, runs through Horace's literary-critical *Satires* and *Epistles*, becoming especially prominent in *Epistles* 1.1, 2.1 (near the end), and 2.2. Horace preferred instead to philosophize, to "chat" with his reader, and these chats, the *Satires* and literary *Epistles*, became the form in which Horace couched his literary criticism and theory.

Principal criticism

Satires 1.4 and 1.10, 35 B.C.
Satire 2.1, 30 B.C.
Epistles 1.1 and 1.19, 20 B.C.
Epistle 2.3, c. 17 B.C. (better known as the *Ars poetica*, or *The Art of Poetry*)
Epistles 2.1 and 2.2, c. 15 B.C.

Other major works and literary forms

In addition to books 1 and 2 of the *Satires* and *Epistles*, Horace wrote several collections of lyric poetry: the *Odes*, in four books (23–13 B.C.), the *Epodes* (c. 30 B.C.), and a commissioned work, the *Carmen saeculare* (17 B.C.).

POETRY
Epodes, c. 30 B.C.
Odes, books 1–3, 23 B.C., book 4, 13 B.C.
Carmen saeculare, 17 B.C.

Further reading

Atkins, John William Hey. *Literary Criticism in Antiquity: A Sketch of Its Development*. Vol. 2, 1934.
Brink, C. O. *Horace on Poetry: Prolegomena to the Literary Epistles*, 1963.
Costa, C. D. N., ed. *Horace*, 1973.
Fraenkel, Eduard. *Horace*, 1957.
Martindale, Charles, and David Hopkins, eds. *Horace Made New: Horatian Influences on British Writing from the Renaissance to the Twentieth Century*, 1993.
Nisbet, R. G., and M. Hubbard, *Commentary on Horace*, 1970–78 (2 volumes).
Rudd, Niall. *The Classical Tradition in Operation: Chaucer / Virgil – Shakespeare / Plautus – Pope / Horace – Tennyson / Lucretius – Pound / Propertius*, 1994.
Russell, D. A. *Criticism in Antiquity*, 1981.
Shackleton, Bailey, D. R. *Profile of Horace*, 1982.
Shapiro, Alan. "Horace and the Reformation of Creative Writing," in *The American Poetry Review*. 21, no. 2 (March–April, 1992), pp. 7–13.
Showerman, Grant. *Horace and His Influence: Our Debt to Greece and Rome*, 1922.

LAURA STONE BARNARD

See also Classical Greek and Roman Literary Theory; Medieval Literary Theory

Hu Shih

Chinese critic

Born: Shanghai, China; December 17, 1891
Died: Nankang, Taiwan; February 24, 1962

Biography

Hu Shih was born in Shanghai on December 17, 1891. The death of his father during Hu's early childhood caused long-term financial difficulties for his family, with the result that the young Hu was educated by relatives in Anhwei province. Having mastered 1,000 Chinese characters by the tender age of four, he was regarded as a prodigy. In 1904 he returned to Shanghai, enrolling in the "new" schools and in the radical China National Institute, where he achieved a sound grasp of English, Western mathematics, and science.

A Boxer Indemnity Scholarship brought Hu in 1910 to Cornell University, where he earned a B.A. in philosophy and membership of Phi Beta Kappa. Moving to Columbia University in 1915, he wrote his dissertation under the direction of John Dewey. Returning to China, he began to teach philosophy at Beijing University. From 1927 to 1930 he taught at Kuanghua University, simultaneously serving as president of the China National Institute, a post that brought conflict with the Nationalist government, eventually forcing his resignation. Between 1931 and 1936, absenting himself only to deliver the Haskell Lectures at the University of Chicago in 1933, he served as dean of Beijing University's College of Arts.

Upon the outbreak of the Sino-Japanese War in 1937, Hu undertook a goodwill tour of the United States, culminating in his appointment as China's ambassador to Washington. Without explanation, he was relieved of this post in 1942. He continued working in the United States until 1946, when he returned to his homeland to serve as chancellor of Peking University. In 1947 he also served as a nonpartisan delegate to China's National Assembly. On the eve of the Communist conquest of China, Hu fled to the United States, where, except for working as a curator at Princeton University's Gest Oriental Library and writing on foreign affairs, he lived in virtual retirement in New York. During a session of the Academia Sinica, which he had served as president since 1958, he was stricken by a heart attack and died in Nankang, Taiwan, on February 24, 1962.

Influence

Hu Shih's lucid advocacy of the use of *pai hua*, the vernacular language of China, as the chief literary medium and as a tool of cultural reform earned for him international recognition as the father of China's literary revolution. Particularly between 1917 and the early 1920s, his clear and unambiguous proposals proved to be of critical importance to large numbers of young Chinese who, with his inspiring writings as a guide, formed the New Culture movement. In unprecedented numbers, this younger generation, distressed by China's impotence and internal disarray in the face of Japanese and Western ambitions and ideas, sought massive remedies for their country's apparent backwardness. Hu's superb Western education, combined with his meticulous scholarly grasp of Chinese traditions, lent special authority to his calls for reform. Through his moderate, decidedly evolutionary, and highly individualistic "revolution," he hastened official acceptance of *pai hua* in educational establishments and transformed it into an increasingly reputable medium of expression for creative writers without divorcing them from their literary heritage.

Analysis

Hu Shih's literary theory, which he propounded most vigorously, specifically, and influentially between 1915 and 1933, is deceptive in its simplicity. Both his boyhood exposure to popular fiction and his incisive classical knowledge convinced him that China's literature had withered and become moribund. Resuscitation of the nation's creative energies, he believed, could only come from a timely literary revolution dedicated to the elevation of *pai hua*, the people's vernacular, to the status of the official, as well as the literary, mode of expression in China. The peaceful revolution that he sought to inspire was consciously reminiscent of efforts undertaken in Europe several centuries earlier to disestablish Latin as the language of privilege in favor of preaching, teaching, and publishing in the common tongue.

In pursuit of this goal, Hu urged creative people, writers and students, to speak only when they had something worthwhile to communicate, to be clear and unequivocal, to address others, particularly officials and the mandarinate, in the lay language, and to avoid the obscurantism of classical phraseology. In his view, classical China was dead. No viable literature, he argued, can spring from an arcane, incomprehensible, and essentially dead language. To the extent that China had enjoyed any genuine literature in the preceding millennium, he contended, it had been phrased in the *pai hua*. Too meticulous a scholar to premise his case on mere assertions, Hu identified, as no one else had, influences of the vernacular in the best poetry and prose of classical periods. Where admired classicists such as Han Yü or Liu Tsungyüan had ignored the *pai hua* in the T'ang era, Hu noted that it was only because the *pai hua* had not yet developed.

Literary revolution, as defined in Hu's critical writings, fits into a broader philosophical perception of change. For him, there are two kinds of historical development. The first is natural and comports with natural tendencies. The second, however, is more revolutionary than evolutionary for it is energized by human efforts. Hu placed *pai hua* in this latter category, for the vernacular had provided a thousand-year-old matrix from which, he believed, literary revolution would spring. In distinction from natural change, this literary revolution would result from self-conscious creativity; indeed, he argued, the *pai hua* revolution, far from being a singular, unstudied, or violent rejection of classicism, actually furnished Chinese literature with a history of its own and only awaited its fulfillment.

Simple in appearance, Hu's proposals would have wide and deep ramifications throughout Chinese society. There is no doubt that his belief in the *pai hua* as the key to the democratization of education was both informed and buttressed by the ideas of John Dewey, although Hu's understanding of Western science, history, and literature in no way left him dependent upon his erstwhile mentor. The theorists agreed, however, upon the importance of linguistic reformation as a requisite for literary reform, and of literary reform as a prerequisite to the circulation of ideas that move people's minds and hearts. These changes, Hu believed, could only be accomplished by language reform that functioned as more than an educational tool; closing the vast gap between the barely literate and the educated elites mandated the production of a literature singular for its liveliness and beauty. In the fullest sense, as Hu explained in his essay on "a constructive literary revolution," China required a literary national language.

Ever the Deweyan experimentalist, Hu, more logically than might at first be manifest, sought to engineer his evolutionary revolution cautiously. Time and the responses of creative writers alone would justify his hypotheses about the *pai hua*. Meanwhile, the matter was open for investigation. In this regard, Hu stood in sharp contrast to some of his earlier supporters who swiftly assumed dogmatic positions and made the call for the *pai hua* a dogma, antitraditionalism an orthodoxy. Ch'en Tu-hsiu argued that toleration of divergent opinions and freedom of expression, at least in reference to literature, were tactically intolerable, merely affording opponents room for discussion. *Pai hua* reformers ought, he believed, to presume the absolute truth of their ideas. Moreover, Ch'en, in a radical vein, wanted to see the classical tradition abandoned as worthless – and old-fashioned scholars along with it.

Hu's unwavering position, however, continued to be that the *pai hua* itself constituted a principal element of the classical tradition, one that China's officials, leaders, educators, and aristocrats either had abandoned or, worse, had ignored. Avoiding the reassuring claim that in previous centuries the Chinese had discovered nearly everything that only more recently had been rediscovered in the West, and refusing to pander to those who denied China's massive backwardness, he cautiously suggested that Chinese traditions, in fact, bore within them the seeds of China's real progress. Where other reformers preoccupied themselves with attacking the past and hence were backward-looking, Hu insisted that if literary reform took place along the lines that he suggested the past would naturally cease to be a burden.

As a scholar who undertook literary and historical analysis of the *I Ching* (c. 500–300 B.C.; *The Book of Changes*) and the works of such thinkers as Confucius, Mo Tih, and the Neo-Moists Chuang-tzu and Hsün-tzu, among others, Hu was aware of the problem of seeming to argue that, as ancient uses of the *pai hua* indicate, the past was rich in creativity, while acknowledging that the past itself had become a manifest cause of China's underdevelopment. Yet what Hu's evidence showed him was that while great beauty and vigor characterized the pre-Confucian and Confucian ages, that past had in fact been drastically altered, distorted, and perverted by the introduction of extraneous influences, with disastrous consequences for those who were unaware of this corruption. Originally, China was a land of simple, unimaginative, unreligious farmers, hardworking and contented with their lot. After the rise of great sages such as Confucius and Meng-tzu and the subsequent founding of states and of the empire, they were reluctantly exposed to urbanization. Basically, as Hu interpreted the past, the common people had sought only good crops and freedom from government interference. Essentially, too, prior to the incursions of Buddhism, Chinese society was divided into farmers and country squires, a fact reflected by its philosophers – Confucius representing the values of the squirearchy and Lao-tzu and Chuang-tzu the laissez-faire outlook of the farmers. Several centuries after Confucius, however, his teachings were being reinterpreted in the light of Buddhist influences. During the twelfth and thirteenth centuries, what once had merely been the attitudes of the country squires came to be enshrined as political principles.

Buddhism, as Hu understood it, taught the abnegation of this world in preparation for the next, and its Chinese proselytes – tragically, he believed – imposed this system upon the realities of Chinese life. He acceded to the view, for it was not his alone, that Chinese society had become lifeless after the twelfth century.

Chinese culture, he concluded, had been locked in one long struggle to divest itself of Buddhism, to little avail. Values sacred to Confucius – life and individuality – were to Buddhists inconsequential. Gone, too, were the familial values integral to Confucianism, displaced by ideals of ascetic monasticism, and gone were the concomitant obligations Confucians believed that they owed to the state. Even Taoism, according to Hu, succumbed to Buddhism, in the sense that in persecuting and boycotting it Taoists had failed to retain the truly colorful and imaginative qualities of the Indian religion. Worse, such neo-Confucians were responsible for the subsequent degradation of women, dramatized by footbinding, which Hu denounced throughout his life in his championship of female emancipation.

As a man of advanced Western education, as an admirer of Dewey, as an experimentalist – that is, as an activist – Hu considered the tendencies of China's recent cultural history to have been disastrous for Chinese literature. China's problems were too monumental, its backwardness too demonstrable, to tolerate arcane esoterica in the world of letters. China's creative writers, its national literature, he believed, should focus upon its corruption, disease, ignorance, and poverty. Real life mandated a progressive literature that pointed the way to a better, more fulfilling existence.

Hu's direct literary influences were partial ones. To be sure, the *pai hua* did rather swiftly displace the language of the elite few and thereby helped fill the gulf between literary language and the language of daily life. Yet a vital new generation of Chinese writers did not arise in his day. Despite his immense abilities and his devotion to his goals, Hu may himself have contributed to this deficiency: while he was skillful in his depiction of the literary scene and the plight of literature, he was not, his few experimental writings aside, a creative writer himself. In this regard, he could never furnish the inspiring example of a great author to those whom he exhorted.

Yet there are ample and accurate grounds for designating Hu the father of the Chinese literary revolution. He was initially the most lucid voice for literary reform. No other scholar-philosopher of his time examined Chinese literary history with comparable textual and historical insight. He was foremost in illuminating the lengthy development of vernacular literature in China, hence in calling attention to the wide dissemination of the Mandarin dialect throughout the country. It is doubtful that anyone else so extensively introduced Western authors, their ideas, and their works to Chinese audiences, or so aptly noted China's immense stimulation from Western contacts during the nineteenth and early twentieth centuries. It was his exegetical labors that revealed the lineage of the great *pai hua* novels, their textual integrity, and their authorship. Though it was developed only through the T'ang dynasty, his history of popular literature remains unsurpassed. Not least, he demonstrated how effectively experimentalist methodology could be employed to resolve obscurities and confusion in cultural issues. While the notoriety that his literary theories and criticisms enjoyed was greatest between 1917 and the end of the 1920s, Hu's contributions and influence have proved enduring.

Principal criticism

"Wen-hsüeh kai-liang ch'u-i," 1917 (in *Hsin Ch'ing*)
"Li-shih-ti wen-hsüeh kuan-nien lun," 1917
"Chien-she ti wen-hsüeh ko-ming lun," 1918
"I-pusheng-chu-i," 1918
"Ch'ing-tai hsüeh-che ti chih-hsüeh fang-fa," 1919
Chung-kuo che-hsüeh shih ta-kang, 1919
The Development of the Logical Method in Ancient China, 1922
Pai-hua wen-hsüeh-shih, shang-chuan, 1928
The Chinese Renaissance, 1934
"Pi-shang liang-shan: Wen-hsüeh ko-ming ti k'ai-shih," 1934
Chung-kuo hsin wen-hsüeh yun-tung hsiao-shih, 1958

Other major works and literary forms

Besides his principal works of literary theory and criticism, Hu Shih published more than two hundred books (several of them multivolume works), chapters in books, and articles. Thus, the corpus of his thought embraces a broad range of subjects of great concern to him and to modern China, including Chinese philosophy, Buddhist influences on Chinese culture, and the tasks of modern religion. He explored the interaction of East and West in such fields as the emancipation and rights of Chinese women, Chinese education in relation to the theories of John Dewey, and the impact of, and Chinese reaction to, Western science. His political writings offered advice to the Nationalist regime of the Kuomintang, criticized "Stalinism" in the People's Republic of China, and discussed Sino-Japanese, Sino-German, and Sino-American political and diplomatic relations. Hu traced the lineage of the great *pai hua* novels and wrote experimental poetry and autobiography. While he initially gained renown chiefly as a revolutionary literary theorist, clearly the bulk of his work deals with other, though not always unrelated, interests.

PLAY
Chung-shen ta-shih, 1919

POETRY
Ch'ang-shih chi, 1919

NONFICTION
Sinological Research at the Present Time, 1925
China's Own Critics, 1931 (with Lin Yu-tang)
My Credo and Its Evolution, 1931
Ssu-shih tzu-shu, 1933
Ts'ang-hui-shih cha-chi, 1939 (4 volumes)
The Conflict of Ideologies, 1941
Historical Foundations for a Democratic China, 1941
China's Place in the Present World Struggle, 1942
My Mother's Betrothal, 1946
China in Stalin's Grand Strategy, 1950
Chung-kuo chung-ku ssu-hsiang-shih ch'ang-pien, 1971
Hu Shih kei Chao Yüan-jen te hsin, 1972
Ting Wen-chiang te chuan-chi, 1973
Hu Shih k'ou-shu tzu-chuan, 1981

Further reading

Boorman, Howard L., ed. *Biographical Dictionary of Republican China*. Vol. 2, 1968.
Creel, Herrlee G. *Chinese Thought from Confucius to Mao*, 1953.
Grieder, Jerome B. *Hu Shih and the Chinese Renaissance*, 1963.
Hsia, C. T. *A History of Modern Chinese Fiction, 1917–1957*, 1961.

CLIFTON K. YEARLEY
KERRIE L. MACPHERSON

See also Chinese Literary Theory

Victor Hugo

French novelist, poet, and playwright

Born: Besançon, France; February 26, 1802
Died: Paris, France; May 22, 1885

Biography

Victor-Marie Hugo was born on February 26, 1802, in Besançon, France, to Joseph-Léopold-Sigisbert Hugo, a career military officer, and his wife, Sophie-Françoise. The Hugo marriage, characterized by long separations and sometimes violent confrontations, eventually ended in a bitter separation. As a child, Victor traveled extensively in Spain and Italy as a consequence of his father's career. In 1816 he moved with his mother, now estranged from Léopold, to Paris. By the age of fifteen he had written two tragedies and a comic opera, and received an honorable mention from the Académie Française for one of his poems. At twenty-one he was granted two pensions from Louis XVIII, one for a collection of poetry, the other for his first novel, *Han d'Islande* (1823; *Hans of Iceland*, 1845). In 1830, after defeating the venerable forces of the classical theater in the famous "battle of *Hernani*," he became a hero among the youthful Romantics and willingly assumed leadership of the new movement. Two years after his 1841 election to the French Academy, the disastrous production of *Les Burgraves* (1843; *The Burgraves*, 1896) effectively ended both his career in the theater and the Romantic movement in France. That same year both his beloved daughter, Léopoldine, and her husband were drowned in a tragic boating accident. Devastated, Hugo published no significant literary work for almost ten years. Meanwhile, his political career flourished. In quick succession, he was named a peer of France in 1841 and was elected to the constituent assembly, then to the legislature.

In 1851 Hugo was exiled after engaging in open opposition to the government of Louis-Napoleon in the national assembly. For the next nineteen years he lived on the island of Guernsey, where, in the calm of Hauteville-House overlooking the sea, he produced many of his greatest works. With the declaration of the Third Republic in December, 1870, Hugo returned triumphantly to France, where he continued to write until his death in 1885. He was buried in the Pantheon in Paris after an official state funeral.

Influence

It has been said that although "the influence of Hugo on nineteenth-century French poetry was deep and pervasive, it is not always an easy one to demonstrate." His influence as a theorist on later French literary theory is equally difficult to document, for he was far more gifted as a practitioner than as a theoretician. The generally unsystematized nature of his critical work, his unyielding tendency toward generalization, and his overwhelming need for synthesis tended to exasperate more than inform his contemporaries. Because Hugo was always most effective when putting theory into practice, it was primarily through his highly revolutionary poetic and fictional work that he was able to rechart the course of French literature in the nineteenth century. Hugo articulated the general concepts of his literary theory in the prefaces to his major fictional works, all of which were widely circulated.

Analysis

During the first quarter of the nineteenth century both French theater and poetry were essentially moribund. Locked into the rigid classical definition of tragedy established by Pierre Corneille and Jean Racine in the seventeenth century, the eighteenth-century theater generated only facile and slavish reproductions of earlier works. Despite limited attempts to break the restrictions of the classical theater (notably by Denis Diderot in his domestic, or bourgeois, drama), the predominant theatrical mode through the turn of the nineteenth century remained that of the classical tragedy, a decaying art whose formulas no longer communicated with a post-Revolutionary audience. In contrast to those who sought to preserve the classical theater, the audiences of the second-class Parisian boulevard theaters flocked to see the new melodramas. This new popular genre was born from a startlingly eclectic marriage of sensational and sentimental materials (often containing incidental "mood" music) which sought to unite the sublime and the comic.

Like the theater, French poetry was caught in the grip of old and dying conventions. The eighteenth-century *philosophes,* adhering to the tenets of the Age of Reason, had preferred to confront critical ideas rather than compose abstract lyrics. In fact, no lyric poetry of merit appeared in France for the nearly three hundred years between the Renaissance and the publication of Alphonse de Lamartine's *Méditations poétiques* in 1820 (*The Poetical Meditations*, 1839).

Despite the dearth of dramatic and poetic activity early in the century, numerous revolutionary theories on the nature of literature were "in the air," as Charles Marie René Leconte de Lisle so often remarked, theories from which eventually blossomed the great Romantic works of Victor Hugo and his contemporaries. With his genius for generalizing the particular and an almost magical ability to make literary theory accessible to a wide public, Hugo skillfully synthesized the diverse ideas of the day and communicated them in an energetic style to a public eager for change and innovation. These ideas, which one might resist calling a "theory of literature" in the light of Hugo's lack of systematic presentation, are most skillfully and boldly expressed in *La Préface de Cromwell* (1827; English translation, 1896). This work is, as René Wellek observes, "the fullest statement of Hugo's early critical views and is deservedly regarded as the main critical text of the French Romantic debate." Hugo's later critical theory appears in a somewhat chaotic presentation entitled *William Shakespeare* (1864; English translation, 1864).

Because of Hugo's genius at synthesizing disparate ideas into a powerful whole, an understanding of the milieu in which Hugo conceived the ideas in *La Préface de Cromwell* is crucial to an assessment of him as literary theorist. The most important influence on literary theory at the time in France was Shakespeare's plays, which had become particularly important as the result of new translations by François Guizot and Alfred de Vigny. An English-cast performance of *Othello*, attended by Hugo, was well received in 1827. In the widely read two-part *Racine et Shakespeare* (1823, 1825; *Racine and Shakespeare*, 1962), Stendhal compared the great French classical dramatist Racine with the English poet. By defining *le romanticisme*, as he called it, as that protean element within a literary work which allows it to satisfy the ever-changing criteria of "ideal beauty" demanded by each generation, Stendhal could call both Racine and Shakespeare "romantics" who differed only in degree. The future of French tragedy, Stendhal concluded, would depend on a willingness to study, as Shakespeare had, "the world in which we live." Building on ideas encountered in the works of Alessandro Manzoni, leader of the Romantic movement in Italy, Stendhal also called for the rejection of the unities of time and place, argued for the use of prose rather than poetry in drama, and insisted on the critical importance of the depiction of great passion onstage. Many of these fundamentally Romantic ideas Hugo freely incorporated into his own literary theory.

In addition to the influence of Shakespeare, Hugo was powerfully affected by August Wilhelm von Schlegel's series of lectures on the Romantic drama translated into French in 1814 as *Cours de littérature dramatique*, in which the German critic admonishes the French dramatists for their blind acceptance of the classical unities of time, place, and action and the absurd restrictions of *les bienséances*, as well as for their refusal to abandon classical themes for modern ones, their strict adherence to the Alexandrine verse form, and their copious use of periphrasis. Schlegel's proposal for a new type of drama which would combine the comic and the tragic and thus mirror more closely the truth of everyday life was an idea enthusiastically embraced by Hugo.

Within this rich milieu, Hugo formulated his theory of the Romantic drama, a synthetic theory which ultimately had wide-ranging implications not only for the theater but also for poetry and "art" in the most general sense.

Hugo's theory of drama is predicated on a grandiose and thus ultimately simplistic ordering of human society into three developmental stages. These stages, which he labels "primitive" (*les temps primitifs*), "ancient" (*les temps antiques*), and "modern" (*les temps modernes*), correspond to the three ages of human life: childhood, adulthood, and old age. Since the evolution of poetry (and thus tragedy, for tragedy is merely dramatic poetry) always parallels that of society, one can discern the character of the former by observing the development of the latter. The primitive era, Hugo assumes, is characterized by the hymn and the poetry implicit in Genesis. In the second stage, the epic dominates, with Homer as its chief exponent. In the final stage, the Christian epoch, the poet sees the world "from a higher and broader perspective." In this modern era, poetry has reached the pinnacle of its development, and this culmination is expressed in the drama, a word whose definition within Hugo's theoretical construct is mercurial at best. Offering example as definition, Hugo maintains that "Shakespeare is drama," for, like Shakespeare, the dramatist melds "the grotesque with the sublime, the frightening with the farcical, the tragic with the comic."

Because the modern era profits from a synthesis of the two preceding eras, it is more capable of accurately representing reality, and thus truth, within its characteristic art form, the drama. Significantly, Hugo observes, the drama was born only after the formulation of the doctrine of Christian dualism, according to which human beings are both mortal and immortal, body and soul. The constant struggle between these opposing natures, between the sublime and the grotesque, defines the fundamental character of the drama, which is the "real" (*le réel*). True poetry, or the reality of drama, for Hugo, is thus found in the "harmony of opposites." It naturally follows that there should be no restrictions on poetry, for all that is permitted in nature is also permitted in art. The ugly, the grotesque are as much a part of art as is beauty; in fact, Hugo insists, the grotesque provides a multitude of possibilities for art because there are so many forms of ugliness, while there is but one form of ideal beauty. The ultimate consequence of the poet's awareness of the creative power implicit in Christian dualism, then, is that the limitations of classical literature give way to the freedom of Romantic literature.

Hugo's insistence on the importance of *le grotesque* remains one of his most important theoretical legacies. Although differing in substantive ways from the concept of the union of good and evil so fundamental to the aesthetic of Charles Baudelaire and the later French Symbolists, Hugo's visualization of the grotesque as the "beastly" side of humanity certainly points toward the very modern concept that the poet's inspiration may originate in either, or both, good and evil, and that the two might, at times, be one and the same. Nevertheless, Hugo does not link the grotesque exclusively to "evil"; rather, the grotesque seems to refer to all those elements of reality, of real life, which had been formally excluded from art by the classical tradition. From the simple acceptance of everyday language (for example, the use of the word "handkerchief" onstage as opposed to some complex circumlocution) to the presentation of the most hideously deformed figure (such as Quasimodo in *Notre-Dame de Paris* (1831; *The Hunchback of Notre Dame*, 1833), Hugo defended absolutely the comprehensive nature of art. It is but a short step from this point to the theory of the congenerous nature of art; the artificial distinctions between traditional literary genre become meaningless and inhibitive in the modern era, when such definitional divisions serve only to limit the potential of art to be wholly inclusive. Thus drama and poetry are one and the same, if not in appearance, certainly in inspiration and intent.

The implications of Hugo's general theory of the drama led him to attack specific conventions of the classical tradition. By first arguing that the arbitrary distinctions between genres are resolved in the drama, he could conclude that, obviously, the drama must be allowed to develop freely, essentially without definition even of its own character. Thus the maintenance of the unities of time and place would be patently absurd because such restrictions are exclusionary and unnatural. Only the unity of action should logically be preserved, for the human eye can adjust to but one perspective at a time. In defending the importance of the thematic integrity of a work, however, Hugo takes care to distinguish between "unity of action" and "simplicity of action." A drama need not omit subplots and intrigues, he insists, so long as they are relevant to the whole: "The unity of the whole is the law of perspective in the theater."

On the more closely focused level of the production of the text, Hugo, like many of his contemporaries, encouraged the use of "local color" to enliven the drama. Yet care must be taken, he warned, to distinguish between the common, superficial splash of color used by some to highlight a character, and that profound, "characteristic" color that penetrates and animates a work like sap coursing through the fibers of a tree. Additionally, the poet should avoid the "common" language of prose and write in verse, not the repetitive Alexandrine verse, however, but a forceful, free, and subtle verse appropriate to the vitality of the modern age. Finally, the poet must perform in a correct yet vibrant idiom, always seeking the evocative and evoking the suggestive powers of language. For Hugo, language was like the sea, constantly changing, unchainable, free.

Hugo produced his major theoretical statements in his early prefaces, and his writings after *La Préface de Cromwell* reflect changes primarily in form not content. Some of his later criticism, however, particularly parts of *William Shakespeare*, indicates a movement toward a more mythic concept of poetry and a definition of literary "types" which critics have linked to Carl Gustav Jung's modern view of "archetypal patterns"; nevertheless, Hugo's concepts remain largely undeveloped. His most significant contributions to the evolution of literary theory must still be found in the familiar territory of his early work: his attempt to order the history of literature into an understandable and informative paradigm, his eloquent condemnation of the obsequious attachment of his contemporaries to the classical tradition, and his emphasis on the harmony of the sublime and the grotesque.

His intuitive awareness of the links between literary evolution and cultural/societal evolution provides useful insights into the age-old debate over the interrelatedness of life and art. His abolition of distinctions between literary genres based on a confidence in the universal "harmony" of all things in the natural world has far-reaching implications, not only in the arts but in all disciplines as well. His battle against the restrictive conventions which had stifled the French lyric spirit for centuries opened the way for modern literature to chart a natural and unimpeded course. Finally, his insistence on the dual nature of humanity and on the importance of resolving in art the opposition of the sublime and the grotesque – which, to some, is suggestive of Erich Auerbach's well-known thesis in his 1946 book, *Mimesis* (English translation, 1953) – effectively destroyed the ancient concepts of high and low style which had always kept comedy at arm's length from tragedy. After Hugo, there would be, as he proclaimed at one point, no more artificial "theories, or poetics, or systems": there would be only "liberty in art."

Principal criticism

La Préface de Cromwell, 1827 (English translation, 1896)
Littérature et philosophie mêlées, 1834
William Shakespeare, 1864 (English translation, 1864)

Other major works and literary forms

Victor Hugo's literary production was prodigious, ranging from poetry to novels, drama, and political essays. To the

French, Hugo has always been first and foremost a poet. In addition to his immense body of poetic work, Hugo wrote nine lengthy novels, two of which, *Notre-Dame de Paris* (1831; *The Hunchback of Notre Dame*, 1833) and *Les Misérables* (1862; English translation, 1862), rank among the greatest novels of French and perhaps world literature. Among his contemporaries, Hugo was as esteemed as a dramatist as he was as a poet and novelist; only a small portion of his theater, however, remains popular. Of particular interest are *Hernani* (1830; English translation, 1830), whose tumultuous first production marked the beginning of the Romantic era in French drama, and *Les Burgraves* (1843; *The Burgraves*, 1896), whose ignominious production announced the imminent death of the French Romantic theater. *Ruy Blas* (1838; English translation, 1890), considered by many critics and a large public to be Hugo's finest play, provides the most fully realized example of his dramatic theories of the apposition of the tragic and the grotesque and of the "confusion of genres."

NOVELS

Han d'Islande, 1823 (*Hans of Iceland*, 1845)
Bug-Jargal, 1826 (*The Noble Rival*, 1845)
Le Dernier Jour d'un condamné, 1829 (*The Last Day of a Condemned*, 1840)
Notre-Dame de Paris, 1831 (*The Hunchback of Notre Dame*, 1833)
Claude Gueux, 1834
Les Misérables, 1862 (English translation, 1862)
Les Travailleurs de la mer, 1866 (*The Toilers of the Sea*, 1866)
L'Homme qui rit, 1869 (*The Man Who Laughs*, 1869)
Quatre-vingt-treize, 1874 (*Ninety-three*, 1874)

PLAYS

Irtamène, written 1816, published 1934 (verse drama)
Inez de Castro, written c. 1818, published 1863 (verse drama)
Cromwell, 1827 (verse drama; English translation, 1896)
Amy Robsart, 1828 (English translation, 1895)
Hernani, 1830 (verse drama; English translation, 1830)
Marion de Lorme, 1831 (verse drama; English translation, 1895)
Le Roi s'amuse, 1832 (verse drama; *The King Amuses Himself*, 1842)
Lucrèce Borgia, 1833 (*Lucretia Borgia*, 1842)
Marie Tudor, 1833 (English translation, 1895)
Angelo, tyran de Padoue, 1835 (*Angelo, Tyrant of Padua*, 1880)
Ruy Blas, 1838 (verse drama; English translation, 1890)
Les Burgraves, 1843 (*The Burgraves*, 1896)
La Grand-mère, 1865
Mille Francs de Récompense, 1866
Torquemada, written 1869, published 1882 (English translation, 1896)
Les Deux Trouvailles de Gallus, 1881
Le Théâtre en liberté, 1886 (includes *Mangeront-ils?*)
The Dramatic Works, 1887
The Dramatic Works of Victor Hugo, 1895–1896 (4 volumes)

POETRY

Odes et poésies diverses, 1822, 1823
Nouvelles Odes, 1824
Odes et ballades, 1826
Les Orientales, 1829 (*Les Orientales: Or, Eastern Lyrics*, 1879)
Les Feuilles d'automne, 1831
Les Chants du crépuscule, 1835 (*Songs of Twilight*, 1836)
Les Voix intérieures, 1837
Les Rayons et les ombres, 1840
Les Châtiments, 1853
Les Contemplations, 1856
La Légende des siècles, 1859–1883 (5 volumes; *The Legend of the Centuries*, 1894)
Les Chansons des rues et des bois, 1865
L'Année terrible, 1872
L'Art d'être grand-père, 1877
Le Pape, 1878
La Pitié suprême, 1879
L'Âne, 1880
Les Quatre Vents de l'esprit, 1881
The Literary Life and Poetical Works of Victor Hugo, 1883
La Fin de Satan, 1886
Toute la lyre, 1888
Dieu, 1891
Les Années funestes, 1896
Poems from Victor Hugo, 1901
Dernière Gerbe, 1902
Poems, 1902
The Poems of Victor Hugo, 1906
Océan, 1942

NONFICTION

Le Rhin, 1842 (*The Rhine*, 1843)
Napoléon le petit, 1852 (*Napoleon the Little*, 1852)
Actes et paroles, 1875–1876
Histoire d'un crime, 1877 (*The History of a Crime*, 1877–1878)
Religions et religion, 1880
Choses vues, 1887 (*Things Seen*, 1887)
En voyage: Alpes et Pyrénées, 1890 (*The Alps and the Pyrenees*, 1898)
France et Belgique, 1892
Correspondance, 1896–1898

MISCELLANEOUS

Œuvres complètes, 1880–1892 (57 volumes)
Victor Hugo's Works, 1892 (30 volumes)
Works, 1907 (10 volumes)
Shadows of a Hand: The Drawings of Victor Hugo, 1998

Further reading

Brombert, Victor. *Victor Hugo and the Visionary Novel*, 1984.
Guerlac, Suzanne. *The Impersonal Sublime: Hugo, Baudelaire, Lautréamont*, 1900.
Halsall, A. W. *Victor Hugo and the Romantic Drama*, 1998.
Houston, John Porter. *Victor Hugo*, 1974.
Ireson, J. *Victor Hugo: A Companion to his Poetry*, 1997.
Masters-Wicks, Karen. *Victor Hugo's "Les Misérables" and the Novels of the Grotesque*, 1994.
Mehlman, Jeffrey. *Revolution and Repetition: Marx / Hugo / Balzac*, 1977.
Richardson, Joanna. *Victor Hugo*, 1976.
Robb, Graham. *Victor Hugo*, 1997.
Souriau, Maurice. Introduction to *La Préface de Cromwell*, 1897.
Wellek, René. "Stendhal and Hugo," in *A History of Modern Criticism: 1750–1950*. Vol. 2, *The Romantic Age*, 1955.

WILLIAM GRIFFIN

See also Baudelaire; Continental Theory; Romanticism; Sainte-Beuve

T. E. Hulme

English poet and theorist

Born: Endon, Staffordshire, England; September 16, 1883
Died: Oost-Duinkerke Bains, the Netherlands; September 28, 1917

Biography

Thomas Earl Hulme was born on September 16, 1883, at the family home of Gratton Hall, near Endon in the northeastern corner of Staffordshire in northern England, a region where the Hulme family had been prominent for more than two centuries as landowners and estate managers. His father was a strict disciplinarian, his mother a robust and independent sportswoman; family life exemplified Victorian earnestness. Hulme attended village schools and the local high school at Newcastle-under-Lyme, where he became known for his zeal for debate. Awarded a scholarship in mathematics, he entered St. John's College, Cambridge University, in 1902; there he marked his presence mainly by avoiding his required studies and engaging all comers in debates on philosophy and art. The college expelled him after two years, apparently for assaulting a policeman during a campus riot. His father then forced him to enroll as a student of biology and physics at University College, London, but he spent two years there principally *in absentia*, attending lectures in philosophy at Cambridge instead.

He then fled to Canada, spending eight months as a farm laborer and lumberjack. Returning to Europe, he settled in Belgium for a year, perfecting his languages and reading widely in current philosophy. In 1908 he settled again in London, setting himself up as champion of the avant-garde in poetry, metaphysics, and the arts. For five years he founded radical groups, contributed to radical journals, and hobnobbed with the radical intelligentsia, notably Ezra Pound and the proto-Imagists. When war broke out in 1914, he threw himself enthusiastically into the cause, believing passionately in the necessity of combating Germany's quest for hegemony in Europe. After being wounded in 1915, he returned to the front in 1917, where he was killed in a random artillery barrage.

Influence

Hulme's significance for the development of many aspects of modernism is immense, quite out of proportion to the amount of his writing and to a degree independent of it. This significance derived primarily from the force of his personality: Hulme, a compulsive talker, dominated the social circles of young artists, writers, political and economic theoreticians, and journalists in prewar London. In these conversations and quasi debates, Hulme urgently promoted his aesthetic and cultural ideas, which called for a radical break with Victorian traditions in art, philosophy, and general culture.

His arguments were not, however, limited to conversation; he recorded them in an influential series of articles, letters, and essays, published mostly in journals of limited circulation. Yet somehow his ideas gained currency, almost as if he became the spokesman for the critical postulates of the World War I generation. His remarks provided a theoretical underpinning for cultural phenomena otherwise as diverse as Imagism, antiromanticism, and modernism in poetry, Symbolism in fiction, abstract impressionism, cubism, and geometrism in art, the Theater of Ideas and Theater of the Absurd in drama, phenomenology and existentialism in philosophy, medievalism and the history of ideas in history, and National Socialism in government. In particular, almost without exception, the poets of the 1920s and 1930s – William Butler Yeats, Ezra Pound, T. S. Eliot, Robert Frost, Wallace Stevens, Stephen Crane, William Carlos Williams, Archibald MacLeish – become more explicable when approached from the perspective of Hulme's ideas.

Analysis

Hulme was neither a systematic thinker nor a systematic writer. Indeed, he once suggested that no one should begin an important philosophical work before the age of forty, and this notion was probably not simply an excuse for his undoubtedly dilatory habits. It is certainly true that at his death he had published only a handful of relatively minor essays and articles in obscure journals. *Speculations* was pieced together from the notebooks and manuscripts left behind. *Further Speculations by T. E. Hulme* collected his published articles and all remaining materials. Some evidence does suggest, however, that during his last few months he was gearing up for more elaborate projects. His "A Notebook on Notebooks" (unpublished), for example, lays out a plan for transforming his compulsive jottings into organized publications. Unfortunately, this outline seems to have been one of his last pieces of work.

In his introduction to *Speculations*, Herbert Read distinguishes six areas which Hulme was developing for studies or series: (1) antihumanism, antiromanticism, and pre-Renaissance philosophy, (2) an introduction to the philosophy of Henri Bergson, (3) Jacob Epstein and the aesthetics of sculpture, (4) the psychology of literature (expression, language, and style), (5) modern theories of art, and (6) an allegory expressing his theories of philosophy. The first category Hulme planned to cover in a series of pamphlets, of which the two essays "Humanism and the Religious Attitude" and "Romanticism and Classicism" would have made parts; these two representative pieces, the best known and most reprinted of his writings, contain many of his root ideas. In 1912 Hulme delivered a series of four lectures on the philosophy of Bergson in London and wrote an introduction to his translation of Bergson's *Introduction à la métaphysique* (1903); these were to form the basis of the second area. Hulme had apparently nearly completed the book on Epstein at his death, but the manuscript disappeared; only fragmentary notes remain. The same is true of category four; his "Notes on Language and Style" was published by Read in *Criterion* (1925) and republished in *Further Speculations by T. E. Hulme*. Materials for the fifth book consist of an outline, numerous notes, and the essay "Bergson's Theory of Art," which appears in *Speculations*. The final category represents much of his thought over a period of at least ten years, but the extensive and extensively emended notes on this subject yield no coherent form or significant content.

Perhaps Hulme's most important work, however, falls into none of these categories and stems from his first return to London. At this time he single-handedly took on himself the reformation of English poetry. Thinking of himself primarily as a poet at that time – almost all of his poetry was written then – he organized the Poets' Club, meeting formally there and informally elsewhere with many of the young generation of poets and hammering out in debate the basic principles of a new theory. He presented an organized statement of these principles in "A Lecture on Modern Poetry," first delivered in 1908 or 1909 and first published in 1938 (reprinted in *Further Speculations by T. E. Hulme*). This liberation of poetry from the constrictions of late Victorianism was an absolute necessity; it laid the foundation for many of the innovations in poetry of the next twenty-five years. It established the theoretical core for Imagism in particular, four years before Pound and F. S. Flint published their tenets in *Poetry*, but it also anticipated Eliot's formulation of the "objective correlative" and Williams' preference for oral to rhetorical meter. Hulme has not usually been credited with this achievement, largely because Pound and Amy Lowell had better publicity, but he truly deserves the credit.

Hulme's essay "Romanticism and Classicism" establishes the groundwork for much of his thinking and writing. His objective is to oust Romanticism from its dominant position in critical theory, to associate the deterioration of modern literature – in fact, of modern life and living – with it, and to argue the need for a revival of classical principles and the recovery of the fancy as the main instrument of literary expression. The argument is typical of Hulme: rather than systematically analyzing the perceived opposition of the two terms and dissecting them with logical precision, he engages in a combination of rhapsodic meditation and rhetorical flourish – a form of discourse closer to a musical theme-and-variations or a soapbox oration than to an unimpassioned, reasoned statement. Further, he expands what is apparently a literary or at most cultural question into ethics and metaphysics.

Thus he attributes the opposed attitudes to two different perceptions of human nature. Romanticism derives from the assumption that humanity is essentially good; classicism holds that it is flawed and limited, but capable of improvement. The basis for the distinction lies in what Hulme calls the "classical" postulate of Original Sin, thus further expanding the argument into religion and theology – and gaining a strong rhetorical advantage. Hulme argues that religion is necessary. When religion is abandoned – as it was by the Romantics – it is perverted where man mistakenly attributes godlike qualities to himself. This lack of restraint makes Romantic poetry simultaneously vague and passive. Classicism, on the other hand, is limited and finite – hard and dry. Hulme does concede that individual Romantics escape his general strictures; his real target is the "modern romantic," the latter-day imitators who merely aped outmoded forms. This target was certainly legitimate. Yet the concession finally weakens his general argument.

Hulme discovered in the work of the French philosopher Bergson what he considered to be metaphysical and epistemological support for his theories in language and poetry. In the process, he became Bergson's major defender in England, but he was less interested in expounding the philosophy than he was in appropriating it for his own uses. Thus he focuses on two of Bergson's fundamental ideas: that reality is a flux unreachable by the intellect, and that action is more important than knowledge. The function of the intellect is to make effective action possible, not to arrive at positive comprehension. Instead of intellectual analysis, Bergson advocates intuition, the power of empathizing with objects, understanding them almost instinctively.

Although Bergson's ideas evoked little enthusiasm among professional philosophers, they proved marvelously fruitful for literature. Hulme quickly grasped their applicability. Since the real target of his attack was the limits placed on literature, art, and culture by scientific rationalism with its progressivist corollaries, he fastened on Bergson's basic antirationalism. Bergson's theory of intuition seemed made for his purposes; it justified his notion of the superior truth of poetry and gave him a counter to intellectual analysis. Without realizing it, Hulme was undermining his own argument, for there seems little difference between Bergson's intuition and the Romantics' celebration of instinct as opposed to mechanical reason. Nevertheless, he used it in support of his contention that the poet stands in a special relation to language: intuition allows him both to identify with his subject in a private way and to discover the unique verbal formulas necessary to give appropriate expression to this identification.

Hulme's own work in philosophy proper – he thought of himself mainly as a metaphysician – is most apparent in his essay "Humanism and the Religious Attitude," although it also appears in some of his articles. As philosophy it is both consistent and curious, for Hulme did not modify his theories much, and his positions are distinctly antirationalistic from start to finish. That is, he considered philosophy an art rather than a science, concerned more with presenting what he called a *Weltanschauung* – a world-view or complex of basic perceptions – than with the systematic examination of premises about the nature of life, and his metaphysics develops accordingly. It consists essentially of an attack on humanism as the source of Romanticism: the notion of humanity as basically good and, therefore, perfectible. He saw this concept as invented by the Renaissance and inherently antagonistic to the formerly prevailing religious view of humanity as limited by its very nature, the tragic but heroic victim of Original Sin. As elsewhere in his work, the object of his distaste is really the liberal humanistic ideas of his own age, but he believed that he had detected their origins in the Renaissance.

Hulme's method may have been flawed, his theories derivative, fragmentary, and repetitive, but he introduced many ideas which have since become commonplaces. One of these was his perception that each historical period defines itself by a network of commonly accepted prevailing ideas constituting its peculiar mind-set; each age creates its own method of viewing life, of which it is largely unconscious. These worldviews are axiomatic for each age, accepted as givens without any internal scrutiny. True history becomes therefore a history of ideas. He saw the Middle Ages as basically religious, the Renaissance as man-centered and consequently flawed. To his mind, making man – and man's mind – the measure of all things was to create false expectations and false hopes. It led finally to the lawlessness of the individual personality, to the promotion of individual freedom, and the eradication of the common good. Hulme thus anticipated many dominant social, political, and psychological theories of the early and middle twentieth century. He also pioneered the discipline of the history of ideas and the belief that only by studying other cultures on their own terms could Western man hope to understand his own.

There remains Hulme's work in aesthetics and the theory of art. This work represents a later adaptation of his central ideas; it proves surprisingly insightful and promises to outlive his earlier work. Here he applies his idea of cultural differentiation to the worlds of art, maintaining that the arts of any culture have to be approached through the norms of that culture rather than being subjected to the foreign standards of the viewer. The art of any period has to be viewed through its own lenses. Like so many of Hulme's ideas, these are derivative, but he freely acknowledges his debts to Wilhelm Worringer, Alois Riegl, and Heinrich Wölfflin. Interested in the philosophy of art rather than in the aesthetic experience itself, he argues that there are two fundamentally distinct approaches to art, the geometrical and the vital. Further, these two approaches are determined by two different perceptions of the relationship between humanity and its physical environment. Vital art grows from the view that humanity can harmonize with its situation, as in the Romantic notion that humanity forms a natural part of the natural order and that it evolved in conjunction with it. Geometrical art perceives the interaction of humans and their environment as hostile and antagonistic, as in the biblical concept of man being required to earn his living by the sweat of his brow. Vital art projects the human into nature; geometrical art abstracts forms from nature.

Hulme denies emphatically that geometrical or abstract art stems from technical disabilities; he takes pains to show that the opposite case is common, for he is chiefly interested in providing a theoretical basis for modern abstract practice. Making abstractionism a matter of preference would create a mode of vision correspondent with prehumanistic theory. It gave modern art philosophical respectability and associated pictorial and representational art with the dregs of sentimentalist theory. Hulme at least succeeded in creating an atmosphere in which unconventional and unfashionable experimentation could be received neutrally.

In all of his work, Hulme operated primarily on attitudes rather than on ideas. In this practice, however, he was consistent with his own beliefs: philosophy is primarily an art; its end is action. The action he recommends repeatedly in his work is twofold: moral reaction and formal innovation. He thus prepared the theoretical atmosphere for the art of the 1920s and 1930s and supplied a reactionary basis for the avant-garde. Hulme is the center of this movement.

Principal criticism

Speculations: Essays on Humanism and the Philosophy of Art, 1924

Further Speculations by T. E. Hulme, 1955

Other major works and literary forms

T. E. Hulme's poems are also of considerable importance, especially because of his influence on the development of Imagism; but they have rarely been accessible. Five of them appeared as "The Complete Poetical Works of T. E. Hulme" in *The New Age* in January, 1912; these were reprinted in that year as an appendix to Ezra Pound's two volumes of poetry, *Ripostes* and *Canzoni*, then reprinted again in *Speculations*. All of his poetry, some thirty-five poems, was finally collected and published by Alun R. Jones in *The Life and Opinions of T. E. Hulme* (1960) – a volume which also printed all Hulme's previously unpublished prose.

TRANSLATION

An Introduction to Metaphysics, 1912 (of Henri Bergson's *Introduction à la métaphysique*)

MISCELLANEOUS

The Life and Opinions of T. E. Hulme, 1960 (Alun R. Jones, editor)

Further reading

Bradbury, Malcolm, and James McFarlane, eds. *Modernism: 1890–1930*, 1976.

Davie, Donald. *Articulate Energy*, 1955.

Isaacs, John. *The Background of Modern Poetry*, 1951.

Kenner, Hugh. *The Pound Era*, 1971.

Kermode, Frank. *Romantic Image*, 1957.

Krieger, Murray. "The Ambiguous Anti-Romanticism of T. E. Hulme," in *Journal of English Literary History*. XX (December, 1953), pp. 300–314.
Levenson, Michael H. *A Genealogy of Modernism: A Study of English Literary Doctrine, 1908–1922*, 1984.
Read, Herbert. *The True Voice of Feeling*, 1952.
Roberts, Michael. *T. E. Hulme*, 1938.
Schwartz, Sanford. *The Matrix of Modernism: Pound, Eliot, and Early Twentieth-Century Thought*, 1985.
Sherry, Vincent. *Ezra Pound, Wyndham Lewis, and Radical Modernism*, 1993.
Wecter, Dixon. "Hulme and the Tragic View of Life," in *Southern Review*. V (Summer, 1939).

JAMES LIVINGSTON

See also Bergson; Pound

Humanism, Renaissance

The term "humanism" has two very different meanings. It is now used to describe the belief that human beings are self-sufficient and have no need for God. In this modern sense, "humanism" can be understood in opposition to religious belief. During the Renaissance, however, humanism was considered perfectly compatible with religion and simply referred to the adaptation of classical learning to the needs of the present world. Renaissance Humanism first took root in northern Italy in the fourteenth century, with the writers and scholars Petrarch and Giovanni Boccaccio, and then Coluccio Salutati, Leonardo Bruni, and many others, assiduously collecting and publishing rhetorical texts, and also modeling their own works on classical rhetoric, historiography, and poetry. At this stage Latin texts formed the foundation of classical learning. Greek studies grew rapidly after Constantinople fell to the Turks in 1453, when many Greek scholars fled to Italy.

Though steeped in Christianity, and often put to the service of the Church, Renaissance Humanism introduced a new and more positive view of humankind, and also a spirit of critical inquiry that would, eventually, lead to a profound questioning of received ideas, and even of the Church itself. Both in form and content, its impact on literature of all kinds was far-reaching.

The Church had in fact played an important role in the growth of Humanism by encouraging the study of classical rhetoric and eloquence. Two eminent Christian theologians, Saint Augustine and Erasmus, argued that a knowledge of pagan literature, rhetoric, and philosophy from ancient Greece and Rome was, in fact, absolutely essential for Christian writers and preachers who wished to present the essential truths of Christianity in an effective and pleasing manner. In his treatise *On Christian Instruction*, Augustine presented a powerful if paradoxical argument. He reminded his reader that when the Jews fled from Egypt, they took with them the Egyptians' gold and used this wealth for purposes more pleasing to God – God had approved of their "stealing the Egyptians' gold." In his work *The Book Against the Barbarians*, Erasmus also justified "stealing the Egyptians' gold." Like Augustine, Erasmus argued that it was essential for Christians to use moral and philosophical insights first made by pagan writers, and especially rhetorical techniques first developed by such influential pagan writers as Aristotle, Cicero, and Quintilian, in order to present more effectively the revealed truths of Christianity. In *The Book Against the Barbarians*, Erasmus even stated that true barbarians were those haughty Christians who denied the relevance of classical learning in their spiritual and intellectual lives.

Educational reforms, which had developed throughout Europe during the sixteenth century, stressed the central role of classical Latin and Greek culture in the intellectual and moral training of students. Despite their very real differences, Erasmus, Saint Ignatius Loyola (who founded the Jesuit order), and Philipp Melanchthon (who implemented Martin Luther's reforms in German schools and universities) all agreed that it was absolutely essential not just for future clergymen but all well-educated people to learn Latin and read the classic texts from ancient Rome in order to become better Christians. Some writers, including Erasmus, the French writers Guillaume Budé and Pierre de Ronsard, and the Spaniard Juan Luis Vives, also recognized the central importance of Greek in education.

It was essential for a wide variety of men and women to possess a solid reading knowledge of classical languages. Clergymen and theologians needed to know Latin so that they could read the works of such eminent Church fathers as saints Augustine, Thomas Aquinas, and Bonaventura, and the Vulgate, the Latin translation of the Bible completed by Saint Jerome. Mastery of Latin enabled clergymen to understand more profoundly how generations of theologians had interpreted the Old and New Testaments. A reading knowledge of Greek was almost as important because the New Testament had been written in Greek and theologians clearly needed to know exactly what the writers of the New Testament had actually said. For lawyers, the study of Latin was absolutely essential because the law in all European countries except England derived from Roman law and all the relevant texts for the study of law had been written in Latin. A lawyer without a sound knowledge of Latin could not read the basic theoretical texts and judicial decisions on which judges would rely in rendering their decisions. Although English law did not derive from Roman law, laws passed by Parliament and English judicial decisions were often published in Latin until well into the seventeenth century. An English lawyer could not adequately defend his clients in civil or criminal cases if he could not read the relevant statutes and judicial rulings. For doctors, Latin was equally important because medicine, as it was then practiced, relied heavily on the writings of classical physicians such as Galen and Hippocrates. When the French writer and physician François Rabelais defended his doctoral dissertation at the medical school of the University of Montpellier, he impressed the examining committee by using the original Greek text of Hippocrates and not a Latin translation: Rabelais clearly believed that his use of original sources of medical works would make him a more effective doctor.

During the sixteenth and seventeenth centuries, Latin was still commonly used by scholars and writers across Europe. Such important writers and scientists as Erasmus, Sir Thomas More, Martin Luther, and Johannes Kepler wrote some or all of their works in Latin. For Luther the choice between German and Latin was determined by his intended audience. For topics related solely to German Lutherans he wrote in German, but when he needed to respond to the Catholic theologian Erasmus' Latin essay *Discourse on the Freedom of the Will* he composed a Latin treatise, *The Bondage of the Will* (*De servo arbitrio*), so that scholars throughout Europe could understand the reasons for his disagreement with Erasmus. Thomas More, as he was awaiting his execution in the Tower of London, wrote his more personal works in English, but he had written his masterpiece, *Utopia*, in Latin. Even writers who chose to write in vernacular languages readily acknowledged the classical sources for their major works. For example, Joachim du Bellay composed in Rome two books of exile poetry (*Les Regrets* and *Les Antiquitez de Rome*, both published 1558), works which clearly constitute a very creative imitation of Ovid's collection of poems *Tristes*, which Ovid had composed in exile on the shores of the Black Sea.

An understanding of the classical sources of Renaissance thought and scholarship allows us to appreciate the profound impact Humanism had on European literature, and to measure the true originality of Renaissance poets, dramatists, and scholars. More specifically, it also allows us to understand the impact Humanism had on literary theory and criticism – a development that came about not only through the study of such theoretical works as Aristotle's *Poetics* (c. 334–323), Cicero's *On Oratory* (55 B.C.), and Horace's *The Art of Poetry* (c. 17 B.C.), but also through the close analysis of classical drama, poetry, and rhetoric.

Further reading

Bady, René. *Humanisme chrétien dans les lettres françaises*, 1972.
Baron, H. *From Petrarch to Leonardi Bruni*, 1968.
Bentley, J. *Humanists and Holy Writ*, 1983.
Bouwsma, William J. *The Interpretation of Renaissance Humanism*, 1959.
Desan, Philippe, ed. *Humanism in Crisis: The Decline of the French Renaissance*, 1991.
Gilmore, Myron P. *The World of Humanism, 1453–1517*, 1962.
Levi, A. H. T., ed. *Humanism in France at the end of the Middle Ages and in the Early Renaissance*, 1970.
Margolin, Jean-Claude. *Erasme: Précepteur de l'Europe*, 1995.
Trinkhaus, C. *The Scope of Renaissance Humanism*, 1983.

EDMUND J. CAMPION

David Hume

Scottish philosopher

Born: Edinburgh, Scotland; May 7, 1711
Died: Edinburgh, Scotland; August 25, 1776

Biography

David Hume was born on May 7, 1711, in Edinburgh, Scotland, son of the laird of Ninewells. His father died when Hume was a child, leaving him to be reared by his mother. Hume began studies at Edinburgh University when he was only twelve years old, as was customary at the time. The natural philosophy of Isaac Newton was taught at Edinburgh, and it is likely that Hume absorbed the teachings of this new science and that its inductive method had a considerable influence on his approach to philosophy.

After leaving Edinburgh University in 1726, Hume experimented briefly with a business enterprise and spent several years supposedly studying law; actually, as he later confessed, he spent most of his time reading classical literature. The intensity of these years of study debilitated Hume psychologically, and in 1729 he suffered a nervous breakdown. After five years of depression, he uprooted himself and settled down in La Flèche, in the French province of Anjou, and there recovered his health. It was in La Flèche that Hume wrote *A Treatise of Human Nature* (1739–1740). He moved to London in 1737 to oversee arrangements for publication of this work and returned to Edinburgh in 1739.

Hume continued to write after his return to Edinburgh, publishing *Essays, Moral and Political* (1741–1742). After standing unsuccessfully in 1744 for the Chair of Ethics and Pneumatical Philosophy at Edinburgh University, Hume went to London, where for a year he was tutor to the Marquess of Annandale. In 1746 Hume was secretary to General James St. Clair, and in 1748 he went with St. Clair as his aide in embassies to Turin and Vienna. Following two years at Ninewells, Hume spent the period between 1751 and 1758 in Edinburgh, after being rejected in 1751 in his candidacy for the Chair of Logic at the University of Glasgow. He also published *An Enquiry Concerning the Principles of Morals* (1751), which he considered to have superseded *A Treatise of Human Nature* as his best work. In 1752 he was named keeper of the Advocates Library and clerk to the faculty of Edinburgh, a position he held for five years while he worked on *The History of England* (1754–1762). He alternated between residences in London and Edinburgh while working on and publishing the six volumes of this work.

Hume went back to France in 1763 as secretary to Lord Hertford in the British embassy. For three years in Paris, Hume enjoyed the company of the philosophes of the Enlightenment, and when he returned to London in 1766 he brought Jean-Jacques Rousseau with him. Hume also met the thirty-eight-year-old Comtesse de Bouffers in Paris, and they eventually became lovers, although she was married and had another lover from the nobility. Returning to Edinburgh in 1769, Hume spent his final years preparing revised editions of his earlier works and enjoying a respected position in intellectual circles. He died on August 25, 1776, after a lingering illness.

Influence

In an advertisement in 1739 for his planned *A Treatise of Human Nature*, Hume announced that, if the first volumes of the treatise were successful, he would "proceed to the examination of *morals*, *politics*, and *criticism*, which will compleat this *Treatise of human nature*." The plan was never followed through, but Hume's intention reveals his keen interest in criticism – or more precisely, aesthetics. Hume is not a major figure in the history of criticism, but his analyses of the role in creative thought of imagination and the association of ideas were in the mainstream of eighteenth-century thought. He deserves recognition for his theoretical contributions to the critical practice of his age.

Analysis

Hume's role in the critical thought of his day can be divided into three parts: his contribution to the associationist psychology that informed eighteenth-century critical theory, his theory of tragedy, and his observations on standards of taste.

Associationist psychology engages one critical problem in aesthetics: do people's standards of beauty derive from innate ideas, or are they a product of mental associations? John Locke had rejected the ancient Platonic and Cartesian faith in the fixed capacities, or innate ideas, of the mind, substituting the doctrine that the mind is a blank slate gradually filled up by sense impressions that come together in patterns of ideas. Neoclassical critics such as the third Earl of Shaftesbury and Edmund Burke scorned the new associationist psychology and clung to a conviction of the mind's innate powers. Prominent among the associationists were Francis Hutcheson and, most influential of them all, David Hume.

In *An Inquiry into the Original of Our Ideas of Beauty and Virtue* (1725), Hutcheson worked out a compromise between the two schools. Hutcheson accepted the notion of an innate instinct which responds equally to aesthetic order and moral virtue. Hutcheson judged the capacity to record impressions of beauty to be as fixed as the responsiveness of the five senses. He attempted to address the question of why people differ in their standards of beauty. His answer was that though the instinct was innate and fixed, the great variety of human experience evokes widely differing associations of ideas. In this way, Hutcheson arrived at an awkward synthesis of the objective and the subjective that accounted for the phenomenon of normally pleasant objects becoming repulsive by personal associations, and vice versa. In effect, Hutcheson made associationist psychology available to neoclassical critical theory. It was Hume, however, who effected the fusion of the schools.

Hume wanted to explain human nature in the same way that Newton had studied physical nature. He began by fragmenting sensory experience into individual perceptions and then postulating three principles of human nature by which these perceptions are associated: resemblance, contiguity, and causality. These principles are essentially self-explanatory. Of resemblance, Hume says that "our imagination runs easily from one idea to any other that resembles it"; regarding contiguity, the imagination will "run along the parts of space and time in conceiving its objects." Cause and effect make up the most powerful principle: "There is no relation, which produces a stronger connection in the fancy, and makes one idea more readily recall another, than the relation of cause and effect between their objects."

From this analysis, Hume derives what he calls the "properties" of human nature. The first of these properties is the linking of ideas through the three modes of association described above – resemblance, contiguity, and causality. The second property is the linking not of ideas but of impressions (that is, passions):

> All resembling impressions are connected together, and no sooner one arises than the rest immediately follow. Grief and disappointment give rise to anger, anger to envy, envy to malice, malice to grief again, till the whole circle be completed.

Finally, the third property is inherent in the coming together of ideas and impressions in double associations, a phenomenon in which the association of ideas and the association of impressions "assist and forward each other."

This joint anatomy of the principles and properties of human nature provides the framework of theory for Hume's understanding of tragedy, as well as of the imagination, the concept of sublimity, and the aesthetic doctrine of the unity of action. The complicated emotional response to tragic spectacles is produced by the mingled associations of pleasing ideas with painful feelings. The artist's genius transforms the pain of tragic scenes into the pleasure which everyone experiences but which few can trace to its source.

The manner by which the mind creates associations acts as a gentle guide in the workings of imagination: "But notwithstanding the empire of the imagination, there is a secret tie or union among particular ideas, which causes the mind to conjoin them more frequently together, and makes the one, upon its appearance, introduce the other." Whereas some earlier thinkers had made the imagination dependent on memory, for Hume the imagination is neither tied to memory nor restrained by judgment.

Hume used his discovery of the interacting association of the ideas and impressions, or passions, to explain sublimity – the awe and admiration felt for objects at a great distance. The experience begins, Hume says, with the excitement of the imagination by the object perceived, and the final satisfying effect is wrought by the subsequent workings of the ideas on the realization of the intervening distance. This is hardly a convincing explanation of the psychology of a familiar experience, but the concept of the sublime was a vexing issue to eighteenth-century aestheticians, and Hume's attempt at an answer should be seen in the context of contemporary discussion.

Hume found in his theory of association a rationalization of the neoclassical rule of dramatic unity of action. If a dramatic work has no unifying structure, then the orderly interassociations of the ideas and the passions are made difficult, and the work will not convey emotional force. Thus, Hume says of the neoclassical strictures:

> These rules are founded on the qualities of human nature: and the quality of human nature, which requires a consistency in every performance, is that which renders the mind incapable of passing in a moment from one passion and disposition to a quite different one.

In his *Four Dissertations* (1757), Hume devotes an entire essay to the question of differences in standards of taste. His remarks on this subject recognize that people often agree on principles but quarrel over particulars, and he hoped to find in the empirical phenomena of individual perceptions some basis for an orderly analysis of what constitutes good taste in art. His conclusion is tentative, acknowledging that individual differences will persist even among the most respected of critics, but he asserts that the intensity of a critic's pleasurable response is one criterion of that critic's taste. The critic's problem is to communicate a sense of his pleasure, and to do that the critic must gain his audience's confidence by a display of good sense and cultural breadth as well as by a consistency of approach that may be summed up in a body of rules. Given these qualities in critics, it is possible to conceive of something like a community of reliable readers whose judgments may be respected.

Hume is not a figure of the first rank in the history of criticism, but he contributed in significant ways to the lively debates of his day. In his attempt to apply empirical observation of human nature to literary theory and practice, he achieved a reconciliation of neoclassical principles with the new doctrines regarding the association of ideas.

Principal criticism

A Treatise of Human Nature: Being an Attempt to Introduce the Experimental Method of Reasoning into Moral Subjects, 1739–1740
Four Dissertations, 1757

Other major works and literary forms

David Hume is generally acknowledged as one of the most distinguished philosophers of the eighteenth century. His major works include *Philosophical Essays Concerning Human Understanding* (1748; best known as *An Enquiry Concerning Human Understanding*), *An Enquiry Concerning the Principles of Morals* (1751), and *Dialogues Concerning Natural Religion* (1779). His multivolume *The History of England* (1754–1762) was widely acclaimed. Hume also published an autobiography, and several volumes of his letters were compiled in the twentieth century.

NONFICTION

Essays, Moral and Political, 1741–1742 (enlarged as *Essays, Moral, Political, and Literary*, 1758)
Three Essays, Moral and Political, 1748
Philosophical Essays Concerning Human Understanding, 1748 (best known as *An Enquiry Concerning Human Understanding*, 1758)
An Enquiry Concerning the Principles of Morals, 1751
Political Discourses, 1752
The History of England, 1754–1762 (6 volumes)
A Concise and Genuine Account of the Dispute Between Mr. Hume and Mr. Rousseau, 1766
The Life of David Hume, Esq., Written by Himself, 1777
Dialogues Concerning Natural Religion, 1779

Further reading

Baier, Annette C. *A Progress of Sentiments: Reflections on Hume's Treatise*, 1991.
Bate, Walter Jackson. *From Classic to Romantic*, 1946.
Brunius, Teddy. *David Hume on Criticism*, 1952.
Capaldi, Nicholas. *David Hume: The Newtonian Philosopher*, 1975.
Cohen, Ralph. "David Hume's Experimental Method and the Theory of Taste," in *English Literary History*. XXV (December, 1958), pp. 270–289.
Deleuze, Gilles. *Empiricism and Subjectivity: An Essay on Hume's Theory of Human Nature*, 1991.
Johnson, Oliver A. *The Mind of David Hume: A Companion to Book I of A Treatise of Human Nature*, 1995.
Kallich, Martin. "The Associationist Criticism of Francis Hutcheson and David Hume," in *Studies in Philology*. XLIII (October, 1946), pp. 644–667.
Mossner, Ernest Campbell. *The Life of David Hume*, 1980 (second edition).
Norton, David Fate, ed. *The Cambridge Companion to Hume*, 1993
Ong, Walter J. "Psyche and the Geometers: Aspects of Associationist Critical Theory," in *Modern Philology*. XLIX (August, 1951), pp. 16–27.
Pears, David. *Hume's System: An Examination of the First Book of His Treatise*, 1991.
Price, John Valdimir. *David Hume*, 1968.

FRANK DAY

See also Johnson; Lord Kames; Neoclassical Literary Theory; Shaftesbury

I

Ideology

The most persistent view of ideology for much of the twentieth century (at least in the Western hemisphere) saw it as a rigid, dogmatic set of ideas, associated with intolerant and programmatic, indeed totalitarian, regimes. According to such a definition, the Soviet Bloc, as well as China, Cuba, and others, were in the grip of "ideology," whereas the liberal democracies of most other Western countries were (and are) ruled by nondogmatic rationalism, where tenets such as "a fair day's pay for a fair day's work" or "a man's home is his castle" were not/are not seen as ideological but as "common sense."

Yet it is clear that it is precisely the most widespread and the least controversial beliefs and values which embody hidden and unquestioned assumptions about social and economic structures, about power relations, in short about politics.

The idea of ideology as related to class interests has been current (though for obvious reasons not uncontested!) since Karl Marx and Friedrich Engels, though this meaning of "ideology" was first developed by the French thinker Antoine Destutt Tracy in 1812. Tracy, against the background of the French Revolution, had inaugurated the study of ideas and their origins as a properly revolutionary unmasking of the class-serving idealism of previous models. This strangely uncelebrated figure, whose *avant-la-lettre* materialism anticipated that of Marx by a few decades, was arguably responsible for coining a word that has been a veritable theoretical battleground and will no doubt remain one.

Though Marx's conception of ideology was always evolving and cannot easily be pinned down to a consistent position, he was nonetheless clear that people's (for Marx, "men's") ways of thinking about the world were shaped by the physical, productive relations entertained with that world. The alienating relations which were the result of capitalism were then, for Marx, at the root of the distorted power relations and of what he sometimes referred to as "false consciousness" which would make it impossible for "men"/people to enjoy direct and egalitarian intercourse as long as capitalism existed. In this sense capitalist society was prey to a "systematic distortion" which precluded unideological thought or relationships.

One consequence of this line of thought led many twentieth-century theorists (many of them no less "Marxist" for all that) to insist that no social formation (even a postcapitalist socialist utopia) would be free of ideology. Indeed, in suggesting that the ways in which we think about the world are "fixed" by our relations (within capitalism), and largely beyond our knowledge, Marx himself (and arguably Tracy before him) had anticipated the "epistemological break" occasioned by Sigmund Freud's "discovery" of the unconscious.

While there remains a strand of writing on ideology which continues to stress the role of conscious ideas (and these certainly have a part to play), the growing emphasis in ideology theory has been on the unconscious nature of ideology. Thus for Antonio Gramsci "habitual behaviour" is one aspect of the hegemonization or legitimization of a dominant group/class's values; similarly, Pierre Bourdieu's *habitus* refers to the internalization of social rules about what is/is not appropriate so that what may seem like an imposition eventually seems "natural." As Terry Eagleton has observed:

> Habitus is thus "history turned into nature," and for Bourdieu it is through this matching of the subjective and the objective, what we feel spontaneously disposed to do and what our social conditions demand of us, that power secures itself.

For a growing number of writers, a key instrument for securing unconscious ideological consent is language. If semiology (semiotics), the study of signs, has sometimes been lampooned for the aridity of its supposedly value-free analyses, its methods have in fact been of great value in exposing the unspoken (ideological) power relations which underlie (any) language. To quote Eagleton again:

> To analyse a form of systematically distorted communication, whether dream or ideology, is thus to reveal how its lacunae, repetitions, elisions and equivocations are themselves significant.

The most ambitious attempt to theorize a synthesis between a Marxist economic model and a model of the individual subject informed by a Freudian/Lacanian unconscious was undertaken by Louis Althusser, for whom the human subject was "always already" within ideology, and there is scarcely any way out: a (some would say overly) pessimistic position. In such a model, ideology is far more than a set of consciously articulable positions or values; it is nothing less than an all-pervasive network of representations (language, discourse, media representations). For Althusser,

> all ideology represents in its necessarily imaginary distortion not the existing relations of production (and the other relations that derive from them), but above all the (imaginary) relationship of individuals to the relations of production and the relations that derive from them.

The difficulty of this strand of ideology theory is due in large part to the obscurity of Jacques Lacan's psychoanalytic theory, in which the "subject," far from being anything like a real person, is a shifting effect of both past and present private and social experiences.

A further complication has been the tendency on the part of some writers (and particularly of popularizations of the concept) to treat ideology as something immutable and monolithic, most notoriously in the formulation "the dominant ideology" (indeed it would generally be better to refer to the less elegant plural "ideologies"). Apart from the Marx-generated debate about whether the end of capitalism would signal an end of ideology (the general view now is that it would not), it is now clear that ideologies can be "dominant," "oppositional," or indeed have some more complex relation to relations of "dominance."

Finally, there is the awkward question raised by any (neo-) Althusserian model: if ideology is everywhere, in all representations and in all discourses, how is it possible to say anything from outside it? Althusser and others speak of "scientific discourse"; but where and how can such discourse originate without being itself formed by its social/political context, without reflecting unspoken assumptions and values, in short without being ideological? And science and technology can scarcely claim to stand outside ideology.

The striving for scientistic rationalism so evident in many theorists of ideology from Tracy and Marx, through Theodor Adorno and Jürgen Habermas to Louis Althusser, Barry Hindess, and Paul Hirst and beyond, has not escaped the critical scrutiny of some sympathetic to their project (most notably Terry Eagleton) and of others for whom the dismantling of logocentrism, of the rationalist base of verbal reasoning, is arguably part of another agenda. For the post-poststructuralist and postmodernist skepticism of Jean-François Lyotard, Richard Rorty, and Jean Baudrillard does more than question enlightenment rationality; it proposes that radical changes in economic systems, forms of media representation, and indeed the very nature of subjectivity mean that the very concept of ideology is losing its relevance. But if ideology is indeed a fluid system of representations, inflected by class and power interests, through which we as human subjects make sense of our world and take our positions in relation to existing relations of power, then what is the function of the postmodernists' proclamation of "the end of ideology"? Could such a position not itself be "ideological"?

Further reading

Althusser, Louis. *Lenin and Philosophy and Other Essays*, 1971, 1977.

Baudrillard, Jean. *Selected Writings*, 1988.

Birnbaum, Norman. "The Sociological Study of Ideology 1940–1960," in *Current Sociology*. Vol. 9 (1960).

Blackburn, Robin, ed. *Ideology in the Social Sciences*, 1972.

Callinicos, Alex. *Against Postmodernism*, 1989.

Eagleton, Terry. *Ideology*, 1991.

Larrain, Jorge. *The Concept of Ideology*, 1979.

Lovell, Terry. *Pictures of Reality*, 1980.

Naess, Arne, et al. *Democracy, Ideology and Objectivity*, 1956.

Williams, Raymond. *Keywords*, 1976.

——. *Marxism and Literature*, 1977.

Jan Udris

See also Althusser; Gramsci; Marxist Theory and Criticism

Indian Literary Theory

Indian philosophy and language theory, which underlie the entire tradition of Indian literary theory, distinguish between theory and practice, conceptualization and *pratibha*, or direct experience. Indian culture has always emphasized the philosophy of *yoga* (union), which posits the interrelation of language, consciousness, and nature, particularly in Sanskrit poetics. Theoretical tenets such as *rasadhvani* – the flavor of suggested sentiments in a text leading toward *moksha* or "liberation" – still permeate India's culture and continue almost by osmosis to influence contemporary writers and critic. Sushil Kumar De has argued that recent Indian literary criticism has neglected the importance of intuition for grasping the unity of language and consciousness and avoiding the preoccupation with formal requirements in literature. But today Indian writing has become multicultural through Islamic and Western influences. Writers such as Salman Rushdie, Anita Desai, and Arundhati Roy present a challenge both to the definition of contemporary literature and to traditional Indian concepts such as unity and transcendentality, calling for new forms and expressions of India's timeless truths.

Indian literary theory has its roots in the sacred texts of the Vedas (*veda* means knowledge), which are the direct cognitions (*shruti*) of Vedic seers. Surendranath Dasgupta notes that the dates of the Vedas have been variously set between 4000 and 1200 B.C. Vedic literature, a vast corpus that derives from and supplies commentary on the four basic Vedas – the *Rig-Veda*, *Sama-Veda*, *Yajur-Veda*, and *Artharva-Veda* – includes the Upanishads, *Brahmanas*, *Ithihasa*, and *Puranas*. The *Ithihasa* consists of the well-known epics the *Ramayana* and the *Mahabharata*, which contains the *Bhagavad-Gita*, considered one of the most authoritative texts of Indian philosophy. Valmiki, the author of the *Ramayana*, is credited with being the first poet and first theorist of poetic form. Sanskrit served as the lingua franca of the Vedic tradition, and because classical Indian literature consists of Sanskrit poetry, Indian literary theory deals primarily with poetic expressions analyzed through various schools of Sanskrit poetics. The first mention of the relation between consciousness and language is in the *Rig-Veda*, and this forms the basis of the earliest surviving account of the relationship between grammar and the structure, rhythm, and effect of Sanskrit poetry, the *Astadhyayi* of Panini, dating from the fifth century B.C.

The *Mundaka Upanishad* describes the difference between conceptualization and direct experience, or aesthetic rapture (*rasa*), in terms of two kinds of knowledge, the higher and the lower. As Max Müller writes: "Two kinds of knowledge must be known, this is what all who know Brahman tell us . . . . The lower knowledge is the *Rig-Veda* [and other forms of Vedic literature]; but the higher knowledge is that by which the Indestructible (Brahman) is [directly] apprehended." Similarly, the *Mandukya Upanishad* defines three common states of consciousness – waking, sleeping, and dreaming (all associated with lower knowledge) – and also a fourth transcendental state (*turiya*) or pure consciousness (associated with higher knowledge). As the unmanifest Absolute, Brahman appears to us through its various manifestations – as in the Great Chain of Being of Western thought, which led from matter through life, mind, and soul to spirit. To quote Sarvepalli Radhakrishnan: "All this is, verily, Brahman. The self [*atman*] is Brahman. This self has four quarters." Moreover, "The fourth [*turiya*] is that which has no elements [consciousness without qualities or content], which cannot be spoken of, into which the world is resolved, benign, non-dual." The earliest Indian criticism was "ritual interpretation" of the "formless and timeless truths" of Vedic texts.

The tenets of Indian literary criticism anticipate much in contemporary Western literary theory, including the debate between humanism and postmodernism. In contrast to the semiology (semiotics) of the twentieth-century Swiss linguist Ferdinand de Saussure, which holds that "in language there are only differences without positive terms," and to postmodern theories of poststructuralism, which question the unity and presence of meaning and the individual self, what distinguishes Indian literary theory is the principle of a natural unity of the self in pure consciousness (*turiya*), and of name and form, sound and meaning, in language. Much in Sanskrit poetics hinges on the correlation between language and *yoga* (union). The degree of unity in language, for instance, depends on the degree of unity in the consciousness of the language user, with the oneness of sound and meaning being apprehended through a glimpse of *turiya*, or pure consciousness. In the absence in Western culture of a knowledge of *yoga* elicited through *rasadhvani*, poststructuralist postmodernism has rejected objective truth, or the "myth of the given" – rejected the foundationalism, essentialism, and transcendentalism that are the key elements of Indian literary theory.

The four main schools of Indian literary theory: the *alankara*, *riti*, *rasa*, and *dhvani* schools

Indian philosophy and literary theory have their roots in the unknown past, but the period of Indian philosophy that stretches for a millennium until the seventeenth century A.D., known as the *sutra* period for its religious and literary hermeneutics, gave birth to several schools of Indian literary criticism. These schools have contributed to what Roman Jakobson, the Russian Formalist, calls "the global science of verbal structure." Four schools that arose during the eighth-century A.D. renaissance in literary theory are of special interest, for they overlap considerably in a move from formalism toward increasing idealism. Indian critics consider the historical development of these schools to be of lesser importance than their special features of poetic integration that evoke the response of aesthetic rapture. The oldest of these schools dealt with poetic figures, *alankaras*, from which it derives its name. Bhamaha, an early theorist of the *alankara* school, lived from the last quarter of the seventh to the middle of the eighth century. The second school concerned itself with *riti*, the poetic arrangement of words. Its two major proponents were Dandin of the first half of the eighth century, and Vamana of the middle of the eighth to the middle of the ninth century. As formalist approaches, the *alankara* (trope) and *riti* (verbal structure) schools resemble Anglo-American New Criticism and Russian Formalism – which played a role in the emergence of structuralism and poststructuralism. The third school emphasized *rasa*, aesthetic mood or flavor, and the fourth school, founded by Anandavardhana, emphasized *dhvani* or the power of suggestion. The *rasa* and *dhvani* schools reacted against the formalism of the two previous schools but did not reject the importance of poetic figures. In their combination of formal and rhetorical elements, the *rasa* (flavor) and *dhvani* (suggestion) schools resemble reception theory, reader-response theory, and phenomenological criticism.

As their dates indicate, any notion of development in Indian literary theory is complicated by the question of chronology, such as whether Dandin, who gave an exhaustive treatment of *alankaras* (tropes), actually followed or preceded Bhamaha of the *alankara* school. All of these schools have their basis in the Vedic theory of language, which posits a natural unity of sound and meaning, name and form (*namarupa*). Language is said to consist of four levels or degrees of unity between sound and meaning which correspond to the levels of knowledge discussed in the Upanishads: the two temporal levels of language (*vaikhari* and *madhyama*) correspond to the lower level of knowledge associated with ordinary waking consciousness, and the two nontemporal levels of language (*pashyanti* and *para*) correspond to the higher level of knowledge associated with pure consciousness or *turiya*. *Para*, defined as the absolute unity of language, is first mentioned in the *Rig-Veda*. The four schools of Indian literary theory, but especially the rhetorical schools of *rasa* and *dhvani*, can be understood as a special use of language intended to evoke *turiya* as an immediate first-hand experience,

Bhamaha, the leading theorist of *alankaras* (tropes), writes in his *Kavyalankara* that the absolute unity of sound and meaning found naturally in language also constitutes the nature of poetry. Later formalist critics also accepted the unity of sound and meaning as a key attribute of poetry. For instance, in his *Srngaraprakasa* of the first half of the eleventh century, Bhoja describes two aspects of linguistic unity, a poetical and a grammatical aspect, and lists their twelve varieties: four poetical and eight grammatical. All poetic unity is also a grammatical unity, but the unity of poetry is of a special type (*visesa*). In the earlier *Natyashastra*, the critic Bharata says that all literary compositions are distinguished from ordinary discourse by at least thirty-six characteristics (*laksanas*) such as poetic figures (*alankaras*), of which he lists only four: simile, metaphor, zeugma, and homophony. In the early eleventh century Abhinavagupta, an influential scholar during the renaissance in Sanskrit poetics, also emphasized the difference between ordinary and poetic expressions. He held that the poet's imagination was "the real secret that elevates an ordinary expression to the position of a poetic expression." But recognizing the limitations of a formalist approach, Abhinavagupta says in anticipation of future schools that because poetic expressions are elevated through the power of the imagination, the poet's imagination is the highest attribute of poetry. The *alankara* school thus begins by focusing on tropes, but then turns to the knower (*rishi*) in a move toward greater emphasis on *turiya* or the unity of pure consciousness.

Nonetheless, the accent on imagination in Indian literary theory did not detract from the emphasis on poetic figures such as similes, metaphors, and symbols. Bhamaha defines poetic figure (*alankara*) as the beautifying principle at the heart of literature. By beautifying principle he means not only the metaphors already found in language, but also the "extraordinary turn" given to an ordinary expression by the author. For Bhamaha, this extraordinary turn, as a striking mode of figurative expression, is that special feature (*visesa*) of unity that defines poetry. The special unity of sound and sense was also noted by the *riti* (rhythm) school as expounded by the critic Vamana, who in his *Vrtti* distinguished *alankaras* from *gunas*, essential qualities such as sweetness and lucidity. *Riti* is a quality of poetry associated with rhythm, the special arrangement of words in a sentence. As an attribute of sound and sense, the *guna* of *riti* constitutes the soul of poetry, while the *alankara* constitutes the body of poetry.

In their emphasis on tropes, sequence, and wholeness, the *alankara* and *riti* schools both resemble and differ from the New Criticism of the 1930s and 1940s. On the one hand these culturally and historically distant schools are strikingly similar in their definition of rhetorical elements – the poem as a "verbal icon," to quote the title of William Wimsatt's best-known book. But ultimately Western formalism collapses the difference between ordinary and poetic language and argues that all language is metaphorical, a field of difference devoid of the unity of sound and meaning, signifier and signified. This emphasis on difference emerges in part through a lack of the systematic experience of the self as pure consciousness or *turiya* in Western culture.

The theory of *rasa* (aesthetic flavor), the third school of Indian literary theory, can be compared to the concept of defamiliarization in Russian Formalism and to the alienation effect of Bertolt Brecht. To defamiliarize means to debunk our habitual perceptions and thus to see the world anew. Through the intervention of *rasa* (flavor), the audience can remain detached from all specific passions and thereby appreciate the whole range of possible responses without running the risk of being overpowered by any one of them. Since the taste of *rasa* involves the tasting of an idealized flavor and not a particular transitory mental state, it differs from the perception of memory or an actual experience. Indian literary theory, unlike post-Saussurean semiotics, is not impressed by the division between signifier and signified, which in Indian theory corresponds to the lower levels of language and knowledge. By invoking the emotional states latent within the mind through direct intuition, *rasa* constitutes an experience of subtler, more unified stages of activity of the mind itself. As in the Russian Formalist notion of defamiliarization, *rasa* strips the veil of familiarity from our perception, not only of the world but also of the self, providing a glimpse of unity or *moksha* (liberation). This freedom, attained through the realization of *turiya*, resembles the *catharsis* of Aristotle's theory of tragedy through which the audience is purged of binding attachments to the emotions. There is also a clear parallel here with the aesthetics of Arthur Schopenhauer. *Rasa* gradually purges one of the three *gunas* – *satva* (happiness), *rajas* (anger), and *tamas* (ignorance or laziness) – which bind the soul to the body.

Without the critical distance from the actuality of emotion provided by *rasa*, the aesthetic purpose of art and literature would be negated. As an aesthetic experience, *rasa* culminates in a spiritual joy (*santa*), which

K. Krishnamoorthy describes as "wild tranquillity" or "passionless passion." Hence, just as in Vedic language theory meaning is ultimately intellectual, a unity of sound and meaning, so in Indian literary theory *rasa* enables one to experience the boundless bliss inherent within the unity of consciousness. As Sushil Kumar De says, "an ordinary emotion (*bhava*) may be pleasurable or painful; but a poetic sentiment (*rasa*), transcending the limitations of the personal attitude, is lifted above such pain and pleasure into pure joy, the essence of which is its relish itself." This awareness of subtler states of purified consciousness, which occurs spontaneously through direct perception, is the nearest realization to the Absolute or *moksha* in Sanskrit poetics. Aesthetic delight thus consists in the bliss of the self savoring its self, an experience described in the *Taittriya Upanishad* as *sat-chit-ananda:* pure being, pure consciousness, pure bliss.

For the experience of *moksha*, however, *rasa* also depends on the theme of a work. If the theme itself deals with the nature and experience of *moksha* then the *rasa* is called *santa*, which relates to *santi*, or peace. As T. P. Ramachandran notes, *santa-rasa* gives one "not only a foretaste of the bliss of *moksha* but also an insight into the nature and source of that bliss."

Although generally thought to be present in literature, *rasa* (flavor) is really the cause and effect of literature. As Krishnamoorthy explains, the poet's emotional complex (*bhava*), which becomes the feeling content embodied in the art form, paradoxically appears subjective to the poet and objective to the critic. If the complex feeling or *bhava* pattern is successful, then it results in the work's unified master-passion or *rasa*, which to the critic appears subjective, but which he or she must analyze in terms of the poet's *bhava* as a "subjective experience objectified." Since the critic infers from his or her experience of *rasa* (aesthetic flavor) toward the poet's experience of *bhava* (emotion), the cause and effect of poetry are both subjective. This *rasabhava* is the soul of poetry, a form of spiritual knowledge attained by transcending the conceptual and rational boundaries of knowledge through an expansion of the heart, which mediates between the intellect and the unity of pure consciousness (*turiya*).

According to the *dhvani* or fourth school of criticism, one of the most important principles of unity is that of suggestion (*vyanjana* or *dhvani*). The reader is thought to receive more delight through the suggested content of a work than through its expressed content. Anandavardhana, the great ninth-century theorist of the *dhvani* school and author of the *Dhvanyaloka*, opposed the older formalist schools of criticism by showing how the suggested content of poetry manifests itself in the form of facts, poetic figures, or emotion. He argued that suggestion more than denotation, connotation, or any other aspect of experience is responsible for conveying *rasa*. Furthermore, suggestion is a power that resides ultimately in the reader's mind in the form of latent impressions (*vasanas*) and beyond that in the structure of pure consciousness itself. The notion of *dhvani* (suggestion) was evolved to explain how the poet's *bhava* (emotion) gives rise to the experience of *rasa* (aesthetic flavor). As defined by Anandavardhana, *dhvani* is that suggested meaning that, in the words of Ramachandran, "flashes into the minds of sympathetic appreciators who perceive the true import (of poetry) when they have turned away from conventional meaning." In addition to suggestion, the element of propriety or the appropriateness of an expression was also considered to be essential to poetic unity. By following the view of Vedic grammarians that an eternal association exists between sound and sense, Indian literary critics set out to ascertain the special features that convert ordinary associations into the extraordinary ones of literature.

Thus, in reacting against Sanskrit formalism, the *rasa* and *dhvani* schools resemble the reader-response and reception theories of Stanley Fish, Wolfgang Iser, and Hans Robert Jauss. With his theory of meaning as a function of a "horizon of expectation" or the history of readers' judgments (a concept taken from Hans-Georg Gadamer), Jauss for example opposed the aesthetics that undermined the unity of self and text. But Jauss' modalities of reception are limited in their affirmative power to recenter the reader. In Indian literary theory, the understanding of reading and reception, the back-and-forth movement between subject and object, reader and text, is potentially much more complete than Jauss and other reader-oriented critics have indicated for it takes into account the distinct levels of language, knowledge, and consciousness. Subjects not only produce the object, as in the reader's filling in textual gaps, but the subject and object, in their underlying connection through *turiya*, are united in very real and pragmatic ways.

Whereas Western literary theories undermine linguistic truth through the free play of the signifier, Indian literary theories find that truth is immanent in language and consciousness, that knowledge changes according to the relation between language and consciousness, both of which have several distinct levels. The eighteenth-century grammarian-philosopher Nagesa notes that poetic unity is not a phenomenal identity between a verbal expression and a sensible thing in the outside world, but an identity between the eternal word unit (*sphota*) and a concept latent within the mind of the subject. Hence the natural unity of name and form (*namarupa*), which in ordinary language involves a correspondence between name and thing, is extended in figurative language to apply to a created or fictional correspondence between name and idea or feeling. The poetic figure enriches the idea and the idea enhances the figure's beauty. But while the figure of speech (signifier) in Sanskrit poetics cannot be replaced, the idea itself (signified) is paradoxically replaceable without detriment to the unity of sound and sense. For in the absolute unity of *para*, all particular meanings connect with the same universal reality on the level of *sat-chit-ananda*, absolute bliss consciousness.

Indian aesthetics

Indian literary theory also has a system of aesthetic value. This system is known as *purusartha* (*artha* – value; *purusha* – human), which, as Ramachandran notes, classifies values into four types: *artha*, *kama*, *dharma*, and *moksha*. These values stem from the universal desire to avoid suffering, the premise being that the purpose of life is the expansion of happiness. *Artha*, which means value in general, also means the economic value needed for survival in the material world. Through *artha* one obtains *kama*, the hedonistic values associated with mundane pleasure such as housing, pleasure, clothing, fame, and power. Duty or social conduct is called *dharma*, which involves self-restraint or self-sacrifice and ensures social coherence. *Moksha*, as we have seen, stands for liberation, the complete freedom from ego and its desires. Indian philosophy divides the four values into a higher and a lower group according to their effectiveness in preventing suffering and bringing lasting happiness: *artha* and *kama* represent the lower level (*adhama*), and *dharma* and *moksha* represent the higher level (*uttama*).

In India there are three views regarding the significance of the appreciation of art (which includes literature). The popular view is that art is a means to *kama* or pleasure. The second view is that of the Sankya system of Indian philosophy and holds that art is an end in itself and does not lead to the expansion of consciousness. The third view, that of the Vedanta system, is the most typical in Indian philosophy and forms the basis of Indian literary theory: art as a means to *moksha*. Indian literary theory thus divides poetry into various categories based on the extent to which they provide a taste (*rasa*) of *moksha*. Anandavardhana, for example, classifies poetry into three major types, *dhvani*, *gunibhutavyangya*, and *citra*, which correspond to the three levels of language, *pashyanti*, *madhyama*, and *vaikhari* respectively. *Dhvani*, the highest type of poetry, consists of a relationship in which the expressed form is subordinated to "a charming suggested content." In the *gunibhutavyangya* type, on the other hand, the suggested content (*dhvani*) is subordinated to its more charming expressed value, yet without the former being completely absent. In the *citra* type of poetry, however, the expressive form and expressed sense completely replace the suggested content. Devoid of a suggested idea that is both charming and meaningful, *citra* is considered not to be real poetry like *dhvani* but merely the imitation of poetry. Subsequent theorists added to these classifications, always emphasizing the value of the suggestive qualities of poetry.

Concluding remarks

Indian literary theory thus presupposes the unity between sound and meaning in language and its special manifestation in poetry. This feature combined with suggestion gives poetry the power to charm the reader on all levels of the mind simultaneously. Because the ultimate suggested meaning (*dhvani*) is the taste (*rasa*) of pure consciousness (*turiya*), the poem will be enigmatic to any approach restricted to ordinary grades of language and the mind. Western literary theory, which generally takes a restricted approach, focuses on the text, author, or reader as isolated contexts, although it recognizes that the contexts determining meaning are infinitely extendible. Indian literary theory, on the other hand, takes a more integral approach that sees the interconnectedness of all contexts and the possibility of discerning timeless truth and meaning. The multicultural context of recent Indian literature has evolved through a "fusion of horizons," in Hans-Georg Gadamer's phrase, between present forms of literary expression and the nontemporal, formless truths of India's neoperennial philosophy and literary theory. As writers such as Bharati Mukherjee and Salman Rushdie enter the historical stream of interpretation, their works enrich the contexts of Indian culture through their innovative forms while simultaneously highlighting their own Indianness and the timeless relevance of *rasadhvani* (the "flavor of suggested sentiments").

Further reading

Aristotle. *Poetics*.

Anandavardhana. *Dhvanyaloka*, 1974. Edited and translated by K. Krishnamoorthy.

Bhamaha. *Kavyalankara*, 1970. Edited and translated by P. V. Nagantha Sastry.

Bharatamuni. *The Natya Shastra*, 1987. Translated by a board of scholars.

Chakrabarti, Tarapada. *Indian Aesthetics and Science of Language*, 1971.

Coomaraswamy, Ananda K. *Christian and Oriental Philosophy of Art*, 1956.

Coward, Harold. *Bhartrhari*, 1976.

——. *The Sphota Theory of Language*, 1980.

Dasgupta, Surendranath. *A History of Indian Philosophy*, 1975.

De, Sushil Kumar. *History of Sanskrit Poetics*, Vols 1 and 2, 1960 (second revised edition).

——. *Sanskrit Poetics as a Study of Aesthetics*, 1963.

Iyengar, K. R. Srinivasa. *Indian Writing in English*, 1962, second edition 1973.

Jauss, Hans Robert. *Toward an Aesthetic of Reception*, 1982.

Krishnamoorthy, K. *Some Thoughts on Indian Aesthetics and Literary Criticism*, 1968.

Müller, Max Friedrich. *The Six Systems of Indian Philosophy*, 1984.

Pandey, K. C. *Abhinavagupta: An Historical and Philosophical Study*, 1963.

Prabhavananda, Swami. *The Spiritual Heritage of India*, 1980.

Radhakrishnan, Sarvepalli, ed. and trans. *The Principle Upanishads*, 1992 (fifth edition).

——, and Charles A. Moore, eds. *A Source Book in Indian Philosophy*, 1957.

Raghavan, V., and Nagendra. *An Introduction to Indian Poetics*, 1970.

Ramachandran, T. P. *The Indian Philosophy of Beauty*, Part One, 1979; Part Two, 1980.

Siegel, Lee. *Laughing Matters: Comic Tradition in India*, 1987.

Tarlekar, G. H. *Studies in the Natyashastra*, 1991 (second revised edition).
Valmiki. *The Ramayana of Valmiki*, 1985 (3 volumes, second edition). Translated by Hari Prasad Shastri.

WILLIAM S. HANEY II

See also Anandavardhana; Bharata; Bhartrhari

Roman Ingarden

Polish philosopher

Born: Kraków, Poland; February 5, 1893
Died: Kraków, Poland; 1970

Biography

Roman Ingarden was born in 1893 in the city of Kraków, the ancient capital and center of higher education of Poland, then under Austrian rule. In his article entitled "Sylwetka filozoficzna Romana Ingardena" (1970; a philosophical silhouette of Roman Ingarden), Narcyz Łubnicki remarks that "philosophy was not only the specialty but also the passion of Roman Ingarden." If this is true, then Ingarden was especially lucky in realizing many opportunities to indulge his passion at the feet of masters. After being under the tutelage of the multitalented analytical philosopher, psychologist, and aesthetician Kazimierz Twardowski in Lvov, Ingarden traveled to Göttingen and Freiburg to study under the famous phenomenologist Edmund Husserl. Among his fellow students were Wilhelm Schapp, Edith Stein, and Fritz Kaufmann. Upon returning to Poland, Ingarden worked as a high school teacher before being called to a professorship at the University of Lvov in 1933, a position which he held until 1941.

The Nazi regime in Germany and the German Occupation of Poland brought years of oppression for Ingarden, whose philosophical system was not favored by the Fascists. After the war his luck did not improve. Ingarden lectured at the famous Jagiellonian University in Kraków, but soon found that his phenomenology was again pushed to the side by Marxist dialectical materialism during the harsh years of the early 1950s. The subsequent ideological thaw gave Ingarden the opportunity to disseminate his theories more freely. Among other honors, Ingarden was a member of the Polish Academy of Science. In 1968 he received the Husserl Award from the University of Vienna. Ingarden's fame in both philosophical and cultural spheres continues to wax even after his death in 1970.

Influence

Ingarden is known for bringing phenomenological theories, which he absorbed from Husserl, into the sphere of literary criticism. His theories on the separation of the world created by the artist from the natural world inhabited by all people are especially prized. For a long time his work (written mostly in Polish, often in German) was appreciated only in his native land and throughout Europe. His career as literary theorist was followed closely by some of the greatest names in contemporary Polish criticism, such as Zygmunt Łempicki, Julian Krzyzanowski, and Manfred Kridl, and his theories have had more than a modicum of influence on the German critic Wolfgang Iser as well. Ingarden is now beginning to attract more notice in the English-speaking world thanks to some recent translations of his work. René Wellek, in his volume entitled *Four Critics* (1981), admits to "learning more from [Ingarden]" on certain questions of literary theory "than from anybody else."

Analysis

Ingarden is a forbiddingly difficult thinker. His complicated, abstruse language is the heritage of a lifetime indulgence of his "passion," philosophy. As René Wellek states in *Four Critics*, "Ingarden remains philosopher and aesthetician, which is nothing to complain about, though it does reduce his usefulness and appeal to a student of concrete literature." Nevertheless, certain aspects of his literary theory are well worth the pain which familiarization with them may cost the student. Four main points of Ingarden's literary theory are especially interesting to the student of literature: the integrity of the literary text and its independence from the phenomenological world, the interlocked aggregates of the literary work (which Ingarden calls its "multilayered structure"), the vital, critical-interpretive process of "concretizing" the literary text under consideration, and the reader's relationship to the literary text.

Ingarden speaks of the literary work as something which defies definition both as an "ideal" and as a "real object." The text cannot be considered an ideal, because a text is created in and subject to the laws of time. There is no guarantee that the text will not someday disappear or be destroyed; it, like all other mortal things, is bound by the laws of decay. Yet it is not merely a real object either, for it is not appreciated as an amalgamation of wood pulp and printer's ink but as a series of verses or sentences which are to be deciphered by eye and ear. According to Wellek, literature "is what phenomenology terms an 'intentional object,' i.e., created by a specific person directed at a specific object." According to Ingarden, the literary work has a life of its own. It is divorced from the real world to which, in some measure, it refers; it is divorced also from the author who created it and from the reader or listener who receives it and deciphers its message.

In its relationship to the world of real objects, the literary text may speak of certain actual happenings in the same way as a history book does. Yet the phrase "Napoleon received the Prussian ambassador at Jena with a dignified, yet patronizing air" might well have a very different nature according to the type of book in which it is found. The literary work, in effect, contains a unique world, entirely different, perhaps, from the one in which humans live, and, therefore, enjoys a special "license" which is not afforded the historical text or newspaper. The idea of "truth" takes on an entirely new meaning in the literary theories of Ingarden.

The world of the literary text is built on what Ingarden calls "quasi-judgments." Quasi-judgments, such as the one mentioned above concerning Napoleon, have little to do with the real world; they are a law unto themselves, their one purpose being the creation and sustenance of the illusory world of the literary text. The difference between a literary text and a historical text is simply the difference between a statement of fact and a quasi-judgment.

In *The Poetics of Roman Ingarden* (1981), Eugene A. Falk underscores the importance of this divorce between the real world and the world of the literary text:

> By establishing that distinction, he has ensured the emancipation of literature as art from other writings and provided literary scholarship with a ground of its own from which a system of essentially related works of literary art can emerge as a distinct branch of knowledge.

What is the literary text and how is this new world constructed? In the preface to his volume *The Literary Work of Art*, Ingarden speaks of the "multilayered structure of the literary text and the related polyphony of these layers which constitute its essential element." The four interlocked layers of the literary text are "sound-units," "meaning-units," schematized aspects, and the new illusory world of the text.

The first of these layers, the sound-units, refers to Ingarden's theory of the "unidealistic-unrealistic" nature of the literary work. The black and white spaces on the printed page are not what constitute the text, rather, the sounds of the language in which the text is composed are the waves upon which the vessels of meaning (meaning-units) are received by the reader. For Ingarden, the sound of the words and sentences in a given text is very important to the correct reception of the text's message. The words "bread," "*pain*," "*chleb*," and "*brot*," for example, although referring to the same substance, all evoke different connotations. Thus, the premise of total translation is challenged: translate a text from one language into another and the meaning of the original text, while it may not be lessened in the transferal, is clearly and unavoidably modified.

The second layer of the text, the meaning-units, are defined as the words and phrases which, colored and shaped by the sound-units, are the vessels of meaning. These two levels, sound-units and meaning-units, allow the reader to enter into the new world of the literary text. Yet these two aspects are not enough to give the entire picture: they only provide the schematized aspects of the new world, its skeletal structure. There remain certain blank spots in the literary work which must be filled in by the individual reader or listener. This process is called concretization. In this step of the reading experience, the reader, who may or may not be familiar with the world described by the literary text, is invited to conjure up familiar scenes and fuse them into the new world to visualize and experience the text better. Wellek repeats Ingarden's example of a novel describing Parisian street life to a reader who has never been to that city. Naturally, the reader's imagination will conjure up images of cities that he or she has visited and people the streets with characters familiar to him or her.

The fourth layer of the text, the new world created by the interaction of the preceding three, refers back to a point made earlier. In reading a literary text, one is not dealing with the world of everyday experience. The world of a literary text may resemble or refer to the phenomenological world, yet it is in every aspect a different, separate universe. Truth, in the literary text, does not mean historical veracity. The truth of a literary work concerns itself with what Wellek terms "objective consistency." To Ingarden, the literary text is "to its own self true."

What, then, is brought to the text by the reader, and in what way is the text separate from the reader's personal concretizations? When one reads a literary work, concretization, or the "filling in" process, goes on continuously and spontaneously. As each reader is an individual, each brings his or her own intellectual baggage to the work, from which he or she extracts the "fill" for the text's blank spaces. Yet it must not be forgotten that the text is a separate entity from the reader; it has its own being and, as such, exerts an influence over the reader, directing the pattern of concretization. As Ingarden sees it, it is the task of criticism to guard the autonomy of the work, interpreting the text correctly and aiding in the transferal process so that the literary work remains intact and valid despite the variety of audiences which it encounters. Criticism, in staving off "false concretizations," is a catalyst, stripping away the accumulation of concretizations from the work.

According to Falk, Ingarden believed that there are two types of reader: the naive reader, who approaches the text in question passively, for the excitement and sheer enjoyment of the reading experience, and the informed, or sensitive, reader, who approaches the text actively, seeking to extract some intellectual value from the work or, what is perhaps more important, to come into contact with the aesthetic quality, or *Gestalt*, of the text:

> The arrangement of aesthetic qualities endows the aesthetic object with a configuration, a *Gestalt*, that is all its own. It is this *Gestalt* that emerges from the functionally inter-related aesthetic qualities of an aesthetic object, but only if we have appropriately concretized a genuine literary work of art.

It is Ingarden's approach to the literary text as a unique, irreplaceable work of art to be savored for its distinct aesthetic qualities, not a mere source of entertainment or an instructive textbook, that makes his theories so important and inviting. Not only do they offer a unique vantage point from which to study a literary text, but they can also heighten a reader's appreciation of literature.

Principal criticism

Das literarische Kunstwerk, 1931 (*The Literary Work of Art*, 1973)
Formy obcowania z dziełow literackich, 1933
O poznawaniu dzieła literackiego, 1937 (revised as *Vom Erkennen des literarischen Kunstwerks*, 1968)
O psychologii i psychologizmie w nauce o literaturze, 1937
O tak zwanej "prawdzie" w literaturze, 1937
O poetyce, 1945
Szkice z filozofii literatury, 1947
"O sztuce tłumaczenia," 1955
Podstawowe twierdzenia o budowie dzieła literackiego, 1960
Poetik und Sprachwissenschaft, 1961
The Cognition of the Literary Work of Art, 1973

Other major works and literary forms

Roman Ingarden is most widely known as a philosopher and aesthetician. A student of Edmund Husserl, Ingarden wrote many works on phenomenology, though he measures swords with his former mentor's theory of transcendental idealism in the two-volume work *Spór o istnienie świata* (1947–1948; the dispute over the existence of the world).

Ingarden's aesthetic theories consider music and the plastic arts, both on their own merits and in relation to literature. His most influential and well-known work in this area is his two-volume collection of essays entitled *Studia z estetyki* (1957–1958; *Selected Papers in Aesthetics*, 1985), in which many of his earlier, most important articles are reedited and presented together.

NONFICTION
Spór o istnienie świata, 1947–1948 (2 volumes)
Studia z estetyki, 1957–1958 (2 volumes; *Selected Papers in Aesthetics*, 1985)

Further reading

Berger, Karol. "Roman Ingarden, the Work of Music and the Problems of Its Identity," in *Journal of the American Musicological Society*. 41, no. 3 (Fall, 1988).
Bostar, L. "Reading Ingarden Read Husserl: Metaphysics, Ontology, and Phenomenological Method," in *Husserl Studies*. 10, no. 3 (1993).
Chrudzimiski, Arkadiusz. "Roman Ingarden: Zur Grundlegang der Erkenntnistheorie (Gesammelte Werke. Bd 7) hrsg und ubersetzt von Włodzimierz Galewicz," in *Journal of the British Society for Phenomenology*. 29, no. 3 (1998).
Falk, Eugene A. *The Poetics of Roman Ingarden*, 1981.
Grabowicz, George. Introduction to *The Literary Work of Art*, 1973.
Haefliger, G. "Ingarden und Husserls transzendentaler Idealismus," in *Husserl Studies.* 7 (1991).
Herman, David. "Ingarden and the Prague School," in *Neophilologus*. 81, no. 4 (1997).
Kocay, Victor. "L'Objet esthétique chez Roman Ingarden: premises et 'valeur,'" in *Canadian Review of Comparative Literature*. 17, nos. 1/2 (1990).
Kuczyński, Janusz. *Fenomenologia Romana Ingardena*, 1977.
Kung, Guido. "Welterkennen und Textinterpretation bei Roman Ingarden und Nelson Goodman," in *Grazer philosophische Studien*. 44 (1993).
Oort, Richard van. "Three Models of Fiction: The Logical, the Phenomenological, and the Anthropological (Searle, Ingarden, Gans)," in *New Literary History*. 29, no. 3 (1998).
Świderski, E. M. "The Problematic Unity of Culture in Ingarden," in *Journal of the British Society for Phenomenology*. 26, no. 2 (1995).
Wellek, René. *Four Critics*, 1981.

CHARLES S. KRASZEWSKI

See also Phenomenological Criticism

Intertextuality

The concept of intertextuality is prevalent in modern critical theory as a means of mapping the interrelationships between texts. The exact degree of interrelationship between any two texts (in the broad sense of cultural artifacts – be they novels, poems, essays, or films) varies enormously: it may be overt, in the sense that quotation from a text is set off from the secondary text and explicitly sourced, or it may amount to a more covert reference – an unacknowledged quotation from another work, an allusion to a well-known plot or character, or a subtle reworking which may be reverential or subversively parodic in its intent.

A concentration on intertextual connections has long underpinned philological inquiries into the sources of or influences upon given literary productions, but the popularity (and not a little of the subversiveness) of the concept in contemporary theory lies in its radical rebuttal of the New Critical belief in the inviolate "autonomy" of the literary work. Any concentration upon the *intertextual* character of a literary work necessarily highlights that text's location in an infinite web of other linguistic products, be they high literary works or the products of popular media such as cinema, television, or advertising. By implication, a work of literature becomes less about itself – in the "pure," New Critical sense – than about the circulation of general cultural types and modes of discourse. The attempt to say something "new" or to express the author's innermost convictions is only ever a metaphysical delusion; the most that can be achieved is the mosaic-like rearrangement of previous utterances and cultural archetypes.

This more specific theoretical sense of the term "intertextuality" develops from the work of the Russian linguist Mikhail Bakhtin, who in his essay "From the Prehistory of Novelistic Discourse" analyzed the finely variegated forms of "direct, half-hidden and completely hidden quoting" found in the literature of the Middle Ages and concluded that their ambiguous textual integration makes it impossible to determine with any finality the author's intention in introducing the quotation:

> The role of the other's word was enormous at that time: there were quotations that were openly and reverently emphasized as such, or that were half-hidden, completely hidden, half-conscious, unconscious, correct, intentionally distorted, unintentionally distorted, deliberately reinterpreted and so forth. The boundary lines between someone else's speech and one's own speech were flexible, ambiguous, often deliberately distorted and confused. Certain kinds of texts were constructed like mosaics out of the texts of others.

Compounding the reduction in authorial status implicit in Bakhtin's work, the Bulgarian-born French linguist and philosopher Julia Kristeva expanded Bakhtin's observations upon specific texts into a general theory of *intertextualité*: the principle that any "new" text can only ever rework and recycle the existing body of literature in a combination specific to itself ("Word, Dialogue, Novel," in *The Kristeva Reader*). In refining Bakhtin's concept in this way for the intellectual milieu of 1960s Parisian poststructuralism, Kristeva explicitly rejects the earlier broad sense of intertextuality as the study of allusion and sources (which may leave the cult of authorial intention unmodified) and instead uses the term to describe the manner in which texts partake in an endless network of difference – signaling their associations with previous or contemporaneous works at the same time as they bespeak their deviations from surrounding texts. Literature is thus liberated from the figure of the individual author and is reconfigured as an autonomous system of discourse, to which the critic – rather than the dethroned author – becomes the interpretive guide.

The figure most closely associated with the use of intertextuality as a device to dislodge the "tyranny" of authorial intention is the French structuralist critic Roland Barthes, whose celebrated essay "The Death of the Author" (1968) heralds in the demise of the authorial presence the liberation of the reader. For Barthes, as for his associate Kristeva, intertextuality is not a characteristic of specific cultural works, but the inescapable medium in which all human discourse must necessarily take place. All that is sayable has, in different forms, been always already articulated:

> The intertextual in which every text is held . . . is not to be confused with some origin of the text: to try to find the "sources," the "influences" of a work is to fall in with the myth of filiation; the citations which go to make up a text are anonymous, untraceable, and yet already read: they are quotations without inverted commas.

The widespread dissemination of Barthes' theories has invigorated literary studies over the last thirty years. His ideas have hastened the collapse of arbitrary hierarchies of "classic" literature over popular culture, and the bypassing of "influence-style" studies of literary tradition by instituting in their place the concept of the web of literary discourse which already encompasses the breadth and variety of literary possibility. Yet the demolition of authorial status championed by Barthes, and subsequently enshrined as a fundamental of poststructuralist thought, has in its turn been contested by exponents of feminist, postcolonial, and gay criticisms, who read in the act of authorship by women, racial minorities, and gay and lesbian writers a potent, identity-based challenge to oppressive literary and political constructs. In the hands of such critics, the concept of intertextuality has acquired a third specific sense, best illustrated by the practice of "writing back" to previous (usually canonical) literary works in order to illustrate the cultural and discursive assumptions which underpin the originals. In this sense, Jean Rhys' novel *Wide Sargasso Sea* (1966) reworks Charlotte Brontë's *Jane Eyre* (1847) from the perspective of the Creole Bertha Mason (the mad first Mrs. Rochester of Brontë's novel), enacting a profound critique of the racial, sexual, and imperial hierarchies encoded in the Victorian text. This practice, recurrent amongst postcolonial writers particularly in relation to "imperial" texts such as William Shakespeare's *The Tempest* (1611) and Daniel Defoe's *Robinson Crusoe* (1719), is by no means restricted to the written medium. In the sphere of gay theory, satirical and intentionally provocative readings have deconstructed such cultural artifacts as the 1970s US television series *Starsky and Hutch* and the cult of Jackie Kennedy Onassis; the Argentinian-Canadian playwright Guillermo Verdecchia in his monologue *Fronteras Americanas* (1993) freewheels through a sly multimedia cross-section of First-World Latino stereotypes; and the Italian semiotician Umberto Eco has unraveled the complex vocabulary of cinematic archetypes and allusions which structures *Casablanca* (1942), making it "not *one* movie, but 'movies'" ("*Casablanca*: Cult Movies and Intertextual Collage," 1984).

The concept of intertextuality encompasses several specific senses useful to differing critical persuasions. But its significance as a structuring principle of twentieth-century literary criticism and theory inheres in its insistence upon the ineluctable interconnectedness of all discourse. By emphasizing the tissue of parallels and contrasts which surrounds individual texts, the concept of intertextuality highlights the linguistic system from which all literary pronouncements derive and in which they take up place.

Further reading

Ashcroft, Bill, Gareth Griffiths, and Helen Tiffin. *The Empire Writes Back: Theory and Practice in Post-Colonial Literatures*, 1989.

Bakhtin, Mikhail. *The Dialogic Imagination: Four Essays*, 1981.

Barthes, Roland. *Image-Music-Text*, 1977.
Eagleton, Terry. *Literary Theory: An Introduction*, 1983.
Eco, Umberto. *Travels in Hyperreality: Essays*, 1986.
Kristeva, Julia. *The Kristeva Reader*, 1986.
Lodge, David, ed. *Modern Criticism and Theory: A Reader*, 1988.
O'Donnell, Patrick, and Robert Con Davis, eds. *Intertextuality and Contemporary American Fiction*, 1989.
Worton, Michael, and Judith Still, eds. *Intertextuality: Theories and Practice*, 1990.

SIMONE MURRAY

See also Bakhtin; Barthes; Kristeva

Luce Irigaray

Belgian-born French psychoanalyst, writer, and critic

Born: Belgium; 1930

Biography

Charting the principal features of Luce Irigaray's personal history is by no means an easy task, partly because she has resisted biographical approaches to her work and in interviews she has discouraged questions which attempt to move from her publications to her private life. Margaret Whitford points out that this reluctance stems from the tendency for biographical criticism to diminish the consequences of intellectual work by women. Biographical commentaries would, Whitford observes, detract from the issues raised in Irigaray's work, and because of this Irigaray generally prefers not to discuss her personal history in interviews.

In spite of this reluctance, some information about Irigaray is known, and some of this information has even been disclosed by Irigaray herself. Her interests lie mainly in the areas of philosophy, linguistics, and psychoanalysis. Following her move from Belgium to France to train to be an analyst, Irigaray carried out research on language and dementia at the Hôpital Sainte Anne (where Michel Foucault and Jacques Lacan had also studied madness) and this research formed the substance of her first book, *Le Langage des déments*, published in 1973. Like many other influential French intellectuals of the 1960s and 1970s, Irigaray attended Lacan's seminars at the eminent École Normale Supérieure in Paris and she later became part of Lacan's École Freudienne de Paris. Irigaray was effectively excommunicated from the École Freudienne in 1974, following the publication of *Spéculum de l'autre femme* (*Speculum of the Other Woman*, 1985, in which she challenges some assumptions about male and female sexuality made by psychoanalysis); her course proposal for the Department of Psychoanalysis at the University of Vincennes (where the École Freudienne was situated) was not accepted (by a commission which consisted of members selected by Lacan) and she lost her teaching position there toward the end of 1974 (despite the fact that she had been teaching at Vincennes since the birth of the university).

Irigaray has doctorates in both linguistics and philosophy and, as an analyst, has her own practice. She is currently a director of research in philosophy at the Centre Nationale de la Recherche Scientifique in Paris and teaches at the Collège Internationale de Philosophie.

Influence

Irigaray's principal contributions to criticism have arisen out of her attempts to theorize and ultimately transform certain assumptions about sexual difference. Much of her earliest work focused on the often ignored (and often implicit) articulation of sexual identity in philosophical and theoretical texts. Irigaray has contributed to debates about the various constructions of masculinity and femininity in psychoanalysis and she has shown how canonical philosophical material (such as Plato's cave analogy in the *Republic*, 388–368 B.C.) subordinates women both by promoting the equation between paternity and authority and by writing the feminine out of social, cultural, and sexual existence.

In more general terms, Irigaray has combined arguments associated with Karl Marx, Friedrich Nietzsche, Sigmund Freud, and Jacques Lacan in order to arrive at alternative ideas about the specific conditions of women's subjectivity. She has contributed to recent debates about the relationship between representation and subjectivity by arguing that women are contained within structures of signification which augment masculine-centered conceptions of identity; because of this some limited correspondences can be discerned between Irigaray's work and the concerns of certain "poststructuralist" thinkers (such as Jacques Derrida, Gilles Deleuze, or Julia Kristeva) who consider the role played by discursive systems in the formation of identity. Irigaray's work is often linked with *l'écriture féminine*, despite the fact that she is not primarily concerned with fictional narratives.

Analysis

Irigaray is mainly concerned with the way that sexual identity forms part of an entrenched hierarchy which she describes as an "economy of men amongst themselves." This structure regulates the distribution of capital and power, but it also circumscribes the nature of female sexuality by excluding any consideration of nonmale characteristics. In this economy women are the objects of men's speech and women are ultimately reduced to the status of commodities which are exchanged between men: women are circulated between and consumed by men, and women exist only insofar as they can foster relations between men (in other words, as wives, daughters, and sisters). Crucially, for Irigaray, discursive operations are largely responsible for the everyday management of this economy: language governs the construction of sexual identity and, consequently, language associates masculinity with authority while simultaneously keeping the feminine in a position of subordination.

Irigaray's preoccupation with the relationship between discourse and cultural power leads her arguments in a number of directions. In general terms, for example, *Ce Sexe qui n'en est pas un* (1977; *This Sex Which is Not One*, 1985) observes that women have their subjectivity constructed and constrained by masculine structures of signification yet remain excluded from the organization of those structures. Women can only represent themselves (and can only enter into relations with other women) through a discursive framework which is controlled by men, and which serves the interests of men. Within this discursive framework women become merely the objects of representation, having their identity and their sexuality signified for them by a language which refuses to allow women any form of self-representation. For Irigaray:

> Women's social inferiority is reinforced and complicated by the fact that woman does not have access to language, except through recourse to 'masculine' systems of representation which disappropriate her from her relation to herself and to other women. The feminine is never to be identified except by and for the masculine.

Men, in contrast, have enjoyed the privilege of actively participating in a linguistic order which has masculinity at its center, and which Irigaray therefore terms "phallogocentrism."

In more specific terms, Irigaray frequently explores the ways that this phallogocentrism manifests itself in psychoanalytic theory and practice. Irigaray certainly supports some of the developments made by psychoanalysis: she defends Freud's comments about women (describing them as a necessary but problematic stage in understanding the relationship between sexuality, language, and knowledge), she claims that the unconscious provides a source for the transformation of cultural power, and her model of ego formation is largely derived from Lacan's notion of the mirror stage. Nevertheless, Irigaray's work plays a decisive role in the critique of psychoanalysis and she, along with other commentators, repeatedly draws attention to the way that psychoanalysis bolsters prevailing ideas about sexual identity.

Irigaray's critique of psychoanalysis draws upon Lacan's claim that the mirror is a crucial factor in the formation of the ego. According to Lacan, subjectivity emerges when a child perceives its body as an image reflected in a mirror; until this perception occurs a state of pre-rational incoherence exists in the child; after this perception the child enters consciousness and construes itself as a unified individual (Lacan calls this process "the imaginary"). For Irigaray, however, the primacy given to the mirror reveals a number of problems in psychoanalytic theory and illustrates its blind spot with regard to women's bodies. Psychoanalysis has, she observes, overemphasized the role of the visible in the formation of subjectivity and it has uncritically adopted a "dominant specularity." In other words, psychoanalysis has relied upon anatomical definitions of identity: it has privileged those anatomical traits which can be seen and it has consequently constructed male physiology (particularly the phallus) as a perceptible presence and female physiology as a lack or absence. Additionally, Irigaray argues, the notion that a mirror impartially reflects these anatomical traits perpetuates this specularized account of the imaginary.

In *Speculum of the Other Woman*, her 1974 philosophy doctoral thesis, Irigaray transforms Lacan's model by claiming that the feminine should be understood not in terms of an image reflected in a flat mirror. Instead, according to Irigaray, a more appropriate mirror can be found in the speculum, the surgical instrument conventionally used to diagnose female sexual maladies. Irigaray focuses on the fact that the speculum is a concave mirror which is specifically designed to reflect female anatomy. More than this, though, the speculum can only produce a different reflection, one which suggests that the perception of women demands an alternative system of representation. Following Lacan's example (while at the same time problematizing some of his assumptions about the relationship between identity and specularity), Irigaray uses the model of the speculum as the basis for a more general approach to sexuality: just as the speculum allows an alternative perception of women's anatomy, it also serves as an example for a different concept of female sexuality and the feminine.

Irigaray makes some suggestions about the forms that these different concepts may take and about how women's specificity may be signified, although in doing so she frequently adopts an elliptical and poeticized style which has resulted in a number of responses to her work. Countering the psychoanalytic characterization of female sexuality as lack, atrophy, or deficiency, Irigaray claims that: "Perhaps it is time to return to that repressed entity, the female imaginary. So woman does not have a sex organ? She has at least two of them, but they are not identifiable as ones. Indeed she has many more. Her sexuality, always double, goes even further: it is *plural . . . woman has sex organs more or less everywhere*." Irigaray develops this notion of the female imaginary by stressing the differences between concepts that accompany phallocentric definitions of subjectivity and concepts that are associated with female sexuality. In particular (and perhaps most notoriously), Irigaray contrasts the singularity of the phallus with the "two lips" of women's bodies: the male imaginary is invested in self-identity, singularity, unity, and coherence, whereas an alternative female imaginary would privilege divided subjectivity and multiplicity.

For Irigaray, then, any effective transformation would only emerge from a systematic recasting of all cultural phenomena, and this would go as far as changing the way that identity is conceptualized. The existing distribution of discursive power and women's subordination would not suddenly disappear if women were allowed equal access to an unaltered phallogocentrism: if women and the feminine are to break free from subordinating phallogocentric structures then, Irigaray argues, an alternative epistemology and an alternative discourse is necessary. In *This Sex Which is Not One* she states that if women "simply reverse the order of things . . . history would repeat itself in the long run, would revert to sameness: to phallocratism." In contrast with some recent theorists of gender and sexuality, however, Irigaray does not conclude that alternative economies and different notions of the body would result in heterogeneous, diverse, and indeterminate identities. Rather, she argues that a transfiguration of sexuality can only begin with a recognition of what she calls "female specificity." Irigaray does not pursue the poststructuralist search for a dissipated and deregulated "sexual otherwise," but begins to define a nonphallic body which can be traced through its (non-) appearance in a dispossessed and disinvested female exteriority. Irigaray, Elizabeth Grosz points out, "is interested in developing accounts of subjectivity and knowledge that acknowledge the existence of two senses, two bodies, two forms of desire and two ways of knowing."

For Irigaray, a second or "other" form of understanding would not characterize women and the feminine with reductive singularities, it would avoid the question "What is Woman?" and it would also avoid the predicative conclusions that such a question provokes. Instead, this alternative paradigm would, according to Irigaray, explore the way that women have been construed as exteriority and deficiency – positions which signal the inscrutability of the feminine within a masculine economy. For Irigaray it is this inscrutability of the feminine which troubles the culture of "men amongst themselves": phallogocentrism constantly strives to represent the feminine yet ultimately fails to do so, and because of this, Irigaray argues, the feminine can only be thought of as a "disruptive excess."

Unsurprisingly, Irigaray's work has provoked controversy and some commentators have criticized a number of her ideas. One of the earliest of these responses can be found in Monique Plaza's essay "'Phallomorphic Power' and the Psychology of 'Woman'"; in this essay Plaza argues that while describing the feminine as both subordinated other and disruptive excess, Irigaray privileges the role of linguistic systems and considers the material subjection of women to be of secondary importance. What Irigaray fails fully to consider, according to Plaza, is that "The notion of 'Woman' is imbricated in the materiality of existence" and "The patriarchal order . . . constitutes a specific, material oppression." In other words, according to this position Irigaray's schematic explorations of a specific female desire leave the actual sociocultural status of women unexamined.

A second, and more prevalent, critique of Irigaray's work arises from her repeated use of terms which appear, on the surface, to refer to physiological properties. Much of Irigaray's work has resulted in the accusation that she relies on biologically essentialist notions of male and female identity. Other theorists (such as Hélène Cixous) attempt to overturn established attitudes toward sexuality by locating feminine attributes in men and, vice versa, by exploring the complicity of women with masculine conventions. Irigaray, on the other hand, seems to locate the feminine entirely within women's bodies, with no possibility that men may exhibit forms of identity which have feminine characteristics. (More often that not, Irigaray argues, men's adoption of a counter-cultural femininity should be understood as an appropriation of women's specificity and, consequently, as a further instance of male narcissism.) In *Sexual/Textual Politics* (1985) Toril Moi, for instance, states that "Irigaray's attempt to establish a theory of femininity that escapes specul(ariz)ation necessarily lapses into a form of essentialism." Irigaray, by her own admission, recognizes that women only have access to "masculine systems of representation" and this would suggest that an alternative language must necessarily emerge out of the dominant symbolic order: women must adopt existing terms and reinscribe their signifying value. For Moi, however, this mimicry might fail because the moment of reinscription may not perceived: instead of overturning "masculine systems of representation," mimesis may simply appear to reproduce an established language. In other words, Irigaray's attempts to transform signifying systems are, according to some commentators, problematic because she necessarily employs those essentializing concepts that she simultaneously disavows.

Other commentators have defended Irigaray's work with equal conviction. For example, Whitford claims that, even if unacknowledged, any mimesis would inevitably transform social and symbolic frameworks. If, as Irigaray claims, women develop symbolic relations of their own and become able to represent themselves then, Whitford points out, the very nature of identity and language will be altered. The culture of "men amongst themselves" would no longer take the same form since its subjection of women would no longer exist. Whitford further argues that the debates surrounding Irigaray's use of biologistic terms has resulted in a productive dialogue between women. According to Whitford, Irigaray has provided "*images of women's bodies* which have become material for symbolic exchange between women, and which therefore have already in a limited domain and to a limited extent exceeded the parameters of patriarchal representations of women . . . what is important about the two lips is not only their literalness, but, above all, *the fact that no one can agree on exactly what they mean*."

Principal criticism

Le Langage des déments, 1973
Spéculum de l'autre femme, 1974 (*Speculum of the Other Woman*, 1985)
Ce Sexe qui n'en est pas un, 1977 (*This Sex Which is Not One*, 1985)
Et L'Une ne bouge pas sans l'autre, 1979
Amante marine. De Friedrich Nietzsche, 1980 (*Marine Lover of Friedrich Nietzsche*, 1991)
Le Corps-à-corps avec la mère, 1981
Passions élémentaires, 1982 (*Elemental Passions*, 1992)
L'Oubli de l'air chez Martin Heidegger, 1983
La Croyance même, 1983
Éthique de la différence sexuelle, 1984 (*An Ethics of Sexual Difference*, 1993)
Parler n'est jamais neutre, 1985
Sexes et parentés, 1987 (*Sexes and Genealogies*, 1993)
Le Temps de la différence: pour une révolution pacifique, 1989 (*Thinking the Difference: For a Peaceful Revolution*, 1994)
Je, tu, nous: pour une culture de la différence, 1990 (*Je, Tu, Nous: Towards a Culture of Difference*, 1993)
J'aime à toi: esquisse d'une félicité dans l'histoire, 1992 (*I Love to You: Sketch for a Felicity within History*, 1996)
Être deux, 1997

Other major works and literary forms

Although much of Luce Irigaray's work is concerned with linguistic and representational issues, it is also concerned with wider ethical and social matters. Indeed, many of her publications during the 1980s and 1990s were concerned less with the relationship between the symbolic and the real than her earlier writings. She has produced several readings of the representation of gender and nature in philosophical texts (by, for example, Nietzsche and Heidegger). Irigaray has paid greater attention to the gendering of ethics, she has explored the relationship between women and the divine in Christianity, and she written extensively about the law and women's rights.

Further reading

Braidotti, Rosi. *Patterns of Dissonance*, 1991.
Butler, Judith. *Gender Trouble: Feminism and the Subversion of Identity*, 1990.
Chanter, Tina. *Ethics of Eros: Irigaray's Rereading of the Philosophers*, 1995.
Grosz, Elizabeth. *Sexual Subversions: Three French Feminists*, 1989.
Moi, Toril. *Sexual/Textual Politics: Feminist Literary Theory*, 1985.
Mortley, Raoul. *French Philosophers in Conversation*, 1991.
Plaza, Monique. "'Phallomorphic Power' and the Psychology of 'Woman,'" in *Feminist Issues*. (Summer, 1980), pp. 71–102.
Whitford, Margaret. *Luce Irigaray: Philosophy in the Feminine*, 1991.

PHILIP LEONARD

See also Cixous; Feminist Criticism; Kristeva; Moi; Psychoanalytic Criticism

Wolfgang Iser

German theorist

Born: Marienberg, Germany; July 22, 1926

Biography

Wolfgang Iser was born in Marienberg, Germany, in 1926, the son of Paul and Else Iser, and he married Lore Reichert, a translator, in 1952. He attended the universities of Leipzig and Tübingen, receiving a doctorate from the University of Heidelberg in 1950. From 1950 to 1967 he taught at the universities of Heidelberg, Glasgow, Würzburg, and Cologne. Then, in 1967, when the University of Constance was founded as a reaction to what was seen as Germany's restrictive, conservative, and elitist educational system, Iser joined the faculty there as a professor of English and comparative literature, later holding a chair at Constance, where he has been a principal member of what has been called the Constance School of Reception Aesthetics, a group of theorists interested in problems of literary reception.

Iser's field of specialization is English literature, and much of his work has been translated into or was originally written in English. Since 1968, when he was at Colgate University in Hamilton, New York, he has spent a significant amount of time in the United States, including Wesleyan University and the University of California at Irvine.

Influence

Iser is a reader-oriented literary theorist and critic concerned with the relationship between literary texts and their readers. With the exception of his colleague at the University of Constance, Hans Robert Jauss, Iser is the only reader-oriented literary theorist and critic from the Constance School, and indeed from most of the European continent, who has had much of an impact on American literary thought. Drawing on Russian Formalism, phenomenology, and other theoretical traditions including speech act theory and Gestalt psychology, Iser has developed a coherent model of reading literary fiction that has been adapted by numerous critics of literary works written by authors ranging from William Shakespeare to John Fowles.

Iser's model is most closely aligned with the phenomenological model of Roman Ingarden, but he differs from Ingarden in wanting to give the reader more creative power in the "concretization" of the literary text. Despite his insistence that the reader is an agent in the production of literary meaning, Iser's theory remains a very conservative reader-oriented theory, since he refuses to dissociate reader and text; indeed, in his model the reader is inscribed within the text and is "instructed" by the text. The meanings the reader produces are not "formulated" by the text, but they are "intended."

The theory is eclectic and expansive, having a remarkable ability to incorporate a variety of theoretical stances from theorists as diverse as Mikhail Bakhtin and J. L. Austin. While this leaves Iser open to criticism such as that levied by Stanley Fish in the journal *Diacritics* in 1981 – Iser, says Fish, is "influential without being controversial, and at a moment when everyone is choosing up sides, he seems to be on no side at all or (it amounts to the same thing) on every side at once" – it also reveals a remarkable breadth of mind and interests.

Analysis

Iser is a reader-oriented literary theorist and critic interested in what happens during an aesthetic literary experience. In his two major theoretical works, *Der implizite Leser: Kommunicationsformen des englischen Romans von Bunyan bis Beckett* (1972; *The Implied Reader: Patterns in Communication in Prose Fiction from Bunyan to Beckett,* 1974) and *Der Akt des Lesens: Theorie ästhetischer Wirkung* (1976; *The Act of Reading: A Theory of Aesthetic Response*, 1978), he takes the two poles of text and reader and develops a model of what occurs between them. In this phenomenological model, the text provides instructions to a reader who activates those instructions, producing a "concretization" of the text as an aesthetic work. This work does not exist unless or until the text is read; it, and its meaning, are "virtual." The relationship between text and reader is thus symbiotic: the text conditions the reader to respond in certain ways, producing an "ideation" of the text, which would not exist without that reader. As a result of this interaction, the reader himself or herself changes.

In his major theoretical statements of the 1970s, Iser considers not actual readers but "implied readers" – that is, readers constituted by the text itself. The implied reader, he writes, is a "textual structure anticipating the presence of a recipient" and designating "a network of response inviting structures, which impel a reader to grasp the text." The implied reader, in other words, is an abstraction, a concept, a set of activities demanded and controlled by a particular text, although Iser implies that there is always a real reader who is taking on this implied reader role.

Later statements by Iser suggest an increased interest in actual readers and spectators. In an interchange with other theorists published in *Diacritics* – "Interview" (1980) and "Talk Like Whales: A Reply to Stanley Fish" (1981) – he comments that he awaits empirical research applying his model to the activities of particular readers reading particular texts (although he does not address the problems of designing a methodology for such studies). Articles about dramatic performances published in the 1980s begin, at least, with a focus on actual spectators, not on what the play asks of these spectators: in "The Art of Failure: The Stifled Laugh in Beckett's Theatre" (1981), for example, he notes that he interviewed several other spectators of Samuel Beckett's plays to find out about the nature of laughter among the audience. His focus in this article remains, however, as it has with all of his theoretical work, on what texts do to readers rather than on the readers themselves.

Iser calls his theory an "aesthetics of reception," thus distinguishing it from that of his colleagues in Constance, such as Hans Robert Jauss, who studies *Rezeptionsästhetik* (reception aesthetics). Where reception aesthetics traces the history of actual readers, Iser primarily concerns himself with a model of what occurs during reception. He is nevertheless interested in literary history, and in *The Implied Reader* he develops his own history of literary prose fiction as a history of changing roles mapped out for readers. The novel begins, he writes, at a point when humans become focused on their own consciousness, and it develops as a form especially suited to entangle its readers in the exploration of reality and of how humans perceive that reality. According to Iser, novels have exerted increasingly less direct control on their readers since the seventeenth century, thus forcing readers to make more connections for themselves and directing their attention to their own interpretive activity, until in the twentieth century novels involved readers in an exploration and critique of the limitations of this interpretive activity.

Since *The Implied Reader*, Iser has become less interested in literary history and more concerned with describing his model of literary reading in more detail. Crucial to this model is the concept of "indeterminacy," by which Iser means the failure of a text to state its own meaning. Because the text does not state its meaning, the reader is stimulated to do so. Comparing the text/reader relationship to any communicative relationship, Iser points out that, as with any communicative interaction, people are limited by the "inexperiencability" of another, the inability to know another's thoughts and intentions. Unlike face-to-face communication, in literary communication readers cannot ask the text for clarification and affirmation, cannot negotiate meaning, and cannot expect the text to adapt to them. Instead, readers must constitute their own meanings. Iser calls this situation the "asymmetry" between reader and text.

In the chapter that concludes *The Act of Reading*, Iser calls this indeterminacy "negativity," explaining that it is the unwritten base of a text, the unformulated double behind the text that conditions the formulations that become the aesthetic work. Metaphorically, negativity is the white space on the page: "In relation to the given positions which it links, negativity traces out what is not given and enables it to be communicated."

Because of this negativity, reading becomes a process of filling in or connecting elements across the spaces, or "gaps," in the text. There are two sorts of gaps – blanks, which ask readers to make connections between them, and negations, which "impel [the reader] to counterbalance these negations by seeking their positive potential." In either case, readers work to build *gestalten*, or unified views of the world represented in the text. Whenever there is a break in what Iser calls "the good continuation" of the text, the reader seeks to transform this break into a consistent view. This consistency-building is a "passive synthesis occurring below the threshold of our consciousness as we read" and is a constant process during reading. As soon as each *gestalt* is built, something new occurs in the text to disconfirm it, demanding that the reader build a new *gestalt.*

Thus, reading becomes a dialectical process. Two particular oppositions come into play, "foreground and background" and "theme and horizon," both of which relate to how different elements of the text interact with the reader. In foregrounding, the reader focuses on different elements of the "repertoire" of the literary text, letting other elements recede into the background of consciousness. This repertoire consists of material taken from the reality outside the text, either from social and cultural and historical reality or from literary conventions. As the reader reads, depending on his or her own knowledge, expectations, and background, he or she focuses on some of these elements rather than on others: thus they are in the foreground. Yet the foregrounded elements are seen against the background of their old natural context in the nontextual world: "The chosen element evokes its original setting, but is to take in a new and as yet unknown function." Because of its new context, it can be seen more distantly and more critically, leading the reader to understand something new about the external world. For example, in reading Tobias Smollett's *Humphrey Clinker* (1771) readers focus on elements of different literary genres – the travelogue, the epistolary novel, the picaresque novel – that are incorporated in the text. Although the reader may be familiar with these forms, in the process of reading them in this new context and in combination with one another, he or she is forced to see both literary conventions and human nature in a new way.

Whereas the foreground/background relation describes a principle of selection of elements from outside the text into the text, the theme/horizon relation describes a principle of combination of elements within the text. There are four basic elements, or perspectives, that may combine: plot, characters, narrator, and reader (as described by the text). While reading, the reader focuses on only one of these elements at a time – this is the current "theme" – and he or she views it against all the other perspectives noticed up until that point – called the "horizon." While noticing this theme in opposition or difference, he or she is forced to make connections, connections that may be undermined by each new perspective afforded by the text. A paradigmatic example of this process occurs in William Faulkner's *The Sound and the Fury* (1929), where the reader must try to make sense of four radically different narrative perspectives: Benjy, Quentin, Jason, and Dilsey. Each new narrator offers a perspective which the reader, through juxtaposition with earlier perspectives, realizes is flawed and which forces the reader to make a sequence of *gestalten*, each of which is subsequently transformed by the next narrator. This transformation occurs both ways: the new perspective or theme is transformed by what occurred previously (the horizon) but so too are the old perspectives transformed by the new theme.

The interchanges between theme and horizon and background and foreground are constant, because with each new focus (theme or foreground) and each new *gestalt* their shadows are carried with them, ready to undermine and transform or even topple the current themes and *gestalten*: "Each gestalt bears with it those possibilities which it has excluded but which may eventually invalidate it. This is the way in which the literary text exploits the consistency-building habit which underlies all comprehension." There is a constant dialectic then between the polysemantic nature of the text and the illusion-making process of the reader. The attempt at balance between these activities is the aesthetic experience, but, says Iser, there must always be an "inherent nonachievement of balance as prerequisite for the very dynamism of the operation."

The reader functions during this process as a wandering viewpoint in the time flow of the novel, his or her consciousness merging memories and expectations. He or she too undergoes a dialectical process. As he or she puts into play the interactions of the text, he or she becomes "decentered," different from him- or herself, alien: "The reader's role . . . is meant to open him up to the workings of the text, so that he will leave behind his individual disposition for the duration of his reading." With that alien self travels the reader's actual self, which has now become "virtual" because it is suppressed in the background. Each of these selves may call into question another, making of the literary reading experience an opportunity for self-discovery and, more importantly, change.

According to Iser, literature has a moral, transcendent purpose that leads to a reorientation of the self. Aesthetic pleasure, he says, derives from two sources: from the experience of exercising one's cognitive and emotional faculties and from the temporary escape from the self. It is this process of losing the particular self, and therefore the "normal" self, giving it up to the structuring activity of the text, that gives readers the distance necessary to examine their world and perceptions and thereby change themselves. Reading, he says, does not simply gratify values and desires; rather, it defines and stimulates them: "The need to decipher gives us the chance to formulate our own deciphering capacity – i.e., we bring to the fore an element of our being of which we are not directly conscious . . . . [Reading literature] entails the possibility that we may formulate ourselves."

Iser is more than a reader-oriented critic. He is a mimetic critic – not in the sense that he believes that literature reflects the world, but because he believes that the process of reading causes a reader to reflect on the world. Most important, he is a moral critic, concerned with the impact of literature on readers' values and beliefs.

Despite Iser's connection with the radical Constance School, in the context of current literary debate Iser is clearly a conservative; indeed, most criticism of Iser centers on the fact that he is not radical enough, that behind his apparent interest in the reader lies a textual critic, even a New Critic. As Steven Mailloux points out in a review published in *Centrum* (1981), Iser is attractive to many American literary theorists because he allows them to "have their text and reader too." Although Iser's model asserts the possibility of multiple readers making multiple meanings of particular texts, he is very interested in how that text controls meaning.

In his critical practice, Iser seems to demonstrate that there is only one correct meaning. Moreover, he seems to insist that there is only one correct way to read – in an active, "productive" manner. Iser has come under attack by many American reader-response critics, including David Bleich and Stanley Fish, for his insistence that textual elements are objectively verifiable, intersubjective "givens," existing prior to an interpretive activity. Both Bleich and Fish, along with Steven Mailloux and Robert Holub, two of Iser's major American analyzers, point out that in fact such givens are already products of an interpreting mind. Underlying all these problems is the fact that Iser never really considers what readers bring to the literary experience. Iser writes, somewhat naively, about the necessity of approaching reading with an open mind, without ideological preconceptions, but in fact his own theory is based on the assumption that readers do not come with an open mind, that in fact they have knowledge, experience, and expectations when they begin to read. Yet Iser never completely considers what knowledge, experience, and expectations they might be or how people with different knowledge, experience, and expectations might interact with the texts he discusses.

Another problem with Iser's theory involves his approach to history. Although he claims to develop a historical theory, he simply develops a reading theory and then uses the texts as a sequence of illustrative examples. His history is an "afterthought," to use the word of Robert Holub, and not an integrated process. Perhaps this is the reason he has such difficulty handling anachronistic reading, that is, reading of literature that is not written by one's contemporaries.

A final problem with Iser is his eclecticism and his tendency to import terms to suit his purposes. Like the literary texts he describes, his own texts seem to import terms from other contexts and place them in new situations. As Holub notes, Iser has an "uncanny ability to merge modernism with more traditional views." Thus, in Iser, ordinary-language philosophy is found side by side with deconstruction. While such juxtapositions may be both stimulating and provocative to Iser's readers, they also lead to a certain amount of ambiguity: what exactly is the difference between "negativity," "polysemantic texts," the "asymmetry between reader and text," and (his most recent term) the "imaginary"? At times Iser seems to substitute elegant variation for explanation, producing texts that are increasingly obtuse.

Whether one sees this eclecticism as a flaw or as a strength, it has certainly been beneficial in one way: Iser has introduced English-speaking theorists and critics to a variety of Continental approaches, especially Ingarden's phenomenology, Russian Formalism, and Czech structuralism. In addition, as Holub notes, "He has forced us to recognize that we cannot forgo an analysis of our own involvement with a text if we are to understand what literature is about."

Principal criticism

Die Weltanschauung Henry Fieldings, 1952 (*The World View of Henry Fielding*, 1952)
Walter Pater: Die Autonomie des Ästhetischen, 1960 (*Walter Pater: The Aesthetic Moment*, 1987)
Die Appelstruktur der Texte: Unbestimmtheit als Wirkungsbeding-ung literarischer Prosa, 1970 ("Indeterminacy and the Reader's Response in Prose Fiction," in *Aspects of Narrative: Selected Papers from the English Institute*, 1971)
Spensers Arkadien: Fiction und Geschichte, 1970
Der implizite Leser: Kommunicationsformen des englischen Romans von Bunyan bis Beckett, 1972 (*The Implied Reader: Patterns of Communication in Prose Fiction from Bunyan to Beckett*, 1974)
Der Akt des Lesens: Theorie ästhetischer Wirkung, 1976 (*The Act of Reading: A Theory of Aesthetic Response*, 1978)
Die Artistik des Misslingens: Ersticktes Lachen im Theater Becketts, 1979 (partially translated as "The Art of Failure: The Stifled Laugh in Beckett's Theatre," 1981)
Funktionen des Fiktiven, 1983 (editor)
"The Dramatization of Double Meaning in Shakespeare's *As You Like It*," 1983
"Feigning in Fiction," 1985
Lawrence Sterne: Tristram Shandy, 1988
Prospecting: From Reader Response to Literary Anthropology, 1989
Das Fiktive und das Imaginäre. Grundzüge einer Literaturanthro-pologie, 1991

Other major works and literary forms

Wolfgang Iser is known primarily as a literary theorist and critic.

Further reading

Bleich, David. "Teleology and Taxonomy in Critical Explanation," in *Bucknell Review*. XXVI, no. 1 (1981), pp. 102–127.
Fish, Stanley. "Why No One's Afraid of Wolfgang Iser," in *Diacritics*. XI (Spring, 1981), pp. 2–13.
Freund, Elizabeth. *The Return to the Reader: Reader-Response Criticism*, 1987.
Holub, Robert C. "Trends in Literary Theory: The American Reception of Reception Theory," in *The German Quarterly*. LV (January, 1982), pp. 80–96.
——. *Reception Theory: A Critical Introduction*, 1984.

Mailloux, Steven. "How to Be Persuasive in Literary Theory: The Case of Wolfgang Iser," in *Centrum*. I (Spring, 1981), pp. 65–73.
——. *Interpretive Conventions: The Reader in the Study of American Fiction*, 1982.
Suleiman, Susan R. "Introduction: Varieties of Audience-Oriented Criticism," in *The Reader in the Text: Essays on Audience and Interpretation*, 1980. Edited by Susan R. Suleiman and Inge Crosman.
Tompkins, Jane P., ed. *Reader-Response Criticism: From Formalism to Post-Structuralism*, 1980.
Wilson, W. Daniel. "Readers in Texts," in *PMLA*. XCVI (October, 1981), pp. 848–863.

JoAnne Liebman Matson

See also Jauss; Reception Theory

Saint Isidore of Seville

Spanish theologian and scholar

Born: Seville, Spain; c. 560
Died: Seville, Spain; April 4, 636

Biography

Isidore's father, Severian, belonged to a Cartagenan noble family, probably of Roman origin. When the Arian Goths destroyed Cartagena, Severian fled to Seville, where Isidore was born about 560. Two of his brothers, Leander and Fulgentius, became, like himself, bishops and eventually saints, and one of his sisters, Florentina, became an abbess who was also eventually canonized. Little is known of Isidore's early life, but after the death of his parents he received an outstanding classical education under the somewhat severe supervision of his older brother Leander. After his theological studies he became a priest and assisted Bishop Leander in ruling the diocese of Seville and in defending Christian orthodoxy against Arianism. Following Leander's death, Isidore became bishop of Seville. During his thirty-six-year episcopate he completed the work begun by his brother of converting the Visigoths from Arianism to Catholicism. He also continued his brother's practice of organizing the Spanish church through councils, the most notable of which were those of Seville in 619 and Toledo in 633. The Fourth Council of Toledo marked the pinnacle of Isidore's career. In religious matters, the council standardized liturgical practices in the Divine Office and the Mass. In political matters, it authorized the union of church and state and political activity by the clergy; it also advocated toleration of the Jews. In educational matters, the council ordered the establishment of cathedral schools in each diocese and raised the qualifications for ordination to the priesthood. This council, over which Isidore presided so successfully, led to a dynamic Spanish church in the heart of a unified Visigothic kingdom.

Throughout his life Isidore was known for his charity, and shortly before his death he distributed his remaining possessions to the poor. He then made his way to his church, where one bishop clothed him in sackcloth while another put ashes on his head. Clad in the symbols of penance, he received the Eucharist, forgave his debtors, and commended himself to the prayers of his people. Upon returning to his home, he peacefully died. He was formally canonized in 1598 and, as the last of the Western Latin Fathers, was declared a Doctor of the Church in 1722.

Influence

Isidore has been called the "Great Schoolmaster of the Middle Ages," an apt characterization, because he helped both to preserve the treasures of a perishing Roman culture and to transmit to the later Middle Ages a vast storehouse of knowledge that he had collected from ancient pagan authors and the Fathers of the Church. He was considered the most learned man of his time, and his *Etymologiae* became the most studied work of the period.

He saw his mission as preserving Spain from decadence, and he helped convert the Arian Goths to Roman Catholicism. He was also influential in uniting church and state in Spain, a mingling of the spiritual and temporal that he found completely natural. The mingling of these two streams can also be seen in his literary work. He was instrumental in preserving much of the Roman literary tradition, and he made this pagan past acceptable to his compatriots by coloring the passages he transcribed with his own spiritual ideas. His own age saw this recasting of the past in spiritual terms as his greatest influence.

Analysis

Although the medieval period was a time of considerable literary creativity, with the rebirth of drama and the flourishing of allegory, satire, and other narrative forms, it was not a time of important literary theory or criticism. Most theoretical energy was directed toward speculative theology, which was quite natural in an essentially theocratic society. This society did not promote literary criticism in the modern sense – that is, as a self-conscious discipline of an individual's verbal imagination. Nevertheless, linguistic analyses were often an element in discussions of widely varying subjects, and Isidore's literary works often have language as their theme.

At the core of Isidore of Seville's literary theory, if one can call it that, lies the insight that the quality of language affects and infects people's spiritual life. Language helps shape both people's social and personal perception of themselves and their relationship with God; it also delimits realms for imagination and forms human values. When the matrix of language is strong, it allows people to contemplate the divine mysteries and to share their insights with other children of God. The communication of spirituality requires a common symbolic language that generates the strength to sacrifice for the common good and to control unruly passions.

Isidore, then, believed deeply in the superior realities of the spiritual world. The boundary between explaining the meaning of words and describing the nature of things, however, is easily violated, especially if one interprets the nature of things scientifically. Isidore, however, was not concerned with scientific but with religious interpretations of things and texts. In his explication of various writings, for example, he extolled the moral and religious, a practice he followed even in interpreting the Roman classics.

Further examples of his approach can be seen in his theological works. *De fide catholica ex Veteri et Novo Testamento contra Iudaeos* (614–615; a treatise on the Catholic faith based on the Old and New Testaments and directed against the Jews) was not written, despite its title, as an apologetic or controversial tract, but as an explication of the great Christological mysteries and their consequences for both Jews and Gentiles. His *Synonyma*, a curious mixture of the linguistic and the theological, is a spiritual meditation in the form of a dialogue between Man and Reason. Isidore wrote it according to the laws of synonymic parallelism, in which equivalent expressions are multiplied to restate and elaborate ideas. In the first book, Man, under the weight of the misfortunes that oppress him, comes to desire his own death, but Reason intervenes to raise his courage and lead him along the path to perfection. In the second book, Reason, continuing this spiritual therapy, counsels Man to resist temptation by practicing prayer, mortification, and vigilance.

Etymologiae is Isidore's longest, most important, and most famous work. In it he concerned himself with the etymological derivations of key words, believing that the knowledge of a word's origin conveyed an insight into the essence of things. These explanations of series of words make Isidore's book essentially an encyclopedia. In its own time, the book was primarily important in keeping the existing fragments of humanistic and scientific knowledge in circulation. In modern times, it remains an interesting and authoritative source for Latin lexicography, and it provides a window into the intellectual world of the early Middle Ages.

Isidore's book on etymologies contains twenty sections, some on the seven traditional liberal arts – both the trivium (grammar, rhetoric, and dialectic) and the quadrivium (arithmetic, geometry, music, and astronomy) – and others on theology, medicine, animals, war, agriculture, and architecture. Though most of these subjects have to do with secular concerns, Isidore found ways to relate worldly knowledge to the divine.

For an understanding of Isidore's literary theory, the most important sections of the *Etymologiae* are the first three books, which discuss the seven liberal arts. He here shows that grammar is the skill of speech, in particular Latin speech, for it was then a living language and all Isidore's works were written in Latin. Indeed, his *De differentiis verborum* (on the differences of words) is basically a grammatical lexicon explaining certain nuances of the Latin language. The grammar in the *Etymologiae* extends far beyond the modern discipline, for Isidore included syntax, etymology, poetic meter, prosody, the explanation of allusions, and even history in his understanding of grammar.

Dialectic, for Isidore, shows how to use words meaningfully. Having learned from grammar how to talk, people learn from dialectic how to talk sense. Philosophy is related to dialectic, for philosophy deals with arguing wisely, proving what is true and disproving what is false. Therefore, at the start of his compendium on dialectics, Isidore discusses the divisions of philosophy. In one of his schemes, he divides speculative philosophy into physics, mathematics, and metaphysics (theology) and practical philosophy into individual ethics, family ethics, and politics. The mixture of science and theology in these divisions is instructive, illustrating once again that for Isidore the only way to articulate knowledge was in the light of the divine.

Much of the material that is now called literary criticism was discussed by Isidore under the rubric of rhetoric. He lived at a time when public speaking was an indispensable skill for every influential person, and so rhetoric was a practical as well as a literary art. Rhetoric's precepts were addressed as much to lawyers as to poets, for both of these concern themselves with the structure and style of speech. Isidore understood poetics as the art of writing Latin verses in classical meters. He knew about classical poetics through both Horace's *Ars poetica* (c. 17 B.C.; *The Art of Poetry*) and Cicero's rhetorical works. He accepted these pagan authors because, as Saint Augustine had shown, their doctrines could be adapted to Christian theology and morals, and Isidore himself showed how the monk's vow of chastity was related to the classical doctrine of temperance.

Having grasped some of the elements of Isidore's literary theory through his analysis of the trivium, one can deepen this understanding through a consideration of his treatment of allegory. Allegories take many forms, from the practical fables of Aesop to the spiritual parables of Christ. Allegory is basically a way of structuring language to produce a linked series of double or multiple meanings. Isidore found it easy to relate allegory to his view of language and reality, since for him all things have a material and a spiritual meaning – often many levels of spiritual meaning. Thus, in Isidore's view, no literal meaning can stand alone, and any valid utterance must have a transcendent meaning, a spiritual surplus beyond the literal level. Following classical tradition, he called allegory an inversion of speech whereby, in saying one thing, a person conveys something else. In his exegetical works, he offered allegorical interpretations of numbers and names of persons and places, and he showed how these secondary (or tertiary or even more remote) senses of the text could be grasped by trained interpreters through a process of creative reflection. God, as an allegorical Poet, encoded multiple meanings into

Scripture, using symbols and iconographic devices. For example, when Isidore read in the Old Testament that Moses raised as a standard a serpent on a staff, he saw a deeper prophetic sense to the text that looked forward to Christ's similarly prophetic words to Nicodemus (in John 3:14): "And as Moses raised up the serpent in the desert, so too must the Son of Man be raised up."

Besides his works on language, Isidore was also well known for his writings on history. In Isidore's hands, dynastic history became a literary genre. His historical writings contain pious dedications, prologues, and epilogues as well as intercalated prayers and speculations about the ultimate fate (Heaven or Hell) of heroes and villains. For him, history is God's story, and the Isidorean economy of history is a pious system in which lives have no meaning until seen as events in the evolution of the City of God. For example, the *Chronica maiora* (major chronicles) contain an overview of the six historical ages of the world from the Creation to the reign of Sisebut, and God's providence is shown to have been responsible for all that happened during that time. In Isidore's scheme, the only events that become history are those that the Church elects to remember and on which it has passed its verdict. Isidore also viewed history as a chronicle of the battles waged against the Catholic church by the Devil through the heretics.

In his treatment of pagan civilizations, Isidore accepted the euhemeristic principle. Euhemerism is a theory linking mythology with real persons; it attributes the origin of gods to the deification of historical heroes. Isidore was part of a tradition that saw pagan civilization as an instrument of God's purpose and a preparation for Christ's coming. He therefore singled out in primitive ages the heroic figures who, from Prometheus onward, had been pioneers and leaders in civilization – the slayers of monsters, the founders of cities, the discoverers of the arts. As benefactors of humanity, these heroes deserved to be held in grateful remembrance, and Isidore ranked them together with biblical patriarchs, judges, and prophets.

Many modern critics have seen Isidore as a compiler utterly lacking in originality who frequently misunderstood his sources or who unjustifiably modified them. Although these criticisms have some validity, they are made from the vantage point of the twentieth century, and Isidore was very much a man of his time, concerned with analogy more than analysis, with the unusual more than the typical, with the encyclopedic more than the specialized. Isidore certainly cannot be considered a first-class literary critic, but his contemporaries regarded him not only as a saint but also as a scholar, someone whose view of the literary works of the past helped elevate Spain's cultural life. As a literary scholar, then, he digested and disseminated what he saw as the best of the past.

As a man who combined in himself the Roman and the Christian traditions, Isidore of Seville wanted the Church to welcome the beauty and wisdom of antiquity into her widened embrace. Indeed, in his life as in his work, he embodied the reconciliation of the Visigothic and the Roman Catholic, the humanities and religion, the pagan and the Christian, Apollo and Christ.

Principal criticism

Etymologiae (partial translation in *An Encyclopedist of the Dark Ages*, 1912)
Libri duo differentiarum (includes *De differentiis verborum* and *De differentiis rerum*)
Synonyma

Other major works and literary forms

Braulio, Bishop of Zaragoza, his earliest editor, and Faustinus Arévalo, his best, maintained that Saint Isidore of Seville left no subject untouched. Great variety also characterized the literary form of his many works in fields as various as theology, mathematics, history, and natural philosophy. In his exegetical works, Isidore sought to interpret Scripture for his age; this exegesis could be at times literal and historical, at times allegorical and moral. In his theological treatises, he dealt with the most profound Christological mysteries as well as the practical business of running church offices. No matter what his genre, his theme was often language and its relationship to reality.

NONFICTION
De fide catholica ex Veteri et Novo Testamento contra Iudaeos, 614–615
De viribus illustribus, c. 615–619
Historia de regibus Gothorum, Vandalorum, et Suevorum, 624 (*History of the Kings of the Goths, Vandals, and Suevi*, 1966)
Mysticorum expositiones sacramentorum seu quaestiones in Vetus Testamentum
Prologus in Librum Canticorum
De ecclesiasticis officiis
Sententiarum libri tres
De Trinitate
De natura rerum
De ordine creaturarum
Chronica maiora
De haeresibus; *De ortu et obitu patrum*

Further reading

Brehaut, E. *An Encyclopedist of the Dark Ages, Isidore of Seville*, 1912.
Brown, R. B. Introduction to *Printed Works of Isidore of Seville*, 1949.
Cazier, P. *Isidore de Seville et la naissance de l'Espagne Catholique*, 1994.
Fontaine, Jacques. *Isidore de Séville et la culture classique dans l'Espagne Wisigothique*, 1959 (2 volumes).
——. "Théorie et pratique du style chez Isidore de Séville," in *Vigiliae Christianae*. XIV (1960), pp. 65–101.
Herrin, J. *The Formation of Christendom*, 1987.
Laistner, Max Ludwig Wolfram. *Thought and Letters in Western Europe*, 1966.
Mullins, P. J. *The Spiritual Life According to St. Isidore of Seville*, 1940.
Séjourné, P. *Le Dernier Père de l'Église: Saint Isidore de Séville*, 1929.

ROBERT J. PARADOWSKI

See also Fulgentius; Medieval Literary Theory

J

Roman Jakobson

Russian-born American linguist and theorist

Born: Moscow, Russia; October 11, 1896
Died: Cambridge, Massachusetts; July 18, 1982

Biography

Roman Jakobson was born on October 11, 1896, in Moscow. After he graduated from the Lazarev Institute of Oriental Languages in 1914, he matriculated at Moscow University to study Slavic philology, receiving his master's degree in 1918. Revolution and civil war prevented him from completing his doctorate there. Meanwhile, in 1915, he had been instrumental in founding the Moscow Linguistic Circle, among the members of which were several young scholars destined to become leaders of the school of literary critics known as the Russian Formalists. In 1920 Jakobson was sent abroad as part of a Soviet Red Cross mission to Czechoslovakia; he was not to return to the Soviet Union until 1956.

In Czechoslovakia Jakobson established the Prague Linguistic Circle, whose works contain some of the classics of modern linguistics. Collaboration in the Circle with N. S. Trubetzkoi, a professor at Vienna, proved especially valuable to Jakobson. In 1930 he received his doctorate from Charles University, Prague, and the following year began teaching at Masaryk University, Brno.

In 1939 Jakobson was obliged to flee the Nazi Occupation, going first to Denmark, then Norway, and then Sweden, continuing his scholarly work under the most difficult circumstances. By 1941 he had made his way to New York, where he was associated with the exiled École Libre des Hautes Études. In 1946 he settled into an American academic career, receiving appointment as T. G. Masaryk Professor of Czechoslovak Studies at Columbia University. In 1949 he moved to Harvard University as Samuel Hazzard Cross Professor of Slavic Languages and Literatures, and in 1957 he received a concurrent appointment as Institute Professor at the Massachusetts Institute of Technology.

Influence

Jakobson's influence radiates in many directions. In his early years as a linguist he led a reaction against the neogrammarian school prevalent at the turn of the century, insisting that in addition to the history of languages (the diachronic axis), equal attention should be paid to their current (synchronic) state, their structure, their operation as a system. Jakobson made vital contributions to general linguistics, among them his discovery, together with Trubetzkoi, of "distinctive features" as the ultimate components of phonemes. In the United States, Jakobson was a central figure in the rapid postwar growth of American Slavistics, and he also played a pivotal role, worldwide, in the development of the general theory of communications, of which linguistics forms a part.

In literary studies, his ideas remained central in the work of the Russian Formalists until their suppression by Joseph Stalin in the 1930s. Much later, after contacts with the Soviet Union were renewed, Jakobson became an active influence on the work of Soviet semioticians, especially the Tartu School – Iurii Lotman and his collaborators. In Czechoslovakia Jakobson was a seminal influence on the development of structuralism in the 1930s, propagating ideas which were taken up with great excitement in the West during the 1960s. Many of his ideas passed over into such fields as cultural anthropology, general semiotics, and psychology.

Analysis

Poetry was a primary concern of Jakobson throughout his life. A lover of poetry and a friend of poets, he believed that the study of poetic language, "language in its aesthetic function," could reveal much about the nature of language itself. Thus Jakobson the linguist and Jakobson the literary theorist are really one and indivisible. Poetry and linguistics interreacted and illuminated each another, and they remained dynamically interlocked throughout his long career.

One of Jakobson's important innovations in both literary and linguistic studies was his insistence on "synchrony." He asked of a poem, or a poet's œuvre, just as he asked of language, not where does it come from (the question that had obsessively dominated nineteenth-century studies in both literature and linguistics), but what is it (now) and how does it work (as a system, a structure). The application of these questions to literature was especially important, since, far more than linguistics, literary scholarship at the turn of the twentieth century was still lost in a wilderness of extraneous concerns – biography, social history, philosophy – with no sense of a "dominant," as Jakobson later put it, that would show the subordination of secondary factors to the primary aesthetic function of literature. "Historians of literature," he wrote, "have mostly been like policemen who, seeking to arrest a particular individual, just in case seize everyone and everything found in an apartment and also people passing by in the street." Instead, "the subject of literary scholarship should not be literature, but literariness," that is, that which makes literature literature. Further, "If literary scholarship wants to be scientific, it must acknowledge the 'device' as its only 'hero.'" These epigrammatic formulations from early Jakobson were among the cornerstones, the basic tenets of Russian Formalism.

In the polemical and iconoclastic spirit of early Formalism, Jakobson and his cohorts sometimes went so far as to deny any connection between art and life: "To incriminate a poet for the ideas and feelings [found in his poetry]," Jakobson wrote, "is as absurd as the behavior of medieval audiences who assaulted the actor who played Judas." According to Jakobson, every artistic school claims to be "truer," that is, to mirror life and reality more faithfully or profoundly than its predecessor did. Therefore all such claims may be dismissed as self-advertisement, and criticism should abandon attempts to assess the "truth" of art. In particular, "realism" in art is to be defined not by its truth, but by the prevalence among realists of metonymy as the dominant trope, whereas among their predecessors, the Romantics, it had been metaphor. Jakobson later retreated from this denial of any epistemological basis for art, but the metaphor/metonymy dichotomy proved very fruitful and was eventually carried over into linguistics and finally into psychology, seen as a fundamental polarity of language and of human thought processes.

In his more mature phase (after 1928, when he published together with Iurii Tynianov the famous "theses" or "Problems in the Study of Literature and Language" which marked the beginning of a transition from Formalism to structuralism), Jakobson himself produced several brilliant explorations of the connection between art and life. Following the suicide of Vladimir Maiakovskii in 1930, he wrote one of his most dazzling articles, "On a Generation That Squandered Its Poets." There he developed – and demonstrated in detail – the notion of a poet's "mythology," that aggregate of imagery, fantasy, transmuted experience, and ideology that makes up the poet's created "world." It is clearly far from being a replica of the real world, but the relationship between the two is a creative and dynamic one. Later Jakobson produced an equally seminal study of Aleksandr Pushkin's mythology ("The Statue in Pushkin's Poetic Mythology").

Thus the mature Jakobson no longer perceived literature as a wholly self-enclosed, self-sufficient system. Its medium, language, contains referents to a real world, and through language these referents become materials for literary art. Nevertheless, the basic Formalist point remains valid: referent and linguistic sign are not identical, and the student of the art whose medium is language must recognize this nonidentity of *signans* (sign) and *signatum* (referent). An important ingredient of verbal art is the *signans* calling attention to itself. Art is not separate from life; it is simply an autonomous sphere of life: "What we stand for is not the separatism of art but the autonomy of the aesthetic function," Jakobson judiciously concluded.

To be sure, verbal art may have values and purposes outside itself, for example, philosophical statements or political exhortations, just as nonpoetic uses of language may have an aesthetic component. (To illustrate the latter point Jakobson once did an elaborate poetic analysis of the slogan "I like Ike.") Literature, however, is not a mechanical agglomeration of equally weighted functions. It can be understood only if it is recognized as a system, a hierarchy, in which one function, the aesthetic one, is dominant over the others: "A poetic work is defined as a verbal message whose aesthetic function is its dominant."

From his studies of Pushkin, especially Pushkin's lyric poetry, Jakobson derived another of his basic notions, later elaborated in "The Poetry of Grammar and the Grammar of Poetry," namely, that poets, whether consciously or unconsciously, manipulate all possible grammatical categories for artistic effects. The popular belief that "imagery" and "ornamentation" are the essence of poetry will simply not work for Pushkin. Setting "stark simplicity" as his ideal, Pushkin consistently "rejects self-sufficient tropes" and emphasizes "precision, dryness, and the informative values of the poetic word." Nor does he seek ostentatious musicality for its own sake: "His sound texture and intonation are closely connected with meaning." What Pushkin's lyrics demonstrate is precisely the "poetry of grammar":

> Often contrasts, affinities, and contiguities of tenses and numbers, of verbal aspects and voices, obtain a directly leading rôle in the composition of particular poems; emphasized by an opposition of grammatical category, they acquire the effectiveness of poetic images.

Later this point was irrefutably demonstrated in a masterful analysis of Pushkin's famous lyric "Ia vas liubil" ("I Loved You Once"), a poem without a single "image," which derives much of its effectiveness from the play of grammatical categories.

Besides his originality, range, and depth as a literary theorist and critic of modern literature, Jakobson was also a distinguished medievalist. He left many important contributions to the study of literary culture in Old Church Slavic, Old Czech, and Old Russian. One of the major enterprises of his middle years was a spirited defense of the authenticity of the twelfth-century East Slavic epic, *Slovo o polku Igoreve* (*The Lay of Igor's Campaign*), which the French Slavist André Mazon had impugned as an eighteenth-century forgery. Jakobson's defense involved not only a massive refutation of Mazon's arguments, but a reconstruction of the text itself in its presumed original form as well, in the process producing a broad picture of the whole cultural ambience of medieval Kiev.

Yet Jakobson's interest in literary theory never died; in fact, it revived and expanded after he became established in American academia. He continued his studies of Slavic metrics, formulating with exceptional clarity the essential laws of Czech and Russian versification. He also pursued metrical research along the diachronic axis, reconstructing prehistoric common Slavic epic verse-forms, these in turn perceived in relation to Vedic Sanskrit and Greek.

During the last two decades of his life Jakobson produced a long series of "readings," now grouped together in the third volume of his *Selected Writings*. These are designed to demonstrate, by close analysis of particular texts, the relevance of the principles set forth in such articles as "Linguistics and Poetics." Explicitly demonstrating that these principles are universally applicable, not limited to any language or family of languages nor to any time and place, these readings extend over an extraordinary range of literatures and periods, including some with which even he could not claim familiarity and for which professional collaborators were required, such as eighth-century Japanese, or Chinese versification during the T'ang Dynasty.

Slavic examples still play a central role in Jakobson's readings, but one of the most important developments of his later years was his undertaking to demonstrate his principles and method with texts taken from other literatures, such as English, French, German, and Italian. Literary scholars other than Slavists might have heard from their linguist colleagues that the name "Jakobson" was very much one with which to conjure in that field; now he boldly invaded the literary scholar's territory with confident studies of poems by such Western eminences as Dante, Friedrich Hölderlin, Bertolt Brecht, Charles Baudelaire, Sir Philip Sidney, William Shakespeare, William Blake, and William Butler Yeats. Perhaps most symbolically significant of all was the article on the poem "Les Chats," by Baudelaire. It was written by Jakobson in collaboration with his old friend Claude Lévi-Strauss, whose own name had already become one with which to conjure in the very field of mythology and magic. Yet Lévi-Strauss had already acknowledged Jakobson as his teacher, and now they appeared together to show what close structural analysis could reveal in a poem by Baudelaire. The specific illustration demonstrated the principles of that structuralism which Lévi-Strauss now wrote large over a much broader domain. Ideas that quickly became the rage among the most up-to-date intellectuals of Paris thus traced their ancestry back to the Prague Linguistic Circle and beyond that to the Moscow Linguistic Circle of 1915.

Principal criticism

Noveyshaia russkaia poeziia, 1921
"O realismu v umění," 1921 ("On Realism in Art," 1971)
O cheshskom stikhe, preimushchestvenno v sopostavlenii s russkim, 1923
"Problemy izucheniia literatury i iazyka," 1928 (with Iurii Tynianov; "Problems in the Study of Literature and Language," 1971)
"O pokolenii, rastrativshem svoikh poetov," 1931 ("On a Generation That Squandered Its Poets," 1973)
"Co je poesie?," 1934 ("What Is Poetry?," 1976)
"Randbemerkungen zur Prosa des Dichters Pasternak," 1936 ("Marginal Notes on the Prose of the Poet Pasternak," 1969)
"Na okraj lyrických básní Puškinnych," 1936 ("Marginal Notes on Pushkin's Lyric Poetry," 1965)
"Socha v symbolice Puškinově," 1937 ("The Statue in Pushkin's Poetic Mythology," 1979)
"Na okraj *Eugena Oněgina*," 1937 ("Marginal Notes on *Eugene Onegin*," 1965)
"K popisu Máchova verše," 1938 ("Towards a Description of Mácha's Verse," 1979)
"On Russian Fairy Tales," 1945
"Slavic Epic Verse: Studies in Comparative Metrics," 1952
"The Kernel of Comparative Slavic Literature," 1953
Fundamentals of Language, 1956 (with Morris Halle)
"Linguistics and Poetics," 1960
"Poeziia grammatiki i grammatika poezii," 1961 ("The Poetry of Grammar and the Grammar of Poetry," 1968)
"'Les Chats' de Charles Baudelaire," 1962 (with Claude Lévi-Strauss; "Charles Baudelaire's 'Les Chats,'" 1971)
"Grammatical Parallelism and Its Russian Facet," 1966
Language in Literature, 1988

Other major works and literary forms

Roman Jakobson produced an enormous output of books and papers on literature and poetics. Almost all have been collected in his seven-volume *Selected Writings*, 1962–1985. In his youth Jakobson published avant-garde poetry (under the pseudonym Alyagrov), and he derived much stimulation, both in Russia and in Czechoslovakia, from his associations with such poets and artists as Velimir Khlebnikov, Vladimir Maiakovskii, Kazimir Malevich, Vítězslav Nezval, and Jaroslav Seifert. Besides literary studies, Jakobson's writings extend over a wide range of subjects, especially within linguistics. They include general linguistic theory, phonology (phonemics), acoustics, morphology, child language, aphasia, and historical and synchronic studies of the Slavic languages, both individually and in their interrelations.

NONFICTION
Six Lectures on Sound and Meaning, 1978
The Sound Shape of Language, 1979 (with Linda R. Waugh)

Brain and Language: Cerebral Hemispheres and Linguistic Structure in Mutual Light, 1980
The Framework of Language, 1980
Dialogues, 1983 (with Krystyna Pomorska)
Russian and Slavic Grammar: Studies, 1931–1981, 1983
Verbal Art, Verbal Sign, Verbal Time, 1985

TRANSLATIONS
La geste du Prince Igor, 1948 (with d'Henri Gregoire and Marc Szeftel)

MISCELLANEOUS
Selected Writings, 1962–1985

Further reading

Armstrong, Daniel, and C. H. van Schooneveld. *Roman Jakobson: Echoes of His Scholarship*, 1977.
Bradford, Richard. *Roman Jakobson: Life, Language, Art*, 1994.
Caton, Steven C. "Contributions of Roman Jakobson," in *Annual Review of Anthropology*. XVI (1987), pp. 223–260.
Culler, Jonathan. *Structuralist Poetics: Structuralism, Linguistics and the Study of Literature*, 1976.
Érlich, Victor. *Russian Formalism: History – Doctrine*, 1981 (third edition).
Holenstein, Elmar. *Roman Jakobson's Approach to Language*, 1976.
Pomorska, Krystyna. "Jákobson, Román Ósipovich," in *Handbook of Russian Literature*, 1985. Edited by Victor Terras.
——. *Russian Formalist Theory and Its Poetic Ambience*, 1968.
Rudy, Stephen. *A Complete Bibliography of Roman Jakobson's Writings, 1912–1982*, 1984.
Waugh, Linda R. *Roman Jakobson's Science of Language*, 1976.

HUGH MCLEAN

See also Metonymy; Prague School; Russian Formalism; Semiotics; Structuralism

Henry James

American novelist and critic

Born: New York, New York; April 15, 1843
Died: London, England; February 28, 1916

Biography

Henry James, Jr., was the second son of a scholar and the younger brother of the United States' first great philosopher. Though born in New York City, James spent most of his childhood abroad and throughout New England. He had an inconsistent education, which included studying art and enrolling briefly at Harvard Law School.

James published his first literary works, a review and a short story (both published anonymously), in 1864. The following year his first signed story appeared in *Atlantic Monthly*. The young James became friends with novelist and editor William Dean Howells. For five years, beginning in 1870, he alternated his residence between the United States and Europe, finally becoming a permanent expatriate in 1875. During this period he wrote prolifically, completing stories, reviews, and his first major novel, *Roderick Hudson* (1875).

For the next four decades, James turned out novels, short stories (or "tales," as he called them), essays, and reviews, making his living by his pen. Focusing on the "international theme" in his literary works, he became a keen observer of American manners both at home and especially in Europe. In 1898 he took up residence at Lamb House in Rye, Sussex. His circle of friends in England included H. G. Wells and Joseph Conrad, and he made the acquaintance of numerous other literary and political figures. In 1915 he became a British subject. A year later, on February 28, he died in Chelsea, London. His ashes were returned to the United States for burial in the family plot in Cambridge, Massachusetts.

Influence

Modern criticism of fiction is greatly indebted to James, both for its popularity and for much of its methodology. He provided many of the terms used to analyze novels and short stories, and his insistence that fiction measure up to aesthetic rather than moral or social standards has become a common-place. His theories caused a revaluation of much of nineteenth-century American and English fiction and shaped both the fiction and the criticism of those who have followed him. No serious writer today can ignore his pronouncements about the preeminence of form and importance of refined sensibility in characterization. Further, James' concern for form, structure, style, and technique was advanced by proponents of the New Criticism, which originated shortly after James died and flourished during the first half of the twentieth century.

Analysis

The distinguished twentieth-century literary theorist René Wellek has called James "by far the best American critic of the nineteenth century." That claim is echoed in remarks by renowned scholar James E. Miller, who considers James "probably the greatest fictional theorist ever to have written." Though there have been detractors – T. S. Eliot and F. R. Leavis among them – who have caviled at James' preoccupation with form over content and his failure to present a coherent critical theory, the preeminence of James as a theorist and exponent of the critic's task in evaluating works of fiction according to aesthetic standards cannot be challenged. His work has been seminal in shaping the modern critical consciousness.

Unfortunately, James wrote no single text in which his theory of fiction or theory of criticism is clearly elucidated. Instead, his pronouncements are scattered throughout writings that spanned half a century. One should not be surprised to find that as James grew older his theories changed, as his ideas about the technical components of fiction became more solidified. Nevertheless, there remains a remarkable consistency of perspective throughout the hundreds of reviews and articles James placed in American and British periodicals during the latter half of the nineteenth century and the first two decades of the twentieth century.

James began his career as a reviewer, and hence much of his early theory is woven into the commentary on specific books about which he had been commissioned to write. Almost always, he has a definite object in focus – a novel, a collection of poems or essays – when he makes some general pronouncement about the aims and methods of the artist. That technique gives him the strength of grounding his theory in specifics, furnishing him with examples to illustrate his ideas about the nature and function of both literature and criticism. Even his most theoretical pieces, such as *The Art of Fiction* (1884) or "The New Novel" (in *Notes on Novelists*, 1914), address topical issues. Though some of his essays were collected during his lifetime, James made no attempt to organize a systematic "defense of fiction" along the lines of Sir Philip Sidney's or Percy Bysshe Shelley's "defenses" of poetry. Much of James' criticism can be seen as a veiled attempt to justify his own creative writing, and his most famous and detailed analyses of the art of fiction are found in his prefaces to the New York edition of his own novels, published by Scribner's between 1907 and 1909.

The significance of James' accomplishment is better understood when one considers it in historical context. At the time James began writing, fiction was not regarded as an important art form. The novel was commonly seen as a sociological document or a means of escapism; subjects were often carefully regulated, and moral conventions played a significant role in determining both the subject and its treatment in many fictional works. The short story was a relatively new genre, made possible by the proliferation of magazines and periodicals both in England and in America. Hence, much of James' effort went toward establishing the place of fiction in the pantheon of the fine arts, calling for its enshrinement beside poetry and drama as a serious medium for exploring the human condition and providing aesthetic pleasure.

Early in his career, James came under the sway of prominent English and French critics and artists, and though he became more independent-thinking as he aged, their influence can be seen even in his latest works. Certainly he admired the works of other reviewers, such as Sir Leslie Stephen and Sir Edmund Gosse. Most prominent among those who formed James' critical sensibilities, however, was the English critic Matthew Arnold. James reviewed Arnold's *Essays in Criticism* (1865) for the *North American Review*; many of Arnold's ideas permeated the younger critic's sensibilities and remained with James throughout his lifetime. Like Arnold, James thought that the English (and their American cousins) were influenced more by moral than by aesthetic impulses (Arnold had called this a penchant for "Hebraism" over "Hellenism"). The tendency to demand strict adherence to a kind of moral code in literature, concurrent with a tendency to reduce all literature to a kind of dichotomous antithesis of "beauty" and "use," made English-speaking readers blind to the technical merits of numerous works and deprived them of the aesthetic pleasures afforded by such compositions. Again like Arnold, James believed that the critic should be rational in evaluating literature, avoiding emotional reactions to works that, on the surface, either confirmed or denied moral or social beliefs.

Perhaps equally important in shaping James' ideas about fiction and criticism were the French writers whom he read avidly during the 1860s and 1870s. Much of James' earliest criticism was devoted to French literary figures: Alfred de Musset, Théophile Gautier, Charles Baudelaire, Honoré de Balzac, George Sand, Gustave Flaubert. He came under the sway of French critics whose analyses of literature seemed to him considerably more dispassionate and substantially less clouded by personal taste than their English counterparts. Notable among such critics were Hippolyte Taine and Charles-Augustin Sainte-Beuve. James preferred Sainte-Beuve over Taine because the former was more systematic in his evaluation of literature while at the same time skeptical about "systems" or formulas for measuring all literature. Sainte-Beuve's reluctance to use critical "templates" against which individual works were to be judged became a cornerstone of James' own methodology.

Unquestionably, despite his insistence on "realism" as a measure for the success of fiction, James was a Romantic in practice. He adopted no outside standard against which works of fiction should be judged. Instead, following the lead of theorists such as Samuel Taylor Coleridge and Edgar Allan Poe, he insisted that a work of art must grow naturally and according to its own internal rules of composition: the subject and the artist's perception of it would determine the form the finished work would take. He expressed his position succinctly in *The Art of Fiction*, using the language of the Romantics directly to make his point:

> A novel is a living thing, all one and continuous, like any other organism, and in proportion as it lives will it be found, I think, that in each of the parts there is something of each of the other parts.

Though he recognized the expectations created in readers by the various "kinds" of literature, James rebelled against the notion that works of literature must be slavishly wrenched into shape by the artist to fit preconceived notions of approved forms.

Central to James' attitudes toward literature is his belief that the artist must be free to choose subjects without regard to the fashion or mores of the day. "We must grant the artist his subject, his idea, his *donnée*," he remarks in *The Art of Fiction*:

> our criticism is applied only to what he makes of it . . . If we pretend to respect the artist at all, we must allow him his freedom of choice, in the face, in particular cases, of innumerable presumptions that the choice will not fructify.

For him, the novel was "the most independent, most elastic, most prodigious of literary forms" (preface to *The Ambassadors*, 1908). The only a priori rules that James would accept for a novel were that it should be "interesting" and that it have "life."

James further insisted that the subject is not the primary factor in determining the greatness of a literary production. In this, he broke away from the mainstream of criticism in his day, a prevailing attitude which demanded, as James' contemporary Sir Walter Besant said, that the novel have a "conscious moral purpose." James did believe that the novelist has an obligation to be moral, but his definition of morality differed from that of Besant and others who equated the term with rectitude, social propriety, and avoidance of subjects that might offend the young and the sheltered. James argued that artists are moral when they present life truly as it appears to them, observing keenly what happens around them and making art from the unstructured reality that passes before their ken. "Morality" is present in a work when the author has rendered the complex human personality in all of its psychological subtleties, truly and plausibly. James was not invoking the dictum of "art for art's sake"; rather, he was insisting that artists have a responsibility to report their observations accurately, filtering them through their imaginations to give them form and meaning. Writers are products of their times, James insisted, and the interaction of the artists with their surroundings is essential to the production of first-rate literature.

The job of the critic is to evaluate the way in which artists create their work, to measure the success of the execution against the standards artists set for themselves within the work itself. Perhaps nowhere else does James make so significant a contribution to the study of literature as he does in his careful presentation of the means by which such an examination can be accomplished. He has added to the critical vocabulary several terms, explaining in detail how the elements of fiction work together to create the sinuous whole of the novel, whose parts are interdependent. He has also provided a framework by which novels, especially those classified as realistic novels, may be judged.

James insisted that, while life appears essentially formless in its passage before any human consciousness, the job of the artist is to give life shape, lucidity, and meaning. The novelist should, in James' view, create the illusion of reality in his or her work. For this reason, he criticized novelists such as Anthony Trollope for including in their works authorial intrusions which blatantly remind readers that the story they are reading is, after all, only make-believe. James was equally harsh on those who believed in the primacy of "plot" or "adventure" in works of fiction. For him, the study of character was of equal, or perhaps even greater, importance. In *The Art of Fiction*, he argues that the union of these two elements is essential to producing great literature: "What is character but the determination of incident? What is incident but the illustration of character?"

Another lasting contribution James made to the theory of fiction lies in his explanation of the various techniques used by writers to achieve this illusion of reality. Foremost among the techniques for which he has provided extensive analysis is point of view. For James, the way in which a story is presented is of equal interest to the story itself: the mind of the character through whom events are narrated to the reader is as crucial to understanding the totality of meaning that a story conveys as are the incidents which are narrated. Not comfortable with first-person narration, James found that the best novels and stories were those in which the principal action is filtered through a single consciousness of an observer who is usually not a main player in the action. In his own fiction, James himself used numerous devices to achieve the illusion he wished to create while still providing essential details needed for the reader to understand both what happens and the significance of events. Most notable among these devices is his use of the *ficelle*, a character whose presence in the story may be only tangential but who functions as a willing auditor or reporter to the central figure narrating the tale.

As important to James as the interaction of subject and character was the concept of form. For him, the way in which a story is narrated – the architecture of the piece – was inseparable from content and characterization. He insisted on a careful balance between dialogue, description, and narration; a novel was not, after all, a drama, nor was it a simple didactic narrative. The reader must be able to see characters in action, picture the scene, and sense that there is much of life going on beneath the surface of events presented in the text.

James' demands on both the artist and the reader are high. He calls on the artist to select details carefully and insists that the reader pay close attention to the text. He insists that great art be "typical," evoking the feeling that its characters are lifelike in their complexity but not quirky or eccentric so as to become caricatures (a fault he finds in the novels of Charles Dickens). Readers, and especially critics, must expend effort to understand the text, to apprehend the life captured only partially in the words of the tale. The role of the critic, James insists, is to interpret a work of art for those of lesser sensibility. Critics must be careful to avoid sentimentality; their judgments must be grounded on a firm analysis of the elements of the text, and their pronouncements must show how those elements work together to create the impression of life that the artist seeks to convey.

Because he wrote for more than half a century and published in some of the leading journals of his day, James influenced, if only to a limited degree, the tastes of the reading public in the late nineteenth century. More significant was his role as a transitional figure between the artists and critics of the expansive, extroverted Victorian period and the intensely introspective decades of the modern era. His keen insights into the role of psychology in shaping characters in fiction were seminal both for the production of future works and for analysis of all forms of literature. Certainly James' observations contributed to the rise of the psychological novels of writers such as James Joyce, William Faulkner, and Virginia Woolf, even if he did not influence them directly. He did have some direct hand in shaping the novels of Edith Wharton and Ford Madox Ford. It would be hard to imagine how, without James' pioneering work in explaining the principles on which such works are constructed, the countless numbers of streamlined modern novels and stories, with their scrupulous attention to point of view and careful understatement of meaning, could have found the comparatively large reading public they enjoy among intellectuals today.

Equally important is James' influence on the direction of literary criticism and literary theory. Though James himself thought that "great criticism seems to us to touch more or less nearly on pure philosophy," he imagined his own brand, like Sainte-Beuve's, to be "pure criticism," which must "be of the small kind." In "A French Critic" (which first appeared in *The Nation* in 1865 and was later collected in *Notes and Reviews*, 1921), he outlines this crucial distinction:

> The philosopher's function is to compare a work with an abstract principle of truth; the critic's is to compare a work with itself, with its own concrete standard of truth. The critic deals, therefore, with parts, the philosopher with wholes.

James' focus was on explaining the effect of the concrete, the individual work of art; all of his theory grows from the discovery of common traits among the great works rather than from the imposition of theory onto single texts. His demand that each work of fiction be judged on its own terms, an inheritance from the Romantics, became the basis upon which the New Critics built their theory of fiction during the 1930s and 1940s. Jamesian principles of analysis are at the heart of Percy Lubbock's *The Craft of Fiction* (1921), a text that shaped the way in which fiction was studied during the twentieth century. James' work has been the subject of much study in academic circles, largely because it yields much to those who take the time to read it carefully. In turn, critics permeated with a sense of James' feel for the interdependence of subject and treatment have reshaped the way in which texts, especially works of fiction, are read. Clarence Arthur Brown's assessment in his introduction to *The Achievement of American Criticism* (1954) expresses James' lasting influence succinctly and accurately: "The criticism of Henry James," Brown says, "has done more than that of any other critic to raise fiction to a fine art and to endow criticism itself with more perceptive principles of form, taste, and method."

Principal criticism

French Poets and Novelists, 1878
Hawthorne, 1879
The Art of Fiction, 1884
Partial Portraits, 1888
Essays in London and Elsewhere, 1893
Picture and Text, 1893
Prefaces to *The Novels and Tales of Henry James*, "*New York Edition*," 1907–1909
Views and Reviews, 1908
Notes on Novelists, 1914
Notes and Reviews, 1921
The Art of the Novel: Critical Prefaces, 1934 (R. P. Blackmur, editor)

Other major works and literary forms

Though known as one of the first great American literary critics, Henry James is even more famous as a novelist and short-story writer. He published more than a score of novels and hundreds of shorter works, many of which he collected into volumes in his own lifetime. He also composed travel essays and prose portraits and was a copious letter writer. Many of the works he scattered in magazines during his lifetime, as well as his letters and private journals, have been published in edited collections.

NOVELS

Roderick Hudson, 1875
The American, 1877
The Europeans, 1878
Daisy Miller, 1878
Washington Square, 1880
The Portrait of a Lady, 1881
The Bostonians, 1886
The Princess Casamassima, 1886
The Tragic Muse, 1890
The Spoils of Poynton, 1897
What Maisie Knew, 1897
The Awkward Age, 1899
The Sacred Fount, 1901
The Wings of the Dove, 1902
The Ambassadors, 1903
The Golden Bowl, 1904

SHORT FICTION

A Passionate Pilgrim and Other Tales, 1875
The Madonna of the Future, 1879
The Siege of London, 1883
Tales of Three Cities, 1884
The Author of Beltraffio, 1885
Stories Revived, 1885
The Aspern Papers, 1888
A London Life, 1889
The Lesson of the Master, 1892
The Real Thing and Other Tales, 1893

The Private Life, 1893
The Wheel of Time, 1893
Terminations, 1895
Embarrassments, 1896
The Two Magics: "The Turn of the Screw" and "Covering End," 1898
The Soft Side, 1900
The Better Sort, 1903
The Novels and Tales of Henry James, 1907–1909 (24 volumes)
The Finer Grain, 1910
A Landscape Painter, 1919
Travelling Companions, 1919
Master Eustace, 1920
Henry James: Selected Short Stories, 1950
Henry James: Eight Tales from the Major Phase, 1958
The Complete Tales of Henry James, 1962–1964 (12 volumes; Leon Edel, editor)

PLAYS
Daisy Miller, 1883
The American, 1891
Theatricals: "Tenants" and "Disengaged," 1894
The Reprobate, 1894
Theatricals, Second Series: "The Album" and "The Reprobate," 1894
Guy Domville, 1895
The High Bid, 1908
The Other House, written 1909, published 1949
The Outcry, written 1909, published 1917
The Saloon, 1911
The Complete Plays of Henry James, 1949 (Leon Edel, editor)

NONFICTION
Transatlantic Sketches, 1875
Portraits of Places, 1883
A Little Tour in France, 1884
William Wetmore Story and His Friends, 1903
English Hours, 1905
The American Scene, 1907
Italian Hours, 1909
A Small Boy and Others, 1913
Notes of a Son and Brother, 1914
The Middle Years, 1917
The Notebooks of Henry James, 1947 (F. O. Matthiessen and Kenneth B. Murdock, editors)
The Scenic Art, 1948 (Allan Wade, editor)
Henry James Letters, 1974–1984 (5 volumes; Edel, editor)

Further reading

Barrett, Laurence. "Young Henry James, Critic," in *American Literature*. XX (January, 1949), pp. 385–400.
Blackmur, R. P. *Studies in Henry James*, 1983.
Coleman, E. "Henry James's Criticism: A Case Study in Critical Inquiry," in *Nineteenth Century Fiction*. XL (December, 1985), pp. 327–344.
Miller, James E., ed. *Theory of Fiction: Henry James*, 1972.
Spilka, Mark. "Henry James and Walter Besant: 'The Art of Fiction,'" in *Towards a Poetics of Fiction*, 1977.
Veedr, William, and Susan M. Griffin, eds. *The Art of Criticism: Henry James on the Theory and the Practice of Fiction*, 1986.
Wellek, René. "Henry James's Literary Theory and Criticism," in *American Literature*. XXX (November, 1958), pp. 293–321.

LAURENCE W. MAZZENO

See also American Literary Theory to 1900; Lubbock; Poe

Fredric Jameson

American critic and theorist

Born: Cleveland, Ohio; April 14, 1934

Biography

Fredric Jameson was educated at Haverford College and Yale University, and in Europe at the universities of Aix, Munich, and Berlin. He taught at Harvard University, the University of California at San Diego and at Santa Cruz, Yale University, and Duke University. In his academic career, Jameson has contributed significantly to the postwar geographical shift of Marxism as a critical theory from the Latin societies to the English-speaking world.

Influence

Jameson is considered one of the most important Marxist literary critics to publish in the United States since World War II. He is distinguished not only for having produced a substantial and significant body of work, one that only Raymond Williams in Britain has been able to match, but also for the lucidity with which he presents difficult material. As Terry Eagleton says in *Against the Grain: Essays, 1975–1985* (1986): "Jameson is a master of coruscating connections and brilliant analogies, whose primary intellectual habit is metaphor." Eagleton also says that if literary criticism is ever to be judged for helping to avert Fascism or nuclear holocaust, Fredric Jameson "is one of the forlornly few names we will stammeringly evoke."

Analysis

In *The Prison-House of Language*, Fredric Jameson demonstrates his skill in description and commentary by making original connections between the various literary theories developed in the twentieth century. Instead of condemning the textually based systems of Russian Formalism and of structuralism for being ahistorical, he shows how their linguistic model can elucidate the mystery of the historical dimension and thus prevent a reader from taking the cultural context of a work for granted. In his historical approach, he says that truth can be understood as "transcoding": the "truth-effect" results from a conceptual operation in which one translates from one code to another – as from the historical to the linguistic. Jameson asserts, however, that linguistic methods and even literature itself must not be taken as ends in themselves but should be used in the process of assembling a more complete theoretical perspective. Just as a verb is part of a larger structure, the sentence or "syntagma," so also the latter is not isolated but part of a unity composed of other syntagmas belonging to a temporal series, that is, to history itself. Although structuralism, which locates meaning in the verbal oppositions within a text, is thought by many critics to repress history, Jameson tries to achieve a synthesis of structural and historical approaches that would preserve the most fruitful insights of both. He notes that "where everything is historical, the idea of history itself has seemed to empty of content." Rather than being a contradiction, then, a synthesis of history and structure would allow for a dialectic between change and nonchange, time and eternity. Jameson's point is that while history reveals the dynamics of change, the laws governing change are universal; thus, "history is the science of the permanent."

Jameson's combined survey and critique of Russian Formalism and structuralism seems to reveal an ambiguity in his relationship to Marxist theory. Is he, as Eagleton questions, participating in the linguistic play of the text, as his metaphorical style sometimes suggests, or is he actually moving through the linguistic mode toward a more complete historical perspective? In defining truth as a transcoding, Jameson does participate in the structuralist analysis of a text without presupposing its content, but he simultaneously frees this analysis from the myth that content can be divorced from its historical context. By seeing the structuralist approach as "nothing but" a temporal project, he opens the "text and analytic process alike to all the winds of history." Jameson thus habitually tries to appropriate all opposing theories for the Marxist purpose of locating a dimension from which their insights can be transformed and harmonized. His work has been criticized for plundering the concepts of other critics without engaging them in any productive dialogue. Nevertheless, Jameson's search for a material condition underlying literary theory is remarkably free from reductive economic determinism and has been persuasive in spite of his occasional tendency to oversynthesize.

One of the greatest influences on Jameson's work is thought to be Georg Lukács' *Geschichte und Klassenbewusstsein* (1923; *History and Class Consciousness*, 1971), especially the chapter on German Idealism, in which Lukács emphasizes the importance of the commodity in philosophical history. In his critique of "commodity fetishism" or "reification," Jameson argues that the main problem with capitalism is its alienating or disconnecting power and that Marxism must reveal how all disconnections are in fact united by an underlying field. Through a Hegelian-Marxist (Idealist) approach, Jameson tends to privilege theoretical *Aufhebung*, or transcendence, over political conflict. This "totalizing" tendency, developed in *The Political Unconscious*, had already been formulated in *Marxism and Form*, in which Jameson explains transcoding as a mediation between literary criticism and sociology, the former spontaneously crossing into the latter so that any statement about a work of art proves equally valid in the social and historical spheres. As Jameson writes,

> at a certain level of concreteness the *thing itself* . . . may be formulated in any one of a number of alternate codes, may be rearticulated in any one of a number of different dimensions: as literary structure, as the lived truth of a determinate social organization, as a certain type of subject-object relationship, as a certain distance of language from its object, as a determinate mode of specialization or of the division of labor, as an implied relationship between classes.

In this way, Jameson attempts to grasp the wholeness of truth in terms of the lived experience of social history, in terms of the mediation between different levels of reality.

The thrust of *The Political Unconscious* is expressed by its first words, "Always historicize." In historicizing Freudian psychoanalytic theory, Jameson argues that Sigmund Freud, far from explaining universal human nature, was actually describing the symptoms resulting from a historical situation – the alienation and fragmentation of life under capitalism. Neither Freudian theory nor the psychological symptoms it describes are permanent or timeless. Jameson locates the cause of Freud's emphasis on human sexuality in the nineteenth-century banishment of the sexual drives from the collective life to the private realm, where they inevitably become food for fantasy. For Jameson, Freud's interpretation of desire in terms of the human libido thus appears to describe a temporary phenomenon rather than the essential nature of desire itself. In a Marxist perspective, Freud's model of the human psyche results from the "universalizing" of what is merely passing and culturally determined. Nevertheless, Freud's theory of interpretation, through which the hidden meanings behind the manifest are brought to light, is very important for Jameson. While Freud studied repression in terms of the individual unconscious, Jameson studies the "political," or collective, unconscious, his focus being the relationship between manifest cultural and ideological structures and repressed historical tendencies that always threaten to erupt.

For Jameson, as William C. Dowling observes in *Jameson, Althusser, Marx: An Introduction to the Political Unconscious* (1984), "the totality is humanity is History, and [this equation] holds in no matter what order the terms are rearranged." In *The Political Unconscious*, Jameson claims the power to resituate meaning historically within the broadest contexts for Marxism, which he calls "that 'untranscendable horizon' that subsumes such apparently antagonistic or incommensurable critical operations, assigning them an undoubted sectoral validity within itself, and thus at once canceling and preserving them." He regards any conceptual system of closure (any ideology such as religion, philosophy, mythology, or aesthetics) as a "strategy of containment" used to deny the intolerable contradictions repressed beneath the social exterior, the "necessity" responsible for the class struggles that turn history into a waking nightmare. The goal of Jameson's criticism is to glimpse the necessity beneath the illusion of invented systems, to confront the intolerable reality of "history" itself, and thereby to win from necessity a freedom that comes only through the truth of demystification.

As a Marxist, Jameson believes that ideology, or the hidden structure of values that underlie supposedly factual statements, functions not only to close off thought from historical truth but also to repress the social contradictions that arise from necessity and history. As an ideological production, literature itself is a strategy of containment that Marxist criticism must subject to a "symptomatic analysis" to determine its complex relation to necessity. This mode of interpretation reveals two things: how the work of art denies or represses history, and, once revealed, what this history is like. Jameson's use of the Freudian notion of repression for resolving oppositions, such as that between historical necessity and literary structure, has its deeper roots in the dialectical process, for each synthesis of a thesis and antithesis is not a final solution but itself becomes a thesis in another opposition leading to a higher synthesis. For Jameson (and for Karl Marx), each successive solution in this historical process is incomplete. Nevertheless, even as strategies of containment, ideologies such as literature still have their own kinds of truth. According to some Marxists, no society can exist without an ideology that expresses the relationship between history and collective consciousness. As a literary critic, Jameson sees literature on the one hand as an ideological expression of the relation between humanity and the real conditions of its existence, and on the other as an expression that looks beyond any prior ideologies or strategies of containment toward its own roots in history and necessity. A non-Marxist criticism, unaware of the "untranscendable horizon," would be an ideology that merely contributes to the process of mystification – a process through which, according to Marxist critics, the capitalist state reproduces itself.

For Jameson, the literary critic is not a marginal figure involved in a leisured pastime. On the contrary, by confronting the text, the literary critic is confronting reality, which always comes encoded in a narrative form. In opposition to textual or linguistic criticism, or any interpretive method that tries to perpetuate its ideology, Jameson's Marxist criticism interprets in a way that moves through increasingly broad mastercodes or ideologies until it reaches the most complete perspective of the social whole. Any literary text, then, has for its unconscious or subtext a History which is always there but which can only be seen indirectly through its symbolic form. History is the unexpressed reality that not only lies beneath the social use of language but is also typically repressed by it. The individual critic, in turn, operates from within history – a process of change from one social formation to another with no orderly progression. For Jameson, this Marxist theory of history subsumes all other theoretical movements. In *The Political Unconscious*, Jameson writes that because "the individual subject is always fully positioned within the social totality," he or she can never be "fully conscious of his or her determination by class." In "the Marxian system, only a collective unity . . . can achieve this transparency." Nevertheless, as a Marxist critic Jameson heightens readers' individual awareness of the "untranscendable horizon" of their historical existence by forcing them to question the theoretical premises of all judgments, including their own.

In *Marxism and Form*, Jameson says, "Even if ours is a critical age, it does not seem to me very becoming in critics to exalt their activity to the level of literary creation." If Marxist criticism is to be truly historical, then the author, the literary text, and the world to which it refers cannot be dispensed with as they are in some postmodern theories of criticism as creation. Jameson thus subordinates aesthetic concerns to a historical and materialist theory of literature as ideological production. The text, moreover, instead of being a static form with a singular meaning, is a complex web of historically specific meanings that continue to build over successive readings. As Jameson demonstrates, the critical enterprise of interpreting a text is always a political enterprise.

Jameson's later work, especially *The Political Unconscious*, is marked by a distinctive style of writing that "shows" as well as "tells" its subject. The tension in his writing between critique and commentary is such, as Eagleton notes, that in transcoding European theory for the Anglo-American audience, he seems to reinvent his materials and become their master instead of mediator. In its attempt to "connect" with an untranscendable horizon of history, Jameson's work can be said to resemble that of the quantum physicists who have posited the existence of a unified field which unites the fundamental forces of nature.

From "Metacommentary" through his later works, Jameson emphasizes the need to move toward a truth of the whole by the act of criticism, a questioning of what it means to write about literature and what the proper goals of culture are. Jameson has also been influential in bringing out the historical connection in literary texts between practice and content, and between the two levels of content, manifest and latent. As he says in "Metacommentary," "The work of art . . . proves to unite a lived experience of some kind, as its content, with an implied question as to the very possibility of Experience itself, as its form." In another influential essay, "Postmodernism: Or, The Cultural Logic of Late Capitalism" (1984), Jameson argues that cultural and aesthetic production today is largely postmodern, that postmodernism has been the cultural dominant since the late 1950s. As defined by Charles Newman in *The Post-Modern Aura: The Act of Fiction in an Age of Inflation* (1985), postmodernism constitutes a shift from economic and political determinisms to an essentially linguistic determinism; it "is an ahistorical rebellion without heroes against a blindly innovative information society." The political aim of postmodernism, according to Jameson, should be a global "cognitive mapping" that closes the gap between life experience (or history) and theoretical understanding.

In *Postmodernism, or, The Cultural Logic of Late Capitalism* (1991), Jameson expresses regret over his complicity with the slogan "postmodern," but considers it too economical and effective to be replaced. In historicizing a condition so ahistorical – not to mention unsystematic – Jameson tries to "outflank it and force a historical way at least of thinking about" it. He defines postmodernism as the "cultural dominant" of our time, and postmodern "theoretical discourse" as "not really theories" at all but "unconscious structures." These are the effects of "postmodern cognitive mapping" (a code word for "class consciousness") whose "media term now passes itself off as this or that philosophical reflection on language, communication, and the media, rather than the manipulation of its figure."

Although literature often tries to repress historical truth, Jameson continues in his literary and cultural analyses to reveal its underlying ideology, namely, its unconscious. In his panorama of contemporary cultural history, Jameson sees the postmodern as a transition from early to late capitalism. Yet even though the latter phase restructures capitalism on a global scale, regulating and dominating the industrialized and developing world, Jameson believes a new international proletariat will eventually reemerge. Indeed, he never ceases to remind us of the Marxian injunction not just to interpret the world but to change it.

Principal criticism

Sartre: The Origins of a Style, 1961
Marxism and Form: Twentieth-century Dialectical Theories of Literature, 1971
The Prison-House of Language: A Critical Account of Structuralism and Russian Formalism, 1972
Fables of Aggression: Wyndham Lewis, the Modernist as Fascist, 1979
The Political Unconscious: Narrative as a Socially Symbolic Act, 1981
The Ideologies of Theory: Essays 1971–1986, 1988 (2 volumes)
Postmodernism and Cultural Theories, 1989
Late Marxism: Adorno, or The Persistence of the Dialectic, 1990
Nationalism, Colonialism, and Literature, 1990 (with Terry Eagleton and Edward Said)
Signatures of the Visible, 1990
Postmodernism, or, The Cultural Logic of Late Capitalism, 1991
The Geopolitical Aesthetic: Cinema and Space in the World System, 1992
The Seeds of Time, 1994
The Cultural Turn: Selected Writings on the Postmodern, 1983–1998, 1998

Other major works and literary forms

In addition to his criticism, Fredric Jameson has published many important articles and essays that have reintroduced Marxist concerns in the field of literary studies. His essay "Metacommentary," which first appeared in *PMLA* in 1971, was awarded the MLA Prize as the best essay of that year.

NONFICTION
"Metacommentary," 1971
"Postmodernism: Or, The Cultural Logic of Late Capitalism," 1984

Further reading

Best, Steven, and Douglas Kellner. *Postmodern Theory: Critical Interrogations*, 1991.
Bullock, Chris, and David Peck, eds. *Guide to Marxist Literary Criticism*, 1980.
Diacritics. XII (Fall, 1982). Special Jameson issue.
Dowling, William C. *Jameson, Althusser, Marx: An Introduction to the Political Unconscious*, 1984.
Eagleton, Terry. "Fredric Jameson: The Politics of Style," in *Against the Grain: Essays, 1975–1985*, 1986.
Kellner, Douglas, ed. *Postmodernism / Jameson / Critique*, 1989.
Ryan, Michael. *Marxism and Deconstruction: A Critical Articulation*, 1983.
Sprinker, Michael. *Imaginary Relations: Aesthetics and Ideology in the Theory of Historical Materialism*, 1987.

William S. Haney II

See also Althusser; American Literary Theory: Twentieth Century; Benjamin; Eagleton; Lukács; Marxist Theory and Criticism; Psychoanalytic Criticism

Japanese Literary Theory

Traditional Japanese literary theory

Japanese written literature dates from the early eighth century A.D. Despite its extensive debt to Chinese literature and culture, which predates it by more than twelve hundred years, Japanese literature developed distinctive features of its own and has its own unique character. The Chinese ideographic writing system is used in the *Kojiki* (712; *Record of Ancient Matters*, 1882), the *Nihon shoki* (720; *Chronicles of Japan*, 1896) – both myth and legend disguised as history – and the *Manyōshū* (759; English translation, 1929–1969). Sounds of fifth- and sixth-century Chinese speech were retained, for the most part, in all three works, except that in the *Chronicles of Japan* some words took the sounds of seventh-century northern pronunciation. It was not until the ninth century that the native Japanese syllabary (*kana*) was invented and became the basis of much literature in the Heian period (794–1185), mostly written by women or by men writing for them.

Between the eighth century and the nineteenth century, Japanese literature was read and written in two languages, Japanese and Chinese (or the Japanese version of Chinese). Chinese verse was called *kanshi* and prose was *kambun*. Reading a text in classical Chinese in Chinese pronunciation (*on'yomi*) was in contrast to reading it in Japanese (*kun'yomi*). *On'yomi* was performed in terms of several Chinese time periods: *go'on* (Wu pronunciation), *kan'on* (Han pronunciation), and *to'an* (T'ang pronunciation). Reading Chinese without changing the word order or inserting Japanese glosses was called *bōyomi*, or "reading [in a straight line like a] stick"; reading for meaning by shifting the word order of the Chinese was termed *kundoku*. A system of signs was used to indicate pronunciation; another system of markings showed the proper word order. Yet another system of signs was used to indicate word inflections and endings.

Despite these ties, the languages of China and Japan are not generically related and have very different sound systems, vocabulary, and grammar. Japanese literature is a world of feeling and sentiment rather than one of thinking and speculation. Moreover, Japanese literature is less inclined to abstraction and systemization and is more concrete than Chinese literature. The history of Japanese literature is largely one of sensitivity to beauty. It is more closely connected to personal and social life than Chinese literature in its concern with metaphysics, history, politics, and ethics.

Poetry is the heart and soul of Japanese culture. To the Japanese, the short lyric – especially *tanka* or *haiku* – best expresses their feelings and passions. The first royally commissioned *waka* anthology, the *Kokinshū* (c. 905; English translation, 1984), consists mostly of short lyrics, the *tanka* (five lines, thirty-one syllables) predominating. It set the poetic standard in Japan from its own time until modern times.

The *Kokinshū* includes two prefaces, one in Japanese vernacular, the other in classical Chinese. The Japanese preface was written by Ki no Tsurayuki (c. 884–945), a leading *waka* poet of the Heian period and the chief editor of the compilation. The Chinese preface was written by Ki no Yoshimochi, a Chinese scholar and a leading poet, who, with Tsurayuki and three other poets, was entrusted in 905 with the task of compiling this first imperial anthology. These prefaces set forth the poetics underlying the editors' criteria. It is evident that both authors owed a considerable debt to the Chinese critical tradition – to Wei Hung's preface to the *Shih ching* (*Book of Songs*), to the chapter on music in the *Li chi*, and to the work of numerous Chinese theorists. The emphases of both prefaces differ, however, from those of the Chinese tradition. Tsurayuki, in particular, stressed those aspects of Japanese poetry which set it apart from Chinese poetry. In short, it may be said that his preface represents the beginning of significant Japanese literary criticism and theory.

In the opening of his preface, Tsurayuki focuses on the native elements which have made Japanese poetry what it is:

> The seeds of Japanese poetry lie in the human heart and grow into leaves of ten thousand words. Many things happen to the people of this world, and all that they think and feel is given expression in description of things they see and hear. When we hear the warbling of the mountain thrush in the blossoms or the voice of the frog in the water, we know every living thing has its song.
>
> It is poetry which, without effort, moves heaven and earth, stirs the feelings of the invisible gods and spirits, smooths the relations of men and women, and calms the hearts of fierce warriors.
>
> Such songs came into being when heaven and earth first appeared. . . . They began with Princess Shitateru, and on earth with the song of Susano-o no mikoto.
>
> In the age of the awesome gods, songs did not have a fixed number of syllables and were difficult to understand because the poets expressed themselves directly, without polish. By the time of the age of humans, beginning with Susano-o no mikoto, poems of thirty-one syllables were composed.

This excerpt summarizes all the fundamental ideas underlying Tsurayuki's poetics. It embraces both the cause of the creation of poetry and the function that poetry performs in human life and society. Tsurayuki's botanical metaphor can be explained as follows. The human heart (mind) constitutes soil (cognition) that contains seeds (emotions). Fertilized by sense experience and watered by emotions, the seeds grow into plants (lyric poems) containing flowers (poetic technique or style) and fruit (matter, substance, content) which provides sustenance (emotional relief and satisfaction to the poet and calming of anxieties of hearers or readers). In sum, Tsurayuki saw poetry as the natural expression of responsive feeling not merely of humans but of all living creatures. Human language, although a socially shared medium, can be used to express personal feelings and can be varied at will, unlike the singing of a thrush or the grunting of a frog. The total form of a poem embraces sentiment, diction, and style (rhythm, manner, imagery, trope, and frame or shape). Tsurayuki sees "true feeling," however, as originating outside the poem rather than being a property inside the poem itself, introduced and developed by the making. According to Tsurayuki, if the poem is a failure, it is a result of the feeling not being "true." On the other hand, in his practical criticism it is clear that he recognizes the importance of poetic technique. In the conclusion of his preface to the *Kokinshū*, Tsurayuki articulates the forward-looking vision that distinguishes Japanese literature and culture from Chinese: "Those who know poetry and who understand the heart of things will look up to the old and admire the new as they look up to and admire the moon in the broad sky."

The novel began in Japan in the second half of the tenth century with the *Utsuho monogatari* (c. 982?; the tale of the hollow tree). Of uncertain authorship, date, and text, it was the world's first full-length novel. It was followed by another, the *Ochikubo monogatari* (992?; *The Tale of the Lady Ochikubo*, 1934). Its authorship and date are similarly uncertain. Both novels, however, are thought to have been written by men for women.

These novels were soon surpassed by one of the world's great masterpieces, the *Genji monogatari* (c. 1004; *The Tale of Genji*, 1925–1976), by Lady Murasaki Shikibu, an attendant at the court of Shōshi, a consort of Emperor Ichyō. Of Lady Murasaki herself little is known. In her great novel, she theorizes about the nature of fiction through the words of her idealized hero, Prince Genji, in his dialogue with Tamakazura, a young girl for whom he is a guardian. Genji finds Tamakazura perusing one of the earlier pictorial novels; he laughs at her for taking falsehood for truth. Seeing her distressed by his remark, however, he apologizes to her and retracts his former words. Now Genji seriously addresses the question of the truth content of fiction. He relates how, in hearing some stories being read aloud, he was surprised to discover that there were two different kinds of narratives: those that proposed characters and events so far removed from ordinary reality that he characterized them as pure fantasy, and those that made him become emotionally involved with the characters and their fortunes to the extent that for him they had the ring of truth. In respect of the second kind, he concluded that a story which could evoke such an illusion must meet two criteria: the rhythm of the story had to conform to that of actual life, and the story had to create a feeling in the listener or reader of deep sympathy toward its characters and their fates.

Furthermore, Genji explains to Tamakazura, people accept history as true, but history records primarily important social or political happenings. It does not attempt to enter into the personal life of an individual to expose his or her soul-life. Hence, Genji argues, history is lacking in truth to the extent that it "records only a fraction of the whole." Laughingly, he remarks, "It is in novels that we find true happenings written in detail." This is a bold statement: Genji is saying that the imaginative truth of fiction is superior to the descriptive truth of history. Indeed, Genji claims, novelists build their accounts primarily on actual happenings which they have either experienced themselves or heard or read about. Moreover, there is not only a truth content to fiction but also an ethical content. The novelist, unlike the historian, does not record facts impartially, but is so moved by the contradiction of the good and the bad in human life that only good things are said of one character and only bad things are revealed about another, according to the author's purpose. Nevertheless, good and bad are part of reality even when distorted by artistry.

Since Buddhism is an important part of the framework of *The Tale of Genji*, Murasaki has Genji compare fictional truth to religious truth. In summing up his position, he asserts that both good novels and the Buddhist *sutras* have the same aim – to come to grips with the contradiction between good and evil and attempt somehow to resolve the duality. In Murasaki's view, this problem represents the greatest issue in human life.

The writing of *renga*, or linked verse, came into vogue about the middle of the Nambokuchō period (1336–1392) as part of a movement to popularize aristocratic court culture. The cultural historian Shuichi Kato has noted that the popularity of *renga* "is an example of a literary form spreading from the top to the bottom of society." Two famous poets, the aristocratic court poet Nijō Yoshimoto (1320–1388) and the Zen priest and poet Gusai (1284?–1378?), a man of humble origin who often collaborated with Yoshimoto, were primarily responsible for starting this new vogue. They showed that *renga* was not merely an idle pastime for the court aristocracy, as it had been since the twelfth century, but an art that could be taken seriously as a team spectacle for the entertainment of a popular audience. Nijō Yoshimoto was both a *waka* and a *renga* poet; he was also a notable theorist. His critical ideas are to be found in such works as *Renga shinshiki* (1372; better known as *Ōan shinshiki*) and *Tsukuba mondō* (1357–1372; *renga* dialogues). He and Gusai collaborated in editing the first collection of *renga*, the *Tsukuba shū* (1356; *renga* anthology). The standard *renga* poem was made up of successive patterned stanzas of *tanka* which were linked sequentially in a pattern called *kusari-renga* (linked-chain *renga*). The *kusari-renga* usually consisted of one hundred stanzas. This sort of poem was not the product of a single poet, but of several, usually three, directed by a leader.

Yoshimoto's poetics stressed that popular art aimed at appealing to the masses. In his view, the primary principle of *renga* composition was "to delight the people present." "Any verse," he proclaimed, "which sounds uninteresting to the audience should be considered mediocre, however insistently the poet may claim to know the secrets of composition." In other words, the *renga* poem exists neither in the mind of the poet nor in the text; it exists only in the minds of the audience. The *renga* poets faced a formidable task: they had to be perfect readers of the stanzas that preceded the one they intended to write, they had to fathom the minds of the poets whose words preceded theirs, and they had to anticipate whether what they wrote would please the audience.

As Makoto Ueda has pointed out, "the theory of linked verse stands directly opposite from that of lyric poetry." *Renga* poets had to suppress their own individuality to serve the unity of the whole poem, and such unity was to be achieved by four means: verse form, progression, tone, and mood. The proper mood was what Yoshimoto called *Yūgen*, or elegance. Yet *Yūgen* had to be balanced by the appearance of something "new." In pursuit of the latter aim, the poet might resort to some unrefined colloquialism which under different circumstances would be considered vulgar.

Several dramatic genres developed in Japan: *Nō*, *Kyōgen*, *Jōruri*, and *Kabuki*. *Nō* were serious and religious in mood, featuring highly stylized plots, elaborate, rich costumes, the use of masks, and much singing and dancing. *Kyōgen* were comic interludes performed between the presentations of *Nō* plays as counterparts to the serious drama. *Jōruri* were puppet plays. *Kabuki*, in striking contrast to the aristocratic *Nō*, were plays for everyone, regardless of social status. None of these Japanese dramatic forms has any counterpart in Western drama. Because of its highly lyrical quality, *Nō* gained such high esteem that it influenced the course of Japanese literary aesthetics. Having originated as a type of popular entertainment some centuries earlier, *Nō* acquired aristocratic status and perfected form under the patronage of the Ashikaga shoguns and the genius of the Namboku *Nō* actor Kan'ami (or Kanze) Kiyotsugu (1333–1384) and his son, the early Muromachi *Nō* actor, playwright, and critic, Zeami (or Kanze) Motokiyo (1363–1443).

Out of his experience as actor, playwright, and theater manager, Zeami composed some twenty treatises on the principles of the *Nō*. The most important one was his first, *Fūshikaden* (1400–1402); among the rest, the following are considered of most importance: *Shikadō* (1420), *Kakyō* (1424), *Nōsakusho* (1423; also known as *Sandō*), and *Sarugaku dangi* (1430; compiled by his second son, Motoyoshi, from his father's teachings). (All these works were first translated into English as "Seami's Sixteen Treatises," in *Monumenta Nipponica*, 1941–1942.) Zeami's basic aesthetic principle seems to have been *monomane* (imitation). He instructed his beginning actors that they should study all objects thoroughly, "because," he said, "imitation is the essence of our art." By imitation, however, he did not mean realism in any Western sense. He had a dual view of reality. For Zeami, *Nō* was a symbolic art meant to reveal not the surface appearances of ordinary reality but true or ultimate reality. *Nō* was a magic art which made visible the invisible mysteries of nature and humanity. True imitation required that the actor become one with an object, become it. Although surface reality might appear beautiful or ugly, complex or simple in structure, true reality underneath was always beautiful and simple. The kind of beauty Zeami desired in the *Nō* he termed *Yūgen*. Although the image he suggested to symbolize *Yūgen* – a swan with a flower in its bill – connotes a beauty that is elegant, delicate, and graceful, there is more to it than that. *Yūgen* is a compound of two words, according to Ueda. *Yū* means "deep, dim, difficult to see"; *gen* means "dark, profound, tranquil color of the universe." In short, *Yūgen* has to do with humanity's effort to penetrate the truth hidden within the mysterious universe. *Yūgen*, therefore, is a beauty not merely of surface appearance: "It is the beauty of the inner nature of things, the beauty of hidden truth."

Zeami saw a *Nō* performance as a process governed by a definite but varied rhythm. To describe this rhythm, he borrowed terms from court music and applied them to the successive phases in the development of a *Nō* drama. The *jo* (preface) was the opening of the process in a smooth, even rhythm. The *ha* (break) called for a change of tone and was the main phase in the development of the play's theme. The *kyū* (fast) was the final phase, in a fast, rhythmic tempo; it was the climax of the play. Zeami came to see *jo-ha-kyū* not only as governing the whole process of a *Nō* drama but also as the universal organizing principle of all things existing in time.

It is evident that Zeami's dramatic theory owed a debt to Tsurayuki's *waka* theory, Yoshimoto's *renga* criticism, and the philosophy and practices of Zen Buddhism. Unlike his father, Kan'ami, who chose his heroes from the masses, dealt with the things of this world, and resorted to no supernatural machinery, Zeami chose his heroes from the warriors of the *Heike monogatari* (c. 1240; *The Tale of the Heike*, 1918–1921) or the courtly personages of Heian culture. Zeami's heroes almost always change from humans into supernatural beings.

The early Edo *Kyōgen* actor and critic, Ōkura Toraaki (1597–1662), wrote the first theoretical treatment of the comic interlude associated with *Nō* drama. His theory of the nature of comedy appeared in his *Warambergusa* (c. 1660; on the nature of *Kyōgen* as a comic art). He pointed out that the comic deals with common human foibles. The comic art exaggerates these faults to make people objects of laughter, yet the people are character-types modeled after real humans. However false in its artistic distortion, comedy also presents the true by revealing the practical truths of human life that are often hidden by surface appearances. Ōkura stressed that "without the true or the real there would be nothing truly comic." Even more important, he maintained that pathos is the ultimate goal of comedy: "All the arts repudiate an attempt to amuse. Everything ends in pathos." Thus, the comic interlude comes full circle: although quite different from the *Nō* in presentation, the final goal of *Kyōgen* is very much the same, and it never ridicules.

The puppet theater grew to maturity in the seventeenth century. It made use of lifelike marionettes that could be made to simulate human actions. The greatest writer of *Jōruri* plays was Chikamatsu Monzaemon (1653–1724), who also wrote outstanding *Kabuki* dramas. Although Chikamatsu wrote no treatise on *Jōruri*, his views of the nature of puppetry were recorded by Hozumi Ikan (1692–1769), a Confucian scholar, in his *Naniwa miyage* (a present from Naniwa).

According to Chikamatsu, art resided "in the thin margin between truth and falsehood." Paradoxically, art was the truth and yet not the truth. According to Chikamatsu, the falseness of art allowed for a necessary distance between art and the actual. Art was effective because it could not be confused with the real; it did not copy life exactly. Indeed, an exact copy of surface reality was repugnant to a spectator. "All puppet plays," Chikamatsu said, "describe facts as they are, but they also contain things that exist only in the sphere of art." In this manner, art presents things which are truer than facts.

Chikamatsu's theory accorded well with the nature of the puppet theater. It was neither realistic like the *Kabuki* nor symbolic like the *Nō*. By using puppets instead of human beings, it refused to copy life. By simulating normal human actions, it avoided symbolic ritual. Indeed, the lifeless puppet could be more convincing than a living actor because it could render dramatic conflicts and basic emotions in a more elementary and plainer way.

Matsuo Bashō (1644–1694) was the greatest master of the *haiku* (abbreviation of *haikai no*). He also composed outstanding *haikai* sequences, essays, and travel diaries. Born into a samurai family, he studied *haikai* poetry under Kitamura Kigin (1624–1705) and Zen Buddhism under Priest Butchō (1642–1715). He opted to become a poet, a traveler, and a teacher, founding the Shofū (or Shōmon) school of poetry. Although Bashō left no treatise on the *haiku*, two of his disciples recorded his teachings: Mukai Kyorai (1651–1704) wrote *Kyorai shō* (1702–1704; Kyorai's recollections of Bashō) and Hattori Dohō (1657–1730) composed *Sanzōshi* (c. 1702; three books).

Bashō maintained that a poet should imitate nature. The vastness of nature evoked a sense of loneliness (*shiori*). A proper poem resulted from the poet's ability to become "unhuman" – to strip himself of personal emotions and to adopt the attitude of loneliness (*sabi*), thereby achieving detachment and objectivity. Such a state could be promoted by the practice of meditation. Bashō preferred poems that evoked an impersonal atmosphere, giving the effect of vastness, quietness, and loneliness.

According to Bashō, there were two ways to write a poem. The wrong way was to write by deliberate calculation, selecting words thought right to convey a personal emotion and observing the conventional rules of versification. The result would be mechanical, flat, and dull. The right way was for poets to be in such a mental state that they allowed the poem to grow spontaneously from the seed of inspiration, watered by their poetic spirit. In this way, the poem would "grow into itself" – that is, it would write itself. The achievement of the proper mental state, according to Bashō, depended on the condition he termed *karumi* (lightness). This lightness of mind came about when poets had emptied themselves of ordinary personal emotions and had released the tensions caused by emotional conflicts. Once their minds were settled and quiet, they entered into the condition of lightness. Under such a circumstance, the "color" of their minds would "grow into a poem."

Bashō perceived two stages in poetic creation. The first stage involved intuitive perception, the second spontaneous, quick, and brief expression. For poets to render merely surface appearance was nothing; they had to render the inner reality of an object, a situation, or an event. To do so, they had to project themselves into them and intuitively perceive their essence. When the poet had transformed personal emotion into the impersonal, the spontaneous growth of the poem required the poet to record it quickly. Since intensity of concentration could be sustained only for a short time, the poet also had to be simple and brief in his or her expression. Obviously, the terse *haiku* form fit Bashō's prescription perfectly.

Motoori Norinaga (1730–1801) was a poet, prose writer, scholar, and critic. As a Shintoist, he was highly critical of Confucian and Buddhist thought, and his literary theory reflects his world-view. His critical views are found mainly in three of his works: *Isonokami sasamegoto* (1793; murmurings of old things), a poetic treatise; *Genji monogatari tama no ogushi* (1796; a little jeweled comb of the '*Genji monogatari*'), in which he applied the concept of pathos to the novel; and *Tamakatsuma* (1801; the beautiful basket), a collection of miscellaneous observations. Norinaga's literary theory was mythological, anti-intellectual, primitivistic, and humanistic.

Norinaga emphasized the limitations of the human mind, the limited extent of human knowledge, and the untrustworthiness of rational thinking. Faced with the irrationalities of human life and the mysteries of the universe, the human intellect was baffled. Furthermore, he declared, the human mind was endowed with merely analytic power and possessed no creative energy.

If the irrationalities of human life and the mysteries of the universe were frustrating to rational thinking, they at least could be made metaphysically comprehensible by making use of the concept of the Shinto gods. The *kami*, presiding spirits inhabiting sky and earth, were the progeny of the sources of all creation, the Sky Father and the Earth Mother. Although human beings are in general subject to the control of the gods, they are free within their status and ability. Modern humanity, Norinaga held, had lost touch with the gods. To be saved, it must return to them to find the true inner heart it had possessed in primeval times.

In other words, according to Norinaga, human nature in his time was corrupt because it had lost its natural sensibility and capacity for true feeling. Certain cultural codes had corrupted the human heart. The chivalric samurai code of Bushido had encouraged its adherents to think lightly of their lives. Confucianism had forced people to accept virtues that ran counter to human nature: to renounce grief over death, for example. Norinaga particularly opposed Bashō's ideal of "unhumanness" through suppression of ordinary human feelings. If people suppress their natural feelings, Norinaga declared, they can become unbearable and harmful to them. How then can modern people recover their original feelings? Norinaga's recommendation was twofold: adopt the concept of the Shinto gods and study the great Japanese classics, which display and evoke a deep feeling for things, a sensibility that he termed *mono no aware*.

Norinaga's idea of *mono no aware* supplied a motive for both the writing and the reading of literature. In writing a poem or novel, writers were purged of the deep feelings and the obsessions that plagued them. By reading good literature, the reader learned to understand and to sympathize with the poet or with the novelist's characters. Good literature reveals human nature. *Mono no aware* is a mode of intuitive perception. If writers know *mono no aware*, they do not have to analyze an object or an event; they take it directly into their hearts, feel it, and understand it. *Mono no aware* instantly penetrates the heart, deeper than the reason or the will. Hence, Norinaga held, the communicative function of *mono no aware* was an important principle for morals as well as for aesthetics.

Modern Japanese literary theory

The modern period begins after the Meiji Restoration of 1868. Even by the time of Norinaga, however, Japanese art and literature had fallen on hard times. Edo popular art and literature – color prints, *Kabuki* theater, *haikai* poetry, and *gesaku* fiction – had become predominant, sending Japanese taste into a tailspin. Actors and prostitutes became the subjects of woodblock color prints as well as of *gesaku* novels and short stories. Despite the impressive quality of the work of such writers as Ihara Saikaku (1643–1693), Hiraga Gennai (1728–1779), Ueda Akinari (1734–1808), and Kyokutei Bakin (1767–1848), by the time of the invasion of Commodore Matthew Perry in 1853, *gesaku* fiction had reached a new low. People of taste still valued *Nō* drama and landscape painting in Chinese style, practiced the tea ceremony, or wrote Chinese poetry. Neo-Confucianism was the official philosophy of the samurai class, whose special idiom was classical Chinese. Even the *gesaku* writers Akinari and Bakin got many of their fictional ideas from Chinese colloquial literature. Hence, Japan entered the modern period, as British historian William G. Beasley has remarked, "with what were in effect two cultures existing side by side, each with rather different aesthetic standards. The 19th century saw the addition of a third, deriving from western Europe."

By the 1880s the reading of Western literature in translation was becoming common. The most notable translators were Oda Jun'ichiro (1851–1919) and Mori Ōgai (1862–1922). In 1879 Oda made the first Japanese translation of a European novel – Edward Bulwer-Lytton's *Ernest Maltravers* (1837) – with considerable success, and other novels by this author followed. Mori did a much-admired 1901 translation of Hans Christian Andersen's *Improvisatoren* (1835; *The Improvisatore*).

Much impressed by the qualities of European and American literature, literary scholar and critic Tsubouchi Shōyō (1859–1935) called for a new and distinctly modern Japanese criticism in his book, *Shōsetsu shinzui* (1885–1886; *The Essence of the Novel*, 1956). He had developed a taste principally for English writers: from Geoffrey Chaucer, William Shakespeare (whose plays he translated), John Milton, to Sir Walter Scott, Edward Bulwer-Lytton, Benjamin Disraeli, and Charles Dickens. He condemned the Confucian principle of *kanzen chō ku* (encouraging virtue and chastising vice), and held that realism – in the sense of strict objectivity, without the imposition of value judgments – was "true art." According to Tsubouchi, the depiction of human feelings (*ninjō shōsitsu*) should be valued for its own sake and should be presented artistically in such a manner as to give the reader a sense of the beautiful (*mono no aware*).

Although Tsubouchi's treatise had a strong influence on other Japanese writers such as his contemporary Futabatei Shimei (1864–1909), who was well grounded in the Russian novels of Ivan Goncharov, Ivan Turgenev, Fedor Dostoevskii, and Lev Tolstoi. He issued the novel *Ukigumo* (1886–1889; English translation, 1967) which portrayed three-dimensional characters, was very realistic, and which was written almost entirely in "colloquial" Japanese of Futabatei's generation. It was, in effect, the first modern Japanese novel.

Nevertheless, many Japanese writers of the Meiji era, although convinced that the novel was the key to a new era in Japanese literature, were of different opinions as to just how to proceed in terms of language, treatment of characters, and the effect to be desired on the reader; indeed, it was questionable whether one should consider such a task a respectable pursuit. For instance, the scholar Seki Naohiko (1857–1920) was deeply impressed by Benjamin Disraeli's novel *Coningsby* (1844); it seemed to him that it was an ideal model to encourage novel-writing in Japan. He reasoned that when people saw that such an eminent man as this famous and well-respected British statesman engaged in writing novels the Japanese scholars and litterateurs would soon vie with one another in writing novels. But there was so much uncertainty that the literary dispute (*fungaku ronsō*) became a prominent feature of modern Japanese criticism. Tsubouchi stressed the importance of presenting "human feelings," by which he meant "love affairs." But other critics took the position that the novels depicted "cheap" rather than "holy" love. In 1893 the literary scholars Kitamura Tokoku (1868–1894) and Yamaji Aizau engaged in a bitter dispute about the proper way to present the characters as "enlightened" or "rational." By "enlightened" Kitamura meant "heroic" and "noble," reckless, ambitious men longing for success and fame who would prove models for the common people; by "rational" he meant the "real" in contrast to the "ideal." Another dispute had to do with the concept of the self relative to other people: was the self an organized configuration that represents a reality, or (as claimed by Buddhism) an aggregate of physical, mental, and volitional factors, the *skandhas*, which are always changing and are without any underlying nature? Kitamura Tokoku wanted the novel to teach the lower classes the facts of life: Yarnaji Aizan wanted the lower classes to be edified by strong leaders and heroes.

The Japanese language also presented a problem for modern writers. To the Japanese, China was to them culturally what Greece and Rome had been to Westerners. Early Japan never devised a written Japanese script: all writing has always been done by various applications of Chinese script, and much early writing was in fact done in Chinese itself. Early Japanese adopted Chinese characters to be used as phonograms, out of which the Japanese evolved two original systems of phonetic writing called *katakava* and *hiragana*, which are abbreviations of standard Chinese characters. Chinese, however, remained the language of high culture – both Natsume Sōseki and Nagai Kafū, for example, received a thorough training in classical Chinese.

But a dramatic change took place in Japan immediately following the Sino-Japanese War (1894–1895), in which Japan won an easy victory. Although the supremacy of Chinese culture had been unquestioned for centuries, the euphoric Japanese now believed that they had surpassed their mentors. Consequently, classical Chinese ceased to be a part of Japanese education. After this time, few educated Japanese had the skill to write a classical Chinese poem. Now the Japanese universities taught English or some other European language. Also, the aftermath of Japan's success in the Russo-Japanese War (1904–1905) led to the naturalist movement in Japan, which would predominate until the outbreak of the Pacific War in 1941.

Naturalism (*shizen*) in Japan developed along different lines from the European variety as laid down by the Frenchman, Émile Zola, from Claude Bernard's work in experimental medi-cine, as Mori Ōgai was to explain in an article in 1889. Himself a doctor, Mori disapproved of the "medical approach" to literature. He insisted that "facts" had to be filtered through a writer's imagination if literary art was to be the result. He also disapproved of Zola's penchant for low life and brutality, declaring that much of Zola's work was immoral and obscene.

In Japan, naturalism was an extension of the realism advocated by Tsubouchi, which simply sought to tell the truth without pretending any scientific detachment and objectivity. It achieved its ultimate purpose in the "I-novels." In other words, naturalism in Japan, while devotedly realistic, had within it a strong romantic strain and retained a focus on the individual in relation to the group.

Naturalistic fiction in Japan was brought to maturity by Shimazaki Tosōn (1872–1943), author of *Hakai* (1906; *The Broken Commandment*, 1974) and Natsume Sōseki (1867–1916), author of the humorous novel, *Wagahai wa neko de aru* (1905–1906; *I Am a Cat*, 1961). He liked to satirize "civilized" society, to examine the solitary, intense, and sometimes demented mind, and to shift from a "subjective examination of the self and an objective examination of others." This last project is seen in his unfinished novel, *Meian* (1916; *Light and Darkness*, 1971). Like Mori Ōgai, he did not consider himself to be a member of the naturalist school.

Nagai Kafū (1879–1959) was a writer of novels and stories as well as a literary theorist. His masterpiece is *Bokutō Kidan* (1937; *A Strange Tale from East of the River*, 1958). The theme he favored was "the ever changing city of Tōkyō and its pleasure quarters." He believed in presenting "the facts of life" in accordance with the carefully selected language chosen by the author. His essay "How to Write a Novel" (*shoset-su*) is especially revealing.

The aftermath of Japan's success in the Russo-Japanese War also led to other changes in the literary scene. Other schools besides the naturalists appeared, including the Ken'yūsha group (Japan's first major literary clique); the Shirakaba; and the Proletarian school (Christian or Marxist). But the most important and popular writers in modern Japan did not belong to any one school. For instance, that master of the short story, Akutagawa Ryūnosuke (1892–1927), who held that genuine literature is based primarily on the meanings and the sounds of words, aimed at conveying "life." He was the author of such masterly stories as "In a Grove" (1952; "*Yabu no maka*," 1922) and "Rashōmon" (1930; "*Rashōmon*," 1915).

With the rise in militarism in Japan in the 1930s, the Proletarian school was suppressed, and writers were forced to renounce Communism. Consequently, there arose what was termed "conversion" (*tenko*) literature. During World War II much patriotic literature was produced, but little of it seems of lasting value. The Japanese surrender in 1945 was followed by many postwar recollections, such as Ibuse Masuji's *Kuroiame* (1967; *Black Rain*, 1969), a novel about the atomic bombing of Hiroshima. With the end of the war, too, leftwing writers were again permitted to publish their work. Under the inspiration of European literature, a spirit of cosmopolitanism began to replace the former naturalism.

When Western influence began to enter Japan after 1868, poetry, like the novel, was in a sorry condition. Interest in serious poetry was revived, however, as translations of European and American poetry were introduced. Nagai Kafū, for example, introduced the Japanese to the French poets Charles Baudelaire, Paul Verlaine, and Stéphane Mallarmé. Language, as well as style and form, however, remained problems for Japanese poets much longer than they did for novelists. Novelists were adopting the colloquial language by the turn of the century. But it was not until Hagiwara Sakutarō (1886–1942) began publishing his poems that colloquial instead of classical Japanese language was used to produce truly modern poetry. Using free verse, he merged his innate lyricism successfully with symbolism to create, as a critic has said, "a world of almost neurotic, haunted beauty." Soon Japanese poets turned not only to Symbolism but also to Dada, Surrealism, and Marxism.

With Japan's defeat in 1945, many poets sank into despair. They searched for human values in poetry, joined leftist movements, accepted European existentialism, evoked the spirit of T. S. Eliot's *The Waste Land* (1922), wrote poems on the atom bomb, and generally displayed their own wounded spirits. By the 1980s, however, Japanese poets had for the most part moved beyond existentialist despair to take up themes of family, sex, feminism, poverty, and other social issues.

Among the leading writers of fiction of the postwar era are Kawabata Yasunari (1899–1972), who was awarded the Nobel Prize for Literature in 1968 and the author of the novels *Yukigani* (1937; *Snow Country*, 1956) and *Senbozuru* (1951; *The Thousand Cranes*, 1959). Kawabata is fond of the theme of the person with high ideals who uses so much energy in his or her quest that they die of exhaustion. Endo Shusaku (1923–), as a Roman Catholic, reminds one of the English novelist Graham Greene and the French writer Georges Bernanos. He is the author of *Chinmoku* (1966; *Silence*, 1979) and *Samurai* (1980; *The Samurai*, 1982). Mishima Yuko (pen name of Haroka Kimitake, 1925–1970) was a thinker and a doer as well as a novelist and expressed himself in his entire life-style. He is especially noted for his philosophical novel *Kinkakuji* (1956; *The Temple of the Golden Pavilion*, 1959). In it a university student named Kashiwagi, who is handicapped by a club foot (as was Lord Byron), excels in the Japanese art of flower arrangement by turning nature's plants from what they *are* into what *they ought to be* and thus creating a small artificial universe. Finally, another unusual writer deserves mention: Abe Kōbō (1924–1993), novelist and playwright, and author of the novel *Suna no Onna* (1962; *The Woman in the Dunes*, 1964). The theme is that life is a trap from which neither man nor woman can escape to any better existence.

Further reading

Benedict, Ruth. *The Chrysanthemum and the Sword: Patterns of Japanese Culture*, 1946.
Bowring, R. J. *Mori Ōgai and the Modernization of Japanese Culture*, 1979.
Hare, T. B. *Zeami's Style: The Noh Plays of Zeami Motokiyo*, 1986.
Hibbett, Howard. *A History of Japanese Literature*, 1991.
Kato, Shuichi. *A History of Japanese Literature*, 1979. Translated by David Chibbett.
Keene, Donald. *Dawn to the West: Japanese Literature of the Modern Era*, 1984 (2 volumes).
Lippet, N. M. *Reality and Fiction in Japanese Literature*, 1980.
Makoto, Ueda. *Modern Japanese Writers and the Nature of Literature*, 1976.
Marks, Alfred H., and Barry D. Bort. *Guide to Japanese Prose*, 1975.
Masao, Mijoshi. *Accomplices of Silence: The Modern Japanese Novel*, 1974.
Miner, Earl, Hiroko Odagiri, and Robert E. Morrel, eds. *The Princeton Companion to Classical Japanese*, 1985.
Rimer, J. Thomas, and Robert E. Morrell. *Guide to Japanese Poetry*, 1975.
Rimer, J. Thomas, *Pilgrimages: Aspects of Japanese Literature and Culture*, 1988.
Ueda, Makorto. *Literary and Art Theories of Japan*, 1967.

RICHARD P. BENTON

See also Kamo No Mabuchi; Motoori Norinaga; Tsurayuki; Yoshimoto

Randall Jarrell

American poet, critic, and teacher

Born: Nashville, Tennessee; May 6, 1914
Died: Chapel Hill, North Carolina; October 14, 1965

Biography

Never separating art from life, Randall Jarrell drew from his biography in all that he wrote. Born in Nashville, Tennessee, he moved with his family to California by his first birthday and spent the next eleven years of his life there. A lifelong melancholy followed his return to Nashville with his mother after she and his father divorced. Particularly painful was his separation from his paternal grandparents, to whom he was very close; when they returned him to Nashville after a year-long visit, he never forgave them or wrote to them again. Later he spoke openly of his love for childhood, fairy tales, and animals, but these were part of a "lost world" abandoned in his youth. Some speculate that his childhood in Long Beach and year in Hollywood – with their proximity to the film industry – nurtured his interest in the "relationship of fantasy and reality." Certainly his later work celebrates a fairy "child driven into exile or setting out on [an] heroic quest," a boy for whom "books were a total existence."

Jarrell's writing career began in his undergraduate years at Vanderbilt where he befriended Robert Lowell and Peter Taylor and was assigned to classes by John Crowe Ransom and Robert Penn Warren. With Lowell he migrated to Kenyon College to study with Warren and Allen Tate. Shaped by the Fugitive poets, Jarrell later explored their forms and ideas in his work, absorbing their anti-Romantic modernism. Having completed a three-year undergraduate degree in psychology, Jarrell turned to English with the zeal of a convert, discussing Anton Chekhov on the sidelines of football games and building a coterie of literary friends.

In 1939 Jarrell accepted a teaching position at the University of Texas, and he and an English Department colleague, Mackie Langham, were married the following year. His first book of poetry was published in 1942, the same year he left Austin to join the Army Air Corps. Although he enlisted as a pilot, Jarrell left the program and spent his service as a flight instructor and navigation tower operator. His second book of poetry was published in 1945. Discharged in 1946, Jarrell accepted an invitation to be a one-year replacement for the literary editor of *The Nation*; while in New York he renewed his academic career, teaching at Sarah Lawrence College. In the fall of 1947 he followed his good friend Peter Taylor to the Woman's College of the University of North Carolina in Greensboro and remained on the permanent faculty there until his death.

Jarrell's third book of poetry was published in 1948 and, like its predecessor, reflected World War II – one of two "major occasions" generally cited for his verse. The second "occasion" was his introduction to German culture in 1948–1949 when he spent part of a Guggenheim Fellowship year teaching "American civilization" in Salzburg. By all accounts, Jarrell was "a born teacher" and always maintained some connection with a university. His fourth book of poetry appeared in 1951, the year he and his wife separated; the following year he took a leave of absence and taught at Princeton University. The summer after, he met Mary von Schrader in southern California, and they were married in November, 1952; he taught at Indiana University and the University of Illinois before returning to Greensboro with Mary and her daughters. While a point has been made of his childlessness, Jarrell remained devoted to the girls.

A professor, lecturer, and reviewer, Jarrell published a volume of criticism in 1953 and then completed his only novel, a satire about a woman's college and a forum for his ideas on progressive education. From 1956 to 1958 Jarrell was poetry consultant to the Library of Congress and then returned again to Greensboro. In 1961 a new collection earned him the National Book Award for poetry, and about that time he turned to the writing of children's books.

Jarrell's last book of poetry to be published during his lifetime came out early in 1965, a difficult time for him. Questions and inconsistencies surround the events in this final year of his life. Some speculate that it was the harshness of the *New York Times*' review of his work that prompted his first suicide attempt in the spring, others mention distancing from his wife. While she claimed that his death was accidental, and what Helen Vendler labels the "decencies of inconclusiveness" are still maintained, it appears that Jarrell walked in front of the car that killed him on the dark night of October 14.

Influence

Jarrell was a poet, critic, novelist, and teacher. It is hyperbole to argue that he was "one of the finest American poets of his generation," as Ashley Brown claims, or "the best critic of poetry in his time," but these offer a starting point to assess his œuvre.

Along with Robert Lowell, John Berryman, and Delmore Schwartz, Jarrell was part of a "Middle Generation" of poets that followed the "Great Modernists" – William Butler Yeats, W. H. Auden, T. S. Eliot, and Ezra Pound. Abandoning the "great impersonal myths" of the modernists, this Middle Generation "forged painfully personal ones" that exacted a terrible toll. This "first generation of poets as academics" was free to practice art full-time, but seeing no boundary between art and life, they lost any respite they might have found from each. While they borrowed themes from the modernists like cultural decline, they shared no artistic credo. Isolation stalked their poems.

Like others of his generation, Jarrell wrote early verse that was derivative of the modernist and Fugitive poetry that followed World War I, in its themes and heavily metered lines; Allen Tate, to whom some of the poems were dedicated, described them as "limp." Over time, by testing the tenets of his teachers, Jarrell developed a poetic voice that was resonant and expansive. If occasionally charged with sentimentalism, he was unafraid to experiment with emotions others found "unmanly," developing, as he did, female personae to present them. In 1942, in a poem that remained unpublished until his death, Jarrell wrote of himself "'Woman,' men say of him, and women, 'man.'"

Helen Vendler conjectures "Jarrell probably saw clearly enough the scope of his own modest poetic talent." Whether he did or not, it seems clear now that his primary gift is in his criticism, and, it may be argued, the balance of his other work – including his poetry – exists to explicate the insights he developed there.

As an educator and critic, Jarrell helped to shape a generation of writers and introduced to them the work of his contemporaries and friends. Suzanne Ferguson assesses Jarrell's gifts as "basically a far-ranging, inquisitive, continually testing intellect; a strong perception of the ironic incongruity of men's ideals with their way of living; a sure feeling for the moral and psychological crises men have in common; and a messianic vocation to show others what he learned and saw in the world." She cites these characteristics to affirm Jarrell's place as a preeminent poet, but they speak directly to his critic's role. In his criticism, as well as his poetry, Jarrell challenged the work of established poets and reinforced the significance of others, attempting to establish aesthetic goals for postmodern poetry. Finally, in assessing Jarrell's lasting influence, one reaches a point of convergence where his work as a teacher, poet, and critic come together.

Analysis

To those who knew him well, Jarrell was "monstrously knowing." To many of the writers of his generation – Lowell, Berryman, and Schwartz among them – he was the critic whose judgment was most unerring, whose eye the most unfailing, who seemed to know instinctively what was genuine and what was not.

Profoundly an educator, Jarrell loved teaching and was fond of saying that if he were a rich man he would pay for the privilege of doing it. German-born American historian Hannah Arendt credited him with teaching her to appreciate English-language poetry; Lowell sought his insight on the Pulitzer Prize-winning poems in *Lord Weary's Castle*. As Jarrell said on one occasion, "the gods who had taken away the poet's audience had given him students," and it was these – including his contemporaries and friends – to whom his messianic energies were addressed.

Although his poetry could be overwhelmed with pity, his criticism was not, often filled instead with indignation at weakness or bad work. As novelist Peter Taylor observed, "If you published something he didn't like, he behaved as though you had been disloyal to him in some way." Vendler adds that he felt the same way "about lapses in books he reviewed, or declines in poets he had admired, like Auden."

Jarrell's challenge to Auden began a break with his literary forebears that was the first of three defining components in his development of a poetic voice. The second was his acknowledgment of a "semifeminine mind," and the third was his espousal of a childlike perspective on literature and the world, which made him, in Lowell's words, as "monstrously innocent" as he was "knowing." These provide a broad outline for an analysis of his criticism.

Invited to launch a career as a critic in 1946 as literary editor for *The Nation*, Jarrell considered himself an appropriate choice because he was not associated with "any particular variety of literary opinion." Implicit in the statement is *The Kenyon Review* edited by Ransom, *The Southern Review* edited by Warren, and *The American Review* edited by Tate; noting that several of his friends were editors, he added, "Their dogmatic convictions and idiosyncrasies and general sectarian leanings hurt their work – a lot." In fact, before he had completed his A.M. degree in 1938 Jarrell had poems published in each of these journals. His intention with the remark was to criticize editorial decisions by Ransom and Warren. As early as 1940 he had begun to question his teachers' "apocalyptic sensibility" even though his poems remained close to it. He had responded to Tate's judgment of his earliest work by asserting, "I'd rather seem limp and prosaic than false and rhetorical." At the same time, he was trying self-consciously to write poems that were postmodern, and found an important model in Auden. His acerbic review "Changes of Attitude and Rhetoric in Auden's Poetry," published in *The Southern Review* in 1941, signaled that a break had begun; by 1946 it was complete.

As a critic, Jarrell was fueled by Auden's Marxism, Tate's classicism, and the modernism of Ransom and Warren; he never lost respect for what they had offered him and continued to maintain that Tate, particularly, was among the best critics of his time. Still, in his criticism he began to take issue with what they represented. "To expect Tate's and Warren's poems to be much influenced by Ransom's is like expecting two nightmares to be influenced by a daydream," he wrote, not so much in support of Ransom's agrarian aesthetic but to set it apart from the work of the other two men. We hear in the quip the kind of "one liner" for which Jarrell's criticism was known, the sharp wit and piercing insight. The comment points, too, to the thing about Warren and Tate that bothered him most – their celebration of violence and evil.

Tate's poems about World War II particularly affected Jarrell. He was different from his friends Lowell and Berryman with his years of war service; his experiences gave rise to his best-known and most anthologized poems. They were criticized for their brutal journalistic details, for the fact that they were overwhelmed with pity, that they were concerned more with "types" than individuals, but they drew from the reality of war as he knew it. He lamented and elegized the indifference of war; he believed that Tate had idealized it. Jarrell never had a sense of the "abyss" of which Warren wrote or the apocalyptic "horror" present in the work of "thousands of others." Evaluating Warren's *Selected Poems* in 1944, he went further, cautioning against the potential political threat inherent to this kind of thinking; "to say that the world is essentially evil and incurable," he argued, "is the only excuse you can find for doing nothing" to change it; to say "that anything you did would only be a silly palliation to hide from yourself the final evil of existence," is to deny responsibility for action.

To many, Jarrell's position seemed harsh, but it reflects the aggressive stance of much of his criticism, often in sharp contrast to the softer "semifeminine" voice of his poetry. While he helped to canonize Lowell's work in *Lord Weary's Castle* as the most important book of poems of the decade, he worked there, too, to expand the range of human emotion and response. In criticism he spoke to the diction, rhythm, and metrics of the poems to mitigate "their savoring of evil and damnation" that emulated the celebration of violence he and Lowell had been taught. Later he responded to the book with a poem of his own. Lowell concludes "where the rainbow ends"; Jarrell's poem begins at "The End of the Rainbow," where his speaker, "on the verge of seeing/ in black and white" is redeemed by turning back to her easel, by the familiar gesture that affirms the "dailiness" of life.

What some call "sentimentality" in Jarrell's work, others call "human truth." Certainly he knew grief and loss; his poems are full of these, but it was his critical and poetic ambition to communicate "difficult ordinary happiness" (a phrase he admired and borrowed from Adrienne Rich), and he worked to achieve it in spite of obvious contradictions. Jarrell was both personal and pointed in his critical observations. His "style of analysis," William Pritchard points out in his biography, "is less analytical than literary and satirical, a 'creative' exaggeration." Vendler adds that one may either see the theoretical or stylistic aim of his remarks or dismiss them as "flippant," "cruel," or "destructive." Both cite as an example Whitman's reference to himself as a "Habitan of Vienna." Jarrell observes: "One has an immediate vision of him as a sort of French-Canadian half-breed to whom the Viennese are offering, with trepidation, through the bars of a zoological garden, little mounds of whipped cream." Pritchard notes, "This is both very funny and eerily right about the line, but is of course not 'analysis' so much as something a novelist or poet might produce as the only adequate response to Whitman's grotesque phrase." Pritchard is also clear in pointing out that Jarrell was capable of profound critical insight and refers to his extended treatment of Auden and Frost for support.

To his earlier assessment of Auden, Jarrell added a second – "Freud to Paul: The Stages of Auden's Ideology" – and both were included in *The Third Book of Criticism* published posthumously in 1969. Like the two volumes of criticism he published in his lifetime, the "Third Book" was a collection of Jarrell's previously published essays and reviews. It included, among others, his observations on "The Collected Poems of Wallace Stevens" and "Robert Frost's Home Burial." Jarrell is generally credited with having "solidified" the reputation of the former and "influentially reassessed" the latter. Of them, Jarrell said, "Frost, along with Stevens and Eliot[,] seems to me the greatest of the American poets of this century. Frost's virtues are extraordinary. No other [poet of his time] has written so well about the actions of ordinary men: his wonderful dramatic monologues or dramatic scenes come out of a knowledge of people that few poets have had, and they are written in verse that uses, sometimes with absolute mastery, the rhythms of actual speech."

This is a resonant voice, missing the frenetic humor generally associated with Jarrell's criticism. Gone is the "consummate performer" continually described "by students, friends, readers, even wives and lovers." Previously, in one of his most entertaining critical observations, he noted that others had been more than just to e. e. cummings' virtues, and he would like to be unjust about his faults: "He is, Alas! A monotonous poet. Everything a poem does is, to old readers, expected. 'Type four,' they murmur. 'Well done!' Then they yawn." If the aggressive stance of some of his essays can seem defensive, the satire that bolsters his reviews can be brutal.

During the last twenty years of his life Jarrell wrote appreciations of poets – William Carlos Williams, Walt Whitman, Frost, and Stevens prominently among them; his poetry never reflected these models. It did, however, have much in common with others whose work he wanted to introduce – Lowell's, as previously discussed, and that of Elizabeth Bishop. The words Jarrell chooses in criticism of Bishop's poems list qualities he wanted to create in his own: "Her work is unusually personal and honest in its wit, perception, and sensitivity – and in its restrictions too; . . . She is morally so attractive . . . because she understands so well that the wickedness and confusion of the age can explain and extenuate other people's wickedness and confusion . . . that morality, for the individual, is usually a small, personal, statistical, but heartbreaking or heart-warming affair of omissions and commissions the greatest of which will seem infinitesimal . . . to those who govern, rationalize, and deplore." For Jarrell, this was not only an anodyne to the violence he saw in Lowell and their literary forebears, but an affirmation, at a time "when many a poem is gruesome occupational therapy for a poet who stays legally innocuous by means of it."

Jarrell's poems do not resemble Bishop's, any more than they do Lowell's, but he felt his life reflected in them, and consequently this criticism offers a valuable insight. As James Longenbach points out, "Bishop's work provided him with a compelling example of his own aesthetic goals (one that he could write about more gracefully than he could write about himself)." Longenbach goes further than the review of Bishop's *North and South*, cited above, and Jarrell's attempt with it to enlist "Bishop in his effort to undermine his teachers' values." He notes that "Bishop was the contemporary poet to whom Jarrell felt closest"; his poems "exemplify Bishop's stylistic ideal of 'a mind thinking' rather than a finished thought," an ideal Jarrell associated "with certain notions of femininity." While male critics complained about his use of female speakers in his poems, female readers – including Bishop – were not impressed with his "understanding and sort-of-over-sympathizing with the lot of women." Jarrell acknowledged he had a "semifeminine mind." In speaking of Ransom, he said he "was writing in an age in which the most natural feeling of tenderness, happiness, or sorrow was likely to be called sentimental," and he "needed a self-protective rhetoric as the most brutal or violent of poets did not." Again, it was himself of whom he spoke.

Late in his career Jarrell turned to female personae to create "the fragile state of childhood domesticity," far from his image of woman as "pythoness" in his earlier poems. Among these speakers is a fourteen-year-old girl, a child of the 1930s, who is much like Jarrell himself, as is the aging and lonely woman obsessed with the ghosts of her past, or the woman feeling "commonplace and solitary" pushing her shopping cart "from Cheer to Joy, from Joy to All."And all of this – impersonation, disguise, experimentation – is essential to understanding the fully mature literary figure Jarrell became. Longenbach adds a critical note: "For Jarrell, the dramatization of a feminine sensibility became inseparable from the exploration of what might be possible in American poetry at the end of the line." And this was the task to which he set himself in criticism.

Finally, there is more to Jarrell's best work than hostile critical assessments and derisive commentary. The childlike quality that informs his late poems affects his critical voice; the unrealized dreams and loneliness of the adult world remain there in counterpoint to the mysteries of childhood. Jarrell loved fairy tales, translated them, and wrote books for children. His late life was, as Hannah Arendt said, as if he "had emerged from the enchanted forests." But these were "sunny/ Inexorable hours," and even as he tried to "gulp from them the dailiness of life," as he wrote in 1965, his "hand [came] back empty."

Vendler concludes that he is "a very touching American minor poet. And when stylishness in critical writing comes back into fashion, Jarrell will once again, in his impish bravado, be an example of the gusto that criticism can evoke." For all of her praise, Brown notes that in 1990 "he does not figure in literary discussions the way that some of his contemporaries do." The timing of his biography is fortunate then (along with a reprint of his *Selected Poems*) in restoring Jarrell to critical discussion. With the reprint of his essays in 2000, one may hope that he will return to the classroom, the critical journal, and the poetry seminar where he was always most at home.

Principal criticism

Poetry and the Age, 1953
A Sad Heart at the Supermarket: Essays and Fables, 1962
The Third Book of Criticism, 1969
Kipling, Auden & Co.: Essays and Reviews, 1935–64, 1980
Jarrell's Letters: An Autobiographical and Literary Selection, 1985 (Mary Jarrell and Stuart Wright, editors)
No Other Books: Selected Essays (editor), to be reprinted, 2000

Other major works and literary forms

It is significant to note that much of the Jarrell œuvre has been published, and republished, posthumously. It is generally held that Jarrell compiled the posthumously published criticism before his death, and that the principal value of the subsequently published *Letters* is to extend his critical premises.

NOVEL
Pictures from an Institution: A Comedy, 1954

SHORT (JUVENILE) FICTION
The Gingerbread Rabbit, 1963
The Bat-Poet, 1964
The Animal Family, 1965
Fly By Night, 1976
A Bat is Born, 1978

POETRY
Blood for a Stranger, 1942
Little Friend, Little Friend, 1945
Losses, 1948
The Seven-League Crutches, 1951
Selected Poems, 1955
Uncollected Poems, 1958
The Woman at the Washington Zoo: Poems and Translations, 1960
Selected Poems, Including The Woman at the Washington Zoo, 1964
The Lost World: New Poems, 1965
Complete Poems, 1968
Death of the Ball Turret Gunner, 1969
The Achievement of Jarrell: A Comprehensive Selection of His Poems, 1970 (Frederick J. Hoffman, editor)
Selected Poems, 1990 (William H. Pritchard, editor)

TRANSLATIONS
The Ghetto and the Jews of Rome, 1948
The Golden Bird and Other Fairy Tales of the Brothers Grimm, 1962
The Rabbit Catcher and Other Fairy Tales of Ludwig Bechstein, 1962
The Three Sisters, 1964
Snow-White and the Seven Dwarfs: A Tale from the Brothers Grimm, 1972
The Juniper Tree and Other Tales from Grimm, 1973
Goethe's Faust, Part I, 1976
The Fisherman and His Wife, 1980

EDITED TEXTS
The Anchor Book of Stories, 1958
The Best Short Stories of Rudyard Kipling, 1961
The English in England, 1962
In the Vernacular: The English in India, 1963
Six Russian Short Novels, 1963

MISCELLANEOUS
Jerome: The Biography of a Poem, 1971

Further reading

Ferguson, Suzanne. *The Poetry of Randall Jarrell*, 1971.
Flynn, Richard. *Randall Jarrell and the Lost World of Childhood*, 1992.
Longenbach, James. "Randall Jarrell's Semifeminine Mind," in *The Southwest Review*. Summer, 1996.
Lowell, Robert, Peter Taylor, and Robert Penn Warren, eds. *Randall Jarrell 1914–1965*, 1967.
Nemerov, Howard. *Poetry and Fiction*, 1963.
Pritchard, William H. *Randall Jarrell: A Literary Life*, 1990.
Quinn, Sister Bernetta. *Randall Jarrell*, 1981.
Rosenthal, M. L. *Randall Jarrell*, American Writers Pamphlet 103, 1972.
Shapiro, Karl. *Randall Jarrell*, 1967.
Vendler, Helen. "The Inconsolable," in *The New Republic*. July 23, 1990.
Williamson, Alan. "Jarrell, The Mother, The Marchen," in *Twentieth Century Literature*. Fall, 1994.

JOAN COREY SEMONELLA

See also American Literary Theory: Twentieth Century

Hans Robert Jauss

German theorist

Born: Göppingen, Germany; December 12, 1921
Died: Constance, Germany; March 1, 1997

Biography

After spending two winters on the Russian front in World War II and having completed one semester in Prague, Hans Robert Jauss began studying Romance philology, history, philosophy, and German studies at the University of Heidelberg in 1948. Both Martin Heidegger and Hans-Georg Gadamer were influential teachers for him during this period of his education. Four years later he received his doctorate with a dissertation on Marcel Proust and later his habilitation with his manuscript on medieval animal literature in 1957. He embarked on an academic career, being hired first as a lecturer at the University of Heidelberg and then as an associate professor two years later at the University of Münster in Westphalia. In 1961 he was promoted to full professor at the University of Giessen, where he stayed until accepting his position at the newly founded University of Constance in 1966. It was in Constance in the late 1960s and early 1970s, during a period of student unrest in Germany, that Jauss began publishing on literary theory and became known as a founder of the Constance School of Reception Aesthetics. Although Jauss also taught as a guest professor at the University of Zürich, the Free University of Berlin, Columbia University, Yale University, the Sorbonne, the University of California at Berkeley, and at the University of Wisconsin at Madison, the center for his academic studies remained in Constance, Germany. Throughout his career he taught countless courses on literary theory, aesthetics, hermeneutics, and Romance literatures in various academic departments and was instrumental in forging the then new academic discipline of *Literaturwissenschaft* (Literary Studies). In 1980 Jauss became a member of the Heidelberg Academy of Science. From his retirement in 1987 to his death in 1997, Jauss lived outside Constance as professor emeritus.

Influence

As one of the two major theorists of the so-called Constance School of Reception Aesthetics, Jauss has had a major impact on the development of European literary scholarship. By broadening critics' understanding of literature to include the aesthetic experience of its readers, Jauss has brought a new dimension to literary analysis and interpretation. His ideas regarding reception aesthetics have also influenced Anglo-American theory in its close relationship to the basic tenets of reader-response criticism.

Analysis

Jauss' prominence as a literary theorist began with his recognition of the need to revolutionize the study of literature. In one of his earlier and often quoted essays, "Paradigmawechsel in der Literaturwissenschaft" (1969; paradigm shift in the study of literature), Jauss presents the study of literature as a study of its changing methods of inquiry. Jauss derived this notion from Thomas Kuhn's influential account of the evolution of scientific knowledge, presented in his book *The Structure of Scientific Revolutions* (1964). Like Kuhn, Jauss sees the growth of academic knowledge as dependent on the continual emergence of new paradigms, of innovative methods of investigation which become generally recognized and accepted by scholars as being effective in solving various academic problems. As in scientific fields, older paradigms compete with and are slowly supplanted by new ones during periods when their effectiveness in providing adequate insights or explanations is questioned. From a brief survey of past literary criticism, Jauss concludes that the study of literature, plagued by a complete lack of methodological consensus, has entered such a revolutionary stage in its development.

From his assessment of major developments in the discipline, he determines that critics have variously applied one of three basic paradigms, all of which Jauss claims are in the process of becoming obsolete. The earliest he terms "classical-humanist," an approach which evaluates artistic works by comparing them to works generally considered masterpieces. The two more recent paradigms he calls the "historicist-positivist" approach, classifying works in terms of their historical or national origins, and the more recent "aesthetic-formalist" paradigm, producing stylistic studies of the "immanent" workings of texts themselves. This approach to literature, influenced by Russian Formalism and promoted in Germany by critics such as Emil Staiger and Wolfgang Kayser, established the tenor of most literary scholarship during the 1960s and 1970s. Jauss detected the stagnation of this paradigm, which regarded literary texts primarily as autonomous systems of poetic devices and stylistic effects, in what he saw as an elitist and politically conservative aesthetic based on a concept of "art for art's sake."

Jauss, writing at a time when the political atmosphere at most German universities had taken a more literary turn, rejected a rationale for literary studies which completely ignored the "socially formative function" of literature. The social and, by extension, historical limitations inherent in such an approach were evident to Jauss and his colleagues at the University of Constance. On the other hand, Jauss claimed that the equally popular and concurrent Marxist literary approach, employing a method resembling the historicist-positivist paradigm, while historically grounded, was at the same time aesthetically naive. Jauss discussed the inadequacy of past paradigms in order to underscore the crisis existing in the discipline of literary study and to provide an orientation to what he then only dimly perceived to be the next stage in this development.

Addressing the European academic community in what has come to be regarded as one of his most influential works, "Literaturgeschichte als Provokation der Literaturwissenschaft" (1967; "Literary History as a Challenge to Literary Theory," 1970), Jauss called for a radical rewriting of literary history. In this proclamation, which has been translated into sixteen languages, Jauss attempts to bridge the gap between the two predominant, yet antithetical literary approaches applied by Formalists and Marxists. Both literary schools, he claims, limit an understanding of literature by restricting their analyses to investigations of either the aesthetic or materialistic aspects involved in the work's representation or production. Jauss objects to the Marxists' overemphasis of art's mimetic function, while commending the Marxists' recognition of the importance of historical contexts. On the other hand, Jauss rejects the strictly textual focus of the Formalists as being too narrow and self-contained, while applauding their reliance on aesthetic analysis as a critical tool. Jauss saw both methods as failing to connect literature with history, aesthetic with historical perceptions.

He sought to unite these distinctions by emphasizing literature's progressive nature. By combining the Formalist assessment of art (as an ongoing transformation of rhetorical systems) with the Marxist concept of history (as a sequence of changing social circumstances), Jauss sought to emphasize literature's dynamic nature. Like Hans-Georg Gadamer, Jauss and other reception theorists opposed previous historians' reliance on historical objectivism, a static view of history as a series of self-evident events existing in a causal relationship to one another. Jauss preferred literary history not to be understood as a mere positivistic compilation of facts about individual authors and works but rather as a "*geschichtlicher Prozess ästhetischer Rezeption und Produktion*," a continual transformation of changing aesthetic perceptions of them.

To avoid contributing to previous static portrayals of literary history, Jauss proposed introducing a new dimension to critical theory, that of the work's reception. This new consideration required a shift in critical awareness from studies concerned with authors and their works exclusively to a third and more important subject of literary investigation: the reader. Reception theorists, such as Jauss and his colleague Wolfgang Iser, consider an investigation of readers' responses to a work to be an indispensable requirement for the interpretation of the literary work itself. Both of these critics, although developing different aspects of reception theory, maintain that a literary text cannot function independently of its readers, that indeed the present relevance of a work is dependent on an audience's interaction with it, on its being received and judged by someone. An appreciation of this complex relationship between reader and text serves as a corrective to the misperception of literary works as permanent receptacles of fixed meanings.

Whereas Iser investigated the typical reader's constitutive role in the reading process, Jauss worked on developing an aesthetic of reception, or *Rezeptionsästhetik*, on analyzing how a literary work is perceived or evaluated by an audience. This aesthetic of reception is concerned not only with recording the effect a given work has or has had on a particular audience but also with analyzing the *Wirkungsbedingungen des Textes*, the parameters responsible for allowing for that effect. The parameter Jauss finds particularly important is the reader's literary preconceptions. Jauss theorizes that readers deduce certain aesthetic conventions of style, theme, and genre from their previous contact with literature and literary topics. A work should be "considered in contrast to the background of works which the author could expect his contemporary public to know either explicitly or implicitly." These previous literary encounters create a frame of reference, or a "horizon of expectation" (*Erwartungshorizont*), for the reader, which affects his or her ultimate aesthetic assessment of the work. By relying on readers' literary experiences instead of their life experiences, Jauss hopes to bypass the difficulty of explaining idiosyncratic reader responses, which he considered to be the result of individual psychological reactions. This concept of readers' "horizons of expectation," which has itself been received with some skepticism, is an elaboration and combination of the phenomenological concept of "horizon" originating in the philosophies of Edmund Husserl and Martin Heidegger and the concept of "expectation" as applied in the fields of sociology and art history.

For the engaged reader, such expectations are continually subjected to a process of adjustment and refinement, *Horizontwandel*, as they are constantly either confirmed, challenged, appended, or disproved by the literary work. Readers engaging in this process of confrontation are engaging in a dialogue with the literary text which, in turn, alters their expectations for subsequent texts. Not only are readers' expectations redefined as the individual work unfolds but their reactions also change according to previous readers' responses. The interaction between one reader and one text Jauss generally defines as "reading," as opposed to "understanding," which involves the reader's comparing his or her reading experience and resulting aesthetic judgments to those of previous readers. By tracing these aesthetic judgments over a period of time, literary historians are able to show that a work's historical relevance is dependent on the responses of successive readers. Only after considering the degree to which a work approximates its audience's expectations – as measured, for example, by its past and present success, rejection, or delayed acceptance – can critics begin to estimate the aesthetic and historic value of an author's work. It is at this point that readers become critics and that Jauss' aesthetic approach to reception takes on a historical dimension.

The proliferation of studies generated in response to Jauss' original challenge attests the impressive impact his work has had on the academic communities of Europe and, to a lesser degree, the United States. Jauss, prompted by the mixed reaction to his work, later published an additional collection of essays, *Ästhetische Erfahrung und literarische Hermeneutik* (1977; *Aesthetic Experience and Literary Hermeneutics*, 1982), which generally modifies his claim that reception theory alone would revolutionize the study of literature. Yet this collection does not minimize the significance of his contribution to the field. Indeed, Jauss' reception theory helped rescue literature from its entrenchment in traditional modes of evaluation. By lending new impetus for a reconsideration of literary history, Jauss' theory prevented the historical relevancy of literary texts from disappearing completely in what was becoming an increasingly meticulous discussion of their poetic devises. No longer were the texts themselves to dominate the spotlight so exclusively, as meaning was now seen to be determined by readers' interaction with the texts, not encapsulated in the works themselves.

Jauss' last book, *Wege des Verstehens* (1994; ways of understanding), a collection of his essays written between 1985 and 1993, defends hermeneutics and rejects what he sees as the dogmatic relativism of poststructuralism and deconstructionism. While limiting the deconstructionists' infinite "play of the signifier" and rejecting the impossibility of "shared meaning," (a concept formulated earlier by his teacher Hans-Georg Gadamer), Jauss also censors the equally dogmatic practice from within hermeneutics of halting dialogue by affixing a single permanent meaning to an artistic work. Instead Jauss espouses the model of a literary hermeneutics that is not monologic, rendering the "other" speechless, but is rather dialogic, crossdisciplinary, and integrative. For him, while always incomplete, the process of understanding emerges out of a dialectic grounded in the hermeneutical category of the ever widening horizon.

Though Jauss' influence is not as widely acknowledged in Anglo-American schools of criticism as is that of his colleague Wolfgang Iser, his impact has nevertheless been significant. The loosely integrated American school of reader-response criticism, including such prominent critics as Stanley Fish and to a lesser degree Michael Riffaterre and Norman Holland, shares several of Jauss' basic assumptions. Jauss also demonstrates an affinity with Paul Ricœur's *critical hermeneutics* in his response to the Gadamer–Habermas debate. In its emphasis on literary and social conventions and the reading community, reception theory has also influenced other critics, such as Peter Bürger, to investigate the role various institutions play in dictating acceptable literary norms and works.

Principal criticism

Zeit und Erinnerung in Marcel Prousts "À la recherche du temps perdu," 1955
Untersuchungen zur mittelalterlichen Tierdichtung, 1959
Genèse de la poésie à allégorique française au moyen âge, 1962
Parallèle des anciens et des modernes en ce qui regarde les arts et les sciences, 1964 (editor)
"Literaturgeschichte als Provokation der Literaturwissenschaft," 1967 ("Literary History as a Challenge to Literary Theory," 1970)
"Paradigmawechsel in der Literaturwissenschaft," in *Linguistische Berichte*. 3 (1969)
Literaturgeschichte als Provokation, 1970
Kleine Apologie der ästhetischen Erfahrung, 1972
Alterität und Modernität der mittelalterlichen Literatur: Gesammelte Aufsätze, 1956–1976, 1977
Ästhetische Erfahrung und literarische Hermeneutik, 1977 (*Aesthetic Experience and Literary Hermeneutics*, 1982)
Pour une esthétique de la réception, 1978 (*Toward an Aesthetic of Reception*, 1982).
Art Social and Art Industrial: Funktionen der Kunst im Zeitalter des Industrialismus, 1987 (edited with Helmut Pfeiffer and Françoise Gaillard)
Studien zum Epochenwandel der ästhetischen Moderne, 1989
Wege des Verstehens, 1994

Other major works and literary forms

Hans Robert Jauss is known primarily for his literary theory and literary criticism.

Further reading

Grimm, Gunter, ed. *Literatur und Leser*, 1975.
——. *Rezeptionsgeschichte: Grundlegung einer Theorie*, 1977.
——. "Beyond Reception Aesthetics," in *New German Critique*. XXVIII (Winter, 1983), pp. 108–146.
Holub, Robert C. *Reception Theory: A Critical Introduction*, 1984.
——. *Crossing Borders: Reception Theory, Poststructuralism, Deconstruction*, 1992.
Rush, Ormond. *The Reception of Doctrine: An Appropriation of Hans Robert Jauss' Reception Aesthetics and Literary Hermeneutics*, 1997.
Suleiman, Susan R., and Inge Crosman, eds. *The Reader in the Text: Essays on Audience and Interpretation*, 1980.
Tompkins, Jane P., ed. *Reader-Response Criticism: From Formalism to Post-Structuralism*, 1980.

JENNIFER HAM

See also Iser; Reception Theory

Samuel Johnson

English writer, editor, and lexicographer

Born: Lichfield, England; September 18, 1709
Died: London, England; December 13, 1784

Biography

Samuel Johnson was born in Lichfield, Staffordshire, England, on September 18, 1709, the son of Michael Johnson and the former Sara Ford. His father was a bookseller who never prospered; his mother came from a Stratford gentry family. As an infant Johnson was accidentally put out to nurse with a tubercular woman. As a result he was, in his own words, "a poor, diseased infant, almost blind." The repercussions were profound: Johnson grew up ungainly, hard of sight, and prey to indolence. Poor health restricted his activity and made him a voracious reader. From 1717 to 1725 he attended the local grammar school, where he excelled in Latin.

Johnson attended Pembroke College, Oxford, as a commoner, for thirteen months (October, 1728 to December, 1729) before lack of money forced him to leave. Suffering from deep depression, Johnson lived for two years at home until his father died. After a brief, unsuccessful attempt at a teaching career, Johnson went to Birmingham, wrote for a newspaper, and, in 1735, published a translation of a travel book. In the same year he married Elizabeth Porter, a widow, and opened a boarding school near Lichfield.

In 1737 Johnson decided to make a career as a writer. He worked steadily and anonymously for *Gentleman's Magazine* and began publishing poetry under his own name. The work was not lucrative, but he made a living and established himself as a recognized author. For eight years (1747–1755) he labored over the massive *A Dictionary of the English Language*, which was published to universal acclaim. His wife died in 1752.

For the next thirty years, Johnson presided over London literary life so remarkably that literary historians label the period "The Age of Johnson." A pension from George III in 1762 allowed Johnson some financial security. He wrote less but reviewed books and talked about literature incessantly. In 1764 he helped found the famed Literary Club with Sir Joshua Reynolds, Edmund Burke, Oliver Goldsmith, and others. He died on December 13, 1784, in London and was buried in Westminster Abbey.

Influence

Johnson is regarded as the last and perhaps greatest neoclassical critic writing in English. He articulated the spirit of neoclassicism, while weaning it from a reductionist reliance upon rules and categories. In place of the superficial critical conventions of his day (which often made criticism a partisan in the political, religious, and social arguments of the time), Johnson urged serious scholarship and lively aesthetic response. Johnson approached reading as an important imaginative act and commentary as the product of research into linguistic, biographical, and historical contexts. Though an imperfect practitioner of his own methods, Johnson was nevertheless a model for subsequent critics. He brought literary criticism to an audience of general readers by giving serious attention to new, popular genres (such as biography and prose fiction) outside the traditional canon.

Analysis

Johnson's writings comment continually on the interdependent topics of authors, books, and critics. Johnson is simultaneously an idealist and a skeptic about the literary world. He perceived a Manichaean world where writers and critics either bring the light of truth to human experience or worship the darkness of ego-induced error.

Ideally, a poet (to use Johnson's word for an imaginative writer) and a critic cooperate in the task of teaching readers to be wise. The poet presents the truths of human existence by adorning them with the graces of art so that the intellect takes "a second view of things hastily passed over or negligently regarded." The critic judges the poet's performance, studies his or her means of pleasing, and recommends the work to contemporaries and to posterity.

Johnson knew equally well the dark side of the literary world. The man beneath the poet's laurels may be no more moral or any wiser about truth; he may write in order to make money rather than to teach. He may care more about his own fanciful graces of art than for enlightening the intellect. The critic may equally pervert his calling through vanity or ignorance. Johnson describes some who take up criticism because they "either imagine it their duty, or make it their amusement, to hinder the reception of every work of genius." Johnson's aim as critic was to show the errors of false criticism and to establish ends and means for true criticism.

Johnson's exemplum of the bad critic is Dick Minim, described in *The Rambler*, issues 60 and 61 (1750). Like others "whom Nature has made weak, and Idleness keeps ignorant," Minim endeavors to "support his vanity by the name of a Critick." He needs only "the common course of puerile studies," the companionship of coffeehouse companions, and memorization of "a few select writers" in order to spout the interpretive clichés of the day. He takes bold-sounding but vague positions: Art copies Nature; all writers have faults as well as beauties; the modern age lacks the literary giants of the past; poetry contains hidden beauties awaiting detection by an ingenious reader. Minim's credentials admit him to a Critical Society wherein he pontificates on the latest poems or plays with a "few favourite epithets" (such as "manly" or "stiff") that have "no settled meaning." He quickly finds grave faults in new writers if "he finds the publick against them." Nothing pleases Minim more than to advise aspiring authors with high-sounding but empty phrases: "read none but the best Authors . . . study his beauties, but avoid his faults . . . catch those moments when he finds his thoughts expanded and his genius exalted, but to take care lest imagination hurry him beyond the bounds of Nature."

Minim's vocabulary is a debased neoclassicism, and his pose a parody of the Augustan man of letters. After the Restoration of Charles II, British literary critics modeled themselves upon Italian and French neoclassicists. These European critics perceived a need to bring order to the literary world by articulating standards which measured the quality of a poet's performance. They based these standards upon the authority of Greek and Roman authors: the theories of Aristotle about tragedy, Horace about poetry, and Quintilian on rhetoric as well as the practice of poets such as Homer, Virgil, and Ovid. On topics on which the ancient authors were silent, the neoclassicists tried to make logical extrapolations.

Neoclassical criticism is built on several basic ideas. First, poetry is an art that copies or imitates Nature, which is an unchanging order or pattern in the world. Since Nature is the same today as in the past, the art of those who first discovered Nature (the ancients) should guide the practice of those who follow (the moderns). Literary works exist in a hierarchical order of genres, ranging from the highest (epic and tragedy) to the lowest (comedy and satire), depending upon whether the genre imitates the best in Nature (godlike heroism) or the worst (human folly). Each genre has distinctive, unalterable rules. Poets win fame insofar as they successfully follow these rules. Poets aim to instruct readers in Nature's truth by pleasing them with artful devices appropriate to each genre.

Dick Minim expresses Johnson's insight that by the mid-1700s neoclassicism had become stagnant. It had degenerated from a noble effort to link the present with the past and inspire modern writers through previous achievement to a mechanical system or mere checklist that any unthinking person might apply under the misapprehension that he or she is a competent judge. Johnson's own criticism is an effort to revitalize neoclassicism by redefining its vaguer terms and expanding its categories.

The earlier English critics most influential upon Johnson are John Dryden (1631–1700), Joseph Addison (1672–1719), and Alexander Pope (1688–1744). Each embodies a virtue that Johnson sees as essential to the task of criticism:

> to establish principles; to improve opinion into knowledge; and to distinguish those means of pleasing which depend upon known causes and rational deduction from the nameless and inexplicable elegancies which appeal wholly to the fancy .... Criticism reduces those regions of literature under the dominion of the sciences, which have hitherto known only the anarchy of ignorance, the caprices of fancy, and the tyranny of prescription.

To Johnson, Dryden is "the father of English criticism, as the writer who first taught us to determine upon principles the merit of composition." Addison improved the public's knowledge of literature by presenting it "in the most alluring form, not lofty and austere, but accessible and familiar." Pope displays in works such as *An Essay on Criticism* (1711) "such extent of comprehension, such nicety of distinction, such acquaintance with mankind, and such knowledge of both ancient and modern learning." The virtues of Dryden, Addison, and Pope are the virtues of Johnson the critic: he proceeds upon principle; he addresses a public, not professional, audience in accessible, familiar forms; he bases his judgments upon a profound knowledge of human experience in general as well as wide reading of ancient and modern literature.

Johnson's revitalization of neoclassical criticism begins with a reaffirmation of one term and the redefinition of two. The term he reaffirms is "truth." Like the poet, the critic must be concerned with truth. Truth for Johnson is, most importantly, religious and moral truth, which guides the choices that people make daily. Believing that "human life is everywhere a state in which much is to be endured, and little to be enjoyed," Johnson knew that an individual had to achieve happiness by an ordered understanding rather than by seeking something outside the self. Poetry and criticism contribute to that ordering process: "The only end of writing is to enable readers better to enjoy life, or better to endure it" Johnson's reaffirmation is striking because few critics before or after so explicitly link individual happiness to truth.

The first term Johnson redefines is "Nature." For most of his contemporaries, "nature" referred to an abstraction: the order, coherence, and pattern of the world. Johnson concretizes this abstract concept in "nature" and "life." Nature, as the philosopher Imlac (often a spokesman for Johnson's opinions), in Johnson's novel *The Prince of Abissinia: A Tale* (1759; later known as *Rasselas*) describes, is the physical world. In "the plants of the garden, the animals of the wood, the minerals of the earth, and the meteors of the sky" the poet finds the images which adorn and make vivid moral or religious truth. By "life" Johnson means the varied states of happiness or of misery in which people of all classes and nations live. In both cases, however, the poet's business is "to examine, not the individual but the species . . . to rise to general and transcendent truth." This redefinition of Nature, concretized into the physical world and human society, gives Johnson a powerful new critical concept: general nature.

The other term Johnson redefines is the "pleasure" that literature gives in addition to instruction. For the traditional neoclassical critic, the explanation of literature's pleasure was never specific. Johnson, however, is eager to appreciate how a reader responds to literature. Readers are moved, he asserts, insofar as they "can more readily adopt the pains or pleasures proposed to [their] minds." This identification is a fiction into which the reader enters knowingly, willingly, and wholeheartedly through the power of the imagination:

> All joy or sorrow for the happiness or calamities of others is produced by an act of the imagination, that realizes the event, however fictitious, or approximates it, however remote, by placing us, for a time, in the condition of him whose fortune we contemplate; so that we feel while the deception lasts, whatever motions would be excited by the same good or evil happening to our selves.

These concepts of truth, general nature, and imaginative identification allow Johnson to rethink or to reject several assumptions of neoclassicism. Johnson incisively evaluates new genres of literature that have no standing in the neoclassical hierarchy yet are steadily replacing the traditional genres. The new genres of the eighteenth century (the novel, the travel book, the biography) are widely read and attract young authors eager for fame. Yet they are not easily discussed in the vocabulary of neoclassical criticism, as Henry Fielding's preface to *Joseph Andrews* (1742) shows.

The novelist's effort to place his new kind of work within the traditional hierarchy ironically hinges on a lost precedent of which no exact details exist.

In *The Rambler*, issue 4 (March, 1750), Johnson has no trouble describing critically the appeal of "modern romances" (the novel). They are clearly preferable to the ancient romances, medieval tales of giants, knights, and castles, because "they exhibit life in its true state, diversified only by accidents that daily happen in the world, and influenced by passions and qualities which are really to be found in conversing with mankind." This premise underlies an important conclusion that anticipates the nineteenth- and twentieth-century debates about the quality of popular fiction. Novels "are written chiefly to the young, the ignorant, and the idle, to whom they serve as lectures of conduct, and introductions into life." Novelists therefore exert great influence over readers, which they can use on behalf of truth or can waste on mere diversion.

In *The Rambler* 60 (October, 1750), Johnson praises the fledgling genre of biography for a similar quality: to present circumstances and images that mirror the reader's own experience. Because it can attract readers, "no species of writing seems more worthy of cultivation, since none can be more delightful or more useful, none can more certainly enchain the heart by irresistable interest, or more widely diffuse instruction to every diversity of condition." By knowing what readers respond to, Johnson can suggest do's and don't's for the biographer: do notice the habits or actions that reveal character; don't merely list the chronology of achievements; do conduct research among the subject's family, friends, and papers.

In *The Idler* 97 (February, 1760), Johnson criticizes the quality of current travel books. Johnson remarks that too many travelers forget that it is their task to please the reader, not the reader's task to find pleasure in whatever is offered. Johnson faults travelers who record the obvious, "who pass a desert and say that it is sandy; who cross a valley and find that it is green." It is the travel writer's task to discover that which will engage the reader's imagination.

Johnson is as skeptical of "ancient rules" as he is eager to admit new genres to the literary pantheon. He argues against rules whenever he thinks they violate truth, nature, life, or the imaginative identification. In *The Idler* 37 (December, 1758), Johnson attacks the practices of contemporary pastoral poetry, which describe the English countryside in the fictions, images, and associations of a mythological golden age. Johnson challenges both the inherent logic and the ancient authority of such affectations. Searching the writings of Virgil, he finds no precedent in authority; he can only find a modern prejudice that, because real peasants could not match Virgil's shepherds in thought or harmonious speech, the poet must set his action in a remote Arcadia. If a prejudice, not truth, underlies a rule, that rule, for Johnson, has no critical authority.

Johnson's most famous confrontation with the rules occurs in the preface to his 1765 edition of William Shakespeare's plays. Reviewing Shakespeare's canon, Johnson observes that the plays are not in "the rigorous and critical sense either tragedies or comedies." Though the ancients could clearly distinguish tragic and comic modes of imitation, Shakespeare's dramas exhibit "the real state of sublunary nature, which partakes of good and evil, joy and sorrow . . . expressing the course of the world in which the loss of one is the gain of another; in which, at the same time the reveler is hasting to his wine, and the mourner is burying his friend." The mingled drama of Shakespeare is admittedly "a practice contrary to the rules of criticism," but "there is always an appeal open from criticism to nature."

By an appeal to nature, Johnson also defends Shakespeare's plays from the charge that they are faulty for failing to observe the unities of time and place which the French neoclassical playwright Pierre Corneille asserted possessed ancient authority. Johnson challenges the logic which holds that unities make drama credible. If the action onstage occurs one moment in Alexandria and the next in Rome, the neoclassical position holds, the spectator will not find the play credible. With magnificent common sense, Johnson rebuts the assumption: "The truth is that the spectators are always in their senses and know from the first act to the last that the stage is only a stage, and that players are only players."

Johnson's critical practice, in fact, calls more than dramatic rules into a new examination. It challenges the training, mental habits, and intellectual categories of contemporary critics. Minim is a bad critic because he is stupid as well as vain. As Alexander Pope's famous couplet warns, "a little learning is a dangerous thing." A few clichés go to a critic's head. Like many contemporaries, Minim ignores the injunction of Pope's second line: "Drink deep, or taste not the Pierian spring."

Johnson, on the other hand, drinks deeply of intellectual springs. His literary criticism stands out because of its intelligence. Johnson replaces the critic's reliance upon a few clichés, a static hierarchy, and a body of rules with linguistic and textual standards as well as biographical and historical methods. Here, too, Johnson goes beyond previous neoclassical notions by defining a concept concretely that Dryden, Addison, and Pope had left abstract. Early-eighteenth-century commentators on literature combined criticism with wit and scorned deliberate or systematic scholarly endeavor. Early in the 1700s, for example, Richard Bentley's efforts to establish reliable texts for ancient writers only made Jonathan Swift and Pope label him a pedant.

The opening sentence of Johnson's first sustained critical writing, *Miscellaneous Observations on the Tragedy of Macbeth* (1745), states a principle that underlies his three major undertakings in criticism, *A Dictionary of the English*

Language (1755), *The Plays of William Shakespeare* (1765), and *Prefaces, Biographical and Critical, to the Works of the English Poets* (1779–1781): "In order to make a true estimate of the abilities and merits of a writer," Johnson asserts, "it is always necessary to examine the genius of his age and the opinions of his contemporaries." Immediately Johnson begins to discuss Renaissance ideas on witchcraft in order to comment on *Macbeth*'s opening scene. In addition to textual commentary based on historical knowledge, Johnson does several things: he relies on the earliest texts, takes cognizance of collateral readings, and restrains conjectures about obscure or disputed passages. This methodology is rare in literary critics of Johnson's time but it is standard for modern scholars.

Johnson knows English literature before 1660 better than his predecessors or his contemporaries. Whether writing his commentary on Shakespeare, finding quotations from the authors "which rose in the time of Elizabeth" to illustrate the definitions in his dictionary, or researching biographical materials for the various prefaces, Johnson demonstrates his self-confessed "zeal for the past." Knowledge of the previous century's manners, superstitions, language, and traditions, as well as its literature, informs Johnson's determination to know the context in which a writer worked. If the critic is to recognize genius so that he may bestow immortality upon it, the critic is curious "to discover the instruments, as well as to survey the workmanship, to know how much is to be ascribed to original powers, and how much to casual and adventitious help."

The reform that Johnson brings to neoclassicism is, in a sense, paradoxical. Even as he urges the critic to appreciate the power of the writer to create an imaginative experience for the reader, he urges the critic to establish principles that may "improve opinion into knowledge."

At the end of the eighteenth century, a Romantic sensibility became prominent. Like other revolutionary ways of thinking, it succeeded by overstating the faults of the preceding concept. In the general reaction against neoclassicism, Johnson was reduced to an opinionated, superficial commentator. To the generation of William Wordsworth, Samuel Taylor Coleridge, and Percy Bysshe Shelley, Johnson became Dick Minim. What the generation overlooked was the debt owed to Johnson. Wordsworth based his *Lyrical Ballads* (1798) on the concept of "general nature." Coleridge noted that the readers' "willing suspension of disbelief" was the central imaginative act, just as Johnson did. Shelley called poets "the unacknowledged legislators of the World," echoing Imlac's description in *Rasselas*.

Until the early twentieth century, Johnson's reputation as a critic languished. Gradually it revived as modern criticism realized how its own methods and principles are prefigured in Johnson's editorial practice and concept of historical context. In many ways, Johnson's work has been superseded. He did not possess the library resources and mechanical aids which today assist the editor in preparing a reliable text. He did not have access to or even know about the document collections which support the modern biographer. He did not have access to libraries filled with old and new editions of the minor as well as major works of Renaissance and Restoration literature. Some of his judgments are admittedly founded on sketchy, even erroneous, evidence.

What is not sketchy or erroneous is the quality of Johnson's thinking. The modern student will find much that is engaging about Johnson's criticism. The first quality is his knowledge of the act of reading. Johnson was a voracious reader who seldom read a book all the way through. He was an eager reader who deeply resented a work or an author that bored him. He was a reader of the Great Books who delighted in popular literature. Johnson the reader always looks over the shoulder of Johnson the critic: he represents the general nature to which criticism's judgments may be appealed.

Johnson's second quality is his knowledge of the act of writing. A poet, dramatist, and fiction writer himself, he knew the ambitions, the struggles, and the hazards which surrounded publication. This experience provides insights into the relationship between the writer's life and texts. *Prefaces, Biographical and Critical, to the Works of the English Poets* is a fascinating work because Johnson feels free to assess frankly a writer's beauties and faults, both as a poet and as a person. His assessment hinges not on a mechanical application of literary or moral rules but on an act of imaginative identification. As Johnson wrote in *The Rambler* 60, "We are all prompted by the same motives, all deceived by the same fallacies, all animated by hope, obstructed by danger, entangled by desire, and seduced by pleasure."

Johnson's third quality is his knowledge of the act of criticizing. For Johnson, criticism was a human activity, equally open to achievement and folly. Often Johnson talks frankly to the reader. For example, he prefaces *A Dictionary of the English Language* with an evaluation of the work's strengths and weaknesses, including an admission that he abridged the work simply to be finished. Then he concludes poignantly, "I have protracted my work till most of those whom I wished to please have sunk into the grave, and success and miscarriage are empty sounds." In the preface to the edition of Shakespeare's plays, he ends his attack on the unities with an admission, "I am almost frightened at my own temerity, and when I estimate the fame and strength of those that maintain the contrary opinion am ready to sink down in reverential silence." Johnson's writings are filled with similar candid remarks that record the critic's hopes and fears about his own profession and his ability to live up to its expectations. Johnson struggled to raise literary criticism to a science, but he practiced it steadily as an art.

Principal criticism

Miscellaneous Observations on the Tragedy of Macbeth, 1745
Essays in *The Rambler*, 1750–1752
A Dictionary of the English Language: To Which Are Prefixed, a History of the Language, and an English Grammar, 1755 (2 volumes)
Essays in *The Idler*, 1758–1760
Preface and notes to *The Plays of William Shakespeare*, 1765 (8 volumes)
Prefaces, Biographical and Critical, to the Works of the English Poets, 1779–1781 (10 volumes; later known as *The Lives of the Poets*)
The Critical Opinions of Samuel Johnson, 1923, 1961 (Joseph Epes Brown, editor)

Other major works and literary forms

Samuel Johnson is the preeminent English man of letters in the latter eighteenth century. In addition to criticism he wrote substantial amounts of poetry and fiction, a play, many essays on moral issues, political pamphlets, a travelogue, several short biographies, and numerous prefaces to the books, plays, and poems of contemporary writers. There is hardly a genre of the age that Johnson did not attempt.

NOVEL
The Prince of Abissinia: A Tale, 1759 (2 volumes; later known as *Rasselas*).

PLAY
Irene: A Tragedy, 1749

POETRY
London: A Poem in Imitation of the Third Satire of Juvenal, 1738
The Vanity of Human Wishes: The Tenth Satire of Juvenal Imitated, 1749
Poems: The Yale Edition of the Works of Samuel Johnson, 1965 (volume 6; E. L. McAdam, Jr., and George Milne, editors)

NONFICTION
Commentary on Pope's "Essay on Man," 1738–1739
Marmer Norfolciense, 1739
A Compleat Vindication of the Licensers of the State, 1739
An Account of the Life of Mr. Richard Savage, Son of the Earl Rivers, 1744
The False Alarm, 1770
Thoughts on Falkland's Islands, 1771
The Patriot, 1774
Taxation No Tyranny, 1775
A Journey to the Western Islands of Scotland, 1775

TRANSLATION
Voyage to Abyssinia, 1735

MISCELLANEOUS
The Works of Samuel Johnson, 1787–1789 (12 volumes; Arthur Murphy, editor, numerous editions)

Further reading

Bate, Walter J. "Johnson as a Critic," in *The Achievement of Samuel Johnson*, 1955.
Brownell, Morris R. *Samuel Johnson's Attitude to the Arts*, 1989.
Damrosch, Leopold, Jr. *The Uses of Johnson's Criticism*, 1976.
——. "Samuel Johnson and Reader-Response Criticism," in *Eighteenth Century: Theory and Interpretation*. XXI (1980), pp. 91–108.
Donner, H. W. "Dr. Johnson as a Literary Critic," in *Samuel Johnson: A Collection of Critical Essays*, 1965. Edited by Donald J. Greene.
Fussell, Paul. *Samuel Johnson's Literary Criticism*, 1952, 1967.
Leavis, F. R. "Johnson as Critic," in *Samuel Johnson: A Collection of Critical Essays*, 1965. Edited by Donald J. Greene.
Piper, William Bowman. "Samuel Johnson as an Exemplary Critic," in *Texas Studies in Language and Literature*. XX (1978), pp. 457–473.
Stock, R. D. *Samuel Johnson and Neo-Classical Dramatic Theory*, 1973.
Tomarken, Edward. *Johnson, Rasselas, and the Choice of Criticism*, 1989.

ROBERT M. OTTEN

See also Dryden; Hume; Neoclassical Literary Theory; Pope

Ben Jonson

English poet, playwright, and critic

Born: London, England; June 11, 1573
Died: London, England; August 6, 1637

Biography

Benjamin Jonson (originally Johnson) was born on June 11, 1573, in or near London, the posthumous son of a minister of Border ancestry who had lost his estate under Mary I. His widowed mother married a bricklayer. Jonson, probably through the patronage of the scholar William Camden, was able to get an excellent classical education at Westminster School, but he was unable to afford university training and was forced for a time to work at his stepfather's occupation, to the great amusement of his detractors. He served briefly in the English army in the Low Countries and later prided himself on having killed one of the enemy in single combat. In 1594 he married, apparently not happily, and soon after became associated with the theater, at first as an actor, but from 1598 onward as a playwright.

In spite of killing a fellow actor in a duel and becoming a recusant (Catholic convert) in prison, Jonson rose rapidly in the world, becoming not only a popular playwright but also a friend of scholars and nobles, a voluminous writer of masques for the court, the recipient of an honorary degree from Oxford University, and England's first poet laureate. Gradually, however, his good fortune declined. Ill health (he suffered a paralytic stroke in 1628), intemperate habits, his quarrelsome nature (he broke with Inigo Jones, who designed the scenery for his highly profitable masques), and changing fashions reduced him to poverty and decay, though he never lacked completely for friends and patrons. He died on August 6, 1637, and was buried in Westminster Abbey.

Influence

As a critic, Ben Jonson might best be described as an early or pioneer neoclassicist. Like John Dryden and Alexander Pope, he believed in imitating the ancients and in following the rules laid down by Aristotle and Horace. In his own time, however, he was a voice crying in the wilderness; in drama, at least, his theory had little influence beyond his immediate circle, the "Sons of Ben." After the Restoration, however, Dryden, who believed that Jonson in his *Discoveries* had given "as many and profitable rules for perfecting the stage as any wherewith the French can furnish us," took up Jonson's rather liberal neoclassicism, which in modified form lasted into the eighteenth century and was reflected in the thought of Samuel Johnson and Sir Joshua Reynolds.

Analysis

In considering Jonson as critic, it must be acknowledged that no major work of criticism that he himself prepared for the press is extant. (A commentary on Horace in dialogue form, in which John Donne appeared as "Criticus," was lost in a fire in Jonson's study.) The *Discoveries*, a substantial work that was published only after Jonson's death, consists largely of passages translated and adapted from classical and neo-Latin critics such as Daniel Heinsius and Joseph Scaliger; it may represent a commonplace book prepared for Jonson's own use or even a collection of loose papers, including rough drafts and lecture notes. It can be accepted as Jonson's own voice because he, after all, made the selections and adapted them to his own time and situation and because he unified them by his own vigorous style. Then there are the *Conversations*, table talk recorded by William Drummond of Hawthornden during Jonson's visit to Scotland, in which Jonson felt it unnecessary to restrain expression of his prejudices and enmities. Finally, various prologues and other miscellaneous pieces, which by their nature express only fragments of his theory, often provide a useful supplement. Taken together, these pieces, though produced at different times and under varying circumstances, reveal not only a unity of style and personality but a unity of principle as well, with only so much inconsistency as would rescue Jonson from a charge of pedantry and rigidity.

Jonson believed in imitating the ancients and in revering the ancient critics, particularly Horace and Aristotle; in the *Discoveries* he calls the latter "the first accurate critic, the truest judge, nay, the greatest philosopher the world has ever had." Yet Jonson clearly does not believe in a slavish imitation or in restricting "a poet's liberty within the narrow limits of laws." The poets, after all, came first; yet what they produced by nature and exercise "Aristotle hath brought into an art, because he understood the causes of things, and what other men do by chance or custom he doth by reason." Yet even Aristotle is not to be made a dictator: "Let Aristotle and others have their dues, but if we can make further discoveries of truth and fitness than they, why are we envied?" (Here Jonson echoes Francis Bacon.) Jonson's classicism is of a flexible and moderate kind. The ancients are "guides, not commanders"; writers should always keep them in sight without necessarily obeying them.

In harmony with his attitude toward the ancients are Jonson's thoughts on the nature of poetic creation, which he represents as springing from a combination of inborn instinct ("a goodness of natural wit") and a self-conscious critical faculty or "art." "Without art, nature can never be perfect, and without art nature can claim no being." Nature alone may produce a William Shakespeare, but art alone can only produce poets who are, in Pope's phrase, "coldly correct and regularly low." Natural wit is, after all, a gift, but art can be cultivated, and much of the *Discoveries* is concerned with the means of cultivation: exercise, imitation, "study and multiplication of reading," and, finally, art proper, the study of the rules of the critics.

The neoclassical fondness for analyzing poetry in terms of dialectical pairs of terms appears in Jonson's conception of the uses of poetry. Echoing Horace and Sir Philip Sidney, Jonson asserts that poetry ought to please and instruct (this formula has no warrant in Aristotle). As he says in the prologue to *Epicoene*, "The ends of all, who for the scene do write,/ Are, or should be, to profit and delight." Jonson, like Sidney, expects much of the poet; if his studies have given him "the exact knowledge of all virtues and their contraries, with ability to render the one loved, the other hated," he can "feign a commonwealth," can "govern it with counsels, strengthen it with laws, correct it with judgments, inform it with religion and morals."

As a follower of Aristotle, Jonson based his theory of poetry on the concept of mimesis, or imitation (not now the imitation of authors, but of nature). "Hence he is called a poet, not he which writeth in measure only, but that feigneth and formeth a fable and writes things like the truth"; the fable and fiction are, as it were, "the form and soul of any poetical work," he says in the *Discoveries*. This fiction is not mere factual truth or what we would call naturalism. As Jonson explains in the prologue to *Epicoene*, "poet never credit gained/ By writing truths, but things like truths, well feigned." "Things like truth" would exclude the kind of imaginative license allowed by Sidney. By making fable – the imitation of an action – the soul of poetry, Jonson seems to limit poetry to the narrative and dramatic kinds; yet this he clearly did not intend to do, for he says that "one alone verse" sometimes makes a perfect poem and maintains that epigrams cannot be narrations. To make his theory complete, he either would have to define "fable" to refer to something more than plot or would have to define a class of poems whose essence is something other than fable, as Ronald S. Crane, a modern Aristotelian, does. It must be remembered, however, that Jonson's theory is incomplete and fragmentary, and that the neoclassical tradition is not generally effective at handling lyric.

It is natural for Jonson as an Aristotelian (and a Horatian) to discuss poems in terms of genres or kinds. Concerning epic, he offers little in the *Discoveries* except an elaborate discussion of the unity of the fable in terms of Aristotle and his commentators. There was much talk at this time of the tangled relations of epic and romance, but although Jonson refers repeatedly to Edmund Spenser, it is generally in terms of disapproval of his stanza form and archaic language. "Yet I would have him read for his matter," but this matter he never discusses beyond reporting some bits of Spenser's allegory. On tragedy he disappoints by ignoring Aristotle's treatment of catharsis. *Sejanus* he admits to be "no true poem" since it lacks a chorus and violates the unity of time; these old conventions are incompatible "with preservation of any popular delight," but the play can be defended for its "truth of argument, dignity of persons, gravity and height of elocution, fulness and frequency of sentence" – standards Aristotelian enough. Comedy is treated more amply, both in the *Discoveries* and in the prologues to the plays. The unities are to be observed (and Jonson did in fact observe them); the plots are to be relatively realistic – "deeds and language such as men do use." On characters, Jonson perhaps goes beyond the type characters of Roman comedy in his theory of the humors. Ultimately, the metaphor is medical, but Jonson uses it to describe what we would call an obsession, Pope's "ruling passion," when "some one peculiar quality" draws a man's "affects, his spirits and his powers . . . all to run one way." Yet the distinction may not be important, for a character such as Morose could illustrate a particular humor while still conforming to a general type. Jonson follows Aristotle, or rather Heinsius, in regarding laughter as a fault in comedy; he is similarly opposed to "injuries to particular persons," since these may interfere with the reforming function of comedy. These late pronouncements are not in accord with Jonson's earlier practice.

Concerning lyric, Jonson left behind no coherent theory but many casual observations, especially in the *Conversations*. Drummond remarks that Jonson "detesteth all other rimes" than couplets and believed that "cross rimes and stanzas" were "all forced." Unless these remarks apply only to narrative poetry, however, they are inconsistent with Jonson's practice. Sonnets he regarded as Procrustean.

Many of Jonson's comments on his contemporaries are too fragmentary and informed with personal animosities to have much theoretical interest, but it is another matter with Donne and Shakespeare, with whom he was on cordial terms, yet toward whose poetry he expressed some ambivalence. According to Drummond, although Jonson "esteemeth John Donne the first poet in the world in some things," he also judged that "Donne, for not keeping of accent, deserved hanging" and "for not being understood, would perish." It is easy to see why Donne's versification and imagery would have offended Jonson's classical taste; it is to be regretted that he was not more specific about the things that made Donne "the first poet." With Shakespeare, the issue is simpler. "He had an open and free nature, had an excellent phantasy, brave notions, and gentle expression" but "wanted art," Jonson told Drummond; "his wit was in his own power; would the rule of it had been too." (The differing opinion expressed in Jonson's verses to Shakespeare is presumably attributable to the occasional nature of the poem.) This conception of Shakespeare persisted for so long that Samuel Taylor Coleridge felt compelled to refute it.

Jonson has often been made the foil of Shakespeare, as he was by Dryden: "I must acknowledge [Jonson] the more correct poet, but Shakespeare the greater wit." Although it would be inadequate to summarize Jonson's achievement merely as "correctness in imitation of the ancients," it is true that he took great pride in his faithfulness to classical tradition. He would surely have been pleased with the eulogy that Dryden put into the mouth of Crites in *Of Dramatic Poesy: An Essay* (1668): "I will produce Father Ben to you, dressed in all the ornaments and colours of the Ancients; you will need no other guide to our party, if you follow him."

Principal criticism

Prologue to *Every Man in His Humour*, 1598
Induction to *Every Man Out of His Humour*, 1599
Preface to *Sejanus His Fall*, 1603 (better known as *Sejanus*)
Prologue to *Volpone: Or, The Fox*, 1606
Prologue to *Epicoene: Or, The Silent Woman*, 1609
"To the Memory of My Beloved, the Author, Mr. William Shakespeare, and What He Hath Left Us," 1623
Timber: Or, Discoveries Made upon Men and Matter, 1641 (better known as *Discoveries*)
Informations by Ben Johnston to W. D. When He Came to Scotland on Foot 1619, 1711 (better known as *Conversations*)

Other major works and literary forms

Ben Jonson is one of those critics whose criticism was incidental to his career as a poet. Most notable are his comedies, of which the best are *Every Man in His Humour* (1598), *Every Man Out of His Humour* (1599), *Volpone* (1606), *Bartholomew Fair* (1614), and *The Alchemist* (1610). Beyond their intrinsic merits, these comedies are of interest because they were consciously written to accord with Jonson's neoclassical principles, including the unities of action, time, and place. They are in the Plautine tradition rather than the romantic tradition associated with William Shakespeare and contain some lively scenes of London low life. Less impressive are his tragedies, *Sejanus His Fall* (1603; better known as *Sejanus*) and *Catiline His Conspiracy* (1611; better known as *Catiline*), which are filled with translations from the Latin historians. Jonson was also the author of some thirty-five masques and the chief English practitioner of this hybrid art. Aside from drama, he wrote a great quantity of satires, epigrams, lyrics, and occasional verse, including the famous verses to Shakespeare and the still-popular "Drink to me only with thine eyes" (1616).

PLAYS
The Isle of Dogs, 1597 (with Thomas Nashe)
The Case Is Altered, 1597
Every Man in His Humour, 1598, 1605
Hot Anger Soon Cold, 1598 (with Henry Chettle and Henry Porter)
Every Man Out of His Humour, 1599
The Page of Plymouth, 1599 (with Thomas Dekker)
Robert the Second, King of Scots, 1599 (with Chettle and Dekker)
Cynthia's Revels: Or, The Fountain of Self-Love, 1600–1601
Poetaster: Or, His Arraignment, 1601
Sejanus His Fall, 1603 (better known as *Sejanus*)
Eastward Ho!, 1605 (with George Chapman and John Marston)
Volpone: Or, The Fox, 1607
Epicoene: Or, The Silent Woman, 1609
The Alchemist, 1610
Catiline His Conspiracy, 1611 (better known as *Catiline*)
Bartholomew Fair, 1614
The Devil Is an Ass, 1616
The Fortunate Isles and Their Union, 1626
The Staple of News, 1626
The New Inn: Or, The Light Heart, 1629
The Magnetic Lady: Or, Humours Reconciled, 1632
A Tale of a Tub, 1633
The Sad Shepherd: Or, A Tale of Robin Hood, 1640

POETRY
Poems, 1601
Epigrams, 1616
The Forest, 1616
Execration Against Vulcan, 1640
Underwoods, 1640

NONFICTION
The English Grammar, 1640

TRANSLATION
Horace His Art of Poetry, 1640 (of *Ars poetica*)

MISCELLANEOUS
The Workes of Benjamin Jonson, 1616
The Works of Benjamin Jonson, 1640–1641 (2 volumes)

Further reading

Atkins, J. W. H. *English Literary Criticism: The Renascence*, 1947.
Cave, Richard Allen. *Ben Jonson*, 1991.
Cave, Richard, Elizabeth Schafer, and Brian Woolland, eds. *Ben Jonson and Theatre: Performance, Practice and Theory*, 1999.
Dutton, Richard. *Ben Jonson, Authority and Criticism*, 1996.
Herford, C. H., Percy Simpson, and Evelyn Simpson. "Commentary on *Discoveries*," in *Ben Jonson*. Vol. 6, 1952.
Leggatt, Alexander. *Ben Jonson: His Vision and Art*, 1981.
Miles, Rosalind. *Ben Jonson: His Life and Work*, 1986.
——. *Ben Jonson: His Craft and Art*, 1990.
Norbrook, David. *Poetry and Politics in the English Renaissance*, 1984.
Riggs, David. *Ben Jonson: A Life*, 1989.
Walker, Ralph S., ed. Introduction to *Timber: Or, Discoveries Made upon Men and Matter*, 1953.

JOHN C. SHERWOOD

See also Puttenham; Renaissance and Restoration Literary Theory; Sidney

K

Lord Kames

(Henry Home, Lord Kames)

Scottish jurist, legal historian, philosopher, and critic

Born: Berwickshire, Scotland; 1696 (exact date unknown)
Died: Edinburgh, Scotland; December 27, 1782

Biography

Henry Home (pronounced and sometimes spelled "Hume") was born in 1696 on the modest family estate of Kames, or Kaims, three miles from the English border in southern Scotland. His father, George Home, was a chronically insolvent country gentleman and Justice of the Peace for the parish of Eccles. His mother was Agnes Walkinshaw of the Barrowfield Walkinshaws. Although he was distantly related to the Earls of nearby Home Castle, legendary participants in centuries of border wars, and to other branches of an illustrious family, Henry inherited neither title nor sufficiency. He suffered from his family's inability to finance his education but benefited from George Home's decision to break with his Jacobite roots and serve with the Hanoverian military against the 1715 Scottish uprising of "the '15." Three decades later, Henry made a similar choice during the final, futile Stuart rebellion of "the '45," and these two demonstrations of loyalty permitted the Crown appointments essential to his judicial career.

Home was tutored ineffectively at home until the age of sixteen or so, at which point he was sent to Edinburgh to apprentice in the law. With his move to Edinburgh, he undertook the lifelong project of his own education, reading widely and incessantly, hiring tutors, attending university lectures and classes, learning languages, discoursing and corresponding with the leading intellectuals of the day. The ambition, self assurance, discipline, and unflagging energy underlying his legal accomplishments crowned his intellectual endeavors as well. In 1723 he was admitted to the Bar as an advocate, a profession he followed successfully until 1752, when he was appointed to the Court of Session, Scotland's highest civil court. This judicial appointment gave him the nonhereditary title of Lord Kames. In 1763 Home became a Commissioner of the High Court of Justiciary, the comparable criminal court. He held both judgeships with distinction until his death.

In 1741, when his father died, he inherited the indebted Kames estate, and later the same year he married Agatha Drummond, with whom he had two children. He instituted numerous agricultural reforms to put the Kames holdings on a sound financial footing, and when Agatha unexpectedly inherited the extensive estate of Blair Drummond in 1766, he applied similarly progressive principles to its management. In giving up Bar for Bench, Home gave up an advocate's chance to make a fortune professionally, so estate management was more than merely a pastime.

Kames' literary career, and his lifetime interest in legal history and jurisprudence, began in 1728 with the publication of *Remarkable Decisions of the Court of Session, from 1716 to 1728*, the first of numerous accounts and analyses of Scottish and British law. In 1751 he published *Essays on the Principles of Morality and Natural Religion*, a reply to David Hume's religious skepticism liberal enough to get him tarred with the same brush of heresy used against his free-thinking friend. A rising circle of moderates within the Kirk led by Alexander Wedderburn, later the first Scottish Lord Chancellor of England, and the historian William Robertson defended Home from excommunication. Although the charges threatened no civil sanctions, fear of obloquy had a moderating influence on Home's subsequent writings and sharpened the growing intellectual distance between him and the irrepressibly iconoclastic Hume.

The year 1762 saw the appearance of the work on which Kames' reputation as a literary critic rests, *Elements of Criticism*, immensely influential in Britain, Europe, and the United States for over a century despite Voltaire's and Samuel Johnson's derisory responses. There are intriguing parallels between the *Elements of Criticism* and Kames' approach to jurisprudence. As an advocate and judge, as well as in his writings, Kames gained a reputation for supplanting bombastic rhetoric and the blind citing of precedents with incisive rational analysis. He placed himself strongly against the unthinking adoption of English common law, which he saw as mired in an inapplicable social history, and he also opposed the feudalism which continued, in shreds and patches, to encroach on Scottish life, especially in the Highlands. He believed that Scottish law should be based on rational and pragmatic principles and rooted more in Roman than English or local medieval traditions. He became his age's strongest advocate for equity, the Court's responsibility to judge right and wrong even in cases where neither statute nor precedent existed.

Kames' six-decade tenure as one of the foremost legal personalities in Edinburgh, his outgoing nature, crusty wit, and lively hospitality, his unquenchable and far-ranging intellectual curiosity, and his penetrating writings on law, history, criticism, farming, education, government, and moral philosophy placed him at the center of the extraordinary flowering of progressive thought in Scotland during the latter half of the eighteenth century. The literati he befriended, patronized, or engaged in dialogue included his distant relative David Hume, Adam Smith, James Boswell, Hugh Blair, Thomas Reid, Elizabeth Montagu, and Benjamin Franklin. Many others knew him as a member of numerous clubs and causes and by the extensive reputation of his works. He was equally at home in the bibulous masculine world of "Auld Reekie," as Edinburgh was fondly termed, and the sexually integrated salons of polite society; he was a firm supporter of education for women and had a number of bluestocking friends. Indeed, in his broad range of interests, faith in rational analysis, tolerance, and middle-of-the-road religious and political ideas, he embodied aspects of Scottish Enlightenment thought responsible for its extraordinary and enduring influence.

Influence

Kames' friendly support of Hume, Smith, Blair, and Reid involved him intimately in the Enlightenment project of applying the lessons of Newtonian science, Lockean epistemology, and associationist psychology to rhetoric and literature as well as other human enterprises. In opposition to the Aristotelianism which dominated school and university education of the day, the "new rhetoricians," to use W. S. Howell's term, sought to ground effective speaking and writing on the principles of scientific psychology; expressive discourse should suit the natural functions of the mind rather than artificial logical and stylistic forms. Kames' *Elements of Criticism* exerted an immediate and lasting influence in Britain, France, and Germany and became, along with Blair's *Lectures on Rhetoric and Belles Lettres* (1783) and George Campbell's *Philosophy of Rhetoric* (1776), one of the central texts in American university curricula throughout most of the nineteenth century. To this day, Kames' *Elements* takes its place with Edmund Burke's *A Philosophical Enquiry into the Origin of our Ideas of the Sublime and Beautiful* (1759) as one of the major British works of critical theory to appear in the long and vibrant period between John Dryden's 1668 *Essay of Dramatic Poesy* and William Wordsworth's preface to the 1800 *Lyrical Ballads.*

Analysis

As William C. Lehmann points out, Scottish Enlightenment thought combined three salient tendencies: (1) the desire to find a "common sense" middle ground between the materialism of Isaac Newton and the immaterialism of George Berkeley and, as well, between the dour Calvinism of the Kirk and the skepticism of Hume and the French *philosophes*; (2) a passion for history that was responsible, for example, for the antiquarian zeal of such works as Lord Monboddo's vast *Of the Origin and Progress of Language* (1773) and Kames' densely allusive *Sketches of the History of Man* (1774); and (3) an inclination to foreground the social side of human nature, as does Kames' *Essays on the Principles of Morality and Natural Religion*, and to explore moral, religious, scientific, metaphysical, and aesthetic issues in terms of pragmatic social implications. The first of these tendencies explains Kames' particular, loose adaptation, in *Elements of Criticism*, of the Newtonian "analytic-synthetic" method of inquiry; the second is evident in the work's vast accumulation of examples and illustrative passages from classical, French, Italian, and British literature; the third underlies its foregrounding of psychological principles understood to be universal and social rather than individually subjective.

For Kames, human consciousness amounts to the awareness, when awake, of "a continued train of perceptions and ideas passing in the mind." Kames sidesteps the daunting question of the relationship between external objects, sensations, and ideas in two ways which ally him to the commonsense philosophy later formalized by his friend Thomas Reid. First, to Kames, mind and nature are obviously and extensively in harmony, a harmony evident in the easy and universal correspondence between sensation and feeling, aesthetic and moral ideas. Second, what is important about the "train of perceptions and ideas passing in the mind" is not so much how they got there but their "ideal presence," the vividness which gives them motive force, and also the manner in which they relate to each other in moving us toward conclusions or actions. Kames places himself firmly within the associationist psychology of his day, but he avoids the epistemological rigor that makes Hume and Berkeley at once compelling and frustrating. Kames asserts mind-world relationships which his colleagues reject as unphilosophical, and he refuses to trace human responses to a single principle such as self-interest.

Since aesthetic activity, for Kames, clearly stands or falls on the emotions, passions, and sentiments it calls up, the "analytical" first volume of *Elements* canvasses and orders the field of such responses and the techniques by which they can be evoked. Emotions, passions, and sentiments share a basis in feeling; a passion is an emotion that evokes a desire, and a sentiment is an emotion with a thought added. The obvious motive force of passions makes them central to the power of the aesthetic. In spite of being handicapped by the abstract nature of words, language comes closer than the visual arts to imitating the natural chain of ideas passing in the mind, and as a result is better at calling up passions and their complex but focused movements. Although it touches on the other arts, including chapters on gardening and architecture, *Elements* is essentially a treatise on literature, evaluated in terms of its capacity to bring to mind an ordered string of passionate responses.

Kames bases the movements of passion on the principles of connection between ideas prominent in Hume's *Enquiry Concerning Human Understanding* (1748): resemblance, contiguity in time or space, and cause and effect. He adds a "principle of order" which helps him explain the importance to literature of such neoclassical values as regularity and congruity. In accord with Kames' commonsense epistemology and the principles of associationism, a work of art must call up vivid images – ideal presences – that stimulate passion and then combine them so as to provide, in Ian Ross' words, "agreeable advance, alternation, and variety" in the service of a unified emotional and moral impression.

Although Kames' easy eliding of the subject-object dichotomy may be philosophically unsatisfying, as it was to Hume, it enables a practical criticism of great clarity and power. Rather than worrying whether beauty resides fundamentally in natural objects or mental responses, Kames treats it as an ideal presence having two varieties, intrinsic and relative. He realizes that the subjective or objective status of intrinsic beauty, the beauty of an object in its own right, can always be argued. On the other hand, relative beauty, deriving from the usefulness or some other associated value of an object, will depend on established social conventions. Gardens possess intrinsic beauty and thus take an untrammeled variety of forms, while architecture must always contend with the relative beauty of buildings, their suitability to designated uses.

Having derived the principles governing the invocation and ordering of the passions, Kames devotes the second volume of *Elements* to synthesizing the rules by which, in literature, "a passion be adjusted to the character, the sentiments to the passion, and the language to the sentiments." Volume Two includes long discussions on the beauties of language and the use of comparisons and figures which amount to a compendium of stylistic principles and precepts. The volume ends with less detailed essays on "Narration and Description," "Epic and Dramatic Compositions," "The Three Unities," "Gardening and Architecture," and "Standard of Taste."

What distinguishes Kames' treatment of style from its classical sources – Aristotle, Cicero, Quintilian, and Longinus – and from more recent French rhetorics with which he shows himself familiar is his incessant stress on "naturalness"; at every step, literary language must mirror and promote the easy, regular, intuitive, "natural" train of ideas in the mind. Kames' treatments of literary genres and types and of the unities are more conventional, and his essay on gardening and architecture is strongly colored by the practice of such contemporaries as William Kent and "Capability" Brown. In the closing essay on the universality of taste, he argues strongly for including the aesthetic under the "common sense of mankind." He points out that the arts benefit greatly from "uniformity of taste" for "without uniformity of taste, there could not be any suitable reward, either of profit or honour, to encourage men of genius to labour in such works."

Not the least of the qualities responsible for the popularity and influence of *Elements of Criticism* was how well Kames' system worked. The combination of vividness, passion, naturalness, and order defined what successive generations of literati, even into the Romantic period, found easy to accept as good taste. Indeed many of Kames' judgments speak persuasively to the modern critic or *cinéaste* – such as, drama benefits from the unmediated nature of its representations; Aristotle is right in emphasizing plot as a completed action and in de-emphasizing the unities of time and space; Voltaire's *Henriade* suffers from its admixture of epic "machinery"; Pierre Corneille and Jean Racine too often lapse into static description; literary genres "run into each other, precisely like colours"; gardens offer glorious opportunities for effects of variety and surprise; Shakespeare is the prince of poets for his comprehensive understanding of human nature. In addition to his judgments, the passages Kames chose for illustration promoted understanding of and a lively appreciation for literature among aspiring writers as far removed from Kames' world as Herman Melville and Emily Dickinson who encountered the ubiquitous *Elements of Criticism* in school curricula and private libraries.

In *Elements of Criticism*, as in his other writings, Kames wears the age's moralism more modestly than Samuel Johnson, its tendentiousness with less spleen than Voltaire, its egoism less arrogantly than Jean-Jacques Rousseau, its artifice less exclusively than Alexander Pope, its indulgence less puerile than James Boswell. As self-conscious postcolonials struggling to rid their writing of dreaded "Scottishisms" and aspiring to the intellectual mainstream, Kames and his circle, even when duped by James Macpherson's Ossianic hoaxes, eschewed the nationalism and snobbery which often stained the work of their English colleagues. It is for this reason, as well as for the quality of their thought, that their writings spoke so long and strongly to the European settlers of America and their heirs. The belief, so important to the modern world, that the country of the mind is a democracy habitable by anyone of sense and energy owes much to Henry Home, Lord Kames, and those who shared with him the enterprise of the Scottish Enlightenment.

Principal criticism

Elements of Criticism, 1762. Kames revised and expanded this work several times. The sixth edition, containing his final alterations, appeared posthumously in 1785.

Other major works and literary forms

Henry Home, Lord Kames, published eleven volumes on English and Scottish law, several of them compilations of and commentaries on court decisions and legal history. Of these the most speculative was *Principles of Equity* (1760). Kames' legal philosophy counts as a crucial building block of the theory of Civil Society formalized in Adam Ferguson's 1764 *Essay on the History of Civil Society* and implicit in Adam Smith's *The Wealth of Nations*, first published in 1776. His writings on law were highly regarded by John Adams, Thomas Jefferson, and James Madison, as well as by his friend Benjamin Franklin; his influence on the constitutional development of the American republic was pervasive and far-reaching.

Other publications outside the field of law include *Introduction to the Art of Thinking* (1761), *Progress of Flax-Husbandry in Scotland* (1766), the encyclopedic *Sketches of the History of Man* (1774), *The Gentleman Farmer* (1776), a work consulted by Thomas Jefferson, and *Loose Hints on Education* (1781), a treatise influenced by Rousseau's *Émile* advocating educational reform.

Further reading

Allen, David. *Virtue, Learning and the Scottish Enlightenment*, 1993.
Chitnis, Anand C. *The Scottish Enlightenment*, 1976.
Howell, Wilbur Samuel. *Eighteenth-Century British Logic and Rhetoric*, 1971.
Lehmann, William C. *Henry Home, Lord Kames, and the Scottish Enlightenment*, 1971.
Potkay, Adam. *The Fate of Eloquence in the Age of Hume*, 1994.
Randall, Helen Whitcomb. *The Critical Theory of Lord Kames*, 1940.
Ross, Ian Simpson. *Lord Kames and the Scotland of his Day*, 1972.

BRYAN C. SHORT

See also Hume; Neoclassical Literary Theory; Warton

Kamo No Mabuchi

Japanese writer and philologist

Born: Hamamatsu, Japan; 1697
Died: Edo, Japan; October 31, 1769

Biography

Kamo no Mabuchi was born in 1697 in Hamamatsu, a town along the Tōkaidō highway which linked the ancient capital of Kyoto with the political center of Edo (modern-day Tokyo). His family had several branches representing Shinto, samurai, and farming traditions; his father's vocation is uncertain. He was taught to read by the niece of the celebrated nativist scholar, Kada no Azumamaro, and as a young man he participated actively in local poetry circles.

In 1733 Mabuchi moved to Kyoto for full-time study in Azumamaro's school; following Azumamaro's death in 1736, Mabuchi moved to Edo, where he developed a reputation as the principal heir to Azumamaro's teachings. From 1746 to 1760 he served in Edo as the tutor in Japanese studies to Tayasu Munetake, the second son of the regnant shogun, Tokugawa Yoshimune. It was while in service to Munetake that Mabuchi began work on his magnum opus, the *Man'yō kō* (1760–1768; on the Manyōshū), a commentary on the twenty-volume poetry anthology *Manyōshū* (759; *Manyōshū*, 1929–1969) which he completed in 1768.

In 1760 Mabuchi retired from Munetake's service and lived the rest of his life in the outskirts of Edo, where he was known by the sobriquet "old man of the fields" (*agatai no ushi*). Mabuchi spent his final years as something of an antiquarian eccentric, lecturing to students on the veranda of his home and devoting himself to writing. He died in Edo on October 31, 1769.

Influence

Mabuchi was the first major nativist critic in Japan to use the philological analysis of ancient verse in order to extrapolate from it what he believed to be the spirit of a natural premoral archaic order which he called the "ancient Way" (*kodō*), and to advocate the emulation of this Way in the present. He had more than three hundred students; the most famous was Motoori Norinaga, who adapted Mabuchi's methodology and applied it to other ancient Japanese classics.

Analysis

During the eighteenth century literary critics in Japan tended to belong to one of two groups: traditional critics who believed that literature's primary purpose was didactic and normative and avant-garde critics who insisted that literature be valued solely for its artistic merits. Mabuchi won his first acclaim during the 1740s by devising a novel compromise between these stances: while literature, especially verse, had no intrinsic moral value, he argued, it nevertheless had the potential to promote social stability by virtue of its capacity to express and thereby to vent powerful emotions which might otherwise prove disruptive to the polity. Mabuchi's later poetics may be regarded as a development and refinement of this basic stance.

Mabuchi regarded verse as the most effective medium for the communication of heartfelt emotion, and he was critical of verse composed in more recent ages on the grounds that it was concerned more with artifice than emotional truth. The more ancient the verse, he argued, the more sincere the emotional expression; thus Mabuchi extolled above all the verses of the *Manyōshū*, Japan's oldest extant poetry anthology, which was compiled in the second half of the eighth century. He claimed that these verses communicated a purely Japanese spirit, unsullied by the Confucian rationalism or Buddhist moralism which he identified with later ages.

The major difficulty with study of the *Manyōshū*, however, was that the text was compiled prior to the invention of the *kana* syllabaries and was written in a highly irregular form of Sino-Japanese which made the work largely unintelligible to readers within a century of its compilation. As late as the seventeenth century, less than 10 percent of the anthology's 4,500 verses were accessible to a literate Japanese. Mabuchi addressed this problem by writing the *Man'yōkō*, a commentary on the anthology which took him twelve years to complete. The quality of Mabuchi's philology was so high that this commentary remains the starting point for most modern research on the *Manyōshū.*

A linguistic purist, Mabuchi believed that certain "truths" about ancient Japan were untranslatable and hence could not be appreciated by his contemporaries reading ancient works written in Chinese. The *Manyōshū*, he argued, presented four advantages as an ancient text. First, even though it was written using Chinese characters, the text was simply a phonetic transcription of ancient songs and so the aural value of the verses was retained. Thus the verses of the *Manyōshū* were linguistically preferable both to those included in other ancient works, such as the verses included in the *Nihon shoki* (720; *Chronicles of Japan*, 1896), and to eighth-century Chinese poems composed by Japanese poets. The second advantage presented by the *Manyōshū*, according to Mabuchi, was that since verse was an intrinsically superior medium for the communication of sincere emotional responses, the "true hearts" (*magokoro*) and spirit of ancient Japanese might best be fathomed through its verses. Here, Mabuchi was comparing the *Manyōshū* primarily with the *Kojiki* (712; *Records of Ancient Matters*, 1882, 1968), Japan's most ancient extant history which posed comparable linguistic hurdles. Third, Mabuchi regarded the composition of ancient verse to have been an essentially spontaneous event in which people sang of their feelings as they arose. Hence he believed that such verses were free of the preoccupation with artistry which he identified with poetry composed after the ninth century. In this regard, Mabuchi asserted that the *Manyōshū* was superior to both the *Kokinshū* (c. 905; English translation, 1984) and *Shin kokinshū* (c. 1205) poetry anthologies which most contemporary poets regarded as the standards against which other anthologies were to be measured, and which Mabuchi criticized for their alleged femininity and obsessive concern with artifice and technique at the expense of emotional expression. Finally, he maintained that since the verses of the *Manyōshū* were composed prior to the introduction from China of Buddhist doctrines and Confucian teachings, mastery of these verses would enable one to learn what was purely and natively "Japanese" about Japan.

Mabuchi claimed that in contrast to all other Japanese anthologies of verse, the poems of the *Manyōshū* were distinguished by their sincerity, directness, vitality, manliness, and naive elegance. Since he regarded the verses as transparent expressions of the hearts of ancient Japanese poets, he attributed the same virtues to his archaic forebears. He declared that persons in ancient Japan possessed hearts which instinctively and spontaneously conformed to what he styled the "natural Way of heaven and earth." As a result, they were capable of being virtuous without moral instruction while living in perfect harmony with the forces and objects of nature about them. He insisted that it was not the case that ancient Japanese never committed wrongdoings, but rather that because they were incapable of duplicity or guile, their wrongdoings were quickly uncovered and resolved. Further, he insisted that since ancient men instinctively worshipped and venerated their emperors and the imperial deities, the ancient polity enjoyed the blessings of social and political order without any laws or theories of government. He claimed that when their emotions reached extreme points, the ancient Japanese vented their concerns in the "natural" rhythms of poetry – rhythms identical to those of heaven and earth – and so a simple and natural order was sustained by the act of versification and prevailed in a seemingly uninterruptible fashion.

This archaic order, however, was disrupted according to Mabuchi by the introduction of Chinese writings from abroad; of all foreign writings, he regarded those of Confucianism as the most pernicious. He believed that Confucian teachings represented "invented" man-made doctrines fashioned to address what he believed to be the specifically Chinese problems of unruliness and insubordination, problems which he claimed arose from an inherent propensity toward wickedness among the people of Japan's formidable continental neighbor. As soon as those writings were introduced into Japan, he claimed, ancient Japanese in their naivete were drawn to this foreign teaching until the people were eventually seduced by its apparent wisdom, fell out of touch with the native Way of heaven and earth, and lost their natural virtues. In response to those Sinophiles who argued that the lack of moral teachings in ancient Japan indicated Japanese cultural backwardness vis-à-vis China, Mabuchi proclaimed that the absence of such teachings demonstrated that the instinctively virtuous Japanese had no need for such teachings and that their introduction had the unintended effect of instructing the ancients in immorality.

The fundamental optimism of Mabuchi's thought and that point at which his poetics melded with his patriotic sentiments lay in his belief that this fall from a primordial state of natural grace was reversible and that the verses of the *Manyōshū* were the key. He maintained that by studying and reciting the ancient verses and then learning to compose verse in archaic modes and styles, a Japanese might assimilate their spirit and literally reanimate his or her dormant "true heart," reclaiming thereby the host of ancient virtues which devolved from it. Accordingly, the composition of verse in imitation of the various styles represented in the *Manyōshū* formed a central part of the instruction Mabuchi imparted to his students, and he himself daily led his students in their recitation.

In certain respects, Mabuchi's teachings were much attuned to certain intellectual and literary trends in his age, but in others, he was seriously at odds with it. His nativist classicism had clear antecedents among the more popular schools of Confucianism in Japan, and his focus on the *Manyōshū* may be regarded as an extension of the gradual awakening of interest in the anthology which had begun a century prior to his birth. On the other hand, his at times xenophobic and anti-Chinese proclamations as well as his disdain for the poetics of later ages were antagonistic to the mainstream opinions of contemporary scholarship and literary criticism. His *Kokuikō* (1765; on the concept of Japan), for example, proved so controversial an essay that rebuttals and defenses of it continued to appear for several decades after Mabuchi's death.

Nevertheless, the quality of his philological scholarship and teaching as well as his undeniable love of the most ancient Japanese classics attracted hundreds of students to him and made him one of the best-known literary scholars of his day. He was greeted by enthusiastic admirers at every stage of a journey he undertook in 1763 to famous sites throughout Japan, and it is significant that despite the overt emphasis on masculinity within his poetics, nearly one-third of his students were women, a figure unmatched by any premodern private academy in Japan.

Perhaps because of the inherent philological difficulty of studying the *Manyōshū*, however, only a handful of Mabuchi's students achieved a measure of acclaim for their work on the anthology. The poetics and literary criticism of Mabuchi's best-known student, Motoori Norinaga, diverged significantly from what Mabuchi taught, though Norinaga's philology owed a considerable amount to Mabuchi's pioneering efforts. During the early decades of the twentieth century, several of Mabuchi's assumptions concerning reverence toward the imperial institution and the innate moral superiority of the Japanese people were incorporated within the ultranationalist ideology which contributed to Japan's involvement in World War II. In the postwar years, attention in Japan has focused more on his poetics and philology than on his nonliterary postulations.

Principal criticism

Ise monogatari koi, 1751
Kanjikō, 1757
Genji monogatari shinshaku, 1758
Man'yō kō, 1760–1768
Bun'ikō, 1762
Kaikō, 1764
Goikō, 1769

Other major works and literary forms

In addition to the above works, Kamo no Mabuchi kept two diaries and wrote several essays on the patriotic and normative value of the study of ancient Japanese writings, of which his most important is *Kokuikō* (1765; on the concept of Japan). He also produced a primer for his students, *Niimanabi* (1765; primary learning) and two major studies of ancient Shinto liturgies and prayers, his *Engishiki norito kai* (1746; explication of the Engishiki liturgies) and *Noritokō* (1768; on liturgies).

NONFICTION
Engishiki norito kai, 1746
Kokuikō, 1765
Niimanabi, 1765
Noritokō, 1768

Further reading

Nosco, Peter. "*Manyōshū* Studies in Tokugawa Japan," in *Transactions of the Asiatic Society of Japan*. 4th series, I (1986), pp. 109–146.
——. "Nature, Invention, and National Learning: The *Kokka hachiron* Controversy, 1742–1746," in *Harvard Journal of Asiatic Studies*. XLI (1981), pp. 75–91.
——. *Remembering Paradise: Nativism and Nostalgia in 18th-Century Japan*, 1990.

PETER NOSCO

See also Japanese Literary Theory; Motoori Norinaga

Immanuel Kant

German philosopher

Born: Königsberg, Prussia; April 22, 1724
Died: Königsberg, Prussia; February 12, 1804

Biography

Immanuel Kant, who effected a "Copernican revolution in philosophy," was born into the family of a poor saddler on April 22, 1724, in Königsberg, Prussia. The family adhered to Pietism, a Protestant current that emphasized spiritual self-examination and serenity. Kant was reared in East Prussia during the period when the regime of Frederick the Great was making "Prussian" a byword for strict discipline and repression of personal desires. The general social atmosphere, Kant's own temperament, and his lifelong poverty combined to make him into a highly self-disciplined man, completely dedicated to his work. In a classic anecdote, the townsfolk of Königsberg were once in consternation when Kant, overwhelmed by reading a work of one of his favorite authors, Jean-Jacques Rousseau, failed to take his daily walk at his scheduled time.

Kant received his entire education in Königsberg, from extremely narrow preparatory work in Latin through his matriculation and later graduate studies at the University of Königsberg. In opposition to the narrowly focused education of his time, Kant sought the broadest possible knowledge of the real world and made contributions to such diverse fields as geology, anthropology, psychology, theology, physics, meteorology, and pedagogy, as well as to philosophy per se. He proved to be a compelling influence at the University of Königsberg, where he lectured steadily from 1754 through 1796. He died in Königsberg on February 12, 1804, having never set foot outside his beloved Prussia.

Throughout his life, Kant was a gentle rebel. The Prussian discipline that infuriated Friedrich Schiller was accepted stoically and turned to good account by Kant. Kant subscribed to the Enlightenment's faith that education would save the world. He never regarded his Spartan personal life as a deprivation. In the words of Ernst Cassirer, Kant's life and work together testified that "the full, compelling power of the universal emerges" only when the personal is suppressed.

Influence

The impact of Kant on the working theories of both critics and writers can scarcely be overestimated. He profoundly influenced the thought of his contemporaries Johann Wolfgang von Goethe and Schiller, the virtual founders of German literature. The Marburg School of philosophy, which in a sense sprang up in order to grapple with (and only partly refute) Kant, inspired seminal thinking on language and culture well into the twentieth century, as represented by Cassirer and Boris Pasternak. The value-free side of Kant's thought and his search for extreme precision, even in a subjective field such as aesthetics, had a definite appeal for the American New Critics of the 1930s and beyond, just as in the early nineteenth century the passionately ethical side of Kant's thought had appealed to the American Transcendentalists. Kant's roots in the French Enlightenment have long made him a compatible contributor to the development of French criticism. Significant studies of Kant have been written in every European language. The Russians adopted him as an honorary member of their academy, both literally (Kant was elected to the St. Petersburg Academy of Sciences in 1794) and indirectly, through the popularizing efforts of Lev Tolstoi, whose credo *Chto takoye iskusstvo* (1898; *What Is Art?*, 1898) reflected Kant's influence.

Analysis

Kant declined to make any detailed critiques of individual writers and artists, despite his intense feelings about art and literature. In his sole but lengthy contribution to criticism, *The Critique of Judgment*, the names of his great contemporaries, Schiller and Goethe, are conspicuous by their total absence. Yet Kant, in his impeccably thorough way, laid the grounds for the practice of modern literary criticism.

In seeking to analyze the universal human attraction to "the Beautiful," Kant scrupulously avoided defining the beautiful in terms of the work of individual artists, lest his absolute analysis be too closely tied to their genius. Instead, Kant looked first to nature as a source of criteria for the beautiful. His assumption is that if one can understand the almost universal response to natural beauty, then the more individual and cultured responses to the beauty of man-made arts and literature can be put on a solid foundation.

In the tradition of the British empiricists (whom he credits), Kant examined the facts of human aesthetic response, insofar as they can be observed. By definition, according to Kant, nothing – whether natural or artificial – inherently contains beauty. Beauty can only be in the beholder's eye. Therefore, every observable human response is relevant to this subject of beauty. Kant refers to the differing responses of Europeans, Asians, and Native Americans to illustrate a purely cultural (and to Kant, superficial) relativity. Not beauty, but the human response to the beautiful, is universal. To a degree, this response is physiological, and Kant analyzed that, though tentatively. As a philosopher, Kant was more interested in the mental component of the aesthetic response, and he began with a certain puzzlement, because "there can be no objective rule of taste by which what is beautiful may be defined by means of [intellectual, logical] concepts." On this dogmatic and somewhat Romantic basis (to which classicists and others might take exception), the whole burden of what is to be judged beautiful and aesthetically valuable falls on the consumer.

Focusing on the human response to beauty, Kant offered several psychological criteria. Indicative that a response is a genuinely aesthetic one, the consumer sees no interest or profit in the thing of beauty but enjoys a "pure delight." Integral to such disinterested enjoyment is "the free play of imagination and understanding" that every beautiful work (whether of humanity or of nature) awakens.

Kant's attitude as a philosopher and logician evolved as he explored his subject. He began by carefully separating "the Beautiful" from both the logical and the good. Yet he ended with a heartfelt analogy verging on the semiotic: that the beautiful is a symbol (on another plane) of the good, as even "common understanding" recognizes. The more closely Kant analyzed emotional response toward the beautiful, the more similarities he found with emotional response toward the good, as if the observing individual were feeling the same thing but in two different modes.

Kant lived at a time when neoclassicism was giving way to Romanticism. Though he referred to neither school (and implicitly takes the position that the ideology of artists is irrelevant, since it is only the consumer's response that matters), Kant's own aesthetic taste, on which he inevitably relied, owed something to both.

In the classical spirit, Kant excoriated sentimentality in literature, honoring it with one of his few directed literary judgments: "Romances, maudlin dramas, shallow homilies . . . make the heart enervated, insensitive to the stern precepts of duty, and incapable of respect for the worth of humanity." In an anachronistic, neoclassical reflex, Kant advised, "Models of taste with respect to the arts of speech must be composed in a dead and learned language . . . to ensure its having a grammar that is not subject to the caprices of fashion." Also in the classical spirit, Kant felt compelled to put the arts into a hierarchy of importance, although he expressed his personal preference reluctantly: "I must confess to the pure delight that I have ever been afforded by a beautiful poem." He justified this weakness by noting that poetry "expands" and "invigorates" the mind.

Kant echoed the Romantic tradition in his strong support of freedom in artistic creation: "By right it is only production through freedom, i.e. through an act of will that places reason at the basis of its action, that should be termed art." He also rejected fixed rules and predictable regularity in art. Formal perfection is inimical to the truly beautiful. Thus, art cannot be evaluated with reference to a formal canon to which the artist faithfully adheres. Kant provided a foundation for the hard-won independent stance of the aesthetic as a value in and of itself.

A strikingly modern aspect of Kant's approach to art is that he accepted the so-called minor and decorative arts, such as landscape gardening, fashion, furniture design, and interior decorating, into a broad discussion of aesthetics in general. The value of the aesthetic, for Kant, was as much independent of any specific art form as it was independent of any specific artist. In his broad encompassing of all the forms of expression from gardening to poetry, Kant anticipated twentieth-century semiotic approaches.

The modern reader will be least receptive to Kant's fundamental assumption that the aesthetic must give "immediate delight" (just as "moral goodness" supposedly does). Modern art and literature often yield a delight that is far from immediate. Kant did make a slight concession to the possibility of the aesthetic being independent of beauty: "Where fine art evidences its superiority is in the beautiful descriptions it gives of things that in nature would be ugly or displeasing." Yet for the most part, Kant's conceptions of the aesthetically powerful are inextricably linked with beauty, empirically measured by the ability to give immediate, but disinterested delight.

Kant became a poet himself in trying to express the effect of purely aesthetic power. The supreme logician settled for a mystical paradox: beauty is that which appears to conform to a law, where there is no law, and possesses a kind of finality, where there is no "end." Kant was conquered, finally, by a truth which does not need logic and yet is true. He became intellectually reconciled with it through semiotics (before semiotics had been invented): beauty, both natural and aesthetic, while not in itself goodness, is the symbol, the semiotic translation, of moral goodness.

While enhancing the perceived worth of all the arts and literature in themselves, Kant deemphasized the artist. Though art cannot be evaluated with reference to any predetermined formal canon, neither can it be evaluated according to criteria that the artist himself proclaims. Instead, the entire burden (and credit) of evaluating art and literature is placed on the consumer, who judges the work solely by how it strikes him or her. For the artist, there is no appeal from the consumer's judgment. (Most avant-garde movements have consisted of artists determined to take – or preferably, wrench – their authority back from the consumer.) The consumer-critic's sole responsibility – and a purely voluntary one, since any morally sound human being is, by definition, capable of responding to the beautiful – is to develop aesthetic taste.

Principal criticism

Kritik der Urteilskraft, 1790 (*The Critique of Judgment*, 1892)

Other major works and literary forms

The contributions of Immanuel Kant span a vast range of knowledge. His work most often takes the form of the philosophical treatise and is crowned by his three critiques, among which *Kritik der reinen Vernunft* (1781; *The Critique of Pure Reason*, 1838) and *Kritik der praktischen Vernunft* (1788; *The Critique of Practical Reason*, 1873) preceded Kant's fundamental analysis of aesthetics, *The Critique of Judgment*. Kant also wrote scholarly works in many scientific fields, such as anthropology and geology, in an essay format that allowed for philosophical digressions. Kant also produced a few works of esoteric intellectual satire aimed at his own fields (and even his own views) of philosophy and ethics, the chief example being *Träume eines Geistersehers erläutert durch Träume der Metaphysik* (1766; *Dreams of a Spirit-Seer, Illustrated by Dreams of Metaphysics*, 1900).

NONFICTION

Der einzig mögliche Beweisgrund zu einer Demonstration des Daseyns Gottes, 1763 (*The Only Possible Ground for Demonstration of the Existence of God*, 1798)

Träume eines Geistersehers erläutert durch Träume der Metaphysik, 1766 (*Dreams of a Spirit-Seer, Illustrated by Dreams of Metaphysics*, 1900)

Allgemeine Naturgeschichte und Theorie des Himmels, 1775 (*The Universal Natural History and Theory of the Heavens*, 1900)

Kritik der reinen Vernunft, 1781 (*The Critique of Pure Reason*, 1838)

Grundlegung zur Metaphysik der Sitten, 1785 (*Fundamental Principles of the Metaphysics of Ethics*, 1895, better known as *Foundations of the Metaphysics of Morals*, 1950)

Kritik der praktischen Vernunft, 1788 (*The Critique of Practical Reason*, 1873)

Die Religion innerhalb der Grenzen der blossen Vernunft, 1793 (*Religion Within the Boundaries of Pure Reason*, 1838)

Further reading

Baldacchino, Lewis. *A Study in Kant's Metaphysics of Aesthetic Experience: Reason and Feeling*, 1991.

Cassirer, Ernst. *Kant's Life and Thought*, 1981.
Crawford, Donald W. *Kant's Aesthetic Theory*, 1974.
Eagleton, Terry. *The Ideology of the Aesthetic*, 1990.
Gulyga, Arsenij. *Immanuel Kant: His Life and Thought*, 1987.
Guyer, Paul. *Kant and the Claims of Taste*, 1979.
Handy, William J. *Kant and the Southern New Critics*, 1963.
Kemal, Salim. *Kant and Fine Art*, 1986.
Sontag, Frederick. *The Existentialist Prolegomena: To a Future Metaphysics*, 1969.

DIANA GOSSELIN NAKEEB

See also Hegel; Romanticism

John Keats

English poet

Born: London, England; October 31, 1795
Died: Rome, Italy; February 23, 1821

Biography

The oldest of a family of four children, John Keats was born on October 31, 1795, to John Thomas and Frances Keats. His father, a manager of a livery stable in a northern London suburb, died when Keats was eight; his mother died when he was fourteen. Keats was educated at the private Clarke's School in Enfield, where he developed an interest in classical art and literature and began a translation of Virgil's *Aeneid* (c. 29–19 B.C.). In 1810 Keats began working as an apprentice to an apothecary-surgeon, after five years of which he entered Guy's Hospital as a student of surgery. In 1816 he was licensed to practice as an apothecary and surgeon. Rather than taking up the profession for which he had been trained, however, Keats decided to devote himself to poetry, and with the help of Leigh Hunt and Percy Bysshe Shelley, he found a publisher. From this time onward, despite discouragements and failure to earn a living as a poet, Keats focused his attention on writing poetry, until, by 1820, he became too weakened with tuberculosis to continue.

Keats' brief literary career can be summarized in an overview of his three most active years as a poet. After the publication in March, 1817, of his first book, *Poems*, he devoted the remainder of the year to the writing of the lengthy (more than four-thousand-line) narrative poem *Endymion* (1818). In the fall and winter of 1817–1818, Keats wrote in his letters to family and friends some of his best-known observations about poetry and poetic theory. From late 1818 through 1819 he composed his greatest poetry: "Hyperion," "The Eve of St. Agnes," "La Belle Dame sans Merci," the odes "On a Grecian Urn," "To a Nightingale," "To Autumn," and *The Fall of Hyperion: A Dream* (1856).

Influence

Keats' poetry – or qualities of it – has influenced major poets since Alfred, Lord Tennyson. Keats' ideas about the creation of poetry and its importance, however, though noted and appreciated by poets and critics, cannot be said to have had a profound direct influence on literary theorists. In part, this is undoubtedly attributable to the difficulty of putting together from Keats' scattered comments in letters a clear literary theory. His ideas have, nevertheless, challenged poets since his time. In *The Use of Poetry and the Use of Criticism: Studies in the Relation of Criticism to Poetry in England* (1933), T. S. Eliot described Keats' letters as "the most notable and most important ever written by any English poet." Eliot also observed, however, that "Keats has no theory, and to have formed one was irrelevant to his interests." Eliot's own insistence on the impersonality of the artist, and what he termed "dissociation of sensibility," might have been influenced by Keats.

Analysis

John Keats cannot in any formal sense be regarded as a literary critic or even a literary theorist. During his brief career, he devoted his attention to the study of poetry and the development of his craft. Fortunately for readers of literature, it was Keats' practice to work on his ideas about the principles of poetry and the qualities of great literature as he wrote letters to family members and friends. The letters in most cases have the abruptness and energy of spontaneous thought. That these letters, collected a generation after the death of Keats, have been studied by serious students of literature as well as by poets is a tribute to the value and compelling expression of Keats' ideas. Keats himself never produced a systematic presentation of his ideas. An even greater obstacle to students of Keats' literary theories, however, is not only that Keats started his literary career with no coherent set of principles but also that even during the time he was producing his most mature work, he entertained conflicting ideas about poetry and how it is produced.

There are, however, some central ideas that inform many of Keats' poems and statements about literature. The most important of these is what he came eventually to call "negative capability." The concept is described in many of his letters and named in a letter begun on December 21, 1817, at the end of a year of intense literary activity, which included his reading of William Shakespeare, John Milton, William Wordsworth, and William Hazlitt, and his completion of *Endymion*. In the letter, he refers to a "disquisition" that he has had with a friend, during which, he reports:

> several things dovetailed in my mind, & at once it struck me, what quality went to form a Man of Achievement especially in Literature & which Shakespeare posessed [*sic*] so enormously – I mean

> *Negative Capability*, that is when man is capable of being in uncertainties, Mysteries, doubts, without any irritable reaching after fact & reason.

In a letter of a month earlier, Keats had commented, "I have never yet been able to perceive how any thing can be known for truth by consequitive reasoning – and yet it must be." The idea being expressed was familiar in Keats' time and common among Romantic poets. It is an argument for the importance of the imagination in the perception of truth, claiming that sequential ("consequitive") reasoning alone is inadequate to one who wants to understand the world around him. In struggling with the logic, or significance, of each detail of an experience in order to guarantee a verifiable conclusion or a claim to understanding, one only asserts his or her character on the elements of the experience, missing the possibility of a truer vision. To arrive at truth, one must, rather, remain open and receptive, absorbing the details of the experience without questioning them or making up one's mind concerning them. For a valid understanding, one must engage the imagination and greet nature through a process involving more of the perceiver than his analytical powers alone.

This process does not, however, challenge the validity or trustworthiness of the human senses or of phenomenal nature, both of which are crucial. The process depends upon the perceiver's active use of his or her imagination, which is described by Keats in his comments about the character of poets. In a letter written on October 27, 1818, Keats observes:

> as to the poetical Character itself . . . it is not itself – it has no self – it is every thing and nothing – It has no character . . . it lives in gusto, be it foul or fair . . . mean or elevated. . . . What shocks the virtuous philosopher delights the camelion Poet. It does no harm from its relish of the dark side of things any more than from its taste for the bright one; because they both end in speculation . . . . A Poet . . . has no Identity – he is continually . . . filling some other Body.

Thus, the process of poetic perception includes the poet's sympathetic identification with natural objects, during moments of intense observation when the poet loses himself in an object, experiencing the details of the object through heightened sense perceptions and intuiting qualities or realities of the object not otherwise perceived. The experience Keats describes is one for which he had a great natural capacity, as evidenced by comments of his friends and by his own writing. Throughout Keats' life, from his childhood, his friends were impressed with his inclination to lose himself in an experience and with the intensity of his imaginative identification with objects around him that interested him. The same inclination made Keats an especially perceptive and impressionable reader of Shakespeare and Milton.

The concept of negative capability, though perhaps never so energetically applied as in Keats' poetry and letters, draws from several intellectual currents well-known to Keats. One of these is objective realism, with its contention that the human mind supplements and shapes its perceptions of objective reality and that what it thus contributes is as valid, and as natural, as the concrete elements of the experience. Knowledge is gained through an exertion of the imagination acting upon sense perceptions. With this idea, Keats is also expressing a notion he shared with other Romantic artists: that reason alone is inadequate for the perception of truth. In a letter written March 13, 1818, Keats wrote of three realities: "Things real – such as existences of Sun Moon & Stars and passages of Shakespeare – Things semireal such as Love, the Clouds &c which require a greeting of the Spirit to make them wholly exist – and Nothings which are made Great and dignified by an ardent pursuit." This emphasis on the significance of the imagination in the grasping of truth was available to Keats from many sources, most notably Wordsworth, Samuel Taylor Coleridge, and Hazlitt.

The influence of the literary criticism of Hazlitt was the most significant among these. Keats had also read, possibly in 1818, the book-length philosophical essay *On the Principles of Human Action* (1805), in which Hazlitt refutes Thomas Hobbes' claim that all human action is motivated by self-love. A moral argument rather than an aesthetic one, Hazlitt's contention is that people are prevented from acting only selfishly through their capacity for sympathetic identification with the natural world. Human imagination, interacting with the elements of the physical world, creates not only the individual's perception of reality but also his bond with it and his concern and sense of responsibility that reach beyond his own ego.

In the period of January through March, 1818, Keats attended a lecture series offered by Hazlitt (published that year as *Lectures on the English Poets*). Like Wordsworth, Hazlitt reflected eighteenth-century English empiricism in his distrust of abstraction and in his confidence in the world of particulars. The individual understands this world through his or her direct perception of it and his or her sympathetic identification, driven and focused by strong emotion, which Hazlitt calls "gusto." "Gusto" is emotion focused outward, toward the phenomenal world. Beauty, as defined by Hazlitt, is found in the intense unifying of the essential qualities of an object, brought about by the perceiver's identification with the object in the spirit of gusto. For Hazlitt, sympathetic imagination takes on a special significance: it is the key not only to the understanding of the phenomenal world but also to the perception of beauty.

Hazlitt was critical of poets whom he regarded as self-absorbed, Wordsworth, Shelley, Lord Byron, who wrote subjective poetry focused not on nature but on their emotional responses to it. The ideal poet, according to Hazlitt, was Shakespeare, who revealed nothing of himself in his work but rather created myriad human characters that owed their reality to the poet's ability to identify imaginatively with a great range of human personalities. In "On Shakespeare and Milton," one of the lectures Keats attended, Hazlitt observed that Shakespeare "was the least of an egotist that it was possible to be."

In the dramatic criticism that Keats wrote in the winter of 1817–1818, echoing many of Hazlitt's observations about drama, Keats commented on the significance of art. Created through the artist's exercise of negative capability, art presents an emotion-charged experience that enables one to perceive the identity of an object through the intense focus on the object's most significant elements. With the elimination of all irrelevancies, art represents beauty and truth. Keats uses *King Lear* (1605–1606) as the ideal model. In watching a performance of *King Lear*, one sees beyond the horror and grief represented to the truth that is revealed regarding human character. The beauty experienced is not mere attractiveness of form or elegance of expression but an insight made possible through a unified, harmonious impression of the essential elements of human nature and the physical world. In this experience is the value of art.

Keats' own poetry can be seen as a progression toward the ideals he was forming for himself in 1817 and 1818. His great odes of 1819 – "To a Nightingale," "On a Grecian Urn," "On Melancholy," and "To Autumn" – are the clearest, most direct, and most intense expressions of these ideals. These odes dramatize the power of the imagination working on an object. In each, the imagination offers a glimpse of beauty and truth, a glimpse that cannot, according to Keats at this time, be sustained for long.

Principal criticism

John Keats wrote no formal works stating his literary theories. His statements about literature and its uses are found in his letters, the most notable of which were written in 1817 and 1818. A complete edition of Keats' letters is *The Letters of John Keats, 1814–1821* (1958), edited by Hyder E. Rollins.

Other major works and literary forms

John Keats' major publications were all books of poetry: *Poems* (1817), *Endymion* (1818), and *"Lamia," "Isabella," "The Eve of St. Agnes," and Other Poems* (1820). Keats also wrote three articles of drama criticism (filling in for a drama critic and friend who was on vacation), published in the *Champion*: the first on December 21, 1817, and the other two on January 4, 1818.

POETRY

Poems, 1817

Endymion, 1818

"Lamia," "Isabella," "The Eve of St. Agnes," and Other Poems, 1820

The Fall of Hyperion: A Dream, 1856

MISCELLANEOUS

Complete Works, 1900–1901 (5 volumes; H. B. Forman, editor)

Further reading

Bates, Walter Jackson. "Negative Capability," in *John Keats*, 1963.

Bush, Douglas. "Keats and His Ideas," in *English Romantic Poets: Modern Essays in Criticism*, 1960. Edited by M. H. Abrams.

Eliot, T. S. "Keats," in *The Use of Poetry and the Use of Criticism*, 1933.

Gittings, Robert. "Numberless Points," in *John Keats*, 1968.

Goldberg, M. A. *The Poetics of Romanticism: Toward a Reading of John Keats*, 1969.

Pettet, E. C. "Keats's Romanticism," in *Critics on Keats*, 1968. Edited by Judith O'Neill.

Sharp, Ronald A. "The Program for Poetry," *Keats, Skepticism, and the Religion of Beauty*, 1979.

Watts, Cedric. "Keats's Views," *A Preface to Keats*, 1985.

DENNIS C. CHOWENHILL

See also Coleridge; Hazlitt; Romanticism; Shelley

Hugh Kenner

Canadian critic

Born: Peterborough, Ontario, Canada; January 7, 1923

Biography

William Hugh Kenner was born on January 7, 1923, in Peterborough, Ontario, Canada, the only child of Henry Rowe Hocking Kenner and the former Mary Williams. His father was a classics teacher who served for decades as the principal of the town's public high school; his mother had taught French and German before her marriage. At the age of five Kenner contracted influenza; as a result, his hearing was severely impaired. The impact of this handicap was lessened by the fact that he had learned to read when he was three. Kenner himself recalls the experience as beneficial: "it threw me back on myself, allowed me to build an enormous self-confidence and an auditory memory that permits me to recall anything interesting at will."

Kenner received his B.A. degree from the University of Toronto in 1945 and his M.A. the following year. After two years of teaching at Assumption College in Windsor, Ontario, he was steered by his older colleague Marshall McLuhan to the doctoral program in English literature at Yale University, receiving his degree in 1950.

In 1947 Kenner married Mary Josephine Waite, with whom he had five children. From 1950 to 1973 Kenner taught in the English department of the University of California at Santa Barbara, also teaching as a visiting professor at several other universities during this period. In 1965, following the death of his first wife the previous year, Kenner married Mary Anne Bittner, with whom he has had two children. In 1973 Kenner moved to The Johns Hopkins University, where he is Andrew W. Mellon Professor of the Humanities.

Influence

Kenner is the preeminent interpreter of the great modernists, Ezra Pound, James Joyce, T. S. Eliot, and Wyndham Lewis. In his studies of these and other innovators (most notably William Butler Yeats, Samuel Beckett, and William Carlos Williams), Kenner has shown how each writer's work dictates a different critical approach, a different critical vocabulary – a lesson that is applicable to writers who have little in common with Kenner's favorite subjects, or indeed with one another, beyond the power and originality of their creations.

Analysis

In the foreword to *Gnomon*, written relatively early in his career, Hugh Kenner outlined his understanding of the nature and purpose of criticism. As an introduction to his characteristic procedures, which differ radically from those of many of his contemporaries, this statement remains useful, particularly in its emphasis on "exegesis." Exegesis, which Kenner identifies as the "foundation of criticism," is most often associated with the exposition of Scripture, based on close reading. The biblical exegete proceeds on the faith that his text coheres. No detail is insignificant; every part has its place in the whole. Such an intuition of order need not be religious; it is expressed in Stewart Brand's aphorism from the back cover of *The Last Whole Earth Catalog* (1971), in the caption for a photograph of the Earth as seen from space: "We can't put it together. It is together." Religiously inspired or not, however, exegesis demands what Kenner in a very early essay described as a "realistic sense of a complex verbal, social, and moral actuality to be explored rather than pinned down."

In its antisystematic character, then, exegesis as practiced by Kenner is not merely distinct from but also opposed to literary theory, at least in the quasi-scientific sense of that term. In his remarkable book *Muses of One Mind: The Literary Analysis of Experience and Its Continuity* (1983), Wesley Trimpi contrasts "'theory' in its older Greek sense of 'viewing' or 'observing' something as a whole in order to understand it" with "the modern connotation of a 'theory' as an idea to be tested, a body of doctrine to be believed, or a program to be instituted." As Trimpi observes, "Arguments in favor of one theory or another . . . tend to be separated from their original contexts, to restrict their attention to methodology and dogma, and, finally, to become the special subject matter of the theorists themselves" – a circumspect but damning summary of fashionable critical discourse in the 1980s.

In contrast, Kenner extols "respect for the concrete fact." This has been a recurring theme, from his first major book, *The Poetry of Ezra Pound*, to his latest works. In an essay, "Pound and Homer," written for a centenary volume edited by George Bornstein (*Ezra Pound Among the Poets*, 1985), Kenner observes:

> The *Iliad* and *Odyssey* were esteemed as a comprehensive curriculum in grammar, rhetoric, history, geography, navigation, strategy, even medicine. But by the mid-nineteenth century A.D. they no longer seemed to contain real information of any kind at all. Had there even been a Trojan War? Scholars inclined to think not.

The solution: literature was redefined "as something that is good for us, however unfactual," and Matthew Arnold pronounced that Homer was Sublime. Yet in 1861, "while British ink was drying on printed copies of Arnold's three lectures on translating Homer, Heinrich Schliemann was nourishing a dream." Within a decade, Schliemann had discovered Troy.

Attention to "the concrete fact" leads Kenner to many illuminating observations which, once he has made them, seem obvious, yet which no one has made before. In *A Colder Eye*, for example, he connects the progressive styles of James Joyce's *Ulysses* (1922) with Joyce's earlier experience as a language teacher in Trieste: "He taught English according to the new Berlitz system, which departed from centuries of custom in forbidding a teacher to use any language in the students' hearing save the one they were learning." The students' experience anticipated that of the reader of *Ulysses*, "a new kind of book altogether, a Berlitz classroom between covers: a book from which we are systematically taught the skills we require to read it." Kenner's mastery of his materials rests on personal experience; convinced of the value of first-hand knowledge, he has met and listened to most of the writers whose works are the subjects of his critical studies and has visited the places about which they have written. While French theorists and their American disciples were explaining that literature is essentially self-referential, Kenner was photographing sites mentioned in the Cantos (1925–1968) of Ezra Pound.

Perhaps the most striking quality of Kenner's criticism, however, is his appropriation of the distinctive styles of his various subjects. Much of the energy of contemporary literary criticism is devoted to the application of metalanguages: the critic is equipped with a toolbox of terms ("logocentrism," "intertextuality," "dialogism," "*écriture féminine*") with which the works of any writer whatsoever can be interpreted, decoded, deconstructed. Kenner's approach is different. "What we ought to have learned from Hugh Kenner," Guy Davenport writes, "is that a literary subject has a geography, a lineage, and a unique nature. The analytical tools for explicating Joyce are a different kit from those needed for Pound."

Those analytical tools, Kenner suggests, are to be found within the writer's own work:

> Styles are possibilities, which artists spend years devising, urged by the soliciting material. The critic who forms his style on that of his author not only does mimetic homage, he avails himself intelligently of the author's principal research: how to write about the pertinent world.

This does not mean that the critic must merely ingest his subject's "ideas"; rather, he must master the writer's unique language, his idiom and syntax and rhythm. Having decided to write a book on Samuel Beckett, Kenner recalls, he had to prepare for eighteen months "until I could command a style sufficiently like his for the purpose. Like, not identical. Beckett couldn't write a book on Beckett." The same deliberate appropriation of his subject's style can be found in Kenner's studies of Pound, Joyce, Eliot, and Lewis, and supremely in his masterpiece *The Pound Era*, where, like Joyce in *Ulysses*, he shifts among a dazzling array of styles.

Reviewers and critics have been slow to recognize this aspect of Kenner's work, and when it has been noticed it has frequently been dismissed as a kind of academic joke. Underlying this reaction is the assumption, sometimes made explicit, that the critic's job is to put things plainly, to which Kenner responds:

> Any linguistic act, including a page of literary explication, is from some points of view as complicated as anything in *Finnegans Wake*. I think people who talk about putting things in plain language should be aware of that: there is no plain language.

What happened to the apostle of "concrete fact" described above? Here, Kenner sounds more like a deconstructionist. This is an important point. It is true that Kenner's vision of order sharply distinguishes him from most poststructuralist critics, an opposition stressed in this account of his work. Yet seen from another perspective, Kenner's work has affinities with that of the poststructuralists.

Kenner, for example, freely concedes that his narratives of literary history are fictions. Noting that some reviewers left-handedly praised *The Pound Era* for its novelistic flair, implying that the book's argument could be discounted, Kenner wonders "what such folk think an acceptable piece of critical writing would be like; there is simply no way not to write a fiction, for reasons embedded in the structure of language itself; sentences hang together grammatically, not semantically, the way a map hangs together geometrically, not geographically."

Kenner is unequivocal in his recognition of the artifice – and the fallibility – entailed in any linguistic act, and it is that recognition which invests with hard-won meaning his affirmation of fidelity to the real. "Pound's great lesson," Kenner wrote, in a memorial piece published in *Saturday Review* after Pound's death in 1972, "was that writing is possible at all: that it is, in fact, possible to nail experiences to the page, that words in sequence can be something more than yatter." To the aggressive defender of common sense, that tribute is an absurdity. ("Who needs to prove that writing is possible? Next they'll be proving that the sky is blue.") The deconstructionist, at least, will acknowledge what is at stake.

In a narrow sense, it is easy to assess Hugh Kenner's influence. His career has coincided with a period of enormous growth in the academic study of literature, particularly the study of modern literature, and his works have made a significant contribution to that development; *The Poetry of Ezra Pound* initiated academic study of its subject. ("Whether that was a service to him or to anyone I have never been sure.") One of the most brilliant figures in an age of brilliant criticism, Kenner has written a shelf-full of books that belie the distinction between critic and creator. Their product is a coherent account (one man's version, but a compelling one) of what he has called "the twentieth-century life of the mind."

No discussion of Kenner's influence, however, can omit consideration of "the case of Ezra Pound": the issues centering on Fascism and anti-Semitism in Pound's life and work. These issues, which remain controversial, have themselves been the subject of many books and articles. They cannot be adequately treated in summary. Nevertheless, several points can be made with regard to the reception of Kenner's work. It is clear that appreciation of Kenner's achievements has been diminished by his apologias for Pound. On the few occasions on which he has directly addressed the questions raised by Pound's Fascism and anti-Semitism, Kenner has evidenced a moral obtuseness the more noticeable in so perceptive a critic. To some extent, then, the critical reaction is justified, yet it must be added that Kenner's "case," like Pound's, is complex, and that for many critics these issues have served as a pretext for dismissing Kenner's entire body of work. That is their loss, for there is no other critic from whom it is possible to learn so much.

Principal criticism

Paradox in Chesterton, 1947
The Poetry of Ezra Pound, 1951
Wyndham Lewis: A Critical Guidebook, 1954
Dublin's Joyce, 1955
Gnomon: Essays on Contemporary Literature, 1958
The Invisible Poet: T. S. Eliot, 1959
Samuel Beckett: A Critical Study, 1961
Flaubert, Joyce, and Beckett: The Stoic Comedians, 1962
Studies in Change: A Book of the Short Story, 1965
The Counterfeiters: An Historical Comedy, 1968
The Pound Era, 1971, 1991
Bucky: A Guided Tour of Buckminster Fuller, 1973
A Reader's Guide to Samuel Beckett, 1973
A Homemade World: The American Modernist Writers, 1975
Joyce's Voices, 1978
Ulysses, 1980
A Colder Eye: The Modern Irish Writers, 1983

The Mechanic Muse, 1987
A Sinking Island: The Modern English Writers, 1988
Mazes: Essays, 1989
Historical Fictions: Essays, 1990
Chuck Jones: A Flurry of Drawings, 1994

Other major works and literary forms

In addition to the books listed above, Hugh Kenner has published several hundred articles, essays, and reviews. While many of these deal with literary topics, others consider such diverse subjects as painting and sculpture, architecture, computers (he has written a user's manual for the Zenith 100 personal computer), and lexicography. Kenner's interest in Buckminster Fuller yielded a technical exposition, *Geodesic Math and How to Use It* (1976).

NONFICTION
Geodesic Math and How to Use It, 1976

EDITED TEXTS
The Art of Poetry, 1959
T. S. Eliot: A Collection of Critical Essays, 1962
Seventeenth Century Poetry: the Schools of Donne and Jonson, 1964
Blast 3, 1984 (with Seamus Cooney, Bradford Morrow, and Bernard Lafourcade)
Desmond Egan, 1990
Selected Poems: Desmond Egan, 1992

Further reading

Bawer, Bruce. "Hugh Kenner: A Sinking Œuvre," in *The New Criterion*. 6, no. 6 (February, 1988), pp. 63–71.
Davenport, Guy. "Hugh Kenner: The Kenner Era," in *National Review*. XXXVII (December 31, 1985), pp. 89–90.
——. "The Critic as Artist," in *Every Force Evolves a Form*, 1987.
The Denver Quarterly. XII (Spring, 1977). Special Kenner issue.
Donoghue, Denis. *Ferocious Alphabets*, 1981.
Goodwin, Will, compiler. *Kenner on Joyce: A Bibliography*, 1991
Hancock, Elise. "Interview with Hugh Kenner," in *Johns Hopkins Magazine*. XXVIII (November, 1977), pp. 10–19.
Rogin, Gilbert. "Out of Adversity Came Diversity," in *Discover*. VII (May, 1986), p. 4.
Sale, Roger. "Hugh Kenner," in *On Not Being Good Enough: Writings of a Working Critic*, 1979.
William Carlos Williams Review. 19, nos. 1–2 (Spring–Fall, 1993), pp. 49–56. Special Kenner issue.

JOHN WILSON

See also American Literary Theory: Twentieth Century

Frank Kermode

English critic and writer

Born: Douglas, Isle of Man; November 29, 1919

Biography

John Frank Kermode was born on November 29, 1919, on the Isle of Man. He has been twice married, in 1947 to Maureen Eccles and in 1976 to Anita Van Vactor. Educated at Liverpool University, Kermode began his academic career at Manchester University (from 1958 to 1965) and Bristol University (from 1965 to 1967). From 1967 to 1974 he was Lord Northcliff Professor at University College, London, and from 1974 until his retirement in 1982 he served as King Edward VII Professor at Cambridge University. He has also held distinguished visiting lectureships at several American institutions: Columbia University, Harvard University, Bryn Mawr College, and the University of California at Irvine. He helped found the *London Review of Books* in 1979. In addition, he has served as general editor since 1964 of Viking's Modern Masters series and since 1984 of the Oxford Authors series of Oxford University Press.

Influence

The world of contemporary British literary criticism was, not so long ago, at once wondrously humane and dismayingly conservative, even reactionary. It was a world in which the well-educated critic spoke gravely and on more or less intimate terms with his audience about issues that were assumed to matter to mankind. It was a criticism as civilized as it was old-fashioned, and as a result British critics in general showed little interest in the revolutions in literature and in literary theory that were attracting so much attention in the United States and Europe in the 1960s and 1970s. In such a more or less staid world, Kermode has performed an especially valuable service, for he has managed to combine the critical mind of a Samuel Johnson and the moral concern of an F. R. Leavis with an attraction to, as well as a certain healthy skepticism about, the newer critical theories of Roland Barthes, Jacques Derrida, and others. Essentially a voice for moderation, Kermode has managed to keep the "great tradition" of British criticism alive by exposing and adapting it to postmodern and poststructuralist influences.

Analysis

In claiming to possess a "limited mind of promiscuous habit," Frank Kermode alludes to, even as he greatly underestimates, those qualities that have made him one of the foremost Anglo-American critics of the twentieth century: moderation, intelligence, and range. Depth and scope, rather than daring, are what distinguish his critical "habit," so much so as to remind one of Edmund Wilson, whose "hard labour," "disciplined commitment," and "volatile curiosity" have drawn Kermode's special approval. Like Wilson, Kermode understands what many academic critics do not, that reviewing is a form of literary criticism and indispensable to "the hygiene of a literary culture." Kermode espouses a critical practice that is accessible to the literary public and that is meditative and evaluative rather than formalist and merely analytical in nature. Although it may be at times difficult to distinguish between art and aesthetic "jokes," it is nevertheless necessary to do so, for art is essentially serious insofar as it helps explain the world – as, for example, John Cage's notorious "4'33"" does not.

Kermode's distaste for the works of Cage and Samuel Beckett is instructive, for what he objects to is their surrender to the very discontinuities against which Kermode has struggled throughout his career. In his first book, *Romantic Image*, he performed a double feat: demolishing the myth of a distinctly modernist breakthrough by establishing the Romantic premise upon which modernism rests, and severely criticizing the Romantics' (and therefore the modernists') efforts to sever poetry and poetic language from life. It is the continuity between art and life that Kermode affirms; thus his choice of a critical method appropriate to his belief: ranging as widely as possible in order to establish essential likenesses. Ranging over Kermode's critical writings, the fruits of his "limited mind of promiscuous habit," one finds a similar scope as well as a sense of development as Kermode continues to search out his critical position. Within this diversity one also notices a remarkable continuity of interests. Thus the discussion which follows will concern three constants within the diversity of Kermode's critical writings: "the problem of schism and continuities," "the human need to make sense through fictions," and the nature of the "classic" and what role the reader plays in determining its meaning.

For Kermode, continuity and all that it implies is precisely what the modern age, including modern literature, has put in doubt. It is harder now, Kermode believes, to have faith in the paradigms one uses – whether literary, religious, political, or social – because it has become so difficult "to imagine a relation between the time of a life and the time of the world." One's sense of time has shrunk to the length of the individual life, and the results of this shrinkage are discontinuity and crisis. What art critic Harold Rosenberg has celebrated as "the tradition of the new" Kermode renders in terms of crisis. Although he rejects the tradition of the new, however, as both illogical and self-defeating (because anarchic), he does recognize the need for a literature (and a criticism) that responds to the changed conditions of modern existence. Working syncretically, first posing an opposition and then resolving the tension between the opposing elements by finding a viable middle ground, he contends that "our stories must recognize mere successiveness without becoming merely successive," and the reason that they must not is that "the survival of the paradigms is as much our business as their erosion." Individual readers will pass away, but the need for paradigms will remain constant. It is this need which makes continuity both possible and real. Writers who evidence this awareness of continuity's essential doubleness draw Kermode's special praise. Jean-Paul Sartre, for example, understands that although there are no givens, no paradigms, not everything can be new. "How to do justice to a chaotic, viscously contingent reality and yet redeem it?" is the question Kermode poses and that Sartre answers, and in answering provides the reader with a "model" text at once complete and provisional.

The tension which Sartre's novel *La Nausée* (1938; *Nausea*, 1949) embodies evidences itself more generally and much more problematically in Kermode's discussion of "the classic" and what the word "classic" means in relation to the *bête noire* of feminist and poststructuralist criticism, "canonicity." As a moderate and a humanist, Kermode wishes to preserve the concept of the classic and the existence of individual classic texts without, however, making any large claims for the intrinsic value of such works. Such claims would run counter to the poststructuralist and existential ideas which, Kermode believes, the modern critic must somehow accommodate, even if not fully accepting them. Moving from the individual text (the focus of the New Criticism), Kermode moves to the larger theoretical question: how does a classic live? How can it be kept alive (that is, continue to be read) in the face of postmodernist doubts? One way is by attempting to determine what such a text meant to its author and his or her contemporary readers – the method favored by literary scholars. Another and better way, Kermode contends, is by a process of accommodation through which the classic is in a sense remade according to the reader's particular culture and literary competence. This latter way implies that there are no distinctions between readings and misreadings. In fact, all readings may be said to be misreadings (and vice versa).

Unlike E. D. Hirsch (*Validity in Interpretation*, 1967), Kermode remains open to the classic's essential plurality of meaning. He is not merely tolerant of this plurality of meanings; Kermode insists that the continued existence of the classic text, or indeed any text, depends on such a plurality. Yet though he rejects Hirsch's conservative position, he does not therefore accept the radical tendency of critics such as Roland Barthes who belittle the classic texts that make up the established literary canon (the result, Barthes contends, of bourgeois taste). Kermode's "classic" text invites and in fact requires the very activity (or quality) that Barthes reserves solely for the most innovative modern texts: the reader must respond "creatively to indeterminacies of meaning inherent in the text and possibly enlarged by the action of time." The "inherent" value of such texts depends not on what is in them but on what is not – on, that is, the existence of the very gaps and inconsistencies which necessitate the reader's imaginative participation in the interpretive process. This kind of interpretive process cannot be reduced to mere philological decoding. Rather, it involves the collaboration of text, reader, and author, whose death Barthes proclaimed but whose resurrection Kermode announces, and it involves as well the acceptance of the incompleteness of all interpretations. Kermode privileges neither text (as did the New Critics) nor author nor reader (Barthes' position), but instead moderates between them. To Barthes' death of the author, Kermode adds the death of the reader and the immortality of the classic text. The text continues to exist, thanks to the reader's efforts, as both the source and the result of all interpretive efforts – efforts that, according to Kermode, would not be made were it not for the fact that the text merits such attention. The "inherent" value of the classic text is nothing more, and nothing less, than its capacity for being misread, which is to say, reread.

In Elizabethan tragedy and more especially in the novel, Kermode has noted, the "end" is less foreseeable, the crisis less tied to some larger design, the plot less deterministic and therefore more open to "the freedom of persons within the plot to choose and so to alter the structure." Kermode's literary theory depends upon the granting of a similar freedom to the reader to interfere in and therefore alter the plot and even the meaning of the text. The reader operates in "the gap between text and meaning" which "is always present and always different in extent." What exists in this "gap" is not some secret to be found out but instead secrecy itself, the fact of the text's irreducible mystery and therefore openness to the misreadings which ensure the text's being reread and reinterpreted. Kermode insists upon the essential openness of the aesthetic text without rejecting, as Barthes and others have, the reader's desire for some one meaning. Readers may not be able to agree as to the meaning of a given text, but they can agree that secrecy does exist at the heart of that text; it is this knowledge that elicits the reader's pleasure and that causes perpetual disappointment over the incompleteness of the meanings that he and other readers assign to the text. Kermode's faith in secrecy as a necessary fiction and in meaning as "a purely anthropomorphic activity" forces him to seek a balanced position that would allow for a plurality of interpretations and still guard against interpretive excess. Whereas Barthes emphasizes the reader's pleasure and liberty, Kermode calls attention to the reader's responsibility in keeping alive the text that, however provisionally and partially, gives his or her life some measure of meaning. In preserving the openness of the text, readers preserve what the openness implies about their own condition, particularly the human need to make meaning.

The interpretive process is, as Kermode has come to realize, both necessary and problematic. It is necessary because "the power to make interpretations is an indispensable instrument of survival in the world." Although he distinguishes between the task of the poet, to make sense of our lives, and that of the critic, "the lesser feat of making sense of the ways we try to make sense of our lives," it becomes clear that the two activities are virtually indentical. Just as the literary work provisionally orders and gives fictive meaning to a purely contingent reality that it both recognizes and supplants, so does criticism deal with the text that forms its reality, a text that has no order or form or meaning except insofar as the critic imagines them. Thus does the line between literary artist and literary critic blur and eventually disappear in the development of Kermode's thought, for each is engaged in an act of the imagination which depends upon an awareness of possibilities and limitations. The critic's task is further complicated by the obligation to justify not only the literary artist's ideas of order but his or her own as well, and part of this obligation necessitates a resistance to all univocal meanings, to all final solutions. The guard against interpretive closure is the knowledge that paradigmatic form must never be divorced from contingent reality. The best literature and the best literary criticism must mediate between the two, and this axiom holds true not only for literary fictions but for political and religious texts as well.

The fact that his is a voice for moderation has made Kermode susceptible to attacks from both the literary left and the literary right. While the former have considered him too provincial and conservative, the latter have judged him nearly nihilistic. Numerous influential younger critics such as David Lodge have acknowledged their indebtedness to Kermode's theories in general and to *The Sense of an Ending* in particular, but many others have been troubled by "a real loss of belief in the value of literature and literary study" which Dame Helen Gardner detected in his work. In *Literature Against Itself: Literary Ideas in Modern Society* (1979), Gerald Graff goes much further, claiming that Kermode in fact denies literature's mimetic function while simultaneously, and therefore inconsistently, making large claims for literature's cognitive uses. How, Graff asks, can anything intelligent be said if one agrees with what Kermode's theory implies, that everything is a fiction, reality and criticism included? How can one fiction be distinguished from any other, literature from reality, for example, since both are fictive? Objections such as Graff's and Gardner's are understandable but by no means convincing. Even if one should agree with Jan Gorak and Frank Lentricchia concerning the self-contradiction within Kermode's criticism, the fact remains that it constitutes less a weakness than a strength, evidence that Kermode's theory, or solution, is by no means final but instead open to further refinement as he continues less to espouse a hard and fast position than to test his own assumptions and those of others in an effort to save both literature and literary criticism from obsolescence on the one hand and inconsequentiality on the other. In its blend of "interpretive ingenuity" and "scholarly caution," Kermode's work represents twentieth-century British criticism at its best.

Principal criticism

Romantic Image, 1957
Wallace Stevens, 1960
Puzzles and Epiphanies: Essays and Reviews, 1958–1961, 1962
The Sense of an Ending: Studies in the Theory of Fiction, 1967
Continuities, 1968
Shakespeare, Spenser, Donne: Renaissance Essays, 1971
D. H. Lawrence, 1973

The Classic, 1975
The Genesis of Secrecy: On the Interpretation of Narrative, 1979
Essays on Fiction, 1971–1982, 1983
Forms of Attention, 1985
History and Value, 1988
An Appetite for Poetry, 1989
Poetry, Narrative, History, 1990
The Uses of Error, 1991

Other major works and literary forms

It might be more appropriate to call Frank Kermode a "critic" rather than a "literary critic." Although he has written chiefly on literary matters, he has brought his critical intelligence to bear upon a wide range of nonliterary subjects, from the Gospels and the visual arts to pop culture and student revolt, and he has published a memoir (*Not Entitled*, 1995). As a critic – literary and otherwise – he has promulgated his views both in the academy and out, in scholarly works as well as in essays and reviews and in programs aired by the British Broadcasting Corporation.

EDITED TEXTS
The Tempest, 1954
The Living Milton: Essays by Various Hands, 1960
Discussions of John Donne, 1962
The Winter's Tale, 1963, revised edition 1988
Four Centuries of Shakespearean Criticism, 1965
William Shakespeare: The Final Plays, 1965
The Metaphysical Poets: Essays on Metaphysical Poetry, 1969
King Lear: A Casebook, 1969
The Oxford Reader: Varieties of Contemporary Discourse, 1971 (with Richard Poirier)
The Literary Guide to the Bible, 1987 (with Robert Alter)
The Way We Live Now, 1994.

ANTHOLOGIES
English Pastoral Poetry From the Beginnings to Marvell, 1952
Seventeenth Century Songs, 1956
Spenser: Selections from the Minor Poems and "The Faerie Queen," 1965
The Oxford Anthology of English Literature, 1973 (with John Hollander et al.)
Selected Prose of T. S. Eliot, 1975
Andrew Marvell, 1990 (with Keith Walker)
The Oxford Book of Letters, 1995 (with Anita Kermode)
Wallace Stevens: Collected Poetry and Prose, 1998

AUTOBIOGRAPHY
Not Entitled, 1995

Further reading

Arac, Jonathan. "History and Mystery: The Criticism of Frank Kermode," in *Salmagundi*. LV (1982), pp. 135–155.
Gorak, Jan. *Critic of Crisis: A Study of Frank Kermode*, 1987.
Graff, Gerald. *Literature Against Itself: Literary Ideas in Modern Society*, 1979.
Lentricchia, Frank. *After the New Criticism*, 1980.
Tudeau-Clayton, Margaret, and Martin Warner, eds. *Addressing Frank Kermode: Essays in Criticism and Interpretation*, 1991.

ROBERT A. MORACE

See also British Literary Theory: Twentieth Century; Leavis

Heinrich von Kleist

German writer and playwright

Born: Frankfurt an der Oder, Prussia; October 18, 1777
Died: Berlin, Prussia; November 21, 1811

Biography

Heinrich von Kleist was born on October 18, 1777, in Frankfurt an der Oder, the eldest son of Captain Joachim Friedrich von Kleist and his second wife, Juliane Ulrike Pannwitz. Following family tradition, Kleist spent seven years in the Prussian army before enrolling at the University of Frankfurt an der Oder. He later attended lectures in Berlin until he left in August, 1800, on a trip that marked his break from family and tradition and freed him to find himself as a writer.

Kleist never married, although he was engaged for two years. He had very unconventional and demanding expectations of female companionship; in words suggested by a description of Friedrich, a character in his drama *Das Käthchen von Heilbronn: Oder, Die Feuerprobe* (1810; *Cathy of Heilbronn: Or, The Trial by Fire*, 1927), the woman capable of loving Kleist probably did not exist.

He tried his hand at four separate publishing ventures: an unsuccessful attempt at his own publishing house in 1807; a literary journal, *Phöbus*, which survived for twelve monthly issues from 1807 to 1808; an unsuccessful attempt at a nationalistic newspaper, *Germania*, in 1809; and finally his *Berliner Abendblätter*, the first Berlin daily newsletter, which survived for 153 issues, from 1810 to 1811.

The last ten years of Kleist's short but productive life were fraught with frustration and disappointment. He had difficulty supporting himself as a writer. Efforts to find acceptable work in the Civil Service failed on several occasions, including at the end of his life, when he hoped for a restored commission in the military. Kleist committed suicide on November 21, 1811, with Henriette Vogel, a terminally ill acquaintance who requested to die by his hand.

Influence

Kleist was brought up in the shadows of Johann Wolfgang von Goethe and Friedrich Schiller, but his sharp insight into human nature, morality, and behavior – and the unrelenting and essentially unfulfilled search for truth – ran quite contrary to the Enlightenment and prevailing attitudes of contemporary Prussian society, as well as to the harmony, balance, and beauty sought by the classical and Romantic literary movements flourishing during the early nineteenth century.

Kleist's perceptions and attitudes were nearly one hundred years ahead of his time. After the turn of the twentieth century, his ideas and perspectives became relevant and appreciated among the existentialists. Kleist's readership has grown substantially since the 1930s, although he is read less as a critic than as a dramatist and a writer of short fiction. His grasp of the human situation and the irony and ambivalence with which he approaches life have endeared him to modern readers.

Analysis

The best collection of Kleist's writings outlining his feelings and theories on the purpose and function of literature is a series of essays appearing in the *Berliner Abendblätter*. These were written near the end of his career and reflect somewhat the posture assumed in his other writings. Kleist's most complete critical statements, however, are made through his poetic works. Together, the plays and short fiction present Kleist's concern with the human condition and the role of literature in developing, delineating, and refining perspectives on the quest for truth.

In the introduction to the first issue of the *Berliner Abendblätter*, Kleist outlines the role and obligation of the literary critic. He camouflages rather weakly his own critical posture in "Prayer of Zarathustra," which was accepted as Kleist's position and policy statement as he started his own daily publication. He explains that whereas humans have god-given abilities, both edifying and demeaning, reveling in their breasts, they frequently think that they are in control of their lives. Yet Kleist believed that humanity is held captive by prejudices and ill-conceived perceptions. Were it not for occasional poetic revelations of humanity's lofty potential, one would have no inkling of the heights from which one could peruse the world. Sophistic education, tradition, and custom often blind people to the truly virtuous.

Fortunately, God occasionally permits the scales to fall from the eyes of a chosen servant so that he or she can see the foolishness and oversights of his or her fellows. With that insight comes the power of the word, enabling this chosen one to move fearlessly and lovingly among his or her fellow humans and awaken them from the curious somnolence in which they find themselves. Kleist suggests that true critics should be moved by the sufferings of their generation and blessed with insight into the superficialities, errors, and hypocrisies that cause the depravity. Kleist allowed Zarathustra to plead for courage that he might cast down the pernicious and the incurable, frighten the wicked, warn the wayward, and nudge the foolish. Beyond the judgmental, Zarathustra asks for guidance in weaving laurels for the virtuous.

Kleist's abiding and unrelenting concern for the role of literature in finding and conveying meaning is perhaps best reflected through another of these essays, "Letter from One Poet to Another." Kleist expresses concern when a colleague commends him on form, meter, rhythm, and harmony in his writing, and he laments that these things would have better accomplished their task had his reader not noticed them at all. Kleist confesses that when communicating, if he could reach into his soul, grasp an idea, and deliver it with open hands to the reader without further embellishment or means of conveyance, then that alone would fulfill the longing of his soul. His reader, too, would benefit from being undistracted by ambiguities arising out of concern for form or structure. All too frequently, however, one busies oneself excessively with the wrappings, and the fruit remains neglected and unappreciated. As poetically satisfying as speech, rhythm, rhyme, and the like are, they are empty detractors, and the able poet can do no better than to make them disappear behind the spirit and meaning of his creation.

Kleist was uncomfortable with both contemporary schools of prevailing literary thought – the classical (or neoclassical), represented almost exclusively by Goethe and Schiller, and the Romantic, whose ideas were gaining recognition throughout Germany. Kleist believed that life could never be as balanced and harmonious and well motivated by such clear delineations of right and wrong, good and bad, as the "noble soul" of the classic represented. Life was too unpredictable, the fate of the individual too uncertain, and the disquieted soul too unknowable for Kleist to find solace with classic constraint. Given his constant, almost oppressive concern with the uncertainty of the purpose and meaning of existence, Kleist can perhaps best be classified as an early forerunner to what has since become known as existentialism.

Like the work of his contemporaries in both schools, his writings reveal a longing for absolute, ultimate truth, truth that will endure all challenges. Yet, uncharacteristic for his time, absolute truth appeared for Kleist to be fleeting, sometimes changing, and ultimately indiscernible. In his poetic works, probings for truth are often linked with a central experience, usually some form of the trial motif, where truth lurks somewhere behind an overwhelming array of empirical, circumstantial contradictions.

Kleist agreed with the Romantics that feeling and sensitive intuition are more dependable revealers of hidden truth than are empirical processes or the physical senses. This idea distanced him from the spirit of the Enlightenment, which pervaded his early education and the tightly structured Prussian society in which he lived. The search for truth always seemed to be ironically distant from apparent physical realities. Thus Kleist developed a chronic distrust of appearances. He perceived an ironic ambivalence in things called good or bad, right or wrong, and their value or essence was frequently quite the opposite from accepted appearances. Whereas the Romantics looked for meaning and fulfillment in a metaphysical paradise beyond the senses, Kleist sought in vain for any semblance of order, fulfillment, or spiritual salvation in some poetic Elysium. Ultimately Kleist mistrusted even the heart, which like the senses could be duped into legitimizing counterfeit perceptions and could thus betray truth.

For Kleist, the classic idealists seemed to ignore the demoniac, unpredictable, and intuitive nature in humankind, and the Romantics overlooked the fact that in spite of one's dreams and ideals, there was a harsh reality that demanded resolution and direction. Kleist perceived the Romantics as living in a self-centered, idealistic world and believed that they ignored the social disruption caused when their idealistic notions clashed with reality. Kleist finds a sort of compromise in his last drama, *Prinz Friedrich von Homburg* (1821; *The Prince of Homburg*, 1875), where he allowed the Romantic nature of Homburg to die and a new self-willed, morally responsible statesman to be resurrected in the service of a moral state.

Kleist believed that humans have lost their pre-Fall innocence and are alone, seeking their way in a confused and decrepit world. In his essay "The Marionette Theater," Kleist represents humankind as having lost grace and harmony through the process of self-knowledge. The door returning to paradise is locked, and the only option is to work one's way through this earthly existence gathering knowledge, insight, and experience as progressive approximations of truth and hoping to find another door open at the other end of life through which to return. One thus faces a lifelong pursuit of gathering wisdom and rehearsing behavior in a quest to regain, and even exceed, the innocence and perfection lost through the Fall. The typically Kleistian enigma of this predicament lies in the inability to ascertain what is truth, or which "truths" will still be intact when one gets to the "other door." One finds oneself in the peculiar and frustrating predicament of being caught in this life between two states of perfection. Before the Fall one was innocent and without blemish because one intuitively did what was right and good. Somewhere up ahead was the hope and dream of returning to this paradise having regained entrance by progressively gathering truth and wisdom and becoming perfect again through omniscience. Thus one stands between the puppet and the god and feels attracted and nourished from both realms, but in this life one can achieve neither.

This idea of paradise lost and regained is not new, but it was central for Kleist. His characters occasionally have dark premonitions of the past and lost innocence and sometimes even anxiously strive to return to it. Adam, in *Der zerbrochene Krug* (1808; *The Broken Jug*, 1930), would prefer to return to bed rather than face his own judgment and the consequences of his "fall." Other noble characters come very close to achieving perfection at the omniscient end, but they either have to die to enter therein or are forced to return, frustrated and despondent, to decrepit mortality. Such glimpses into the intuitive perfection of the pre-Fall condition, or into the anticipated Elysium after death, provide hope for humankind's quest, but they are always transitory and one must always face the brutality of the real world. They provide a vision of what life could be, or should be, but unfortunately never will be.

For Kleist, humanity's progression is either from or toward perfection. Ironically, Kleist teaches in his essay "Thoughts on the Way of the World" that civilizations generally regress rather than improve substantially. He illustrates how the civilizations of Rome and Greece were first heroic, which represented the peak of their goodness. When they ran out of genuine champions of virtue, they created new ones through the arts. When the artistic heroes disappeared, they developed rules and laws in an attempt to mimic their lost grandeur. When the rules became prolific, confusing, and contradictory, they summarized the wisdom of life, and when they were finished with that, they became corrupt. The poignant contrast between the idyllic vision and the vain reality provides Kleist's sharpest criticism of social, legal, and military institutions and practices of his day.

Much of Kleist's literary work was not published until fifteen years after his death, with the first edition of his collected works edited by Ludwig Tieck (*Heinrich von Kleists gesammelte Schriften*, 1826). His dramas *The Broken Jug*, one of the most successful German comedies of all time, and *The Prince of Homburg* appear regularly on the German stage. Other works, *Die Marquise von O . . .* (1810; *The Marquise of O . . .*, 1960) and *Michael Kohlhaas* (1810; English translation, 1844) in particular have enjoyed considerable success as films.

Principal criticism

Phöbus: Ein Journal für die Kunst, serial 1807–1808, book 1861

Essays in the *Berliner Abendblätter*, 1810–1811 (collected in *An Abyss Deep Enough: Letters of Heinrich von Kleist, with a Selection of Essays and Anecdotes*, 1982): "Gebet des Zoroaster" ("Prayer of Zarathustra"), "Betrachtungen über den Weltlauf" ("Thoughts on the Way of the World"), "Allerneuster Erziehungsplan" ("The Very Last Word in Modern Educational Theory"), "Brief eines jungen Dichters an einen jungen Maler" ("Letter from a Young Writer to a Young Painter"), "Von der Überlegung" ("On Thinking Things Over"), "Ein Satz aus der höheren Kritik" ("A Thought on Higher Criticism"), "Über das Marionettentheater" ("The Marionette Theater"), and "Brief eines Dichters an einen Andern" ("Letter from One Poet to Another")

Other major works and literary forms

Heinrich von Kleist is primarily recognized for his dramas and novellas. In addition, he wrote a comparatively short collection of lyric poetry and epigrams, mostly didactic, political, or nationalistic in nature, and about twenty-five published anecdotes. His shorter prose works and essays can be grouped into those dealing with literature and the arts, political and nationalistic essays written during a relatively brief period around 1809, and editorials and news commentaries for his daily newsletters. He was a prolific letter writer; more than two hundred of his letters have been preserved and published.

NOVELS

Michael Kohlhaas, 1810 (novella; English translation, 1844)

SHORT FICTION
Erzählungen, 1810–1811 (2 volumes; *The Marquise of O, and Other Stories*, 1960)

PLAYS
Die Familie Schroffenstein, 1803 (*The Schroffenstein Family*, 1916)
Amphitryon, 1807 (English translation, 1962)
Penthesilea, 1808 (English translation, 1959)
Der zerbrochene Krug, 1808 (*The Broken Jug*, 1930)
Robert Guiskard, 1808 (English translation, 1962)
Das Käthchen von Heilbronn: Oder, Die Feuerprobe, 1810 (*Cathy of Heilbronn: Or, The Trial by Fire*, 1927)
Die Hermannsschlacht, 1821
Prinz Friedrich von Homburg, 1821 (*The Prince of Homburg*, 1875)

MISCELLANEOUS
Heinrich von Kleists gesammelte Schriften, 1826 (Ludwig Tieck, editor)
Selected Writings, 1997 (English translation)

Further reading

Allan, Sean D. *The Plays of Heinrich von Kleist: Ideals and Illusions*, 1996.
Brown, Hilda Meldrum. *Heinrich von Kleist: The Ambiguity of Art and the Necessity of Form*, 1998.
Cooke, Raymond. *Heinrich von Kleist: A Critical Study*, 1987.
Dyer, Denys. *The Stories of Kleist: A Critical Study*, 1977.
Ellis, John Martin. *Heinrich von Kleist: Studies in the Character and Meaning of His Writings*, 1979.
Gearey, John. *Heinrich von Kleist: A Study in Tragedy and Anxiety*, 1968.
Graham, Ilse. *Heinrich von Kleist: Word into Flesh, a Poet's Quest for the Symbol*, 1977.
Grandin, John M. *The Influence of Heinrich von Kleist on Franz Kafka*, 1987.
Hamburger, Michael. *Reason and Energy*, 1957.
Hohendahl, Peter Uwe. *A History of German Literary Criticism, 1730–1980*, 1988.
Maass, Joachim. *Kleist: A Biography*, 1983. Translated by Ralph Manheim.
Reeve, William C. *In Pursuit of Power: Heinrich von Kleist's Machiavellian Protagonists*, 1987.
Sembdner, Helmut. *Kleist-Bibliographie, 1803–1862*, 1966.
Ugrinsky, Alexej. *Heinrich von Kleist Studies*, 1980.

JOSEPH O. BAKER

See also Goethe; Grillparzer; Romanticism; Schiller

L. C. Knights

English critic and scholar

Born: Grantham, England; May 15, 1906
Died: Cambridge, England; March 8, 1997

Biography

Lionel Charles Knights was born in Grantham, Lincolnshire, and educated at Selwyn College, Cambridge, where he read history and English and graduated with first-class honors in 1928. He taught for a short period and then returned to Cambridge as Adelaide Stoll Bachelor Fellow at Christ's College. There, as a contemporary of William Empson, he studied under I. A. Richards. He was the Charles Oldham Shakespeare Scholar in 1928, and winner of the Members' Prize in 1929. He gained his M.A. in 1931. Knights began lecturing in English at the University of Manchester in 1933, and was awarded his Ph.D. in 1936 for work which would subsequently be published as a critical study of Ben Jonson's drama. He was appointed professor of English at Sheffield University in 1947, and became the Winterstoke Professor of English at Bristol University in 1953. He was the Andrew Mellon Visiting Professor at the University of Pittsburgh from 1961 to 1962 and in 1966, and the Beckman Visiting Professor at Berkeley in 1970. He delivered the Clark Lectures for 1970–1971 at Trinity College, Cambridge. In 1965 he had returned to Cambridge as Edward VII Professor of English Literature at Queens College, where he remained until his retirement in 1973. In 1932 Knights cofounded the critical periodical *Scrutiny*, and he was a member of its editorial board until 1953 when it ceased publication. He was awarded honorary degrees from the universities of York and Manchester, and was an Honorary Fellow of Selwyn College, Cambridge. He married Elizabeth Mary Barnes in 1936, and they had two children.

Influence

By far Knights' best-known work is the book-length essay *How Many Children Had Lady Macbeth?* (1933), which attacked A. C. Bradley's work on Shakespearean characters. It was a critique of what Knights and other contributors to *Scrutiny* in the 1930s perceived as an outmoded, nineteenth-century attitude to literary criticism that was still being widely practiced. Knights' achievement in the essay was to have argued for an appraisal of William Shakespeare's tragedies as "dramatic poetry" to be analyzed in a modern critical method, rather than a Bradleyan character-oriented method, in which collections of characters would be studied individually, divorced from the poetic whole. He prepared the way for new methods of metaphorical interpretation in Shakespeare criticism which reacted against Bradley's more literal stance; other modern critics such as Dover Wilson, E. E. Stoll, and G. Wilson Knight were to produce work that analyzed Shakespeare's consistent use of imagery and symbols throughout individual plays and play sequences. Ultimately, this reaction against Bradley was tempered with time, and the enduring value of his criticism was to reassert itself; Knights and his fellow proponents of this modern school of Shakespeare criticism may be seen to have established an historically inevitable – if overzealous – rebuttal of the emphasis of Bradley's work. Some of Knights' criticism shows a strong sociological interest, a flirtation with Marxism that was very much of its time in academic circles in the 1930s. Knights was always insistent upon his indebtedness to the criticism and teaching of I. A. Richards and F. R. Leavis, and the lasting influence that they had on his own work. He wrote toward the end of his life that "Leavis was the most important intellectual influence of my life in young adulthood; without his influence a large part of me might have remained dormant."

Analysis

Knights' first publication was the ironically entitled *How Many Children Had Lady Macbeth?*. It was an unreserved attack on what he regarded as a misguided emphasis on characterization and the rationalization of dramatic events as the ultimate criteria for judging literary works, particularly Shakespearean drama. In the essay, Knights claims to perceive in early-twentieth-century Shakespeare criticism (of which he suggests there is an overabundance) a tendency to presume that the "main business" of a writer is to create characters. In fact, Shakespeare had long been celebrated in English letters largely for his genius in the creation of vivid and rounded characters, and Knights and other *Scrutiny* writers were adamant in dismissing this kind of literary appraisal as a relic of nineteenth-century criticism. In *How Many Children Had Lady Macbeth?* Knights portrays the critical obsession with characters as fallacious and widespread: he regrets that schoolchildren in his day are understood to have fully "appreciated" a drama if they feel impelled to discuss and analyze its characters. He goes on to argue that the character-oriented conception of literature is an imbalanced view which had long since "invaded" the criticism of another literary form – the novel. He takes issue with Hugh Walpole's claim in *The Waverley Pageant* (1932) that "The test of a character in any novel is that it should have existed before the book that reveals it to us began and should continue after the book is closed." Knights' response is forthright:

> It should be obvious that a criterion for the novel by which we should have to condemn *Wuthering Heights*, *Heart of Darkness*, *Ulysses*, *To the Lighthouse* and the bulk of the work of D. H. Lawrence does not need to be very seriously considered.

Knights' approval of the emphasis on the authorial characteristics exhibited by these novels, rather than simply the dramatic characters of the fiction, signals his own affiliations as a critic raised in the modernist, postwar era of New Criticism. He implicitly claims Shakespeare for modernist poetics and analysis by demonstrating the amenability of his play texts to modern critical methods, and in doing so Knights is a true inheritor of the criticism of I. A. Richards. He goes on to survey the prioritization of the construction of character in some recent critical works on Shakespeare's drama, before identifying the epitome of such criticism ("the most illustrious example") to be A. C. Bradley's influential volume *Shakespearean Tragedy* (1904). Knights regards Bradley's literalism with regard to the characters and events of Shakespeare's drama as wrong-footed, a method in which "the detective interest supersedes the critical." It is against Bradley's general approach that Knights takes aim.

A. B. Walkley's essay "Professor Bradley's Hamlet" (*Times Literary Supplement*, April 7, 1905) had already argued against Bradley's insistence upon regarding Shakespeare's characters as fully realized human personalities by countering it with a reassertion of the practical considerations of the dramatist who must construct a workable and commercial entertainment. A. J. A. Waldock's *Hamlet: A Study in Critical Method* (1931) considered Bradley's attempt to reconstruct what takes place "behind the scenes" of *Hamlet* (in order to elucidate the main character's psychology) to be flawed for similar reasons. Waldock had insisted that "Drama is not history." Knights' approach is allied to that of the earlier Bradleyan dissenters, but rather than examining the practicalities and contingencies of a dramatic production in order to undermine Bradley's idealistic concentration upon Shakespeare's characters, he asserts that Shakespearean tragedy is not primarily – or merely – a delineation of temporalized personalities, but rather it is "dramatic poetry" – authorial verse literature in its own right. Knights' textual method in this study is thus intentionally regardless of the practicalities of dramatic production, and minimizes the "abstraction" of characters from the work by insisting upon the apprehension of a play as a unified poetic whole:

> In the mass of Shakespeare criticism there is not a hint that "character" – like "plot," "rhythm," "construction" and all our other critical counters – is merely an abstraction from the total response in the mind of the reader or spectator, brought into being by written or spoken words, and that our duty as critics is to examine first the words of which the play is composed, then the total effect which this combination of words produces in our mind. This applies equally to the novel or any other form of art which uses language as its medium.

Knights is arguing for a middle path: *How Many Children Had Lady Macbeth?* is an objection to the overemphasis on Shakespeare's characters, but it is not ultimately an assertion that conceiving of a play as a unified linguistic whole is the only critical approach. His succeeding publication would demonstrate this stance by examining the economic conditions in Renaissance England in some detail and relating them to the dramatic texts of the period.

There is a case that Knights was being somewhat reductive and generalized in his apprehension of Bradley's argument in *Shakespearean Tragedy*. For example, Bradley had made it clear that in *Macbeth* many of the minor characters are "sketched lightly . . . seldom developed further than the strict purposes of the action required" and that this makes *Macbeth* in practice a superior drama to *King Lear*, if slightly inferior as a "dramatic poem." Here, Bradley's terms and concerns are very close to those which permeate Knights' study, and his conclusions are not dissimilar. In fact, he exhibits an alertness to dramatic practicalities that many subsequent critics felt he lacked. It does not appear to be the case that Bradley simply mistakes Shakespeare's characters for real people, as he was regularly charged. It is fair to conclude that Knights invokes Bradley as an icon of tendencies in Shakespeare studies that predate the New Criticism, placing him in a school supposedly resistant to metaphorical and symbolic readings of drama; in doing so, Knights simplifies Bradley's work into opposition.

Drama and Society in the Age of Jonson (1937) was based on Knights' doctoral thesis which was completed in the preceding year. It was his first full-length critical book, and sets out to examine, within the Elizabethan and Jacobean period, a subject just as pertinent to the social and political climate of the 1930s: "the relation between economic activities and general culture." From the opening of the study Knights exhibits a detailed interest in Marx and Engels' ideas combined with a dissatisfaction with the tendency of Marxist-oriented critics to oversimplify the relationship between the methods of production and "cultural consciousness" or "spiritual processes." Knights states that his aim is to avoid the "intellectual flag-waving" and "exasperating haziness" of much politically affiliated criticism, and to be rigorous in his description and analysis of the economic culture of the period. Knights establishes Ben Jonson as focus of his study, and aims to prove that Jonson is "the greatest dramatist . . . handling social themes" in English Renaissance drama. Knights' method is to incorporate materialist concerns by acknowledging the plays to be social products, but not by limiting his study – as others had done – to those plays and dramatists that had made contemporary economics and culture their subject. Knights suggests that Jonson is something of a proto-Marxist himself. The dramatist can be depicted as a clear-sighted social critic from an earlier, preindustrial epoch:

> the standards of judgement that [Jonson and his contemporaries] brought to bear were not formed in that new world of industrial enterprise. They belonged to an older world which was still "normal", a world of small communities in which . . . human problems can be truly perceived.

Knights suggests that Jonson's satiric representation of contemporary life derives its forcefulness from the contrast with "the traditional economic morality" which had existed in the Middle Ages, and which was being corrupted by the new mercantile, urban economy. But Knights simultaneously argues that a rigidly Marxist, "economic" approach can be irrelevant and imprecise. Elizabethan and Jacobean drama was a popular medium, enjoyed by all classes, yet it was maintained by the patronage of a hereditary, landowning governing class which was feeling the encroachment of a new commerce and industry. For Knights, questions of ideological representation and economic necessity in the drama of the period are necessarily complex, but he ultimately chooses to place economic concerns within a wider, literary context. Although the plays are clearly "means" with various social and economic purposes, Knights refuses that the writers themselves or the contemporary critic should not consider them as cultural "ends" as well, in the light of which his own apprehension of the plays as "dramatic poetry" is the fullest and most inclusive approach. By grounding his critical study within a detailed analysis of their social and economic milieu, Knights attempts to demonstrate the astuteness and vigor of dramatists such as Jonson, Thomas Dekker, and Thomas Middleton. He identifies an engagement with major social developments within their work, a depiction (and arguably a critique) of their culture. Knights is by no means a Marxist critic per se, yet it is this work that exhibits most sharply his continuing – if unadventurous – interest in the relevance of Marx and Engels' writings when examining the potential for writers to depict or analyze the political realities of their own epoch.

Some Shakespearean Themes (1959) and *An Approach to Hamlet* (1960) are two contrasting Shakespearean studies which appear later in Knights' career; the former is a result of thirty years of work on seventeenth-century literature and Shakespeare's drama in particular; the latter is a close analysis of *Hamlet*, and its eponymous lead character, which artfully falls short of becoming a Bradleyan endeavor. *Some Shakespearean Themes* outlines Knights' author-centered approach to Shakespeare's work on a grand scale, and it is based on Knights' conviction that "Shakespeare's plays form a coherent whole, that they stem from and express a developing 'attitude to life.'" Knights maintains this belief while acknowledging that Shakespeare's plays were also written as a "response to outside demands," including the practical demands of writing to an audience. *Some Shakespearean Themes* pursues the approach to drama as poetry that Knights had employed in his first critical work. Here, it is "the strength, integrity and coherence of [Shakespeare's] poetic thought, that makes his work something properly described as a philosophic achievement." This conception of Shakespeare's œuvre as an aesthetically and ideologically consistent work in its own right has many affinities with the criticism of G. Wilson Knight, Knights' contemporary, and a fellow successor to I. A. Richards. In his books *The Imperial Theme* (1931), *The Wheel of Fire* (1949), and *The Crown of Life* (1958), Wilson Knight examined the epic poetics of Shakespeare's histories and tragedies according to their highly consistent use of metaphor and symbol in the portrayal of the morality of personal and political machinations.

In *An Approach to Hamlet* Knights addresses Shakespeare's philosophically problematic play and character in a similar manner, but with a keen awareness that "critics are in danger of finding reflected what they bring with them to the task of interpretation." His analysis is tentative and exploratory, and rests upon concepts that recall Leavis' analyses such as "maturity" and "integration of attitude." Knights relates Hamlet to Lear (as two characters that epitomize the poetic themes of their respective plays) by suggesting that both are "studies of the mind's engagement with the world." Thus Lear learns to "see better" by means of a purgatorial experience, while Hamlet embodies an "intermediate stage of spirit" and cannot break out of a cycle of "loathing and self-contempt." Knights' endeavor in both of these books is to examine Shakespeare's characters strictly as focal elements for the overall thematic qualities of the dramatic work; Hamlet and Lear are thus conduits for what Knights sees as Shakespeare's wide-reaching "poetic thought," rather than realizable characters that are capable of isolation from their dramatic poetic context.

Public Voices (1971) collects the Clark Lectures that Knights delivered at Trinity College, Cambridge, from 1970 to 1971, and sees him returning to the political background of seventeenth-century literature that he had explored in *Poetry, Politics and the English Tradition* (1954) and *Shakespeare's Politics* (1957). For the purposes of illustration and reference, Knights draws direct parallels between the political literature of the period and contemporary political language, and sees a correlation between the efficacy of a political regime and the general literacy of the population. He divides public language into four categories, and his general thesis is that "there should be some connexion – however complex and difficult to define – between the first three kinds (speech, manifesto, political theory) and the fourth (art)." His lectures are incidentally polemical in as far as he argues, after Noam Chomsky's *American Power and the New Mandarins* (1969), that contemporary public language prevents a subtlety of thought and debate, that it is actually "narrowing the range of the thinkable." At the same time, his aim is to analyze literature of various kinds from the period of Shakespeare to John Dryden by judging its "tone and manner" in a literary critical manner reminiscent of Leavis, ultimately searching for "the authentic voice of reason, humanity and common sense." His survey is thus a fusion of historical, political, and literary methods, and its main criteria are "tone," "manner," and "sympathy."

Many of Knights' essays were collected during his career in the *Explorations* volumes, the majority of them concentrating on seventeenth-century drama and poetry. It is for his claiming of Shakespeare for modern analysis and his work on *Scrutiny* that he continues to be best known.

Principal criticism

How Many Children Had Lady Macbeth? An Essay in the Theory and Practice of Shakespeare Criticism, 1933
Drama and Society in the Age of Jonson, 1937
Explorations: Essays in Criticism, Mainly on the Literature of the Seventeenth Century, 1946
Literature and the Study of Society, 1948
Poetry, Politics and the English Tradition, 1954
Shakespeare's Politics, with Some Reflections on the Nature of Tradition, 1957
Some Shakespearean Themes, 1959
An Approach to Hamlet, 1960
William Shakespeare: The Histories: Richard III, King John, Richard II, Henry V, 1962
Further Explorations, 1965
Public Voices: Literature and Politics with Special Reference to the Seventeenth Century, 1971
Explorations III, 1976
"Hamlet" and Other Shakespearean Essays, 1979

Other major works and literary forms

L. C. Knights was a prolific essayist and a large amount of his uncollected criticism may be found in *Scrutiny*.

EDITED TEXTS
Metaphor and Symbol, 1960 (with Basil Cottle)
Myth and Symbol: Critical Approaches and Applications, 1964

MISCELLANEOUS
"*Scrutiny* and F. R. L.: A Personal Memoir," in *The Leavises: Recollections and Impressions*, 1984. Edited by Denys Thompson

Further reading

Bryant, J. A., Jr. "L. C. Knights and *Explorations*," in *Sewanee Review*. 93, no. 3 (Summer, 1985), pp. 446–456.
Cooke, Katharine. *A. C. Bradley and His Influence in Twentieth-Century Shakespeare Criticism*, 1972.
Nuttall, A. D. "The Argument about Shakespeare's Characters," in *Critical Quarterly*. VII, no. 2 (1965), pp. 107–119.

MICHAEL BRETT

See also Bateson; Bradley; British Literary Theory: Twentieth Century; Leavis; Richards

Annette Kolodny

American critic

Born: Brooklyn, New York; August 21, 1941

Biography

Annette Kolodny was born in 1941 in Brooklyn, New York, the eldest of three daughters of a middle-class Jewish family. Educationally, she benefited from the publicly funded schooling system in the district, attending Erasmus Hall High School and later Brooklyn College of the City University of New York, from which she graduated in 1962 with a B.A. *magna cum laude* with honors in English. After a brief – though eye-opening – stint as associate to the editor of *Newsweek*'s international editions, Kolodny returned to academic pursuits, hoping to encourage awareness of the power of words in forming public opinion.

From 1963 until 1969 Kolodny was a masters and later a doctoral student at the University of California, Berkeley. In 1970, having been awarded her Ph.D. for a thesis entitled "The Pastoral Impulse in American Writing, 1590–1850," Kolodny married the novelist and biographer Daniel Peters. The political ferment of the period and its prevailing ethos of identity politics saw Kolodny become involved in civil-rights politics and, toward the late 1960s, the emergent women's liberation movement. This early consciousness-raising in feminist politics has energized all of her subsequent academic work. Her explicit commitment to women's politics caused considerable friction in her professional life, most notably in her five-year sexual discrimination suit in the 1970s against the University of New Hampshire. Kolodny won the case and was awarded the then highest damages payment in compensation for the university's obstruction of her promotion and appointment to tenure, lending what Kolodny describes as a personal "legal nightmare" wider political and institutional resonance.

Kolodny's career flourished in the wake of her two best-known works, *The Lay of the Land: Metaphor as Experience and History in American Life and Letters* (1975) and *The Land Before Her: Fantasy and Experience of the American Frontiers, 1630–1860* (1984), both re-readings of American expansionism from feminist and psychoanalytic perspectives. Her important synthesis of second-wave feminist literary studies, the essay "Dancing through the Minefield: Some Observations of the Theory, Practice and Politics of a Feminist Literary Criticism," won the 1979 Florence Howe Essay Prize and has since been much anthologized. In 1983 she was appointed professor of literature at the Rensselaer Polytechnic Institute, and in 1988 she took up an appointment as dean of the University of Arizona's College of Humanities. Her experience of academic administration during the free-market driven 1980s and 1990s forms the substructure of her book *Failing the Future: A Dean Looks at Higher Education in the Twenty-First Century* (1998), a plea for diversity, participatory democracy, and equality of access in the American higher education sector.

Influence

Kolodny's writing exemplifies the politically engaged approach to literary criticism which has flourished over the past thirty years. By demonstrating the role of traditional criticism in normalizing and perpetuating existing power relations in society, Kolodny reveals how alternative ways of interpreting the written word might, in turn, initiate changes in the wider world. The connection between literary criticism and politics is fundamental to Kolodny's work, contrasting her analysis with the work of less materially and socially focused feminist critics, such as those associated with French psychoanalytic feminisms. Kolodny's analytical position insists upon a pluralistic perspective, drawing connections between women's marginalized literary status and other radical causes, such as the environmental movement, the position of ethnic minorities, and gay and lesbian identities. Her literary-critical ideal, as expressed in the conclusion to "Dancing through the Minefield," is not for feminists to "establish our own 'party line,'" but to "camp . . . out, on the far side of the minefield, with all the other pluralists and pluralisms."

Kolodny's critical work is characterized by an influential melding of theory and practice: commonly her books and articles develop a theoretical position and then proceed to demonstrate how such an approach might be used to recover new readings from established works. In *The Land before Her*, arguably her most influential book, this two-pronged approach is further expanded. In this work Kolodny not only traces a specifically female response to America's frontier history, but she in addition documents it by quoting from often little-known materials – the diaries, letters, and occasional journals of nineteenth-century pioneering women. Kolodny's readiness to rethink literary critical practice – in terms of source materials, analysis, and theory – has been profoundly influential on academic criticism, initiating a heightened awareness of critics' own power in determining the "natural" meaning of any literary work.

Analysis

It is possible to construct a framework for understanding the recurrent themes in Kolodny's diverse critical output by focusing on three propositions enumerated in her 1979 essay "Dancing through the Minefield." In this summary of academic feminist literary criticism's evolution over its first decade, Kolodny posits, firstly, that literary history as we have come to know it is a fiction; secondly, that all critical methodologies have political investments which should be analyzed as such; and, thirdly, that the critical techniques derived from already canonical texts precondition the reception of newer writing. The cumulative force of these three literary-critical tenets is the advocacy of a new transparency in literary studies: a frank acknowledgment that there is nothing "natural" or "objective" about the verdicts literary criticism casts on individual texts, and the development of the alternative practice of metacriticism, in which critics' writings themselves comprise the object of literary study.

The most fundamental of Kolodny's structuring principles – her belief that all literary criticism is political in its implication – has been advanced consistently in her writing, in particular in her work since "Dancing through the Minefield." In using the term "political," Kolodny refers not so much to the concept of party politics within the nation state, but the looser conception of politics first articulated in Kate Millett's important radical feminist analysis *Sexual Politics* (1970), in which "politics" is used to connote any social relationship based on an inequality of power. Literary criticism is therefore *political* in the way that it appears to naturalize power imbalances in society, be they racial, sexual, linguistic, or class-based. Yet criticism's importance for Kolodny, as for other critics of the left, is its potential to subvert those very power hierarchies it has thus far generally functioned to reinforce. Thus critical reading tactics may be developed to read "against the grain of a text," refusing those values which the text appears to support and valorizing those subject positions which at surface level it denigrates. When read in the light of a sympathetic critical schema, writing from marginalized social groups – for example black writers or women writers – may initiate not only personal affirmation in readers from these groups but also, Kolodny contends, social change in the outside world.

Kolodny's conviction that any standard record of literary history can only ever amount to a selective view underpins her criticism of the American critic Harold Bloom's much-discussed theory of the anxiety of influence. Bloom contends in *The Anxiety of Influence: A Theory of Poetry* (1973) and *A Map of Misreading* (1975) that poets are locked in an Oedipal-style struggle with their literary forefathers, whose work they must wilfully "misread" in order to dislodge its status as definitive, and thus clear cultural space for their own literary productions. Kolodny takes issue with the unexamined Freudian psychoanalysis which structures Bloom's apparently universalist pronouncements in her articles "A Map for Rereading: Or, Gender and the Interpretation of Literary Texts" (1980) and "The Influence of Anxiety: Prolegomena to a Study of the Production of Poetry by Women" (1987). Not only does the male-focused psychodrama of Bloom's schema admit no place for the woman writer, but moreover, Kolodny suggests, the recurrent motif in women's writing is not the rejection of literary forebears, so much as the search for a *female* writerly tradition into which women writers might insert themselves. The implications of Kolodny's challenge to Bloom's would-be universalism are far-reaching. Her radical critique suggests that critics of literature find in texts the patterns which they set out to find.

Kolodny's work faces squarely the implications of her proposition that literary history can only ever be, at best, a partial construct. In place of the old certainties, Kolodny proposes a dual strategy for the writing of criticism which aims to be more than simply the self-projection of the individual critic. Self-consciousness is vital to Kolodny's conception of politically informed criticism, in the sense that critics must strive to be alert to and explicit about the motivations which underpin their writing. Secondly, critics should aim for a productive pluralism which draws connections between critical approaches old and new and which provides the benefits of a multidisciplinary outlook. In endorsing such an approach, Kolodny perhaps reveals the influence of her training in older Leavisite and New Critical methodologies – concepts which comprised the critical orthodoxy during her undergraduate and postgraduate years. For she proposes that women, having mastered the critical reading techniques and appreciation of literary styles taught by older critical schools, should not jettison these wholesale as irredeemably tainted by their male origins. Instead, feminist critics should make use of all the sophisticated reading tools they have to hand, but should aim to apply these with a political sensitivity and openness to literary innovation:

> The overriding task of an intellectually vigorous feminist criticism as I see it, therefore, must be to school itself in rigorous methods for analyzing style and image and then without preconception or preconceived conclusions to apply those methodologies to individual works.

The broader aim of a self-conscious and pluralistic feminist criticism is, in Kolodny's terms, to reinscribe a "humanistic" world-view which appreciates the variety of human experience and affirms the worth of individual human life. Feminism's adherence to a humanistic code of values is presented as a check on the potential of any revolutionary movement to merely replace an existing power structure (for example, that of white masculinity) with an alternative one (for example, that of women or Chicano/Chicana). Kolodny's alertness to the potential pitfalls of adopting a critic-focused theoretical approach led her to decry early second-wave feminist criticism's tendency to assume that white, middle-class women's experiences were shared by women from other social and ethnic groups – an assumption not widely acknowledged in feminist circles until the early- to mid-1980s.

Yet Kolodny's advocacy of a humanistic pluralist feminist agenda has led to criticism of her position from other feminist critics who read her work as too ready to reinscribe the humanist notion of the autonomous, rational individual. Poststructuralist-influenced critics similarly diagnose in Kolodny's assertion of a "real world" beyond the text an unexamined assumption that texts refer to external "realities," rather than simply to an endless series of other texts. Tania Modleski, in a review essay about feminist literary criticism in the 1980s, discerns a fundamental tension between Kolodny's faith in pluralism (which posits an unconstrained individual) and feminism (which starts from the position that women have been socialized into constricting behavioral patterns by society). Modleski, along with radical feminist critics such as Judith Kegan Gardiner and Elly Bulkin, claims that Kolodny underestimates the ease with which the introduction of feminist criticism into a newly "pluralist" academy could leave social and economic power structures unaltered. Kolodny has, however, in her more recent work tackled precisely this problem of the academy's tendency to contain and coopt radical agendas. In an essay to mark the tenth anniversary of "Dancing through the Minefield" – allusively titled "Dancing between Left and Right: Feminism and the Academic Minefield in the 1980s" (1988) – Kolodny analyzes a new minefield faced by feminist critics, one caused by the divorce of feminist theory from any conception of feminist politics. Speaking very much as a critic of feminism's activist second wave, Kolodny asserts uncompromisingly (and, for the time, somewhat unfashionably) that "theory devoid of activist politics isn't feminism but, rather, pedantry and moral abdication."

The third of the interrelated principles which structure Kolodny's work is the belief that literary criticism has, until the late 1960s, been a largely self-perpetuating exercise. Critics have tended to develop reading techniques from a highly selective body of canonical texts. These techniques have gradually ossified into a paradigm against which the reading of new texts is governed, with the inhibiting result that innovative contemporary works are read so as to accord with preexisting critical conventions and criticized when they fail to do so. Kolodny has explored this dynamic in her first published book, *The Lay of the Land*, which examines the pattern of European male responses to the "New World" of America as one of desire for erotic conquest of "virgin" territory. Early American literature's repeated metaphoric representation of the land as female patterns a response to landscape in which the (male) author positions himself in the role of lover, son, or conquistador – a linguistically inscribed relationship which Kolodny maintains still powerfully preconditions modern Americans' response to the landscape. Kolodny's subsequent book, *The Land before Her* – the second in a projected trilogy about the evolving fantasies of the American landscape – demonstrates how inherited critical paradigms for interpreting the American pastoral tradition might be subverted by looking at texts written from a marginalized group such as women, and by a critical readiness to upend received notions of what constitutes "American literature." In this work Kolodny traces the development of a specifically female response to the nation's landscape in which the conquering and taming preoccupations of the frontiersman are replaced by the desire to build communities and gardens in a wilderness perceived as vulnerable to human encroachment and industrialization.

Having demonstrated in her own work how a dominant tradition may be denominated, and subsequently subverted to make audible excluded voices, Kolodny has proceeded in recent work to suggest a new paradigm for American literary studies. In the essay "Letting Go Our Grand Obsessions: Notes toward a New Literary History of the American Frontiers" (1992), published in the year of celebrations and protests marking the five-hundredth anniversary of Columbus' "discovery" of the Americas, Kolodny proposes that critics of American literature focus their analyses upon the tensions of cross-cultural encounters throughout the continent's history. She maintains that any investigation of territorial conflict must recognize that the territories at stake are both literal and figurative, and must avoid the inherited overtones of racial supremacy associated with the doctrine of manifest destiny. Such an approach, based as it is upon examining inter- and intracultural tensions, posits language, race, sexuality, and region as its chief concerns, and therefore cannot *but* be political in the broader sense Kolodny has consistently championed:

> In effect, in my reformulation the term "frontier" comes to mean what we in the Southwest call *la frontera*, or the borderlands, that liminal landscape of changing meanings on which distinct human cultures first encounter one another's "otherness" and appropriate, accommodate, or domesticate it through language.

Similarly, in the sphere of contemporary women's writing Kolodny has championed heterogeneity, innovation, and textual resistance, although here her emphasis has been specifically on the avant-garde critic as avant-garde reader. In her essays "Some Notes on Defining a 'Feminist Literary Criticism'" (1975) and "The Lady's Not for Spurning: Kate Millett and the Critics" (1976), Kolodny asserts that women have no biologically given or socially learnt skill at reading experimental women's fiction, but that the project of constructing a female literary tradition demands readers who are sophisticated at interpreting formally inventive and nontraditional works. Just as writers must piece together a female tradition in literature by appropriating existing techniques for new ends, so the individual reader approaching an experimental and initially confusing woman writer's text should assume a highly active and resourceful reading position – drawing out meaning from the work by active participation in its writerly processes. Women writers' attempts to bend established traditions in order to record experiences which have hitherto eluded the domain of "high" literature will inevitably seem peculiar to readers trained only in the old critical orthodoxies. Thus the freeing of writers depends upon a simultaneous freeing of readers, so that literary criticism may move beyond self-perpetuating pronouncements and relate its critical practice to a concrete world of changing political realities.

The principles of textual politics, pluralism, and critical self-consciousness which Kolodny has championed in her writing have never, of course, derived solely from her own thought. They have been culturally pervasive during the periods in which she has written – an interpenetration of external political realities and individual literary critical practice precisely illustrating Kolodny's own concept of the progressive critic. But in the elegance and conceptual sophistication of her writing, in her willingness to synthesize vibrant and complex critical debates, and in her realization that only a self-conscious and inclusivist criticism can buttress the humanities' claim to continued educational relevance, Kolodny has contributed vitally to the development of an engaged and revivified critical practice.

Principal criticism

The Lay of the Land: Metaphor as Experience and History in American Life and Letters, 1975
"Some Notes on Defining a 'Feminist Literary Criticism,'" in *Critical Inquiry*. 2 (1975), pp. 75–92
"'Stript, shorne and made deformed': Images on the Southern Landscape," in *South Atlantic Quarterly*. 75 (1976), pp. 55–73
"The Lady's Not for Spurning: Kate Millett and the Critics," in *Contemporary Literature*. 17 (1976), pp. 541–562
"Dancing through the Minefield: Some Observations of the Theory, Practice and Politics of a Feminist Literary Criticism," [1979] in *Feminist Studies*. 6 (1980), pp. 1–25
"A Map for Rereading: Or, Gender and the Interpretation of Literary Texts," in *New Literary History*. 11 (1980), pp. 451–467
"Turning the Lens on 'The Panther Captivity': A Feminist Exercise in Practical Criticism," in *Critical Inquiry*. 8, no. 2 (Winter, 1981), pp. 329–345
Introduction to *The Blithedale Romance* by Nathaniel Hawthorne, 1983
The Land before Her: Fantasy and Experience of the American Frontiers, 1630–1860, 1984
"The Integrity of Memory: Creating a New Literary History of the United States," in *American Literature*. 57, no 2 (May, 1985), pp. 291–307
"The Influence of Anxiety: Prolegomena to a Study of the Production of Poetry by Women," in *A Gift of Tongues: Critical Challenges in Contemporary American Poetry*, 1987 (Marie Harris and Kathleen Aguero, editors)
"Dancing between Left and Right: Feminism and the Academic Minefield in the 1980s," in *Literature, Language and Politics*, 1988 (Betty Jean Craige, editor)
"Letting Go Our Grand Obsessions: Notes toward a New Literary History of the American Frontiers," in *American Literature*. 64, no. 1 (March, 1992), pp. 1–18
"Among the Indians: The Uses of Captivity," in *New York Times Book Review*. 31 January, 1993, pp. 1, 26–28
"Unearthing Herstory: An Introduction," in *The Ecocriticism Reader: Landmarks in Literary Ecology*, 1996 (Cheryll Glotfelty and Harold Fromm, editors)

Other major works and literary forms

NONFICTION
Failing the Future: A Dean Looks at Higher Education in the Twenty-First Century, 1998

MISCELLANEOUS
Border Crossings, 1978 (fictionalized account of Kolodny's struggles as a feminist academic within conservative university English departments written by her husband, Daniel Peters)

Further reading

Gardiner, Judith Kegan, Elly Bulkin, Rena Grasso Patterson, and Annette Kolodny. "An Interchange on Feminist Criticism on 'Dancing through the Minefield,'" in *Feminist Studies*. 8, no. 3 (Fall, 1982), pp. 629–675.
Jones, A. G. "A Landscape of Her Own," in *American Quarterly*. 37 (1985), pp. 615–626.
Koppelman, Susan. "Annette Kolodny," in *Dictionary of Literary Biography*, Vol. 67, 1988.
Lussier, Mark, and Peggy McCormack. "An Interview with Annette Kolodny," in *New Orleans Review*. 13, no. 4 (1986), pp. 50–58.
Modleski, Tania. "Feminism and the Power of Interpretation: Some Critical Readings," in *Feminist Studies: Critical Studies*, 1986. Edited by Teresa de Lauretis.
Moi, Toril. *Sexual/Textual Politics: Feminist Literary Theory*, 1985.

SIMONE MURRAY

See also American Literary Theory: Twentieth Century

Murray Krieger

American critic

Born: Newark, New Jersey; November 27, 1923

Biography

Murray Krieger was born November 27, 1923, in Newark, New Jersey, the son of Isidore Krieger and his wife, Jennie (née Glinn). He has a brother, Leonard, to whom he has dedicated one book; he has also listed his parents, wife, children, teacher, and colleagues in his dedications. Krieger married Joan Alice Stone on June 15, 1947; they have two children, Catherine Leona and Eliot Franklin. Joan Krieger is a graphic artist and has supplied important emblems for a number of her husband's publications, most notably the figure for the presence/absence paradox on the title page of *Poetic Presence and Illusion* and the plates for *Arts on the Level*.

Krieger began college at Rutgers University, which he attended from 1940 to 1942. He then served in the United States Army from 1942 to 1946. He received a master's degree from the University of Chicago in 1948, then worked as an instructor of English at Kenyon College before completing his Ph.D. at Ohio State University in 1952. Krieger also taught during his last year of study at Ohio State, where his dissertation formed the basis for his later, major study of New Criticism. Krieger's first book was coedited with the man he credits as "his master," the scholar who "forcefully shaped" his study of theory, Eliseo Vivas. They worked together on *The Problems of Aesthetics: A Book of Readings* (1953), and Krieger followed that project with a profound tribute to Vivas in the preface to his acclaimed theoretical study *The New Apologists for Poetry*. Krieger's contribution to a later Vivas Festschrift has been reprinted in *Poetic Presence and Illusion*.

Krieger's first professorship was at the University of Minnesota, from 1952 to 1958. In 1956 he received a promotion from assistant to associate professor. He then took a position as full professor with the University of Illinois, Urbana (1958–1963). There he published *The Tragic Vision*, first drafted on a 1956 Guggenheim Fellowship, and *A Window to Criticism*, part of which Krieger wrote while he was an Associate of the University of Illinois Center for Advanced Study (1961–1962). Krieger's last appointment in the Midwest was as M. F. Carpenter Professor of Literary Criticism at the University of Iowa (1963–1966). Krieger received an additional Guggenheim in 1961–1962 and a postdoctoral fellowship from the American Council of Learned Societies (1966–1967); during the latter year, he collected the essays that summarize the first half of his career in *The Play and Place of Criticism*.

Krieger began his association with the University of California in 1966, moving to the Irvine campus to assume a professorship in the Department of English and Comparative Literature. Since his arrival at Irvine, the program in criticism of which Krieger took charge has developed into an international center for literary scholarship, with a faculty that includes such luminaries as Jacques Derrida and Wolfgang Iser. In 1973 Krieger added a position at the Los Angeles campus to his responsibilities, which developed in 1974 into his current status as university professor. The second phase of Krieger's professional career was accompanied by a shift in his critical attitude, first expressed in 1971 in *The Classic Vision*. In the next year, 1971–1972, Krieger began the historical project of interpreting the tradition of literary criticism from a humanistic perspective under the auspices of a grant from the National Endowment for the Humanities. This study would eventually produce what stands as Krieger's major work of contemporary significance, *Theory of Criticism*, which culminates in a response to deconstruction that reveals Derrida's skeptical work as a complement to the tensions charted by Kantian aesthetics.

At Irvine, Krieger also founded, with Hazard Adams, the School for Criticism and Theory, a summer program that involves intensive study for young scholars with the leading figures of literary scholarship. Krieger directed the school alone from 1977 to 1981; it has since moved to Northwestern and Dartmouth (where in 1987 Michael Riffaterre succeeded Geoffrey Hartman as its executive officer). Krieger returned to lecture at the school in 1987, presenting a major unpublished work on literary and theatrical aesthetics called "Representation in Words and in Drama: The Illusive Naturalization of the Literary Sign." Krieger delivered a series of lectures at the University of Tennessee, the John C. Hodges lectures, that were written on a 1978 fellowship from the Rockefeller Humanities Research program, published in 1981 as *Arts on the Level*. He has also produced two lengthy volumes of occasional lectures, *Poetic Presence and Illusion* and *Words About Words About Words*, both of which continue his exploration and evaluation of poststructuralist critical theory.

Influence

Krieger's impact upon the history and study of literary theory comes from the success and variety of his undertakings. As a theorist proper, Krieger provides the best summary and first important criticism of the New Critical orthodoxy in America. He has also supplied the most compelling defense of traditional aesthetic criticism to the challenge of deconstruction. As an editor, he has shaped the reception of such important figures as Northrop Frye, and he has provided a graphic summary of the problems of aesthetics that stood as a guidepost for thirty years. As an educator, Krieger has produced an impressive number of contemporary theorists from the excellent graduate programs that he has taught within or administered. Krieger has also had important influence as a founder of institutions, such as the vital School for Criticism and Theory and the University of California Institute for the Humanities.

Analysis

In his first major critical work, *The New Apologists for Poetry*, Murray Krieger began to deal with the critical issues that would not animate the general debate in the theory of literature for at least a decade to come: the apparent logocentrism of the New Criticism, with its poetics of absolute closure. Krieger does not anticipate Derrida's coinage, but he does trace – in the paradoxical terms that characterize his own discourse – the problematic position of the poem between a system of language that is entirely open and an experience of a self-contained discourse:

> The poem must in one sense, as a special form of discourse, be nonreferential, even as it must be referential to be any form of discourse at all. It must, as organic, be autonomous, even as it illuminates human experience. If it is to be the ground of the integrated, disinterested, even selfless experience I would denominate as aesthetic, the poem must be distinguished by what have been termed "immanent meanings," even though these cannot be discovered if I do not bring to the poem clearly specified meanings from the outside.

In keeping with the artist/object/perceiver model of the artistic transaction that he formulated with Eliseo Vivas in the introduction to *The Problems of Aesthetics*, Krieger charts this problematic in three areas: the "psychology of poetic creativity," the "structure of the poem as aesthetic object," and the "definition of aesthetic experience." Krieger, perhaps taking a cue from Stephen Pepper, describes the New Critical aesthetic as "contextualist," but in the end his confrontations with the difficulties of closure and reference are more than a summary of New Criticism; they constitute an attempt to write an original poetics based on a fresh appreciation of the paradoxical relations and effects of the "facts of his experience of poetry."

Krieger then develops these existential "facts" into a related but separate kind of critical project, the "thematics" of *The Tragic Vision*: "thematics as the study of the experiential tensions which, dramatically entangled in the literary work, become an existential reflection of that work's aesthetic complexity." Krieger takes as his focus those tensions generated by the "Manichaean" or "Dionysian" character within a number of modern novels. This project, too, anticipates Krieger's later response to deconstruction, for the character's "tragic vision" in these novels is a kind of absolute of difference, experienced as the absolute "particularity" of the Kierkegaardian individual, which is then absorbed and reintegrated into the system of ethical values by the containing form of the artwork. Krieger makes the containment of the tragic vision the specific concern of a companion study, *The Classic Vision*, in which he examines a number of other works, from the eighteenth century to the period following World War II, from the standpoint of their ability to acknowledge but withstand the irruptive force of absolute difference. Krieger recognizes that the being-in-itself of the tragic impulse is essentially a form of skepticism just as extreme as the deconstructive impulse, and that both can be answered with a similar strategy.

In his study of William Shakespeare's sonnets, *A Window to Criticism*, Krieger devises a metaphor that expresses the paradoxical function of language in poetry. He notes three ways that language can work: referentially as a "window to the world"; formally, through a closure activity of "endlessly faceted mirrors ever multiplying itself but finally shut up within itself"; and through a miraculous simultaneity whereby the mirror "miraculously becomes window again after all." Here closure is still not quite illusory, as it would be theorized in Krieger's later works, but it is transparent, a glass wall made such by the application of a "both/and" logic that embraces the paradoxical experience of poetry outlined in *The New Apologists for Poetry*. Krieger then applies this metaphor to the whole body of Shakespearean sonnets in one of the most extended, detailed displays of his sensitive critical practice. His essay isolates

> Shakespeare's brilliant method of creating constitutive symbols in one sonnet and, having earned his right to them there, transferring them whole to another sonnet, with their full burden of borrowed meaning, earned elsewhere, taken for granted. Thus a creative symbol in one sonnet becomes a sign, part of the raw materials, in another.

This move takes Krieger beyond his "thematic" attitudes to a notion of the intertext that is completely in accord with his insistence upon the integrity of each individual poem, culminating in a trope of "poetic effigy." Here the poem becomes an object of willed "transubstantiation," like the actor who is character made flesh, a vivified language structure that is both not present and not not present.

Krieger develops a similar metaphor and paradoxical resolution in the essay that he has indicated provides a key to his work, "The Ekphrastic Principle and the Still Movement of Poetry: Or, Laokoon Revisited," in *The Play and Place of Criticism*. Here Krieger changes his own critical attitude slightly, for rather than argue against the New Critical theory by which a poem is granted presence, Krieger applies a strict formal analysis of his own, based on paradox, to the central problem of "the poem's achieving a formal and linguistic self-sufficiency." Krieger notes how language acquires not only stability through the growth of the poetic utterance but movement as well. He summarizes this double effect in his use of the word "still,"

> as adjective, adverb and verb; as still movement, still moving, and more forcefully, the stilling of movement: so "still" movement as quiet, unmoving movement; "still" moving as a forever-now movement, always in process, unending; and the union of these meanings at once twin and opposed in the "stilling" of movement, an action that is at once the quieting of movement and the perpetuation of it, the making of it, like Eliot's wheel and Chinese jar, a movement that is still and is still with us, that is – in his words – "forever still."

The ekphrastic inspiration for this insight is provided by that kind of verse – Keats' "Ode: To a Grecian Urn" being one example – which translates the artistic effect and impression of one kind of art form into another. Krieger does not extend the metaphysical potential of the "effigy" figure, but rather returns to the formal contingencies of time and space, the basic assumptions of all relativist thought, and explains how the poem has special powers to resolve the retreat of time and space in a way that is not "real" by any material or discursive standard, but instead captures those categories by which one defines reality in the momentary illusion of stability: "The poem can uniquely order spatial stasis within its temporal dynamics because through its echoes and its texture it can produce – together with the illusion of progressive movement – the illusion of an organized simultaneity." Krieger confutes the phenomenological insistence that such a liberation can occur only in the mind, claiming the objective status of poetry in the "well-wrought, well-lighted place of aesthetics."

By emphasizing the positive powers of illusion, Krieger sets the stage for his confrontation with structuralist (and especially deconstructive) criticism. Krieger voices two major objections to the proponents of structuralism, both of which are unique to the French interpretation of the structuralist heritage. In the first place, Krieger points out that the structuralists, with their generally leveling insistence upon difference as an absolute, refuse to acknowledge the difference between poetry and other kinds of language. He outlines this problem in *Theory of Criticism* and then adopts it as his main concern in *Arts on the Level*. Krieger maintains that the French structuralists have taken the legacy of Ferdinand de Saussure in general linguistics and have applied it indiscriminately to the deviational uses of language found in poetry. Krieger points out, in terms that beat structuralism with its own stick, that

> for all the demythifications that structuralist method may have produced – they [the French structuralists] are themselves guilty of the grossly naive myth of reifying their own terms, of confounding their language with reality, projecting the former upon the latter: that is, they limit what can exist (in this case the kinds of operations of which language is capable) by what their terms, and the system of differentiation permitted by their terms, permit to exist.

Krieger excludes such critics as Roman Jakobson and the Prague School of Linguistics from his broadside, for in those cases the differentiation between referential and aesthetic uses of language provides the basis for a semiotic poetics. The force of Krieger's argument, and his confidence in maintaining the special status of poems, doubtless derives from the conviction he maintained from his first book, that there is something unique about his own experience of poetry as opposed to other discourse, and the feeling he experiences from poetry requires some acknowledgment in any adequate poetics.

Krieger's second major objection to the influence of structuralism has to do with what he interprets as the negative attitude, the destructive force, of deconstruction. Krieger interprets Derrida's description of the word as the trace of absence as a rephrasing, from a different value, of his description of the poem as all illusion of presence; he and Derrida "represent, respectively, the positive print and the negative of a photograph, both seeming to have the same reality (or unreality) but with reverse emphases, the lights of one being the darks of the other." Krieger notes a similar, even more pronounced negativity in the depressed attitude of Paul de Man, who grasps the failure of language to create absolute, real presence as an opportunity to emphasize his "existential thematics," like the dark vision of the tragic character in Krieger's second book. Krieger finds the negative potential of deconstruction to have considerable validity in its application to philosophical discourse. In a coup of the first order, however, Krieger shows how Derrida's central term, the word that figures the whole process and project of deconstruction, is a poetic construction of a transcendental signifier:

> In Derrida's own discourse, the very word "différ*a*nce," with or without my emendation, is surely and in a profound sense a word behaving most *un*deferentially. The decentering use to which he puts it does not alter our sense of the need he has for the word's capacity to contain its divergent meanings. How much more undeferential – how much more self-assertive – would it be if it was serving a . . . poem!

Krieger then goes on to point out how his own version of poetic presence, with its emphasis upon the illusion of closure and stasis, protects the poem from making any real truth claims that might be made the object of deconstruction.

Having met and absorbed the challenge of deconstruction to his own project of an ongoing, cumulative poetics, Krieger has written both applied and theoretical criticism with a new assurance; the defensive posture of *Theory of Criticism* has been superseded in his work by the confidence of such essays as "Literature as Illusion, as Metaphor, as Vision," in *Poetic Presence and Illusion*, wherein Krieger reasserts his old affection for paradox and simultaneity in the context of his critical rite of passage:

> I have tried to speak firmly, definitively, about the will-o'-the-wisp literature, whose very being undoes this mode of dealing with it. Its duplicitous way of functioning makes a myth of every claim. In taking itself lightly as discourse, it forces all discourse – even the theoretical – to take itself lightly in pursuit of literature.

Similar magic occurs in other essays, as Krieger's critical style, sometimes condemned for its complexity and often misread because of its difficulty, becomes more and more like the poetry he defends. In an essay that is less lyrical yet more like a miracle of concise summation, "An Apology for Poetics" in *Words About Words About Words*, Krieger isolates six distinct schools or trends in contemporary critical practice, and demonstrates the particular and shared inadequacy of each of them to delimit a poetics that accounts for the social facts of poetry as it is written and perceived. For this failure of poetics Krieger apologizes; poetry itself, making few claims and providing such intense experience, needs no excuses.

Principal criticism

The New Apologists for Poetry, 1956
The Tragic Vision: Variations on a Theme in Literary Interpretation, 1960
A Window to Criticism: Shakespeare's Sonnets and Modern Poetics, 1964
The Play and Place of Criticism, 1967
The Classic Vision: The Retreat from Extremity in Modern Literature, 1971
Theory of Criticism: A Tradition and Its System, 1976
Poetic Presence and Illusion: Essays in Critical History and Theory, 1979
Arts on the Level: The Fall of the Elite Object, 1981
"Representation in Words and in Drama: The Illusive Naturalization of the Literary Sign," 1987

Words About Words About Words: Theory, Criticism, and the Literary Text, 1988
A Reopening of Closure: Organicism Against Itself, 1989
Ekphrasis: The Illusion of the Natural Sign, 1992
The Ideological Imperative: Repression and Resistance in Recent American Theory, 1993
The Institution of Theory, 1994

Other major works and literary forms

Murray Krieger is known primarily as a literary critic and theorist.

EDITED TEXTS
The Problems of Aesthetics: A Book of Readings, 1953 (with Eliseo Vivas)
Northrop Frye in Modern Criticism, 1966
Literature and History: Papers Read at the Clark Library Seminar, March 3, 1973, 1974 (with Ralph Cohen)
Directions for Criticism: Structuralism and Its Alternatives, 1977 (with L. S. Dembo)
The Aims of Representation, 1987

Further reading

Berg, Richard, ed., and Hazard Adams, introd. "The Theory and Practice of Murray Krieger: A Special Section," in *New Orleans Review*. 10, no. 1 (Spring, 1983), pp. 4–78.
Bolling, Doug, ed. *Philosophy and Literature*, 1987.
Clark, Michael, ed. *The Revenge of the Aesthetic*, 1999.
Free, William J. "Murray Krieger and the Place of Poetry," in *The Georgia Review*. 22 (Summer, 1968), pp. 236–246.
Harris, Paul A. "The Time of Possibilities: Murray Krieger and Literary Theory," in *Anglistik*. 8, no. 2 (September, 1997), pp. 69–79).
Henricksen, Bruce, ed. *Murray Krieger and Contemporary Critical Theory*, 1986.
Herring, Henry D. "Literature, Concepts, and Knowledge," in *New Literary History*. 18 (Autumn, 1968), pp. 171–190.
Kartiganer, Donald M. "The Criticism of Murray Krieger: The Expansions of Contextualism," in *Boundary*. 2, no. 2 (Spring, 1974), pp. 584–607.
Lentricchia, Frank. *After the New Criticism*, 1980.
Morris, Wesley. *Toward a New Historicism*, 1972.
Webster, Grant. *The Republic of Letters: A History of Postwar American Literary Opinion*, 1979.
Wimsatt, William K. *Day of the Leopards*, 1976.

MICHAEL L. QUINN

See also American Literary Theory: Twentieth Century

Julia Kristeva

Bulgarian-born French critic and theorist

Born: Bulgaria; 1941

Biography

Born in Bulgaria in 1941, Julia Kristeva received her early education from a French religious order and her college training at the University of Sofia. She arrived in Paris in 1966 to begin studies toward a doctoral degree; this step turned into a permanent emigration for her, and her professional life in effect began in Paris. In 1967 her articles began to appear in the leading intellectual journals, *Critique*, *Langages*, and *Tel Quel*. Owing to her close association with the latter, Kristeva tended to be grouped with the post-structuralist school of thought about language and culture. She had, however, a distinctive voice from the very first. Having been introduced to Western literature through the innovative Russian critic Mikhail Bakhtin, she arrived prepared to make a unique contribution at the moment when Paris was most receptive to nontraditional, non-Western approaches to Western culture.

After defending her doctoral dissertation, *Revolution in Poetic Language*, Kristeva was appointed to a chair in linguistics at the University of Paris VII. She served on the editorial board of *Tel Quel* from 1970 to 1983. With a group from *Tel Quel*, she made a three-week visit to China in 1974; from this experience came her perceptive study *About Chinese Women* (1977). Kristeva married the French novelist and theorist Philippe Sollers in 1970 and had a son in 1976. She has completed professional training in psychoanalysis, opening her own practice in 1979. While retaining her position at the Sorbonne, she lectures at Columbia University in approximately alternate years.

Influence

In the esoteric world of French avant-garde criticism, the influence of its leaders, such as Kristeva, Roland Barthes, and Jacques Derrida, was mutual and acknowledged as such. The effort to create a radically new approach, encompassing the entire history of human (though predominantly Western) culture, of necessity required the moral support and broad erudition of a brilliant, highly committed group. In 1968 they produced a jointly written credo, *Théorie d'ensemble*.

Kristeva began as a theorist accessible only to specialists, and developed into writer with a less convoluted style, who increasingly reaches a broader public. She has contributed to an intellectual climate in which a wide range of cultural phenomenon can be reexamined dynamically, with a sense that they form a continuous whole. Much of her influence is indirect and unacknowledged, but her revitalization of Greek mythology and biblical motifs has born fruit in the popular media that apply, with new sophistication, such symbols as Narcissus and Gemorah to modern culture and consciousness.

Analysis

Kristeva's work has broader goals than literary criticism in the strict sense. While it gives tantalizing glimpses of her impeccable taste in literature, her writing is not concerned with the qualitative grading of individual authors. Kristeva's work treats literature itself as a psychological, historical, and political phenomenon. Individual works and authors serve only as details of a much larger picture. While her range of erudition is multicultural, her focus is most often on French literature, with Russian a significant secondary source. James Joyce heads the wide-ranging list of literary sources outside the Russian and French.

The first stage of Kristeva's critical writings, roughly from the years 1967 through 1974, includes *Séméiotiké: Recherches pour une sémanalyse* (1969), *Le Texte du roman* (1970), and *Revolution in Poetic Language* (1984). In this stage, Kristeva is concerned with elaborating the tools of criticism. She validates Bakhtin's concept of literary polyphony as an important stage in the novel and his understanding of "poetic language" as a concept much broader than poetry. She validates Barthes' insights into the existential "negativity" of language and the preeminence of history and politics over literature. She expands the inventory of critical terminology with numerous new terms, such as "intertextuality," "paragram," "genotext," and "phenotext." (Of these, "intertextuality" has gained the widest acceptance; it refers to the transposition of one system of signs into another, refreshing the connotations of both.) She affirms the application, begun by colleagues such as Barthes and Derrida, of semiotics to literature; in so doing, she emphasizes that the semiotic approach is a post-Symbolist approach and carefully distinguishes between the traditional symbols and the innovative concept of "signs" in literature. In this first stage, Kristeva's approach is at its most severely technical or structuralist. For example, she applies calculus in her definition of an omniscient narrator opening a story with a description of a hero in the third person:

> The subject of utterance (S_d) coincides with the zero degree of the subject of enunciation (S_r), which can be designated either by the "he/she" non-person pronoun or a proper name. This is the simplest technique found at the inception of the narrative.

An anthology of her early writings taken from many sources and available only in English, *Desire in Language* (1980), puts Kristeva's approach into focus. She clarifies her goals in relating semiotics to literature: "One of the problems for semiotics is to replace the formal, rhetorical division of genres with a typology of texts." For her, the most important genre in need of semiotic redefinition is the novel, particularly in its subversive role, from François Rabelais to Louis-Ferdinand Céline, as the carrier of what Bakhtin called the "carnivalesque" (joyous, sensual, mocking) impulse in Western culture. She views the novel dynamically, as a process or operation. The importance of the differing stylistic and psychological threads weaving through the novel is emphasized as the real key to the distinctness of the genre. She sounds a distinct extraliterary note in a chapter entitled "The Ethics of Linguistics": both linguistic and literary analysis deserve a larger role in the interpretation of history and culture than has previously been seen. In semiotic fashion, a parallel is assumed among all manifestations of culture, with literary and language codes participating in the same processes as, for example, ethical and legal codes. In the late nineteenth century "something quite new [entered] . . . Western society and discourse . . . subsumed in the names of Marx, Nietzsche, and Freud." She finds a parallel between these thinkers' shattering of various codes and the code-shattering of such twentieth-century writers as the Russian Futurists and Céline. In Kristeva's words, "a code . . . must be shattered in every revolutionary beginning."

In its subsequent stages, Kristeva's literary theory becomes indissolubly integrated with her contributions to psychology, philosophy, and fine arts criticism. She continues to analyze the creative processes of individual writers, but with the goal of illuminating universal creative and psychological processes, in writer and nonwriter alike. *Strangers to Ourselves* (1991) is a fully matured example of Kristeva's integration of literary history, psychology, and philosophy. It is full of brilliant insights and erudition in all three fields. In terms of literary history, it brings a fresh look to a range of writers, both ancient and modern, with particular strength in classical French literature. However, the literary aspects of her analysis at times suffer because of subordination to other fields. Thus, the chapter "Love-Hatred in a Couple" exhaustively treats William Shakespeare's *Romeo and Juliet* from the standpoint of a case history "covering the full range of sadomasochism," with no reference to literary values. More successful is Kristeva's analysis of the parallel status of women, foreigners, Jews, and, ultimately, modern man in general; she brings these parallels into relief through Greek myth, biblical motifs, and Freudian psychology.

Strangers to Ourselves is Kristeva's most personal work, arising from a mastery of her own status as a Bulgarian exile adapting to France, and from a heroic determination to make her complex experience useful to all. This work also leads into a political dimension:

> Freud does not speak of foreigners; he teaches us how to detect foreignness in ourselves . . . .
>
> The ethics of psychoanalysis implies a politics: it would involve a cosmopolitanism of a new sort that, cutting across governments, economies, and markets, might work for a mankind whose solidarity is founded on the consciousness of its unconscious – desiring, destructive, fearful, empty, impossible.

The strengths and weaknesses of Kristeva's multidisciplinary approach to literary criticism are apparent in her monograph on the French writer who has come to challenge her interest the most. She invites the reader to learn about Marcel Proust, though not just to know Proust (*Time and Sense: Proust and the Experience of Literature*, 1994). The reader's own experience, as implied by the title, will play an important role.

This study of Proust begins with the enchanting metaphor of the talking statue as having been the model for all literary characters, both mythical and realistic, from the time of the ancient Greeks up until Proust. And while Proust departs radically from his antecedents, Kristeva nonetheless covers them in meticulous detail, because she is even more convinced than most critics of the importance of literary background in the upbringing of an author. Kristeva also returns to her early background as a virtuoso of linguistic analysis, producing a masterful technical study of an archetypal Proustian sentence from *Remembrance of Things Past.*

However, as Kristeva proceeds with her psychological analysis of the author, her study intermingles details from the author's works and life on an equal footing, in opposition to the caveat of Proust himself and of many other critics, that a writer's biography must not be literally equated with the writer's creative life. Kristeva then appeals to the reader's personal psychological experience, at times in a hypnotically suggestive tone, to verify the universality of phenomena such as sadomasochism and the Oedipal complex:

> that consummate archaic apparition where mother and child begin to cultivate the glorification and profanation of the lover and the beloved. Talent brings all its taste and effort to this attempt to give an infectious shape to this experience . . . .
>
> Meanwhile, the mother is dead, I have killed her, my grief turns to remorse, I speak of her to another woman, I speak to myself, I speak – and everything is regained.

In *Visions Capitales* (1998), Kristeva focuses on a recurring image in painting and sculpture, which, throughout the ages, proves to have rich adumbrations: the severed head. Inasmuch as severed heads also enter literature through the myth of Medusa, through the Bible, and their many literary reflections, this work represents an interesting contribution to literary as well as art history. Evaluations of literary quality, however, are tangential to the critic's tracing the theme of sadomasochism.

Principal criticism

Le Texte du roman, 1970
La Révolution du langage poétique, 1974 (*Revolution in Poetic Language*, 1984)
Pouvoirs de l'horreur, 1980 (*Powers of Horror: An Essay on Abjection*, 1982)
Desire in Language: A Semiotic Approach to Literature and Art, 1980
Histoires d'amour, 1983 (*Tales of Love*, 1987)
Strangers to Ourselves, 1991
Time and Sense: Proust and the Experience of Literature, 1994
Visions Capitales, 1998

Other major works and literary forms

In addition to literary criticism, Julia Kristeva has written important works in other fields which touch on literature tangentially. Her essay *Des Chinoises* (1974; *About Chinese Women*, 1977) focuses on cultural history in the broad sense. From time to time, she returns to her early interest in linguistics. From the 1980s onward her work shows increasing interest in depth psychology, politics, and fine art. The 1990s are marked by her new career as a published novelist.

NOVELS
Les Samurai, 1990 (*The Samurai*, 1992)
Le vieil homme et les loups, 1991 (*The Old Man and the Wolves*, 1994)
Possessions, 1996; (*Possessions*, 1998)

NONFICTION
Séméiotiké: Recherches pour une sémanalyse, 1969
"The System and the Speaking Subject," 1973
Des Chinoises, 1974 (*About Chinese Women*, 1977)
"Psychoanalysis and the Polis," 1983
Langage, cet inconnu, 1981 (*Language – the Unknown: An Initiation Into Linguistics*, 1989)
Au commencement était l'amour: Psychanalyse et foi, 1985 (*In the Beginning Was Love: Psychoanalysis and Faith*, 1988)
Lettre ouverte a Harlem Desir, 1990 (*Nations Without Nationalism*, 1993)
Novelles maladies de l'ame, 1993 (*New Maladies of the Soul*, 1995)

EDITED TEXT
La Sémiotique/Semiotics, 1974

Further reading

Jones, Ann Rosalind. "Julia Kristeva on Femininity: The Limits of a Semiotic Politics," in *Feminist Review*. XVIII (Winter, 1984), pp. 56–63.
Lechte, John. *Julia Kristeva*, 1990.
Moi, Toril. Introduction to *The Kristeva Reader*, 1986.
Oliver, Kelly. *Reading Kristeva: Unraveling the Double-bind*, 1993.
Pajaczkowska, Claire. "Introduction to Kristeva," in *Masculin/féminin*. nos. 5/6 (1981), pp. 149–157.
Payne, Michael. *Reading Theory: An Introduction to Lacan, Derrida, and Kristeva*, 1993.
Roudiez, Léon S. Introduction to *Desire in Language*, 1980.
——. Introduction to *Powers of Horror*, 1982.
Smith, Anne-Marie. *Julia Kristeva: Speaking the Unspeakable*, 1998.

DIANA GOSSELIN NAKEEB

See also Feminist Criticism; French Literary Theory: Twentieth Century; Intertextuality; Irigaray; Lacan; Moi; Psychoanalytic Criticism; Semiotics